Psychology: The Science of Mind and Behaviour

Psychology: The Science of Mind and Behaviour
European edition

Michael Passer, Ronald Smith, Nigel Holt, Andy Bremner, Ed Sutherland, Michael L. W. Vliek

**McGraw-Hill
Higher Education**

London   Boston   Burr Ridge, IL   Dubuque, IA   Madison, WI   New York   San Francisco
St. Louis   Bangkok   Bogotá   Caracas   Kuala Lumpur   Lisbon   Madrid   Mexico City   Milan
Montreal   New Delhi   Santiago   Seoul   Singapore   Sydney   Taipei   Toronto

Psychology: The Science of Mind and Behaviour
Michael Passer, Ronald Smith, Nigel Holt, Andy Bremner, Ed Sutherland, Michael L. W. Vliek
ISBN-13 978-0-07-711836-5
ISBN-10 0-07-711836-7

Published by McGraw-Hill Education
Shoppenhangers Road
Maidenhead
Berkshire
SL6 2QL
Telephone: 44 (0) 1628 502 500
Fax: 44 (0) 1628 770 224
Website: www.mcgraw-hill.co.uk

British Library Cataloguing in Publication Data
A catalogue record for this book is available from the British Library

Library of Congress Cataloging in Publication Data
The Library of Congress data for this book has been applied for from the Library of Congress

Acquisitions Editor: Ruben Hale
Development Editor: Hannah Cooper
Marketing Manager: Mark Barratt
Head of Production: Beverley Shields

Text Design by Hard Lines
Cover design by Ego Creative
Printed and bound in Italy by Rotolito, Lombarda

Nigel Holt
For Katie, my lifeline, and for Vic and Wendy who have made absolutely everything possible

Andy Bremner
To Bea, Wad-wad, Gavin, Maggie & Miranda (in alphabetical order)

Ed Sutherland
To Siobhan, Samuel and Elayna (sorry for the moods and the late nights)
and also to Bruce and Janice

Michael Vliek
To Ina & Leo, for their love

Brief table of contents

Detailed table of contents

Preface

Mind and behaviour: It is difficult to think of anything more fascinating. But we didn't all recognize this when we began university. The original authors of the US edition of this textbook, Michael Passer and Ronald Smith were destined for lifetimes in physics and journalism when they embarked upon their studies. Nigel Holt entered university to study Economics, whereas Michael Vliek and Andy Bremner turned up at university having chosen Psychology but weren't really sure why. But each of us took an introductory psychology course, and suddenly our life-paths changed. Because of instructors who brought the subject to life, we were hooked, and that initial enthusiasm has never left us.

Now, through this textbook, we have the pleasure and privilege to share our enthusiasm with today's lecturers and students. The original US version of this text is an extremely strong text and one which we as the adapting authors felt privileged to take on. As is the case with the original version, we have endeavoured to put together a thoughtfully integrated book and multimedia package of uncompromising student friendliness and scientific integrity – a teaching tool that introduces students to psychology as a science while highlighting its relevance to their lives and to society. Indeed, the reason that we have embarked upon this adaptation of the original US text was to ensure that the material is especially relevant to those who will use this book. By focusing on examples and research geared towards a more international audience, we want to help students to experience, as we did, the intellectual excitement of studying the science of mind and behaviour. We also seek to help students sharpen their critical-thinking skills and dispel commonly held myths. All of this is done within the simple conceptual framework emphasized in the original US text; the structured explanation of relationships between biological, psychological, and environmental levels of analysis.

THIS ADAPTATION

The original version of this textbook was written by Michael Passer and Ronald Smith to be relevant to North American students, and to facilitate the type of courses which their instructors would convene. Many teachers outside the US saw the great strengths of Michael and Ronald's approach and have been using the American version of the text in their universities across Europe, South Africa and Australasia. However, teaching and learning is better facilitated by using examples and research which is more relevant to the students' and teachers' cultures. And so with this goal in mind, we have developed this adaptation to be more relevant to an international audience of students and teachers. A comparison of this text and the original US book will also show a very significant change in how the book has been laid out. The publisher proposed these changes to us following careful research into the existing books on the European and South African markets. Notable changes to bring this book more in line with psychology teaching in these parts of the world include the subdivision of the life-span development chapter into two chapters, the first on physical and cognitive development and the second focusing on social-emotional development. Additionally, the original chapter on biological approaches to psychology has been subdivided into one chapter on genetic and evolutionary research, and a second on the neural bases of psychology. Overall we feel that the open, clear layout of this book will provide readers with a pleasant, fresh and uncluttered reading experience. We have not replaced everything from the original book. After all, 'if it ain't broke, don't fix it'! However, we have updated references and used examples that European and South African readers would expect to see, better reflecting the academic environments in those countries. An adaptation like this is much more than altering the spelling and adding a few references; it is concerned with tailoring a successful textbook to the needs of a slightly different audience. This, the end-product of a 3 year project, will provide you the reader with focused access to relevant psychological thought and research at the beginning of your university career. We hope also that you will keep your copy of our book on your shelf for years to come. We often find ourselves reaching for the introductory text we used as undergraduate students as it forms a familiar, friendly reference from which to begin our research and writing.

We are particularly excited about the unique way in which this textbook is integrated with its supplements. This integration results in a learning package that 'uses science to teach science.' This approach draws on research (e.g., Hamilton, 1985; Moreland et al., 1997; Thiede & Anderson, 2003) showing that recall of textual material is significantly enhanced by asking students to summarize material they have just read and by presenting focus questions and learning objectives that serve as retrieval cues and help students identify important information. Marginal Focus Questions integrated into each chapter of this textbook serve these purposes and help students assess their mastery of the material. But well beyond that, these Focus Questions provide a comprehensive learning framework for the supplements.

What you will find throughout the supplements is a carefully developed integration of the in-text Focus Questions with Learning Objectives. Instructors and students alike will be guided by the Learning Objectives, as they form the cornerstone of the Instructor's Manual, Online Learning Centre, In-Psych interactive programme and Test Banks. Items in the Test Bank are keyed specifically to the Focus Questions and Learning Objectives.

Let's take a closer look at the features of our edition of this tried and tested textbook:

THE BIG PICTURE: A SIMPLE UNIFYING FRAMEWORK THAT EASILY ADAPTS TO THE INSTRUCTOR'S PREFERENCES

Psychology is a vibrant but sprawling discipline, and the tremendous diversity of issues covered in the introductory course can lead students to perceive psychology as a collection of unrelated topics. To reduce this tendency and also help students become more sophisticated in their everyday understanding of behaviour, we present a simple unifying framework that is applied throughout the book. This framework, called *Levels of Analysis* (LOA), emphasizes how psychologists examine *biological, psychological, and environmental factors* in their quest to understand behaviour. The LOA framework is easy for students to understand and remember; is consistently applied in every chapter; accurately portrays the focus of modern psychology; supports critical thinking; and also helps students understand how biological, psychological, and environmental factors are related to one another.

Although we carry the LOA framework throughout the book in textual discussion and schematics, we are careful to apply it selectively so that it does not become overly repetitious for students or confining for instructors. Indeed, one of the beauties of the LOA framework is that it stands on its own and thus instructors can easily adapt it to their personal teaching preferences.

For example, some adopters of the book have told us that they never bring up the LOA framework explicitly in class. Instead, they emphasize their own preferred theoretical perspective in lectures while resting assured that, behind the scenes, each textbook chapter illustrates for students how behaviour can be studied from multiple angles, that is, from different levels of analysis. Other instructors consistently incorporate a levels-of-analysis approach into their lectures. Finally, as we do in our own courses, instructors can explicitly bring the LOA framework into their lectures only for selected topics, once again knowing that for other topics the textbook will round out their students' conceptual exposure.

READABILITY, RIGOUR, AND RELEVANCE

A textbook has long-term educational value only if students read it, understand its content, and find that content to be worthwhile. We have worked diligently to develop a narrative that will excite students and draw them into the fascinating world of mind and behaviour. We have made every attempt to use clear prose, careful explanations, engaging and relevant examples, and supporting artwork to make the book and multimedia accessible to our students. The students at our own institutions form a fairly representative cross-section of those who may use the book. And so, as we wrote with our own students in mind, we hope that this will mean that those who read it will find the approach helpful. More broadly, we hope to portray psychology as the rigorous and keenly relevant discipline that it is. The following elements support these goals.

- **Focus on Scientific Psychology:** Throughout the narrative we portray *psychology as a contemporary science* without becoming excessively formal or terminological. And because we live in an era in which students (along with everyone else) are bombarded with scientific information and misinformation, we focus not only on principles derived from research, but also on how good research is done.

- **Focus on Personal and Societal Applications:** Everyday examples are used throughout the narrative not only to illustrate psychological principles and concepts, but also to engage students and personalize their learning experience. We also highlight numerous ways in which psychological knowledge has been used to enhance the welfare of society.

- **Focus on Relations between Basic Science and Application:** Whether in the context of their personal lives or of larger societal issues, we emphasize that many questions studied from a basic science perspective are inspired by real-world questions and issues, and that basic research findings often guide solutions to individual and societal problems.

- **Focus on Helping Students to Think Critically and Dispel Misconceptions:** In diverse ways, we strongly emphasize critical thinking as a skill for students to learn and practise. In the general narrative throughout the text, we repeatedly address basic critical-thinking issues, such as the importance of identifying alternative explanations and recognizing that correlation does not establish causation. We emphasize that many faulty inferences – in everyday life as well as in science – are made by failing to pay attention to basic critical-thinking principles.

- **Integrated and Featured Coverage of Cultural and Gender Issues:** Cultural and gender issues are at the forefront of contemporary psychology, and rather than isolating this material within dedicated chapters, we integrate it throughout the text. Our levels-of-analysis approach conceptualizes culture as an environmental factor and also as a psychological factor that reflects the internalization of cultural influences. In addition to coverage of cultural and gender issues throughout the narrative, these topics are addressed via features such as the *Research Close-Ups* and *What Do You Think?* exercises. Notable in this regard are sections in Chapter 10 (Intelligence) on sex differences in cognitive abilities and the effects of stereotypes on math performance, in Chapter 16 (Health Psychology: Adjusting to Life) on possible reasons why women live longer than men, and in Chapter 18 (Treatment of Psychological Disorders) on cultural and gender issues in psychotherapy.

- **New Artwork:** Many of the images and figures in this new adaptation have been changed to make them more relevant to the proposed audience.

- **Updated coverage:** This edition is rich in discussions of research and new references – hundreds of the book's citations are from the years 2000 to 2008, and a good deal of the cited research reflects the research interests of the countries in which the focus audience work and study.

Guided tour

Focus arrows

These appear in the margins of the book adjacent to important material. They are designed to function as study guides, retrieval cues, and self-tests.

Focus 2.3
Explain the major drawback of hindsight understanding. What approach to understanding do scientists prefer? Why?

Focus 2.4
Describe some characteristics of a good theory.

Key terms and concepts

These are highlighted and defined in the margins, with a summary at the end of each chapter so that they can be found quickly and easily. An ideal tool for last minute revision or to check definitions as your read.

pheromones
chemical signals found in natural body scents

menstrual synchrony
the tendency of women who live together or are close friends to become more similar in their menstrual cycles

Figures and tables

Each chapter provides a number of figures, illustrations and photos to help you to visualize key psychological theories and studies.

Sensation and Perception Chapter Five 173

FIGURE 5.5
Demonstrating visual adaptation.
(a) To create a stabilised retinal image, a person wears a contact lens with a tiny projector attached. Despite tiny eye movements, images are cast on the same region of the retina. (b) Under these conditions, the stabilized image is clear at first and then begins to fade and reappear in meaningful segments as the receptors fatigue and recover.
SOURCE: adapted from Pritchard, 1961.

What do you think? and Beneath the surface boxes

These exercises challenge you to think critically in evaluating popular truisms, scientific and pseudoscientific claims, and psychology's relevance to your own life.

WHAT DO YOU THINK?

TWO MINDS IN ONE BRAIN? (p. 155)

Let us consider the second question first. How is it that the s life? Would not two independent minds get in the way of on brain patients could function adequately because they had le hemispheres. For example, they could scan the visual enviro visual fields got into both hemispheres. Where personal ide seemed to connect present and future with the past in a man emerging and tripping over one another. Some 'psychologis self resides in the left hemisphere, because consciousness an and present (Ornstein, 1997). The exotic 'split-mind' phenot because patients with a rare biological feature were tested u specifically designed to isolate the functions of the two hem research were so dramatic that they led some people (and ev brain functions as being highly localized and restricted to or about education programmes directed at developing the 'un there is some degree of localization of brain functions, but a normal brain, most functions involve many areas (and both brain is an exquisitely integrated system, not a collection of

In review boxes

These boxes provide quick recaps of material presented throughout the chapter, to consolidate your understanding as you work through the book.

IN REVIEW

- The brain is divided structurally into the hindbrain, the midbrain and the forebrain. This organization reflects the evolution of increasingly more complex brain structures related to behavioural capabilities.
- Major structures within the hindbrain include the medulla, which monitors and controls vital body functions; the pons, which contains important groups of sensory and motor neurons; and the cerebellum, which is concerned with motor co-ordination.
- The reticular formation, located in the midbrain, plays a vital role in consciousness, attention and sleep. Activity of the ascending reticular formation excites higher areas of the brain and prepares them to respond to stimulation. The descending reticular formation acts as a gate, determining which stimuli enter into consciousness.
- The forebrain consists of two cerebral hemispheres and a number of subcortical structures. The cerebral hemispheres are connected by the cornus

Research close-up boxes

In each chapter, this feature uses a scientific-journal format to provide an inside look at a research study and engage students in a process of critical thinking about the research question.

RESEARCH CLOSE-UP

INSIDE THE BRAIN OF A KILLER

SOURCE: J. Stoddard, A. Raine, S. Bihrle and M. Buchsbau lacking psychosocial deficits. In A. Raine, P.A. Brennan, *Biosocial bases of violence*. New York: Plenum.

INTRODUCTION

What stops us from impulsively killing an irritating neighbou coat we would like to own? The answer may lie, at least in pa a civilized person – self-control, judgement, foresight, reason executive functions of your prefrontal cortex. As seen in the the brain can reduce those civilizing inhibitions.
    Until recently, researchers could only infer that impulsively had reduced prefrontal activity, for they could not look direct That changed with the development of brain-imaging proced Jacqueline Stoddard and her co-workers applied PET technol people who had committed savage acts of violence. They also environmental factors in this violence-prone population.

METHOD

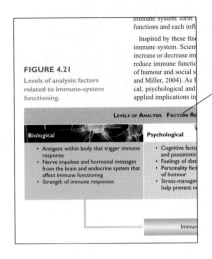

Levels of analysis

The book's basic LOA framework emphasizes how psychologists carefully study behaviour from diverse angles, reinforces the core concept that behaviour typically has multiple causes, and encourages you to be wary of overly simplistic explanations.

Applying psychological science boxes

In each chapter, this feature brings a key concept into the realm of personal or social real-life application.

In-Psych icon

Look out for the In-Psych icon throughout the text to refer you to view online video clips that demonstrate the themes and research presented in the chapter.

Technology to enhance learning and teaching

Online Learning Centre (OLC)

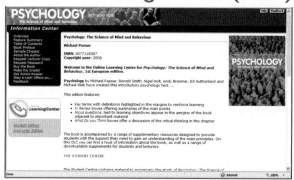

After completing each chapter, log on to the supporting Online Learning Centre website. Take advantage of the study tools offered to reinforce the material you have read in the text, and to develop your knowledge of psychology in a fun and effective way.

Resources for students include:
- *Glossary (including local language versions)*
- *Weblinks*
- *Self-test multiple choice, true/false and essay questions*
- *Link to Silvius*
- *In-Psych interactive tool, with video clips linked to chapter topics*

Also available for lecturers:
- *Instructor's Manual*
- *PowerPoint presentations*
- *Image library*
- *BPS course matching guidelines*
- *PrepCenter*

Test Bank available in McGraw-Hill EZ Test Online

A test bank of over 1800 questions is available to lecturers adopting this book for their module. A range of questions is provided for each chapter including multiple choice, true or false, and short answer or essay questions. The questions are identified by type, difficulty and topic to help you to select questions that best suit your needs and are accessible through an easy-to-use online testing tool, **McGraw-Hill EZ Test Online**.

McGraw-Hill EZ Test Online is accessible to busy academics virtually anywhere – in their office, at home or while travelling – and eliminates the need for software installation. Lecturers can chose from question banks associated with their adopted textbook or easily create their own questions. They also have access to hundreds of banks and thousands of questions created for other McGraw-Hill titles. Multiple versions of tests can be saved for delivery on paper or online through WebCT, Blackboard and other course management systems. When created and delivered though EZ Test Online, students' tests can be immediately marked, saving lecturers time and providing prompt results to students.

To register for this FREE resource, visit www.eztestonline.com

Custom Publishing Solutions:
Let us help make our **content** your **solution**

At McGraw-Hill Education our aim is to help lecturers to find the most suitable content for their needs delivered to their students in the most appropriate way. Our **custom publishing solutions** offer the ideal combination of content delivered in the way which best suits lecturer and students.

Our custom publishing programme offers lecturers the opportunity to select just the chapters or sections of material they wish to deliver to their students from a database called Primis at www. primisonline.com

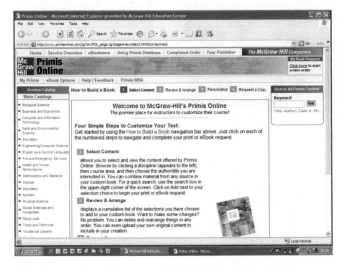

Primis contains over two million pages of content from:
- textbooks
- professional books
- case books – Harvard Articles, Insead, Ivey, Darden, Thunderbird and BusinessWeek
- Taking Sides – debate materials

Across the following imprints:
- McGraw-Hill Education
- Open University Press
- Harvard Business School Press
- US and European material

There is also the option to include additional material authored by lecturers in the custom product – this does not necessarily have to be in English.

We will take care of everything from start to finish in the process of developing and delivering a custom product to ensure that lecturers and students receive exactly the material needed in the most suitable way.

With a Custom Publishing Solution, students enjoy the best selection of material deemed to be the most suitable for learning everything they need for their courses – something of real value to support their learning. Teachers are able to use exactly the material they want, in the way they want, to support their teaching on the course.

Please contact your local McGraw-Hill representative with any questions or alternatively contact Warren Eels **e-mail:** warren_eels@mcgraw-hill.com.

Make the grade!

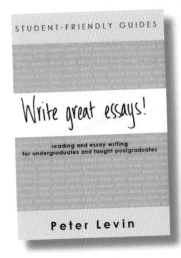  

Acknowledgements

Our thanks go to the following reviewers for their comments at various stages in the text's development:

Proposal reviewers
Trevor Archer, University of Gothenburg
Fredrik Bjorklund, Lund University
Mark Blades, University of Sheffield
Mieke Donk, Vrije University, Amsterdam
Catrin Finkenauer, Vrije University, Amsterdam
Kirston Greenop, Witwatersrand University
Kathy Grieve, UNISA
Phil Higham, University of Southampton
Mary Ivers, University College, Dublin
Matt Jarvis, University of Southampton
Gert Kruger, University of Johannesburg
Brendan McGonigle, University of Edinburgh
Liz Milne, University of Sheffield
Padraic Monaghan, University of York
Aidan Moran, University College, Dublin
Catriona Morrison, University of Leeds
Karen Mortier, Vrije University, Amsterdam
Anna O'Reilly-Trace, University College, Cork
Peter Starreveld, Vrije University, Amsterdam
Frode Svartdal, Tromso University
Arie van der Lugt, Maastricht University
Frank van Overwalle, Vrije Universiteit Brussels

Manuscript reviewers
Chris Armitage, University of Sheffield
Stella Bain, Glasgow Caledonian
Paul Bennett, University of Cardiff
Paul Bishop, University of Glasgow
Herbert Bless, University of Mannheim
Jonathan Cole, University of Liverpool
Peter de Vries, Twente University
John de Wit, Utrecht University
Derek Dorris, University College, Cork
Patrick Green, Heriot Watt University
Steve Kilpatrick, University of Northampton
Jurek Kirakowski, University College, Cork
Bonaventura Majolo, University of Lincoln
Andrea Mechelli, King's College, London
Christine Mohn, University of Oslo
Alice Sawyerr, Royal Holloway, University of London
Adrian Scott, University of Bath
David Shanks, UCL
Ian Stewart, University of Galway
Clifford Stott, University of Liverpool
Dick Terry, University of Stirling
Ian Walker, University of Bath

Thomas Webb, University of Sheffield
Barbara Zwirs, Erasmus University, Rotterdam

We would also like to thank the following people for their contribution to the online resources:

Philip Beaman, University of Reading
Viv Brunsden, Nottingham Trent University
Marie Cahillane
Sandie Taylor, Bath Spa University
Ian Walker, University of Bath
Lance Workman, Bath Spa University

Author's acknowledgements

We would like to thank the following people for their guidance at various stages in writing this adaptation. Lance Workman provided many hours of stimulating discussion on evolutionary psychology and his direction in that area has been invaluable. Paul Dockree, at Trinity College, Dublin gave his neuroscience expertise freely, and we are very grateful to him. Dr David Wilde of the Law Department in Reading provided advice on how best to describe the relationship psychology has with the legal system.

Countless other researchers and academics have given their time freely and have been at the end of a telephone when information and clarification was needed at short notice, and we would like to thank them for their help. These include the academics of the Department of Psychology at Goldsmiths, academics at the University of Amsterdam, academics at the Surrey Sleep Research Centre, academics at the University of Leeds, Peter Bailey at York, Anna Weighall at Sheffield, Philip Beaman at Reading, Ian Walker at Bath and Ken Manktelow at Wolverhampton.

We would like to thank the following for permission to reprint images:

Alamy Images
Corbis
Science Photo Library
Hux Records
Football.co.uk
www.cartoonstock.com
Bonnie Waitzkin
UCL Institute of Cognitive Neuroscience
University of Groningen Donald Smits Center for Information Technology
USGS National Wetlands Research Center
University of Heidelberg
Florida Atlantic University College of Education
UK Department for Transport Think! Campaign

Every effort has been made to trace and acknowledge ownership of copyright and to clear permission for material reproduced in this book. The publishers will be pleased to make suitable arrangements to clear permission with any copyright holders whom it has not been possible to contact.

Cover image © Antony Gormley
Reprinted with kind permission of the Artist, White Cube Gallery and The Arts Council Collection

You may recognise the cover image as part of the Field collection by British artist, Antony Gormley. This was chosen as we wanted an image that would encapsulate both the individual and group nature of the topics in the text and reflect the distinguished academic reputation of the book, but with a fun element to demonstrate its accessibility. Another factor in our decision was the desire to have a cover that is instantly recognisable as belonging to Passer et al. – so whether you love it, loathe it, or are simply intrigued by it, we hope you will discover that the material behind those little people staring down from your bookshelf will help get you through your psychology course!

About the authors

NIGEL J. HOLT, D.Phil.

Nigel Holt is a senior lecturer in psychology at Bath Spa University in Somerset, UK. Bath Spa University is one of Britain's youngest Universities, gaining full University status in 2005. It is a 'teaching led' university meaning that it aims to provide courses of the highest quality, whose content and delivery are informed by teaching excellence and focused scholarship. Dr Holt's first degree from the University of Reading was followed by a D.Phil. from the University of York where he investigated the perceptual lateralization of audio-visual stimuli. A brief spell in industry provided him with clear evidence that teaching and research in a university environment were the place for him. His current post followed a post-doc in speech perception. His University roles include convening and leading a compulsory module at level 1. He also has the opportunity to teach a level 2 course on cognitive psychology, and a final year option which he calls Hearing, Speech and Language, where he has the chance to indulge his interests in the auditory system. Outside University, he examines at a senior level for a major exam board, is an external university examiner, and is a commissioning editor for a popular psychology magazine in between writing other books. He does his best to find time to research speech perception and how sound and other areas of cognition interact.

ANDREW J. BREMNER, D.Phil.

Andy completed his first degree in Experimental Psychology at the University of Oxford and then decided to stay and submit a D.Phil. (three years later) on 'Object representation in infancy and early childhood' under the supervision of Professor Peter Bryant. Following two post-doctoral appointments in London and Brussels in which he undertook further research into cognitive development in early life, Andy took up the position of lecturer in psychology at Goldsmiths, University of London, where he has now been for three years. Andy conducts research into a variety of questions surrounding perceptual and cognitive development and cognitive neuroscience. Particular research interests include object recognition in infancy, the development of memory and cognitive control in the early preschool years, the development of spatial representations of the body and the environment in infancy and childhood, and the development of multisensory perceptual processes. He also gets out to the pub in the evening as much as he can.

MICHAEL L. W. VLIEK, Ph.D.

Michael is a lecturer at the University of Amsterdam. After finishing his Masters at the University of Amsterdam, he decided to stay at the University of Amsterdam to work on his Ph.D. thesis on the subject of social comparison processes, followed by a position as lecturer at the same university (where he has now been for over ten years). Michael has also been a visiting scholar at the University of Sussex, England. His main research interests include social comparison and the dynamics of self-evaluation, intra-group processes and the influence of time in motivational processes.

ED SUTHERLAND

Ed completed his first degree at the University of Bangor and his Ph.D. at the University of Wolverhampton under the supervision of Prof. Ken Manktelow. He then filled the next few years with a research post at the University of Reading and his first lectureship at the University of Derby. He is currently lecturer in cognitive psychology at the University of Leeds where he has been for nearly ten years. His current research interests are on the role of emotion in reasoning and on affective computing. When not working he spends his time with his family and on the river bank.

CHAPTER ONE

THE SCIENCE OF PSYCHOLOGY

CHAPTER OUTLINE

Perhaps the most fascinating and mysterious universe of all is the one within us.

CARL SAGAN

In the early 1920s a group of intrepid explorers, headed by Howard Carter, set off to Egypt to seek fame, fortune and the final resting place of one of history's most enigmatic kings. The expedition was funded by Lord Carnarvon and they were to discover the site of King Tutankhamun's tomb in the Valley of the Kings, near Luxor, opening it together on 17 February 1923. This was the beginning of a strange story of myth and legend, centring on a curse discovered in the tomb that those to disturb the resting place would suffer a swift death. Carnarvon died in the spring of 1923, bitten by a mosquito, and as he did so the lights of Cairo are said to have inexplicably gone out. The press exploded with stories of mysterious deaths of people, and animals, related to the expedition. Howard Carter's pet canary was allegedly bitten by a snake and died, and Carnarvon's dog is said to have dropped dead at 2 a.m., on the morning following his master's death. George Benedite of the Louvre in Paris and Arthur C. Mace from the Metropolitan Museum of Art in New York died shortly after exhibiting the contents of the tomb at their museums, and Howard Carter's secretary also died, as did his secretary's father. All these were blamed on the now legendary curse of the mummy's tomb.

...

Waiting in a queue for their tickets at the theatre, Jonathan put his arms around Marie and kissed her cheek. 'Do you remember that party where we met last year?' he asked. 'You caught my eye the moment you walked into the room.' 'Of course I remember!' Marie laughed. 'You were so shy that your friends had to drag you over to talk to me! You're lucky I'm so outgoing.' Jonathan knew he was shy, especially around women, but he was not sure why. He had been too nervous to enjoy the few dates he had been on while in school. During his first year at university he met a few women he really liked but was too afraid to ask them out. He did not make many male friends either, and by winter he was becoming very lonely. He became a little depressed, he could not sleep well and his work suffered. During his Easter holiday at home with his family, Jonathan decided that enough was enough, and determined to turn things around. He worked hard when he returned to university and did well on his coursework and examinations. He also made friends with people in his halls of residence. His mood improved, and towards the end of the year he met Marie who was herself attracted to Jonathan. Sensing both his shyness and his interest, Marie took the initiative and asked Jonathan out. Jonathan has now been going out with Marie for a year and is doing well at university. He is happy and self-confident, and has even talked to Marie about getting married after they complete their degrees.

THE NATURE OF PSYCHOLOGY

Why are some individuals shy and others outgoing? What causes people, such as Marie and Jonathan, to become attracted to one another and fall in love? Can we predict which relationships will last? Why is it that we remember a first date from long ago yet forget information during a test that we studied for only hours before? Where in the brain are memories stored? Why did Jonathan become depressed? Was it his lack of a social life, or was something else going on? And in the case of Tutankhamun's 'curse', is it possible that a psychological factor – a culturally based belief in something akin to 'voodoo' – could have affected biological functioning and actually brought about the demise of the adventurers and their colleagues? We will return to the mystery of 'voodoo' later in the chapter.

Welcome to psychology, the discipline that studies all of these questions and countless more. We can define **psychology** as the scientific study of behaviour and the mind. The term *behaviour* refers to actions and responses that we can directly observe, whereas the term *mind* refers to internal states and processes – such as thoughts and feelings – that cannot be seen directly and that must be inferred from observable, measurable responses. For example, we cannot directly see Jonathan's feeling of loneliness. Instead, we must infer how Jonathan feels based on his verbal statement that he is lonely.

Because behaviour is so complex, its scientific study poses special challenges. As you become familiar with the kinds of evidence necessary to validate scientific conclusions, you will become a better informed consumer of the many claims made in the name of psychology. The study of behaviour takes many forms, and psychology, like other disciplines, follows trends and fashions, with different schools in different countries and regions favouring and championing different approaches at different times in history. For instance, the biological basis of behaviours and the study of neuropsychology are driving research and explanations of behaviour in this, the beginning of the twenty-first century, whereas the psychodynamic school of Sigmund Freud and his followers still has its champions, but does not currently form the focus of much research in psychology. This course will teach you that many widely held beliefs about behaviour are inaccurate. Can you distinguish the valid claims from the invalid ones in Table 1.1?

Perhaps even more important than the concepts you learn in this course will be the habits of thought that you acquire – habits that involve *critical thinking*. Critical thinking involves taking an active role in understanding the world around you, rather than merely receiving information. It is important to reflect on what that information means, how it fits in with your experiences, and its implications for your life and society. Critical thinking also means evaluating the validity of something presented to you as fact. For example, when someone tells you a new 'fact', ask yourself the following questions:

What exactly are you asking me to believe?

How do you know? What is the evidence?

Are there other possible explanations?

What is the most reasonable conclusion?

We hope that after completing this course you will be more cautious about accepting psychological claims and less likely to form simplistic judgements about why people behave and think as they do. These critical-thinking skills will serve you well in many areas of your life.

In this book we hope to share with you our enthusiasm for psychology. As you will see, psychology relates to virtually every aspect of your life. Psychological research provides us with a greater understanding of ourselves and with powerful tools to improve our lives and to promote human welfare.

Focus 1.1

What is psychology's focus? In science and daily life, what does critical thinking involve, and why is it important? (These focus questions will help you identify key concepts as you read, study, and review; they also tie in with the 'Learning Objectives' in the Online Learning Centre and other supplements.)

psychology
the scientific study of behaviour and the mind

TABLE 1.1 WIDELY HELD BELIEFS ABOUT BEHAVIOUR: FACT OR FICTION?

Directions	Decide whether each statement is true or false
1.	Most people with exceptionally high IQs are well adjusted in other areas of their life
2.	In romantic relationships, opposites usually attract
3.	Overall, married adults are happier than adults who are not married
4.	In general, we only use about 10 per cent of our brain
5.	A person who is innocent of a crime has nothing to fear from a lie detector test
6.	People who commit suicide usually have signalled to others their intention to do so
7.	If you feel that your initial answer on a multiple-choice test is wrong, leave it alone; students usually lose points by changing answers
8.	On some types of mental tasks, people perform better when they are 70 years old than when they are 20 years old
9.	Usually, it is safe to awaken someone who is sleepwalking
10.	A schizophrenic is a person who has two or more distinct personalities, hence the term *split personality*

Answers: Items 1, 3, 6, 8 and 9 are supported by psychological research. The remaining items are false. (If you correctly answered 9 or 10 of these items, you have done significantly better than random guessing.)

basic research
reflects the quest for knowledge purely for its own sake

applied research
designed to solve specific, practical problems

Focus 1.2
How do basic and applied research differ? Explain how knowledge from basic research helps solve practical problems.

PSYCHOLOGY AS A BASIC AND APPLIED SCIENCE

The global nature of psychology means that it draws on, and extends material from a wide variety of sources. The discipline can certainly be considered as a science. Science involves two types of research: **basic research**, which reflects the quest for knowledge purely for its own sake, and **applied research**, which is designed to solve specific, practical problems. For psychologists, most basic research examines how and why people behave, think and feel the way they do. Basic research may be carried out in laboratories or real-world settings, with human participants or other species. Psychologists who study other species usually attempt to discover principles that ultimately will shed light on human behaviour, but some study animal behaviour for its own sake. In applied research, psychologists often use basic scientific knowledge to design, implement and assess intervention programmes. Consider the following example.

Robber's Cave and the Jigsaw Classroom

How does hostility and prejudice develop between groups, and what can be done to reduce it? In today's multicultural world, where religious and ethnic groups often clash, this question has great importance.

To provide an answer, psychologists conduct basic research on factors that increase and reduce intergroup hostility. In one experiment, researchers divided 11-year-old boys into two groups when the boys arrived at a summer camp in Robber's Cave, Oklahoma (Sherif et al., 1961). The groups, named the 'Eagles' and 'Rattlers', lived in separate cabins but did all other activities together. Initially, they got along well.

To test the hypothesis that competition would breed intergroup hostility, the researchers began to pit the Eagles and Rattlers against one another in athletic and other contests. As predicted, hostility soon developed between the groups. Next the researchers examined whether conflict could be reduced by having the two groups share enjoyable activities, such as watching movies together. Surprisingly, these activities only bred more taunting and fighting. The researchers then created several small emergencies to test a final hypothesis – that placing hostile groups in situations requiring co-operation to attain important, common goals would reduce intergroup conflict. In one 'emergency', a heavy lorry bringing food to the hungry boys supposedly stalled, forcing the Eagles and Rattlers to pool their strength and tow it with a rope to get it started. This and other co-operative experiences gradually reduced hostility between the groups, and many new friendships developed.

The Robber's Cave study, which has since become a classic (that is, an older but widely known and influential study), represents basic research because its goal was to discover general principles of intergroup conflict, not to solve some pre-existing problem. Prejudice between the Eagles and Rattlers did not exist from the outset; rather, the researchers created it. They showed that hostility could be bred by competition and reduced by making hostile groups dependent on one another to reach a common goal. But could this principle, derived from basic research, also be applied to real-life situations?

Focus 1.3
Identify the major goals of psychology.

Years later psychologist Elliot Aronson and his co-workers (1978) developed and evaluated a classroom procedure called the 'jigsaw program'. The motivation for this programme was the desegregation of schools in the area. Ethnic groups were mixed in the classroom for the first time. This programme, which is now widely used to foster co-operation among children, involves creating multi-ethnic groups of five or six children who are assigned to prepare for an upcoming test on, for example, the life of Abraham Lincoln. Within the groups, each child is given a piece of the total knowledge to be learned. One child has information about Lincoln's childhood, another about his political career, and so on. To pass the test, group members must fit their knowledge pieces together as if working on a jigsaw puzzle. Each child must teach the others his or her piece of knowledge. Like the children at Robber's Cave, students learn that to succeed they must work together (Fig. 1.1).

The jigsaw technique and other *co-operative learning programmes* have been evaluated in hundreds of classrooms, with encouraging results (Johnson, 2000). Children's liking for one another generally increases, prejudice decreases, and self-esteem and school achievement improve. Co-operative learning programmes show how basic research, such as the Robber's Cave experiment, provide a foundation for designing intervention programmes. We will see many other examples of how basic research provides knowledge that not only satisfies our desire to understand our world, but also can be applied to solve practical problems.

FIGURE 1.1

The jigsaw classroom, designed by psychologist Elliot Aronson, was inspired by basic research that showed how mutual dependence and co-operation among hostile groups can reduce intergroup hostility. Aronson's applied research had similar positive effects within racially integrated classrooms.

THE GOALS OF PSYCHOLOGY

As a science, psychology has five central goals:

1. To *describe* how people and other species behave
2. To *understand* the causes of these behaviours
3. To *predict* how people and animals will behave under certain conditions
4. To *influence* behaviour through the control of its causes
5. To *apply* psychological knowledge in ways that enhance human welfare

In the Robber's Cave study, the researchers carefully observed the boys' behaviour under various conditions (description). They believed that competition would cause intergroup hostility and that co-operation could reduce it (tentative understanding). To test whether their understanding was correct, they predicted that competition would create hostility between the Eagles and Rattlers and that co-operation would reduce this conflict (prediction). Next they controlled the camp setting, first by pitting the Eagles and Rattlers against one another in contests, and then by arranging situations that forced the groups to co-operate (influence). As predicted, competition produced hostility and co-operation reduced it, suggesting that the researchers' understanding was correct. Later, when Aronson and his co-workers sought to reduce racial hostility within newly integrated schools, they had a scientific basis for predicting what might work. They were able to apply their knowledge successfully in the form of the jigsaw programme (application).

PSYCHOLOGY'S BROAD SCOPE: A LEVELS-OF-ANALYSIS FRAMEWORK

The scope of modern psychology stretches from the borders of medicine and the biological sciences to those of the social sciences (Fig. 1.2). Because we are biological creatures living in a complex social world, psychologists study an amazing array of factors to understand why people behave, think and feel as they do, including neuropsychological and biopsychological explanations. At times, this diversity of factors may seem a bit overwhelming, but we would like to provide you with a framework that will greatly simplify matters. We call it *levels of analysis*: behaviour and its causes can be examined at the *biological level* (e.g., brain processes, genetic influences), the *psychological level* (e.g., our thoughts, feelings and motives) and the *environmental level* (e.g., past and current physical and social environments to which we are exposed).

Here are two brief examples of how the levels-of-analysis framework can be applied. First, consider a behaviour that you engage in every day: eating (Fig. 1.3). At the biological level of analysis we may turn to neuroscience to help us address the various chemicals, neural circuits and structures in your brain that respond to bodily signals and help regulate whether you feel hungry or full. At the psycho-

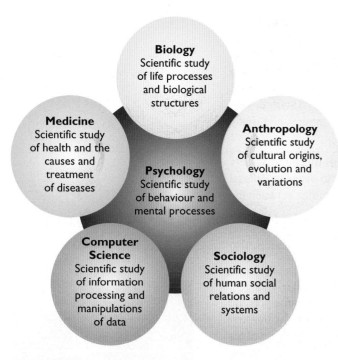

FIGURE 1.2

Psychology as a scientific hub.

Psychology links with and overlaps many sciences.

FIGURE 1.3

(*Left*) **Biological level.**

As we (or rats) eat, hunger decreases as certain brain regions regulate the sensation of becoming full. Those regions in this rat's brain have been damaged, causing it to over-eat and become obese.

(*Centre*) **Psychological level.**

At times we may eat out of habit, stress or boredom.

(*Right*) **Environmental level.**

Grubs are eaten by traditional populations worldwide. Cultural norms influence food preferences.

logical level of analysis, your moods, food preferences and motives affect eating. Do you ever eat when you are not hungry, perhaps because you feel stressed or bored? The environmental level of analysis calls attention to specific stimuli (such as the appearance or aroma of different food) that may trigger eating and to cultural customs that influence our food preferences. Does the aroma of fresh bread ever make your stomach growl? How about the sight of duck feet or a mound of fish gills on a plate? To most westerners, duck feet and fish gills may not be appetizing, to Chinese consumers, they may be regarded rather differently.

Now let us apply the levels-of-analysis framework to a rare and seemingly mysterious event, 'voodoo' death, or perhaps the curse of Tutankhamun. How can we explain something like this without invoking supernatural powers?

Whereas the curse of Tutankhamun is a special case, voodoo-like practices are common in several regions of the world. Decades ago, physiologist Walter Cannon (1942) suggested a possible mechanism for death by 'magic curses'. Cannon drew on his own research on severe stress responses in animals, as well as eyewitness reports by cultural anthropologists of deaths by magic curses. One such account described the practice of 'boning', the placing of a death curse by pointing a sacred bone at the victim:

> The man who discovers that he is being boned by any enemy is, indeed, a pitiable sight.... His cheeks blanch and his eyes become glassy.... His body begins to tremble and the muscles twitch involuntarily ... soon after he writhes as if in mortal agony. Unless help is forthcoming in the shape of a countercharm administered by the ... medicine-man, his death is only a matter of a comparatively short time. (Basedow, 1925, pp. 178–9)

Cannon noted that in cases of death by magic curses, the victim firmly believed that he or she was doomed. For the victim, this belief represents the psychological level of analysis. At the environmental level, this belief was supported by the victim's family, friends, enemies and culture. At the biological level of analysis, Cannon speculated that the victim's beliefs triggered a profound and persistent stress response – a flood of stress hormones (chemicals released by glands in the body) – sending the victim into physiological shock. Cannon's research had shown that one aspect of such shock is a rapid and often fatal drop in blood pressure as stress hormones allow fluid to leak out of veins and capillaries. He noted that normal autopsy procedures would not detect this mechanism of death, making it appear, as in the case of the young woman, that there was no natural cause.

Mind–Body and Nature–Nurture Interactions

Cannon's hypothesis is a plausible alternative to supernatural explanations and is consistent with research showing that negative thoughts about a stressful situation can quickly trigger the secretion of stress hormones (Borod, 2000). This work illustrates what traditionally have been called *mind–body interactions* – the relations between mental processes in the brain and the functioning of other bodily systems. Mind–body interactions focus our attention on the fascinating interplay between the psychological and biological levels of analysis. This topic has a long history within psychology and, as you will see throughout the textbook, it remains one of psychology's most exciting frontiers.

The levels-of-analysis framework also addresses an issue that has been debated since antiquity: is our behaviour primarily shaped by nature (our biological endowment) or by nurture (our environment and learning history)? The pendulum has swung towards one end or the other at different times in history, but today growing interest in cultural influences and advances in genetics and brain research keep the nature–nurture pendulum in a more balanced position.

Perhaps most important, modern research increasingly reveals that nature and nurture interact (Jaffee et al., 2003). Just as our biological capacities affect how we behave and experience the world, our experiences influence our biological capacities. For humans and rats alike, continually depriving a newborn of physical contact, or providing a newborn with an enriched environment in which to grow, can influence its brain functioning and biological development (Rosenzweig, 1984). Thus, while it may be tempting to take sides, 'nature or nurture?' usually is the wrong question. As the levels-of-analysis framework implies, nature, nurture and psychological factors must all be taken into account to gain the fullest understanding of behaviour.

Later in the chapter we provide a more detailed example of how looking at behaviour from multiple levels enhances our understanding. For now, in concluding our discussion of psychology's scope, we would like you to think critically about Cannon's mind–body explanation for voodoo death.

WHAT DO YOU THINK?

DEATH BY CURSE

Why might a 'cursed' person die? Do you believe that this hypothesis is reasonable? Can you think of other explanations for death other than the curse? (Think about it, then see page 35.)

IN REVIEW

- Psychology is the scientific study of behaviour and the mind. The term *behaviour* refers to actions and responses that can be observed and measured directly. In contrast, mental processes such as thoughts and feelings must be inferred from directly observable responses.

- Basic research reflects the quest for knowledge for its own sake. Applied research focuses on solving practical problems.

- The primary goals of psychological science are to describe, understand predict and influence behaviour, and to apply psychological knowledge to enhance human welfare.

- To understand more fully why people act, think and feel as they do, psychologists examine behaviour at the biological, the psychological and the environmental levels of analysis.

PERSPECTIVES ON BEHAVIOUR

The fact that psychologists study biological, psychological and environmental factors that influence behaviour is not new; it has been an integral part of psychology's history. But just how did psychology's scope become so broad? In part, it happened because psychology has roots in such varied disciplines as philosophy, medicine, and the biological and physical sciences. As a result, different ways of viewing people, called *perspectives*, became part of psychology's intellectual traditions (Fig. 1.4).

If you have ever met someone who views the world differently from the way you do, you know that perspectives matter. Perspectives serve as lenses through which psychologists examine and interpret behaviour. In science, new perspectives are an engine of progress. Advances occur as existing beliefs are challenged, a debate ensues, and scientists seek new evidence to resolve the debate. Sometimes, the best-supported elements of contrasting perspectives are merged into a new framework, which in turn will be challenged by still newer viewpoints.

Psychology's major perspectives guide us through its intellectual traditions and address timeless questions about human nature. To better understand how these perspectives evolved, let us briefly examine psychology's roots.

PSYCHOLOGY'S INTELLECTUAL ROOTS

Humans have long sought to understand themselves, and at the centre of this quest lies an issue that has tested the best minds of the ages, the so-called *mind–body problem*. Is the mind – the inner agent of consciousness and thought – a spiritual entity separate from the body, or is it a part of the body's activities?

FIGURE 1.4

Youth and beauty? Or maturity and wisdom?

What we perceive depends on our perspective. If you examine this drawing, you will see either a young woman or an old one. Now try changing your perspective. The ear and necklace of the young woman are the left eye and mouth of the old woman.

Many early philosophers held a position of **mind–body dualism**, the belief that the mind is a spiritual entity not subject to physical laws that govern the body. But if the mind is not composed of physical matter, how could it become aware of bodily sensations, and how could its thoughts exert control over bodily functions? French philosopher, mathematician and scientist René Descartes (1596–1650) proposed that the mind and body interact through the tiny pineal gland in the brain. Although Descartes placed the mind within the brain, he maintained that the mind was a spiritual, non-material entity. Dualism implies that no amount of research on the physical body (including the brain) could ever hope to unravel the mysteries of the nonphysical mind.

An alternative view, **monism** (from the Greek word *monos*, meaning 'one'), holds that mind and body are one and that the mind is not a separate spiritual entity. To monists, mental events are simply a product of physical events in the brain, a position advocated by English philosopher Thomas Hobbes (1588–1679). Monism helped set the stage for psychology because it implied that the mind could be studied by measuring physical processes within the brain. The stage was further set by John Locke (1632–1704) and other philosophers from the school of **empiricism**, which held that all ideas and knowledge are gained empirically – that is, through the senses. According to the empiricists, observation is a more valid approach to knowledge than is reason, because reason is fraught with the potential for error. This idea bolstered the development of modern science, whose methods are rooted in empirical observation.

Discoveries in physiology (an area of biology that examines bodily functioning) and medicine also paved the way for psychology's emergence. By 1870 European researchers were electrically stimulating the brains of laboratory animals and mapping the surface areas that controlled various body movements. During this same period, medical reports linked damage in different areas of patients' brains with various behavioural and mental impairments. For example, damage to a specific region on the brain's left side impaired people's ability to speak fluently.

Mounting evidence of the relation between brain and behaviour supported the view that empirical methods of the natural sciences could also be used to study mental processes. Indeed, by the mid-1800s, German scientists were measuring people's sensory responses to many types of physical stimuli (for example, how the perceived loudness of a sound changes as its physical intensity increases). Their experiments established a new field called *psychophysics*, the study of how psychologically experienced sensations depend on the characteristics of physical stimuli.

mind–body dualism
the belief that the mind is a spiritual entity not subject to physical laws that govern the body

Focus 1.4
Discuss psychology's philosophical and scientific roots, earliest schools of thought, and founders.

 In-Psych

To learn more about the historical approaches to studying human behaviour and treating mental illness, watch the video in Chapter 1 in the In-Psych programme online.

monism
holds that mind and body are one and that the mind is not a separate spiritual entity

empiricism
held that all ideas and knowledge are gained empirically – that is, through the senses

Around this time, Charles Darwin's (1809–82) theory of evolution generated shock waves that are still felt today. His theory, which we discuss later, was vigorously opposed because it seemed to contradict philosophical and religious beliefs about the exalted nature of human beings. Evolution implied that the human mind was not a spiritual entity but, rather, the product of a biological continuity between humans and other species. Moreover, Darwin's theory implied that scientists might gain insight about human behaviour by studying other species. By the late 1800s, a convergence of intellectual forces provided the impetus for psychology's birth.

EARLY SCHOOLS: STRUCTURALISM AND FUNCTIONALISM

The infant science of psychology emerged in 1879, when Wilhelm Wundt (1832–1920) established the first experimental psychology laboratory at the University of Leipzig. Wundt, who helped train the first generation of scientific psychologists, wanted to model the study of the mind after the natural sciences (Fig. 1.5). He believed that the mind could be studied by breaking it down into its basic components, as a chemist might do in studying a complex chemical compound. One of his graduate students, Englishman Edward Titchener (1867–1927), later established a psychology laboratory in the USA at Cornell University. Like Wundt, Titchener attempted to identify the basic building blocks, or structures, of the mind. Wundt and Titchener's approach came to be known as **structuralism**, the analysis of the mind in terms of its basic elements.

structuralism

the analysis of the mind in terms of its basic elements

FIGURE 1.5

At the University of Leipzig in 1879, Wilhelm Wundt (*far right*) established the first laboratory of experimental psychology to study the structure of the mind.

Focus 1.5

Describe the psychodynamic perspective. Contrast Freud's psychoanalytic theory with modern psychodynamic theories.

In their experiments, structuralists used the method of *introspection* ('looking within') to study sensations, which they considered the basic elements of consciousness. They exposed participants to all sorts of sensory stimuli – lights, sounds, tastes – and trained them to describe their inner experiences. Although this method of studying the mind was criticized and died out after a few decades, the structuralists left an important mark on the infant field of psychology by establishing a scientific tradition for the study of cognitive processes.

functionalism

which held that psychology should study the functions of consciousness rather than its structure

In the USA, structuralism eventually gave way to **functionalism**, which held that psychology should study the functions of consciousness rather than its structure. Here is a rough analogy to explain the difference between structuralism and functionalism: consider your arms and hands. A structuralist would try to explain their movement by studying how muscles, tendons and bones operate. In contrast, a functionalist would ask, 'Why do we have arms and hands? How do they help us adapt to our environment?' The functionalists asked similar questions about mental processes and behaviour. In part, they were influenced by Darwin's evolutionary theory, which stressed the importance of adaptation in helping organisms survive and reproduce in their environment. Functionalists did much of the early research on learning and problem solving.

William James (1842–1910), a leader in the functionalist movement, was a 'big-picture' person who taught courses in physiology, psychology and philosophy at Harvard University (Fig. 1.6). James's broad functionalist approach helped widen the scope of psychology to include the study of various biological processes, mental processes and behaviours.

Although functionalism no longer exists as a school of thought within psychology, its tradition endures in two modern-day fields: *cognitive psychology*, which studies mental processes, and *evolutionary psychology*, which emphasizes the adaptiveness of behaviour.

THE PSYCHODYNAMIC PERSPECTIVE: THE FORCES WITHIN

Have you ever been mystified by why you behaved or felt a certain way? Recall the case of Jonathan, the student described at the beginning of the chapter who could not understand why he was so shy. The **psychodynamic perspective** searches for the causes of behaviour within the inner workings of our personality (our unique pattern of traits, emotions, and motives), emphasizing the role of unconscious processes. Sigmund Freud (1856–1939) developed the first and most influential psychodynamic theory (Fig. 1.7). His legacy was developed by others, including Melanie Klein (1882–1960) who began work as an analyst in the early part of the twentieth century (Fig. 1.8).

FIGURE 1.6

William James, a leader of functionalism. His multivolume book *Principles of Psychology* (1950, first published 1890) greatly expanded the scope of psychology.

psychodynamic perspective

searches for the causes of behaviour within the inner workings of our personality (our unique pattern of traits, emotions, and motives), emphasizing the role of unconscious processes

FIGURE 1.7

Sigmund Freud founded psychoanalysis. For more than 50 years, he probed the hidden recesses of the mind.

FIGURE 1.8

Melanie Klein (1882–1960), the great European psychoanalyst.

Psychoanalysis: Freud's Great Challenge

Late in the nineteenth century, as a young physician in Vienna, Freud was intrigued by the workings of the brain. He was confronted with patients who experienced physical symptoms such as blindness, pain or paralysis without any apparent bodily cause. Over time he treated patients who had other problems, such as *phobias* (intense unrealistic fears). Because no disease or bodily malfunction could explain these conditions, Freud reasoned that the causes must be psychological. Moreover, if his patients were not producing their symptoms consciously, Freud reasoned that the causes must be hidden from awareness – they must be unconscious. At first Freud treated his patients by using hypnosis. Later he used a technique called *free association*, in which the patient expressed any thoughts that came to mind. To Freud's surprise, his patients eventually described painful and long-'forgotten' childhood experiences, often sexual in nature. Often, after recalling and figuratively reliving these traumatic childhood experiences, the patients' symptoms improved.

psychoanalysis

the analysis of internal and primarily unconscious psychological forces

defence mechanisms

psychological techniques that help us cope with anxiety and the pain of traumatic experiences

Freud became convinced that an unconscious part of the mind profoundly influences behaviour, and he developed a theory and a form of psychotherapy called **psychoanalysis** – the analysis of internal and primarily unconscious psychological forces. He also proposed that humans have powerful inborn sexual and aggressive drives and that, because these desires are punished in childhood, we learn to fear them and become anxious when we are aware of their presence. This leads us to develop **defence mechanisms**, which are psychological techniques that help us cope with anxiety and the pain of traumatic experiences. Repression, a primary defence mechanism, protects us by keeping unacceptable impulses, feelings and memories in the unconscious depths of the mind. All behaviour, whether normal or 'abnormal', reflects a largely unconscious and inevitable conflict between the defences and internal impulses. This ongoing psychological struggle between conflicting forces is dynamic in nature, hence the term *psychodynamic*. To explain Jonathan's extreme shyness around women, Freud might have explored whether Jonathan is unconsciously afraid of his sexual impulses and therefore avoids putting himself into dating situations where he would have to confront those hidden impulses.

Freud's theory became a lightning rod for controversy. Some of his own followers strongly disagreed with aspects of the theory, especially its heavy emphasis on childhood sexuality. Other psychologists viewed the theory as difficult to test. Indeed, Freud opposed laboratory research on psychoanalytic theory, believing that his clinical observations were more valid. Nevertheless, Freud's ideas did stimulate research on topics such as dreams, memory, aggression and mental disorders. A review of more than 3000 scientific studies examining Freud's ideas found support for some aspects of his theory, whereas other aspects were unsupported or contradicted (Fisher and Greenberg, 1996). But even where Freud's theory was not supported, the research it inspired led to important discoveries. In addition, Freud's work forever broadened the face of psychology to include the study and treatment of psychological disorders.

Another prominent thinker in this area was Carl Jung (1875–1961), a student of Freud, who became a regular correspondent and friend. Their ways parted in the early 1900s as Jung began to disagree with Freud's focus on the libido and his views on religion, but Freud had greatly influenced Jung. Jung's contribution to psychoanalysis centred on his construction of what he called 'concepts', including the concepts of introversion and extroversion, and his idea of the 'complex'. By this he meant a build-up of feelings in the subconscious that analysis can help identify. It is this 'complex' that can account for a person's odd or difficult to understand behaviour. Jung courted controversy just before and during the Second World War, when he was labelled as having Nazi sympathies. Jung later denied this, and explained that his endorsement of Hitler's *Mein Kampf* as reading for psychoanalysts served to keep psychoanalysis, as a movement founded by Freud, a Jewish intellectual, alive during this dangerous time. He also made his friendship and respect for Freud very clear at the end of the war.

Modern Psychodynamic Theory

object relations theories

focus on how early experiences with caregivers shape the views that people form of themselves and others

Modern psychodynamic theories continue to explore how unconscious and conscious aspects of personality influence behaviour. However, they downplay the role of hidden sexual and aggressive motives and focus more on how early family relationships, other social factors and our sense of 'self' shape our personality (Kohut, 1977). For example, psychodynamic **object relations theories** focus on how early experiences with caregivers shape the views that people form of themselves and others (Kernberg, 1984; 2000). In turn, these views unconsciously influence a person's relationships with other people throughout life. To explain Jonathan's shyness, a modern psychodynamic psychologist might examine Jonathan's conceptions of himself and his parents. Jonathan's shyness may stem from a fear of rejection of which he is unaware. This fear may be based on conceptions that he developed of his parents as being rejecting and disapproving, views that now unconsciously shape his expectations of how relationships with women and men will be.

The psychodynamic perspective dominated thinking about personality, mental disorders and psychotherapy for the first half of the twentieth century, and it continues to influence applied and academic psychology Psychoanalysis remains a major force in psychology, particularly in Europe.

Links with psychodynamic concepts can be found within several areas of psychological science. For example, biologically oriented psychologists have identified brain mechanisms that can produce emotional reactions of which we are consciously unaware (Davidson et al., 2000), and cognitive scientists have shown that many aspects of information processing occur outside of awareness (Chartrand and Bargh, 2002). Thus, while most contemporary psychological scientists reject Freud's version of the unconscious mind, many support the concept that behaviours can be triggered by non-conscious processes.

THE BEHAVIOURAL PERSPECTIVE: THE POWER OF THE ENVIRONMENT

The **behavioural perspective** focuses on the role of the external environment in governing our actions. From this perspective, our behaviour is jointly determined by habits learned from previous life experiences and by stimuli in our immediate environment.

Origins of the Behavioural Perspective

The behavioural perspective is rooted in the philosophical school of empiricism, which held that all ideas and knowledge are gained through the senses. According to the early empiricist, John Locke, at birth the human mind is a *tabula rasa* – a 'blank tablet' or 'slate' – upon which experiences are written. In this view, human nature is shaped purely by the environment.

In the early 1900s, experiments by Russian physiologist Ivan Pavlov (1849–1936) revealed one way in which the environment shapes behaviour: through the association of events with one another. Pavlov found that dogs automatically learned to salivate to the sound of a new stimulus, such as a tone, if that stimulus was repeatedly paired with food. Meanwhile, Edward Thorndike (1874–1949) was examining how organisms learn through the consequences of their actions. According to Thorndike's (1911) *law of effect*, responses followed by satisfying consequences become more likely to recur, and those followed by unsatisfying consequences become less likely to recur. Thus learning is the key to understanding how experience moulds behaviour.

Behaviourism

Behaviourism, a school of thought that emphasizes environmental control of behaviour through learning, began to emerge in 1913. John B. Watson (1878–1958), who led the new movement, strongly opposed the 'mentalism' of the structuralists, functionalists and psychoanalysts (Fig. 1.9). He argued that the proper subject matter of psychology was observable behaviour, not unobservable inner consciousness. Human beings, he said, are products of their learning experiences. So passionately did Watson hold this position that in 1924 he issued the following challenge:

> Give me a dozen healthy infants, well-formed, and my own specialised world to bring them up in and I'll guarantee you to take any one of them at random and train him to become any type of specialist I might select – doctor, lawyer, artist, merchant-chief and, yes, even beggarman and thief, regardless of his talents, penchants, tendencies, abilities, vocations, and race of his ancestors. (p. 82)

behavioural perspective
focuses on the role of the external environment in governing our actions

Focus 1.6
What are the behavioural perspective's origins and focus? Contrast radical behaviourism with cognitive behaviourism.

behaviourism
school of thought that emphasizes environmental control of behaviour through learning

FIGURE 1.9

John B. Watson founded the school of behaviourism. He published *Psychology as the Behaviorist Views It* in 1913.

FIGURE 1.10

B.F. Skinner, a leading behaviourist, argued that mentalistic concepts were not necessary to explain behaviour and that learning principles could be used to enhance human welfare.

Behaviourists sought to discover the laws that govern learning, and in accord with Darwin's theory of evolution, they believed that the same basic principles of learning apply to all organisms. B.F. Skinner (1904–90) was the leading modern figure in behaviourism (Fig. 1.10). Although Skinner did not deny that thoughts and feelings occur within us, he maintained that 'No account of what is happening inside the human body, no matter how complete, will explain the origins of human behaviour' (1989b, p. 18). Skinner believed that the real causes of behaviour reside in the outer world and insisted that 'A person does not act upon the world, the world acts upon him' (1971, p. 211). His research, based largely on studies of rats and pigeons under controlled laboratory conditions, examined how behaviour is shaped by the rewarding and punishing consequences that it produces.

In the case of our university student, Jonathan, a behaviourist might explain his shyness around women by examining his past experiences. In high school, the first time Jonathan invited a girl out he was turned down. Later, he had a crush on a girl and they went out once, after which she turned him down. Though nervous, he asked out a few girls after that but was turned down each time. Such punishing consequences decreased the likelihood that Jonathan would ask someone out in the future. Fortunately, Marie asked Jonathan out, and the positive consequences they experienced on their first date reinforced their behaviour, increasing the odds that they would go out again.

Skinner believed that society could harness the power of the environment to change behaviour in beneficial ways and that the chief barrier to creating a better world through 'social engineering' is an outmoded conception of people as free agents. Skinner's approach, known as *radical behaviourism*, was considered extreme by many psychologists, but he was esteemed for his scientific contributions and for focusing attention on how environmental forces could be used to enhance human welfare. In the 1960s, behaviourism inspired powerful techniques known collectively as *behaviour modification*. These techniques, aimed at decreasing problem behaviours and increasing positive behaviours by manipulating environmental factors, are still used widely today.

Behaviourism's insistence that psychology should focus only on observable stimuli and responses resonated with many who wanted this young science to model itself on the natural sciences. Behaviourism dominated much research on learning into the 1960s, and challenged psychodynamic views about the causes of psychological disorders, and led to highly effective treatments for some disorders. But radical behaviourism's influence waned after the 1970s as interest in studying mental processes expanded (Robins et al., 1999). Nevertheless, behaviourists continue to make important contributions to basic and applied psychology, and their discovery of basic laws of learning was one of the greatest contributions to psychology in the twentieth century.

Cognitive Behaviourism

In the 1960s and 1970s, a growing number of psychologists showed that cognitive processes such as attention and memory could be rigorously studied by using sophisticated experiments. This led some behaviourists to challenge radical behaviourism's view that mental life was off-limits as a topic for scientific study. They developed a modified view called **cognitive behaviourism**, which proposes that learning experiences and the environment influence our expectations and other thoughts, and in turn our thoughts influence how we behave (Bandura, 1969; 2002a; 2002b). Cognitive behaviourism remains an influential viewpoint to this day (Fig. 1.11).

A cognitive behaviourist might say that Jonathan's past dating rejections were punishing and led him to expect that further attempts at romance would be doomed. In turn, these expectations of social rejection inhibited him from asking women out and even from making male friends. While at home for a spring break, family discussions helped Jonathan think about his situation in a new light. This helped Jonathan to modify his behaviour, become more outgoing and improve his social relationships.

cognitive behaviourism

proposes that learning experiences and the environment influence our expectations and other thoughts, and in turn our thoughts influence how we behave

FIGURE 1.11

FIGURE 1.11

Albert Bandura has played a key role in developing cognitive behaviourism, which merges the behavioural and cognitive perspectives.

WHAT DO YOU THINK?

ARE STUDENTS LAZY?

Imagine that you are a school teacher. Whenever you try to engage your students in a class discussion, they gaze into space and hardly say anything. You start to think that they are just a bunch of lazy kids. From a radical behavioural perspective, is your conclusion reasonable? How might you improve the situation? (Think about it, then see page 36).

THE HUMANISTIC PERSPECTIVE: SELF-ACTUALIZATION AND POSITIVE PSYCHOLOGY

In the mid-twentieth century, as the psychodynamic and behavioural perspectives vied for intellectual dominance within psychology, a new viewpoint arose to challenge them both. Known as the **humanistic perspective** (or **humanism**), it emphasized free will, personal growth and the attempt to find meaning in one's existence.

Humanists rejected psychodynamic concepts of humans as being controlled by unconscious forces. They also denied behaviourism's view of humans as reactors moulded by the environment. Instead, humanistic theorists such as Abraham Maslow (1908–70) proposed that each of us has an inborn force towards *self-actualization*, the reaching of one's individual potential (Fig. 1.12). When the human personality develops in a supportive environment, the positive inner nature of a person emerges. In contrast, misery and pathology occur when environments frustrate our innate tendency towards self-actualization. Humanists emphasized the importance of personal choice and responsibility, personality growth and positive feelings of self-worth. They insisted that the meaning of our existence resides squarely in our own hands.

humanistic perspective (or humanism)

emphasized free will, personal growth and the attempt to find meaning in one's existence.

Focus 1.7

How does humanism's conception of human nature differ from that advanced by psychodynamic theory and behaviourism?

FIGURE 1.12

The humanistic perspective emphasizes the human ability to surmount obstacles in the drive toward self-actualization.

Thinking about Jonathan's shyness and loneliness, a humanist might say that no matter how many rejections Jonathan has had in the past, he must take personal responsibility for turning things around. A humanist also might wonder whether, in his first year as an undergraduate, Jonathan's happiness and sense of self-worth were resting too heavily on his hope for a good romantic relationship. By focusing on building a few friendships, Jonathan wisely found another way to satisfy what Maslow (1954) called 'belongingness', our basic human need for social acceptance and companionship.

Focus 1.8
Describe the focus and the origins of the cognitive perspective and some areas of modern cognitive science.

positive psychology movement
emphasizes the study of human strengths, fulfilment and optimal living

cognitive perspective
examines the nature of the mind and how mental processes influence behaviour

Gestalt psychology
examined how elements of experience are organized into wholes

FIGURE 1.13

This painting illustrates the Gestalt principle that the whole is greater than the sum of its parts. The individual elements are sea creatures, but the whole is perceived as a portrait of a face. *The Water*, by Arcimboldo, from Kunsthistorisches Museum, Vienna.

Few early humanists were scientists and, historically, humanism has had a more limited impact on mainstream psychological science than have other perspectives. Still, it has inspired important areas of research. Humanist Carl Rogers (1902–87) pioneered the scientific study of psychotherapy. In the 1940s and 1950s his research group was the first to audiotape counselling sessions and analyse their content. Rogers (1967) identified key processes that led to constructive changes in clients. As another example, psychologists have conducted many studies of self-concept over the past 30 years, and much of this work incorporates humanistic ideas (Verplanken and Holland, 2002).

Humanism's focus on self-actualization and growth is also seen in today's growing **positive psychology movement**, which emphasizes the study of human strengths, fulfilment and optimal living (Diener and Seligman, 2004). In contrast to psychology's long-standing focus on 'what's wrong with our world' (e.g., mental disorders, conflict, prejudice), positive psychology examines how we can nurture what is best within ourselves and society to create a happy and fulfilling life.

THE COGNITIVE PERSPECTIVE: THE THINKING HUMAN

Derived from the Latin word *cogitare* ('to think'), the **cognitive perspective** examines the nature of the mind and how mental processes influence behaviour. In this view, humans are information processors whose actions are governed by thought.

Origins of the Cognitive Perspective

As discussed earlier, structuralism and functionalism arose as two of psychology's earliest schools of thought. The structuralists attempted to identify the basic elements, or structure, of consciousness by using the method of introspection. In contrast, functionalists explored the purposes of consciousness. Other pioneering cognitive psychologists, such as Hermann Ebbinghaus (1850–1909) studied memory.

By the 1920s German scientists had formed a school of thought known as **Gestalt psychology**, which examined how elements of experience are organized into wholes. The word *gestalt* may be translated roughly as 'whole' or 'organization'. Instead of trying to break consciousness down into its elements, Gestalt psychologists argued that our perceptions are organized so that 'the whole is greater than the sum of its parts'. Consider the painting in Figure 1.13. Many people initially perceive it as a whole – as a portrait of a strange-looking person – rather than as a mosaic of individual sea creatures. Gestalt psychology stimulated interest in cognitive topics such as perception and problem solving.

Renewed Interest in the Mind

Interest in cognition grew in a number of different areas. For example, a theory developed by Swiss psychologist Jean Piaget (1896–1980), which explained how children's thinking processes become more sophisticated with age, gained widespread recognition in the psychological community worldwide (Fig. 1.14). Lev Semenovich Vygotsky (1886–1934) provided a slightly different, but just as important, perspective on cognitive development. Vygotsky was a Russian, studying in the then Soviet Republic, in the 1920s. He died, tragically, of tuberculosis, aged just 48, but his work has had a pronounced impact. Vygotsky believed that language and thought were closely linked. He also felt that the environment in which children developed, the social and cultural factors they were exposed to had an important impact on their development.

In the 1950s several factors contributed to a renewed interest in studying cognitive processes. In part, this interest stemmed from psychologists' involvement during the Second World War in designing information displays, such as gauges in aeroplane cockpits, that enabled military personnel (e.g., pilots) to recognize experiments that reflected an information-processing approach.

FIGURE 1.14

Swiss psychologist Jean Piaget was a master of observation. Many of his conclusions about cognitive development came from carefully watching children solve problems.

Computer technology, which was in its infancy at that time, provided new information-processing concepts and terminology that psychologists began to adapt to the study of memory and attention (Broadbent, 1958). A new metaphor was developing – the mind as a system that processes, stores and retrieves information. The information-processing approach to studying the mind continues to be influential.

On another front in the 1950s, a heated debate arose between behaviourists and linguists about how children acquire language. The behaviourists, led by B.F. Skinner, claimed that language is acquired through basic principles of learning. The linguists, led by Noam Chomsky (b. 1928), argued that humans are biologically 'pre-programmed' to acquire language and that children come to understand language as a set of 'mental rules'. This debate convinced many psychologists that language was too complex to be explained by behavioural principles and that it needed to be examined from a more cognitive perspective. Overall, psychologists' interest in mental processes swelled by the 1960s and 1970s – a period that sometimes is referred to as the 'cognitive revolution'.

The Modern Cognitive Perspective

Cognitive psychology, which focuses on the study of mental processes, embodies the cognitive perspective. Cognitive psychologists study the processes by which people reason and make decisions, devise solutions to problems, form perceptions and mental images, and produce and understand language. They study the nature of knowledge and expertise. Some, such as Allan Baddeley have greatly expanded our understanding of memory and of factors that influence it (Fig. 1.15). Cognitive psychologists continue to explore the nature of attention and consciousness, and have become increasingly interested in how non-conscious processes influence behaviour.

Cognitive neuroscience, which uses sophisticated electrical recording and brain-imaging techniques to examine brain activity while people engage in cognitive tasks, is a rapidly growing area that represents the intersection of cognitive psychology and the biological perspective within psychology. Cognitive neuroscientists seek to determine how the brain goes about its business of learning language, acquiring knowledge, forming memories, and performing other cognitive activities (Rajah and McIntosh, 2005). Advances in technology have played an important role in the advance of neuropsychology to its now prominent position within the discipline.

Social constructivism, an influential cognitive viewpoint, maintains that what we consider 'reality' is largely our own mental creation, the product of a shared way of thinking among members of social groups (Gergen, 2000). Constructivists would maintain, for example, that the

FIGURE 1.15

Cognitive psychologist Alan Baddeley has provided important insights into the structure of memory.

cognitive psychology
focuses on the study of mental processes

cognitive neuroscience
uses sophisticated electrical recording and brain-imaging techniques to examine brain activity while people engage in cognitive tasks

social constructivism
maintains that what we consider 'reality' is largely our own mental creation

long-standing conflict between, Israeli Jews and Palestinian Arabs reflect immense differences in how they perceive God's plan for them and how they interpret the history of the land where they live (Rouhana and Bar-Tal, 1998).

From a cognitive perspective, we might examine Jonathan's shyness in terms of how he pays attention to and processes information, his perceptions and his memory. The few times that he went on dates, Jonathan's nervousness may have caused him to focus on even the slightest things that were not going well, while failing to notice other cues that suggested his date was having a good time. Jonathan's interpretation of his past dating failures may also be based on faulty reasoning. Jonathan may believe he was rejected because of his personal qualities ('I'm not attractive or interesting enough') and therefore expects that future dating attempts will also be unsuccessful. If Jonathan correctly attributed the rejections to some temporary or situational factor ('She was already interested in someone else'), then he would not necessarily expect other women to reject him in the future. A cognitive psychologist also might ask whether Jonathan's memories of his past dating experiences are accurate or have become distorted over time. Jonathan may be remembering those events as much more unpleasant than they actually were.

THE SOCIOCULTURAL PERSPECTIVE: THE EMBEDDED HUMAN

Humans are social creatures. Embedded within a culture, each of us encounters ever-changing social settings that shape our actions and values, our sense of identity, our very conception of reality. The **sociocultural perspective** examines how the social environment and cultural learning influence our behaviour, thoughts and feelings.

Cultural Learning and Diversity

Culture refers to the enduring values, beliefs, behaviours, and traditions that are shared by a large group of people and passed from one generation to the next. All cultural groups develop their own social **norms**, which are rules (often unwritten) that specify what behaviour is acceptable and expected for members of that group. Norms exist for all types of social behaviours, such as how to dress, respond to people of higher status, or act as a woman or man (Fig. 1.16). For culture to endure, each new generation must internalize, or adopt, the norms and values of the group as their own. **Socialization** is the process by which culture is transmitted to new members and internalized by them.

Focus 1.9

Explain the sociocultural perspective. What are culture, norms, socialization and individualism-collectivism?

sociocultural perspective

examines how the social environment and cultural learning influence our behaviour, thoughts and feelings

culture

the enduring values, beliefs, behaviours, and traditions that are shared by a large group of people and passed from one generation to the next

norms

rules (often unwritten) that specify what behaviour is acceptable and expected for members of that group

socialization

the process by which culture is transmitted to new members and internalized by them

FIGURE 1.16

Social norms differ across cultures and over time within cultures. The idea of women engaging in traditionally male-dominated pastimes such as football, or occupations such as pilot would be less acceptable in some cultures and times than others.

In word if not in deed, psychologists have long recognized culture's impact in shaping who we are. The behaviourists, Neil Miller and John Dollard, noted in 1941 that

> no psychologist would venture to predict the behaviour of a rat without knowing [where in a maze] the feed or the shock is placed. It is no easier to predict the behaviour of a human being without knowing the conditions of his 'maze,' i.e. the structure of his social environment. Culture … is a statement of the design of the human maze, of the type of reward involved, and of what responses are to be rewarded. (p. 5)

Yet despite acknowledging culture's importance, throughout much of the twentieth century psychological research largely ignored non-western groups. Such cross-cultural work usually was left to anthropologists. Even within western societies, for decades participants in psychological research typically were white and came from middle- or upper-class backgrounds. This situation was so common that in 1976, African-American psychologist Robert Guthrie published a book titled *Even the Rat Was White: A Historical View of Psychology*. There were important exceptions, however, such as research by Kenneth Clark (1914–2005) and Mamie Clark (1917–83) and others, examining how discrimination and prejudice influenced the personality development of African-American children (Clark and Clark, 1947; Fig. 1.17).

Over time, psychologists increasingly began to study diverse ethnic and cultural groups. Today the growing field of **cultural psychology** (sometimes called cross-cultural psychology) explores how culture is transmitted to its members and examines psychological similarities and differences among people from diverse cultures.

One important difference among cultures is the extent to which they emphasize *individualism* versus *collectivism* (Triandis and Suh, 2002). Most industrialized cultures of northern Europe promote **individualism**, an emphasis on personal goals and self-identity based primarily on one's own attributes and achievements. In contrast, many cultures in Asia, Africa and South America nurture **collectivism**, in which individual goals are subordinated to those of the group and personal identity is defined largely by the ties that bind one to the extended family and other social groups. This difference is created by social learning experiences that begin in childhood and continue in the form of social customs. In school, for example, Japanese children more often work in groups on a common assignment, whereas European children more often work alone on individual assignments.

Thinking about Jonathan's lonely first year at university, the sociocultural perspective leads us to ask how his cultural upbringing and other social factors contributed to his shy behaviour. Throughout his teenage years, cultural norms for male assertiveness may have put pressure on Jonathan. His shyness may have evoked teasing and other negative reactions from his school peers, increasing his feelings of inadequacy by the time he reached university. As for Jonathan and Marie's relationship, we might examine how norms regarding courtship and marriage differ across cultures.

In each chapter of this book, we provide you with condensed, in-depth looks at important studies, paralleling the format of research articles published in psychological journals. We give you background information about the studies, describe its method and key results, and discuss and evaluate key aspects of the work. Our first 'Research close-up' examines cross-cultural attitudes about love and marriage.

FIGURE 1.17

Psychologists Kenneth B. Clark and Mamie P. Clark studied the development of racial identity among African-American children. Kenneth Clark also wrote books on the psychological impact of prejudice and discrimination.

cultural psychology
explores how culture is transmitted to its members and examines psychological similarities and differences among people from diverse cultures

individualism
an emphasis on personal goals and self-identity based primarily on one's own attributes and achievements

collectivism
individual goals are subordinated to those of the group and personal identity is defined largely by the ties that bind one to the extended family and other social groups

Focus 1.10
How does the 'Research close-up' illustrate cultural psychology's goals and importance?

RESEARCH CLOSE-UP

LOVE AND MARRIAGE IN 11 CULTURES

SOURCE: R. Levine, S. Sato, T. Hashimoto and J. Verma (1995) Love and marriage in eleven cultures, *Journal of Cross-Cultural Psychology*, vol. 26, pp. 554–71.

INTRODUCTION

Would you marry someone you did not love? According to one theory, people in individualistic cultures are more likely to view romantic love as a requirement for marriage because love is a matter of personal choice (Goode, 1959). In collectivistic cultures, concern for the extended family plays a larger role in marriage decisions.

Psychologist Robert Levine and his colleagues (1995) examined college students' views about love and marriage. Whereas previous research focused on American students, these authors studied students from 11 countries. They also examined whether students from collectivistic and economically poorer countries would be less likely to view love as a prerequisite to marriage.

METHOD

The researchers administered language-appropriate versions of the same questionnaire to 1163 female and male college students from 11 countries. The key question was, 'If someone had all the other qualities you desired, would you marry this person if you were not in love with him/her?' The students responded 'No', 'Yes', or 'Not sure'. The researchers determined each country's economic status and collectivistic versus individualistic orientation from data gathered by previous cross-cultural investigators.

RESULTS

Within each country, the views of female and male students did not differ significantly. In contrast, beliefs across countries varied strongly (Table 1.2). In India, Thailand and Pakistan most students said they would marry or at least consider marrying someone they did not love. In the Philippines and Japan, a sizeable minority – just over a third – felt the same way. In contrast, students from the other countries overwhelmingly rejected the notion of marrying somebody they did not love. Overall, students from collectivistic and economically poorer countries were less likely to view love as a prerequisite to marriage.

DISCUSSION

Among most of our own students, the notion that you marry someone you love is a truism. They are surprised – as perhaps you are – that many students in other countries would consider marrying someone they did not love. This study reminds us that as members of a particular culture, it is easy to mistakenly assume that 'our way' is the 'normal way'.

As in all research, we must interpret the results carefully. For example, among those students who said they would marry someone without being in love, would it be accurate to conclude that they view love as irrelevant to marriage? Not necessarily, because other research has found that 'mutual attraction/love' is viewed across most cultures as a desirable quality in a mate (Buss, 1989). Thus the results of the Levine et al. study suggest only that in some cultures love is not viewed as an *essential prerequisite* to enter into marriage.

Focus 1.11

Describe the biological perspective and the focus of behavioural neuroscience and behaviour genetics.

THE BIOLOGICAL PERSPECTIVE: THE BRAIN, GENES AND EVOLUTION

The **biological perspective** examines how brain processes and other bodily functions regulate behaviour. Biological psychology has always been a prominent part of the field, but its influence has increased dramatically over recent decades.

TABLE 1.2 LOVE AND MARRIAGE IN 11 CULTURES

If someone had all the other qualities you desired, would you marry this person if you were not in love with him/her?

Country	No %	Yes %	Not sure %
India	24	49	27
Thailand	34	19	47
Pakistan	39	50	11
Philippines	64	11	25
Japan	64	2	34
Hong Kong	78	6	16
Australia	80	5	15
Mexico	83	10	7
England	84	7	9
Brazil	86	4	10
USA	86	4	10

SOURCE: Levine et al., 1995.

Behavioural Neuroscience

Jonathan and Marie are in love. They study and eat together. They hold hands and kiss. Yet a year earlier, Jonathan was afraid to ask women out and became depressed. What brain regions, neural circuits and brain chemicals enable us to feel love, pleasure, fear and depression? To read, study and feel hunger? How do hormones influence behaviour? These questions are the province of **behavioural neuroscience** (also called *physiological psychology*), which examines brain processes and other physiological functions that underlie our behaviour, sensory experiences, emotions and thoughts (Robinson et al., 2005).

The study of brain–behaviour relations was in its infancy as psychology entered the twentieth century. Two pioneers of biological psychology, Karl Lashley (1890–1958) and Donald O. Hebb (1904–85), studied the brain's role in learning. Lashley trained rats to run through mazes and then measured how surgically produced lesions (damage) to various brain areas affected the rats' learning and memory. His research inspired other psychologists to map the brain regions involved in specific psychological functions (Fig. 1.18).

Hebb (1949) proposed that changes in the connections between nerve cells in the brain provide the biological basis for learning, memory and perception. His influential theory inspired much research, continuing to this day, on

biological perspective
examines how brain processes and other bodily functions regulate behaviour

behavioural neuroscience
examines brain processes and other physiological functions that underlie our behaviour, sensory experiences, emotions and thoughts

FIGURE 1.18

Karl Lashley was a pioneer of physiological psychology (behavioural neuroscience). He examined how damage to various brain regions affected rats' ability to learn and remember.

how the brain's neural circuitry changes as we learn, remember and perceive. This research led to the discovery of **neurotransmitters**, which are chemicals released by nerve cells that allow them to communicate with one another. The study of neurotransmitters' role in normal behaviour and mental disorders represents an important area of current neuroscience research.

Because behavioural neuroscience focuses on processes that are largely invisible to the naked based brain-imaging techniques and devices that record brainwaves, psychologists can watch activity in specific brain areas as people experience emotions, perceive stimuli and perform tasks (Fig. 1.19). These advances have led to new areas of study that forge links between various psychological perspectives. For example, cognitive neuroscience – the study of brain processes that underlie attention, reasoning, problem solving and so forth – represents an intersection of cognitive psychology and behavioural neuroscience. As a whole, however, behavioural neuroscience is broader than cognitive neuroscience. Behavioural neuroscientists, for example, also study the biology of hunger, thirst, sex, body-temperature regulation, emotion, movement, and sensory processes such as vision, hearing and taste. This area of research, more than any other is gaining focus and popularity at this time. Advances in scanning technology are playing their part in driving forward this exciting area of research, with researchers in neuroscience forming part of the vanguard of the psychology of today.

neurotransmitters

chemicals released by nerve cells that allow them to communicate with one another

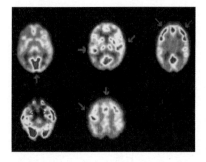

FIGURE 1.19A

Behavioural neuroscientists use positron-emission tomography (PET) scans to measure brain activity as people perform various tasks. Viewed from above, each image pictures a horizontal slice of the brain with the front of the brain at the top. Yellow and red indicate regions of greatest activity: (*top left*) visual task, (*top centre*) auditory task, (*top right*) cognitive task, (*bottom left*) memory task and (*bottom right*) motor task.

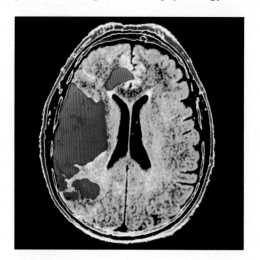 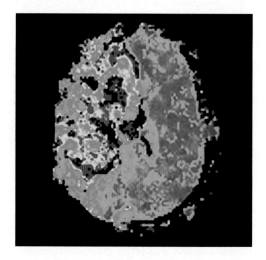

FIGURE 1.19B

Magnetic resonance imaging (MRI) (*left*) provides detailed images of living brains, and functional magnetic resonance imaging (fMRI) (*right*) allows researchers to see how activity in the brain changes to different stimuli and during different behaviours.

behaviour genetics

the study of how behavioural tendencies are influenced by genetic factors

FIGURE 1.20

Selective breeding can produce physical and behavioural characteristics. This tiny horse was produced by selectively breeding very small horses over a number of generations.

Behaviour Genetics

Psychologists have had a long-standing interest in **behaviour genetics**, the study of how behavioural tendencies are influenced by genetic factors (Miles and Carey, 1997). As we all know, animals can be selectively bred for physical traits (Fig. 1.20). But they can also be bred for behavioural traits such as aggression and intelligence. This is done by allowing highly aggressive or very bright males and females to mate with one another over generations. In Thailand, where gambling on fish fights is a national pastime, the selective breeding of winners has produced the highly aggressive Siamese fighting fish. The male of this species will instantly attack his own image in a mirror.

Human behaviour also is influenced by genetic factors. Identical twins, who result from the splitting of a fertilized egg and therefore have the same genetic make-up, are far more similar to one another on many behavioural traits than are fraternal twins, who result from two different fertilized eggs and therefore are no more similar genetically than are non-twin siblings. This greater degree of similarity is found even when the identical twins have been reared in different homes and dissimilar environments (Plomin and Caspi, 1999).

Thinking about Jonathan, a behaviour geneticist would consider the extent to which heredity contributes to differences in shyness among people. Some infants display an extremely shy, inhibited emotional style that seems to be biologically based and persists through childhood into adulthood (Kagan, 1989; Newman et al., 1997). Perhaps Jonathan inherited a tendency to be shy, and dating rejections in school reinforced his natural reluctance to ask women out.

Evolutionary Psychology

Charles Darwin published his theory of evolution in 1859 (Fig. 1.21). He was not the first to suggest that organisms evolve, but his theory was the best documented. His ideas were stimulated by a five-year voyage aboard a British research vessel that explored coastal regions around the globe. Darwin was struck by the numerous differences between seemingly similar species that lived in different environments. He began to view these differences as ways in which each species had adapted to its unique environment.

Darwin noted that the individual members of given species differ naturally in many ways. Some possess specific traits to a greater extent than other members do. Through a process he called **natural selection**, if an inherited trait gives certain members an advantage over others (such as increasing their ability to attract mates, escape danger, or acquire food), these members will be more likely to survive and pass these characteristics on to their offspring. In this way, species evolve as the presence of adaptive traits increases within the population over generations. In contrast, traits that put certain members at a disadvantage tend to become less common within a species over time because members having these traits will be less likely to survive and reproduce.

As the environment changes, the adaptiveness of a trait may increase or decrease. Thus, through natural selection, the biology of a species evolves in response to environmental conditions (Fig. 1.22). Darwin assumed that the principle of natural selection could be applied to all living organisms, including humans.

FIGURE 1.21

Charles Darwin, a British naturalist, formulated a theory of evolution that revolutionized scientific thinking.

natural selection

if an inherited trait gives certain members an advantage over others these members will be more likely to survive and pass these characteristics on to their offspring

Focus 1.12

What is natural selection? Explain the focus of evolutionary psychology.

FIGURE 1.22

Natural selection pressures result in physical changes. Over many generations, peppered moths who live in polluted urban areas have become darker, not from the pollution but because moths who inherited slightly darker colouration blended better into their grimy environment. Thus they were more likely to survive predators and pass their 'darker' genes on to their offspring.

evolutionary psychology

a growing discipline that seeks to explain how evolution shaped modern human behaviour

Evolutionary psychology is a growing discipline that seeks to explain how evolution shaped modern human behaviour (Workman and Reader, 2008). Evolutionary psychologists stress that through natural selection, human mental abilities and behavioural tendencies evolved along with a changing body. Consider how the brain evolved over millions of years, with the greatest growth occurring in brain regions involving higher mental processes.

According to one theory, as our humanlike ancestors developed new physical abilities (such as the ability to walk upright, thus freeing the use of the arms and hands), they began to use tools and weapons and to hunt and live in social groups (Workman and Reader, 2008). Certain psychological abilities – memory, thought, language, and the capacity to learn and solve problems – became more important to survival as our ancestors had to adapt to new ways of living.

Within any generation, genetically based variations in brain structure and functioning occur among individuals. Ancestors whose brain characteristics better supported adaptive mental abilities were more likely to survive and reproduce. Thus, through natural selection, adaptations to new environmental demands contributed to the development of the brain, just as brain growth contributed to the further development of human behaviour.

Evolutionary psychologists also attempt to explain the evolution of human social behaviours. For example, recall that Jonathan and Marie are contemplating marriage. As a species, why have we evolved to seek out a long-term bond with a mate? And why is it that across the world, on average, men desire a younger mate and attach greater importance than women to a potential mate's physical attractiveness, whereas women tend to seek an older mate and attach more importance than men to a potential mate's ambition? Whereas sociocultural psychologists argue that socialization and gender inequality in job opportunities cause most sex differences in mate preferences, some evolutionary psychologists propose that through natural selection men and women have become biologically predisposed to seek somewhat different qualities in a mate (Buss, 2005; Workman and Reader, 2008).

IN REVIEW

- Psychology's intellectual roots lie in philosophy, biology and medicine. Several major perspectives have shaped psychology's scientific growth. In the late 1800s Wundt and James helped found psychology. Structuralism, which examined the basic components of consciousness, and functionalism, which focused on the purposes of consciousness, were psychology's two earliest schools of thought.

- The psychodynamic perspective calls attention to unconscious motives, conflicts, and defence mechanisms that influence our personality and behaviour. Freud emphasized how unconscious sexual and aggressive impulses and childhood experiences shape personality. Modern psychodynamic theories focus more on how early family relationships and our sense of self unconsciously influence our current behaviour.

- The behavioural perspective emphasizes how the external environment and learning shape behaviour. Behaviourists such as Watson and Skinner believed that psychology should only study observable stimuli and responses, not unobservable mental processes. Behaviourists discovered basic laws of learning through controlled research with laboratory animals and applied these principles to enhance human welfare. Cognitive behaviourists believe that learning experiences influence our thoughts, which in turn influence our behaviours.

- The humanistic perspective emphasizes personal freedom and choice, psychological growth and self-actualization. Humanism has contributed to research on the self, the process of psychotherapy and today's positive psychology movement.

- The cognitive perspective, embodied by the field of cognitive psychology, views humans as information processors who think, judge and solve problems. Its roots lie in the early schools of structuralism, functionalism and Gestalt psychology. Cognitive neuroscience examines the brain processes that occur as people perform mental tasks. Social constructivism maintains that much of what we call reality is a creation of our own mental processes.

- The sociocultural perspective examines how the social environment and cultural learning influence our behaviour and thoughts. Cultural psychologists study how culture is transmitted to its members and examine similarities and differences among people from various cultures. An orientation towards individualism versus collectivism represents one of many ways in which cultures vary.

With roots in physiology, medicine, and Darwin's theory of evolution, the biological perspective examines how bodily functions regulate behaviour. Behavioural neuroscientists study brain and hormonal processes that underlie our behaviour, sensations, emotions and thoughts. Behaviour geneticists study how behaviour is influenced by our genetic inheritance. Evolutionary psychologists examine the adaptive functions of behaviours and seek to explain how evolution has biologically predisposed modern humans towards certain ways of behaving.

USING LEVELS OF ANALYSIS TO INTEGRATE THE PERSPECTIVES

As summarized in Table 1.3, psychology's major perspectives (presented in the order we have discussed them) provide us with differing conceptions of human nature. Fortunately, we can distil the essence of these perspectives into the simple three-part framework that we briefly

TABLE 1.3 COMPARISON OF SIX MAJOR PERSPECTIVES ON HUMAN BEHAVIOUR

	Psychodynamic	Behavioural	Humanistic	Cognitive	Sociocultural	Biological
Conception of human nature	The human as controlled by inner forces and conflicts	The human as reactor to the environment	The human as free agent, seeking self-actualization	The human as thinker	The human as social being embedded in a culture	The human animal
Major causal factors in behaviour	Unconscious motives, conflicts, and defences; early childhood experiences and unresolved conflicts	Past learning experiences and the stimuli and behavioural consequences that exist in the current environment	Free will, choice and innate drive towards self-actualization; search for personal meaning of existence	Thoughts, anticipations, planning, perceptions, attention, and memory processes	Social forces, including norms, social interactions, and group processes in one's culture and social environment	Genetic and evolutionary factors; brain and biochemical processes
Predominant focus and methods of discovery	Intensive observations of personality processes in clinical settings; some laboratory research	Study of learning processes in laboratory and real-world settings, with an emphasis on precise observation of stimuli and responses	Study of meaning, values and purpose in life; study of self-concept and its role in thought, emotion and behaviour	Study of cognitive processes, usually under highly controlled laboratory conditions	Study of behaviour and mental processes of people in different cultures; experiments examining people's responses to social stimuli	Study of brain–behaviour relations; role of hormones and biochemical factors in behaviour; behaviour genetics research

introduced earlier in the chapter: Behaviour can be understood at biological, psychological and environmental levels of analysis.

First, we can analyse behaviour and its causes in terms of brain functioning and hormones, as well as genetic factors shaped over the course of evolution. This is the *biological level of analysis*. The biological level can tell us much, but not everything. For example, we may know that certain thoughts and emotions are associated with activity in particular brain regions, but this does not tell us what those thoughts are. Thus we must also examine the *psychological level of analysis*. Here we might look to the cognitive perspective and analyse how thought, memory and planning influence behaviour. Borrowing from the psychodynamic and humanistic perspectives, we also can examine how certain motives and personality traits influence behaviour. Finally, we must also consider the *environmental level of analysis*. Here we can use the behavioural and sociocultural perspectives to examine how stimuli in the physical and social environment shape our behaviour, thoughts, and feelings.

Realize that a full understanding of behaviour often moves us back and forth between these three levels. Consider Jonathan and Marie. When we describe aspects of the culture in which they were raised, such as its religious values and social customs, we are operating at the environmental level of analysis. However, once Jonathan and Marie adopted those cultural values as their own, those values became an essential part of their identities, which represent the psychological level of analysis. Similarly, we might describe a family environment as highly abusive, but an abused child's tendency to worry and feel anxious – and the chemical changes in the brain that underlie this anxiety – move us to the psychological and biological levels of analysis.

AN EXAMPLE: UNDERSTANDING DEPRESSION

To appreciate how the levels-of-analysis framework can help us understand behaviour, let's examine a common but complex psychological problem in our culture: depression. Most people experience sadness, grief, or the blues at some time in their lives. Recall that Jonathan was lonely during his first year at college and became mildly depressed for a short time. These feelings often are normal responses to significant negative events or losses that we have experienced. However, when these emotions are intense, persist over a long period, and are accompanied by thoughts of hopelessness and an inability to experience pleasure, we have crossed the boundary between a normal reaction and clinical depression.

To better understand depression, let us begin at the biological level of analysis. First, genetic factors appear to predispose some people towards developing depression (Neumeister et al., 2004). In one study, relatives of people who had developed major depression before age 20 were eight times more likely to become depressed at some point than were relatives of non-depressed people (Weissman et al., 1984).

Biochemical factors also play a role. Recall that neurotransmitters are chemicals that transmit signals between nerve cells within the brain. For many depressed people certain neurotransmitter systems do not operate normally, and the most effective antidepressant drugs restore neurotransmitter activity to more normal levels.

From an evolutionary perspective, ancestors who developed effective ways to cope with environmental threats increased their chances of surviving and passing on their genes. At times, the psychological and physical ability to withdraw and conserve one's resources was undoubtedly the most adaptive defence against an environmental stressor, such as an unavoidable defeat or personal loss. Some evolutionary theorists view depression (and its accompanying disengagement and sense of hopelessness) as an exaggerated form of this normally adaptive, genetically based withdrawal process (Gilbert, 2001).

Moving to a psychological level of analysis, we find that depression is associated with a thinking style in which the person interprets events pessimistically (Seligman and Isaacowitz, 2000).

Focus 1.13

Use the three-level framework to integrate psychology's perspectives and discuss causes of depression.

In-Psych

IP

How would you apply the three levels of analysis to another psychological condition, an eating disorder? Consider this question as you watch the video in Chapter 1 in the In-Psych programme online.

Depressed people can find the black cloud that surrounds every silver lining. They tend to blame themselves for negative things that occur and take little credit for the good things that happen in their lives; they generally view the future as bleak and may have perfectionistic expectations that make them overly sensitive to how other people evaluate them (Bieling et al., 2004).

Are some personality patterns more prone to depression than others? Many psychodynamic theorists believe that severe losses, rejections or traumas in childhood help create a personality style that causes people to overreact to setbacks, setting the stage for future depression. In support of this notion, studies show that depressed people are more likely than non-depressed people to have experienced parental rejection, sexual abuse or the loss of a parent through death or separation during childhood (Bowlby, 2000).

Finally, at the environmental level of analysis, behaviourists propose that depression is a reaction to a non-rewarding environment. A vicious cycle begins when the environment provides fewer rewards for the person. As depression intensifies, some people feel so bad that they stop doing things that ordinarily give them pleasure, which decreases environmental rewards still further. To make things worse, depressed people may complain a lot and seek excessive support from others. These behaviours eventually begin to alienate other people, causing them to shy away from the depressed person. The net result is a worsening environment with fewer rewards, reduced support from others and hopeless pessimism (Lewinsohn et al., 1985; Nezlek et al., 2000).

Sociocultural factors also affect depression. As noted above, abusive family environments and other traumatic social experiences increase children's risk for depression later in life. Moreover, although depression is found in virtually all cultures, its symptoms, causes and prevalence may reflect cultural differences (Kleinman, 2004). For reasons still unknown, in the USA, Canada and other western nations, women are twice as likely as men to report feeling depressed; no such sex difference is found in developing countries (Culbertson, 1997).

Figure 1.23 organizes causal factors in depression into three classes: biological, psychological and environmental. Keep in mind, however, that the specific causes of depression and the

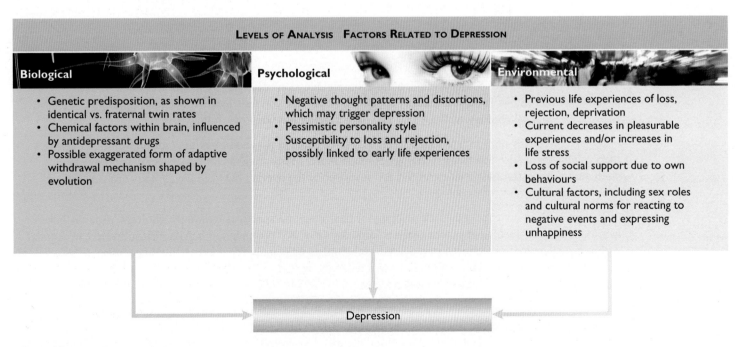

FIGURE 1.23

Levels of analysis: factors related to depression.

interaction

the way in which one factor influences behaviour depends on the presence of another factor

way in which they combine or interact may differ from case to case. **Interaction** means that the way in which one factor influences behaviour depends on the presence of another factor. For example, someone who experiences a minor setback in life may become depressed if she or he has a strong biological predisposition for depression. The same setback might barely faze a person with a weak biological predisposition for depression; only a catastrophic loss might cause this other person to become depressed. Thus the intensity of life stress and strength of biological predisposition would interact to influence behaviour. Just as boiling water softens celery and hardens an egg, the same environment can affect two people differently.

SUMMARY OF MAJOR THEMES

Our excursion through psychology's major perspectives and levels of analysis reveals several principles that you will encounter repeatedly as we explore the realm of behaviour:

1. As a science, psychology is empirical. It favours direct observation over pure intuition or reasoning as a means of attaining knowledge about behaviour.
2. Although committed to studying behaviour objectively, psychologists recognize that our personal experience of the world is subjective.
3. Behaviour is determined by multiple causal factors, including our biological endowment ('nature'), the environment and our past learning experiences ('nurture'), and psychological factors that include our thoughts and motives.
4. Behaviour is a means of adapting to environmental demands; capacities have evolved during each species' history because they facilitated adaptation and survival.
5. Behaviour and cognitive processes are affected by the social and cultural environments in which we develop and live.

Focus 1.14

Discuss five major themes identified in this chapter.

BENEATH THE SURFACE

WHAT DID YOU EXPECT?

We would like you to reflect for a moment on a simple question: what have you learned so far about psychology that differs from your initial expectations? We ask you this question because, up to now, we have focused on what psychology is. We would now like to point out what psychology is not.

Perhaps like many of our own students you may have equated psychology with counselling or therapy. If so, then you have already seen that psychology is much more. Many students do not expect psychologists to study brain processes and genetics; others are surprised at the overlap between psychology and disciplines such as sociology and anthropology.

Perhaps you did not expect the rich diversity of theoretical perspectives within psychology. You may have heard of Sigmund Freud and psychoanalysis, or possibly of B.F. Skinner and behaviourism. Indeed, in popular cartoons, psychologists are often stereotyped as therapists who analyse patients lying on couches, or as researchers in white lab coats studying rats in a maze. Now you know that other major perspectives are important parts of psychology's past and present.

Given psychology's theoretical diversity, perhaps you did not expect how environmental, psychological and biological factors intertwine to influence behaviour. And, with regard to influencing behaviour, we hasten to dispel the notion that psychology is about mind control. Psychology's goal is not to control people's minds in the sense that *control* means inducing people to think or do things against their will. Rather, psychologists conduct basic research to learn how people behave, think and feel; many also apply that knowledge to promote positive changes for individuals, groups and society as a whole.

We have observed that some students mistakenly expect psychology to be just plain common sense. After all, each of us has spent much of our lives interacting with other people, and we all form notions about human behaviour and why people act as they do. For many reasons (which we explore in later chapters) our common sense often misleads us. For example, we usually do not subject our common-sense notions to a careful test. Perhaps when you took the true–false test in Table 1.1 you found that some of your common-sense answers were not consistent with the scientific findings.

Finally, we have found that many students underestimate the amount of work required to succeed in this course and therefore mistakenly expect introductory psychology to be easy. However, because of the breadth of topics and the nature of the concepts and information covered in this course, you may find that it takes a lot more effort than you anticipated to gain a true understanding of the material.

In the coming chapters, you will read about many research findings that are likely to contradict your expectations and many popular misconceptions about behaviour. We look forward to helping you explore our exciting and important branch of science.

IN REVIEW

- Factors that influence behaviour can be organized into three broad levels of analysis. The biological level examines how brain processes, hormonal and genetic influences, and evolutionary adaptations underlie behaviour. The psychological level focuses on mental processes and psychological motives and how they influence behaviour. The environmental level examines physical and social stimuli, including cultural factors, that shape our behaviour and thoughts.

- To understand behaviour, we often move back and forth between these levels of analysis. For example, when as children we are first exposed to cultural norms, those norms reflect a characteristic of our environment. However, once we adopt norms as our own, they become a part of our world view and now represent the psychological level of analysis.

- Biological, psychological and environmental factors contribute to depression. These factors can also interact. A mild setback may trigger depression in a person who has a strong biological predisposition towards depression, whereas a person who has a weak biological predisposition may become depressed only after suffering a severe setback.

PSYCHOLOGY TODAY

To many people, when you say the word *psychologist*, the first image that comes to mind is that of a therapist. This is understandable, as a large number of psychologists are indeed *clinical psychologists*, who diagnose and treat people with psychological problems in clinics, hospitals and private practice. Yet many clinical psychologists also are scientists who conduct research on the causes of mental disorders and the effectiveness of various kinds of treatment. Moreover, there are many other types of psychologists who have no connection with therapy and instead work as basic or applied researchers.

A GLOBAL SCIENCE AND PROFESSION

As a science and a profession, psychology today is more diversified and robust than ever before. Because of psychology's enormous breadth, no psychologist can be an expert on all aspects of behaviour. As in other sciences, many areas of specialization have emerged. Table 1.4 describes some of psychology's major subfields, but note that psychological research often cuts across subfields. For example, developmental, social, clinical and physiological psychologists might all study the causes of antisocial behaviour among children.

Modern psychology is also geographically, ethnically and gender diversified. A century ago, psychological research was conducted almost entirely in Europe, North America and Russia by white males. Today these regions remain scientific powerhouses, but you will find women and men from diverse backgrounds conducting psychological research and providing psychological services around the globe. Founded in 1951 to support psychology worldwide, the International Union of Psychological Science consists of major psychological organizations from 70 countries (IUPsyS, 2005). Moreover, across the world, students are eagerly studying psychology both at university and, increasingly, in pre-university education. At university, students will learn about a number of key areas in psychology. Each of these key areas have subtopics that may or may not be included in the courses. Different professional bodies scrutinize the provision of psychology courses in their particular countries, and may require that certain topics are covered, maintaining parity and quality across institutions.

Besides its fascinating subject matter, psychology attracts many people with its rich variety of career options. Table 1.5 shows the major settings in which psychologists work. Many psychol-

TABLE 1.4 KEY AREAS WITHIN PSYCHOLOGY

Specialty	Subtopics
Biological psychology	Biological bases of behaviour, hormones and behaviour, behavioural genetics, neuropsychology, sociobiology and evolutionary psychology
Cognitive psychology	Perception, learning, memory, thinking, language, consciousness and cognitive neuropsychology
Developmental psychology	Childhood, adolescence and lifespan development, development of attachment, social relations, cognitive and language development, social and cultural contexts of development
Personality and individual differences	Abnormal and normal personality, psychological testing, intelligence, cognitive style, emotion, motivation and mood
Social psychology	Social cognition, attribution, attitudes, group processes and intergroup relations, close relationships and social constructionism
Research methods	Research design, the nature and appropriate statistical analysis of data, psychometrics and measurement techniques, and quantitative and qualitative methods

Focus 1.15

Describe some of psychology's major subfields and professional organizations.

TABLE 1.5 WORK SETTINGS OF PSYCHOLOGISTS

Occupation	%
Administrative and secretarial	20.8
Managers and senior officials	7.4
Professional	16.2
Associate professional and technical	22.5
Personal and protective service	15.9
Sales and customer service	11.6
Others	5.6

SOURCE: HESA Standard Occupational Classification (SOC) Psychology Graduates, 2003.

ogists teach, engage in research or apply psychological principles and techniques to help solve personal or social problems. Practising as a psychologist depends partly on the type of psychology being conducted, and partly on the country in which the professional lives. For more information on careers in psychology, visit the Online Learning Centre (OLC) that accompanies this book

PSYCHOLOGY AND PUBLIC POLICY

Modern society faces a host of complex social problems. Psychology, as a science and profession, is poised to help solve them. Through basic research, psychologists provide fundamental knowledge about behaviour. In applied research, they use this knowledge to design, implement and assess intervention programmes. Together, basic research and applied research are pillars for *evidence-based public policies* that affect the lives of millions of people.

Psychologists can help influence national policy by helping politicians develop legislation dealing with a host of social issues, from preventing AIDS and obesity to enhancing childcare and homeland security. Moreover, their influence is not limited to the USA. School bullying, for example, is a serious problem in several countries. Norwegian psychologist, Dan Olweus, a leading researcher on bullying, developed a prevention programme that the Norwegian government makes available to all its public schools (Olweus, 2004).

PSYCHOLOGY AND YOUR LIFE

We are biased, of course, but to us psychology is the most fascinating subject around, and we hope that some of this enthusiasm rubs off on you. We also hope that as you learn new concepts in your psychology course, you will reflect on how they relate to your own experiences. Psychological principles can not only help solve societal problems, but also enhance your own life. For example, research by behavioural, cognitive and educational psychologists on learning and memory provides guidelines that can improve your academic performance.

Focus 1.16

How can psychology help shape public policy?

Focus 1.17

Describe scientifically based strategies that can enhance students' learning and academic performance.

APPLYING PSYCHOLOGICAL SCIENCE

HOW TO ENHANCE YOUR ACADEMIC PERFORMANCE

University life presents many challenges, and work-skills can be as important for meeting those challenges as working hard. The following strategies can help you increase your learning and academic performance (Fig. 1.24).

EFFECTIVE TIME MANAGEMENT

If you efficiently allocate the time needed for study, you will have a clear conscience when it is time for recreational activities and relaxation. First, *develop a written schedule*. This forces you to decide how to allocate your time and increases your commitment to the plan. Begin by writing down your class meetings, your seminars, your lectures and other responsibilities. Then block in periods of study, avoiding times when you are likely to be tired. Distribute study times throughout the week, and schedule some study times immediately before enjoyable activities, which you can use as rewards for studying.

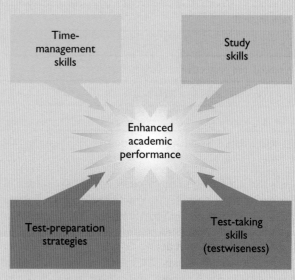

FIGURE 1.24

Improving academic performance.

Academic performance-enhancement methods include strategies for managing time, studying more effectively, preparing for tests and taking tests.

Second, *prioritize your tasks*. Most of us tend to procrastinate by working on simple tasks while putting off the toughest tasks until later. This can result in never getting to the major tasks (such as writing a term paper or studying for an examination) until too little time remains. Ask yourself, each day, 'What is the most important thing to get done?' Do that task first, then move to the next most important task, and so on.

Third, *break large tasks into smaller parts* that can be completed at specific times. Important tasks often are too big to complete all at once, so break them down and define each part in terms of a specific but realistic goal (e.g., number of pages to be read or amount of material to be studied). Successfully completing each goal is rewarding, strengthens your study skills and increases your feelings of mastery.

STUDYING MORE EFFECTIVELY

After planning your study time, use that time effectively. *Choose a study place where there are no distractions and where you do nothing but study*, say, a quiet library rather than a busy cafeteria. In time, you will learn to associate that location with studying, and studying there will become even easier (Watson and Tharp, 1997).

How you study is vital to your academic success. Do not read material passively and hope that it will just soak in. Instead, *use an active approach to learning* (Glaser and Bassok, 1989). For example, when reading a textbook chapter, first look over the chapter outline, which will give you a good idea of the information you are going to be processing. As you read the material, think about how it applies to your life or how it relates to other information that you already know.

USE FOCUS QUESTIONS TO ENHANCE ACTIVE LEARNING

You can also increase active learning by using the focus questions that appear in the margins of this book. These questions call attention to major concepts and facts. Use them to help you anticipate key points before you read a section, and use them again after you have read each section to test your understanding of the material. This will require you to stop and think about the content. Research shows that responding to these types of questions promotes better recall (Moreland et al., 1997).

Realize that these questions focus on only a portion of the important material. We could have written more questions, but just because some sections do not have focus questions does not mean that you can skip the material. In fact, you will learn even more if you supplement our questions with ones of your own – especially for sections that do not already have focus questions. Answering the focus questions and writing questions of your own will require more effort than passive reading does, but it will result in better learning (Estes and Vaughn, 1985; Hamilton, 1985).

PREPARING FOR TESTS

Contrary to what some students believe, introductory psychology is not an easy course. It covers a lot of diverse material, and many new concepts must be mastered. Many students who are new to university do not realize that the academic demands far exceed those of secondary school. Moreover, many students do not realize how hard high achievers actually work. In one study, researchers found that failing students spent only one-third as many hours studying as did students who regularly achieved the highest grades (who studied about two hours for every hour spent in class). Yet the failing students *thought* they were studying as much as anyone else, and many wondered why they were not doing well (Watson and Tharp, 1997).

A written study schedule helps spread your test preparation over time and helps avoid last-minute cramming. Cramming is less effective because it is fatiguing, taxes your memory and may increase test anxiety, which interferes with learning and test performance (Sarason and Sarason, 1990). Ideally, as the examination day nears, you should already understand the material. Then use the time before the test to refine your knowledge. Using the focus questions can pay big dividends in the final days before an examination.

TEST-TAKING STRATEGIES

Some students are more effective test-takers than others. They know how to approach different types of tests (e.g., multiple choice or essay) to maximize their performance. Such skills are called *testwiseness* (Fagley, 1987). Here are some strategies that testwise students use:

1. Use time wisely. Check your progress occasionally during the test. Answer the questions you know first (and, on essay examinations, the ones worth the most points). Do not get bogged down on a question you find difficult. Mark it and come back to it later.

2. On essay examinations, outline the points you want to make before you begin writing, then cover the key points in enough detail to communicate what you know.

3. On multiple-choice tests, read each question and try to answer it before reading the answer options. If you find your answer among the alternatives, that alternative is probably the correct one. Still, read all the other alternatives to make sure that you choose the best one.

4. Many students believe that they should not change answers on multiple-choice tests because the first guess is most likely to be correct. Eighty years of research shows that this belief is false (Kruger et al., 2005). As Figure 1.25 shows, changing an answer is far more likely to result in a wrong answer becoming a correct one than vice versa. Do not be reluctant to change an answer if you are fairly sure that the alternative is better.

5. Some multiple-choice questions have 'all of the above' as an alternative. If one of the other answers is clearly incorrect, eliminate the 'all of the above' option; if you are sure that at least two of the other answers are correct but are not sure about the third, choose 'all of the above'.

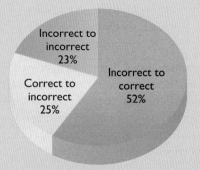

FIGURE 1.25

Changing answers on multiple-choice tests.

Researchers analysed the eraser marks on 6412 examinations taken by introductory psychology students. Contrary to popular wisdom, changing an answer was twice as likely to result in gaining points rather than losing points.

SOURCE: based on Kruger et al., 2005.

Time management, study skills, test-preparation strategies and testwiseness are not acquired overnight; they require effort and practice.

IN REVIEW

- Psychologists today conduct research and provide services around the globe.

- Psychologists specialize in various subfields and work in many settings. They teach, conduct research, perform therapy and counselling, and apply psychological principles to solve personal and social problems.

- You can use principles derived from psychological science to enhance your learning and increase your likelihood of performing well on tests. These include time-management principles, strategies for studying more effectively, test-preparation strategies, and techniques for taking tests.

KEY TERMS AND CONCEPTS

Each term has been boldfaced and defined in the chapter on the page indicated in parentheses.

applied research (p. 4)

basic research (p. 4)

behaviour genetics (p. 22)

behavioural neuroscience (p. 21)

behavioural perspective (p. 13)

behaviourism (p. 13)

biological perspective (p. 21)

cognitive behaviourism (p. 14)

cognitive neuroscience (p. 17)

cognitive perspective (p. 16)

cognitive psychology (p. 17)

collectivism (p. 19)

cultural psychology (p. 19)

culture (p. 18)

defence mechanisms (p. 12)

empiricism (p. 9)

evolutionary psychology (p. 24)

functionalism (p. 10)

Gestalt psychology (p. 16)

humanistic perspective (humanism) (p. 15)

individualism (p. 19)

interaction (p. 27)

mind–body dualism (p. 9)

monism (p. 9)

natural selection (p. 23)

neurotransmitters (p. 22)

norms (p. 18)

object relations theory (p. 12)

positive psychology movement (p. 16)

psychoanalysis (p. 12)

psychodynamic perspective (p. 11)

psychology (p. 3)

social constructivism (p. 17)

socialization (p. 18)

sociocultural perspective (p. 18)

structuralism (p. 10)

WHAT DO YOU THINK?

THE CASE OF DEATH BY CURSE (p. 8)

According to Cannon's hypothesis, the belief in voodoo or curses may drive someone to experience persistent, excessive stress. In the example of Tutankhamun's curse the increasing death toll may well have resulted in increasing terror among the survivors, which may well have culminated in shock and death caused themselves by physiological changes associated with fright.

Does this explanation seem reasonable to you? In forming your answer, one issue to consider is whether any good evidence supports Cannon's explanation. Cannon's research with animals suggested that a persistent, intense stress response could cause death in a way that would not be easily detectable upon autopsy, and more recent psychological and medical research points to negative effects that stress (caused by fear, worry or other factors) can have on bodily functioning. However, we also need to consider other possible explanations for the death.

First, in many cases, certainly in the case of voodoo, victims often refuse all food and drink after they feel that they have been cursed, and prolonged severe dehydration may be the cause of death (Barber, 1961). However, in other documented cases, food and drink restriction can be ruled out.

Second, curse victims often seem to surrender psychologically; they feel helpless and hopeless, believing that there is no place to hide from impending death (Cohen, 1985). Some scientists argue that this hopelessness increases victims' susceptibility to disease, which then leads to death (Lester, 1972). Others propose that this hopelessness has a more direct effect, triggering bodily responses that eventually decrease one's heart rate and cause death (Richter, 1957). Note that all of these explanations, although different from Cannon's, still illustrate mind–body interactions, and they support the general point that psychological beliefs can trigger responses that – one way or another – impair health.

Finally, even without the curse, perhaps the victims would have died anyway. Sudden death is relatively rare, and the link between the victims would have been an amazing coincidence, but we cannot completely rule out a physical condition that was undetected.

In our opinion, Cannon's explanation seems plausible, but as a critical thinker you should keep the bottom line in mind: we cannot say for sure why the victims died. For obvious ethical reasons, researchers do not expose people to curses in controlled experiments to carefully examine whether and how they die! Instead, scientists obtain clues from natural cases of death by voodoo and other curses, and from research on stress and mind–body interactions and, then, try to formulate the most plausible explanation.

ARE STUDENTS LAZY? (p. 15)

It may be tempting to blame the students' unresponsiveness on laziness, but a radical behaviourist would not focus on internal mental states to explain their inaction. First, to say that students are unresponsive *because* they are lazy does not explain anything. Consider this reasoning: how do we know that the students are lazy? Answer: because they are unresponsive. Therefore, if we say that students are lazy because they are unresponsive and then conclude that students are unresponsive because they are lazy, all we are really saying is that 'students are unresponsive because they are unresponsive'. This is not an explanation at all but, rather, an example of circular reasoning.

From a behavioural perspective, people's actions are shaped by the environment and learning experiences. Put yourself in the hypothetical role of the school teacher: You may not realize it, but when students sit quietly, you smile and seem more relaxed. When students participate in class discussions, you are quick to criticize their ideas. In these ways you may have taught your students to behave passively.

To change their behaviour, you can modify their educational environment so that they will learn new responses. Reward behaviours that you want to see (raising hands, correctly answering questions, and so on). For example, praise students not only for giving correct answers but also for participating. If an answer is incorrect, point this out in a non-punitive way while still reinforcing the student's participation.

Modifying the environment to change behaviour is often not as easy as it sounds, but this example illustrates one way a behaviourist might try to rearrange the environmental consequences rather than jump to the conclusion that the situation is hopeless.

CHAPTER TWO

STUDYING BEHAVIOUR SCIENTIFICALLY

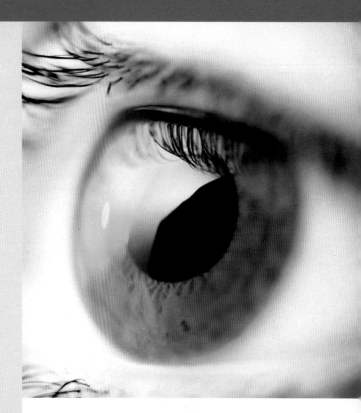

CHAPTER OUTLINE

I have no special talents. I am only passionately curious.

ALBERT EINSTEIN

At 7.15 on Friday the 25th of May 2007, Adam Morgan was severely injured by armed robbers during a raid on Rayleigh railway station in Essex, England. He had been trying to assist a female security guard when he was shot. Mr Mapleson's parents were understandably very upset by the news. They told a reporter 'knowing Adam as we do, although we were shocked to discover that he had been shot, we were not surprised to hear that he received his injuries trying to protect another'. (*BBC News 24*, Saturday, 26 May 2007, 18:59 GMT)

…

In March 1964, 28-year-old Kitty Genovese was stabbed repeatedly and raped by a knife-wielding assailant as she returned from work to her New York City apartment at about 3 a.m. The attack lasted about 30 minutes, during which time her screams and pleas for help were heard by at least 38 neighbours. Many went to their windows to find out what was happening. Yet nobody assisted her, and by the time anyone called the police, she had died. The incident drew international attention from a shocked public, and commentators expressed outrage over 'bystander apathy' and people's refusal to 'get involved'.

Science frequently has all the mystery of a good detective story. Consider the psychological puzzle of bystander intervention. If you were in trouble and needed help from bystanders, would you receive it? Ordinary citizens like Adam Mapleson often act decisively to help someone in need (Fig. 2.1). But, as the Kitty Genovese murder and similar tragedies illustrate, people do not always come to the aid of others. Why do bystanders sometimes risk injury and death to assist a stranger yet at other times fail to intervene – even when helping or calling the police entails little personal risk? We will return to this puzzle shortly.

In this chapter we explore principles and methods that form the foundation of psychological science. These principles also promote a way of thinking – critical thinking – that can serve you well in many aspects of your life.

SCIENTIFIC PRINCIPLES IN PSYCHOLOGY

Science is about discovery. At its core, science is an approach to asking and answering questions about the universe around us. Certainly, there are other ways we learn about our world and ourselves: through philosophy and reason; religion and spirituality; art, music and literature; the teachings of family, friends and others; and intuition and common sense. What distinguishes science from these approaches is a process guided by certain principles.

SCIENTIFIC ATTITUDES

Curiosity, scepticism and open-mindedness are driving forces behind scientific inquiry. Like a child who constantly asks 'Why?' the good scientist has an insatiable curiosity. And like a master detective, the good scientist is an incurable sceptic. Each claim is met with the reply, 'Show me your evidence'. Scientists also must remain open-minded to conclusions that are supported by facts, even if those conclusions refute their own beliefs.

Following the Kitty Genovese murder, two psychologists, John Darley and Bibb Latané, met for dinner. They were so curious about how 38 people could witness a violent crime and not even call the police that they decided to investigate further.

Darley and Latané also were sceptical of the 'bystander apathy' explanation offered by the media; they believed it was unlikely that every one of the 38 bystanders could have been apathetic. As social psychologists, they understood that the social environment powerfully influences behaviour, even though people may be unaware of its influence. They noted that the bystanders could see that other neighbours had turned on their lights and were looking out of their windows. Each bystander might have been concerned about Kitty Genovese's plight but assumed that someone else surely would help or call the police.

Darley and Latané reasoned that the presence of multiple bystanders produced a *diffusion of responsibility*, a psychological state in which each person feels decreased personal responsibility for intervening. They performed several experiments to test their explanation but had to remain open-minded to the possibility that the findings would not support their point of view.

GATHERING EVIDENCE: STEPS IN THE SCIENTIFIC PROCESS

Figure 2.2 shows how scientific inquiry often proceeds. Curiosity sparks the first step: scientists observe something noteworthy and ask a question about it. Darley and Latané observed that nobody helped Kitty Genovese and then asked the question 'Why?'

At the second step, scientists examine whether any studies, theories and other information already exist that might help answer their question, and then they formulate a tentative explanation. Noting that many bystanders had been present and that each one probably knew that others were witnessing Genovese's plight, Darley and Latané combined these clues to arrive at a possible explanation: a diffusion of responsibility reduced the likelihood that any one bystander would feel responsible for helping. This tentative explanation is then translated into a

FIGURE 2.1

What determines whether a bystander will help a victim?

Focus 2.1

Describe three key scientific attitudes and how they guided Darley and Latané's response to the Genovese murder.

STEPS IN THE SCIENTIFIC PROCESS

1. Initial observation or question

Kitty Genovese incident. Why did no one help?

2. Gather information and form hypothesis

A diffusion of responsibility may have occurred.
Hypothesis: IF multiple bystanders are present, THEN each bystander's likelihood of intervening will decrease

3. Test hypothesis (conduct research)

• Create 'emergency' in controlled setting.
• Manipulate perceived number of bystanders.
• Measure helping.

4. Analyse data and draw tentative conclusion

Helping decreases as the perceived number of bystanders increases. The hypothesis is supported.
(If data do not support the hypothesis, revise and retest.)

5. Report findings to scientific community

Researchers submit report to a scientific journal. If expert reviewers favourably evaluate the study, it is published. Fellow scientists learn about the research and may challenge, support or expand on it

6. Further research and theory building

Additional studies support the hypothesis. A theory of social impact is developed based on these and other findings

7. New hypotheses derived from theory

The theory is tested directly by deriving new hypotheses and conducting new research

FIGURE 2.2

The scientific process.

This sequence represents one common path to scientific understanding. In other cases, scientists begin with an observation or question, gather background information, and proceed directly to research without testing hypotheses or trying to build theories.

hypothesis

a specific prediction about some phenomenon or other

Focus 2.2

Use Darley and Latané's research or another study to illustrate seven major steps in the scientific process.

hypothesis, a specific prediction about some phenomenon or other that often takes the form of an 'If–Then' statement: 'In an emergency, IF multiple bystanders are present, THEN the likelihood that any one bystander will intervene is reduced.'

The third step is to test the hypothesis by conducting research. Darley and Latané (1968) staged an 'emergency' in their laboratory and observed people's responses. Undergraduate participants were told that they would be discussing 'personal problems faced by college students'. They were also told that to ensure privacy, they would be in separate rooms and communicate through an intercom system and that the experimenter would not listen to their conversation. Participants understood that they would take turns speaking for several rounds. In each round, a participant would have 2 minutes to speak, during which time the others would be unable to interrupt or be heard, because their microphones would be turned off.

As the discussion began over the intercom, a speaker described his difficulties adjusting to college life and disclosed that he suffered from seizures. During the next round of conversation, this same speaker began to gasp and stammer, saying: '"… Could somebody-er-er – help … [choking sounds] … I'm gonna die-er-er – I'm gonna die-er – help … seizure' [chokes, then silence]' (Darley and Latané, 1968, p. 379).

Unbeknown to the participants, they were actually listening to a tape recording. This ensured that all of them were exposed to the identical 'emergency'. To test how the number of bystanders influences helping, Darley and Latané manipulated the number of other people that each participant believed to be present and listening over the intercom. Participants were assigned to one of three conditions on a random basis. Each participant actually was alone but was led to believe that (1) they were alone with the victim, (2) there was another listener present, or (3) there were four other listeners present. Participants believed that the seizure was real and serious. But did they help?

At the fourth step of scientific inquiry, researchers analyse the information (called *data*) they collect and draw tentative conclusions. As Figure 2.3 shows, Darley and Latané found that all participants who thought they were alone with the victim helped within 3 minutes of the seizure. As the number of presumed bystanders increased, the proportion of actual participants who helped decreased, and those who helped took longer to respond. These findings support the diffusion-of-responsibility explanation and illustrate how research can contradict common-sense adages such as 'There's safety in numbers'. As you will see throughout this book, many common-sense beliefs have not survived the cutting edge of psychological research.

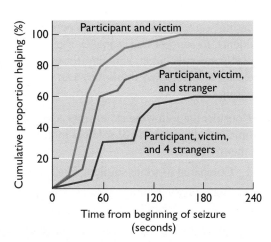

FIGURE 2.3

Helping in an emergency.

Participants who believed that they were the only bystander who could hear a seizure victim's plea for help were more likely to take action than were participants who believed that either one or four additional bystanders were listening.

SOURCE: data from Darley and Latané, 1968.

At the fifth step, scientists communicate their findings to the scientific community. Darley and Latané submitted an article describing their research to a scientific journal. Expert reviewers favourably evaluated the quality and importance of their bystander research, so the journal published the article. Scientists may also present their research at professional conferences, in books and more recently in journals designed specifically for use online, such as *Philica*. Disseminating research is essential to scientific progress. It allows fellow scientists to learn about new ideas and findings, to scrutinize the research and to challenge or expand on it.

At the sixth step, scientists conduct more research. As additional evidence comes in, scientists attempt to build theories. A **theory** is a set of formal statements that explains how and why certain events are related to one another. Theories are broader than hypotheses. For example, dozens of experiments revealed that diffusion of responsibility occurred across a range of situations. Latané then combined the principle of diffusion of responsibility with other principles of group behaviour to develop a broader *theory of social impact*, which he and others have since used to explain a variety of human social behaviours (Latané and Bourgeois, 2001).

> **theory**
>
> a set of formal statements that explains how and why certain events are related to one another

Finally, at the seventh step, scientists use the theory to develop new hypotheses, which are then tested by conducting additional research and gathering new evidence. In this manner the scientific process becomes self-correcting. If research consistently supports the hypotheses derived from the theory, confidence in the theory becomes stronger. If the predictions made by the theory are not supported, then it will need to be modified or, ultimately, discarded. Accurately and carefully communicating the methodology applied in the research is a very important part of science. It allows others to replicate findings, extend their research and take it further. Replication of research is also an extremely important component in developing support for the hypothesis and developing confidence in the theory under investigation, and we describe this a little later in the chapter.

TWO APPROACHES TO UNDERSTANDING BEHAVIOUR

Humans have a strong desire to understand why things happen. Why do scientists favour the preceding step-by-step approach to understanding behaviour over the approach typically involved in everyday common sense: hindsight?

Hindsight (After-the-Fact Understanding)

Many people erroneously believe that psychology is nothing more than common sense. 'I knew that all along!' or 'They had to do a study to find that out?' are common responses to some psychological research. It is always easy to arrive at an explanation to account for a statement you may hear. For instance, if you heard that when people wear seatbelts they drive more responsibly you might explain this by saying 'this is clearly because the seatbelt reminds them of the danger they and others are in, and so their driving reflects this'. When you are told that

Focus 2.3

Explain the major drawback of hindsight understanding. What approach to understanding do scientists prefer? Why?

wearing seatbelts does *not* make a person drive more responsibly, but in fact there is contested evidence to suggest that it makes them drive *faster* then it is not difficult to arrive at just as suitable an explanation. You may, for instance say 'of course people drive faster. They feel safer wearing a seatbelt, so think they can drive faster and still be as safe as when they were not wearing one'.

Consider the following statements adapted from Stouffer et al. (1949a; 1949b), who looked at attitudes and behaviours of soldiers in the Second World War. How would you account for each of them?

1. Compared to white soldiers, black soldiers were less motivated to become officers.
2. During basic training, soldiers from rural areas had higher morale and adapted better than soldiers from large cities.
3. Soldiers were more motivated to return home while the fighting was going on than they were after the war ended.

You should have no difficulty explaining these results. Typical reasoning might go something like this: (1) Owing to widespread prejudice, black soldiers knew that they had little chance of becoming officers. Why should they torment themselves wanting something that was unattainable? (2) It is obvious that the rigours of basic training would seem easier to people from farm settings, who were used to hard work and rising at the crack of dawn. (3) Any sane person would have wanted to go home while bullets were flying and people were dying.

What happens of we reverse the statements.

1. Compared to white soldiers, black soldiers were more motivated to become officers.
2. During basic training, soldiers from rural areas had lower morale and adapted worse than soldiers from large cities.
3. Soldiers less motivated to return home while the fighting was going on than they were after the war ended.

Try and arrive at explanations for the statements now. You should find that it is just as simple as it was the first time you did it. After-the-fact explanations for almost any result are easy to arrive at.

In everyday life, *hindsight* (after-the-fact explanation) is probably our most common method of trying to understand behaviour. The Danish philosopher Søren Kierkegaard noted, 'Life is lived forwards, but understood backwards'. The major limitation of relying solely on hindsight is that past events usually can be explained in many ways, and there is no sure way to know which – if any – of the explanations is correct. Despite this drawback, after-the-fact understanding can provide insights and is often the foundation on which further scientific inquiry is built. For example, Darley and Latané's diffusion-of-responsibility explanation was initially based on after-the-fact reasoning about the Kitty Genovese murder.

Understanding through Prediction, Control and Theory Building

Whenever possible, scientists prefer to test their understanding of 'what causes what' more directly. If we truly understand the causes of a given behaviour, then we should be able to predict the conditions under which that behaviour will occur in the future. Furthermore, if we can control those conditions (e.g., in the laboratory), then we should be able to produce that behaviour.

Darley and Latané's research illustrates this approach. They predicted that owing to a diffusion of responsibility, the presence of multiple bystanders during an emergency would reduce individual helping. Next, they carefully staged an emergency and controlled participants' beliefs about the number of bystanders present. Their prediction was supported. Understanding through prediction and control is a scientific alternative to after-the-fact understanding.

Theory building is the strongest test of scientific understanding, because good theories generate an integrated network of predictions. A good theory has several important characteristics.

1. It incorporates existing knowledge within a broad framework; that is, it organizes information in a meaningful way.

2. It is testable. It generates new hypotheses whose accuracy can be evaluated by gathering new evidence (Fig. 2.4).

3. The predictions made by the theory are supported by the findings of new research.

4. It conforms to the *law of parsimony*: if two theories can explain and predict the same phenomenon equally well, the simpler theory is the preferred one.

"IT MAY VERY WELL BRING ABOUT IMMORTALITY, BUT IT WILL TAKE FOREVER TO TEST IT."

Even when a theory is supported by many successful predictions, it is never regarded as an absolute truth. It is always possible that some future observation will contradict it or that a newer and more accurate theory will take its place. The displacement of old beliefs and theories by newer ones is the essence of scientific progress.

Finally, although scientists use prediction as a test of 'understanding', this does not mean that prediction requires understanding. Based on experience, even a child can predict that thunder will follow lightning without knowing why it does so. But prediction based on understanding (i.e., theory building) has advantages: it satisfies our curiosity and generates principles that can be applied to new situations that we have not yet directly experienced.

DEFINING AND MEASURING VARIABLES

Psychologists study variables and the relations among them. A **variable**, quite simply, is any characteristic or factor that can vary. Gender is a variable: Some people are female, others male. People's age, weight and typing speed are variables, as are concepts such as intelligence and stress. There were three major variables in Darley and Latané's bystander experiment: (1) the number of other bystanders that the real participants thought were present, (2) whether a participant helped the victim or not, and (3) for those who helped, how many seconds passed before they responded.

Because any variable (such as stress) may mean different things to different people, scientists must define their terms clearly. When conducting research, scientists do this by defining variables operationally. An **operational definition** defines a variable in terms of the specific procedures used to produce or measure it. Operational definitions translate abstract terms into something observable and measurable that the rest of the scientific community can understand clearly.

For example, suppose we want to study the relation between stress and academic performance among university students. How shall we operationally define our concepts? 'Academic performance' could mean a single test score, a grade for a module, or one's overall average. So, for our study, let us define it as students' final examination scores in an introductory chemistry course. As for 'stress', before or during the examination we could measure students' levels of muscle tension or stress hormones, or ask them to report how worried they feel. During the test we might observe their frequency of nail biting. We also could define stress in terms of environmental conditions, such as whether the examination questions and grading scale are easy or difficult. Figure 2.5 summarizes how we might operationally define examination stress at the biological, psychological and environmental levels.

FIGURE 2.4

Is this a testable hypothesis? Yes – if people drink it but still die at some point, then we have refuted the hypothesis – therefore it is testable. It is, however, impossible to absolutely prove true. If a person drinks the potion, then no matter how long she or he lives – even a million years – she or he might die the next day. Thus we cannot prove that the potion can make you live forever. Copyright © 2004 by Sidney Harris. ScienceCartoonsPlus.com. Reprinted.

Focus 2.4
Describe some characteristics of a good theory.

variable
any characteristic or factor that can vary

operational definition
defines a variable in terms of the specific procedures used to produce or measure it

Focus 2.5
Why are operational definitions important? Identify four major ways to measure behaviour and explain a limitation of each one.

LEVELS OF ANALYSIS : MEASURING EXAM STRESS		
Biological	**Psychological**	**Environmental**
• Stress-hormone levels measured at rest and during an examination • Measures of heart rate and respiration rate • Physiological measures of muscle tension and sweating	• General achievement anxiety measured by self-report personality test • Preexam questionnaire ratings of worry, tension and anxiety • Behavioural observations of 'nervous habits' during exam (e.g. fingernail biting, foot wiggling, hair pulling)	• Aspects of immediate environment that create stress (e.g. difficulty of examination, time pressure, noise and heat levels) • Easy or difficult course grading standards set by instructor • Achievement expectations set by parents or lecturer

Examination Stress

FIGURE 2.5

Levels of analysis: measuring examination stress.

To define a concept operationally, we must be able to measure it. Measurement is challenging because psychologists study incredibly varied and complex processes. Some processes are directly observable, but others are not. Fortunately, psychologists have numerous measurement techniques at their disposal (Fig. 2.6). There are often a number of different ways to operationalize a variable, and different members of the scientific community may have a preference for a particular method. For instance, a psychologist working in a biological field may choose to operationalize their variable differently from a psychologist investigating the same topic from a psychophysical perspective.

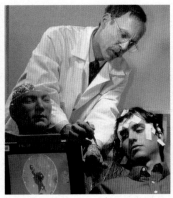

FIGURE 2.6

(a) Self-report, (b) physiological and (c) behavioural measures are important scientific tools for psychologists.

Self-Reports and Reports by Others

Self-report measures ask people to report on their own knowledge, attitudes, feelings, experiences or behaviour. This information can be gathered in several ways, such as through interviews or questionnaires. The accuracy of self-reports hinges on people's ability and willingness to respond honestly. Especially when questions focus on sensitive topics, such as sexual habits or drug use, self-reports may be distorted by *social desirability bias*, i.e. the tendency to respond in a socially acceptable manner rather than according to how one truly feels or behaves. Researchers try to minimize this bias by establishing rapport with participants and allowing them to respond confidentially or anonymously. Questionnaires can also be designed to reduce social desirability bias.

We also can get information about someone's behaviour by obtaining *reports made by other people*, such as parents, spouses, and teachers who know the person. University students might be asked to rate their class-mates' personality traits, and job supervisors might be asked to rate a worker's competence. As with self-reports, researchers try to maximize participants' honesty in reporting about other people.

Observations of Behaviour

Another measurement approach is to *observe and record overt (i.e., directly visible) behaviour*. In an animal learning experiment, we might measure how often a rat follows the correct path in a maze. In Darley and Latané's (1968) bystander emergency experiment, they recorded whether college students helped a seizure victim. Psychologists also develop *coding systems* to record different categories of behaviour. If we observe how a parent behaves while a child performs a task, we might code each instance of parental behaviour into categories such as 'praises child', 'assists child', 'criticizes child', and so forth. Once a coding system is developed, observers are trained to use it properly so that their measurements will be *reliable* (i.e., consistent). If two observers watching the same behaviours repeatedly disagree in their coding (e.g., one says the parent 'praised' and another says the parent 'assisted'), then the data are unreliable and of little use.

Humans and other animals may behave differently when they know they are being observed. To counter this problem, researchers may camouflage themselves or use **unobtrusive measures**, which record behaviour in a way that keeps participants unaware that they are being observed. A person's choice of words in a conversation may reveal something about them, and something about their true feelings and meanings. Careful analysis of a discussion (called discourse analysis) is an example of an unobtrusive measure.

Psychologists also gather information about behaviour by using **archival measures**, which are records or documents that already exist. For example, researchers assessing a programme to reduce drunk driving could examine police records to measure how many people were arrested for driving while drunk before and after the programme was implemented.

unobtrusive measure
record behaviour in a way that keeps participants unaware that they are being observed

archival measures
records or documents that already exist

Psychological Tests

Psychologists develop and use specialized tests to measure many types of variables. For example, *personality tests*, which assess people's personality traits, often contain series of questions that ask how a person typically feels or behaves (e.g., 'True or False: I prefer to be alone rather than in social gatherings.'). In essence, such tests are specialized self-reports. Other personality tests present a series of ambiguous stimuli (e.g., pictures that could have different meanings), and personality traits are judged based on how a person interprets these stimuli.

Other psychological tests consist of performance tasks. For example, *intelligence tests* may ask people to assemble objects or solve arithmetic problems. *Neuropsychological tests* help diagnose normal and abnormal brain functioning by measuring how well people perform mental and physical tasks, such as recalling lists of words or manipulating objects. As you will learn in Chapter 9, developing a good psychological test takes a tremendous amount of technical work.

Physiological Measures

Although psychologists use self-reports to measure people's subjective experiences, they also record physiological responses to assess what people are experiencing. Measures of heart rate, blood pressure, respiration rate, hormonal secretions, and electrical and biochemical processes in the brain have long been the mainstay of researchers working within the biological perspective, but these measures have become increasingly important in many other areas of psychology.

Physiological responses can have their own interpretive problems. For example, if a person shows increased heart rate and brain activity in a particular situation, what emotion or thought is being expressed? The links between specific patterns of physiological activity and particular mental events are far from being completely understood.

In sum, psychologists can measure behaviour in many ways, each with advantages and disadvantages. To gain greater confidence in their findings, researchers may use several types of measures within a single study.

IN REVIEW

- Curiosity, scepticism and open-mindedness are key scientific attitudes. The scientific process proceeds through several steps: (1) asking questions based on some type of observation, (2) formulating a tentative explanation and a testable hypothesis, (3) conducting research to test the hypothesis, (4) analysing the data and drawing a tentative conclusion, (5) reporting one's findings to the scientific community, (6) building a theory and (7) using the theory to generate new hypotheses, which are tested by more research.

- In everyday life we typically use hindsight to explain behaviour. Hindsight is flawed because there may be many possible explanations and no way to assess which is correct. Psychologists prefer to test their understanding through prediction, control and theory building.

- A good theory organizes known facts, gives rise to additional hypotheses that are testable, is supported by the findings of new research and is parsimonious.

- An operational definition defines a concept or variable in terms of the specific procedures used to produce or measure it.

- To measure behaviour, psychologists obtain people's self-reports and reports from others who know the participants, directly observe behaviour, use unobtrusive measures, analyse archival data, administer psychological tests and measure physiological responses.

ETHICAL PRINCIPLES IN RESEARCH

When conducting research, scientists must weigh the knowledge and possible applications to be gained against potential risks to research participants. To safeguard the rights of participants, researchers must adhere to ethical standards set by government regulations and national psychological organizations (Fig. 2.7). Animal subjects must also be treated in accordance with established ethical guidelines. At academic and research institutions, it is a growing practice that special committees review the ethical issues involved in research proposals. If a proposed study is considered ethically questionable, it must be modified or the research cannot be conducted.

The British Psychological Society, as well as the Irish, Danish, Finnish, Norwegian, Scandinavian and South African psychological associations all adhere to ethical considerations. Some take the guidelines outlined by the American Psychological Association as their starting point, but essentially the codes all describe principles of conduct when conducting research in psychology. It seems that professional bodies the world over consider ethical conduct as being extremely important. All have subtle differences, but the principles laid out by the British Psychological Society are representative, and are as follows:

FIGURE 2.7

Ethical standards are designed to protect the welfare of both humans and non-humans in psychological research.

Focus 2.6

Identify major ethical issues in human and animal research.

1. *Competence*: maintenance of high levels of training, and operation within boundaries of ability
2. *Responsibility*: performing professional duties with utmost care
3. *Integrity*: being honest and accurate
4. *Respect*: respecting people's dignity and rights to confidentiality and self-determination

ETHICAL STANDARDS IN HUMAN RESEARCH

These *ethics codes* also provide specific guidelines for psychological activities, including research. According to the ethical standard of **informed consent**, before people agree to participate in research they should be informed about:

- the study's purpose and procedures
- the study's potential benefits
- potential risks to participants
- the right to decline participation and withdraw at any time without penalty
- whether responses will be confidential and, if not, how privacy will be safeguarded.

When children, or other vulnerable people, such as those with mental illnesses, who cannot give true informed consent are involved, consent must be obtained from parents, guardians or, in some cases, doctors. To safeguard a participant's right to privacy, researchers typically gather and report data in ways that keep participants' identity anonymous or confidential, often referring to specific cases or individuals by numbers or initials rather than names.

Deception, which occurs when participants are misled about the nature of a study, is controversial. Consider the Darley and Latané (1968) bystander experiment. Participants were not told that the study was going to examine how they would respond to an emergency, nor were they informed that the procedure (someone presumably having a seizure) might cause them stress.

Deception violates the principle of informed consent, but its proponents argue that when studying certain types of behaviours, deception is the only way to obtain natural, spontaneous responses from participants. Darley and Latané's participants, for example, had to believe that the emergency was significant and real.

Guidelines may permit deception only when no other feasible alternative is available and the study has scientific, educational or applied benefits that clearly outweigh the ethical costs of deceiving participants. When deception is used, the true purpose of the study should be explained to participants after it is over. The overwhelming majority of psychological studies do not involve deception.

informed consent

before people agree to participate in research they should be informed about

- the study's purpose and procedures
- the study's potential benefits
- potential risks to participants
- the right to decline participation and withdraw at any time without penalty
- whether responses will be confidential and, if not, how privacy will be safeguarded.

ETHICAL STANDARDS IN ANIMAL RESEARCH

In a minority of experimental procedures in psychology, animals are used as subjects. This includes research done in the wild and in more controlled settings. Rodents and birds comprise 90 per cent of the animals studied; nonhuman primates comprise another 5 per cent.

Some psychologists study animals to discover principles that shed light on human behaviour, and some do so to learn more about other species. As in medical research, some studies expose animals to conditions considered too hazardous for humans. This topic is controversial, with some believing that animals should never be used in research. Most psychologists though feel that careful animal research is an important route to scientific progress in psychology.

Ethics guidelines require that animals be treated humanely and that the potential importance of the research clearly justify the risks to which they are exposed. This determination, however, is not always easy to make, and people often disagree. For example, should researchers be allowed to inject a drug into an animal in order to learn whether that drug might permanently impair memory? Before animal research can be conducted, it must be reviewed and approved by panels that often include non-scientists.

Animal research is debated both outside and within the psychological community (Herzog, 2005). Psychologists agree that it is morally wrong to subject animals to needless suffering. Many scientists, however, do not agree with anti-vivisectionists who maintain that animals should never be used in research 'which is not for the benefit of the animals involved' (Goodman, 1982, p. 61). Proponents point to important medical and psychological advances made possible by animal research. For example, had Louis Pasteur not subjected some dogs to suffering, he could not have developed the rabies vaccine, which has saved the lives of countless humans as well as animals. They ask, 'Does the prospect of finding a cure for cancer or of identifying harmful drug effects or the causes of psychological disorders justify exposing some animals to harm?'

Other research using animals in captivity is focused on how animals behave. A healthy, psychologically sound animal is more likely to behave 'normally' and as such their welfare is extremely important. Legislation to ensure animal welfare of this kind is carefully monitored by groups such as the International Fund for Animal Welfare (IFAW). In 1956 the Treaty of Rome was signed to set up the European Union. The treaty did not include any legislation to account for animal welfare, but in 1997 it was amended to take this into account. The 'Treaty of Amsterdam' became effective in 1999.

Although animal research has declined slightly in recent decades, the ethical questions remain as vexing as ever. What is most encouraging is that the welfare of animals in research is receiving the careful attention it deserves.

IN REVIEW

- Psychological research follows extensive ethical guidelines. In human research, key issues are the use of informed consent, the participants' right to privacy, potential risks to participants and the use of deception.

- Ethical guidelines require that animals be treated humanely and that the risks to which they are exposed be justified by the potential importance of the research. As in human research, before animal research can be conducted it must be reviewed and approved, often by ethics review boards that include non-scientists.

METHODS OF RESEARCH

Like detectives searching for clues to solve a case, psychologists conduct research to gather evidence about behaviour and its causes. The research method chosen depends on the problem being studied, the investigator's objectives, and ethical principles.

DESCRIPTIVE RESEARCH: RECORDING EVENTS

The most basic goal of science is to describe phenomena. In psychology, **descriptive research** seeks to identify how humans and other animals behave, particularly in natural settings. It provides valuable information about the diversity of behaviour, can be used to test hypotheses and may yield clues about potential cause–effect relations that are later tested experimentally. Case studies, naturalistic observation and surveys are common descriptive methods.

Case Studies: Victor – the Wild Child of Aveyron

A **case study** is an in-depth analysis of an individual, group, or event. By studying a single case in great detail, the researcher typically hopes to discover principles of behaviour that hold true for people or situations in general. Data may be gathered through observation, interviews, psychological tests, physiological recordings or task performance.

One advantage of a case study is that when a rare phenomenon occurs, this method enables scientists to study it closely. A second advantage is that a case study may challenge the validity of a theory or widely held scientific belief. Perhaps the biggest advantage of a case study is that it can be a vibrant source of new ideas that may subsequently be examined using other research methods. History is littered with famous case studies that have hugely influenced our understanding of science and behaviour. These case studies have often informed the progression of science. Consider this important example.

In 1797 a boy was captured in the woods near Aveyron in France. He had been spotted many times by the locals, but was finally captured. He escaped, and was recaptured twice more before taking a decision to walk from the woods into 'captivity' in 1800. He could not speak and his age was unknown, but those who saw him and worked around him estimated him as being approximately 12 years old, certainly old enough to be able to talk under normal circumstances. After some investigation from a local biologist, Victor was taken in and studied by a medical student called Jean Marc Gaspard Itard (see Fig. 2.8)

Gaspard ensured that Victor could hear. His responses to loud sounds and his ability to mimic rhythms with a drum assured Gaspard of this. Victor could also make rudimentary sounds, but Gaspard was still unsure of whether speech could be possible. Gaspard's thinking was interesting. His theory was that the difference between animals and humans lay in an ability with language and an understanding of empathy. If he could just show that speech was possible, this would provide evidence that Victor was not beyond help, and that he possessed abilities not available to animals.

Victor showed some early progression, with a very basic, extremely limited vocabulary of two phrases: 'lait' meaning 'milk' and 'Oh Dieu' meaning 'Oh God'. This was the limit of his linguistic ability. One day though, Gaspard's housekeeper, Madame Guerin, with whom Victor spent some considerable time, was upset at the loss of her husband. Victor consoled her, showing empathy – one of Gaspard's uniquely human traits. He was, after all, capable of human-like behaviour.

This case study is unique in its details, but bears some resemblance to other similar studies, Genie (Curtiss, 1977) is a more modern example, and there are more. Collectively these cases are described as 'feral children' and you should not have any trouble finding information about them in libraries or on the web.

descriptive research
seeks to identify how humans and other animals behave, particularly in natural settings

Focus 2.7
Discuss three types of descriptive research, and explain the advantages and disadvantages of each.

case study
an in-depth analysis of an individual, group, or event

FIGURE 2.8

Jean Marc Gaspard Itard, a medical student, who studied Victor, the so-called 'wild-boy' of Aveyron.

The major limitation of a case study is that it is a poor method for determining cause–effect relationships. In most case studies, explanations of behaviour occur after the fact and there is little opportunity to rule out alternative explanations. The fact that Victor's problems with language co-occurred with his not having spent his earlier childhood with humans could have been pure coincidence. He may perhaps have had a head injury which could have been responsible for his lack of language.

Another potential drawback concerns the *generalizability* of the findings: will the principles uncovered in a case study hold true for other people or in other situations? The question of generalizability pertains to all research methods, but drawing broad conclusions from a case study can be particularly risky. The key issue is the degree to which the case under study is representative of other people or situations. One thing that Gaspard's study showed was Victor's inability to gain the ability to speak. This may indicate that speech can only be obtained if done so before a particular age, which Victor had already passed. This is a 'critical-period' hypothesis, and Victor's case and some of the feral children cases that followed provides support for this idea.

A third drawback is the possible lack of objectivity in the way data are gathered and interpreted. Such bias can occur in any type of research, but case studies can be particularly worrisome because they are often based largely on the researcher's subjective impressions. In science, a sceptical attitude requires that claims based on case studies be followed up by more comprehensive research methods before they are accepted. In everyday life we should adopt a similar sceptical view. When you encounter claims based on case examples or anecdotes, keep in mind that the case may be atypical or that the person making the claim may be biased. Try to seek out other evidence to support or refute the claim.

Naturalistic Observation: Chimpanzees, Tool Use and Cultural Learning

In **naturalistic observation**, the researcher observes behaviour as it occurs in a natural setting. Naturalistic observation is used extensively to study animal behaviour (Fig. 2.9). Jane Goodall gained fame for her observations of African chimpanzees in the wild. Goodall (1986) and other researchers found that chimpanzees display behaviours, such as making and using tools, that were formerly believed to lie only within the human domain. Goodall's careful, detailed observations were vital in making her work accessible, and acceptable, to an initially sceptical scientific community.

> **naturalistic observation**
> the researcher observes behaviour as it occurs in a natural setting

FIGURE 2.9

Researcher Jane Goodall uses naturalistic observation to study the behaviour of wild chimpanzees.

Swiss researcher Christophe Boesch (1991) has observed a 'hammer/anvil' tool-use technique among wild African chimpanzees. A chimp places a nut on a hard surface (the anvil) and then hammers it several times with a stone or a fallen branch until it cracks. Some nuts with hard shells are tricky to open, and it may take several years for chimps to perfect their hammering. Especially fascinating is Boesch's observation that mothers seem to intentionally teach their young how to use this technique. Consider this interaction between a chimp named Ricci and her 5-year-old daughter, Nina:

Nina … tried to open nuts with the only available hammer, which was of an irregular shape. As she struggled unsuccessfully … Ricci joined her and Nina immediately gave her the hammer…. Ricci, in a very deliberate manner, slowly rotated the hammer into the best position with which to pound the nut effectively…. With Nina watching her, she then proceeded to use the hammer to crack 10 nuts … then Ricci left and Nina resumed cracking. Now, by adopting the same hammer grip as her mother, she succeeded in opening four nuts in 15 min…. In this example the mother corrected an error in her daughter's behaviour. (Boesch, 1991, p. 532)

For evolutionary and cultural psychologists, such naturalistic observations can provide clues about the possible origins of human behaviour. As in human cultures, these chimpanzees developed a method for using tools and appeared to teach it to their young. These findings support the view that the mechanisms by which human cultures are formed – such as the intentional transmission of information across generations – may have an evolutionary basis (Workman and Reader, 2008).

The excerpt about Ricci and Nina illustrates how naturalistic observation can provide a rich description of behaviour. Numerical data, such as the frequency of various behaviours, may be recorded and analysed. Naturalistic observation is also used to study human behaviour. For example, developmental psychologists observe children in natural settings to learn about their co-operative play, aggression and friendships.

Like case studies, naturalistic observation does not permit clear conclusions about the causal relations between variables. In the real world, many variables simultaneously influence behaviour, and they cannot be disentangled with this research technique. There also is the possibility of bias in the way that researchers interpret the behaviours they observe. Finally, observers must try to avoid influencing the participants being studied. Even the mere presence of a human observer may disrupt a person's or animal's behaviour, at least initially. As time passes, people and other animals typically adapt to and ignore the presence of an observer.

This adaptation process is called *habituation*. The knowledge that animals habituate in this way is of particular use in developmental psychology where, it turns out, infants show similar behaviour. This allows experiments to be designed to make use of this habituation, or to account for it in experimental procedures. It is worth noting that researchers often use a mixture of techniques in their work. For instance, both naturalistic and experimental methods have been used in the field of tool use in primates. It is important to use the correct tool for the job, and that includes the research methods tools available to the researcher!

Survey Research: How Well Do You Sleep?

In **survey research**, information about a topic is obtained by administering questionnaires or interviews to many people. Surveys typically ask about participants' attitudes, opinions and behaviours. For example, do you ever have difficulty falling or staying asleep? Are you ever so sleepy during the day that it interferes with your activities? The 'Enough sleep' project began in 2005, and is a collaboration between a number of universities and research institutions in Finland, Holland, Sweden and Switzerland. The aim of the project is to investigate how we regulate sleep. Sleep is a vital part of life and is terribly important for our well-being. The project will look at a data-set of 9000 people gathered in Finland in the year 2000. How is it possible to make an accurate estimate of the problems of almost all those adults that have disturbed sleep based on this relatively small data-set of only 9000 people?

Two key concepts in survey research are population and sample. A **population** consists of all the individuals that we are interested in drawing a conclusion about, such as 'Finnish adults' in the sleep survey example. Because it is often impractical to study the entire population, we would administer the survey to a **sample**, which is a subset of individuals drawn from the larger population.

To draw valid conclusions about a population from the results of a single survey, the sample must be representative: A **representative sample** is one that reflects the important characteristics of the population (Fig. 2.10). A sample composed of 80 per cent males would not be representative of the student body at a college where only 50 per cent of the students are men. To obtain a representative sample, survey researchers typically use a procedure called **random sampling**, in which every member of the population has an equal probability of being chosen to participate in the survey. A common variation of this procedure, called

survey research
information about a topic is obtained by administering questionnaires or interviews to many people

population
all the individuals that we are interested in drawing a conclusion about

sample
a subset of individuals drawn from the larger population

representative sample
reflects the important characteristics of the population

random sampling
in which every member of the population has an equal probability of being chosen to participate in the survey

FIGURE 2.10

Surveys and sampling.

A representative sample possesses the important characteristics of the population in the same proportions. Data from a representative sample are more likely to generalize to the larger population than are data from an unrepresentative sample.

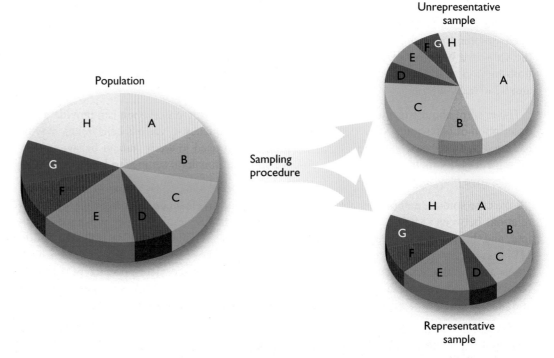

Focus 2.8

What is random sampling and why do survey researchers use it? What problems can occur when conducting surveys?

stratified random sampling, is to divide the population into subgroups based on characteristics such as gender or ethnic identity. Suppose the population is 55 per cent female. In this case, 55 per cent of the spaces in the sample would be allocated to women and 45 per cent to men. Random sampling is then used to select the individual women and men who will be in the survey.

When a representative sample is surveyed, we can be confident (though never completely certain) that the findings closely portray the population as a whole. This is the strongest advantage of survey research. Modern political opinion polls typically use such excellent sampling procedures that, just prior to elections, they can reasonably predict from a sample of about 1000 people who will win or if the result is too evenly balanced to confidently make a prediction.

In contrast, unrepresentative samples can produce distorted results. It is better to have a smaller representative sample than a larger, unrepresentative one. If the sample that you choose does not relate to the population in general, then you may live to regret your prediction. Newspapers regularly set two different front pages at election time to ensure that they will have an appropriate story whoever wins. They know that making a prediction on an exit poll (people leaving the voting stations) is fraught with danger, and these polls often get their predictions very wrong because of an inappropriate sample. Bad sample, bad prediction. In sum, always consider the nature of the sample when interpreting survey results. Another way of looking at this is to think about where data used in psychology come from. Banyard and Hunt (2000) investigated papers published in two journals, and discovered that a significant proportion of the data were provided by university students. Not only that, but a large number of them were obliged by their course requirements to participate in these experiments. We could infer from this that a large proportion of samples are *students who are forced to participate*. This is hardly representative of the general population and, as such, care should be taken when interpreting some of these results. Of course, careful design of experiments means that this rather restricted sample may not be a problem at all, but the point is worth making here.

In scientific research, surveys are an efficient method for collecting a large amount of information about people's opinions and lifestyles, and they can reveal changes in people's beliefs and habits over many years but there are several major drawbacks to surveys. First, survey data cannot be used to draw conclusions about cause and effect. Second, surveys rely on participants' self-reports, which can be distorted by factors such as social desirability bias, interviewer bias or people's inaccurate perceptions of their own behaviour. Third, unrepresentative samples can lead to faulty generalizations about how an entire population would respond. And, finally, even when surveys use proper random sampling procedures, once in a while – simply by chance – a sample that is randomly chosen will turn out not to be representative of the larger population. In most good professional and scientific surveys this happens less than 5 per cent of the time ... but it does happen. Thus for several reasons even well-crafted surveys can yield inaccurate estimates.

WHAT DO YOU THINK?

SHOULD YOU TRUST INTERNET AND POPULAR MEDIA SURVEYS?

Tom fills out a political-attitude survey posted on the Internet. Claire mails in a marital-satisfaction survey that came in a fashion magazine to which she subscribes. Sam responds to a local television news phone-in survey on a tax issue ('Call our number, press "1" to agree, "2" to disagree'). For each survey, can the results be trusted to reflect the general public's attitudes? Think about it, then see page 81.

CORRELATIONAL RESEARCH: MEASURING ASSOCIATIONS BETWEEN EVENTS

What factors distinguish happily married couples from those headed for divorce? Do first-born children differ in personality from later-born children? Is monetary wealth related to happiness? These and countless other psychological questions ask about associations between naturally occurring events or variables. To examine such relationships, scientists typically conduct **correlational research**, which in its simplest form has three components:

1. The researcher measures one variable (X), such as people's age.
2. The researcher measures a second variable (Y), such as self-reported daytime sleepiness.
3. The researcher statistically determines whether X and Y are related.

Keep in mind that correlational research involves *measuring* variables, not *manipulating* them.

Naturalistic observation and surveys are often used not only to describe events but also to study associations between variables. Imagine we needed to investigate the relationship between how the sale of ice cream changes with temperature. Our data may look something like those shown in Table 2.1. Here the *association* between the two variables (*temperature* and *volume of ice cream sold*) is shown as a positive relationship. As one variable increases (it gets hotter) more ice-cream is sold. You might also use correlation in other types of research as our 'Research close-up' section illustrates.

correlational research
measures one variable (X), measures a second variable (Y), statistically determines whether X and Y are related

Focus 2.9
Describe three components of correlational research and how they are illustrated by the study of very happy people.

RESEARCH CLOSE-UP

SEASONAL AFFECTIVE DISORDER

SOURCE: P.P.A. Mersch, H.M. Middendorp, A.L. Bouhuys, D.G.M. Beersma and R.H. van den Hoofdakker (1999). Seasonal affective disorder and latitude: a review of the literature. *Journal of Affective Disorders*, Vol. 53, pp. 35–48.

INTRODUCTION

The long winter nights of Northern Europe give way to glorious sunshine (hopefully!) in April, May and June. We spend more time outside because the weather is warm and the days are longer. The countryside is heavy with summertime smells and the promise of spring. It is a wonderful time of the year. Spending time outside, and in the sunshine, for some reason makes us feel happy. A relaxing summer holiday on a wonderful beach in Greece or Spain perhaps, recharges our batteries, both physically and psychologically. The summer makes way to darker, shorter days in September and October. It rains more, and we spend more time indoors, huddled around our fires and television sets. We leave for our places of work or study in the dark in the morning, and arrive home in the dark in the evening.

For some reason, we feel less good in ourselves than we did in the summer. People have known this for a long time. But relatively recently, a psychological disorder has been described that indicates why some of us suffer more with these changes in happiness, or feelings of well-being as the seasons change. It is called *seasonal affective disorder (SAD)* and was described by Rosenthal et al. in 1984. Among those suffering with this problem, there appears to be a strong correlation between feeling of well-being and exposure to sunshine. In this paper, Mersch et al. have reviewed literature that looks at how the *latitude (how far North) at which we live* may influence our feeling of well-being, as measured here by incidence of seasonal affective disorder. Lower SAD means a generally better feeling among the population studied. Previous work from Lingjaerde et al. (1986) in Norway and Potkin et al. (1986) in the USA had shown just such a relationship, and a meta-analysis (see later in this chapter for an explanation of this term) of the available data would help Mersch et al. see any patterns that might reveal support for the hypothesis.

METHOD

Mersch et al. looked at many papers that investigated SAD in different seasons. These papers used different methods to assess SAD and were carried out on different samples and populations. By looking for patterns in the data Mersch et al. hoped to be able to either confirm or deny a relationship between latitude and incidence of SAD. To do this two variables were collected: latitude and percentage of those with SAD symptoms. These were then plotted on a scatterplot, like those seen in Figure 2.12.

RESULTS

The results were a little confusing. Mersch et al. found that the relationship between latitude and SAD in the USA was significant. In Europe the relationship was not significant. In other words, people that live at the same latitude were more likely to show SAD symptoms if they lived in America than if they lived in Europe. How could this be?

DISCUSSION

It seems that the relationship between latitude and SAD is not clear. Something else may be playing a part in the incidence of SAD, or the level of well-being we feel. It makes perfect sense to think that living further North means that there is generally less sunshine and less light, and that this would account for the greater incidence of SAD. It seems though that a third variable may be playing a part, one which we may not have accounted for. Living in America, for whatever reason, seems to mean that SAD is more likely, when latitude is taken into consideration, than living in Europe. So what is going on here? Mersch et al. suggest that *climate* may be the mystery factor. Even though they are at the same latitude, Madrid and New York have very different climates. The weather in New York has extremes of cold and hot, and is much harsher than Madrid's weather pattern. They also point out that social and cultural patterns and factors should be considered. Admitting a psychological problem in a questionnaire or interview may be more acceptable in some cultures than others. Also, genetic factors may influence the data. It could be that a weakness to suffer from SAD may be passed genetically, and for some reason may become more prominent as the generations go by. It could be that Americans have a genetic predisposition to show these symptoms, whereas Europeans may not. Another issue in the prevalence of SAD may be the general knowledge of the diagnosis in the population. It may be that in the American surveys the samples used had a greater awareness that SAD existed than did the European samples, and would be more likely to answer positively if asked about symptoms. Finally, the difference in US and European data may have been something to do with the samples used in the original studies. It might be that the samples were not representative of the general population, and that the test used to measure whether the person showed SAD symptoms may not have been valid for all groups of people.

We can conclude then that the relationship between latitude and SAD is not terribly clear. It is different in the USA than in Europe and this may be due to all sorts of factors. A new study that collects new data rather than looking at existing data taking all the factors Mersch et al. identified would help us clear up this interesting area of research.

TABLE 2.1 ICE CREAM SALES AND TEMPERATURE

The relationship between sales of ice cream and the weather. C.f. Cohen et al., 2001.

Temperature	Litres of ice cream sold
2 °C	5
22 °C	36
32 °C	52

Correlation and Causation

It is tempting to conclude from studies of seasonal affective disorder that spending time outside in the sun causes people to have an increased feeling of well-being, but we have seen from Mersch et al.'s work that correlational research does not allow us to draw clear conclusions like this. First, the direction of causality could be just the opposite. Perhaps feeling good in ourselves causes people to want to get out more. In correlational research, you must consider the possibility that variable X (spending time outside) has caused variable Y (feeling of well-being), that Y has caused X, or that both variables have influenced each other. This interpretive problem is called the *bidirectionality* (i.e., *two-way causality*) *problem* (Fig. 2.11b).

Second, the association between time spend outside and our feeling of well-being may be artificial, or what scientists call *spurious* (not genuine). Although the two are statistically related, it may be that neither variable has any causal effect on the other. A third variable, Z, may really be the cause of why some people spend time outside. In general, people with a more outgoing and agreeable personality tend to worry less about how others perceive them. They may not think twice about putting on a swimsuit and strolling to the beach on a hot day, whereas shy people or those with a more negative body image would not experience the sunshine in the same way because of a lack of confidence. In this case it is a personality style that means that people enjoy

Focus 2.10

Explain why scientists cannot draw causal conclusions from correlation research. Discuss an example.

FIGURE 2.11

Correlation and causation.

(a) Why does an association occur between spending more time outdoors and having an increased sense of well-being? (b) Spending more time outside could cause people to feel better or, conversely, feeling better in themselves could make people feel like going out more. This is the bidirectionality problem. (c) There may be no causal link at all. Other variables, such as personality traits, may be part of the true common origin of how we feel in ourselves, and whether we enjoy spending time outdoors. This is the third-variable problem.

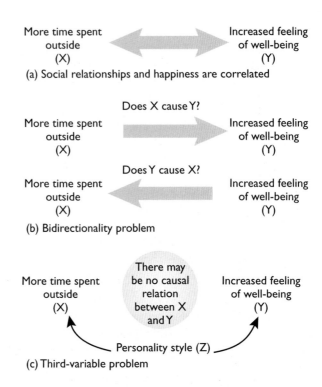

(a) Social relationships and happiness are correlated

Does X cause Y?

Does Y cause X?

(b) Bidirectionality problem

There may be no causal relation between X and Y

Personality style (Z)

(c) Third-variable problem

more time outdoors, and experience more sunshine. At the same time, this style may help people soak up more joy from life and therefore feel happier in themselves. Thus on the surface it looks as if time spent outside and feeling of well-being are causally linked, but in reality this may only be due to Z (in this case, personality style).

This interpretive problem is called the *third-variable problem*: Z is responsible for what looks like a relation between X and Y (Fig. 2.11c). As Z varies, it causes X to change. As Z varies, it also causes Y to change. The net result is that X and Y change in unison, but this is caused by Z – not by any direct effect of X or Y on each other. In sum, we cannot draw causal conclusions from correlational data, and this is the major disadvantage of correlational research.

WHAT DO YOU THINK?

DOES EATING ICE CREAM CAUSE PEOPLE TO DROWN?

Nationally, ice cream consumption and drownings are positively correlated. Over the course of the year, on days when more ice cream is consumed, there tend to be more drownings. Are these two variables causally related? What causal possibilities should you consider? The data in Table 2.1 may give you a clue! Think about it, then see page 81.

correlation coefficient

a statistic that indicates the direction and strength of the relation between two variables

positive correlation

higher scores on one variable are associated with higher scores on a second variable

The Correlation Coefficient

A **correlation coefficient** is a statistic that indicates the direction and strength of the relation between two variables. You can only do correlations if you have numerical measures on two or more variables from a number of different individuals. The correlation coefficient is arrived at using some relatively straightforward mathematics. Variables can be correlated either positively or negatively. A **positive correlation** means that higher scores on one variable are associated with higher scores on a second variable. Thus social relationships and happiness are positively correlated such that more satisfying relationships are associated with higher levels of happiness. Similarly, people's height and weight are positively correlated (i.e., in general, taller people tend to weigh more), as are hours of daylight and average daily temperature (overall, the longer days of spring and summer have higher average temperatures than do the shorter days of autumn and winter).

A **negative correlation** occurs when higher scores on one variable are associated with lower scores on a second variable. Job satisfaction and job turnover are negatively correlated, which means that workers who are more satisfied with their jobs tend to have lower rates of turnover (e.g., quitting, being fired). Likewise, students' test anxiety and examination performance are negatively correlated (students with higher levels of test anxiety tend to perform more poorly in examinations), as are hours of daylight and time spent indoors (overall, on the longer days of the year we spend less time indoors).

Correlation coefficients range from values of +1.00 to −1.00. The plus or minus sign tells you the direction of a correlation (i.e., whether the variables are positively or negatively correlated). The absolute value of the statistic tells you the strength of the correlation. The closer the correlation is to +1.00 (a perfect positive correlation) or −1.00 (a perfect negative correlation), the more strongly the two variables are related. Therefore a correlation of −.59 indicates a stronger association between X and Y than does a correlation of +.37. A zero correlation (0.00) means that X and Y are not related statistically: As scores on X increase or decrease, scores on Y do not change in any orderly fashion. Figure 2.12 illustrates three **scatterplots**, graphs that show the correlation between two variables.

negative correlation

when higher scores on one variable are associated with lower scores on a second variable

scatterplots

graphs that show the correlation between two variables

Focus 2.11

Explain positive and negative correlation coefficients and scatterplots. How does correlation facilitate prediction?

FIGURE 2.12

Scatterplots depicting correlations.

A scatterplot depicts the correlation between two variables. The horizontal axis represents variable **X**, the vertical axis variable **Y**. Each data point represents a specific pair of **X** and **Y** scores. The three scatterplots show (a) a strong positive correlation, (b) a zero correlation (0.00) and (c) a strong negative correlation for hypothetical sets of data.

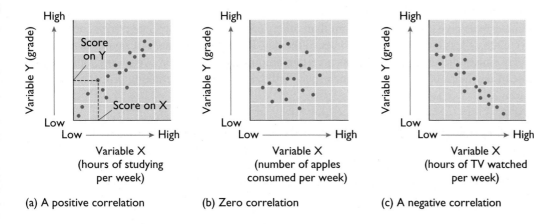

(a) A positive correlation (b) Zero correlation (c) A negative correlation

Correlation as a Basis for Prediction

Why conduct correlational research if it does not permit clear cause–effect conclusions? One benefit is that correlational research can help establish whether relations found in the laboratory generalize to the outside world. For example, suppose that laboratory experiments show that talking on a telephone while operating a driving simulator causes people to get into more simulated crashes. Correlational studies, while not demonstrating cause–effect, can at least establish whether there is a real-world association between driver mobile-phone usage and automobile accident rates. A second benefit is that correlational research can be conducted before experiments to discover associations that can then be studied under controlled laboratory conditions. Third, for practical or ethical reasons some questions cannot be studied with experiments but can be examined correlationally. We cannot experimentally manipulate how religious someone is, but we can measure people's religiousness and determine if it is associated with other variables, such as personality traits.

Another benefit is that correlational data allow us to make predictions. If two variables are correlated, either positively or negatively, knowing the score of one variable helps us estimate the score on the other variable. For example, the space drivers afford to cyclists when overtaking them at different times of day (Walker, 2006; 2007), as the scatterplot in Figure 2.13 shows.

FIGURE 2.13

Correlation of time of day with space between bicycle and car in an overtaking procedure.

This scatterplot represents data for a sample of 50 students. The horizontal axis represents variable X, time of day. The vertical axis represents variable Y, space between car and bicycle in an overtaking procedure. Variables X and Y are moderately correlated.

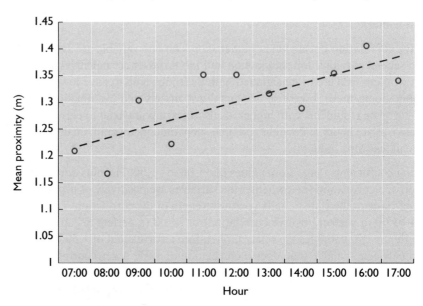

These data suggest that the later the time of day, the more room drivers give cyclists when overtaking (Walker, 2007). The scatterplot shows that this positive correlation is not perfect. Some drivers give cyclists more room than others early on in the day; conversely, some drivers give cyclists less space than others later in the day. Remember, we are not saying that the time of day causes drivers to give cyclists a certain amount of space when overtaking, only that the time of day helps us predict how much space will be given in an overtaking procedure.

EXPERIMENTS: EXAMINING CAUSE AND EFFECT

In contrast to descriptive and correlational methods, experiments are a powerful tool for examining cause-and-effect relations. Suppose we conduct an experiment to examine whether noise influences university students' ability to learn new information. Each student is placed alone in a room, has 30 minutes to study five pages of textbook material, and then takes a 20-item multiple-choice test.

An **experiment** has three essential characteristics:

experiment

manipulates one or more variables, measures whether this manipulation influences other variables, attempts to control extraneous factors that might influence the outcome of the experiment

1. The researcher manipulates one or more variables. In the noise example, the researcher manipulates (i.e., controls) one variable – the amount of noise in the room. Some students (participants) are placed in a noisy room; others are placed in a quiet room. These would represent the groups (conditions) of the experiment (i.e., noise condition, no-noise condition).

2. The researcher measures whether this manipulation influences other variables (i.e., variables that represent the participants' responses). In the noise experiment, the researcher uses the multiple-choice test to measure whether the amount of learning differs in the noise condition versus the no-noise condition. We might find, for example, that participants in the noise condition perform less well on the multiple-choice test than do participants in the no-noise condition.

3. The researcher attempts to control extraneous factors that might influence the outcome of the experiment. For example, we would not want one group to do better because it had easier textbook material or test questions. So every participant will read the same material and take the same test. The room temperature and lighting will be kept constant, and the researcher will be courteous to everyone.

The logic behind this approach is straightforward:

1. Start out with equivalent groups of participants.
2. Treat them equally in all respects except for the variable that is of particular interest (in this case, noise).
3. Isolate this variable and manipulate it (creating the presence or absence of noise).
4. Measure how the groups respond (in this case, the amount they learn).

If the groups respond differently, then the most likely explanation is that these differences were caused by the manipulated variable (Fig. 2.14).

Focus 2.12

What is the major advantage of experiments? Identify the key characteristics and logic of experiments.

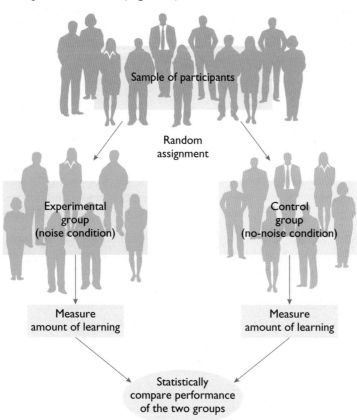

FIGURE 2.14

The logic of designing an experiment.

The experimenter manipulates the amount of noise to which participants are exposed, measures their learning, and attempts to treat them equally in every other way. This creates an experimental group and a control group.

Independent and Dependent Variables

The term **independent variable** refers to the factor that is manipulated by the experimenter. In our example, noise is the independent variable. The **dependent variable** is the factor that is measured by the experimenter and may be influenced by the independent variable. In this experiment, the amount of learning is the dependent variable.

An easy way to keep this distinction clear is to remember that the dependent variable depends on the independent variable. Presumably, students' learning will depend on whether they were in a noisy or quiet room. The independent variable is the cause, and the dependent variable is the effect.

We have described the independent and dependent variables at a general level, but recall that when doing research we must also define our variables operationally. 'Noise' could mean many things, from the roar of a jet engine to the annoying drip of a tap. 'Learning' could mean anything from memorizing a list of words to acquiring the skill to ride a bicycle. In our experiment, we could operationally define our variables as in Table 2.2:

independent variable
the factor that is manipulated by the experimenter

dependent variable
the factor that is measured by the experimenter and may be influenced by the independent variable

Focus 2.13

What are independent and dependent variables? Experimental and control groups?

Focus 2.14

How and why are random assignment and counterbalancing used to design experiments?

TABLE 2.2 OPERATIONALLY DEFINING VARIABLES

	Independent variable (cause)	Dependent variable (effect)
Conceptual level	Noise	Learning
Operational level	Recording of street sounds played at 60 decibels for 30 minutes (versus quiet room)	Number of multiple-choice questions, based on five pages of text, answered correctly

Our noise experiment thus far has only one dependent variable, but we could have many. We could measure how quickly participants read the material, their stress during the task, and so on. This way, we could gain more knowledge about how noise affects people. To test your understanding, identify the independent and dependent variables in Darley and Latané's bystander experiment (pp. 39–41). See the answer on page 66.

Experimental and Control Groups

The terms *experimental group* and *control group* are often used when discussing experiments. An **experimental group** is the group that receives a treatment or an active level of the independent variable. A **control group** is not exposed to the treatment or receives a zero-level of the independent variable. The purpose of the control group is to provide a standard of behaviour with which the experimental group can be compared. In our experiment, the participants in the noise condition represent the experimental group (or experimental condition), and the participants in the no-noise condition represent the control group (or control condition).

Experiments often include several experimental groups. In our study on noise, we could play the recording of street sounds at three different volume levels, creating high-noise, moderate-noise, and low-noise experimental conditions. The no-noise condition would still represent the control group. In some experiments, however, the concept of a control group does not apply. For example, in a taste-test experiment in which participants taste and then rate how much they like Coca-Cola versus Pepsi, each drink represents an experimental condition, and participants simply make a direct comparison between the two drinks.

Two Basic Ways to Design an Experiment

One common way to design an experiment is to have different participants in each condition. To draw meaningful conclusions, the various groups of participants must be equivalent at the start of the study. For example, suppose that in our experiment the noise group performed substantially worse on the multiple-choice test than the no-noise group. If the students in the noise group, on average, happened to be poorer readers or more anxious than the students in the no-noise group, then these factors – not the noise – might have been why they performed more poorly.

To address this issue, researchers typically use **random assignment**, a procedure in which each participant has an equal likelihood of being assigned to any one group within an experiment. Thus a participant would have a 50 per cent chance of being in the noise group and a 50 per cent chance of being in the no-noise group; that determination would be made randomly. This procedure does not eliminate the fact that participants differ from one another in reading ability, anxiety or other characteristics. Instead, random assignment is used to balance these differences across the various conditions of the experiment. It increases our confidence that, at the start of an experiment, participants in the various conditions are equivalent overall.

A second way to design experiments is to expose each participant to all the conditions. We could measure how much the same people learn when exposed to noise and when placed in a quiet room. By doing so, factors such as the participants' reading ability and general anxiety are

---

experimental group

the group that receives a treatment or an active level of the independent variable

control group

is not exposed to the treatment or receives a zero-level of the independent variable

In-Psych

How was the experimental method used to measure people's level of acceptance of authority? To find out, watch the video, 'Obedience to Authority', in Chapter 2 of the In-Psych programme online.

In-Psych

Watch the 'Conformity' video in Chapter 2 of the In-Psych programme online to see another classic study using the experimental method.

random assignment

procedure in which each participant has an equal likelihood of being assigned to any one group within an experiment

held constant across the no-noise and noise conditions, and therefore we can rule them out as alternative explanations for any results we obtain. However, this approach creates problems if not used properly.

For one thing, it would make little sense to have our participants read the same textbook pages and take the same multiple-choice questions twice. Instead, we would have to develop two equally difficult reading tasks and have participants perform each task only once. Most important, suppose that every participant were exposed to the no-noise condition first. If they then learned more poorly in the noise condition, what would be the cause? The noise? Perhaps. But perhaps the participants were bored or fatigued by the time they performed the second task. To avoid this problem, researchers use **counterbalancing**, a procedure in which the order of conditions is varied so that no condition has an overall advantage relative to the others. Half the participants would be exposed to the no-noise condition first and the noise condition second. For the remaining participants, this order would be reversed.

counterbalancing
procedure in which the order of conditions is varied so that no condition has an overall advantage relative to the others

Manipulating One Independent Variable: Effects of Environmental Stimulation on Brain Development

In a hospital, a massage therapist gently strokes a tiny premature baby who was exposed to cocaine while in its mother's womb. This procedure is repeated several times each day. Why is the infant receiving this treatment?

The answer partially lies in landmark experiments by physiological psychologist Mark Rosenzweig (1984) and his co-workers, who manipulated the degree of environmental stimulation to which infant rats (called 'pups') were exposed. This independent variable – environmental stimulation – was operationally defined by creating two conditions: an experimental condition in which some pups lived in a stimulating environment containing toys and other pups with whom they could interact, and a control condition in which other pups lived alone in standard cages (Fig. 2.15). The pups came from several litters, so to create equivalent groups at the outset the researchers randomly assigned some pups from each litter to the enriched and standard environments.

After the rats had lived in these environments for several months, the dependent variable – brain development – was measured. Brain development was operationally defined by several measures, such as the weight of the rats' brains and the concentrations of brain chemicals involved in learning. The rats raised in the enriched environment were superior on each measure and performed better on learning tasks than did the control-group rats. More recent research found that physical stimulation and the environment in which the newborn rat lives can significantly influence its long-term development and behaviour (Pryce and Feldon, 2003). A not insubstantial, and growing body of research indicates that touch and massage can significantly influence a child's development.

Developmental psychologist Tiffany Field and other researchers have found that, like the rat pups, newborn human infants benefit from stimulation (Field, 2001). In one experiment, the researchers manipulated one independent variable, randomly assigning premature infants either to receive three daily massage sessions for 10 days or to receive standard care and contact. The researchers measured several dependent variables and found that the massaged infants had fewer health problems, more mature

FIGURE 2.15

At birth, rat pups from several litters were randomly assigned to experimental and control groups. The experimental group were given toys and playmates. Control-group pups were raised alone in standard laboratory cages. In this experiment, the difference in the environmental conditions represented the independent variable. Brain development was the main dependent variable.

FIGURE 2.16

Experiments by psychologist Tiffany Field and others reveal that massage therapy improves the health and enhances the physical development of premature infants. It also shortens their hospital stay, thus reducing medical costs.

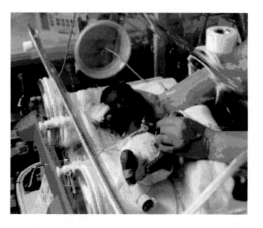

movement patterns and greater weight gain (Fig. 2.16). Because massage enhances their health, premature infants can leave the hospital sooner, reducing heath-care costs. Full-term infants also benefit from massage. They display better development than infants who are simply held and rocked for the same amount of time.

These areas of research helped revolutionize thinking about how experience affects brain development. They also show, once again, how basic research – including animal experiments – can have human applications.

Manipulating Two Independent Variables: Effects of Alcohol and Expectations on Sexual Arousal

To better capture the complexity of behaviour, researchers often study several causal factors within a single experiment by manipulating simultaneously two or more independent variables. They assess the separate influence of each variable on behaviour and examine whether combinations of variables produce distinct effects.

Consider that many men and women report that alcohol enhances their sexual arousal. Why might this be? Perhaps alcohol's chemical properties directly influence sexual arousal. Or maybe the cause is psychological – that is, if people simply believe that alcohol will enhance their sexual arousal, then perhaps this expectation by itself can bring about increased sexual responsiveness.

How can we separate the purely physiological effects of drinking from the psychological ones? The answer emerged in an ingenious procedure developed more than 25 years ago (Rohsenow and Marlatt, 1981). The researchers created two drinks that people could not tell apart by taste: one with tonic water and a squirt of lime juice, the other with vodka added to this mix. Then they designed an experiment with two independent variables. The first independent variable manipulated participants' expectations: they were told either that their drink contained alcohol or that it did not. The second independent variable was whether participants received the alcoholic or non-alcoholic drink.

As Figure 2.17a shows, when these two independent variables are combined within the same experiment, four different conditions are created. Condition 1 is expect alcohol/receive alcohol. This is the normal state of affairs when people drink; they expect that they are drinking alcohol and actually are. Changes in sexual arousal that occur in this condition could reflect either the chemical effects of alcohol, psychological expectations or a combination of both. Condition 2 is expect no alcohol/receive alcohol. This condition assesses physiological effects alone. Because participants believe they are not receiving alcohol, changes in sexual arousal would presumably be due to alcohol's chemical effects. Condition 3 is expect alcohol/receive no alcohol. Because no alcohol is consumed, changes in sexual arousal, if any, would have to be caused by participants' expectations about drinking alcohol. Finally, condition 4 is expect no alcohol/receive no alcohol. This condition creates a control group having neither alcohol nor alcohol expectations.

Participants in the four conditions are then shown identical sexually stimulating materials (e.g., slides or films) or are led to anticipate that they will be viewing such materials. The dependent variable, sexual arousal, may be assessed by self-report ratings on questionnaires or by physiological measures, in this case the increase in the diameter of the penis, as the men became aroused.

Focus 2.15

Explain the advantage of manipulating two independent variables in the same experiment.

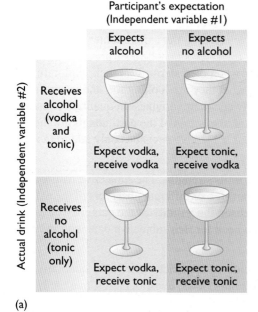

Participant's expectation
(Independent variable #1)

(a)

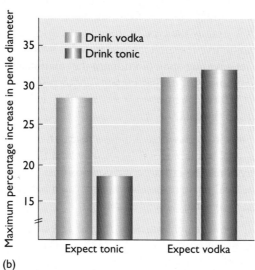

(b)

FIGURE 2.17

Alcohol, expectations, and sexual arousal.

(a) Simultaneously manipulating two independent variables – participant's expectation and actual drink content – creates four conditions in this design. (b) In one experiment, male participants in these four conditions were shown sexually explicit films. The dependent variable, sexual arousal, was measured by a device that recorded changes in the size of each man's penis. Regardless of what they actually drank, men who believed they had consumed alcohol became more aroused than men who believed they had not consumed alcohol. Among men who believed they drank alcohol, those who drank only tonic were just as aroused as those who actually drank alcohol.

SOURCE: data adapted from Wilson and Lawson, 1976.

Most researchers have studied men, in part due to an interest in the issue of alcohol consumption and rape, which primarily is committed by men. (We will discuss the findings with women later.) Overall, as Figure 2.17b shows, men who believe that they have consumed low to moderate doses of alcohol – regardless of whether they actually drank alcohol – feel more aroused and show greater physiological arousal to sexual stimuli than men who believe that they have consumed only tonic water. Among men, the *mere expectation* that one is drinking alcohol also weakens sexual inhibitions and impairs judgement in recognizing coercive sexual behaviour towards women (Gross et al., 2001). Alcohol is a depressant drug; it suppresses neural activity. At low to moderate doses that produce blood-alcohol levels of about .04 or less, men's expectations about alcohol contribute to their enhanced sexual arousal. At higher doses, the chemical effects of alcohol take over and decrease men's sexual arousal and ability to reach orgasm.

This research illustrates how studying several independent variables simultaneously can help unravel some of the complexity of behaviour. It also reinforces one of our main themes: behaviour (in this case, sexual arousal) results from an interplay of factors that are psychological (beliefs and expectations), environmental (the presence of sexual stimuli) and physiological (chemical effects of alcohol at certain doses).

QUALITATIVE RESEARCH

Up to this point we have discussed research that might be described, as 'quantitative'. This means that measures of variables are made, with representative samples from the population. 'Qualitative' research is a slightly different approach, but one which is very popular in some areas, and one which is extremely useful in many areas of psychology. Consider market research for instance. Here we look at the underlying reasons behind people's behaviour and ask why people behave as they do and how. The samples we might choose for qualitative research uses sample populations that might be from a particular group rather than a random sample. For instance, we may want to know the decision process involved in choosing a career as a firefighter. This risky, not terribly well paid, job attracts all sorts of people and we might want to know how to attract more. Careful qualitative research can help us try and find patterns in people's behaviour. A qualitative report focuses on these patterns. One way that you might think of the difference between the two types of research is that qualitative research is exploratory, digging out patterns to reveal reasons why decisions were made. Quantitative research might be described as more conclusive, in that decisions about cause and effect are made more often (Denzin et al., 2005).

Another way to think of qualitative research is that it can involve the analysis of words in discussions or interviews, images in books or in a video, or even objects and artefacts. Quantitative research involves analysis of numbers. In qualitative research the experimenter has an idea of the area they wish to study, but the commentary in interviews may be a surprise, they may not know exactly the type of thing they are looking for when they start off on their exploration. In quantitative research the researchers know exactly what they are looking for, and is careful not to let anything spoil (confound) the relationship between their variables. In qualitative research the opinions of the participants are terribly important, the words of the participants are the data that inform the investigation. How they feel and their subjective decisions only add to the richness of the data.

One problem with qualitative research is also one of its strengths. The subjective nature of the material available for analysis may be difficult to interpret, or different observers of the material may come to very different conclusions. For this reason the validity of the data may be at risk. The qualitative researcher must try and balance the need for rich subjective data with the problem associated with interpreting it.

If the research warrants it, and researchers decide to approach their topic qualitatively, a number of options are open to them. These include interviews, questionnaires, and analysis of text and video material. It is from the data gathered from the qualitative methods chosen that the researchers glean evidence upon which to draw conclusions and develop their research further. Whereas qualitative research is certainly exploratory, it is important to highlight the evidence based quality of the process.

Questionnaires are used for all manner of topics. It is common for us to experience market research, or other work that may be questionnaire based, on almost a daily basis. Interviews may take a number of different forms. They can be unstructured, where the participant is encouraged to speak and present data in their own time and organized in any way they feel appropriate. The researcher organizes the topic, either recording responses electronically or taking notes. The interviews may be semi-structured, where there are no fixed questions, but the researcher guides the discussion, perhaps through a series of predetermined topics. Finally, the interview may be structured. In this case the researcher asks each participant the same set of carefully organized questions.

Analysing documents and media recordings of material can achieve extremely rich data. In these cases the researcher seeks to find evidence and data, usually with a predetermined set of research criteria. If the data are language based, perhaps political speeches or transcripts of conversations held in government debates, then the researcher can be said to be using discourse analysis. The relationships between the different speakers may be analysed, as well as many issues such as the use of language in developing a hierarchy or power structure.

In qualitative research the researchers themselves are an integral part of the analysis process. They decide on the way in which data will be collected, be it using questionnaires or interviews or other methods. They go on to design the questionnaires that go to participants. They conduct the long interviews, carefully guiding questions so as to help the interviewee develop a train of thought relevant to the research project. Once this is done, the researchers themselves analyse the data. They themselves take the answers in the completed questionnaires and interpret them, using criteria they themselves may have developed for the process. They take the videotapes, or audio recordings of interviews and analyse the often subtle opinions expressed, forming patterns which they later develop into a series of concluding remarks. In short their input is central, and must be as objective as possible. This can be extremely hard to do well, and in recent years an exciting development in qualitative research has been in establishing methods that attempt to set objective standards for the research process. In quantitative research the data are analysed following well-understood and agreed statistical procedures, and only then does the researcher engage in inferential remarks.

Table 2.3 summarizes key features of the research methods we have discussed, as well as some limitations which we discuss next.

TABLE 2.3 AN OVERVIEW OF RESEARCH METHODS

Method	Primary features	Main advantages	Main disadvantages
Case study	An individual, group, or event is examined in detail, often using several techniques (e.g., observations, interviews, psychological tests)	Provides rich descriptive information, often suggesting hypotheses for further study. Can study rare phenomena in depth	Poor method for establishing cause–effect. The case may not be representative. Often relies on the researcher's subjective interpretations
Naturalistic observation	Behaviour is observed in the setting where it naturally occurs	Can provide detailed information about the nature, frequency, and context of naturally occurring behaviours	Poor method for establishing cause–effect relations. Observer's presence, if known, may influence participants' behaviour
Survey	Questions or tests are administered to a sample drawn from a larger population	A properly selected, representative sample typically yields accurate information about the broader population	Unrepresentative samples may yield misleading results. Interviewer bias and social desirability bias can distort the findings
Correlational study	Variables are measured and the strength of their association is determined. (Naturalistic observation and surveys are often used to examine associations between variables)	Correlation allows prediction. May help establish how well findings from experiments generalize to more natural settings. Can examine issues that cannot be studied ethically or practically in experiments	Correlation does not imply causation, due to the bidirectionality problem and the third-variable problem (which creates a confounding of variables)
Experiment	Independent variables are manipulated, and their effects on dependent variables are measured	Optimal method for examining cause–effect relations. Ability to control extraneous factors helps rule out alternative explanations	Confounding of variables, demand characteristics, placebo effects and experimenter expectancies can threaten the validity of causal conclusions
Qualitative study	More open data gathering techniques, such as interviews, self-report questionnaires and analysis of video material are used and analysed looking for patterns laid down by the researcher	The data are rich, unrestricted and unpredictable. The method allows for opinion and subjective commentary and may reveal patterns not identifiable with stricter, quantitative methods	The samples may be unrepresentative, Subjective opinions may be badly analysed with subjective misinterpretations

IN REVIEW

- Descriptive research describes how organisms behave, particularly in natural settings. Case studies involve the detailed study of a person, group or event. They often suggest ideas for further research, but are a poor method for establishing cause–effect relations.

- Naturalistic observation gathers information about behaviour in real-life settings. It can yield rich descriptions of behaviour and allows the examination of relations between variables. Researchers must avoid influencing the participants that they observe.

- Surveys involve administering questionnaires or interviews to many people. Most surveys study a sample that is randomly drawn from the larger population the researcher is interested in. Representative samples allow for reasonably accurate estimates of the opinions or behaviours of the entire population. Unrepresentative samples can lead to number of inaccurate estimates. Interviewer bias and bias in participants' self-reports can distort survey results.

- Correlational research measures the relation between naturally occurring variables. A positive correlation means that higher scores on one variable are associated with higher scores on a second variable. A negative correlation occurs when higher scores on one variable are associated with lower scores on a second variable.

- Causal conclusions cannot be drawn from correlational data. Variable X may cause Y, Y may cause X or some third variable (Z) may be the true cause of both X and Y. Nevertheless, if two variables are correlated, then knowing the scores of one variable will help predict the scores of the other.

- A well-designed experiment is the best way to examine cause–effect relations. Experiments have three essential characteristics: (1) one or more variables are manipulated, (2) their effects on other variables are measured, and (3) extraneous factors are eliminated or reduced so that cause effect conclusions can be drawn.

- Manipulated variables are called independent variables. Dependent variables are measured, not manipulated. The independent variable is viewed as the cause, the dependent variable as the effect.

- The experimental group receives a treatment or an active level of the independent variable, whereas the control group does not.

- In some experiments different participants are randomly assigned to each condition. In other experiments the same participants are exposed to all the conditions, but the order in which the conditions are presented is counterbalanced.

- Researchers can study several causal factors within one experiment by simultaneously manipulating two or more independent variables. They assess the separate influence of each variable on behaviour and examine whether combinations of variables produce distinct effects.

Answer to question on p. 60.

The independent variable in the Darley and Latané experiment was the number of other bystanders presumed to be present (0, 1 or 4). The dependent variables were the percentage of participants who aided the victim and the speed of response.

THREATS TO THE VALIDITY OF RESEARCH

Although the experimental approach is a powerful tool for examining causality, researchers must avoid errors that can lead to faulty conclusions. **Internal validity** represents the degree to which an experiment supports clear causal conclusions. For example, because Darley and Latané's bystander experiment had proper controls, we can be confident that it was the independent variable (i.e., the number of bystanders) that caused the differences in the dependent variable (i.e., whether a bystander helped the victim). Thus the experiment had high internal validity. However, if an experiment contains important flaws it will have low internal validity because we can no longer be sure what caused the differences in the dependent variable.

CONFOUNDING OF VARIABLES

Consider a fictitious experiment in which Dr Starr examines how listening to different types of music influences people's feelings of relaxation. The independent variable is the type of music: classical, country or rock. Sixty university students are randomly assigned to listen to one of the three types of music for 20 minutes. Afterwards, they rate how relaxed they feel on a questionnaire.

Dr Starr believes that the experiment will be more realistic if the classical music is played at a low volume, the country music at a moderate volume and the rock music at a loud volume. The results show that students who listened to the classical music felt most relaxed, while those who listened to the rock music felt least relaxed. Dr Starr concludes that, of the three types of music, classical music is the most relaxing.

What is wrong with Dr Starr's conclusion that the type of music caused the differences in how relaxed students felt? Stated differently, can you identify another major factor that could have produced these results? Perhaps students who listened to classical music felt most relaxed because their music was played at the lowest, most soothing volume. Had they listened to it at a high volume, maybe they would have felt no more relaxed than the students who listened to the rock music. We now have two variables that, like the strands of a rope, are intertwined: the independent variable (the type of music) that Dr Starr really was interested in and a second variable (the volume level) that Dr Starr was not interested in but foolishly did not keep constant (Table 2.4).

Confounding of variables means that two variables are intertwined in such a way that we cannot determine which one has influenced a dependent variable. In this experiment the music's volume level is called a *confound* or a *confounding variable*.

The key point to remember is that this confounding of variables prevents Dr Starr from drawing clear causal conclusions, thereby ruining the internal validity of the experiment. Dr Starr can eliminate this problem by keeping the volume level constant across the three music conditions.

Confounding, by the way, is a key reason why causal conclusions cannot be drawn from correlational research. Recall the 'third-variable' problem (see page 56). If variables X (e.g., feeling of well-being) and Y (e.g., time spent outside) are correlated, a third variable, Z (e.g., personality style) may be mixed up with X and Y, so we cannot tell what has caused what. Thus Z is just another type of confounding variable.

internal validity
the degree to which an experiment supports clear causal conclusions

Focus 2.16
What is internal validity? Why do confounding of variables and demand characteristics decrease internal validity?

confounding of variables
two variables are intertwined in such a way that we cannot determine which one has influenced a dependent variable

TABLE 2.4 INDEPENDENT VARIABLES AND POSSIBLE CONFOUNDING VARIABLES

	Group 1	Group 2	Group 3
Independent variable (type of music)	Classical	Country	Rock
Confounding variable (volume level)	Low	Moderate	High

DEMAND CHARACTERISTICS

In unfamiliar situations, it is natural for us to search for clues about how we are expected to act. **Demand characteristics** are cues that participants pick up about the hypothesis of a study or about how they are supposed to behave (Orne, 1962). Consider the experiments on alcohol and sexual arousal discussed earlier. Some participants are told that they are drinking alcohol but in reality are given non-alcoholic drinks. Suppose that after a few drinks a participant does not feel intoxicated and concludes that the drinks are non-alcoholic. At this point the researchers' statement that the drinks are alcoholic is a cue – a demand characteristic – that may tip off the participant about the hypothesis being tested ('Hmm, maybe they're trying to see how I behave if I simply believe I'm drinking alcohol.'). This damages the experiment's internal validity because it can distort participants' true responses. Most people want to be good participants and may respond in ways that they think the experimenter wants (Fig. 2.18).

demand characteristics

cues that participants pick up about the hypothesis of a study or about how they are supposed to behave

placebo

a substance that has no pharmacological effect

placebo effect

people receiving a treatment show a change in behaviour because of their expectations, not because the treatment itself had any specific benefit

"WHAT IT COMES DOWN TO IS YOU HAVE TO FIND OUT WHAT REACTION THEY'RE LOOKING FOR, AND YOU GIVE THEM THAT REACTION."

FIGURE 2.18

Demand characteristics provide participants with clues about how they 'should' behave during a study. This may cause participants to alter their natural responses, thereby ruining the internal validity of the experiment. Copyright © by Sidney Harris. ScienceCartoonsPlus.com. Reprinted with permission.

Skilled researchers try to anticipate demand characteristics and design studies to avoid them. For example, if careful procedures are used, participants given non-alcoholic drinks can be convinced that they have consumed moderate to high amounts of alcohol (MacDonald et al., 2000).

PLACEBO EFFECTS

In medical research, the term **placebo** refers to a substance that has no pharmacological effect. In experiments testing the effectiveness of new drugs for treating diseases, one group of patients – the *treatment group* – receives the actual drug (e.g., through pills or injections). A second group, the *placebo control group*, only receives a placebo (e.g., pills composed of inactive ingredients or injections of saline). Typically, participants are told that they will be given either a drug or a placebo, but they are not told which one.

The rationale for using placebos is that patients' symptoms may improve solely because they expect that a drug will help them. If 40 per cent of patients receiving the actual drug improve but 37 per cent of the placebo control patients show similar improvement, then we have evidence of a **placebo effect**: people receiving a treatment show a change in behaviour because of their expectations, not because the treatment itself had any specific benefit (Fig. 2.19).

Placebo effects decrease internal validity by providing an alternative explanation for why responses change after exposure to a treatment. This problem applies to evaluating all types of treatments, not just those that test the effectiveness of drugs. For example, suppose that depressed patients improve (i.e., become less depressed) while receiving psychotherapy. Is this due to the specific procedures and content of the psychotherapy itself, or might it merely be a placebo effect resulting from their positive expectations that the therapy would help them? Experiments that include the proper control groups can examine this question, as we discuss in Chapter 18.

FIGURE 2.19

Placebo effects have fostered the commercial success of many products that had no proven physiological benefit. Herbal medicines are one of today's health crazes. Do they really work? The best way to answer this question is through experiments that include placebo control groups.

Focus 2.17

What are placebo effects and experimenter expectancy effects? How can they be minimized?

EXPERIMENTER EXPECTANCY EFFECTS

Researchers typically have a strong commitment to the hypothesis they are testing. In psychology, the term **experimenter expectancy effects** refers to the subtle and unintentional ways researchers influence their participants to respond in a manner that is consistent with the researcher's hypothesis. Scientists can take several steps to avoid experimenter expectancy effects. For example, researchers who interact with participants in a study or who record participants' responses are often kept blind to (i.e., not told about) the hypothesis or the specific condition to which a participant has been assigned. This makes it less likely that these researchers will develop expectations about how participants 'should' behave.

The **double-blind procedure**, in which both the participant and experimenter are kept blind as to which experimental condition the participant is in, simultaneously minimizes participant placebo effects and experimenter expectancy effects. In research testing drug effects, each participant receives either a real drug or a placebo but does not know which. People who interact with the participants (e.g., those who dispense the drugs or measure participants' symptoms) also are kept unaware of which participants receive the drug or placebo. This procedure minimizes the likelihood that the researchers will behave differently towards the two groups of participants, and it reduces the chance that participants' own expectations will influence the outcome of the experiment (Fig. 2.20).

"IT WAS MORE OF A 'TRIPLE-BLIND' TEST. THE PATIENTS DIDN'T KNOW WHICH ONES WERE GETTING THE REAL DRUG, THE DOCTORS DIDN'T KNOW, AND I'M AFRAID, NOBODY KNEW"

REPLICATING AND GENERALIZING THE FINDINGS

Let us return to our finding that university students in a noisy room learned textbook material more poorly than did students in a quiet room. Because our study was done properly, it has high internal validity and thus we are confident that the noise, and not some other factor, caused students to perform more poorly. There remain, however, other questions that we must ask. Would the results be similar with other types of participants (e.g., children, adults not at university) or with different tasks (e.g., learning music or sports skills)? Does noise impair learning in real-world settings?

These questions focus on **external validity**, which is the degree to which the results of a study can be generalized to other populations, settings and conditions. Judgements about external validity typically do not focus on the exact responses of the participants. For example, the fact that students in noisy versus quiet rooms correctly answered, say, 48 per cent versus 83 per cent of the questions is not the issue. Rather, *we are concerned about the external validity of the underlying principle*: does noise decrease learning?

To determine external validity, either we or other scientists will need to replicate our experiment. **Replication** is the process of repeating a study to determine whether the original findings can be duplicated. If our findings are successfully replicated – especially in experiments that study other types of participants (e.g., children), noise (e.g., aeroplanes flying overhead) and learning tasks (e.g., learning a sports skill) – we become more confident in concluding that noise impairs learning. Although straight replications are rarely published, lack of replication can eventually cast doubt on the claims of scientists Replications are usually done as part of the process of extending the findings of one study into a new area or into a wider context.

experimenter expectancy effects
subtle and unintentional ways researchers influence their participants to respond in a manner that is consistent with the researcher's hypothesis

double-blind procedure
both the participant and experimenter are kept blind as to which experimental condition the participant is in

Focus 2.18
What is external validity? Why is replication important? Apply these concepts to paranormal claims.

FIGURE 2.20

The double-blind procedure is useful, but scientists try to avoid the infamous 'triple-blind procedure'. Copyright © 2000 by Sidney Harris.

external validity
the degree to which the results of a study can be generalized to other populations, settings and conditions

replication
process of repeating a study to determine whether the original findings can be duplicated

FIGURE 2.21

Workman and Reader (2008) report Ekman's research (1967; 1969; 1971) describing the universality of emotional facial expressions. Cross-cultural patterns such as these provide evidence allowing us to generalize the hypothesis that there are six basic emotional expressions of the face: happiness, anger, sadness, fear, surprise, disgust/ contempt.

Dianne van Hemert (2003) from Tilburg explains how careful analysis of cross-cultural data from many different sources and pieces of research can help us determine patterns. This type of analysis is called *meta-analysis* and we return to it later in this chapter. The patterns and similarities across cultures increase our confidence in the generalizability of our findings (Fig. 2.21).

Research findings that fail to replicate often lead to important discoveries. For example, we have seen that men's belief that they have consumed a few alcoholic drinks (even if the drinks are non-alcoholic) increases their sexual arousal to explicit sexual materials. But experiments have found that women's expectation of having consumed a few alcoholic drinks does not increase their sexual responsiveness (Crowe and George, 1989; Norris, 1994). Scientists are still exploring why this gender difference occurs.

In contrast, studies that consistently fail to replicate the original results of earlier research suggest that the original study may have been flawed or that the finding was a fluke. Even so, the scientific process has done its job and prevented us from getting caught in a blind alley. To see why replication is such an important component of the scientific process, let us look at the following 'Beneath the surface'.

BENEATH THE SURFACE

SCIENCE, PSYCHICS, AND THE PARANORMAL

Do you believe – or know people who believe – in psychic phenomena (Fig. 2.22), such as mental telepathy (transmitting thoughts between individuals) and precognition (foretelling the future)? There is widespread belief in the paranormal the world over. Adopting a scientific attitude means we should approach this issue with open-minded scepticism; that is, we should apply rigorous standards of evaluation, as we do to all phenomena (Cardeña et al., 2000). The ability of independent investigators to replicate initial research findings is one of those standards.

When tested under controlled conditions in well-designed experiments and replications, claim after claim of psychic ability has evaporated. The Koestler Parapsychology unit at Edinburgh University investigates these beliefs scientifically. The unit consists of psychologists, other scientists, philosophers and magicians expert in the art of fakery. To conclude that a phenomenon is psychic we must rule out presently known natural physical or psychological explanations.

Tricking members of the public by playing on their belief, or desire to believe, in the paranormal has a long history. It was relatively common at the turn of the nineteenth century to attend a party where you might join in with a seance, or experience so called 'psychic' phenomena such as 'table-tipping' where furniture moved apparently at the command of mysterious spirits. These psychics were, obviously, fakes and charlatans, but

FIGURE 2.22

Many people believe in the paranormal, despite an overwhelming lack of reliable scientific evidence.

there are still those in this day and age who profess to have psychic powers of the type alluded to all those years ago. It seems that criminals also know of the public's desire to believe in the paranormal. In November 2005 the BBC reported a fraud where conmen in the Thames valley in the south of England were offering, for a small fee, to protect the public from 'evil' in the form of the paranormal.

In the 1990s a report in a major scientific journal provided evidence of mental telepathy from 11 studies using the *ganzfeld procedure* (Bem and Honorton, 1994). In this approach, a participant (the 'receiver') listens to a hissing sound played through earphones and sees red light through translucent goggles. Parapsychologists believe this procedure makes the receiver more sensitive to mental telepathy signals. In another shielded room, the 'sender' concentrates on one of four different visual forms presented in random order. In these studies, the receivers reported the correct form on 32 per cent of the trials, a statistically significant increase above the chance level of 25 per cent.

Does the ganzfeld procedure – which involves many rigorous controls – provide the first solid evidence of a psychic phenomenon? Some scientists suggest that the original ganzfeld studies may not have fully prevented the receivers from detecting extremely subtle cues that could have influenced their responses (Hyman, 1994). Although several parapsychology researchers have reported successful replications (Parker, 2000), psychologists Julie Milton and Richard Wiseman (1999) analysed 30 ganzfeld studies conducted by seven independent laboratories and concluded that 'the ganzfeld technique *does not* at present offer a replicable method for producing ESP in the laboratory' (p. 387, italics added). As newer studies and reviews are published, scientists continue to debate the status of the ganzfeld findings (Palmer, 2003).

Critical thinking requires us to have a reasoned scepticism that demands solid scientific evidence, but not a blind scepticism that rejects the unknown as impossible. In our opinion, at present there is no generally accepted scientific evidence to support the existence of paranormal phenomena. Research continues, and while the burden of proof lies with those who believe in the paranormal, evaluations of their claims should be based on scientific evidence rather than on preconceived positive or negative expectations.

IN REVIEW

- An experiment has high internal validity when it is designed well and permits clear causal conclusions.

- Confounding occurs when the independent variable becomes mixed up with an uncontrolled variable. This ruins internal validity because we can no longer tell which variable caused the changes in the dependent variable.

- Internal validity is weakened by: (1) demand characteristics, which are cues that tip off participants as to how they should behave; (2) placebo effects, in which the mere expectation of receiving a treatment produces a change in behaviour; and (3) experimenter expectancy effects, which are the subtle ways a researcher's behaviour influences participants to behave in a manner consistent with the hypothesis being tested.

- The double-blind procedure prevents placebo effects and experimenter expectancy effects from biasing research results.

- External validity is the degree to which the findings of a study can be generalized to other populations, settings, and conditions. By replicating (repeating) a study under other circumstances, researchers can establish its external validity.

Focus 2.19

What are some things you can do to be a critical consumer of statistics?

ANALYSING AND INTERPRETING DATA

Around election time, do you feel like you're swimming in a sea of statistics from endless voter polls and political advertisements? As a student, you live in a world of grade point averages. And in newspapers and television shows that cover sports and finances, you will find loads of statistics about athletes, teams, the economy and stock prices.

Statistics are woven into the fabric of modern life, and they are integral to psychological research. We will explain why statistics are important by focusing on a few basic concepts.

BEING A SMART CONSUMER OF STATISTICS

Suppose that a group in your home town wants your support for a new crime-watch programme. To convince you, the group quotes statistics from a nearby town, showing that this programme will reduce your chance of being robbed by a whopping 50 per cent. Sounds impressive, but would you be impressed if you learned that in 2006 this town had two robberies and that after adopting the crime-watch programme in 2007 they had only one? Because the number of robberies was so low to begin with, this percentage change does not mean much. In everyday life, it helps to ask about the number of cases or observations that stand behind percentages.

Now consider a fictitious consumer study that asked 1000 people to taste three cola drinks from competing companies and choose the one they liked best. The two *bar graphs* in Figure 2.23 show the same results but make a different visual impression. It is always wise to look at the fine print, including the scale of measurement, that accompany graphs and charts.

Finally, imagine that you apply for a consulting job at Honest Al's Consulting Firm. You ask Al how much money his consultants make. Al replies, 'Our consultants' average salary is €75 000'. 'Wow', you think to yourself. Now look at the list of 10 salaries in Table 2.5. Is the job still as attractive to you? This is another example of why it is important to think critically about statistics. Honest Al was indeed being honest, but as you will now see, by asking questions about a few other statistics, you come away with a more accurate understanding of the situation.

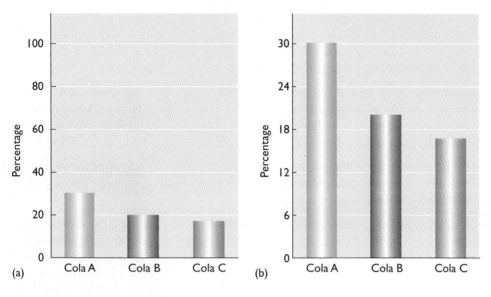

Percentage of people in taste test who prefer each cola

FIGURE 2.23

Manipulating visual impressions of data.

Of 1000 taste testers, suppose that 33 per cent had no preference (thus their results are not placed in the graph), 30 per cent preferred Cola A, 20 per cent preferred Cola B, and 17 per cent preferred Cola C. Look at the Y-axis (the vertical axis) of each graph. The left-hand graph (a), where the Y-axis scale goes from 0 to 100 per cent, makes this difference seem small. The right-hand graph (b), with a Y-axis scale of 0 to 30 per cent, makes this difference seem substantial. As the marketing director for Cola A, which graph would you put in your advertisements?

USING STATISTICS TO DESCRIBE DATA

In contrast to the information in Table 2.5, psychological research often involves a large number of measurements. Typically it is difficult to make much sense out of the *data* (i.e., the information collected) by examining the individual scores of each participant. **Descriptive statistics** allow us to summarize and describe the characteristics of a set (or distribution) of data. You are already familiar with one descriptive statistic – the correlation coefficient, which we discussed on pages 56–58. Now we introduce two other types of descriptive statistics.

descriptive statistics
allow us to summarize and describe the characteristics of a set (or distribution) of data

TABLE 2.5 SALARIES OF 10 CONSULTANTS AT HONEST AL'S CONSULTING FIRM

Consultant	Annual salary (€)
Al's brother	263 000
Al's sister	263 000
Smith	30 500
Rodriguez	29 500
Müller	29 000
van-Noorden	28 000
Johansson	27 500
Carter	27 500
James	26 500
Watson	26 000
Total	*750 000*

mode – 263 000
(most frequent salary)

median – 28 500
(middle salary)

mode – 75 000
(middle salary)

Total salary
_____
number of salaries

Focus 2.20

Describe three measures of central tendency and two measures of variability.

mode

the most frequently occurring score in a distribution

median

the point that divides a distribution of scores in half when those scores are arranged in order from lowest to highest

mean

the arithmetic average of a set of scores

range

the difference between the highest and lowest scores in a distribution

standard deviation

takes into account how much each score in a distribution differs from the mean

Measures of Central Tendency

Given a set of data, *measures of central tendency* address the question, 'What's the typical score?' One measure, the **mode**, is the most frequently occurring score in a distribution. At Honest Al's the modal salary is €263 000. While the mode is easy to identify, it may not be the most representative score. Clearly, €263 000 is not the typical salary of the 10 consultants.

A second measure of central tendency is the **median**, the point that divides a distribution of scores in half when those scores are arranged in order from lowest to highest. Half of the scores lie above the median, half below it. In Table 2.3, because there is an even number of scores, the median is €28 500 – the point halfway between employee 5 (€29 000) and employee 6 (€28 000).

Finally, the **mean** is the arithmetic average of a set of scores. To determine the mean you simply add up all the scores in a distribution and divide by the number of scores. The €75 000 average that Honest Al quoted was the mean salary.

Note that the mean has a disadvantage: it is affected by extreme scores. The €263 000 salaries of Al's brother and sister inflate the mean, making it less representative of the typical salary. The median, in contrast, is not affected by extreme scores. Changing the top salary to €1 million does not change the median but further inflates the mean. Still, the mean has a key advantage over the median and mode: it captures information from every score. In Table 2.3, if Johnson and Rodriguez each received a €50 000 salary increase, the median and mode would not change. However, the mean would increase and reflect the fact that Honest Al was now paying some of his employees a better salary.

Because the mean takes all the information in a set of scores into account, it is the most commonly used measure of central tendency in research, and perhaps in everyday life as well. But keep in mind that extreme scores will distort the mean. When you go for that job interview, also ask about the median and modal salaries. Although all these ways of measuring central tendency are well understood and agreed upon, there is no automatic decision procedure as to which is most appropriate. The researcher in the end has to use their knowledge of statistics to employ the best method of describing the data that makes a true statement and does not distort the picture they are trying to present.

Measures of Variability

To describe a set of data, we want to know not only the typical score, but also whether the scores cluster together or vary widely. *Measures of variability* capture the degree of variation, or spread, in a distribution of scores. Look at Table 2.6, which lists Honest Al's salaries alongside those of 10 consultants from Claire's Consulting Firm. The mean salary is the same at both firms, but notice how Claire's salaries are closer to one another – less variable – than are Al's. The simplest but least informative measure of variability is the **range**, which is the difference between the highest and lowest scores in a distribution. At Honest Al's, the salary range is €237 000; at Claire's the range is only €11 000.

A more important statistic, the **standard deviation**, takes into account how much each score in a distribution differs from the mean. At Honest Al's, the standard deviation is €94 009; at Claire's it's only €3000. We need not be concerned here with how the standard deviation is calculated. Rather, the key point is that it uses information from every score, whereas the range only takes into account the highest and lowest scores.

USING STATISTICS TO MAKE INFERENCES

Descriptive statistics allow researchers to summarize data efficiently, but researchers typically want to go beyond mere description and draw *inferences* (conclusions) from their data. To illustrate, let us return to our experiment examining how noise affects students' learning. Suppose that 80 college students agree to participate in our study. We randomly assign 40 students to the noise condition

Focus 2.21

What is the purpose of inferential statistics? What is statistical significance?

TABLE 2.6 ANNUAL SALARIES OF 10 CONSULTANTS AT TWO CONSULTING FIRMS (€)

Honest Al's firm		Claire's firm
263 000		81 000
263 000		78 000
30 500		76 000
29 500		76 000
29 000		76 000
28 000		75 000
27 500		73 000
27 000		73 000
26 500		72 000
26 000		70 000
75 000	Mean	75 000
237 000	Range	11 000
94 009	Standard deviation	3000

and 40 to the quiet condition. They study the identical textbook material for 30 minutes and then take a 20-item multiple-choice test. We find that, on average, students in the noisy room perform more poorly (mean = 8.20 correct answers) than students in the quiet room (mean = 12.50).

At this point we would like to make a general inference: Noise impairs students' learning of textbook material. However, we must first wrestle with a key issue: even if our experiment had all the proper controls and there were no confounding variables, perhaps the noise really had no effect on performance, and our findings were merely a chance outcome. Perhaps, for example, just by random chance we happened to end up with 40 students in the noisy room who would have performed this poorly anyway, even if they had been in a quiet room.

For all types of research, **inferential statistics** allow us to make inferences about a population from data provided by a sample of that distribution. In our case, they help determine the probability that we would obtain similar results if our experiment were repeated over and over with other samples drawn from the same population of college students. Inferential statistics tell researchers whether their findings are *statistically significant*. **Statistical significance** means that it is very unlikely that a particular finding occurred by chance alone. Psychologists typically consider results to be statistically significant only if the results could have occurred by chance alone fewer than five times in 100.

Keep in mind that *statistical significance* does not mean that a finding is scientifically or socially important. If thousands of students took our 20-item test in either a noisy or quiet room, and if the variability (the standard deviation) within each condition was small, then even a tiny difference between the average test performance of these groups might be statistically significant but trivial for practical purposes. Yet a psychological technique that helps athletes run or swim faster by one-hundredth of a second might make the difference between winning the gold medal or no medal at the Olympics. Statistical significance only means it is unlikely that the results of study are due to chance. The scientific or social significance of the findings must be judged within a broader context.

inferential statistics
allow us to make inferences about a population from data provided by a sample of that distribution

statistical significance
is very unlikely that a particular finding occurred by chance alone

META-ANALYSIS: COMBINING THE RESULTS OF MANY STUDIES

As research on a topic accumulates, scientists must reach overall conclusions about how variables are related. We described earlier how meta-analyses of this kind is a useful technique in cross-cultural psychology. Experts on a topic often will review the number and quality of studies that support, or fail to support, a particular relation and then draw conclusions that they believe are best supported by the facts.

Increasingly, these expert reviews are being supplemented by **meta-analysis**, a statistical procedure for combining the results of different studies that examine the same topic. In a typical research study, the responses of each participant are analysed. In a meta-analysis, however, each study is treated as a 'single participant', and its overall results are analysed with those of other studies. A meta-analysis will tell researchers about the direction and statistical strength of the relation between two variables.

For example, would you expect that exercising during the day helps people sleep better at night? One meta-analysis combined the results of 38 studies and concluded that the overall relation is weak (Youngstedt et al., 1997). On average, people slept only about 10 minutes longer when they had exercised that day, and they fell asleep only about 1 minute faster.

Researchers who use meta-analysis must decide which studies to include and describe their common limitations. The authors of the meta-analysis on exercise and sleep cautioned that most studies only examined young adults who slept well. Many researchers consider meta-analysis to be the most objective way to integrate the findings of multiple studies and reach overall conclusions about behaviour.

meta-analysis
a statistical procedure for combining the results of different studies that examine the same topic

Focus 2.22

Describe the purpose of meta-analysis.

IN REVIEW

- Statistics can be misleading if they are based on very few observations or are distorted by extreme scores. Understanding basic statistical concepts can help you be a smarter citizen and consumer.

- Descriptive statistics summarize the characteristics of a set of data.

- Measures of central tendency identify the typical score in a distribution. The mode is the most frequent score. The median is the halfway point in a distribution of scores arranged in numerical order; half of the scores are above and half are below. The mean is the arithmetic average of the scores.

- Measures of variability assess whether scores are clustered together or spread out. The range is the difference between the highest and lowest scores. The standard deviation takes into account how much each score differs from the mean.

- Inferential statistics allow researchers to determine whether their findings reflect a chance occurrence. The term *statistical significance* means that it is very unlikely that a particular finding occurred by chance alone.

- Meta-analysis statistically combines the results of many studies that examine the same variables. It calculates the direction and strength of the overall relation between those variables.

CRITICAL THINKING IN SCIENCE AND EVERYDAY LIFE

In today's world we are exposed to a great deal of information about human behaviour – some of which is accurate and much of which is not. Especially in the popular media, we encounter oversimplifications, overgeneralizations and *pseudoscientific misinformation* – nonsense and jargon that is made to sound scientific. To be an informed consumer, you must be able to critically evaluate research and identify factors that limit the validity of conclusions. Critical-thinking skills can also help you avoid being misled by claims made in everyday life, such as those in advertisements. Thus, enhancing your critical-thinking skills is an important benefit that you can derive from your psychology course.

Throughout this chapter you have seen how critical thinking, a healthy dose of scepticism and the scientific method help scientists solve puzzles of mind and behaviour. As critical thinkers, we should recognize that our beliefs and emotions can act as psychological blinders that allow us to accept inadequate evidence uncritically, especially when this evidence supports our current views. This does not mean that we should be so sceptical of everything that we end up believing nothing at all. Rather, we need to balance open-mindedness with a healthy scepticism and evaluate evidence for what it is worth (Fig. 2.24).

Focus 2.23

What critical thinking questions can be used to evaluate claims made in everyday life?

FIGURE 2.24

Modern society bombards us with scientific and pseudoscientific claims. Critical thinking often can help us tell good science from junk science. This journal, which promotes healthy scepticism and critical thinking, is published by the Committee for the Scientific Investigation of Claims of the Paranormal. Another organization, the Skeptics Society, publishes *Skeptic*.

APPLYING PSYCHOLOGICAL SCIENCE

EVALUATING CLAIMS IN RESEARCH AND EVERYDAY LIFE

To exercise your critical-thinking skills, read the following descriptions of a research study, an advertisement, and a newspaper article. Have some fun and see if you agree with the claims made.

Write down your answers and compare them with the answers provided at the end of the box. You can facilitate critical thinking by asking yourself the following questions:

1. What claim is being made?

2. What evidence is being presented to support this claim?

3. What is the quality of the evidence? Are there any other plausible explanations for the conclusions being drawn?

4. What additional evidence would be needed to reach a clearer conclusion?

5. What is the most reasonable conclusion to draw?

SOME INTERESTING CLAIMS

Example 1: a lot of bull

Deep inside the brain of humans and other mammals is a structure called the *caudate nucleus*. Years ago, a prominent researcher hypothesized that this part of the brain is responsible for turning off aggressive behaviour. The scientist was so confident in his hypothesis that he bet his life on it. A microelectrode was implanted inside the caudate nucleus of a large, aggressive bull. The researcher stood before the bull and, like a Spanish matador, waved a cape to incite the bull to charge. As the bull thundered towards him, the researcher pressed a button on a radio transmitter that he held in his other hand. This sent a signal that caused the microelectrode to stimulate the bull's caudate nucleus. Suddenly, the bull broke off its charge and stopped. Each time this sequence was repeated, the bull stopped its charge. The researcher concluded that the caudate nucleus was the 'aggression-off' centre of the brain.

Stimulating the caudate nucleus caused the bull to stop charging, but does this demonstrate that the caudate nucleus is an aggression-off centre? Why or why not? (*Hint:* What other bodily functions might the caudate nucleus help regulate that would cause the bull to stop charging?)

Example 2: holidays and burglaries

Consider the following scenario. A newspaper advertisement appeared in several countries. The headline 'While You Are Taking Your Summer Holiday, Burglars Go to Work' was followed by this statement: 'According to police statistics, over 26 per cent of home burglaries take place between 1 June and 30 September'. The advertisement then offered a home security system at a special, summer-only price of €500, a reduction of €250. In sum, the advertisement implied that burglaries are particularly likely to occur while people are away on summer holiday. How do you feel about this claim and its supporting evidence?

Example 3: will staying up late cause you to forget what you have studied?

The headline of a newspaper article read, 'Best Way to Retain Complex Information? Sleep on It, Researcher Says'. The article began, 'Students who work hard from Monday to Friday and then party all night on weekends may lose much of what they learned during the week, according to a sleep researcher'. The researcher was then quoted as saying, 'It appears skewing the sleep cycle by just two hours can have this effect. Watching a long, late movie the night following a class and then sleeping in the next morning will make it so you're not learning what you thought. You'll not lose it all – just about 30 per cent'.

Next, the experiment was described. University students learned a complex logic game and then were assigned to one of four sleep conditions. Students in the control condition were allowed to have a normal night's sleep. Those in condition 2 were not allowed to have any sleep, whereas students in conditions 3 and 4 were awakened only when they went into a particular stage of sleep. (We learn about sleep stages in Chapter 5.) A week later everyone was tested again. Participants in conditions 3 and 4 performed 30 per cent worse than the other two groups.

Re-examine the experimental conditions, then identify what's wrong with the claims in the first paragraph.

CRITICAL ANALYSES OF THE CLAIMS

Analysis 1: a lot of bull

Perhaps the caudate nucleus plays a role in vision, memory or movement, and stimulating it momentarily caused the bull either to become blind, to forget what it was doing or to alter its movement. Perhaps the bull simply became dizzy or experienced pain. These are all possible explanations for why the bull stopped charging. In fact, the caudate nucleus helps regulate movement; it is not an aggression-off centre in the brain.

Analysis 2: holidays and burglaries

First, how much is 'over 26 per cent'? We do not know for sure but can assume that it is less than 27 per cent, because it would be to the advertiser's advantage to state the highest number possible. The key problem is that the time period between 1 June and 1 September typically represents between 25 per cent of the days of the year. Therefore about 26 per cent of burglaries occur during about 25 per cent of the year. Wow! Technically the advert is correct: burglars do go to work in the summer while you are on holiday. But the advert also may have misled people. Burglars seem to be just as busy at other times of the year.

Analysis 3: will staying up late cause you to forget what you have studied?

It could be true that going to bed and waking up later than usual might cause you to forget more of what you have studied. However, the article does not provide evidence for this claim. Look at the four conditions carefully. To test this claim, an experiment would need to include a condition in which participants went to bed later than usual, slept through the night and then awakened later than usual. But in this experiment the control group slept normally, and the three experimental conditions examined only the effects of getting no sleep or losing certain types of sleep.

When you read newspaper or magazine articles, look beyond the headlines and think about whether the claims are truly supported by the evidence. Were you able to pick out some flaws in these claims before you read the analyses? Critical thinking requires practice, and you will get better at it if you keep asking yourself the five critical-thinking questions listed previously.

IN REVIEW

- Critical thinking is an important life skill. We should also be open-minded to new ideas that are supported by solid evidence.

- In science and everyday life, critical thinking can prevent us from developing false impressions about how the world operates and from being duped in everyday life by unsubstantiated claims.

- When someone presents you with a claim, you should consider the quality of the evidence, whether there are other plausible explanations for the conclusions being drawn, and whether additional evidence is needed to reach a clearer conclusion. Then ask yourself whether the claim is the most reasonable conclusion to draw.

KEY TERMS AND CONCEPTS

Each term has been boldfaced and defined in the chapter on the page indicated in parentheses.

archival measures (p. 45)

case study (p. 49)

confounding of variables (p. 67)

control group (p. 60)

correlation coefficient (p. 56)

correlational research (p. 53)

counterbalancing (p. 61)

demand characteristics (p. 68)

dependent variable (p. 59)

descriptive research (p. 49)

descriptive statistics (p. 73)

double-blind procedure (p. 69)

experiment (p. 58)

experimental group (p. 60)

experimenter expectancy effects (p. 69)

external validity (p. 69)

hypothesis (p. 40)

independent variable (p. 59)

inferential statistics (p. 75)

informed consent (p. 47)

internal validity (p. 67)

mean (p. 74)

median (p. 74)

meta-analysis (p. 76)

mode (p. 74)

naturalistic observation (p. 50)

negative correlation (p. 57)

operational definition (p. 43)

placebo (p. 68)

placebo effect (p. 68)

population (p. 51)

positive correlation (p. 56)

random assignment (p. 60)

random sampling (p. 51)

range (p. 74)

replication (p. 69)

representative sample (p. 51)

sample (p. 51)

scatterplots (p. 57)

standard deviation (p. 74)

statistical significance (p. 75)

survey research (p. 51)

theory (p. 41)

unobtrusive measures (p. 45)

variable (p. 43)

WHAT DO YOU THINK?

SHOULD YOU TRUST INTERNET AND POPULAR MEDIA SURVEYS? (p. 53)

Recall the *Literary Digest* survey we just discussed. Even with 2 million people responding, the survey was inaccurate because the sample did not represent the overall population.

Typical Internet, magazine and phone-in surveys share two major problems. First, people who choose to respond are entirely *self-selected* (rather than selected by the researcher), and the resulting samples likely do not even represent the entire population of people who use the Internet, subscribe to that magazine or watch that television show, respectively. Perhaps those who respond are more motivated, have a more helpful personality, or differ in some other important way from those who don't respond.

Second, it is unlikely that samples of Internet users, magazine subscribers and television news viewers represent the population at large (e.g., our adult population). Although this may be a stereotype, the majority of users of the Internet are relatively young. Those that respond to Internet questionnaires then, may not include people from a very wide age-range. Do you think that the readers of *Cosmopolitan*, *Playboy*, *Hello* or any magazine typify the general population? Because Internet and popular media surveys do not use random sampling, they are likely to generate samples that are not representative of the broader population.

Surely, many news organizations sponsor high-quality surveys conducted by professional pollsters. The key is that these surveys, such as political polls, use appropriate random sampling procedures to obtain representative samples.

Finally, be aware that some psychologists – especially those who study people's personality and social behaviours – are increasingly using the Internet to collect research data. As users surf the Web, they may find a site that invites them to participate in an experiment or take a psychological test. These studies are not surveys that critically depend on having representative samples of the broader population. Rather, they typically examine relations among variables and underlying psychological principles. Some researchers question the validity of such Internet-based studies, but proponents have shown that most of these concerns are unfounded. More research is needed, but thus far it seems that Internet-based studies of this type yield findings that are consistent with those obtained from more traditional types of methods (Best et al., 2001; Gosling et al., 2004).

DOES EATING ICE CREAM CAUSE PEOPLE TO DROWN? (p. 56)

Just because two variables are correlated, we cannot conclude that they are causally related. First, consider the bidirectionality problem. We do not see any likely way that drownings could cause the rest of the public to eat more ice cream, so let us rule that out. Can we conclude, then, that more ice cream consumption causes more drownings? We suppose that in a few cases gorging on ice cream soon before swimming might enhance the risk of drowning. But nationally, how often is this likely to happen?

Now consider the third-variable problem. What other factors might cause people to eat more ice cream and also lead to an increase in drownings? The most obvious third variable is 'daily temperature' (or 'month of the year'). Summer months bring hotter days, and people eat more ice cream in hot weather. Likewise, on hotter days drownings increase simply because so many more people go swimming. In short, the most reasonable conclusion is that the ice cream–drowning correlation is due to a third variable.

CHAPTER THREE

GENES, ENVIRONMENT AND BEHAVIOUR

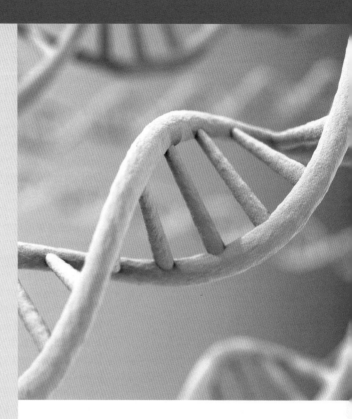

CHAPTER OUTLINE

The interaction of nature and circumstances is very close, and it is impossible to separate them with precision . . . (but) . . . we are perfectly justified in attempting to appraise their relative importance.

SIR FRANCIS GALTON

After being born in Trinidad, Oskar Stohr and Jack Yufe were raised rather differently. Jack remained in the Caribbean with his father, and was brought up as a Jew. He even lived for a time in Israel. Oskar, on the other hand, was brought up by his grandmother in Germany, as a Catholic and a Nazi, joining the Hitler Youth as a boy. Two different environments could hardly be imagined, but the similarities when they were reunited in their sixties were quite astonishing. They found that both kept elastic bands on their wrists, both had a habit of falling asleep in front of the television, both enjoyed spicy food, both enjoyed dipping buttered toast in their coffee and both had the habit of flushing the toilet before using it. Other twins also show amazing similarities even though not raised in the same environment.

…

Jim Lewis and Jim Springer first met in 1979 after 39 years of being separated. They had grown into adulthood oblivious to the existence of one another until Jim Lewis felt a need to learn more about his family of origin. After years of searching through court records, Jim Lewis finally found his twin brother, Jim Springer. When they met, Lewis described it as 'like looking into a mirror', but the similarities went far beyond their nearly identical appearance. When they shared their stories, they found that both had childhood dogs named Toy. Both had been nail biters and fretful sleepers, suffered from migraine headaches and had high blood pressure. Both Jims had married women named Linda, had been divorced and married second wives named Betty. Lewis named his first son James Allen, Springer named his James Alan. For years, they both had taken holidays at the same Florida beach. Both of the Jims worked as sheriff's deputies. They both drank Miller Lite, smoked Salem cigarettes, loved stock car racing, hated baseball, left regular love notes to their wives, made doll's furniture in their basements, and had constructed unusual circular benches around the trees in their backyards (see Fig. 3.1).

FIGURE 3.1

Jim Springer and Jim Lewis are identical twins who were separated when four weeks old and raised in different families. When reunited in adulthood, they showed striking similarities in personality, interests and behaviour.

Jim Springer and Jim Lewis became the first participants in a landmark University of Minnesota study of twins who had been separated early in life and reared apart. The Minnesota researchers found that the twins' habits, facial expressions, brainwaves, heartbeats and handwriting were nearly identical. When given a series of psychological tests, they were strikingly similar in intelligence and personality traits (Tellegen et al., 1988).

How can we explain the behavioural similarities in Jim Springer and Jim Lewis? In fact, they had been brought up quite differently; the Minnesota researchers found that the adoptive families of the Jim twins differed in important ways. What the Jims did have in common, however, were their identical genes. Although it is always possible that the behavioural commonalities of the Jim twins were coincidental, the Minnesota researchers found that other identical-twin pairs separated early in life also showed striking similarities. For example, when a pair of twin housewives from England met one another in Minneapolis for their week-long battery of psychological and medical tests, they found to their amazement that each was wearing seven rings, two bracelets on one wrist, and a watch and bracelet on the other. Whether raised together or apart, the identical twins were far more similar in personality and intelligence test scores than were siblings (including non-identical twins) raised in the same families (Tellegen et al., 1988). For psychologists, the connections between the twins' biological and behavioural similarities raise fascinating questions about factors that underlie human development.

It has been said that each of us is (1) what all humans are, (2) what some other humans are, and (3) what no other human in the history of the world has been, is or will be (Kluckhohn and Murray, 1953). In this chapter we examine important biological and environmental factors that produce the behavioural commonalities and differences among humans. First, we examine the role of the genes passed on to you at conception by your parents. Next, we explore how learning helps you adapt to your environment and how it is related to culture and evolution. We see that genetic and environmental factors interact to influence many of your psychological characteristics, including intelligence and personality. Finally, we explore the role of evolutionary forces that, millions of years before your birth, helped forge some of what you are today. We will see that biological and environmental factors interacted in complex ways, setting into place the pieces of the puzzle that is the human being and helping to account for both our similarities and our differences.

As we see throughout the book, this biological level of analysis provides us with key insights into behaviour and its causes. The knowledge gained in this chapter will give you the background needed to understand many behaviours in the chapters that follow.

GENETIC INFLUENCES ON BEHAVIOUR

From antiquity, humans have wondered how physical characteristics are transmitted from parents to their offspring. The answer was provided in the 1860s by Gregor Mendel (see Bateson, 1909), an Austrian monk trained in both physics and plant physiology. Mendel, renowned as a plant breeder, was fascinated with the variations he saw in plants of the same species. For example, the garden pea can have either white or purple flowers, yellow or green seeds, wrinkled or smooth skins, and different pod shapes (Fig. 3.2). Best of all from his research perspective, pea plants (which normally fertilize themselves) could be artificially cross-fertilized to combine the features of plants that differed in physical characteristics. In a series of elegantly controlled experiments, Mendel did exactly that, carefully recording the features of the resulting offspring. His beautifully conducted experiments showed that heredity must involve the passing on of specific organic factors, not a simple blending of the parents' characteristics. For example, if he fertilized a plant with purple flowers with pollen from a white-flowered plant, he did not get offspring with light purple flowers, but various percentages of purple and white-flowered plants. Moreover, these specific

FIGURE 3.2

The elegant experiments performed by Gregor Mendel revolutionized scientific thinking and spurred the development of the science of genetics. His research was done on the inheritance of physical characteristics in garden peas.

Focus 3.1
Differentiate between genotype and phenotype. How do genes regulate biological structures and functions?

genotype
the specific genetic make-up of the individual

phenotype
the individual's observable characteristics

chromosome
a double-stranded and tightly coiled molecule of deoxyribonucleic acid (DNA)

genes
the biological units of heredity

FIGURE 3.3

The ladder of life.

Chromosomes consist of two long, twisted strands of DNA, the chemical that carries genetic information. With the exception of red blood cells, every cell in the body carries within its nucleus 23 pairs of chromosomes, each containing numerous genes that regulate every aspect of cellular functioning.

factors might produce visible characteristics in the offspring, or they might simply be carried for possible transmission to another generation. In any case, Mendel showed that in the humble pea plant, as in humans, the offspring of one set of parents do not all inherit the same traits, as is evident in the differences we see among brothers and sisters.

Early in the twentieth century, geneticists made the important distinction between **genotype**, the specific genetic make-up of the individual, and **phenotype**, the individual's observable characteristics. A person's genotype is like the commands in a computer software program. At a biological level, genes direct the process of development by programming the formation of protein molecules, which can vary in an infinite fashion. Some of the genes' directives are used on one occasion, some on another. Some are never used at all, either because they are contradicted by other genetic directives or because the environment never calls them forth. For example, geneticists discovered that chickens have retained the genetic code for teeth (Kollar and Fisher, 1980). Yet because the code is prevented from being phenotypically expressed (converted into a particular protein), there is not a chicken anywhere that can sink its teeth into a postal worker. Genotype is present from conception, but phenotype can be affected both by other genes and by the environment. Thus, genotype is like the software commands in your word processing program that allow you to type an email; phenotype is like the content of the email that appears on your computer screen.

CHROMOSOMES AND GENES

What exactly are Mendel's 'organic factors' and how are they transmitted from parents to offspring? The egg cell from the mother and sperm cell from the father carry within their nuclei the material of heredity in the form of rod-like units called *chromosomes*. A **chromosome** is a double-stranded and tightly coiled molecule of deoxyribonucleic acid (DNA). All of the information of heredity is encoded in the combinations of four chemical bases – adenine, thymine, guanine and cytosine – that occur throughout the chromosome. Within each DNA molecule, the sequence of the four letters of the DNA alphabet – A, T, G and C – creates the specific commands for every feature and function of your body. Human DNA has about 3 billion chemical base pairs, arranged as A-T or G-C units (Human Genome Project, 2007). The ordering of 99.9 per cent of these bases is the same in all people.

The DNA portion of the chromosome carries the **genes**, the biological units of heredity (Fig. 3.3). The average gene has about 3000 ATGC base pairs, but sizes vary greatly; the largest gene has 2.4 million bases. Each gene carries the ATGC codes for manufacturing specific proteins, as well as the codes for when and where in the body they will be made. These proteins can take many forms and functions, and they underlie every bodily structure and chemical process. It is estimated that about half of all genes target brain structure and functions (Kolb and Whishaw, 2003). Every moment of every day, the strands of DNA silently transmit their detailed instructions for cellular functioning.

Each chromosome contains numerous genes, segments of DNA that contain instructions to make proteins – the building blocks of life

One chromosome of every pair is from each parent

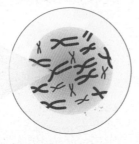

Each nucleus contains 46 chromosomes, arranged in 23 pairs

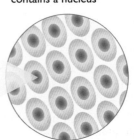

Each human cell (except red blood cells) contains a nucleus

The human body contains 100 trillion cells

With one exception, every cell with a nucleus in the human body has 46 chromosomes. The exception is the *sex cell* (the egg or sperm), which has only 23. At conception, the 23 chromosomes from the egg combine with the 23 corresponding chromosomes from the sperm to form a new cell, the *zygote*, containing 46 chromosomes. Within each chromosome, the corresponding genes received from each parent occur in matched pairs. Every cell nucleus in your body contains the genetic code for your entire body, as if each house in your community contained the architect's plans for every building and road in the entire city.

Dominant, Recessive and Polygenic Effects

Alternative forms of a gene that produce different characteristics are called **alleles**. Thus, there is an allele that produces blue eyes and a different one that produces brown eyes. However, genotype and phenotype are not identical because some genes are dominant and some are recessive. If a gene in the pair received from both the mother and father is **dominant**, the particular characteristic that it controls will be displayed. If, however, a gene received from one parent is **recessive**, the characteristic will not show up unless the partner gene inherited from the other parent is also recessive. In humans, for example, brown eyes are dominant over blue eyes. A child will have blue eyes only if both parents have contributed recessive genes for blue eyes. If a child inherits a dominant gene for brown eyes from one parent and a recessive gene for blue eyes from the other, he will have brown eyes and the blue-eyed trait will remain hidden in his genotype. Eventually, the brown-eyed child may pass the recessive gene for blue eyes to his own offspring.

In a great many instances, a number of gene pairs combine their influences to create a single pheno-typic trait. This is known as **polygenic transmission**, and it complicates the straightforward picture that would occur if all characteristics were determined by one pair of genes. It also magnifies the number of possible variations in a trait that can occur. Despite the fact that about 99.9 per cent of human genes are identical among people, it is estimated that the union of sperm and egg can result in about 70 trillion potential genotypes, accounting for the great diversity of characteristics that occurs even among siblings.

The Human Genome

At present, our knowledge of phenotypes greatly exceeds our understanding of the underlying genotype, but that may soon change. In 1990, geneticists began the Human Genome Project, a co-ordinated effort to map the DNA, including all the genes, of the human organism. The genetic structure in every one of the 23 chromosome pairs has now been mapped by methods that allow the investigators to literally disassemble the genes on each chromosome and study their specific sequence of bases (A, T, G and C; see Fig. 3.3).

The first results of the genome project provided a surprise: The human genome consists of approximately 25 000 genes rather than the 100 000 previously estimated (Human Genome Project, 2007). That result told geneticists that gene interactions are even more complex than formerly believed and that it is highly unlikely that a single gene could account for a complex problem such as anorexia or schizophrenia. Even given this reduced number of genes, the 3.1 billion ATGC combinations in the entire human genome, if printed consecutively, would add about 150 000 pages to this book.

The 'book of life' revealed by the Human Genome Project has given us greater knowledge of which specific genes or gene combinations are involved in normal and abnormal characteristics (McGuffin et al., 2005). The location and structure of more than 80 genes that contribute to hereditary diseases have already been identified through gene mapping (Human Genome Project, 2007). On another front, behavioural scientists are exploring the gene combinations that underlie behaviour and, in some cases, are modifying those genes.

---

alleles
alternative forms of a gene that produce different characteristics

dominant
the particular characteristic that it controls will be displayed

recessive
the characteristic will not show up unless the partner gene inherited from the other parent is also recessive

Focus 3.2
Describe dominant, recessive and polygenic influences on phenotype.

polygenic transmission
when a number of gene pairs combine their influences to create a single phenotypic trait

A Genetic Map of the Brain

The mouse's brain is 99 per cent identical with the human brain and is therefore frequently used by neuroscientists to study human brain function. Using a robotic system to analyse 16 000 paper-thin brain slices per week, scientists have determined where in the brain 21 000 genes are turned on, or expressed, and a genetic atlas of the brain that is now available to all scientists online. (You can view the atlas at www.brain-map.org.) Almost every cell in the mouse body contains the full genotype. What a particular cell will become and how it will function is determined by which genes are switched on, so that a liver cell will look and function differently than will a skin cell, or a brain cell. The Allen Institute researchers discovered that about 80 per cent of all mouse genes are switched on somewhere in the brain, and that there are probably more cell types within the brain than in all the other organs of the body combined (Allen Institute for Brain Science, 2006). Using human cadaver brains and bits of living tissue removed by brain surgeons during tumour removal or aneurism repair, researchers next plan to develop a genetic map of the human cerebral cortex, the seat of our higher mental functions. Knowing where and how genes are switched on in the brain will provide new insights on both normal brain functions and diseases of the brain, and may herald the development of revolutionary new treatment and prevention techniques.

BEHAVIOURAL GENETICS

The activities of genes lie behind every structure and process in the body, and behaviour reflects a continuous interplay between a biological being and the environment in which it operates. Researchers in the field of **behavioural genetics** study how heredity and environmental factors influence psychological characteristics. In contrast to evolutionary psychologists who are interested in the genetic commonalities among people, behavioural geneticists try to determine the relative influence of genetic and environmental factors in accounting for individual differences in behaviour. For example, a behavioural geneticist might ask, 'How important are genetic factors in aggression, intelligence, personality characteristics and various types of psychological disorders?'

> **behavioural genetics**
> how heredity and environmental factors influence psychological characteristics

The degree of relatedness to one another tells us how genetically similar people are. Recall that children get half of their genetic material from each parent. Thus the probability of sharing any particular gene with one of your parents is 50 per cent, or .50. If you have brothers and sisters, you also have a .50 probability of sharing the same gene with each of them, since they get their genetic material from the same parents. Of course, as we have seen, if you are an identical twin, you have a 1.00 probability of sharing any particular gene with your twin. And what about a grandparent? Here, the probability of a shared gene is .25 because, for example, your maternal grandmother passed half of her genes on to your mother, who passed half of hers on to you. Thus the likelihood that you inherited a specific gene from your grandmother is $.50 \times 50$, or .25. The probability of sharing a gene is also .25 for half-siblings, who share half of their genes with the common biological parent but none with the other parent. If you have a first cousin, you share 12.5 of your genes with him or her. Theoretically, an adopted child differs genetically from his or her adoptive parents, and the same is true for unrelated people. These facts about genetic similarity give us a basis for studying the role of genetic factors in physical and behavioural characteristics. If a characteristic has higher **concordance**, or co-occurrence, in people who are more closely related to one another, this points to a possible genetic contribution, particularly if the people have lived in different environments.

> **concordance**
> co-occurrence

Adoption and Twin Studies

Knowing the level of genetic similarity among family and kin provides a basis for estimating the relative contributions of heredity and environment to a physical or psychological characteristic. As discussed earlier, family members and relatives differ in the percentages of genes they share. Many studies have shown that the more similar people are genetically, the more similar they are likely to be psychologically, although this level of similarity differs depending on the characteristic in question.

One research method used to estimate the influence of genetic factors is the **adoption study**, in which people who were adopted early in life are compared on some characteristic with both their biological parents, with whom they share genetic endowment, and with their adoptive parents, with whom they share no genes. If adopted people are more similar to a biological parent (with whom they share 50 per cent of their genes) than to an adoptive parent (with whom they share a common environment but no genes), a genetic influence on that trait is indicated. If they are more similar to their adoptive parents, environmental factors are judged to be more important for that particular characteristic.

In one such study, Kety and co-workers (1978) identified adoptees who were diagnosed with schizophrenia in adulthood. They then examined the backgrounds of the biological and adoptive parents and relatives to determine the rate of schizophrenia in the two sets of families. The researchers found that 12 per cent of biological family members had also been diagnosed with schizophrenia, compared with a concordance rate of only 3 per cent of adoptive family members, suggesting a hereditary link.

Twin studies, which compare trait similarities in identical and fraternal twins, are one of the more powerful techniques used in behavioural genetics. Because *monozygotic*, or identical, twins develop from the same fertilized egg, they are genetically identical (Fig. 3.4). Approximately one in 250 births produces identical twins. *Dizygotic*, or fraternal, twins develop from two fertilized eggs, so they share 50 per cent of their genetic endowment, like any other set of brothers and sisters. Approximately one in 150 births produces fraternal twins.

Twins, like other siblings, are usually raised in the same familial environment. Thus, we can compare **concordance rates**, or trait similarity, in samples of identical and fraternal twins.

Focus 3.3

How are adoption and twin studies used to estimate genetic and environmental determinants of behaviour?

adoption study

people who were adopted early in life are compared on some characteristic with both their biological parents, with whom they share genetic endowment, and with their adoptive parents, with whom they share no genes

twin studies

compare trait similarities in identical and fraternal twins

concordance rates

trait similarity

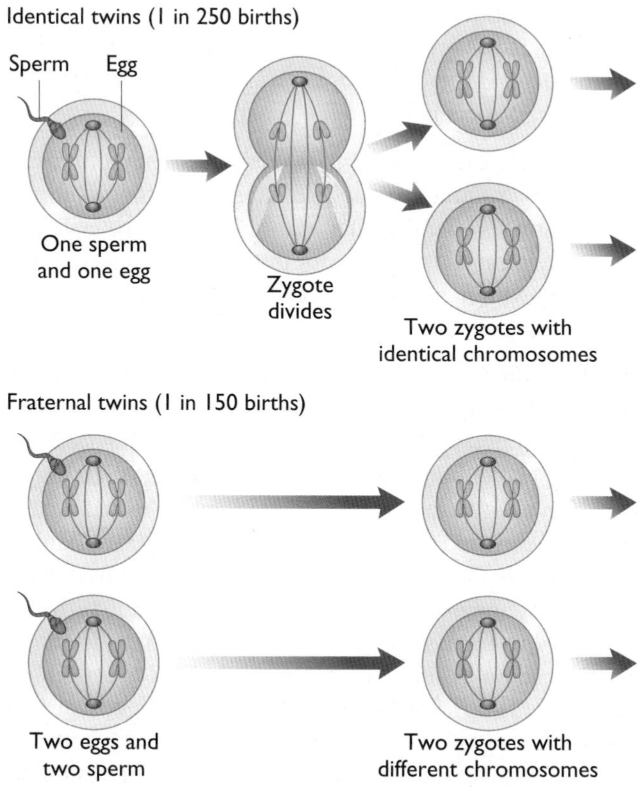

Identical twins (1 in 250 births)

Sperm   Egg

One sperm and one egg

Zygote divides

Two zygotes with identical chromosomes

Fraternal twins (1 in 150 births)

Two eggs and two sperm

Two zygotes with different chromosomes

FIGURE 3.4

Identical (monozygotic) twins come from a single egg and sperm as a result of a division of the zygote. They have all of their genes in common. Fraternal (dizygotic) twins result from two eggs fertilized by two sperm. They share only half of their genes as a result.

We assume that if the identical twins are far more similar to one another than are the fraternal twins in a specific characteristic, a genetic factor is likely to be involved. Of course, the drawback is the possibility that because identical twins are more similar to one another in appearance than fraternal twins are, they are treated more alike and therefore share a more similar environment. This could partially account for greater behavioural similarity in identical twins.

To rule out this environmental explanation, behavioural geneticists have adopted an even more elegant research method. Sometimes, as in the University of Minnesota study in which the Jim twins participated, researchers are able to find and compare sets of identical and fraternal twins who were separated very early in life and raised in *different* environments (Bouchard et al., 1990). By eliminating environmental similarity, this research design permits a better basis for evaluating the respective contributions of genes and environment.

As we shall see, many (but not all) psychological characteristics, including intelligence, personality traits and certain psychological disorders, have a notable genetic contribution (Bouchard, 2004). Adopted children are typically found to be more similar to their biological parents than to their adoptive parents on these measures, and identical twins tend to be more similar to one another than are fraternal twins, even if they were separated early in life and reared in different environments (Loehlin, 1992; Lykken et al., 1992; Plomin and Spinath, 2004). On the other hand, identical twins reared together still tend to be somewhat more similar for some characteristics than those reared apart, indicating that the environment also makes a difference.

Heritability: Estimating Genetic Influence

Using adoption and twin studies, researchers can apply a number of statistical techniques to estimate the extent to which differences among people are due to genetic differences. A **heritability coefficient** estimates the extent to which the differences, or variation, in a specific phenotypic characteristic within a group of people can be attributed to their differing genes. For example, propensity for divorce is relatively high, around 50 per cent. It is important that you understand what this .50 heritability coefficient does *not* mean. This result does *not* mean that 50 per cent of a particular person's propensity for divorce is due to genetic factors and the other 50 per cent to the environment. Heritability applies only to differences *within particular groups* (and estimates can and do vary, depending on the group).

Table 3.1 shows the wide range of heritability that has been found for a range of physical and psychological characteristics. Subtracting each heritability coefficient from 1 provides an estimate of the proportion of group variability that is attributable to the environment in which people develop. For height, environment accounts for only about 1 minus .9, a proportion of .1 (or 10 per cent), of the variation within groups, but for religious attitudes, environment accounts for virtually all differences among people.

Even while they try to estimate the contributions of genetic factors, behavioural geneticists realize that genes and environment are not really separate determinants of behaviour. Instead, they operate as a single, integrated system. Gene expression is influenced on a daily basis by the environment. For example, two children of equal intellectual potential may have differences in intelligence quotients (IQs) as great as 15 to 20 points if one is raised in an impoverished environment and the other in an enriched one (Plomin and Spinath, 2004). And high or low environmental stress can be responsible for turning on or off genes that regulate the production of stress hormones (Taylor, 2006a). Neumeister et al. (2004) have shown that the genetic influence on certain psychological disorders can be very significant indeed, and it is our genetics that provide some of us with a predisposition to suffer with a problem. This is certainly true of depression. Weissman et al. (1984) showed that having relatives that have suffered from depression before the age of 20 means that you are significantly (eight times) more likely to suffer yourself at some point in your life. Of course, as we see elsewhere in the book, a predisposition (or diathesis) to

heritability coefficient
estimates the extent to which the differences, or variation, in a specific phenotypic characteristic within a group of people can be attributed to their differing genes

TABLE 3.1 HERITABILITY ESTIMATES FOR VARIOUS HUMAN CHARACTERISTICS

Trait	Heritability estimate
Height	.80
Weight	.60
Likelihood of being divorced	.50
School achievement	.40
Activity level	.40
Preferred characteristics in a mate	.10
Religious attitudes	.00

SOURCES: Bouchard et al., 1990; Dunn and Plomin, 1990.

suffer with something does not mean that you certainly will, just that it may happen given the correct experiences, and environment.

Caspi et al. (2002) looked at how the environment and genetics interacted. The gene they were interested in was the MAOA gene, which they thought may relate to violent or aggressive behaviour. They genotyped a number of men from New Zealand. The reason they did this was that there had been previous evidence of violent behaviour in a Dutch family who had an MAOA mutation, so looking specifically at this gene made sense. The results were very interesting. They showed that the MAOA genotype did not, in itself, correlate with violent activity, but if low MAOA activity was coupled with a history of child abuse while younger, then the men were four times more likely to be convicted of a violent crime before the age of 24: nature (genetics) and nurture (the environment) interacting.

Focus 3.4
Define heritability. How are heritability coefficients estimated?

IN REVIEW

- Hereditary potential is carried in the genes, whose commands trigger the production of proteins that control body structures and processes. Genotype (genetic structure) and phenotype (outward appearance) are not identical, in part because some genes are dominant while others are recessive. Many characteristics are polygenic in origin, that is, they are influenced by the interactions of multiple genes.

- Behavioural geneticists study how genetic and environmental factors contribute to the development of psychological traits and behaviours. Adoption and twin studies are the major research methods used to disentangle hereditary and environmental factors. Especially useful is the study of identical and fraternal twins who were separated early in life and raised in different environments. Identical twins are more similar on a host of psychological characteristics, even when reared apart. Many psychological characteristics have appreciable heritability.

ADAPTING TO THE ENVIRONMENT: THE ROLE OF LEARNING

We encounter changing environments, each with its unique challenges, from the moment we are conceived. Some challenges, such as acquiring food and shelter, affect survival. Others, such as deciding where to go on a date, do not. But no matter what the challenge, we come into this world with biologically based abilities to respond adaptively. These mechanisms allow us to perceive our world, to think and problem solve, to remember past events and to profit from our experiences. If evolution can be seen as *species adaptation* to changing environments, then we can view learning as a process of *personal adaptation* to the circumstances of our lives. Learning allows us to use our biological heredity to profit from experience and adapt to our environment.

HOW DO WE LEARN? THE SEARCH FOR MECHANISMS

For a long time, the study of learning proceeded along two largely separate paths, guided by two different perspectives on behaviour: *behaviourism* (see Chapter 1) and *ethology* (Bolles and Beecher, 1988). Within psychology, behaviourism dominated learning research from the early 1900s through to the 1960s. Behaviourists assumed that there are laws of learning that apply to virtually all organisms. For example, each species they studied – whether birds, reptiles, rats, monkeys or humans – responded in predictable ways to patterns of reward or punishment.

Behaviourists treated the organism as a *tabula rasa*, or 'blank tablet', on which learning experiences were inscribed. Most of their research was conducted with non-human species in controlled laboratory settings. Behaviourists explained learning solely in terms of directly observable events and avoided speculating about an organism's mental state (as cognitive psychologists later did).

WHY DO WE LEARN? THE SEARCH FOR FUNCTIONS

While behaviourism flourished in early- to mid-twentieth-century America, a specialty area called *ethology* arose in Europe within the discipline of biology (Lorenz, 1937; Tinbergen, 1951). Ethologists focused on animal behaviour in the natural environment viewing the organism as much more than a blank tablet, arguing that because of evolution, every species comes into the world biologically prepared to act in certain ways. However, this is not to say that the ethologists denied that learning occurs. They rather focused on the *functions* of behaviour, particularly its **adaptive significance**, how a behaviour influences an organism's chances of survival and reproduction in its natural environment.

An example of the kinds of behaviours which the ethologists studied is that of young herring gulls' pecking behaviour. Newly hatched gulls beg for food by pecking at a red mark on their parents' bills. Parents respond by regurgitating food, which the hatchlings ingest. Seeing the red mark and long shape of a parent's bill automatically triggers the chicks' pecking. This behaviour is so strongly pre-wired that chicks will peck just as much at long inanimate models or objects with red dots or stripes (Fig. 3.5). Ethologists call this instinctive behaviour a **fixed action pattern**, an unlearned response automatically triggered by a particular stimulus.

adaptive significance
how a behaviour influences an organism's chances of survival and reproduction in its natural environment

fixed action pattern
an unlearned response automatically triggered by a particular stimulus

Focus 3.5
Contrast the behaviouristic and ethological assumptions regarding the development of behaviour.

FIGURE 3.5

A herring gull hatchling will peck most frequently at objects that are long and have red markings, even if they are inanimate models and do not look like adult gulls. This innate fixed action pattern is present from birth and does not require learning. The stimuli that trigger a fixed action pattern, such as the red markings on the inanimate objects and on the beak of the real herring gull shown here, are called releaser stimuli.

SOURCE: adapted from Hailman, 1969.

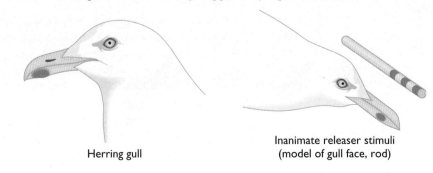

Herring gull

Inanimate releaser stimuli
(model of gull face, rod)

As ethology research proceeded, several things became clear. First, some fixed action patterns are modified by experience. Unlike herring gull hatchlings, older chicks have learned what an adult gull looks like and will not peck at an inanimate object unless it resembles the head of an adult gull (Hailman, 1967). Second, in many cases what appears to be instinctive behaviour actually involves learning. For example, the indigo bunting is a songbird that migrates between North and Central America. As if by pure instinct, it knows which direction to fly by using the North Star to navigate. (The North Star is the only stationary star in the Northern Hemisphere that maintains a fixed compass position.) In autumn, the buntings migrate south by flying away from the North Star; they return in the spring by flying towards it.

To study whether any learning was involved in the buntings' navigational behaviour, Emlen (1975) raised birds in a planetarium with either a true sky or a false sky in which a star other than the North Star was the only stationary one. In the autumn, the buntings became restless in their cages as migration time approached. When the birds raised in the planetarium with the true sky were released, they flew away in the direction opposite the North Star. In contrast, those exposed to the false sky ignored the North Star and instead flew away in the direction opposite the 'false' stationary star. Emlen concluded that although the indigo bunting is genetically pre-wired to navigate by a fixed star, it has to learn through experience which specific star in the night sky is stationary.

LEARNING, CULTURE AND EVOLUTION

The separate paths of behaviourism and ethology have increasingly converged (Papini, 2002), reminding us that the environment shapes behaviour in two fundamental ways: through *species adaptation* and through *personal adaptation*. Our personal adaptation to life's circumstances occurs through the laws of learning that the behaviourists and other psychologists have examined, and it results from our interactions with immediate and past environments.

When you drive or go out on a date, your behaviour is influenced by the immediate environment (e.g., traffic, your girlfriend's or boyfriend's smiles) and by capabilities you acquired through past experiences (e.g., driving skills, social skills). Because culture plays an ongoing role in shaping our present and past experiences, it strongly affects what we learn. Cultural socialization influences our beliefs and perceptions, our social behaviour and sense of identity, the skills that we acquire, and countless other characteristics (Fig. 3.6).

FIGURE 3.6

People in different cultures learn specific behaviours in order to adapt to their environment. Even the same general skill will take on different forms, depending on unique environmental features and demands.

The environment also influences species adaptation. Over the course of evolution, environmental conditions faced by each species help shape its biology. This does not occur directly. Learning, for example, does not modify an organism's genes, and therefore learned behaviours do not pass genetically from one generation to the next. But through natural selection, genetically based characteristics that enhance a species' ability to adapt to the environment – and thus to survive and reproduce – are more likely to be passed on to the next generation. Eventually, as physical features (e.g., the red mark on the adult gull's beak) and behavioural tendencies (e.g., the chick pecking the mark) influenced by those genes become more common, they become a part of a species' very nature.

Focus 3.6

Discuss the relation of evolution and culture to learning. What are the basic adaptive things that organisms must learn?

Theorists propose that as the human brain evolved, it acquired adaptive capacities that enhanced our ability to learn and solve problems (Chiappe and MacDonald, 2005; Cosmides and Tooby, 2002). In essence, we have become pre-wired to learn. Of course, so have other species. Because all species face some common adaptive challenges, we might expect some similarity in their library of learning mechanisms. Every environment is full of events, and each organism must learn:

- which events are, or are not, important to its survival and well-being
- which stimuli signal that an important event is about to occur
- whether its responses will produce positive or negative consequences.

These adaptive capacities are present to varying degrees in all organisms. Even the single-celled paramecium can learn to jerk backward in its avoidance pattern in response to a vibration that has been paired with electric shock (Hennessey et al., 1979). As we move up the phylogenetic scale from simpler to more complex animals, learning abilities become more sophisticated, reaching their highest level in humans. Learning is the mechanism through which the environment exerts its most profound effects on behaviour, and we explore learning processes in depth in Chapter 7. For now, let's explore a few key concepts surrounding environmental influences.

Shared and Unshared Environments

Environment is a very broad term, referring to everything from the pre-natal world of the womb and the simplest physical environment to the complex social systems in which we interact with multiple people, places and things. Some of these environments, such as our family household or school classroom, are shared with other people, such as our siblings and class-mates. This is called a **shared environment** because the people who reside in these experience many of their features in common. Siblings living in the same home are exposed to a common physical environment, the availability or unavailability of books, a television or a computer. They share the quality of food in the home, exposure to the attitudes and values transmitted by parents, and many other experiences. However, each of us also has experiences that are unique to us, or an **unshared environment**. Even children living in the same home have their own unique experiences, including distinct relationships with their parents and siblings.

shared environment

the people who reside in these experience many of their features in common

unshared environment

experiences that are unique to us

Focus 3.7

How large a factor is heritability in individual differences in intelligence?

Twin studies (especially those that include twins raised together and apart) are particularly useful in estimating the extent to which genotype, shared environment and unshared environment contribute to group variance on a particular characteristic (see Fig. 3.7). As we shall see, such studies have provided new insights on the factors that influence a wide range of human characteristics.

FIGURE 3.7

Behavioural genetics research methods permit the estimation of three sources of variation in a group's scores on any characteristics. It is therefore possible to estimate from results of twin and adoption studies the contributions of genetic factors and of shared and unshared environmental factors.

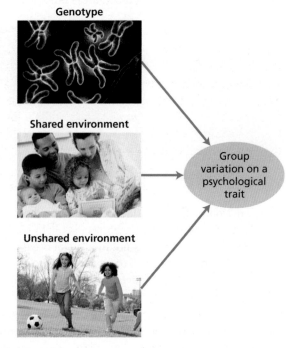

Genotype

Shared environment

Unshared environment

Group variation on a psychological trait

> ## IN REVIEW
>
> - The environment exerts its effects largely through processes of learning that are made possible by innate biological mechanisms. Humans and other organisms can learn which stimuli are important and which responses are likely to result in goal attainment.
>
> - Since learning always occurs within environments, it is important to distinguish between different kinds of environments. Behavioural genetics researchers make an important distinction between shared and unshared environmental influences.

BEHAVIOURAL GENETICS, INTELLIGENCE AND PERSONALITY

Of the many psychological characteristics that we possess, few if any are more central to our personal identity and our successful adaptation than intelligence and personality. Although we consider these topics in much greater detail in Chapters 10 and 15, respectively, intelligence and personality are particularly relevant to our current discussion because the genetic and environmental factors that influence them have been the subject of considerable research.

GENES, ENVIRONMENT AND INTELLIGENCE

To what extent are differences in intelligence (as defined by an IQ score derived from a general intelligence test) due to genetic factors? This seemingly simple question has long been a source of controversy and, at times, bitter debate. The answer has important social as well as scientific consequences.

Heritability of Intelligence

Let us examine the genetic argument. Suppose that intelligence were totally heritable, that is, suppose that 100 per cent of the intellectual variation in the population were determined by genes. (No psychologist today would maintain that this is so, but examining the extreme view can be instructive.) In that case, any two individuals with the same genotype would have identical intelligence test scores, so the correlation in IQ between identical (monozygotic) twins would be 1.00. Non-identical brothers and sisters (including fraternal twins, who result from two fertilized eggs) share only half of their genes. Therefore, the correlation between the test scores of fraternal twins and other siblings should be substantially lower. Extending the argument, the correlation between a parent's test scores and his or her children's scores should be about the same as that between siblings, because a child inherits only half of his or her genes from each parent.

What do the actual data look like? Table 3.2 summarizes the results from many studies. As you can see, the correlation between the test scores of identical twins is substantially higher than any other correlations in the table (but they are not 1.00). Identical twins separated early in life and reared apart are of special interest because they have identical genes but experienced different environments. Note that the correlation for identical twins raised apart is nearly as high as that for identical twins reared together. It is also higher than that for fraternal twins raised together. This pattern of findings is a powerful argument for the importance of genetic factors (Bouchard et al., 1990; Plomin et al., 2007).

Adoption studies are also instructive. As Table 3.2 shows, IQs of adopted children correlate as highly with their biological parents' IQs as they do with the IQs of the adoptive parents who reared them. Overall, the pattern is quite clear: the more genes people have in common, the more

TABLE 3.2 CORRELATIONS IN INTELLIGENCE AMONG PEOPLE WHO DIFFER IN GENETIC SIMILARITY AND WHO LIVE TOGETHER OR APART

Relationship	Percentage of shared genes	Correlation of IQ scores
Identical twins reared together	100	.86
Identical twins reared apart	100	.75
Non-identical twins reared together	50	.57
Siblings reared together	50	.45
Siblings reared apart	50	.21
Biological parent – offspring reared by parent	50	.36
Biological parent – offspring not reared by parent	50	.20
Cousins	25	.25
Adopted child–adoptive parent	0	.19
Adopted children reared together	0	.32

SOURCES: based on Bouchard and McGue, 1981; Bouchard et al., 1990; Scarr, 1992.

similar their IQs tend to be. This is very strong evidence that genes play a significant role in intelligence, accounting for 50 to 70 per cent of group variation in IQ (Petrill, 2003; Plomin and Spinath, 2004). However, analysis of the human genome shows that there clearly is not a single 'intelligence' gene (Plomin and Craig, 2002). The diverse abilities measured by intelligence tests are undoubtedly influenced by large numbers of interacting genes, and different combinations seem to underlie specific abilities (Luciano et al., 2001; Plomin and Spinath, 2004).

Environmental Determinants

Because genotype accounts for only 50 to 70 per cent of the IQ variation among individuals, genetics research provides a strong argument for the contribution of environmental factors to intelligence (Plomin and Spinath, 2004). Good places to look for such factors are in the home and school environments.

Shared family environment   How important to intelligence level is the shared environment of the home in which people are raised? If home environment is an important determinant of intelligence, then children who grow up together should be more similar than children who are reared apart. As Table 3.2 shows, siblings who are raised together are indeed more similar to one another than those reared apart, whether they are identical twins or biological siblings. Note also that there is a correlation of .32 between unrelated adopted children reared in the same home. Overall, it appears that between a quarter and a third of the population's individual differences in intelligence can be attributed to shared environmental factors.

Focus 3.8

Describe the shared and unshared environmental influences on intelligence.

The home environment clearly matters, but there may be an important additional factor. Recent research suggests that differences within home environments are much more important at lower socio-economic levels than they are in upper-class families. This may be because lower socio-economic families differ more among themselves in the intellectual richness of the home environment than do upper-class families (Turkheimer et al., 2003). Indeed, a lower-income family that has books in the house, cannot afford video games and encourages academic effort may be a very good environment for a child with good intellectual potential.

Environmental enrichment and deprivation Another line of evidence for environmental effects comes from studies of children who are removed from deprived environments and placed in middle- or upper-class adoptive homes. Typically, such children show a gradual increase in IQ on the order of 10 to 12 points (Scarr and Weinberg, 1977; Schiff and Lewontin, 1986). Conversely, when deprived children remain in their impoverished environments, they either show no improvement in IQ or they actually deteriorate intellectually over time (Serpell, 2000). Scores on general intelligence tests correlate around .40 with the socio-economic status of the family in which a child is reared (Lubinski, 2004).

Educational experiences As we might expect, educational experiences, perhaps best viewed as a non-shared variable, can also have a significant impact on intelligence. Many studies have shown that school attendance can raise IQ and that lack of attendance can lower it. A small decrease in IQ occurs over summer holidays, especially among low-income children. Intelligence quotient scores also drop when children are unable to start school on time owing to teacher shortages or strikes, natural disasters, or other reasons (Ceci and Williams, 1997). It appears that exposure to an environment in which children have the opportunity to practice mental skills is important in solidifying those skills.

Where intelligence is concerned, we have seen that genetic factors, shared environment and unique experiences all contribute to individual differences in intelligence. Do the same factors apply to personality differences?

PERSONALITY DEVELOPMENT

'Like father, like son' is a saying which young and even quite old men hear very often. But if this old saying has validity, what causes similarities in personality between fathers and sons (and mothers and daughters)? Is it genes, environment, or both?

Heritability of Personality

Behavioural genetics studies on personality have examined genetic and environmental influences on relatively broad personality traits. One prominent personality trait theory is called the five factor model (see Chapter 15). Five factor theorists like Robert McCrae and Paul Costa (2003) believe that individual differences in personality can be accounted for by variation along five broad personality dimensions or traits known as the Big Five: (1) *extraversion–introversion* (sociable, outgoing, adventuresome, spontaneous versus quiet, aloof, inhibited, solitary), (2) *agreeableness* (co-operative, helpful, good natured versus antagonistic, uncooperative, suspicious); (3) *conscientiousness* (responsible, goal-directed, dependable versus undependable, careless, irresponsible); (4) *neuroticism* (worrying, anxious, emotionally unstable versus well adjusted, secure, calm); and (5) *openness to experience* (imaginative, artistically sensitive, refined versus unreflective, crude and boorish, lacking in intellectual curiosity).

Focus 3.9

Describe the heritability of personality and the role of shared and unshared environmental influences on personality differences.

What results are obtained if we compare the Big Five traits, described above, in identical and fraternal twins who were raised together and those who were raised apart? Table 3.3 shows heritability estimates of the Big Five personality factors described above. These results are consistent with studies of other personality variables as well, indicating that between 40 and 50 per cent of the personality variations among people are attributable to genotype differences (Bouchard, 2004). Although personality characteristics do not show as high a level of heritability as the .70 figure found for intelligence, it is clear that genetic factors account for a significant amount of personality difference.

Environment and Personality Development

If genetic differences account for only about 40 to 50 per cent of variations in personality, then surely environment is even more important than it is in the case of intelligence. Researchers

TABLE 3.3 HERITABILITY OF THE BIG FIVE PERSONALITY FACTORS BASED ON TWIN STUDIES

Trait	Heritability coefficient
Extraversion	.54
Neuroticism	.48
Conscientiousness	.49
Agreeableness	.42
Openness to experience	.57

SOURCE: Bouchard, 2004.

expected that the shared environment might be even more important for personality than it is for intelligence. Over the years, virtually every theory of personality has embraced the assumption that experiences within the family, such as the amount of love expressed by parents and other child-rearing practices, are critical determinants of personality development. Imagine, therefore, the shock waves generated by the findings from twin studies that shared features of the family environment account for little or no variance in major personality traits (Bouchard et al., 2004; Plomin, 1997). The key finding was that twins raised together and apart, whether identical or fraternal, did not differ in their degree of personality similarity (although identical twins were always more similar to one another than were fraternal twins). In fact, researchers have found that pairs of children who are raised within the same family are as different from one another as are pairs of children who are randomly selected from the population (Plomin and Caspi, 1999).

Adoption studies support a similar conclusion. In adoption studies, the average correlation for personality variables between adopted siblings who are genetically dissimilar but do share much of their environment, including the parents who raise them, the schools they attend, the religious training they receive, and so on, is close to .00 (Plomin et al., 2007). Except at child-rearing extremes, where children are abused or seriously neglected, parents probably get more credit when children turn out well personality-wise – and more blame when they do not – than they deserve (Scarr, 1992).

However, the surprising findings concerning shared environments does not mean that experience is not important. Rather than the general family environment, it seems to be the individual's unique or unshared environment, such as his or her unique school experiences (for example, being in Mr Jones's classroom, where conscientiousness and openness to experience were stressed) and interactions with specific peers (such as Jeremy, who fostered extraverted relationships with others) that account for considerable personality variance. Even within the same family, we should realize, siblings have different experiences while growing up, and each child's relationship with his or her parents and siblings may vary in important ways. It is these unique experiences that help shape personality development. Whereas behavioural geneticists have found important shared-environment effects in intelligence, attitudes, religious beliefs, occupational preferences, notions of masculinity and femininity, political attitudes, and health behaviours such as smoking and drinking (Larson and Buss, 2007), these shared-environment effects do not extend to general personality traits such as the Big Five. At this point, we do not know whether there are some crucial unshared-environmental variables that researchers have missed because of their preoccupation with shared-environmental factors, or whether there are countless small variables that make the difference. This question is of key importance to personality research.

IN REVIEW

- Intelligence has a strong genetic basis, with heritability coefficients in the .50 to .70 range. Shared family environment is also important (particularly at lower socio-economic levels), as are educational experiences.

- Personality also has a genetic contribution, though not as strong as that for intelligence. In contrast to intelligence, shared family environment seems to have no impact on the development of personality traits. Unshared individual experiences are far more important environmental determinants.

GENE–ENVIRONMENT INTERACTIONS

Genes and environment both influence intelligence, personality and other human characteristics. But, as we've stressed throughout this chapter, they rarely operate independently. Even the pre-natal environment can influence how genes express themselves, as when the mother's drug use or malnutrition retards gene-directed brain development. In the critical periods following birth, enriched environments, including the simple touching or massaging of newborns, can influence the unfolding development of premature infants (Field, 2001) and the future 'personality' of young monkeys (Harlow, 1958). Although they cannot modify the genotype itself, environmental conditions can influence how genetically based characteristics express themselves phenotypically throughout the course of development (Plomin et al., 2007).

Just as environmental effects influence phenotypic characteristics, genes can influence how the individual will experience the environment and respond to it (Hernandez and Blazer, 2007; Plomin and Spinath, 2004). Let us examine some of these interactions between genes and experience.

HOW THE ENVIRONMENT CAN INFLUENCE GENE EXPRESSION

First, genes produce a range of potential outcomes. The concept of *reaction range* provides one useful framework for understanding gene–environmental interactions. The **reaction range** for a genetically influenced trait is the range of possibilities – the upper and lower limits – that the genetic code allows. For example, to say that intelligence is genetically influenced does not mean that intelligence is fixed at birth. Instead, it means that an individual inherits a *range* for potential intelligence that has upper and lower limits. Environmental effects will then determine where the person falls within these genetically determined boundaries.

At present, genetic reaction ranges cannot be measured directly, and we do not know if their sizes differ from one person to another. The concept has been applied most often in the study of intelligence. There, studies of IQ gains associated with environmental enrichment and adoption programmes suggest that the ranges could be as large as 15 to 20 points on the IQ scale (Dunn and Plomin, 1990). If this is indeed the case, then the influence of environmental factors on intelligence would be highly significant. A shift this large can move an individual from a below-average to an average intellectual level, or from an average IQ that would not predict college success to an above-average one that would predict success.

Some practical implications of the reaction range concept are illustrated in Figure 3.8. First, consider persons B and H. They have identical reaction ranges, but person B develops in a very deprived environment and H in an enriched environment with many cultural and educational advantages. Person H is able to realize her innate potential and has an IQ that is 20 points higher than person B's. Now compare persons C and I. Person C actually has greater intellectual potential than person I but ends up with a lower IQ as a result of living in an environment that does

reaction range
the range of possibilities – the upper and lower limits – that the genetic code allows

Focus 3.10
Describe reaction range and its hypothesized effects on the genetic expression of intelligence.

FIGURE 3.8

Reaction range is an example of how environmental factors can influence the phenotypic expression of genetic factors. Genetic endowment is believed to create a range of possibilities within which environment exerts its effects. Enriched environments are expected to allow a person's intelligence to develop to the upper region of his or her reaction range, whereas deprived environments may limit intelligence to the lower portion of the range. Where intelligence is concerned, the reaction range may cover as much as 15 to 20 points on the IQ scale.

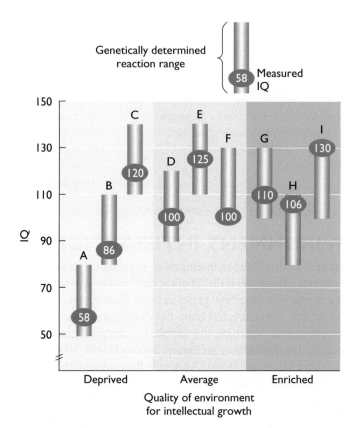

not allow that potential to develop. Finally, note person G, who was born with high genetic endowment and reared in an enriched environment. His slightly-above-average IQ of 110 is lower than we would expect, suggesting that he did not take advantage of either his biological capacity or his environmental advantages. This serves to remind us that intellectual growth depends not only on genetic endowment and environmental advantage, but also on interests, motivation and other personal characteristics that affect how much we apply ourselves or take advantage of our gifts and opportunities.

As noted earlier, heritability estimates are not universal by any means. They can vary, depending on the sample being studied, and they may be influenced by environmental factors. This fact was brought home forcefully in research by Turkheimer and colleagues (2003), mentioned previously. They found in a study of 7-year-old identical and fraternal twins that the proportions of IQ variation attributable to genes and environment varied by social class. In impoverished families, fully 60 per cent of the IQ variance was accounted for by the shared (family) environment, and the contribution of genes was negligible. In affluent families, the result was almost the reverse, with shared environment accounting for little variance and genes playing an important role. Clearly, genes and social-class environment seem to be interacting in their contribution to IQ.

It seems quite likely that there are genetically based reaction ranges for personality factors as well. This would mean that, personality-wise, there are biological limits to how malleable, or changeable, a person is in response to environmental factors. However, this hardly means that biology is destiny. Depending on the size of reaction ranges for particular personality characteristics – and even, perhaps, for different people – individuals could be quite susceptible to the impact of unshared environmental experiences.

HOW GENES CAN INFLUENCE THE ENVIRONMENT

Reaction range is a special example of how environment can affect the expression of genetically influenced traits. But there are other ways in which genetic and environmental factors can interact with one another. Figure 3.9 shows three ways in which genotype can influence the environment, which, in turn, can influence the development of personal characteristics (Scarr and McCartney, 1983).

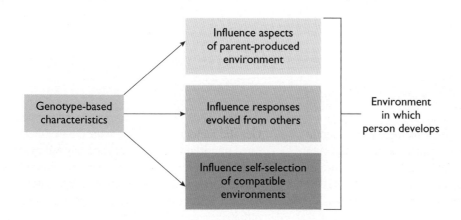

FIGURE 3.9

Three ways in which a person's genotype can influence the nature of the environment in which the person develops.

SOURCE: based on Scarr and McCartney, 1983.

First, genetically based characteristics may influence aspects of the environment to which the child is exposed. For example, we know that intelligence has strong heritability. Thus, a child born to highly intelligent parents is also likely to have good intellectual potential. If, because of their own interests in intellectual pursuits, these parents provide an intellectually stimulating environment with lots of books, educational toys, computers, and so on, this environment may help foster the development of mental skills that fall at the top of the child's reaction range. The resulting bright child is thus a product of both the genes shared with the parents and of his or her ability to profit from the environment they provide.

A second genetic influence on the environment is called the **evocative influence**, meaning that a child's genetically influenced behaviours may evoke certain responses from others. For example, some children are very cuddly, sociable and outgoing almost from birth, whereas others are more aloof, shy and do not like to be touched or approached. These characteristics are in part genetically based (Kagan, 1999; Plomin et al., 2007). Think of how you yourself would be most likely to respond to these two types of babies. The outgoing children are likely to be cuddled by their parents and evoke lots of friendly responses from others as they mature, creating an environment that supports and strengthens their sociable and extraverted tendencies. In contrast, shy, aloof children typically evoke less positive reactions from others, and this self-created environment may strengthen their genotypically influenced tendency to withdraw from social contact.

In both of these examples, genotype helped create an environment that reinforces already existing biologically based tendencies. However, a behaviour pattern can also evoke an environment that counteracts the genetically favoured trait and discourages its expression. We know, for example, that activity level has moderate heritability of around .40 (Table 3.1). Thus, parents of highly active 'off the wall' children may try to get them to sit still and calm down, or those of inactive children may press the child into lots of physical activities designed to increase physical well-being, in both instances opposing the natural tendencies of the children. Thus, the environment may either support or discourage the expression of a person's genotype.

evocative influence
a child's genetically influenced behaviours may evoke certain responses from others

Focus 3.11
Describe three ways that genotype can affect environmental influences on behaviour.

Finally, people are not simply passive responders to whatever environment happens to come their way. We actively seek out certain environments and avoid others. Genetically based traits may therefore affect the environments that we select, and these environments are likely to be compatible with our traits. Thus, a large, aggressive boy may be attracted to competitive sports with lots of physical contact, a highly intelligent child will seek out intellectually stimulating environments, and a shy, introverted child may shun social events and prefer solitary activities or a small number of friends. These varied self-selected environments may have very different effects on subsequent development. We therefore see that how people develop is influenced by both biology and experience, and that these factors combine in ways that are just beginning to be understood.

IN REVIEW

- Genetic and environmental factors rarely operate alone; they interact with one another in important ways. Genetic factors may influence how different people experience the same environment, and the environment can influence how genes express themselves.

- Genetic factors can influence the environment in three important ways. First, genes shared by parents and children may be expressed in the parents' behaviours and the environment they create. Second, genes may produce characteristics that influence responses evoked from others. Finally, people may self-select or create environments that are consistent with their genetic characteristics.

GENETIC MANIPULATION AND CONTROL

Focus 3.12

Describe some of the gene modification methods used to study causes of behaviour.

Until recently, genetics researchers had to be content with studying genetic phenomena occurring in nature. Aside from selectively breeding plants and animals for certain characteristics or studying the effects of genetic mutations, they had no ability to influence genes directly. Today, however, technological advances have enabled scientists not only to map the human genome but also to duplicate and modify the structures of genes themselves (Aldridge, 1998).

Some gene-manipulation research involves transplanting genes from one species into another. Such studies have shown how closely we humans are related to other living creatures. For example, both humans and insects have eyes; although the eyes differ markedly in their structural characteristics (see Fig. 3.10). Some years ago, geneticists identified a human gene called *Pax6*

FIGURE 3.10

When the human *Pax6* gene that initiates eye development in people is implanted in the fruit fly *Drosophila*'s side, it produces a multifaceted eye that looks like the eye of the insect itself, showing how the biological environment in which a gene operates can influence its expression. This demonstration also shows the relatedness of species as dissimilar as insects and humans.

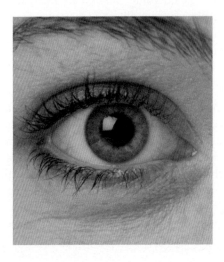
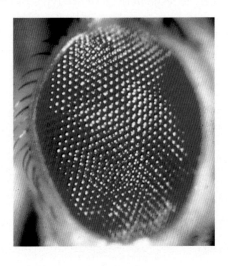

that is responsible for eye development. If this gene is not switched on at a critical time in development, people do not develop eyes. What do you think would happen if we were to transplant human *Pax6* genes at various locations along the body of a fruit fly and let them express themselves within that biological environment? Amazingly, numerous small eyes that looked just like the multifaceted eye of the insect itself appeared on the fruit fly's body, demonstrating how the biological environment in which a gene resides can determine its phenotypic expression (Hartwell et al., 2008). Studies of many other genes have shown that organisms as different as fruit flies and humans use the same genes to turn on the development of structures that may differ phenotypically but retain their ancestral roots.

The importance of finding relatedness and unity across a wide range of organisms cannot be overstated. It means that in many cases, the experimental manipulation of organisms known as *model organisms* can shed light on important processes in humans. Human functions cannot only be studied in such model organisms as rats, mice and monkeys, but also in such distant organisms as fruit flies.

In another gene-manipulation approach, researchers use certain enzymes (proteins that create chemical reactions) to cut the long threadlike molecules of genetic DNA into pieces, combine it with DNA from another organism, and insert it into a host organism such as a bacterium. Inside the host, the new DNA combination continues to divide and produce many copies of itself. Researchers can also insert new genetic material into viruses that can infiltrate the brain and modify the genetic structure in brain tissue.

Recent gene-modification research by psychologists has focused on processes such as learning, memory, emotion and motivation. One procedure done with animals (typically mice) is to alter a specific gene in a way that prevents it from carrying out its normal function. This is called a **knockout procedure** because that particular function of the gene is knocked out, or eliminated. The effects on behaviour are then observed. For example, psychologists can insert genetic material that will prevent neurons from responding to a particular brain chemical, or neurotransmitter. They can then measure whether the animal's ability to learn or remember is subsequently affected. This can help psychologists determine the importance of particular transmitters in relation to the behaviours of interest (Jang et al., 2003; Thomas and Palmiter, 1997). Researchers can also use a **knock-in procedure** to insert a new gene into an animal during the embryonic stage and study its impact on behaviour. Gene-modification techniques may one day enable us to alter genes that contribute to psychological disorders, such as depression and schizophrenia (McGuffin et al., 2005). Behavioural geneticists Robert Plomin and John Crabbe (2000) proclaim, '[We] predict that DNA will revolutionize psychological research and treatment early in the twenty-first century' (p. 806).

knockout procedure
that particular function of the gene is knocked out, or eliminated

knock-in procedure
insert a new gene into an animal during the embryonic stage and study its impact on behaviour

Focus 3.13
Describe some of the ethical and societal issues that attend the use of genetic screening and counselling.

APPLYING PSYCHOLOGICAL SCIENCE

THINKING CRITICALLY ABOUT GENETIC SCREENING

Technical advances in the field of molecular genetics allow the direct analysis of a person's genes. A DNA sample can be obtained from any tissue, including blood (Pupecki, 2006). Using an automated DNA sequencer (Fig. 3.11), it is possible to analyse the one copy of a gene present in a single cell, including a sperm cell that might be used in artificial insemination or one from a human embryo that has not yet been implanted in a woman. This technology allows the detection of many human traits, including the advance diagnosis of diseases such as sickle-cell anaemia, cystic fibrosis and Down syndrome, which produces mental

FIGURE 3.11

An automated DNA sequencer is used to analyse an individual's genotype. A modern sequencer like this one can analyse about 350 000 DNA base pairs per day. Typically, specific genes are targeted for screening. More than 900 specific genetic screens are now available through testing laboratories.

retardation, and Huntington's disease, a degenerative brain disorder that kills within five to 15 years after symptoms appear. By detecting mutated base sequences in a person's genome, genetic screening provides a means of identifying people, born and unborn, who are genetic carriers of the trait in question. But this capability brings with it some serious practical, ethical and life-altering issues that may confront you in your lifetime. Here are a few of them.

1. *What are the potential benefits of genetic screening?* There are at present more than 900 genetic tests available from testing laboratories (Human Genome Project, 2007). Proponents argue that screening can provide information that will benefit people. Early detection of a treatable condition can save lives. For example, were you to find through genetic screening that you have a predisposition to develop heart disease, you could alter your lifestyle with exercise and dietary measures to improve your chances of staying healthy. Screening could also affect reproductive decisions that reduce the probability of having children affected by a genetic disease. In a New York community, Hasidic Jews from Eastern Europe had a high incidence of Tay-Sachs disease, a fatal, genetically based neurological disorder. A genetic screening programme allowed rabbis to counsel against child-bearing in marriages involving two carriers of the abnormal allele, virtually eliminating the disease in offspring.

2. *Should private employers and insurance carriers be allowed to test their employees and clients?* Some employers say they would like to screen their employees in order to place them into job positions that would reduce risks of occupational diseases. Critics of employee screening see a more ominous motive behind the screening, including non-hiring or exclusion of employees whose future health might reduce company productivity. Likewise, insurance companies might well deny coverage to people whose screens indicate the presence of inherited medical disorders, or even a slightly increased likelihood of developing such disorders. This is exactly what occurred when test results from a genetic screening programme for the presence of the sickle-cell anaemia allele was made available to employers and insurance companies in the early 1970s. Many medical ethicists recommend the passing of laws that ensure that genetic information be confidential, disclosed only at the discretion of the tested person. France is one country which has already passed such a law.

3. *How accurate are the screens?* Another issue is whether an inaccurate screen may result in fateful decisions. Although screens for various diseases exceed 90 per cent accuracy, it is still possible that there can be a false positive result (an indication that a genetic predisposition to a disorder is present when it is not). Thus, a person may decide not to have children on the basis of an erroneous test that indicates a high risk of having a mentally retarded child. Alternatively, a false negative test may indicate that a predisposition is not present when in fact it is. Moreover, some tests, called *susceptibility tests*, simply tell you that you are more likely than others to develop a particular disorder, with no assurance that that will indeed occur.

4. *How should people be educated and counselled about test results?* Because of the importance of decisions that might be made on the basis of genetic screening, there is strong agreement that clients should be educated and counselled by specially trained counsellors. In the sickle-cell anaemia screening of the 1970s, follow-up education was inadequate, the result being that some African-American men who were informed that they were carriers of the sickle-cell allele elected to remain childless because they were not told that the disorder would not occur in their offspring if their mates were non-carriers of the allele. The genetic counsellor's role is to help the person, couple or family to decide whether to be screened, to help them to fully understand the meaning of the test results, and to assist them during what might well be a difficult and traumatic time.

As you can see, many complex issues swirl around the area of genetic screening. What kinds of guidelines would you like to see established to ensure that information gained from genetic screening is used appropriately? Such guidelines may well affect you at some time in the future as the tools of molecular genetics are more broadly applied.

IN REVIEW

- Genetic and environmental factors interact in complex ways to influence phenotypic characteristics. Genetic reaction range sets upper and lower limits for the impact of environmental factors. Where intelligence is concerned, environmental factors may create differences as large as 20 IQ points. Genotype can influence the kind of environments to which children are exposed, as when intelligent parents create an enriched environment. Genetically influenced behaviour patterns also have an evocative influence, influencing how the environment responds to the person. Finally, people often select environments that match genetically influenced personal characteristics.

- Genetic manipulation allows scientists to duplicate and alter genetic material or, potentially, to repair dysfunctional genes. These procedures promise ground-breaking advances in understanding genetic mechanisms and in treating physical and psychological disorders. Moreover, our ability to analyse people's genotypes allows for genetic screening and raises a host of practical and ethical issues.

EVOLUTION AND BEHAVIOUR: INFLUENCES FROM THE DISTANT PAST

In the misty forests and verdant grasslands of past eons, our early human ancestors faced many environmental challenges as they struggled to survive. If even one of your ancestors had not behaved effectively enough to survive and reproduce, you would not be here to contemplate your existence. In this sense, each of us is an evolutionary success story. As descendants of those successful fore-bears, we carry within us genes that contributed to their adaptive and reproductive success.

The vast majority (99.9 per cent) of genes we share with all other humans creates the 'human nature' that makes us like all other people. We enter the world with innate **biologically based mechanisms** that enable and predispose us to perceive, behave, feel, and think in certain ways (Stearns and Hoekstra, 2005). In humans, these inborn capacities allow us to learn, to remember, to speak a language, to perceive certain aspects of our environment at birth, to respond with universal emotions, and to bond with other humans. Most scientists view these biological

biologically based mechanisms
enable and predispose us to perceive, behave, feel, and think in certain ways

FIGURE 3.12

These days, evolutionary principles are widely discussed.

FIGURE 3.12

These days, evolutionary principles are widely discussed.

evolution

a change over time in the frequency with which particular genes – and the characteristics they produce – occur within an interbreeding population

mutations

random events and accidents in gene reproduction during the division of cells

natural selection

characteristics that increase the likelihood of survival and reproduction within a particular environment will be more likely to be preserved in the population and therefore will become more common in the species over time

FIGURE 3.13

Human-initiated selective breeding over a number of generations produced this tiny horse. A similar process could occur through natural selection if for some reason a particular environment favoured the survival and reproductive ability of smaller members of the equine population.

characteristics as products of an evolutionary process. Evolutionary theorists (see Fig. 3.12) also believe that important aspects of social behaviour, such as aggression, altruism, sex roles, protecting kin, and mate selection are influenced by biological mechanisms that have evolved during the development of our species. Evolutionary psychologist David Buss says: 'Humans are living fossils – collections of mechanisms produced by prior selection pressures' (1995, p. 27).

EVOLUTION OF ADAPTIVE MECHANISMS

Evolution is a change over time in the frequency with which particular genes – and the characteristics they produce – occur within an interbreeding population. As particular genes become more or less frequent in a population, so do the characteristics they influence. Some genetic variations arise in a population through **mutations**, random events and accidents in gene reproduction during the division of cells. If mutations occur in the cells that become sperm and egg cells, the altered genes will be passed on to offspring. Mutations help create variation within a population's physical characteristics. It is this variation that makes evolution possible.

Natural Selection

Long before Charles Darwin published his theory of evolution in 1859, people knew that animals and plants could be changed over time by selectively breeding members of a species that shared desired traits (see Fig. 3.13). A visit to a dog show illustrates the remarkably varied products of selective breeding of pedigree animals.

Just as plant and animal breeders 'select' for certain characteristics, so too does nature. According to Darwin's principle of **natural selection**, characteristics that increase the likelihood of survival and reproduction within a particular environment will be more likely to be preserved in the population and therefore will become more common in the species over time. As environmental changes produce new and different demands, various new characteristics may contribute to survival and the ability to pass on one's genes (Barrow, 2003). In this way, natural selection acts as a set of filters, allowing certain characteristics of survivors to become more common. Conversely, characteristics of non-survivors become less common and, perhaps, even extinct over time. The filters also allow neutral variations that neither facilitate nor impede fitness to be preserved in a population. These neutral variations, sometimes called *evolutionary noise*, could conceivably become important in meeting some future environmental demand. For example, people differ in their ability to tolerate radiation (Vral et al., 2002). In today's world, these variations are of limited importance, but they clearly could affect survivability if future nuclear war were to increase levels of radioactivity around the world. As those who could tolerate higher levels of radiation survived and those who could not perished, the genetic basis for high-radiation tolerance would become increasingly more common in the human species. Thus, for natural selection to work, there must be individual variation in a species characteristic that influences survival or the ability to reproduce (Workman and Reader, 2008).

Principles of natural selection in psychology   The histories of evolutionary theory and psychology are inextricably intertwined. In addition to his works on natural selection, Darwin also wrote an 1877 paper entitled 'A biographical sketch of the infant'. This represents an early, observational study in developmental psychology. Darwin was influential to, and himself influenced by, early psychologists.

However, the application of principles of natural selection to psychology has not been without controversy. For example, E.O. Wilson's *Sociobiology* (1975) describes research in which the behaviours of humans and non-humans are investigated in terms of their functionality or usefulness. Evolutionary theory suggests that if something is not useful or functional then it will not occur with such frequency in later generations. The controversy in Wilson's work in was applying explanations of non-human animal behaviour to humans. Explanations of promiscuity in a male as a means of ensuring the progression of his genetic make-up may not be easy reading for people who feel that reason or morality underlies their behaviour.

There is a great danger in the misapplication of Darwin's thinking. For example, Francis Galton argued that certain traits which might have been functional and useful in the past were not so in modern Victorian England. He coined the term 'eugenics' to describe a practice of improving the human race by encouraging 'desirable' human traits through selective breeding. Those who had these 'desirable' traits should be encouraged to have children; those who did not (criminals) should be discouraged or prevented. Bitter experience has taught us that the principles of eugenics can be taken even further with horrifying consequences; Hitler's attempts to improve society with eugenics resulted in the death of millions in Nazi Germany (see later 'Beneath the surface').

It is clear, then, that the relationships between evolution, and evolutionary psychology have been entwined with controversy. Nonetheless, it is also clear that the principles of evolution are not only extremely interesting, but one of the greatest scientific contributions ever made.

Evolutionary adaptations   The products of natural selection are called **adaptations**, physical or behavioural changes that allow organisms to meet recurring environmental challenges to their survival, thereby increasing their reproductive ability. In the final analysis, the name of the natural selection game is to pass on one's genes, either personally or through kin who share at least some of them (Dawkins, 2006). Evolutionary theorists believe this is why animals and humans may risk, or even sacrifice, their lives in order to protect their kin and the genes they carry.

In the animal kingdom, we find fascinating examples of adaptation to specific environmental conditions. For example, the tendency for one species of cannibalistic spider to eat its own kind decreases markedly if other food supplies are available. Genetically identical butterflies placed in different environments can take on completely different physical appearances depending on local climactic conditions during the larval stage of development. And in several species of tropical fish, imbalances in the ratio of males to females can actually result in males changing

Focus 3.14
Define evolution and explain how genetic variation and natural selection produce adaptations.

adaptations
physical or behavioural changes that allow organisms to meet recurring environmental challenges to their survival, thereby increasing their reproductive ability

into females or females into males (Schaller, 2006). If environmental factors can trigger such profound changes in insects and fish, should we be surprised if a species as remarkably flexible as humans would also adapt to environmental changes and evolve over time?

Applying concepts of natural selection and adaptation to human evolution begins with the notion that an organism's biology determines its behavioural capabilities, and that its behaviour (including its mental abilities) determines whether or not it will survive. In this sense, a discussion of the evolution of our biology, and our neurobiology, directly relates to the evolution of behaviour.

One theory is that when dwindling vegetation in some parts of the world forced ape-like animals down from the trees and required that they hunt for food on open, grassy plains, chances for survival were greater for those capable of *bipedal locomotion* (walking on two legs). By freeing the hands, bipedalism fostered the development and use of tools and weapons that could kill at a distance (Lewin, 1998). Hunting in groups and avoiding dangerous predators encouraged social organization, which required the development of specialized social roles (such as 'hunter and protector' in the male and 'nurturer of children' in the female) that still exist in most cultures. These environmental challenges also favoured the development of language, which enhanced social communication and the transmission of knowledge. In this manner, successful human behaviour evolved together with a changing body (Geary, 2005; Tooby and Cosmides, 1992).

Brain evolution   Tool use, bipedal locomotion and social organization put new selection pressures on many parts of the body. These included the teeth, the hands and the pelvis, all of which changed over time in response to the new dietary and behavioural demands. But the greatest pressure was placed on the brain structures involved in the abilities most critical to the emerging way of life: attention, memory, language and thought. These mental abilities became important to survival in an environment that required quick learning and problem solving. In the evolutionary progression from *Australopithecus* (an early human ancestor who lived about 4 million years ago) through *Homo erectus* (1.6 million to 100 000 years ago) to the human subspecies Neanderthal of 75 000 years ago, the brain tripled in size, and the most dramatic growth occurred in the parts of the brain that are the seat of the higher mental processes (Fig. 3.14). Thus, evolved changes in behaviour seem to have contributed to the development of the brain, just as the growth of the brain contributed to evolving human behaviour (Striedter, 2005).

Surprisingly, perhaps, today's human brain does not differ much from the Stone Age brain of our ancient ancestors. Yet the fact that we perform mental activities that could not have been imagined

FIGURE 3.14

The human brain evolved over a period of several million years. The greatest growth occurred in those areas concerned with the higher mental processes, particularly memory, thought, and language. Current thought is that Neanderthal man took a different evolutionary route from Homo erectus, and is thus not our ancestor.

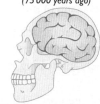

Neanderthal
(75 000 years ago)

The skull more closely resembles that of modern humans

Australopithecus
(4 million years ago)

The brain capacity ranges from 450 to 650 cubic centimetres (cc)

Homo erectus
(1.6 million to 100 000 years ago)

Further development of the skull and jaw are evident, and brain capacity is 900 cc

Homo sapiens

The deeply convoluted brain reflects growth in areas concerned with higher mental processes

in those ancient times tells us that human capabilities are not solely determined by the brain; cultural evolution is also important in the development of adaptations. From an evolutionary perspective, culture provides important environmental inputs to evolutionary mechanisms (Boyd and Richerson, 2005). It is still debated, but there is general agreement among evolutionists that during early evolution, after *Homo erectus*, there came two separate strands in the evolutionary path. *Homo sapiens* took one path, and Neanderthal man another such that Neanderthals are not our evolutionary ancestor, but rather an evolutionary 'cousin' with whom we shared a common ancestor. Quite why Neanderthal man became extinct is unknown. Perhaps their abilities to adapt to climate changes and other environmental pressures were not as robust as those skills in *Homo sapiens*.

In a study of brain size across a variety of primate species Robin Dunbar (1993) observed that the average size of the neocortex in a given species is strongly related to the size of the social group that species can maintain. Dunbar thus suggests that the main reason for evolving larger brain is in order to maintain larger social groups. As part of his 'social brain hypothesis' he formulated a value called *Dunbar's Number* which describes the theoretical maximum size of social group that an individual can maintain. The number in humans is 150. Dunbar says that we can, theoretically at least, have, and maintain, a social grouping of up to 150 people in which we can fully understand their relationships with others in the group. Dunbar thus suggests that our social lives are constrained by the size of our neocortex (Dunbar, 1993).

Evoked culture   According to the evolutionary concept of **evoked culture**, cultures may themselves be the product of biological mechanisms that evolved to meet specific adaptation challenges faced by specific groups of people in specific places at specific times. Through this process, a culture could develop in a setting in which survival depended on the male's success in hunting game that differed in important ways from a culture in a farming community in which women shared the 'breadwinner' role (Gangestad et al., 2006). In the shared-breadwinner culture, we might expect less sharply defined sex roles. Once established by successful adaptation, a culture is transmitted to future members through social learning, as has occurred for all of us in our own process of development. This serves to remind us of another truism: the creation of new environments through our own behaviour is another important part of the evolutionary equation (Boyd and Richerson, 2005). Through our own behaviours, humans can create environments that influence subsequent natural selection of biological traits suited to the new environment (Bandura, 1997).

> **evoked culture**
> the product of biological mechanisms that evolved to meet specific adaptation challenges faced by specific groups of people in specific places at specific times

WHAT DO YOU THINK?

NATURAL SELECTION AND GENETIC DISEASES

If Darwin was right about natural selection, then why do we have so many harmful genetic disorders? Consider, for example, cystic fibrosis, a hereditary disorder of European origin that clogs one's lungs with mucus and prevents digestion, typically causing death before age 30. Another example is sickle-cell anaemia, which causes early deaths in many people of African descent. Can you reconcile the existence of such disorders with 'survival of the fittest'? Think about it, then see p. 121.

EVOLUTION AND HUMAN NATURE

To evolutionary psychologists, what we call human nature is the expression of inborn biological tendencies that have evolved through natural selection. There exists a vast catalogue of human characteristics and capabilities that unfold in a normally developing human being. Consider, for example, this brief preview of commonalities in human behaviour that are discussed in greater detail in later chapters.

1. Infants are born with an ability to acquire any language spoken in the world (see Chapter 9). The specific languages learned depend on which ones they are exposed to. Deaf children have a similar ability to acquire any sign language, and their language acquisition pattern parallels the learning of spoken language. Language is central to human thought and communication.

2. Newborns are pre-wired to perceive specific stimuli (see Chapter 5). For example, they are more responsive to pictures of human faces than to pictures of the same facial features arranged in a random pattern (Johnson et al., 1991). They are also able to discriminate the odour of their mother's milk from that of other women (McFarlane, 1975). Both adaptations improve human bonding with caregivers.

3. At one week of age, human infants show primitive mathematical skills, successfully discriminating between two and three objects. These abilities improve with age in the absence of any training. The brain seems designed to make 'greater than' and 'less than' judgements, which are clearly important in decision making (Geary, 2005).

4. According to Robert Hogan (1983), establishing co-operative relationships with a group was critical to the human species' survival and reproductive success. Thus humans seem to have a need to belong and strongly fear being ostracized from the group (see Chapter 11). Social anxiety (fear of social disapproval) may be an adaptive mechanism to protect against doing things that will prompt group rejection (Baumeister and Tice, 1990).

5. As a species, humans tend to be altruistic and helpful to one another, especially to children and relatives (see Chapter 14). Research shows that altruism increases with degree of relatedness. Evolutionary theorists suggest that helping family members and relatives increases the likelihood that those people will be able to pass on the genes they share with you. People are also more likely to help younger people than older ones (Burnstein et al., 1994), perhaps because, from a species perspective, younger people have more reproductive value than do older people.

6. As we will see in Chapter 11, there is much evidence for a set of basic emotions that are universally recognized (Ekman, 1973). Smiling, for example, is a universal expression of happiness and goodwill that typically evokes positive reactions from others (Fig. 3.15). Emotions are important means of social communication that trigger mental, emotional and behavioural mechanisms in others (Ketellar, 1995).

7. In virtually all cultures, males are more violent and more likely to kill others (particularly other males) than are females. The differences are striking, with male–male killings outnumbering female–female killings, on average, by about 30 to one (Daly and Wilson, 1988). Evolutionary researchers suggest that male–male violence is rooted in hunting, establishing dominance hierarchies and competing successfully for the most fertile mates, all of which enhanced personal and reproductive survival as our species evolved.

Focus 3.16

How have evolutionary principles been used to account for diverse cultures?

Focus 3.17

Do genetically based diseases provide an argument against natural selection?

FIGURE 3.15

The human smile seems to be a universal expression of positive emotion and is universally perceived in that way. Evolutionary psychologists believe that expressions of basic emotions are hard-wired biological mechanisms that have adaptive value as methods of communication.

Having sampled from the wide range of behavioural phenomena that have been subjected to an evolutionary analysis, let us focus in greater detail on two areas of current theorizing that relate to both commonalities and differences among people – sex and self. Before doing so, however, we should emphasize a most important principle: *behaviour does not occur in a biological vacuum; it always involves a biological organism acting within (and often, in response to) an environment*. That environment may be inside the body in the form of interactions with other genes, influencing how genes and the protein molecules through which they operate express themselves. It may be inside the mother's womb, or it may be 'out there', in the form of a physical environment or a culture. Although everyone agrees that biological and environmental factors interact with one another, most of the debates in evolutionary psychology concern two issues: (1) how general or specific are the biological mechanisms that have evolved? and (2) how much are these mechanisms influenced in their expression by the environment?

Focus 3.18
Describe examples of human behaviour that suggest innate evolved mechanisms. Differentiate between remote and proximate causal factors.

Sexuality and Mate Preferences

The purpose of evolution is to continue the species, and the only way this can occur is through reproduction. In order to pass on one's genes and maintain the species, people must mate. We should not be surprised, therefore, that evolutionary theorists and researchers have devoted great attention to sexuality, differences between men and women, and mate-seeking. This topic also has generated considerable debate about the relative contributions of evolutionary and sociocultural factors to this domain of behaviour.

One of the most important and intimate ways that humans relate to one another is by seeking a mate. Marriage seems to be universal across the globe (Buss and Schmitt, 1993). In seeking mates, however, women and men display different mating strategies and preferences. Compared with women, men typically show more interest in short-term mating, prefer a greater number of short-term sexual partners, and have more permissive sexual attitudes and more sexual partners over their lifetimes (Schmitt et al., 2001). In one study of 266 undergraduates, two-thirds of the women said that they desired only one sexual partner over the next 30 years, but only about half of the men shared that goal (Pedersen et al., 2002). These attitudinal differences also extend to behaviour. In research done at three different universities, Russell Clark and Elaine Hatfield (1989; Clark, 1990) sent male and female research assistants of average physical attractiveness out across the campus. Upon seeing an attractive person of the opposite sex, the assistant approached the person, said he or she found the person attractive, and asked, 'Would you go to bed with me tonight?'

Women approached in this manner almost always reacted very negatively to the overture and frequently dismissed the assistants as 'sleaze' or 'pervert'. Not a single woman agreed to have sex. In contrast, three in every four men enthusiastically agreed, some asking why it was necessary to wait until that night. Other findings show that men think about sex about three times more often than women do, desire more frequent sex and initiate more sexual encounters than do women (Baumeister et al., 2001; Laumann et al., 1994). Men also are much more likely to interpret a woman's friendliness as a sexual come-on, apparently projecting their own sexual desires onto the woman (Johnson et al., 1992).

Despite these differences, most men and women make a commitment at some point in their lives to a long-term mate. What qualities do women and men seek in such a mate? Once again, we see sex differences. Men typically prefer women somewhat younger than themselves, whereas women prefer somewhat older men. This tendency is exaggerated in the 'trophy wives' sometimes exhibited by wealthy and famous older men. In terms of personal qualities, Table 3.4 shows the overall results of a worldwide study of mate preferences in 37 cultures (Buss et al., 1990). Men and women again show considerable overall agreement, but some differences emerge. Men place greater value on a potential mate's physical attractiveness and domestic skills, whereas women place greater value on a potential mate's earning potential, status and ambitiousness. But why might this be? Evolutionary psychologists have an answer.

TABLE 3.4 CHARACTERISTICS OF A MATE

Women and men rated each characteristic on a 4-point scale. From top to bottom, the following numbers represent the order (rank) of most highly rated to least highly rated items for Buss's worldwide sample. How would you rate their importance?

Characteristic desired in a mate	Rated by	
	Women	Men
Mutual attraction/love	1	1
Dependable character	2	2
Emotional stability/maturity	3	3
Pleasing disposition	4	4
Education/intelligence	5	6
Sociability	6	7
Good health	7	5
Desire for home/children	8	8
Ambition	9	11
Refinement	10	9
Similar education	11	14
Good financial prospect	12	13
Good looks	13	10
Social status	14	15
Good cook/housekeeper	15	12
Similar religion	16	17
Similar politics	17	18
Chastity	18	16

SOURCE: Based on Buss et al., 1990.

sexual strategies theory (and a related model called **parental investment theory**) mating strategies and preferences reflect inherited tendencies, shaped over the ages in response to different types of adaptive problems that men and women faced

According to an evolutionary viewpoint called **sexual strategies theory** (and a related model called **parental investment theory**), mating strategies and preferences reflect inherited tendencies, shaped over the ages in response to different types of adaptive problems that men and women faced (Buss and Schmitt, 1993; Trivers, 1972). In evolutionary terms, our most successful ancestors were those who survived and passed down the greatest numbers of their genes to future generations. Men who had sex with more partners increased the likelihood of fathering more children, so they were interested in mating widely. Men also may have taken a woman's youth and attractive, healthy appearance as signs that she was fertile and had many years left to bear his children (Buss, 1989).

In contrast, ancestral women had little to gain and much to lose by mating with numerous men. They were interested in mating wisely, not widely. In humans and other mammals, females typically make a greater investment than males: they carry the foetus, incur health risks and possible birth-related death, and nourish the newborn. Engaging in short-term sexual relationships with multiple males can in the end create uncertainty about who is the father, thereby decreasing a male's willingness to commit resources to helping a mother raise the child. For these reasons, women maximized their reproductive success – and the survival chances of themselves and their offspring – by being selective and choosing mates who were willing and able to commit time, energy and other resources (e.g., food, shelter, protection) to the family. Women increased their likelihood of passing their genes into the future by mating wisely, and men by mating widely. Through natural selection, according to evolutionary psychologists, the differing qualities that maximized men's and women's reproductive success eventually became part of their biological nature (Buss, 2007).

Focus 3.19
Contrast sexual strategies and social structure explanations for mate preferences, citing results from cross-cultural research.

Steven Gangestad, Martie Haselton, and David Buss (2006) found that some of these mate preference patterns are more pronounced in parts of the world with historically high levels of pathogens (disease-causing germs) that endangered survival than in areas that had historically low levels of pathogens. Where diseases like malaria, plague and yellow fever are more prevalent, male factors such as physical attractiveness and robustness, intelligence and social dominance – all presumably signs of biological fitness – seem especially important to women even today. Gangestad et al. suggest that in such environments, women seem willing to sacrifice some degree of male investment in their offspring in favour of a mate who has a higher probability of giving them healthy children. To men, a woman's attractiveness and healthiness (and that of her family) also is more important in high-pathogen environments, presumably because these historically were signs of a woman who would be more likely to give birth to healthy children and live long enough to rear them.

Not all scientists have bought into this evolutionary explanation for human mating patterns and other social behaviours. Again, the disagreement revolves around the relative potency of interacting biological and environmental factors. In the case of mate selection, proponents of **social structure theory** maintains that men and women display different mating preferences not because nature impels them to do so, but because society guides them into different social roles (Eagly and Wood, 1999; 2006). Adaptive behaviour patterns may have been passed from parents to children not through genes but through learning. Social structure theorists point out that despite the shift over the past several decades towards greater gender equality, today's women still have generally less power, lower wages and less access to resources than do men. In a two-income marriage, the woman is more likely to be the partner who switches to part-time work or becomes a full-time homemaker after childbirth. Thus, society's division of labour still tends to socialize men into the breadwinner role and women into the homemaker role.

social structure theory
men and women display different mating preferences not because nature impels them to do so, but because society guides them into different social roles

Given these power and resource disparities and the need to care for children, it makes sense for women to seek men who will be successful wage earners and for men to seek women who can have children and fulfil the domestic-worker role. An older male–younger female age gap is favourable because older men are likely to be further along in earning power and younger women are more economically dependent, and this state of affairs conforms to cultural expectations of marital roles. This division-of-labour hypothesis does not directly address why men emphasize a mate's physical attractiveness more than women do, but Alice Eagly and Wendy Wood (1999) speculate that attractiveness is viewed as part of what women 'exchange' in return for a male's earning capacity (see Fig. 3.16).

FIGURE 3.16

Marriages in which the woman is much younger than the man are far more common than are marriages in which the woman is far older. Is the tendency for woman to marry men older than themselves a remnant of evolutionary influences or a product of sociocultural forces?

We now have two competing explanations for sex differences in mating behaviour: the evolution-based sexual strategies approach and the social structure view. Our 'Research close-up' looks at one attempt to compare predictions derived from the two theories.

RESEARCH CLOSE-UP

SEX DIFFERENCES IN THE IDEAL MATE: EVOLUTION OR SOCIAL ROLES?

SOURCES: D.M. Buss (1989) Sex differences in human mate preferences: evolutionary hypotheses tested in 37 cultures, *Behavioral and Brain Sciences*, Vol. 12, pp. 1–49; A. Eagly and W. Wood (1999) The origins of sex differences in human behavior: evolved dispositions versus social roles, *American Psychologist*, Vol. 54, pp. 408–23.

INTRODUCTION

How can we possibly test the hypothesis that, over the ages, evolution has shaped the psyches of men and women to be inherently different? Evolutionary psychologist David Buss proposes that, as a start, we can examine whether gender differences in mating preferences are similar across cultures. If they are, this would be consistent with the view that men and women follow universal, biologically based mating strategies that transcend culture. Based on principles of evolutionary psychology, Buss hypothesized that *across cultures*, men will prefer to marry younger women because such women have greater reproductive capacity; men will value a potential mate's attractiveness more than women will because men use attractiveness as a sign of health and fertility; and women will place greater value than men on a potential mate's earning potential because this provides survival advantages for the woman and her offspring.

METHOD

Buss's team of 50 scientists administered questionnaires to women and men from 37 cultures around the globe. Although random sampling could not be used, the sample of 10 047 participants was ethnically, religiously and socio-economically diverse. Participants reported the ideal ages at which they and a spouse would marry, rank-ordered (from 'most desirable' to 'least desirable') a list of 13 qualities that a potential mate might have, and rated the importance of 18 mate qualities on a second list (see Table 3.4).

Alice Eagly and Wendy Wood wondered if men's and women's mate preferences might be influenced by a third variable, namely, cultural differences in gender roles and power differentials. To find out, they reanalysed Buss's data, using the United Nations Gender Empowerment Measure to assess the degree of gender equality in each of the cultures. This measure reflects women's earned income relative to men's, seats in parliament, and share of administrative, managerial, professional and technical jobs.

RESULTS

In all 37 cultures, men wanted to marry younger women. Overall, they believed that the ideal ages for men and women to marry were 27.5 and 24.8 years, respectively. Similarly, women preferred older men, reporting on average an ideal marriage age of 28.8 for husbands and 25.4 for wives. In every culture, men valued having a physically attractive mate more than women did, and in 36 of 37 cultures, women attached more importance than men did to a mate's earning potential.

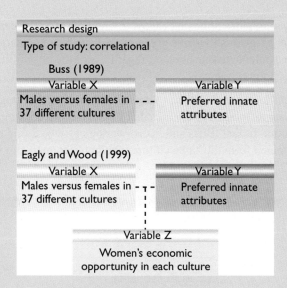

EVOLUTIONARY AND SOCIAL ROLES INTERPRETATIONS

David Buss concluded that the findings strongly supported the predictions of evolutionary (sexual strategies) theory. Subsequently, Alice Eagly and Wendy Wood analysed Buss's data further in order to test two key predictions derived from their social structure theory:

1. Men place greater value than women on a mate's having good domestic skills because this is consistent with culturally defined gender roles.

2. If economic and power inequalities cause men and women to attach different values to a mate's age, earning potential and domestic skills, then these gender differences should be smaller in cultures where there is less inequality between men and women.

As reported by Buss, the potential-mate characteristic 'good cook/housekeeper' produced large overall gender differences, with men valuing it more highly. Could this overall trend, however, depend on differences in cultural roles or power differentials? As predicted by the social structure model, Eagly and Wood found that in cultures with greater gender equality, men showed less of a preference for younger women, women displayed less of a preference for older men, and the gender gap decreased in mate preferences for a 'good cook/housekeeper' and 'good financial prospect'. On the other hand, cultural gender equality did not influence the finding that men value physical attractiveness more than women; that gender difference was *not* smaller in cultures with greater gender equality.

DISCUSSION

Both Buss (Gangestad et al., 2006) and Eagly and Wood (2006) share an interactionist perspective on mate selection that simultaneously takes nature and nurture into account. They differ, however, on how specific and strongly programmed the biological dispositions are thought to be. When Buss found remarkably consistent sex differences in worldwide mate preferences, he interpreted this cross-cultural consistency as evidence that men and women follow universal, biologically based mating strategies. Yet Eagly and Wood (1999; 2006) insist that consistency in behaviour across cultures does not, by itself, demonstrate *why* those patterns occur. They view the mate selection preferences not as biologically pre-programmed, but rather as reflecting evolved but highly flexible dispositions that depend heavily on social input for their expression. In support of this position, they found that a commonly found social condition across cultures, gender inequality, accounts for some – but not all – of the sex differences in mating preferences.

In science, such controversy stimulates opposing camps to find more sophisticated ways to test their hypotheses. Ultimately, everyone's goal is to arrive at the most plausible explanation for behaviour. This is why scientists make their data available to one another, regardless of the possibility that their peers may use the data to bolster an opposing point of view.

Although men and women differ in some of their mating preferences and strategies, the similar overall order of mate preferences shown in Table 3.4 indicates that we are talking once again about shades of the same colour, not different colours. In fact, Buss and his co-workers (1990) found that 'there may be more similarity between men and women from the same culture than between men and men or women and women from different cultures' (p. 17).

evolutionary personality theory

looks for the origin of presumably universal personality traits in the adaptive demands of our species' evolutionary history

Focus 3.20

How does evolutionary theory account for the universal nature of the Big Five personality traits and of variation on each of them?

Evolutionary Approaches To Personality

Personality is an especially interesting topic to consider from an evolutionary perspective because traditionally, evolutionary approaches are geared to explaining the things we have in common. An approach called **evolutionary personality theory** looks for the origin of presumably universal personality traits in the adaptive demands of our species' evolutionary history. It asks the basic question, 'Where did the personality traits exhibited by humans come from in the first place?' The focus here is on the traits that we (and other animals) have in common. But evolutionary personality theory also tries to account for the core question in the field of personality: why do we differ from one another in these personality traits?

Previously in this chapter, we described the five factor model of personality, the leading current trait theory. Because these five trait dimensions – extraversion, agreeableness, conscientiousness, neuroticism and openness to experience – have been found in people's descriptions of themselves and others in virtually all cultures, some theorists regard them as universal among humans (Nettle, 2006). And because evolutionary theory addresses human universals, the Big Five traits have been the major focus of evolutionary personality theory.

Why should these traits be found so consistently in the languages and behaviours of cultures around the world? According to David Buss (1999), they exist in humans because they have helped us achieve two overriding goals: physical survival and reproductive success. Traits such as extraversion and emotional stability would have been helpful in attaining positions of dominance and mate selection. Conscientiousness and agreeableness are important in group survival, as well as in reproduction and the care of children. Finally, because openness to experience may be the basis for problem solving and creative activities that could affect the ultimate survival of the species, there has always been a need for intelligent and creative people. Evolutionary theorists therefore regard the behaviours underlying the Big Five as sculpted by natural selection until they ultimately became part of human nature.

The five personality factors also may reflect the ways in which we are biologically programmed to think about and discriminate among people. Lewis Goldberg (1981) suggests that over the course of evolution, people have had to ask some very basic questions when interacting with another person, questions that have survival and reproductive implications:

1. Is person X active and dominant or passive and submissive? Can I dominate X, or will I have to submit to X?

2. Is X agreeable and friendly or hostile and uncooperative?

3. Can I count on X? Is X conscientious and dependable?

4. Is X sane (stable, rational, predictable) or crazy (unstable, unpredictable, possibly dangerous)?

5. How smart is X, and how quickly can X learn and adapt?

Not surprisingly, according to Goldberg, these questions relate directly to the Big Five factors. He believes that this is the reason analyses of trait ratings reveal Big Five consistency across very diverse cultures.

So much for commonalities in the personality traits that people exhibit. But what about the individual differences in these traits that we witness every day, and that define individual personalities? If natural selection is a winnowing process that favours certain personal characteristics over others, would we not expect people to become more alike over time and personality differences to be minimal? Here we turn to another important evolutionary concept called **strategic pluralism**, the idea that multiple – even contradictory – behavioural strategies (for example, introversion and extraversion) might be adaptive in certain environments and would therefore be maintained through natural selection. Thus, Daniel Nettle (2006) theorizes that we see variation in the Big Five traits because all of them have adaptive trade-offs (a balance of potential benefits and costs) in the outcomes they may produce.

Take extraversion, for example. Nettle (2006) reviewed research showing that scores on personality tests that measure extraversion are positively related to the number of sexual partners that males have and to their willingness to abandon sexual relationships with women in order to pursue a more desirable partner. These behaviours should increase the prospects for reproducing lots of offspring. Compared with introverts, extraverts also have more social relationships, more positive emotions, greater social support, and are more adventurous and risk-taking, all of which can have benefits. The trade-offs, however, are greater likelihood of risk-produced accidents or illnesses, and a higher potential for antisocial behaviour (which in the ancestral environment might have resulted in ostracism or even death and in the current environment, imprisonment). For a woman, the outgoing demeanour of the extravert may facilitate attracting a mate, but also may lead to impulsive sexual choices that are counterproductive for her and her offspring. The trait of agreeableness brings with it the benefits of harmonious social relationships and the support of others, but also the risks of being exploited or victimized by others. Another potential cost of agreeableness arises from not sufficiently pursuing one's own personal interests; a little selfishness can be adaptive. Even neuroticism, which is generally viewed as a negative trait, has both costs and benefits that could relate to survival. On the cost side, neuroticism involves anxiety, depression and stress-related illness that could shorten the lifespan and drive potential mates away. But the fitness trade-off of neuroticism is a vigilance to potential dangers that could be life-saving, as well as fear of failing and a degree of competitiveness that could have adaptive achievement outcomes. Nettle believes that these trade-offs favour evolutionary variation in the Big Five traits and that the specific environment in which our ancestors evolved made it more or less adaptive to be an extravert or an introvert, agreeable or selfish, fearful or fearless, conscientious or immoral, and so on. This would help account for genes favouring individual differences on personality dimensions and for the great diversity we see in personality trait patterns.

Evolutionary theorists also account for individual differences in personality traits by focusing on gene–environment interactions. Evolution may provide humans with species-typical behaviour patterns, but environmental inputs influence how they are manifested. For example, dominance may be the behaviour pattern encouraged by innate mechanisms in males, but an individual male who has many early experiences of being subdued or dominated may develop a submissive personality. For evolutionists who assume that the innate female behaviour pattern is submissiveness, an individual female who has the resources of high intelligence and physical strength may be quite willing and able to behave in a competitive and dominant fashion.

strategic pluralism
the idea that multiple – even contradictory – behavioural strategies might be adaptive in certain environments and would therefore be maintained through natural selection

Focus 3.21
Describe some of the fallacies that can arise from misinterpreting evolutionary theory.

FIGURE 3.17

Levels of analysis: interacting biological, environmental, and psychological factors.

As we have seen throughout this chapter, genetic factors underlie evolutionary changes, and they strongly influence many aspects of our human behaviour. Genes do not act in isolation, however, but in concert with environmental factors, some of which are created by nature and some of which are of human origin. Together, these forces have forged the human psychological capabilities and processes that are the focus of psychological science. Figure 3.17 shows how the causes of behaviour can be studied at biological, psychological and environmental levels of analysis.

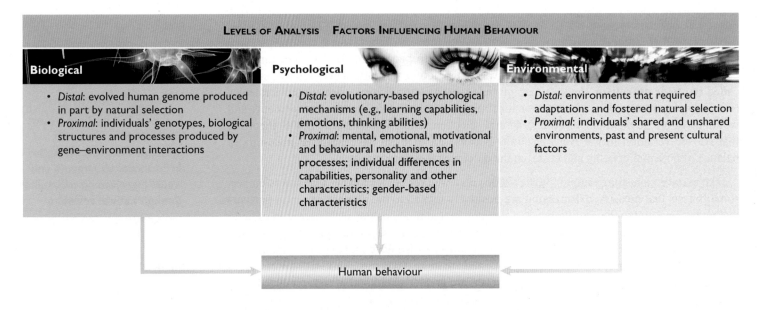

LEVELS OF ANALYSIS   FACTORS INFLUENCING HUMAN BEHAVIOUR

Biological
- *Distal*: evolved human genome produced in part by natural selection
- *Proximal*: individuals' genotypes, biological structures and processes produced by gene–environment interactions

Psychological
- *Distal*: evolutionary-based psychological mechanisms (e.g., learning capabilities, emotions, thinking abilities)
- *Proximal*: mental, emotional, motivational and behavioural mechanisms and processes; individual differences in capabilities, personality and other characteristics; gender-based characteristics

Environmental
- *Distal*: environments that required adaptations and fostered natural selection
- *Proximal*: individuals' shared and unshared environments, past and present cultural factors

Human behaviour

BENEATH THE SURFACE

HOW *NOT* TO THINK ABOUT EVOLUTIONARY THEORY

Evolutionary theory is an important and influential force in modern psychology. However, as we have seen, it is not without its controversial issues, which are both scientific and philosophical in nature. There also exist some widespread misconceptions about evolutionary theory.

First, some scientific issues. One has to do with the standards of evidence for or against evolutionary psychology. Adaptations are forged over a long period of time – perhaps thousands of generations – and we cannot go back to prehistoric times and determine with certainty what the environmental demands were. For this reason, evolutionary theorists are often forced to infer the forces to which our ancestors adapted, leading to after-the-fact speculation that is difficult to prove or disprove. A challenge for evolutionary theorists is to avoid the logical fallacy of circular reasoning: 'Why does behavioural tendency X exist?' 'Because of environmental demand Y.' 'How do we know that environmental demand Y existed?' 'Because otherwise behaviour X would not have developed.'

Evolutionary theorists also remind us that it is fallacious to attribute every human characteristic to natural selection (Clark and Grunstein, 2005; Lloyd and Feldman, 2002). In the distant past, as in the present, people created environments that shape behaviour, and those behaviours are often passed down through cultural learning instead of through natural selection. Likewise, a capability that evolved in the past for one reason may now be adaptive for something else. For example, the ability to discern shapes was undoubtedly advantageous for prehistoric hunters trying to spot game in the underbrush. Today, however, few humans in our culture need to hunt in order to survive, but those shape-discriminating capabilities are critical in perceiving letters and learning to read.

Evolutionary theorists have sometimes been accused of giving insufficient weight to cultural learning factors, and many debates about evolutionary explanations centre around this issue (Regal, 2005). Witness, for example, the dizzying changes that have occurred in world culture in the past 50 years as humans have altered their own environment. Modern evolutionary theorists acknowledge the role both of *remote causes* (including past evolutionary pressures that may have prompted natural selection) and *proximate* (more recent) *causes*, such as cultural learning and the immediate environment, that influence current behaviour. Human culture evolves as both a cause and an effect of brain and behavioural evolution (Boyd and Richerson, 2005). In other words, genes and environment affect one another over time.

In thinking about behaviour from an evolutionary point of view, it is important to avoid two other fallacies. One is **genetic determinism**, the idea that genes have invariant and unavoidable effects that cannot be altered. It makes no sense to conclude that because something in nature (such as males' greater tendency to be violent) is influenced by our genes, it is either unavoidable, natural or morally right. Although evolutionary theorists themselves argue against this view, it has been used to defend the status quo and also to conclude that if 'survival of the fittest' (a term actually coined by Herbert Spencer, not by Darwin) is the rule of nature, then those at the top of the social ladder are somehow the most fit of all and therefore 'the best people'. This notion of genetic superiority has had destructive consequences, not the least of which was the *eugenics* movement of the early twentieth century to prevent the 'less biologically fit' (particularly immigrants) from breeding, and Nazi Germany's programme of selective breeding designed to produce a 'master race'. As for the notion that genetically based behaviours are unalterable and therefore must be accepted, we should remember that all behaviours are a function of both the person's biology and the environment. In many cases, what we consider to be self-control or morality requires that we override 'natural' biologically based inclinations. Our ability to regulate our own behaviour and to exercise moral control is often just as important to our survival (i.e., as adaptive) as are our biological tendencies. Likewise, we can choose to alter the environment in order to override undesired behavioural tendencies, and many of the laws and sanctions that societies enact serve exactly that purpose.

The second fallacy is the view that evolution is purposive, or 'has a plan'. There is, in fact, no plan in evolutionary theory; there is only adaptation to environmental demands and the natural selection process that results. The 'nature's plan' concept has sometimes been used to support the morality of certain acts, even destructive ones. The usual strategy is for proponents of some idea to find an example of what they believe to be a comparable behaviour occurring in the natural world and to use that example to support their own behaviour or cause as 'in accord with nature'. To use this argument to define what is ethically or morally correct is not appropriate. Although there are regularities in natural events that define certain 'laws of nature', judgements of morality are most appropriately based on cultural standards and philosophical considerations, and not on biological imperatives.

genetic determinism
the idea that genes have invariant and unavoidable effects that cannot be altered

IN REVIEW

- Evolutionary psychology focuses on biologically based mechanisms sculpted by evolutionary forces as solutions to the problems of adaptation faced by species. Some of these genetically based mechanisms are general (e.g., the ability to learn from the consequences of our behaviour), whereas others are thought to be domain-specific, devoted to solving specific problems, such as mate selection.

- Evolution is a change over time in the frequency with which particular genes, and the characteristics they produce, occur within an interbreeding population. Evolution represents an interaction between biological and environmental factors.

- The cornerstone of Darwin's theory of evolution is the principle of natural selection. According to this principle, biologically based characteristics that contribute to survival and reproductive success increase in the population over time because those who lack the characteristics are less likely to pass on their genes. The concept of evoked culture implies that cultures also develop in response to adaptive demands specific to various human populations.

- Among the aspects of human behaviour that have received evolutionary explanations are human mate selection and personality traits. In research on mate selection, evolutionary explanations have been tested against hypotheses derived from social structure theory, which emphasizes the role of cultural factors.

- Critical thinking helps counter circular reasoning about evolutionary causes and effects, and challenges genetic determinism. We should also recognize that harmful genetically based behaviour tendencies can be overridden by human decision and self-control.

KEY TERMS AND CONCEPTS

Each term has been boldfaced and defined in the chapter on the page indicated in parentheses.

adaptations (p. 107)

adaptive significance (p. 92)

adoption study (p. 89)

alleles (p. 87)

behavioural genetics (p. 87)

biologically based
  mechanisms (p. 105)

chromosome (p. 86)

concordance (p. 87)

concordance rates (p. 89)

dominant gene (p. 87)

evocative influence (p. 101)

evoked culture (p. 109)

evolution (p. 106)

evolutionary personality
  theory (p. 116)

fixed action pattern (p. 92)

genes (p. 86)

genetic determinism
  (p. 119)

genotype (p. 86)

heritability coefficient
  (p. 90)

knock-in procedure (p. 103)

knockout procedure (p. 103)

mutations (p. 106)

natural selection (p. 106)

phenotype (p. 86)

polygenic transmission
  (p. 87)

reaction range (p. 99)

recessive gene (p. 87)

sexual strategies/parental
  investment theory (p. 112)

shared environment (p. 94)

social structure theory
  (p. 113)

strategic pluralism (p. 117)

twin studies (p. 89)

unshared environment
  (p. 94)

WHAT DO YOU THINK?

NATURAL SELECTION AND GENETIC DISEASES (p. 109)

Genetics research shows that in most cases, there's not a one-to-one relation between a particular gene and a particular trait. Most traits involve the influence of many genes, and a given gene can contribute to many traits. Traits, therefore, come in packages, with some of the traits in the package being adaptive and others maladaptive. In fact, cystic fibrosis (CF) is one such example. Cystic fibrosis is the most commonly inherited disorder among people of European descent. Why would such a damaging genetic trait survive in the gene pool? Geneticists have found that people with CF also have a trait that slows the release of salts into the intestine. Some scientists believe that this related trait might have helped save carriers from severe dehydration and death from the diarrhoeal diseases that killed seven out of every 10 newborns in medieval Europe. Perhaps CF was preserved in the population because another part of the trait package made carriers more likely to survive and pass on their genes.

Let us consider sickle-cell anaemia. Many people of African descent suffer from this genetically caused blood disorder that lowers life expectancy. Why would a disorder that decreases survival be preserved in a population? The answer may be that despite its negatives, the sickle cell gene has an important redeeming quality: it makes people more resistant to malaria, the most lethal disease in the African environment. Because it enhanced survival from malaria, the sickle cell trait became more common among Africans and can therefore be seen as a product of natural selection. This example shows us that we should be careful not to oversimplify the concept of adaptation and assume that any trait that survives, whether physical or psychological, is of immediate benefit to the species.

CHAPTER FOUR

THE BRAIN AND BEHAVIOUR

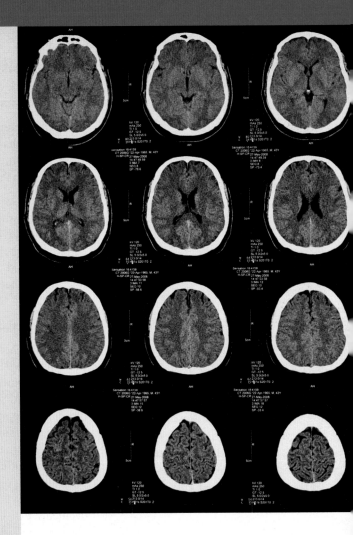

The brain is the last and grandest biological frontier, the most complex thing we have yet discovered in our universe. It contains hundreds of billions of cells interlinked through trillions of connections. The brain boggles the mind.

JAMES WATSON, NOBEL PRIZE RECIPIENT

The year was 1848. As the Vermont winter approached, a railroad construction crew hurried to complete its work on a new track. The men could not know that they were about to witness one of the most celebrated incidents in the annals of neuroscience.

As a blasting crew prepared its charges, the dynamite accidentally exploded. A 13-pound (5.9 kg) spike more than 3 feet (0.9 m) long was propelled through the head of Phineas Gage, a 25-year-old foreman. The spike entered through the left cheek, passed through the brain, and emerged through the top of the skull (Fig. 4.1). Dr J.M. Harlow, who treated Gage, described the incident:

> The patient was thrown upon his back by the explosion, and gave a few convulsive motions of the extremities, but spoke in a few minutes. He … seemed perfectly conscious, but was becoming exhausted from the hemorrhage, … the blood pouring from the top of his head.… He bore his sufferings with firmness, and directed my attention to the hole in his cheek, saying, 'the iron entered there and passed through my head.' (1868, pp. 330–2)

Miraculously, Gage survived, but not unscathed.

> His physical health is good, and I am inclined to say that he has recovered. Has no pain in his head, but says it has a queer feeling that he is not able to describe.… His contractors, who regarded him as the most efficient and capable foreman in their employ previous to his injury, considered the change in his mind so marked that they could not give him his place again. The equilibrium or balance, so to speak, between his intellectual faculties and animal propensities, seems to have been destroyed. He is fitful, irreverent, indulging at times in the grossest profanity (which was not previously his custom), manifesting but little deference for his fellows, impatient of restraint or advice when it conflicts with his desires … devising many plans of future operations, which are no sooner arranged than they are abandoned in turn for others.… His mind is radically changed, so decidedly that his friends and acquaintances say that he is 'no longer Gage.' (Harlow, 1868, pp. 339–40)

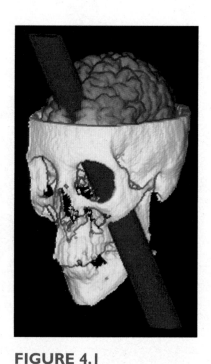

FIGURE 4.1

The brain damage suffered by Phineas Gage seemed to change him into a new person. The red image shows the path of the spike that shot through Gage's brain.

Mind and body, body and mind. The tragic story of Phineas Gage illustrates the intimate connection between brain, mind and behaviour. Physical damage to Gage's brain changed his thinking and behaviour so radically that he became, psychologically, a different person, 'no longer Gage'. Is our personal identity so thoroughly locked inside our skull? Is who we are and what we do reducible to the electrochemical activities of the nervous system? Most neuroscientists would not hesitate to answer, 'Yes'.

The evolutionary history of our species, the genes you inherited from your parents and your life experiences have shaped who you are. From a psychological perspective, your most important physical organ is your brain, a grapefruit-sized mass of tissue that feels like jelly and has the gnarled appearance of a greyish walnut. One of the true marvels of nature, the brain has been termed 'our three-pound universe', for every experience is represented within our skull (Hooper and Teresi, 1986). To understand how the brain controls our experience and behaviour, we must first understand how its individual cells function and how they communicate with one another.

NEURONS

Specialized cells called **neurons** are the basic building blocks of the nervous system. The estimated 100 billion nerve cells in your brain and spinal cord are linked together in circuits, not unlike the electrical circuits in a computer. Each neuron has three main parts: a cell body, dendrites, and an axon (Fig. 4.2). The cell body, or *soma*, contains the biochemical structures needed to keep the neuron alive, and its nucleus carries the genetic information that determines how the cell develops and functions. Emerging from the cell body are branch-like fibres called **dendrites** (from the Greek word meaning 'tree'), specialized receiving units like antennae that collect messages from neighbouring neurons and send them on to the cell body. There, the incoming information is combined and processed. The many branches of the dendrites can receive input from 1000 or more neighbouring neurons. The surface of the cell body also has receptor areas that can be directly stimulated by other neurons. All parts of a neuron are covered by a protective membrane that controls the exchange of chemical substances between the inside and outside of the cell. These exchanges play a critical role in the electrical activities of nerve cells.

neurons
the basic building blocks of the nervous system

dendrites
specialized receiving units like antennae that collect messages from neighbouring neurons and send them on to the cell body

FIGURE 4.2

The neuron and its structural elements.

Stimulation received by the dendrites or soma (cell body) may trigger a nerve impulse, which travels down the axon to stimulate other neurons, muscles or glands. Some axons have a fatty myelin sheath interrupted at intervals by the nodes of Ranvier. The myelin sheath helps increase the speed of nerve conduction.

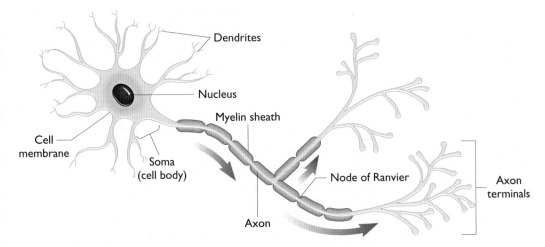

axon
conducts electrical impulses away from the cell body to other neurons, muscles or glands

Extending from one side of the cell body is a single **axon**, which conducts electrical impulses away from the cell body to other neurons, muscles or glands. The axon branches out at its end to form a number of *axon terminals* – as many as several hundred in some cases. Each axon terminal may connect with dendrites from numerous neurons, making it possible for a single neuron to pass messages to as many as 50 000 other neurons (Simon, 2007). Given the structure of the dendrites and axons, it is easy to see how there can be trillions of interconnections in the brain, making it capable of performing the complex activities that are of interest to psychologists.

THE ELECTRICAL ACTIVITY OF NEURONS

Neurons do two important things. Like tiny batteries, they generate electricity that creates nerve impulses. They also release chemicals that allow them to communicate with other neurons and with muscles and glands.

Let us first consider how nerve impulses occur. Nerve activation involves three basic steps:

1. At rest, the neuron has an electrical *resting potential* due to the distribution of positively and negatively charged chemical ions inside and outside the neuron.
2. When stimulated, a flow of ions in and out through the cell membrane reverses the electrical charge of the resting potential, producing an *action potential*, or nerve impulse.
3. The original ionic balance is restored, and the neuron is again at rest.

Let us now flesh out the details of this remarkable process. Like other cells, neurons are surrounded by body fluids and separated from this liquid environment by a protective membrane. This cell membrane is a bit like a selective sieve, allowing certain substances in the body fluid to pass through *ion channels* into the cell, while refusing or limiting passage to other substances.

The chemical environment inside the neuron differs from its external environment in significant ways, and the process whereby a nerve impulse is created involves the exchange of electrically charged atoms called *ions*. In the salty fluid outside the neuron are positively charged sodium ions (Na^+) and negatively charged chloride ions (Cl^-). Inside the neurons are large negatively charged protein molecules (*anions*, or A^+) and positively charged potassium ions (K^-). The high concentration of sodium ions in the fluid outside the cell, together with the negatively charged protein ions inside, results in an uneven distribution of positive and negative ions that makes the interior of the cell negative compared to the outside (Fig. 4.3a). This internal difference of around 70 millivolts (mV) is called the neuron's **resting potential**. At rest, the neuron is said to be in a state of *polarization*.

Nerve Impulses: The Action Potential

In research that won them the 1963 Nobel Prize, neuroscientists Alan Hodgkin and Andrew Huxley found that if they stimulated the neuron's axon with a mild electrical stimulus, the interior voltage differential shifted instantaneously from ⁻70 millivolts to ⁺40 millivolts. This electrical shift, which lasts about a millisecond (1/1000 of a second), is called the **action potential**, or nerve impulse.

What happens in the neuron to cause the action potential? Hodgkin and Huxley found that the key mechanism was the action of sodium and potassium ion channels in the cell membrane. Figure 4.3 shows what happens. In a resting state, the neuron's sodium and potassium channels are closed, and the concentration of Na^+ ions is 10 times higher outside the neuron than inside it (see Fig. 4.3a). But when a neuron is stimulated sufficiently, nearby sodium channels open up. Attracted by the negative protein ions inside, positively charged sodium ions flood into the axon, creating a state of *depolarization* (see Fig. 4.3b). In an instant, the interior now becomes positive (by about 40 millivolts) in relation to the outside, creating the action potential. In a reflex action to restore the resting potential, the cell closes its sodium channels, and positively charged potassium ions flow out through their channels, restoring the negative resting potential (see Fig. 4.3c). Eventually, the excess sodium ions flow out of the neuron, and the escaped potassium ions are recovered. The resulting voltage changes are shown in Figure 4.3d.

Once an action potential occurs at any point on the membrane, its effects spread to adjacent sodium channels, and the action potential flows down the length of the axon to the axon terminals. Immediately after an impulse passes a point along the axon, however, there is a recovery period as the K^+ ions flow out of the interior. During this **absolute refractory period**, the membrane is not excitable and cannot discharge another impulse. This places an upper limit

---

Focus 4.1

What chemical actions create the neuron's resting potential? What chemical changes cause the action potential?

In-Psych

Why are neurotransmitters critical to our ability to experience stress, relaxation, pain and pleasure? To find out, watch the video, 'Functions of Neurotransmitters', in Chapter 4 of the In-Psych programme online.

resting potential

internal difference of around 70 millivolts (mV)

action potential

electrical shift, which lasts about a millisecond (1/1000 of a second)

absolute refractory period

the membrane is not excitable and cannot discharge another impulse

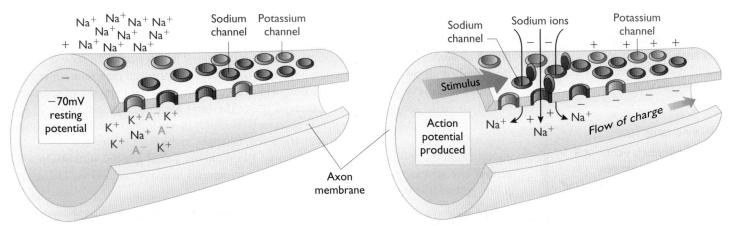

(a) The 10:1 concentration of sodium (Na^+) ions outside the neuron and the negative protein (A^-) ions inside contribute to a resting potential of $-70mV$.

(b) If the neuron is sufficiently stimulated, sodium channels open and sodium ions flood into the axon. Note that the potassium channels are still closed.

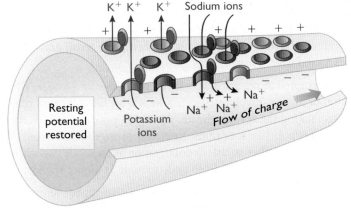

(c) Sodium channels that were open in (b) have now closed and potassium channels behind them are open, allowing potassium ions to exit and restoring the resting potential at that point. Sodium channels are opening at the next point as the action potential moves down the axon.

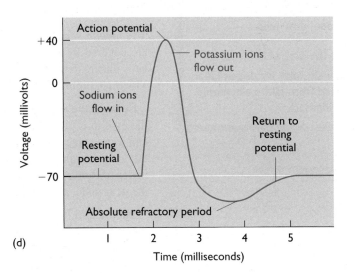

(d)

FIGURE 4.3

Nerve impulses: from resting potential to action potential.

When a neuron is not being stimulated, a difference in electrical charge of about –70 millivolts (mV) exists between the interior and the surface of the neuron. (a) This resting potential is caused by the uneven distribution of positively and negatively charged ions, with a greater concentration of positively charged sodium ions kept outside the cell by closed sodium channels and the presence of negatively charged protein (A^-) ions inside the cell. In addition, the action of sodium-potassium pumps helps maintain the negative interior by pumping out three sodium (Na^+) ions for every two positively charged potassium (K^+) ions drawn into the cell. (b) Sufficient stimulation of the neuron causes an action potential. Sodium channels open for an instant and Na^+ ions flood into the axon, reversing the electrical potential from –70 mV to +40 mV. (c) Within a millisecond, the sodium channels close and many K^+ ions flow out of the cell through open potassium channels, helping to restore the interior negative potential. As adjacent sodium channels are opened and the sequence in (b) and (c) is repeated, the action potential moves down the length of the axon. (d) Shown here are the changes in electrical potential that would be recorded from a particular point on the axon. After a brief absolute refractory period during which the neuron cannot be stimulated, another action potential can follow.

Focus 4.2

What is the nature and importance of the myelin sheath? Which disorder results from damage to it?

all-or-none law

action potentials occur at a uniform and maximum intensity, or they do not occur at all

graded potentials

changes in the negative resting potential that do not reach the ‑50 millivolt action potential threshold

myelin sheath

a whitish, fatty insulation layer derived from glial cells during development

on the rate at which nerve impulses can occur. In humans, the limit seems to be about 300 impulses per second (Kolb and Whishaw, 2005).

It's all or nothing   One other feature of the action potential is noteworthy. In accordance with the so-called **all-or-none law**, action potentials occur at a uniform and maximum intensity, or they do not occur at all. Like firing a gun, which requires that a certain amount of pressure be placed on the trigger, the negative potential inside the axon has to be changed from ‑70 millivolts to about ‑50 millivolts (the *action potential threshold*) by the influx of sodium ions into the axon before the action potential will be triggered. Changes in the negative resting potential that do not reach the ‑50 millivolt action potential threshold are called **graded potentials**. Under certain circumstances, graded potentials caused by several neurons can add up to trigger an action potential in the postsynaptic neuron.

For a neuron to function properly, sodium and potassium ions must enter and leave the membrane at just the right rate. Drugs that alter this transit system can decrease or prevent neural functioning. For example, local anaesthetics such as Novocain and Xylocaine attach themselves to the sodium channels, stopping the flow of sodium ions into the neurons. This stops pain impulses from being sent by the neurons (Ray and Ksir, 2004).

The myelin sheath   Any axons that transmit information throughout the brain and spinal cord are covered by a tube-like **myelin sheath**, a whitish, fatty insulation layer derived from glial cells during development. Unmyelinated axons are grey in colour, hence the term, *grey matter*. Myelinated fibres are sometimes called *white matter*.

Because the myelin sheath is interrupted at regular intervals by the *nodes of Ranvier*, where the myelin is either extremely thin or absent, myelinated axons look a bit like sausages placed end to end (see Fig. 4.2). In axons lacking the myelin sheath, the action potential travels down the axon length in a point-to-point fashion like a burning fuse. But in myelinated axons, the nodes of Ranvier are close enough to one another so that depolarization at one node can activate the next node, allowing electrical conduction to jump from node to node at higher speeds.

The myelin sheath is most commonly found in the nervous systems of higher animals. In many neurons, the myelin sheath is not completely formed until some time after birth. The resulting efficiency of neural transmission is partly responsible for the gains that infants exhibit in muscular co-ordination and cognitive functioning as they grow older (Cabeza et al., 2005).

Damage to the myelin coating can have tragic effects. In people afflicted with multiple sclerosis, the person's own immune system attacks the myelin sheath, disrupting the delicate timing of nerve impulses to the muscles. The result is increasingly jerky and uncoordinated movements and, in the final stages, paralysis (Toy, 2007).

We have now seen how nerve impulses are created. However, the activity of a single neuron means little unless it can communicate its message to other neurons. This is where the chemical activities of neurons come into play.

HOW NEURONS COMMUNICATE: SYNAPTIC TRANSMISSION

The nervous system operates as a giant communications network, and its action requires the transmission of nerve impulses from one neuron to another. Early in the history of brain research, scientists thought that the tip of the axon made physical contact with the dendrites or cell bodies of other neurons, passing electricity directly from one neuron to the next. With the advent of the electron microscope, however, researchers discovered a **synaptic space**, a tiny gap between the axon terminal and the next neuron. This discovery raised new and perplexing questions: If neurons do not physically touch the other neurons to which they send signals, how does communication occur? If the action potential does not cross the synapse, what does? What carries the message?

synaptic space

a tiny gap between the axon terminal and the next neuron

NEUROTRANSMITTERS

We now know that in addition to generating electricity, neurons produce **neurotransmitters**, chemical substances that carry messages across the synaptic space to other neurons, muscles or glands. This process of chemical communication involves five steps: synthesis, storage, release, binding and deactivation. In the *synthesis* stage, the transmitter molecules are formed inside the neuron. The molecules are then *stored* in **synaptic vesicles**, chambers within the axon terminals. When an action potential comes down the axon, these vesicles move to the surface of the axon terminal and the molecules are *released* into the fluid-filled space between the axon of the *presynaptic* (sending) neuron and the membrane of the *postsynaptic* (receiving) neuron. The molecules cross the synaptic space and *bind* themselves to **receptor sites**, large protein molecules embedded in the receiving neuron's cell membrane. Each receptor site has a specially shaped surface that fits a specific transmitter molecule, just as a lock accommodates a single key (Fig. 4.4).

neurotransmitters
chemical substances that carry messages across the synaptic space to other neurons, muscles or glands

synaptic vesicles
chambers within the axon terminals

receptor sites
large protein molecules embedded in the receiving neuron's cell membrane

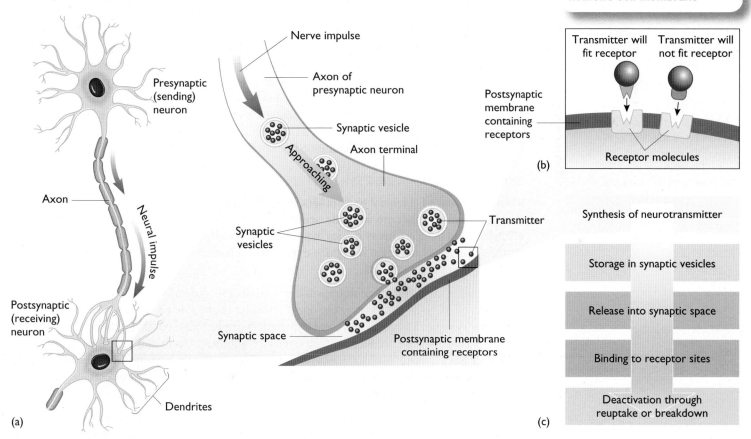

FIGURE 4.4

A synapse between two neurons.

The action potential travels to the axon terminals, where it stimulates the release of transmitter molecules from the synaptic vesicles. (a) These molecules travel across the synaptic space and bind to specially keyed receptor sites on the cell body or dendrite of the postsynaptic neuron. (b) The lock and-key nature of neurotransmitters and receptor sites means that only transmitters that fit the receptor sites will influence membrane potentials. (c) The sequence of neurotransmitter activity moves from synthesis to deactivation. If the neurotransmitter has an excitatory effect on the neuron, the chemical reaction that occurs creates a graded or an action potential. If the transmitter substance is inhibitory, it increases the negative potential inside the neuron and makes it more difficult to fire it.

Focus 4.3

Describe five important steps in neurotransmitter function. How do transmitters produce excitation and inhibition? How are they deactivated?

When a transmitter molecule binds to a receptor site, a chemical reaction occurs. This reaction can have two different effects on the receiving neuron. When an *excitatory* transmitter is at work, the chemical reaction causes the postsynaptic neuron's sodium channels to open. As sodium ions flood into the cell and depolarize it, they create either a graded potential or an action potential as just described. An *inhibitory* neurotransmitter will do the opposite. It may cause positive potassium ions to flow out of the neuron or negative chloride ions from the exterior to flow into it through chloride channels in the membrane, increasing the neuron's negative potential and making it harder to fire the neuron. The action of an inhibitory neurotransmitter from one presynaptic neuron may prevent the postsynaptic neuron from firing an action potential even if it is receiving excitatory stimulation from other neurons at the same time.

If the nervous system is to function properly, it must maintain a fine-tuned balance between excitation and inhibition. Even such a simple act as bending your arm requires excitation of your biceps muscles and simultaneous inhibition of your triceps so those muscles can relax.

Once a neurotransmitter molecule binds to its receptor, it continues to excite or inhibit the neuron until it is *deactivated*, or shut off. This occurs in two major ways (Simon, 2007). Some transmitter molecules are deactivated by other chemicals located in the synaptic space that break them down into their chemical components. In other instances, the deactivation mechanism is **re-uptake**, in which the transmitter molecules are taken back into the presynaptic axon terminals. Some antidepressant medications inhibit re-uptake of the excitatory transmitter serotonin, allowing serotonin to continue to excite neurons and thereby reduce depression.

re-uptake
the transmitter molecules are taken back into the pre-synaptic axon terminals

SPECIALIZED TRANSMITTER SYSTEMS

Through the use of chemical transmitters, nature has found an ingenious way of dividing up the brain into systems that are uniquely sensitive to certain messages. There is only one kind of electricity, but there are many shapes that can be assumed by transmitter molecules. Because the various systems in the brain recognize only certain chemical messengers, they are immune to cross-talk from other systems.

There are many different neurotransmitter substances, some of which can coexist within the same neuron. A given neuron may use one transmitter at one synapse and a different transmitter at another synapse. Moreover, different transmitters can be found within the same axon terminal or in the same synapse, adding another layer of complexity (Kolb and Whishaw, 2005). Each substance has a specific excitatory or inhibitory effect on certain neurons. Some neurotransmitters (for example, norepinephrine) can have either excitatory or inhibitory effects, depending on which receptor sites they bind to.

Table 4.1 lists several of the more important neurotransmitters that have been linked to psychological phenomena. We'll encounter all of these substances in this and future chapters. For the moment, we focus on **acetylcholine (ACh)**, a neurotransmitter involved in muscle activity and memory, to illustrate the diversity of neurotransmitter mechanisms.

acetylcholine (ACh)
a neurotransmitter involved in muscle activity and memory

Underproduction of ACh is an important factor in Alzheimer's disease, a degenerative brain disorder that afflicts 5 to 10 per cent of people over 65 years of age (Morris and Becker, 2005). Reductions in acetylcholine weaken or deactivate neural circuitry that stores memories, creating profound memory impairments. Acetylcholine is also an excitatory transmitter at the synapses where neurons activate muscle cells, helping to account for the severe motor impairments found in the later stages of Alzheimer's disease.

Drugs that block the action of ACh can prevent muscle activation and cause paralysis. One example occurs in botulism, a serious type of food poisoning that can result from improperly canned food. The toxin formed by the botulinum bacteria blocks the release of ACh from the axon terminal, resulting in a potentially fatal paralysis of the muscles, including those of the

TABLE 4.1 SOME NEUROTRANSMITTERS AND THEIR EFFECTS

Neurotransmitter	Major function	Disorders associated with malfunctioning	Additional discussion
Acetylcholine (ACh)	Excitatory at synapses involved in muscular movement and memory	Alzheimer's disease (undersupply); paralysis (absence); violent muscle contractions and convulsions (oversupply)	Chapter 8
Noradrenaline (known as norepinephrine in the USA)	Excitatory and inhibitory functions at various sites, involved in neural circuits controlling learning, memory, wakefulness and eating	Depression (undersupply); stress and panic disorders (overactivity)	Chapters 6, 18
Serotonin	Inhibitory or excitatory; involved in mood, sleep, eating and arousal, and may be an important transmitter underlying pleasure and pain	Depression; sleeping and eating disorders (undersupply); obsessive-compulsive disorder (overactivity)	Chapters 6, 11, 14, 17, 18
Dopamine	Excitatory; involved in voluntary movement, emotional arousal, learning, memory and experiencing pleasure or pain	Parkinson's disease and depression (undersupply); schizophrenia (overactivity)	Chapters 6, 7, 11, 12, 17, 18
GABA (gamma-aminobutyric acid)	Inhibitory transmitter in motor system	Destruction of GABA-producing neurons in Huntington's disease produces tremors and loss of motor control, as well as personality changes	Chapters 6, 17, 18
Endorphin	Inhibits transmission of pain impulses (a neuromodulator)	Insensitivity to pain (oversupply); pain hypersensitivity, immune problems (undersupply)	Chapters 11, 16

respiratory system. A mild form of the toxin, known as Botox, is used cosmetically to remove skin wrinkles by paralysing the muscles whose contraction causes them.

The opposite effect on ACh occurs with the bite of the black widow spider. The spider's venom triggers a torrent of ACh, resulting in violent muscle contractions, convulsions and possible death. Some chemical agents, such as the deadly sarin gas released into the Tokyo subway system by terrorists in 1995, also raise havoc by allowing ACh to run wild in the nervous system. Sarin and similar nerve gas agents prevent the activity of an enzyme that normally degrades ACh at the synapse. The result is uncontrolled seizures and convulsions that can kill.

Most neurotransmitters have their excitatory or inhibitory effects only on specific neurons that have receptors for them. Others, called **neuromodulators**, have a more widespread and generalized influence on synaptic transmission. These substances circulate through the brain

neuromodulators

have a more widespread and generalized influence on synaptic transmission

Focus 4.4

Describe the roles played by acetylcholine and the consequences that occur when its functioning is disrupted.

psychoactive drugs

chemicals that produce alterations in consciousness, emotion and behaviour

and either increase or decrease (i.e., modulate) the sensitivity of thousands, perhaps millions, of neurons to their specific transmitters. The best known neuromodulators are the *endorphins*, which travel through the brain's circulatory system and inhibit pain transmission while enhancing neural activity that produces pleasurable feelings. Other neuromodulators play important roles in functions such as eating, sleeping and coping with stress.

Knowledge about neurotransmitter systems has many important applications. For one thing, it helps us understand the mechanisms that underlie the effects of **psychoactive drugs**, chemicals that produce alterations in consciousness, emotion and behaviour. The following 'Applying psychological science' feature focuses on mechanisms of drug effects within the brain.

APPLYING PSYCHOLOGICAL SCIENCE

UNDERSTANDING HOW DRUGS AFFECT YOUR BRAIN

Drugs affect consciousness and behaviour by influencing the activity of neurons. If you have had a soft drink or a cup of coffee, taken an aspirin or smoked a cigarette, you have ingested a drug. A 2006 report from the European Monitoring Centre for Drugs and Drug Addiction describes how widespread illegal drug use is in Europe. The report provides statistics for drug use in Europe in a number of categories. In the year 2005–6 22.5 million European adults took cannabis, 3.5 million took cocaine, 3 million took ecstasy and 2 million took amphetamines. In addition to this, in 70 per cent of acute drug deaths, opioids were found in the body, and of those treated for drug problems, 60 per cent were related to opioid (e.g. heroin) abuse. Countless students ingest caffeine in coffee, chocolate, cocoa and soft drinks. Perhaps you have wondered exactly how these drugs exert their diverse effects.

Most psychoactive drugs produce their effects by either increasing or decreasing the synthesis, storage, release, binding or deactivation of neurotransmitters. An **agonist** is a drug that increases the activity of a neurotransmitter. Agonists may (1) enhance a neuron's ability to synthesize, store or release neurotransmitters; (2) mimic the action of a neurotransmitter by binding with and stimulating postsynaptic receptor sites; (3) bind with and stimulate postsynaptic receptor sites; or (4) make it more difficult for neurotransmitters to be deactivated, such as by inhibiting re-uptake.

An **antagonist** is a drug that inhibits or decreases the action of a neurotransmitter. An antagonist may (1) reduce a neuron's ability to synthesize, store or release neurotransmitters; or (2) prevent a neurotransmitter from binding with the postsynaptic neuron by fitting into and blocking the receptor sites on the postsynaptic neuron.

With the distinction between agonist and antagonist functions in mind, let us consider how some commonly used drugs work within the brain. Alcohol is a depressant drug having both agonist and antagonist effects. As an agonist, it stimulates the activity of the inhibitory transmitter GABA, thereby depressing neural activity. As an antagonist, it decreases the activity of glutamate, an excitatory transmitter (Levinthal, 2007). The double-barrelled effect is a neural slowdown that inhibits normal brain functions, including clear thinking, emotional control and motor co-ordination. Sedative drugs, including barbiturates and tranquilizers, also increase GABA activity, and taking them with alcohol can be deadly when their depressant effects on neural activity are combined with those of alcohol.

agonist

a drug that increases the activity of a neurotransmitter

antagonist

a drug that inhibits or decreases the action of a neurotransmitter

Focus 4.5

How do agonist and antagonist functions underlie the neural and behavioural effects of psychoactive drugs?

Caffeine is a stimulant drug that increases the activity of neurons and other cells. It is an antagonist for the transmitter adenosine. Adenosine inhibits the release of excitatory transmitters. By reducing adenosine activity, caffeine helps produce higher rates of cellular activity and more available energy. Although caffeine is a stimulant, it is important to note that contrary to popular belief, caffeine does *not* counteract the effects of alcohol and sober people up. What your drunken friend needs is a ride home with a driver who is sober – not a cup of coffee.

Nicotine is an agonist for the excitatory transmitter acetylcholine. Its chemical structure is similar enough to ACh to allow it to fit into ACh binding sites and create action potentials. At other receptor sites, nicotine stimulates dopamine activity, which seems to be an important chemical mediator of energy and pleasure. This may help account for nicotine's powerful addictive properties. Researchers are working to develop medications that could wean people off cigarettes and other tobacco products by blocking or occupying the specific receptor sites that trigger dopamine release.

Amphetamines are stimulant drugs that boost arousal and mood by increasing the activity of the excitatory neurotransmitters dopamine and norepinephrine. They do so in two major ways. First, they cause presynaptic neurons to release greater amounts of these neurotransmitters. Second, they inhibit re-uptake, allowing dopamine and noradrenaline to keep stimulating postsynaptic neurons (Ksir et al., 2008). Cocaine produces excitation, a sense of increased muscular strength and euphoria. Like amphetamines, cocaine increases the activity of noradrenaline and dopamine, but it does so in only one major way: it blocks their re-uptake. Thus amphetamines and cocaine have different mechanisms of action on the dopamine and noradrenaline transmitter systems, but both drugs produce highly stimulating effects on mood, thinking and behaviour.

We should comment on two other drugs that, unfortunately, are also found in society. Rohypnol (flunitrazepam) and GHB (gamma hydroxybutyrate) are so-called date rape drugs. Partygoers sometimes add these drugs to punch and other drinks in hopes of lowering drinkers' inhibitions and facilitating non-consensual sexual conquest. The drugs are powerful sedatives that suppress general neural activity by enhancing the action of the inhibitory transmitter GABA (Lobina et al., 1999). Rohypnol is about 10 times more potent than Valium. At high doses or when mixed with alcohol or other drugs, these substances may lead to respiratory depression, loss of consciousness, coma and, even, death. Rohypnol also attacks neurotransmission in areas of the brain involved in memory, producing an amnesia effect that may prevent users from remembering the circumstances under which they ingested the drug or what happened to them afterwards. GHB, which makes its victim appear drunk and helpless, is now a restricted drug, and slipping it into someone's drink is a criminal act. The bottom line is that these drugs are good neither to give nor to receive (Fig. 4.5). Increasingly, women are being advised against accepting an opened drink from a fellow reveller or leaving their own drink unattended at parties. In another misuse of these drugs, Selina Hakki was found guilty in England of using the drugs not for sex, but to rob men of valuables. She used the promise of sex to gain entrance to their homes, then drugged and robbed them.

FIGURE 4.5

Partying can alter brain activity. Nicotine from cigarette smoke activates acetylcholine and dopamine neurons, increasing neural excitation. Alcohol stimulates the activity of the inhibitory transmitter GABA and decreases the activity of an excitatory transmitter, glutamate, thus depressing brain functions. Drinks can also be spiked with one of the powerful and potentially deadly date-rape sedative drugs.

IN REVIEW

- Each neuron has dendrites, which receive nerve impulses from other neurons; a cell body, which controls the vital processes of the cell; and an axon, which conducts nerve impulses to adjacent neurons, muscles and glands.

- Psychoactive drugs such as caffeine, alcohol, nicotine and amphetamines produce their effects by either increasing or decreasing the action of neurotransmitters. Agonists can mimic or increase the action of neurotransmitters, whereas antagonists inhibit or decrease the action of neurotransmitters.

- Neural transmission is an electrochemical process. The nerve impulse, or action potential, is a brief reversal in the electrical potential of the cell membrane from negative to positive as sodium ions from the surrounding fluid flow into the cell through sodium ion channels. The action potential obeys the all-or-none law, firing completely or not at all. The myelin sheath increases the speed of neural transmission.

sensory neurons
carry input messages from the sense organs to the spinal cord and brain

motor neurons
transmit output impulses from the brain and spinal cord to the body's muscles and organs

interneurons
perform connective or associative functions within the nervous system

peripheral nervous system
contains all the neural structures that lie outside the brain and spinal cord

somatic nervous system
consists of sensory neurons that are specialized to transmit messages from the eyes, ears, and other sensory receptors, and motor neurons that send messages from the brain and spinal cord to the muscles that control our voluntary movements

Focus 4.6

Name the two divisions of the peripheral nervous system. How does the autonomic system maintain homeostasis?

THE NERVOUS SYSTEM

The nervous system is the body's control centre. Three major types of neurons carry out the system's input, output and integration functions. **Sensory neurons** carry input messages from the sense organs to the spinal cord and brain. **Motor neurons** transmit output impulses from the brain and spinal cord to the body's muscles and organs. Finally, there are neurons that link the input and output functions. These **interneurons**, which far outnumber sensory and motor neurons, perform connective or associative functions within the nervous system. For example, interneurons would allow us to recognize a friend by linking the sensory input from the visual system with the memory of that person's characteristics stored elsewhere in the brain. The activity of interneurons makes possible the complexity of our higher mental functions, emotions and behavioural capabilities.

The nervous system can be broken down into several interrelated subsystems (Fig. 4.6). The two major divisions are the peripheral and central nervous systems.

THE PERIPHERAL NERVOUS SYSTEM

The **peripheral nervous system** contains all the neural structures that lie outside the brain and spinal cord. Its specialized neurons help carry out (1) the input functions that enable us to sense what is going on inside and outside our bodies and (2) the output functions that enable us to respond with our muscles and glands. The peripheral nervous system has two major divisions: the somatic nervous system and the autonomic nervous system.

The Somatic Nervous System

The **somatic nervous system** consists of sensory neurons that are specialized to transmit messages from the eyes, ears, and other sensory receptors, and motor neurons that send messages from the brain and spinal cord to the muscles that control our voluntary movements. The axons of sensory neurons group together like many strands of a rope to form *sensory nerves*, and motor-neuron axons combine to form *motor nerves*. As you read this page, sensory neurons in your eyes are sending impulses into a complex network of specialized visual tracts that course through your brain. (Inside the brain and spinal cord, nerves are called *tracts*.) At the same time, motor neurons are stimulating the eye movements that allow you to scan the lines of type and turn the pages. The somatic system thus allows you to sense and respond to your environment.

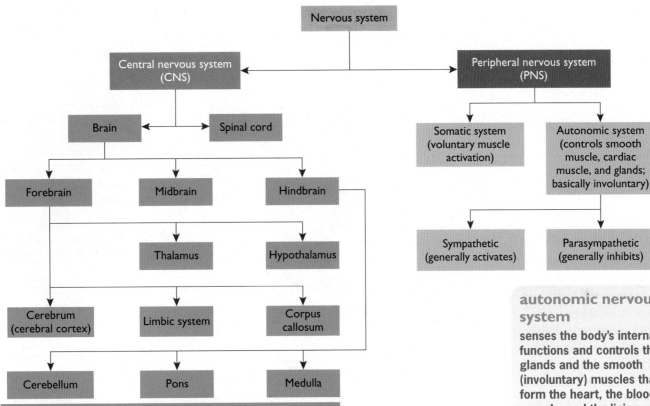

FIGURE 4.6

Structural organization of the nervous system.

The Autonomic Nervous System

The body's internal environment is regulated largely through the activities of the **autonomic nervous system**, which senses the body's internal functions and controls the glands and the smooth (involuntary) muscles that form the heart, the blood vessels, and the lining of the stomach and intestines. The autonomic system is largely concerned with involuntary functions, such as respiration, circulation and digestion; it is also involved in many aspects of motivation, emotional behaviour and stress responses. It consists of two subdivisions: the *sympathetic nervous system* and the *parasympathetic nervous system* (Fig. 4.7). Typically, these two divisions affect the same organ or gland in opposing ways.

The **sympathetic nervous system** has an activation or arousal function, and it tends to act as a total unit. For example, when you encounter a stressful situation, your sympathetic nervous system helps you confront the stressor in several ways. It speeds up your heart rate so that it can pump more blood to your muscles, dilates your pupils so that more light can enter the eye and improve your vision, slows down your digestive system so that blood can be transferred to the muscles, increases your rate of respiration so that your body can get more oxygen and, in general, mobilizes your body. This is sometimes called the *fight-or-flight response*.

Compared with the sympathetic branch, which tends to act as a unit, the **parasympathetic nervous system** is far more specific in its opposing actions, affecting one or a few organs at a time. In general, it slows down body processes and maintains a state of tranquillity. Thus your sympathetic system speeds up your heart rate; your parasympathetic system slows it down. By working together

autonomic nervous system

senses the body's internal functions and controls the glands and the smooth (involuntary) muscles that form the heart, the blood vessels, and the lining of the stomach and intestines

sympathetic nervous system

has an activation or arousal function, and it tends to act as a total unit

parasympathetic nervous system

is far more specific in its opposing actions, affecting one or a few organs at a time. In general, it slows down body processes and maintains a state of tranquillity

Focus 4.7

What are the three major types of neurons in the nervous system? What are their functions?

Focus 4.8

What are the two main structures in the central nervous system?

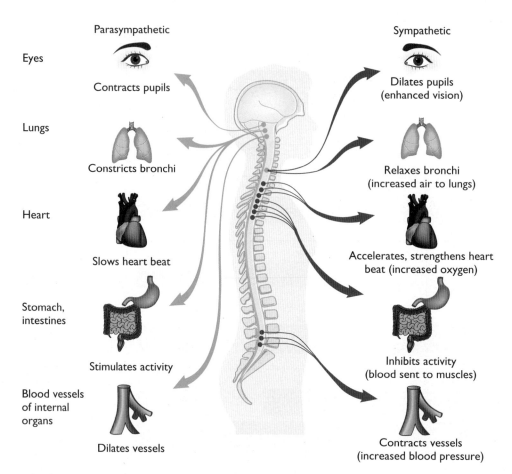

FIGURE 4.7

Autonomic nervous system.

The sympathetic branch of the autonomic nervous system arouses the body and speeds up its vital processes. The parasympathetic division, which is more specific in its opposing actions, slows down body processes. The two divisions work in concert to maintain equilibrium within the body.

homeostasis

a delicately balanced or constant internal state

central nervous system

contains the brain and the spinal cord, which connects most parts of the peripheral nervous system with the brain

to maintain equilibrium in our internal organs, the two divisions can maintain **homeostasis**, a delicately balanced or constant internal state. In addition, sympathetic and parasympathetic activities sometimes co-ordinate to enable us to perform certain behaviours. For example, sexual function in the male involves penile erection (through parasympathetic dilation of blood vessels) followed by ejaculation (a primarily sympathetic function; Masters et al., 1988).

THE CENTRAL NERVOUS SYSTEM

More than any other system in our body, the central nervous system distinguishes us from other creatures. This **central nervous system** contains the brain and the spinal cord, which connects most parts of the peripheral nervous system with the brain.

The Spinal Cord

Most nerves enter and leave the central nervous system by way of the spinal cord, a structure that in a human adult is 16 to 18 inches (40.5 to 45.5 cm) long and about 1 inch (2.5 cm) in diameter. The vertebrae (bones of the spine) protect the spinal cord's neurons. When the spinal cord is viewed in cross section (Fig. 4.8), its central portion resembles an H or a butterfly. The H-shaped portion consists largely of grey-coloured neuron cell bodies and their interconnections. Surrounding the grey matter are white-coloured myelinated axons that connect various levels of the spinal cord with each other and with the higher centres of the brain. Entering the back side of the spinal cord along its length are sensory nerves. Motor nerves exit the spinal cord's front side.

Some simple stimulus–response sequences, known as *spinal reflexes*, can be triggered at the level of the spinal cord without any involvement of the brain. For example, if you touch something hot, sensory receptors in your skin trigger nerve impulses in sensory nerves that flash into

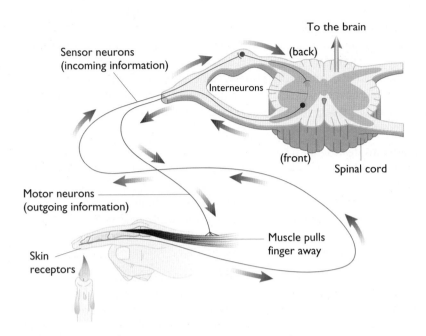

FIGURE 4.8

The spinal cord.

Sensory and motor nerves enter and exit the spinal cord on both sides of the spinal column. Interneurons within the H-shaped spinal gray matter can serve a connective function, but in many cases, sensory neurons can also synapse directly with motor neurons. At this level of the nervous system, reflex activity is possible without involving the brain.

your spinal cord and synapse inside with interneurons. The interneurons then excite motor neurons that send impulses to your hand, so that it pulls away (see Fig. 4.8). Other interneurons simultaneously carry the 'Hot!' message up the spinal cord to your brain. But it is a good thing that you do not have to wait for the brain to tell you what to do in such emergencies. Getting messages to and from the brain takes slightly longer, so the spinal cord reflex system significantly reduces reaction time and, in this case, potential tissue damage.

The Brain

The three pounds of protein, fat and fluid that you carry around inside your skull is the real you. It is also the most complex structure in the known universe and the only one that can wonder about itself. As befits this biological marvel, your brain is the most active energy consumer of all your body organs. Although your brain accounts for only about 2 per cent of your total body weight, it consumes about 25 per cent of your body's oxygen and 70 per cent of its glucose. Moreover, the brain never rests; its rate of energy metabolism is relatively constant day and night. In fact, when you dream, the brain's metabolic rate actually increases slightly (Simon, 2007).

How can this rather nondescript blob of greyish tissue discover the principle of relativity, build the Hubble space telescope, and produce great works of art, music and literature? Answering such questions requires the ability to study the brain and how it functions. To do so, neuroscientists use a diverse set of tools and procedures.

Unlocking the Secrets of the Brain

Because of scientific and technical advances, more has been learned about the brain in the past four decades than was known throughout all the preceding ages. Neuroscientists use a number of methods to study the brain's structures and activities.

Neuropsychological tests Psychologists have developed a variety of *neuropsychological tests* to measure verbal and non-verbal behaviours of people who may have suffered brain damage through accident or disease (Strauss et al., 2006). They are also important research tools. For example, Figure 4.9 shows a portion of a Trail Making Test, used to test memory and planning. Scores on the test give an indication of a person's type and severity of brain damage. Neuropsychological tests of this kind have provided much information about brain behaviour relations. They are also used to assess learning disabilities and developmental disorders.

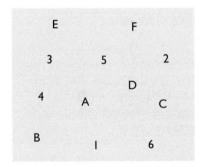

FIGURE 4.9

A neuropsychological test.

The trail making test is used by psychologists to assess brain functioning. It consists of randomly scattered numbers and letters, which the patient must connect consecutively with a continuous line or 'trail' (i.e., A to 1 to B to 2 to C to 3, and so on). People with certain kinds of brain damage have trouble alternating between the numbers and letters because they cannot retain a plan in memory long enough.

Focus 4.9

Describe four methods used to study brain–behaviour relations.

In-Psych

IP

To discover how brain researchers are harnessing the power of new technologies to better understand how the brain functions, view the video, 'Brain Structures and Imaging Methods', in Chapter 4 of the In-Psych programme online.

Focus 4.10

How are CAT scans, PET scans and MRIs produced, and what kinds of information does each provide?

electroencephalograph (EEG)

measures the activity of large groups of neurons through a series of large electrodes placed on the scalp

computerized axial tomography (CT, or CAT) scans

use X-ray technology to study brain structures

magnetic resonance imaging (MRI)

creates images based on how atoms in living tissue respond to a magnetic pulse delivered by the device

Destruction and stimulation techniques   Experimental studies are another useful method of learning about the brain (Tatlisumak and Fisher, 2006). Researchers can produce brain damage (lesions) in which specific nervous tissue is destroyed with electricity, with cold or heat, or with chemicals. They can also surgically remove some portion of the brain and study the consequences. Most experiments of this kind are performed on animals, but humans can also be studied when accident or disease produces a specific lesion or when abnormal brain tissue must be surgically removed.

An alternative to destroying neurons is chemically or electrically stimulating them, which typically produces effects opposite to destruction. In chemical stimulation, a tiny tube, or *cannula*, is inserted into a precise area of the brain so that chemicals, including neurotransmitters, can be delivered directly and their effects on behaviour studied. A specific region of the brain can also be stimulated by a mild electric current. Electrodes can be permanently implanted so that the region of interest can be stimulated repeatedly. Some electrodes are so tiny that they can stimulate individual neurons.

In a recent electrical-stimulation study, placement of electrodes on a specific region of the brain's outer surface above the right ear produced a surprising effect. The woman experienced herself as floating in the air above her body (Blanke et al., 2002). Neuroscientists wonder if the researchers may have accidentally discovered a neural basis for 'near death' and other so-called paranormal out-of-body experiences that have been reported by many people.

Electrical recording   Because electrodes can record brain activity as well as stimulate it, scientists can eavesdrop on the electrical 'conversations' occurring within the brain. Neurons' electrical activity can be measured by inserting small electrodes in particular areas of the brain or even in individual neurons.

In addition to measuring individual 'voices' scientists can tune in to 'crowd noise'. The **electroencephalograph (EEG)** measures the activity of large groups of neurons through a series of large electrodes placed on the scalp (Fig. 4.10(a) and (b)). Although the EEG is a rather nonspecific measure that taps the electrical activity of thousands of neurons in many parts of the brain, specific EEG patterns correspond to certain states of consciousness, such as wakefulness and sleep. Clinicians also use the EEG to detect abnormal electrical patterns that signal the presence of brain disorders.

Brain imaging   The newest tools of discovery are imaging techniques that permit neuroscientists to peer into the living brain (Fig. 4.10c). The most important of these are *CT scans*, *PET scans*, *MRIs* and *fMRIs*. CT scans and MRIs are used to visualize brain structure, whereas PET scans and fMRIs allow scientists to view brain activity (Bremner, 2005).

Developed in the 1970s, **computerized axial tomography (CT, or CAT) scans** use X-ray technology to study brain structures. A highly focused beam of X-rays takes pictures of narrow slices of the brain. A computer analyses the X-rayed slices and creates pictures of the brain's interior from many different angles (Fig. 4.10d). Pinpointing where deterioration or injuries have occurred helps clarify relations between brain damage and psychological functioning. CT scans are 100 times more sensitive than standard X-ray procedures, and the technological advance was so dramatic that its developers, Cormack and Hounsfield, were awarded the 1979 Nobel Prize for medicine.

Magnetic resonance imaging (MRI) creates images based on how atoms in living tissue respond to a magnetic pulse delivered by the device. When the magnetic field is shut off, the magnetic energy absorbed by the atoms in the tissue emits a small electrical voltage that is relayed to a computer for analysis. MRI provides colour images of the tissue and can make out details one-tenth the size of those detected by CT scans (Fig. 4.10e).

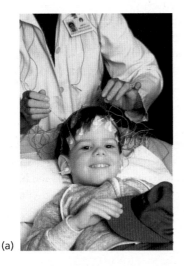

(a)

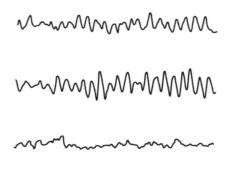

(b)

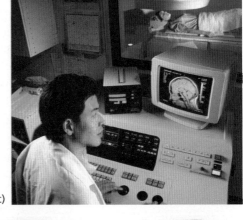

(c)

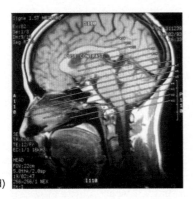

(d)

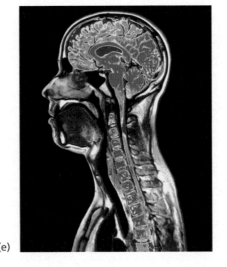

(e)

(f)

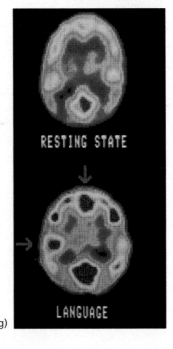

(g)

FIGURE 4.10

Measuring brain activity.

(a) The EEG records the activity of large groups of neurons in the brain through a series of electrodes attached to the scalp. (b) The results appear on an EEG readout. (c) Various brain scanning machines produce a number of different images. (d) The CT scan uses narrow beams of X-rays to construct a composite picture of brain structures. (e) MRI scanners produce vivid pictures of brain structures. (f) Functional MRI (fMRI) procedures take images in rapid succession, showing neural activity as it occurs. (g) PET scans record the amount of radioactive substance that collects in various brain regions to assess brain activity.

Whereas CT scans and MRIs provide pictures of brain structures, **positron-emission tomography (PET) scans** measure brain activity, including metabolism, blood flow and neurotransmitter activity. Glucose, a natural sugar, is the major nutrient of neurons, so when neurons are active, they consume more glucose. To prepare a patient for a PET scan, a radioactive (but harmless) form of glucose is injected into the bloodstream and travels to the brain, where it circulates in the blood supply. The PET scan measures the energy emitted by the radioactive substance, and the data, fed into a computer, produce a colour picture of the brain on a display screen (Fig. 4.10g). If the patient is performing a reasoning task, for example, a researcher can tell by the glucose concentration pattern which parts of the brain are most heavily activated.

positron-emission tomography (PET) scans
measure brain activity, including metabolism, blood flow and neurotransmitter activity

functional MRI (fMRI)

can produce pictures of blood flow in the brain taken less than a second apart

The conventional MRI yields pictures taken several minutes apart. An important advance in MRI technology is **functional MRI (fMRI)**, which can produce pictures of blood flow in the brain taken less than a second apart. Researchers can now, quite literally, watch live presentations as different regions of the brain light up when participants perform various tasks (Fig. 4.10f). Active brain tissue uses more oxygen; thus scanning the oxygen concentration of blood in the brain provides a vivid picture of brain activity without the need to inject a radioactive substance into the brain (Huettel et al., 2005).

Advances in brain research represent an important frontier of psychology. Driven by its intense desire to 'know thyself', the brain is beginning to yield its many secrets. Yet many important questions remain. This should not surprise us, for as one observer noted, 'If the brain were so simple that we could understand it, we would be so simple that we couldn't' (Pugh, 1977).

BENEATH THE SURFACE

IT'S A MIRACLE! PSYCHOLOGISTS OUT OF A JOB NOW THAT WE CAN 'SEE INTO' THE BRAIN?

When you get home from university, or wherever it is that you are studying with this book, you will become sensitive to hearing people's opinions of psychology and psychologists. The regular one, of course, is that you may find that the friends and acquaintances you knew before you embarked upon your study in psychology may act slightly differently towards you. It is even worse with strangers. There is a certain suspicion in their faces, and it is routed in their lack of understanding of exactly what psychology is. They feel that you are 'analysing' them somehow, reading things into their every word. They may think that you have almost magical powers of knowing things about them which comes from your study of the mind and how it works. It is entertaining, sometimes, to let people think that this really is the case, but eventually it wears a little thin, and you spend quite a lot of your time explaining to people that this is not possible, and enter into a discussion of what psychology really is.

A similar situation is seen in relation to scanning techniques. There is a belief that because we now have access to fabulous technology that provides wonderful, and often very detailed images of activity in the brain, then we no longer have need for psychologists. Clearly, if we want to know what happens to us when we experience something, all we need to do is stick our heads in an MRI scanner, and wait for the images to roll off the printer. You would be surprised at how many people actually have this opinion. The controversy lies essentially in whether 'brain' and 'mind' are the same thing. It also lies in opinions of what actually happens in the 'brain' when we have a thought, or an emotion.

The press often reveals exciting research about the presence in the brain of a 'God-spot' for instance, an area of the brain that when stimulates produces hallucinations of sorts, which are then interpreted as mystical or spiritual experiences. The evidence for such a 'module' is debated (Ramachandran and Blakeslee, 1999). Whether a part of the brain lights up when a 'religious' experience is experienced is, though, potentially misleading. In the same way, seeing a familiar face, or the image of a long-lost loved one will generate a pattern of stimulation in the brain. The danger is that a scan such as an MRI concentrates very much on localized activity. This is extremely useful in itself, and makes the work of the cognitive neuropsychologist more quantifiable, but localized activity is of limited use in our greater and deeper understanding pf psychology. Concentrating on localized activity ignores a significant component of the brain's design, that of interconnectivity. It is the distribution of function and the complex network in the brain that allows us, and indeed makes us think, feel and behave as we do. Algorithms that help the software to interpret the images are advancing though, and they are now beginning to address interactivity within the brain – things are certainly improving.

The precision offered by an MRI or an fMRI, although improving, is not terribly good. The images and blobs that appear indicate activity in small regions of the brain, but these 'small' regions are still very large in terms of neurology. Greater accuracy will come with the technology though, and we await it with great anticipation.

Finally, 'Popular Press-friendly' coverage of headline-grabbing stunts with an MRI scanner do not help the public's understanding of how an MRI scan, although useful, does have limited utility sometimes, particularly in psychology. Famously, one report showed that the amygdala (an area of the brain involved in emotion) lit up when men look at Ferraris, and one looked at whether people actually prefer Coke to Pepsi. This process has been called 'neuromarketing' and is much more widespread than you may think. These incredibly expensive machines are being used by marketing companies to see what consumers actually think about their products. The problem is that the words 'brain' and 'mind' are used interchangeably, but should they be? Just because a part of a person's brain lights up when you show him a photograph of the holocaust does not tell us what the thought process is, and how that person's experiences of life have led him to produce this brain activity.

The take-home message is clear. Scanning is a powerful and extraordinarily expensive tool that is getting more useful, more powerful and less expensive. For now though, there is still demand for us psychologists, because the images cannot tell us about thinking or logic, or indeed how it actually feels to feel something whether physically or as an emotion.

IN REVIEW

- The nervous system contains sensory neurons, motor neurons and interneurons. Its two major divisions are the central nervous system, consisting of the brain and spinal cord, and the peripheral nervous system. The peripheral system is divided into the somatic system (which is responsible for sensory and motor functions) and the autonomic nervous system (which directs the activity of the body's internal organs and glands).

- The autonomic nervous system consists of sympathetic and parasympathetic divisions. The sympathetic system has an arousal function and tends to act as a unit. The parasympathetic system slows down body processes and is more specific in its actions. Together, the two divisions maintain a state of homeostasis, or internal balance.

- The spinal cord contains sensory neurons and motor neurons. Interneurons inside the spinal cord serve a connective function between the two. Simple stimulus–response sequences can occur as spinal reflexes.

- Neuropsychological tests, destruction and stimulation techniques, electrical recording and brain imaging have facilitated discoveries about brain–behaviour relations. Recently developed methods for producing computer-generated pictures of structures and processes within the living brain include the CT scan, PET scan, MRI and fMRI.

THE HIERARCHICAL BRAIN: STRUCTURES AND BEHAVIOURAL FUNCTIONS

In an evolutionary sense, your brain is far older than you are, for it represents perhaps 500 million years of evolutionary development and fine-tuning. The human brain is like a living archaeological site, with the more recently developed structures built on top of structures from the distant evolutionary past (Striedter, 2005). The structures at the brain's core, which we share with all other vertebrates, govern the basic physiological functions that keep us alive, such as breathing and heart rate. Built upon these basic structures are newer systems that involve progressively more complex functions – sensing, emoting, wanting, thinking and reasoning. Evolutionary theorists believe that as genetic variation sculpted these newer structures over time, natural selection favoured their retention because animals who had them were more likely to survive in changing environments. The crowning feature of brain development is the *cerebral cortex*, the biological seat of Einstein's scientific genius, Mozart's creativity, Saddam Hussein's brutality, Mother Teresa's compassion and that which makes you a unique human being.

The major structures of the human brain, together with their psychological functions, are shown in Figure 4.11. The brain has traditionally been viewed as having three major subdivisions: the hindbrain, the midbrain, which lies above the hindbrain, and the forebrain.

Focus 4.11

Which behavioural functions are controlled by the medulla, the pons and the cerebellum? What is the consequence of damage to these structures?

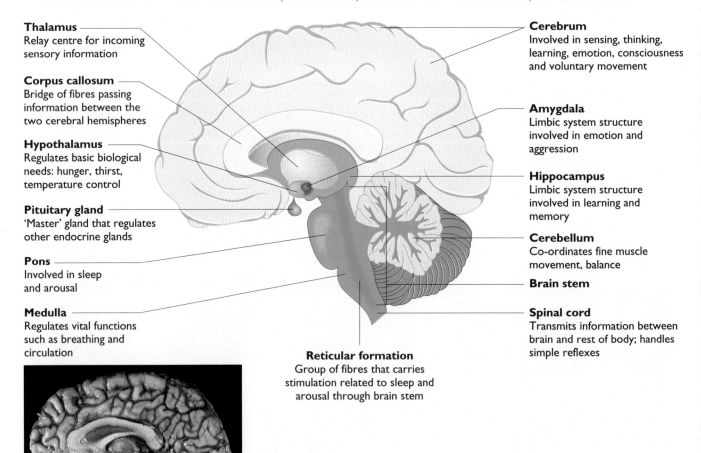

Thalamus
Relay centre for incoming sensory information

Corpus callosum
Bridge of fibres passing information between the two cerebral hemispheres

Hypothalamus
Regulates basic biological needs: hunger, thirst, temperature control

Pituitary gland
'Master' gland that regulates other endocrine glands

Pons
Involved in sleep and arousal

Medulla
Regulates vital functions such as breathing and circulation

Cerebrum
Involved in sensing, thinking, learning, emotion, consciousness and voluntary movement

Amygdala
Limbic system structure involved in emotion and aggression

Hippocampus
Limbic system structure involved in learning and memory

Cerebellum
Co-ordinates fine muscle movement, balance

Brain stem

Spinal cord
Transmits information between brain and rest of body; handles simple reflexes

Reticular formation
Group of fibres that carries stimulation related to sleep and arousal through brain stem

FIGURE 4.11

Interior of the brain.

The photograph shows the human brain sectioned at its midline. The drawing shows the brain structures as they would appear if the left side of the brain were transparent, permitting a view to the midline.

THE HINDBRAIN

The **hindbrain** is the lowest and most primitive level of the brain. As the spinal cord enters the brain, it enlarges to form the structures that compose the stalk-like brain stem. Attached to the brain stem is the other major portion of the hindbrain, the *cerebellum*.

The Brain Stem: Life-Support Systems

The structures of the **brain stem** support vital life functions. Included are the *medulla* and the *pons*. The 1.5-inch-long (3.8 cm) medulla is the first structure above the spinal cord. Well developed at birth, the **medulla** plays an important role in vital body functions such as heart rate and respiration. Because of your medulla, these functions occur automatically. Damage to the medulla usually results in death or, at best, the need to be maintained on life-support systems. Suppression of medulla activity can occur at high levels of alcohol intoxication, resulting in death by heart or respiratory failure (Blessing, 1997).

The medulla is also a two-way thoroughfare for all the sensory and motor nerve tracts coming up from the spinal cord and descending from the brain. Most of these tracts cross over within the medulla, so the left side of the brain receives sensory input from and exerts motor control over the right side of the body, and the right side of the brain serves the left side of the body. Why this crossover occurs is one of the unsolved mysteries of brain function.

The **pons** (meaning 'bridge' in Latin) lies just above the medulla and carries nerve impulses between higher and lower levels of the nervous system. The pons also has clusters of neurons that help regulate sleep. Like the medulla, the pons helps control vital functions, especially respiration, and damage to it can produce death.

The Cerebellum: Motor Co-ordination Centre

Attached to the rear of the brain stem, the cerebellum ('little brain' in Latin) does indeed look like a miniature brain. Its wrinkled *cortex*, or covering, consists mainly of grey cell bodies (grey matter). The **cerebellum** is concerned primarily with muscular movement co-ordination, but it also plays a role in learning and memory.

Specific motor movements are initiated in higher brain centres, but their timing and co-ordination depend on the cerebellum (De Zeeuw and Circirata, 2005). The cerebellum regulates complex, rapidly changing movements that require precise timing, such as those of a ballet dancer or a competitive diver. Within the animal kingdom, cats have an especially well developed cerebellum, helping to account for their ability to move gracefully (Altman and Bayer, 1996).

The motor-control functions of the cerebellum are easily disrupted by alcohol, producing the co-ordination difficulties that some police forces look for in roadside sobriety tests. Intoxicated people may be unable to walk a straight line or touch their nose with their index finger (Fig. 4.12). Physical damage to the cerebellum results in severe motor disturbances characterized by jerky, uncoordinated movements, as well as an inability to perform habitual movements such as walking.

hindbrain
the lowest and most primitive level of the brain

brain stem
supports vital life functions

medulla
plays an important role in vital body functions such as heart rate and respiration

pons
lies just above the medulla and carries nerve impulses between higher and lower levels of the nervous system

cerebellum
concerned primarily with muscular movement co-ordination, but it also plays a role in learning and memory

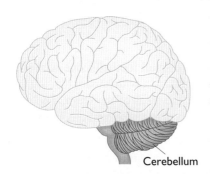

Cerebellum

FIGURE 4.12

Balance and co-ordination.

The cerebellum's movement-control functions are easily disrupted by alcohol. This provides the neural basis for a test of sobriety administered in some parts of the world by the police.

THE MIDBRAIN

Lying just above the hindbrain, the **midbrain** contains clusters of sensory and motor neurons. The sensory portion of the midbrain contains important relay centres for the visual and auditory systems. Here, nerve impulses from the eyes and ears are organized and sent to forebrain structures involved in visual and auditory perception (Nolte, 2002). The midbrain also contains motor neurons that control eye movements.

The Reticular Formation: The Brain's Gatekeeper

Buried within the midbrain is a finger-shaped structure that extends from the hindbrain up into the lower portions of the forebrain. This structure receives its name from its resemblance under a microscope to a *reticulum*, or net. The **reticular formation** acts as a kind of sentry, both alerting higher centres of the brain that messages are coming and then either blocking those messages or allowing them to go forward. The reticular formation has an *ascending* part, which sends input to higher regions of the brain to alert it, and a *descending* portion, through which higher brain centres can either admit or block out sensory input.

The reticular formation plays a central role in consciousness, sleep, and attention. Without reticular stimulation of higher brain regions, sensory messages do not register in conscious awareness even though the nerve impulses may reach the appropriate higher areas of the brain. It is as if the brain is not awake enough to notice them. In fact, some general anaesthetics work by deactivating neurons of the ascending reticular formation so that sensory impulses that ordinarily would be experienced as pain never register in the sensory areas of the brain (Simon, 2007).

The reticular formation also affects sleep and wakefulness. In a classic series of experiments in the late 1940s, researchers discovered that electrical stimulation of different portions of the reticular formation can produce instant sleep in a wakeful cat and sudden wakefulness in a sleeping animal (Marshall and Magoun, 1997). Severe damage to the reticular formation can produce a permanent coma (Pendlebury, 2007).

Attention is an active process during which only important or meaningful sensory inputs get through to our consciousness. Other inputs have to be toned down or completely blocked out or we'd be overwhelmed by stimulation. The descending reticular formation plays an important part in this process, serving as a kind of gate through which some inputs are admitted while others are blocked out by signals coming down from higher brain centres (Van Zomeren and Brouwer, 1994).

THE FOREBRAIN

The **forebrain** is the brain's most advanced portion from an evolutionary standpoint. Its major structure, the **cerebrum**, consists of two large hemispheres, a left side and a right side, that wrap around the brain stem as the two halves of a cut grapefruit might wrap around a large spoon. The outer portion of the forebrain has a thin covering, or cortex. Within are a number of important structures buried in the central regions of the hemispheres.

The Thalamus: The Brain's Sensory Switchboard

The *thalamus* is located above the midbrain. It resembles two small footballs, one within each cerebral hemisphere. The **thalamus** has sometimes been likened to a switchboard that organizes inputs from sensory organs and routes them to the appropriate areas of the brain. The visual, auditory, and body senses (balance and equilibrium) all have major relay stations in the thalamus (Jones, 2006).

Because the thalamus plays such a key role in routing sensory information to higher brain regions, individuals with disrupted functioning in the thalamus often experience a highly con-

---

midbrain

contains clusters of sensory and motor neurons

reticular formation

acts as a kind of sentry, both alerting higher centres of the brain that messages are coming and then either blocking those messages or allowing them to go forward

Focus 4.12

Describe the roles played by the ascending and descending reticular formation. What occurs with damage to this structure?

forebrain

the brain's most advanced portion from an evolutionary standpoint

cerebrum

consists of two large hemispheres, a left side and a right side

thalamus

has sometimes been likened to a switchboard that organizes inputs from sensory organs and routes them to the appropriate areas of the brain

Focus 4.13

Describe the structural characteristics and functions of the thalamus and the hypothalamus.

fusing world. MRIs from 39 schizophrenic men were compared with those of 47 normal male volunteers. The brain images showed specific abnormalities in the thalamus of the schizophrenic brains, suggesting that the thalamus may have been sending garbled sensory information to the higher regions of the brain and creating the confusing sensory experiences and hallucinations reported by many patients (Andreason et al. 1994).

The Hypothalamus: Motivation and Emotion

The *hypothalamus* (literally, 'under the thalamus') consists of tiny groups of neuron cell bodies that lie at the base of the brain, above the roof of the mouth. The **hypothalamus** plays a major role in many aspects of motivation and emotion, including sexual behaviour, temperature regulation, sleeping, eating, drinking, and aggression. Damage to the hypothalamus can disrupt all of these behaviours (Toy, 2007). For example, destruction of one area of a male's hypothalamus results in a complete loss of sex drive; damage to another portion produces an overwhelming urge to eat that results in extreme obesity (Morrison, 2006).

The hypothalamus has important connections with the *endocrine system*, the body's collection of hormone-producing glands (discussed later in this chapter). Through its connection with the nearby *pituitary gland* (the master gland that exerts control over the other glands of the endocrine system), the hypothalamus directly controls many hormonal secretions that regulate sexual development and sexual behaviour, metabolism and reactions to stress.

The hypothalamus is also involved in our experiences of pleasure and displeasure. The discovery of this fact occurred quite by accident. In 1953 psychologist James Olds was conducting an experiment to study the effects of electrical stimulation in a rat's midbrain reticular formation. One of the electrodes missed the target and was mistakenly implanted in the hypothalamus. Olds noticed that whenever this rat was stimulated, it repeated whatever it had just done, as if it had been rewarded for that behaviour. Olds then implanted electrodes in the hypothalamus of other animals and exposed them to a variety of learning situations. He found that they also learned and performed behaviours in order to receive what was clearly an electrical reward. In fact, some of the rats pressed a pedal up to 5000 times in an hour until they dropped from exhaustion. Stimulation of other nearby areas produced just the opposite effect – a tendency to stop performing any behaviour that was followed by stimulation, as if the animal had been punished. Olds and other researchers who replicated his work concluded that they had discovered what they called 'reward and punishment areas' in the brain, some of which were in the hypothalamus. The reward areas are rich in neurons that release dopamine, which seems to be an important chemical mediator of pleasure (Kolb and Whishaw, 2005).

Humans who have had electrodes implanted in their brains to search for abnormal brain tissue have reported experiencing pleasure when these reward regions were electrically stimulated. One patient reportedly proposed marriage to the experimenter while being so stimulated (Heath, 1972). Thus a misplaced electrode in James Olds's laboratory led to a discovery that neural events occurring in the hypothalamus and adjacent areas have important roles in motivation.

The Limbic System: Memory, Emotion and Goal-Directed Behaviour

As we continue our journey up through the brain, we come to the *limbic system*, a set of structures lying deep within the cerebral hemispheres (Fig. 4.13). The **limbic system** helps co-ordinate behaviours needed to satisfy motivational and emotional urges that arise in the hypothalamus. It is also involved in memory.

Two key structures in the limbic system are the *hippocampus* and the *amygdala*. The **hippocampus** is involved in forming and retrieving memories. Damage there can result in severe memory impairment for recent events (Isaacson, 2002). The **amygdala** (from the Greek word for 'almond') organizes motivational and emotional response patterns, particularly those linked to aggression and fear (LeDoux, 1998). Electrically stimulating certain areas of the amygdala

hypothalamus

plays a major role in many aspects of motivation and emotion, including sexual behaviour, temperature regulation, sleeping, eating, drinking and aggression

limbic system

helps co-ordinate behaviours needed to satisfy motivational and emotional urges that arise in the hypothalamus. It is also involved in memory

hippocampus

involved in forming and retrieving memories

amygdala

organizes motivational and emotional response patterns, particularly those linked to aggression and fear

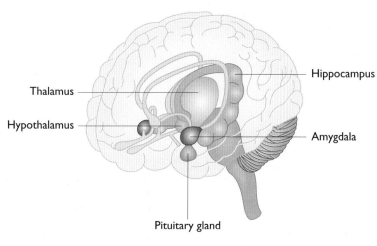

(b)

FIGURE 4.13

Limbic system structures.

(a) The amygdala and hippocampus are major structures of the limbic system. The hippocampus is important in the establishment of memories. (b) Electrical stimulation of the amygdala, which organizes emotional responses, can evoke an immediate aggressive response.

Focus 4.14

What roles do the hippocampus and amygdala play in psychological functions?

cerebral cortex

¼-inch-thick (0.63 cm) sheet of grey (unmyelinated) cells that form the outermost layer of the human brain

causes animals to snarl and assume aggressive postures (see Fig. 4.13b), whereas stimulation of other areas results in a fearful inability to respond aggressively, even in self-defence. For example, a normally aggressive and hungry cat will cower in fear from a tiny mouse placed in its cage. The amygdala can also produce emotional responses without the higher centres of the brain 'knowing' that we are emotionally aroused, providing a possible explanation for unconscious emotional responses (LeDoux, 1998).

The amygdala is a key part of a larger control system for anger and fear that also involves other brain regions (Siegel, 2005). It has important interconnections with the hippocampus, and amygdala stimulation is important in the hippocampus's creation of emotional memories. Without amygdala activity, emotional memories are not well established. One patient whose amygdala was removed could not recall emotional scenes from movies seen a day earlier, although he was able to remember the non-emotional scenes.

Finally, like the hypothalamus, the limbic system contains reward and punishment areas that have important motivational functions. Certain drugs, such as cocaine and marijuana, seem to induce pleasure by stimulating limbic reward areas that use dopamine as their neurotransmitter (LeMoal, 1999).

The Cerebral Cortex: Crown of the Brain

The **cerebral cortex**, a ¼-inch-thick (0.63 cm) sheet of grey (unmyelinated) cells that form the outermost layer of the human brain, is the crowning achievement of brain evolution. Fish and amphibians have no cerebral cortex, and the progression from more primitive to more advanced mammals is marked by a dramatic increase in the proportion of cortical tissue. In humans, the cortex constitutes fully 80 per cent of brain tissue (Simon, 2007).

The cerebral cortex is not essential for physical survival in the way that the brain stem structures are, but it is essential for human functioning. How much so is evident in this description of patients who, as a result of an accident during pre-natal development, were born without a cerebral cortex:

> Some of these individuals may survive for years, in one case of mine for twenty years. From these cases, it appears that the human [lacking a cortex] sleeps and wakes; … reacts to hunger, loud sounds, and crude visual stimuli by movement of eyes, eyelids, and

facial muscles; … may see and hear, … may be able to taste and smell, to reject the unpalatable and accept such food as it likes.... [They can] utter crude sounds, can cry and smile, showing displeasure when hungry and pleasure, in a babyish way, when being sung to;[they] may be able to perform spontaneously crude [limb] movements. (Cairns, 1952, p. 109)

Because the cortex is wrinkled and convoluted, like a wadded-up piece of paper, a great amount of cortical tissue is compressed into a relatively small space inside the skull. If we could remove the cortex and smooth it out, the tissue would cover an area roughly the size of a pillow-case. Perhaps 75 per cent of the cortex's total surface area lies within its *fissures*, or canyon-like folds. Three of these fissures are important landmarks. One large fissure runs lengthwise across the top of the brain, dividing it into a right and a left hemisphere. Within each hemisphere, a *central fissure* divides the cerebrum into front and rear halves, and a third fissure runs from front to rear along the side of the brain. On the basis of these landmarks, neurologists have divided each hemisphere into four lobes: *frontal, parietal, occipital* and *temporal*. A fist made with your right hand (with the side of your thumb facing you) can serve as a rough orientation to these lobes. The bend in your fingers represents the frontal lobe, your knuckles the parietal lobe, your wrist area the occipital lobe, and your thumb the temporal lobe of the left hemisphere.

As shown in Figure 4.14, each of the cerebral lobes is associated with particular sensory and motor functions, as well as with speech understanding and speech production (Biller et al. 2006). The large areas in Figure 4.14 that are not associated with sensory or motor functions (about three fourths of the cortex) make up the *association cortex*, involved in mental processes such as thought, memory, and perception. (We will discuss the association cortex in more detail shortly.)

Focus 4.15
Describe the locations of the four lobes of the brain and the organization of the motor, sensory, and association cortexes.

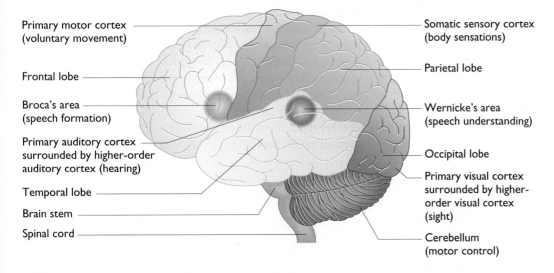

Primary motor cortex (voluntary movement)

Frontal lobe

Broca's area (speech formation)

Primary auditory cortex surrounded by higher-order auditory cortex (hearing)

Temporal lobe

Brain stem

Spinal cord

Somatic sensory cortex (body sensations)

Parietal lobe

Wernicke's area (speech understanding)

Occipital lobe

Primary visual cortex surrounded by higher-order visual cortex (sight)

Cerebellum (motor control)

FIGURE 4.14

Lobes of the brain.

Division of the brain into frontal (blue), parietal (green), occipital (purple) and temporal (yellow) lobes, showing localization of sensory, motor and some important language functions in the cortex. The remainder is primarily association cortex, consisting of interneurons involved in complex psychological functions, such as perception and reasoning.

The motor cortex The **motor cortex** controls the 600 or more muscles involved in voluntary body movements. It lies at the rear of the frontal lobes adjacent to the central fissure. Because the nerve tracts from the motor cortex cross over at the level of the medulla, each hemisphere governs movement on the opposite side of the body. Thus severe damage to the right motor cortex would produce paralysis in the left side of the body. The left side of Figure 4.15 shows the relative organization of function within the motor cortex. As you can see, specific body areas are represented in upside-down fashion within the motor cortex, and the amount of cortex devoted to each area depends on the complexity of the movements that are carried out by the body part. For example, the amount of cortical tissue devoted to your fingers is far greater than that devoted to your torso, even though your torso is much larger. If we electrically stimulate a particular point on the motor cortex, movements occur in the muscles governed by that part of the cortex.

motor cortex

controls the 600 or more muscles involved in voluntary body movements

The sensory cortex   Specific areas of the cortex receive input from our sensory receptors. With the exception of taste and smell, at least one specific area in the cortex has been identified for each of the senses.

The **somatic sensory cortex** receives sensory input that gives rise to our sensations of heat, touch and cold, and to our senses of balance and body movement (kinaesthesis). It lies at the front portion of the parietal lobe just behind the motor cortex, separated from it by the central fissure. As in the case of the motor system, each side of the body sends sensory input to the opposite hemisphere. Like the motor area next to it, the somatic sensory area is basically organized in an upside-down fashion, with the feet being represented near the top of the brain. Likewise, the amount of cortex devoted to each body area is directly proportional to that region's sensory sensitivity. The organization of the sensory cortex is shown on the right side of Figure 4.15, as is the proportion of cortex devoted to each body area. As far as your sensory cortex is concerned, you are mainly fingers, lips and tongue. Notice also that the organization of the sensory cortex is such that the body structures it serves lie side by side with those in the motor cortex, an arrangement that enhances sensory-motor interactions in the same body area.

The senses of hearing and sight are well represented in the cortex. As shown in Figure 4.14, the auditory area lies on the surface of the temporal lobe at the side of each hemisphere. Each ear sends messages to the auditory areas of both hemispheres, so the loss of one temporal lobe has little effect on hearing. The primary sensory area for vision lies at the rear of the occipital lobe. Here, messages from the eyes are analysed, integrated and translated into sight. As in the auditory system, each eye sends input to both hemispheres.

Within each sensory area, neurons respond to particular aspects of the sensory stimulus; they are tuned into specific aspects of the environment. Thus certain cells in the visual cortex fire only when we look at a particular kind of stimulus, such as a vertical line or a corner (Hubel and Wiesel, 1979). In the auditory cortex, some neurons fire only in response to high tones, whereas others respond only to tones having some other specific frequency. Many of these neuronal responses are present at birth, suggesting that we are pre-wired to perceive many aspects of our sensory environment (Noback et al., 2005). Nonetheless, the sensory cortex, like other parts of the brain, is also sensitive to experience. For example, when people learn to read Braille, the area in the sensory cortex that receives input from the fingertips increases in size, making the person more sensitive to the tiny sets of raised dots (Pool, 1994).

> **somatic sensory cortex**
>
> **receives sensory input that gives rise to our sensations of heat, touch and cold, and to our senses of balance and body movement (kinaesthesis)**

FIGURE 4.15

Cortical organization.

Both the motor cortex and the somatic sensory cortex are highly specialized so that every site is associated with a particular part of the body. The amount of cortex devoted to each body part is proportional to the sensitivity of that area's motor or sensory functions. Both the motor cortex and somatic sensory cortex are arranged in an upside down fashion and serve the opposite side of the body.

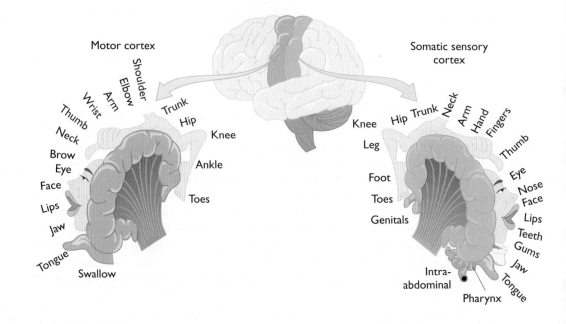

Speech comprehension and production   Two specific areas that govern the understanding and production of speech are also located in different lobes of the left hemisphere (see Fig. 4.14). **Wernicke's area**, in the temporal lobe, is primarily involved in speech comprehension. Damage to this cortical region leaves patients unable to understand written or spoken speech. Scott Moss, a psychologist who suffered temporary aphasia from a left hemisphere stroke (blockage or bursting of blood vessels in the brain that resulted in death of neurons from lack of oxygen) described his experience: 'I recollect trying to read the headlines of the Chicago Tribune but they didn't make any sense to me at all. I didn't have any difficulty focusing, it was simply that the words, individually or in combination, didn't have meaning' (Moss, 1972, p. 4).

Broca's area, in the frontal lobe, is mainly involved in the production of speech through its connections with the motor cortex region that controls the muscles used in speech. Damage to this area leaves patients with the ability to comprehend speech but not to express themselves in words or sentences. These two speech areas normally work in concert when you are conversing with another person. They allow you to comprehend what the other person is saying and to express your own thoughts.

Association cortex   The **association cortex** is involved in many important mental functions, including perception, language and thought. These areas are sometimes referred to as 'silent areas' because electrically stimulating them does not give rise to either sensory experiences or motor responses. Damage to specific parts of the association cortex causes disruption or loss of functions such as speech, understanding, thinking and problem-solving. As we might expect, if the association cortex is involved in higher mental processes, the amount of association cortex increases dramatically as we move up the brain ladder from lower animals to human beings. It constitutes about 75 per cent of the human cerebral cortex and accounts for people's superior cognitive abilities. One scientist has described our mass of association cortex as 'evolution's missing link' (Skoyles, 1997). He suggests that its flexibility and learning capacity have allowed us to acquire new mental skills specific to our human way of life, such as reading and mathematics, far more quickly than could have occurred through natural selection alone.

The importance of the association cortex is demonstrated in people who suffer from *agnosia*, the inability to identify familiar objects. One such case is described by the neurologist Oliver Sacks (1985).

Dr P. (one of Sacks's patients) was a talented and accomplished musician whose behaviour was quite normal with one glaring exception: although his vision was perfect, he often had difficulty recognizing familiar people and objects. He would chat with pieces of furniture and wonder why they did not reply, or pat the tops of fire hydrants, thinking they were children. One day, while visiting Sacks's office for an examination, Dr P. looked for his hat as he was ready to depart. Suddenly he reached out and grabbed his wife's head, trying to lift it. He had mistaken his wife for his hat! His wife smiled tolerantly as she had become accustomed to such actions on his part. Dr P. had suffered brain damage that left him unable to connect the information sent to the visual cortex with information stored in other cortical areas that concerned the nature of objects. The associative neurons responsible for linking the two types of information no longer served him.

The frontal lobes: the human difference   Some neuroscientists suggest that the entire period of human evolutionary existence could well be termed the age of the frontal lobe (Krasnegor et al., 1997). This brain region hardly exists in mammals such as mice and rats. The frontal lobes compose about 3.5 per cent of the cerebral cortex in the cat, 7 per cent in the dog, and 17 per cent in the chimpanzee. In a human, the frontal lobes constitute 29 per cent of the cortex. The frontal lobes the site of such human qualities as self-awareness, planning, initiative and responsibility are in some respects the most mysterious and least understood part of the brain.

Wernicke's area
in the temporal lobe, is primarily involved in speech comprehension

Broca's area
in the frontal lobe, is mainly involved in the production of speech through its connections with the motor cortex region that controls the muscles used in speech

Focus 4.16
Where are Wernicke's and Broca's areas? How are they involved in speech?

association cortex
is involved in many important mental functions, including perception, language and thought

Focus 4.17
Describe the role of the frontal cortex in higher mental (including executive) functions.

Much of what we know about the frontal lobes comes from detailed studies of patients who have experienced brain damage. Frontal-lobe damage results not so much in a loss of intellectual abilities as in an inability to plan and carry out a sequence of actions, even when patients can verbalize what they should do. This can result in an inability to correct actions that are clearly erroneous and self-defeating (Shallice and Burgess, 1991).

The frontal cortex is also involved in emotional experience. In people with normal brains, PET scans show increased activity in the frontal cortex when people are experiencing feelings of happiness, sadness or disgust (Lane et al., 1997). In contrast, patients with frontal-lobe damage often exhibit attitudes of apathy and lack of concern. They simply do not seem to care about anything. Consider the following episode reported by a neurologist who was testing a patient with frontal-lobe damage:

> Testing left-right discrimination was oddly difficult, because she said left or right indifferently. When I drew her attention to this, she said, 'Left/right. Right/left. Why the fuss? What's the difference?'
>
> 'Is there a difference?' I asked.
>
> 'Of course,' she said with a chemist's precision.... 'But they mean nothing to me. They're no different *for me*. Hands.... Doctors.... Sisters,' she added, seeing my puzzlement. 'Don't you understand? They mean nothing – nothing to me. *Nothing means anything*, at least to me.'
>
> Mrs. B, though acute and intelligent, was somehow not present – 'desouled' – as a person. (Sacks, 1985, p. 174)

A region of the frontal lobe has received increasing attention in recent years. The **prefrontal cortex**, located just behind the forehead, is the seat of the so-called executive functions. Executive functions are mental strategic planning, and impulse control – that allow people to direct their behaviour in an adaptive fashion. Deficits in executive functions seem to underlie a number of problem behaviours. People with prefrontal-cortex disorders seem oblivious to the future consequences of their actions and seem to be governed only by immediate consequences (Zald and Rauch, 2008). As you may have guessed by now, Phineas Gage, the railroad foreman described in our chapter-opening case, suffered massive prefrontal damage when the spike tore through his brain (see Fig. 4.1). Thereafter he exhibited classic symptoms of disturbed executive functions, becoming behaviourally impulsive and losing his capacity for future planning.

A more ominous manifestation of prefrontal dysfunction – the capacity to kill – was recently discovered by researchers using PET-scan technology. We describe this landmark study in the following 'Research close-up'.

HEMISPHERIC LATERALIZATION: THE LEFT AND RIGHT BRAINS

The left and right cerebral hemispheres are connected by a broad white band of myelinated nerve fibres. The **corpus callosum** is a neural bridge consisting of white myelinated fibres that acts as a major communication link between the two hemispheres and allows them to function as a single unit (see Fig. 4.11). Despite the fact that they normally act in concert, there are important differences between the psychological functions of the two cerebral hemispheres (Hugdahl and Davidson, 2005). **Lateralization** refers to the relatively greater localization of a function in one hemisphere or the other.

Medical studies of patients who suffered various types of brain damage provided the first clues that certain complex psychological functions were lateralized on one side of the brain or the other. The deficits observed in people with damage to either the left or right hemisphere

prefrontal cortex

located just behind the forehead, is the seat of the so-called executive functions

corpus callosum

is a neural bridge consisting of white myelinated fibres that acts as a major communication link between the two hemispheres and allows them to function as a single unit

lateralization

refers to the relatively greater localization of a function in one hemisphere or the other

Focus 4.18

What is hemispheric lateralization, and what functions are localized in the left and right hemispheres?

RESEARCH CLOSE-UP

INSIDE THE BRAIN OF A KILLER

SOURCE: J. Stoddard, A. Raine, S. Bihrle and M. Buchsbaum (1997). Prefrontal dysfunction in murderers lacking psychosocial deficits. In A. Raine, P.A. Brennan, D.P. Farrington and S.A. Mednick (eds), *Biosocial bases of violence*. New York: Plenum.

INTRODUCTION

What stops us from impulsively killing an irritating neighbour, a disloyal friend, or a total stranger wearing a coat we would like to own? The answer may lie, at least in part, in our frontal lobes. Much of what makes you a civilized person – self-control, judgement, foresight, reasoning, delaying gratification – is regulated by the executive functions of your prefrontal cortex. As seen in the case of Phineas Gage, damage in this region of the brain can reduce those civilizing inhibitions.

Until recently, researchers could only infer that impulsively violent people without obvious brain damage had reduced prefrontal activity, for they could not look directly into the brain and see how it was functioning. That changed with the development of brain-imaging procedures, particularly the PET scan. In this study, Jacqueline Stoddard and her co-workers applied PET technology to examine brain functioning in a group of people who had committed savage acts of violence. They also examined the possible contribution of environmental factors in this violence-prone population.

METHOD

The researchers studied 41 individuals (39 men and two women) who had been tried for murder or manslaughter in California. All had pleaded not guilty by reason of insanity or were judged mentally incompetent to stand trial. Each killer was paired with a non-violent control participant matched for age, sex and ethnicity. A radioactive glucose substance was injected into the participants, and this nutrient travelled to the brain. Positron-emission tomography (PET) scans were then taken to assess brain activity while the participants worked on a mental performance task that is known to require frontal-lobe involvement.

To assess the potential role of environmental factors that might foster violent tendencies, the records of the murderers were independently reviewed by two raters for degree of psychosocial deprivation. 'Deprivation' was defined as stressful histories of physical or sexual abuse, severe family conflict, neglect or being raised in a broken home. There was high agreement between the two raters, who knew nothing about the murderers' PET data.

RESULTS

On the basis of the psychosocial history ratings, the murderers were divided into a deprived group, numbering 26, who clearly had grown up under adverse circumstances, and a second group of 12 whose histories showed no evidence of deprivation. (The other three murderers had only minor deprivation and were not included in the comparisons.) These groups were compared with the non-violent controls in glucose metabolic rates, which measure the activity of neurons in the brain. The glucose recordings from the prefrontal areas of the left and right hemispheres are shown in Figure 4.16.

The murderers with no history of psychosocial deprivation differed significantly from their non-violent controls, the lower glucose readings indicating reduced activity in the prefrontal area. Although their prefrontal readings were also lower, the murderers with adverse environmental histories did not differ significantly from the non-violent controls.

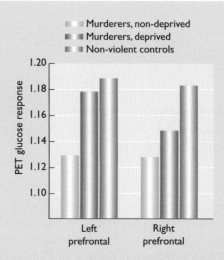

FIGURE 4.16

Prefrontal cortical activity.

Prefrontal cortical activity measured by PET scans in (a) murderers with no history of psychosocial conditions predictive of aggressive behaviour, (b) murderers with a history of psychosocial deprivation, and (c) a non-violent control group. Murderers with no history of deprivation showed notable prefrontal dysfunction.

SOURCE: data from Stoddard et al., 1997.

DISCUSSION

This study illustrates the value of brain-imaging techniques for studying brain–behaviour relations. Prior research using PET technology had suggested that violent individuals have reduced prefrontal activity (Raine et al., 1997), and other research using fMRI with non-violent people showed that the prefrontal cortex lit up when people were made to feel guilty or embarrassed, suggesting the role of this structure in the inhibition of unacceptable behaviour (Takahashi et al., 2004).

The study by Stoddard and her co-workers is particularly significant because it took into account not only brain functioning, but also environmental effects known to be associated with the development of violent behaviour. The researchers reasoned that both biological and environmental factors can prime people to become violent. In the absence of being raised in an environment that would be expected to foster impulsive violence, a brain abnormality that affected the executive functions of the prefrontal cortex would be a likely biological suspect. In accord with the researchers' hypothesis, the murderers who did not have a history of adverse environmental experiences were the ones who showed the greatest prefrontal dysfunction.

Other questions remain, however. First, the 41 murderers were not only violent people, but they were also psychologically disturbed enough to plead not guilty by reason of insanity. Although these people are obviously an important and dangerous subset of murderers, the findings can be applied to differences only between disturbed murderers and non-violent populations who are not psychologically disturbed. In this study, it would have been ideal to have a second control group that was non-violent but psychologically disturbed so that we could be more certain that the group differences were related to violent tendencies and not simply to mental illness. Also needed to flesh out the links between brain and violence are future studies of prefrontal functioning in other populations that engage in impulsive, poorly planned violence, such as certain types of juvenile delinquents or violent children. However, no single study can address all these questions, and this study is an excellent start towards understanding brain mechanisms responsible for violence and how they might interact with environmental factors.

suggested that for most people, verbal abilities and speech are localized in the left hemisphere, as are mathematical and logical abilities (Springer, 1997). When Broca's or Wernicke's speech areas in the left hemisphere are damaged, the result is **aphasia**, the partial or total loss of the ability to communicate. Depending on the location of the damage, the problem may lie in recognizing the meaning of words, in communicating verbally with others, or in both functions. We should note, however, that women are less likely to suffer aphasia when their left hemisphere is damaged, suggesting that for women, language is represented in both hemispheres to a greater extent than for men (Rossell et al., 2002).

When the right hemisphere is damaged, the clinical picture is quite different. Language functions are not ordinarily affected, but the person has great difficulty perceiving spatial relations. A patient may have a hard time recognizing faces and may even forget a well-travelled route or, as in the case of Dr P., mistake his wife for a hat (Sacks, 1985). It appears that mental imagery, musical and artistic abilities, and the ability to perceive and understand spatial relations are primarily right-hemisphere functions (Biller et al., 2006).

The two hemispheres differ not only in the cognitive functions that reside there but also in their links with positive and negative emotions. EEG studies have shown that the right hemisphere is relatively more active when negative emotions such as sadness and anger are being experienced. Positive emotions such as joy and happiness are accompanied by relatively greater left-hemisphere activation (Marshall and Fox, 2000).

THE SPLIT BRAIN: DIVIDING THE HEMISPHERES

Despite the lateralization of specific functions in the two cerebral hemispheres, the brain normally functions as a unified whole because the two hemispheres communicate with one another through the corpus callosum. But what would happen if this communication link were cut? Would we, in effect, produce two different and largely independent minds in the same person? A series of Nobel Prize-winning studies by Roger Sperry (1970) and his associates addressed this question. Sperry and his co-workers studied people whose corpora callosa had been severed to stop epileptic seizures from spreading throughout the brain.

Split-brain research was made possible by the way in which our visual input to the brain is organized. To illustrate, extend your two hands straight out in front of you, separated by about 1 foot (30 cm). Now focus on the point between them. You will find that you can still see both hands in your peripheral vision and that you have a unified view of the scene. It therefore might surprise you to know that your left hand is being 'seen' only by your right hemisphere and your right hand only by your left hemisphere. To see how this occurs, examine Figure 4.17, which shows that some of the fibres of the optic nerve from each eye cross over at the *optic chiasma* and travel to the opposite brain hemisphere.

FIGURE 4.17

The split brain.

The visual system's anatomy made studies of split brain subjects possible. Images entering the eye are reversed by the lens, so that light waves from the right visual field fall on the left side of the retina and those from the left visual field fall on the right side of the retina. Optic nerve fibres from the inner portion of the retina (towards the nose) cross over at the optic chiasma, whereas the fibres from the outer portion of the retina do not. As a result, the right side of the visual field projects to the visual cortex of the left hemisphere, whereas the left visual field projects to the right hemisphere. When the corpus callosum is cut, the two hemispheres no longer communicate with each other. By presenting stimuli to either side of the visual fixation point, researchers can control which hemisphere receives the information.

aphasia
the partial or total loss of the ability to communicate

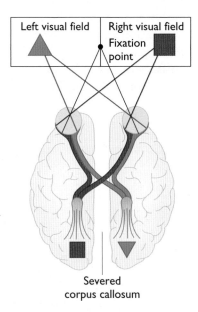

Severed
corpus callosum

Despite this arrangement, we experience a unified visual world (as you did when you looked at your hands), rather than two half-worlds, because our hemispheres' visual areas are connected by the corpus callosum. When the corpus callosum is cut, however, visual input to only one hemisphere can be accomplished by projecting the stimulus to either the right side of the visual field, in which case the image goes only to the left hemisphere, or to the left side of the visual field, which sends it to the right hemisphere.

In Sperry's experiments, split-brain patients basically did what you did with your hands: they focused on a fixation point, a dot on the centre of a screen, while slides containing visual stimuli (words, pictures, and so on) were flashed to the right or to the left side of the fixation point (Fig. 4.18).

FIGURE 4.18

A split-brain patient.

A split-brain patient focuses on the fixation point in the centre of the screen.
(a) A picture of a hairbrush is briefly projected to the left side of the visual field, thus sending the information to the right hemisphere. (b) The patient is asked to report what she saw. She cannot name the object. (c) She is then asked to select the object she saw and quickly finds it with her left hand. What would happen if the object were to be transferred to her right hand or if the word were to be projected to the right side of the visual field? In either case, the information would be sent to the language-rich left hemisphere, and she would be able to name the object.

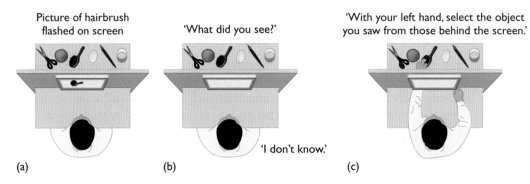

(a) Picture of hairbrush flashed on screen

(b) 'What did you see?' 'I don't know.'

(c) 'With your left hand, select the object you saw from those behind the screen.'

Sperry found that when words were flashed to the right side of the visual field, resulting in these being sent to the language-rich left hemisphere, patients could verbally describe what they had seen. They could also write what they had seen with their right hand (which is controlled by the left hemisphere). However, if words were flashed to the left side of the visual field and sent on to the right hemisphere, the patients could not describe what they had seen on the screen. This pattern of findings indicates that the right hemisphere does not have well-developed verbal expressive abilities.

The inability to describe stimuli verbally did not mean, however, that the right hemisphere was incapable of recognizing them. If a picture of an object (e.g., a hairbrush) was flashed to the right hemisphere and the left hand (controlled by the right hemisphere) was allowed to feel different objects behind the screen, the person's hand would immediately select the brush. As long as the person continued to hold the brush in the left hand, sending sensory input about the object to the 'non-verbal' right hemisphere, the person was unable to name it. However, if the brush was transferred to the right hand, the person could immediately name it. In other words, until the object was transferred to the right hand, the left hemisphere had no knowledge of what the right hemisphere was experiencing.

Later research showed the right hemisphere's definite superiority over the left in the recognition of patterns. In one study, three split-brain patients were presented with photographs of similar looking faces projected in either the left or right visual fields. On each trial, they were asked to select the photo they had just seen from a set of 10 cards. In this task, the spatially oriented right hemisphere was far more accurate than the linguistic left hemisphere in correctly identifying the photos. Apparently, the faces were too similar to one another to be differentiated very easily by left-hemisphere verbal descriptions, but the pattern-recognition abilities of the right hemisphere allowed discrimination among them (Gazzaniga and Smylie, 1983). Split-brain research firmly established the different abilities of the two hemispheres.

WHAT DO YOU THINK?

TWO MINDS IN ONE BRAIN?

Sperry's split-brain studies caused a sensation in neuroscience and in the popular press. Soon *left brain* and *right brain* became part of the popular vernacular, and educational programmes were proposed to unearth the unrealized potential of the right brain. Do you believe that this left brain/right brain concept and programmes based on it are justified by Sperry's findings? How can you explain the fact that the split-brain patients were able to function in daily life? Think critically about these questions, then see the discussion on p. 164.

IN REVIEW

- The brain is divided structurally into the hindbrain, the midbrain and the forebrain. This organization reflects the evolution of increasingly more complex brain structures related to behavioural capabilities.

- Major structures within the hindbrain include the medulla, which monitors and controls vital body functions; the pons, which contains important groups of sensory and motor neurons; and the cerebellum, which is concerned with motor co-ordination.

- The reticular formation, located in the midbrain, plays a vital role in consciousness, attention and sleep. Activity of the ascending reticular formation excites higher areas of the brain and prepares them to respond to stimulation. The descending reticular formation acts as a gate, determining which stimuli enter into consciousness.

- The forebrain consists of two cerebral hemispheres and a number of subcortical structures. The cerebral hemispheres are connected by the corpus callosum.

- The thalamus acts as a switchboard through which impulses originating in sense organs are routed to the appropriate sensory-projection areas. The hypothalamus plays a major role in many aspects of motivational and emotional behaviour. The limbic system seems to be involved in organizing the behaviours involved in motivation and emotion.

- The cerebral cortex is divided into frontal, parietal, occipital and temporal lobes. Some areas of the cerebral cortex receive sensory input, some control motor functions, and others (the association cortex) are involved in higher mental processes in humans. The frontal lobes are particularly important in such executive functions as planning, voluntary behaviour and self-awareness.

- Although the two cerebral hemispheres ordinarily work in co-ordination with one another, they appear to have different functions and abilities. Studies of split-brain patients, whose corpora callosa have been cut, indicate that the left hemisphere commands language and mathematical abilities, whereas the right hemisphere has well developed spatial abilities but a generally limited ability to communicate through speech. Positive emotions are linked to relatively greater left hemisphere activation and negative emotions to relatively greater right-hemisphere involvement. Despite hemispheric localization, however, most behaviours involve interactions between both hemispheres; the brain normally operates as a highly integrated system.

PLASTICITY IN THE BRAIN: THE ROLE OF EXPERIENCE AND THE RECOVERY OF FUNCTION

Learn to walk, acquire speech, begin to read or fall in love, and your brain changes in ways that make you a different person from who you were before. Learning and practicing a mental or physical skill may change the size or number of brain areas involved and alter the neural pathways used in the skill (Adams and Cox, 2002; Posner and Rothbart, 2007a). This process of brain alteration begins in the womb and continues throughout life. It is governed in important ways by genetic factors but is also strongly influenced by the environment.

Neural plasticity refers to the ability of neurons to change in structure and function (Huttenlocher, 2002). Two aspects of neural plasticity – the effects of early experience on brain development and recovery from brain damage – are at the forefront of current research.

Neural plasticity

the ability of neurons to change in structure and function

HOW EXPERIENCE INFLUENCES BRAIN DEVELOPMENT

Brain development is programmed by complex commands from our genes, but how these genetic commands express themselves can be powerfully affected by the environment in which we develop, including the environment we are exposed to in the womb (Fenichel, 2006). Consider the following research findings:

1. For the foetus in the womb, exposure to high levels of alcohol ingested by the pregnant mother can disrupt brain development and produce the lifelong mental and behavioural damage seen in foetal alcohol syndrome. Drinking during the first weeks of pregnancy – sometimes before a woman is even aware that she's pregnant – is particularly risky in this regard (Streissguth et al., 1985).

2. Compared with those of normally reared rats, the brains of rat pups raised in a stimulating environment weighed more and had larger neurons, more dendritic branches and greater concentrations of acetylcholine, a neurotransmitter involved in motor control and in memory (Rosenzweig, 1984).

3. Prematurely born human infants who were caressed and massaged on a regular basis showed faster neurological development than did those given normal care and human contact (Field et al., 1986).

4. MRI recordings revealed that experienced violinists and other string-instrument players who do elaborate movements on the strings with their left hands had a larger right hemisphere somato-sensory area devoted to these fingers than did non-musicians. The corresponding left-hemisphere (right-hand) cortical areas of the musicians and non-musicians did not differ. The earlier in life the musicians had started playing their instruments, the greater the cortical differences (Elbert et al., 1995).

5. Chronic alcoholism inhibits the production of new neural connections in the hippocampus, thereby impairing learning, memory and other cognitive functions. After weeks of abstinence, the process of neural regeneration is reinstated (Nixon and Crews, 2004).

6. Some theorists believe that life stress has a similar negative effect on neuron formation in the brain, thereby causing or maintaining clinical depression. Antidepressant medications increase serotonin action in the brain, and serotonin increases neuron production in the brain (Jacobs, 2004).

7. Cultural factors may affect brain development as well. For example, the Chinese language uses complex pictorial images (rather than words) to represent objects or concepts. Because pictorial stimuli are processed in the right hemisphere, we might expect less left hemisphere lateralization of language among speakers of Chinese than among people who speak English or other alphabet-based languages. There is evidence to support this hypothesis in the areas of reading and writing (Tzeng et al., 1979).

These and other findings show that in a very real sense, each person's brain goes through its own personal evolutionary process. The brain changes and adapts as it is sculpted by life experiences (Posner and Rothbart, 2007b).

Studies using the electron microscope help explain why such plasticity is possible early in life. The 1- to 2-year-old child has about 50 per cent more brain synapses than mature adults do (Lomber and Eggermont, 2006). This greater availability of synapses may help explain why children can recover from brain damage more quickly and completely than adults. But, sadly, the days of synaptic riches do not last forever. Unused or weaker synapses deteriorate with age, so that the brain loses some of its plasticity (Huttenlocher, 2002). Moreover, cell death is programmed into every neuron by its genes, and what some neuroscientists refer to as the neuron's 'suicide apparatus' is activated by a lack of stimulation from other neurons and by many other factors that are not yet known. As a result, adults actually have fewer synapses than do children, despite their more advanced cognitive and motor capabilities. However, the remaining neurons form new connections in response to experiences and the formation of new memories. This plasticity, and ability to form new connections is extremely useful, but can be influenced. Nicotine, for example, has been shown to help concentration, and cognition, and has been seen to show beneficial effects in those with Parkinson's disease, but recent work has shown that it actually reduces the plasticity of cells in the frontal lobes (Couey et al., 2007).

HEALING THE NERVOUS SYSTEM

When nerve tissue is destroyed or neurons die as part of the ageing process, surviving neurons can restore functioning by modifying themselves either structurally or biochemically. They can alter their structure by sprouting enlarged networks of dendrites or by extending axons from surviving neurons to form new synapses (Shepherd, 1997). Surviving neurons may also make up for the loss by increasing the volume of neurotransmitters they release (Robinson, 1997). Moreover, research findings have disproved the long-standing assumption of brain scientists that dead neurons cannot be replaced in the mature brain (McMillan et al., 1999). The production of new neurons in the nervous system is called **neurogenesis**. Neurogenesis occurs in both the immature and the adult brain. In the adult brain, the birth of new cells has been established only in the hippocampus so far, but it may occur in other areas as well. The study of neurogenesis is an exciting research frontier.

Ian Robertson's research group in Trinity, Dublin, are looking at a number of different strands of research surrounding rehabilitation, and degeneration. Among a raft of other things, their work on brain plasticity has included investigations in Alzheimer's disease and traumatic brain injuries. They are also part of pioneering exciting work on another aspect of neuropsychology called cognitive neurogenomics. Cognitive neurogenomics refers to the genetic make-up of cognitive function. It typically involves the search for neuropsychological or biological markers for clinical disorders (i.e., ADHD, Autism, etc.) linked to known genetic patterns. For example, genetic variation within the DAT1 genotype, that helps distribute the neurotransmitter dopamine, can influence the development of prefrontal cortex. It has been found that children possessing two copies of the DAT-associated risk allele had significantly poorer sustained attention than those ADHD children who did not possess this risk component. This is a high priority for the health service because drugs like ritalin may only have an influence on a certain subset (proportion) of ADHD children who show the appropriate genotypic response to the drug. On one hand, this is not good news for the pharmaceutical companies because a greater understanding of the linkage between gene, drug action and cognitive function will mean that fewer drugs will be prescribed, and only to the target subset. On the other hand, it has potential to help generate revenue for the more ethically minded pharmaceutical companies who will be striving to design drugs with a careful focus that actually work. The research is providing exciting possibilities for combining focused drug treatments for disorders with behavioural and cognitive techniques that may significantly improve the quality of life of those with these neuropsychological problems.

neurogenesis
the production of new neurons in the nervous system

Focus 4.19
What is neural plasticity? How do age, environment and behaviour affect plasticity?

Focus 4.20
Describe the ways in which neural function can be restored following damage.

neural stem cells

immature 'uncommitted' cells that can mature into any type of neuron or glial cell needed by the brain

One revolutionary neurogenesis technique involves the transplantation into the brain of **neural stem cells**, immature 'uncommitted' cells that can mature into any type of neuron or glial cell needed by the brain. These cells, found in both the developing and adult nervous systems, can be put into a liquid medium and injected directly into the brain. Once in the brain, they can travel to any of its regions, especially developing or degenerating areas. There they can detect defective or genetically impaired cells and somehow convert themselves into healthy forms of the defective cells. Stem cells have been successfully transplanted into the spinal cords of injured animals, where they have taken hold and organized themselves into neural networks (Tzeng, 1997). This success may herald an eventual ability to do what has never before been possible: repair the severed spinal cord.

The fact that transplanted stem cells can apparently go anywhere in the brain and become any kind of cell suggests the possibility of revolutionary treatments for diseases involving neural degeneration and dysfunction. These include Alzheimer's disease, multiple sclerosis, strokes, mental disorders and genetically based birth defects, all of which have serious psychological consequences (Wernig and Brustle, 2002). Stem cells may also hold the key to countering the effects of ageing on brain functioning. In one study, human stem cells transplanted into the brains of aged rats migrated to the hippocampus and cortex. Four weeks later, these rats showed improved performance in a water-maze task, suggesting improved learning and memory ability (Qu et al., 2001). Much more research is needed, but, at long last, we may be on the threshold of being able to heal the damaged brain and restore lost psychological functions (Brazel and Rao, 2004). A key to doing so will be to discover why it is that stem cells, which have the potential to produce new neurons and are found throughout the adult brain, are not utilized more widely by the brain to repair itself. It may be that altering stem cells through pharmacological or genetic interventions will increase their ability to repair the damaged brain (Kempermann, 2005).

BENEATH THE SURFACE

DO WE REALLY USE ONLY 10 PER CENT OF OUR BRAIN CAPACITY?

How often have you heard that we only use 10 per cent of our brain capacity? Is there any truth to this notion?

Let us apply what we have learned in this chapter to critically evaluate that statement. One principle of critical thinking is to test an idea by trying to find evidence against it. The reason is that we can find something to support almost any statement, even if it is false. In contrast, one disconfirming piece of evidence tells us the statement is not true as is.

First, let us consider what we know about brain activity from PET and fMRI imaging studies. Do they show that only 10 per cent of the brain is active at any time? Certainly not. Instead, the brain exhibits widespread activity even during sleep. Although certain functions may use only a small part of the brain at one time, any sufficiently complex set of activities or thought patterns involves many parts of the brain. For any given activity, such as eating, watching television, walking or reading this book, you may use a few specific parts of your brain. Over the course of a whole day, however, just about all of the brain is used at one time or another. Thus, brain activity data fly in the face of the 10 per cent truism.

Next, we might consider what we know about brain damage. Does the 10 per cent principle mean that we would be just fine if 90 per cent of our brain were removed? Hardly. It is well known that damage to a relatively small area of the brain, such as that caused by a stroke, can cause devastating disabilities.

Yet the damage caused by such a condition is far less than what would occur if 90 per cent of the brain were removed. As a prominent neurologist told us, 'If a surgeon tells you he or she is going to remove the 90 per cent of the brain you don't need, run like hell'.

We might also apply what we have learned about neural development, particularly the 'use it or lose it' principle. The process of brain development involves pruning synapses that are not used, thereby fine-tuning brain functioning. Many studies have shown that if the input to a particular neural system is eliminated, then neurons in this system will not function properly. If we were really using only 10 per cent of the brain, we could expect the other 90 per cent to atrophy over time. Where did the 10 per cent idea come from in the first place? Perhaps it was inspired in part by the work of psychologist Karl Lashley in the 1920s and 1930s. Lashley removed large areas of the cerebral cortex in rats and found that these animals could still relearn specific tasks. This did not mean, however, that other functions were not severely affected. But psychics and other 'human potential' marketeers found the idea intriguing and have kept it alive over the decades. After all, if we use only 10 per cent of our brain, imagine the untapped psychic abilities that lie dormant, just waiting to be released using their methods. Psychics often attribute their special, if fraudulent, gifts to the release of neural potential that other people have not accessed.

This does not mean that we do not have untapped potentials; it is just that, if realized, they would be represented in the form of new synapses within brain tissue that you are already using. A final reason why the myth persists is that it has been repeated so often over the years in the mass media that it has become a part of popular culture, an unquestioned factoid that has taken on a life of its own. However, there is no question that the 10 per cent principle is a myth without scientific foundation.

IN REVIEW

- Neural plasticity refers to the ability of neurons to change in structure and function. Environmental factors, particularly early in life, have notable effects on brain development. There are often periods during which environmental factors have their greatest (or only) effects on plasticity.

- A person's ability to recover from brain damage depends on several factors. Other things being equal, recovery is greatest early in life and declines with age.

- When neurons die, surviving neurons can alter their structure and functions to recover the ability to send and receive nerve impulses. Neurons can also increase the amount of neurotransmitters they release. Recent findings suggest that the brains of mature primates and humans are capable of producing new neurons (neurogenesis).

- Current advances in the treatment of neurological disorders include experiments on neurogenesis and the injection of neural stem cells into the brain, where they find and replace diseased or dead neurons.

endocrine system

consists of numerous hormone-secreting glands distributed throughout the body

hormones

chemical messengers that are secreted from its glands into the bloodstream

Focus 4.21

How does the endocrine system differ from the nervous system? How do hormones affect development and behaviour?

THE NERVOUS SYSTEM INTERACTS WITH THE ENDOCRINE AND IMMUNE SYSTEMS

The nervous system interacts with two other communication systems within the body, namely, the endocrine and immune systems. These interactions have major influences on behaviour and on psychological and physical well-being.

INTERACTIONS WITH THE ENDOCRINE SYSTEM

The **endocrine system** consists of numerous hormone-secreting glands distributed throughout the body (Fig. 4.19). Like the nervous system, the endocrine system's function is to convey information from one area of the body to another. Rather than using nerve impulses, however, the endocrine system conveys information in the form of **hormones**, chemical messengers that are secreted from its glands into the bloodstream. Just as neurons have receptors for certain neurotransmitters, cells in the body (including neurons) have receptor molecules that respond to specific hormones from the endocrine glands (Porterfield and White, 2007). Many of the hormones secreted by these glands affect psychological development and functioning.

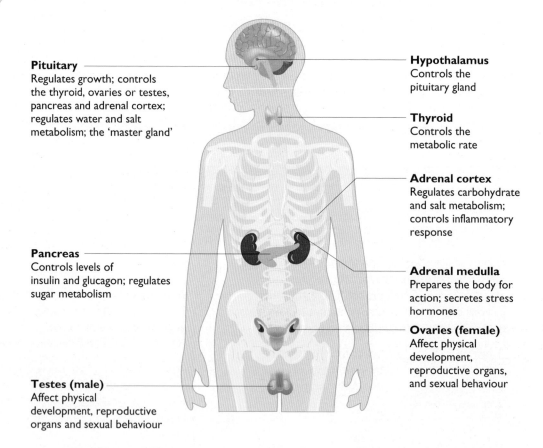

FIGURE 4.19

The endocrine system.

The location of the glands that comprise the endocrine system and the effects of their hormones on bodily functions.

Pituitary
Regulates growth; controls the thyroid, ovaries or testes, pancreas and adrenal cortex; regulates water and salt metabolism; the 'master gland'

Pancreas
Controls levels of insulin and glucagon; regulates sugar metabolism

Testes (male)
Affect physical development, reproductive organs and sexual behaviour

Hypothalamus
Controls the pituitary gland

Thyroid
Controls the metabolic rate

Adrenal cortex
Regulates carbohydrate and salt metabolism; controls inflammatory response

Adrenal medulla
Prepares the body for action; secretes stress hormones

Ovaries (female)
Affect physical development, reproductive organs, and sexual behaviour

Endocrine messages trigger responses in the brain, and mental processes within the brain can affect endocrine functioning. For example, negative thoughts about a stressful situation can quickly trigger the secretion of stress hormones within the body (Borod, 2000).

The nervous system transmits information rapidly, with the speed of nerve impulses. In contrast, the endocrine system is much slower because the delivery of its messages depends on the rate of blood flow. Nonetheless, hormones travel throughout the body in the bloodstream and can reach billions of individual cells. Thus, when the brain has important information to transmit, it has the choice of sending it quickly and directly in the form of nerve impulses to a relatively small number of neurons or indirectly by means of hormones to a large number of cells. Often both communication networks are used, resulting in both immediate and prolonged stimulation.

Hormones begin to influence our development, capacities and behaviour long before we are born. In the third to fourth month of pregnancy, genetically programmed releases of sex hormones in the foetus determine sex organ development, as well as differences in the structure and function of several parts of the nervous system, including the hypothalamus. One area of the hypothalamus affected in this manner continues to influence hormonal release in later life, such as the cyclic pattern of hormonal release during the female menstrual cycle.

Aside from reproductive structures and sexual behaviours, pre-natal hormones affect a variety of other characteristics including sex differences in aggressiveness and longevity; males tend to be more aggressive than females, and females live longer than men (Nelson and Luciana, 2001). Pre-natal hormones also produce differences in brain structures in males and females. Females have a greater density of neurons in language-relevant areas of the temporal lobe, which may contribute to the small overall superiority they manifest in verbal skills (Collins and Kimura, 1997). They also tend to have a relatively larger corpus callosum than males, which may help account for the fact that language functions are less localized in the left hemisphere in females (Rossell et al., 2002). These sex differences are discussed in greater detail in Chapter 9.

Of special interest to psychologists are the **adrenal glands**, twin structures perched on top of the kidneys that serve, quite literally, as hormone factories, producing and secreting about 50 different hormones that regulate many metabolic processes within the brain and other parts of the body. The adrenals produce the neurotransmitter dopamine, as well as several stress hormones. In an emergency, the adrenal glands are activated by the sympathetic branch of the autonomic nervous system. Stress hormones are then secreted into the bloodstream, mobilizing the body's emergency response system. Because hormones remain in the bloodstream for some time, the action of these adrenal hormones is especially important under conditions of prolonged stress. If not for the long-term influence of hormones, the autonomic nervous system would have to produce a constant barrage of nerve impulses to the organs involved in responding to stress.

INTERACTIONS INVOLVING THE IMMUNE SYSTEM

The nervous and endocrine systems interact not only with one another but also with the immune system (Chrousos et al., 2006). A normal, healthy immune system is a wonder of nature. At this moment, microscopic soldiers patrol every part of your body, including your brain. They are on a search-and-destroy mission, seeking out biological invaders that could disable or kill you. Programmed into this legion of tiny defenders is an innate ability to recognize which substances belong to the body and which are foreign and must be destroyed. Such recognition occurs because foreign substances known as **antigens** (meaning *anti*body *gen*erators) trigger a biochemical response from the immune system. Bacteria, viruses, abnormal cells, and many chemical molecules with antigenic properties start the wars that rage inside our bodies every moment of every day (Fig. 4.20).

The immune system has a remarkable memory. Once it has encountered one of the millions of different antigens that enter the body, it will recognize the antigen immediately in the future and produce the biochemical weapons, or *antibodies*, needed to destroy it (Nossal and Hall, 1995). This memory is the basis for developing vaccines to protect people and animals from some diseases; it is also the reason we normally catch diseases such as mumps and chicken pox only once in our lives. Unfortunately, though the memory may be perfect, our body's defences may not be. Some bacteria and viruses evolve so rapidly that they can change just enough over time to slip past the sentinels in our immune system and give us this year's cold or flu.

adrenal glands
twin structures perched on top of the kidneys that serve, quite literally, as hormone factories, producing and secreting about 50 different hormones

antigens
foreign substances that trigger a biochemical response from the immune system

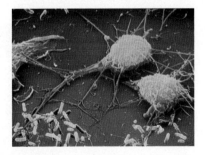

FIGURE 4.20

An immune-system cell reaches out to capture bacteria, shown here in yellow. The bacteria that have already been pulled to the surface of the cell will be engulfed and devoured.

Focus 4.22

What evidence exists that the nervous, endocrine, and immune systems communicate with and influence one another?

The immune system, like the nervous system, has an exquisite capacity to receive, interpret and respond to specific forms of stimulation. It senses, learns, remembers and reacts; in other words, it behaves. Despite these similarities, research on the nervous and immune systems proceeded along independent paths for many years, with only a few visionaries suggesting that the two systems might be able to communicate and influence each others' activities. We now know that the nervous, endocrine and immune systems are all parts of a communication network that so completely underlies our every mental, emotional and physical action that neuroscientist Candace Pert (1986), one of the pioneers in this area of research, has dubbed this network 'bodymind'.

Pieces of this communication puzzle began to fall into place with several key discoveries. First, researchers found that electrical stimulation or destruction of certain sites in the hypothalamus and cerebral cortex resulted in immediate increases or decreases in immune-system activity. Conversely, activating the immune system by injecting antigens into the body resulted in increased electrical activity in several brain regions (Saphier, 1992). Clearly, the nervous and immune systems were communicating with and influencing one another.

Later research showed that the nervous and immune systems are chemically connected as well. Immune-system cells contain receptors keyed to specific neurotransmitter substances, meaning that the action of immune cells can be directly influenced by chemical messengers from the brain (Maier and Watkins, 1999). An equally startling discovery was that immune cells can actually produce hormones and neurotransmitters, allowing them to directly influence the brain and endocrine system (Felton and Maida, 2000). In sum, the brain, endocrine glands and immune system form a complete communication loop, with each having sensory and motor functions and each influencing and being influenced by one another.

Inspired by these findings, many researchers began to study psychological influences on the immune system. Scientific investigations soon revealed a host of psychosocial factors that can increase or decrease immunity. For example, chronic stress, depression and pessimistic thinking reduce immune functioning, whereas stress management skills, an optimistic outlook, a sense of humour and social support help preserve immunity (Kiecolt-Glaser et al., 2002; Segerstrom and Miller, 2004). As Figure 4.21 shows, immune functioning is now being studied at biological, psychological and environmental levels of analysis. We examine these findings and their applied implications in greater depth in Chapter 14.

FIGURE 4.21

Levels of analysis: factors related to immune-system functioning.

LEVELS OF ANALYSIS FACTORS RELATED TO IMMUNE-SYSTEM FUNCTIONING		
Biological	**Psychological**	**Environmental**
• Antigens within body that trigger immune response • Nerve impulses and hormonal messages from the brain and endocrine system that affect immune functioning • Strength of immune responses	• Cognitive factors, including optimistic and pessimistic thinking • Feelings of distress and depression • Personality factors, including a sense of humour • Stress-management coping skills that help prevent negative effects of stress	• Environmental stressors and significant losses decrease immune functioning • Social support when stressed enhances immune function

Immune functioning

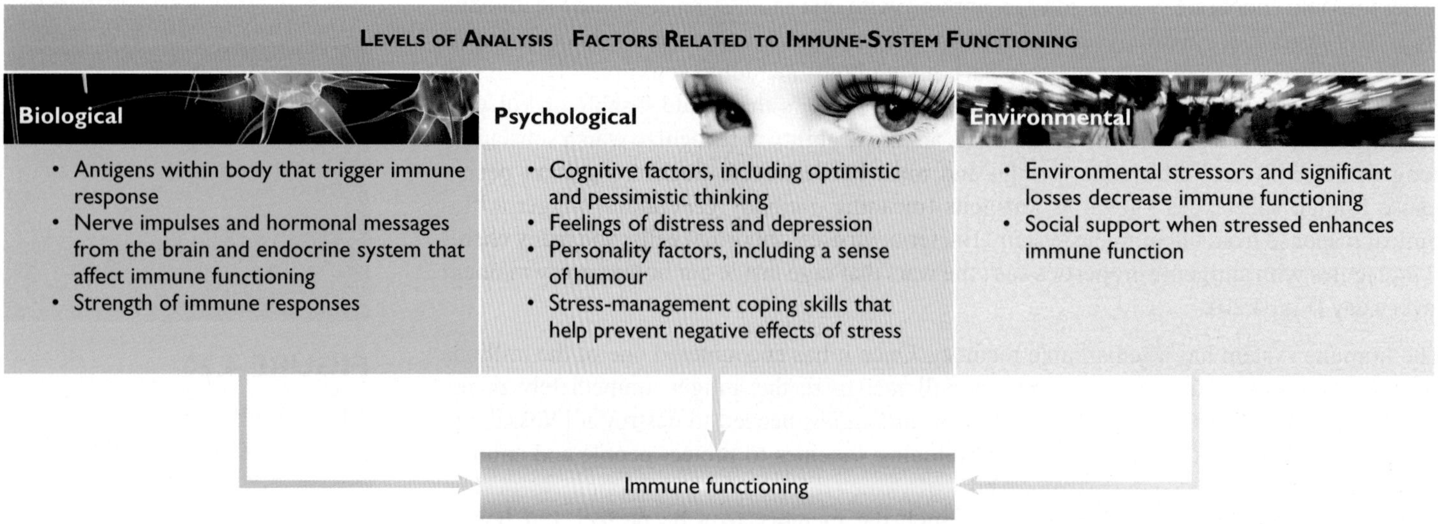

IN REVIEW

- The nervous, endocrine and immune systems have extensive neural and chemical means of communication, and each is capable of affecting and being affected by the others.

- The endocrine system secretes hormones into the bloodstream. These chemical messengers affect many body processes, including those associated with the central and autonomic nervous systems. Because of the adrenal glands' relation to functions of the nervous system, they are of particular interest to psychologists. Hormonal effects in the womb may produce brain differences in males and females that influence sex differences in certain psychological functions.

- The immune system interacts extensively with the central and autonomic nervous systems and with the endocrine system. As a behaving entity, the immune system has the capacity to sense, interpret and respond to specific forms of stimulation.

KEY TERMS AND CONCEPTS

Each term has been boldfaced and defined in the chapter on the page indicated in parentheses.

absolute refractory period (p. 125)

acetylcholine (Ach) (p. 130)

action potential (p. 125)

adrenal glands (p. 161)

agonist (p. 132)

all-or-none law (p. 128)

amygdala (p. 145)

antagonist (p. 132)

antigens (p. 161)

aphasia (p. 153)

association cortex (p. 149)

autonomic nervous system (p. 135)

axon (p. 125)

brain stem (p. 143)

Broca's area (p. 149)

central nervous system (p. 136)

cerebellum (p. 143)

cerebral cortex (p. 146)

cerebrum (p. 144)

computerized axial tomography (CT, or CAT) scans (p. 138)

corpus callosum (p. 150)

dendrites (p. 125)

electroencephalograph (EEG; p. 138)

endocrine system (p. 160)

forebrain (p. 144)

functional MRI (fMRI) (p. 140)

graded potentials (p. 128)

hindbrain (p. 143)

hippocampus (p. 145)

homeostasis (p. 136)

hormones (p. 160)

hypothalamus (p. 145)

interneurons (p. 134)

lateralization (p. 150)

limbic system (p. 145)

magnetic resonance imaging (MRI) (p. 138)

medulla (p. 143)

midbrain (p. 144)

motor cortex (p. 147)

motor neurons (p. 134)

myelin sheath (p. 128)

neural plasticity (p. 156)

neural stem cells (p. 158)

neurogenesis (p. 157)

neuromodulators (p. 131)

neurons (p. 125)

neurotransmitters (p. 129)

parasympathetic nervous system (p. 135)

peripheral nervous system (p. 134)

pons (p. 143)

positron-emission tomography (PET) scans (p. 139)

prefrontal cortex (p. 150)

psychoactive drugs (p. 132)

receptor sites (p. 129)

resting potential (p. 125)

reticular formation (p. 144)

re-uptake (p. 130)

sensory neurons (p. 134)

somatic nervous system (p. 134)

somatic sensory cortex (p. 148)

sympathetic nervous system (p. 135)

synaptic space (p. 128)

synaptic vesicles (p. 129)

thalamus (p. 144)

Wernicke's area (p. 149)

WHAT DO YOU THINK?

TWO MINDS IN ONE BRAIN? (p. 155)

Let us consider the second question first. How is it that the split-brain patients could function in everyday life? Would not two independent minds get in the way of one another? It appears that in daily life, the split-brain patients could function adequately because they had learned to compensate for their disconnected hemispheres. For example, they could scan the visual environment so that input from both the left and right visual fields got into both hemispheres. Where personal identity was concerned, the linguistic left hemisphere seemed to connect present and future with the past in a manner that prevented two different personalities from emerging and tripping over one another. Some 'psychologists' have suggested that what we call the conscious self resides in the left hemisphere, because consciousness is based on our ability to verbalize about the past and present (Ornstein, 1997). The exotic 'split-mind' phenomena shown in Sperry's laboratory emerged because patients with a rare biological feature were tested under experimental conditions that were specifically designed to isolate the functions of the two hemispheres. Nonetheless, the results of split-brain research were so dramatic that they led some people (and even some scientists) to promote a conception of brain functions as being highly localized and restricted to one hemisphere or the other. Even today, we hear about education programmes directed at developing the 'untapped potentials of the right brain'. Certainly, there is some degree of localization of brain functions, but a far more important principle is that, in the normal brain, most functions involve many areas (and both hemispheres) of the brain working together. The brain is an exquisitely integrated system, not a collection of isolated functions.

CHAPTER FIVE

SENSATION AND PERCEPTION

CHAPTER OUTLINE

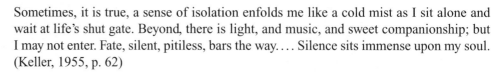

All our knowledge has its origins in our perceptions.

LEONARDO DA VINCI

Sometimes, it is true, a sense of isolation enfolds me like a cold mist as I sit alone and wait at life's shut gate. Beyond, there is light, and music, and sweet companionship; but I may not enter. Fate, silent, pitiless, bars the way.... Silence sits immense upon my soul. (Keller, 1955, p. 62)

So wrote Helen Keller, deprived of both vision and hearing by an acute illness she suffered at the age of 19 months (Fig. 5.1). For those of us who enjoy and take for granted the use of these senses, it is hard to imagine what it would be like to sink into a dark and silent universe, cut off from all sight and sound. Helen Keller worked closely with her teacher, Anne Sullivan, who tried day after day to communicate with her by tapping signs onto the little girl's palm. One day, Anne tapped *water* onto Helen's palm as she placed the child's hand under the gushing spout of a pump. Communication was at last possible.

That living word awakened my soul, gave it light, hope, joy, set it free! That was because I saw everything with a strange new sight that had come to me.... It would have been difficult to find a happier child than I was. (p. 103)

FIGURE 5.1

Helen Keller (*left*) 'hears' her teacher, Anne Sullivan, by reading Sullivan's lips with her fingers.

synaesthesia
literally, 'mixing of the senses'

Helen Keller went on to write her celebrated book, *The Story of My Life* (1955). She became an inspirational advocate for people with disabilities.

Nature gives us a marvellous set of sensory contacts with our world. If our sense organs are not defective, we experience light waves as brightness and colours, air vibrations as sounds, chemical substances as odours or tastes, and so on. However, such is not the case for people with a rare condition called **synaesthesia**, which means, quite literally, 'mixing of the senses' (Cytowic, 2002; Harrison and Baron-Cohen, 1997). Individuals with synaesthesia may experience sounds as colours, or tastes as touch sensations of different shapes.

Russian psychologist A.R. Luria (1968) studied a highly successful writer and musician whose life was a perpetual stream of mixed-up sensations. On one occasion Luria asked him to report on his experiences while listening to electronically generated musical tones. In response to a medium-pitched tone, the man experienced a brown strip with red edges, together with a sweet and sour flavour. A very high-pitched tone evoked the following sensation: 'It looks something like a fireworks tinged with a pink-red hue. The strip of colour feels rough and unpleasant, and it has an ugly taste – rather like that of a briny pickle.... You could hurt your hand on this.' Mixed sensations like these frequently occurred in the man's daily life, and they were sometimes disconcerting. On one occasion, the man asked an ice-cream vendor what flavours she sold. 'But she answered in such a tone that a whole pile of coals, of black cinders, came bursting out of her mouth, and I couldn't bring myself to buy any ice cream after she answered that way.'

Sensory-impaired people like Helen Keller and those who are not impaired, but experience synaesthesia, provide glimpses into different aspects of how we sense and understand our world. These processes, previewed in Figure 5.2, begin when specific types of stimuli activate specialized sensory receptors. Whether the stimulus is light, sound waves, a chemical molecule or pressure, your sensory receptors must translate the information into nerve impulses. Once this translation occurs, specialized neurons break down and analyse the specific features of the stimulus. At the next stage, these numerous stimulus features are reconstructed into a neural representation that is then compared with previously stored information, such as our knowledge of how particular objects look, smell or feel. This matching of a new stimulus with our internal store of knowledge allows us to recognize the stimulus and give it meaning. We then consciously experience a perception.

Helen Keller could not detect light waves or sound waves, the stimuli for sight and hearing. But for her, the sense of touch helped make up for this deficit, giving her a substitute window to her world. In contrast, for synesthetes something goes wrong at the level of either feature detection or the recombining of the elements of a stimulus so that light waves might give rise to an experience of a sound or texture (Cytowic, 2002).

In some ways, sensation and perception blend together so completely that they are difficult to separate, for the stimulation we receive through our sense organs is quickly organized and transformed into the experiences that we refer to as perceptions. There is, however, a distinction in psychology. **Sensation** is the stimulus detection process by which our sense organs respond to and translate environmental stimuli into nerve impulses that are sent to the brain. **Perception** involves making 'sense' of what our senses tell us. It is the active process of organizing this stimulus input and giving it meaning (Goldstein, 2007; Pashler and Yantis, 2002).

Because perception is an active and creative process, the same sensory input may be perceived in different ways at different times. For example, read the two sets of symbols in Figure 5.3. The middle symbols in both sets are exactly the same, and they sent identical input to your brain, but you probably perceived them differently. Your interpretation, or perception, of the characters was influenced by their context – that is, by the characters that preceded and followed them and by your learned expectation of what normally follows the letter A and the number 12. This is a simple illustration of how perception takes us a step beyond sensation.

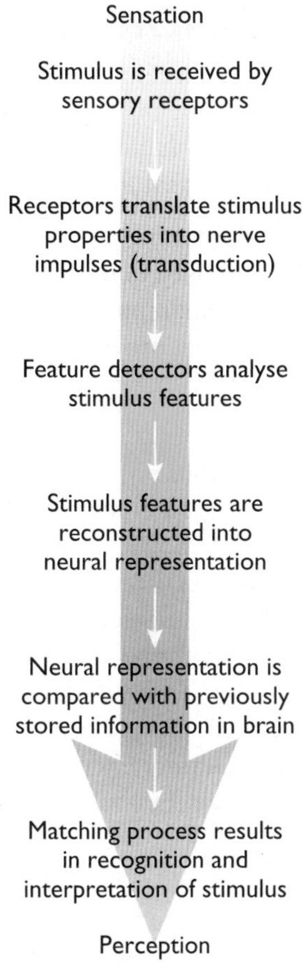

Sensation

Stimulus is received by sensory receptors

Receptors translate stimulus properties into nerve impulses (transduction)

Feature detectors analyse stimulus features

Stimulus features are reconstructed into neural representation

Neural representation is compared with previously stored information in brain

Matching process results in recognition and interpretation of stimulus

Perception

FIGURE 5.2

Sensation becomes perception.

Sensory and perceptual processes proceed from the reception and translation of physical stimuli into nerve impulses. The brain then receives the nerve impulses, organizes and confers meaning on them, and constructs a perceptual experience.

sensation

the stimulus detection process by which our sense organs respond to and translate environmental stimuli into nerve impulses that are sent to the brain

perception

making 'sense' of what our senses tell us. It is the active process of organizing this stimulus input and giving it meaning

ABC
12 13 14

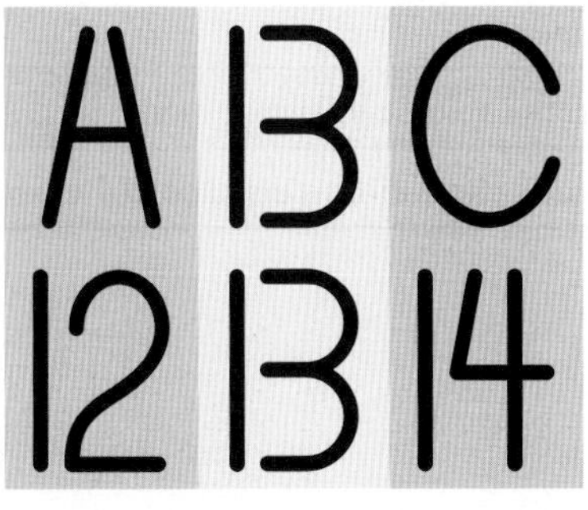

FIGURE 5.3

Context and perception.

Quickly read these two lines of symbols out loud. Your perception of the middle symbol in each line is influenced by the symbols that surround it.

SENSORY PROCESSES

Your brain cannot 'understand' light waves, sound waves or the other types of stimuli that make up the language of the environment. Certain neurons have developed into specialized sensory receptors that can transform and translate these energy forms into the code language of nerve impulses that the brain can understand and work with.

As a starting point, we might ask how many senses there are. If you think about it, you might be surprised to reach the conclusion that there appear to be more than the five classical senses: vision, audition (hearing), gustation (taste), olfaction (smell) and touch. For example, there are senses that provide information about balance and body position. Also, the sense of touch can be subdivided into separate senses of pressure, pain and temperature. Receptors deep within the brain monitor the chemical composition of our blood.

Like those of other organisms, human sensory systems are designed to extract from the environment the information that we need to function and survive. Although our survival does not depend on having eyes like owls, noses like bloodhounds or ears as sensitive as cats', we do have specialized sensors that can detect many different kinds of stimuli with considerable sensitivity. The scientific area of **psychophysics**, which studies the relationship between the physical characteristics of stimuli and sensory capabilities, is concerned with *two* kinds of sensitivity. The first concerns the absolute limits of sensitivity. For example, the dimmest light, the faintest sound or the weakest salt solution that humans can detect. The second kind of sensitivity has to do with differences between stimuli. The smallest difference between two tones that we can detect, or the tiniest difference between two shades of grey.

STIMULUS DETECTION: THE ABSOLUTE THRESHOLD

How intense must a stimulus be before we can detect its presence? Researchers answer this question by systematically presenting stimuli of varying intensities to people and asking whether they can detect them. Researchers designate the **absolute threshold** as the lowest intensity at which a stimulus can be detected 50 per cent of the time. Thus the lower the absolute threshold, the greater the sensitivity. From studies of absolute thresholds, we can estimate the general limits of human sensitivity for the five major senses. Some examples are presented in Table 5.1. As you can see, many of our absolute thresholds are surprisingly low. Yet some other species have sensitivities that far surpass those of humans. For example, a female silkworm moth who is ready to mate needs to release only a billionth of an ounce of an attractant chemical molecule per second to attract every male silkworm moth within a mile (1.6 km) radius.

TABLE 5.1 SOME APPROXIMATE ABSOLUTE THRESHOLDS FOR HUMANS

Sensory modality	Absolute threshold
Vision	Candle flame seen at 50 kilometres on a clear, dark night
Hearing	Tick of a watch under quiet conditions at 20 feet (6 metres)
Taste	1 teaspoon of sugar in 7.5 litres of water
Smell	1 drop of perfume diffused into the entire volume of a large room
Touch	Wing of a fly or bee falling on a person's cheek from a distance of 1 centimetre

SOURCE: based on Galanter, 1962.

Focus 5.1

Describe the six stages in the sensory processing and perception of information. Differentiate between sensation and perception.

psychophysics

studies the relationship between the physical characteristics of stimuli and sensory capabilities

In-Psych

What do researchers know about how perception occurs? Watch the 'Sensory Processes and Brain Integration' video in Chapter 5 of the In-Psych programme online.

absolute threshold

the lowest intensity at which a stimulus can be detected 50 per cent of the time

Focus 5.2

Define the absolute threshold from traditional and signal detection perspectives.

SIGNAL DETECTION THEORY

Perhaps you can remember lying in bed as a child, in the dark after seeing a frightening film or reading a story that gave you a scare. You may recall straining your ears in an attempt to detect any unusual sound that might signal the presence of a monster or intruder in the house. You may even have detected the occasional faint and ominous sound that would have probably gone unnoticed had you just watched a comedy or read one of your school books.

At one time scientists thought that although some people have greater sensory acuity than others, each person has a more or less fixed level of sensitivity for each sense. But psychologists who study stimulus detection found that an individual's apparent sensitivity can fluctuate quite a bit. The concept of a fixed absolute threshold is inaccurate because there is no single point on the intensity scale that separates non detection from detection of a stimulus. There is instead a range of uncertainty, and people set their own **decision criterion**, a standard of how certain they must be that a stimulus is present before they will say they detect it. The decision criterion can also change from time to time, depending on such factors as fatigue, expectation (e.g., having watched a horror movie), and the potential significance of the stimulus. **Signal detection theory** (Green and Swets, 1974) is concerned with the factors that influence sensory judgements.

In a typical signal-detection experiment, participants are told that after a warning light appears, a barely perceptible tone may or may not be presented. Their task is to tell the experimenter whether or not they hear the tone. Under these conditions, there are four possible outcomes, as shown in Figure 5.4. When the tone is in fact presented, the participant may say 'yes' (a hit) or 'no' (a miss). When no tone is presented, the participant may also say 'yes' (a false alarm) or 'no' (a correct rejection).

At low stimulus intensities, both the participant's and the situation's characteristics influence the decision criterion (Methot and Huitema, 1998; Pitz and Sachs, 1984. Bold participants who frequently say 'yes' have more hits, but they also have more false alarms than do conservative participants. Researchers can influence participants to become bolder or more conservative by manipulating the rewards and costs for giving correct or incorrect responses. Increasing the rewards for hits or the costs for misses results in lower detection thresholds (more 'yes' responses at low intensities). Thus a Navy radar operator may be more likely to notice a faint blip on the radar screen during a wartime mission – when a miss could have disastrous consequences – than during a peacetime voyage. Conversely, like physicians who will not perform a risky medical procedure without strong evidence to support their diagnosis, participants become more conservative in their 'yes' responses as costs for false alarms are increased, resulting in higher detection thresholds (Irwin and McCarthy, 1998). Signal-detection research shows us that perception is, in part, a decision.

SUBLIMINAL STIMULI: CAN THEY AFFECT BEHAVIOUR?

A **subliminal stimulus** is one that is so weak or brief that although it is received by the senses, it cannot be perceived consciously. There is little question that subliminal stimuli can register in the nervous system (Kihlstrom, 1999; MacLeod, 1998), but can such stimuli affect attitudes and behaviour without our knowing it? The answer appears to be yes – to a limited extent.

In the late 1950s, James Vicary, a public relations executive, arranged to have subliminal messages flashed on a cinema screen during a movie. The messages urged the audience to drink Coca-Cola and eat popcorn. Vicary's claim that the subliminal messages increased popcorn sales by 50 per cent and soft drink sales by 18 per cent aroused a public furore. Consumers and scientists feared the possible abuse of subliminal messages to covertly influence the buying habits of consumers; they were concerned such messages might be used for mind-control and brainwashing purposes.

decision criterion

a standard of how certain they must be that a stimulus is present before they will say they detect it

signal detection theory

is concerned with the factors that influence sensory judgements

	Stimulus	
	Present	Absent
Participant's response 'Yes'	Hit	False alarm
'No'	Miss	Correct rejection

FIGURE 5.4

Signal-detection research.

This matrix shows the four possible outcomes in a signal-detection trial in which participants decide whether a stimulus has been presented or not. The percentages of responses that fall within each category can be affected by both characteristics of the participants and the nature of the situation.

subliminal stimulus

is so weak or brief that although it is received by the senses, it cannot be perceived consciously

The outcries were, in large part, false alarms. Several attempts to reproduce Vicary's results under controlled conditions failed, and many other studies conducted in laboratory settings, on television and radio, and in cinemas indicated that there is little reason to be concerned about significant or widespread control of consumer behaviour through subliminal stimulation (Dixon, 1981; Drukin, 1998). Years later, Vicary admitted that his study was a hoax designed to revive his floundering advertising agency. Nonetheless, his false report stimulated a great deal of useful research on the power of subliminal stimuli to influence behaviour. Where consumer behaviour is concerned, the conclusion is that persuasive stimuli above the perceptual threshold are far more influential than subliminal attempts to sneak into our subconscious mind.

Although subliminal stimuli cannot control consumer behaviour, research suggests that such stimuli do affect more subtle phenomena, such as perceptions and attitudes (Greenwald and Banaji, 1995). In one study, college students who were exposed to subliminal presentations of aggressively toned words like 'hit' and 'attack' later judged ambiguous behaviours of others as more aggressive. They also were more likely to behave aggressively than were participants who had been exposed to subliminal non-aggressive words (Todorov and Bargh, 2002). Although the original fears about brainwashing with subliminal stimuli may be unfounded, there is little doubt that subliminal stimuli can have subtle effects on attitudes, judgements and behaviour. Mayer and Merkelbach (1999) have further investigated the use of subliminal information in unconscious processes and anxiety, so it seems that even though we may not consciously perceive a stimulus because it is presented below our threshold (*sub-threshold*) we may still be acting on it somehow, and the implications for this are potentially very significant. Begg et al. (1993) have investigated one of the most famous and intriguing examples of supposed subliminal messages. In their study, participants were asked to indicate whether a message played backwards matched a comparison message played forwards. People could do this, but they could not, if played in isolation, identify any details of the reversed message. The idea for the experiment came from the assertion that some rock bands had hidden messages in their music and that these reversed messages were being processed by the unsuspecting listeners. The controversy was that the alleged messages were often satanic, or said to encourage suicide. Begg et al. showed clearly that even though people may expect a certain speech pattern, and therefore find the reversed speech pattern more familiar, the identity of the message was unavailable to the listeners. Some people believe that subliminal information can also be a means to self-improvement. The following 'Beneath the surface' feature discusses this issue.

Focus 5.3

How do subliminal stimuli affect consumer behaviour, attitudes and self-improvement outcomes?

BENEATH THE SURFACE

ARE SUBLIMINAL SELF-HELP PRODUCTS EFFECTIVE?

Consumers spend millions on subliminal CDs that promise to help them lose weight, stop smoking, conquer fears, feel better about themselves, or achieve other self-improvement goals. But do these aids work?

In fact, many people believe they do. Why are these products effective? Do they programme the subconscious mind to make changes? Or is it possible that people make changes because they believe in the tapes? Can you think of a way to test these two possibilities?

Let us suppose you have a research group of people who want to change in one of two ways. Some want to improve their memory and others want to increase their self-esteem. You then pre-test them on both a memory task and a psychological test measuring self-esteem so that you can determine later whether they have improved. You are now ready for your critical experiment.

You have purchased two commercial subliminal CDs, one for memory improvement, the other to increase self-esteem. Each person who comes for memory improvement is given a CD labelled 'memory improvement' and told to use it once a day for a month. What they will not know is that half of the memory-improvement participants will actually be given the self-esteem-improvement recording. Similarly, the self-esteem seekers are each given a CD labelled 'self-esteem improvement', but half of them will actually receive the recording containing subliminal memory-improvement messages. This experimental design lets you control for participants' expectations.

A month later you bring the people back and retest them on the memory and self-esteem measures. Theoretically, if change is being produced by the subliminal messages, people should improve only in the area addressed by the tape they actually heard. What do you expect to find?

Social psychologist Anthony Greenwald and co-workers (1991) conducted an experiment exactly like this. They found that people generally improved in both self-esteem and memory, regardless of which recording they heard. More significantly, self-esteem improvement was actually greater for those who listened to the memory-improvement tape, and those who listened to the self-esteem tape improved more in memory than they did in self-esteem. Thus the power of an expectancy, or a placebo effect, explains the results better than does the power of subliminal programming of the unconscious mind. And the bottom line is that while subliminal products may appeal to some people as a relatively effortless way to bring about change, they remain unproven scientifically, especially in comparison with other behaviour-change methods. Personally, we have much greater faith in the effectiveness of the techniques presented in this book's 'Applying psychological science' features, because they are backed by scientific evidence.

THE DIFFERENCE THRESHOLD

Distinguishing between stimuli can sometimes be as important as detecting stimuli in the first place. When we try to match the colours of paints or clothing, small stimulus differences can be very important. Likewise, a slight variation in taste might signal that food is tainted or spoiled. Professional wine tasters and piano tuners make their living by being able to make subtle discriminations.

The **difference threshold** is defined as the smallest difference between two stimuli that people can perceive 50 per cent of the time. The difference threshold is sometimes called the *just noticeable difference (jnd)*. German physiologist and arguably the father of psychophysics Ernst Weber discovered in the 1830s that there is some degree of lawfulness in the range of sensitivities within our sensory systems. **Weber's law** states that the difference threshold, or jnd, is directly proportional to the magnitude of the stimulus with which the comparison is being made and can be expressed as a *Weber fraction*. For example, the jnd value for weights is a Weber fraction of approximately 1/50 (Teghtsoonian, 1971). This means that if you lift a weight of 50 grams, a comparison weight must be at least 51 grams in order for you to be able to judge it as heavier. If the weight were 500 grams, a second weight would have to be at least 510 grams (i.e., 1/50 = 10g/500g) for you to discriminate between them.

Although Weber's law breaks down at extremely high and low intensities of stimulation, it holds up reasonably well within the most frequently encountered range, thereby providing a useful barometer of our abilities to discern differences in the various sensory modalities. Later, Gustav Theodor Fechner (1801–87) used Weber's ideas to measure just noticeable differences in perception. That is, he identified how much brighter something has to be to be noticeable, or how much louder it has to be to be identified as such. This pioneering work marked Europe as the birthplace of experimental psychology. Table 5.2 lists Weber fractions for the various senses. The

Focus 5.4

What is the difference threshold? What is Weber's law, and why is it important?

difference threshold

defined as the smallest difference between two stimuli that people can perceive 50 per cent of the time

Weber's law

states that the difference threshold, or jnd, is directly proportional to the magnitude of the stimulus with which the comparison is being made

smaller the fraction, the greater the sensitivity to differences. As highly visual creatures, humans show greater sensitivity in their visual sense than they do in, for example, their sense of smell. Undoubtedly many creatures who depend on their sense of smell to track their prey would show quite a different order of sensitivity. Weber fractions also show that humans are highly sensitive to differences in the pitch of sounds but far less sensitive to loudness differences.

More recent research has been produced by Mather and Smith (2002) at Sussex University. They showed that the perception of blurred edges depends on how the edges were defined. They used Weber's fractions to show (among other things) how much easier a blurred edge between a black and white surface was to see than a blurred edge between two differently textured surfaces. This nineteenth-century research is still in active use in today's labs.

SENSORY ADAPTATION

From a survival perspective, it is important to know when a change in the environment requires your attention. If you were relaxing outdoors, you would want to be aware of the buzz of an approaching wasp. Because changes in our environment are often important, sensory systems are finely attuned to changes in stimulation (Rensink, 2002). Sensory neurons are engineered to respond to a constant stimulus by decreasing their activity, and the diminishing sensitivity to an unchanging stimulus is called **sensory adaptation**.

Adaptation is a part of everyday experience. After a while, monotonous background sounds go largely unnoticed. Many of us are very familiar with sitting at a personal computer for long periods but it's only when you turn the machine off that you realize quite how noisy it was. We become less aware of the feel of a wristwatch against the skin the longer we wear it. When you dive into a swimming pool, the water may feel cold at first because your body's sensors respond to the change in temperature. Over time, however, you become used to the water temperature.

Adaptation occurs in all sensory modalities, including vision. Indeed, were it not for tiny involuntary eye movements that keep images moving about the retina, stationary objects would simply fade from sight if we stared at them. In an ingenious demonstration of this type of adaptation, R.M. Pritchard (1961) attached a tiny projector to a contact lens worn by each participant (Fig. 5.5a). This procedure guaranteed that visual images presented through the projector would maintain a constant position on the retina, even when the eye moved. When a stabilized image was projected through the lens onto the retina, participants reported that the image appeared in its entirety for a time and then began to vanish and reappear as parts of the original stimulus (Fig. 5.5b). We also produce

sensory adaptation

the diminishing sensitivity to an unchanging stimulus

TABLE 5.2 WEBER FRACTIONS FOR VARIOUS SENSORY MODALITIES

Sensory modality	Weber fraction
Audition (tonal pitch)	1/333
Vision (brightness, white light)	1/60
Kinaesthesis (lifted weights)	1/50
Pain (heat produced)	1/30
Audition (loudness)	1/20
Touch (pressure applied to skin)	1/7
Smell (India rubber)	1/4
Taste (salt concentration)	1/3

SOURCE: Based on Teghtsoonian, 1971.

three different types of purposive eye movements. *Saccades* are eye movements that occur all the time as we experience the visual field about us. *Saccades* may be purposive, where you shift vision quickly from one point to another, as you do when you skip from one part of a page to the next when reading, or from one place on a painting to the next when looking at art. *Pursuit movements* are tracking movements. We use them when following an object such as a runner or a car as they move across our field of vision. *Conjugate movements* are those that allow us to keep the same image on the appropriate parts of the retina in each eye. If you hold a pencil up in front of you, imagine where on each retina the image is. Now, move the pencil towards you and away from you. The movements your eyes make to keep focus on the pencil, and to keep its image on corresponding parts of each retina are conjugate movements.

Although sensory adaptation may reduce our overall sensitivity, it is adaptive, for it frees our senses from the constant and the mundane, allowing them to pick up informative changes in the environment that could be important to our well-being or survival.

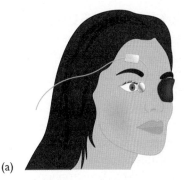

(a)

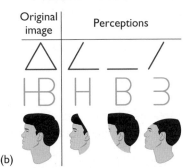

(b)

FIGURE 5.5

Demonstrating visual adaptation.

(a) To create a stabilised retinal image, a person wears a contact lens with a tiny projector attached. Despite tiny eye movements, images are cast on the same region of the retina. (b) Under these conditions, the stabilized image is clear at first and then begins to fade and reappear in meaningful segments as the receptors fatigue and recover.
SOURCE: adapted from Pritchard, 1961.

IN REVIEW

- Sensation is the process by which our sense organs receive and transmit information, whereas perception involves the brain's processing and interpretation of the information.

- Psychophysics is the scientific study of how the physical properties of stimuli are related to sensory experiences. Sensory sensitivity is concerned in part with the limits of stimulus detectability (absolute threshold) and the ability to discriminate between stimuli (difference threshold). The absolute threshold is the intensity at which a stimulus is detected 50 per cent of the time. Signal detection theory is concerned with factors that influence decisions about whether or not a stimulus is present.

- Research indicates that subliminal stimuli, which are not consciously perceived, can influence perceptions and behaviour in subtle ways, but not strongly enough to justify concerns about the subconscious control of behaviour through subliminal messages. The use of subliminal self-help materials sometimes results in positive behaviour changes that may be a product of expectancy factors rather than the subliminal messages themselves.

- The difference threshold, or just noticeable difference (jnd), is the amount by which two stimuli must differ for them to be perceived as different 50 per cent of the time. Studies of the jnd led to Weber's law, which states that the jnd is proportional to the intensity of the original stimulus and is constant within a given sense modality.

- Sensory systems are particularly responsive to changes in stimulation, and adaptation occurs in response to unchanging stimuli.

THE SENSORY SYSTEMS

The particular stimuli to which different animals are sensitive vary considerably. The sensory equipment of any species is an adaptation to the environment in which it lives. Many species have senses that humans lack altogether. Carrier pigeons, for example, use the Earth's magnetic field to find their destination on cloudy nights when they cannot navigate by the stars. Sharks sense electric currents leaking through the skins of fish hiding in undersea crevices, and rattle-snakes find their prey by detecting infrared radiation given off by small rodents. Whatever the source of stimulation, its energy must be converted into nerve impulses and transmitted to the appropriate parts of the brain. Transduction refers to the changing of one type of information into another. A microphone, for instance, transduces movement at a sensitive membrane, into electricity, which can be understood by the amplifier. In this context, **Transduction** is the process whereby the characteristics of a stimulus are converted into nerve impulses. We now consider the range of stimuli to which humans and other mammals are attuned and the manner in which the various sense organs carry out the transduction process.

> **transduction**
>
> **the process whereby the characteristics of a stimulus are converted into nerve impulses**

VISION

Light travels in waves of electromagnetic energy. These waves are measured in nanometres (nm), or one billionth of a metre. In addition to the tiny portion of light waves that humans can perceive, the electromagnetic spectrum encompasses X-rays, television and radio signals, and infrared and ultraviolet rays (Fig. 5.6). Bees are able to see ultraviolet light, and rattlesnakes, as mentioned above, can detect infrared energy. Our visual system is sensitive only to wavelengths extending from about 700 nanometres (red) down to about 400 nanometres (blue-violet). '**R**ichard **O**f **Y**ork **G**ave **B**attle **I**n **V**ain' is a favourite phrase used to remember the order, as is '**R**owntrees **O**f **Y**ork **G**ave **B**est **I**n **V**alue' – Red, Orange, Yellow, Green, Blue, Indigo, Violet.

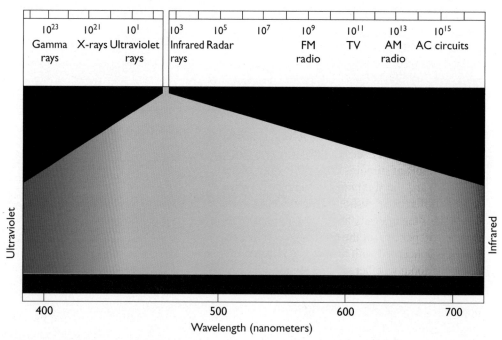

FIGURE 5.6

Light energy.

Of the full spectrum of electromagnetic radiation, only the narrow band between 400 and 700 nanometres (nm) is visible to the human eye. One nanometre equals one 1 000 000 000th of a metre.

The Human Eye

Light waves enter the eye through the *cornea*, a transparent protective structure at the front of the eye (Fig. 5.7). Behind the cornea is the *pupil*, an adjustable opening that can dilate (get wider) or constrict to control the amount of light that enters the eye. The pupil's size is controlled by muscles in the coloured *iris* that surrounds the pupil. Low levels of illumination cause the pupil to dilate, letting more light into the eye to improve optical clarity; bright light makes the pupil constrict.

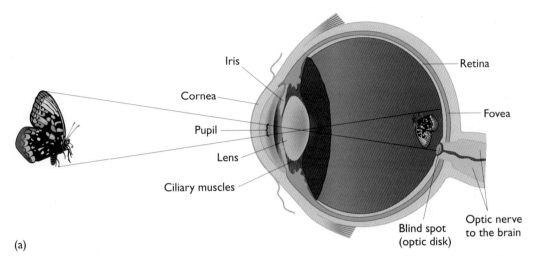

(a)

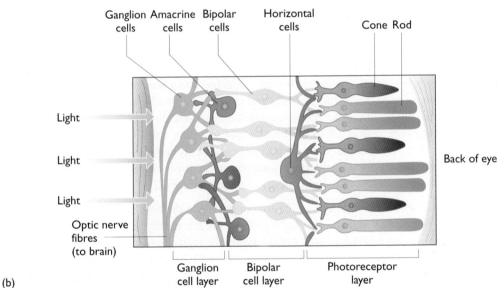

(b)

FIGURE 5.7

The human eye.

(a) The iris controls the size of the pupil. The ciliary muscles control the shape of the lens. The image entering the eye is reversed by the lens and cast on the retina, which contains the rod and cone photoreceptor cells. The optic disk, where the optic nerve exits the eye, has no receptors and produces a blind spot, as demonstrated in Figure 5.8. (b) Photoreceptors in the retina, the rods and cones, synapse with bipolar cells, which in turn synapse with ganglion cells whose axons form the optic nerve. The horizontal and amacrine cells allow sideways integration of retinal activity across areas of the retina.

Behind the pupil is the **lens**, an elastic structure that becomes thinner to focus on distant objects and thicker to focus on nearby objects. Just as the lens of a camera focuses an image on a photosensitive material (film), so the lens of the eye focuses the visual image on the **retina**, a multilayered light-sensitive tissue at the rear of the fluid-filled eyeball. As seen in Figure 5.7a, the lens reverses the image from right to left and top to bottom when it is projected upon the retina, but the brain reverses the visual input into the image that we perceive.

The ability to see clearly depends in part on the lens's ability to focus the image directly onto the retina, and is known as *accommodation*. If you have good vision for nearby objects but have difficulty seeing faraway objects, you probably suffer from *myopia* (nearsightedness). In nearsighted people, the lens focuses the visual image in front of the retina (or too near the lens), resulting in a blurred image for faraway objects. This condition generally occurs because the eyeball is longer (front to back) than normal. In contrast, some people have excellent distance vision but have difficulty seeing close-up objects clearly. *Hyperopia* (farsightedness) occurs when the lens does not thicken enough and the image is therefore focused on a point behind the retina (or too far from the lens). Glasses and contact lenses are designed to correct for the natural lens's inability to focus the visual image directly onto the retina.

lens

an elastic structure that becomes thinner to focus on distant objects and thicker to focus on nearby objects

retina

multilayered light-sensitive tissue at the rear of the fluid-filled eyeball

Focus 5.5

How does the lens affect visual acuity, and how does its dysfunction cause myopia and hyperopia?

Photoreceptors: The Rods and Cones

rods

function best in dim light, are primarily black-and-white brightness receptors

cones

colour receptors, function best in bright illumination

fovea

small area in the centre of the retina that contains no rods but many densely packed cones

optic nerve

ganglion cells, whose axons are collected into a bundle to form the optic nerve

Focus 5.6

How are the rods and cones distributed in the retina, and how do they contribute to brightness perception, colour vision, and visual acuity?

visual acuity

ability to see fine detail

FIGURE 5.8

Find your blind spot.

Close your left eye and, from a distance of about 12 inches (30 cm), focus steadily on the dot with your right eye as you slowly move the book toward your face. At some point the image of the X will cross your optic disk (blind spot) and disappear. It will reappear after it crosses the blind spot. Note how the checkerboard remains wholly visible even though part of it falls on the blind spot. Your perceptual system fills in the missing information.

The retina, with its specialized sensory neurons, can be regarded as an extension of the brain (Bullier, 2002). It contains two types of light-sensitive receptor cells, called *rods and cones* because of their shapes (see Fig. 5.7b). There are about 120 million rods and 6 million cones in the human eye.

The **rods**, which function best in dim light, are primarily black-and-white brightness receptors. They are about 500 times more sensitive to light than are the cones, but they do not give rise to colour sensations. The retinas of some nocturnal creatures, such as owls, contain only rods, giving them exceptional vision in very dim light but no colour vision (Dossenbach and Dossenbach, 1998). The **cones**, which are colour receptors, function best in bright illumination. Some creatures that are active only during the day, such as pigeons and chipmunks, have only cones in their retinas, so they see the world in living colour but have very poor night vision (Dossenbach and Dossenbach, 1998). Animals that are active both day and night, as humans are, have a mixture of rods and cones. In humans, rods are found throughout the retina except in the **fovea**, a small area in the centre of the retina that contains no rods but many densely packed cones. Cones decrease in concentration the farther away they are from the centre of the retina, and the periphery of the retina contains mainly rods.

Rods and cones send their messages to the brain via two additional layers of cells. The rods and cones have synaptic connections with *bipolar cells*, which, in turn, synapse with a layer of about 1 million ganglion cells, whose axons are collected into a bundle to form the **optic nerve**. Thus input from more than 126 million rods and cones is eventually funnelled into only 1 million traffic lanes leading out of the retina towards higher visual centres. Figure 5.7b shows how the rods and cones are connected to the bipolar and ganglion cells. One interesting aspect of these connections is the fact that the rods and cones not only form the rear layer of the retina, but their light-sensitive ends actually point away from the direction of the entering light so that they receive only a fraction of the light energy that enters the eye.

The manner in which the rods and cones are connected to the bipolar cells accounts for both the greater importance of rods in dim light and our greater ability to see fine detail in bright illumination, when the cones are most active. Typically, many rods are connected to the same bipolar cell. They can therefore combine, or funnel, their individual electrical messages to the bipolar cell, where the additive effect of the many signals may be enough to fire it. That is why we can more easily detect a faint stimulus, such as a dim star, if we look slightly to one side so that its image falls not on the fovea but on the peripheral portion of the retina, where the rods are packed most densely.

Like the rods, the cones that lie in the periphery of the retina share bipolar cells. In the fovea, however, the densely packed cones each have their own dedicted link to a single bipolar cell. As a result, our **visual acuity**, or ability to see fine detail, is greatest when the visual image projects directly onto the fovea. Such focusing results in the firing of a large number of cones and their private-line bipolar cells. Some birds of prey, such as eagles and hawks, are have two foveas in each eye, contributing to a visual acuity that allows them to see small prey on the ground as they soar hundreds of feet above the earth (Tucker, 2000). The optic nerve formed by the axons of the ganglion cells exits through the back of the eye not far from the fovea, producing a blind spot where there are no photoreceptors. You can demonstrate the existence of your blind spot by following the directions in Figure 5.8. Ordinarily, we are unaware of the blind spot because our perceptual system fills in the missing part of the visual field (Rolls and Deco, 2002).

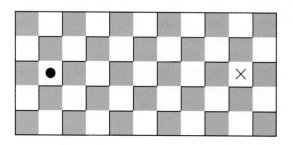

Visual Transduction: From Light Waves to Nerve Impulses

Rods and cones translate light waves into nerve impulses through the action of protein molecules called **photopigments** (Stryer, 1987; Wolken, 1995). The absorption of light by the photopigments produces a chemical reaction that changes the rate of neurotransmitter release at the receptor's synapse with the bipolar cells. The greater the change in transmitter release, the stronger the signal passed on to the bipolar cell and, in turn, to the ganglion cells whose axons form the optic nerve. If a stimulus triggers nerve responses at each of the three levels (rod or cone, bipolar cell and ganglion cell), the message is instantaneously sent to the visual relay station in the thalamus and from there to the visual cortex of the brain.

Brightness Vision and Dark Adaptation

As noted earlier, rods are far more sensitive than cones under conditions of low illumination. Nonetheless, the sensitivity of both the rods and the cones to light intensity depends in part on the wavelength of the light. Rods have a much greater sensitivity than cones throughout the colour spectrum except at the red end, where rods are relatively insensitive. Cones are most sensitive to low illumination in the greenish-yellow range of the spectrum. In the USA, these findings have prompted many city authorities to change the colour of their fire engines from the traditional red (to which rods are relatively insensitive) to a greenish yellow in order to increase the vehicles' visibility to both rods and cones in dim lighting.

Although the rods are by nature sensitive to low illumination, in certain circumstances they behave rather unexpectedly, and let us down. Perhaps you have had the embarrassing experience of entering a dark cinema on a sunny day, stumbling around in the darkness, and finally sitting down in someone's lap. Although one can meet interesting people this way, most of us prefer to stand in the rear of the cinema until our eyes adapt to the dimly lit interior.

Dark adaptation is the progressive improvement in brightness sensitivity that occurs over time under conditions of low illumination. After absorbing light, a photoreceptor is depleted of its pigment molecules for a short period of time. If the eye has been exposed to conditions of high illumination, such as bright sunlight, a substantial amount of photopigment will be depleted. During dark adaptation, the photopigment molecules are regenerated and the receptor's sensitivity slowly increases.

Vision researchers have plotted the course of dark adaptation as people move from conditions of bright light into darkness (Carpenter and Robson, 1999). By focusing light flashes of varying wavelengths and brightness on the fovea (which contains only cones) or on the periphery of the retina (where rods reside), they discovered the two-part curve shown in Figure 5.9. The first part of the curve is due to dark adaptation of the cones. As you can see, the cones gradually become sensitive to fainter lights as time passes, but after about 5 to 10 minutes in the dark, their sensitivity has reached its maximum. The rods, whose photopigments regenerate more slowly, do not reach their maximum sensitivity for about half an hour. It is estimated that after complete adaptation, rods are able to detect light intensities 1/10 000 as great as those that could be detected before dark adaptation began (Stryer, 1987).

photopigments
rods and cones translate light waves into nerve impulses through the action of protein molecules called photopigments

Focus 5.7
How does the transduction process occur in the photoreceptors of the eye?

Focus 5.8
What is the physiological basis for dark adaptation and for the two components of the dark adaptation curve?

dark adaptation
the progressive improvement in brightness sensitivity that occurs over time under conditions of low illumination

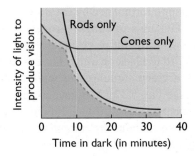

FIGURE 5.9

Adapting to the dark.

The course of dark adaptation is graphed over time. The curve has two parts, one for the cones and one for the rods. The cones adapt completely in about 10 minutes, whereas the rods continue to increase their sensitivity for another 20 minutes.

FIGURE 5.10

Working in red light keeps the rods in a state of dark adaptation because rods are quite insensitive to that wavelength. Therefore they retain high levels of photopigment and remain sensitive to low illumination.

During the Second World War, psychologists familiar with the process of dark adaptation provided a method for enhancing night vision in pilots who needed to take off at a moment's notice and see their targets under conditions of low illumination. Knowing that the rods are important in night vision and relatively insensitive to red wavelengths, they suggested that fighter pilots either wear goggles with red lenses or work in rooms lit only by red lights while waiting to be called for a mission. Because red light stimulates only the cones, the rods remain in a state of dark adaptation, ready for immediate service in the dark. That highly practical principle continues to be useful to this day (Fig. 5.10).

Colour Vision

We are blessed with a world rich in colour. The majesty of a glowing sunset, the rich blues and greens of our coasts and the brilliant colours of autumn are all visual delights. Human vision is finely attuned to colour; our difference thresholds for light wavelengths are so small that we are able to distinguish an estimated 7.5 million hue variations (Backhaus et al., 1998). Historically, two different theories of colour vision have tried to explain how this occurs.

The trichromatic theory   At the beginning of the nineteenth century it was discovered that any colour in the visible spectrum could be produced by some combination of the wavelengths that correspond to the colours blue, green and red in what is known as additive colour mixture (Fig. 5.11a). This fact was the basis for an important trichromatic (three-colour) theory of colour vision advanced by the physicist, Thomas Young, and the physiologist, Hermann von Helmholtz. According to the **Young–Helmholtz trichromatic theory**, there are three types of colour receptors in the retina. Although all cones can be stimulated by most wavelengths to varying degrees, individual cones are most sensitive to wavelengths that correspond to either blue, green or red (Fig. 5.12). Presumably, each of these receptor classes sends messages to the brain, based on the extent to which they are activated by the light energy's wavelength. The visual system then combines the signals to recreate the original hue. If all three cones are equally activated, pure white is perceived (see the centre of Fig. 5.11a).

Although the Young–Helmholtz theory was consistent with the laws of additive colour mixture, there are several facts that did not fit the theory. Take our perception of yellow, for example. According to the theory, yellow is produced by the activity of red and green receptors. Yet certain people with red–green colour blindness, who are unable to perceive either colour, are somehow able to experience yellow. A second phenomenon that posed problems for the trichromatic theory was the colour afterimage, in which an image in a different colour appears after a colour stimulus has been viewed steadily and then withdrawn. To experience an afterimage, follow the instructions for Figure 5.13. Trichromatic theory cannot account for what you will see.

Opponent-process theory   A second influential colour theory, formulated by Ewald Hering in 1870, also assumed that there are three types of cones. **Hering's opponent-process theory** proposed that each of the three cone types responds to two different wavelengths. One type responds to blue or yellow, another to red or green and a third to black or white. For example, a red–green cone responds with one chemical reaction to a green stimulus and with its other chemical reaction (opponent process) to a red stimulus (see Fig. 5.12). You have experienced one of the phenomena that support the existence of opponent processes if you did the exercise in Figure 5.13. The afterimage that you saw in the blank space contains the colours specified by opponent-process theory: the green portion of the flag appeared as red; the black, as white; and

Young–Helmholtz trichromatic theory

there are three types of colour receptors in the retina

Focus 5.9

Summarize the trichromatic, opponent-process and dual-process theories of colour vision. What evidence supports each theory?

Hering's opponent-process theory

each of the three cone types responds to two different wavelengths

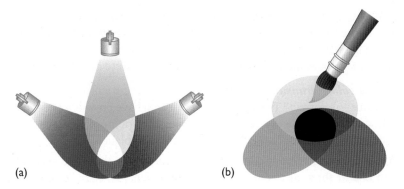

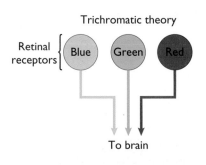

FIGURE 5.11

Two kinds of colour mixtures.

Additive and subtractive colour mixtures are different processes. (a) In additive colour mixture, a beam of light of a specific wavelength directed onto a white surface is perceived as the colour that corresponds to that wavelength on the visible spectrum. If beams of light that fall at certain points within the blue, green or red colour range are directed together onto the surface in the correct proportions, a combined, or additive, mixture of wavelengths will result, with the possibility of producing any colour in the visible spectrum (including white at the point where all three colours intersect). The Young–Helmholtz trichromatic theory of colour vision assumes that colour perception results from the additive mixture of impulses from cones that are sensitive to blue, green and red. (b) In subtractive colour mixture, mixing pigments or paints produces new colours by subtraction – that is, by removing (i.e., absorbing) other wavelengths. Paints absorb (subtract) colours different from themselves while reflecting their own colour. For example, blue paint mainly absorbs wavelengths that correspond to non-blue hues. Mixing blue paint with yellow paint (which absorbs wavelengths other than yellow) will produce a subtractive mixture that emits wavelengths between yellow and blue (i.e., green). Theoretically, certain wavelengths of the three primary colours of blue, yellow (not green, as in additive mixture) and red can produce the whole spectrum of colours by subtractive mixture. Thus in additive colour mixture, the primary colours are blue, green and red; in subtractive colour mixture they are blue, yellow and red.

FIGURE 5.12

The Young–Helmholz trichromatic theory and Hering's opponent process theory.

The Young–Helmholtz trichromatic theory proposed three different receptors, one for blue, one for green and one for red. The ratio of activity in the three types of cones facilitates our experience of a particular hue, or colour. Hering's opponent-process theory also assumed that there are three different receptors: one for blue–yellow, one for red–green, and one for black–white. Each of the receptors can function in two possible ways, depending on the wavelength of the stimulus. Again, the pattern of activity in the receptors yields our perception of the hue.

FIGURE 5.13

Opponent processes at work.

Negative colour afterimages demonstrate opponent processes occurring in the visual system. Stare steadily at the centre of the white square for about a minute, then look quickly at a blank piece of white paper. The opponent colours should appear.

the yellow, as blue. According to opponent-process theory, as you stared at the green, black and yellow colours, the neural processes that register those colours became fatigued. Then when you cast your gaze on the white surface, which reflects all wavelengths, a rebound opponent reaction occurred as each receptor responded with its opposing red, white or blue reactions.

Dual processes in colour transduction   Which theory – the trichromatic theory or the opponent-process theory – is correct? Two centuries of research have provided verifying evidence for each theory. Today's **dual-process theory** combines the trichromatic and opponent-process theories to account for the colour transduction process (Knoblauch, 2002).

The trichromatic theorists Young and Helmholtz were right about the cones. The cones do indeed contain one of three different protein photopigments that are most sensitive to wavelengths roughly corresponding to the colours blue, green and red (Abramov and Gordon, 1994). Different ratios of activity in the blue-, green- and red-sensitive cones can produce a pattern of neural activity that corresponds to any hue in the spectrum (Backhaus et al., 1998).

Hering's opponent-process theory was also partly correct, but opponent processes do not occur at the level of the cones, as he maintained. When researchers began to use microelectrodes to record from single cells in the visual system, they discovered that ganglion cells in the retina, as well as neurons in visual relay stations and the visual cortex, respond in an opponent-process fashion by altering their rate of firing (Knoblauch, 2002). For example, if a red light is shone on the retina, an opponent process ganglion cell may respond with a high rate of firing, but a green light will cause the same cell to fire at a very low rate. Other neurons respond in a similar opponent fashion to blue and yellow stimuli.

The red–green opponent processes are triggered directly by input from the red- or green-sensitive cones in the retina (Fig. 5.14). The blue-yellow opponent process is a bit more complex.

> **dual-process theory**
>
> **combines the trichromatic and opponent-process theories to account for the colour transduction process**

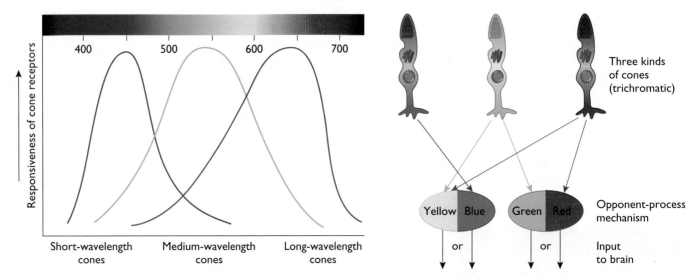

FIGURE 5.14

Dual colour vision processes.

Colour vision involves both trichromatic and opponent processes that occur at different places in the visual system. Consistent with trichromatic theory, three types of cones are maximally sensitive to short (blue), medium (green) and long (red) wavelengths, respectively. However, opponent processes occur further along in the visual system, as opponent cells in the retina, visual relay stations, and the visual cortex respond differentially to blue versus yellow, red versus green and black versus white stimuli. Shown here are the inputs from the cones that produce the blue–yellow and red–green opponent processes.

Activity of blue-sensitive cones directly stimulates the blue process further along in the visual system. And yellow? The yellow opponent process is triggered not by a yellow-sensitive cone, as Hering proposed, but rather by simultaneous input from the red- and green-sensitive cones (Abramov and Gordon, 1994).

Colour-deficient vision   People with normal colour vision are referred to as *trichromats*. They are sensitive to all three systems: blue–yellow, red–green and black–white. However, about 7 per cent of the male population and 1 per cent of the female population have a deficiency in the blue–yellow system, the red–green system or both. This deficiency is caused by an absence of hue-sensitive photopigment in certain cone types. A *dichromat* is a person who is colour-blind in only one of the systems (blue–yellow or red–green). A *monochromat* is sensitive only to the black–white system and is totally colour-blind. Most colour-deficient people are dichromats and have their deficiency in the red–green system. Typically, colour-blindness tests employ sets of coloured dots such as those in Figure 5.15. Depending on the type of deficit, a colour-blind person cannot discern the number embedded in one of the two circles.

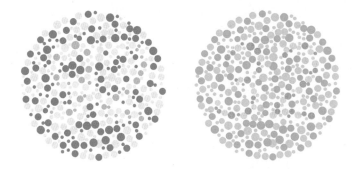

Analysis and Reconstruction of Visual Scenes

Once the transformation of light energy to nerve impulses occurs, the process of combining the messages received from the photoreceptors into the perception of a visual scene begins. As you read this page, nerve impulses from countless neurons are being analysed and the visual image that you perceive is being reconstructed. Moreover, you know what these black squiggles on the page mean. How does this occur?

From the retina, the optic nerve sends impulses to a visual relay station in the thalamus, the brain's sensory switchboard. From there, the input is routed to various parts of the cortex, particularly the primary visual cortex in the occipital lobe at the rear of the brain. Microelectrode studies have shown that there is a point-to-point correspondence between tiny regions of the retina and groups of neurons in the visual cortex. This is called retinotopic mapping. As you might expect, the fovea, where the one-to-one synapses of cones with bipolar cells produce high visual acuity, is represented by a disproportionately large area of the visual cortex. Somewhat more surprising is the fact that there is more than one retinotopic cortical map; there are many retinotopic maps and not all are exact duplicates of one another.

Groups of neurons within the primary visual cortex are organized to receive and integrate sensory nerve impulses originating in specific regions of the retina. Some of these cells, known as **feature detectors**, fire selectively in response to visual stimuli that have specific characteristics (Kanwisher, 1998). Discovery of these feature detectors won David Hubel and Torsten Wiesel of Harvard University the 1981 Nobel Prize. Using tiny electrodes to record the activity of individual cells of the visual cortex of animals (Fig. 5.16), Hubel and Wiesel found that certain neurons fired most frequently when lines of certain orientations were presented. One neuron might fire most frequently when a horizontal line was presented; another neuron in response to a line of a slightly different orientation; and so on 'around the clock'. For example, the letter A

Focus 5.10
What kinds of feature detectors exist in the visual system? What is parallel processing of sensory information?

FIGURE 5.15

Test your colour vision.

These *Ishihara disks*, are named after the Japanese scientist, *Shinobu Ishihara*. They were first published in 1917. The left one tests for blue–yellow colour blindness, the right one for red–green colour blindness. Because the dots in the picture are of equal lightness, colour is the only available cue for perceiving the numbers in the circles. Can you see them? You should be able to read '92' in the blue disk and '32' in the predominantly green disk.

feature detectors
fire selectively in response to visual stimuli that have specific characteristics

FIGURE 5.16

A partially anaesthetized monkey views an image projected on the screen while an electrode embedded in its visual cortex records the activity of a single neuron. This research by Hubel and Wiesel led to the discovery of feature detectors that analyse visual stimulus features such as contours and shapes, movement and colour.

FIGURE 5.17

A Bill Clinton feature detector?

Single-neuron electrical recording in a patient's amygdala (which receives extensive visual input) revealed a neuron that responded to depictions of Bill Clinton but not to 47 other pictures showing other presidents, celebrities, objects, landscapes, and geometric shapes. This neuron was apparently part of a neuronal network that had learned to recognize and represent the former president.

SOURCE: Koch, 2004.

could be constructed from the response of feature detectors that responded to three different line orientations: /, \, and −. Within the cortex, this information is integrated and analysed by successively more complex feature-detector systems to produce our perception of objects (Palmer, 2002).

Other classes of feature detectors respond to colour, to depth, or to movement (Livingstone and Hubel, 1994). These feature-detector 'modules' subdivide a visual scene into its component dimensions and process them simultaneously. Thus, as a red, white, and green beach ball sails towards you, separate but overlapping modules within the brain are simultaneously analysing its colours, shape, distance and movement by engaging in parallel processing of the information and constructing a unified image of its properties (Hubel and Wiesel, 2005). The final stages in the process of constructing a visual representation occur when the information analysed and recombined by the primary visual cortex is routed to other cortical regions known as the *visual association cortex*, where features of the visual scene are combined and interpreted in light of our memories and knowledge (Grossberg et al., 2005). If all goes correctly, a process that began with nerve impulses from the rods and cones now ends with our recognizing the beach ball for what it is and catching it. Quite another conscious experience and response would probably occur if we interpreted the oncoming object as a water balloon.

Recently, scientists have discovered that neurons in the brain respond selectively not only to basic stimulus characteristics like corners and colours, but also to complex stimuli that have acquired special meaning through experience. For example, recording from single neurons in the amygdala of a brain-damaged patient, scientists have found a neuron that responded electrically to only three of 50 visual scenes. The three scenes differed significantly, but all involved former President of the United States, Bill Clinton. One was a portrait, another a group picture that included Clinton, and the third was a cartoonist's representation of the president. Pictures of other celebrities, animals, landscapes and geometric forms evoked no response (Fig. 5.17). This neuron was likely part of a neural circuit that was created within the brain to register this particular individual (Koch, 2004). The firing of the single cell would be insufficient to represent all of Clinton, but a group of cells, the 'neural circuit' would be enough, firing together to produce the percept.

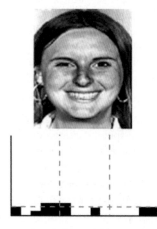

Neuron's Electrical Response

Face Perception

Faces are a particularly important and salient stimulus. We know both from experience and research that infants find the face extremely compelling. The face can provide the infant and mother, or caregiver a means of communicating before language can be shared. Pascalis and de Haan (2002) have shown that infants are in fact more sensitive to changes in faces that older humans. Their research indicates that infants can even tell the difference in faces from different species, an ability that becomes dulled, or is lost entirely in older humans, who become focused on or tuned to the type of face most important to them, the human face. Face processing is though of as a special process, different from our perceptions of other items and objects.

The importance of 'features' Bruce and Young (1984) say that basic information about the person is perceived, including gender and age. Facial expression features are then processed. The model of the face that is produced is consigned to memory where personal identity is coded along with these features. This is the *feature theory* of face perception. When the person experiences a face again, the appropriate 'face-recognition unit' is activated, and we realize that we have seen the face before, we have recognition. Some features may be more important than others though. Sadr et al. (2003) have suggested that the eyebrows are extremely important. They had participants identify celebrity faces with various features removed. The pictures with the eyebrows missing were significantly harder to identify than those with the eyes removed. However, different features are more reliable in different situations. If features are presented in isolation (without the rest of the face) then the eyes are the most reliable indicator of gender (Burton et al., 1993). It seems then that features distinguish faces from one another, but there are general rules that help us identify more global differences, such as gender. Bruce et al. (1987) for instance, showed that gender is very quickly identified, quicker even than familiarity. The features of a face that distinguish gender include the shape and length of the nose, and how the brows and eyes are set (males have deeper set eyes, and more prominent brows, altering a relatively large portion of the visual array).

Emotion Bruce and Young (1986) show that extremely important information is available from faces, not least our perception of others' emotions. Women, it seems, are better at identifying emotions from facial expressions than men. The gender difference extends through childhood into adulthood, with all females showing better performance than males of their own age group (McClure, 2000). There are other interesting factors associated with gender in face perception. During the menstrual cycle, women change their preference for male faces, preferring a more masculine face when in the follicular stage (Penton-Voak and Perrett, 2000). It is at this stage that conception is most likely following sexual intercourse. In terms of evolutionary psychology, we might describe this as a desire to choose a father who shows certain attributes that the woman sees as beneficial. These attributes might be the stereotypical masculine traits described in a face as a strong jaw, deep set eyes, etc. Other research, however, has indicated that the behaviour of the male can also significantly influence his attractiveness to the female at different times in her menstrual cycle (Gangstad et al., 2005).

Attractiveness The concept of attractiveness is very subjective. It is widely regarded that what we find attractive may depend on our culture, but research suggests that it may not. Our treatment of people we regard as attractive is, it seems, independent of culture, according to Langlois et al. (2000), who showed startling cross-cultural agreement on attractiveness ratings of pictures of individuals. They also showed that attractive people were treated better than unattractive people in the cultures they tested. The youthfulness of the face has been identified as a factor in attractiveness (Ishi et al. 2004). Researchers used a technique to blend faces into one another, and change, or morph, the faces they used to look more youthful. Their results showed that the younger faces, and those that had been made to look more feminine (feminized) were judged as more attractive than the older or more masculine faces. Evolution suggests that the perceived attractiveness of a face is related to the pressure to produce young of optimal genetic make-up. The perceived health-iness of the face is also a factor in attractiveness ratings, and healthiness has obvious evolutionary advantages. Rhodes (2006) has shown that more attractive faces were rated as healthier. But what about the features that people find attractive? People are constantly engaged in complex, costly and painful plastic surgery in pursuit of the ideal face, but what is it that makes a face ideal? Perrett et al. (1994) show that faces are consistently rated as more attractive if they have larger eyes and higher cheeks relative to the size and shape of the face. In their experiment, Perrett and colleagues morphed faces together and had them rated in attractiveness by a panel. They then produced the average of the most attractively rated faces and enhanced them, to make them 'highly attractive'. Their participants rated this 'highly attractive' composite face higher in attractiveness than a simi-larly produced 'average' composite face, suggesting that enhancing some features does indeed produce a more attractive face. In contrast to this Bruce et al. (1994) showed that faces with aver-age features are rated as more attractive than those with more pronounced features. In evolution-ary terms this makes sense. An average face means a mate that is of familiar genetic construction. This means less risk to the genetic make-up of the offspring.

Recognizing faces   Sometimes people lose the ability to recognize faces. In these cases we say that the person has a form of *prospagnosia*. This is usually caused by a traumatic brain injury of some kind. Imagine not being able to process faces, not knowing who you have met previously and whether you should recognize someone you see. Face perception is indeed an extremely important part of our social world. You can find more on this in Chapter 3. Recognition is extremely important, and there is evidence (Bruce et al., 2001; Burton et al., 1999) that match-ing clear faces to even very degraded images is much easier if you know the person. This is use-ful to people who use closed-circuit television (CCTV). When a witness identifies someone on an often very degraded CCTV image as someone they know, then the likelihood of this being a correct identification is much higher than if the person in the image is not known to the witness.

Object recognition

Recognizing the objects around us is the most important goal of the visual perceptual process. You will not be surprised to hear that there are a number of theories that explain how this hap-pens. In the next section we introduce two approaches. First, David Marr's ground-breaking computational model and, second, Biederman's recognition-by-components theory which fol-lowed it.

A Computational Model of Visual Processing

In 1982, David Marr produced an extremely influential model of visual perception. In his *compu-tational model*, he proposes that vision is a three-stage process, which takes the perceiver from an extremely basic two-dimensional (2D) view of the item being perceived, through to a more com-plex, three-dimensional (3D) representation. You can see this illustrated in Figure 5.18.

FIGURE 5.18

Marr's computational model.

(a) Primal sketch – here edges of the object, a result of processing light and shade, are represented. (b) 2½D sketch – shading and texture provide more information, and binocular information is also used to give information about depth. (c) The final 3D model: All the information is combined. The viewpoint is irrelevant. The relationship between all the constituent parts of the object are considered and built into a rich 3D model (redrawn from Marr (1982)).

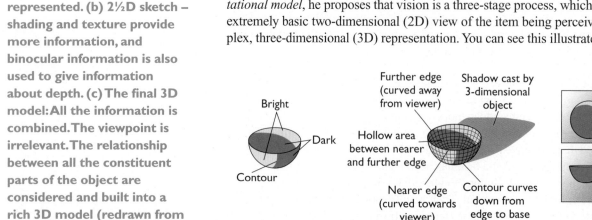

(a)   (b)   (c)

The first thing we see is a basic, or *primal sketch*. All we have of the object so far are patterns of light and shade. Which once processed provide us with information about edges. Next, information is developed into what Marr calls a *2½ D sketch*. Information from the shading is built into the new representation, providing information regarding relative distances from us of the different parts of the object. This is what the object actually looks like from our (the perceiver's) perspective. Finally we develop a *three-dimensional model*. Here we have internalized a visual model of the item we are observing, free of the constraints of viewpoint. We have developed an understanding of what the reverse of the object should look like for instance.

Recognition by Components

Biedeman's (1987; 1990) *recognition-by-components* (RBC) theory can be seen as a development of Marr's work. Biederman describes the visual world as being made up of a number of basic shapes. Some examples of these shapes, can be seen in Figure 5.19. These are called *geons*. Take a moment and look at the images in Figure 5.20 and identify the *geons* in each item.

The telephone, for instance, can be made up of a sausage shape laid on top of a wedge shape. A cup might be made up of a funnel shape with the sausage-shaped geon as the handle. Let us take a step back for a moment. We have the idea of geons and RBC theory, that items might be identified by how their component geons are arranged, but how do we identify the geons in the first place? Biederman indicates that *edge detection* is central to this theory. The first thing that must be done is to parse, or chop up the object into geons, and we do this through information from the edges we can identify. Biederman identifies five invariant (unchanging) properties of edges, that in different combinations allow us to identify the different geons. These are *curvature* (points on the edge are on a curve), *parallel* (points are in parallel), *cotermination* (edges end at the same point), *symmetry* and *co-linearity* (points are in a straight line).

This provides Biederman's theory with a real strength. Even though we may not be able to see the entire object, perhaps because it is obscured somehow, we know that these properties exist, and they do not change. We may only need to see a small part of an edge to know how it will behave for the rest of the partially obscured object. Only a small part of many objects need to be seen at all to identify them, and as such much of the object is redundant anyway as far as its identity is concerned. This means that the viewpoint of the observer, so important in Marr's theory, becomes irrelevant here as long as the geons can be identified. Tarr and Bülthoff (1998) however say that viewpoint is important in analysis of the visual scene. They showed that participants made more errors and were slower at recognizing familiar objects shown from unfamiliar viewpoints, indicating that viewpoint was very important, and thereby supporting Marr's computational model.

In summary, then, Marr's model gives us an understanding of how systematic processes might be used in the representation of our visual world. The computational theory begins from basics, and is in that sense a bottom-up process. One criticism that might be made of the theory is that the role of expectation, a top-down component of perceptual processing, is not developed in the theory. Also, how we reach the 3D representation from the 2½D stage is not well explained. Biederman's later recognition-by-components analysis indicates that visual objects can be made up of a combination of simple shapes, or geons. These geons can be identified simply from our knowledge of edges, and even if partially obscured, we should still be able to pick them out of the scene, eliminating the importance of the viewpoint of the observer. Tarr and Bülthoff (1998) show that viewpoint *is* an issue though. One criticism that has been levied at both theories is that neither allow subtle distinctions. They may allow us to identify a cup, or a mug or a cat, but neither allow us to identify whether the object we see is our favourite cup or mug, or whether the animal is our pet cat.

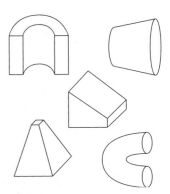

FIGURE 5.19

Geons: Biederman's (1987) recognition by components theory proposes that objects are made up of 36 basic shapes, which he calls *geons*. Here are five of them.

FIGURE 5.20

Identify the geons seen in these pictures.

IN REVIEW

- The senses may be classified in terms of the stimuli to which they respond. Through the process of transduction, these stimuli are transformed into nerve impulses.

- The normal stimulus for vision is electromagnetic energy, or light waves. Light-sensitive visual receptor cells are located in the retina. The rods are brightness receptors, and the less numerous cones are colour receptors. Light energy striking the retina is converted into nerve impulses by chemical reactions in the photopigments of the rods and cones. Dark adaptation involves the gradual regeneration of photopigments that have been depleted by brighter illumination.

- Colour vision is a two-stage process having both trichromatic and opponent-process components. The first stage involves the reactions of cones that are maximally sensitive to blue, green and red wavelengths. In the second stage, colour information from the cones is coded through an opponent-process mechanism further along in the visual system.

- Visual stimuli are analysed by feature detectors in the primary visual cortex, and the stimulus elements are reconstructed and interpreted in light of input from the visual association cortex.

- Marr and Biederman provide us with two influential theories that help explain how we identify and recognize objects. Marr's computational theory describes how simple representations are developed into more complex 3D models, and Biederman's recognition-by-components theory says that all objects can be made up of simple shapes called geons.

Focus 5.11

Describe the two physical characteristics of sound waves and their relation to auditory experience.

FIGURE 5.21

Auditory stimuli.

Sound waves are a form of mechanical energy. As the tuning fork vibrates, it produces successive waves of compression and expansion of air molecules. The number of maximum compressions per second (cycles per second) is its frequency, measured in hertz (Hz). The height of the wave represents the sound's amplitude. Frequency determines pitch; amplitude determines loudness, measured in decibels (dB).

AUDITION

The stimuli for our sense of hearing are sound waves, a form of mechanical energy. What we call *sound* is actually pressure waves in air, water or some other conducting medium. When a stereo's volume is high enough, you can actually see cloth speaker covers moving in and out. If you balance a tiny piece of paper or a table tennis ball on a speaker cone, you will see it moving with the music, as the cone pushes it into the air. The resulting vibrations cause successive waves of compression and expansion among the air molecules surrounding the source of the sound. These sound waves have two characteristics: frequency and amplitude (Fig. 5.21).

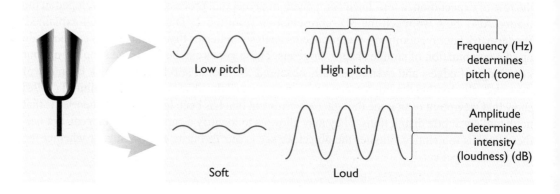

Frequency is the number of sound waves, or cycles, per second. **Hertz (Hz)** is the measure of cycles per second; 1 hertz equals 1 cycle per second. The sound waves' frequency (how often – how *frequent* the cycles are) is related to the perceived pitch of the sound; the higher the frequency (hertz), the higher the perceived pitch. Humans are capable of detecting sound frequencies from 20 to 20 000 hertz (20–20 kilohertz [kHz]). As a rule, the younger we are, the higher the frequency we can perceive. Among musical instruments, the piano can play the widest range of frequencies, from 27.5 hertz at the low end of the keyboard to 4186 hertz at the high end.

Amplitude refers to the vertical size of the sound waves – the depth between the peaks and the troughs in the sound wave. The sound wave's amplitude is the primary determinant of the sound's perceived loudness. Differences in amplitude are expressed in **decibels (dB)**, a measure of the physical pressures that occur at the eardrum. Zero decibels is designated as our minimum absolute threshold, any quieter and we cannot hear it. Each increase of 10 decibels represents a tenfold increase in loudness. Table 5.3 shows various sounds scaled in decibels.

frequency

the number of sound waves, or cycles, per second

Hertz (Hz)

the measure of cycles per second; 1 hertz equals 1 cycle per second

amplitude

the vertical size of the sound waves – The depth between the peaks and the troughs in the sound wave

decibels (dB)

measure of the physical pressures that occur at the eardrum

TABLE 5.3 DECIBEL SCALING OF COMMON SOUNDS

Level in decibels (dB)	Common sounds	Threshold levels
140	Jet fighter taking off 25 metres away, Formula 1 car at 1 metre	Potential damage to auditory system
130	Loud metal workshop	Human pain threshold
120	Rock-and-roll band, jet aircraft at 166 metres overhead	
110	Car horn at 1 metre	
100	Crosscut saw at position of operator	
90	Kitchen blender	Hearing damage with prolonged exposure
80	Vacuum cleaner at 1 metre	
70	Motorway traffic	
60	A busy city street	
50	Restaurant	
40	Quiet suburban street	
30	Quiet bedroom or theatre	
20	Recording studio, whispered speech	
10	Breathing	
0	A fly at 3 metres	Minimum threshold of hearing

NOTE: The decibel scale relates a *physical quantity* – sound intensity – to *the human perception* of that quantity – sound loudness. It is a *logarithmic scale* – that is, each increment of 10 dB represents a tenfold increase in loudness. The table indicates the decibel ranges of some common sounds as well as thresholds for hearing, hearing damage and pain.

Auditory Transduction: From Pressure Waves to Nerve Impulses

The transduction system of the ear is made up of tiny bones, membranes and liquid-filled tubes designed to translate pressure waves into nerve impulses (Fig. 5.22). Sound waves travel into an auditory canal leading to the *eardrum*, a membrane that vibrates in response to the sound waves. Beyond the eardrum is the *middle ear*, a cavity housing three tiny bones (the smallest in the body, in fact). The vibrating activity of these bones – the *hammer (malleus)*, *anvil (incus)* and *stirrup (stapes)* – amplifies the sound waves more than 30 times. The first bone, the hammer, is attached firmly to the eardrum, and the stirrup is attached to another membrane, the *oval window*, which forms the boundary between the middle ear and the inner ear.

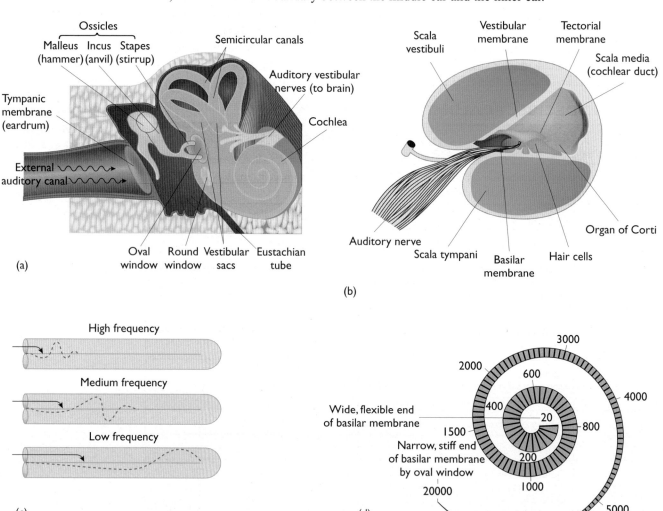

FIGURE 5.22

The ear.

(a) A cross-section of the ear shows the structures that transmit sound waves from the auditory canal to the cochlea. The semicircular canals and vestibular sacs of the inner ear contain components that provide us with our sense of balance. (b) Cross section of cochlea, sound waves are translated into waves that stimulate hair cells in the organ of Corti. The resulting nerve impulses reach the brain via the auditory nerve. (c) Different waves are created by different sound frequencies. (d) Varying frequencies maximally stimulate different areas of the basilar membrane. High-frequency waves peak quickly and stimulate the membrane close to the oval window.

The outer ear is the visual part of the ear (*the pinna*) and the auditory canal, the part that contains wax, which many people use cotton-buds to remove. The role of the pinna is partly to catch the sound. If you cup your hand behind your pinna you will catch more sound, helping you to hear voices across a busy table, or in a noisy room. The pinna also has a role in sound localization which we will describe in a moment.

Next comes the middle ear, containing three tiny bones, called the hammer, anvil and stirrup – the ossicles. The role of the ossicles is something called *impedance matching*. Sound travels through air, which has a very low *impedance* by which we mean that it does not impede the wave very much. It does not get in the way of the sound very much at all. The inner ear is extremely sensitive, so evolution has seen fit to put the ossicles between the air (low impedance) and the cochlea (extremely low impedance) to ensure that sound caught by the pinna does not damage the sensitive organ of Corti. The bones translate the sound, reducing it in energy and transferring it to the inner ear. The ossicles *match the impedance of the air to that of the cochlea*. They provide a safety mechanism to help avoid damage to the sensitive inner ear.

The inner ear contains the **cochlea**, a coiled, snail-shaped tube about 3.5 cm in length that contains the **basilar membrane**, a sheet of tissue that runs its length. Resting on the basilar membrane is the **organ of Corti**, which contains thousands of tiny hair cells that are the actual sound receptors. The tips of the hair cells contain even tinier protrusions called cilia, which lie beneath another membrane, the *tectorial membrane*, that overhangs the basilar membrane along the entire length of the cochlea. As the basilar membrane flexes, the hair cells also move. This movement in turn produces a movement of the cilia. It is this bending motion that causes the hair cell to fire. The hair cells pass information with the neurons of the auditory nerve, which in turn send impulses via the thalamus to the temporal lobe's auditory cortex.

Sound waves strike the eardrum and pressure is created at the oval window by the ossicles. The waves that result vibrate the basilar membrane and the tectorial membrane, causing a bending of the hair cells in the organ of Corti (see Fig. 5.22b). This bending of the hair cells triggers the release of neurotransmitters into resulting in nerve impulses that are sent to the brain. Within the auditory cortex are feature-detector neurons that respond to specific kinds of auditory input, much as occurs in the visual system (Goldstein, 2002).

Coding of Pitch and Loudness

The auditory system transforms the sensory qualities of wave amplitude and frequency (experienced by us as loudness and pitch) into nerve impulses. In the case of intensity, high-amplitude sound waves cause the hair cells to bend more and release more neurotransmitter substance at the point where they synapse connect) with auditory nerve cells, resulting in a higher rate of firing within the auditory nerve. Also, certain receptor neurons have higher thresholds than others, so that they will fire only when the hair cells bend considerably in response to an intense sound. What we experience as loudness is coded in terms of both the *rate* of firing in the axons of the auditory nerve and also the *specific hair cells* that are sending messages (Carney, 2002).

The coding of wave frequency that produces our perception of pitch also involves two different processes, one for frequencies below about 1000 hertz and another for higher frequencies. Historically, as in the case of colour vision, two competing theories were proposed to account for our perception of pitch. According to the **frequency theory of pitch perception**, nerve impulses sent to the brain match the frequency of the sound wave. Thus a 30-hertz (30 cycles per second) sound wave from a piano should send 30 volleys of nerve impulses per second to the brain.

Unfortunately, frequency theory encounters a major problem. Because neurons are limited in their rate of firing, individual impulses or volleys of impulses fired by groups of neurons cannot produce high enough frequencies of firing to match sound-wave frequencies above 1000 hertz. How then do we perceive higher frequencies, such as a 4000-hertz note from the same piano?

cochlea
coiled, snail-shaped tube about 3.5 cm in length

basilar membrane
sheet of tissue that runs its length

organ of Corti
contains thousands of tiny hair cells that are the actual sound receptors

Focus 5.12
Describe how the middle and inner ear structures are involved in the auditory transduction process.

Focus 5.13
Describe the frequency and place theories of pitch perception. In what sense are both theories correct?

frequency theory of pitch perception
nerve impulses sent to the brain match the frequency of the sound wave

Experiments conducted by Georg von Békésy (1957) uncovered a second mechanism for coding pitch that earned him the 1961 Nobel Prize. His pioneering work in the 1940s famously involved the cochleae of an elephant that died at Budapest Zoo. He heard of the demise of the animal and excitedly dispatched his research assistant to retrieve the cochleae. On his return Békésy was disappointed to find that the cochleae were missing, and that his assistant had removed the outer ears only, slicing through the auditory canal. His mistake was in not realizing that the auditory canal of the elephant is approximately 20 cm in length. All was not lost. He returned to the glue-factory to which the elephant had been sent and returned with the prized cochleae. Békésy discovered that high-frequency sounds produced an abrupt fluid wave (Fig. 5.22c) that peaked close to the oval window, whereas lower-frequency vibrations produced a slower fluid wave that peaked farther down the cochlear canal. Békésy's observations supported a **place theory of pitch perception**, suggesting that the specific point in the cochlea where the fluid wave peaks and most strongly bends the hair cells serves as a frequency coding cue (Fig. 5.22d). Researchers later found that similar to the manner in which the retina is mapped onto the visual cortex (retinotopic mapping), the auditory cortex has a tonal frequency map (tonotopic mapping) that corresponds to specific areas of the cochlea. By analysing the specific location of the cochlea from which auditory nerve impulses are being received, the brain can code individual pitches, like those produced by tuning forks and the individual strings of a piano.

Thus, like trichromatic and opponent–process theories of colour vision, which were once thought to contradict one another, frequency and place theories of pitch perception both proved applicable in their own ways. At low frequencies, frequency theory holds true; at higher frequencies, place theory provides the mechanism for coding the frequency of a sound wave.

> **place theory of pitch perception**
> the specific point in the cochlea where the fluid wave peaks and most strongly bends the hair cells serves as a frequency coding cue

Sound Localization

Have you ever wondered why you have two ears, one located on each side of your head? As is usually the case in nature's designs, there is a good reason. Our very survival can depend on our ability to locate objects that emit sounds. The nervous system uses information concerning the time and intensity differences of sounds arriving at the two ears to locate the source of sounds in space (Moore, 1997).

Sounds arrive first and loudest at the ear closest to the sound. When the source of the sound is directly in front of us, the sound wave reaches both ears at the same time and at the same intensity, so the source is perceived as being straight ahead. Our binaural (two-eared) ability to localize sound is amazingly sensitive. For example, a sound 3 degrees to the right arrives at the right ear only 300 millionths of a second before it arrives at the left ear, and yet we can tell which direction the sound is coming from (Yin and Kuwada, 1984). Our outer ear (pinnae) also provide us with some sense of the height, or *the elevation* of an object. The folds of your ears are unique to you. Sounds arriving from a particular elevation are given a 'shape' by these folds, that your brain recognizes. It is the folds in your ears that code the elevation of the sound.

Other animals have even more exotic sound localization systems. For example, the barn owl comes equipped with ears that are exquisitely tailored for pinpoint localization of its prey during night hunting. Its right ear is directed slightly upward, its left ear slightly downward. This allows it to localize sounds precisely both vertically and horizontally, thereby allowing it to zero in on its prey with deadly accuracy.

Hearing Loss

If you had to make the unwelcome choice of being blind or being deaf, which impairment would you choose? When asked this question, most people say that they would rather be deaf. Yet hearing loss can have more devastating social consequences than blindness does. Helen Keller, who was both blind and deaf, considered deafness to be more socially debilitating. She wrote, 'Blindness cuts people off from things. Deafness cuts people off from people'.

WHAT DO YOU THINK?

NAVIGATING IN FOG: PROFESSOR MAYER'S TOPOPHONE

The device shown in Figure 5.23 is called a *topophone*. It was used in the late 1880s to help sailors locate sounds while navigating in thick fog. Based on what you have learned about the principles of sound localization, can you identify two features of this instrument that would assist sailors in detecting and locating sounds? Think about it, then see p. 222.

FIGURE 5.23

An early 'hearing aid'.

The topophone, used in the late 1800s by sailors to increase their ability to locate sounds while navigating in thick fog, assisted in two ways. Can you identify the relevant principles?

Focus 5.14

What are the two kinds of deafness, and how can they be treated?

The vast majority of people who suffer from hearing loss were born with normal hearing These individuals suffer from two major types of hearing loss. **Conduction deafness** (also known as **conductive hearing loss**) involves problems with the mechanical system that transmits sound waves to the cochlea. For example, a punctured eardrum or a loss of function in the tiny bones of the middle ear can reduce the ear's capacity to transmit vibrations. Use of a hearing aid, which amplifies the sounds entering the ear, may correct many cases of conduction deafness.

An entirely different matter is **nerve deafness** (also known as **sensorineural hearing loss**), caused by damaged receptors within the inner ear or damage to the auditory nerve itself. This cannot be helped by a hearing aid because the problem does not lie in the transmission of sound waves to the cochlea. Although ageing and disease can produce sensorineural hearing loss, exposure to loud sounds is one of its leading causes. Repeated exposure to loud sounds of a particular frequency (as might be produced by a machine in a factory) can eventually cause the loss of hair cells at a particular point on the basilar membrane, thereby causing hearing loss for that frequency.

Extremely loud music can also take a serious toll on hearing (West and Evans, 1990). Figure 5.24 shows the devastating results of a guinea pig's exposure to a sound level approximating that of loud rock music heard through earphones. As shown in Table 5.3, even brief exposure to sounds exceeding 140 decibels can cause irreversible damage to the receptors in the inner ear, as can more continuous sounds at lower decibel levels.

conduction deafness (also known as conductive hearing loss)

involves problems with the mechanical system that transmits sound waves to the cochlea

nerve deafness (also known as sensorineural hearing loss)

caused by damaged receptors within the inner ear or damage to the auditory nerve itself

FIGURE 5.24

Danger! Hearing loss.

Exposure to loud sounds can destroy auditory receptors in the inner ear. These pictures, taken through an electron microscope, show the hair cells of a guinea pig before (*left*) and after (*right*) exposure to 24 hours of noise comparable to that of a loud rock concert.

SOURCE: Micrographs by Robert E. Preston, courtesy of Professor J. E. Hawkins, Kresge Hearing Research Institute, University of Michigan.

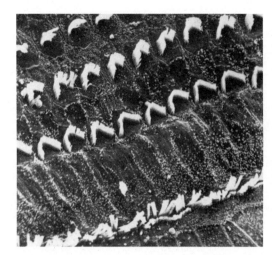 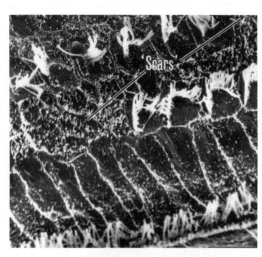

gustation

sense of taste

olfaction

sense of smell

Focus 5.15

Describe the stimuli and the receptors involved in gustation and olfaction.

taste buds

chemical receptors concentrated along the tip, edges, and back surface of the tongue

TASTE AND SMELL: THE CHEMICAL SENSES

Gustation, the sense of taste, and **olfaction**, the sense of smell, are chemical senses; their receptors are sensitive to chemical molecules rather than to some form of energy. These senses are so intertwined that some scientists consider them a 'common chemical sense' (Halpern, 2002). Enjoying a good meal usually depends on the simultaneous activity of taste and odour receptors, as becomes apparent when we have a stuffy nose and our food tastes bland. People who lose their sense of smell typically believe they have lost their sense of taste as well (Beauchamp and Bartoshuk, 1997). It seems then that 'holding your nose' when forced to take an unpleasant tasting medicine really does have something to be said for it.

Gustation: The Sense of Taste

You may be surprised to learn that your sense of taste responds to only four qualities: sweet, sour, salty and bitter. Every taste experience combines these qualities and those of other senses, such as smell, temperature and touch. For example, part of the taste of popcorn includes its complex texture, its crunchiness and its odour. In addition to its chemical receptors, the tongue is richly endowed with tactile (touch) and temperature receptors.

Taste buds are chemical receptors concentrated along the tip, edges, and back surface of the tongue (Fig. 5.25). Each taste bud is most responsive to one or two of the basic taste qualities but responds weakly to the others as well. An additional mysterious taste sensation, called *umani*, increases the intensity of other taste qualities. This sensory response is activated by certain proteins, as well as by monosodium glutamate, a substance used by some restaurants to enhance the flavour of their food.

Humans have about 9000 taste buds, each consisting of several receptor cells arranged like the segments of an orange. A small number of receptors are also found in the roof and back of the mouth, so that even people without a tongue can taste substances. Hair-like structures project from the top of each cell into the taste pore, an opening to the outside surface of the tongue. When a substance is taken into the mouth, it interacts with saliva to form a chemical solution that flows into the taste pore and stimulates the receptor cells. A taste results from complex patterns of neural activity produced by the four types of taste receptors (Halpern, 2002).

The sense of taste not only provides us with pleasure but also has adaptive significance in discriminating between nutrients and toxins (Scott, 1992). Our response to some taste qualities is innate. For example, newborn infants respond positively to sugar water placed on the tongue and negatively to bitter substances such as quinine (Davidson and Fox, 1988). Many poisonous substances in nature have bitter tastes, so this emotional response seems to be hardwired into

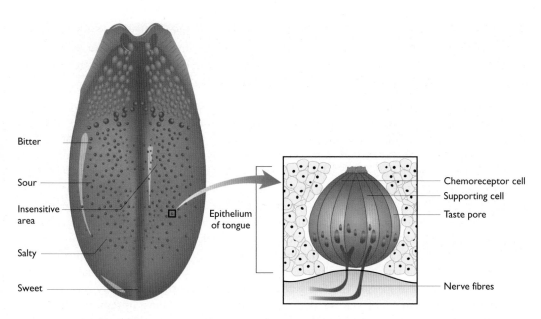

Bitter

Sour

Insensitive area

Salty

Sweet

Epithelium of tongue

Chemoreceptor cell

Supporting cell

Taste pore

Nerve fibres

FIGURE 5.25

Taste organs.

The receptors for taste are specialized cells located in the tongue's 9000 taste buds, found on the tip, back, and sides of the tongue. As this figure shows, certain areas of the tongue are especially sensitive to chemical stimuli that produce particular taste sensations. However, these different sensitivities are a matter of degree, as all kinds of taste buds are found in most areas of the tongue. The centre of the tongue is relatively insensitive to chemical stimuli for taste.

our physiology. In nature, sweet substances are more likely to occur in high-calorie (sugar-rich) foods. Unfortunately, many humans now live in an environment that is different from the food-scarce environment in which preferences for sweet substances evolved (Scott and Giza, 1993). As a result, people in affluent countries over-consume sweet foods that are good for us only in small quantities.

Olfaction: The Sense of Smell

The sense of smell (olfaction) is of great importance for many species. Humans are more orientated to sound and vision. Bloodhounds, for example, have relatively poor eyesight but a highly developed olfactory sense that is about 2 million times more sensitive than ours (Thomas, 1974). A bloodhound can detect a person's scent in a footprint that is four days old, something no human could do. Recent research has shown that dogs need the olfactory trace of only five human steps to determine the direction the person has walked (Porter et al., 2007). People who are deprived of other senses often develop a highly sensitive olfactory sense. Helen Keller, though blind and deaf, exhibited a remarkable ability to smell her environment. With uncanny accuracy, she could tell when a storm was brewing by detecting subtle odour changes in the air. She could also identify people (even those who bathed regularly and did not wear scents of any kind) by their distinctive odours (Keller, 1955).

The receptors for smell are long cells that project through the lining of the upper part of the nasal cavity and into the mucous membrane. Humans have about 40 million olfactory receptors, and 350 different types of them; dogs about 1 billion receptors. Unfortunately, our ability to discriminate among different odours is not well understood. Olfactory receptors have structures that resemble neurotransmitter binding sites on neurons. Any of the thousands of potential odour molecules can lock into sites that are tailored to fit them (Buck and Axel, 1991). The receptors that fire send their input to the **olfactory bulb**, a forebrain structure immediately above the nasal cavity. Each odorous chemical excites only a limited portion of the olfactory bulb, and odours are apparently coded in terms of the specific area of the olfactory bulb that is excited (Dalton, 2002).

The social and sexual behaviour of animals is more strongly regulated by olfaction than is human behaviour (Alcock, 2002). For example, many species use urine to mark their territories; we humans find other ways, such as erecting fences or spreading our belongings over the table we are using in the library. Nonetheless, like animals, we have special receptors in the nose that send impulses to a separate olfactory area in the brain that connects with brain structures

olfactory bulb

forebrain structure immediately above the nasal cavity

pheromones
chemical signals found in natural body scents

menstrual synchrony
the tendency of women who live together or are close friends to become more similar in their menstrual cycles

involved in social and reproductive behaviour. Some researchers believe that **pheromones**, chemical signals found in natural body scents, may affect human behaviour in subtle ways (Beauchamp and Bartoshuk, 1997) and E.O. Wilson, the sociobiologist, has said that pheromones are the most important signals used by organisms of all kinds (Wyatt, 2003).

One interesting phenomenon known as **menstrual synchrony** is the tendency of women who live together or are close friends to become more similar in their menstrual cycles. Psychologist Martha McClintock (1971) tested 135 college women and found that during the course of an academic year, room-mates moved from a mean of 8.5 days apart in their periods to 4.9 days apart. Another study of 51 women who worked together showed that close friends had menstrual onsets averaging 3.5 to 4.3 days apart, whereas those who were not close friends had onsets that averaged 8 to 9 days apart (Weller et al., 1999). Are pheromones responsible for synchrony? In one experiment, 10 women with regular cycles were dabbed under the nose every few days with underarm secretions collected from another woman. After three months, the recipients' cycles began to coincide with the sweat donor's cycles. A control group of women who were dabbed with an alcohol solution rather than sweat showed no menstrual synchrony with a partner (Preti et al., 1986). In other studies, however, menstrual synchrony was not found for cohabiting lesbian couples or for Bedouin women who spent most of their time together, indicating that prolonged and very intensive contact may not be conducive to menstrual synchrony (Weller and Weller, 1997; Weller et al., 1999). The jury here is still out, with Stern and McClintock (1998) showing that the cycle can be shortened by the smell of a secretion from the underarm of other women at certain points of their menstrual cycle. Research from Wang et al. (2002) appear to indicate that there is also a gender difference in sensitivities to odours. Women appear more sensitive, with lower thresholds than men for certain smells.

Do odours make us sexually attractive? The marketers of various 'pheromone' perfumes tell us they do. It is clear that animals find the scents of the opposite sex irresistible when ready to mate. However, researchers have yet to find any solid evidence to back the claims of commercial products promising instant sexual attraction. For humans, it appears that a pleasant personality and good grooming are a better bet than artificially applied pheromones when it comes to finding a mate. A strong scent was certainly important to Napoleon, who famously instructed his lover Josephine not to wash before his arrival. A little known malady is the loss of the sense of smell, known as *anosmia* which can clearly cause significant perceptual and social problems. The causes may be a result of head injury (Smith and Seiden, 1991) or, perhaps, infection. Either way, the loss of the sense of smell can be extremely debilitating. The treatments for the problem stem from courses of drugs to more significant surgical intervention. Surgery might be used, for instance, to develop the nasal cavities or to remove any obstructions that may be there. Treatment for anosmia as a result of head injury often requires different drugs, and the success rate appears to be less than perfect, but reports (Duncan and Seiden, 1995) indicate that while complete recovery may not happen, treatment can help improve matters. An interesting, although unpleasant effect of the treatment has been reported by some sufferers who report *phantosmias, or phantom-smells* or *parosmia – a distortion of smell*. Smell is, to some extent the 'forgotten' sense, but it should not be.

THE SKIN AND BODY SENSES

The skin and body senses include the senses of touch, **kinaesthesis** (muscle movement) and equilibrium. The last two are called *body senses, and collectively as proprioception (the felt, or perceived position of the body in space)*, because they inform us of the body's position and movement. They tell us, for example, if we are running or standing still, lying down or sitting up.

kinaesthesis
sense of muscle movement

The Tactile Senses

Touch is important to us in many ways. Sensitivity to extreme temperatures and to pain enables us to escape external danger and alerts us to disorders within our body. Tactile sensations are also a source of many of life's pleasure. As discussed in Chapter 2, massage can enhance new-born babies' development (Cigales et al., 1997; Field, 2000). Conversely, it has been shown that a lack of tactile contact with a caretaking adult can significantly delay physical, social and emotional development (Harlow, 1958).

Humans are sensitive to at least four tactile sensations: pressure (touch), pain, warmth and cold. These sensations are conveyed by receptors in the skin and in our internal organs. Mixtures of these four sensations form the basis for all other common skin sensations, such as itching.

Considering the Importance of Our Skin Senses

The skin, a multilayered elastic structure that covers 2 square yards (6 square metres) and weighs between 2.7 and 4.5 kilograms, is the largest organ in our body. As shown in Figure 5.26, it contains a variety of receptor structures, but their role in specific sensations is less clear than for the other senses. Many sensations probably depend on specific patterns of activity in the various receptors (Goldstein, 2002). We do know that the primary receptors for pain and temperature are the *free nerve endings*, simple nerve cells beneath the skin's surface that resemble bare tree branches (Gracely et al., 2002). *Basket cell fibres* situated at the base of hair follicles are receptors for touch and light pressure (Heller and Schiff, 1991).

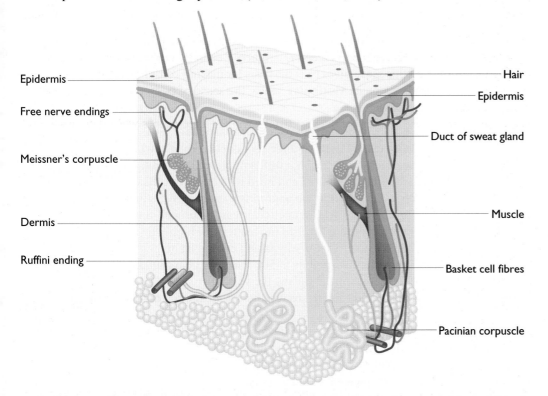

Focus 5.16

Describe the receptors and processing mechanisms for the tactile senses.

FIGURE 5.26

Skin receptors.

A variety of sensory receptors in the human skin and internal tissues allow us to sense touch and temperature. Basket cell fibres around hair follicles detect bending of the hair in light touch, and Meissner's corpuscles provide the same information in hairless areas. Pacinian corpuscles and Ruffini endings provide deeper touch sensations, and the free nerve endings respond to temperature and painful stimuli.

SOURCE: adapted from Smith, 1998.

The brain can locate sensations because skin receptors send their messages to the point in the somatosensory cortex that corresponds to the area of the body where the receptor is located. As we saw in Chapter 4, the amount of cortex devoted to each area of the body is related to that part's sensitivity. Our fingers, lips and tongue are well represented, accounting for their extreme sensitivity to stimulation (Fig. 5.27; see also Fig. 4.21).

Sometimes the brain 'locates' sensations that cannot possibly be present. This occurs in the puzzling phantom-limb phenomenon, in which amputees experience vivid sensations coming

Focus 5.17

What are the two major body senses? Where are their receptors?

FIGURE 5.27

World-renowned percussionist Evelyn Glennie became deaf many years ago. She now uses her tactile sense to detect distinct vibrations that correspond with individual tones. Though deaf, she is capable of extremely accurate tonal discrimination.

Focus 5.18

What sensory principles underlie sensory prosthetics for the blind and the hearing impaired?

proprioception

the sense of kinaesthesis, which provides us with feedback about our muscles' and joints' positions and movements

vestibular sense

the sense of body orientation, or equilibrium and balance

FIGURE 5.28

Kinaesthesis and the vestibular sense are especially well developed in some people – and essential for performing actions like this one.

from the missing limb (Warga, 1987). Apparently an irritation of the nerves that used to originate in the limb fools the brain into interpreting the resulting nerve impulses as real sensations. Joel Katz and Ronald Melzack (1990) studied 68 amputees who insisted that they experienced pain from the amputated limb that was as vivid and real as any pain they had ever felt. This pain was not merely a recollection of what pain used to feel like in the limb; it was actually experienced in the present. The phantom-limb phenomenon can be quite maddening. Imagine having an intense itch that you can never scratch or an ache that you cannot rub. When amputees are fitted with prosthetic limbs and begin using them, phantom pain tends to disappear (Gracely et al., 2002).

Pain is one of the most intriguing of the skin senses. The sensory and perceptual aspects of pain are topics of great theoretical and research interest to psychologists (Pappagallo, 2005; Watkins and Maier, 2003). Because of pain's relevance to stress and health, we will focus on this sensory modality in greater detail in Chapter 16.

The Body Senses

We would be totally unable to co-ordinate our body movements were it not for **proprioception**, the sense of *kinaesthesis*, which provides us with feedback about our muscles' and joints' positions and movements. Kinaesthetic receptors are nerve endings in the muscles, tendons and joints. The information this sense gives us is the basis for making co-ordinated movements. Co-operating with kinaesthesia is the **vestibular sense**, the sense of body orientation, or equilibrium and balance (Fig. 5.28).

The vestibular receptors are located in the vestibular apparatus of the inner ear (see Fig. 5.21). One part of the balance system consists of three semicircular canals, which contain the receptors for head movement. Each canal lies in a different plane: left–right, backward–forward or up–down. These canals are filled with fluid and lined with hair-like cells that function as receptors. When the head moves, the fluid in the appropriate canal shifts, stimulating the hair cells and sending messages to the brain. The semicircular canals respond only to acceleration and deceleration; when a constant speed is reached (no matter how high), the fluid and the hair cells return to their normal resting state. That is why taking off and landing in an aeroplane gives us a sense of movement whereas cruising along at 500 miles per hour (800 km per hour) does not. Located at the base of the semicircular canals, the vestibular sacs also contain hair cells that respond to the position of the body and tell us whether we are upright or tilted at an angle. These structures form the second part of the body-sense system. If this balance system becomes damaged, or infected, the result can be extremely uncomfortable, with almost constant nausea and the perception of unsteadiness, dizziness and vertigo. A particularly nasty problem of this sort is an illness called labyrinthitis, where a virus attacks the labyrinth-like structure that supports and houses the vestibular components of the inner ear.

You have now learned a considerable amount about the principles underlying stimulus detection and transduction. As the following 'Applying psychological science' section shows, these principles have not only informational value for understanding how our sensory systems operate, but also applied value in helping people with sensory impairments.

APPLYING PSYCHOLOGICAL SCIENCE

SENSORY PROSTHETICS: 'EYES' FOR THE BLIND, 'EARS' FOR THE HEARING IMPAIRED

Millions of people suffer from blindness and deafness, living in sightless or soundless worlds. A promising development combines psychological research on the workings of the sensory systems with technical advances in bioengineering. The result is **sensory prosthetic devices** which provide sensory input that can, to some extent, substitute for what cannot be supplied by the person's sensory receptors. In considering these devices, we should remind ourselves that we do not see with the eyes, hear with the ears or taste with the taste buds; we see, hear and taste with our brain. The nerve impulses sent from the retina or the organ of Corti or the taste buds are no different from those sent from anywhere else in the body. Sight, hearing or taste is simply the brain's adaptation to the input it receives.

> **sensory prosthetic device**
>
> provide sensory input that can, to some extent, substitute for what cannot be supplied by the person's sensory receptors

SEEING WITH THE EARS

One device, known as a Sonicguide, provides new 'eyes' through the ears, capitalizing on principles of auditory localization (Kay, 1982). The Sonicguide (Fig. 5.29) works on the same principle as *echolocation*, the sensory tool used by bats to navigate in total darkness. A headset contains a transmitter that emits high-frequency sound waves beyond the range of human hearing. These waves bounce back from objects in the environment and are transformed by the Sonicguide into sounds that can be heard through earphones. Different sound qualities match specific features of external objects, and the wearer must learn to interpret the sonic messages. For example, the sound's pitch tells the person how far away an object is; a low pitch signals a nearby object and becomes higher as the distance to the object increases. The loudness of the sound tells how large the object is, and the clarity of the sound (ranging from a static-like sound to a clear tone) signals the texture of the object, from very rough to very smooth. Finally, the sound-localization principle described earlier tells the person where the object is located in the environment by means of differences in the time at which sounds arrive at the two ears.

FIGURE 5.29

The Sonicguide allows a blind person to perceive the size, distance, movement, shape, and texture of objects through sound waves that represent the visual features of objects.

In the first laboratory tests of the Sonicguide, psychologists Aitken and Bower (1982) used the apparatus with six blind babies who ranged in age from 5 to 16 months. Within hours or days, all of the babies using the Sonicguide could reach for objects, walk or crawl through doorways, and follow the movement of their hands and arms as they moved them about. Moreover, abilities such as reaching for objects, recognizing favourite toys, and reaching out to be picked up when mother (but not someone else) approached seemed to occur on the same developmental timetable as in sighted children. Aitken and Bower concluded that blind infants can extract the same information from sonic cues as sighted babies do from visual cues.

Older children and adults can learn to use the device too, but not as easily as babies can. Older children trained with the device can easily find objects, such as water fountains and specific toys. They can thread their way through crowded school corridors and can even play hide-and-seek. The Sonicguide is now being used by visually impaired children in schools and other natural settings, as well as by adults (Hill et al., 1995).

THE SEEING TONGUE

Paul Bach-y-Rita has developed a tactile tongue-based, electrical input sensor as a substitute for visual input. The tongue seems an unlikely substitute for the eye, hidden as it is in the dark recess of the mouth. Yet in many ways it may be the second-best organ for providing detailed input, for it is densely packed with tactile receptors, thus allowing the transmission of high resolution data. Moreover, its moist surface is a good conducting medium for electricity, meaning that minimum voltage is required to stimulate the receptors.

Researchers have built an experimental prototype of a device that eventually will be small enough to be invisibly attached directly to the teeth. The current stimulator, shown in Figure 5.30a, receives digital data from a camera and provides patterns of stimulation to the tongue through a 144-electrode array. The array can transmit shapes that correspond to the main features of the visual stimulus. Initial trials with blindfolded sighted people and blind people show that with about nine hours of training, users can 'read' the letters of a Snellen eye chart with an acuity of 20/430, a modest but noteworthy beginning (Simpaio et al., 2001).

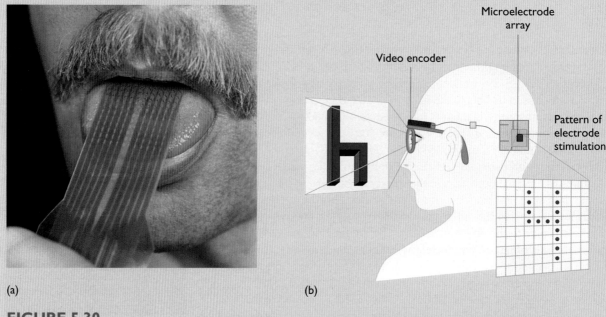

(a)   (b)

FIGURE 5.30

Two approaches to providing artificial vision for the blind.

(a) Bach-y-Rita's device converts digitized stimuli from a camera to a matrix of electrodes, which stimulate tactile receptors in the tongue to communicate spatial information to the brain. (b) Tiny electrodes implanted into individual neurons in the visual cortex produce patterns of phosphenes that correspond to the visual scene observed through the video camera and encoder. Note how the cortical image is reversed as in normal visual input.

With continued development, a miniature camera mounted in spectacles will transmit data to a more densely packed electrode array attached to a device worn in the mouth as you would wear a retainer.

CORTICAL IMPLANTS

A different approach to a visual prosthesis is being investigated. Researchers have developed a device to stimulate the visual cortex directly (Normann et al., 1999). When cells in the visual cortex are stimulated electrically, discrete flashes of light called *phosphenes* are experienced by both sighted and blind people. Because sensory neurons in the visual cortex are arranged in a manner that corresponds to the organization of the retina, a specific pattern of stimulation applied to individual neurons in the cortex can form a phosphene pattern that conforms to the shapes of letters or objects. The acuity of the pattern depends on the area of the visual cortex that is stimulated (the portion receiving input from the densely packed fovea produces greatest acuity) and on the number of stimulating electrodes in the array.

Building on this approach, researchers have developed the device shown in Figure 5.29b. The Utah Intracortical Electrode Array consists of a silicon strip containing thousands of tiny stimulating electrodes that penetrate directly into individual neurons in the visual cortex, where they can stimulate phosphene patterns. Eventually, a tiny television camera mounted in specially designed spectacles will provide visual information to a microcomputer that will analyse the scene and then send the appropriate patterns of electrical stimulation through the implanted electrodes to produce corresponding phosphene patterns in the visual cortex. The researchers have shown that sighted participants who wear darkened goggles that produce phosphene-like patterns of light flashes like those provided by cortical stimulation can quickly learn to navigate through complex environments and are able to read text at about two-thirds their normal rate (Normann et al., 1996; 1999). Blind people who have had the stimulating electrodes implanted in their visual cortex have also been able to learn a kind of cortical Braille for reading purposes.

COCHLEAR IMPLANTS

People with hearing impairments have also been assisted by the development of prosthetic devices. The cochlear implant, a device that can restore hearing in people suffering from nerve deafness (sensorineural hearing loss), has helped many. Instead of amplifying sound like a conventional hearing aid (people with nerve deafness cannot be helped by mere sound amplification), the cochlear implant sorts out useful sounds and converts them into electrical impulses, bypassing the disabled hair cells in the cochlea and stimulating the auditory nerve directly (Fig. 5.31). With a cochlear implant, patients can hear everyday sounds such as sirens, and many wearers can understand speech (Meyer et al., 1998; Parkinson et al., 1998). Sounds heard with currently developed implants tend to be a little muffled, so patients should not expect their hearing to be restored to 'normal'. Training and practice with the implant is required to get used to the sound and to make the most of the additional stimulation it provides. Electrical recording of cortical responses to sounds revealed that hearing-impaired people provided with a cochlear implant show a more widespread pattern of neural activity in the auditory cortex than do people with normal hearing, perhaps helping to account for their poorer sound discrimination (Ito et al., 2004).

Sensory prosthetics illustrate the ways in which knowledge about sensory phenomena such as phosphenes, the organization of the visual cortex, sound localization and the place theory of pitch perception can provide the information needed to take advantage of new technological advances. Yet even with all our ingenuity, prosthetic devices are not substitutes for our normal sensory systems, a fact that should increase our appreciation for what nature has given us.

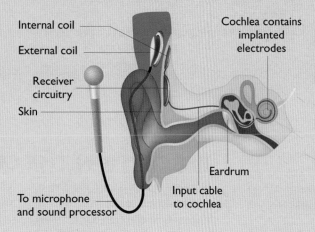

FIGURE 5.31

Cochlear implants.

Cochlear implants provide direct stimulation of the auditory nerve in people whose hair cells are too damaged to respond to fluid waves in the cochlea. Sound enters a microphone and is sent to a processor that breaks the sound down into its principal frequencies and sends electrical signals to external and internal coils. The receiver circuitry stimulates electrodes implanted in cochlear areas associated with particular frequencies.

IN REVIEW

- Sound waves, the stimuli for audition, have two characteristics: frequency, measured in terms of cycles per second, or hertz (Hz); and amplitude, measured in terms of decibels (dB). Frequency is related to pitch, amplitude to loudness. The receptors for hearing are hair cells in the organ of Corti of the inner ear.

- Loudness is coded in terms of the number and types of auditory nerve fibres that fire. Pitch is coded in two ways. Low-frequency tones are coded in terms of corresponding numbers of nerve impulses in individual receptors or by volleys of impulses from a number of receptors. Frequencies above 4000 hertz are coded according to the region of the basilar membrane that is displaced most by the fluid wave in the cochlear canal.

- Hearing loss may result from conduction deafness (conductive hearing loss), produced by problems involving the structures of the ear that transmit vibrations to the cochlea, or from nerve deafness (sensorineural hearing loss), in which the receptors in the cochlea or the auditory nerve are damaged.

- The receptors for taste and smell respond to chemical molecules. Taste buds are responsive to four basic qualities: sweet, sour, salty and bitter. The receptors for smell (olfaction) are long cells in the upper nasal cavity. Natural body odours produced by pheromones appear to account for a menstrual synchrony that may occur among women who live together or are close friends.

- The skin and body senses include touch, kinaesthesis, and equilibrium. Receptors in the skin and body tissues are sensitive to pressure, pain, warmth and cold. Kinaesthesis functions by means of nerve endings in the muscles, tendons, and joints. The sense organs for equilibrium are in the vestibular apparatus of the inner ear.

- Principles derived from the study of sensory processes have been applied in developing sensory prosthetics for the blind and the hearing impaired. Examples include the Sonicguide, which uses auditory input; a device that provides visual information through tactile stimulation of the tongue; direct electrical stimulation of the visual cortex; and cochlear implants.

Focus 5.19

Compare bottom-up and top-down processing of sensory information.

bottom-up processing

system takes in individual elements of the stimulus and then combines them into a unified perception

top-down processing

sensory information is interpreted in light of existing knowledge, concepts, ideas and expectations

PERCEPTION: THE CREATION OF EXPERIENCE

Sensory systems provide the raw materials from which experiences are formed. Our sense organs do not select what we will be aware of or how we will experience it; they merely transmit information through our nervous system. Yet our experiences are not simply a one-to one reflection of what is external to our senses. Different people may experience the same sensory information in radically different ways, because perception is an active, creative process in which raw sensory data are organized and given meaning.

To create our perceptions, the brain carries out two different kinds of processing functions (Fig. 5.32). In **bottom-up processing**, the system takes in individual elements of the stimulus and then combines them into a unified perception. Your visual system operates in a bottom-up fashion as you begin to 'read' letter shapes on a page. Its feature detectors analyse the elements in each letter of every word and then recombine them into your visual perception of the letters and words. In **top-down processing**, sensory information is interpreted in light of existing knowledge, concepts, ideas and expectations. Top-down processing is occurring as you interpret the words and sentences constructed by the bottom-up process. Here you make use of higher-order knowledge, including what you have learned about the meaning of words and sentence construction. Indeed, a given sentence may convey a different personal meaning to you than to another person if you relate its content to some unique personal experiences. Top-down processing accounts for many psychological influences on perception, such as the roles played by our motives, expectations, previous experiences and cultural learning. My personal favourite example of top-down processing is the alleged 'message' that Led Zeppelin 'hid' in their song 'Stairway to Heaven', an example of a supposed subliminal message (see earlier in this chapter). Famously, reversing the music is supposed to reveal sinister alternative lyrics about the devil. The problem is, the 'alternative' lyrics are not really there at all. It is only when you know what you are looking for, when you have an expectation of what you should be perceiving, that the lyrics reveal themselves to you. Top-down processing in action.

PERCEPTION IS SELECTIVE: THE ROLE OF ATTENTION

As you read these words, 100 million sensory messages may be clamouring for your attention. Only a few of these messages register in awareness; the rest you perceive either dimly or not at all. But you can shift your attention to one of those unregistered stimuli at any time. (For example, how does the big toe of your right foot feel right now?) Attention, then, involves two processes: (1) focusing on certain stimuli and (2) filtering out other incoming information. Much of the pioneering work on selective attention was produced by Donald Broadbent (1926–93). He worked at, and eventually directed the Applied Psychology Research Unit in Cambridge, the same unit that was set up in 1944 at the suggestion of Sir Fredrick Bartlett, the great experimental psychologist. At this time, Broadbent was interested in how we select items to attend to. His 'filter theory' tells us how selection is facilitated quite early on in the perception process, before our expectations have begun to play a role. For this reason his is known as an 'early' selection theory. The 'cocktail-party' effect of Cherry (1953) is an example of how some information, even though presented at a very low level, can make it through to our attention systems. Cocktail parties are rather unusual events these days, but you get the idea. Imagine yourself in a busy, speech-laden environment; a café perhaps. I imagine you have experienced the phenomenon of someone mentioning your name among this cacophony, and your attention being drawn immediately in the direction of the source. This is the cocktail-party effect, and is used as evidence for a selective filtering mechanism that allows through certain important, salient information such as your name, meriting conscious, immediate experience.

These processes have been studied experimentally through a technique called *shadowing*, or as Broadbent described them more accurately, *dichotic listening tasks*. Participants wear earphones and listen simultaneously to two messages, one sent through each earphone. They are asked to repeat (or shadow) one of the messages word for word as they listen. Most participants can do this quite successfully, but only at the cost of not remembering what the other message was about. Shadowing experiments demonstrate that we cannot attend completely to more than one thing at a time. But we can shift our attention rapidly back and forth between the two messages, drawing on our general knowledge to fill in the gaps (Bonnel and Hafter, 1998; Sperling, 1984).

Inattentional Blindness

Electrical recording and brain-imaging studies have shown that unattended stimuli register in the nervous system but do not enter into immediate experience (Itti and Rees, 2005). In the visual realm, scientists have coined the term **inattentional blindness** to refer to the failure of unattended stimuli to register in consciousness (Mack, 2003). We can look right at something without 'seeing' it if we are attending to something else. In one study, several experienced pilots training on flight simulators were so intent on watching the landing instruments, such as the airspeed indicator on the plane's windshield, that they directed their plane onto a runway containing another aircraft (Haines, 1991). In another instance, research participants who were counting the number of passes made during a videotaped basketball game did not notice a man wearing a gorilla suit who stopped to thump his chest as he walked across the court, even though he remained in clear sight for more than five seconds (Simons and Chabris, 1999). Inattentional

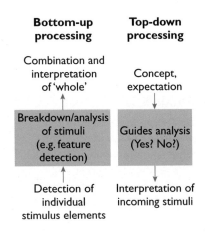

FIGURE 5.32

Perceptual processing.

Bottom-up perceptual processing builds from an analysis of individual stimulus features to a unified perception. Top-down processing begins with a perceptual whole, such as an expectation or an image of an object, and then determines the degree of fit with the stimulus features.

inattentional blindness
the failure of unattended stimuli to register in consciousness

blindness is surely relevant to findings that cell phone conversations significantly reduce driving performance in experimental studies (e.g., Golden et al., 2003). It really is a bad idea to drive and talk on the phone at the same time, and not just because of the obvious 'two-hands-on-the-wheel' reason either. We may extend from this research to suggest that *any* task in addition to driving may result in some disruption of attention away from the primary task of controlling the car. Perhaps even singing along to music, tuning your radio or even speaking to passengers.

Environmental and Personal Factors in Attention

Attention is strongly affected by both the nature of the stimulus and by personal factors. Stimulus characteristics that attract our attention include intensity, novelty, movement, contrast and repetition. Advertisers use these properties in their commercials and packaging (Fig. 5.33). Internal factors, such as our motives and interests, act as powerful filters and influence which stimuli in our environment we will notice. For example, when we are hungry, we are especially sensitive to food-related cues, another good reason for not doing your weekly food shop when hungry. A botanist walking through a park is especially attentive to the plants; a landscape architect attends primarily to the layout of the park; musicians or audiologists attends more closely to the detail in the music or sounds they hear.

People are especially attentive to stimuli that might represent a threat to their well-being, a tendency that would clearly have biological survival value (Izard, 1989; Oehman et al., 2001). A study by Christine and Ranald Hansen (1988) illustrates this tendency. They presented slides showing groups of nine people. In half of the pictures, all the people looked either angry or happy. In the other half, there was one discrepant face, either an angry face in a happy crowd or a happy face in an angry crowd. Participants were asked to judge as quickly as possible whether there was a discrepant face in the crowd, then press 'yes' or 'no' buttons attached to electrical timers. The dependent variable was the length of time required to make this judgement, measured in milliseconds (thousandths of a second).

The results, summarized in Figure 5.34, showed that participants were much faster at detecting a single angry face in an otherwise happy crowd than at finding a happy face in an angry crowd. It was as if the angry face, which the experimenters assumed to have threat value, jumped out of the crowd when the stimuli were scanned. Ulf Dimberg (1997) also believes that humans are biologically programmed to detect threatening faces, and he has shown via high-speed photography that emotional facial responses to such stimuli occur in observers within one-third of

Focus 5.20

What two complementary processes occur in attention? What is inattentional blindness? What kinds of external and internal factors influence attention?

FIGURE 5.33

Advertisers use attention-attracting stimuli in their advertisements. Personal characteristics of potential customers are also important. What kinds of individuals do you suppose would be most attentive to this advertisement from a Europe-based retailer?

In-Psych

We each interpret incoming stimuli based on previous experiences and associations. Thus, while individuals may have very similar sensory experiences, their perceptual experiences differ. Consider this as you view the 'Perceptual Integration' video in Chapter 5 of the In-Psych programme online.

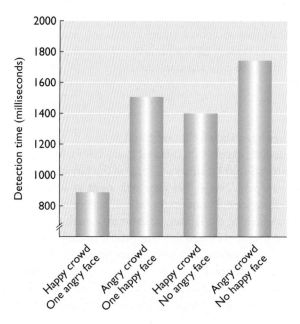

FIGURE 5.34

Primed to perceive threat.

Perceptual vigilance to threatening stimuli is shown in the finding that people required less time to detect an angry face in a happy crowd than to detect a happy face in an angry crowd or to determine if there was any discrepant face in a happy or an angry crowd.

SOURCE: based on Hansen and Hansen, 1988.

a second. Attentional processes are thus based both on innate biological factors and on past experiences that make certain stimuli important or meaningful to us.

Advertisers are adept at using attention-getting stimuli to attract potential customers to their products. However, sometimes the process backfires as in the case of a particularly popular car advert in the UK where a model disrobes as she walks towards the car, finally dropping her underwear out of the window before driving off. Reports indicated that although people remembered the advert very well, the brand of the car could be recalled by very few.

PERCEPTIONS HAVE ORGANIZATION AND STRUCTURE

Have you ever stopped to wonder why we perceive the visual world as being composed of distinct objects? After all, the information sent by the retina reflects nothing but an array of varying intensities and frequencies of light energy. The light rays reflected from different parts of a single object have no more natural 'belongingness' to one another than those coming from two different objects. Yet we perceive scenes as involving separate objects, such as trees, buildings and people. These perceptions must be a product of an organization imposed by our nervous system (Jenkin and Harris, 2005; Tarr and Vuong, 2002). This top-down process of perceptual organization occurs so automatically that we take it for granted. But Dr Richard, a prominent psychologist who suffered brain damage in an accident, no longer does. His story makes fascinating reading and is reported here by Oliver Sacks.

> There was nothing wrong with his eyes, yet the input he received from them was not put together correctly. Dr Richard reported that if he saw a person, he sometimes would perceive the separate parts of the person as not belonging together in a single body. But if all the parts moved in the same direction, Dr Richard then saw them as one complete person. At other times, he would perceive people in crowds wearing the same colour clothes as 'going together' rather than as separate people. He also had difficulty putting sights and sounds together. Sometimes, the movement of the lips did not correspond to the sounds he heard, as if he were watching a badly dubbed foreign movie. Dr Richard's experience of his environment was thus disjointed and fragmented. (Sacks, 1985, p. 76)

Another, more extreme example of perceptual organization gone awry is synaesthesia, which we described at the beginning of this chapter. It is important to point out that synaesthesis is not a sensory impairment comparable to deafness or blindness, but it is extremely interesting none the less. What, then, are the processes whereby sensory confusion or nonsense begins to make perceptual sense?

Gestalt Principles of Perceptual Organization

Early in the twentieth century, Gestalt psychologists set out to discover how we organize the separate parts of our perceptual field into a unified and meaningful whole. *Gestalt* is the German term for 'pattern', 'whole', or 'form'. Gestalt theorists were early champions of top-down processing, arguing that the wholes we perceive are often more than (and frequently different from) the sum of their parts. Thus your perception of the photograph in Figure 5.35 is likely to be more than people on a field.

The Gestalt theorists emphasized the importance of **figure–ground relations**, our tendency to organize stimuli into a central or foreground figure and a background. In vision, the central figure is usually in front of or on top of what we perceive as background. It has a distinct shape and is more striking in our perceptions and memory than the background. We perceive borders or contours wherever there is a distinct

Focus 5.21
Which Gestalt psychology principles and laws underlie perceptual organization?

figure–ground relations

our tendency to organize stimuli into a central or foreground figure and a background

FIGURE 5.35

As Gestalt psychologists emphasize, what we perceive (in this case, the famous Palm development in Dubai) is more than simply the sum of its individual parts; much more than a collection of islands.

FIGURE 5.36

What do you see?

Figure–ground relations are important in perceptual organization. Here the artist, Bev Doolittle, has created great similarity between figure and ground in this representation of natural camouflage, yet enough figural cues remain to permit most people to detect the ponies. *Pintos*, by Bev Doolittle, 1979. The Greenwich Workshop, Trumbull, Connecticut.

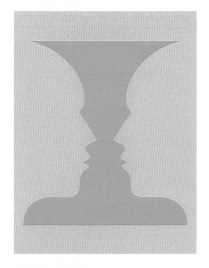

FIGURE 5.37

One stimulus, two perceptions.

This reversible figure illustrates alternating figure-ground relations. It can be seen as a candlestick/vase or as two people facing one another. Whichever percept exists at the moment is seen as figure against background.

Gestalt laws of perceptual organization
similarity, proximity, closure and continuity

change in the colour or lightness (illumination level) of a visual scene, but we interpret these contours as part of the figure rather than background. Likewise, we tend to hear instrumental music as a melody (figure) surrounded by other chords or harmonies (ground).

Separating figure from ground or background can be challenging (Fig. 5.36), yet our perceptual systems are usually equal to the task. Sometimes, however, what is figure and what is ground is not completely obvious, and the same stimulus can give rise to two different perceptions. Consider Figure 5.37, for example. If you examine it for a while, two alternating but equally plausible perceptions will emerge, one based on the inner portion and the other formed by the two outer portions. When the alternative perception occurs, what was previously the figure becomes the background.

In addition to figure–ground relations, the Gestalt psychologists were interested in how separate stimuli come to be perceived as parts of larger wholes. They suggested that people group and interpret stimuli in accordance with four **Gestalt laws of perceptual organization**: similarity, proximity, closure and continuity. These organizing principles are illustrated in Figure 5.38. What is your perception of Figure 5.38a? Do you perceive 16 unrelated dots or two triangles formed by different-sized dots? If you see triangles, your perception obeys the Gestalt *law of similarity*, which says that when parts of a configuration are perceived as similar, they will be perceived as belonging together. The *law of proximity* says that elements that are near each other are likely to be perceived as part of the same configuration. Thus most people perceive Figure 5.38b as three sets of two lines rather than six separate lines. Illustrated in Figure 5.38c is the *law of closure*, which states that people tend to close the open edges of a figure or fill in gaps in an incomplete figure, so that their identification of the form (in this case, a circle) is more complete than what is actually there. Finally, the *law of continuity* holds that people link individual elements together so they form a continuous line or pattern that makes sense. Thus Figure 5.38d is far more likely to be seen as combining components a–b and c–d rather than a–d and c–b, which have poor continuity. Or consider Fraser's spiral, shown in Figure 5.39, which is not really a spiral at all! (To demonstrate, trace one of the circles with a pencil.) We perceive the concentric circles as a spiral because, to our nervous system, a spiral gives better continuity between individual elements than does a set of circles. The spiral is created by us, not by the stimulus.

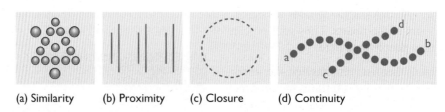

(a) Similarity   (b) Proximity   (c) Closure   (d) Continuity

FIGURE 5.38

Gestalt perceptual laws.

Among the Gestalt principles of perceptual organisation are the laws of (a) similarity, (b) proximity, (c) closure, and (d) continuity. Each principle causes us to organize stimuli into wholes that are greater than the sums of their parts.

FIGURE 5.39

A spiral that is not.

Fraser's spiral illustrates the Gestalt law of continuity. If you follow any part of the 'spiral' with a pencil, you will find that it is not a spiral at all but a series of concentric circles. The 'spiral' is created by your nervous system because that perception is more consistent with continuity of the individual elements.

PERCEPTION INVOLVES HYPOTHESIS TESTING

Recognizing a stimulus implies that we have a **perceptual schema** – a mental representation or image containing the critical and distinctive features of a person, object, event or other perceptual phenomenon. Schemas provide mental templates that allow us to classify and identify sensory input in a top-down fashion.

Imagine, for example, that a person approaches you and calls out your name. Who is this person? If the stimuli match your internal schemas of your best friend's appearance and voice closely enough, you identify the person as your friend (McAdams and Drake, 2002). Many political cartoonists have an uncanny ability to capture the most noteworthy facial features of famous people so that we can easily recognize the person represented by even the simplest line sketch.

Perception is, in this sense, an attempt to make sense of stimulus input, to search for the best interpretation of sensory information we can arrive at based on our knowledge and experience. Likening perception to the scientific process described in Chapter 2, Gregory (1966; 2005) suggested that each of our perceptions is essentially a hypothesis about the nature of the object or, more generally, the meaning of the sensory information. The perceptual system actively searches its gigantic library of internal schemata for the interpretation that best fits the sensory data.

An example of how effortlessly our perceptual systems build up descriptions or hypotheses that best fit the available evidence is found in the comic strips created by Gustave Verbeek in the early 1900s. The Sunday *New York Herald* told Verbeek that his comic strip had to be restricted to six panels. Verbeek wanted 12 panels, so he ingeniously created 12-panel cartoons in only six panels by drawing pictures like that shown in Figure 5.40a. The reader viewed the first six

> **perceptual schema**
> a mental representation or image containing the critical and distinctive features of a person, object, event or other perceptual phenomenon

> **Focus 5.22**
> What roles do perceptual schemas and perceptual sets play in our sensory interpretations?

(a)

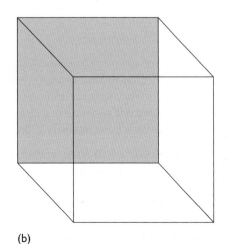

(b)

FIGURE 5.40

Reversible perceptions.

Here are two examples of how the same stimulus can give rise to different perceptions. (a) After viewing this comic strip panel by Gustave Verbeek, turn it upside down for a different spin on the story. (b) Stare at this Necker cube for a while; the front of the cube will suddenly become the back, and it will appear as if you are viewing the cube from a different angle.

panels, then turned the newspaper upside down to read the last six and finish the story. Try this yourself on the panel shown in the figure, and you will find that a bird story becomes story about a fish. The point is that you do not see an upside-down bird; you see an entirely different picture because the stimuli created by the new orientation match other perceptual schemas.

In some instances, sensory information fits two different internal representations, and there is not enough information to permanently rule out one of them in favour of the other. For example, examine the Necker cube, shown in Figure 5.40b. If you stare at the cube for a while, you will find that it changes before your very eyes as your nervous system tries out a new perceptual hypothesis.

PERCEPTION IS INFLUENCED BY EXPECTATIONS: PERCEPTUAL SETS

There are occasions where your expectation of a scene may significantly influence your perception of it. In times of war, for instance, tragic mistakes have been made. The modern parlance is 'friendly fire' where death is caused by fire from allied forces. The press is often full of such cases. In 1988, the USS *Vincennes* shot down an airliner containing 290 passengers, which it had mistaken for an F-14 fighter-plane. The death of Lance-Corporal Matty Hull in Afghanistan in March 2003 is another example. Why might these terrible events have happened? Psychologists have identified a phenomenon known as perceptual set. Just as the central unit in each line in Figure 5.3 depends on the context in which it is presented – on the identity of the flanking items, so too can our perception of a scene be influenced by the context in which the scene is viewed. We might describe those who pulled the triggers, or released the bombs and missiles, in the many friendly fire incidents that have occurred as having had a **perceptual set** – a readiness to perceive stimuli in a particular way. Sometimes, believing is seeing.

STIMULI ARE RECOGNIZABLE UNDER CHANGING CONDITIONS: PERCEPTUAL CONSTANCIES

When a closed door suddenly swings open, it casts a different image on our retina, but we still perceive it as a door. Our perceptual hypothesis remains the same. Were it not for **perceptual constancies**, which allow us to recognize familiar stimuli under varying conditions, we would have to literally rediscover what something is each time it appeared under different conditions. Thus you can recognize a tune even if it is played in a different octave or register, or even by another instrument, as long as the relations among its notes are maintained. You can detect the flavour of a particular spice even when it occurs in foods having very different tastes.

In vision, several constancies are important. *Shape constancy* allows us to recognize people and other objects from many different angles. Take a look at an nearby door, as it is opened the image arriving at your perceptual systems changes, but you still perceive the door as door-shaped, nearly always a rectangle! Sitting close to the screen in a cinema can make it appear, at first a little distorted. After a while the visual system corrects for the distortion and objects on the screen look normal again.

Because of *lightness constancy*, the relative lightness of objects remains the same under different conditions of illumination (brightness), such as full sunlight and shade. Lightness constancy occurs because the ratio of light intensity between an object and its surroundings is usually constant. The actual brightness of the light that illuminates an object does not matter, as long as the same light intensity illuminates both the object and its surroundings.

When we take off in an aeroplane, we know that the cars and buildings below are not shrinking as we climb away from them. *Size constancy* is the perception that the perceived size of objects remains relatively constant even though images on our retina change in size with variations in distance. Thus a man who is judged to be 6 feet (1.83 m) tall when standing 5 feet (1.5 m) away is not perceived to be 3 feet (0.9 m) tall at a distance of 10 feet (3 m), even though the size of his image on the retina is reduced to half its original size (Fig. 5.41).

perceptual set
a readiness to perceive stimuli in a particular way

perceptual constancies
allow us to recognize familiar stimuli under varying conditions

Focus 5.23
What factors account for shape, lightness and size constancy in vision?

FIGURE 5.41

Who's bigger?

Size constancy based on distance cues causes us to perceive the person in the background as being of normal size. When the same stimulus is seen in the absence of the distance cues, size constancy breaks down.

WHAT DO YOU THINK?

WHY DOES THAT RISING MOON LOOK SO BIG?

Just before bedding down for the night on a backpacking trip, a friend of ours poked his head outside his tent and gasped to his wife, 'Look at the moon! Just look at that moon!' Indeed, a bright-red full moon had just come over the horizon, and it was so enormous that it dwarfed the mammoth peaks surrounding them. The couple gazed at it in wonder for a few minutes and then retired into their tent. Later that night, they looked outside again and were puzzled to see a rather small, ordinary full moon approaching the zenith. You too may have exclaimed over the size of a rising moon, only to notice later that the moon, well above the horizon, seemed to have shrunk. What can explain this phenomenon? Think about it, then see p. 222.

IN REVIEW

- Perception involves both bottom-up processing, in which individual stimulus fragments are combined into a perception, and top-down processing, in which existing knowledge and perceptual schemas are applied to interpret stimuli.

- Attention is an active process in which we focus on certain stimuli while blocking out others. We cannot attend completely to more than one thing at a time, but we are capable of rapid attentional shifts. Inattentional blindness refers to a failure to perceive certain stimuli when attending to other stimulus elements. Attentional processes are affected by the nature of the stimulus and by personal factors such as motives and interests. The perceptual system appears to be especially vigilant to stimuli that denote threat or danger.

- Gestalt psychologists identified a number of principles of perceptual organization, including figure-ground relations and the laws of similarity, proximity, closure and continuity. Gregory suggested that perception is essentially a hypothesis about what a stimulus is, based on previous experience and the nature of the stimulus.

- Perceptual sets involve a readiness to perceive stimuli in certain ways, based on our expectations, assumptions, motivations and current emotional state.

- Perceptual constancies allow us to recognize familiar stimuli under changing conditions. In the visual realm, there are three constancies: shape, lightness and size.

FIGURE 5.42

The demands faced by a work-class tennis player in judging the speed, distance and movements of a service within thousandths of a second underscore the capabilities of the visual perceptual system.

> **monocular depth cues**
> (one eye)
>
> **binocular depth cues**
> (both eyes)

PERCEPTION OF DEPTH, DISTANCE AND MOVEMENT

The ability to adapt to a spatial world requires that we make fine distinctions involving distances and the movement of objects within the environment. Humans are capable of great precision in making such judgements. Consider, for example, the perceptual task faced by a tennis player (Fig. 5.42). A service in tennis can reach in excess of 190 km/h. This gives the receiver a split second to react. A slower service of, say, 170 km/h will reach the receiver a little later. To adequately return the service and stand a good chance of winning the point the receiver must judge speed and point of arrival moments after the ball has been struck. If any of the judgements are wrong the ball may well be mis-hit, or the point lost through a poor return. The perceptual demands of such a task are imposing indeed – as are the salaries earned by those who can perform this task consistently. How does the visual perception system make such judgements?

DEPTH AND DISTANCE PERCEPTION

One of the more intriguing aspects of visual perception is our ability to perceive depth. The retina receives information in only two dimensions (length and width), but the brain translates these cues into three-dimensional perceptions. It does this by using both **monocular** *(one eye)* **depth cues**, and **binocular** *(both eyes)* **depth cues**.

Monocular Depth Cues

Judging the relative distances of objects is one important key to perceiving depth. When artists paint on a flat canvas, they depend on a variety of monocular cues to create perceptions of depth in their pictures. One such cue is *patterns of light and shadow*. Twentieth-century artist M.C. Escher skilfully used light and shadow to create the three-dimensional effect shown in Figure 5.43. The depth effect is as powerful if you close one eye as it is when you use both.

FIGURE 5.43

Patterns of light and shadow can serve as monocular depth cues, as shown in *Drawing Hands,* by M.C. Escher.

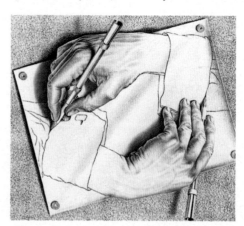

Another cue, *linear perspective*, refers to the perception that parallel lines converge, or angle towards one another, as they recede into the distance. Thus if you look down rail tracks, they appear to angle towards one another with increased distance, and we use this as a depth cue as in Figure 5.46a. The same occurs with the edges of a highway or the sides of an elevator shaft. *Interposition*, in which objects closer to us may cut off part of our view of more distant objects, provides another cue for distance and depth.

An object's *height in the horizontal plane* provides another source of information. For example, a ship 10 kilometres offshore appears in a higher plane and closer to the horizon than does one that is only 2 kilometres from shore. *Texture* is a fifth cue, because the texture or grain of an object appears finer as distance increases. Likewise, *clarity* can be an important cue for judging distance; we can see nearby hills more clearly than ones that are far away, especially on hazy days.

Relative size is yet another basis for distance judgements. If we see two objects that we know to be of similar size, then the one that looks smaller will be judged to be farther away. For example, this cue may figure prominently in the moon illusion.

None of these monocular cues involve movement of the object(s), but a final monocular cue, *motion parallax*, tells us that if we are moving, nearby objects appear to move faster in the opposite direction than do those further away. Like the other monocular cues, motion provides us with information that we can use to make judgements about distance and therefore about depth.

Figure 5.44 illustrates all of the monocular cues just described, with the exception of motion parallax. Linear perspective is produced by the converging lines of the plank. The people and objects in the background are smaller than those in the foreground (relative size). The background is in a higher horizontal plane than in the foreground. The objects in the background are less detailed than the 'closer' ones (texture and clarity). The people and objects in the foreground cut off parts of those 'behind' them in the background (interposition). Light and shadow are also used to create a depth effect.

FIGURE 5.44

In this mural the artist has skilfully used seven monocular depth cues to create a striking three-dimensional depth effect.

Focus 5.24

Describe the major monocular and binocular depth/distance cues, as well as the bases for movement perception.

binocular disparity

each eye sees a slightly different image

convergence

produced by feedback from the muscles that turn your eyes inward to view a close object

Binocular Depth Cues

The most dramatic perceptions of depth arise with binocular depth cues, which require the use of both eyes. For an interesting binocular effect, hold your two index fingers about 6 inches (15 cm) in front of your eyes with their tips about 1 inch (2.5 cm) apart. Focus on your fingers first, then focus beyond them across the room. Doing so will produce the image of a third finger between the other two. This third finger will disappear if you close either eye.

Most of us are familiar with the delightful depth experiences provided by View-Master slides and 3-D movies watched through special glasses. These devices make use of the principle of **binocular disparity**, in which each eye sees a slightly different image. Within the brain, the visual input from the two eyes is analysed by feature detectors that are attuned to depth (Howard, 2002; Livingstone and Hubel, 1994). Some of the feature detectors respond only to stimuli that are either in front of or behind the point on which we are fixing our gaze. The responses of these depth-sensitive neurons are integrated to produce our perception of depth (Goldstein, 2002).

A second binocular distance cue, **convergence**, is produced by feedback from the muscles that turn your eyes inward to view a close object. You can experience this cue by holding a finger about 1 foot (30 cm) in front of your face and then moving it slowly towards you. Messages sent to your brain by the eye muscles provide it with a depth cue.

PERCEPTION OF MOVEMENT

The perception of movement is a complex process, sometimes requiring the brain to integrate information from several different senses. To demonstrate, hold a pen in front of your face. Now, while holding your head still, move the pen back and forth. You will perceive the pen as moving. Now hold the pen still and move your head back and forth at the same rate of speed. In both cases, the image of the pen moved across your retina in about the same way. But when you moved your head, your brain took into account input from your proprioceptive and vestibular systems and concluded that you were moving but the pen was not.

The primary cue for perceiving motion is the movement of the stimulus across the retina (Sekuler et al., 2002). Under optimal conditions, a retinal image need move only about one-fifth the diameter of a single cone for us to detect movement (Nakayama and Tyler, 1981). The relative movement of an object against a structured background is also a movement cue (Gibson, 1979). For example, if you fixate on a bird in flight, the relative motion of the bird against its background is a strong cue for perceived speed of movement.

The illusion of smooth motion can be produced if we arrange for the sequential appearance of two or more stimuli. Gestalt psychologist Max Wertheimer (1912) demonstrated this in his studies of **stroboscopic movement**, illusory movement produced when a light is briefly flashed in darkness and then, a few milliseconds later, another light is flashed nearby. If the timing is just right, the first light seems to move from one place to the other in a manner indistinguishable from real movement.

Stroboscopic movement (termed the 'phi phenomenon' by Wertheimer) has been used commercially in numerous ways. For example, think of the strings of successively illuminated lights on railway platforms or electronic noticeboards that seem to move endlessly around the border or that spell out messages in a moving script. Stroboscopic movement is also the principle behind motion pictures, which consist of a series of still photographs, or frames, that are projected on a screen in rapid succession with dark intervals in between (Fig. 5.45). The rate at which the frames are projected is critical to our perception of smooth movement. Early films, such as the silent films of the 1920s, projected the stills at only 16 frames per second, and the movements appeared fast and jerky. Today the usual speed is 24 frames per second, which more perfectly produces an illusion of smooth movement. Television presents at 30 images per second.

ILLUSIONS: FALSE PERCEPTUAL HYPOTHESES

Our analysis of perceptual schemas, hypotheses, sets and constancies allows us to understand some interesting perceptual experiences known as **illusions**, compelling but incorrect perceptions. Such perceptions can be understood as erroneous perceptual hypotheses about the nature of a stimulus. Illusions are not only intriguing and sometimes delightful visual experiences, but also provide important information about how our perceptual processes work under normal conditions (Gregory, 2005).

Ironically, most visual illusions can be attributed to perceptual constancies that ordinarily help us perceive more accurately (Frisby, 1980). For example, size constancy results in part from our ability to use distance cues to judge the size of objects. But as we saw in the discussion of the moon illusion, distance cues can sometimes fool us. In the Ponzo illusion, shown in Figure 5.46a, the depth cues of linear perspective (the tracks converging) and height of the horizontal plane provide distance cues that make the upper bar appear farther away than the lower bar. Because it seems farther away, the perceptual system concludes that the bar in the background must be larger than the bar in the foreground, despite the fact that the two bars cast retinal images of the same size. The same occurs in the vertical arrangement seen in Figure 5.46b.

---

stroboscopic movement

illusory movement produced when a light is briefly flashed in darkness and then, a few milliseconds later, another light is flashed nearby

FIGURE 5.45

Stroboscopic movement is produced in moving pictures as a series of still photographs projected at a rate of 24 per second.

illusions

compelling but incorrect perceptions

Focus 5.25

What is an illusion? How are constancies and context involved in visual illusions?

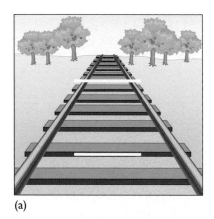
(a)

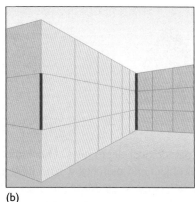
(b)

FIGURE 5.46

Two examples of the Ponzo illusion.

Which lines in (a) and (b) are longer? The distance cues provided by the converging rail tracks and the walls affect size perception and disrupt size constancy. You may also notice that the bars and 'fins' at their ends, formed by the walls and panels in the picture resemble the different parts of the Müller-Lyer illusion shown in Figure 5.55.

Distance cues can be manipulated to create other size illusions. To illustrate this, Adelbert Ames constructed a special room. Viewed through a peephole with one eye, the room's scene presents a startling size reversal (Fig. 5.47a). Our perceptual system assumes that the room has a normal rectangular shape because, in fact, most rooms do. Monocular depth cues do not allow us to see that, in reality, the left corner of the room is twice as far away as the right corner (Fig. 5.47b). As a result, size constancy breaks down, and we base our judgement of size on the sizes of the retinal images cast by the two people.

(a)

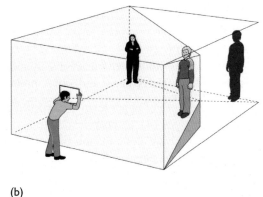
(b)

FIGURE 5.47

A size illusion.

(a) The Ames Room produces a striking size illusion because it is designed to appear rectangular. (b) The room, however, is actually a trapezoid, and the figure on the left is actually much farther away from the viewer than the one on the right and thus appears smaller.

The study of perceptual constancies shows that our perceptual hypotheses are strongly influenced by the context, or surroundings, in which a stimulus occurs. Figure 5.48 shows some examples of how context can produce illusory perceptions.

Some of the most intriguing perceptual distortions are produced when monocular depth cues are manipulated to produce a figure or scene whose individual parts make sense but whose overall organization is 'impossible' in terms of our existing perceptual schemas. Figure 5.49 shows three impossible figures. In each case, our brain extracts information about depth from the individual features of the objects, but when this information is put together and matched with our existing schemas, the percept that results simply does not make sense. The 'devil's tuning fork', for example, could not exist in our universe. It is a two-dimensional image

The long lines are actually parallel, but the small lines make them appear crooked.

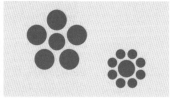
Which inner circle is larger? check and see.

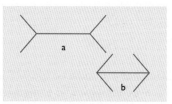
The Müller-Lyer illusion. Which line, a or b, is longer? Compare them with a ruler.

FIGURE 5.48

Context-produced geometric illusions.

FIGURE 5.49

Things that could not be.

Monocular depth cues are cleverly manipulated to produce an impossible triangle, a never-ending staircase, and the 'devil's tuning fork'.

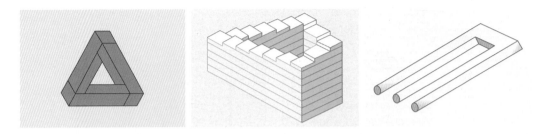

containing paradoxical depth cues. Our brain, however, automatically interprets it as a three-dimensional object and matches it with its internal schema of a fork – which turns out to be a bad fit. The never-ending staircase provides another compelling example of an impossible scene that seems perfectly reasonable when we focus only on its individual elements.

Illusions are not only personally and scientifically interesting, but they can have important real-life implications. Our 'Research close-up' describes one scientist's search for an illusion having life-and-death implications.

WHAT DO YOU THINK?

EXPLAIN THIS STRIKING ILLUSION

We would like you to experience a truly interesting illusion. To do so, all you need is a piece of fairly heavy paper and a little patience.

Fold the piece of paper lengthwise down the middle and set it on a table with one of the ends facing you like an open tent. Close one eye and, from slightly above the object, stare at a point midway along the top fold of the paper. At first the object looks like a tent, but after a while the paper will suddenly 'stand up' and look like a corner viewed from the inside. When this happens, gently move your head back and forth while continuing to view with one eye. The movement will produce a striking perception. Can you explain what you now see? For a discussion of this illusion, see p. 222.

RESEARCH CLOSE-UP

STALKING A DEADLY ILLUSION

SOURCE: C.L. Kraft (1978) A psychophysical contribution to air safety: simulator studies of illusions in night visual approaches, in H.L. Pick, Jr., H.W. Leibowitz, J.E. Singer, A. Steinschneider, and H.W. Stevenson (eds), *Psychology: From Research to Practice*. New York: Plenum.

INTRODUCTION

When the Boeing Company introduced the 727 jet airliner in the mid-1960s, it was the height of technology and design in aviation technology. The plane performed well in test flights, but four fatal crashes soon after it was placed in service raised fears that there might be a serious flaw in its design.

The first accident occurred as a 727 made its approach to Chicago's airport over Lake Michigan on a clear night. The plane plunged into the lake 19 miles (30 km) offshore. About a month later, another 727 glided in over the Ohio River to land in Cincinnati. Unaccountably, it struck the ground about 12 feet (4 m) below the runway elevation and burst into flames. The third accident occurred as an aircraft approached Salt Lake City over dark land. The lights of the city twinkled in the distance, but the plane made too rapid a descent and crashed short of the runway. Months later, a Japanese airliner approached Tokyo at night. The flight ended tragically as the plane, its landing gear not yet lowered, struck the waters of Tokyo Bay, 6 miles (9.5 km) from the runway.

Analysis of these four accidents, as well as others, suggested a common pattern. All occurred at night under clear weather conditions, so the pilots were operating under visual flight rules rather than performing instrument landings; by this we mean that the pilots were watching the real horizon, monitoring the aeroplane's performance by visually checking flight orientation and position through the windows, not only by using the dials. In each instance, the plane was approaching city lights over dark areas of water or land. In all cases, the lights in the background terrain sloped upward to varying degrees. Finally, all the planes crashed short of the runway. These observations led a Boeing industrial psychologist, Conrad L. Kraft, to suspect that the cause of the crashes might be pilot error based on some sort of visual illusion.

METHOD

To test this possibility, Boeing engineers constructed an apparatus to simulate night landings (Fig. 5.50). It consisted of a cockpit and a miniature lighted city named Nightertown. The city moved towards the cockpit on computer-controlled rollers, and it could be tilted to simulate various terrain slopes. The pilot could control simulated air speed and rate of climb and descent, and the Nightertown scene was controlled by the pilot's responses just as a true visual scene would be.

FIGURE 5.50

Conrad Kraft, a Boeing psychologist, created an apparatus to study how visual cues can affect the simulated landings of airline pilots. Pilots approached Nightertown in a simulated cockpit. The computer-controlled city could be tilted to reproduce the illusion thought to be responsible for fatal air crashes.

The participants were 12 experienced Boeing flight instructors who made virtual-reality landings at Nightertown under systematically varied conditions created by the computerized simulator. All their landings were visual landings so as to be able to test whether a visual illusion was occurring. Every aspect of their approach and the manner in which they controlled the aircraft were measured precisely.

RESULTS

The flight instructors' landings were nearly flawless until Kraft duplicated the conditions of the fatal crashes by having the pilots approach an upward-sloping distant city over a dark area. When this occurred, the pilots were unable to detect the upward slope, assumed that the background city was flat, and consistently overestimated their approach altitude. On a normal landing, the preferred altitude at 4.5 miles (7 km) from the runway is about 1240 feet (377 m). As Figure 5.51 shows, the pilots approached at about this altitude when the simulated city was in a flat position. But when it was sloped upward, 11 of the 12 experienced pilot instructors crashed about 4.5 miles (7 km) short of the runway.

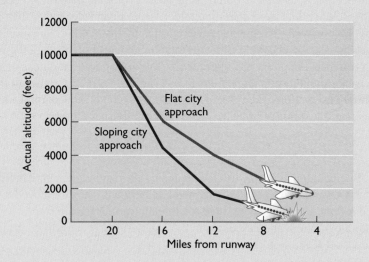

FIGURE 5.51

Misperceptions of experienced pilots.

The illusion created by upward-sloping city lights caused even highly experienced pilots to overestimate their altitude, and 11 of the 12 flight instructors crashed short of the runway. When the lights were flat, all the pilots made perfect approaches.

SOURCE: based on Kraft, 1978.

CRITICAL DISCUSSION

This study shows the value of studying behaviour under highly controlled conditions and with precise measurements. By simulating the conditions under which the fatal crashes had occurred, Kraft identified the visual illusion that was the source of pilot error. He showed that the perceptual hypotheses of the flight instructors, like those of the pilots involved in the real crashes, were tragically incorrect. It would have been ironic if one of the finest jetliners ever built had been removed from service because of presumed mechanical defects while other aircraft remained aloft and at risk for tragedy.

Kraft's research not only saved the 727 from months – or perhaps years – of needless mechanical analysis but, more important, it also identified a potentially deadly illusion and the precise conditions under which it occurred. On the basis of Kraft's findings, Boeing recommended that pilots attend carefully to their instruments when landing at night, even under perfect weather conditions. Today, commercial airline pilots are required to make instrument landings not only at night but also during the day.

IN REVIEW

- Monocular cues to judge distance and depth include linear perspective, relative size, height in the horizontal plane, texture and clarity. Depth perception also occurs through the monocular cues of light and shadow patterns, interposition and motion parallax.

- Binocular disparity occurs as slightly different images are viewed by each eye and acted on by feature detectors for depth. Convergence of the eyes provides a second binocular cue.

- The basis for perception of movement is absolute movement of a stimulus across the retina or relative movement of an object in relation to its background. Stroboscopic movement is illusory.

- Illusions are erroneous perceptions. They may be regarded as incorrect perceptual hypotheses. Perceptual constancies help produce many illusions, including the moon illusion and a variety of other context-produced illusions.

EXPERIENCE, CRITICAL PERIODS AND PERCEPTUAL DEVELOPMENT

Development of sensory and perceptual systems results from the interplay of biological and experiential factors. Genes play a very significant role in biological development, but this development is also influenced by environmental experiences. For example, if you were to be blinded in an accident and later learned to read Braille, the area of the somatosensory cortex that is devoted to the fingertips would enlarge over time as it borrowed other neurons to increase its sensitivity (Pool, 1994). By the time they are old enough to crawl, children placed on a 'visual cliff' formed by a glass-covered table that suddenly drops off beneath the glass will not ordinarily venture over the edge (Fig. 5.52). This aversion may result from the interaction of innate depth-perception abilities and previous experience (Gibson and Walk, 1960).

FIGURE 5.52

Eleanor Gibson and Richard Walk constructed this 'visual cliff' with a glass-covered drop-off to determine whether crawling infants and newborn animals can perceive depth. Even when coaxed by their mothers, young children refuse to venture onto the glass over the cliff. Newborn animals also avoid the cliff.

What might a lifetime of experience in a limited environment do to perceptual abilities that seem innate? Sometimes, conditions under which people live create natural experiments that help provide answers. For example, the Ba Mbuti pygmies, who live in the rainforests of Central Africa, spend their lives in a closed-in green world of densely packed trees without open spaces. Turnbull (1961) once brought a man named Kenge out of the forest to the edge of a vast plain. A herd of buffalo grazed in the distance. To Turnbull's surprise, Kenge remarked that he had never seen insects of that kind. When told that they were buffalo, not insects, Kenge was deeply offended and felt that Turnbull was insulting his intelligence. To prove his point, Turnbull drove Kenge in his jeep towards the animals. Kenge stared in amazement as the 'insects' grew into buffalo before his eyes. To explain his perceptual experience to himself, he concluded that witchcraft was being used to fool him. Kenge's misperception occurred as a failure in size constancy. Having lived in an environment without open spaces, he had no experience in judging the size of objects at great distances.

FIGURE 5.53

A challenging world.

Inverted vision would create a world that looks like this. How would you make your way around in this upside-down environment where right is left and left is right? Adaptation to such a world is possible but challenging.

Focus 5.26

What evidence shows that cultural factors can influence perceptual interpretations, constancies and susceptibility to illusions?

As noted earlier, when light passes through the lens of the eye, the image projected on the retina is reversed, so that right is left and up is down. What would happen if you were to wear a special set of glasses that undid this natural reversal of the visual image and created a world like that in Figure 5.53? In 1896 perception researcher George Stratton did just that, possibly becoming the first human ever to have a right-side-up image on his retina while standing upright. Reversing how nature and a lifetime of experience had fashioned his perceptual system disoriented Stratton at first. The ground and his feet were now up, and he had to put on his hat from the bottom up. He had to reach to his left to touch something he saw on his right. Stratton suffered from nausea and could not eat or get around for several days. Gradually, however, he adapted to his inverted world, and by the end of eight days he was able to successfully reach for objects and walk around. Years later, people who wore inverting lenses for longer periods of time did the same. Some were able to ski down mountain slopes or ride motorcycles while wearing the lenses, even though their visual world remained upside down and never became normal for them. When they removed the inverting lenses, they had some initial problems but soon readapted to the normal visual world (Dolezal, 1982).

CROSS-CULTURAL RESEARCH ON PERCEPTION

As far as we know, humans come into the world with the same perceptual abilities, regardless of where they are born. From that point on, however, the culture they grow up in helps determine the kinds of perceptual learning experiences they have. Cross-cultural research can help identify which aspects of perception occur in all people, regardless of their culture, as well as perceptual differences that result from cultural experiences (Deregowski, 1989). Although there are far more perceptual similarities than differences among the peoples of the world, the differences that do exist show us that perception can indeed be influenced by experience.

Consider the perception of a picture that depends on both the nature of the picture and characteristics of the perceiver. In Figure 5.54a, what is the object above the woman's head? In one study, most Europeans instantly identified it as a window. They also tended to see the family sitting inside a dwelling. But when the same picture was shown to East Africans, nearly all perceived the object as a basket or box that the woman was balancing on her head. To them, the family was sitting outside under a tree (Gregory and Gombrich, 1973). These interpretations were more consistent with their own cultural experiences.

In our earlier discussion of monocular depth cues, we used paintings such as that in Figure 5.43 to illustrate monocular depth perception. In western culture, we have constant exposure to

FIGURE 5.54

Does culture influence perception?

(a) What is the object above the woman's head? East Africans had a far different answer than did North Americans and Europeans. (b) Cultural differences also occurred when people were asked which animal the archer was about to shoot.

SOURCES: (a) adapted from Gregory and Gombrich, 1973; (b) adapted from Hudson, 1960.

(a)

(b)

two-dimensional pictures that our perceptual system effortlessly turns into three-dimensional perceptions. Do people who grow up in cultures where they are not exposed to pictures have the same perceptions? When presented with the picture in Figure 5.54b and asked which animal the hunter was about to shoot, tribal African people answered that he was about to kill the 'baby elephant'. They did not use the monocular cues that cause westerners to perceive the man as hunting the antelope and to view the elephant as an adult animal in the distance (Hudson, 1960).

Illusions occur when one of our common perceptual hypotheses is in error. Previously we showed you the Müller-Lyer illusion (see Fig. 5.48), in which a line appears longer when the V-shaped lines at its ends radiate outward rather than inward. Westerners are very susceptible to this illusion. They have learned that in their 'carpentered' environment, which has many corners and square shapes, inward-facing lines occur when corners are closer and outward-facing lines occur when they are farther away (Fig. 5.55). But when people from other cultures who live in more rounded environments are shown the Müller-Lyer stimuli, they are more likely to correctly perceive the lines as equal in length (Segall et al., 1966). They are less likely to fall prey to a perceptual hypothesis that normally is correct in an environment like ours that is filled with sharp corners but wrong when applied to the lines in the Müller-Lyer illusion (Deregowski, 1989).

Cultural learning affects perceptions in other modalities as well. Our perceptions of tastes, odours and textures are strongly influenced by our cultural experiences. A taste that might produce nausea in one culture may be considered delicious in another. The taste and gritty texture experienced when chewing a large raw insect or the rubbery texture of a fish eye may appeal far less to you than it would to a person from a culture in which that food is common or considered a delicacy.

CRITICAL PERIODS: THE ROLE OF EARLY EXPERIENCE

The examples in the preceding section suggest that experience is essential for the development of perceptual abilities. For some aspects of perception, there are also **critical periods** during which certain kinds of experiences must occur if perceptual abilities and the brain mechanisms that underlie them are to develop normally. If a critical period passes without the experience occurring, it is too late to undo the deficit that results.

Earlier we saw that the visual cortex has feature detectors composed of neurons that respond only to lines at particular angles. What would happen if newborn animals grew up in a world in which they saw some angles but not others? In a classic experiment, Blakemore and Cooper (1970) created such a world for newborn kittens. The animals were raised in the dark except for a five-hour period each day, during which they were placed in round chambers that had either vertical or horizontal stripes on the walls. Figure 5.56a shows one of the kittens in a vertically

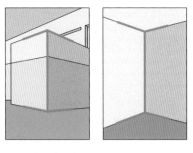

FIGURE 5.55

Which vertical line is longer?

Perceptual experiences within our 'carpentered' environment make us susceptible to the Müller-Lyer illusion (see Fig. 5.48), which appears here in vertical form. Again, the vertical lines are the same physical length.

critical periods

during which certain kinds of experiences must occur if perceptual abilities and the brain mechanisms that underlie them are to develop normally

FIGURE 5.56

Effects of visual deprivation.

(a) Kittens raised in a vertically striped chamber such as the one shown here lacked cortical cells that fired in response to horizontal stimuli. (b) The kittens' perceptual 'holes' are easily seen in this diagram, which shows the orientation angles that triggered nerve impulses from feature detectors.

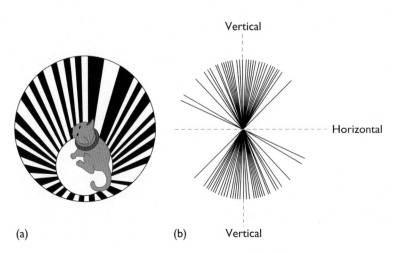

(a)   (b)

striped chamber. A special collar prevented the kittens from seeing their own bodies while they were in the chamber, guaranteeing that they saw nothing but stripes.

When the kittens were 5 months old, Blakemore and Cooper presented them with bars of light at differing angles and used microelectrodes to test the electrical responses of individual feature detector cells in their visual cortex. The results for the kittens raised in the vertically striped environment are shown in Figure 5.56b. As you can see, the kittens had no cells that fired in response to horizontal stimuli, resulting in visual impairments. They also acted as if they could not see a pencil when it was held in a horizontal position and moved up and down in front of them. However, as soon as the pencil was rotated to a vertical position, the animals began to follow it with their eyes as it was moved back and forth.

As you might expect, the animals raised in the horizontally striped environment showed the opposite effect. They had no feature detectors for vertical stimuli and did not seem to see them. Thus the cortical neurons of both groups of kittens developed in accordance with the stimulus features of their environments.

Other visual abilities also require early exposure to the relevant stimuli. Sugita (2004) raised infant monkeys in rooms illuminated with only monochromatic light. As adults, these monkeys were clearly deficient in colour perception. They had particular difficulty with colour constancy, being unable to recognize the same colours under changing levels of brightness.

Some perceptual abilities are influenced more than others by restricted stimulation. In other research, monkeys, chimpanzees and kittens were raised in an environment devoid of shapes. The animals distinguished differences in size, lightness and colour almost as well as normally reared animals do, but for the rest of their lives they performed poorly on more complex tasks, such as distinguishing different types of objects and geometric shapes (Riesen, 1965).

RESTORED SENSORY CAPACITY

Suppose it had been possible to restore Helen Keller's vision when she reached adulthood. What would she have seen? Could she have perceived visually the things that she had learned to identify through her other senses?

Unfortunately, it was not possible to provide Helen Keller with the miracle of restored vision. However, scientists have studied the experiences of other visually impaired people who acquired the ability to see later in life. For example, people born with cataracts grow up in a visual world without form. The clouded lenses of their eyes permit them to perceive light but not patterns or shapes. One such person was Virgil, who had been almost totally blind since childhood. He read Braille, enjoyed listening to sports on the radio and conversing with other people, and had adjusted quite well to his disability. At the urging of his fiancée, Virgil agreed to undergo surgery to remove his thick cataracts. The day after the surgery, his bandages were removed. Neurologist Oliver Sacks (1999) recounts what happened next.

> There was light, there was colour, all mixed up, meaningless, a blur. Then out of the blur came a voice that said, 'Well?' Then, and only then ... did he finally realize that this chaos of light and shadow was a face – and, indeed, the face of his surgeon.... His retina and optic nerve were active, transmitting impulses, but his brain could make no sense of them. (p. 132)

Virgil was never able to adjust to his new visual world. He had to touch objects in order to identify them. He had to be led through his own house and would quickly become disoriented if he deviated from his path. Eventually, Virgil lost his sight once again. This time, however, he regarded his blindness as a gift, a release from a sighted world that was bewildering to him.

Virgil's experiences are characteristic of people who have their vision restored later in life. Marius von Senden (1960), compiled data on patients born with cataracts who were tested soon

Focus 5.27

How do studies of restricted stimulation and restored vision illustrate the role of critical periods in perceptual development?

after their cataracts were surgically removed in adulthood. These people were immediately able to perceive figure–ground relations, to scan objects visually and to follow moving targets with their eyes, which suggests that such abilities are innate. However, they could not visually identify objects, such as eating utensils, that they were familiar with through touch; nor were they able to distinguish simple geometric figures without counting the corners or tracing the figures with their fingers.

After several weeks of training, the patients were able to identify simple objects by sight, but their perceptual constancies were very poor. Often they were unable to recognize the same shape in another colour, even though they could discriminate between colours. Years later, some patients could identify only a few of the faces of people they knew well. Many also had great difficulty judging distances. Apparently, no amount of subsequent experience could make up for their lack of visual experience during the critical period of childhood.

All of these – cross-cultural perceptual differences, animal studies involving visual deprivation and observations of congenitally impaired people whose vision has been restored – suggest that biological and experiential factors interact in complex ways. Some of our perceptual abilities are at least partially present at birth, but experience plays an important role in their normal development. How innate and experiential factors interact promises to be a continued focus of perception research. Perception is very much a biopsychological process whose mysteries are best explored by examining them from biological, psychological and environmental levels of analysis (Fig. 5.57).

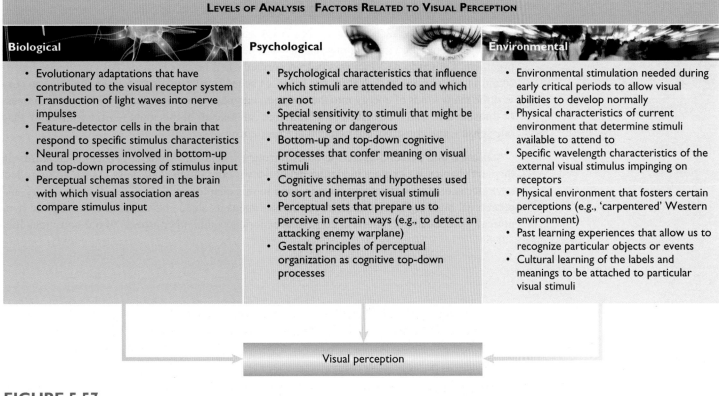

LEVELS OF ANALYSIS   FACTORS RELATED TO VISUAL PERCEPTION

Biological

- Evolutionary adaptations that have contributed to the visual receptor system
- Transduction of light waves into nerve impulses
- Feature-detector cells in the brain that respond to specific stimulus characteristics
- Neural processes involved in bottom-up and top-down processing of stimulus input
- Perceptual schemas stored in the brain with which visual association areas compare stimulus input

Psychological

- Psychological characteristics that influence which stimuli are attended to and which are not
- Special sensitivity to stimuli that might be threatening or dangerous
- Bottom-up and top-down cognitive processes that confer meaning on visual stimuli
- Cognitive schemas and hypotheses used to sort and interpret visual stimuli
- Perceptual sets that prepare us to perceive in certain ways (e.g., to detect an attacking enemy warplane)
- Gestalt principles of perceptual organization as cognitive top-down processes

Environmental

- Environmental stimulation needed during early critical periods to allow visual abilities to develop normally
- Physical characteristics of current environment that determine stimuli available to attend to
- Specific wavelength characteristics of the external visual stimulus impinging on receptors
- Physical environment that fosters certain perceptions (e.g., 'carpentered' Western environment)
- Past learning experiences that allow us to recognize particular objects or events
- Cultural learning of the labels and meanings to be attached to particular visual stimuli

Visual perception

FIGURE 5.57

Levels of analysis: factors related to visual perception.

IN REVIEW

- Perceptual development involves both physical maturation and learning. Some perceptual abilities are innate or develop shortly after birth, whereas others require particular experiences early in life in order to develop.

- Cultural factors can influence certain aspects of perception, including picture perception and susceptibility to illusions. However, many aspects of perception seem constant across cultures.

- Visual-deprivation studies, manipulation of visual input and studies of restored vision have shown that the normal biological development of the perceptual system depends on certain sensory experiences at early periods of development.

SOME FINAL REFLECTIONS

Suppose someone were to be born cut off not only from sight and sound, as Helen Keller was, but from all internal and external sensory stimulation. What would that person's conscious life be like? With the brain deprived of all sensory input from world and body, what mental processes could exist? What knowledge could accrue? What memories could form? Would the brain itself atrophy as it was deprived of the sensory input needed for neuronal development and synaptic network formation?

As far as we know, such a scenario has never occurred. However, imagining such a condition does bring home the vital role our sensory and perceptual systems play in being a functioning organism. Leonardo da Vinci was indeed correct when he proclaimed, 'All knowledge has its origin in our perceptions'. Nature has given us specialized sensors that allow the brain to convert the many kinds of energy into the common language of nerve impulses through the process of transduction, and it has given us a brain that can take all of this input – often from more than one sense – and construct our perceptual experiences.

Sensation and perception are the basis for our existence as sentient, conscious creatures. In the next chapter, we explore in greater detail the varieties of consciousness. As we do so, reflect back occasionally on what you have learned in this chapter and ask yourself what sensory and perceptual building blocks underlie such phenomena as sleep and wakefulness, drug and hypnotically produced alterations in conscious experience, and other aspects of our conscious life.

KEY TERMS AND CONCEPTS

Each term has been boldfaced and defined in the chapter on the page indicated in parentheses.

absolute threshold (p. 168)

amplitude (p. 187)

basilar membrane (p. 189)

binocular depth cues (p. 208)

binocular disparity (p. 209)

bottom-up processing (p. 200)

cochlea (p. 189)

conduction deafness (conduction hearing loss) (p. 191)

cones (p. 176)

convergence (p. 209)

critical periods (p. 217)

dark adaptation (p. 177)

decibels (dB) (p. 187)

decision criterion (p. 169)

difference threshold (p. 171)

dual-process theory (p. 180)

feature detectors (p. 181)

figure–ground relations (p. 203)

fovea (p. 176)

frequency (p. 187)

frequency theory of pitch perception (p. 189)

Gestalt laws of perceptual organization (p. 204)

gustation (p. 192)

Hering's opponent-process theory (p. 178)

hertz (Hz) (p. 187)

illusions (p. 210)

inattentional blindness (p. 201)

kinaesthesis (p. 194)

lens (p. 175)

menstrual synchrony (p. 194)

monocular depth cues (p. 208)

nerve deafness (sensorineural hearing loss) (p. 191)

olfaction (p. 192)

olfactory bulb (p. 193)

optic nerve (p. 176)

organ of Corti (p. 189)

perception (p. 167)

perceptual constancies (p. 206)

perceptual schema (p. 205)

perceptual set (p. 206)

pheromones (p. 194)

photopigments (p. 177)

place theory of pitch perception (p. 190)

proprioception (p.196)

psychophysics (p. 168)

retina (p. 175)

rods (p. 176)

sensation (p. 167)

sensory adaptation (p. 172)

sensory prosthetic devices (p. 197)

signal detection theory (p. 169)

stroboscopic movement (p. 210)

subliminal stimulus (p. 169)

synaesthesia (p. 166)

taste buds (p. 192)

top-down processing (p. 200)

transduction (p. 174)

vestibular sense (p. 196)

visual acuity (p. 176)

Weber's law (p. 171)

Young–Helmholtz trichromatic theory (p. 178)

WHAT DO YOU THINK?

NAVIGATING IN FOG: PROFESSOR MAYER'S TOPOPHONE (p. 191)

The device shown in Figure 5.22 made use of two principles of sound localization. First, because the two ear receptors were much larger than human ears, they could capture more sound waves and funnel them to the sailor's ears. Second, the wide spacing between the two receptors increased the time difference between the sound's arrival at the two human ears (the inter-aural time difference), thus increasing directional sensitivity.

WHY DOES THAT RISING MOON LOOK SO BIG? (p. 207)

To begin with, let us emphasize the obvious: the moon is not actually larger when it is on the horizon. Photographs show that the size of the image cast on the retina is exactly the same in both cases. So what psychologists call the moon illusion must be created by our perceptual system. Though not completely understood, the illusion seems to be a false perception caused by cues that ordinarily contribute to maintaining size constancy. The chief suspect is apparent distance, which figures importantly in our size judgements. One theory holds that the moon looks bigger as it is rising over the horizon because we use objects in our field of vision, such as trees, buildings and landscape features to estimate its distance. Experiments have shown that objects look farther away when viewed through filled spaces than they do when viewed through empty spaces (such as the sky overhead). Filled space can make objects look as much as 2.5 to 4 times farther away. According to the theory, the perceptual system basically says, 'If the size of the retinal image is the same but it's farther away, then it must be bigger'.

   This explanation cannot be the whole story, however, because some people perceive the moon on the horizon as being closer, rather than farther away. If something the same size seems closer, it will look larger even though it is not. It may be that there are individual differences in the size-judgement processes that cause the illusion, so that no single explanation applies to everybody.

EXPLAIN THIS STRIKING ILLUSION (p. 212)

To analyse your experience, it is important to understand that both the 'tent' and the 'corner' cast identical images on your retina. After perceiving the tent for a while, your brain shifted to the second perceptual hypothesis, as it did in response to the Necker cube shown in Figure 5.39. When the object looked like a tent, all the depth information was consistent with that perception. But when you began to see it as a corner and then moved your head slowly back and forth, the object seemed to twist and turn as if it were made of rubber. This occurred because when you moved, the image of the near point of the fold moved across your retina faster than the image of the far point. This is the normal pattern of stimulation for points at different depths and is known as motion parallax. Thus when you were seeing a tent, the monocular cue of motion parallax was consistent with the shape of the object. But when the object was later seen as standing upright, all the points along the fold appeared to be the same distance away, yet they were moving at different rates of speed! The only way your brain could maintain its 'corner' perception in the face of the motion parallax cues was to see the object as twisting and turning. Again, as in other illusions, forcing all of the sensory data to fit the perceptual hypothesis produced an unusual experience.

CHAPTER SIX
CONSCIOUSNESS

Our normal waking consciousness is but one special type of consciousness, whilst all about it, parted from it by the filmiest of screens, there lie potential forms of consciousness entirely different.

Three unrelated people, whom we will call Sondra, Katrien and Jason, sought treatment for an unusual problem: eating while asleep. They would rise from bed several times each night and sleepwalk to the kitchen. Sondra would

> consume cat food or salt sandwiches, buttered cigarettes and odd concoctions prepared in a blender.... She frequently binged on large quantities of peanut butter, butter, salt and sugar.... Once she awakened while struggling to open a bottle of ammonia cleaning fluid, which she was prepared to drink on account of being thirsty. (Schenck et al., 1991, p. 430)

While sleepwalking, Jason and Katrien also consumed odd foods (such as raw bacon), and sometimes Jason spoke coherently with his wife. Upon awakening, they could not remember their experiences, but empty packages and half-eaten food indicated that something was amiss.

After evaluation by sleep specialists, Sondra was treated with medication and Jason was referred to his primary physician. Neither drugs nor psychotherapy helped Katrien, so a new plan was tried: locking the kitchen door before turning in, putting the key in a hard-to-find location, and placing crackers and a pitcher of water by the bed. Usually, when Katrien wakes in the morning, the crackers and water are gone, and she has no memory of having consumed them (c.f. Whyte and Kavey, 1990).

...

At age 34, DF lost consciousness and suffered brain damage from carbon-monoxide exposure. As psychologist Melvin Goodale (2000) describes, when DF regained consciousness,

> she was unable to recognize the faces of her relatives and friends or identify the visual form of common objects. In fact, she could not even tell the difference between simple geometric shapes such as a square and a triangle. At the same time, she had no difficulty recognizing people from their voices or identifying objects placed in her hands; her perceptual problems appeared to be exclusively visual. (p. 367)

DF's condition is called **visual agnosia**, an inability to visually recognize objects. Visual agnosia is not blindness. DF can see, and brain imaging has revealed that her primary visual cortex is largely undamaged. Regions that are damaged have left her, according to Goodale (2000), without the ability to perceive the size, shape and orientation of objects.

But how, then, is DF able to walk across a room while easily avoiding obstacles? And if she cannot consciously perceive the difference in shape and size between, say, a spoon and a glass, how does she know to open her hand to the proper width to grasp objects? On a laboratory task, how is DF able to insert an object into a tilted rectangular slot when, just moments before, she could not consciously recognize the slot's orientation (see Fig. 6.1)?

visual agnosia
an inability to visually recognize objects

FIGURE 6.1

Perception without conscious awareness.

A rectangular slot was rotated to different angles on a series of trials. When asked simply to hold and tilt a rectangular card to match the slot's angle, DF performed poorly. She could not consciously recognize the orientation of the slot. Despite this, when asked to rapidly insert the card into the slot, as illustrated here, she performed well.

SOURCE: Goodale, 1995.

Sondra, Jason and Katrien's sleep-eating and DF's visual agnosia are clear departures from our normal state of conscious awareness. Yet their experiences contain features that are not as far removed from our daily existence as we might think.

How can someone be asleep yet find the kitchen and prepare food? Well, consider this: why don't you fall out of bed at night? You are not consciously aware of your many postural shifts when you are sound asleep, yet a part of you somehow knows where the edge of the bed is. And what of DF's ability, while awake, to avoid obstacles and grasp objects without conscious awareness of their shape or size? Again, consider this: have you ever lost concentration while driving because you were deeply engrossed in thought? Suddenly you snap out of it, with no memory of the miles you have just driven. While you were consciously focused inward, some part of you – without conscious awareness – kept track of the road and controlled your hand movements at the wheel.

Philosopher David Chalmers (1995) notes that consciousness is the most mysterious thing in the world while at the same time being the most familiar. As we now explore, its mysteries range from normal waking states to sleep and dreams, drug-induced experiences, and beyond (Fig. 6.2).

(a)

(b)

FIGURE 6.2

During a Sufi religious ceremony in Istanbul, Turkey, whirling dervishes perform a spinning dance – a prayer in motion –that induces an altered state of consciousness. (b) Buddhists believe that meditation produces inner peace, facilitates insight and enlightenment, and opens the path to different dimensions of consciousness.

THE PUZZLE OF CONSCIOUSNESS

What is consciousness, and how does it arise within our brain? When psychology was founded in the late 1800s, its 'great project' was to unravel some of the puzzles of consciousness (Natsoulas, 1999). This interest waned during behaviourism's mid-twentieth-century dominance, but a resurgence of the cognitive and biological perspectives has led us to rethink long-standing conceptions about the mind. Rethinking these conceptions has led psychologists to address the puzzle of consciousness in a number of different ways, and we describe them in the chapter that follows.

CHARACTERISTICS OF CONSCIOUSNESS

In psychology, **consciousness** is often defined as our moment-to-moment awareness of ourselves and our environment. Among its characteristics, consciousness is:

- *subjective and private.* Other people cannot directly know what reality is for you, nor can you enter directly into their experience.
- *dynamic (ever changing).* We drift in and out of various states throughout each day. Moreover, though the stimuli of which we are aware constantly change, we typically experience consciousness as a continuously flowing stream of mental activity, rather than as disjointed perceptions and thoughts (James, 1950).

consciousness
our moment-to-moment awareness of ourselves and our environment

Focus 6.1

Describe the basic characteristics of consciousness. How are states of consciousness measured?

selective attention

the process that focuses awareness on some stimuli to the exclusion of others

- *self-reflective and central to our sense of self*. The mind is aware of its own consciousness. Thus no matter what your awareness is focused on – a lovely sunset or an itch on your back – you can reflect on the fact that you are the one who is conscious of it.

- *intimately connected with the process of selective attention*, discussed in Chapter 4. William James noted that 'the mind is at every stage a theatre of simultaneous possibilities. Consciousness consists in … the selection of some, and the suppression of the rest by the … agency of Attention' (1879, p. 13). **Selective attention** is the process that focuses awareness on some stimuli to the exclusion of others. If the mind is a theatre of mental activity, then consciousness reflects whatever is illuminated at the moment – the bright spot on the stage – and selective attention is the spotlight or mechanism behind it (Baars, 1997).

MEASURING STATES OF CONSCIOUSNESS

Scientists who study consciousness must operationally define private inner states in terms of measurable responses. *Self-report measures* ask people to describe their inner experiences. They offer the most direct insight into a person's subjective experiences but are not always verifiable or possible to obtain. While asleep, most of us (thankfully) do not speak; nor can we fill out self-report questionnaires.

Behavioural measures record, among other things, performance on special tasks. By examining DF's performance on the card-slot task under different conditions (see Fig. 6.1), researchers concluded that despite being unable to consciously perceive the slot's orientation, her brain nonetheless processed this information. Behavioural measures are objective, but they require us to infer the person's state of mind. Figure 6.3 illustrates another clever behavioural measure.

FIGURE 6.3

Gordon Gallup (1970) exposed four chimpanzees to a mirror. By day 3 they used it to inspect hard-to-see parts of their own bodies and began making odd faces at themselves in the mirror. To further test whether the chimps knew the mirror image was their own reflection, Gallup anaesthetized them and put a red mark on each of their foreheads. Later, with no mirror, the chimps rarely touched the red mark. But upon seeing it when a mirror was introduced, they touched the red spot on their forehead almost 30 times in 30 minutes, suggesting that the chimps had some self-awareness. Using a similar test in which a red mark was placed on the tip of infants' noses, researchers found that infants begin to recognize themselves in a mirror around 18 months of age.

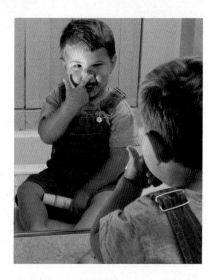

Physiological measures establish the correspondence between bodily processes and mental states. Through electrodes attached to the scalp, the electroencephalograph (EEG) measures brainwave patterns that reflect the ongoing electrical activity of large groups of neurons. Different patterns correspond to different states of consciousness, such as whether you are alert, relaxed, or in light or deep sleep. Brain-imaging techniques allow scientists to more specifically examine brain regions and activity that underlie various mental states. Physiological measures cannot tell us what a person is experiencing subjectively, but they have been invaluable for probing the inner workings of the mind. The problem with consciousness is that it cannot be seen, it is difficult to describe, and quite how one thought leads to another, and how an opinion, image or a stimulus of some other kind can influence our behaviour is not easily described at all. Consider the issue of brain imaging for instance. A researcher presenting a picture of a politician to a person in an MRI scanner will be rewarded with a brain scan. Interpreting what it was about the image that generated the activation seen in the scan is neither simple nor possible. Yes, portions of the brain that deal with visual images, perhaps familiar or famous faces may have responded, but the person's political opinion, memories of past experiences as a once politically active student, or the fact that the politician looks a little like the person's great aunt who is expected for dinner at the weekend will not be coded in the scan. In short, our consciousness cannot be 'read'. As Papanicolaou (1998) points out, no one currently would be likely to insist that statements such as 'the subject just saw this red nose, then he felt an itch on his forehead and, while raising his hand to scratch, a fleeting image of another red nose went through his mind's eye' (p. 129), could possibly be correct. Functional imaging techniques cannot presently accomplish feats such as these, although whether this may be possible in the future is open to debate.

LEVELS OF CONSCIOUSNESS

Much of what occurs within your brain is beyond conscious access. You do not consciously perceive the brain processes that lull you to sleep, wake you or regulate your body temperature. You are aware of your thoughts but not of how your brain creates them. What else lies outside of conscious awareness?

The Freudian Viewpoint

In 1900 Sigmund Freud (1953) proposed that the human mind consists of three levels of awareness. The *conscious* mind contains thoughts and perceptions of which we are currently aware. *Preconscious* mental events are outside current awareness but can easily be recalled under certain conditions. For instance, you may not have thought about a friend for years, but when someone mentions your friend's name, you become aware of pleasant memories. *Unconscious* events cannot be brought into conscious awareness under ordinary circumstances. Freud proposed that some unconscious content – such as unacceptable sexual and aggressive urges, traumatic memories and threatening emotional conflicts – is *repressed*; that is, it is kept out of conscious awareness because it would arouse anxiety, guilt or other negative emotions.

Focus 6.2

Contrast the psychodynamic and cognitive views of the mind, and controlled versus automatic processing.

Behaviourists roundly criticized Freud's ideas. After all, they sought to explain behaviour without invoking conscious mental processes, much less unconscious ones. Cognitive psychologists and many contemporary psychodynamic psychologists also take issue with specific aspects of Freud's theory. As psychodynamic psychologist Drew Westen (1998) notes, 'Many aspects of Freudian theory are indeed out of date, and they should be. Freud died in 1939, and he has been slow to undertake further revisions' (p. 333), although the non-scientific nature of Freud's work has been defended by some, including Grünbaum (1986), who said that strong statements and claims made by Freud for the power of psychoanalysis lend themselves strongly to testing, and attempts at disproving them. If a more suitable form of therapy is available, then the proposal that psychotherapy is the most appropriate form of therapy has been disproved. In this way Freud's theory can be seen as following a 'scientific' method of sorts. In addition to this, research supports Freud's general premise that unconscious processes can affect behaviour. The work of Lloyd Siverman has provided a research paradigm for investigating psychoanalytic theory. Silverman has used a method called SPA (subliminal psychodynamic activation). A phrase is presented subliminally to a participant and their performance on a task is measured. Silverman found that presenting male dart-throwers with the sentence 'Beating dad is OK' drew better performance than the sentence 'Beating dad is wrong' leading him to conclude that the oedipal wish to compete with and beat the father figure is activated and sanctioned by the 'Beating dad is OK' sentence. Additional work has led Silverman and Weinberger (1985) to conclude that the sentence 'Mommy and I are one' is extremely important as it taps an unconscious desire for a state where the person finds him or herself at one with their mother figure. Silverman and

Weinberger say that fulfilling this wish can influence the person in some way. The researchers reported a reduction in the symptoms experienced by a range of clinical groups, including schizophrenics and neurotics. Evidence, say the researchers for the role of the subconscious in modifying our behaviour.

The Cognitive Viewpoint

Cognitive psychologists reject the notion of an unconscious mind driven by instinctive urges and repressed conflicts. Rather, they view conscious and unconscious mental life as complementary forms of information processing that work in harmony (Reisberg, 2001). To illustrate, consider how we perform everyday tasks.

Many activities, such as planning a holiday or studying, require **controlled (conscious, or explicit) processing**, the conscious use of attention and effort. Other activities involve **automatic (unconscious, or implicit) processing** and can be performed without conscious awareness or effort.

Automatic processing occurs most often when we carry out routine actions or very well-learned tasks, particularly under familiar circumstances (Ouellette and Wood, 1998). In everyday life, learning to write, drive, ride a bicycle and type on a computer keyboard all involve controlled processing; at first you have to pay a lot of conscious attention to what you are doing as you learn. With practice, performance becomes more automatic and certain brain areas involved in conscious thought become less active (Jansma et al., 2001). Through years of practice, athletes and musicians programme themselves to execute highly complex skills with a minimum of conscious thought.

Automatic processing, however, has a key disadvantage because it can reduce our chances of finding new ways to approach problems (Langer, 1989). Controlled processing is slower than automatic processing, but it is more flexible and open to change. Still, many well-learned behaviours seem to be performed faster and better when our mind is on autopilot, with controlled processing taking a back seat. Tasks ranging from putting a golf ball to playing video games, in experiments suggest that too much self-focused thinking can damage task performance and cause people to make a mistake under pressure (Beilcock and Carr, 2001).

Automatic processing also facilitates **divided attention**, the capacity to attend to and perform more than one activity at the same time. We can talk while we walk, type as we read, and so on. Yet divided attention has limits and is more difficult when two tasks require similar mental resources. For example, we cannot fully attend to separate messages delivered simultaneously through two earphones.

UNCONSCIOUS PERCEPTION AND INFLUENCE

The concept of unconscious information processing is widely accepted among psychologists today, but this was not always the case. It has taken painstaking research to demonstrate that stimuli can be perceived without conscious awareness and in turn can influence how we behave or feel. Let us look at some examples.

Visual Agnosia

Studies of people with brain damage can provide scientists with important insights into how the mind works. Recall that DF, the woman with visual agnosia, could not consciously perceive the shape, size or orientation of objects, yet she had little difficulty performing a card-insertion task and avoiding obstacles when she walked across a room. In order to perform these tasks so easily, her brain must have been processing accurate information about the shape, size and angles of objects. And if she professed no conscious awareness of these properties, then this information processing must have occurred at an unconscious level (Goodale, 2000).

---

controlled (conscious, or explicit) processing
the conscious use of attention and effort

automatic (unconscious, or implicit) processing
can be performed without conscious awareness or effort

divided attention
the capacity to attend to and perform more than one activity at the same time

In-Psych

According to Freud, dreams are a key to the unconscious. Watch the video, 'Freudian Interpretation of Dreams', in Chapter 6 of the In-Psych programme online to learn more about this theory.

Focus 6.3

How do visual agnosia, blindsight and priming illustrate unconscious processing?

There are many types of visual agnosia. For example, people with *prosopagnosia* can visually recognize objects but not faces. When some of these patients look in the mirror, they do not recognize their own faces. Despite this lack of conscious awareness, in laboratory tests the patients display different patterns of brain activity, autonomic arousal and eye movements when they look at familiar rather than unfamiliar faces. (Bauer and Verfaellie, 1988). In other words, their brain is recognizing and responding to the difference between familiar and unfamiliar stimuli, but this recognition does not reach the level of conscious awareness.

In 1987, Glyn Humphreys and Jane Ridoch, two researchers from London, published an important case study of their patient 'John', or HJA as he was also known in the many papers that preceded their book, and followed it. HJA's visual agnosia began with a stroke. Objects with which he was previously very familiar seemed strange to him. His wife Iris was unrecognizable to him and even his own image in a mirror appeared as a stranger. The map of HJA's world was also confused because of this inability to recognize his environment, and he got lost very easily, often within very familiar surroundings such as his own house. What makes the case all the more interesting is that HJA was able to recognize objects by touch, and by sound. It seemed that removing the visual component of an object's identity removed, or helped with, his problem. Even though he did not recognize things, when Humphreys and his co-workers asked him to copy the item, HJA could do so very well. His memory for objects was, then, undamaged, and he had a very good knowledge of how objects should appear and behave. Both of these skills are very important to us when perceiving items. HJA was unable to recognize objects, but he was able to see them. There are, however, situations where some processing of objects is available even though they cannot be seen at all. This is true in the case of blindsight.

Blindsight

People with agnosia are not blind, but those with a rare condition called **blindsight** are blind in part of their visual field yet in special tests respond to stimuli in that field despite reporting that they cannot see those stimuli (Weiskrantz, 2002). For example, owing to left-hemisphere damage from an accident or disease, a blindsight patient may be blind in the right half of the visual field. A stimulus (e.g., a horizontal line) is flashed on a screen so that it appears in one of several locations within the patient's blind visual field. On trial after trial, the patient reports seeing nothing, but when asked to point to where the stimulus was, she or he guesses at rates much higher than chance. On other tasks, different colours or photographs of facial expressions are projected to the blind visual field. Again, despite saying that they cannot see anything, patients guess the colour or facial expression at rates well above chance. On some tasks, guessing accuracy may reach 80 to 100 per cent (Weiskrantz, 2002). The first study was a patient identified by Weiscrantz as DB, who had had his occipital cortex removed because of a tumour. Amazingly, DB showed very strong performance in discriminating things in his visual field. He could tell different orientations of things from one another, and if something was moving or not. All this without being able to 'see' the items (Fig. 6.4; Weiskrantz et al., 1974). DB was the focus of

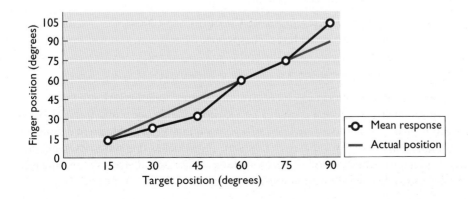

blindsight
blind in part of their visual field yet in special tests respond to stimuli in that field despite reporting that they cannot see those stimuli

FIGURE 6.4

Blindsight.

The portion of the brain marked in red has been damaged or removed. Part of their right visual field is therefore missing. Despite this, and despite saying that they cannot 'see' things in the missing area, those with blindsight are still able to discriminate between objects and identify their position when presented there. The graph shows the results of an experiment whereby an item was presented in the damaged visual field of DB, a blindsight suffer.

SOURCE: data redrawn from Wieskrantz et al., 1974.

many studies in the following years, providing Weiskrantz and his UK-based teams with much invaluable insight into the condition. Blindsight was further differentiated into Type 1 blindsight and Type 2 blindsight (Weiskrantz, 2002). With Type 1 blindsight, discriminations are possible in the 'blind' area but the person feels nothing at all. With Type 2 blindsight, rapid motion or changes in orientation are experienced as some kind of 'feeling'. DB continues to work with researchers looking into his condition, and work from Trevethan et al. (2004) is continuing this by asking whether the properties of blindsight are different, or in some way superior to 'normal' sight. Their research has shown that DB is actually better at discriminating between different objects and images in his blind field than in his sighted field. This rich vein of research has produced many important and fascinating results and it looks set to continue.

Priming

Here's a simple task. Starting with the two letters *ho_____* (this is called a *word stem*), what is the first word that comes to your mind? Was it *hot, how, home, house, hope, hole* or *honest*? Clearly, you had these and many other words to choose from.

Now imagine that just before completing this word stem you had looked at a screen on which the word *hose* (or perhaps a picture of a hose) was presented *subliminally* (it was displayed so rapidly or weakly that it was below your threshold for conscious perception).

Suppose we conduct an experiment with many participants and many word stems (e.g., *ho_____, gr_____, ma_____*, etc.). We find that compared to people who are not exposed to subliminal words such as *hose, gripe* and *manage*, people who are subliminally exposed are more likely to complete the word stems with those particular words. This provides evidence of a process called **priming**: exposure to a stimulus influences (i.e., primes) how you subsequently respond to that same or another stimulus. Thus even without consciously seeing *hose*, the subliminal word or image primes people's response to *ho_____*.

Subliminal stimuli can prime more than our responses to word stems. For example, when people are shown photographs of a person, the degree to which they evaluate that person positively or negatively is influenced by whether they have first been subliminally exposed to pleasant images (e.g., smiling babies) or unpleasant images (e.g., a face on fire; Krosnick et al., 1992). Likewise, being subliminally exposed to words with an aggressive theme causes people to judge another person's ambiguous behaviour as being more aggressive (Todorov and Bargh, 2002).

WHY DO WE HAVE CONSCIOUSNESS?

Given our brain's capacity to process information unconsciously, why have we evolved into conscious beings? What functions does consciousness serve? Surely the subjective richness of your life might evaporate if you lost the ability to consciously reflect on nature's beauty or on your feelings, thoughts and memories. But what about survival? How does consciousness help us adapt to, and survive in, our environment?

In his book, *The Quest for Consciousness*, Christof Koch (2004) notes that, 'evolution gave rise to organisms with subjective feelings. These convey significant survival advantages, because consciousness goes hand-in-hand with the ability to plan, to reflect upon many possible courses of action, and to choose one' (p. 205).

Koch suggests that consciousness serves a summarizing function. At any instant, your brain is processing numerous external stimuli (e.g., sights, sounds, etc.) and internal stimuli (e.g., bodily sensations). Conscious awareness provides a summary – a single mental representation – of what is going on in your world at each moment, and it makes this summary available to brain regions involved in planning and decision-making. Other scientists agree that consciousness facilitates the distribution of information to many areas of the brain (Baars, 2002).

priming
exposure to a stimulus influences (i.e., primes) how you subsequently respond to that same or another stimulus

On another front, a lack of self-awareness would compromise your ability to override potentially dangerous behaviours governed by impulses or automatic processing. Without the capacity to reflect, you might lash out after every provocation. Without the safety net of consciousness, Sondra almost drank ammonia during a sleepwalking episode. Under the control of unconscious, autopilot processing, other sleepwalkers have fallen down stairs or have cooked foods and then burned themselves severely while grabbing red-hot pans.

Unconscious processing also is poorly equipped to deal with novelty, such as when we have to learn new tasks or work out how to handle new situations. Consciousness allows us to deal flexibly with novel situations and helps us plan responses to them (Koch, 2004; Langer, 1989). Self-awareness – coupled with communication – also enables us to express our needs to other people and co-ordinate actions with them.

THE NEURAL BASIS OF CONSCIOUSNESS

Within our brains, where does consciousness arise? And if no individual brain cell is conscious (as far as we know), then how does brain activity produce consciousness? Psychologists and other scientists who study the brain are in hot pursuit of answers to these difficult questions (see Vaitl et al., 2005, for an excellent overview). A neural basis of consciousness simply describes a neurological state that correlates with a particular state of consciousness, or one that directly generates consciousness. This idea is also enriched and supported by a number of philosophers including Daniel Dennett. Neurons and synaptic connections form very quickly and increase in number after birth to a maximum number at about 6 months of age. From this point on synaptic pruning takes place where unused connections are removed, leaving only those that are needed. The term 'Neural Darwinism' came from Edelman (1987), and explains how the brain loses the weakest or least used connections, and retains the strongest and most useful. Hence the Darwinian, 'survival of the fittest' analogy.

Windows to the Brain

Some researchers have examined the brain functioning of patients who have visual agnosia, blindsight, or other disorders that impair conscious perception. Let us return to the case of DF. Brain imaging revealed that DF's primary visual cortex was largely undamaged from carbon-monoxide exposure. Why then, could she not consciously recognize objects and faces?

The answer builds on prior research in which psychologists discovered multiple brain pathways for processing visual information (Ungerleider and Mishkin, 1982). One pathway, extending from the primary visual cortex to the parietal lobe, carries information to support the unconscious guidance of movements (Milner and Dijkerman, 2001). A second pathway, extending from the primary visual cortex to the temporal lobe, carries information to support the conscious recognition of objects (Fig. 6.5). Consistent with this view, imaging of DF's brain

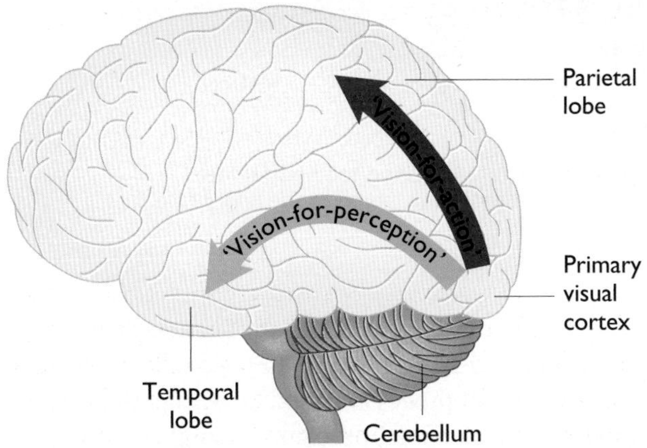

Focus 6.4

What are some adaptive functions of consciousness?

FIGURE 6.5

Action and perception.

The neural pathway shown in red is sometimes called the *vision-for-action pathway* as it carries information used in the visual control of movement. The pathway shown in green is sometimes called the *vision-for-perception pathway* because it carries information that helps us recognize objects (Koch, 2004; Milner and Dijkerman, 2001). Both pathways ultimately make connections to the prefrontal cortex.

Focus 6.5

How do scientists identify brain pathways involved in conscious versus unconscious processing? Describe the global-workspace view of consciousness.

indicated that parts of this second visual pathway were badly damaged (Goodale, 2000). Although other parts of DF's brain were also damaged, studies of humans and monkeys with more localized brain damage support the existence of these different visual pathways.

Scientists have also studied the neural basis of consciousness in other creative ways. Some have explored conscious perceptions that are created when specific brain areas are electrically stimulated, while others have tried to determine how consciousness is lost when patients are put under anaesthesia (Flohr, 2000). Still others have used a procedure called *masking* (Fig. 6.6) to control whether people perceive a stimulus consciously or unconsciously. In experiments, participants undergo brain imaging while exposed to masked and unmasked stimuli. This enables scientists to assess how brain activity differs depending on whether the same stimuli (e.g., photographs of angry faces) are consciously or unconsciously perceived.

Building on this technique, neuroscientists have found that emotionally threatening stimuli are processed consciously and unconsciously through different neural pathways. The pathway that produces conscious recognition involves the prefrontal cortex and several other brain regions that are bypassed in the pathway for unconscious processing (Morris and Dolan, 2001).

Technological advances present us with tantalizing possibilities. Scanning for instance, is allowing us to see things happening in the brain in a way that we could hardly have imagined until relatively recently. A word of warning here though. We have already discussed in a previous chapter how the use of MRI and other scanning methods could be over-interpreted, and the area of consciousness is no different. It is extremely tempting to infer that people are thinking of an 'experience' when we can see that a stimulus generates a patch of activity in the brain, but conscious experience is more that a localized area of stimulation, so beware. Papanicolaou (2007) points out that we must be careful. A particular pattern of brain activity does not allow us to infer anything about a particular experience. Careful investigation can provide us with evidence that the person is experiencing a particular *kind* of experience. The scan allows us to infer things about general concepts not the individual experiences themselves.

FIGURE 6.6

An example of masking.

(a) If a picture of an angry face is flashed on a screen for 30 milliseconds, people report seeing it. (b) If the angry face is immediately followed by a photograph of a neutral face shown for a longer time (e.g., 45 milliseconds), people report seeing the neutral face but not the angry face. In this approach – called *backward masking* – the presentation of the second photograph masks the conscious perception of the first photograph. Masking works with many types of stimuli, not just photographs of faces.

SOURCE: adapted from Morris and Dolan, 2001.

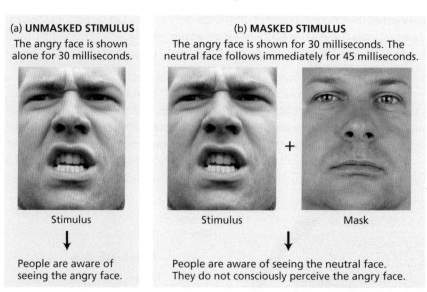

(a) **UNMASKED STIMULUS**
The angry face is shown alone for 30 milliseconds.

Stimulus

People are aware of seeing the angry face.

(b) **MASKED STIMULUS**
The angry face is shown for 30 milliseconds. The neutral face follows immediately for 45 milliseconds.

Stimulus   Mask

People are aware of seeing the neutral face. They do not consciously perceive the angry face.

Consciousness as a Global Workspace

Neuroscience research has led many investigators to the same conclusion: There appears to be no single place in the brain that gives rise to consciousness. Instead, they view the mind as a collection of largely separate but interacting information-processing modules that perform tasks related to sensation, perception, memory, movement, planning, problem-solving, emotion, and so on. The modules process information in parallel – that is, simultaneously and largely independently. However, there also is cross-talk between them, as when the output from one module is carried by neural circuits to provide input for another module. For example, a formula recalled from memory can become input for problem-solving modules that allow you to compute answers during a mathematics examination.

According to this view, consciousness is a *global workspace* that represents the unified activity of multiple modules in different areas of the brain (Baars, 2002; Dehaene and Naccache, 2001). In essence, of the many brain modules and connecting circuits that are active at any instant, a particular subset becomes joined in unified activity that is strong enough to become a conscious perception or thought (Dehaene and Naccache, 2001; Koch, 2004). The specific modules and circuits that make up this dominant subset can vary as our brain responds to changing stimuli – sights, sounds, smells, and so on – that compete for conscious attention.

Subjectively, of course, we experience consciousness as unitary, rather than as a collection of modules and circuits. This is akin to listening to a choir sing. We are aware of the integrated, harmonious sound of the choir rather than the voice of each individual member. As we now see, many factors influence these modules and, in so doing, alter our consciousness.

Neural States of Consciousness – a Different View

Of course, the description of a neural state of consciousness, as a neurological state that generates a conscious state of some kind is very compelling. After all, none of us need a scanner to know that it is somewhere north of the neck that thinking happens. There are, though, proponents of a theory called 'enactive' consciousness that have introduced an interesting dimension to the debate. The basic premise is that consciousness is not something that just happens to us, it is something that we do. Let us consider 'perception'. The generally held view by science is that perception involves internal representations and that we interact with the world as guided by these. An 'enactive' explanation does not necessarily deny that there may be representations in the brain, but theorists such as Alva Noë (2004) say that our brains do not necessarily construct models based on what we perceive. Our perceptual world is an integration of the skills we have developed. Perception, then, is a skill, and it depends on our actions and how we carry them out, how we *enact* them. Consciousness in general can be considered in the same way. Whatever consciousness is, it is not something that happens to us, it is something that we ourselves do. In this way, the neural basis of consciousness can be questioned and given another dimension. It is not the brain that provides us with consciousness, it is our actions and our behaviour that generates our consciousness.

IN REVIEW

- Consciousness refers to our moment-to-moment awareness of ourselves and the environment. It is subjective, dynamic, self-reflective and central to our sense of identity.

- Scientists use self-report, behavioural and physiological measures to define states of consciousness operationally.

- Freud believed that the mind has conscious, preconscious and unconscious levels. He viewed the unconscious as a reservoir of unacceptable desires and repressed experiences. Cognitive psychologists view the unconscious mind as an information-processing system and distinguish between controlled and automatic processing.

- Research on visual agnosia, blindsight and priming reveals that information processed unconsciously can influence people's responses. Emotional and motivational processes also can operate unconsciously and influence behaviour.

- Consciousness enhances our ability to adapt to our environment. It makes information available to brain regions involved in planning and decision-making. It also helps us to cope with novel situations and to override impulsive and autopilot behaviours. You will find more on the roles of different brain structures, including the amygdala and thalamus, elsewhere in the book.

- Brain-imaging studies of healthy and brain-damaged people have discovered separate neural circuits for conscious versus unconscious information processing.

- Many theorists propose that the mind consists of separate but interacting information-processing modules. Global-workspace models propose that consciousness arises from the unified, co-ordinated activity of multiple modules located in different brain areas.

CIRCADIAN RHYTHMS: OUR DAILY BIOLOGICAL CLOCKS

circadian rhythms
daily biological cycles

Like other animals, humans have adapted to a world with a 24-hour day–night cycle. The word circadian finds its origin in 'circa' meaning 'around' and 'dias' meaning 'day'. The circadian rhythm is a steady rhythmic state that lasts for 24 hours. During this 24 hours our body temperature, certain hormonal secretions, and other bodily functions undergo a steady rhythmic change that affects our alertness and readies our passage back and forth between waking consciousness and sleep (Fig. 6.7). These daily biological cycles are called **circadian rhythms**.

FIGURE 6.7

Circadian rhythms.

(a) Changes in our core body temperature, (b) levels of melatonin in our blood, and (c) degrees of alertness are a few of the bodily functions that follow a cyclical 24-hour pattern called a *circadian rhythm*. Humans also have longer and shorter biological cycles, such as the 28-day female menstrual cycle and a roughly 90-minute brain activity cycle during sleep.

SOURCE: adapted from Monk et al., 1996.

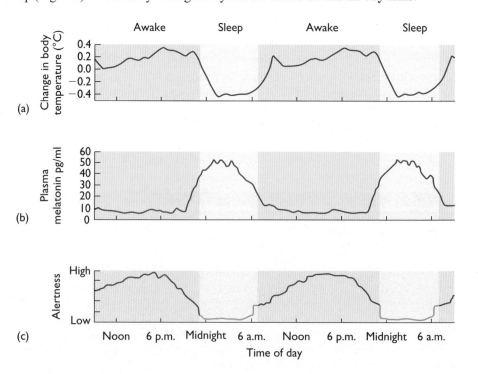

KEEPING TIME: BRAIN AND ENVIRONMENT

As Figure 6.8 shows, most circadian rhythms are regulated by the brain's **suprachiasmatic nuclei (SCN)**, located in the hypothalamus. These SCN neurons have a genetically programmed cycle of activity and inactivity, functioning like a biological clock. They link to the tiny pineal gland, which secretes **melatonin**, a hormone that has a relaxing effect on the body. The SCN neurons become active during the daytime and reduce the pineal gland's secretion of melatonin, raising body temperature and heightening alertness. At night SCN neurons are inactive, allowing melatonin levels to increase and promoting relaxation and sleepiness (Zhdanova and Wurtman, 1997).

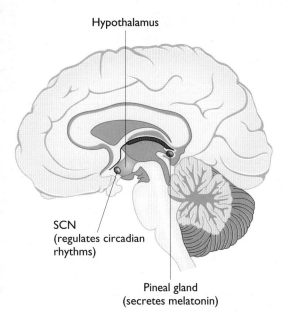

Hypothalamus

SCN
(regulates circadian
rhythms)

Pineal gland
(secretes melatonin)

FIGURE 6.8

The master circadian clock.

The suprachiasmatic nuclei (SCN) are the brain's master circadian clock. Neurons in the SCN have a genetically programmed cycle of activity and inactivity, but daylight and darkness help regulate this cycle. The optic nerve links our eyes to the SCN, and SCN activity affects the pineal gland's secretion of melatonin. In turn, melatonin influences other brain systems governing alertness and sleepiness.

suprachiasmatic nuclei (SCN)

most circadian rhythms are regulated by

melatonin

hormone that has a relaxing effect on the body

Our circadian clock is biological, but environmental cues such as the day–night cycle help keep SCN neurons on a 24-hour schedule. Your eyes have neural connections to the SCN, and after a night's sleep, the light of day increases SCN activity and helps reset your 24-hour biological clock. What would happen, then, if you lived in a laboratory or an underground cave without clocks and could not tell whether it was day or night outside? In experiments in which people did just that, most participants drifted into a natural wake–sleep cycle, called a *free-running circadian rhythm*, that is longer than 24 hours (Mills et al., 1974).

For decades, research suggested that our free-running rhythm was about 25 hours long. In these studies, however, the bright room lights that participants kept on artificially lengthened their circadian rhythms. Under more controlled conditions, the free-running rhythm averages around 24.2 hours (Lavie, 2000). Yet even this small deviation from the 24-hour day is significant. If you were to follow your free-running rhythm, two months from now you would be going to bed at noon and waking at midnight.

Focus 6.6

How do the brain and environment regulate circadian rhythms? What are free-running circadian rhythms?

Early Birds and Night Owls

Circadian rhythms also influence our tendency to be a morning person or a night person (Duffy et al., 2001). Compared to night people ('night owls'), morning people ('early birds') go to bed and rise earlier, and their body temperature, blood pressure and alertness peak earlier in the day. As Figure 6.9 shows, a study of university students found that early birds are more likely than night owls to enrol in and perform better in early (8 a.m.) classes.

Cultures may differ in their overall tendency towards 'morningness'. Carla Smith and her co-workers (2002) used questionnaires to measure the degree of morningness among college

FIGURE 6.9

Course grades of early birds and night owls.

In a study of 454 of university students, 'night owls' struggled in their 8 a.m. classes, as compared with 'early birds'. In later classes the two groups performed more similarly. Stated differently, early birds did slightly better in their earliest class than in later classes, whereas night owls did better in their later classes rather than their earliest class.

SOURCE: based on Guthrie et al., 1995.

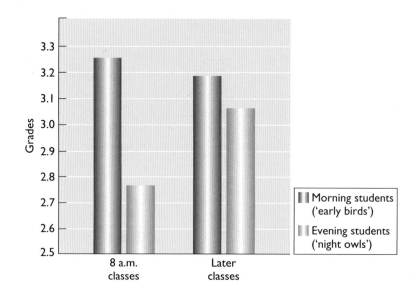

students from six countries. They predicted and found that students from Colombia, India and Spain – regions with warmer annual climates – exhibited greater morningness than students from England, the USA and the Netherlands (Table 6.1). In addition to this, a person may inherit the tendency and may be influenced by their physiology to be a morning or evening person (Vink et al., 2001). As with many things, both nature and nurture are likely to play a role in this aspect of a person's behaviour.

TABLE 6.1 MORNINGNESS AMONG COLLEGE STUDENTS FROM SIX COUNTRIES

Country	Morningness score
Colombia	42.4
India	39.4
Spain	33.9
England	31.6
USA	31.4
Netherlands	30.1
NOTE: Scores can range from 13 ('extreme evening type') to 55 ('extreme morning type').	

SOURCE: Smith et al., 2002.

WHAT DO YOU THINK?

EARLY BIRDS, CLIMATE AND CULTURE

Is this cross-cultural study of morningness correlational or experimental? Why might people from warmer regions display greater morningness? What factors other than climate might explain these results? Think about it, then see p. 278.

ENVIRONMENTAL DISRUPTIONS OF CIRCADIAN RHYTHMS

Our circadian rhythms are vulnerable to disruption by both sudden and gradual environmental changes. Jet lag is a sudden circadian disruption caused by flying across several time zones in one day. Flying east, you lose hours from your day; flying west extends your day to more than 24 hours. Jet lag, which often causes insomnia and decreased alertness, is a significant concern for business people, athletes, airline crews and others who frequently travel across many time zones (Ariznavarreta et al., 2002). The body naturally adjusts about one hour or less per day to time-zone changes. Typically, people adjust faster when flying west, presumably because lengthening the travel day is more compatible with our natural free-running circadian cycle.

Night-shift work, affecting millions of full-time workers around the globe, is the most problematic circadian disruption for society. Imagine having to begin an eight-hour work shift at 11 p.m. or midnight, a time when your biological clock is promoting sleepiness. After work you head home in morning daylight, making it harder to alter your biological clock. Like many night workers, if you go to bed in the late morning or early afternoon, you may get only two to four hours of sleep (Kogi, 1985). Over time you may become fatigued, stressed and more accident-prone (Garbarino et al., 2002). On your days off, reverting to a typical day–night schedule to spend time with family and friends will disrupt any hard-earned circadian adjustments you have made. And, if you work for a company that requires employees to rotate shifts every few days or weeks, then after adapting to night work, you will have to switch to a day or evening shift and readjust your biological clock once again.

These circadian disruptions, combined with fatigue from poor daytime sleep, can be a recipe for disaster. Job performance errors, fatal traffic accidents, and engineering and industrial disasters peak between midnight and 6 a.m. (c.f. Folkard and Tucker, 2003). In some cases, night operators at nuclear power plants have been found asleep at the controls. On-the-job sleepiness is also a major concern among long-distance truck drivers, airline crews, doctors and nurses, and others who work at night.

Seasonal affective disorder (SAD) is a cyclic tendency to become psychologically depressed during certain seasons of the year. Some people become depressed in spring and summer; however, in the vast majority of cases, SAD begins in autumn or winter, when there is less daylight, and then lifts in spring (Rosenthal and Wehr, 1992). The circadian rhythms of SAD sufferers may be particularly sensitive to light, so as sunrises occur later in winter, the daily onset time of their circadian clocks may be *delayed* to an unusual degree, altering the beginning time of the person's 'biological' morning. On late-autumn and winter mornings, when many people must rise for work and school in darkness, SAD sufferers remain in sleepiness mode long after the morning alarm clock sounds.

Where you live may influence SAD. Mersch et al. (1999) suggested that the prevalence of seasonal affective disorder increases in the USA, with latitude. The higher the latitude (Fig. 6.10), the fewer hours of daylight. This relationship was not seen in Europe, although there is some disagreement in the literature (Eagles, 2003). It seems that climate, genetics and sociocultural context all influence SAD.

Focus 6.7

Describe environmental disruptions of circadian rhythms.

seasonal affective disorder (SAD)

a cyclic tendency to become psychologically depressed during certain seasons of the year

Focus 6.8

Describe ways to minimize circadian disruptions involved in jet lag, night-shift work and SAD.

FIGURE 6.10

The latitude at which you live may influence levels of SAD, but other factors need to be considered, including a possible genetic influence, climate and your sociocultural environment.

APPLYING PSYCHOLOGICAL SCIENCE

OUTSMARTING JET LAG, NIGHT-WORK DISRUPTIONS AND WINTER DEPRESSION

Circadian research provides important insights on the nature of consciousness. It also offers several treatments for circadian disruptions affecting millions of people.

CONTROLLING EXPOSURE TO LIGHT

Reducing jet lag

When you fly east across time zones, your body's internal clock falls behind the time at your destination. This alters the onset time of your 'biological' morning. Exposure to outdoor light in the morning – and avoiding light late in the day – moves the circadian clock forward and helps it catch up to local time. (Think of morning light as jump-starting your circadian clock at a time when you would be asleep back home.) Flying west, your body clock moves ahead of local time. So to reduce jet lag, you want to delay your circadian cycle by avoiding bright light in the morning and exposing yourself to light in the afternoon or early evening. These are general rules, but the specific timing and length of exposure to light depend on the number of time zones crossed (Houpt et al., 1996). For jet travellers, spending time outside (even on cloudy days) is the easiest way to get the needed exposure to light.

Adjusting to night work

When night employees go home after work, their circadian adjustment can be increased by (1) keeping the bedroom dark and quiet to foster daytime sleep and (2) maintaining a schedule of daytime sleep even during days off (Boulos, 1998). Day sleepers are advised to install light-blocking window shades, unplug the phone and use earplugs. Wearing sunglasses is also recommended when the night-worker travels home in the morning.

Treating SAD

Many experts believe that phototherapy can be useful in treating the effects of winter depression and winter SAD. This involves properly timed exposure to specially prescribed bright artificial lights (Leppämäki et al., 2002). Several hours of daily phototherapy, especially in the early morning, can shift circadian rhythms by as much as two to three hours per day (Neumeister, 2004). The fact that phototherapy effectively treats SAD is the strongest evidence that SAD is triggered by winter's lack of sunlight rather than by its colder temperatures (Fig. 6.11).

FIGURE 6.11

For many people, the depression from SAD can be reduced by daily exposure to bright fluorescent lights.

MELATONIN TREATMENT: USES AND CAUTIONS

The hormone melatonin is a key player in the brain's circadian clock. Melatonin also exists in pill or capsule form; it is a prescription drug in some countries and is unavailable to the public in others. In the USA it is a non-prescription dietary supplement. Depending on when it is taken, oral melatonin can shift some circadian cycles forward or backward by as much as 30 to 60 minutes per day of use. Melatonin treatment has been used with some success to decrease jet lag, help employees adapt to night-shift work and alleviate SAD (Arendt et al., 1997). For shift-workers, it may indeed be beneficial to take melatonin just before going to bed after a night shift. However, if the worker is working shifts, that is to say, three night shifts followed by two day shifts then delaying the phase of the circadian rhythm in this way may cause additional problems for the worker when moving from night to day shift.

But there is reason for caution. Doses of 0.1 to 0.5 milligrams are often sufficient to produce circadian shifts, but tablet doses are often 3 to 5 milligrams, producing melatonin levels in the blood that are over 10 times the normal concentration (Sack et al., 1997). Melatonin use is supervised during research, but individuals who self-administer it may do themselves more harm than good. Taking melatonin at the wrong time can backfire and make circadian adjustments more difficult. Daytime use may decrease alertness (Graw et al., 2001). Some experts are also concerned that millions of people are using melatonin tablets as a nightly sleeping aid even though possible side effects of long-term use have not been adequately studied.

It is not only melatonin that needs to be administered at the correct time to optimize the wanted effects, and limit the unwanted ones. Both light and meltonin follow similar *phase-responses*. Their actions are to advance or delay the phase of the rhythm depending on when they are administered. If melatonin is taken in the person's 'biological' morning, the circadian rhythm is delayed. If it is taken in the person's 'biological' evening, the phase of the circadian rhythm is advanced. The effects of bright light are the opposite. If bright light is administered in the 'biological' morning, the phase of the circadian rhythm is advanced, if administered in the 'biological' evening the phase is delayed.

REGULATING ACTIVITY SCHEDULES

Properly timed physical exercise may help shift the circadian clock (Mistlberger et al., 2000). For example, compared with merely staying up later than normal, exercising when you normally go to bed may help push back your circadian clock, as you would want to do when flying west (Baehr, 2001). To reduce jet lag, you can also begin synchronizing your biological clock to the new time zone in advance. To do so, adjust your sleep and eating schedules by 30 minutes to 1 hour per day, starting several days before you leave. Schedule management can also apply to night-shift work. For workers on rotating shifts, circadian disruptions can be reduced by a forward-rotating shift schedule – moving from day to evening to night shifts – rather than a schedule that rotates backward from day to night to evening shifts (Knauth, 1996). The forward schedule takes advantage of our free-running circadian rhythms. When work shifts change, it is easier to extend the waking day than to compress it.

IN REVIEW

- Circadian rhythms are 24-hour biological cycles that help regulate many bodily processes and influence our alertness and readiness for sleep. The suprachiasmatic nuclei (SCN) are the brain's master circadian clock.

- Our free-running circadian rhythm is roughly 24.2 hours, but environmental factors such as the day–night cycle help reset our daily clocks to a 24-hour schedule.

- Circadian rhythms influence our tendency to be either a morning person or a night person, but cultural factors may also play a role.

- In general, our alertness is lowest in the early morning hours between 12 a.m. and 6 a.m. Job performance errors, major industrial accidents and fatal road traffic accidents peak during these hours.

- Jet lag, night-shift work and seasonal affective disorder (SAD) involve environmental disruptions of circadian rhythms. Treatments include controlling one's exposure to light, taking oral melatonin and regulating one's daily activity schedule.

SLEEP AND DREAMING

Sweet, refreshing, mysterious sleep. We spend much of our lives in this altered state, relinquishing conscious control of our thoughts, entering a world of dreams, and remembering so little of it upon awakening. Yet sleep, like other behaviours, can be studied at biological, psychological and environmental levels.

STAGES OF SLEEP

From 1968, sleep researchers have classified sleep as presented in the following section. In 2007, the American Academy of Sleep Medicine (AASM) altered the classification of sleep stages. Those that are accredited by the AASM will use the new classification system, but everyone else can continue to use the old system described here.

Circadian rhythms promote a readiness for sleep by decreasing alertness, but they do not directly regulate sleep. Instead, roughly every 90 minutes while asleep, we cycle through different stages in which brain activity and other physiological responses change in a generally predictable way (Dement, 1974; Kleitman, 1963).

Sleep research is often carried out in specially equipped laboratories where sleepers' physiological responses are recorded (Fig. 6.12). Electroencephalogram recordings of your brain's electrical activity would show a pattern of **beta waves** when you are awake and alert. Beta waves have a high frequency (of about 15 to 30 cycles per second, or cps) but a low amplitude, or height (Fig. 6.13). As you close your eyes, feeling relaxed and drowsy, your brainwaves slow down and **alpha waves** occur at about 8 to 12 cps.

beta waves

when you are awake and alert

alpha waves

feeling relaxed and drowsy, your brainwaves slow down

Focus 6.9

What brainwave patterns distinguish waking states and the stages of sleep? Describe the characteristics of REM sleep.

FIGURE 6.12

The sleep laboratory.

Electrodes attached to the scalp record the person's EEG brainwave patterns. Electrodes attached beside the eyes record eye movements during sleep. Electrodes attached to the jaw record muscle tension. A neutral electrode is attached to the ear.

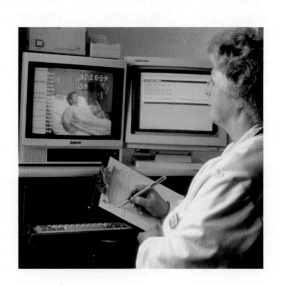

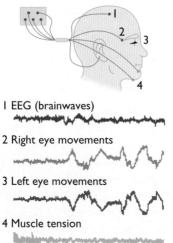

1 EEG (brainwaves)

2 Right eye movements

3 Left eye movements

4 Muscle tension

Stage 1 through Stage 4

As sleep begins, your brainwave pattern becomes more irregular, and slower *theta waves* (3.5 to 7.5 cps) increase. You are now in *stage 1*, a form of light sleep from which you can easily be awakened. You will probably spend just a few minutes in stage 1, during which time some people experience dreams, vivid images and sudden body jerks. As sleep becomes deeper, *sleep spindles* – periodic 1- to 2-second bursts of rapid brainwave activity (12 to 15 cps) – begin to appear. Sleep spindles indicate that you are now in *stage 2* (see Fig. 6.13). Your muscles are more relaxed, breathing and heart rate are slower, dreams may occur, and you are harder to awaken.

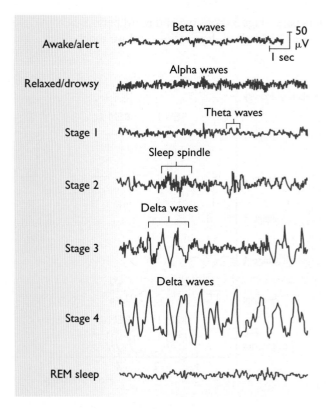

FIGURE 6.13

Stages of sleep.

Changing patterns of brain-wave activity help define the various stages of sleep. Note that brain waves become slower as sleep deepens from stage 1 through stage 4.

SOURCE: adapted from Hauri, 1982.

Sleep deepens as you move into *stage 3*, marked by the regular appearance of very slow (0.5 to 2 cps) and large **delta waves**. As time passes, they occur more often, and when delta waves dominate the EEG pattern, you have reached *stage 4*. Stage 3 and stage 4 together are often referred to as **slow-wave sleep**. Your body is relaxed, activity in various parts of your brain has decreased, you are hard to awaken, and you may have dreams. After 20 to 30 minutes of stage-4 sleep, your EEG pattern changes as you go back through stages 3 and 2, spending a little time in each. Overall, within 60 to 90 minutes of going to sleep, you have completed a cycle of stages: 1–2–3–4–3–2. At this point, a remarkably different sleep stage ensues.

REM Sleep

In 1953 Eugene Aserinsky and Nathaniel Kleitman struck scientific gold when they identified a unique sleep stage called **REM sleep (or 'R')**, characterized by rapid eye movements (REM), high arousal and frequent dreaming. They found that every half minute or so during REM sleep, bursts of muscular activity caused sleepers' eyeballs to vigorously move back and forth beneath their closed eyelids. Moreover, sleepers awakened from REM periods almost always reported a dream – including people who swore they 'never had dreams'. At last, scientists could examine dreaming more closely. Wait for REM, awaken the sleeper, and catch a dream.

delta waves
very slow (0.5 to 2 cps) and large

slow-wave sleep
stage 3 and stage 4 together

REM sleep (or 'R')
rapid eye movements (REM), high arousal and frequent dreaming

During REM sleep, physiological arousal may increase to daytime levels. The heart rate quickens, breathing becomes more rapid and irregular, and brainwave activity resembles that of active wakefulness. Regardless of dream content (most dreams are not sexual), men have penile erections and women experience vaginal lubrication. The brain also sends signals making it more difficult for voluntary muscles to contract. As a result, muscles in the arms, legs and torso lose tone and become relaxed. These muscles may twitch, but in effect you are paralysed, unable to move. This state is called *REM sleep paralysis*, and because of it REM sleep is sometimes called *paradoxical sleep*: your body is highly aroused, yet it looks like you are sleeping peacefully because there is so little movement.

Although each cycle through the sleep stages takes an average of 90 minutes, Figure 6.14 shows that as the hours pass, stage 3 drops out and REM periods become longer. There has been research on the effects of REM sleep deprivation, and we touch on that in a section following shortly.

FIGURE 6.14

Cycling through a night's sleep.

This graph shows a record of a night's sleep. The REM stages are shown in blue. People typically average four to five REM periods during the night, and these tend to become longer as the night wears on. On this night, the REM 5 period has been cut short because the person awakened.

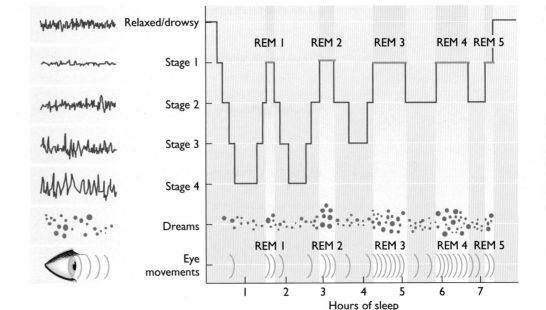

GETTING A NIGHT'S SLEEP: FROM BRAIN TO CULTURE

The brain steers our passage through sleep, but it has no single 'sleep centre'. Various brain mechanisms control different aspects of sleep, such as falling asleep and REM sleep. Moreover, falling asleep is not just a matter of turning off brain systems that keep us awake. There are separate systems that turn on and actively promote sleep.

Certain areas at the base of the forebrain (called the *basal forebrain*) and within the brain stem regulate our falling asleep. Other brain stem areas – including where the reticular formation passes through the pons (called the *pontine reticular formation*) – play a key role in regulating REM sleep (Hobson et al., 2000). This region contains neurons that periodically activate other brain systems, each of which controls a different aspect of REM sleep, such as eye movement and muscular paralysis.

Brain images taken during REM sleep reveal intense activity in limbic system structures, such as the amygdala that regulate emotions – a pattern that may reflect the emotional nature of many REM-sleep dreams (Fig. 6.15). The primary motor cortex is active, but its signals for movement are blocked and do not reach our limbs. Association areas near the primary visual cortex are active, which may reflect the processing of visual dream images. In contrast, decreased activity

In-Psych

What is the function of REM sleep? View the video, 'REM Sleep', in Chapter 6 of the In-Psych programme online to explore an REM-sleep debate among researchers and theorists.

Focus 6.10

What factors regulate nightly sleep and differences in people's sleep behaviour? How does sleep change with age?

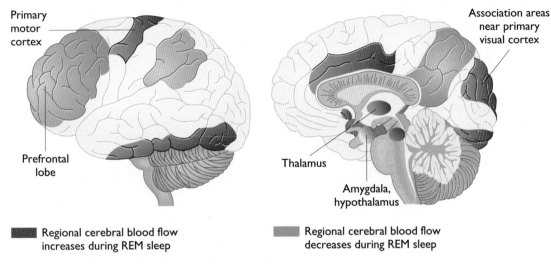

The brain during REM sleep

Primary motor cortex

Prefrontal lobe

Association areas near primary visual cortex

Thalamus

Amygdala, hypothalamus

▆▆▆ Regional cerebral blood flow increases during REM sleep

▆▆▆ Regional cerebral blood flow decreases during REM sleep

FIGURE 6.15

Brain activity during REM sleep.

As compared to the waking brain, during REM sleep several brain regions display markedly decreased (blue) and increased (rust) activity. Note the decreased activation in certain prefrontal lobe regions and increased activity in parts of the amygdala and hypothalamus, thalamus, primary motor cortex, and association areas near the primary visual cortex in the occipital lobe.

SOURCE: Schwartz and Maquet, 2002.

occurs in regions of the prefrontal cortex involved in high-level mental functions, such as planning and logical analysis. This may indicate that our sleeping mind does not monitor and organize its mental activity as carefully as when awake, enabling dreams to be illogical and bizarre (Hobson et al., 2000).

Environmental factors, such as changes in season, also affect sleep. In fall and winter, most people sleep about 15 to 60 minutes longer per night. Shift work, stress at work and school, and night-time noise can decrease sleep quality (Bronzaft et al., 1998).

Several aspects of sleep, such as its timing and length, vary across cultures (Sauter et al., 2002). One study of 818 Japanese and Slovak adolescents found that, on average, the Japanese teenagers went to sleep later at night and slept for a shorter time than their Slovak peers (Iwawaki and Sarmany-Schuller, 2001). Many people, particularly those living in cultures in tropical climates, enjoy the traditional ritual of a one- to two-hour midday nap and reduce the length of night-time sleep (Kribbs, 1993).

Cultural norms also influence several behaviours related to sleep. Do you sleep on a cushioned bed? In some cultures people sleep on floors or suspended in hammocks (Fig. 6.16). *Co-sleeping*, in which children sleep with their parents in the same bed or room, is not common in the USA, as children's sleeping alone is seen as a way to foster independence. But in most cultures, co-sleeping is the norm (Rothrauff et al., 2004).

HOW MUCH DO WE SLEEP?

The question seems simple enough, as does the answer for many of us: not enough! In reality, the issue is complex. First there are substantial differences in how much people sleep at various ages (Fig. 6.17). Newborn infants average 16 hours of sleep a day, and almost half of their sleep time is in REM (De Weerd and van den Bossche, 2003). But as we age, three important changes occur:

1. We sleep less; 19-to-30-year-olds average around seven to eight hours of sleep a night, and elderly adults average just under six hours.

2. REM sleep decreases dramatically during infancy and early childhood but remains relatively stable thereafter.

3. Time spent in stages 3 and 4 declines. By old age we get relatively little slow-wave sleep.

FIGURE 6.16

In warmer regions of the Americas, the use of hammocks for sleeping has been common among various indigenous peoples for centuries. This photograph shows a Mayan family in the Yucatan, Mexico.

Focus 6.11

How do different types of sleep deprivation affect mood and behaviour?

FIGURE 6.17

Ageing and sleep.

Daily total sleep time and the percentage of sleep time in REM and non-REM sleep change with age.

SOURCE: adapted from Roffwarg, H.P., Muzio, J.N. and Dement, W.C. (1966) Ontogenic development of human dream-sleep cycle, *Science*, vol. 152, p. 604, FIGURE 1. Copyright © American Association for the Advancement of Science. Reprinted with permission.

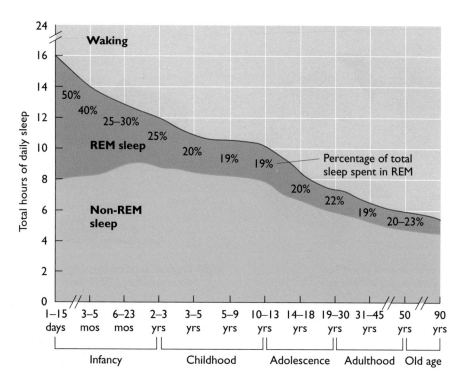

Second, individual differences in the amount of sleep occur at every age. Sleep surveys indicate that about two thirds of young adults sleep between 6.5 and 8.5 hours a night (Webb, 1992). About 1 per cent sleep more than 10 hours a night and 1 per cent less than five hours. Similarly, our sleep habits change with age, with some teenagers, for instance falling asleep later, and waking later if allowed to remain in their beds (DeWeerd et al., 2003).

Do We Need Eight Hours of Nightly Sleep?

Sleep surveys, of course, describe how much sleep people believe they get, not how much they need. Still, it appears that the old adage, 'everyone needs eight hours of sleep a night', is not true (Monk et al., 2001). Indeed, laboratory studies reveal that a few people function well on very little sleep. Researchers in London examined a healthy, energetic 70-year-old woman who claimed to sleep less than one hour a night (Meddis et al., 1973). Over five consecutive nights at the sleep lab, she averaged 67 minutes of sleep a night and showed no ill effects. Such extreme short-sleepers, however, are rare.

What accounts for differences in how much we sleep? Part of the answer appears to reside in our genes. Surveys of thousands of twins in Finland and Australia reveal that identical twins have more similar sleep lengths, bedtimes and sleep patterns than do fraternal twins (Heath et al., 1990). Using selective breeding, researchers have developed some genetic strains of mice that are long- versus short-sleepers, other strains that spend more or less time in REM and still others that spend more or less time in slow-wave sleep (Ouyang et al., 2004).

The twin studies indicate that differences in sleep length and sleep patterns are also affected by non-genetic factors. Working day versus night jobs, having low-key versus high-pressure lifestyles, and sleeping in quiet versus noisy environments are among the many factors contributing to the variability in people's sleep.

SLEEP DEPRIVATION

Sleep deprivation is a way of life for many students and other adults. Pilcher and Huffcutt (1996) meta-analysed 19 studies in which participants underwent either 'short-term total sleep deprivation' (up to 45 hours without sleep), 'long-term total sleep deprivation' (more than 45 hours without sleep), or 'partial deprivation' (being allowed to sleep no more than five hours a night for one or more consecutive nights). The researchers measured participants' mood (e.g., irritability) and responses on mental tasks (e.g., logical reasoning, word memory) and physical tasks (e.g., manual dexterity, treadmill walking).

What would you predict? Would all types of deprivation affect behaviour, and which behaviours would be affected the most? In fact, all three types of sleep deprivation impaired functioning. Combined across all studies, the typical sleep-deprived person functioned only as well as someone in the bottom 9 per cent of non-deprived participants. Overall, mood suffered most, followed by cognitive and then physical performance, although sleep loss significantly impaired *all three* behaviours.

But what about students who pull all-nighters or cut back their sleep, claiming they still perform as well as ever? June Pilcher and Amy Walters (1997) found that university students deprived of one night's sleep performed more poorly on a critical-thinking task than students allowed to sleep – yet they incorrectly perceived that they had performed better. The authors concluded that students underestimate the negative effects of sleep loss on performance.

Most total-sleep-deprivation studies with humans last less than five days, but 17-year-old Randy Gardner set a world record (since broken) of staying awake for 11 days for his 1964 high school science-fair project in San Diego. Grateful sleep researchers received permission to study him (Gulevich et al., 1966). Contrary to a popular myth that Randy suffered few negative effects, at times during the first few days he became irritable, forgetful and nauseated. By the fifth day he had periods of disorientation and mild hallucinations. Over the last four days he developed finger tremors and slurred speech. Still, in his final day without sleep he beat sleep researcher William Dement 100 consecutive times at a pinball-type game. When Randy finally went to bed, he slept almost 15 hours the first night and returned to his normal amount of sleep within a week. In general, it takes several nights to recover from extended sleep deprivation, and we do not make up all the sleep time that we have lost. Dinges and Kribbs (1991) say that those deprived of sleep and those that are rested function similarly at baseline level. However, sleep-deprived people have the occasional lapses of attention where their functioning suffers. This has become known as the 'lapse hypothesis'. However, later research from Dinges et al. (1997) has suggested that the more hours of sleep that are lost the more variable people's reactions become on a typical task that measures the participants' ability to watch out for a target on a screen and respond to it quickly. This variation would not be predicted by the lapse hypothesis.

So what happens when a person is sleep deprived? There is some evidence that sleep deprivation can alter people's confidence of how well they have performed a task that requires them to think critically and be vigilant. The effects of the sleep loss can depend on the type of task being performed, for example, whether it is complex or simple, whether the person is familiar with it, or whether it is novel, and whether the person is motivated or not. For instance, a complex, novel task with little or no motivation will not be performed well under conditions of sleep deprivation. Leproult et al. (1997) indicate that speed of processing information reduces with the amount of time spent awake. Attention also suffers similarly. Chee and Choo (2004) indicate that memory, and in particular working memory, tasks are harder as we begin to lose sleep.

WHY DO WE SLEEP?

Given that we spend almost a third of our lives sleeping, it must serve an important purpose. But what might that purpose be?

Sleep and Bodily Restoration

According to the **restoration model**, sleep recharges our run-down bodies and allows us to recover from physical and mental fatigue (Hess, 1965). Sleep-deprivation research strongly supports this view, indicating that we need sleep to function at our best.

restoration model

sleep recharges our run-down bodies and allows us to recover from physical and mental fatigue

If the restoration model is correct, activities that increase daily wear on the body should increase sleep. Evidence is mildly supportive. A study of 18- to 26-year-old ultramarathon runners found that they slept much longer and spent a greater percentage of time in slow-wave sleep on the two nights following their 57-mile run (Shapiro et al., 1981). For the rest of us mere mortals, a meta-analysis of 38 studies found that we tend to sleep longer by about 10 minutes on days we have exercised (Youngstedt et al., 1997).

What is it that gets restored in our bodies while we sleep? Are vital chemicals depleted during the day and replenished at night? Does waking activity produce toxins that are purged during sleep? We don't have precise answers, but many researchers believe that a cellular waste product called *adenosine* plays a role (Alanko et al., 2004). Like a car's exhaust emissions, adenosine is produced as cells consume fuel. As adenosine accumulates, it inhibits brain circuits responsible for keeping us awake, thereby signalling the body to slow down because too much cellular fuel has been burned. During sleep, however, our adenosine levels decrease.

Sleep as an Evolved Adaptation

Evolutionary/circadian sleep models emphasize that sleep's main purpose is to increase a species' chances of survival in relation to its environmental demands (Webb, 1974). Our prehistoric ancestors had little to gain – and much to lose – by being active at night. Hunting, food gathering and travelling were accomplished more easily and safely during daylight. Leaving the protection of one's shelter at night would have served little purpose other than to become dinner for night-time predators.

Over the course of evolution, each species developed a circadian sleep–wake pattern that was adaptive in terms of its status as predator or prey, its food requirements, and its methods of defence from attack. For small prey animals such as mice and squirrels, which reside in burrows or trees safely away from predators, spending a lot of time asleep is adaptive. For large prey animals such as horse, deer and zebra, which sleep in relatively exposed environments and whose safety from predators depends on running away, spending a lot of time asleep would be hazardous (Fig. 6.18). Sleep may also have evolved as a mechanism for conserving energy. Our body's overall metabolic rate during sleep is about 10 to 25 per cent slower than during waking rest (Zhang et al., 2002). The restoration and evolutionary theories highlight complementary functions of sleep, and both contribute to a two-factor model of why we sleep (Webb, 1994).

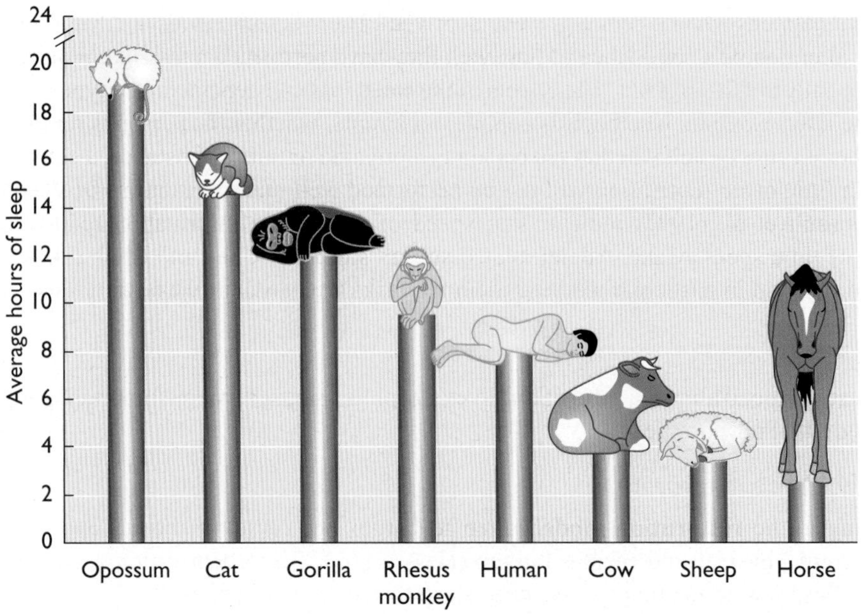

evolutionary/circadian sleep models

sleep's main purpose is to increase a species' chances of survival in relation to its environmental demands

Focus 6.12

Explain the restoration, evolutionary/circadian and memory-consolidation models of sleep.

FIGURE 6.18

Daily hours of sleep.

The average daily hours of sleep vary across species.

Sleep and Memory Consolidation

When a person is deprived of REM sleep, by regularly waking them when REM is detected their sleep patterns following the period of disruption are altered. Lavie et al. (1984) indicate that even though it may seem counterintuitive, the consequences of REM disruption are not terribly significant. Patients who have suffered brain injury that results in reduced periods of REM or no REM at all have gone on to perform extremely well both academically and professionally.

So, do specific sleep stages have special functions? To answer this question, imagine volunteering for a sleep-deprivation study in which we will awaken you only when you enter REM sleep; you will be undisturbed through the other sleep stages. How will your body respond? First, on successive nights, we will have to wake you more often, because your brain will fight back to get REM sleep (Fig. 6.19a). Second, when the study ends, for the first few nights you probably will experience a *REM-rebound effect*, a tendency to increase the amount of REM sleep after being deprived of it (Fig. 6.19b).

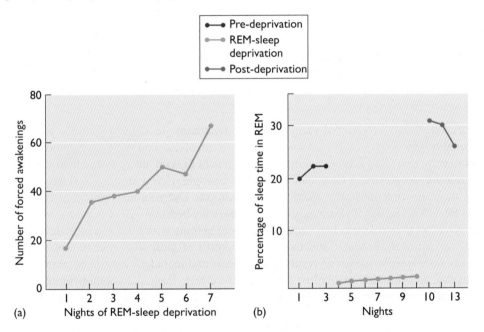

FIGURE 6.19

REM-sleep deprivation.

(a) In REM-sleep-deprivation studies, participants start to go into REM periods more times with each passing night, as the brain tries to get REM sleep. (b) After REM deprivation ends, the sleeper spends more time than usual in REM sleep for a few nights. This is the REM rebound effect.

SOURCE: adapted from Agnew et al., 1967.

This suggests that the body needs REM sleep (similar effects are found for slow-wave sleep). But for what purpose? Many theorists believe that the high level of brain activity in REM sleep helps us remember important events by enhancing **memory consolidation**, a gradual process by which the brain transfers information into long-term memory (Smith et al., 2004; Winson, 1990). There have been many experiments on this topic, including brain-imaging studies, but despite much supportive evidence, the issue remains controversial (Vertes and Eastman, 2003). For example, the consolidation hypothesis is contradicted by the fact that although many antidepressant drugs greatly suppress or nearly eliminate REM sleep, patients taking these drugs for long periods of time do not show impaired abilities to remember new information or experiences.

In contrast to the memory-consolidation view, some researchers argue that the function of REM sleep is purely biological. The periodic high activation of REM sleep keeps the brain healthy during sleep and offsets the periods of low brain arousal during restful slow-wave sleep (Vertes and Eastman, 2003). At present, the unique functions of REM and other sleep stages are still debated.

memory consolidation

a gradual process by which the brain transfers information into long-term memory

SLEEP DISORDERS

As the sleepeating cases of Sondra, Jason, and Ellen illustrate, the processes that regulate sleep are complex and can go wrong in many ways. Almost 75 per cent of American adults feel that they have some type of sleep problem (National Sleep Foundation, 2002).

Insomnia

insomnia
chronic difficulty in falling asleep, staying asleep or experiencing restful sleep

True or false: someone who falls asleep easily can still have insomnia. The statement is true because **insomnia** refers to chronic difficulty in falling asleep, staying asleep or experiencing restful sleep. If you occasionally have trouble getting a good night's sleep, do not worry. Almost everyone does. People with true insomnia have frequent and persistent sleep troubles.

Many people with insomnia overestimate how much sleep they lose and how long it takes them to fall asleep. To some, 20 minutes of lying awake may seem like an hour. Still, insomnia is the most common sleep disorder, experienced by 10 to 40 per cent of the population of various countries (Ohayon and Lemoine, 2004). Some people, however, display *paradoxical insomnia*; they complain of insomnia but sleep normally when examined in the laboratory.

Some people are genetically predisposed towards insomnia. Moreover, medical conditions, mental disorders such as anxiety and depression, and many drugs can disrupt sleep, as can general worrying, stress at home and work, poor lifestyle habits, and circadian disruptions such as jet lag and night-shift work.

Psychologists have pioneered many non-drug treatments to reduce insomnia and improve sleep quality. One treatment, called *stimulus control*, involves conditioning your body to associate stimuli in your sleep environment (such as your bed) with sleep, rather than with waking activities and sleeplessness (Bootzin, 2002). For example, if you are having sleep difficulties, do not study, watch television or snack in your bedroom. Use your bed only for sleeping. If you cannot fall asleep within 10 minutes, get up and leave the bedroom. Do something relaxing until you feel sleepy, then return to bed. Other methods of helping with insomnia include the application of relaxation techniques, and the careful control of your sleep habits (known as sleep hygiene). Poor sleep hygiene can result in poor sleep, and includes the habit of taking naps during the day, and drinking alcohol or caffeine before bed. Table 6.2 contains more guidelines from sleep experts regarding good sleep hygiene for reducing insomnia and achieving better sleep. In some cases, sleep restriction therapy has been found to be useful. Essentially this means staying awake even if you feel sleepy. This can help the person suffering from insomnia reduce the amount of time they spend awake in their bed trying to fall asleep. By restricting sleep, the insomniac can become tired and fall asleep naturally, at the correct time.

Narcolepsy

narcolepsy
extreme daytime sleepiness and sudden, uncontrollable sleep attacks that may last from less than a minute to an hour

About one out of every 2000 people suffers not from an inability to sleep but from an inability to stay awake (Ohayon and Lemoine, 2004). **Narcolepsy** involves extreme daytime sleepiness and sudden, uncontrollable sleep attacks that may last from less than a minute to an hour. No matter how much they rest at night, individuals with narcolepsy may experience sleep attacks at any time, with hypnagogic (dream-like) hallucinations and sleep paralysis being common among sufferers.

Focus 6.13
Describe the symptoms, causes and treatment of major sleep disorders.

When a sleep attacks occurs, they may go right into a REM stage. People with narcolepsy also may experience attacks of *cataplexy*, a sudden loss of muscle tone often triggered by excitement and other strong emotions. In severe cases, the knees buckle and the person collapses, conscious but unable to move for a few seconds to a few minutes. Cataplexy is an abnormal version of the normal muscular paralysis that takes place during night-time REM sleep, and some experts view narcolepsy as a disorder in which REM sleep intrudes into waking consciousness.

TABLE 6.2 HOW TO IMPROVE THE QUALITY OF YOUR SLEEP

Sleep experts recommend a variety of procedures to reduce insomnia and improve the general quality of sleep:

- Maintain a regular sleep–wake pattern to establish a stable circadian rhythm.
- Get the amount of sleep you need during the week, and avoid sleeping in on weekends, as doing so will disrupt your sleep rhythm. Even if you sleep poorly or not at all one night, try to maintain your regular schedule the next.
- If you have trouble falling asleep at night, avoid napping if possible. Evening naps should be especially avoided because they will make you less sleepy when you go to bed.
- Avoid stimulants. This includes not just tobacco products and coffee but also caffeinated soft drinks and chocolate (sorry), which contains caffeine. It can take the body four to five hours to reduce the amount of caffeine in the bloodstream by 50 per cent.
- Avoid alcohol and sleeping pills. As a depressant, alcohol may make it easier to go to sleep, but it disrupts the sleep cycle and interferes with REM sleep. Sleeping pills also impair REM sleep, and their constant use can lead to dependence and insomnia.
- Try to go to bed in a relaxed state. Muscle-relaxation techniques and meditation can reduce tension, remove worrisome thoughts and help induce sleep.
- Avoid physical exercise before bedtime because it is too stimulating. If you are unable to fall asleep, do not use exercise to try and wear yourself out.
- If you are having sleep difficulties, avoid performing non-sleep activities in your bedroom.

SOURCES: Bootzin, 2002; King et al., 2001.

Narcolepsy can be devastating. People with narcolepsy are more prone to accidents, feel that their quality of life is impaired and may be misdiagnosed by doctors as having a mental disorder rather than a sleep disorder (Kryger et al., 2002). Some people may be genetically predisposed towards developing narcolepsy. It can be selectively bred in dogs (Fig. 6.20). In humans, if one identical twin has narcolepsy, the other has a 30 per cent chance of developing it (Mignot, 1998). Narcolepsy is today perceived as an auto-immune disorder – as it has been linked to some specific human antigen variants. An area in the hypothalamus which produces a neurotransmitter called 'hypocretine' seems to be specifically affected. Thus, patients suffering from narcolepsy typically have very low levels of hypocretine in their cerebrospinal fluid.

At present there is no cure for narcolepsy, but stimulant drugs and daytime naps often reduce daytime sleepiness, and antidepressant drugs (which suppress REM sleep) can decrease attacks of cataplexy.

FIGURE 6.20

This dog lapses suddenly from alert wakefulness into a limp sleep while being held by sleep researcher William Dement. Using selective breeding, researchers at Stanford's Sleep Disorders Center have established a colony of narcoleptic canines.

REM-Sleep Behaviour Disorder

Kaku Kimura and his colleagues in Japan (1997) reported the case of a 72-year-old woman who, during a night in a sleep laboratory, repeatedly sang and waved her hands during REM sleep. One episode lasted three minutes. She was experiencing **REM-sleep behaviour disorder (RBD)**, in which the loss of muscle tone that causes normal REM-sleep paralysis is absent. If awakened, RBD patients often report dream content that matches their behaviour, as if they were acting out their dreams: 'A 67-year-old man . . . was awakened one night by his wife's yelling as he was choking her. He was dreaming of breaking the neck of a deer he had just knocked down' (Schenck et al., 1989, p. 1169).

REM-sleep behaviour disorder sleepers may kick violently, throw punches or get out of bed and move about wildly, leaving the bedroom in shambles. Many RBD patients have injured themselves or their sleeping partners. Research suggests that brain abnormalities may interfere with signals from the brain stem that normally inhibit movement during REM sleep, but in many cases the causes of RBD are unknown (Zambelis et al., 2002). REM-sleep behaviour disorder has also been associated with other degenerative diseases such as Parkinson's disease.

Sleepwalking

Unlike RBD, sleepwalking typically occurs during a stage-3 or stage-4 period of slow-wave sleep (Guilleminault et al., 2001). Sleepwalkers often stare blankly and are unresponsive to other people. Many seem vaguely conscious of the environment as they navigate around furniture, yet they can injure themselves accidentally, such as by falling down stairs. Some go to the bathroom or – like Sondra, Jason and Ellen – find something to eat. The pattern, however, is variable. Recall that Jason, while eating during his sleepwalking episodes, could have intelligible conversations with his wife. People who sleepwalk often return to bed and wake in the morning with no memory of the event.

About 10 to 30 per cent of children sleepwalk at least once, but less than 5 per cent of adults do. If you did not sleepwalk as a child, the odds are less than 1 per cent that you will do so as an adult (Hublin et al., 1997).

A tendency to sleepwalk may be inherited, and daytime stress, alcohol, and certain illnesses and medications can increase sleepwalking (Hublin et al., 2001), with the most likely thing to bring on a bout of sleepwalking in those that suffer from it being a period of sleep deprivation. Treatments may include psychotherapy, hypnosis and waking children before the time they typically sleepwalk (Frank et al., 1997). But for children, the most common approach is simply to wait for the child to outgrow it while creating a safe sleep environment to prevent injury. Contrary to common belief, waking people who sleepwalk is not harmful, although they may be confused for a few minutes.

Nightmares and Night Terrors

Nightmares are bad dreams, and virtually everyone has them. Like all dreams, they occur more often during REM sleep. Arousal during nightmares typically is similar to levels experienced during pleasant dreams.

Night terrors are frightening dreams that arouse the sleeper to a near-panic state. In contrast to nightmares, night terrors are most common during slow-wave sleep (stages 3 and 4), are more intense and involve greatly elevated physiological arousal; the heart rate may double or triple. In some cases the terrified sleeper may suddenly sit up, let out a scream or flee the room – as if trying to escape from something. Come morning the sleeper usually has no memory of the episode. If brought to full consciousness during an episode – which is hard to do – the person may report a sense of having been choked, crushed or attacked (Fisher et al., 1974).

REM-sleep behaviour disorder (RBD)

the loss of muscle tone that causes normal REM-sleep paralysis is absent

---

night terrors

frightening dreams that arouse the sleeper to a near-panic state

Up to 6 per cent of children, but only 1 to 2 per cent of adults, experience night terrors (Ohayon et al., 1999). In most childhood cases, treatment is simply to wait for the night terrors to diminish with age.

Sleep Apnea

An *apnea* is a period of 10 seconds or more when a person stops breathing. People with **sleep apnea** repeatedly stop and restart breathing during sleep. Stoppages usually last 20 to 40 seconds but can continue for one to two minutes. In severe cases they occur 400 to 500 times a night. Obstructive sleep apnea is most commonly caused by an obstruction in the upper airways, such as sagging tissue as muscles lose tone during sleep. The chest and abdomen keep moving, but no air gets through to the lungs in obstructive apnea. Finally, reflexes kick in and the person gasps or produces a loud, startling snore, followed by a several-second awakening. The person typically falls asleep again without remembering having been awake. In *central apnea* the chest and abdomen do not continue to move.

About 1 to 5 per cent of people have some form of sleep apnea, and the obstructive type is most common among overweight, middle-aged males. Surgery may be performed to remove the obstruction, and sleep apnea sometimes is treated by having the sleeper wear a mask that continuously pumps air to keep the air passages open, a CPAP – continuous positive airway pressure device (Sage et al., 2001). It is often the partner of a person with sleep apnea – repeatedly woken by the gasps, loud snores and jerking body movements – who encourages the person to seek treatment.

sleep apnea
repeatedly stop and restart breathing during sleep

THE NATURE OF DREAMS

Dreams play a key role in the social fabric of many traditional cultures, such as the Timiar (Senoi) of Malaysia (Greenleaf, 1973). To the Timiar, dreams provide a link to the spirit world, and dream interpretation, particularly when performed by shamans, is highly valued. Although western societies attach less importance to dreams than do many cultures, dreams remain a source of endless curiosity in everyday life.

When Do We Dream?

Mental activity occurs throughout the sleep cycle. Some of our students say they experience vivid images soon after going to bed and ask if this is unusual. It is not. When Jason Rowley and his colleagues (1998) woke college students merely 45 seconds after sleep onset, about 25 per cent of the students reported that they had been experiencing visual hallucinations (visual images that seemed real). As this *hypnagogic state* – the transitional state from wakefulness through early stage-2 sleep – continued, mental activity became less 'thoughtlike' and more 'dreamlike'. By five minutes after sleep onset, visual hallucinations were reported after 40 per cent of awakenings.

Throughout the night we dream most often during REM sleep, when activity in many brain areas is highest. Awaken a REM sleeper and you have about an 80 to 85 per cent chance of catching a dream. In contrast, people awakened from non-REM (NREM) sleep report dreams about 15 to 50 per cent of the time. Also, our REM dreams are more likely to be vivid, bizarre and storylike than NREM dreams. Some researchers attribute this to the fact that REM dreams typically are longer, allowing more time for vivid content to unfold (Domhoff, 1999). But like the proverbial chicken and the egg, other researchers argue that it is the greater richness of REM dreams that causes them to be longer (Hobson et al., 2000).

Despite these REM–NREM differences, do not believe the fallacy (often reinforced by the popular media) that dreaming only happens during REM sleep. Figure 6.21 shows an analysis of 1576 reports collected from 16 college students woken from various sleep stages (Fosse et al., 2001). Even during NREM sleep, hallucinatory images were more common than non-dreamlike thoughts. By some estimates, about 25 per cent of the vivid dreams we have each night actually occur during NREM periods (Solms, 2002).

Focus 6.14
When do dreams occur, and what are common characteristics of dream content? How can science explain 'psychic' dreams?

FIGURE 6.21

Mental activity during sleep.

This graph shows the percentage of verbal reports that reflected thoughts and visual hallucinations recorded during active and quiet wakefulness and when awakened during sleep onset, REM sleep and NREM sleep.

SOURCE: adapted from Fosse et al., 2001.

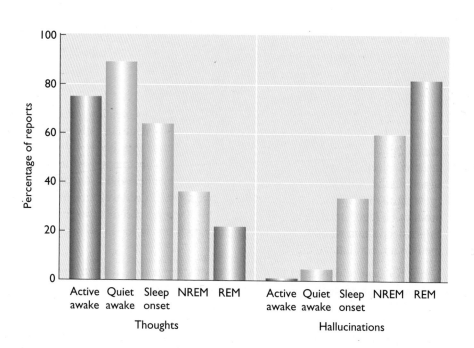

What Do We Dream About?

Much of our knowledge about dream content derives from 40 years of research using a coding system developed by Calvin Hall and Robert Van de Castle (1966). Analysing 1000 dream reports (mostly from college students), they found that although some dreams certainly are bizarre, dreams overall are not nearly as strange as they are stereotyped to be. Most take place in familiar settings and often involve people we know.

Given the stereotype of 'blissful dreaming', it may surprise you that most dreams contain negative content. In their research, Hall and Van de Castle (1966) found that 80 per cent of dream reports involved negative emotions, almost half contained aggressive acts and a third involved some type of misfortune. They also found that women dreamt almost equally about male and female characters, whereas about two-thirds of men's dream characters were male. Although the reason for this gender difference is not clear, a similar pattern has been found across several cultures and among teenagers and pre-adolescents.

Our cultural background, life experiences, and current concerns can shape dream content (Domhoff, 2001). Pregnant women, for example, have dreams with many pregnancy themes, and Palestinian children living in violent regions of the Gaza Strip dream about persecution and aggression more often than do their peers living in non-violent areas (Punamäki and Joustie, 1998). In the weeks following the 11 September 2001 terrorist attacks, a study of 1000 residents of Manhattan found that one in 10 experienced distressing dreams about the attacks (Galea et al., 2002). Overall, it appears that up to half of our dreams contain some content reflecting our recent experiences (Harlow and Roll, 1992).

Why Do We Dream?

Questions about the purpose and meaning of dreams have intrigued humankind for ages. Let us examine a few viewpoints. It is during REM sleep that the majority of dreaming occurs, and we have already described the role of REM in memory consolidation. According to *evolutionary theory* for instance, the function of dreams might be to prepare us for a hostile environment. Revonsuo (2000) indicates that most dreams have a negative emotional content. It could be that this allows us to experience a dangerous environment in the safety of our dreams.

BENEATH THE SURFACE

WHEN DREAMS COME TRUE

'Last summer, I had a dream that my sister was hurt in an accident. A week later, she was seriously injured in a bicycle crash! Why does this happen? Are some dreams psychic?'

Have you ever had a dream that came true? Many of our students say they have, and they often ask us whether this has some special meaning. As critical thinkers, let us consider a few issues. First, what are we being asked to believe? Two things really: (1) that a dream foretold the future and (2) that this signifies something special or psychic.

Second, what is the evidence? Well, the evidence is that a dream supposedly came true. So let us think about this. Did the dream really come true? In the example above, what type of accident did the dream involve? A car, train, plane, boat, home, sports or work accident? If it was not a bicycle accident, then the dream really did not come true.

'Come on', you might say, 'that's being too picky. After all, the dream was "close" – the main theme was that the sister was injured.' Well, in that case, suppose you picked a number from 1 to 1000, we bet you 1000 euro that we could guess it, and we guessed 625. You actually picked 638, but we said, 'Our prediction came true. We were very close'. Would you agree and pay us 1000 euro? If not, then why set a sloppy standard for accuracy when it comes to deciding whether a dream comes true? Nonetheless, for the sake of argument let us assume that the dream did involve a bicycle accident and came true a week later.

Third, what is the most plausible explanation? Given all the dreams that we recall, some of them are bound to come true simply by sheer coincidence. If you consider how many dreams you have had that *did not* come true, you will realize this. By some estimates we have dozens of dreams nightly, most of which we forget; but let us suppose we remember one dream every two nights. Between the ages of 15 and 75 we will have almost 11 000 opportunities for a remembered dream to come true the same day, 77 000 opportunities for a remembered dream to come true within a week, and so on. Thus a good number of our dreams should come true simply by coincidence. Collectively, if you consider that hundreds of millions of people may recall a dream each day, the odds are that someone, somewhere, by sheer coincidence will have had a recent dream come true. This is especially true given that ongoing events or issues in our lives can influence the content of our dreams.

In short, we do not need to resort to mystical phenomena to explain why some dreams come true. Rather, we need only consider the likelihood that certain events will occur periodically by chance and coincidence alone.

Freud's psychoanalytic theory   Sigmund Freud (1953) believed that the main purpose of dreaming is **wish fulfilment**, the gratification of our unconscious desires and needs. These desires include sexual and aggressive urges that are too unacceptable to be consciously acknowledged and fulfilled in real life. Freud distinguished between (1) a dream's *manifest content*, the surface story that the dreamer reports and (2) its *latent content*, which is its disguised psychological meaning. Thus a dream about being with a stranger on a train that goes through a tunnel (manifest content) might represent a hidden desire for sexual intercourse with a forbidden partner (latent content).

Dream work was Freud's term for the process by which a dream's latent content is transformed into the manifest content. It occurs through symbols (e.g., train = penis; tunnel = vagina) and by

Focus 6.15

Contrast the psychoanalytic, activation-synthesis and cognitive dream theories.

wish fulfilment

the gratification of our unconscious desires and needs

creating individual dream characters who combine features of several people in real life. This way, unconscious needs can be fulfilled and, because they are disguised within the dream, the sleeper does not become anxious and can sleep peacefully.

Although dreams often reflect ongoing emotional concerns, many researchers reject the specific postulates of Freud's theory. They find little evidence that dreams have disguised meaning or that their general purpose is to satisfy forbidden, unconscious needs and conflicts (Domhoff, 1999). Critics of dream analysis say that it is highly subjective; the same dream can be interpreted differently to fit the particular analyst's point of view.

Modern psychodynamic psychologists emphasize that beyond the types of unconscious processing discussed earlier, emotional and motivational processes also operate unconsciously and influence behaviour (Westen, 1998). At times these hidden processes can cause us to feel and act in ways that mystify us. Consider the case of a 47-year-old amnesia patient who could not remember new personal experiences. One day, as Swiss psychologist Edouard Claparède (1911) shook this woman's hand, he intentionally pricked her hand with a pin hidden between his fingers. Later, Claparède extended his hand to shake hers again. The woman could not consciously recall the pinprick or even having met Claparède, but despite her amnesia, she suddenly withdrew her hand. Apparently, an unconscious memory of the painful experience influenced her behaviour.

Numerous experiments support the view that unconscious processes can have an emotional and motivational flavour (LeDoux, 2000). For example, have you ever been in a bad or a good mood and wondered why you were feeling that way? Perhaps it is because you were influenced by events in your environment of which you were not consciously aware.

In one study, Tanya Chartrand and her colleagues (2002) subliminally presented college students with nouns that were either strongly negative (e.g., *cancer*, *cockroach*), mildly negative (e.g., *Monday*, *worm*), mildly positive (e.g., *parade*, *clown*), or strongly positive (e.g., *friends*, *music*). Later, students rated their mood on psychological tests. Although not consciously aware of seeing the nouns, students shown the strongly negative words reported the saddest mood, whereas those who had seen the strongly positive words reported the happiest mood.

Activation-synthesis theory   Is it possible that dreams serve no special purpose? In 1977, J. Allan Hobson and Robert McCarley proposed a physiological theory of dreaming.

activation-synthesis theory

dreams do not serve any particular function – they are merely a by-product of REM neural activity

According to the **activation-synthesis theory**, dreams do not serve any particular function – they are merely a by-product of REM neural activity. When we are awake, neural circuits in our brain are activated by sensory input – sights, sounds, tastes, and so on. The cerebral cortex interprets these patterns of neural activation, producing meaningful perceptions. During REM sleep the brain stem bombards our higher brain centres with random neural activity (the activation component). Because we are asleep, this neural activity does not match any external sensory events, but our cerebral cortex continues to perform its job of interpretation. It does this by creating a dream – a perception – that provides the best fit to the particular pattern of neural activity that exists at any moment (the synthesis component).

This helps to explain the bizarreness of many dreams, as the brain is trying to make sense of random neural activity. Our memories, experiences, desires and needs can influence the stories that our brain develops, and therefore dream content may reflect themes pertaining to our lives. In this sense, dreams can have meaning, but they serve no special function (McCarley, 1998).

Critics claim that activation-synthesis theory overestimates the bizarreness of dreams and pays too little attention to NREM dreaming (Solms, 2002). Nevertheless, this theory revolutionized dream research by calling attention to a physiological basis for dreaming, and it remains a dominant dream theory (Hobson et al., 2000).

Cognitive theories   According to **problem-solving dream models**, because dreams are not constrained by reality, they can help us find creative solutions to our problems and ongoing concerns (Cartwright, 1977). Self-help books and numerous websites promote this idea, and history offers some intriguing examples of inventors, scientists and authors who allegedly came upon creative ideas or solutions to problems in a dream (Fig. 6.22). But critics argue that because so many of our dreams do not focus on personal problems, it is difficult to see how problem solving can be the broad underlying reason for *why* we dream. They also note that just because a problem shows up in a dream does not mean that the dream involved an attempt to solve it. Moreover, we may think consciously about our dreams after waking and obtain important new insights; in this sense dreams may indeed help us work through ongoing concerns. However, this is not the same as solving problems *while* dreaming (Squier and Domhoff, 1998).

problem-solving dream models

because dreams are not constrained by reality, they can help us find creative solutions to our problems and ongoing concerns

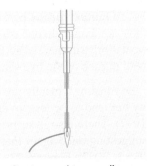

Hand-held needle   Spears in Howe's dream   Sewing machine needle

FIGURE 6.22

Dreams and problem solving.

In 1846 American inventor Elias Howe patented a sewing machine. He had struggled unsuccessfully for years to figure out how to get a machine to stitch using a needle with the threading hole in the back (blunt) end – as in a traditional hand-held needle. Allegedly, one night he had a dream that he was being pursued by spear-throwing tribesmen. In the dream he saw that each spearhead had a hole in it. When Howe woke, he recognized that for a sewing machine to work, the threading hole needed to be at the front (sharp) end of the needle, as it had been on the spears.

Cognitive-process dream theories focus on the process of how we dream and propose that dreaming and waking thought are produced by the same mental systems in the brain (Foulkes, 1982). For example, research indicates that there is more similarity between dreaming and waking mental processes than was traditionally believed (Domhoff, 2001). Consider that one reason many dreams appear bizarre is because their content shifts rapidly. 'I was dreaming about an examination and all of a sudden, the next thing I knew, I was in Hawaii on the beach.' (Don't we wish!) Yet if you reflect on the contents of your waking thoughts – your stream of consciousness – you will realize they also shift suddenly. About half of REM dream reports involve rapid content shifts, but when people are awake and placed in the same environmental conditions as sleepers (a dark, quiet room), about 90 per cent of their reports involve rapid content shifts (Antrobus, 1991). Thus rapid shifting of attention is a process common to dreaming and waking mental activity.

cognitive-process dream theories

propose that dreaming and waking thought are produced by the same mental systems in the brain

Towards integration   Although there is no agreed-on model of why or even of how we dream, theorists are developing models that integrate several perspectives. In general, these models propose that dreaming involves an integration of perceptual, emotional, motivational and cognitive processes performed by various brain modules. For example, *neurocognitive models* (such as the activation-synthesis model) bridge the cognitive and biological perspectives by

Focus 6.16

What functions do daydreams serve? How are they different from and similar to night-time dreams?

attempting to explain how various subjective aspects of dreaming correspond to the physiological changes that occur during sleep (Hobson et al., 2000). And, as noted previously, these models allow for the possibility that motivational factors – our needs and desires – can influence how the brain goes about its business of attaching meaning to the neural activity that underlies our dreams.

DAYDREAMS AND WAKING FANTASIES

Our dreams and fantasy lives are not restricted to the nocturnal realm. Daydreams are a significant part of waking consciousness, providing stimulation during periods of boredom and letting us experience a range of emotions (Hartmann et al., 2001). In *The Secret Life of Walter Mitty*, author James Thurber (1942) portrayed the fictional Mitty as a person who transformed his humdrum existence into an exhilarating fantasy world of adventure. Like Mitty, people who have a **fantasy-prone personality** often live in a vivid, rich fantasy world that they control, and most are female. In one study, about three-quarters of fantasy-prone people were able to achieve sexual orgasm merely by fantasizing about sex, and all could experience fantasies 'as real as real' in each of the five senses (Wilson and Barber, 1982).

fantasy-prone personality

often live in a vivid, rich fantasy world that they control

Daydreams typically involve greater visual imagery than other forms of waking mental activity but tend to be less vivid, emotional and bizarre than night-time dreams (Kunzendorf et al., 1997). There also is surprising similarity in the themes of daydreams and night-time dreams, suggesting once again that nocturnal dreams may be an extension of daytime mental activity (Beck, 2002). Figure 6.23 summarizes some of the biological, psychological and environmental factors that contribute to our understanding of sleep and dreaming.

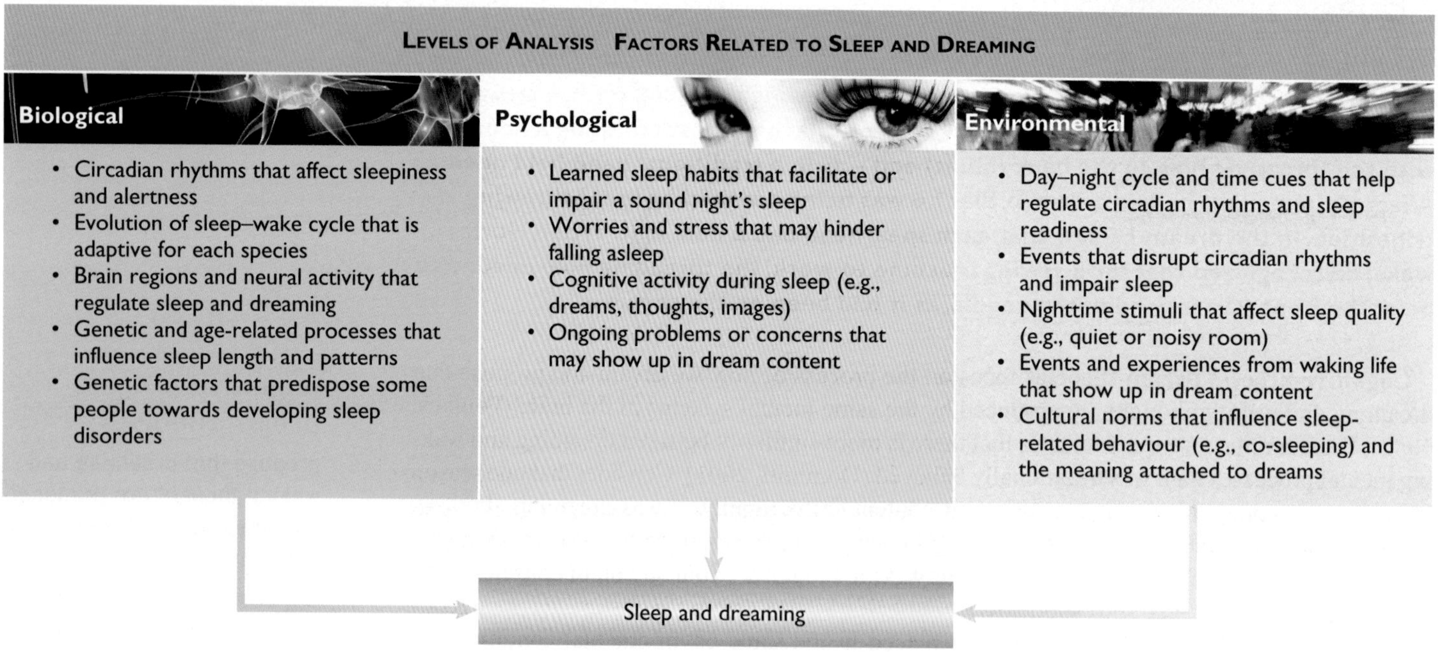

LEVELS OF ANALYSIS   FACTORS RELATED TO SLEEP AND DREAMING

Biological	**Psychological**	**Environmental**
• Circadian rhythms that affect sleepiness and alertness • Evolution of sleep–wake cycle that is adaptive for each species • Brain regions and neural activity that regulate sleep and dreaming • Genetic and age-related processes that influence sleep length and patterns • Genetic factors that predispose some people towards developing sleep disorders	• Learned sleep habits that facilitate or impair a sound night's sleep • Worries and stress that may hinder falling asleep • Cognitive activity during sleep (e.g., dreams, thoughts, images) • Ongoing problems or concerns that may show up in dream content	• Day–night cycle and time cues that help regulate circadian rhythms and sleep readiness • Events that disrupt circadian rhythms and impair sleep • Nighttime stimuli that affect sleep quality (e.g., quiet or noisy room) • Events and experiences from waking life that show up in dream content • Cultural norms that influence sleep-related behaviour (e.g., co-sleeping) and the meaning attached to dreams

Sleep and dreaming

FIGURE 6.23

Levels of analysis: factors related to sleep and dreaming.

IN REVIEW

- Sleep has five main stages. Stages 1 and 2 are lighter sleep, and stages 3 and 4 are deeper, slow-wave sleep. High physiological arousal and periods of rapid eye movement characterize the fifth stage, REM sleep.

- Several brain regions regulate sleep, and the amount we sleep changes as we age. Genetic, psychological and environmental factors affect sleep duration and quality.

- Sleep deprivation negatively affects mood and performance. The restoration model proposes that we sleep to recover from physical and mental fatigue. Evolutionary/circadian models state that each species developed a sleep–wake cycle that maximized its chance of survival.

- Insomnia is the most common sleep disorder, but less common disorders such as narcolepsy, REM-sleep behaviour disorder and sleep apnea can have serious consequences. Sleepwalking typically occurs during slow-wave sleep, whereas nightmares most often occur during REM sleep. Night terrors create a near-panic state of arousal and typically occur in slow-wave sleep.

- Dreams occur throughout sleep but are most common during REM periods. Unpleasant dreams are common. Our cultural background, current concerns and recent events influence what we dream about.

- Freud proposed that dreams fulfil unconscious wishes that show up in disguised form within our dreams. Activation-synthesis theory regards dreaming as the brain's attempt to fit a story to random neural activity. Cognitive-process dream theories emphasize that dreaming and waking thought are produced by the same mental systems.

- Daydreams and nocturnal dreams often share similar themes. People with fantasy-prone personalities have especially vivid daydreams.

DRUG-INDUCED STATES

Like sleep and dreaming, drug-induced states have mystified humans for ages. Three thousand years ago, the Aztecs considered hallucinogenic mushrooms to be a sacred substance for communicating with the spirit world. Today drugs are a cornerstone of medical practice and, as Figure 6.24 shows, a pervasive part of social life. They alter consciousness by modifying brain chemistry, but drug effects are also influenced by psychological, environmental and cultural factors (Julien, 2005).

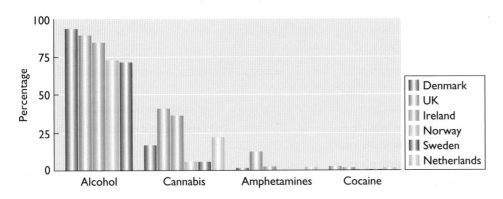

FIGURE 6.24

Drug use among students.

This graph illustrates non-medical drug use among students from a number of different countries. The percentage of those using each drug is shown. (The figure for alcohol consumption in the Netherlands is not available.)

SOURCE: Smart and Ogbourne, 2000.

DRUGS AND THE BRAIN

Like any cell, a neuron is essentially a fragile bag of chemicals, and it takes a delicate chemical balancing act for neurons to function properly. Drugs work their way into the bloodstream and are carried throughout the brain by an extensive network of small blood vessels called capillaries. These capillaries contain a **blood-brain barrier**, a special lining of tightly packed cells that lets vital nutrients pass through so neurons can function. The blood-brain barrier screens out many foreign substances, but some, including various drugs, can pass through. Once inside they alter consciousness by facilitating or inhibiting synaptic transmission (Julien, 2005).

(a) Synthesis, storage, release (b) Binding (c) Re-uptake

Agonistic drugs

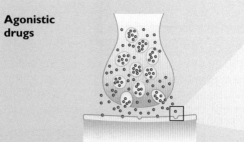
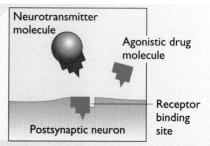
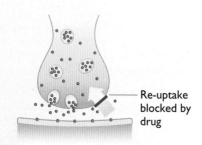

Drug causes neuron to synthesize more transmitter molecules, store them more safely, or release them.

Drug and neurotransmitter have similar structure. Drug binds with receptor site and activates it.

Drug blocks re-uptake. More transmitter molecules remain in synapse, available to activate receptor sites.

Antagonistic drug

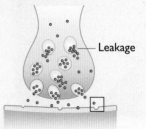

Drug impairs neuron's ability to synthesize, store, or release transmitter. Molecules may leak and degrade prematurely.

Drug binds with receptor site but is not similar enough to transmitter to activate site. Blocks transmitter from activating site.

FIGURE 6.25

How drugs affect neurotransmitters.

(*Top*) Agonistic drugs increase the activity of a neurotransmitter. **(*Bottom*)** Antagonistic drugs decrease the activity of a neurotransmitter.

How Drugs Facilitate Synaptic Transmission

Recall from Chapter 4 that synaptic transmission involves several basic steps. First, neurotransmitters are synthesized inside the pre-synaptic (sending) neuron and stored in vesicles. Next, neurotransmitters are released into the synaptic space, where they bind with and stimulate receptor sites on the postsynaptic (receiving) neuron. Finally, neurotransmitter molecules are deactivated by enzymes or by re-uptake.

An **agonist** is a drug that increases the activity of a neurotransmitter. Figure 6.25 shows that agonists may

- enhance a neuron's ability to synthesize, store, or release neurotransmitters
- bind with and stimulate postsynaptic receptor sites (or make it easier for neurotransmitters to stimulate these sites)
- make it more difficult for neurotransmitters to be deactivated, such as by inhibiting re-uptake.

Consider two examples. First, *opiates* (such as morphine and codeine) are effective pain relievers. Recall that the brain contains its own chemicals, endorphins, which play a major role in pain relief. Opiates have a molecular structure similar to that of endorphins. They bind to and activate receptor sites that receive endorphins. To draw an analogy, think of trying to open a lock with a key. Normally an endorphin molecule acts as the key, but owing to its similar shape, an opiate molecule can fit into the lock and open it.

Second, *amphetamines* boost arousal and mood by causing neurons to release greater amounts of dopamine and norepinephrine and by inhibiting re-uptake. During re-uptake, neurotransmitters in the synapse are absorbed back into pre-synaptic neurons through special channels. As shown in Figure 6.25c, amphetamine molecules block this process. Therefore, dopamine and norepinephrine remain in the synaptic space longer and keep stimulating postsynaptic neurons.

How Drugs Inhibit Synaptic Transmission

An **antagonist** is a drug that inhibits or decreases the action of a neurotransmitter. As Figure 6.25 shows, an antagonist may

- reduce a neuron's ability to synthesize, store or release neurotransmitters, or
- prevent a neurotransmitter from binding with the postsynaptic neuron, such as by fitting into and blocking the receptor sites on the postsynaptic neuron, or degradation in the synapse.

Consider the action of drugs called *antipsychotics* used to treat *schizophrenia*, a severe psychological disorder whose symptoms may include hallucinations (e.g., hearing voices) and delusions (clearly false beliefs, such as believing you are Joan of Arc). These symptoms are often associated with overactivity of the dopamine system. To restore dopamine activity to more normal levels, pharmaceutical companies have developed drugs with a molecular structure similar to dopamine, but not too similar. Returning to the lock-and-key analogy, imagine finding a key that fits into a lock but will not turn. The key's shape is close enough to the real key to get in but not to open the lock. Similarly, antipsychotic drugs fit into dopamine receptor sites but not well enough to stimulate them. While they occupy the sites, dopamine released by presynaptic neurons is blocked and cannot get in, and the schizophrenic symptoms usually decrease.

DRUG TOLERANCE AND DEPENDENCE

When a drug is used repeatedly, the intensity of effects produced by the same dosage level may decrease over time. This decreasing responsivity to a drug is called **tolerance**. As it develops, the person must take increasingly larger doses to achieve the same physical and psychological effects. Tolerance stems from the body's attempt to maintain a state of optimal physiological balance, called *homeostasis*. If a drug changes bodily functioning in a certain way, by, say, increasing heart rate, the brain tries to restore balance by producing **compensatory responses**, which are reactions opposite to that of the drug (e.g., reactions that decrease heart rate).

What happens when drug tolerance develops and the person suddenly stops using the drug? The body's compensatory responses may continue and, no longer balanced out by the drug's effects, the person can experience strong reactions opposite to those produced by the drug. This occurrence of compensatory responses after discontinued drug use is known as **withdrawal**. For example, in the absence of alcohol's sedating and relaxing effects, a chronic drinker may experience anxiety and hypertension. One of the consequences of abrupt drug withdrawal is called 'rebound insomnia'. This happens with a class of drugs called 'hypnotics' that are designed to help a patient sleep. Stopping these drugs abruptly can cause the patient to suffer with insomnia, which was why they were taking the hypnotic in the first place. The result is that the 'rebound insomnia' is seen by the patient as a reoccurrence of their original insomnia. They believe that they still need the drug, and the habit persists, as the patient lapses and begins taking the drug once more. The person is now showing the symptoms of drug dependency.

antagonist
a drug that inhibits or decreases the action of a neurotransmitter

tolerance
decreasing responsivity to a drug

compensatory responses
reactions opposite to that of the drug

withdrawal
occurrence of compensatory responses after discontinued drug use

Focus 6.17
How are tolerance, compensatory responses, withdrawal and dependence related? How does learning affect tolerance?

FIGURE 6.26

Conditioned drug responses and overdose.

Environmental stimuli that are repeatedly paired with the use of a drug can eventually trigger compensatory responses on their own. If the same drug dose is now taken in a new setting, compensatory responses will not be at full strength, thereby increasing the risk of an 'overdose' reaction.

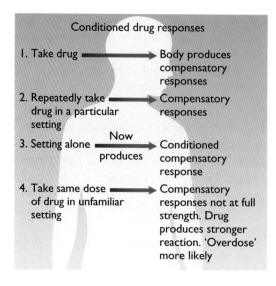

Conditioned drug responses

1. Take drug → Body produces compensatory responses

2. Repeatedly take drug in a particular setting → Compensatory responses

3. Setting alone Now produces → Conditioned compensatory response

4. Take same dose of drug in unfamiliar setting → Compensatory responses not at full strength. Drug produces stronger reaction. 'Overdose' more likely

Learning, Drug Tolerance and Overdose

Tolerance for various drugs depends partly on the familiarity of the drug setting. Figure 6.26 illustrates how environmental stimuli associated with repeated drug use begin to elicit compensatory responses through a learning process called *classical conditioning*. As drug use continues, the physical setting triggers progressively stronger compensatory responses, increasing the user's tolerance. This helps explain why drug addicts often experience increased cravings when they enter a setting associated with drug use. The environmental stimuli trigger compensatory responses that, without drugs to mask their effect, cause the user to feel withdrawal symptoms (Duncan et al., 2000).

There is a hidden danger in this process, particularly for experienced drug users. Compensatory responses serve a protective function by physiologically countering part of the drug's effects. If a user takes his or her usual high dose in a familiar environment, the body's compensatory responses are at full strength – a combination of compensatory reactions to the drug itself and also to the familiar, conditioned environmental stimuli. But in an *unfamiliar* environment, the conditioned compensatory responses are weaker, and the drug has a stronger physiological net effect than usual (Siegel et al., 2000).

Shepard Siegel (1984) interviewed people addicted to heroin who experienced near-fatal overdoses. He found that in most cases they had not taken a dose larger than their customary one. Rather, they had injected a normal dose in an unfamiliar environment. Siegel concluded that the addicts were not protected by their usual compensatory responses, resulting in an 'overdose' reaction.

Drug Addiction and Dependence

Drug addiction, which is formally called **substance dependence**, is a maladaptive pattern of substance use that causes a person significant distress or substantially impairs that person's life. Substance dependence is diagnosed as occurring with *physiological dependence* if drug tolerance or withdrawal symptoms have developed. The term *psychological dependence* is often used to describe situations in which people strongly crave a drug because of its pleasurable effects, even if they are not physiologically dependent. However, this is not a diagnostic term, and some drug experts feel it is misleading. Drug cravings do have a physical basis; they are rooted in patterns of brain activity (Sun and Rebec, 2005).

Misconceptions about substance dependence   Many people mistakenly believe that if a drug does not produce tolerance or withdrawal, one cannot become dependent on it. In reality, neither tolerance nor withdrawal is needed for a diagnosis of substance dependence.

The popular media image of a shaking alcoholic desperately searching for a drink or a heroin junkie looking for a fix reinforces another misconception, namely, that the motivation to avoid or end withdrawal symptoms is the primary cause of addiction. Such physiological dependence contributes powerfully to drug dependence, but consider these points:

- People can become dependent on drugs, such as cocaine, that produce only mild withdrawal (Kampmann et al., 2002). The drug's pleasurable effects – often produced by boosting dopamine activity – play a key role in causing dependence.

substance dependence

maladaptive pattern of substance use that causes a person significant distress or substantially impairs that person's life

- Many drug users who quit and make it through withdrawal eventually start using again, even though they are no longer physiologically dependent.

- Many factors influence drug dependence, including genetic predispositions, personality traits, religious beliefs, family and peer influences, and cultural norms.

DEPRESSANTS

Depressants decrease nervous system activity. In moderate doses, they reduce feelings of tension and anxiety, and produce a state of relaxed euphoria. In extremely high doses, depressants can slow down vital life processes to the point of death.

Alcohol

Alcohol is the most widely used recreational drug in many cultures. The World Health Authority indicate that the European region has the highest alcohol consumption of all its regions, with consumption levels twice those of the world average (Fig. 6.27). Alcohol is a major cause of death in Europe, whether directly, or because of its role in fatal accidents. In 2002, for instance, 600 000 Europeans died in alcohol-related deaths. Over 16 000 of these were young people aged between 15 and 29. In addition to this, continued consumption of alcohol can cause other problems. Tolerance develops gradually and can lead to physiological dependence. Alcohol dampens the nervous system by increasing the activity of GABA, the brain's main inhibitory neurotransmitter, and by decreasing the activity of glutamate, a major excitatory neurotransmitter (Anton, 2001). Why, then, if alcohol is a depressant drug, do many people initially seem less inhibited when they drink and report getting a high from alcohol? In part, the weakening of inhibitions occurs because alcohol's neural slowdown depresses the action of inhibitory control centres in the brain. As for the subjective high, alcohol boosts the activity of several neurotransmitters, such as dopamine, that produce feelings of pleasure and euphoria (Lewis, 1996; Tupala and Tiihonen, 2004). At higher doses, however, the brain's control centres become increasingly disrupted, thinking and physical co-ordination become disorganized, and fatigue may occur as blood alcohol level (BAL) rises (Table 6.3). For reference, the BAL deemed legal for driving in Europe ranges between 0.2mg/ml to 0.8mg/ml. In Turkey, it is illegal to have consumed any alcohol at all, when taking passengers in your car. In South Africa the limit is 0.2mg/ml if you are a professional driver, or if you are carrying paying customers, such as a taxi driver might be; otherwise the limit of 0.5mg/ml.

depressants
decrease nervous system activity

Focus 6.18
How do depressants affect the brain? How does alcohol intoxication affect decisions about drinking and driving?

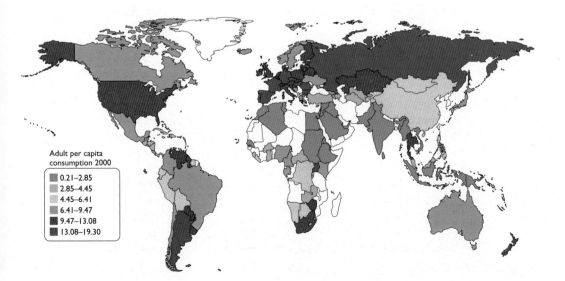

Adult per capita
consumption 2000

- 0.21–2.85
- 2.85–4.45
- 4.45–6.41
- 6.41–9.47
- 9.47–13.08
- 13.08–19.30

FIGURE 6.27

Adult per capita alcohol consumption in the world measured in pure alcohol consumption per person per year.

Alcohol consumption across the world varies. The level in Europe is almost twice that of the world average.

SOURCE: World Health Organization, 2005.

TABLE 6.3 BEHAVIOURAL EFFECTS OF ALCOHOL

BAL	Hours to leave body	Behavioural effects
.03	1	Decreased alertness, impaired reaction time in some people
.05	2	Decreased alertness, impaired judgement and reaction time, good feeling, release of inhibitions
.10	4	Severely impaired reaction time, motor function and judgement; lack of caution
.15	10	Gross intoxication, worsening impairments
.25	?	Extreme sensory and motor impairment, staggering
.30	?	Stuporous but conscious, cannot comprehend immediate environment
.40	?	Lethal in over 50 per cent of cases

Alcohol consumption can significantly influence judgement and performance. *Blood-alcohol level* is a measure of alcohol concentration in the body. Elevated BALs impair reaction time, co-ordination and decision making, and increase risky behaviours. The problem is very serious, so much so that the European Union has set itself a target to halve deaths in road traffic; 40 000 people were killed and over 1.7 million people injured in accidents where alcohol was involved (Eurocare, 2003).

Why do intoxicated people often act in risky ways that they would not when sober? It is not simply a matter of lowered inhibitions. Alcohol also produces what Steele and Josephs (1990) call **alcohol myopia**, short-sighted thinking caused by the inability to pay attention to as much information as when sober. People who drink start to focus only on aspects of the situation (cues) that stand out. In the absence of strong cautionary cues (such as warnings) to inhibit risky behaviour, they do not think about long-term consequences of their actions as carefully as when they are sober. Our 'Research close-up' illustrates this effect.

> **alcohol myopia**
> **short-sighted thinking caused by the inability to pay attention to as much information as when sober**

RESEARCH CLOSE-UP

DRINKING AND DRIVING: DECISION MAKING IN ALTERED STATES

SOURCE: T.K. MacDonald, M.P. Zanna and G.T. Fong (1995) Decision making in altered states: effects of alcohol on attitudes towards drinking and driving, *Journal of Personality and Social Psychology*, vol. 68, pp. 973–85.

INTRODUCTION

Most people have negative attitudes about drunk driving and say they would not do it. They realize that the cons (e.g., risk of accident, injury, death and police arrest) far outweigh the pros (e.g., not having to ask someone for a lift). Why, then, do so many people decide to drive after becoming intoxicated?

Based on alcohol-myopia principles, Tara MacDonald and her colleagues reasoned that when intoxicated people decide whether to drive, they may focus on the pros or the cons but do not have the attentional capacity to focus on both. If a circumstance that favours driving (a *facilitating cue*) is called to the intoxicated person's attention (e.g., 'It's only a short distance'), she or he will latch on to it and fail to consider the cons. But in general situations that do not contain facilitating cues, intoxicated people's feelings about driving should remain as negative as when they were sober.

The authors made two predictions. First, intoxicated and sober people will have equally negative *general attitudes* and intentions towards drinking and driving. Second, intoxicated people will have fewer negative attitudes and greater intentions towards drinking and driving than sober people in situations that contain a facilitating cue.

METHOD

Laboratory experiment

Fifty-seven male introductory psychology students, all regular drinkers who owned cars, participated. They were randomly assigned to either the sober condition, in which they received no alcohol, or the alcohol condition, in which they received three alcoholic drinks within an hour (the average BAL was .074 per cent, just below the .08 per cent legal driving limit in Ontario, Canada).

Participants then completed a drinking-and-driving questionnaire. Some items asked about general attitudes and intentions (e.g., 'I will drink and drive the next time that I am out at a party or bar with friends'). Other items contained a facilitating cue, a special circumstance that suggested a possible reason for drinking and driving ('If I had only a short distance to drive home … / If my friends tried to persuade me to drink and drive … I would drive while intoxicated.'). Participants rated each item on a 9-point scale (1 = 'strongly disagree'; 9 = 'strongly agree').

Party/bar diary study

Fifty-one male and female college students recorded a telephone diary while at a party or bar where they were going to drink alcohol. Some were randomly assigned to record the diary when they first arrived; others, just before they left. To record the diary, participants opened up a packet containing the same drinking-and-driving questionnaire described above, called a number on the packet, and recorded their responses on the researchers' answering machine. Based on participants' descriptions of how much alcohol they had consumed, the researchers estimated their BAL and identified two groups: 'sober participants' (average BAL .01) and 'intoxicated participants' (average BAL .11).

RESULTS

The findings from both studies supported the predictions. Sober participants and intoxicated participants both expressed negative general attitudes about drinking and driving, and indicated they would not drive when intoxicated. But, as Figure 6.28 shows, when the questions presented a special circumstance, intoxicated participants expressed more favourable attitudes and a greater intention to drive than sober participants.

DISCUSSION

This study nicely illustrates how a person's physiological state (sober versus intoxicated) and an environmental factor (general situation versus special circumstance) interact to influence psychological functioning (attitudes and decision making). However, let us think critically about the results. Was it really narrowed attention – leading to a failure to consider negative consequences – that caused the results? The authors anticipated two alternative explanations. First, perhaps people who drink do not realize how

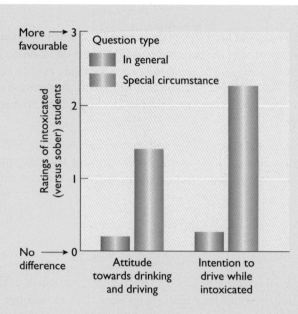

FIGURE 6.28

Intoxicated and sober people's attitudes towards drinking and driving.

When general attitudes and intentions towards drinking and driving are measured, intoxicated and sober participants have similar negative reactions. But when questioned about situations involving special circumstances (facilitating cues), intoxicated participants have more favourable attitudes and greater intentions to drive after drinking than do sober participants.

intoxicated they are. Second, perhaps intoxicated people overestimate their driving ability, a belief called *drunken invincibility*. The authors tested and ruled out these explanations. Intoxicated participants believed they were *more* intoxicated than they actually were and estimated that they would drive *more poorly* than the average person.

Is it possible that the findings were caused by participants' expectations about alcohol rather than its chemical effects? The authors conducted a placebo control experiment in which some participants were convincingly misled to believe they were intoxicated. Results showed that the alcohol-myopia effect occurred only for participants who truly had consumed alcohol. It was not caused by participants' expectations.

What practical value do these findings have? The researchers suggest that a sign saying 'Drinking and Driving Kills', or a large photograph of a police officer administering a Breathalyser test, be made highly visible near the exit of a bar. Alcohol myopia should cause intoxicated people to narrow their focus of attention to these *inhibiting cues*, causing them to rethink any decision to drink and drive. In subsequent research, MacDonald and co-workers (2003) found that making strong inhibiting cues salient did indeed lead intoxicated people to behave more cautiously.

Barbiturates and Tranquillizers

Physicians sometimes prescribe barbiturates (sleeping pills) and tranquillizers (antianxiety drugs, such as Valium) as sedatives and relaxants. Like alcohol, they depress the nervous system by increasing the activity of the inhibitory neurotransmitter GABA (Nishino et al., 2001).

Mild doses of drugs belonging to the benzodiazapine group are effective as sleeping pills but are highly addictive. As tolerance builds, addicted people may take up to 50 sleeping pills a day. At high doses, barbiturates trigger initial excitation, followed by slurred speech, loss of co-ordination, depression and memory impairment. Overdoses, particularly when taken with alcohol, may cause unconsciousness, coma and, even, death. Barbiturates and tranquillizers are widely overused, and tolerance and physiological dependence can occur. Users often do not recognize that they have become dependent until they try to stop and experience serious withdrawal symptoms, such as anxiety, insomnia, and, possibly, seizures. It must be said, though, that more modern hypnotics (drugs that help people sleep) do not cause people to suffer quite so badly with these side effects.

Some doctors prescribe other drugs for insomnia, such as antidepressants and antihistamines, as these have a sedative effect, but avoid the problem of tolerance.

STIMULANTS

Stimulants increase neural firing and arouse the nervous system. They increase blood pressure, respiration, heart rate and overall alertness. While they can elevate mood to the point of euphoria, they also can heighten irritability.

Amphetamines

Amphetamines are powerful stimulants prescribed to reduce appetite and fatigue, decrease the need for sleep and reduce depression. Unfortunately, they are widely overused to boost energy and mood (Anthony et al., 1997).

Amphetamines increase dopamine and noradrenaline (aka norepinephrine) activity. Tolerance develops, and users may crave their pleasurable effects. Eventually, many heavy users start injecting large quantities, producing a sudden surge of energy and rush of intense pleasure. With frequent injections, they may remain awake for a week, their bodily systems racing at breakneck speed. Injecting amphetamines greatly increases blood pressure and can lead to heart failure and cerebral haemorrhage (stroke); repeated high doses may cause brain damage (Diaz, 1997).

There is an inevitable crash when heavy users stop taking the drug. They may sleep for one to two days, waking up depressed, exhausted and irritable. This crash occurs because the neurons' noradrenaline (norepinephrine) and dopamine supplies have become depleted. Amphetamines tax the body heavily.

Cocaine

Cocaine is a powder derived from the coca plant, which grows mainly in Western South America. Usually inhaled or injected, it produces excitation, a sense of increased muscular strength and euphoria. Cocaine increases the activity of noradrenaline (norepinephrine) and dopamine by blocking their re-uptake.

At various times in history, cocaine has been hailed as a wonder drug and branded as a menace. It was once widely used as a local anaesthetic in eye, nose and throat surgery. Novocain, a synthetic form of cocaine, is still used in dentistry as an anaesthetic. Owing to its stimulating effects, cocaine found its way into potions sold to the public to enhance health. In 1885 John Pemberton developed Coca-Cola by mixing cocaine with the kola nut and syrup (Fig. 6.29).

> **stimulants**
> increase neural firing and arouse the nervous system

(a)

(b)

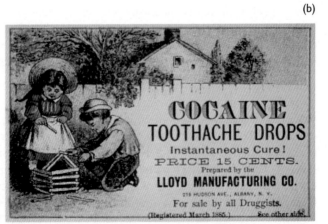

FIGURE 6.29

(a) When Coca-Cola was first produced, there was a clear reason why it 'relieved fatigue': it contained cocaine. (b) Before it was made illegal, cocaine was found in a variety of medicinal products.

Focus 6.19

How do amphetamines, cocaine and Ecstasy affect the brain? Why can their use lead to a 'crash'?

Focus 6.20

Describe the major effects and dangers of opiates, hallucinogens and marijuana.

In large doses, cocaine can produce vomiting, convulsions and paranoid delusions (Boutros et al., 2002). A depressive crash may occur after a cocaine high. Tolerance develops to many of cocaine's effects, and chronic use has been associated with an increased risk of cognitive impairments and brain damage (Franklin et al., 2002). Crack is a chemically converted form of cocaine that can be smoked, and its effects are faster and more dangerous. Overdoses can cause sudden death from cardiorespiratory arrest.

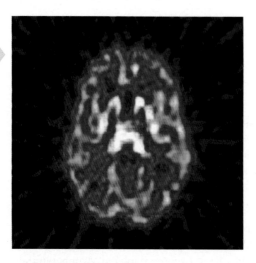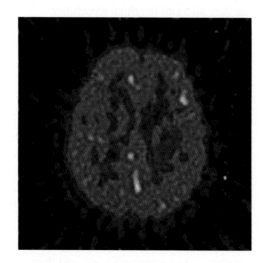

FIGURE 6.30

Frequent Ecstasy use and the brain.

(*Left*) This PET-scan image shows the brain of a person who never used Ecstasy. (*Right*) This image shows the brain of a person who used Ecstasy 70 times or more over a period of at least 1.5 years but who stopped using the drug for several weeks before these images were taken. Areas of lighter colour indicate a higher density of special proteins (called *transporters*) necessary for normal serotonin re-uptake. The darker image of the brain on the right suggests that there is damage to the serotonin re-uptake system.

SOURCE: McCann et al., 1998.

Ecstasy (MDMA)

Ecstasy, also known as MDMA (methylenedioxymethamphetamine), is artificially synthesized and has a chemical structure that partly resembles both methamphetamine (a stimulant) and mescaline (a hallucinogen). Ecstasy produces feelings of pleasure, elation, empathy and warmth. In the brain, it primarily increases serotonin functioning, which boosts one's mood but may cause agitation. After the drug wears off, users often feel sluggish and depressed – a rebound effect partly due to serotonin depletion (Travers and Lyvers, 2005). They may have to take increasingly stronger doses to overcome tolerance to Ecstasy.

Ecstasy is called a *rave drug* because it is used at nightclubs and rave parties. It causes locomotor activity and can cause hyperthermia, which when used in hot nightclubs can in some cases lead to death (Green et al., 2004) In experiments with laboratory rats, Ecstasy has produced long-lasting damage to the axon terminals of neurons that release serotonin (Mechan et al., 2002). Human studies of habitual Ecstasy users suggest a similar possibility (Fig. 6.30), but it is not clear whether such damage is permanent. In the long run, Ecstasy may produce consequences that are anything but pleasurable. Continued use has been associated with impaired memory, sleep difficulties and a diminished capacity to experience sexual pleasure (Parrott, 2001).

OPIATES

Opium is a product of the opium poppy. Opium and drugs derived from it, such as morphine, codeine and heroin, are called **opiates**. Opiates have two major effects: they provide pain relief and cause mood changes which may include euphoria. Opiates stimulate receptors normally activated by endorphins, thereby producing pain relief. Opiates also increase dopamine activity, which may be one reason they induce euphoria (Bardo, 1998).

In medical use, opiates are the most effective agents known for relieving intense pain. Heroin was developed in 1889 by the Bayer company (which today produces aspirin). Initially thought to be a non-addictive painkiller, heroin is, like other opiates, highly addictive. In the 1920s it was made illegal in the USA.

Heroin users feel an intense rush within several minutes of an injection, but they often pay a high price for this transient pleasure. High doses may lead to respiratory depression, which can be fatal, and coma, and overdoses can cause death (Julien, 2005).

HALLUCINOGENS

Hallucinogens are powerful mind-altering drugs that produce hallucinations. Many are derived from natural sources; mescaline, for example, comes from the peyote cactus. Natural hallucinogens have been considered sacred in many tribal cultures because of their ability to produce unearthly states of consciousness and contact with spiritual forces (Fig. 6.31). Other hallucinogens, such as LSD (lysergic acid diethylamide, or 'acid') and phencyclidine ('angel dust') are synthetic.

Hallucinogens distort sensory experience and can blur the boundaries between reality and fantasy. Users may speak of having mystical experiences and of feeling exhilarated. They may also experience violent outbursts, paranoia and panic, and have flashbacks after the trip has ended. The mental effects of hallucinogens are always unpredictable, even if they are taken repeatedly. This unpredictability constitutes their greatest danger.

LSD is a powerful hallucinogen that causes a flooding of excitation in the nervous system. Tolerance develops rapidly but decreases quickly. It increases the activity of serotonin and dopamine at certain receptor sites, but scientists still do not know precisely how LSD produces its effects (Nichols and Sanders-Bush, 2002).

MARIJUANA

Marijuana, a product of the hemp plant (*Cannabis sativa*), is the most widely used and controversial illegal drug which has found a prominent role in popular culture over the years (Fig. 6.32). **THC (tetrahydrocannabinol)** is marijuana's major active ingredient, and it binds to receptors on neurons

opiates
opium and drugs derived from it, such as morphine, codeine and heroin

hallucinogens
powerful mind-altering drugs that produce hallucinations

FIGURE 6.31

In some cultures, hallucinogenic drugs are thought to have spiritual powers. Under the influence of peyote, this Indian shaman prepares to conduct a religious ceremony.

THC (tetrahydrocannabinol)
marijuana's major active ingredient

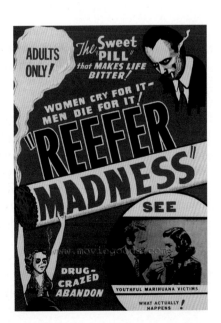

FIGURE 6.32

Marijuana has features prominently in popular culture for a very long time. Films like *Reefer Madness* (1936) were clearly propaganda focused on those considering the use of the drug. Other media used popular myths about marijuana to sensational effect. Books such as *The Marijuana Mob* by James Hadley Chase (1950), and *Reefer Girl* by Jane Manning (1956) were just two of many.

throughout the brain. But why does the brain have receptor sites for a foreign substance such as marijuana? The answer is that the brain produces its own THC-like substances called *cannabinoids* (Kirkham, 2004). With chronic use, THC may increase GABA activity, which slows down neural activity and produces relaxing effects (Diaz, 1997). THC also increases dopamine activity, which may account for some of its pleasurable subjective effects (Maldonado and Rodriguez de Fonseca, 2002). THC has been shown to have some therapeutic potential, for example in cases of chemotherapy-induced nausea, in some pain conditions and as a drug that may alleviate some symptoms of multiple sclerosis (Carlimi, 2004).

Misconceptions about Marijuana

One misconception about marijuana is that chronic use causes people to become unmotivated and apathetic towards everything, a condition called *amotivational syndrome*. Another misconception is that marijuana causes people to start using more dangerous drugs. Neither statement is supported by scientific evidence (Diaz, 1997; Rao, 2001). A third misconception is that using marijuana has no significant dangers. In fact, marijuana smoke contains more cancer-causing substances than does tobacco smoke. At high doses, users may experience negative changes in mood, sensory distortions, and feelings of panic and anxiety. While users are high, marijuana can impair their reaction time, thinking, memory, learning and driving skills (Lane et al., 2005).

Another misconception is that users cannot become dependent on marijuana. Actually, repeated marijuana use produces tolerance and, at typical doses, some chronic users may experience mild withdrawal symptoms, such as restlessness. People who use chronically high doses and suddenly stop may experience vomiting, disrupted sleep and irritability. About 5 to 10 per cent of people who use marijuana develop dependence (Coffey et al., 2002).

FROM GENES TO CULTURE: DETERMINANTS OF DRUG EFFECTS

Table 6.4 summarizes some typical drug effects, but a user's reaction depends on more than the drug's chemical structure.

Biological Factors

Animal research indicates that genetic factors influence sensitivity and tolerance to drugs' effects (Boehm et al., 2002). The most extensive research has focused on alcohol. Rats and mice can be genetically bred to inherit a strong preference for drinking alcohol instead of water. Even in their first exposure to alcohol, these rats show greater tolerance than normal rats.

Among humans, identical twins have a higher concordance rate for alcoholism than do fraternal twins (Heath et al., 1997). Scientists have also identified a gene that is found more often among alcoholics and their children than among non-alcoholics and their offspring (Noble, 1998). No one claims that this is an 'alcoholism gene'; rather, it may influence how the brain responds to alcohol.

People who grow up with alcoholic versus non-alcoholic parents respond differently to drinking alcohol under laboratory conditions. Adults who had alcoholic parents typically display faster hormonal and psychological reactions as blood-alcohol levels rise, but these responses drop off more quickly as blood-alcohol levels decrease (Newlin and Thomson, 1997). Compared with other people, they must drink more alcohol over the course of a few hours to maintain their feeling of intoxication. Overall, many scientists see evidence for a genetic role in determining responsiveness and addiction to alcohol (Knopik et al., 2004).

Psychological Factors

At the psychological level, people's beliefs and expectancies can influence drug reactions (George et al., 2000). Experiments show that people may behave as if drunk if they simply think they have consumed alcohol but actually have not. If a person's fellow drinkers are happy and

Focus 6.21

Explain how drug reactions depend on biological, psychological and environmental factors.

TABLE 6.4 EFFECTS OF SOME MAJOR DRUGS

Class	Typical effects	Risks of high doses and/or chronic use
Depressants		
Alcohol	Relaxation, lowered inhibition, impaired physical and psychological functioning	Disorientation, unconsciousness, possible death at extreme doses
Barbiturates, tranquillizers	Reduced tension, impaired reflexes and motor functioning, drowsiness	Shallow breathing, clammy skin, weak and rapid pulse, coma, possible death
Stimulants		
Amphetamines, cocaine, Ecstasy	Increased alertness, pulse, and blood pressure; elevated mood; suppressed appetite; agitation; sleeplessness	Hallucinations, paranoid delusions, convulsions, long-term cognitive impairments, brain damage, possible death
Opiates		
Opium, morphine, codeine, heroin	Euphoria, pain relief, drowsiness, impaired motor and psychological functioning	Shallow breathing, convulsions, coma, possible death
Hallucinogens		
LSD, mescaline, phencyclidine	Hallucinations and visions, distorted time perception, loss of contact with reality, nausea	Psychotic reactions (delusions, paranoia), panic, possible death
Marijuana	Mild euphoria, relaxation, enhanced sensory experiences, increased appetite, impaired memory and reaction time	Fatigue, anxiety, disorientation, sensory distortions, possible psychotic reactions, exposure to carcinogens

gregarious, he or she may feel it is expected to respond the same way. Personality factors also influence drug reactions and usage. People who have difficulty adjusting to life's demands or whose contact with reality is marginal may be particularly vulnerable to severe and negative drug reactions and to drug addiction (Ray and Ksir, 2004).

Environmental Factors

The physical and social setting in which a drug is taken can strongly influence a user's reactions. As noted earlier, merely being in a familiar drug-use setting can trigger compensatory physiological responses and cravings. Moreover, the behaviour of other people who are sharing the drug experience provides important cues for how to respond, and a hostile environment may increase the chances of a bad trip with drugs such as LSD (Palfai and Jankiewicz, 1991).

Cultural learning also affects how people respond to a drug (Bloomfield et al., 2002). In many western cultures, increased aggressiveness and sexual promiscuity are commonly associated with drunken excess. In contrast, members of the Camba culture of Bolivia customarily drink large quantities of a 178-proof beverage, remaining cordial and non-aggressive between episodes of passing out. In the 1700s, Tahitians introduced to alcohol by European sailors reacted at first with pleasant relaxation when intoxicated, but after witnessing the violent aggressiveness exhibited by drunken sailors, they too began behaving aggressively (MacAndrew and Edgerton, 1969).

FIGURE 6.33

Levels of analysis: factors related to the effects of drugs.

Cultural factors also affect drug consumption. Traditionally, members of the Navajo tribe do not consider drinking any amount of alcohol to be normal, whereas drinking wine or beer is central to social life in some European countries (Tanaka-Matsumi and Draguns, 1997). In some cultures, hallucinogenic drugs are feared and outlawed, whereas in others they are used in medicinal or religious contexts to seek advice from spirits. Figure 6.33 summarizes some of the biological, environmental and psychological factors that may influence drug experiences.

LEVELS OF ANALYSIS   FACTORS RELATED TO THE EFFECTS OF DRUGS

Biological
- Agonistic or antagonistic effects on neurotransmission
- Neural pathways and brain centres affected by drug action
- Compensatory responses and tolerance to drug intake
- Genetic factors that influence biological reactivity to specific drugs

Psychological
- Attitudes towards the drug and drug use
- Expectations concerning drug effects
- Individual's level of personal adjustment, which can influence the likelihood of a negative response

Environmental
- Cultural norms and experiences that affect user expectations
- Physical setting and presence of conditioned compensatory stimuli
- Social context and behaviour of other drug users who are present

Drug-induced states of consciousness

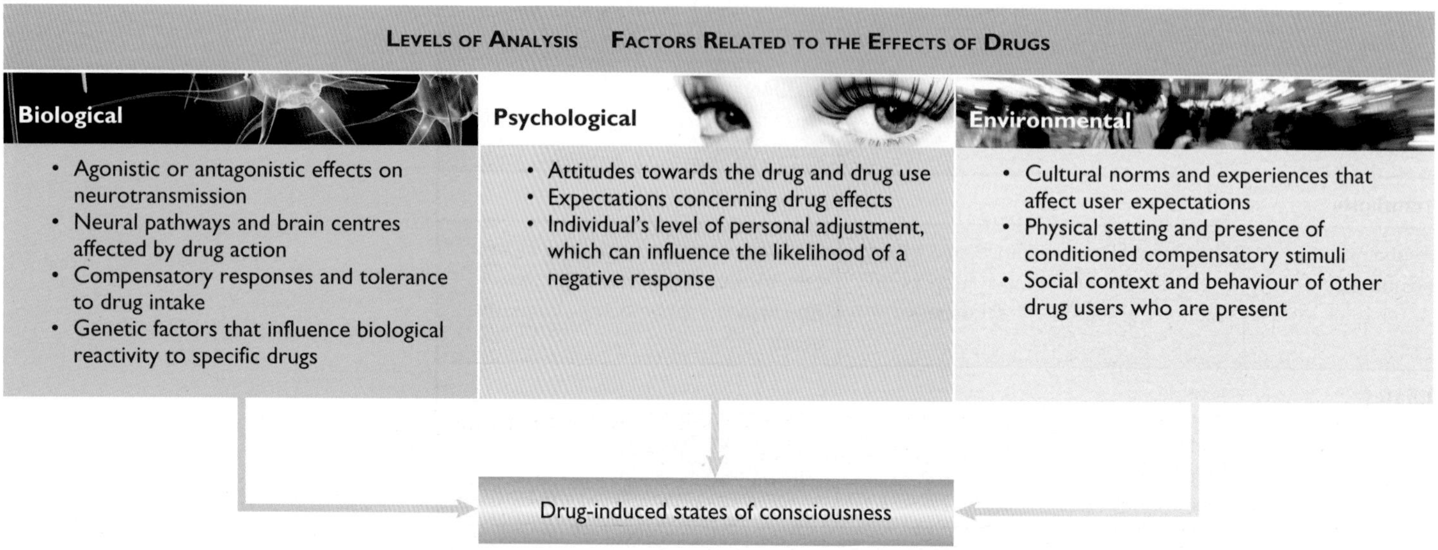

IN REVIEW

- Drugs alter consciousness by modifying neurotransmitter activity. Agonists increase the activity of a neurotransmitter, whereas antagonists decrease it.

- Tolerance develops when the body produces compensatory responses to counteract a drug's effects. When drug use is stopped, compensatory responses continue and produce withdrawal symptoms.

- Substance dependence is a maladaptive pattern of drug use. It can occur with or without physiological dependence.

- Depressants, such as alcohol, barbiturates and tranquillizers, decrease neural activity. The weakened inhibitions often associated with low alcohol doses partly occur because alcohol depresses inhibitory brain centres.

- Amphetamines and cocaine are stimulants that increase arousal and boost mood. Ecstasy produces elation but can also cause agitation. A depressive crash can occur after these drugs wear off. Repeated use may produce serious negative psychological effects and bodily damage.

- Opiates increase endorphin activity, producing pain relief and mood changes that may include euphoria. Opiates are important in medicine but are highly addictive.

- Hallucinogens, such as LSD, powerfully distort sensory experience and can blur the line between reality and fantasy.

- Marijuana produces relaxation at low doses but can cause anxiety and sensory distortions at higher doses. It can impair thinking and reflexes.

- A drug's effect depends on its chemical actions, the physical and social setting, cultural norms and learning, as well as the user's genetic predispositions, expectations and personality.

HYPNOSIS

In eighteenth-century Vienna, physician Anton Mesmer gained fame for using magnetized objects to cure patients. He claimed that illness was caused by blockages of an invisible bodily fluid and that his technique of 'animal magnetism' (later named *mesmerism* in his honour) would restore the fluid's normal flow. A scientific commission discredited mesmerism, but its use continued. Decades later, Scottish surgeon James Braid investigated the fact that mesmerized patients often went into a trance in which they seemed oblivious to their surroundings. Braid concluded that mesmerism was a state of 'nervous sleep' produced by concentrated attention, and he renamed it *hypnosis*, after Hypnos, the Greek god of sleep.

THE SCIENTIFIC STUDY OF HYPNOSIS

Hypnosis is a state of heightened suggestibility in which some people are able to experience imagined situations as if they were real. Hypnosis draws great interest because many therapists use it in treating mental disorders. Hypnosis is not just a stage act. Many universities across Europe, and indeed across the world, offer modules and courses in hypnosis with scientists exploring whether hypnosis is a unique state of altered consciousness, putting its claims to rigorous test.

Hypnotic induction is the process by which one person (a researcher or hypnotist) leads another person (the subject) into hypnosis. A hypnotist may ask the subject to sit down and gaze at an object on the wall, and then, in a quiet voice, suggest that the subject's eyes are becoming heavy. The goal is to relax the subject and increase her or his concentration.

Contrary to popular belief, people cannot be hypnotized against their will. Even when people want to be hypnotized, they differ in how susceptible (i.e., responsive) they are to hypnotic suggestions. **Hypnotic susceptibility scales** contain a standard series of pass–fail suggestions that are read to a subject after a hypnotic induction (Table 6.5). The subject's score is based on the number of passes. About 10 per cent of subjects are completely non-responsive, 10 per cent pass all or nearly all of the items, and the rest fall in between (Hilgard, 1977).

HYPNOTIC BEHAVIOURS AND EXPERIENCES

Does hypnosis alter people's psychological functioning and behaviour? Let us examine some claims.

Involuntary Control and Behaving against One's Will

Hypnotized people *subjectively experience* their actions to be involuntary (Kirsch, 2001). For example, look at the second item in Table 6.5. To hypnotized subjects, it really feels like their hands are being pushed apart by a mysterious force, rather than by their conscious control.

If behaviour seems involuntary under hypnosis, then can a hypnotist make people perform acts that are harmful to themselves or others? Martin Orne and Frederick Evans (1965) found that hypnotized subjects could be induced to dip their hands briefly in a foaming solution they were told was acid and then to throw the 'acid' in another person's face. This might appear to be a striking example of the power of hypnosis to get people to act against their will. However, Orne and Evans tested a control group of subjects who were asked to simply pretend that they were hypnotized. These subjects were just as likely as hypnotized subjects to put their hands in the 'acid' and throw it at someone.

In Chapter 17 you will learn about experiments in which researchers induced hundreds of 'normal' adults to keep giving what they believed were extremely painful electric shocks to an innocent man with a heart condition who begged them to stop (Milgram, 1974). Not one participant was hypnotized; they were simply following the researcher's orders. Hypnosis does not involve a unique power to get people to behave against their will (Kirsch and Braffman, 2001). A legitimate authority figure can induce people to commit out-of-character and dangerous acts whether they are hypnotized or not.

hypnosis

a state of heightened suggestibility in which some people are able to experience imagined situations as if they were real

hypnotic susceptibility scales

a standard series of pass–fail suggestions that are read to a subject after a hypnotic induction

TABLE 6.5 SAMPLE TEST ITEMS FROM THE STANFORD HYPNOTIC SUSCEPTIBILITY SCALE, FORM C

Focus 6.22

Evaluate claims that hypnosis can produce involuntary behaviour, amazing feats, pain relief and altered memory.

Item	Suggested behaviour	Criterion for passing
Lowering arm	Right arm is held out; subject is told arm will become heavy and drop	Arm is lowered by 6 inches (15 cm) in 10 seconds
Moving hands apart	With hands extended and close together, subject is asked to imagine a force pushing them apart	Hands are 6 or more inches (15 cm or more) apart in 10 seconds
Mosquito hallucination	It is suggested that a mosquito is buzzing nearby and lands on subject	Any grimace or acknowledgement of mosquito
Post-hypnotic amnesia	Subject is woken and asked to recall suggestions after being told under hypnosis that he or she will not remember the suggestions	Three or fewer items recalled before subject is told, 'Now you can remember everything'

SOURCE: Based on Weitzenhoffer and Hilgard, 1962.

FIGURE 6.34

The human-plank demonstration, a favourite of stage hypnotists, seems to demonstrate the power of hypnosis. Are you convinced?

Amazing Feats

Have you seen or heard about stage hypnotists who get an audience member to perform an amazing physical feat, such as the 'human plank' (Fig. 6.34)? A subject, usually male, is hypnotized and lies outstretched between two chairs. He is told that his body is rigid and then, amazingly, another person successfully stands on the subject's legs and chest.

Similarly, hypnosis can have striking physiological effects. Consider a classic experiment involving 13 people who were strongly allergic to the toxic leaves of a certain tree (Ikemi and Nakagawa, 1962). Five of them were hypnotized, blindfolded and told that a leaf from a harmless tree to which they were not allergic was touching one of their arms. In fact, the leaf really was toxic, but four out of the five hypnotized people had no allergic reaction. Next, the other arm of each hypnotized person was rubbed with a leaf from a harmless tree, but he or she was falsely told that the leaf was toxic. All five people responded to the harmless leaf with allergic reactions.

Should we attribute the human-plank feat and the unusual responses of the allergic people to unique powers of hypnosis? Here is where a healthy dose of critical thinking is important.

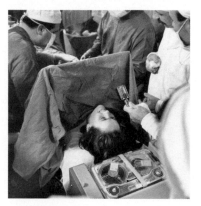

FIGURE 6.35

This patient is having her appendix removed with hypnosis as the sole anaesthetic. Her verbal reports that she feels no pain are being recorded.

Pain Tolerance

Scottish surgeon James Esdaile performed more than 300 major operations in the mid-1800s using hypnosis as the sole anaesthetic (Fig. 6.35). Experiments confirm that hypnosis often increases pain tolerance and that this is not due to a placebo effect (Montgomery et al., 2000). For patients who experience chronic pain, hypnosis can produce relief that lasts for months or even years (Patterson, 2004). Brain-imaging research reveals that hypnosis modifies neural activity in brain areas that process painful stimuli, but non-hypnotic techniques, such as mental imagery and performing distracting cognitive tasks, also alter neural functioning and reduce pain (Petrovic and Ingvar, 2002).

We do not know exactly how hypnosis produces its painkilling effects. It may influence the release of endorphins, decrease patients' fear of pain, distract patients from their pain or somehow help them separate the pain from conscious experience (Barber, 1998).

Hypnotic Amnesia

You may have seen television shows or films in which hypnotized people are given a suggestion that they will not remember something (such as a familiar person's name), either during the session itself (*hypnotic amnesia*) or after coming out of hypnosis (*post-hypnotic amnesia*). A reversal cue also is given, such as a phrase ('You will now remember everything') that ends the amnesia once the person hears it. Is this Hollywood fiction?

WHAT DO YOU THINK?

HYPNOSIS AND AMAZING FEATS

In the case of the human-plank and in the allergy experiment, what additional evidence do you need to determine whether these amazing feats and responses really are caused by hypnosis? How could you gather this evidence? Think about it, then see p. 278.

Research indicates that about 25 per cent of hypnotized college students can be led to experience amnesia (Kirsch, 2001). Although researchers agree that hypnotic and post-hypnotic amnesias occur, they debate the causes. Some feel it results from voluntary attempts to avoid thinking about certain information; others believe it is caused by an altered state of consciousness that weakens normal memory systems (Kihlstrom, 1998; Spanos, 1986).

Hypnosis, Memory Enhancement and Eyewitness Testimony

In contrast to producing forgetting, can hypnosis enhance memory? Law enforcement agencies sometimes use hypnosis to aid the memory of eyewitnesses to crimes. In a famous 1977 case in California, a bus carrying 26 children and its driver disappeared without a trace. The victims, buried underground in an abandoned trailer truck by three kidnappers, were later found alive. After the rescue, a police expert hypnotized the bus driver and asked him to recall the ordeal. The driver formed a vivid image of the kidnappers' white van and could 'read' all but one digit on the van's licence plate. This information allowed the police to track down the kidnappers.

Focus 6.23

Contrast dissociation and social cognitive theories of hypnosis. What does research on the hypnotized brain reveal?

Despite occasional success stories like this one, controlled experiments find that hypnosis does not reliably improve memory. In some experiments, participants watch videotapes of simulated bank robberies or other crimes. Next, while hypnotized or not, they are questioned by police investigators or criminal lawyers. Hypnotized people display better recall than non-hypnotized people in some studies but no better recall in others (Lynn et al., 2001). In still other experiments, hypnotized participants perform more poorly than non-hypnotized controls; they recall more information, but much of that extra recall is inaccurate (Burgess and Kirsch, 1999).

Another concern is that some memories recalled under hypnosis may be *pseudomemories*, false memories *created* during hypnosis by statements or leading suggestions made by the examiner. In some experiments, hypnotized and non-hypnotized subjects are intentionally exposed to false information about an event (e.g., about a bank robbery). Later, after the hypnotized subjects have been brought out of hypnosis, all participants are questioned. Highly suggestible people who have been hypnotized are most likely to report the false information as being a true memory, and often are confident that their false memories are accurate (Sheehan et al., 1992).

Although some psychologists are exploring ways to minimize hypnosis-induced memory errors, at present, many courts have banned or limited testimony obtained under hypnosis

(Wagstaff et al., 2004). The increased suggestibility of hypnotized people makes them particularly susceptible to memory distortion caused by leading questions, and they may honestly come to believe facts that never occurred (Scoboria et al., 2002). Similarly, if a therapist uses hypnosis to help patients recall long-forgotten memories of sexual abuse, what shall we conclude? Are the horrible memories real, or are they pseudomemories created during therapy? We explore this issue in Chapter 8.

THEORIES OF HYPNOSIS

Hypnos may have been the Greek god of sleep, but studies of brain physiology reveal that hypnosis definitely *is not* sleep. What is hypnosis, and how does it produce its effects?

Dissociation Theories

> **dissociation theories**
>
> view hypnosis as an altered state involving a division (dissociation) of consciousness

Several researchers propose **dissociation theories** that view hypnosis as an altered state involving a division (dissociation) of consciousness. Ernest Hilgard (1977; 1991) proposed that hypnosis creates a division of awareness in which the person simultaneously experiences two streams of consciousness that are cut off from one another. One stream responds to the hypnotist's suggestions, while the second stream – the part of consciousness that monitors behaviour – remains in the background but is aware of everything that goes on. Hilgard refers to this second part of consciousness as the *hidden observer*.

Suppose a hypnotized subject is given a suggestion that she will not feel pain. Her arm is lowered into a tub of ice-cold water for 45 seconds, and every few seconds she reports the amount of pain. In contrast to non-hypnotized subjects, who find this experience moderately painful, she probably will report feeling little pain. But suppose the procedure is done differently. Before lowering the subject's arm, the hypnotist says, 'Perhaps there is another part of you that is more aware than your hypnotized part. If so, would that part of you report the amount of pain'. In this case, the subject's other stream of consciousness, the hidden observer, will report a higher level of pain (Fig. 6.36).

FIGURE 6.36

Hypnosis and the hidden observer.

(a) This hypnotized woman's hand is immersed in painfully cold ice water. Placing his hand on her shoulder, Ernest Hilgard contacts her dissociated hidden observer. (b) This graph shows pain-intensity ratings given by a woman when she is not hypnotized, when she is under hypnosis and by her hidden observer in the same hypnotic state. The hidden observer reports more pain than the hypnotized woman but less than the subject when she is not hypnotized.

SOURCE: based on Hilgard, 1977.

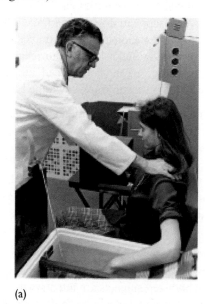

(a)

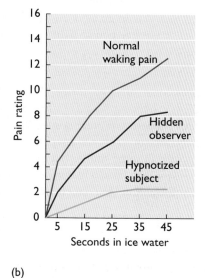

(b)

For Hilgard, this dissociation explained why behaviours that occur under hypnosis seem involuntary or automatic. Given the suggestion that 'your arm will start to feel lighter and will begin to rise', the subject intentionally raises his or her arm, but only the hidden observer is aware of this. The main stream of consciousness that responds to the command is blocked from this awareness and perceives that the arm is rising all by itself.

Social Cognitive Theories

To other theorists, hypnosis does not represent a special state of dissociated consciousness. Instead, **social cognitive theories** propose that hypnotic experiences result from expectations of people who are motivated to take on the role of being hypnotized (Kirsch, 2001; Spanos, 1991). Most people believe that hypnosis involves a trance-like state and responsiveness to suggestions. People motivated to conform to this role develop a readiness to respond to the hypnotist's suggestions and to perceive hypnotic experiences as real and involuntary.

In a classic study, Martin Orne (1959) illustrated the importance of expectations about hypnosis. During a classroom demonstration, college students were told that hypnotized people frequently exhibit spontaneous stiffening of the muscles in the dominant hand. (Actually, this rarely occurs.) An accomplice of the lecturer pretended to be hypnotized and, sure enough, he 'spontaneously' exhibited hand stiffness. When students who had seen the demonstration were later hypnotized, 55 per cent of them exhibited stiffening of the hand without any suggestion from the hypnotist. Control-group participants saw a demonstration that did not mention or display hand stiffening. Not one of these students exhibited hand stiffening when they were hypnotized.

Does social-cognitive theory imply that hypnotized people are faking or play-acting? Not at all. Role theorists emphasize that when people immerse themselves in the hypnotic role, their responses are completely real and may indeed represent altered experiences (Kirsch, 2001). Our expectations strongly influence how the brain organizes sensory information. Often, we literally see what we expect to see. According to social-cognitive theory, many effects of hypnosis represent an extension of this principle. The hypnotized subject whose arm automatically rises in response to a suggestion genuinely perceives the behaviour to be involuntary because this is what the subject expects and because attention is focused externally on the hypnotist and the hypnotic suggestion.

THE HYPNOTIZED BRAIN

Can peering inside the brain help us determine the nature of hypnosis? To find out, take a look at the coloured drawing and the grey-scale drawing in Figure 6.37. Now, do two simple tasks:

1. Look at the coloured drawing again, form a mental image of it, and try to drain the colour out of it. In other words, try to visualize it as if it were a grey-scale figure.

2. Next, look at the grey-scale drawing, form a mental picture of it, and try to add colour to it. In other words, visualize it as if it were a coloured figure.

 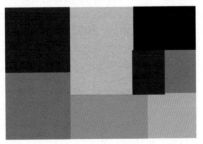

social cognitive theories

propose that hypnotic experiences result from expectations of people who are motivated to take on the role of being hypnotized

FIGURE 6.37

Colour perception and the hypnotized brain.

These colour and greyscale drawings are similar to those used by Kosslyn and his colleagues (2000).

Stephen Kosslyn and co-workers (2000) identified eight people who scored high in hypnotic susceptibility and who reported they could successfully drain away or add colour to their mental images of such drawings. Subjects then performed these tasks (in varying order) while inside a PET scanner. On some trials they were hypnotized, and on other trials they were not hypnotized.

The PET scans revealed that whether subjects were hypnotized or not, an area in the right hemisphere that processes information about colour was more active when subjects visualized the grey drawing as having colour (Task 2) than when they visualized the colour drawing as grey (Task 1). In other words, this right-hemisphere region actually responded to mental images involving colour, and subjects did not need to be hypnotized for this brain activity to occur. In the left hemisphere, however, visualizing the grey drawing as having colour increased brain activation in one particular region only when the subjects were hypnotized. As the researchers noted, 'The right hemisphere appeared to respond to imagery per se, whereas the left required the additional boost provided by hypnosis' (Kosslyn et al., 2000, p. 1283).

The results of brain-imaging studies converge with other physiological findings in leading to an important conclusion: hypnotized people are not faking it but rather are experiencing an altered state of brain activation that matches their verbal reports (Raz and Shapiro, 2002). In this study, when hypnotized subjects mentally added colour to the drawing and drained colour from it, their brain activity changed in ways beyond those brought about by mental imagery in a non-hypnotized state. Likewise, other studies reveal that giving hypnotized subjects pain-reducing suggestions not only decreases their subjective report of pain but also decreases activity in several brain regions that process pain signals (Petrovic and Ingvar, 2002). But do these findings indicate that hypnosis is an altered state of dissociation?

Social cognitive theorists would argue that these findings do not resolve the issue (Kirsch, 2001). They note that hypnotic experiences are subjectively real, and the fact that brain activity patterns under hypnosis differ from those of simple mental imagery does not contradict their position that people's expectations are what lead them to become hypnotized in the first place. In sum, cognitive neuroscience is providing us with fascinating insights into the hypnotized brain, but it will take more research to resolve the debate about hypnosis.

I'M INTOXICATED, NO MATTER WHAT YOU SAY!

To close our discussion of hypnosis and altered states, consider the behaviour of a college student in the 'Research close-up' experiment on drinking and driving. (Nobody was hypnotized in this study.) This student consumed three non-alcoholic drinks, but through taste and smell cues, he was convincingly led to believe that they were alcoholic. Prior to taking a Breathalyser test, he estimated his blood-alcohol level to be .07, just below the .08 legal driving limit where he lived. He felt intoxicated, and when told the drinks were non-alcoholic, he argued that there had to be a mistake. When shown his true Breathalyser result of .000, he claimed it was rigged and refused to drive home until the effects of his drinks wore off (MacDonald et al., 1995).

This example, together with topics previously covered (e.g., voodoo spells, placebo effects), suggests that we have a remarkable capacity to alter our own state of consciousness without being aware that we ourselves are responsible for causing the change. The popular belief is that a hypnotist places the subject under a mysterious spell or into a trance, but this is a myth (Kirsch, 2001; Raz and Shapiro, 2002). Rather, like a guide on a wilderness hike, the hypnotist may point the way, but the subject is doing the actual mental work and ultimately altering her or his own state of consciousness.

IN REVIEW

- Hypnosis involves an increased receptiveness to suggestions. Hypnotized people experience their actions as involuntary, but hypnosis has no unique power to make people behave against their will, alter their physiological reactions or perform amazing feats. Hypnosis increases pain tolerance, as do other psychological techniques.

- Some people can be led to experience hypnotic amnesia and post-hypnotic amnesia. The use of hypnosis to improve memory is controversial. Hypnosis increases the danger that people will develop distorted memories about events in response to leading questions asked by a hypnotist or examiner.

- Dissociation theories view hypnosis as an altered state of divided consciousness. Social cognitive theories state that hypnotic experiences occur because people have strong expectations about hypnosis and are highly motivated to enter a hypnotized role.

- Brain imaging reveals that hypnotized people display changes in neural activity consistent with their subjectively reported experiences. This supports the view that hypnosis involves an altered state, but whether it is a dissociated state and the extent to which people's expectations bring about this state are still unclear.

KEY TERMS AND CONCEPTS

Each term has been boldfaced and defined in the chapter on the page indicated in parentheses.

activation-synthesis theory (p. 254)

agonist (p. 258)

alcohol myopia (p. 262)

alpha waves (p. 240)

antagonist (p. 259)

automatic (unconscious, or implicit) processing (p. 228)

beta waves (p. 240)

blindsight (p. 229)

blood-brain barrier (p. 258)

circadian rhythms (p. 234)

cognitive-process dream theories (p. 255)

compensatory responses (p. 259)

consciousness (p. 225)

controlled (conscious, or explicit) processing (p. 228)

delta waves (p. 241)

depressants (p. 261)

dissociation theories (of hypnosis) (p. 274)

divided attention (p. 228)

evolutionary/circadian sleep models (p. 246)

fantasy-prone personality (p. 256)

hallucinogens (p. 267)

hypnosis (p. 271)

hypnotic susceptibility scales (p. 271)

insomnia (p. 248)

melatonin (p. 235)

memory consolidation (p. 247)

narcolepsy (p. 248)

night terrors (p. 250)

opiates (p. 267)

priming (p. 230)

problem-solving dream models (p. 255)

REM sleep (or 'R') (p. 241)

REM-sleep behaviour disorder (RBD) (p. 250)

restoration model (p. 245)

seasonal affective disorder (SAD) (p. 237)

selective attention (p. 226)

sleep apnea (p. 251)

slow-wave sleep (p. 241)

social cognitive theories (of hypnosis) (p. 275)

stimulants (p. 265)

substance dependence (p. 260)

suprachiasmatic nuclei (SCN) (p. 235)

THC (tetrahydrocannabinol) (p. 267)

tolerance (p. 259)

wish fulfilment (p. 253)

withdrawal (p. 259)

WHAT DO YOU THINK?

EARLY BIRDS, CLIMATE, AND CULTURE (p. 236)

As a critical thinker, it is important to keep in mind that correlation does not establish causation. This is a correlational study, not an experiment. The major variables (climate of country, students' degree of morningness) were not manipulated; they were only measured. The association between climate and morningness suggests the possibility of a causal relation, but we must consider other possible explanations.

First, why might climate affect morningness? The researchers (who were from India, Spain, Wales and the USA) hypothesized that to avoid performing daily activities during the hottest part of the day, people who live in warmer climates adapt to a pattern of rising early in the morning, a finding consistent with a prior study that revealed strong tendencies towards morningness among Brazilians (Benedito-Silva et al., 1989).

Second, as the authors note, these results could be due to factors other than climate. The Netherlands, England and the USA share a northern-European heritage, and perhaps some aspect of this common background predisposes people towards less morningness. Yet, say the authors, India's cultural traditions are distinct from those of Spain and Colombia, so it is difficult to apply the 'common cultural heritage' argument to explain the greater morningness found among students from these countries. If not cultural heritage, perhaps the greater industrialization and use of air-conditioned environments in the Netherlands, England and the USA to avoid summer heat reduce the necessity for residents to adapt circadian cycles to local climatic conditions. Strip away the air-conditioning from homes, workplaces, food markets, shopping centres, and cars, buses and trains, and it would be interesting to see whether people would gradually shift towards greater morningness in hot weather. Aware of the limitations of the study, the authors suggest that climate may be just one of several factors that contribute to cross-cultural differences in morningness.

HYPNOSIS AND AMAZING FEATS (p. 273)

No matter what the claim, as critical thinkers, it is always important to think about the concept of control groups. Thus, you should keep this question in mind: what would have happened anyway, even without this special treatment or intervention, or condition? Applied to hypnosis, the key question is whether people can exhibit these same amazing feats when they are not hypnotized. When a stage hypnotist gets someone to perform the human plank, the audience indeed attributes this feat to the hypnotic trance. What the audience does not know is that an average man suspended in this manner can support 300 pounds on his chest with little discomfort and no need of a hypnotic trance. Indeed, Figure 6.34 shows The Amazing Kreskin, a professional performer and self-proclaimed 'mentalist', standing on someone who is not hypnotized.

As for the allergy experiment, the findings are impressive, but we must ask whether allergic people might show the same reactions if they were not hypnotized. For this reason, the researchers properly designed their experiment to measure the responses of eight non-hypnotized control participants (Ikemi and Nakagawa, 1962). When blindfolded and exposed to a toxic leaf but misled to believe that it was harmless, seven out of the eight non-hypnotized people did not show an allergic response. Conversely, when their arm was rubbed with a harmless leaf but they were falsely told it was toxic, all eight had an allergic reaction. In short, the non-hypnotized people responded the same way as the hypnotized subjects.

Other research shows that under hypnosis, vision in near-sighted people can be improved, warts can be cured and stomach acidity can be increased. However, well-controlled studies show that non-hypnotized subjects can exhibit these same responses (Spanos and Chaves, 1988). As we have already seen when discussing placebo effects and other mind–body interactions, people's beliefs and expectations can produce real physiological effects.

CHAPTER SEVEN

LEARNING: *THE ROLE OF EXPERIENCE*

CHAPTER OUTLINE

A man who carries a cat by the tail learns something he can learn in no other way.

MARK TWAIN

Thanks to six sessions with a clinical psychologist, Michelle's life is normal again. She is now free from the intense fear of something many of us do without a qualm every day: riding in a car. Michelle was severely injured in a car crash and hospitalized for months. A year later, she described to a clinician how the fear began when her husband came to take her home from the hospital.

> As we walked towards the new car he had bought, I began to feel uneasy. I felt nervous all the way home. It started to get worse after that. I found myself avoiding riding in the car, and couldn't drive it at all. I stopped visiting friends and tried to get them to come to our house.... After a while, even the sight of a car started to make me nervous.... You know, this is the first time I've left the house in about four months.

To help Michelle, the clinical psychologist used a highly successful procedure based, in part, on century-old principles of learning discovered in laboratory investigations of salivating dogs.

…

On a high street in a suburb of London, a woman volunteers her time soliciting donations for a local charity. Though cold, wet and tired, she remains upbeat and thanks each person who drops money in her collection tin. Inside an amusement arcade on the same street, a man has been playing the slot machines all day. He is exhausted and down to his last few pounds, having fed the machine coins all day long for the past six days. The till attendant mutters under his breath, 'I'll never understand what keeps these guys going'.

…

A judge in New York City prohibited two teenage brothers from watching professional wrestling on television because they were becoming too violent. The boys vigorously practised body slams and choke holds, repeatedly injuring one another. Their frightened mother reported that her 13-year-old son tried to apply a 'sleeper hold' on her as she was cooking in the kitchen. Fortunately, she broke free before losing consciousness. The judge told the mother that either she had to prohibit the boys from watching wrestling or he would have the family's television set removed and might place the boys in foster homes (*Sporting News, U.S.*, 1985).

Although vastly different, the behaviours in these examples share an important characteristic: they are all learned. Our genetic endowment creates the potential for these behaviours to occur, but we are not biologically programmed to fear cars, solicit donations, bet on horses or wrestle people by applying sleeper holds.

Focus 7.1
What is learning?

Reflect for a moment on how much of your behaviour is learned. You had to learn how to tell the time, how to get dressed, when to go to the toilet, how to ride a bike, how to read, how to play music and sports; the list is virtually endless. As we shall see, beyond our skills such as those listed above, learning affects our emotional reactions, physiological responses and, even, our perceptions. Through experience, we learn to think, act and feel in ways that contribute richly to our individual identities.

Learning is a *process by which experience produces a relatively enduring and adaptive change in an organism's capacity for behaviour*. Importantly, this definition specifies that learning is a change in the *capacity* for behaviour. This highlights a distinction made by psychologists: that between 'learning' and 'performance'. The distinction between learning and performance is especially important, as it highlights that changes in behaviour do not always mean that we have learned something. For example, an increase in our searching for food is usually due to our physiological hunger, rather than our having learned something. The challenge for psychologists researching learning is to disentangle when measured changes in behaviour (performance) are actually due to learning. For example, when we observe two boys applying choke holds to each other (a change in performance), this could be due to their having watched a wrestling match on television earlier in the day (learning), but it could also be simply due to their aggressive personalities or to an argument about what to watch next on television.

learning
process by which experience produces a relatively enduring and adaptive change in an organism's capacity for behaviour

In this chapter we explore five basic learning processes. The first two, *habituation* and *sensitization* are the simplest, involving changes in behaviour that result merely from repeated exposure to a stimulus. Next, we look in depth at two types of *associative learning* or *conditioning*, which involve learning associations between events. *Classical conditioning* occurs when two stimuli become associated with each other (e.g., being inside a car and being severely burned) such that one stimulus (being in a car) now triggers a response (intense fear) that previously was triggered by the other stimulus (being burned). In *operant conditioning*, organisms learn to associate their behavioural responses with specific consequences (e.g., asking for a charitable donation leads to a monetary gift). Finally, we consider *observational learning*, in which observers imitate the behaviour of a model (e.g., children imitate choke holds performed by wrestlers on television).

This chapter focuses on how environmental experiences modify behaviour and knowledge, but you will see that biological and cognitive factors also play important roles in learning. You will also find many examples of how psychologists have creatively applied learning principles to enhance human welfare.

Focus 7.2
Describe habituation and sensitization. What is the adaptive significance of these forms of learning?

ADAPTING TO THE ENVIRONMENT

The concept of learning, like that of evolution, calls attention to the importance of adapting to the environment. As noted in Chapter 3, evolutionary theory focuses on species adaptation. Over the course of evolution, environmental conditions faced by each species help shape that species' biology. Through natural selection, genetically based characteristics that enhance a species' ability to adapt to its environment and thus to survive and reproduce, are more likely to be passed on to the next generation. With passing generations, as the physical or behavioural characteristics influenced by those genes appear with greater frequency in the population, they become a part of that species' nature.

LEARNING AS PERSONAL ADAPTATION

Whereas evolution focuses on species' adaptations passed down biologically across generations, learning represents a process of personal adaptation. That is, learning focuses on how an organism's behaviour changes in response to environmental stimuli encountered during its lifetime. Although specific behaviours that each organism learns may be unique to its species – we have yet to encounter a deer that has learned to order take-away food – all animal species face some common adaptive challenges, such as finding food. Because environments contain many events, each organism must learn: (1) which events are, or are not, important to its survival and well-being, (2) which stimuli signal that an important event is about to occur, and (3) whether its responses will produce positive or negative consequences. The learning processes examined in this chapter enable humans and other species to respond to one or more of these adaptive challenges. First, we consider the simplest forms of learning in which we change our responses to just one stimulus over time: *habituation* and *sensitization*

HABITUATION AND SENSITIZATION

Imagine that you are a participant in an experiment. You're sitting alone in a quiet laboratory when suddenly (as part of the experiment) a loud sound startles you. Your body jerks slightly, you become aroused, and you look towards the source of the sound. Over time, as you hear it again and again, your startle response diminishes until eventually you ignore the sound. You have habituated to the noise.

Habituation is a decrease in the strength of response to a repeated stimulus. It occurs across species ranging from humans to dragonflies to sea snails. Touch the skin of a sea snail in a certain location, and it will reflexively contract its gill. With repeated touches, this response habituates. This is a simple form of learning in that it occurs in response to only a single stimulus (in contrast to more complex forms of learning, discussed later in the chapter, in which two or more stimuli are associated in some way).

Now imagine that you are sitting in your college hall taking an examination. Five minutes in, an examination invigilator walks down the aisle to provide someone with extra paper. The examination invigilator is wearing high heels and her shoes make a quite audible sound as she walks though the examination hall. Initially you think nothing of the sound and get underway with your first essay. However, people keep raising their hands for extra paper, and one hour into the examination you are so aggravated by the repeated noise that you can no longer concentrate on writing. You have sensitized to the sound of the invigilator's shoes.

Sensitization is an increase in the strength of response to a repeated stimulus. Like habituation, sensitization is also classified as a simple learning mechanism as it occurs in response to only a single stimulus. Also like habituation, sensitization serves an adaptive function. There are some aspects of the environment to which it is important for us to attend. Often, these stimuli are harmful to us in some way. When a stronger tactile stimulus is applied to sea snails, on repeated presentation they will respond by withdrawing more parts of their body than they did initially (Kandel, 2004). The strength of their response increases on repeated presentation of the stimulus.

But what determines whether we habituate or sensitize to a stimulus? Groves and Thompson (1970) proposed that both sensitization and habituation happen at the same time, and compete to determine our behaviour. Figure 7.1 shows how their theory worked. In situations where a stimulus creates more arousal (e.g., when it is more painful or more complex), sensitization wins (Fig. 7.1(B)). But in situations where the stimulus creates less arousal, habituation wins (Fig. 7.1(A)). Here we can clearly see the distinction between learning and performance. The two separate systems, habituation and sensitization, are learning, whereas behavioural performance is the net result of these two learning processes.

habituation

a decrease in the strength of response to a repeated stimulus

sensitization

an increase in the strength of response to a repeated stimulus. Like habituation, sensitization is also classified as a simple learning mechanism as it occurs in response to only a single stimulus

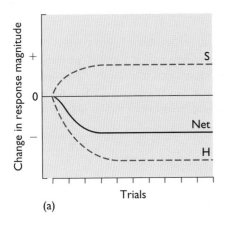
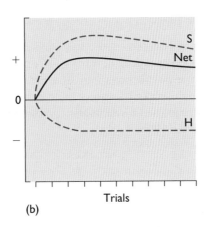

FIGURE 7.1

Groves and Thompson (1970) described behaviour in relation to repeated stimuli as the net outcome of both habituation (H) and sensitization (S) working at the same time and independently of one another. Panel A displays a situation where habituation has the greatest effect on behaviour (perhaps where the stimulus is unthreatening), and panel B shows a situation where sensitization has the greatest effect (perhaps where the stimulus is threatening).

But why do we need habituation and sensitization? Both processes serve key adaptive functions. If an organism responded to every stimulus in its environment, it would rapidly become overwhelmed and exhausted. By learning not to respond (habituating) to uneventful familiar stimuli, organisms conserve energy and can attend to other stimuli that are important. However, there are clearly some situations where it is not useful for us to ignore stimuli – when we are learning a lot from them (e.g., when watching an interesting television programme) or when they are a threat to our survival (e.g., when accidentally walking on glass with bare feet).

IN REVIEW

- Learning is a process by which experience produces a relatively enduring change in an organism's behaviour or capabilities. Learning is measured by changes in performance.

- The environment influences adaptation in two major ways: species adaptation, which occurs through natural-selection pressures that guide evolution, and personal adaptation, which occurs through learning.

- Habituation and sensitization are increases and decreases in the strength of a response to a repeated stimulus. These are simple forms of learning and allow organisms to attend appropriately in situations where the repeated stimulus is important or threatening (sensitization) or when other stimuli are more important (habituation).

CLASSICAL CONDITIONING: ASSOCIATING ONE STIMULUS WITH ANOTHER

Life is full of interesting associations. Do you ever hear songs on the radio or find yourself in places that instantly make you feel good because they are connected to special times you have had? When you smell the aroma of popcorn or freshly baked cakes, does your mouth water or your stomach growl? These examples illustrate a learning process called **classical conditioning**, in which an organism learns to associate two stimuli (e.g., a song and a pleasant event), such that one stimulus (the song) comes to elicit a response (feeling happy) that was originally elicited only by the other stimulus (the pleasant event). Like habituation and sensitization, classical conditioning is a basic form of learning that occurs across numerous species. In contrast to habituation and sensitization however, classical condition involves changing behaviour in response to associations between stimuli. Its discovery dates back to the late 1800s and an odd twist of fate.

classical conditioning

an organism learns to associate two stimuli such that one stimulus comes to elicit a response that was originally elicited only by the other stimulus

Focus 7.3

Describe Pavlov's research and how a classically conditioned response is acquired. Explain spontaneous recovery and extinction.

FIGURE 7.2

Pavlov's method of measuring salivation in dogs.

(a) Ivan Pavlov (*with the white beard*) is shown here with colleagues and one of his canine subjects. (b) In his early research, Pavlov measured salivation using a simple device similar to the one shown here. In later research, a collection tube was inserted directly into the salivary gland.

unconditioned stimulus (UCS)

a stimulus that elicits a reflexive or innate response (the UCR) without prior learning

unconditioned response (UCR)

a reflexive or innate response that is elicited by a stimulus (the UCS) without prior learning

PAVLOV'S PIONEERING RESEARCH

In the 1860s, Ivan Pavlov was studying theology in a Russian seminary when his plans to join the priesthood unexpectedly changed. A new government policy allowed the translation of western scientific publications into Russian. Pavlov read Darwin's theory of evolution and other works, which sparked a strong interest in the sciences (Windholz, 1997). As a result, Pavlov became a renowned physiologist, conducting research on digestion in dogs that won him the Nobel Prize in 1904.

To study digestion, Pavlov presented food to dogs and measured their salivary response (Fig. 7.2). As often occurs in science, Pavlov made an accidental but important discovery. He noticed that with repeated testing, the dogs began to salivate before the food was presented, such as when they heard the footsteps of the approaching experimenter.

(a)

(b)

Further study by Pavlov's (1928) research team confirmed this observation. Dogs have a natural reflex to salivate to food but not to tones. Yet when a tone or other stimulus that ordinarily did not cause salivation was presented just before food powder was squirted into a dog's mouth, soon the sound of the tone alone made the dog salivate. This process of learning by association came to be called *classical*, or *Pavlovian*, *conditioning*. Many psychologists regard Pavlov's discovery as one of the most important in psychology's history (Wills, 2005). But why was the discovery that dogs can learn to salivate to tones so important?

This question raises a widely misunderstood point about basic scientific research: it is the *underlying principle* – not the specific behavioural findings – that is paramount. Classical conditioning is a basic learning process that performs a key adaptive function: it alerts organisms to stimuli that signal the impending arrival of an important event. As Pavlov noted, if salivation could be conditioned, so might bodily processes that affect diseases and mental disorders.

BASIC PRINCIPLES

What factors influence the acquisition and persistence of conditioned responses? Let us examine some basic principles of conditioning.

Acquisition

Acquisition refers to the period during which a response is being learned. Suppose we wish to condition a dog to salivate to a tone. Sounding the tone may initially cause the dog to prick up its ears but not to salivate. At this time, the tone is a *neutral stimulus* because it does not elicit salivation (Fig. 7.3). If, however, we place food in the dog's mouth, the dog will salivate. This salivation response to food is *reflexive* – it is what dogs do by nature. Because no learning is required for food to produce salivation, the food is an **unconditioned stimulus (UCS)**, a stimulus that elicits a reflexive or innate response (the UCR) without prior learning. Salivation is an **unconditioned response (UCR)**, a reflexive or innate response that is elicited by a stimulus (the UCS) without prior learning.

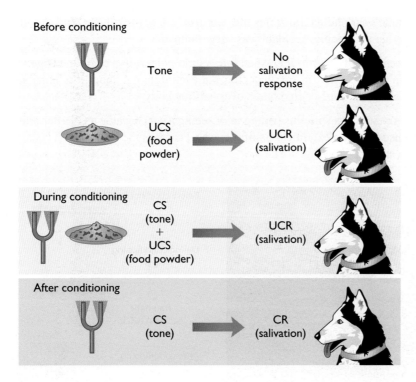

FIGURE 7.3

The classical conditioning process.

In classical conditioning, after a neutral stimulus such as a tone is repeatedly associated with food (unconditioned stimulus), the tone becomes a conditioned stimulus capable of eliciting a salivation response (conditioned response).

conditioned stimulus (CS)

a stimulus that, through association with a UCS, comes to elicit a conditioned response similar to the original UCR

conditioned response (CR)

a response elicited by a conditioned stimulus

Next the tone and the food are paired – each time they are paired is called a *learning trial* – and the dog salivates. After several learning trials, if the tone is presented by itself, the dog salivates even though there is no food. The tone has now become a **conditioned stimulus (CS)**, a stimulus that, through association with a UCS, comes to elicit a conditioned response similar to the original UCR. Because the dog is now salivating to the tone, salivation has become a **conditioned response (CR)**, a response elicited by a conditioned stimulus. Notice that when the dog salivates to food, this natural (unconditioned) reflex is called a UCR. But when it salivates to a tone, this learned (conditioned) response is called a CR.

During acquisition, a CS (e.g., a tone) typically must be paired multiple times with a UCS (e.g., food) to establish a strong CR (see the red line in Fig. 7.4). But Pavlov also found that a tone became a CS more rapidly when it was followed by greater amounts of food, so the *intensity of the* UCS also matters. Indeed, when the UCS is intense and aversive – such as an electric shock or a traumatic event – conditioning may require only one CS–UCS pairing (Richard et al.,

FIGURE 7.4

Acquisition, extinction and spontaneous recovery.

The strength of the CR (salivation) increases during the acquisition phase as the CS (tone) and the UCS (food) are paired on each trial. This is represented by the red line. During the extinction phase, only the CS is presented, and the strength of the CR decreases and finally disappears. This is represented by the blue line. After a rest period following extinction, presentation of the CS elicits a weaker CR (spontaneous recovery) that extinguishes more quickly than before. This is represented by the green line.

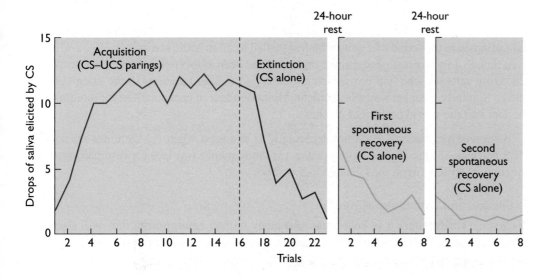

2000). Michelle's car phobia illustrates this *one-trial (single-trial) learning.* As she explains to the therapist, her automobile accident was very traumatic.

> My car went out of control. It crashed into a light pole, rolled over, and began to burn. I … couldn't get out … I'm sorry, doctor, but even thinking about it is horrible. I had a broken pelvis and third-degree burns over half my body.

In Michelle's example, a stimulus (riding in or seeing a car) became a CS after only one pairing with an intense UCS (an extremely painful crash). Fear was the UCR, and it became a CR triggered by the sight of cars (Fig. 7.5).

FIGURE 7.5

Classical conditioning and Michelle's car phobia.

It is likely that Michelle's phobia of cars was acquired through classical conditioning.

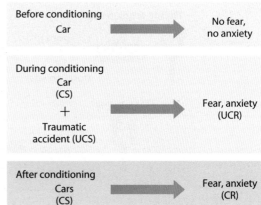

The sequence and time interval of the CS–UCS pairing also affects conditioning. Learning usually occurs most quickly with *forward pairing* in which the CS (tone) appears first and is still present when the UCS (food) appears. Because UCSs are typically very pertinent to survival (e.g., food, traumatic accident), the ability to learn a forward pairing has particular adaptive value; one learns that the CS signals the impending arrival of the UCS. Typically, presenting the CS and UCS at the same time (*simultaneous pairing*) produces less rapid conditioning, and learning is slowest when the CS is presented after the UCS (*backward pairing*). In *forward short-delay pairing* the CS (tone) appears first and is still present when the UCS (food) appears. Forward short-delay pairing is typically the most effective form of forward pairing. In *forward trace pairing*, the tone sounds and then stops, and afterwards the food is presented. In forward pairing, it is often optimal for the CS to appear no more than two or three seconds before the UCS (Klein and Mowrer, 1989).

Once a CR is established, it may persist for a long time. In one study, hospitalized US Navy veterans who had seen combat aboard ships in the Second World War showed strong physiological responses to the sound of a gong which signalled a call to battle stations on US naval vessels, even though 15 years had passed since this gong had been associated with danger. Hospitalized US Army veterans who had not served on ships had weaker reactions to the gong (Edwards, 1962). Similarly, after her horrible accident, Michelle's fear of cars persisted for months despite the fact that she was in no further crashes.

To summarize, classical conditioning usually is strongest when (1) there are repeated CS-UCS pairings, (2) the UCS is more intense, (3) the sequence involves forward pairing, and (4) the time interval between the CS and UCS is short.

Extinction and Spontaneous Recovery

extinction

a process in which the CS is presented repeatedly in the absence of the UCS, causing the CR to weaken and eventually disappear

If classical conditioning is to help organisms adapt to their environment, they will also need a way to eliminate the CR when it is no longer appropriate. This form of learning can also be observed. **Extinction** is a process in which the CS is presented repeatedly in the absence of the

UCS, causing the CR to weaken and eventually disappear. Each occurrence of the CS without the UCS is called an *extinction trial*. When Pavlov repeatedly presented the tone without the food, the dogs eventually stopped salivating to the tone (see Fig. 7.4). Occasional re-pairings of the CS (e.g., tone) and the UCS (e.g., food) are usually required to maintain a CR.

Perhaps it seems inconsistent to you that Pavlov's dogs would eventually stop salivating to the tone if food was no longer presented with it, whereas Michelle's phobia of cars persisted for months even though she was not in any additional crashes. How can we explain this?

Focus 7.4

Explain stimulus generalization, discrimination, higher-order conditioning and their adaptive significance.

WHAT DO YOU THINK?

WHY DID MICHELLE'S CAR PHOBIA PERSIST?

Reread the definition of extinction carefully. In Michelle's case, identify the CS, UCS, and CR. Can you explain why her fear of cars did not extinguish on its own? Think about it, then see p. 329.

Even when a CR extinguishes, not all traces of it are necessarily erased. Suppose we condition a dog to salivate to a tone. Then we repeatedly present the tone without food, and the dog eventually stops salivating to the tone. Later, if we present the tone alone, the dog may salivate once again. This is called **spontaneous recovery**, the reappearance of a previously extinguished CR after a rest period and without new learning trials. As Figure 7.4 shows, the spontaneously recovered CR is usually weaker than the initial CR and extinguishes more rapidly in the absence of the UCS. Spontaneous recovery tells us something important about conditioning and extinction. If a conditioned response can suddenly reappear after extinction, then the initial learned pairing of UCS and CS must still exist. In turn, this must also mean that *extinction is not a process of unlearning the CR, but rather of inhibiting the CR* (see Fig. 7.6).

spontaneous recovery
reappearance of a previously extinguished CR after a rest period and without new learning trials

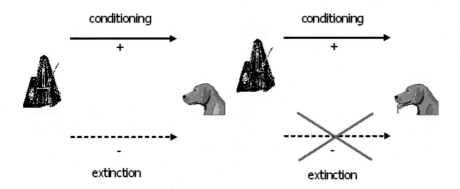

Generalization and Discrimination

Thus far we have explained Michelle's car phobia as a case of one-trial conditioning in which being in a car was paired with a traumatic experience. But why would Michelle fear other cars when it was her old car – now long gone – that was in the accident?

Pavlov found that once a CR is acquired, the organism often responds not only to the original CS but also to stimuli that are similar to it. The greater the stimulus similarity, the greater the chance that a CR will occur. A dog that salivates to a medium-pitched tone is more likely to

FIGURE 7.6

Spontaneous recovery.

Pavlov reasoned that because the CR can spontaneously re-emerge after extinction has taken place, then extinction must represent a learned inhibition of the CR, rather than an unlearning of the CR. Panel A shows a dog whose conditioned salivation response to a metronome is counteracted by a learned inhibition (following extinction). Panel B shows how the CR can spontaneously recover, if the inhibition is removed.

stimulus generalization

stimuli similar to the initial CS elicit a CR

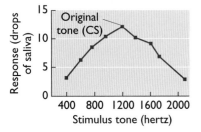

FIGURE 7.7

Stimulus generalization.

An animal will salivate most strongly to the CS that was originally paired with the UCS. Progressively weaker conditioned responses occur as stimuli become less similar to the CS, as seen here with tones of lower or higher frequencies (pitch).

discrimination

when a CR occurs to one stimulus but not to others

higher-order conditioning

a neutral stimulus becomes a CS after being paired with an already established CS

salivate to a new tone slightly different in pitch than to a very low- or high-pitched tone. Learning theorists call this **stimulus generalization**: stimuli similar to the initial CS elicit a CR (Fig. 7.7).

Stimulus generalization serves critical adaptive functions. An animal that ignores the sound of rustling bushes and then is attacked by a hidden predator will (assuming it survives) become alarmed by the sound of rustling bushes in the future. If stimulus generalization did not occur, then the next time the animal heard rustling it would become alarmed only if the sound was identical to the rustling that preceded the earlier attack. This would be of little value to the animal's survival. Through stimulus generalization, however, the animal develops an alarm response to a range of rustling sounds. Some will be false alarms, but safe is better than sorry.

Unfortunately, maladaptive responses can occur when generalization spreads too far. The car involved in Michelle's crash was gone, but after leaving the hospital her fear immediately generalized to the new car her husband bought. Over time, stimulus generalization continued, though the fear was weaker:

Michelle: After a while, even the sight of a car started to make me nervous.
Therapist: As nervous as riding in one?
Michelle: No, but still nervous. It's so stupid. I'd even turn off the TV during scenes involving car crashes.

To prevent stimulus generalization from running wild, organisms must be able to discriminate between irrelevant stimuli and those that may signal danger. An animal that became alarmed at every sound it heard would exhaust itself from stress. In classical conditioning, **discrimination** is demonstrated when a CR (such as an alarm reaction) occurs to one stimulus (a sound) but not to others. Michelle's fear of cars was widespread, but it did not occur when she saw bicycles, trains or aeroplanes.

When my mother was a girl a large dog bit her several times. From then on, she was afraid of dogs. Years later, when my brother wanted a dog, my mother would have none of it. But he pleaded endlessly. How could our family satisfy my brother's wish yet not trigger my mother's fear? The solution: get a dog as dissimilar as possible to the large dog that bit her, in the hope that my mother's fear would display stimulus discrimination. So we adopted a tiny Chihuahua puppy. The plan was half successful. My mother was not afraid and adored the dog. Alas, my brother's fondness for big dogs failed to generalize to Chihuahuas, and he repeatedly called it a 'yippity oversized rat'.

Higher-Order Conditioning

Imagine that we expose a dog to repeated tone–food pairings and the tone becomes a CS that elicits a strong salivation response. Next, suppose that we present a neutral stimulus, such as a black square, and the dog does not salivate. Now, we present the black square just prior to the tone, but we do not present any food. After repeated square–tone pairings, the square will become a CS and elicit salivation by itself (Fig. 7.8). This process is called **higher-order conditioning**: a neutral stimulus becomes a CS after being paired with an already established CS. Typically, a higher-order CS produces a CR that is weaker and extinguishes more rapidly than the original CR: The dog will salivate less to the black square than to the tone, and its response to the square will extinguish sooner.

Higher-order conditioning greatly expands the influence of conditioned stimuli and can affect what we come to value, fear, like or dislike (Gerwitz and Davis, 2000). For example, political candidates try to get voters to like them by associating themselves with patriotic symbols, cuddly babies, famous people and other conditioned stimuli that already trigger positive emotional reactions.

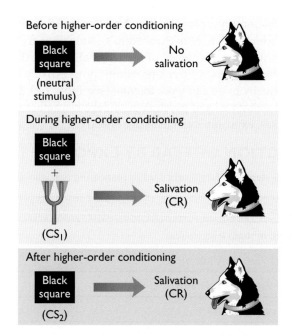

Before higher-order conditioning

Black square → No salivation

(neutral stimulus)

During higher-order conditioning

Black square + (tuning fork) → Salivation (CR)

(CS₁)

After higher-order conditioning

Black square → Salivation (CR)

(CS₂)

FIGURE 7.8

Higher-order conditioning.

Once a tone has become a conditioned stimulus that triggers salivation, we can now use it to condition a salivation response to a new neutral stimulus: a black square. The tone is the CS1. The black square becomes the CS2.

APPLICATIONS OF CLASSICAL CONDITIONING

Pavlov's belief that salivation was merely the tip of the classical conditioning iceberg has proven correct. Conditioning principles discovered in laboratory research – much of it with non-human species – help us understand diverse human behaviours and problems.

Acquiring and Overcoming Fear

Building on Pavlov's discoveries, pioneering behaviourist John B. Watson challenged Freud's view of the causes of mental disorders, such as phobias. To explain Michelle's car phobia, no assumptions about hidden unconscious conflicts or repressed traumas are needed. Instead, from the behaviourist viewpoint, cars have become a fear-triggering CS due to a one-trial pairing with the UCS (crash) and stimulus generalization.

Does this explanation seem reasonable? It may, but almost any explanation can seem plausible with hindsight. Therefore, John B. Watson and Rosalie Rayner (1920) set out to obtain stronger evidence that fear could be conditioned. They studied an 11-month-old infant named Albert. One day, as Little Albert played in a hospital room, Watson and Rayner showed him a white rat. Albert displayed no sign of fear. Later, knowing that Albert was afraid of loud noises, they hit a steel bar with a hammer, making a loud noise as they showed Albert the rat. The noise scared Albert and made him cry. After several rat-noise pairings, the sight of the white rat alone made Albert cry.

To examine stimulus discrimination and generalization, Watson and Rayner exposed Albert to other test stimuli several days later. Albert displayed no fear when shown coloured blocks, but furry white or grey objects, such as a rabbit and a bearded Santa Claus mask, made him cry (Fig. 7.9). By the time Albert's mother took him from the hospital, he had not been exposed to any treatment designed to extinguish his fear. Unfortunately, we do not know what became of Albert after that.

Two other sources of evidence suggest that at least some fears are conditioned. First, laboratory experiments convincingly show that animals become afraid of neutral stimuli that are paired with electric shock (Ayres, 1998). Second, in humans, behavioural treatments partially based on classical conditioning principles are among the most effective psychotherapies for phobias (Wolpe and Plaud, 1997). The key assumption is that if phobias are learned, they can be unlearned.

In 1924 a psychologist called Mary Cover Jones successfully treated a boy named Peter who had a strong fear of rabbits. Jones gradually extinguished Peter's fear. Her approach was a

Focus 7.5

How is classical conditioning relevant to fear acquisition and treatment, attraction and aversion, and health?

FIGURE 7.9

John Watson and Rosalie Rayner examine how Little Albert reacts to a furry mask.

exposure therapies

a patient is exposed to a stimulus (CS) that arouses an anxiety response (such as fear) without the presence of the UCS, allowing extinction to occur

forerunner of current behaviour therapies, discussed in Chapter 15. Collectively, they are called **exposure therapies**, in which a patient is exposed to a stimulus (CS) that arouses an anxiety response (such as fear) without the presence of the UCS, allowing extinction to occur. In this particular case Cover Jones increased Peter's proximity progressively over a number of steps such that he became gradually more and more tolerant (see Table 7.1). In reality, the origin of a patient's phobia is often unknown, and psychologists debate whether all phobias are learned. But, even so, in most cases, exposure treatments are effective.

TABLE 7.1 REDUCTION OF FEAR BY EXPOSURE TRAINING

This table lists 10 of the 17 steps, in Mary Cover Jones's pioneering exposure training procedure.

Step	Peter's progress
1.	Rabbit anywhere in room triggers fear
2.	Rabbit 12 feet (3.7 m) away tolerated
4.	Rabbit 3 feet (0.9 m) away tolerated
5.	Rabbit close in cage tolerated
6.	Rabbit free in room tolerated
8.	Rabbit touched when free in room
10.	Rabbit allowed on tray of high chair
12.	Holds rabbit on lap
16.	Fondles rabbit affectionately
17.	Lets rabbit nibble his fingers

SOURCE: adapted from Jones, 1924.

Mental imagery, real-life situations, or both can be used to present the phobic stimulus. In one approach called *systematic desensitization*, the patient learns muscle-relaxation techniques and then is gradually exposed to the fear-provoking stimulus (Wolpe, 1958). Another approach, sometimes called *flooding*, immediately exposes the person to the phobic stimulus (Nesbitt, 1973). In Michelle's case, her therapist extinguished the car phobia in six sessions of flooding. He asked her to imagine vivid scenes in which she drove in motorway traffic and travelled at high speeds on narrow mountain roads. As Michelle's initially strong anxiety decreased, she was able to sit in her car and eventually drive it. Exposure therapies are highly effective and represent one of behaviourism's important applied legacies (Taylor, 2004). More recent exposure therapies have used virtual reality technology to help patients confront their fears (Rothbaum et al., 2002; see also Fig. 7.10).

FIGURE 7.10

Virtual reality technology has been successfully used as exposure therapies. Here we see patients undergoing virtual reality therapy for (a) fear of heights (acrophobia), (b) fear of dogs and (c) fear of flying

(a)

(b)

(c)

WHAT DO YOU THINK?

WAS THE 'LITTLE ALBERT' STUDY ETHICAL?

Research ethics committees did not exist in the 1920s. Would you have approved Watson and Rayner's request to conduct the Little Albert study? Why or why not? Think about it, then see p. 329.

Attraction and Aversion

Classical conditioning influences what attracts and pleasurably arouses us. Consider sexual arousal. The comment, 'It really turns me on when you wear that', reflects how a garment or scent of a partner's perfume can become a CS for arousal. People, fish, birds and rats become more sexually aroused to originally neutral stimuli after those stimuli have been paired with a naturally arousing UCS (Domjan, 2000b).

Classical conditioning can also decrease our arousal and attraction to stimuli. This principle is used in **aversion therapy**, which attempts to condition an aversion (a repulsion) to a stimulus that triggers unwanted behaviour by pairing it with a noxious UCS. Aversion therapies have been used to reduce maladaptive and socially undesirable behaviours. Clinicians have attempted to treat paedophiles by pairing pictures of children with strong electric shocks, and to reduce alcoholics' attractions to alcohol through administering them with a drug which induces severe nausea when alcohol is consumed (Nathan, 1985). Aversion therapy was famously described in Anthony Burgess's *A Clockwork Orange* (later made into a film by Stanley Kubrick (see Fig. 7.11). However, aversion therapies have generally yielded mixed results, often producing short-term changes in behaviour which extinguish over time.

Conditioned attraction and aversion also influence our attitudes. By repeatedly pairing a CS with pleasant or unpleasant stimuli, we may develop a favourable or unfavourable attitude towards that CS. Advertising executives carefully link products to attractive and famous people, humour and pleasurable interactions with family, friends and the opposite sex (Fig. 7.12). Marketing experiments show that the products become conditioned stimuli that elicit favourable consumer attitudes (Priluck and Till, 2004).

> **aversion therapy**
> attempts to condition an aversion (a repulsion) to a stimulus that triggers unwanted behaviour by pairing it with a noxious UCS

FIGURE 7.11

Alex, portrayed in Stanley Kubrick's *A Clockwork Orange* by Malcolm McDowell, is administered with aversion therapy. In order to reduce his aggressive behaviour, clinical psychologists administered him with a nausea-inducing drug while he was forced to watch violent acts on a film screen.

FIGURE 7.12

Advertisers attempt to classically condition favourable consumer attitudes to products by associating the products with other positive stimuli, such as physically attractive models.

Sickness and Health

Through classical conditioning, our bodies can learn to respond in ways that either promote or harm our health. Let us look at three examples.

Allergic reaction   Classical conditioning often can account for the appearance of physical symptoms that do not seem to have a medical cause. For example, by consistently pairing a neutral stimulus (e.g., a distinct odour) with a substance that naturally triggers an allergic reaction, the odour can become a CS that elicits a similar allergic response (Irie et al., 2001). Also consider the case of an asthma patient who experienced wheezing attacks whenever she saw goldfish. To confirm this, doctors showed her a live goldfish in a bowl: 'Under our eyes she developed a severe asthmatic attack with loud wheezing.... During the next experiment the goldfish was replaced by a plastic toy fish which was easily recognized as such ... but a fierce attack resulted' (Dekker and Groen, 1956, p. 62). For the asthma patient, goldfish appeared to be conditioned stimuli that triggered wheezing attacks, and her response to the plastic fish indicated stimulus generalization.

Anticipatory nausea and vomiting   Chemotherapy and radiation therapy save countless lives in the fight against cancer but often cause nausea and vomiting. Many cancer patients eventually develop **anticipatory nausea and vomiting (ANV)**; they become nauseated and may vomit anywhere from minutes to hours *before* a treatment session.

Anticipatory nausea and vomiting is a classically conditioned response (Stockhorst et al., 2000). Initially neutral stimuli, such as hypodermic needles, the hospital room or even the sight of a hospital, become associated with the treatment (the UCS) and act as conditioned stimuli that trigger nausea and vomiting (the UCR). Fortunately, just as they can condition fear psychological treatments can help patients unlearn the ANV response (Edser, 2002). The patient may first be taught how to physically relax, and then the conditioned stimuli that trigger the ANV are paired with relaxation and pleasant mental imagery.

The immune system   As psychologist Robert Ader (2001; Ader and Cohen, 1975) discovered decades ago, even the immune system can be classically conditioned, affecting susceptibility to disease and fatal illness. As Figure 7.13 shows, when rats drink sweetened water (a neutral stimulus) that is paired with injections of a drug (the UCS) that suppresses immune activity (the UCR), the sweetened water becomes a CS that suppresses immune activity.

Conversely, conditioning can also increase immune functioning (DeMoranville et al., 2000). German researchers gave sweet sherbet to an experimental group of volunteers, together with an injection of epinephrine (i.e., adrenaline), which increases the activity of immune-system cells that attack tumours. Compared with control groups, people receiving the sherbet–epinephrine pairings subsequently reacted to the sherbet alone with a stronger immune response (Buske-Kirschbaum et al., 1992; 1994).

This suggests that classical conditioning can help fight disease. Indeed, one experiment by Robert Ader investigated whether classical conditioning can help mice suffering from a normally fatal illness that caused their immune systems to attack their own bodies (Ader and Cohen, 1982). By classically conditioning a sweet taste (CS) to trigger immune suppression (CR), the researchers reduced the mice's mortality rate. Later, a similar conditioning procedure was used together with drug therapy to successfully treat an 11-year-old-girl who had a life-threatening disease in which her immune system was overactive (Olness and Ader, 1992).

---

anticipatory nausea and vomiting (ANV)

become nauseated and may vomit anywhere from minutes to hours before a treatment session

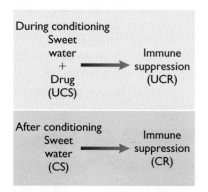

FIGURE 7.13

The immune system can be classically conditioned.

After being paired with an immune suppressant drug, sweet water becomes a CS that triggers a reduced immune response.

Focus 7.6

Describe how Thorndike and Skinner pioneered the study of operant conditioning.

IN REVIEW

- Classical conditioning involves pairing a neutral stimulus with an unconditioned stimulus (UCS) that elicits an unconditioned response (UCR). Through repeated pairing, the neutral stimulus becomes a conditioned stimulus (CS) that evokes a conditioned response (CR) similar to the original UCR.

- The acquisition phase involves pairing the CS with the UCS. Extinction, the disappearance of the CR, occurs when the CS is presented repeatedly in the absence of the UCS.

- Sometimes spontaneous recovery occurs after a rest period, and the CS will temporarily evoke a response even after extinction has taken place. Spontaneous recovery indicates that extinction occurs through the formation of an inhibition of the CR, rather than the unlearning of the CR.

- Stimulus generalization occurs when a CR is evoked by a stimulus similar to the original CS. Discrimination occurs when a CR occurs to one stimulus but not another.

- In higher-order conditioning, once a stimulus (e.g., a tone) becomes a CS, it can be used in place of the original UCS (food) to condition other neutral stimuli.

- A wide range of bodily and psychological responses can be classically conditioned, including fears, sexual attraction, and positive and negative attitudes. Techniques based on classical conditioning are highly successful in treating fears and phobias.

- Cancer patients may develop anticipatory nausea and vomiting (ANV) to stimuli that are paired with their chemotherapy. Anticipatory nausea and vomiting is a classically conditioned response. Classical conditioning also can increase or decrease immune-system responses.

OPERANT CONDITIONING: LEARNING THROUGH CONSEQUENCES

For all its power to affect our emotions, attitudes, physiology and health, classical conditioning cannot explain how animals and humans learn *new* patterns of behaviour. Classical conditioning cannot explain how a dog learns to sit on command. Nor can it account for how we learn to drive cars, or use computers. Unlike salivating to a tone, these are not *elicited responses* automatically triggered by some stimulus. Rather, they are *emitted (voluntary) responses*, and they are learned in a different way.

THORNDIKE'S LAW OF EFFECT

While Pavlov was studying classical conditioning, American psychology student Edward L. Thorndike (1898) was exploring how animals learn to solve problems. He built a special cage, called a *puzzle box*, that could be opened from the inside by pulling a string or stepping on a lever (Fig. 7.14). Thorndike placed a hungry animal, such as a cat, inside the box. Food was put outside, and to get it the animal had to learn how to open the box. The cat scratched and pushed the bars, paced and tried to dig through the floor. By chance, it eventually stepped on the lever, opening the door. Thorndike observed that cat's performance slowly improved with repeated trials (i.e., each time the cat was placed in the box) and eventually the cat learned to press the lever soon after the door was shut.

Because performance improved slowly, Thorndike concluded that the animals did not attain *insight* into the solution. Rather, with trial and error, they gradually eliminated responses that failed to open the door and became more likely to perform the actions that worked. Thorndike

FIGURE 7.14

Thorndike's puzzle box.

Through trial and error, a cat eventually learns to open Thorndike's puzzle box in order to obtain food.

SOURCE: based on Thorndike, 1898; 1911.

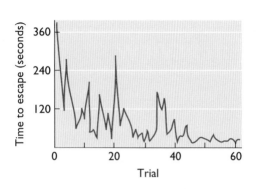

---

law of effect

in a given situation, a response followed by a satisfying consequence will become more likely to occur and a response followed by an annoying consequence will become less likely to occur

operant conditioning

a type of learning in which behaviour is influenced by the consequences that follow it

Skinner box

a special chamber used to study operant conditioning experimentally

reinforcement

is when a response is strengthened by an outcome that follows it

---

(1911) called this process *instrumental learning* because an organism's behaviour is instrumental in bringing about certain outcomes. He also proposed the **law of effect**, which states that in a given situation, a response followed by a satisfying consequence will become more likely to occur and a response followed by an annoying consequence will become less likely to occur.

SKINNER'S ANALYSIS OF OPERANT CONDITIONING

Harvard psychologist B.F. Skinner, who built on and expanded Thorndike's work, was America's leading proponent of behaviourism throughout much of the twentieth century. Skinner coined the term *operant behaviour* to denote an organism *operating* on its environment in some way.

Operant conditioning is a type of learning in which behaviour is influenced by the consequences that follow it (Skinner, 1938; 1953). Skinner designed what has come to be known as a **Skinner box**, a special chamber used to study operant conditioning experimentally. A lever on one wall is positioned above a small cup. Sometimes when the lever is depressed, a food pellet automatically drops into the cup. As shown in Figure 7.15, a hungry rat is put into the chamber and, as it moves about, it accidentally presses the lever. A food pellet clinks into the cup, and the rat eats it. We record the rat's behaviour on a cumulative recorder, which shows that the rat presses the bar more frequently over time.

Skinner identified several types of consequences. For now, we will focus on two: *reinforcement* and *punishment*. With **reinforcement**, a response is strengthened by an outcome that follows it. Typically, the term *strengthened* is operationally defined as an increase in the frequency of a response. The outcome (a stimulus or event) that increases the frequency of a response is a called a *reinforcer*. Food pellets are reinforcers because they increase the rat's frequency of lever

---

FIGURE 7.15

Measuring and reinforcing an operant response.

A light inside an operant experimental chamber (Skinner box) is switched on. A rat, also inside the Skinner box, rises up and presses a lever). A food reinforcer is automatically delivered by the apparatus to the left of the box, and the rat's performance is displayed on a cumulative recorder.

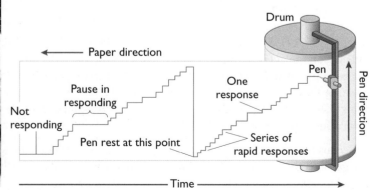

pressing. Once a response becomes established, reinforcers maintain it: The rat keeps pressing the lever because it continues to receive food.

In contrast to reinforcement, **punishment** occurs when a response is weakened by outcomes that follow it. Take our lever-pressing rat. Suppose we change things so that pressing the lever delivers a brief electric shock rather than food. If lever pressing decreases (which it will), then the electric shock represents a *punisher*, a consequence that weakens the behaviour. Notice that reinforcers and punishers are defined in terms of their observable effects on behaviour. If the food does not increase lever pressing, then it is not a reinforcer for this rat in this situation.

Following Darwin's notion of natural selection, which applies to species adaptation, Skinner viewed operant conditioning as a type of natural selection that facilitates an organism's personal adaptation to the environment. Through operant conditioning, organisms generally learn to increase behaviours that are followed by favourable consequences and reduce behaviours that are followed by unfavourable consequences, a pattern consistent with Thorndike's law of effect.

Skinner's analysis of operant behaviour involves three kinds of events that form a three-part contingency: (1) *antecedents*, which are stimuli that are present before a behaviour occurs, (2) *behaviours* that the organism emits, and (3) *consequences* that follow the behaviours. Thus

IF antecedent stimuli are present (IF I say, 'Sit!')
AND behaviour is emitted (AND my dog Rover sits),
THEN consequences will occur (THEN Rover will receive a treat).

The relationship between the behaviour and the consequence is called a *contingency*. After I say, 'Sit!' the consequence of receiving food is contingent on Rover's response of sitting.

Distinguishing Operant from Classical Conditioning

Despite accurately learning all of the terms involved in classical and operant conditioning, some students still have difficulty distinguishing between these two types of learning. As we explore operant conditioning more closely, keep in mind these differences between classical and operant conditioning:

1. Classical conditioning focuses on *elicited* behaviours: the conditioned response (e.g., salivation) is triggered involuntarily, almost like a reflex, by the conditioned stimulus (e.g., a tone). Operant conditioning focuses on *emitted* behaviours: in a given situation, the organism generates responses (e.g., pressing a lever) that are under its physical control.

2. In classical conditioning, learning occurs through CS–UCS pairings. In other words, one stimulus (e.g., a tone) becomes associated with another stimulus (e.g., food). In operant conditioning, behaviour changes when responses made by the organism (e.g., pressing a lever) become associated with certain consequences (e.g., receiving food).

3. In classical conditioning the CS (e.g., tone) occurs before the CR (e.g., salivation) and triggers it. In operant conditioning, the reinforcing or punishing consequences occur *after* a response is made. Table 7.2 summarizes these differences.

It is also important to realize that, although classical and operant conditioning are different processes, many learning situations involve both. Have you ever had a teacher who squeaked chalk when writing on a blackboard? The mere sight of the teacher raising the chalk to the board can become a CS that automatically triggers a CR of shivers up the spine. It is also an effective signal for the students to put their fingers in their ears (an operant response), which was reinforced by the consequence of reducing the squeaking sound. Thus, one stimulus (raising the chalk) can have classical as well as operant functions in behaviour.

punishment
occurs when a response is weakened by outcomes that follow it

Focus 7.7
Contrast classical and operant conditioning. Why are antecedent stimuli important in operant conditioning?

TABLE 7.2 SOME DIFFERENCES BETWEEN CLASSICAL AND OPERANT CONDITIONING

Question	Classical conditioning	Operant conditioning
What type of behaviour is involved?	Elicited: CR is a reflex-like response (e.g., salivation, fear) triggered by CS (e.g., tone, sight of cars)	Emitted: response (e.g., lever pressing, sitting down) operates on the environment and is under the organism's control
How does learning occur?	Through CS–UCS pairings, one stimulus (CS; tone) is associated with another stimulus (UCS; food)	Organism's responses are associated with reinforcing, punishing or neutral consequences
What is the sequence of events?	The CS occurs before the CR and triggers it (e.g., tone triggers salivation; sight of car triggers fear)	Consequences follow an organism's response (e.g., food is delivered after a lever is pressed); antecedent stimuli may set the occasion for emitting certain responses

ANTECEDENT CONDITIONS: IDENTIFYING WHEN TO RESPOND

In operant conditioning, the antecedent may be a general situation or a specific stimulus. Let us return to our lever-pressing rat. At present, simply being in the Skinner box is the antecedent condition. In this situation, the rat will press the lever. Suppose we place a light on the wall above the lever. When the light is on, pressing the lever dispenses food, but when the light is off, no food is given. The rat will soon learn to press the lever only when the light is on. The light becomes a **discriminative stimulus**, a signal that a particular response will now produce certain consequences. Discriminative stimuli set the occasion for operant responses. The sight of the teacher raising chalk to the blackboard is – in operant conditioning terms – a discriminative stimulus signalling it is time for the students to put their fingers in their ears.

Discriminative stimuli guide much of your everyday behaviour. Food on your plate, school bells, the words people speak to you, and the sight of a friend's face are all discriminative stimuli that set the occasion for you to make certain responses.

CONSEQUENCES: DETERMINING HOW TO RESPOND

Behaviour is governed by its consequences. Two major types of reinforcement strengthen responses, and two major types of punishment weaken them. Operant behaviour also is weakened by extinction. Figure 7.16 shows these processes.

Positive Reinforcement

Positive reinforcement occurs when a response is strengthened by the subsequent presentation of a stimulus. A rat receives food pellets when it presses a lever and eventually begins to press the lever more often. A new employee, praised by her boss for completing a small project quickly, begins to complete more of her projects on time. The stimulus that follows and strengthens the response is called a *positive reinforcer*. Food, drink, comforting physical contact, attention, praise and money are common positive reinforcers. In our chapter-opening vignette, we might choose to explain the charity worker's behaviour of soliciting money for charity as being positively reinforced by each donation, by the praise of fellow charity workers at the charity and by her feeling of pride in helping people.

The term *reward* is often misused as a synonym for the term *positive reinforcer*. Behaviourists prefer *positive reinforcer* because it focuses on how consequences affect behaviour. In many

discriminative stimulus

signal that a particular response will now produce certain consequences

positive reinforcement

occurs when a response is strengthened by the subsequent presentation of a stimulus

Focus 7.8

Explain and illustrate positive and negative reinforcement, operant extinction, aversive punishment and response cost.

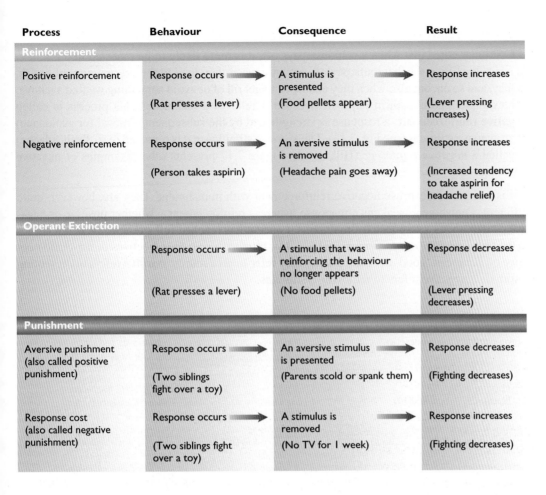

Process	Behaviour	Consequence	Result
Reinforcement			
Positive reinforcement	Response occurs ➡ (Rat presses a lever)	A stimulus is presented ➡ (Food pellets appear)	Response increases (Lever pressing increases)
Negative reinforcement	Response occurs ➡ (Person takes aspirin)	An aversive stimulus is removed ➡ (Headache pain goes away)	Response increases (Increased tendency to take aspirin for headache relief)
Operant Extinction			
	Response occurs ➡ (Rat presses a lever)	A stimulus that was reinforcing the behaviour no longer appears ➡ (No food pellets)	Response decreases (Lever pressing decreases)
Punishment			
Aversive punishment (also called positive punishment)	Response occurs ➡ (Two siblings fight over a toy)	An aversive stimulus is presented ➡ (Parents scold or spank them)	Response decreases (Fighting decreases)
Response cost (also called negative punishment)	Response occurs ➡ (Two siblings fight over a toy)	A stimulus is removed ➡ (No TV for 1 week)	Response increases (Fighting decreases)

FIGURE 7.16

Five major operant processes.

instances rewards do not function as positive reinforcers. Parents may give a child a reward (such as a new toy) for cleaning her room, but if the child does not clean her room in the future, then the toy was not a positive reinforcer for that behaviour.

Primary and secondary reinforcers Psychologists distinguish between two broad types of positive reinforcers: **Primary reinforcers** are stimuli, such as food and water, that an organism naturally finds reinforcing because they satisfy biological needs. **Secondary (conditioned) reinforcers** are stimuli that acquire reinforcing properties through their association with primary reinforcers. Money is a conditioned reinforcer. Similarly, chimpanzees learn to value, work for and, even, hoard tokens (a secondary reinforcer) that they can place into a vending machine to obtain raisins.

Secondary reinforcers illustrate how behaviour often depends on both classical and operant conditioning. Consider dog training. Correct responses, such as sitting on command, initially are operantly reinforced with food. But just before delivering food, the trainer enthusiastically says, 'Good Dog!' At first the phrase 'Good Dog!' is just meaningless sounds to the dog. But by repeatedly pairing 'Good Dog!' with food each time the dog sits, 'Good Dog!' becomes a classically conditioned stimulus that elicits excitement (salivation, tail wagging). Now the trainer can use the phrase 'Good Dog!' as a secondary reinforcer, instead of always having to carry and provide food.

primary reinforcers
stimuli, such as food and water, that an organism naturally finds reinforcing because they satisfy biological needs

secondary (conditioned) reinforcers
stimuli that acquire reinforcing properties through their association with primary reinforcers

Negative Reinforcement

B.F. Skinner noted that when a response pays off, it is more likely to be repeated in the future. In everyday life, our behaviours pay off not only when they lead to the presentation of praise, money, and so on, but also when they enable us to get rid of or avoid something we find aversive. For example, taking aspirin pays off because it relieves a headache. This process is called **negative reinforcement**: a response is strengthened by the subsequent removal (or avoidance) of an aversive stimulus (see Fig. 7.13). The aversive stimulus that is removed (e.g., the headache) is called a *negative reinforcer* (Hill, 1963). Figure 7.17 presents other examples of negative reinforcement.

It is common to confuse negative reinforcement with punishment. They are, however, quite different; Punishment weakens a response, whereas reinforcement – whether positive or negative – strengthens a response (or maintains it once it has reached full strength). When it comes to the terms *positive reinforcement* and *negative reinforcement*, the adjectives *positive* and *negative* do not mean 'good' or 'bad'. Rather they refer to procedures: *positive* refers to presenting a stimulus; *negative* refers to removing a stimulus.

negative reinforcement

a response is strengthened by the subsequent removal (or avoidance) of an aversive stimulus

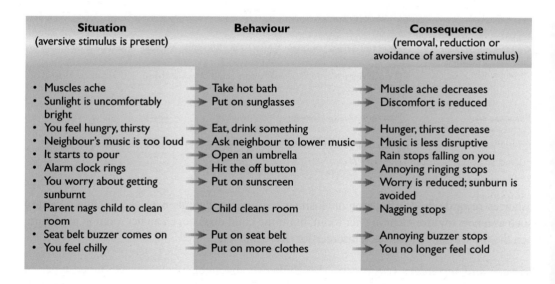

FIGURE 7.17

Negative reinforcement in everyday life.

Here are some common examples of negative reinforcement. In each case, the consequence strengthens the behaviour. There are countless other examples. Can you think of a few more?

Negative reinforcement plays a key role in helping us learn to escape from and avoid aversive situations. While showering, have you ever heard someone flush a toilet, only to have your shower water turn scalding hot? Your response of backing away is negatively reinforced – strengthened – by the escape from (i.e., removal of) the scalding water. Soon the mere sound of the flush becomes a signal – a discriminative stimulus – for you to back away. You successfully avoid the scalding water, which negatively reinforces your response of backing away as soon as you hear the flush.

Operant Extinction

Operant extinction is the weakening and eventual disappearance of a response because it is no longer reinforced. When previously reinforced behaviours no longer pay off, we are likely to abandon and replace them with more successful ones. If pressing a lever no longer results in food pellets, the rat will eventually stop making this response.

The degree to which non-reinforced responses persist is called *resistance to extinction*. Non-reinforced responses may stop quickly (low resistance), or they may keep occurring hundreds or thousands of times (high resistance). People who solicit charitable donations, like the London charity worker, do not stop just because 100 passers-by in a row fail to give money. As we

operant extinction

the weakening and eventual disappearance of a response because it is no longer reinforced

explain later, resistance to extinction is strongly influenced by the pattern of reinforcement that has previously maintained the behaviour.

Operant extinction often provides a good alternative to punishment as a method for reducing undesirable behaviours. Consider the following hypothetical example: Mrs Jeffries sought help at a child guidance clinic because her 4-year-old son, Kieran, delighted in misbehaving. She had tried to reason with him. Then she resorted to yelling. When that failed, Mrs. Jeffries began smacking Kieran. Even that did not work.

The intended punishments probably failed because they actually reinforced Kieran with what he wanted most: some attention. In many situations behavioural psychologists might advise Mrs Jeffries, that, difficult as it might be at times, the best solution would be to ignore Kieran when he misbehaves, thereby depriving him of the attention he craves. In addition, behavioural psychologists might also advise Mrs Jeffries to reinforce Kieran's desirable behaviours by paying attention to him when he acts accordingly. The hope is that Kieran will become a model citizen through operant extinction and positive reinforcement.

Aversive Punishment

Like reinforcement, punishment comes in two forms. One involves actively *applying* aversive stimuli, such as painful slaps, electric shock and verbal reprimands. This is called **aversive punishment** (also called **positive punishment** or **punishment by application**): a response is weakened by the subsequent presentation of a stimulus. Smacking and telling off a child for misbehaving are obvious examples, but so is a child's touching a hot stovetop burner. The pain delivered by the burner makes it less likely that the child will touch it in the future. Likewise, if a woman wears a new blouse, and her friends' facial expressions indicate their distaste for it, she is less likely to wear that blouse in future.

Aversive punishment can produce rapid results, an important consideration when it is necessary to stop a particularly dangerous behaviour, such as an animal or person attacking someone. Although aversive punishment often works, the use of smacking and other forms of physical punishment for disciplinary purposes is controversial. Let us explore this issue.

aversive punishment (also called **positive punishment** or **punishment by application**)
a response is weakened by the subsequent presentation of a stimulus

Focus 7.9
Discuss the corporal punishment debate, considering the limitations of punishment and reinforcement.

BENEATH THE SURFACE

SPARE THE ROD AND SPOIL THE CHILD?

As a child, were you smacked for misbehaving? And, as someone who may one day become a parent or may already be one, do you believe that there are times when parents should smack their children? The answers you give to these questions are likely to vary according to which country you come from, as global opinion is divided on this issue. Sweden banned corporal (i.e., physical) punishment of children in 1979. Austria, Denmark, Norway and Germany as well as at least 11 other countries in Europe to date have all since passed similar bans. In the UK, parents are allowed to smack, so long as no mark is left. However the practice of corporal punishment is widely accepted in France and the USA. In one national survey of American parents, 94 per cent reported that by the time their children reached the age of 4, they had smacked them (Straus and Stewart, 1999).

THE CORPORAL PUNISHMENT DEBATE

Corporal punishment is clearly a controversial issue. Let us consider the question of whether parents should physically punish their children's misbehaviour, with reference to what psychologists have taught us about learning.

The notion that sparing the rod spoils the child comes from the Bible (Proverbs 13–24), and has clearly been upheld as part of the conventional received wisdom of child-rearing. But what is the evidence that smacking helps? Psychologist Elizabeth Gershoff (2002a) conducted a meta-analysis of 88 studies on parental use of corporal punishment, involving about 36 000 participants. Five of these studies examined whether corporal punishment was effective in temporarily suppressing children's misbehaviour. Overall the answer was yes, but Gershoff cautioned that this result was inconsistent because it was found in only three of the five studies.

In contrast, the other major outcomes that Gershoff studied consistently showed unfavourable associations with child corporal punishment. These outcomes, based almost entirely on correlational studies, included:

- decreased quality of the parent–child relationship

- poorer internalization of moral standards during childhood

- increased aggressive behaviour during childhood and, later, during adulthood

- increased delinquent and antisocial behaviour (e.g., truancy, stealing) during childhood and adulthood

- poorer mental health during childhood and adulthood

- increased childhood risk of physical abuse

- increased risk, upon becoming an adult, of physically abusing one's own children or spouse.

Gershoff (2002a) emphasizes that these findings 'do not imply that all children who experience corporal punishment turn out to be aggressive or delinquent.... Corporal punishment may make certain behaviours more likely but clearly not inevitable' (p. 551). Remember, most people who are smacked do not grow up to be violent or antisocial adults.

What are the alternative explanations? As a critical thinker, recall that correlation does not prove causation. To see why, let us examine the association between corporal punishment and child aggression. Before reading further, can you identify three possible causal explanations for this correlation? (If you have trouble, refer back to Fig. 2.11 on p. 56.)

One possibility is that corporal punishment causes children to behave more aggressively. Many psychologists have expressed this concern because physical punishment amounts to control by aggression and may send a message to the child that aggression is appropriate and effective. Moreover, laboratory experiments indicate that children learn aggressive behaviours by watching aggressive adult models (Bandura, 1965).

We must also consider the bidirectionality problem. Perhaps children who are more aggressive cause their parents to be more physically punitive. Thus greater misbehaviour may lead to greater punishment. And, finally, we must consider the third-variable problem. Maybe something else – an inherited or environmental factor – causes children to behave more aggressively and causes parents to punish more aggressively (i.e., physically), making it seem like aggression and corporal punishment are directly related when in fact they are not.

What additional evidence would be helpful? After child corporal punishment was banned in Sweden, did new generations of children grow up to become poorly socialized teenagers? Examining national statistics from 1975 through 1996, Joan Durrant (2000) found that after the corporal punishment ban, teenage rates of theft, rape, narcotics trafficking, drug use and suicide all declined. Durrant points out that economic, social and other national factors likely influenced these results, so we cannot conclude that banning corporal punishment caused these changes. Yet whatever the cause, the direction of the findings runs counter to 'spare the rod, spoil the child'. As Durrant notes, 'Swedish youth have not become more unruly, under socialized, or self-destructive following the ... ban. In fact, most measures demonstrated a substantial improvement in youth well being' (2000, p. 451).

What should we conclude? The study of Swedish youth and Gershoff's meta-analysis converge on the same point: causality is unclear, but the direction of the association runs counter to traditional wisdom; it appears that using the rod – rather than sparing it – may be associated with poorer child-development outcomes. Still, some psychologists cite evidence that mild to moderate spanking has its place, such as a backup technique when other types of discipline fail with young children who have behaviour problems (Baumrind et al., 2002).

WOULD YOU BAN CORPORAL PUNISHMENT?

Decisions about banning child corporal punishment involve more than scientific evidence. Parents' belief in their entitlement to use corporal punishment is deeply embedded in cultural history, religion and beliefs about the privacy of the family (Holden, 2002).

After examining the preceding evidence, what are your thoughts about the appropriateness of smacking?

Response Cost

The second form of punishment is **response cost**. As many parents who do not use corporal punishment might tell you, 'Just because you don't smack doesn't mean you have to let your kids have their own way all of the time. You can still set limits'. Indeed, groundings, loss of privileges and monetary fines represent another approach to modifying behaviour. They take away something that an individual finds satisfying. In response cost (also called **negative punishment** or **punishment by removal**), a response is weakened by the subsequent removal of a stimulus (i.e., 'that'll cost you'). A popular child-rearing practise is to punish children who misbehave by making them sit quietly (possibly in isolation) for a period of time, temporarily removing opportunities to play, watch television, or participate in other enjoyable activities. Response cost, of course, is not limited to disciplining children or teenagers. Adults are often punished by monetary fines (e.g., after a speeding offence), as the removal of money is a powerful incentive to adhere to the law. One example of response cost is the sin-bin penalty applied in rugby in which, following a minor infraction, a player is made to serve a time penalty on the bench (Fig. 7.18).

response cost (also called **negative punishment** or **punishment by removal**)

response is weakened by the subsequent removal of a stimulus

FIGURE 7.18

Response cost in action. Rugby players sent to the 'sin-bin'.

Many psychologists and clinicians who counsel parents on modifying children's behaviour favour using time-out as a punishment technique (Baumrind et al., 2002). Still, as disciplinary techniques, aversive punishment and response cost have limitations. They suppress behaviour but do not cause an organism to forget how to make the response. Because they tell us what not to do but do not necessarily help us learn what to do, it is important to use positive reinforcement to strengthen desirable alternative responses directly. Finally, punishment of any type may arouse negative emotions, such as fear and anger, that can produce dislike and avoidance of the person delivering the punishment.

Skinner (1953) believed that punishing behaviour was not an effective way to produce long-term change. Indeed, try imagining the effect of punishing the rat when it does not press the lever instead of rewarding it when it does. The rat would probably get confused and fearful without necessarily linking this punishment to the fact that it did not press the lever according to the experimenter's wishes. It would likely never learn to press the lever. Yet research indicates that under the proper conditions, punishment can promote enduring changes, particularly if it occurs after every instance of the behaviour being punished (Domjan, 2000a).

Immediate, Delayed and Reciprocal Consequences

Focus 7.10

How do immediate, delayed and reciprocal consequences affect learning?

In general, a consequence that occurs immediately after a behaviour has a stronger effect than when it is delayed. Training animals typically requires immediate reinforcement so that they associate the correct response, rather than a subsequent behaviour, with the reinforcer.

Because humans can imagine future consequences, our behaviour is less rigidly controlled by the timing of consequences than that of other species. Still, the power of immediate reinforcement helps explain why many people continue to engage in behaviours with maladaptive long-term consequences. Chronic drug users usually find it difficult to stop because the immediate reinforcing consequences of the drug override the delayed benefits of not using the drug (e.g., being healthier, living longer). With many drugs, such as cocaine, use is positively reinforced by feelings of pleasure that seem to result from enhanced dopamine activity (Julien, 2005). Powerful negative reinforcers also play a role. Chronic cigarette smokers experience increased tension as the nicotine level in their blood drops after their last cigarette. When they smoke again, the tension decreases. Thus smoking is negatively reinforced by the removal of unpleasant tension.

Finally, it is important to realize that under ecological circumstances learning is frequently a reciprocal process involving a sequence of responses *between* organisms. Whether it is friends socializing or a tiger chasing a gazelle, each response by one organism may reinforce, punish, help extinguish or classically condition the other organism's behaviour.

WHAT DO YOU THINK?

CAN YOU EXPLAIN THE 'SUPERMARKET TANTRUM'?

At the supermarket, a child asks his dad to buy sweets. His dad refuses. The child screams and will not stop. Soon the father cannot stand it, buys the sweets and the child's tantrum ends. A week later this scene repeats, but the father gives in as soon as the tantrum starts. The next time the child asks for sweets, the father just says, OK. Use concepts of reinforcement and punishment to explain this sequence of events. Then see p. 330.

SHAPING AND CHAINING: TAKING ONE STEP AT A TIME

Mark is a 4-year-old who attends pre-school. He does not play much with other children, rarely engages in physical activity, and during outdoor break spends most of his time sitting in the sandbox. His teachers and parents would like him to be more active. How can we use operant conditioning to try to change Mark's behaviour?

First, let us set a specific goal: getting Mark to play on the monkey bars. Second, let us select a positive reinforcer: attention. Now, all we need to do is reinforce Mark with attention when he plays on the monkey bars. The problem is, we will be waiting a long time because Mark rarely displays this behaviour.

Fortunately, Skinner discovered a powerful process for overcoming this problem. We begin by reinforcing Mark with attention every time he stands up in the sandbox. This is the first approximation towards our final goal. Once this response is established, we reinforce him only if he stands up and walks from the sandbox towards the monkey bars. This is the second approximation. Then we reinforce him only when he stands next to the bars and, finally, only when he is on the bars and moving. This process, known as **shaping** (also called the method of successive approximations), involves reinforcing successive approximations towards a final response. Using a shaping procedure similar to the one just described, researchers found that they could get Mark to play on the monkey bars in only a little time (Johnston et al., 1966).

Even when behaviours can be learned through trial and error – such as a rat learning to press a lever for food – shaping can speed up the process. By reinforcing successive approximations – such as standing near the lever, raising a front paw, touching the lever and, finally, depressing the lever – acquisition time is reduced.

Another procedure, **chaining**, is used to develop a sequence (a chain) of responses by reinforcing each response with the opportunity to perform the next response. For example, suppose that a rat has learned to press a lever to receive food when a light is on. Next we place a bell nearby. By accident, the rat eventually bumps into and rings the bell, which turns on the light. Seeing the light, the rat runs to and presses the lever. Over time, the rat will learn to ring the bell because this response is reinforced by the light turning on, which provides the opportunity to press the lever for food. As in this example, chaining usually begins with the final response in the sequence and works backward towards the first response (Catania, 1998). Figure 7.19 shows another example of chaining.

The behaviours that we display in everyday life often develop through shaping and chaining. Recall the father who initially refused his child's request for sweets, then gave in after a lengthy

Focus 7.11

Explain how behaviours develop through shaping and chaining. Describe operant generalization and discrimination.

shaping (also called **method of successive approximations**) involves reinforcing successive approximations towards a final response

chaining used to develop a sequence (a chain) of responses by reinforcing each response with the opportunity to perform the next response

FIGURE 7.19

Chaining a sequence of responses.

Through chaining, this rat has learned to climb a ladder to reach a string, pull on the string to raise the ladder, and then climb the ladder again to reach food at the top. Typically, you begin this training with the last step in the chain. Then, working backwards, each prior step in the chain is reinforced by the opportunity to perform the next step.

tantrum, then gave in as soon as a tantrum started and, finally, just said OK to the request. In essence, his eventual response of agreeing immediately was shaped. Instructors who teach musical, athletic and academic skills often shape their students' performance by starting with a simple response and reinforcing progressively closer approximations to the complex response that is ultimately desired.

GENERALIZATION AND DISCRIMINATION

As in classical conditioning, operant responses may generalize to similar antecedent situations. A dog taught by its owner to 'Sit' will likely start sitting when other people give the command. A young child who touches a hot stovetop burner learns to avoid touching not only that burner but other hot burners as well. Thus in **operant generalization**, an operant response occurs to a new antecedent stimulus or situation that is similar to the original one.

Through experience, we also learn to discriminate between antecedent conditions. Children learn to raid the biscuit jar only when the parents are not in the kitchen. We learn to board buses and trains marked by specific symbols (79: Express) and avoid otherwise identical vehicles with different symbols (78: Local). **Operant discrimination** means that an operant response will occur to one antecedent stimulus but not to another. These antecedent stimuli – parents' presence or absence, bus markings – are discriminative stimuli. A behaviour that is influenced by discriminative stimuli is said to be under **stimulus control**. The sight of a police car exerts stimulus control over most people's driving behaviour.

The concept of operant discrimination gives science a powerful tool for examining the perceptual and cognitive abilities of human infants and non-human species. We cannot ask infants and animals to tell us if they can distinguish between different colours, sounds, faces, and so on. But by using a procedure called *operant discrimination training*, we can teach an organism, for example, that pressing a lever when a red light is on produces a food reinforcer. Now all we have to do is change the colour of the light and not reinforce any response when that light is on. If the organism learns to respond to one colour and not the other, we infer that it can discriminate between them.

SCHEDULES OF REINFORCEMENT

In daily life, reinforcement comes in different patterns and frequencies. These patterns, referred to as *schedules of reinforcement*, have strong and predictable effects on learning, extinction and performance (Ferster and Skinner, 1957). The most basic distinction is between continuous and partial reinforcement. With **continuous reinforcement**, every response of a particular type is reinforced. Every press of the lever results in food pellets. Every euro deposited in the drinks machine results in a can of cool, bubbly drink. With **partial (intermittent) reinforcement**, only a portion of the responses of a particular type is reinforced. (Hereafter, when discussing reinforcement schedules, we simply use the term *response* to refer to the particular behaviour of interest.)

Partial reinforcement schedules can be categorized along two important dimensions. The first is ratio versus interval schedules. On *ratio schedules*, a certain percentage of responses are reinforced. For example, we might decide to reinforce only 50 per cent of the rat's lever presses with food. The key factor is that ratio schedules are based on the number of responses: more responses, more reinforcement. On *interval schedules*, a certain amount of time must elapse between reinforcements, regardless of how many responses might occur during that interval. We might reinforce lever pressing only once per minute, whether the rat presses the lever five, 10 or 60 times. The key factor is that interval schedules are based on the passage of time.

The second dimension is fixed versus variable schedules. On a *fixed schedule*, reinforcement always occurs after a fixed number of responses or after a fixed time interval. On a *variable*

---

operant generalization

an operant response occurs to a new antecedent stimulus or situation that is similar to the original one

operant discrimination

an operant response will occur to one antecedent stimulus but not to another

stimulus control

a behaviour that is influenced by discriminative stimuli

---

continuous reinforcement

every response of a particular type is reinforced

partial (intermittent) reinforcement

only a portion of the responses of a particular type is reinforced

---

Focus 7.12

Describe and illustrate schedules of reinforcement. How do they affect performance, learning rates and extinction?

schedule, the required number of responses or the time interval between them varies at random around an average. Combining these two dimensions creates four types of reinforcement schedules (Fig. 7.20).

Reinforcement Schedules, Learning and Extinction

Continuous reinforcement has an important advantage over partial reinforcement: It produces more rapid learning because the association between a behaviour and its consequences is easier to perceive. However, it also has a disadvantage: continuously reinforced responses extinguish more rapidly, because it is easier to perceive when reinforcement is withdrawn, as there is a sudden change between reinforcement on every trial and no reinforcement on any trial.

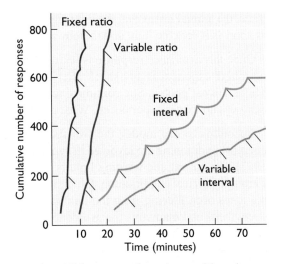

Partial reinforcement produces behaviour that is learned more slowly but is more resistant to extinction. Especially when reinforcement has been unpredictable in the past, it takes longer to learn that it is gone forever. People do not continue to drop coins into a drinks machine that does not deliver, because vending machines are supposed to operate on a continuous schedule. But it would take many pulls on a fruit machine to recognize that it had stopped paying out completely. To sum up, the best way to promote fast learning and high resistance to extinction is to begin reinforcing a desired behaviour on a continuous schedule until the behaviour is well established and then shift to a partial (preferably variable) schedule that is gradually made more demanding.

ESCAPE AND AVOIDANCE CONDITIONING

Behaviour often involves escaping from or avoiding aversive situations. Escape occurs when we take medications to relieve pain or put on more clothes when we are cold. Avoidance occurs when we put on sunscreen to prevent sunburn or obey traffic laws to avoid tickets. You can probably think of many more examples.

In **escape conditioning**, the organism learns a response to terminate an aversive stimulus. Escape behaviours are acquired and maintained through negative reinforcement. If you are cold, putting on a sweater is negatively reinforced by the desirable consequence that you no longer shiver. Taking a pain reliever is negatively reinforced by the reduction of pain. In **avoidance conditioning**, the organism learns a response to avoid an aversive stimulus. We learn to dress warmly to avoid feeling cold in the first place.

Escape and avoidance conditioning can be demonstrated experimentally (Solomon and Wynne, 1953; Van der Borght et al., 2005). For example, researchers may place an animal in a *shuttlebox*, a rectangular chamber divided into two compartments and connected by a doorway (Fig. 7.21). The floor is a grid through which electric shock can be delivered to either compartment. When the animal receives a shock in its compartment, it attempts to escape. Eventually, it runs through the door and into the other compartment where there is no electric shock. When the situation is reversed and shock is delivered to that compartment, the animal can escape by running back to the original side. Running through the door removes the shock, which negatively reinforces this escape behaviour. Over a few trials, the animal learns to escape as soon as the shock is administered.

To study avoidance conditioning experimentally, researchers introduce a discriminative stimulus – a warning signal such as a light – that precedes the shock by a few seconds. After a few

---

FIGURE 7.20

Partial reinforcement schedules affect performance.

Each type of positive reinforcement schedule produces a typical cumulative response curve. The hash marks indicate the delivery of a reinforcer. Ratio schedules produce a high rate of responding, as shown in the steep slopes of the curves. Variable schedules typically produce a steadier rate of responding than fixed schedules.

escape conditioning
the organism learns a response to terminate an aversive stimulus

avoidance conditioning
the organism learns a response to avoid an aversive stimulus

Focus 7.13
Describe and illustrate escape and avoidance conditioning. Explain the two-factor theory of avoidance learning.

FIGURE 7.21

A shuttlebox.

Researchers use the shuttlebox to study escape and avoidance learning.

trials, the animal learns that the light signals impending shock. It runs to the other compartment as soon as it sees the light and thereby avoids being shocked.

Once this avoidance response is learned, it often is hard to extinguish, even when the animal no longer experiences any shock after the light is turned on. We saw the same situation with Michelle's car phobia. She continued to avoid cars even though the intense pain from her accident was no longer experienced. What makes avoidance so resistant to extinction?

According to one model, the **two-factor theory of avoidance learning**, both classical and operant conditioning are involved in avoidance learning (Mowrer, 1947; Rescorla and Solomon, 1967). For our rat, the warning light is initially a neutral stimulus paired with a shock (UCS). Through classical conditioning, the light becomes a CS that elicits fear. Now operant conditioning takes over. Fleeing from the light is negatively reinforced by the termination of fear. This strengthens and maintains the avoidance response. Now if we permanently turn off the shock, the avoidance response prevents extinction from taking place. Seeing the light come on, the animal will not hang around long enough to learn that the shock no longer occurs.

In similar fashion, Michelle's fear of cars was classically conditioned. The mere sight of a car (like the light for the rat) elicits fear and she flees, thereby avoiding riding in or driving the car. This avoidance is negatively reinforced by fear reduction, so it remains strong (Fig. 7.22). Extinction is difficult because Michelle doesn't give herself the opportunity to be in the car without experiencing physical pain and trauma. This is why exposure therapies for phobias are so effective. By preventing avoidance responses, they provide the key ingredient for extinction: exposure to the CS (car) in the absence of the UCS (pain, trauma).

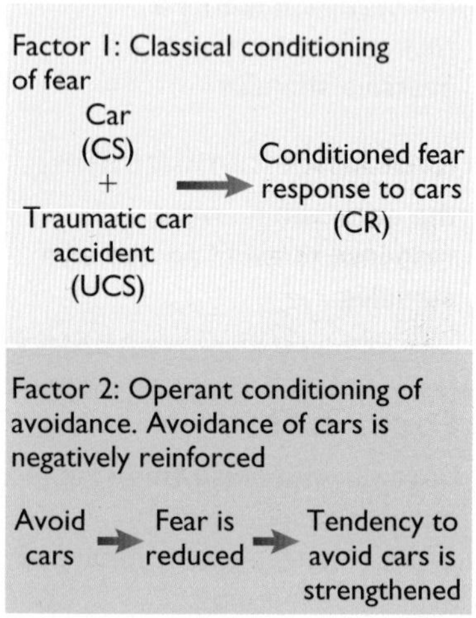

The two-factor theory helps us understand how many avoidance behaviours develop (Baron and Perone, 2001). However, it has trouble explaining some aspects of avoidance, such as why people and other animals develop phobic avoidance to some stimuli (e.g., snakes) more easily than to others (e.g., flowers). As we shall explore later, other factors also regulate our avoidance responses.

APPLICATIONS OF OPERANT CONDITIONING

In his best-selling books *Walden Two* (1948) and *Beyond Freedom and Dignity* (1971), Skinner set forth his utopian vision of how a 'technology of behaviour' based on positive reinforcement could end war, improve education and solve other social problems. To his critics, Skinner's ideas conjured up images of people being manipulated like rats. But Skinner's point was that social influence is a natural part of human existence (see also Chapter 14, 'Social psychology'). Parents and children influence each other, as do employees and employers, teachers and students, friends and romantic partners. To behaviourists, individual and societal problems are created by the all-too common *haphazard* use of reinforcement and over-reliance on punishment (Catania, 2001).

Today, many of Skinner's ideas have been put into action. Walk into your local computer shop, and you are likely to find shelves of educational software, teaching everything from mathematics to foreign languages. The effectiveness of computerized instruction rests on two principles championed by Skinner: *immediate performance feedback* and *self-paced learning*. Today, personal computers have made Skinner's vision an educational reality. Computer-assisted instruction also is found in business, industry and the military (Parchman et al., 2000). *Educational software typically quizzes the student and provides immediate feedback*. In addition, students who do not learn the material the first time can repeat steps, those who do can advance to the next set of information; exemplifying Skinner's principle of self-paced learning.

Skinner's shaping and training procedures have also been utilized in order to teach animals to perform some truly remarkable behaviours. Some are trained to be television, film or circus performers, whereas others learn to assist people with disabilities (Fig. 7.23). Police dogs assist

---

two-factor theory of avoidance learning

both classical and operant conditioning are involved in avoidance learning

---

Focus 7.14

How have operant principles been applied to education, the workplace, animal training and solving problem behaviours?

Factor 1: Classical conditioning of fear

Car (CS) + Traumatic car accident (UCS) → Conditioned fear response to cars (CR)

Factor 2: Operant conditioning of avoidance. Avoidance of cars is negatively reinforced

Avoid cars → Fear is reduced → Tendency to avoid cars is strengthened

FIGURE 7.22

Two-factor theory of avoidance learning.

The two-factor theory of avoidance learning would account for Michelle's car phobia in terms of two sets of learning processes: Classical conditioning of a fear response and the negative reinforcement of avoidance of cars through fear reduction.

FIGURE 7.23

(*Left*) A trainer uses a laser to point out an object for the monkey to pick up. (*Right*) Because of injuries suffered in an accident, this woman cannot move her arms or legs. The monkey has been operantly trained to assist her with basic aspects of day-to-day living, such as eating.

officers on routine patrol, and other dogs learn to use their sense of smell to help locate hidden bombs, illegal drugs and missing persons. The US Navy trains sea lions to dive and retrieve sunken test weapons, and dolphins learn to patrol waters around nuclear submarine bases and search for underwater intruders (Morrison, 1988). Operantly trained dolphins also patrolled the waters around some US ships during the Vietnam and Persian Gulf Wars.

Operant conditioning demonstrates the environment's power in shaping behaviour. But this does not mean we are at its mercy. The following 'Applying psychological science' describes how you can use your knowledge of learning principles to gain greater control over your own behaviour.

Focus 7.15

Describe the five main steps in a behavioural self-regulation programme.

APPLYING PSYCHOLOGICAL SCIENCE

USING OPERANT PRINCIPLES TO MODIFY YOUR BEHAVIOUR

People often blame the inability to overcome bad habits or maladaptive behaviours on vague concepts such as poor willpower and lack of self-control. Behaviourists prefer the more optimistic assumption that we can acquire *self-regulation*, which implies that we can use learning principles to change our behaviour (Kanfer and Goldstein, 1991). This approach has helped people overcome addictions, lose excess weight, reduce their risk of heart disease and improve their lives in many other ways. Let us examine how a college student could use self-regulation principles to increase the amount and effectiveness of studying.

STEP 1: SPECIFY THE PROBLEM

The first step in a self-regulation programme is to pinpoint the behaviours you want to change (Watson and Tharp, 1997). This may be more challenging than it sounds, because we often use vague words to describe our problems. Here is how one of our students described her study problem: 'I'm just not motivated to study hard.' With a little help, she redefined her problem in more specific behavioural terms: 'Between 7 and 10 p.m. I don't spend enough time at my desk reading and outlining my textbook.'

Whenever possible, design your programme to positively reinforce desirable behaviours (i.e., studying) rather than punish undesirable ones (i.e., not studying). Therefore we define this student's *target behaviour* (the specific goal) as follows: 'Four nights a week, between 7 and 10 p.m., spend 2½ hours studying.'

STEP 2: COLLECT BASELINE DATA

The next step is to collect *baseline (preintervention) data* on your behaviour. Baseline data provide information about how frequently the target behaviour currently occurs. Without it, you have no way of measuring how much you change after starting your programme. The most effective approach is to plot data on a graph. Figure 7.24 shows data collected by a student.

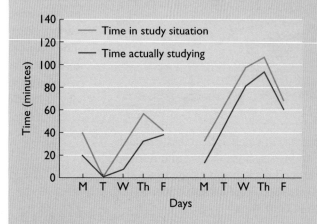

FIGURE 7.24

Using self-reinforcement to increase study time.
This student graphed the amount of time he spent in the study environment and the time he actually spent studying. Study time increased when he began to self-reinforce study behaviour in the second week.

STEP 3: IDENTIFY ANTECEDENTS AND CONSEQUENCES

While you collect baseline data, try to identify *antecedent* factors that disrupt study behaviour, such as friends phoning you or stopping by (Watson and Tharp, 1997). Also focus on the *consequences* of your behaviour. Does studying produce outcomes that are satisfying?

STEP 4: DEVELOP A PLAN TO MODIFY THE ANTECEDENTS AND CONSEQUENCES

Once you have identified key antecedents and consequences, you are in position to modify either or both.

Altering the antecedents

You can modify the environment so that different stimuli control your behaviour. To increase studying, select a specific place where you do nothing but study. If your attention wanders, get up and leave the study area. Your objective is to condition yourself to study in response to the stimuli present in the study area. B.F. Skinner used this technique throughout his own career: he did all of his writing at a particular desk and did nothing else there.

Altering the consequences

Consequences determine whether a behaviour will be repeated. Fortunately, we have the power to arrange many of our own consequences. Self-administered *positive reinforcement* should be the cornerstone of most programmes. Find an effective reinforcer that you can control, and make it available only if you engage in the desired behaviour. Almost any activity or object you enjoy can serve as a reinforcer, but it must be potent enough to maintain the desired behaviour. Awarding yourself a penny for each hour of study time is unlikely to modify your behaviour, whereas a 30-minute credit towards a recreational activity might be very effective. After selecting a reinforcer, decide how to use it. Draw up and sign a contract with yourself. The contract should precisely state:

- how often or how long you must perform the target behaviour (or refrain from performing it if the goal is to reduce an undesirable behaviour)

- the kind and amount of reinforcement you will receive for specific achievements.

Use reinforcers effectively

Immediately reinforce the target behaviour whenever possible. If your reinforcer cannot be available immediately, use tokens that can later be converted into a reinforcer. One student who wanted to increase her study time awarded herself one point per 15 minutes of study time. Points were redeemed for rewards that varied in their reinforcement value. For example, one point was worth 15 minutes of television viewing, but 15 points earned the right to 'do anything I want to, all day'. Behaviour analysts have used these '*token economies*' successfully with workers, children, patients in mental hospitals, prison inmates and other groups (Swain and McLaughlin, 1998).

Use shaping

If you collect good baseline data, you will know the level at which you currently perform your target behaviour. Begin at this level or slightly beyond it and move *slowly* towards your final goal, reinforcing yourself at each step. For example, begin by reinforcing yourself for each 10-minute increase in study time. If you have trouble, reduce the size of your steps. Attaining each small goal along the way can be reinforcing and provides motivation to continue (Locke and Latham, 2002). The goal is to bring about gradual change while enjoying plenty of reinforcers, as well as the satisfaction that comes from increasing self-mastery. *The way you arrange reinforcement contingencies is the most critical determinant of whether you will achieve your goal.*

STEP 5: IMPLEMENT THE PROGRAMME AND KEEP MEASURING BEHAVIOUR

Most people experience occasional setbacks or plateaus when progress seems to stop. If this happens repeatedly, it is not a sign of weak willpower but rather a need to modify the programme. Yes, self-regulation programmes can fail, but failure calls for resourcefulness rather than despair. If need be, change the terms of your contract, but always operate under a specific contract. Keep recording and graphing the target behaviour. This is the only way to identify your progress accurately.

This five-step process is one of several behavioural approaches to gaining greater control of our lives. Psychologists continue to design and test methods to increase self-regulation, adding new meaning to the phrase 'Power to the people'.

IN REVIEW

- Thorndike's law of effect states that responses followed by satisfying consequences will be strengthened, whereas those followed by annoying consequences will be weakened.

- Skinner analysed operant conditioning in terms of relations between antecedents, behaviours and consequences. Discriminative stimuli are antecedents that signal the likely consequences of particular behaviours in a given situation.

- Reinforcement occurs when a response is strengthened by an outcome (a reinforcer) that follows it. With positive reinforcement, a response is strengthened by the presentation of a stimulus that follows it. With negative reinforcement, a response is strengthened by the removal of an aversive stimulus.

- Operant extinction is the weakening and eventual disappearance of a response because it no longer is reinforced.

- Punishment occurs when a behaviour is weakened by an outcome (a punisher) that follows it. With aversive punishment, the behaviour becomes weaker when it is followed by the presentation of an aversive stimulus. With response cost, the behaviour becomes weaker when it is followed by the removal of a stimulus.

- The use of corporal punishment with children is controversial and is correlated with several negative outcomes for children's development.

- Shaping, which uses the method of successive approximations, involves reinforcing behaviours that increasingly resemble the final desired behaviour. Chaining is used to develop a sequence of responses by reinforcing each response with the opportunity to perform the next response.

- Operant generalization occurs when behaviour changes in one situation due to reinforcement or punishment, and the new response then carries over to similar situations. In contrast, operant discrimination occurs when an operant response is made to one discriminative stimulus but not to another.

- On a continuous reinforcement schedule, every response is reinforced. Partial reinforcement may occur on a ratio schedule, in which a certain percentage of responses are reinforced, or on an interval schedule, in which a certain amount of time must pass before a response gets reinforced. In general, ratio schedules produce higher rates of performance than interval schedules.

- On a fixed-ratio schedule, reinforcement occurs after a fixed number of responses; on a fixed interval schedule, it occurs after a fixed time interval. On variable schedules, the required number of responses or interval of time between them varies around some average.

- Escape conditioning and avoidance conditioning result from negative reinforcement. According to the two-factor theory, fear is created through classical conditioning. This fear motivates escape and avoidance, which are then negatively reinforced by fear reduction.

- Operant conditioning principles can enhance human performance in educational and work settings, reduce a wide array of behaviour problems, and help people self-regulate their behaviour. Animals can be operantly trained to perform many specialized tasks.

CHALLENGES TO BEHAVIOURISM

Behaviourists built much of the foundation on which our knowledge of learning principles rests, and behaviourism remains influential today (Leslie, 2002). Over the years, however, psychologists who viewed behaviour from biological and cognitive perspectives enriched our understanding of learning by challenging some of behaviourism's key assumptions.

BIOLOGICAL CONSTRAINTS: EVOLUTION AND PREPAREDNESS

Behaviourists never suggested that a rat could learn to fly, but for decades they assumed that they could condition virtually any behaviour an organism was physically capable of performing. Yet evidence mounted that 'conditioned' animals did not always respond as they were supposed to. The behaviourist assumption was wrong because it ignored a key principle discussed both at the outset of this chapter and in Chapter 3: behaviour is influenced by an organism's evolutionary history, and this places biological constraints on learning.

Martin Seligman's (1970) concept of *preparedness* captures this idea. **Preparedness** means that through evolution, animals are biologically predisposed (pre-wired) to learn some associations more easily than others. In general, behaviours related to a species' survival are learned more easily than behaviours contrary to an organism's natural tendencies. Let us consider some examples.

preparedness

through evolution, animals are biologically predisposed (pre-wired) to learn some associations more easily than others

Focus 7.16

How does research on learned taste aversions and fear conditioning support the concept of biological preparedness?

Constraints on Classical Conditioning: Learned Taste Aversions

Imagine eating or drinking something, then becoming sick and vomiting. Perhaps it is a case of the flu, or it could be food poisoning. When a food is associated with nausea or vomiting, that particular food can become a CS that triggers a **conditioned taste aversion**, a conditioned response in which the taste (and sometimes the sight and smell) of a particular food becomes disgusting and repulsive (Garcia et al., 1985). The very thought of it may even make us feel queasy, and we learn to avoid it. During pregnancy many women experience nausea and vomiting, and they may develop aversions to foods associated with these symptoms (Bayley et al., 2002). Cancer patients may develop aversions to foods they eat before chemotherapy or radiation therapy sessions, even when they know that the food did not cause their post-treatment stomach upset. Like other conditioned responses, the aversion develops involuntarily.

Psychologist John Garcia pioneered numerous taste-aversion experiments that challenged two basic assumptions of classical conditioning. First, behaviourists had assumed that the CS–UCS time interval had to be relatively short: usually a few seconds. Garcia showed that animals learned taste aversions even though the food (CS) was consumed up to several hours – or even a day – before they became ill (in this case, the UCS).

Second, in a classic experiment, Garcia illustrated how biological preparedness influences learned aversions (Garcia and Koelling, 1966). Whenever rats licked a drinking tube, they were simultaneously exposed to three neutral stimuli: sweet-tasting water, a bright light and a buzzer (Fig. 7.25). The rats were then divided into two conditions. In one condition, the rats were

> **conditioned taste aversion**
>
> a conditioned response in which the taste (and sometimes the sight and smell) of a particular food becomes disgusting and repulsive

Stage 1: All Rats
When rats touch the drinking tube, sweet water is delivered and a light and buzzer turn on.

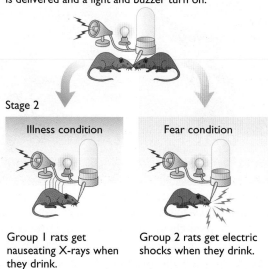

Stage 2

Illness condition	Fear condition

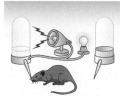 

Group 1 rats get nauseating X-rays when they drink.

Group 2 rats get electric shocks when they drink.

Stage 3

Group 1 rats avoid the sweet water and prefer the plain water with the light and buzzer.

Group 2 rats still drink the sweet water, but avoid the plain water with the light and buzzer.

FIGURE 7.25

Biological preparedness in classical conditioning.

This figure illustrates the design and main results of Garcia and Koelling's (1966) aversion experiment.

exposed to X-rays upon drinking the water, which later made them ill (UCS). Would the rats develop an aversion to all three neutral stimuli? No, they avoided the sweet water but not the light or buzzer. Why did only the sweet taste become a CS? Because rats are biologically primed to form taste–illness associations, which means that in nature they most easily identify poisonous or bad food by its taste (or smell). In nature, sounds and lights do not make rats sick.

When rats in the second condition licked the tube, the light, buzzer and sweet taste were all paired with an electric shock. Would these rats learn to fear all three neutral stimuli? No, they avoided the light and buzzer but kept drinking the sweet water. This also makes adaptive sense. In nature, sights and sounds – but not how food and drink taste – signal fear-provoking situations (e.g., a cat about to pounce).

The same principle applies to humans. When a food makes us violently sick, we may develop an aversion to it but not to the friends we ate with. Further, seeing the food again may repulse us but not make us afraid.

Psychologists have applied knowledge about conditioned aversions to save animals' lives. To prevent coyotes from killing farmers' sheep, scientists (Gustavson et al., 1974) laced pieces of meat with lithium chloride, a nausea-inducing drug. They wrapped the meat in sheep hide and left it out for coyotes to eat. The coyotes ate it, became ill, and developed an aversion to the meat, thereby becoming less likely to kill sheep. This saved the livelihoods of the farmers, saved the lives of sheep – and of the coyotes, who otherwise would have been shot by the farmers. Figure 7.26 illustrates nature's own wildlife management based on learned taste aversions.

FIGURE 7.26

A conditioned aversion in nature.

This blue jay has never eaten a monarch butterfly but does not pass up an easy meal. Soon, toxins in the butterfly cause food poisoning. The jay feels discomfort, vomits and develops a conditioned aversion triggered by the sight of the monarch's brightly patterned wings. From now on, it will leave monarchs alone.

SOURCE: Photographs courtesy of Lincoln P. Brower.

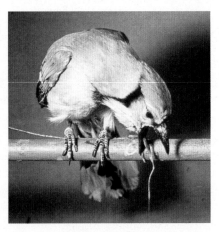

Applying taste-aversion principles to children with cancer, psychologists gave young patients an unusual-tasting sweet before their chemotherapy sessions (Broberg and Bernstein, 1987). As hypothesized, the sweet acted as a scapegoat and protected the children from developing aversions to their normal foods. Thus the sweet – rather than their normal food – became the aversive CS.

Are We Biologically Prepared to Fear Certain Things?

Seligman (1971) proposes that like other animals, humans are biologically prepared to acquire certain fears more readily than others. In one case, a 4-year-old girl saw a snake in a park but was not frightened by it (Marks, 1977). Soon thereafter she returned to the family car and accidentally trapped her hand in the car door. She subsequently developed a phobia not of car doors or cars, but of snakes.

In the laboratory, Swedish psychologists showed people pictures of various stimuli, flashing each picture on a screen and pairing it with electric shock (the UCS). Next, they measured people's physiological responses when those stimuli were presented alone (Öhman and Soares, 1998). When the pictures showed snakes, spiders or angry faces, people quickly acquired conditioned fear responses to these stimuli, even when the pictures were flashed too briefly to be consciously perceived. But participants who received shocks while looking at slides of flowers, houses or happy faces displayed much weaker fear conditioning.

Humans develop phobias to many stimuli, but most often we fear things that seem to have greater evolutionary significance: snakes, spiders, and potentially dangerous animals and places (Hofmann et al., 2004). Is this the result of evolution-based biological preparedness, or might it be due to learning experiences that teach us to expect that some stimuli can be dangerous? Multiple factors may affect human fear conditioning, but one thing is clear: as with taste aversions, fear can be conditioned much more easily to some stimuli than to others.

Constraints on Operant Conditioning: Animals that 'Won't Shape Up'

Two of B.F. Skinner's students, Keller and Marian Breland (Breland and Breland, 1961; 1966), became famous animal trainers. They successfully used shaping and chaining to train thousands of animals for circuses, television shows and films, but sometimes the animals simply refused to behave according to the laws of operant conditioning.

On one occasion, the Brelands tried to train a chicken to play baseball. A small ball would roll towards home plate, and the chicken would pull a chain to swing a small metal bat. If the ball was hit, a bell would ring and the chicken was supposed to run to first base to get a food reinforcer. The Brelands easily trained the chicken to pull the chain that swung the bat and to run to first base when it heard the bell. But when the ball was introduced into the game, utter chaos ensued. If the chicken hit the ball, instead of running to first base it chased the ball all over the field, pecking at it furiously and flapping its wings. Try as they might, the Brelands could not extinguish these behaviours. This brought an end to the training and the chicken's baseball career. This and other similar cases suggest that in operant conditioning (as in classical conditioning), organisms are biologically prepared to learn some types of behaviours more readily than others.

The Brelands also found that once a particular stimulus came to represent food, animals began to act as if it were food. The chicken pecked at the ball as if it were something to eat. In another case, raccoons had learned to deposit tokens into a box to receive a food reinforcer. But soon, instead of depositing the tokens, the raccoons kept rubbing them as if they were washing real food. This washing behaviour was so deeply rooted that it simply overrode the conditioning procedure. The Brelands called this **instinctive drift**, the tendency for a conditioned response to drift back towards instinctive behaviour.

Research provides other evidence of instinctive drift. For example, wild rats trained to press a lever for food will often drift back to instinctive behaviours and instead scratch and bite the lever (Powell and Curley, 1976).

Instinctive drift also has practical importance. People who adopt wild animals as pets or who train them for circuses face some personal risk no matter how hard they try to train these animals (Fig. 7.27).

COGNITION AND CONDITIONING

Early behaviourists believed that learning involves the relatively automatic formation of bonds between stimuli and responses. This viewpoint came to be known as *S-R (stimulus-response) psychology*. Behaviourists opposed explanations of learning that went beyond observable stimuli and responses. They did not deny that people had thoughts and feelings, but argued that behaviour could be explained without referring to such mentalistic concepts (Skinner, 1953; 1990).

Focus 7.17

How does instinctive drift illustrate preparedness, and why is it important?

instinctive drift

the tendency for a conditioned response to drift back towards instinctive behaviour

FIGURE 7.27

Instinctive drift in action.

There are some instinctive behaviours which are impossible to remove completely through training.

FIGURE 7.28

Some psychologists who challenged behaviourism's S-R model argued that to best explain human and animal behaviour (though, obviously, not the activity of amoebae), the organism's cognitive representations must be taken into account.

insight
the sudden perception of a useful relationship that helps to solve a problem

Focus 7.18
Discuss how research on insight and cognitive maps challenged behaviourist views of learning.

THE FAR SIDE® By GARY LARSON

"Stimulus, response! Stimulus, response! Don't you ever *think?*"

Even in psychology's early years, some learning theorists challenged the S-R model, arguing that in between stimulus and response there is something else: the organism's (O) cognitive representation of the world (Fig. 7.28). This came to be known as the *S-O-R*, or *cognitive, model of learning*. Today the cognitive perspective represents an important force in learning theory.

Early Challenges to Behaviourism: Insight and Cognitive Maps

In the 1920s, German psychologist Wolfgang Köhler (1925) challenged Thorndike's behaviourist assumption that animals learn to perform tasks only by trial and error. Köhler exposed chimpanzees to novel learning tasks and concluded that they were able to learn by **insight**, the sudden perception of a useful relationship that helps to solve a problem. Figure 7.29 shows how one of his apes solved the problem of how to retrieve bananas that were dangling beyond reach. Köhler emphasized that the apes often spent time staring at the bananas and available tools, as if they were contemplating the problem, after which the solution suddenly appeared.

FIGURE 7.29

Sultan seems to study the hanging bananas that are out of reach. After looking around, Sultan suddenly grabs some crates, stacks them and obtains his tasty reward.

Behaviourists argued that insight actually represents the combining of previously learned responses (Epstein et al., 1984). Imagine a pigeon placed inside a chamber where a miniature model of a banana dangles from the ceiling, out of reach. A small box sits in the corner of the chamber. Similar to Köhler's apes, the pigeon looks around, goes to the box, moves it under the banana by pushing it with its beak, then stands on the box and pecks the banana. Without knowing the pigeon's behavioural history (just as we do not know the entire behavioural history of Köhler's apes), we might conclude that this is a novel behaviour reflecting remarkable insight. But instead, the pigeon has simply combined several independent behaviours (e.g., pushing a box, stepping onto a box) that researchers had operantly conditioned using reinforcement.

Recent research with New Caledonian Crows, is reigniting the argument for the existence of unreinforced insightful behaviour in animals. Animal behaviour experts at Oxford University (Weir et al. 2002) report the observation that a female caledonian crow ('Betty') spontaneously manufactured a hook by bending a straight piece of wire. Betty then used the manufactured hook to successfully retrieve food by lifting a bucket from the bottom of a vertical pipe (Fig. 7.30). Importantly Weir and colleagues state that the animals had very little prior experience with pliant (bendable) material before the observation, and this experience had been with pipe-

FIGURE 7.30

Betty using the hook tool she has manufactured in order to pull up food in a bucket from the bottom of a vertical pipe.

cleaners and not the wire used in the experiment. The debate about insight rages, and Weir and colleagues' work with crows has reinvigorated Köhler's ideas and the argument for cognitive learning.

Another cognitive pioneer, American learning theorist Edward Tolman, studied spatial learning in rats. Look at the maze in Figure 7.31a. A rat runs to an open circular table, continues across and follows the only path available to a goal box containing food. After 12 trials, the rat easily negotiates the maze. Next, the maze is changed. The rat runs its usual route and reaches a dead end (Fig. 7.31b). What will the rat do? Tolman found that rats returned to the table, briefly explored most of the 18 new paths for just a few inches, and then chose one. By far, the largest number – 36 per cent – chose the fourth path to the right of their original route, which took them closest to where the goal box had been. In short, the rats behaved as you would, given your advantage of seeing the maps.

Focus 7.19

Describe the role of cognition in classical and operant conditioning. How did Tolman illustrate latent learning?

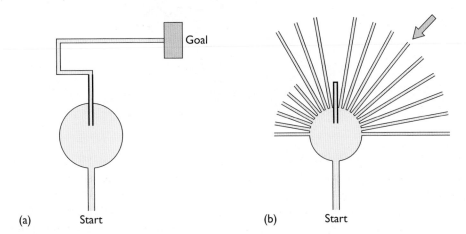

(a)   Start   (b)   Start

Goal

FIGURE 7.31

Cognitive maps in rats.

(a) Rats first learned to run the simple maze. (b) When the maze was switched, many rats chose the fourth path to the right of the original route. Tolman proposed that the rats had developed a cognitive map of the maze.

SOURCE: adapted from Tolman, 1948.

It is difficult for reinforcement theory to explain this behaviour. Tolman (1948) suggested that the rats had developed a **cognitive map**, a mental representation of the spatial layout. The concept of cognitive maps supported Tolman's belief that learning does not merely represent stimulus response associations. Rather, he argued that learning provides knowledge, and based on their knowledge, organisms develop an expectancy; a cognitive representation, of 'what leads to what'.

Behaviourists disagreed with Tolman's interpretations and, as with insight, the debate over cognitive maps continues. Nevertheless, Tolman's concept of expectancy remains a cornerstone of today's cognitive approaches to classical and operant conditioning.

cognitive map

a mental representation of the spatial layout

Latent learning   Tolman's research illustrated in Figure 7.31 suggested that the rats developed cognitive maps when they were reinforced with food for running a maze. Tolman also believed that cognitive maps could be learned without reinforcement, posing an even greater challenge to the behaviourist viewpoint. In one experiment, three groups of rats learned the correct path through a complex maze (Tolman and Honzik, 1930). Rats in the first group found food each time they reached the goal box. Rats in the second group found the goal box empty each time they reached it. Rats in the third group found no food at the end of the maze for the first 10 days but did find food in the goal box starting on the eleventh day.

The results are shown in Figure 7.32, and the key finding is this: on day 11, the rats in the third group discovered food in the goal box for the first time. By the very next day, they were performing just as well as the first group, which had been reinforced all along. What could explain this significant, sudden performance improvement? According to Tolman, during days 1 to 10, rats in the third group were learning the spatial layout of the maze as they wandered about. They were not being reinforced by food, but they gained knowledge and developed their cognitive maps. This learning remained *latent* (hidden) until the rats discovered a good reason on day 11 to get to the goal box quickly; it was then immediately displayed in performance the next day. Tolman's experiments support the concept of **latent learning**, which refers to learning that occurs but is not demonstrated until later, when there is an incentive to perform (Blodgett, 1929). In other words, we may learn how to do something at one time but not display that knowledge until we perform a task at a future time.

latent learning

learning that occurs but is not demonstrated until later, when there is an incentive to perform

FIGURE 7.32

Tolman's demonstration of latent learning.

Rats had one trial in the maze per day. Group R was reinforced with food every time they reached the end of the maze. Group NR never received reinforcement. The critical group, NR-R, received food reinforcement on day 11. Their immediate performance improvement suggested that they had learned the maze prior to the introduction of reinforcement.

SOURCE: Tolman and Honzik, 1930.

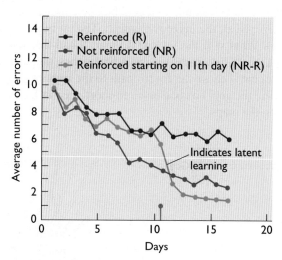

Cognition in Classical Conditioning

Expectancy in classical conditioning   Early American behaviourists such as Hull (1943) believed that classical conditioning created a direct reflex like connection between the CS (e.g., tone) and CR (e.g., salivation). Interestingly, Pavlov held a different view, proposing that a neural bond is formed between the CS and the UCS. Thus for Pavlov's dogs, the tone triggered an association with food, which then triggered salivation.

Cognitive learning theorists also believe that classical conditioning forms a CS–UCS link. In cognitive terminology, the link is an expectancy that the CS will be followed by the UCS (Hollis, 1997). *Expectancy models* states that the most important factor in classical conditioning is not how often the CS and the UCS are paired, but how well the CS predicts (i.e., signals) the appearance of the UCS (e.g., Pearce and Hall, 1980; Rescorla and Wagner, 1972).

Expectancy models came to the fore owing to the necessity of having to explain some phenomena which had been observed in adaptations of traditional Pavlovian conditioning experiments. One important finding made by Robert Rescorla (1968), was that the number of times which a CS and US are paired together does not determine whether learning occurs. Rescorla (1968) conducted a fear conditioning experiment in which rats were divided into one of two learning conditions. Rats in one condition received electric shocks (UCS), and each shock was preceded by a tone. As usual, the tone soon became a CS that elicited a fear response when presented alone. In the second condition, rats received the same number of tone–shock pairings as the first group, but they also received as many shocks that were not preceded by the tone. Would the tone become a CS for fear? According to traditional learning theory, the answer should be yes, because the number of tone–shock pairings was the same as in the first group. But the expectancy model predicts no, because the tone does not reliably predict when the shock will occur. Rescorla's (1968) results supported the expectancy model: The tone did not elicit a fear response for the second group.

This CS–UCS inconsistency also explains why we do not become conditioned to all the neutral stimuli that are present just before a UCS appears. For example, when Pavlov's dogs were presented with tone–food pairings, there was light in the room. Why did the dogs not learn to salivate whenever they saw light? The key is that when the room was lit, the dogs often were *not* receiving food. When a neutral stimulus does not consistently predict the arrival of the UCS, it is less likely to become a CS. This is highly adaptive; if it were not the case, you and I (along with Pavlov's dogs) would be twitching, salivating and exhibiting all sorts of reflexive responses to so many stimuli that it would be difficult to function.

Other evidence supports the expectancy model. For example, recall that forward pairing (e.g., a tone followed by food) typically produces the strongest learning, whereas backward pairing (e.g., food followed by a tone) produces the weakest learning. This makes sense based on the expectancy model. In forward pairing, the tone predicts the imminent arrival of the food; it is a signal that something meaningful is about to happen. In backward pairing, the tone has no predictive value because the food has already arrived. In sum, the expectancy model has been highly influential and provides good evidence that cognition plays a role in classical conditioning (Siegel and Allan, 1996).

Blocking   Another important phenomenon which emerged at about the same time as Rescorla's findings was the 'blocking effect'. This was first documented in experiments conducted by Leon Kamin (1968; 1969). Like Rescorla, Kamin used a fear conditioning procedure. Rats were divided into two experimental groups (Fig. 7.33). In the experimental condition the rat is first given trials in which CS A (e.g., light) is presented before the UCS (shock). Then, in phase two, the experimental group of rats are given trials in which both CS A (e.g., light) and CS B (e.g., a noise) are presented before the shock. In the control group the rats only receive phase 2 training in which both light and sound are presented with the shock. Kamin found that only the control group showed evidence of having learned the association between CSB and the shock (by demonstrating the fear response to the noise). Kamin proposed that the previous pairing of the light with the shock 'blocked' the rats' acquisition of an association between the sound and the shock.

blocking
obstruction of conditioning of a CR, because that response has already been conditioned to a different stimulus

FIGURE 7.33

The blocking procedure.

This comprises three phases in which the experimenter examines rats conditioning to two CSs (in this case the UCS is an electric shock, the UCR is the fear response, and the two CSs are a light, and a sound). In the experimental group the rat is first given trials in which the light is presented before the UCS (shock), and then, in phase 2, given trials in which both the light and the noise are presented with the shock. In the control group the rats only receive phase 2 training in which both light and sound are presented with the shock. Prior presentation of the light stimuli in the first phase prevents the experimental group from learning about the relationship between the sound and the shock.

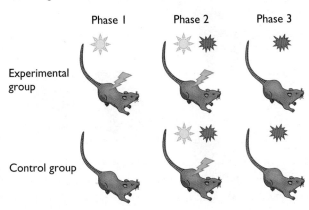

Phase 1   Phase 2   Phase 3

Experimental group

Control group

The phenomenon of blocking again demonstrates how associative learning is not simply due to the number of times which a CS and a UCS have been presented together. Rather, animals and indeed humans (e.g., Oades et al., 1996) appear to examine how well the CS predicts the UCS. Here is an example to make it clearer how blocking works in an everyday situation. Imagine you have just been introduced to a new social group; a group of friends who always drink in the same pub. As a newcomer you are trying to ascertain what relationships the group comprises. You have seen Amy arrive at the pub closely followed by Lawrence several times, and have formed the association that they are a couple. However, a few weeks later you see Amy arrive with Jane and then Lawrence. Do you then start to think that Jane and Lawrence may be an item? This seems an irrational conclusion, as you already have strong evidence that it is Amy who is seeing Lawrence.

The Rescorla–Wagner theory of classical conditioning   The blocking effect led researchers to argue that the strength of the association formed in classical conditioning was determined by how surprising the UCS was, or how unexpected it was. To go back to Kamin's experiment, by the time the rat in the experimental condition reaches phase 2 it has already learned to expect the light following the shock so it will no longer be surprised when the shock is administered – it will expect the shock. Rescorla and Wagner (1972) argue that no association is formed between the sound and the shock, because the shock is already expected – thus there is no surprise. They formalized this idea into a mathematical model of classical conditioning and accurately predicted a number of conditioning phenomena, including blocking, on the basis of how surprising or unexpected the UCS is in the learning episode. The take-home message of their model was that if the UCS (e.g., a shock) is surprising or unexpected, then it will be more strongly associated with a CS (e.g. a noise). If the shock is unsurprising or expected, for instance when it has already been predicted by a prior event, then it will not form so strong an association. Rescorla and Wagner's (1972) model was very influential because it was the first formalized model of conditioning which went beyond a simple associative explanation, like that used by the S-R theorists, by considering the mediating role of cognitive processes in learning; in this case the expectancy of the UCS.

Latent inhibition and attentional theories of conditioning   However, as is the process in scientific method, researchers set out to test the Rescorla–Wagner model, and identified a number of learning phenomena which were difficult for it to explain. **Latent inhibition**, described by Lubow and Moore (1959), is probably the most notable of these phenomena. Latent inhibition is the weakening of classical conditioning due to the prior presentation of the CS on its own. Lubow and Moore (1959) showed sheep and goats either a light flash *or* a spinning rotor. They then trained them to expect a shock after seeing both of these (Figure 7.34). They found that the

Rescorla–Wagner theory

a theory of classical conditioning which states that the strength of conditioning is determined by how surprising the UCS is

latent inhibition

the weakening of classical conditioning due to the prior presentation of the CS on its own

FIGURE 7.34

Latent inhibition experiment.

In Lubow and Moore's (1959) latent inhibition experiment, goats were first pre-exposed to one of two stimuli, and then trained to associate a shock with each of the stimuli in turn. So in the training phase, the goats were trained to expect a shock following both novel and familiar stimuli (the rotor is novel if pre-exposed to the light, and vice versa). They found that goats were slower to learn UCS associations with the CS which was familiar to them than with the CS which was novel to them. Latent inhibition of the familiar CS had occurred.

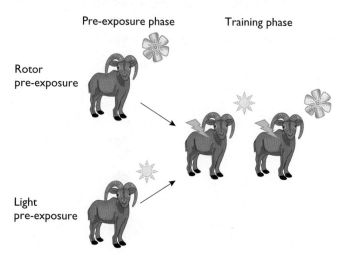

animals were slower to learn an association between the shock (UCS) and the stimulus to which they had already been exposed. So just the fact of having seen a particular CS before slowed their learning down.

Latent inhibition has also been observed in humans, and makes a lot of adaptive sense. If there are stimuli in our environment all the time, it would make little sense to associate these with novel unconditioned stimuli. For example, imagine a plate of food in front of you. The plate contains vegetables you are used to, some bread and some unidentified seafood which you have never sampled before. After eating your meal, you are violently sick. Do you develop a taste aversion to vegetables and bread? No. Sensibly, you develop an aversion to the novel unidentified seafood which you have eaten, and latent inhibition has prevented you from forming an aversion to bread and vegetables. Latent inhibition helps us to filter out spurious associations from our learning. However, it is clearly difficult for the Rescorla–Wagner model to explain. The UCS (shock) is only introduced after the pre-exposure phase. It is just as surprising whether the goat has been pre-exposed to CS or not so, according to Rescorla–Wagner, latent inhibition should not occur.

The most influential accounts of why latent inhibition occurs are those which suggest that the amount of attention which is paid to a CS determines how well we learn a new stimulus pairing. British psychologists, Neil Mackintosh (1975) and, later, John Pearce and Geoffrey Hall (1980) developed models of classical conditioning which suggest that the strength of the learned associations is determined by how much attention is paid to the CS during the learning episode. The amount of attention paid to the CS is said to be determined by factors such as how novel it is, and how well it predicts the UCS.

These **attentional theories of classical conditioning** explain latent inhibition by suggesting that the effect of presenting the CS (e.g., a light) in the absence of the UCS (e.g., a shock) is to habituate the animal to the CS. As we learned at the beginning of the chapter, habituation is a simple process whereby repeated presentation of a single stimulus reduces our response towards it. If we consider attention to be an orienting response to a stimulus, then we can see that the effect of presenting the CS on its own can habituate our attention towards the CS. Thus, attentional theories of classical conditioning suggest that the decreased attention towards the CS caused by habituation during pre-exposure reduces the strength of the association formed once the UCS is presented. To go back to Lubow and Moore's (1959) demonstration (see Fig. 7.34), the goats were pre-exposed to either a rotor or a light, having the effect of habituating these groups to these particular stimuli. The attentional models of conditioning by Mackintosh (1975) and Pearce and Hall (1980) propose that because the animals are now paying less attention to one CS (e.g., the rotor), they will be more likely to attend to the other CS (e.g., the light) when it is presented during the training phase, and thus more likely to learn an association between it and the UCS (the shock).

> **attentional theories of classical conditioning**
> state that the strength of conditioning is determined by how much attention is paid to the CS during the learning episode

In addition to *latent inhibition*, attentional theories can explain a wide variety of other phenomena in classical conditioning. For example, they explain blocking (see Fig. 7.33) by suggesting that attention is paid to a CS when it is a good predictor of the UCS; thus because a CS (e.g., a light) is already a good predictor of the UCS following phase 1 of a blocking experiment, more attention is paid to it at phase 2, at the expense of the newly introduced CS (e.g., a sound), and thus little association is formed between the sound and the UCS.

IN REVIEW

- An organism's evolutionary history prepares it to learn certain associations more easily than others, and this places biological constraints on learning. Thus organisms show faster classical conditioning when a CS has evolutionary significance.

- It is difficult to operantly condition animals to perform behaviours that are contrary to their evolved natural tendencies. Instinctive drift occurs when a conditioned behaviour is abandoned in favour of a more natural response.

- Studies of animal insight (such as Köhler's work with chimpanzees) and Tolman's research on cognitive maps suggested that cognition plays a role in learning. Tolman emphasized that learning is based on knowledge and an expectation of 'what leads to what'.

- Cognitive learning theorists view operant conditioning as the development of an expectancy that certain behaviours will produce certain consequences under certain conditions. Research on latent learning indicates that learning can occur without reinforcement.

- Cognitive interpretations of classical conditioning propose that organisms learn an expectancy that the CS will be followed by the UCS.

- There has been much debate concerning what determines how well an association, or expectancy is learned in classical conditioning. Rescorla and Wagner (1972) argue that the strength of the association is determined by how surprising the UCS is. This theory can explain the phenomenon of 'blocking'. On the other hand, Mackintosh (1975) and Pearce and Hall (1980) argue that the strength of the association is determined by how much attention is paid to the CS during the learning episode. These theories can explain both 'blocking' and 'latent inhibition'.

OBSERVATIONAL LEARNING: WHEN OTHERS SHOW THE WAY

observational learning
learning that occurs by observing the behaviour of a model

Focus 7.20
What is the adaptive significance of observational learning? Describe Bandura's theory and the four steps in the modelling process.

How did you learn to write, dance and drive a car, or spread peanut butter evenly across a piece of bread? Reinforcement was certainly involved, but so was **observational learning**, the learning that occurs by observing the behaviour of a model. Teachers, parents and trainers often help us learn by intentionally demonstrating skills. But observational learning extends beyond such contexts. We also learn fears, prejudices, likes and dislikes, and social behaviours by watching others (Olsson and Phelps, 2004). Through observation we may learn desirable responses, or like the two boys in our opening vignette who overenthusiastically emulated their television wrestling heroes, we may acquire undesirable behaviours. If parents who swear in front of their children complain to one another, 'Why do our kids use that damn language?' observational learning can help us answer their question.

Observational learning can be highly adaptive. By observing others, an organism can learn which events are important, which stimuli signal that such events are about to occur, and which responses are likely to produce positive or negative consequences. For example, hens may learn which other hens they can safely pick a fight with, and which ones they should avoid, by observing the hens that emerge as victors and losers in battles (Hogue et al., 1996). And monkeys may learn adaptive fears – such as a fear of snakes – by observing other monkeys react with fear (Öhman and Mineka, 2001).

Humans' capacity to learn by observation, which is also called *modelling*, far outstrips that of other creatures. It helps us bypass the potentially time-consuming and dangerous learning process of trial and error. For example, we would not want each new generation of brain surgeons or airline pilots to learn their craft only through trial and error!

BANDURA'S SOCIAL-COGNITIVE THEORY

As you have seen, research on biological preparedness and cognitive factors in conditioning challenged behaviourism's S-R view of learning. Psychologist Albert Bandura's pioneering research and theorizing on observational learning also helped carry forward the S-O-R challenge to behaviourism. Bandura's **social-cognitive theory**, also known by its former name **social-learning theory**, emphasizes that people learn by observing the behaviour of models and acquiring the belief that they can produce behaviours to influence events in their lives (Bandura, 1969; 2004).

The Modelling Process and Self-Efficacy

Bandura views modelling as a four-step process that includes several cognitive factors:

1. *Attention:* we must pay attention to the model's behaviour.
2. *Retention:* we must retain that information in memory so that it can be recalled when needed.
3. *Reproduction:* we must be physically capable of reproducing the model's behaviour or something similar to it.
4. *Motivation:* we must be motivated to display the behaviour.

According to Bandura, **self-efficacy**, which represents people's belief that they have the capability to perform behaviours that will produce a desired outcome, is a key motivational factor in observational learning. Recall that at the beginning of the chapter we defined learning as a change in an organism's behaviour or capabilities based on experience. According to Bandura, the knowledge or capability to perform a behaviour may be acquired at one time but not displayed until a later time when the motivational conditions are favourable.

Tolman's research on latent learning in rats demonstrated this point, and a classic experiment by Bandura (1965) on modelling demonstrated the learning-versus-performance distinction in humans. In this experiment, children watched a film in which a model acted aggressively towards a 'Bobo doll' (an inflatable plastic clown), punching, kicking and hitting it with a mallet. One group saw the model rewarded with praise and candy, a second group saw the model reprimanded for aggression and a third group saw no consequences for the model. After the film, each child was placed in a room with various toys, including a Bobo doll (Fig. 7.35).

Children who saw the model punished performed fewer aggressive actions towards the Bobo doll than did children in the other two groups. Does this mean that this group failed to learn how to respond aggressively? To find out, the experimenter later offered the children attractive prizes if they could do what the model had done. All of the children quickly reproduced the model's aggressive responses. Note that just as Tolman showed that rats apparently learned the layout of a maze while they were not receiving reinforcement, Bandura demonstrated that regardless of whether the model was reinforced or punished, children had indeed learned the model's behaviour.

> **social-cognitive theory** (also known by its former name **social-learning theory**) emphasizes that people learn by observing the behaviour of models and acquiring the belief that they can produce behaviours to influence events in their lives

> **self-efficacy** people's belief that they have the capability to perform behaviours that will produce a desired outcome

In-Psych

'Why Are We Violent?' This video in Chapter 7 of the In-Psych programme online presents a landmark researcher's view on this question.

FIGURE 7.35

In Bandura's (1965) experiment, most children who watched an aggressive model attack a Bobo doll later imitated that behaviour.

Imitation of Aggression and Pro-social Behaviour

Bandura's work helped stir a societal controversy that was brewing in the 1960s and continues to this day: what effect does viewing aggressive models on television or in films have on our attitudes and behaviour? We discuss this issue, and violent video games, more fully in Chapter 14. In brief, research strongly suggests that viewing media violence:

- decreases viewers' concerns about the suffering of victims
- habituates us to the sight of violence
- provides aggressive models that increase viewers' tendency to act aggressively (Eron, 2000; Huesmann et al., 2003).

If watching media violence can enhance our tendency to act aggressively, might watching pro-social models (models who do good deeds) increase our tendency to help others? Psychologist Joyce Sprafkin and her colleagues (1975) conducted one of the first experiments on this issue. They found that by exposing children to a television show in which an action hero helps save a young puppy, the children became more likely to help what they believed were real puppies in danger, even though helping meant giving up the opportunity to win prizes at a game. Many studies similarly indicate that exposure to pro-social models enhances people's helping behaviour (Hearold, 1986).

APPLICATIONS OF OBSERVATIONAL LEARNING

Focus 7.21

Describe applications of social-cognitive theory to solve large-scale societal problems.

In everyday life we learn many skills from observing models. Elementary school teachers model how to write, pronounce and use words. In college, foreign-language instructors do the same. Parents, teachers, business managers and athletic coaches model how to solve problems and perform tasks. If you play sports or video games, you may have picked up strategies or moves by watching other players.

Psychologists have also used observational learning to enhance pro-social behaviour. For example, researchers showed secondary school students an audio-visual programme that featured models (other students) who donated blood. Subsequently donations to a blood bank increased by 17 per cent (Sarason et al., 1991).

More ambitiously, observational learning has been used to address global social problems. In 1975, Miguel Sabido, a vice-president in charge of research at one of Mexico's largest media companies, used Bandura's theory to help develop the first project to tackle an important social problem (in this case high levels of illiteracy) with social-cognitive theory (Smith, 2002). When a national literacy programme in Mexico failed to draw a good turnout, Sabido created a television soap opera to give the literacy programme a boost. The popular soap opera aired for a year and featured a literate female character who, as part of the national programme, organized a self-study group for teenagers and adults who struggled with illiteracy.

Sabido hoped that by showing soap opera characters learning to read, this would provide viewers with positive role models, increase viewers' self-efficacy that they could learn to read, and motivate viewers to enrol in the literacy programme. His hope bore fruit. After one episode in which viewers were directly asked to enrol, 'about 25,000 people descended on the distribution center in Mexico City to get their reading materials' (Bandura, 2002a, p. 224). New annual enrolments in the literacy programme jumped from 100 000 in the previous year to over 900 000 in the year the soap opera aired and decreased to about 400 000 the year after the soap opera ended.

Mass media programmes incorporating social-cognitive learning principles have since tackled social problems all over the world. Our 'Research close-up' describes an experiment that implemented and evaluated one of these programmes.

USING SOCIAL-COGNITIVE THEORY TO PREVENT AIDS: A NATIONAL EXPERIMENT

SOURCE: P.W. Vaughan, E.M. Rogers, A. Singhal and R.M. Swalehe (2000) Entertainment-education and HIV/AIDS prevention: a field experiment in Tanzania, *Journal of Health Communication*, vol. 5, pp. 81–100.

INTRODUCTION

In the 1990s, the African nation of Tanzania, like many countries, faced a growing AIDS crisis that was fuelled by risky sexual practices and widespread misinformation about HIV transmission. Many Tanzanians believed that HIV was spread by mosquitoes or the lubricant on condoms. Some men believed that AIDS could be cured by having sex with a virgin (Bandura, 2002a). HIV/AIDS was widely spread through heterosexual contact between truck drivers and prostitutes who frequented the areas where truckers made stops.

To combat this crisis and other societal problems, the Tanzanian government and Radio Tanzania produced and aired 208 episodes of a radio soap opera over several years. The content of this series was carefully designed by educators, government officials, members of the clergy and other consultants to take advantage of principles from social-cognitive theory. In this five-year study, Peter Vaughan and his colleagues (2000) measured the effects of the radio programme on listeners' attitudes and sexual practices.

METHOD

The soap opera featured three types of role models. Positive role models were knowledgeable about HIV/AIDs, minimized risky sex and ultimately attained rewarding social outcomes. Transitional role models began by acting irresponsibly but eventually adopted safer sexual practices. Negative role models, such as a major character named Mkwaju, engaged in risky sex that led to punishing outcomes. Mkwaju was a promiscuous, married truck driver who had unprotected sex with many girlfriends and ignored warnings about HIV/AIDS. During the series his wife, fearing infection, leaves him. Later, Mkwaju contracts HIV and dies of AIDS.

The programme's content was designed to (1) make listeners realize that they were at risk for contracting HIV/AIDS, (2) increase listeners' self-efficacy by showing them how to control the risk, and (3) get listeners to reduce their number of sexual partners and use condoms when having sex. This prime-time soap opera was broadcast twice weekly to six geographic regions (e.g., the experimental regions) of Tanzania for five years. A seventh geographic region served as a control region for the first three years and received the radio programme for only the final two years. Each year interviewers gathered information about participants' attitudes, sexual behaviours, and personal characteristics. One or more family members from roughly 2750 randomly chosen households participated.

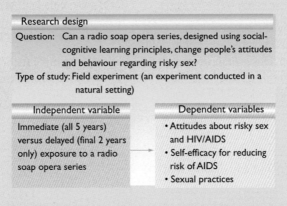

Research design

Question: Can a radio soap opera series, designed using social-cognitive learning principles, change people's attitudes and behaviour regarding risky sex?

Type of study: Field experiment (an experiment conducted in a natural setting)

Independent variable	Dependent variables
Immediate (all 5 years) versus delayed (final 2 years only) exposure to a radio soap opera series	• Attitudes about risky sex and HIV/AIDS • Self-efficacy for reducing risk of AIDS • Sexual practices

RESULTS

Just over half of the participants living in the six experimental regions listened to the soap opera, a remarkably high figure given that many Tanzanians did not own radios. The typical listener heard 108 of the 204 episodes, and about 80 per cent said that the programme helped them learn about preventing HIV/AIDS. Compared with people who were not exposed to the programme, those who tuned in became more likely to believe that they were at risk of contracting HIV/AIDS but could control this risk through safer sexual practices. Listeners identified with the soap opera's positive role models, spoke more often with their partners about HIV/AIDS, reduced their number of sexual partners and increased their use of condoms. These findings were replicated in the seventh geographic region after it was switched from being a control group to an experimental group.

DISCUSSION

This study illustrates how a scientific theory can guide the development of a treatment programme that addresses a major societal problem. The project had several features of an experiment. There was an independent variable (exposure/no exposure to the programme) and many dependent variables (participants' attitudes and sexual behaviours). By cleverly turning the comparison region into an experimental region after three years, the researchers were able to test whether their initial findings were due to social learning from the radio programme, or to a more global change in behaviour across society.

Still, conducting large-scale research in the real world presents difficult challenges that can threaten a study's internal validity. Within each experimental region, the researchers could not control who tuned into the radio programmes. Indeed, listeners and non listeners differed in several ways (e.g., listeners were somewhat better educated and wealthier). To minimize the chance that such factors would distort the results, the researchers statistically adjusted for these factors when they analysed the data.

The study also relied heavily on participants' self-reports. One drawback of self-reports is that participants may distort their answers in a socially desirable way, especially when answering sensitive questions. However, by gathering some objective data, such as increases in the number of condoms distributed in these regions, the researchers were able to corroborate some of the self-report measures. In sum, this project was an ambitious attempt to change people's attitudes and behaviour on a national level.

IN REVIEW

- Observational learning occurs by watching the behaviour of a model

- Bandura's social-cognitive theory proposes that modelling involves four steps: attention, retention, reproduction, and motivation. Observing successful models can increase people's self-efficacy and thus motivate them to perform the modelled behaviour.

- Children can learn aggressive and pro-social behaviours by watching models. Even when viewing an aggressive model who is punished, children may learn the behaviour and display it at a later time.

- Modelling is often a key instructional technique in everyday skill-learning situations. Psychologists have applied modelling concepts to increase people's pro-social behaviour.

- Social-cognitive theory has helped stimulate intervention programmes to address social problems, such as illiteracy and HIV/AIDS.

THE ADAPTIVE BRAIN

We began this chapter by noting that learning represents your personal adaptation to the circumstances you encounter throughout your life. To close the chapter, we would like to emphasize that your ability to learn and adapt depends not only on networks of brain structures and circuits, but also on the brain's own ability to adapt – to modify its structure and functioning – in response to experience.

LEARNING THROUGH CONNECTIONS

How do these modifications take place? In the 1800s, the prevalent view was that new memories are formed through the growth of new cells in the brain. However, Spanish physiologist, Santiago Ramon y Cajal (see Fig. 7.36a), proposed that learning might occur through changes in the strengths of connection between nerve cells. In the mid-twentieth century, Donald Hebb (1949) took this idea a step further by proposing that these changes in connection strength may be caused by concurrent activity across a connection or synapse in the brain. This mechanism has become known as the Hebb rule. Can simple mechanisms like this explain how learning happens in the brain? Modern day 'neural network modellers' attempt to understand how learning and memory can be instantiated in the neurons and synapses in our central nervous systems. They construct **neural network (or connectionist) models** which learn new information through changes in the connections between mathematically simulated neurons (or 'nodes'). Figure 7.36c shows a very simple neural network which illustrates how the Hebb rule could lead to the kind of learning which occurs in classical conditioning. The fact that the node responding to the CS and the cell controlling salivation are active at the same time during conditioning means that the connection between them is strengthened. Later the tone node will activate the salivation node on its own. Similar processes could be happening in the neurons and synapses of a dog's brain while it takes part in a Pavlovian conditioning experiment. Neural network and connectionist modellers usually focus on more complex forms of learning such as the ability to

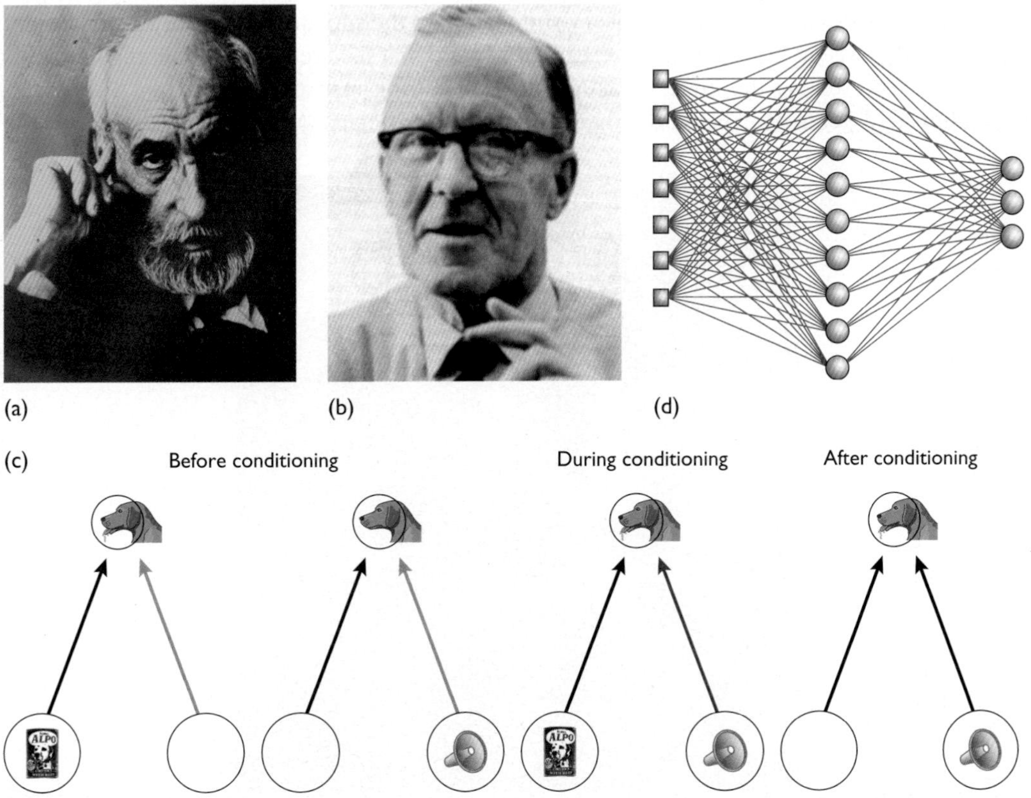

> **neural network (or connectionist) models**
> learn new information through changes in the connections between mathematically simulated neurons

FIGURE 7.36

Our brains learn new information by altering the connections between different neurons. This mechanism was first proposed by Santigo Ramon y Cajal (a). Donald O. Hebb (b) proposed a specific mechanism where simultaneous activity across a synapse (or connection) would increase the strength of that connection. The very simple connectionist model illustrated in (c), illustrates how experience and Hebb's rule can interact to lead to new behaviour (in this case Pavlovian conditioning of salivation to a tone). Black arrows indicate strong connections. Grey arrows indicate weak connections. Red arrows indicate a connection which is strengthening. In this example, the connection between the unit perceiving a tone and the salivation unit strengthens during conditioning because both units are active at once. More complex kinds of learning have been modelled with much larger neural networks (d).

(a) (b) (d)

(c) Before conditioning During conditioning After conditioning

learn to read words (McClelland and Rumelhart, 1986). These kinds of learning require more complicated neural networks containing more nodes and more connections (Fig. 7.36d). We return to the role of connections when we discuss the neural basis of memories in the next chapter (Chapter 8, 'Memory').

WHERE DOES LEARNING HAPPEN IN THE BRAIN?

No single part of the brain controls learning. For example, the hypothalamus and neural pathways involving dopamine play a key role in regulating our ability to experience reward (Olds, 1958; Rolls, 2000). Humans report pleasure when specific areas of the hypothalamus are electrically stimulated, and both humans and rats will learn to repeatedly press a button or lever to receive these electrical reinforcers. The cerebellum plays an important role in acquiring some classically conditioned movements, such as conditioned eyeblink responses, whereas the amygdala is centrally involved in acquiring conditioned fears (Schafe and LeDoux, 2002). We take a closer look at brain processes that underlie learning when we discuss memory in the next chapter.

Biology affects learning, but learning also influences brain functioning (Fanselow and Poulos, 2005). As we noted in the previous chapter, in a new task, as you make the transition from inexperienced novice to experienced master, your brain is able to rely less on conscious processing and instead process more information without consciousness. Highly trained athletes and musicians can execute incredibly complex skills with a minimum of conscious thought. No doubt you can think of skills that seem almost automatic to you now (perhaps driving a car or typing on a keyboard) but which required considerable effort when you first learned them. As we gain experience at novel tasks, the brain's frontal lobes – the seat of executive functions such as decision making and planning – tend to exercise less control and become less active (Eliassen et al., 2003). Indeed, notice in Figure 7.37 how a video-game player's brain activity generally decreased after practising the game.

Learning also etches its imprints on the brain's physical structure. During countless hours of practice and performance, a violinist makes continuous, precise movements with the fingers of his or her left hand while the right hand moves the bow (Fig. 7.38). This constant fingering of the strings provides a great deal of sensory stimulation to the somatosensory cortex of the right hemisphere. By using brain imaging, researchers found that the area in this brain region that is devoted to representing the fingers was larger among string-instrument musicians (who averaged almost 12 years of experience) than among non-musicians. Moreover, the earlier in life

Focus 7.22

How does learning influence the brain? Summarize biological, psychological and environmental factors involved in learning.

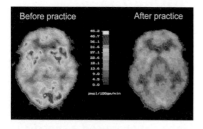

Before practice   After practice

FIGURE 7.37

While learning a computer game, the brain of a novice player is highly active and uses a lot of energy, as indicated by the large yellow and red areas in the left PET scan. As the right scan shows, energy consumption decreases with experience.

FIGURE 7.38

The precise, constant left-hand movements involved in fingering the strings provides a great deal of sensory stimulation to this violinist's right-hemisphere somatosensory cortex.

that the musicians had started to play their instruments, the greater the size of this brain area. In contrast, the left-hemisphere somatosensory area representing the right-hand fingers of the musicians and non-musicians did not differ (Elbert et al., 1995).

Because these findings are correlational, they cannot clearly establish cause and effect. Perhaps it was not playing music that caused the brain differences. Maybe it was the other way around: pre-existing brain differences helped these individuals become musicians. Yet controlled experiments with animals do indeed show that learning leaves its mark not only on the somatosensory cortex but on other parts of the brain as well. For example, when monkeys and rats learn skilled movements that require them to use their fingers or paws, the representations of these body parts in their motor cortex change (Kleim et al., 2002).

A recent topic of interest in learning research is our ability to improve our skills while we are not actually practising them – *offline learning* or *consolidation*. A number of laboratories are now uncovering evidence that some large improvements in ability at certain learned skills such as perceptual discriminations and sequential finger movements (as when learning a new piece on the violin) are observable after we have been asleep (Robertson et al., 2004). In addition, these improvements have been found to be linked to the amount of time we spend in particular stages of sleep. In particular, increased time spent in sleep stage II (see Chapter 6) is implicated in improvements in motor skill (Walker et al., 2002). It seems that active processes in our brain consolidate what we have learned while we sleep.

Learning's effects on the brain occur throughout the life cycle. Compared with newborn rats that grow up in standard cages, litter mates that grow up in enriched environments – with toys and greater opportunities to learn – develop heavier brains whose neurons have more dendrites and synapses and greater concentrations of various neurotransmitters (Rosenzweig, 1984). In turn, this increased brain development enables animals to perform better on subsequent learning tasks (Meaney et al., 1991). And in humans, exposure to stimulating environments and new learning opportunities during late adulthood seems to slow declines in brain functioning, as measured by better performance on intellectual and perceptual tasks (Goldstein et al., 1997; Schaie, 2005). In a sense, then, every day you are alive your brain adapts and continues its own personal evolution; its neural networks and patterns of activity are affected not only by your genetic endowment but by your learning experiences as well.

In closing, Figure 7.39 summarizes some of the environmental, psychological, and biological factors that play key roles in learning. As you study the learning concepts we've covered, try to apply them to your own behaviour. Think about the roles that classical conditioning, operant conditioning, and observational learning play in developing and maintaining important behaviours in your life.

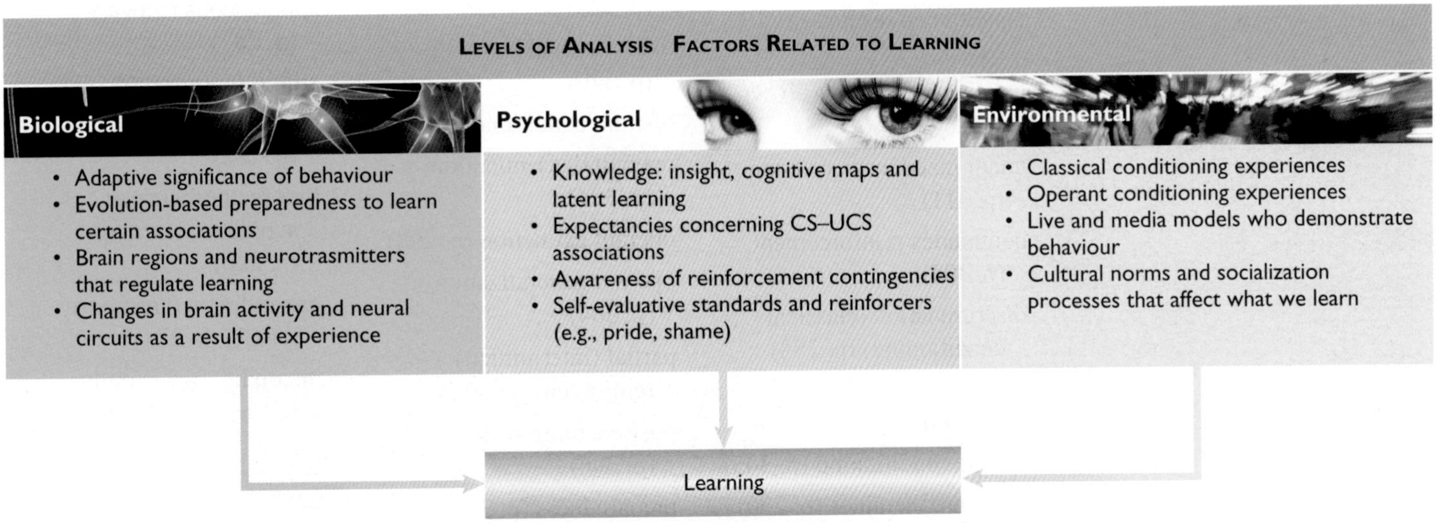

FIGURE 7.39

Levels of analysis: factors related to learning.

LEVELS OF ANALYSIS FACTORS RELATED TO LEARNING		
Biological	**Psychological**	**Environmental**
• Adaptive significance of behaviour • Evolution-based preparedness to learn certain associations • Brain regions and neurotransmitters that regulate learning • Changes in brain activity and neural circuits as a result of experience	• Knowledge: insight, cognitive maps and latent learning • Expectancies concerning CS–UCS associations • Awareness of reinforcement contingencies • Self-evaluative standards and reinforcers (e.g., pride, shame)	• Classical conditioning experiences • Operant conditioning experiences • Live and media models who demonstrate behaviour • Cultural norms and socialization processes that affect what we learn

Learning

IN REVIEW

- The brain's ability to adapt and modify itself in response to experience underlies our ability to learn.

- No single part of the brain regulates all learning. The hypothalamus and dopamine pathways play a role in enabling us to experience reward. The cerebellum and the amygdala are involved in acquiring different types of classically conditioned responses.

- Studies examining the brains of people and animals who have learned specific skills, as well as environmental-enrichment experiments with animals, support the conclusion that learning alters the brain.

KEY TERMS AND CONCEPTS

Each term has been boldfaced and defined in the chapter on the page indicated in parentheses.

anticipatory nausea and vomiting (ANV) (p. 292)

attentional theories of classical conditioning (p. 319)

aversion therapy (p. 291)

aversive punishment (positive punishment, punishment by application) (p. 299)

avoidance conditioning (p. 305)

chaining (p. 303)

classical conditioning (p. 283)

cognitive map (p. 315)

conditioned response (CR) (p. 285)

conditioned stimulus (CS) (p. 285)

conditioned taste aversion (p. 311)

continuous reinforcement (p. 304)

discrimination (classical conditioning) (p. 288)

discriminative stimulus (p. 296)

escape conditioning (p. 305)

exposure therapies (p. 290)

extinction (classical conditioning) (p. 286)

habituation (p. 282)

higher-order conditioning (p. 288)

insight (p. 314)

instinctive drift (p. 313)

latent inhibition (p. 318)

latent learning (p. 316)

law of effect (p. 294)

learning (p. 281)

negative reinforcement (p. 298)

neural network (or connectionist) models (p. 325)

observational learning (p. 320)

operant conditioning (p. 294)

operant discrimination (p. 304)

operant extinction (p. 298)

operant generalization (p. 304)

partial (intermittent) reinforcement (p. 304)

positive reinforcement (p. 296)

preparedness (p. 310)

primary reinforcers (p. 297)

punishment (p. 295)

reinforcement (p. 294)

response cost (negative punishment, punishment by removal) (p. 301)

secondary (conditioned) reinforcers (p. 297)

self-efficacy (p. 321)

sensitization (p. 282)

shaping (p. 303)

Skinner box (p. 294)

social-cognitive theory (social-learning theory) (p. 321)

spontaneous recovery (p. 287)

stimulus control (p. 304)

stimulus generalization (p. 288)

two-factor theory of avoidance learning (p. 306)

unconditioned response (UCR) (p. 284)

unconditioned stimulus (UCS) (p. 284)

WHAT DO YOU THINK?

WHY DID MICHELLE'S CAR PHOBIA PERSIST? (p. 287)

We cannot know for sure why Michelle's anxiety reaction failed to extinguish, but a strong possibility is that she was not exposed to sufficient extinction trials. The key to extinction is the presentation of the CS (car) without the UCS (events of the crash). If Michelle avoided cars after her accident, then there was little opportunity for the CS to occur without the UCS. This is the unfortunate irony of phobias: people avoid the stimulus they fear, thereby depriving themselves of an opportunity to reduce their fear (extinction trials). Thus, the key ingredient to extinction is not the mere passage of time but repeated presentation of the CS without the UCS.

Applying this same principle, can you explain why the US Navy veterans who heard the battle gong automatically showed a strong alarm reaction 15 years after the war's end? Again, we cannot know for sure, but once the combat ended, the sailors most likely had insufficient opportunities to experience extinction trials. In other words, the way to extinguish their fear would be to sound the battle gong (CS) repeatedly without the associated danger of manning battle stations and preparing for combat (UCS).

WAS THE 'LITTLE ALBERT' STUDY ETHICAL? (p. 291)

In forming your judgement, did you consider the ethical criteria discussed in Chapter 2 (pp. 46–8)? With those criteria in mind, let us imagine that we are reviewing this research proposal in the early 1900s.

(1) If you initially thought that you would not approve a study like this, then consider the following:

- Suppose the experimenters promise to obtain informed consent from Albert's parents and keep everyone's identity confidential.
- Although Albert will experience some short-term stress, consider the enormous potential benefits of this study. If we can classically condition phobias in humans, this may revolutionize thinking about how phobias develop and could lead to faster, more effective treatments. These treatments could benefit countless people with phobias.
- Suppose that the experimenters promise to use procedures based on learning theory to extinguish Albert's phobia after the study, so that he will not suffer any negative long-term consequences.

Under these conditions and with these issues in mind, would you now approve the study?

(2) If your initial judgement (or new judgement) is that you would approve this study, then consider the following:

- Would it be ethical to proceed with the study if the parents did not give informed consent?
- Based on learning theory, is there not a risk that the phobia will generalize to other stimuli? Consider the short-term and long-term psychological risks associated with this possibility if Albert's phobia persists.
- If a phobia is successfully conditioned, what about the treatment to eliminate it? What steps are in place to guarantee that Albert will receive this treatment? Has the treatment been scientifically tested with humans? What is the failure rate? If there already is good evidence that the treatment is effective, then why conduct this study?

Applying today's ethical standards to the 'Little Albert' study, we believe it clearly would have been rejected. Even with informed consent and a secure system in place to guarantee that an infant would receive treatment afterward, the risks would have been considered too high. At the time of the actual experiment, there was insufficient evidence to clearly support the effectiveness of the extinction treatment with humans. An alternative, more ethical approach would have been to study whether learning-based treatments are effective with patients who already have phobias.

CAN YOU EXPLAIN THE 'SUPERMARKET TANTRUM'? (p. 302)

The father's initial refusal to buy sweets is followed by an aversive stimulus (the tantrum). This punishes the father's response, and after two tantrums he no longer refuses the request. When the father eventually gives in, this removes the aversive stimulus (the tantrum), which negatively reinforces (strengthens) the response of giving in. Thus the father's response of refusing to buy sweets is weakened by punishment, and the response of giving in is strengthened by negative reinforcement. Just as importantly, however, the child has learned that throwing a tantrum pays off. The tantrum was positively reinforced by the consequence of getting sweets.

CHAPTER EIGHT

MEMORY

The charm, one might say the genius of memory, is that it is choosy, chancy, and temperamental.

ELIZABETH BOWEN

Some people are famous for their extraordinary remembering; others for their extraordinary forgetting. Consider Rajan Mahadevan, who at age 5 sauntered outside his home in India one day while his parents entertained about 40 to 50 guests at a party. Rajan studied the guests' parked cars, returned to the party and then recited all the licence plate numbers from memory, matching each to the proper guest in the order they had parked. While in college, Rajan set a world record by flawlessly recalling the first 31811 digits of pi. He averaged 3.5 digits per second!

How does Rajan perform such amazing feats? When memory researchers at Kansas State University (where Rajan was a student) asked him this very question, he said 'that being asked to describe how he learned numbers was like being asked to describe how he rode a bicycle. He knew how to do both tasks, but he found it difficult to describe either process' (Thompson et al., 1993, p. 13).

In most other ways, Rajan's memory is ordinary. Indeed, he uses a shopping list to remember what to buy at the supermarket. As he notes, 'Unless I put my glasses, wallet and keys together near the door before I leave to start my day, I will surely forget them' (Harris, 2002).

...

You are about to meet HM, who at age 27 had most of his hippocampus and surrounding brain tissue surgically removed to reduce his severe epileptic seizures. The operation succeeded, but it unexpectedly left HM with *amnesia*, or memory loss.

When you talk with HM, he can discuss his childhood, teens and early twenties, for those memories are intact. Indeed, for the most part, at age 27 HM's amnesia did not rob him of his past. Rather, it robbed him of his future.

HM lost the ability to form new memories that he can consciously recall. Typically, once an experience or fact leaves his immediate train of thought, he cannot remember it. Spend the day with HM, depart and return minutes later, and he will not recall having met you. He reads magazines over and over as if he has never seen them before. A favourite uncle has died, but HM cannot remember. Thus every time HM asks how his uncle is, he experiences shock and grief as though it were the first time he learned of his uncle's death.

HM's surgery took place in 1953, and researchers have studied him for over 50 years (Skotko et al., 2004). No matter how many years pass, HM's memory for events contains little after 1953. Even his sense of identity is frozen in time. HM recalls himself looking like a young man but cannot remember the ageing image of himself that he sees in the mirror.

Memory refers to the processes that allow us to record, store, and later retrieve experiences and information. Memory adds richness and context to our lives, but even more fundamentally, it allows us to learn from experience and thus adapt to changing environments. From an evolutionary standpoint, without the capacity to remember we would not have survived as a species.

As the cases of Rajan and HM illustrate, memory is complex. How did Rajan remember over 31 000 digits of pi? Why is it, as Figure 8.1 shows, that HM can remember the skilled movements needed to perform a new task yet swear each time he encounters the task that he has never even seen it before (Milner, 1965)? In this chapter we explore the fascinating nature of memory.

(a)

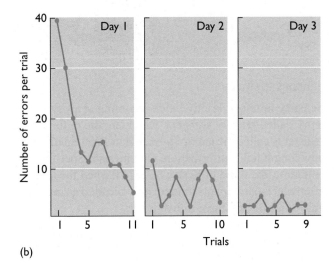

(b)

FIGURE 8.1

Learning without consciously remembering.

(a) On this complex task, a participant traces a pattern while looking at its mirror image, which also shows the writing hand moving in the direction opposite to its actual movement. (b) HM's performance on this task rapidly improved over time – he made fewer and fewer errors – indicating that he had retained a memory of how to perform the task. Yet each time he performed it, he stated that he had never seen the task before and had to have the instructions explained again.

SOURCE: adapted from Milner, 1965.

MEMORY AS INFORMATION PROCESSING

Psychological research on memory has a rich tradition, dating back to late-nineteenth-century Europe. By the 1960s, computer advances and the cognitive revolution in psychology led to a new metaphor that continues to guide memory research: the mind as a processing system that encodes, stores and retrieves information. **Encoding** refers to getting information into the system by translating it into a neural code that your brain processes. This is a little like what happens when you type on a computer keyboard; your keystrokes are translated into an electrical code that the computer can understand and process. **Storage** involves retaining information over time. Once in the system, information must be filed away and saved, as happens when a computer stores information temporarily in RAM (random access memory) and more permanently on a hard drive. Finally, **retrieval** refers to processes that access stored information. On a computer, retrieval occurs when you give a software command (e.g., 'open file') that transfers information from the hard drive back to RAM and the screen, where you can scroll through it. Keep in mind, however, that this analogy between human and computer is crude. For one thing, people routinely forget and distort information, and sometimes 'remember' events that never occurred (Loftus and Bernstein, 2005). Human memory is highly dynamic, and its complexity cannot be fully captured by any existing information-processing model.

Encoding, storage and retrieval represent what our memory system does with information. Before exploring these processes more fully, let us examine some basic components of memory.

memory
the processes that allow us to record, store, and later retrieve experiences and information

encoding
getting information into the system by translating it into a neural code that your brain processes

storage
retaining information over time

retrieval
processes that access stored information

Focus 8.1

What is memory, and how is it like an information-processing system?

FIGURE 8.2

The three-stage model of memory.

In this model, memory has three major components: (1) sensory memory, which briefly holds incoming sensory information; (2) working (short-term) memory, which processes certain information received from sensory memory and information retrieved from long-term memory; and (3) long-term memory, which stores information for longer periods of time.

SOURCE: adapted from Atkinson and Shiffrin, 1968.

sensory memory
briefly holds incoming sensory information

A THREE-STAGE MODEL

The model in Figure 8.2, developed by Atkinson and Shiffrin (1968) and subsequently modified, depicts memory as having three major components: sensory memory working (short-term) memory and long-term memory. Other models have been proposed, but this three-stage framework has been the most influential.

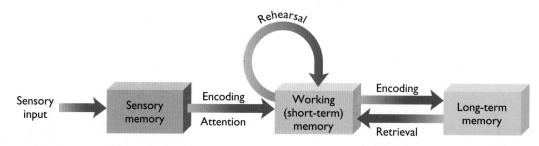

Sensory Memory

Sensory memory briefly holds incoming sensory information. It comprises different subsystems, called *sensory registers*, which are the initial information processors. Our visual sensory register is called the *iconic store*, and in 1960 Sperling conducted a classic experiment to assess how long it holds information. On one task, Sperling arranged 12 letters in three rows and four columns, like those in Figure 8.3. He flashed the array on a screen for a twentieth of a second, after which participants immediately recalled as many letters as they could. Typically, they were able to recall only three to five letters.

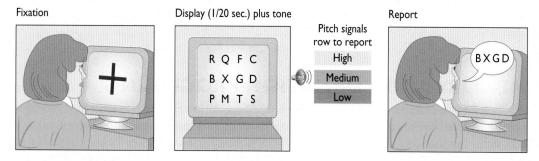

FIGURE 8.3

Sperling's classic study of iconic memory.

After a participant fixates on a screen, a matrix of letters is flashed for a twentieth of a second. In one condition, participants do not hear any tone and must immediately report as many letters as they can. In another condition, a high-, medium- or low-pitched tone signals the participant to report either the top, middle or bottom row. If the tone occurs just as the letters are flashed off, participants typically can report three or all four letters, no matter which row is signalled.

Why was recall so poor? Did participants have too little time to scan all the letters, or had they seen the whole array, only to have their iconic memory fade before they could report all the letters? To find out, Sperling conducted another experimental condition. This time, just as the letters were flashed off, participants heard either a high-, medium- or low-pitched tone, which signalled them to report either the top, middle or bottom row of letters.

In this case, participants often could report all four letters in whichever row was signalled. Their not knowing which row would be signalled ahead of time implies that their iconic memory had stored an image of the whole array, and they now had time to 'read' their iconic image of any one line before it rapidly disappeared. If this logic is correct, then participants should

Focus 8.2

Describe sensory memory. How long does information remain in iconic memory, and how did Sperling determine this?

have done poorly if the signalling tone was delayed. Indeed, with just a 1-second delay, performance was no better than without the tone. As Figure 8.4 illustrates, it is difficult, perhaps impossible, to retain complete information in purely visual form for more than a fraction of a second. In contrast, our auditory sensory register, called the *echoic store*, can hold information about the precise details of a sound for several seconds (Winkler et al., 2002).

Working/Short-Term Memory

Most information in sensory memory rapidly fades away. But according to the original three-stage model, through selective attention some information enters **short-term memory**, a memory store that temporarily holds a limited amount of information.

Focus 8.3

Discuss the limits of short-term/working memory. What are the four major components of working memory?

Memory codes   Once information leaves sensory memory, it must be represented by some type of code if it is to be retained in short-term memory. For example, the words that someone just spoke to you ('I like your new haircut') must somehow become represented in your mind. **Memory codes** are mental representations of some type of information or stimulus, and they can take various forms. We may try to form mental images (*visual codes*), code something by sound (*phonological codes*) or focus on the meaning of a stimulus (*semantic codes*). For physical actions, such as learning sports or playing musical instruments, we code patterns of movement (*motor codes*).

The form of a memory code often does not correspond to the form of the original stimulus. As you read these words (visual stimuli) you are probably not storing images of the way the letters look. Rather, you are likely forming phonological codes (as you say the words silently) and semantic codes (as you think about their meaning). Thus when people are presented with lists of words or letters and asked to recall them immediately, they often make phonetic errors. They might mistakenly recall a *V* as a *B* because of the similarity in how the letters sound (Conrad, 1964).

Capacity and duration   Short-term memory can hold only a limited amount of information at a time. Depending on the stimulus, such as a series of unrelated numbers or letters, most people can hold no more than five to nine meaningful items in short-term memory, leading George Miller (1956) to set the capacity limit at 'the magical number seven, plus or minus two'. To demonstrate this, try administering the digit-span test in Table 8.1 to some people you know.

If short-term memory capacity is so limited, how can we remember and understand sentences as we read? For a partial answer, read the letters below (one per second); then cover them up and write down as many letters as you can remember, in the order presented.

B I R C D E R Y K A E U Q S A S A W T I

Did you have any trouble? Now, with the order of the letters reversed (and a few spaces added), try to remember all 20 letters.

IT WAS A SQUEAKY RED CRIB

short-term memory

memory store that temporarily holds a limited amount of information

memory codes

mental representations of some type of information or stimulus

TABLE 8.1 DIGIT-SPAN TEST

Directions: Starting with the top sequence, read these numbers at a steady rate of one per second. Immediately after saying the last number in each series, signal the person to recall the numbers in order. Most people can recall a maximum sequence of five to nine digits.

8 3 5 2
4 3 9 3 1
7 1 4 9 3 7
5 4 6 9 2 3 6
1 5 2 4 8 5 8 4
9 3 2 6 5 8 2 1 4
6 8 1 3 1 9 4 7 3 5
4 2 4 6 9 5 2 1 7 4 3
3 7 9 8 4 6 1 7 2 4 9 5

chunking

combining individual items
into larger units of meaning

No doubt you found the second task much easier. The limit on short-term storage capacity concerns the number of meaningful *units* that can be recalled, and the 20 letters have been combined into six meaningful units (words). Combining individual items into larger units of meaning is called **chunking**, which aids recall.

Short-term memory is limited in duration as well as capacity. Have you ever been introduced to someone and then, moments later, realized that you have forgotten her or his name? Without rehearsal, information in short-term memory generally has a shelf life of up to 20 seconds (Fig. 8.5; Peterson and Peterson, 1959). However, by rehearsing information – such as when you look up a telephone number and keep saying it to yourself while waiting to use a phone – you can extend its duration in short-term memory.

FIGURE 8.5

Rapid forgetting of non-rehearsed information in working memory.

Participants who were prevented from rehearsing three letter syllables in working memory showed almost no recall of the letters within 18 seconds, illustrating the rapid forgetting of information in working memory.

SOURCE: based on Peterson and Peterson, 1959.

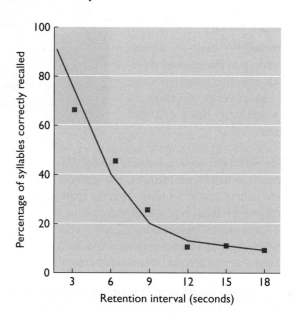

working memory

a limited-capacity system that
temporarily stores and
processes information

Putting short-term memory to work   The original three-stage model viewed short-term memory as a temporary holding station along the route from sensory to long-term memory. Information that remained in short-term memory long enough presumably was transferred into more permanent storage. Cognitive scientists now reject this view as too passive. Instead, they view short-term memory as **working memory**, a limited-capacity system that temporarily stores and processes information (Baddeley, 2002). In other words, working memory is a mental workspace that stores information, actively manipulates it, and supports other cognitive functions such as problem solving and planning.

Components of working memory   According to one influential model, working memory has several components, as shown in Figure 8.6 (Baddeley, 2002; Baddeley and Hitch, 1974). One component, the *phonological loop*, briefly stores mental representations of sounds. The phonological loop is active when you listen to a spoken word or when you sound out a word to yourself as you read. Silently repeating the name of person to whom you are being introduced will briefly refresh the acoustic codes stored in the phonological loop. Baddeley and Hitch (1974) proposed that the phonological loop consists of two components, namely, a phonological store and an articulatory rehearsal system. It is the articulatory rehearsal system that is used to silently repeat the information that you are trying to hold in the phonological store.

A second component, the *visuospatial sketchpad*, briefly stores visual and spatial information, as occurs when you form a mental image of someone's face or of the spatial layout of your bedroom. Note that the phonological loop and visuospatial sketchpad can be active simultaneously. For example, you can silently repeat the word *sunset* while at the same time holding a mental image of a sun-

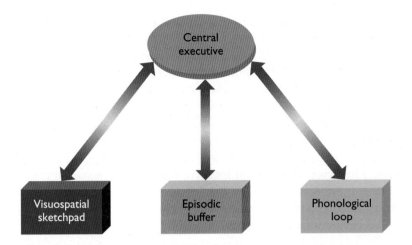

FIGURE 8.6

Components of working memory.

According to Baddeley's most recent model, working memory has four components.

SOURCE: adapted from Baddeley, 2002.

set or, for that matter, of an elephant. This notion has important implications for much of the research that has utilized the concept of working memory (see 'Research close-up' box).

These two subsystems of the working memory model are often referred to as the 'slave systems' as it is proposed that they are controlled by the central executive (see below). There has been a great deal of influential research on the components of the working memory model and much of the early work focused on the phonological loop and the visuospatial sketchpad.

Conrad and Hull (1964) found that participants' immediate serial recall of similar sounding letter strings – *V, P, D, C, G, B* was poorer than that for a string of dissimilar sounding items – *R, X, N, Y, H, F*. It is believed that this finding reflects the phonological nature of the store. However, similarity of meaning does not have any effect in immediate recall (Baddeley, 1966), suggesting that there is no semantic processing within the store.

A final important finding with regard to the phonological loop is that of the word length effect (Baddeley, Thomson and Buchanan (1975). For example there is better immediate serial recall of strings of short words (car, bit, rag, mat, see, top) than strings of long words (aeroplane, relationship, sacrifice, presentation, television). This effect clearly demonstrates that what can be held in store in the phonological loop is dependent on the time that it takes to rehearse those items in the articulatory rehearsal system. The phonological loop has also been implicated in language learning both in children and in adults learning a second language (Baddeley, Gathercole and Papagno, 1998).

A third component, called the *episodic buffer*, provides a temporary storage space where information from long-term memory and from the phonological and/or visuospatial subsystems can be integrated, manipulated and made available for conscious awareness (Baddeley, 2002). For example, after reading or hearing me say 'How much is 87 plus 36?' your phonological loop initially maintains the acoustic codes for the sounds of 87 and 36 in working memory. Your visuospatial sketchpad also might maintain a mental image of the numbers. But to do this task, the rules for performing addition must be retrieved from your long-term memory and temporarily stored in the episodic buffer, where they are integrated with (i.e., applied to) information from the phonological and visuospatial subsystems. This creates the ingredients for the conscious perceptions that you experience as you perform the mental addition (e.g., '7 + 6 = 13, carry the 1…').

The episodic buffer also comes into play when you chunk information. British psychologist Alan Baddeley (2002) notes that despite the phonological loop's very limited acoustic storage capacity, people can routinely listen to and then repeat novel sentences that are 15 or 16 words long. It is within the episodic buffer, he proposes, that groups of words are chunked into meaningful phrases and stored (and phrases can be further chunked into sentences), enabling us to recall relatively long sections of prose.

The fourth component of working memory, called the *central executive*, directs the overall action. When solving arithmetic problems, for example, the central executive does not store the numbers or rules of addition. Instead, it plans and controls the sequence of actions that need to be performed, divides and allocates attention to the other subsystems and integrates information within the episodic buffer. It also may monitor the progress as interim steps are completed (DeStefano and LeFevre, 2004).

Long-Term Memory

long-term memory

our vast library of more durable stored memories

Long-term memory is our vast library of more durable stored memories. Perhaps there have been times in your life, such as periods of intensive study during final examinations, when you have felt as if there is no room for storing so much as one more new fact inside your brain. Yet as far as we know, long-term storage capacity essentially is unlimited, and once formed, a long-term memory can endure for up to a lifetime.

Focus 8.4

Describe long-term memory and its limits. Based on the three-stage model, why does the serial position effect occur?

Are short-term and long-term memory really distinct? Case studies of amnesia victims such as HM suggest so. If you told HM your name or some fact, he could remember it briefly but could not form a long-term memory of it. Experiments in which people with normal memory learn lists of words also support this distinction. Suppose that we present you with a series of 15 unrelated words, one word at a time. Immediately after seeing or hearing the last word, you are to recall as many words as you can, in any order you wish. As Figure 8.7 illustrates, most experiments find that words at the end and beginning of a list are the easiest to recall. This U-shaped pattern is called the **serial position effect**, meaning that the ability to recall an item is influenced by the item's position in a series. The serial position effect has two components: a *primacy effect*, reflecting the superior recall of the earliest items, and a *recency effect*, representing the superior recall of the most recent items.

serial position effect

the ability to recall an item is influenced by the item's position in a series

FIGURE 8.7

The serial position effect.

Immediate recall of a word list produces a serial position curve, where primacy and recency effects are both evident. However, even a delay of 15 to 30 seconds in recall (during which rehearsal is prevented) eliminates the recency effect, indicating that the later items in the word list have disappeared from short-term memory.

SOURCE: adapted from Glanzer and Cunitz, 1966.

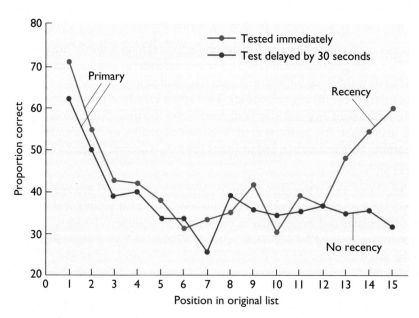

What causes the primacy effect? According to the three-stage model, as the first few words enter short-term memory, we can quickly rehearse them and transfer them into long-term memory. However, as the list gets longer, short-term memory rapidly fills up and there are too many words to keep repeating before the next word arrives. Therefore, beyond the first few words, it is harder to rehearse the items and they are less likely to get transferred into long-term memory. If this hypothesis is correct, then the primacy effect should decrease if we are prevented from rehearsing the early words, say, by being presented the list at a faster rate. Indeed, this is what happens (Glanzer, 1972).

As for the recency effect, the last few words still linger in short-term memory and have the benefit of not being bumped out by new information. Thus if we try to recall the list immediately, all we have to do is recite the last words from short-term memory before they decay (i.e., fade away). In sum, according to the three-stage model, the primacy effect is due to the transfer of early words into long-term memory, whereas the recency effect is due to the continued presence of information in short-term memory.

If this explanation is correct, then it must be possible to wipe out the recency effect – but not the primacy effect – by eliminating the last words from short-term memory. This happens when the recall test is delayed, even for as little as 15 to 30 seconds, *and* we are prevented from rehearsing the last words. To prevent rehearsal, we might be asked to briefly count a series of numbers immediately after the last word is presented (Glanzer and Cunitz, 1966; Postman and Phillips, 1965). Now by the time we try to recall the last words, they will have faded from short-term memory or been bumped out by the numbers task (6 … 7 … 8 … 9 …). Figure 8.7 shows that under delayed conditions, the recency effect disappears while the primacy effect remains.

Having examined some basic components of memory, let us now explore more fully how information is encoded, stored and retrieved.

IN REVIEW

- Memory involves three main processes (encoding, storage and retrieval) and three components (sensory memory, working/short-term memory and long-term memory).

- Sensory memory briefly holds incoming sensory information. Some information reaches working memory and long-term memory, where it is mentally represented by visual, phonological, semantic or motor codes.

- Working memory actively processes a limited amount of information and supports other cognitive functions. It has phonological, visuospatial, episodic and executive (co-ordinating) components.

- Long-term memory stores large amounts of information for up to a lifetime. Research on amnesia and on the serial position effect support the distinction between working- and long-term memory.

ENCODING: ENTERING INFORMATION

The holdings of your long-term memory, like those of a library, must be organized if they are to be available when you wish to retrieve them. The more effectively we encode material into long-term memory, the greater the likelihood of retrieving it (Fig. 8.8). Let us explore two basic types of encoding and then examine some ways to optimize encoding quality.

EFFORTFUL AND AUTOMATIC PROCESSING

Think of the parade of information that you have to remember every day: names, meeting times and mountains of university work. Remembering it all

"The matters about which I'm being questioned, Your Honor, are all things I should have included in my long-term memory but which I mistakenly inserted in my short-term memory."

FIGURE 8.8

Ineffective encoding can have practical as well as theoretical significance.

involves *effortful processing*, encoding that is initiated intentionally and requires conscious attention (Hasher and Zacks, 1979). When you rehearse information, make lists and take notes, you are engaging in effortful processing.

In contrast, have you ever been unable to answer an examination question and thought, 'I should know this! I can even picture the diagram on the upper corner of the page!' In this case, you have apparently transferred information about the diagram's location on the page (which you were not trying to learn) into your long-term memory through *automatic processing*, encoding that occurs without intention and requires minimal attention.

Information about the frequency, spatial location and sequence of events is often encoded automatically (Jimenez and Mendez, 2001).

LEVELS OF PROCESSING: WHEN DEEPER IS BETTER

Imagine that you are participating in a laboratory experiment and are about to be shown a list of words, one at a time. Each word will be followed by a question, and all you have to do is answer yes or no. Here are three examples:

1. POTATO 'Is the word in capital letters?'
2. HORSE 'Does the word rhyme with *course*?'
3. TABLE 'Does the word fit in the sentence, "The man peeled the _____"?'

Each question requires effort but differs from the others in an important way. Question 1 requires superficial *structural encoding*, as you only have to notice how the word looks. Question 2 requires a little more effort. You must engage in *phonological* (also called *phonemic*) *encoding* by sounding out the word to yourself and then judging whether it matches the sound of another word. Question 3 requires *semantic encoding* because you must pay attention to what the word means.

Like the three examples above, the words you are about to be presented with in this experiment will be followed by a question that requires either structural, phonological or semantic encoding. Unexpectedly, you will then be given a memory test in which you will be shown a list of words and asked to identify which words were presented earlier. Which group of words will you recognize most easily? Those processed structurally, phonologically, or semantically?

According to the concept of **levels of processing**, the more deeply we process information, the better we will remember it (Craik and Lockhart, 1972). Thus you should best remember those words that you processed semantically, as shown in Figure 8.9. Merely perceiving the structural properties of the words (e.g., uppercase versus lowercase) involves shallow processing, and phonemically encoding words is intermediate. Semantic encoding, however, involves the deepest processing because it requires us to focus on the meaning of information.

Although many experiments have replicated this finding, at times depth of processing can be difficult to measure. If some students prepare for an examination by creating hierarchical outlines while others create detailed flashcards, which method involves deeper processing? If the first group performs better, should we assume that they processed the information more deeply? To

Focus 8.5

Contrast effortful and automatic processing, and discuss the levels-of-processing model.

levels of processing

the more deeply we process information, the better we will remember it

Focus 8.6

Contrast maintenance and elaborative rehearsal. Describe ways to use organization and imagery to enhance encoding.

FIGURE 8.9

Depth of processing and memory.

Participants were shown words and asked questions that required (1) superficial structural processing, (2) somewhat deeper phonemic processing, or (3) deeper semantic processing of each word. Depth of processing increased later recognition of the words in a larger list.

SOURCE: based on Craik and Tulving, 1975.

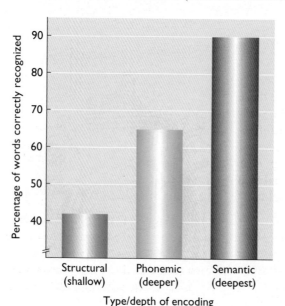

do so, warns Baddeley (1990), is to fall into a trap of circular reasoning. Still, the levels-of-processing model has stimulated much research (Clifford, 2004). There are situations where few would argue with at least a broad distinction between shallow and deep processing. Here is one of them.

EXPOSURE AND REHEARSAL

Years ago one of our students sought advice after failing an examination. He said that he had been to all the lectures and read each chapter three times. Yet not a word in his textbook had been underlined or highlighted. When asked whether he took notes as he read the text or paused to reflect on the information, he said no. Instead, he read and reread each chapter quickly, much like a novel, and assumed that the information would somehow sink in.

Unfortunately, mere exposure to a stimulus without focusing on it represents shallow processing. To demonstrate, try drawing from memory a picture of the smallest-value coin in your country (e.g., a UK penny), accurately locating all the markings. Few people can do this. Even thousands of shallow exposures to a stimulus do not guarantee long-term retention.

Rehearsal goes beyond mere exposure. When we rehearse information, we are thinking about it. But not all rehearsals are created equal. Have you ever seen a live performance of a play and been amazed at the actors' flawless recall of volumes of material in front of live audiences? You may picture the actors reading the script and saying the words over and over, day after day, until they have memorized their lines. This approach, called **maintenance rehearsal**, involves simple, rote repetition, and some students rely on it to learn their course material.

Maintenance rehearsal keeps information active in working memory, as when someone tells you a phone number and you repeat it to yourself as you place the call. However, rote memorization usually is not an optimal method to transfer information into long-term memory.

What, then, is a better method? Professional actors begin not by memorizing but by studying the script in great depth, trying to get into the mindset of their characters. Based on detailed research, Noice and Noice (2002a) note that actors, 'before they gave any thought to memorization, stressed the notion of understanding the ideas behind the utterances, and the reasons the characters used those words to express those ideas' (p. 9). The techniques actors use are examples of **elaborative rehearsal**, which involves focusing on the meaning of information or expanding (i.e., elaborating) on it in some way.

If your study habits include (1) organizing and trying to understand the material rather than just memorizing it, (2) thinking about how it applies to your own life and (3) relating it to concepts or examples you already know, then you are using elaboration. According to Craik and Lockhart (1972), elaborative rehearsal involves deeper processing than maintenance rehearsal, and experiments show that it is more effective in transferring information into long-term memory (Benjamin and Bjork, 2000).

ORGANIZATION AND IMAGERY

JC is an awe-inspiring restaurant waiter. Perhaps you would like a filet mignon, medium-rare, a baked potato, and Thousand Island dressing on your salad? Whatever you order, it represents only one of over 500 options (7 entrees × 5 serving temperatures × 3 side dishes × 5 salad dressings) available at the restaurant where JC works. Yet you and 20 of your friends can place your selections with JC, and he will remember them perfectly without writing them down.

Ericsson and Polson (1988) studied JC and found that he invented an organizational scheme to aid his memory. He divided customers' orders into four categories (entree, temperature, side dish, dressing) and used a different system to encode the orders in each category. For example, he encoded dressings by their initial letter, so orders of Thousand Island, oil and vinegar, blue cheese, and oil and vinegar would become TOBO. Organizational schemes are an excellent way to enhance memory.

maintenance rehearsal
simple, rote repetition

elaborative rehearsal
focusing on the meaning of information or expanding (i.e., elaborating) on it in some way

Hierarchies and Chunking

Organizing material in a *hierarchy* takes advantage of the principle that memory is enhanced by associations between concepts (Bower et al., 1969). A logical hierarchy enhances our understanding of how individual items are related; as we proceed from top to bottom, each category serves as a cue that triggers our memory for the items below it. Because hierarchies have a visual organization, imagery can be used as a supplemental memory code. The hierarchy in Figure 8.10, for example, may help you remember some concepts about encoding.

FIGURE 8.10

Meaningful hierarchical organization enhances memory.

Placing information into a meaningful hierarchy enhances encoding and memory. This hierarchy could be developed further by adding a fifth level of boxes under 'Organization' labelled *Hierarchies, Chunking, Acronyms* and *Rhymes*. A box labelled *Method of Loci* could be added under 'Imagery', although it also organizes information.

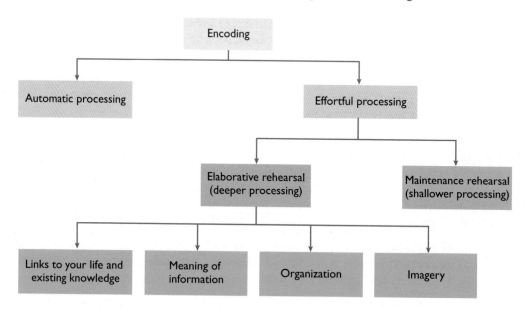

As noted earlier, chunking refers to combining individual items into larger units of meaning. To refresh your memory, read the letters below (one per second), then try to recall as many as you can in the same sequence.

    I R S Y M C A I B M C I A F B I

If you recalled five to nine letters in order, you did well. Now let us reorganize these 16 letters into five larger, more meaningful chunks: IRS, YMCA, IBM, CIA and FBI. These chunks are easier to rehearse, keep active in working memory, and transfer into long-term memory. When learning a new telephone number (e.g., 123-456-7890), you probably encode it in chunks.

Visual Imagery

What did your Year 6 class-mates look like? To answer this question, you might construct mental images in your working memory, based on information that you draw out of long-term memory.

Allan Paivio (1969) proposes that information is stored in long-term memory in two forms: verbal codes and visual codes. According to his **dual coding theory**, encoding information using both verbal and visual codes enhances memory because the odds improve so that at least one of the codes will be available later to support recall. Dual coding, however, is harder to use with some types of stimuli than it is with others. Try to construct a mental image of (1) a fire truck and (2) jealousy. You probably found the second task more difficult because jealousy represents an abstract concept rather than a concrete object (Paivio et al., 2000).

Memory experts recommend using imagery to dual-code information. The ancient Greeks developed the **method of loci** (*loci* is Latin for 'places'), a memory aid that associates information with mental images of physical locations. To use this technique, imagine a place that has distinct locations, such as your campus. Next, link each location with an item you are trying to

dual coding theory

encoding information using both verbal and visual codes enhances memory because the odds improve that at least one of the codes will be available later to support recall

method of loci

a memory aid that associates information with mental images of physical locations

remember. For example, to remember the components of working memory, imagine walking to the administration building (central executive), an art studio (visuospatial sketchpad), a music room (phonological loop) and the campus newspaper room (episodic buffer). It may take some practice to use this imagery technique effectively, but many studies support its effectiveness (Wang and Thomas, 2000).

Other Mnemonic Devices

The term *mnemonics* (*nee-MON-iks*) refers to the art of improving memory, and a **mnemonic device** is a memory aid. Mnemonic devices reorganize information into more meaningful units and provide extra cues to help retrieve information from long-term memory. Hierarchies, chunking, visual imagery and the method of loci are mnemonic devices. So are *acronyms*, which combine one or more letters (usually the first letter) from each piece of information you wish to remember. For example, many students learn the acronym ROY G. BIV to help remember the hues in the visible spectrum (the colours of the rainbow: red, orange, yellow, green, blue, indigo, violet).

Even putting information in a rhyme may enhance memory. As memory researcher Paul Whalen (2003) humorously noted: 'I once had the greatest difficulty remembering the name of a woman I had met named Gisa, until it later occurred to me that her name rhymed with both a leaning tower and a credit card' (p. 240). Some of our students use rhyming when they study, and advertisers often include rhyming jingles in their messages. In one experiment, adults listened to a 10-minute radio programme into which researchers had inserted an advertisement for a fictitious mouth rinse (Cavoloss). The advertisement either contained a rhyme ('Toss the floss, use Cavoloss') or presented the same information without a rhyme. Tested one week later, participants exposed to the rhyme remembered more product information and showed better brand-name recall (Smith and Phillips, 2001).

HOW PRIOR KNOWLEDGE SHAPES ENCODING

Can you recall the paragraph you just read word for word? Typically, when we read, listen to someone speak or experience some event, we do not precisely encode every word, sentence or moment. Rather, we usually encode the *gist* – the general theme (e.g., 'rhymes can enhance memory') – of that information or event.

Schemas: Our Mental Organizers

The themes that we extract from events and encode into memory are often organized around *schemas*. A **schema** is a mental framework – an organized pattern of thought – about some aspect of the world (Bartlett, 1932; Koriat et al., 2000). For example, the concepts 'dog', 'shopping' and 'love' serve as schemas that help you organize your world. To see more clearly what a schema is and how it can influence encoding, read the following paragraph.

> The procedure is actually quite simple. First you arrange things into different groups. Of course, one pile may be sufficient depending on how much there is to do. If you have to go somewhere else due to lack of facilities, that is the next step; otherwise you are pretty well set … it is better to do too few things at once than too many. In the short run this might not seem important, but complications can easily arise. A mistake can be expensive as well.… After the procedure is completed, one arranges the materials into different groups again. Then they can be put into their appropriate places. Eventually they will be used once more, and the whole cycle will have to be repeated. (Bransford and Johnson, 1972, p. 722)

Asked to recall the details of the preceding paragraph, you would probably have trouble. However, suppose we tell you that the paragraph is about a common activity: washing clothes. Now if you read the paragraph again, you will find that the abstract and seemingly unrelated details suddenly make sense. Thus, your schema for 'washing clothes' helps you organize and encode these details as a meaningful pattern and thus remember more of them.

Focus 8.7

How do schemas affect encoding? What role do schemas and mnemonic devices play in expertise and exceptional memory?

mnemonic device
a memory aid

schema
a mental framework – an organized pattern of thought – about some aspect of the world

Schemas, Encoding and Expertise

When most people look at a musical score, they see sheets of uninterpretable information. In contrast, musicians see organized patterns that they can easily encode. In music, as in other fields, acquiring *expertise* is a process of developing schemas that help encode information into meaningful patterns (Boschker et al., 2002).

Chase and Simon (1973) demonstrated this point in an intriguing study. Three chess players – an expert ('master'), an intermediate player and a beginner – were allowed 5 seconds to look at a chessboard containing about 25 pieces. Then they looked away and, on an empty board, attempted to reconstruct the placement of the pieces from memory. This was repeated over several trials, each with a different arrangement of pieces. On some trials, the chess pieces were arranged in *meaningful positions* that actually might occur in game situations. With only a 5-second glance, the expert typically recalled 16 pieces, the intermediate player eight, and the novice only four. But when the pieces were in *random positions*, each player did poorly, accurately recalling only two or three pieces.

How would you explain these results? We have to reject the conclusion that the expert had better overall memory than the other players, because he performed no better than they did with the random arrangements. But the concepts of schemas and chunking do explain the findings (Gobet and Simon, 2000). When the chess pieces were arranged in meaningful positions, the expert could apply well-developed schemas to recognize patterns and group pieces together. For example, he would treat as a unit all pieces that were positioned to attack the king. The intermediate player and especially the novice, who did not have well-developed chess schemas, could not construct the chunks and had to try to memorize the position of each piece.

However, when the pieces were not in positions that would occur in a real game, they were no more meaningful to the expert than to the other players. When that happened, the expert lost the advantage of schemas and had to approach the task on a piece-by-piece basis just as the other players did. Similarly, football coaches show much better recall than novices do after looking at diagrams of football plays (patterns of Xs and Os), but only when the plays are logical (Fig. 8.11).

FIGURE 8.11

Schemas, expertise, and memory.

When chess players of varying ability are required to recall mid-game positions after just five seconds exposure it is clear that masters (M) are at an advantage over Class A (A) players and Beginners (B). However, when the pieces are placed randomly then there is no difference in recall between players of different ability.

SOURCES: Chase and Simon, 1973; www.joshwaitzkin.com/images/J2.jpg.

ENCODING AND EXCEPTIONAL MEMORY

A **mnemonist** (or **memorist**) is a person who displays extraordinary memory skills, and it is tempting to assume that mnemonists like the waiter JC or pi-master Rajan Mahadevan have an innate, photographic memory. But Ericsson and his colleagues (Ericsson and Chase, 1982; Ericsson et al., 2004) argue that exceptional memory is a highly learned skill that involves prior knowledge, meaningful associations, efficient storage and retrieval, and extensive practice.

Mnemonists take advantage of basic memory principles. Many create visual images or stories to help them encode information. They often chunk information into larger units, combine smaller chunks into larger ones, and elaborate on the material by associating chunks with other meaningful information. Thus, 194473862001 might become '1944 = Second World War; 73 and 86 = two old people; 2001 = famous movie'. Combining techniques like these with 190 hours of practice, a college student with average memory became capable of remembering strings of up to 80 numbers on a digit-span test (Ericsson et al., 1980).

How, then, did Rajan learn 31 811 digits of pi? Rajan said that he did not have a photographic memory, and psychologists Charles Thompson and co-workers (1993), who studied Rajan intensively, agreed. Instead, they found that Rajan used chunking; the mathematical tables of pi that he studied grouped digits in chunks of 10, so Rajan did the same. But surprisingly, Rajan did not associate the chunks with meaningful material. Rather, beyond basic chunking, Rajan relied primarily on the brute force of rote memorization and extensive practice. How much practice? Thompson and co-workers estimated that it took Rajan over a year to learn the digits of pi.

Realize that just because rote memorization *can* transfer information into long-term memory, it is not necessarily the best way. Mnemonists (including the person who broke Rajan's record by recalling 42 195 digits of pi) often use elaborative rehearsal. Moreover, rote memorization is better suited to learning a string of numbers than to learning material that has meaning. When Rajan applied his rote strategy to memory tasks that involved meaningful stimuli (e.g., written stories), he performed more poorly or no better than college students in a control group.

So, is exceptional memory a learned skill? After a year of practice, could the average person really remember 32 000 digits of pi? Thompson and co-workers (1993) believe that in memory, as in sports and music, endless skilled practice will not enable most people to rise to the top unless they also have the requisite innate ability. Yet Ericsson and co-workers (1993; 2004) disagree, arguing that 'many characteristics once believed to reflect innate talent are actually the result of intense practice' (1993, p. 363).

mnemonist (or memorist)

a person who displays extraordinary memory skills

 In-Psych

How does a mnemonist develop superior memory abilities? View the video, 'Mnemonic Strategies in Memory', in Chapter 8 of the In-Psych programme online.

Focus 8.8

Contrast associative network models and neural network models of memory, and explain priming.

WHAT DO YOU THINK?

WOULD PERFECT MEMORY BE A GIFT OR A CURSE?

If you could have a perfect memory, would you want it? What might be the drawbacks? Think about it, then see p. 379.

IN REVIEW

IN REVIEW

- Effortful processing involves intentional encoding and conscious attention. Automatic processing occurs without intention and requires minimal effort.

- Deep processing enhances memory. Elaborative rehearsal provides deeper processing than maintenance rehearsal. Hierarchies, chunking, dual coding that includes visual imagery, and other mnemonic devices facilitate deeper encoding.

- Schemas are mental frameworks that shape how we encode information. As we become experts in any given field, we develop schemas that allow us to encode information into memory more efficiently.

- People who display exceptional memory take advantage of sound memory principles and mnemonic devices.

STORAGE: RETAINING INFORMATION

At a moment's notice you can recall an incredible wealth of information, from the name of Russia's capital to how you spent your most recent holiday. This ability to rapidly access diverse facts, concepts and experiences has influenced many cognitive models of how information is stored and organized in memory.

MEMORY AS A NETWORK

We noted that memory is enhanced by forming associations between new information and other items already in memory. The general principle that memory involves associations goes to the heart of the *network* approach.

associative network

a massive network of associated ideas and concepts

Associative Networks

One group of theories proposes that long-term memory can be represented as an **associative network**, a massive network of associated ideas and concepts (Collins and Loftus, 1975). Figure 8.12 shows what a tiny portion of such a network might be like. In this network, each concept or unit of information – 'fire engine', 'red', and so on – is represented by a *node* somewhat akin to each knot in a huge fishing net. The lines in this network represent associations between concepts, with shorter lines indicating stronger associations. For simplicity, Figure 8.12 shows only a few connections extending from each node, but there could be hundreds or more. Notice that items within the same category – types of flowers, types of fruit, colours, and so on – generally have the strongest associations and therefore tend to be clustered closer together. In essence, an associative network is a type of schema; it is a mental framework that represents how we have organized information and how we understand the world (Roediger and McDermott, 2000).

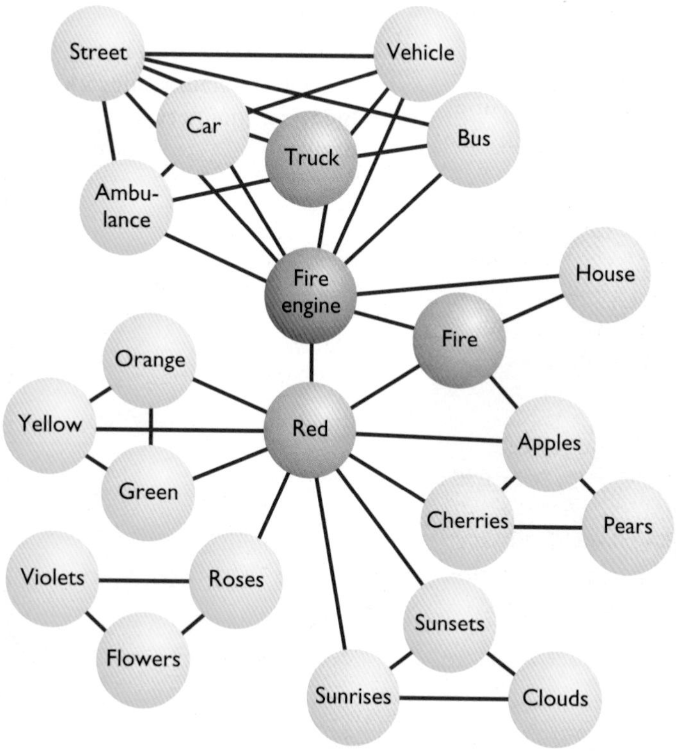

FIGURE 8.12

Semantic networks.

Each node in this semantic network represents a concept. The lines represent associations between concepts, with shorter lines indicating stronger associations.

SOURCE: adapted from Collins and Loftus, 1975.

Collins and Loftus (1975) theorize that when people think about a concept, such as 'fire engine', there is a *spreading activation* of related concepts throughout the network. For example, when you think about a 'fire engine', related concepts such as 'truck', 'fire' and 'red' should be partially activated as well. The term **priming** refers to the activation of one concept (or one unit of information) by another. Thus 'fire engine' primes the node for 'red', making it more likely that our memory for this colour will be accessed (Chwilla and Kolk, 2002).

The notion that memory stores information in an associative network helps explain how hints and mnemonic devices stimulate recall (Reisberg, 1997). For example, when you hear 'Name the colours of the rainbow', the nodes for 'colour' and 'rainbow' jointly activate the node for 'ROY G. BIV', which in turn primes your recall for 'red', 'orange', 'yellow', and so forth.

Neural Networks

Neural network models take a different approach to explain why spreading activation and priming occur (Chappell and Humphreys, 1994). Neural network models are computer models whose programming incorporates principles taken from the operation of the nervous system. A neural network has nodes (often called *units*) that are linked to each other, but unlike the nodes in associative network models, each node in a neural network model does not contain an individual unit of information. There is no single node for 'red', no single node for 'fire engine', and so on. Instead, each node in a neural network is more like a small information-processing unit. As an analogy, think of each neuron in your brain as a node. A neuron processes inputs and sends outputs to other neurons, but as far as we know, the concepts of 'red' and 'fire engine' are not stored within any single neuron.

Recall that in the brain, neurons have synaptic connections with many other neurons, receive and send signals that can be excitatory (increasing the likelihood that a neuron will fire) or inhibitory (decreasing the likelihood of firing), and will fire if the overall input they receive moves their electrical potential to a certain threshold point (see Chapter 4). Similarly, nodes in neural network models have connections with many other nodes, are programmed to receive and transmit excitatory or inhibitory signals, and become activated when the input they receive reaches a certain threshold strength. Just as learning experiences modify the brain's neural circuitry, in computer simulations neural networks 'gain experience' by processing different bits of information, such as sounds or visual patterns. As they do, connections among various nodes become stronger or weaker (reflected by changes in the mathematical weight assigned to each connection) and the network learns to recognize and distinguish between different types of stimuli (e.g., images of faces, spoken words, and so on).

In trying to model how memory operates, if concepts such as 'red' and 'fire engine' are not stored in their own individual nodes, then where are they stored? In **neural network (connectionist) models**, each memory is represented by a unique pattern of interconnected and simultaneously activated nodes. When node 4 is activated simultaneously (i.e., in parallel) with nodes 95 and 423, the concept 'red' comes to mind. But when node 4 is simultaneously activated with nodes 78 and 901, the concept of 'fire engine' enters our thoughts.

As we look across the entire neural network, various nodes *distributed* throughout the network fire in parallel at each instant and simultaneously spread their activation to other nodes. In this manner, certain nodes prime other nodes, and concepts and information are retrieved. For this reason, neural network (connectionist) models are often called **parallel distributed processing (PDP) models** (Rumelhart et al., 1986). Increasingly, scientists in many fields are using the neural network approach to model learning, memory, and other cognitive processes such as perception and decision making (Vogel, 2005).

priming
the activation of one concept (or one unit of information) by another

neural network (connectionist) models
each memory is represented by a unique pattern of interconnected and simultaneously activated nodes

parallel distributed processing (PDP) models
neural network (connectionist) models

declarative memory
factual knowledge

episodic memory
knowledge concerning personal experiences: when, where, and what happened in the episodes of our lives

semantic memory
general factual knowledge about the world and language, including memory for words and concepts

Focus 8.9
Contrast and illustrate declarative versus procedural memory and explicit versus implicit memory.

FIGURE 8.13

Multiple long-term memory systems.

Some theorists propose that we have separate but interacting declarative and procedural memory systems. Episodic and semantic memories are declarative; their contents can be verbalized. Procedural memory is non-declarative; its contents cannot readily be verbalized.

procedural (non-declarative) memory
reflected in skills and actions

TYPES OF LONG-TERM MEMORY

Research with amnesia patients, brain-imaging studies, and animal experiments indicate that the brain houses several long-term memory systems (Park and Gutchess, 2005). Think back, for example, to HM's amnesia. Once new facts or new personal experiences leave his immediate train of thought, he is unable to consciously remember them. Yet with practice, HM can retain the skills needed to perform new tasks even though he cannot recall having seen the tasks before (Milner, 1965).

Declarative and Procedural Memory

Declarative memory involves factual knowledge and includes two subcategories (Fig. 8.13). **Episodic memory** is our store of knowledge concerning personal experiences: when, where, and what happened in the episodes of our lives. Your recollections of childhood friends, a favourite film, and what you ate this morning represent episodic memories. **Semantic memory** represents general factual knowledge about the world and language, including memory for words and concepts. You know that Mount Everest is the world's tallest peak and that $e = mc^2$. Episodic and semantic memories are called *declarative* because to demonstrate our knowledge, we typically have to declare it: We tell other people what we know.

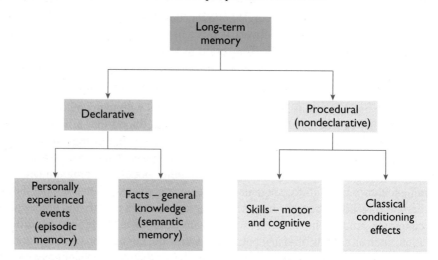

HM's brain damage impaired both components of his declarative memory. He could not remember new personal experiences, nor could he remember new general facts. For example, HM retained good memory for words that he had learned growing up (Kensinger et al., 2001). Yet no matter how many times he was told their definition, he could not remember the meaning of new words (e.g., *Xerox*, *biodegradable*) that entered the English language in the years after his operation. In contrast, some brain-injured children cannot remember their daily personal experiences but can remember new factual knowledge, enabling them to learn language and attend mainstream schools (Vargha-Khadem et al., 1997).

Procedural (non-declarative) memory is reflected in skills and actions (Gupta and Cohen, 2002). One component of procedural memory consists of skills that are expressed by doing things in particular situations, such as typing or riding a bicycle. HM formed a new procedural memory when he learned how to perform the mirror-tracing task.

Classically conditioned responses also reflect procedural memory. After a tone was repeatedly paired with a puff of air blown towards HM's eye, he began to blink involuntarily to the tone alone (Woodruff-Pak, 1993). Although HM could not consciously remember undergoing this procedure (i.e., he did not form a declarative memory), his brain stored a memory for the tone–air puff association, and thus he blinked when subsequently exposed to the tone alone (i.e., he formed a procedural memory).

Explicit and Implicit Memory

Many researchers distinguish between *explicit* and *implicit memory*. **Explicit memory** involves conscious or intentional memory retrieval, as when you consciously recognize or recall something. *Recognition* requires us to decide whether a stimulus is familiar, as when an eyewitness is asked to pick out a suspect from a police line-up or when students take multiple-choice tests. In recognition tasks, the target stimuli (possible suspects or answers) are provided to you. *Recall* involves spontaneous memory retrieval, in the sense that you must retrieve the target stimuli or information on your own. This occurs when you are briefly shown a list of words and then asked to recall them. With *cued recall*, hints are given to stimulate memory. If you cannot recall the word *hat* from the list, we might say, 'It rhymes with *bat*'. As a student, you are no doubt familiar with test items that involve recall or cued recall, such as essay, short-answer and fill-in-the-blank questions.

Implicit memory occurs when memory influences our behaviour without conscious awareness (May et al., 2005). HM was able to form a procedural memory for performing the mirror-tracing task, although he had no conscious awareness of having learned it. His memory for the task (in this case, procedural memory) was implicit. In Chapter 6 we encountered another amnesia patient, whose hand Edouard Claparède (1911) intentionally pricked with a pin during a handshake. Shortly thereafter the patient could not consciously recall this incident, but despite her amnesia, she showed implicit memory of their encounter by withdrawing her hand when Claparède offered to shake it again.

In less dramatic ways, each of us demonstrates memory without conscious awareness. Riding a bicycle, driving or performing any well-learned skill are common examples. Cycling to class, you may be consciously thinking about an upcoming examination while your implicit, procedural memory enables you to keep pedalling and to maintain your balance.

Consider another example of implicit memory. Suppose that as part of an experiment you read a list of words (one word per second) that includes *kitchen*, *moon* and *defend*. Days, weeks or, even, a year later, you participate in another, seemingly unrelated study. The experimenter rapidly shows you many word stems, some of which might be *KIT—*, *MO—* and *DE—*, and asks you to complete each stem to form a word. You are not aware that this is a memory test, but compared with people not given the original list of words, you will be more likely to complete the stems with words on the original list (e.g., *MOon*, rather than *MOther* or *MOney*). This represents one of many types of *priming tasks*: the word stems have activated, or primed, your stored mental representations of the original complete words. This suggests that information from the original list is still in your memory and is implicitly influencing your behaviour even though you may have no explicit, conscious recall of the original words (Schacter, 1992).

---

explicit memory
conscious or intentional memory retrieval, as when you consciously recognize or recall something

implicit memory
when memory influences our behaviour without conscious awareness

---

IN REVIEW

- Associative network models view long-term memory as a network of associated nodes, with each node representing a concept or unit of information.

- Neural network models propose that each piece of information in memory is represented not by a single node but by multiple nodes distributed throughout the brain. Each memory is represented by a unique pattern of simultaneously activated nodes.

- Declarative long-term memories involve factual knowledge and include episodic memories (knowledge concerning personal experiences) and semantic memories (facts about the world and language). In contrast, procedural memory is reflected in skills and actions.

- Explicit memory involves conscious or intentional memory retrieval, whereas implicit memory influences our behaviour without conscious awareness.

retrieval cue
a stimulus, whether internal or external, that activates information stored in long-term memory

Focus 8.10

How do retrieval cues assist memory? What is the benefit of having multiple, self-generated cues and distinctive cues?

Focus 8.11

Are emotionally arousing events, including those that produce flashbulb memories, remembered differently from other events? How are confidence and memory accuracy related?

RETRIEVAL: ACCESSING INFORMATION

Storing information is useless without the ability to retrieve it. A **retrieval cue** is a stimulus, whether internal or external, that activates information stored in long-term memory. If I ask you, 'Have you seen Sonia today?' the word *Sonia* is intended to serve as a retrieval cue. Likewise, a yearbook picture can act as a retrieval cue that triggers memories of a class-mate. Priming is another example of how a retrieval cue (*MO—*) can trigger associated elements (*MOon*) in memory, presumably via a process of spreading activation (Chwilla and Kolk, 2002).

THE VALUE OF MULTIPLE CUES

Experiments by Mäntylä (1986) vividly show the value of having multiple retrieval cues. In one, Swedish college students were presented with a list of 504 words. Some students were asked to think of and write down one association for each word, while others produced three associations per word. To illustrate, what three words come to your mind when I say *banana*? Perhaps you might think of *peel*, *fruit* and *ice cream*.

The students had no idea that their memory would be tested, and after finishing the association task they were given an unexpected recall test for 252 of the original words. For some words, students were first shown the one or three associations they had just generated. As a control, for other words they were first shown one or three associations another participant had generated. Then they tried to recall the original word.

The results were remarkable. When the associations (i.e., retrieval cues) were self-generated, students shown one cue recalled 61 per cent of the words and those shown three cues recalled 91 per cent. In contrast, when students were shown cues that someone else had generated, recall with one cue dropped to 11 per cent and with three cues to 55 per cent. Further, when given another surprise recall test one week later on the remaining 252 words, students still remembered 65 per cent of the words when they were first provided with three self-generated retrieval cues.

Why does having multiple, self-generated retrieval cues maximize recall? On the encoding side, generating your own associations involves deeper processing than does being presented with associations generated by someone else. Similarly, generating three associations involves deeper processing than generating only one. On the retrieval side, these self-generated associations become cues that have personal meaning. And with multiple cues, if one fails, another may activate the memory. The implication for studying academic material is clear. Think about the material you are studying, and draw one or (preferably) more links to ideas, knowledge, or experiences that have meaning for you.

THE VALUE OF DISTINCTIVENESS

To demonstrate a simple point, here is a brief self-test. A list of words appears below. Say each word to yourself (one per second); then when you see the word *WRITE*, look away and write down as many words as you can recall, in any order. Here's the list:

sparrow, eagle, nest, owl, feather, goose, crow, artichoke, rooster, fly, robin, parrot, chirp, hawk, pigeon, WRITE.

If you are like most of our own students, you probably recalled *artichoke* even though it appeared in the middle of the list. The other words all relate to birds, but *artichoke* is a food: It's distinctive. In general, distinctive stimuli are better remembered than nondistinctive ones (Ghetti et al., 2002).

In school, when all the material starts looking the same, you can make it more distinctive by associating it with other information that is personally meaningful to you. According to Mäntylä (1986), this is one reason why students who generated their own three-word associations remembered almost all of the original 504 words. The associations formed a distinctive set of cues.

Distinctive events stand a greater chance of etching long-term memories that seem vivid and clear. In one study, college students listed their three clearest memories (Rubin and Kozin, 1984). Distinctive events such as weddings, romantic encounters, births and deaths, holidays and accidents were among the most frequently recalled. In another study, university students watched a videotape of a guest lecturer who engaged in some distinctive, atypical behaviours (e.g., ate crisps, burped) and some typical ones (e.g., sat down, took off jacket). On a memory test a week later, students correctly remembered about 80 per cent of all the lecturer's behaviours, but they were more likely to report having a clear image of the distinctive ones (Neuschatz et al., 2002).

AROUSAL, EMOTION AND MEMORY

Many experiences in our lives, such as romantic encounters, deaths, graduations, accidents, and local or world events may be better remembered not only because they were distinctive, but also because they stirred up our emotions and aroused us (Fig. 8.14). In experiments, people shown arousing and neutral stimuli (e.g., pictures of happy, fearful, or neutral faces; violent or neutral film scenes) typically remember the arousing stimuli best, even when tested several weeks later (Matlin and Stang, 1978; Putman et al., 2004) or even up to one year later (Bywaters et al., 2004).

FIGURE 8.14

A memory of an emotionally arousing, distinctive event can seem so vivid and clear that we feel we can picture it as if it were a snapshot of a moment in time. Researchers call this a *flashbulb memory*.

Why do emotionally arousing stimuli wind their way more deeply into memory? By physiologically monitoring people during these tasks, researchers have found that arousing stimuli trigger the release of stress hormones. This causes neurotransmitters to increase activation of the amygdala, a brain structure that helps encode the emotional aspects of experiences into longer-term memories (McGaugh and Roozendaal, 2002). Injecting rats with drugs that stimulate or inhibit stress hormone activity will, respectively, boost or impair the rats' ability to remember responses that they are learning or have recently learned.

Outside the laboratory, researchers have found that emotional arousal enhances **autobiographical memories**, memory for the events of one's life (Conway and Rubin, 1993). When people are asked to record their unique daily experiences in a diary and rate the emotional pleasantness and intensity of each event (e.g., say, on a seven-point scale ranging from 'extremely unpleasant' to 'extremely pleasant'), it typically is the more intense events that they recall most vividly when tested days, months or years later. Over time, however, the emotionality of most pleasant and unpleasant memories may fade a bit, as Richard Walker and his colleagues (1997) found when they asked college students to (1) remember diary events that were experienced during the prior month or year and (2) rate how pleasant or unpleasant each event 'feels to you now'.

autobiographical memories

memory for the events of one's life

Interestingly, even though the students originally rated their pleasant and unpleasant events as equally arousing when the events happened, the intensity of memories for the pleasant events faded a little less rapidly over time. This slower emotional fading of positive memories, combined with cross-cultural findings that most people express positive life satisfaction, led Walker, Skowronski and Thompson (2003) to proclaim that 'life is pleasant – and memory helps to keep it that way!' (p. 203). Of course, as they emphasize, life surely is not pleasant for everyone, and some people do not exhibit these memory effects. They found, for example, that among mildly depressed students, the intensity of pleasant and unpleasant memories faded at the same rate (Walker, Skowronski, Gibbons, Vogl and Thompson, 2003). Moreover, some people's memories of traumatic experiences may remain emotionally intense for years.

Overall, then, distinctive and emotionally arousing events are recalled most easily or vividly over time. But just because a memory seems vivid does not guarantee its accuracy. In the experiment where a guest lecturer ate chips, burped, and performed other odd behaviours, some students vividly remembered events (e.g., the lecturer zipped up his pants) that actually never occurred. Do similar errors occur when we retrieve memories of even more distinctive, dramatic real-world events – events that we seemingly remember like it was just yesterday? Let us take a look in the following 'Beneath the surface' segment.

flashbulb memories

recollections that seem so vivid, so clear, that we can picture them as if they were snapshots of moments in time

BENEATH THE SURFACE

DO WE REALLY REMEMBER IT LIKE IT WAS YESTERDAY?

Can you picture the tragic moment on 11 September 2001, when you first heard or saw that jetliners had crashed into the World Trade Center and the Pentagon? Perhaps you can picture the moment when you learned that Diana, Princess of Wales had been killed in a car crash in Paris, or that a massive tsunami had struck Southeast Asia. Your authors, like others of our generation, can vividly recall the moment over 15 years ago when we heard that UK Prime Minister Margaret Thatcher had resigned.

Flashbulb memories are recollections that seem so vivid, so clear, that we can picture them as if they were snapshots of moments in time and we are able to recall information about the *reception event*, where we were, who told us and our emotional response to the news. They are most likely to occur for distinctive events that evoke strong emotional reactions and that are repeatedly recalled in conversations with other people (Brown and Kulik, 1977).

FLASHBULB MEMORIES: FOGGING UP THE PICTURE?

Because flashbulb memories seem vivid and are easily recalled, we often feel confident of their accuracy. But are they accurate? Hornstein et al. (2003) reported a study of long-term memory for the death of Diana Princess of Wales and found that at testing periods of both three months and 18 months after the event recollection of the reception event was still highly accurate, suggesting that memories for such shocking events are robust and immune to the forgetting seen in normal everyday memories. However, in 1986 the space shuttle *Challenger* exploded shortly after takeoff, killing all on board. The next day, Ulric Neisser and Nicole Harsch (1993) asked college students to describe how they learned of the disaster, where they were, who they were with, and so on. Reinterviewed three years later, about half of the students remembered some details correctly but recalled other details inaccurately. One-quarter of the students completely misremembered all the major details and were astonished at how inaccurate their memories were after reading their original descriptions.

Conway et al. (1994) noted that in order for flashbulb memories to be formed the original event must be both surprising and consequential for the individual, something that may not have been the case for those recalling the *Challenger* disaster. In order to study the importance of these factors they investigated the formation of flashbulb memories for the resignation of the British Prime Minister Margaret Thatcher, comparing the recall of UK and non-UK participants. Conway et al. reported that over 86 per cent of the UK participants had flashbulb memories 11 months after the event and these participants were able to produce detailed and accurate accounts of the reception event. However, only 29 per cent of non-UK participants had flashbulb memories and their accounts typically contained errors and there was a significant amount of forgetting. Here is how one student's recollection of the event altered over time:

[Initial test] I was taking my study break in my dorm and was switching the TV channels. It was on the news and I almost turned right past it. I finally figured out what was being said and realised what was going on.

[Retest – 11 months later] I was walking to class with my boyfriend and he brought it up. I couldn't believe that I hadn't heard; how cut off from the news had I been. I was surprised but when I thought about how many other countries were having a change in government I didn't find it that strange. (Conway et al., 1994, p. 342)

It seems to be important that both surprise and consequences must be present for the formation of flashbulb memories. This is why Conway et al. found higher incidence of flashbulb memory in their UK participants – the event had greater consequences for this group than it did for the non-UK participants.

CONFIDENCE AND MEMORY ACCURACY

If people are highly confident in their memory, is it likely to be accurate? After the car crash that killed Princess Diana in 1997, a study in England found that 44 per cent of participants said that they had seen a videotape on the television news showing the crash take place. No such tape was ever shown, yet they were as confident in their memory as people who said they never saw such a tape (Ost et al., 2002). Similarly, a few weeks after the 9/11 terrorist attacks, Kathy Pezdek (2003) asked students attending college in New York City (Manhattan), Southern California, and Hawaii: 'On September 11, did you see the videotape on television of the first plane striking the first tower?' Overall, 73 per cent of the students said yes. Yet this was impossible, because a videotape of the first plane crashing was not broadcast until after 11 September. Moreover, students who incorrectly responded yes were more confident in their memory than the students who correctly said no!

Indeed, one day after 9/11, Jennifer Talarico and David Rubin (2003) asked Duke University students to report the personal details (e.g., where were you, who were you with) for two events: (1) the moment they learned about the 9/11 terrorist attacks and (2) a typical college event of their choice that they had recently experienced (e.g., a party, sports event, studying). A week, six weeks and 32 weeks later, the students did not display any more accurate autobiographical memory for 9/11 than for the everyday personal event, even though they rated 9/11 as a more emotionally intense event. As Figure 8.15a shows, students' recall for both events, though still good, became less accurate (i.e., less consistent with their original reports) over time. The key difference: For the everyday event, over time students said that they were less confident in their memory and that it was less vivid, but not so for 9/11. After 32 weeks, students were as confident in their memory and said it was as vivid (e.g., 'I feel as though I am reliving the experience') as the day after the attacks happened (Fig. 8.15b). Similarly, another study asked people to report personal details surrounding 9/11 within two days after the attacks; over the next year, respondents remained highly confident of their memories despite the fact that those memories actually became less accurate (Weaver and Krug, 2004).

Memory researchers have studied the relation between confidence and accuracy with children and adults, inside and outside the laboratory, and for many types of events. Overall, confidence and accuracy are weakly related (Busey et al., 2000). People accurately recall many events – even after years pass – and typically are very confident when they do. But people often swear by inaccurate memories. In general, distinctive and emotionally arousing events in our lives have a memory advantage. However, even for such events, a memory can feel like it happened just yesterday when, in truth, it is foggy.

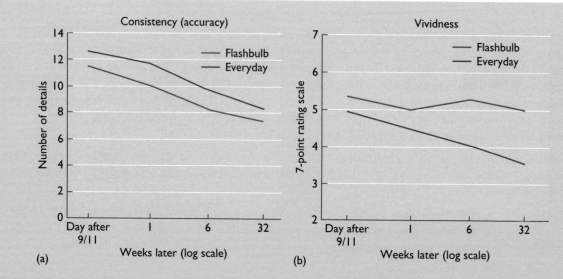

FIGURE 8.15

Flashbulb memories of 9/11.

(a) During the 32 weeks following the terrorist attacks of 9/11, students' recall of personal details for 9/11 (e.g., where they were, who they were with) and for an everyday event became less consistent with their initial reports made on 12 September. (b) Despite this decrease in memory accuracy, students continued to report a vivid memory of 9/11, whereas the memory of the everyday event became progressively less vivid.

SOURCE: Talarico and Rubin, 2003.

THE EFFECTS OF CONTEXT, STATE AND MOOD ON MEMORY

encoding specificity principle

memory is enhanced when conditions present during retrieval match those that were present during encoding

context-dependent memory

it typically is easier to remember something in the same environment in which it was originally encoded

Focus 8.12

Describe and illustrate encoding specificity, context- and state-dependent memory, and mood-congruent recall.

Our ability to retrieve a memory is influenced not only by the nature of the original stimulus (such as its distinctiveness) but also by environmental, physiological and psychological factors. Years ago, two Swedish researchers reported the case of a young woman who was raped while out for a jog (Christianson and Nilsson, 1989). When found by a passer-by, she was in shock and could not remember the assault. Over the next three months, the police took her back to the crime scene several times. Although she could not recall the rape, she became emotionally aroused, suggesting implicit memory of the event. While jogging one day shortly thereafter, she consciously recalled the rape.

Why did her memory return? One possibility is based on the **encoding specificity principle**, which states that memory is enhanced when conditions present during retrieval match those that were present during encoding (Tulving and Thomson, 1973). When stimuli associated with an event become encoded as part of the memory, they may later serve as retrieval cues.

Context-Dependent Memory: Returning to the Scene

Applying the encoding specificity principle to *external* cues leads us to **context-dependent memory**: it typically is easier to remember something in the same environment in which it was originally encoded. Thus visiting your high school or old neighbourhood may trigger memories of teachers, class-mates and friends. As with the Swedish jogger, police detectives may take an eyewitness or crime victim back to the crime scene, hoping to stimulate the person's memory.

In a classic experiment, Duncan Godden and Alan Baddeley (1975) asked scuba divers to learn some lists of words underwater and some on dry land. When the divers were later retested

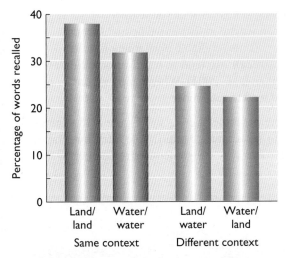

FIGURE 8.16

Context-dependent memory.

Scuba divers who learned lists of words while under water later recalled them best while under water, whereas words they learned on land were best recalled on land. Recall was poorer when the learning and testing environments were mismatched.

SOURCE: adapted from Godden and Baddeley, 1975.

in both environments, lists learned underwater were recalled better underwater and those learned on land were better recalled on land (Fig. 8.16). Other studies, spanning diverse environments, have replicated this finding (Smith and Vela, 2001).

Consider the relevance of context-dependent memory to college life. In one experiment, when randomly assigned college students studied material in either a quiet or noisy room, they later displayed better memory on short-answer and multiple-choice questions when tested in a similar (quiet or noisy) environment (Grant et al., 1998). Thus if you take examinations in quiet environments, try to study in a quiet environment.

State-Dependent Memory: Arousal, Drugs and Mood

Moving from external to internal cues, the concept of **state-dependent memory** proposes that our ability to retrieve information is greater when our internal state at the time of retrieval matches our original state during learning. The Swedish jogger who was raped consciously remembered her assault for the first time while jogging. In her case, both context-dependent cues (similar environment) and state-dependent cues (arousal while jogging) may have stimulated her memory.

Diverse experiments support this effect. Many students on the campus gym read course materials while exercising on a bicycle, treadmill or stair-climber machine. Christopher Miles and Elinor Hardman (1998) found that material learned while we are aroused during aerobic exercise is later recalled more effectively if we are once again aerobically aroused, rather than at rest. Conversely, material learned at rest is better recalled at rest.

Many drugs produce physiological effects that directly impair memory, but state-dependent memory also explains why events experienced in a drugged state may be difficult to recall later while in a drug-free state (Fig. 8.17). Experiments examining alcohol, marijuana, amphetamines and other drugs have often found that information recall is poorer when there is a mismatch between the person's states during learning and testing (Carter and Cassaday, 1998). This *does not* mean, by the way, that drugs improve memory relative to not taking drugs during initial learning.

state-dependent memory

our ability to retrieve information is greater when our internal state at the time of retrieval matches our original state during learning

FIGURE 8.17

State-dependent memory.

In the film *City Lights*, a drunken millionaire befriends and spends the evening partying with Charlie Chaplin after Chaplin saves his life. The next day, in a sober state, the millionaire does not remember Chaplin and considers him an unwanted pest. After getting drunk again, he remembers Chaplin and treats him like a good buddy.

Does state-dependent memory extend to mood states? Is material learned while we are in a happy mood or a sad mood better recalled when we are in that mood again? Inconsistent findings suggest that such *mood-dependent memory* is not a reliable phenomenon. Instead, there is more consistent evidence of **mood-congruent recall**: we tend to recall information or events that are congruent with our current mood (Fiedler et al., 2001). When happy we are more likely to remember positive events, and when sad we tend to remember negative events.

Thus far we have focused on how information is remembered, and Figure 8.18 summarizes some of the factors involved. We have more to say about the brain's role later, but first, in the next two sections we examine why we forget and why we sometimes remember events that never occurred.

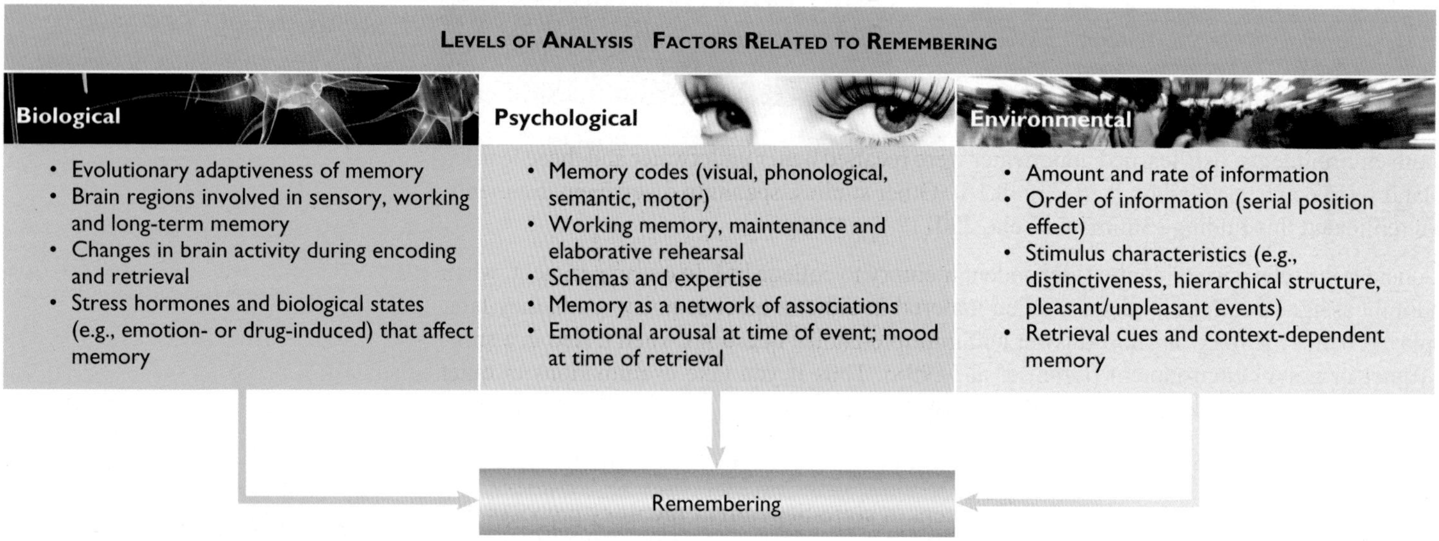

mood-congruent recall

we tend to recall information or events that are congruent with our current mood

LEVELS OF ANALYSIS   FACTORS RELATED TO REMEMBERING

Biological

- Evolutionary adaptiveness of memory
- Brain regions involved in sensory, working and long-term memory
- Changes in brain activity during encoding and retrieval
- Stress hormones and biological states (e.g., emotion- or drug-induced) that affect memory

Psychological

- Memory codes (visual, phonological, semantic, motor)
- Working memory, maintenance and elaborative rehearsal
- Schemas and expertise
- Memory as a network of associations
- Emotional arousal at time of event; mood at time of retrieval

Environmental

- Amount and rate of information
- Order of information (serial position effect)
- Stimulus characteristics (e.g., distinctiveness, hierarchical structure, pleasant/unpleasant events)
- Retrieval cues and context-dependent memory

Remembering

FIGURE 8.18

Levels of analysis: factors related to remembering.

IN REVIEW

- Retrieval cues activate information stored in long-term memory. Memory retrieval is more likely to occur when we have multiple cues, self-generated cues and distinctive cues.

- We experience flashbulb memories as vivid and clear snapshots of an event and are confident of their accuracy. However, over time many flashbulb memories become inaccurate. Overall, memory accuracy and memory confidence are only weakly related.

- The encoding specificity principle states that memory is enhanced when cues present during retrieval match cues that were present during encoding. Typically it is easier to remember a stimulus when we are in the same environment (context-dependent memory) or same internal state (state-dependent memory) as when the stimulus was originally encoded.

- Mood states provide an exception to encoding specificity. In general, we tend to recall stimuli that are congruent with our current mood.

FORGETTING

Some very bright people are legendary for their memory failures. The eminent French writer, Voltaire, began a passionate letter, 'My Dear Hortense', and ended it, 'Farewell, my dear Adele'. The splendid absentmindedness of English nobleman Canon Sawyer once led him, while welcoming a visitor at a railroad station, to board the departing train and disappear (Bryan, 1986). Indeed, how we forget is as interesting a scientific question as how we remember.

THE COURSE OF FORGETTING

German psychologist Hermann Ebbinghaus (1964) pioneered the study of forgetting by testing only one person – himself (Fig. 8.19). He created over 2000 *nonsense syllables*, meaningless letter combinations (e.g., *biv, zaj, xew*), to study memory with minimal influence from prior learning, as would happen if he used actual words. In one study, Ebbinghaus performed over 14 000 practice repetitions trying to memorize 420 lists of nonsense syllables.

Ebbinghaus typically measured memory by using a method called *relearning* and then computing a savings percentage. For example, if it initially took him 20 trials to learn a list but only half as many trials to relearn it a week later, then the savings percentage was 50 per cent. In one series of studies, he retested his memory at various time intervals after mastering several lists of nonsense syllables. As Figure 8.20a shows, forgetting occurred rapidly at first and slowed noticeably thereafter.

Focus 8.13
Describe Ebbinghaus's research, its value and its limitations.

Focus 8.14
Explain why we forget based on concepts of encoding failure, decay and interference.

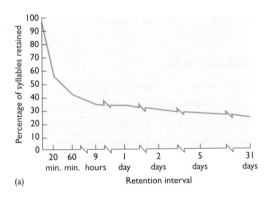
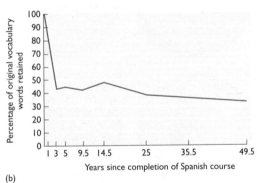

FIGURE 8.20

Forgetting over time.

(a) Hermann Ebbinghaus's forgetting curve shows a rapid loss of memory for nonsense syllables at first and then a more gradual decline. The rapid decline is probably due to the meaningless nature of the nonsense syllables. (b) The forgetting of vocabulary from high school Spanish language classes follows a similar curve, except that the time frame is in years, not days.
SOURCES: based on (a) Ebbinghaus, 1964, and (b) Bahrick, 1984.

FIGURE 8.19

Hermann Ebbinghaus was a pioneering memory researcher.

Do we indeed forget most of what we learn so quickly? Ebbinghaus studied so many lists of nonsense syllables that his ability to distinguish among them undoubtedly suffered. If you learned just a few lists, the shape of your forgetting curve might resemble Ebbinghaus's, but the amount you forgot would likely be less. Moreover, when material is meaningful (unlike nonsense syllables), we are likely to retain more of it over time (Bahrick, 2005).

Consider the forgetting curve in Figure 8.20b, based on a study examining the vocabulary retention of people who had studied Spanish in school anywhere from three to 50 years earlier and then rarely used it (Bahrick, 1984). Once again, forgetting occurred more rapidly at first, but notice that the Spanish-retention study employed a time frame of years rather than hours and days as in Ebbinghaus's studies.

WHY DO WE FORGET?

If some memories last a lifetime, why do we forget so much? Explanations for normal memory loss emphasize difficulties in encoding, storage and retrieval.

Encoding Failure

Many memory failures result not from forgetting information that we once knew, but from failing to encode the information into long-term memory in the first place. Perhaps you had the radio or television on this morning while eating breakfast, but chances are you can recall only those songs or stories that you found especially interesting. Much of what we sense simply is not processed deeply enough to commit to memory.

We noted earlier that few people can accurately draw a coin from memory. Even when the task is made easier by requiring only recognition, as in Figure 8.21, most people cannot identify the correct coin (Nickerson and Adams, 1979). Can you? The details of a coin's appearance are not meaningful to most of us, and we may not notice them, no matter how often we see coins.

> **decay theory**
>
> with time and disuse the long-term physical memory trace in the nervous system fades away

(a)   (b)   (c)   (d)

FIGURE 8.21

Which coin portrays a real pound?

If you want to try your skill at picking it out, do it before reading further. Most people have difficulty choosing the correct one because they have never bothered to encode all of the features of a real pound coin. The correct coin is (d).

We may notice information but fail to encode it deeply because we turn our attention to something else. Brad Bushman and Angelica Bonacci (2002) randomly assigned 328 adults to watch either a sexually explicit, violent or neutral television programme. Nine commercial advertisements (e.g., for snacks, cereal, laundry detergent) appeared during each programme. Immediately afterward and again a day later, the researchers tested viewers' memory for the advertisements. At both times, viewers who watched the sexually explicit and violent programmes remembered the fewest number of advertisements (Fig. 8.22). Several factors might account for this, and as the researchers proposed, one of them is encoding failure: All the viewers clearly saw the advertisements, but those watching the sexually explicit and violent programmes likely were the most preoccupied with thoughts about the content of the shows.

Decay of the Memory Trace

Information in sensory memory and short-term memory decays quickly as time passes. Do long-term memories also decay? One early explanation for forgetting was **decay theory**, which proposed that with time and disuse the long-term physical memory trace in the nervous system fades away. Decay theory soon fell into disfavour because scientists could not locate physical memory traces nor measure physical decay. In recent decades, however, scientists have begun to unravel how neural circuits change when a long-term memory is formed. This has sparked new interest in examining how these changes might decay over time (Villarreal et al., 2002).

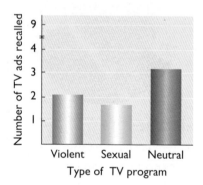

FIGURE 8.22

Violence, sex and memory for television commercials.

In one study, television viewers who watched programmes with violent or sexual content recalled fewer commercials than viewers who watched a neutral programme.

SOURCE: based on Bushman and Bonacci, 2002.

Unfortunately, decay theory's prediction – the longer the time interval of disuse between learning and recall, the less should be recalled – is problematic. Some professional actors display perfect memory for words they had last spoken on stage two years earlier – this despite having moved on to new acting roles and scripts (Noice and Noice, 2002b). Moreover, when research participants learn a list of words or a set of visual patterns and are retested at two different times, they sometimes recall material during the second testing that they could not remember during the first. This phenomenon, called *reminiscence*, seems inconsistent with the concept that a memory trace decays over time (Greene, 1992). In sum, scientists still debate the validity of decay theory.

Interference

According to *interference theory*, we forget information because other items in long-term memory impair our ability to retrieve it (Postman and Underwood, 1973). Figure 8.23 illustrates two major types of interference. **Proactive interference** occurs when material learned in the past interferes with recall of newer material. Suppose that Kim changes residences, gets a new phone number, and memorizes it. That night, when a friend asks Kim for her new number, she can recall only three digits and instead keeps remembering her old phone number. Memory of her old phone number is interfering with her ability to retrieve the new one.

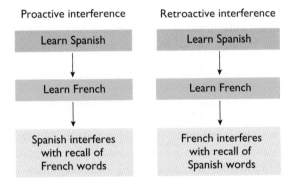

Retroactive interference occurs when newly acquired information interferes with the ability to recall information learned at an earlier time. Suppose Kim has now had her new phone number for two months and recalls it perfectly. If we ask her, 'What was your old number?' Kim may have trouble recalling it, perhaps mixing up the digits with her new number. In general, the more similar two sets of information are, the more likely it is that interference will occur. Kim (or you) would probably experience little interference in recalling highly dissimilar material, such as her new phone number and French vocabulary.

Why does interference occur? It takes time for the brain to convert short-term memories into long-term memories, and some researchers propose that when new information is entered into the system, it can disrupt (i.e., retroactively interfere with) the conversion of older information into long-term memories (Wixted, 2005). Others believe that once long-term memories are formed, retroactive and proactive interference are caused by competition among retrieval cues (Anderson and Neely, 1996). When different memories become associated with similar or identical retrieval cues, confusion can result and accessing a cue may call up the wrong memory. Retrieval failure also can occur because we have too few retrieval cues or the cues may be too weak.

Almost all of us have experienced a retrieval problem called the **tip-of-the-tongue (TOT) state**, in which we cannot recall something but feel that we are on the verge of remembering it. When Bennett Schwartz (2002) asked 56 college students to record a diary for four weeks, he found that they averaged just over one TOT experience per week. Most often, TOT states aroused emotion and were triggered by the inability to remember the name of an acquaintance, a famous person or an object. Sooner or later, the answer often popped into the mind spontaneously, but in many cases students had to consult a book or another person.

proactive interference

occurs when material learned in the past interferes with recall of newer material

Focus 8.15

Why is motivated forgetting a controversial concept? Describe some types and causes of amnesia and the nature of prospective memory.

FIGURE 8.23

Interference and forgetting.

Interference is a major cause of forgetting. With proactive interference, older memories interfere with the retrieval of newer ones. With retroactive interference, newer memories interfere with the retrieval of older ones.

retroactive interference

occurs when newly acquired information interferes with the ability to recall information learned at an earlier time

tip-of-the-tongue (TOT) state

we cannot recall something but feel that we are on the verge of remembering it

WHAT DO YOU THINK?

IS IT REALLY ON THE TIP OF YOUR TONGUE?

Suppose you're having a TOT experience. Should you assume that it is a retrieval problem? What else might explain your inability to come up with an answer? Think about it, then see p. 380.

Motivated Forgetting

Psychodynamic and other psychologists propose that, at times, people are consciously or unconsciously motivated to forget. Sigmund Freud often observed that during therapy, his patients remembered long-forgotten traumatic or anxiety-arousing events. One of his patients suddenly remembered with great shame that while standing beside her sister's coffin she had thought, 'Now my brother-in-law is free to marry me'. Freud concluded that the thought had been so shocking and anxiety arousing that the woman had *repressed* it – pushed it down into her unconscious mind, there to remain until it was uncovered years later during therapy. **Repression** is a motivational process that protects us by blocking the conscious recall of anxiety-arousing memories.

The concept of repression is controversial. Some evidence supports it, and other evidence does not (Karon, 2002). People certainly do forget unpleasant events – even traumatic ones – yet they also forget very pleasant events. If a person cannot remember a negative experience, is this due to repression or to normal information-processing failures (Epstein and Bottoms, 2002)? Overall, it has been difficult to demonstrate experimentally that a special process akin to repression is the cause of memory loss for anxiety-arousing events (Holmes, 1990). We will return to this topic shortly.

FORGETTING TO DO THINGS: PROSPECTIVE MEMORY

Have you ever forgotten to mail a letter, turn off the oven, keep an appointment or purchase something at the market? In contrast to *retrospective memory*, which refers to memory for past events, **prospective memory** concerns remembering to perform an activity in the future. That people forget to do things as often as they do is interesting, because prospective memories typically involve little content. Often we need only recall that we must perform some event-based task ('Remember, on your way out, mail the letter.') or time-based task ('Remember, take your medication at 4 p.m.'). Successful prospective memory, however, draws on other cognitive abilities, such as planning and allocating attention while performing other tasks.

During adulthood, do we become increasingly absentminded about remembering to do things, as a common stereotype suggests? Numerous laboratory experiments support this view (Vogels et al., 2002). Typically, participants perform a task that requires their ongoing attention while trying to remember to signal the experimenter at certain time intervals or whenever specific events take place. Older adults generally display poorer prospective memory, especially when signalling is time based. However, when prospective memory is tested outside the laboratory using tasks such as simulated pill-taking, healthy adults in their sixties to eighties often perform as well as or better than adults in their twenties (Rendell and Thomson, 1999). Perhaps older adults are more motivated to remember in such situations, or they rely more on habit and setting up a standard routine (Anderson and Craik, 2000).

repression

a motivational process that protects us by blocking the conscious recall of anxiety-arousing memories

prospective memory

remembering to perform an activity in the future

AMNESIA

As HM's case illustrates, the most dramatic instances of forgetting occur in amnesia. The term *amnesia* commonly refers to memory loss due to special conditions, such as brain injury, illness or psychological trauma. However, as we will see shortly, there is one type of amnesia that all of us experience.

Retrograde and Anterograde Amnesia

Amnesia takes several forms. **Retrograde amnesia** represents memory loss for events that took place sometime in life before the onset of amnesia. For example, HM's brain operation, which took place at age 27, caused him to experience mild memory loss for events in his life that had occurred during the preceding year or two (i.e., when he was 25 to 26 years old). Football players experience retrograde amnesia when they are knocked out by a concussion, regain consciousness and cannot remember the events just before being hit.

Anterograde amnesia refers to memory loss for events that occur after the initial onset of amnesia. HM's brain operation, and particularly the removal of much of his hippocampus, produced severe anterograde amnesia and robbed him of the ability to consciously remember new experiences and facts. Similarly, the woman whose hand was pinpricked by Swiss psychologist Edouard Claparède during a handshake also suffered from anterograde amnesia; moments later she could not consciously remember the episode. Unlike HM's anterograde amnesia, hers was caused by *Korsakoff's syndrome*, which can result from chronic alcoholism and may also cause severe retrograde amnesia.

Dementia and Alzheimer's Disease

Dementia refers to impaired memory and other cognitive deficits that accompany brain degeneration and interfere with normal functioning. There are more than a dozen types and causes of dementia, and although it can occur at any point in life, dementia is most prevalent among elderly adults.

Alzheimer's disease (AD) is a progressive brain disorder that is the most common cause of dementia among adults over the age of 65, accounting for about 50 to 60 per cent of such cases. Overall, 2 to 4 per cent of elderly adults are estimated to have AD.

The early symptoms of AD, which worsen gradually over a period of years, include forgetfulness, poor judgement, confusion and disorientation. Often, memory for recent events and new information is especially impaired. By itself, forgetfulness is not necessarily a sign that a person is developing AD. However, memory is the first psychological function affected, as AD initially attacks subcortical temporal lobe regions – areas near the hippocampus and then the hippocampus itself – that help convert short-term memories into long-term memories.

Alzheimer's disease spreads across the temporal lobes and to the frontal lobes and other cortical regions (Fig. 8.24). As German physician, Alois Alzheimer, first noticed a century ago,

retrograde amnesia
memory loss for events that took place sometime in life before the onset of amnesia

anterograde amnesia
memory loss for events that occur after the initial onset of amnesia

dementia
impaired memory and other cognitive deficits that accompany brain degeneration and interfere with normal functioning

Alzheimer's disease (AD)
a progressive brain disorder that is the most common cause of dementia among adults over the age of 65

The progression of Alzhelmer's disease

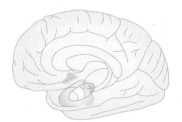
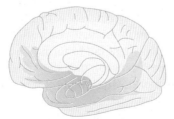

Preclinical AD   Mild to moderate AD   Severe AD

Blue indicates areas affected at various stages of AD

FIGURE 8.24

The progression of Alzheimer's disease.

SOURCE: National Institutes of Health, 2002.

patients with this disease have an abnormal amount of plaques and tangles in their brain. *Plaques* are clumps of protein fragments that build up on the outside of neurons, whereas *tangles* are fibres that get twisted and wound together within neurons (Cattabeni et al., 2004). Neurons become damaged and die, brain tissue shrinks and communication between neurons is impaired as AD disrupts several neurotransmitter systems, especially the acetylcholine system. Acetylcholine plays a key role in synaptic transmission in several brain areas involved in memory, and drugs that help maintain acetylcholine functioning have had some temporary success in improving AD patients' cognitive functioning (Ritchie et al., 2004).

Working memory and long-term memory worsen as AD progresses. If you read a list of just three words to healthy 80-year-old adults and then test their recall after a brief time delay, they will typically remember two or all three words. Patients with AD, however, typically recall either no words or one word (Chandler et al., 2004). Anterograde and retrograde amnesia become more severe, and procedural, semantic, episodic and prospective memory can all be affected. Patients may lose the ability to learn new tasks or remember new information or experiences, forget how to perform familiar tasks and have trouble recognizing even close family members.

What causes AD and its characteristic plaques and tangles? Scientists have identified several genes that contribute to early-onset AD, an inherited form of the disease that develops before the age of 65 (and as early as age 30) but accounts for only 5 to 10 per cent of Alzheimer's cases (Cattabeni et al., 2004). The precise causes of the more typical, late-onset AD remain elusive, but researchers have identified one genetic risk factor. This gene helps direct the production of proteins that carry cholesterol in the blood plasma, and high cholesterol and other risk factors for cardiovascular disease may likewise increase the risk of developing AD. Indeed, a recent study found that even healthy elderly adults who carried this particular gene, as compared to peers who did not, performed more poorly on a prospective memory task (Driscoll et al., 2005).

If you know someone who has AD, then you are aware that it involves much more than memory loss. Patients experience language problems, disorganized thinking, and mood and personality changes. Ultimately, they may lose the ability to speak, walk, and control bladder and bowel functions. We have more to say about the psychological, physical and social aspects of dementia and ageing in Chapter 12.

Infantile (Childhood) Amnesia

There is one type of amnesia that almost all of us encounter: an inability to remember personal experiences from the first few years of our lives. Even though infants and pre-schoolers can form long-term memories of events in their lives (Peterson and Whalen, 2001), as adults we typically are unable to recall these events consciously. This memory loss for early experiences is called **infantile amnesia** (also known as *childhood amnesia*). Our memories of childhood typically do not include events that occurred before the age of 3 or 4, although some adults can partially recall major events (e.g., the birth of a sibling, hospitalization or a death in the family) that happened before the age of 2 (Eacott and Crawley, 1998).

What causes infantile amnesia? One hypothesis is that brain regions that encode long-term episodic memories are still immature in the first years after birth. Another is that we do not encode our earliest experiences deeply and fail to form rich retrieval cues for them. Additionally, because infants lack a clear self-concept, they do not have a personal frame of reference around which to organize rich memories (Harley and Reese, 1999).

infantile amnesia

memory loss for early experiences

IN REVIEW

- Forgetting tends to occur most rapidly soon after initial learning, but the time frame and degree of forgetting can vary widely depending on many factors.

- We often cannot recall information because we never encoded it into long-term memory in the first place. Decay theory proposes that physical memory traces in long-term memory deteriorate with disuse over time.

- Proactive interference occurs when material learned in the past impairs recall of newer material. Retroactive interference occurs when newly acquired material impairs the ability to recall information learned at an earlier time.

- Psychodynamic theorists propose that we may forget anxiety-arousing material through repression, an unconscious process of motivated forgetting.

- Whereas retrospective memory refers to memory for past events, prospective memory refers to our ability to remember to perform some activity in the future.

- Retrograde amnesia is memory loss for events that occurred before the onset of amnesia. Anterograde amnesia refers to memory loss for events that occur after the initial onset of amnesia. Alzheimer's disease produces both types of amnesia and is the leading cause of dementia among elderly adults. Infantile amnesia is our inability to remember experiences from the first few years of our lives.

MEMORY AS A CONSTRUCTIVE PROCESS

Retrieving information from long-term memory is not like viewing a digital replay. Our memories are often incomplete or sketchy. We may literally *construct* (or, as some say, *reconstruct*) a memory by piecing together bits of stored information in a way that seems real and accurate. Yet, as our discussion of flashbulb memories illustrated, we may be highly confident of memories that in fact are inaccurate.

Memory construction can be amusing at times. Many of us have a tendency to recall the world through slightly rose-tinted glasses, which helps us feel good about ourselves. For example, when college students in one study recalled their high school grades, the worse the grade was, the less often students remembered it accurately. Students correctly recalled almost all of their As, but only a third of their Ds (Fig. 8.25). Most important, errors were positively biased; students usually misremembered their Bs as having been As, their Cs as Bs, and their Ds as Cs (Bahrick et al., 1996). As we will see, however, memory construction also can have serious personal and societal consequences.

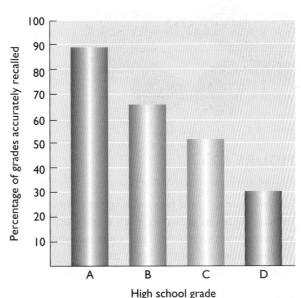

FIGURE 8.25

Rosy recall of high school grades.

The lower the grade, the less likely students were to accurately recall it. When students incorrectly recalled a grade, they almost always overestimated how well they did.

SOURCE: adapted from Bahrick et al., 1996.

MEMORY DISTORTION AND SCHEMAS

Decades ago, Sir Frederick Bartlett (1932) asked residents of Cambridge, England, to read stories and then retell them days or months later. One story, a Pacific Northwest Indian tale called 'The War of the Ghosts', describes two young men who go down to a river to hunt seals. While there, warriors in canoes come up the river, and one of the young men agrees to join them for a raid on a town. During the raid, the man discovers that his companions are ghosts, and later he dies a mysterious death.

Bartlett's participants were twentieth-century residents of England, not eighteenth-century Native Americans. When they retold the story, they partly reconstructed it in a way that made sense to them. A day after reading the story, one participant shortened it by almost half, described the hero as fishing rather than as hunting seals, and substituted the word *boat* for *canoe*. Bartlett found that the longer the time interval between the reading and retelling of the story, the more the story changed to fit English culture.

Bartlett, who coined the term *schema*, believed that people have generalized ideas (schemas) about how events happen, which they use to organize information and construct their memories. Recall, for example, the laundry-washing description. Schemas, however, often distort our memories by leading us to encode or retrieve information in ways that make sense and fit in with our pre-existing assumptions about the world.

Quite literally, memory construction extends to how we visualize the world (Intraub, 2002). As Figure 8.26 illustrates, when college students in one study looked at photographs that had a main object within a scene and then drew what they saw from memory, they consistently displayed *boundary extension*; they remembered the scene as more expansive (in this case, wider-angled) than it really was (Intraub et al., 1996). In real life, objects usually occur against an expansive background, creating a schema for how we expect scenes to look. Thus when we remember close-up images, our schemas lead us to recall a broader scene than the one we saw. The following 'Research close-up' offers some insight into how schemas can lead us to remember things that never happened.

Focus 8.16

Discuss examples of memory construction, and explain how schemas influence this process.

Focus 8.17

How did the 'Research close-up' studies investigate false memories? What might have caused the false memories?

(a)

(b)

FIGURE 8.26

Boundary extension: What you see . . . what you remember.

Helene Intraub and her colleagues (1996) have found that when people (a) briefly look at close-up pictures, such as this one of a teddy bear, and then (b) draw the pictures from memory, they unknowingly convert the image into a wide-angle scene in which the size of the main object shrinks. This effect is less likely to occur if the original picture is already a wide-angle scene.

SOURCE: images courtesy of Helene Intraub.

RESEARCH CLOSE-UP

MEMORY ILLUSIONS: REMEMBERING THINGS THAT NEVER OCCURRED

STUDY 1: COLLEGE STUDENTS REMEMBERING WORD LISTS

SOURCE: H.L. Roediger III and K. McDermott (1995) Creating false memories: remembering words not presented in lists, *Journal of Experimental Psychology: Learning, Memory, and Cognition*, vol. 21, pp. 803–14.

Introduction

In this famous experiment, Henry Roediger III and Kathleen McDermott examined how often false memories occurred while people performed a simple task: remembering lists of words. They also investigated whether people experience false memories as being vivid and clear.

Method

Building on previous research (Deese, 1959), the researchers created lists of 15 words. Each list contained words that, to varying degrees, were associated with a central organizing word. To illustrate, look at the following list:

sour, candy, sugar, bitter, good, taste, tooth, nice, honey, soda, chocolate, heart, cake, tart, pie

The word *sweet* does not occur in the list, yet it is associated with these items. The central word (*sweet*) is called a *critical lure*.

Thirty-six college students each listened to 16 lists. For some lists, students' recall was measured as soon as each list ended. Then, after hearing all 16 lists, students performed a recognition task. They were given a sheet of paper with 96 words, half of which actually had been on the lists. The other words were critical lures and filler items. Students identified whether each word had been on the lists they heard. If they selected a word, they also reported whether they had a vivid memory of having heard it or, instead, were sure that they had heard it but lacked a vivid memory.

Results

Students correctly recalled 62 per cent of the real words but falsely recalled almost as many (55 per cent) of the critical lures. On the recognition task, they correctly identified 62 per cent of the actual words but falsely identified 72 per cent of the critical lures. And in just over half of the cases where students falsely recognized a critical lure, they reported having a vivid memory of it.

Discussion

Although critical lures were never presented, students falsely recalled them half the time and falsely recognized them almost three quarters of the time. Moreover, students often reported having a clear memory of the nonexistent critical lure. Many researchers have replicated this finding.

What causes these false memories? Roediger and McDermott (1995; 2000) argue that hearing the words activates an associative network – a schema – for the critical lure.

For some people, the words *sour*, *candy*, *sugar*, etc. may consciously trigger a thought of 'sweet'. For others, spreading activation from the words unconsciously primes the concept of 'sweet'. Either way, the critical lure is activated, so that during retrieval people may misinterpret the source of activation and falsely remember the lure as being on the list (Fig. 8.27a).

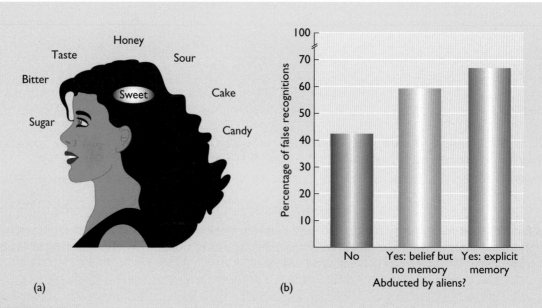

(a)   (b)

FIGURE 8.27

Memory illusion.

(a) After listening to a list of related words, people often remember hearing a critical lure (sweet) that was never presented. (b) This graph shows the degree of false recognition of critical lures among three groups of participants.

SOURCE: based on Clancy et al., 2002.

   In your view, are these findings relevant to memory in the real world? Critics argue that the research context – college students learning word lists – may have little relevance to situations involving memory for important events. Yet Roediger and McDermott argue that this context makes the findings more impressive. Students knew it was a memory test and that inaccurate memories would be spotted. Further, memory was tested soon after hearing each list. If people can be confident of their false memories in this straightforward situation, then what might happen in real-world contexts where conditions for remembering events are more complex and not as optimal?

STUDY 2: PERSISTANT DÉJÀ VECU

SOURCE: C.J.A. Moulin, M.A. Conway, R.G. Thompson, N. James and R. Jones (2005) Disordered memory awareness: recollective confabulation in two cases of persistent déjà vecu, *Neuropsychologia*, vol. 43, pp. 1362–78.

Introduction

There are many studies involving difficulties with memory and the vast majority of them focus on problems with recalling information. However, these are not the only disorders of memory that may be observed. In this interesting study Chris Moulin and his colleagues report the cases of two individuals who claimed to have the sensation of having previously lived through the present moment, or persistent déjà vecu. Moulin et al. define déjà vecu as an error of recollection rather than the strange sensation of familiarity that is sometimes, temporarily experienced as déjà vu. One of their patients (AKP) was found to have atrophy to the temporal lobes and the hippocampus with greater loss of cells to the left hemisphere while the other (MA) had a diagnosis of Alzheimer's disease.

Method

Moulin et al. conducted a range of tests on AKP and MA and compared them to a group of control participants. These tests included tests of source memory (where something was learned) and recognition tests including both words and faces as material. They also took a measures of metacognition; this involves assessing whether the patients are able to make accurate judgements about the contents of their memory.

Results and discussion

The main findings from their three experiments were that the two patients made far more judgements of remembering for items that were not present in tests of memory than the control participants did. What is important here is that the level of these false positives (claiming to remember items that were not presented in the learning phase) was higher than for the control participants and that the patients frequently considered that they *remembered* the items rather than just considered them to be familiar (which is more often the case with controls). Thus it seems that the patients had *recollective experience* for items that they had not learned, and that this recollective experience seemed to be more likely with items that were rare (such as low frequency words). Interestingly, both patients were able to make accurate assessments of their memory as shown by the metacognitive tasks employed.

Moulin et al. argued that the explanation for the experiences that the patients have is that there is a problem with inhibiting output from long-term memory. Memories are activated by the cues they receive but they do not reach conscious awareness. However, their level of activation is sufficient to cause the recollective experience, and this is uncontrolled because of the brain damage. Looking at the pattern of brain damage that their patients had and from the findings of related research they argued that it is damage to fronto-temporal circuits that causes the difficulties that their patients reported.

MISINFORMATION EFFECTS AND EYEWITNESS TESTIMONY

If memories are constructed, then information that occurs *after* an event may shape that construction process. This **misinformation effect**, the distortion of a memory by misleading post-event information, has frequently been investigated in relation to mistaken eyewitness testimony. In one celebrated case, Father Bernard Pagano, a Roman Catholic priest, was positively identified by seven eyewitnesses as the perpetrator of a series of armed robberies in the Wilmington, Delaware, area. He was saved from almost certain conviction when the true robber, dubbed the 'gentleman bandit' because of his politeness and concern for his victims, confessed to the crimes. You can see in Figure 8.28 that there was little physical resemblance between the two men.

misinformation effect
the distortion of a memory by misleading post-event information

Focus 8.18
Describe the misinformation effect, why it occurs, and how it affects memory accuracy in children and adults.

FIGURE 8.28

Seven eyewitnesses to armed robberies committed by Ronald Clouser (*left*) mistakenly identified Father Bernard Pagano (*right*) as the robber, probably as a result of information from police that influenced their memory reconstructions.

In-Psych

Watch the video, 'When Eyes Deceive', in Chapter 8 of the In-Psych programme online to see a research experiment illustrating the unreliability of eyewitness testimony.

FIGURE 8.29

A misinformation effect.

College students' memory of how fast two cars were moving just before an accident varied significantly depending on how the question was phrased.

SOURCE: adapted from Loftus and Palmer, 1974.

source confusion

our tendency to recall something or recognize it as familiar but to forget where we encountered it

Two key factors may have distorted the witnesses' memory. First, the polite manner of the robber is consistent with the schema many people have of priests. Second, before presenting pictures of suspects to the eyewitnesses, the police let it be known that the suspect might be a priest. Father Pagano was the only suspect wearing a clerical collar (Tversky and Tuchin, 1989).

Even one or two words can produce a misinformation effect while questioning an eyewitness. Imagine that after witnessing a two-car crash, a police officer takes your statement and asks you, 'About how fast were the cars going when they *contacted* each other?' In one experiment, college students viewed films of car accidents and then judged how fast the cars were going. As Figure 8.29 shows, the judged speed increased by up to 33 per cent when the word *contacted* was changed to *hit*, *bumped into*, *collided with*, or *smashed into* (Loftus and Palmer, 1974).

How fast were the two cars going when they _____ each other?	
Words	Perceived speed
Smashed into	41 mph
Collided with	39 mph
Bumped into	38 mph
Hit	34 mph
Contacted	31 mph

Source Confusion

Misinformation effects also occur because of **source confusion** (also called source monitoring error), our tendency to recall something or recognize it as familiar but to forget where we encountered it. Suppose an eyewitness to a crime looks through a series of photographs and reports that none of the individuals in the photographs is the perpetrator. Several days later, the eyewitness is brought back to view a live line-up and is asked to identify the person who committed the crime. In reality, none of the people in the line-up did, but one suspect was pictured in a photograph that the eyewitness had seen days earlier. 'That's the person', says the eyewitness. Source confusion occurs because the eyewitness recognizes the individual's face but fails to remember that this recognition stems from the photograph. Instead, the witness mistakenly assumes that he or she saw the familiar-looking suspect committing the crime.

In an experimental analogue to this situation, 29 per cent of participants who witnessed a staged event and later viewed photographs misidentified *innocent* suspects as having been involved in the event because of source confusion (Brown et al., 1977). Source confusion also occurs when people witness an event (e.g., a video of an unarmed home burglar) and then are exposed to misleading, suggestive statements about it (e.g., that the burglar had a gun). They may forget that the source of the misinformation was a question or statement made by someone else and then come to believe it was part of the event they had witnessed (Mitchell and Zaragoza, 2001).

Researchers have begun to use brain-imaging techniques to study the neural activity that occurs when false memories are created by misinformation (Okado and Stark, 2005), but the debate over whether misinformation permanently alters a witness's original memory is far from resolved. Still, researchers overwhelmingly agree that misinformation can distort eyewitness reports. Results like these have raised concerns about the reliability of eyewitness testimony not only from adults but also from children in cases of alleged physical and sexual abuse.

THE CHILD AS EYEWITNESS

In cases of alleged child sexual abuse, there is often no conclusive corroborating medical evidence and the child is usually the only witness (Bruck et al., 1998). If the charges are true, failing to convict the abuser and returning the child to an abusive environment is unthinkable. Conversely, if the charges are false, the consequences of convicting an innocent person are equally distressing.

Accuracy and Suggestibility

A single instance of suggestive questioning can distort some children's memory, but suggestive questioning most often leads to false memories when it is repeated. Young children are typically more susceptible to misleading suggestions than older children (Ceci et al., 2000).

In one experiment by Michelle Leichtman and Stephen Ceci (1995), 3- to 6-year-old children were told about a man named Sam Stone. Over several weeks, some children were repeatedly told stories that portrayed Sam as clumsy. Later Sam visited their classroom, was introduced, and behaved innocuously. The next day, the children were shown a ripped book and soiled teddy bear, things for which Sam was not responsible. Over the next 10 weeks they were interviewed several times, and some were asked suggestive questions about Sam (e.g., 'When Sam Stone tore the book, did he do it on purpose, or was he being silly?'). Two weeks later a new interviewer asked all the children to describe Sam's visit to the classroom.

Children who had heard suggestive information about Sam – whether before, after, or especially before *and* after Sam's appearance – made more false reports about Sam's behaviour than a control group that had never heard suggestive information. One child stated that after soaking the teddy bear in the bath, Sam smeared it with a crayon. These findings are troubling, because during many sexual-abuse investigations, the child initially denies being abused, but then after repeated suggestive questioning during therapy or police interviewing, the child acknowledges the abuse (Bruck et al., 1998). Was the child understandably reluctant to open up at first, or did suggestive questions produce a false allegation?

Recall of traumatic events   How well do children remember traumatic events? Elaine Burgwyn-Bailes and co-workers (2001) interviewed 3- to 7-year-olds a few days, six weeks, and one year after the children underwent emergency plastic surgery for facial lacerations. At each interview, children accurately remembered most of the details of their operations, but they also mistakenly agreed with about 15 per cent of leading questions ('Did the doctor's helper use any needles?') and suggestive questions ('The lady took off your watch, didn't she?') about events that never occurred. Compared to older children, younger children remembered fewer true details and agreed more often to leading and suggestive questions.

True Versus False Reports: Can Professionals Tell Them Apart?

Can professionals reliably distinguish between children's accurate and false reports? The answer appears to be no, at least when false reports are caused by repeated, suggestive questioning. Mental health workers, social workers, prosecutors, and judges shown videotapes of children's reports in the Sam Stone experiment often rated false reports as highly credible. Perhaps many children who make false reports are credible because they are not intentionally lying; rather, they believe their memories are accurate. After suggestive questioning, children are as confident of their false memories as they are of their accurate ones (Roebers, 2002).

What should society do? Like adults, young children accurately remember a lot, but they also misremember and are susceptible to repeated suggestive questioning. Thanks to psychological research, law enforcement officials, mental health workers and legal professionals are now paying more attention to how children's admissions of abuse are elicited, and training programmes are helping practitioners minimize suggestive interviewing techniques (Sternberg et al., 2002).

The goal is not to discredit children's allegations of abuse. On the contrary, the hope is that by minimizing the risk of false allegations, non-suggestive interviewing will elicit allegations judged as even more compelling, thereby helping to ensure that justice is done.

THE RECOVERED MEMORY CONTROVERSY

In 1997 a woman from Illinois settled a lawsuit against two psychiatrists and their hospital for $10.6 million. She alleged that her psychiatrists used hypnosis, drugs and other treatments that led her to develop false memories of having been a high priestess in a sexually abusive satanic cult (*APA Monitor*, 1997). Yet only years earlier, there had been a wave of cases in which adults – usually in the course of psychotherapy – began to remember long-forgotten childhood sexual abuse and sued their parents, other family members and former teachers for the alleged trauma (Fig. 8.30).

The scientific controversy over the validity of recovered memories of childhood trauma involves two issues. First, when a recovered memory of sexual abuse occurs, is it accurate? Second, if the abuse really happened, what caused the memory to be forgotten – repression or another psychological process? Let us briefly examine the second issue. Many scientists and therapists question Freud's concept of repression. Repression implies a special psychological mechanism that actively pushes traumatic memories into the unconscious mind, and we have already noted that researchers have had difficulty demonstrating it experimentally.

Recovered memories of childhood sexual abuse or other traumas cannot be taken as automatic evidence of repression. Memory loss may have occurred because of ordinary sources of forgetting or because the victim intentionally avoided thinking about the abuse or reinterpreted the trauma to make it less upsetting (Epstein and Bottoms, 2002). But beyond these factors, other researchers and many therapists believe that repression is a valid concept (Brewin, 2004). This controversy will not be resolved soon.

What about the more basic question? Can someone forget childhood sexual abuse, by whatever psychological mechanism, and then recover that memory as an adult? Indeed, some survivors of natural disasters, children who witness the violent death of a parent, victims of rape, combat veterans, and victims of sexual and physical abuse have shown limited or no memory of their traumas (Epstein and Bottoms, 2002). Some victims of documented child sexual abuse do not recall their trauma when they are adults, and accurate memories of the abuse can indeed return after many years of post-trauma forgetting (Kluft, 1999). Yet memory loss after psychological trauma is usually far shorter, with memory returning over weeks, months or, perhaps, a few years. In many cases of trauma, the victim's primary problem is not memory loss but rather an *inability* to forget, which may involve involuntary nightmares or flashbacks (Berntsen, 2001).

Experiments reveal that when exposed to suggestive questioning, American college students developed false memories of personal childhood events that never happened (e.g., being hospitalized overnight), and residents of Moscow developed false memories for fictitious details (e.g., the presence of injured animals) of a 1999 terrorist bombing in their city (Nourkova et al., 2004). Such studies may not tap the intense trauma of directly experiencing sexual abuse, and for ethical reasons experimenters do not test whether false memories of sexual abuse can be implanted. Nevertheless, say many researchers and clinicians, add these findings to everything science has taught us about forgetting and constructive memory, and the conclusion is that we should not take the accuracy of recovered memories at face value (Pickrell et al., 2003). They are especially concerned that in recovered-memory therapy, therapists repeatedly suggest the possibility of abuse to people who are already emotionally vulnerable.

The message from science is not that all claims of recovered traumatic memories should be dismissed. Rather, it is to urge caution in unconditionally accepting those memories, particu-

Focus 8.19

Discuss the recovered memory controversy, the two key issues involved and relevant evidence.

FIGURE 8.30

In a famous 1990 case, George Franklin was convicted of the 1969 murder of 8-year-old Susan Nason. Franklin's 28-year-old daughter Eileen (*shown here*), who had been Susan's childhood friend, provided the key evidence. During therapy Eileen recovered memories of her father sexually assaulting and killing Susan. A judge overturned the conviction after learning that Eileen's memories had been recovered under hypnosis.

Focus 8.20

Illustrate how culture influences memory construction.

larly when suggestive techniques are used to recover the memories (Brandon et al., 1998). Some day it may be scientifically possible to separate true memories from false ones; researchers have begun to examine whether some types of true versus false memories are associated with different patterns of brain activity. But at present, these findings cannot be used to determine reliably whether any individual memory is true or false (Pickrell et al., 2003).

CULTURE AND MEMORY CONSTRUCTION

Culture and memory have a reciprocal relation. On the one hand, cultural survival depends on transmitting knowledge and customs from one generation to the next. Without our capacity to remember events and information, culture simply could not exist (nor could we, as a species).

At the same time, culture influences memory. Our cultural upbringing shapes the schemas that we acquire and use to perceive ourselves and the world. For example, as we discussed in Chapter 1, most people living in northern Europe and North America learn to view the world through a relatively *individualistic* lens in which self-identity is based primarily on one's own attributes and achievements. People living in many Asian, African and South American cultures tend to see the world through a more *collectivistic* framework in which personal identity is defined largely by ties to the extended family and other social groups. If cultural socialization influences our schemas and our schemas influence how we encode and reconstruct events, then people from different cultures may recall events in somewhat distinct ways.

Let us consider an example: our earliest memories. In one study, Qi Wang (2001) asked over 200 college students from Harvard University and Beijing University to describe their earliest memories (Fig. 8.31). He predicted and found that the Americans were more likely than their Chinese counterparts to recall events that focused on individual experiences and self-determination (e.g., 'I was sorting baseball cards when I dropped them. As I reached down to get them, I knocked over a jug of iced tea.'). In contrast, Chinese students were more likely than American students to recall memories that involved family or neighbourhood activities (e.g., 'Dad taught me ancient poems. It was always when he was washing vegetables that he would explain a poem to me.').

Wang also found that American college students dated their earliest personal memory back to the time when they were, on average, 3 years old. Students in China, however, reported memories that, on average, dated to the time they were almost 4 years old. Although the reason is not

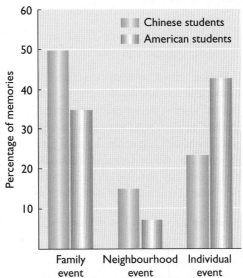

FIGURE 8.31

Culture and our earliest memories.

What is your earliest memory? In one study, Chinese students recalled events that, overall, were more family and neighbourhood oriented than events recalled by American students. How else might our cultural upbringing and worldview influence memory?

SOURCE: based on Wang, 2001.

clear, it may relate to American students' greater tendency to report earliest memories of single, distinctive events that involved greater emotionality, whereas Chinese students were more likely than Americans to report more routine events that involved collective activity. Other researchers also have found cross-cultural differences in age of earliest memories. When Shelley MacDonald and co-workers (2000) studied New Zealand European, New Zealand Asian, New Zealand Maori, and Chinese adults, they found that Maori adults – whose traditional culture strongly values the past – recalled the earliest personal memories.

IN REVIEW

- Our schemas may cause us to misremember events in ways that fit with our pre-existing concepts about the world; they also may lead us to recall events that never occurred.

- Misinformation effects occur when our memory is distorted by misleading postevent information, and they often occur because of source confusion – our tendency to recall something or recognize it as familiar but to forget where we encountered it.

- Like adults, children experience misinformation effects. Vulnerability is greatest among younger children and when suggestive questions are asked repeatedly. Experts cannot reliably tell when children are reporting accurate memories versus sincerely believed false memories.

- Psychologists debate whether recovered memories of child abuse are accurate and whether they are forgotten through repression or other psychological processes. Concern about the possibility of false memory has led many experts to urge caution in unconditionally accepting the validity of recovered memories.

MEMORY AND THE BRAIN

Focus 8.21

Describe brain structures involved in memory and how changes in neural circuitry may underlie memory formation.

Where in your brain are memories located? How were they formed? The quest for answers has taken some remarkable twists. Psychologist Karl Lashley spent decades searching for the *engram* – the physical trace that presumably was stored in the brain when a memory was formed. Lashley (1950) trained animals to perform tasks, such as running mazes, and later removed or damaged (lesioned) specific regions of their cortexes to see if they would forget how to perform the task. No matter what small area was lesioned, memories remained intact. Lashley never found the engram and concluded that a memory is stored throughout the brain.

Perhaps most striking was James McConnell's (1962) discovery of 'memory transfer'. He classically conditioned flatworms to a light that was paired with electric shock, eventually causing the worms to contract to the light alone. Next he chopped them up and fed the RNA (ribonucleic acid) from their cells to untrained worms. Amazingly, the untrained worms showed some conditioning to the light, suggesting that RNA might be a memory molecule that stores experiences. Some scientists replicated these findings, but others were unable to, and McConnell eventually gave up on the idea (Rilling, 1996). Yet despite the inevitable dead ends, scientists have learned a great deal about memory processes in the brain.

WHERE ARE MEMORIES FORMED AND STORED?

To answer this question, scientists examine how damage to different brain regions affects the memory of human patients and laboratory animals; they also peer into the healthy human brain as research participants perform various memory tasks. These lines of research reveal that memory involves many interacting brain regions. Figure 8.32 shows a few of the major regions.

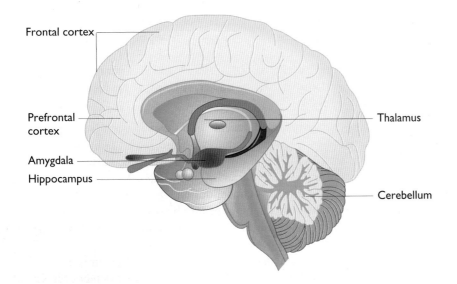

Frontal cortex

Prefrontal cortex

Amygdala

Hippocampus

Thalamus

Cerebellum

FIGURE 8.32

Some brain regions involved in memory.

Many areas of the brain, such as the regions shown here, play key roles in memory.

Sensory and Working Memory

Sensory memory depends on our visual, auditory, and other sensory systems to detect stimulus information (e.g., the sounds of 'Hi, my name is Carlos'), transform it into neural codes, and send it to the brain, where sensory areas of the cerebral cortex initially process it. As working memory becomes involved in different types of tasks – remembering a person's name and face, recalling a list of numbers or learning and rehearsing a concept in your textbook – a network of cortical areas located across different lobes of the brain becomes more active (Zhang et al., 2004). For example, using visuospatial working memory to form a mental image of an object will activate some of the same areas of the visual cortex and other brain regions that become more active when looking at the actual object (Ganis et al., 2004).

The frontal lobes – especially the prefrontal cortex – play key roles in working memory. The frontal lobes generally become more active during tasks that place greater demands on working memory. In one brain-imaging experiment, students had to pay attention to the meaning of words (i.e., deep, semantic encoding) or to whether the words were in capital or lowercase letters (i.e., shallow, perceptual encoding). Deeper encoding produced better memory for the words and, as Figure 8.33 shows, also produced greater activity in specific areas of the left prefrontal cortex (Gabrieli et al., 1996). Other imaging studies have found that spatial working-memory tasks produce somewhat greater activation in the right prefrontal cortex than verbal tasks do (Walter et al., 2003).

The frontal lobes seem to be particularly important in supporting central-executive functions, such as allocating attention to the other components of working memory. This does not mean, however, that the central executive resides exclusively within the frontal lobes. Frontal-lobe damage often – but not always – impairs central-executive functions of working memory. Moreover, patients with intact frontal lobes but damage in other brain areas may exhibit central-executive impairments (Adrés, 2003). Thus even the 'master control' executive functions of working memory depend on a network of neural activity that connects regions across the brain.

Long-Term Memory

Where are long-term memories formed and stored? Once again, multiple brain areas are involved, but the hippocampus and its adjacent areas appear to play important roles in encoding certain types of long-term memories (Squire et al., 2004).

Declarative memory Like HM, many patients with extensive hippocampal damage retain the use of their short-term memory but cannot form new, explicit long-term declarative memories –

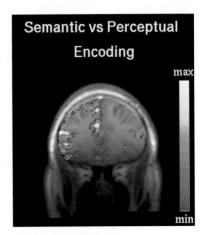

Semantic vs Perceptual Encoding

max

min

FIGURE 8.33

Depth of processing and the prefrontal lobes.

Four participants in one experiment performed shallow perceptual (i.e., structural) encoding and deep (semantic) encoding tasks while undergoing functional magnetic resonance imaging (fMRI). The results, shown here for one participant, revealed that semantic encoding was accompanied by greater neural activity in specific regions of the left prefrontal cortex.

SOURCE: photo courtesy of John Gabrieli.

memories for new personal experiences and facts. For example, one patient could recall the names of presidents elected before his brain injury occurred but not the names of presidents elected after his injury (Squire, 1987). The hippocampus does not seem to be the site where long-term declarative memories are permanently stored, which explains why HM retained his long-term memories acquired earlier in life. Rather, it helps to gradually convert short-term memories into permanent ones.

According to one view, the diverse components of an experience – where something happened, what the scene or people looked like, sounds we heard, the meaning of events or information, and so on – are processed initially in different regions of the cortex and then gradually bound together in the hippocampus (Squire and Zola-Morgan, 1991). This hypothetical and gradual binding process is called **memory consolidation**. Once a memory for a personal experience is consolidated, its various components appear to be stored across wide areas of the cortex, although we retrieve and reintegrate these components as a unified memory. Semantic memories (factual information) also appear to be stored across wide-ranging areas of the brain. As John Gabrieli (1998) notes, 'knowledge in any domain [e.g., for pictures or words] ... is distributed over a specific, but extensive, neural network that often extends over several lobes' (p. 94). Several brain regions, including portions of the prefrontal cortex and hippocampus, appear to be involved in consciously retrieving declarative memories (LePage et al., 1998; Tulving, 2002).

> **memory consolidation**
> hypothetical and gradual binding process

Although we have focused on the frontal lobes and hippocampus, memory formation also depends on other brain areas. For example, damage to the thalamus – the brain's major sensory relay station – can impair both the encoding of new memories and the retrieval of old ones (Van Der Werf et al., 2003). In one famous case, a young US Air Force technician named NA was injured in a freak accident (Squire, 1987). While his room-mate was practising thrusts with a miniature fencing foil, NA suddenly turned around in his seat and was stabbed through the right nostril, piercing his brain and damaging a portion of his thalamus. The damage permanently limited his ability to form new declarative memories. In many cases, thalamic damage also can cause permanent retrograde amnesia.

The amygdala encodes emotionally arousing aspects of stimuli and plays an important role in helping us form long-term memories for events that stir our emotions (McGaugh, 2004). As we discussed earlier, in laboratory experiments, most people remember emotionally arousing stimuli (e.g., film clips, slides) better than neutral ones. Damage to the amygdala eliminates much of this 'memory advantage' from arousing stimuli (LaBar and Phelps, 1998).

Procedural memory   Along with other parts of the brain, the cerebellum plays an important role in forming procedural memories. This helps explain why HM, whose cerebellum was not damaged by the operation, showed improved performance at various hand–eye co-ordination tasks (e.g., mirror tracing) even though he was unable to consciously remember having performed the tasks.

Richard Thompson (1985) and co-workers have examined another type of procedural memory. Studying rabbits, they repeatedly paired a tone (CS) with a puff of air to the eyes (UCS), and soon the tone alone caused the rabbits to blink. As the rabbits learned this conditioned response, electrical recordings revealed increased activity in the cerebellum. Later Thompson found that removing a tiny portion of the cerebellum completely abolished the memory for the *conditioned* eye-blink but did not affect the rabbits' general (unconditioned) eye-blink response. Similarly, eye-blink conditioning fails to work with human patients who have a damaged cerebellum (Green and Woodruff-Pak, 2000).

HOW ARE MEMORIES FORMED?

How does the nervous system form a memory? The answer appears to lie in chemical and physical changes that take place in the brain's neural circuitry.

Synaptic Change and Memory

Eric Kandel (2001) and his co-workers have studied a marine snail, *Aplysia californica*, for over 25 years – work for which Kandel received a Nobel Prize in 2000. *Aplysia* is no mental giant, but it can learn, form memories, and has only about 20 000 neurons (compared with our 100 billion) that are larger and easier to study than ours. For example, *Aplysia* retracts its gill slightly in self-defence when a breathing organ on top of the gill is gently squirted with water. But if a squirt is paired with electric shock to its tail, *Aplysia* covers up its gill with a protective flap of skin. After repeated pairings, *Aplysia* acquires a classically conditioned response and will cover its gill with the protective flap when the water is squirted alone. In other words, *Aplysia* forms a simple procedural memory.

Kandel and his co-workers have traced the formation of this procedural memory to a series of biochemical events that occur between and within various sensory neurons and motor neurons. How long these events last seems to be one key in determining whether short-term memories become long-term memories. If a single shock is paired with the squirt of water, certain chemical reactions shut off after a brief period and no permanent memory is formed. But with repeated pairings, these chemical reactions persist and a long-term memory forms. Days later, a squirt of water will still trigger a conditioned response.

During the conditioning procedure, various sensory neurons become densely packed with neurotransmitter release points, and postsynaptic motor neurons (which cause the protective flap to cover the gill) develop more receptor sites. These structural changes result in a greater ease of synaptic transmission that may be the basis for memory consolidation (Abel and Kandel, 1998).

Long-Term Potentiation

A different line of research, involving rats and other species with more complex nervous systems, supports the hypothesis that synaptic changes may be the basis for memory consolidation. Here, researchers try to mimic (albeit very crudely) a process of long-term memory formation by stimulating specific neural pathways with rapid bursts of electricity (say, 100 impulses per second for several seconds). They find that once this rapid stimulation ends, the neural pathway becomes stronger – synaptic connections are activated more easily – for days or even weeks (Martinez et al., 1998). This enduring increase in synaptic strength is called **long-term potentiation (LTP)**. Long-term potentiation has been studied most extensively in regions of the hippocampus where neurons send and receive using glutamate, the most abundant neurotransmitter in the brain.

For LTP to occur, complex biochemical events must take place inside and between these neurons. Administering drugs that inhibit these events will block LTP. Moreover, mice can be genetically bred to be deficient in certain proteins required for LTP. These mice not only have impaired long-term potentiation but also display memory deficits on a variety of learning tasks (Schimanski and Nguyen, 2005).

How, then, does LTP occur? At least in some cases, it appears that when neural pathways are sufficiently stimulated, the postsynaptic neurons alter their structure so that they become more responsive to glutamate. For example, postsynaptic neurons may change the shape of some receptor sites, or they may increase the number of receptor sites by developing additional tiny branches (spines) on their dendrites. This means that in the future, pre-synaptic neurons will not need to release as much glutamate in order to stimulate postsynaptic neurons to fire. In sum, the

long-term potentiation (LTP)
enduring increase in synaptic strength

formation of a long-term memory seems to involve long-lasting changes in synaptic efficiency that result from new or enhanced connections between pre-synaptic and postsynaptic neurons (Kandel, 2001).

In closing, we hope that this chapter has piqued your interest in understanding why we remember, forget and sometimes misremember. Figure 8.34 summarizes some factors involved in forgetting and memory distortion. We also hope that the chapter has applied value for you. Following the 'In review' summary, our 'Applying psychological science' feature describes some ways to enhance your own memory and academic learning.

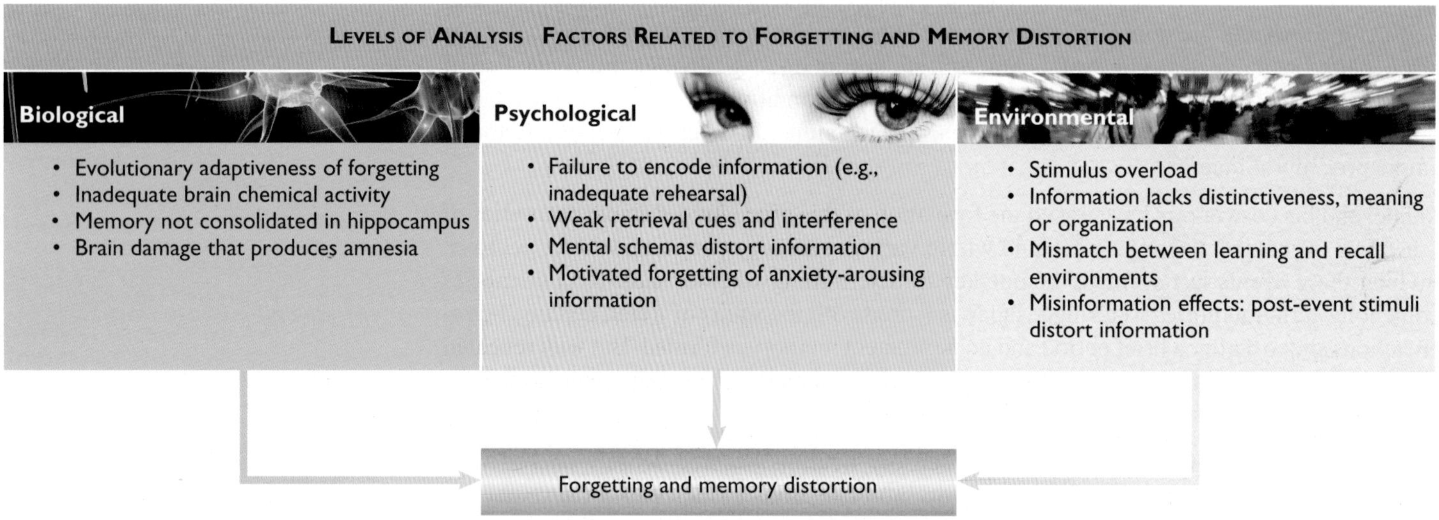

Focus 8.22

Identify practical principles for enhancing memory.

LEVELS OF ANALYSIS FACTORS RELATED TO FORGETTING AND MEMORY DISTORTION

Biological
- Evolutionary adaptiveness of forgetting
- Inadequate brain chemical activity
- Memory not consolidated in hippocampus
- Brain damage that produces amnesia

Psychological
- Failure to encode information (e.g., inadequate rehearsal)
- Weak retrieval cues and interference
- Mental schemas distort information
- Motivated forgetting of anxiety-arousing information

Environmental
- Stimulus overload
- Information lacks distinctiveness, meaning or organization
- Mismatch between learning and recall environments
- Misinformation effects: post-event stimuli distort information

Forgetting and memory distortion

FIGURE 8.34

Levels of analysis: factors related to forgetting and memory distortion.

IN REVIEW

- Memory involves numerous interacting brain regions. Sensory memory depends on input from our sensory systems and sensory areas of the cortex that initially process this information.

- Working memory involves a network of brain regions. The frontal lobes play a key role in performing the executive functions of working memory.

- The hippocampus helps consolidate long-term declarative memories. The cerebral cortex stores declarative memories across distributed sites.

- The amygdala encodes emotionally arousing aspects of events, and the cerebellum helps form procedural memories. Damage to the thalamus can produce severe amnesia.

- Research with sea snails and studies of long-term potentiation in other species indicate that as memories form, complex chemical and structural changes that enhance synaptic efficiency occur in neurons.

APPLYING PSYCHOLOGICAL SCIENCE

IMPROVING MEMORY AND ACADEMIC LEARNING

There are no magical or effortless ways to enhance memory, but psychological research offers many principles that you can put to your advantage. Memory-enhancement strategies fall into three broad categories:

- *external aids*, such as shopping lists, notes and appointment calendars
- *general memory strategies*, such as organizing and rehearsing information
- *formal mnemonic techniques*, such as acronyms, the method of loci and other systems that take practice to be used effectively.

Memory researchers strongly recommend using external aids and general strategies to enhance memory (Park et al., 1990). Of course, during closed-book university examinations, external aids may land you in the dean's office! The following principles can enhance memory.

USE ELABORATIVE REHEARSAL TO PROCESS INFORMATION DEEPLY

Elaborative rehearsal – focusing on the meaning of information – enhances deep processing and memory (Benjamin and Bjork, 2000). Put simply, if you are trying to commit information to memory, make sure that you understand what it means. You may think we are daft for stating such an obvious point, but many students try to learn material by rote memorization rather than by making an effort to understand it. Students who find material confusing sometimes try to bypass their confusion with rote memorization – an approach that often fails – whereas they should be seeking assistance to have the material explained. The learning objectives and practice tests that appear in the Online Learning Centre (OLC) can help you process the course material more deeply by helping you focus on and think about key points.

LINK NEW INFORMATION TO EXAMPLES AND ITEMS ALREADY IN MEMORY

Once you understand the material, process it more deeply by associating it with information you already know. This creates memory 'hooks' onto which you can hang new information. Because you already have many memorable life experiences, make new information personally meaningful by relating it to your life.

Pay attention to examples, even if they are unrelated to your own experiences. In one study, participants read a 32-paragraph essay about a fictitious African nation. Each paragraph contained a topic sentence stating a main theme, along with zero, one, two or three examples illustrating that theme. The greater the number of examples, the better the participants recalled the themes (Palmere et al., 1983).

ORGANIZE INFORMATION

Organizing information keeps you actively thinking about the material and makes it more meaningful. Before reading a chapter, look at its outline or headings to determine how the material is logically developed. When studying, take notes from a chapter and use outlining to organize the information. This hierarchical structure forces you to arrange main ideas above subordinate ones, and it becomes an additional retrieval cue that facilitates recall (Bower et al., 1969).

USE IMAGERY

As dual coding theory predicts, images provide a splendid additional 'cognitive hook' on which to hang and retrieve information (Paivio et al., 2000). Instead of writing down customers' orders, some restaurant waiters and waitresses form images, such as visualizing a man who has ordered a margarita as turning light green.

As one waitress remarked, 'After a while, customers start looking like drinks' (Bennett, 1983, p. 165). Be creative. For example, to help you remember that flashbulb memories often are less accurate than people think, imagine a camera flashbulb with a big red X through it.

OVERLEARN THE MATERIAL

overlearning
continued rehearsal past the point of initial learning, and it significantly improves performance on memory tasks

Overlearning refers to continued rehearsal past the point of initial learning, and it significantly improves performance on memory tasks (Driskell et al., 1992). Moreover, much of this memory boost persists for a long time after overlearning ends. In short, just as elite athletes keep practising their already honed skills and professional actors continue to rehearse scripts they already know, keep studying material after you have first learned it (Noice and Noice, 2002a).

DISTRIBUTE LEARNING OVER TIME AND TEST YOURSELF

You have finished the readings and organized your notes for an upcoming test. Now it is time to study and review. Are you better off with *massed practice*, a marathon session of highly concentrated learning, or with *distributed practice*, several shorter sessions spread out over a few days? Research indicates that you will retain more information with distributed practice and that periodically testing yourself on the material before an examination can further enhance learning (Cull, 2000). Distributed practice can reduce fatigue and anxiety, both of which impair learning. Testing yourself ahead of time (e.g., using practice items, if available, or questions such as those in the margins of this textbook) helps you to further rehearse the material and to identify content that you do not understand.

MINIMIZE INTERFERENCE

Distributed practice is effective because rest periods between study sessions reduce interference from competing material. However, when you need to study for several examinations on the same or consecutive days, there really are few rest periods. There is no simple solution to this problem. Suppose you have a psychology examination on Thursday and a sociology examination on Friday. Try to arrange several sessions of distributed practice for each examination over the preceding week. On Wednesday, limit your studying to psychology if possible. Once your psychology examination is over, return your attention to studying sociology. This way, the final study period for each course will occur as close as possible to test time and minimize interference from other cognitive activities.

Studying before you go to sleep may enhance retention by temporarily minimizing interference, but if you are carrying a typical college course load, you will likely have to contend with interference much of the time. This is why you are advised to study the material beyond the point where you feel you have learned it.

KEY TERMS AND CONCEPTS

Each term has been boldfaced and defined in the chapter on the page indicated in parentheses.

Alzheimer's disease (AD) (p. 361)

anterograde amnesia (p. 361)

associative network (p. 346)

autobiographical memories (p. 351)

blocking (p. 317)

chunking (p. 336)

context-dependent memory (p. 354)

decay theory (p. 358)

declarative memory (p. 348)

dementia (p. 361)

dual coding theory (p. 342)

elaborative rehearsal (p. 341)

encoding (p. 333)

encoding specificity principle (p. 354)

episodic memory (p. 348)

explicit memory (p. 349)

flashbulb memories (p. 352)

implicit memory (p. 349)

infantile amnesia (p. 361)

levels of processing (p. 340)

long-term memory (p. 338)

long-term potentiation (LTP) (p. 375)

maintenance rehearsal (p. 341)

memory (p. 333)

memory codes (p. 335)

memory consolidation (p. 374)

method of loci (p. 342)

misinformation effect (p. 367)

mnemonic device (p. 343)

mnemonist (memorist) (p. 345)

mood-congruent recall (p. 356)

neural network (connectionist) models (p. 347)

overlearning (p. 378)

parallel distributed processing (PDP) model (p. 347)

priming (p. 347)

proactive interference (p. 359)

procedural (non-declarative) memory (p. 348)

prospective memory (p. 360)

repression (p. 360)

Rescorla–Wagner theory (p. 318)

retrieval (p. 333)

retrieval cue (p. 350)

retroactive interference (p. 359)

retrograde amnesia (p. 361)

schema (p. 343)

semantic memory (p. 348)

sensory memory (p. 334)

serial position effect (p. 338)

short-term memory (p. 335)

source confusion (p. 368)

state-dependent memory (p. 355)

storage (p. 333)

tip-of-the-tongue (TOT) state (p. 359)

working memory (p. 336)

WHAT DO YOU THINK?

WOULD PERFECT MEMORY BE A GIFT OR A CURSE? (p. 345)

No doubt, perfect memory would have advantages, but were you able to think of any liabilities? Russian newspaper reporter S.V. Shereshevski – arguably the most famous mnemonist in history – had a remarkable capacity to remember numbers, poems in foreign languages, complex mathematical formulas, nonsense syllables, and sounds. Psychologist Aleksandr Luria (1968), who studied 'S' for decades, describes how S was tyrannized by his seeming inability to forget meaningless information. Almost any stimulus might unleash a flood of trivial memories that dominated his consciousness and made it difficult for him to concentrate or think abstractly.

S's experience may have been atypical, but perfect memory could indeed clutter up our thinking with trivial information. Moreover, perfect memory would deprive us of one of life's blessings: the ability to forget unpleasant experiences from our past. As illustrated in this chapter, imperfect memory allows us to view our past through slightly rose-tinted glasses (Bahrick et al., 1996).

Would a perfect memory help you perform better on examinations? On test questions calling only for definitions, formulas, or facts, probably so. But on questions asking you to apply concepts, synthesize ideas, analyse issues, and so forth, perfect memory might be of little benefit unless you also understood the material. In his graduate school classes,

> Rajan had a tendency to try to commit the reading assignments to memory and reproduce them on tests. The strategy ... is counterproductive in graduate courses where students are asked to apply their knowledge and understanding to new situations.... When taking tests, Rajan would write furiously ... in hopes that the correct answer was somewhere in his response.... As he progressed in our graduate program, he tended to rely less on the strategy of memorizing everything and more on trying to understand and organize the information (Thompson et al.,1993, p. 15).

Rajan's extraordinary memory for numbers did not extend to reading or visual tasks, but even if yours did, it still might tempt you to focus too heavily on sheer memorization and cause you to neglect paying attention to the meaning of the material. In sum, although imperfect memory can be frustrating and have serious consequences (as when eyewitnesses identify the wrong suspect), we should also appreciate how our memory system is balanced between the adaptiveness of remembering and the benefits of forgetting.

(By the way, in case you are curious, the current record for recalling pi is 42 195 digits. In 1999, Sim Pohann of Malaysia recalled 67 053 digits, but he made 15 errors. To put this feat in perspective, imagine the next 12 pages of this textbook filled up with nothing but numbers!)

IS IT REALLY ON THE TIP OF YOUR TONGUE? (p. 360)

Please try to answer the following questions:

1. What is the name of the only kind of living reptile that flies?

2. What is the name of the only type of cat native to Australia?

3. What is the name of the planet Mercury's moon?

Did you feel like the answer to any of these questions was on the tip of your tongue? If you did not, that is OK. We just want to illustrate some of the questions that Bennett Schwartz (1998) asked college students in a clever TOT study.

Schwartz asked students 100 questions, but 20 of them – like the ones above – were unanswerable (e.g., Mercury has no moon). If there was no correct answer, then students could not have a true retrieval problem, because there was no stored information to retrieve. Yet nearly one-fifth of the students felt that the answer was on the tip of their tongue when they were contemplating these questions. Schwartz obtained similar findings in another experiment.

Schwartz calls these experiences 'illusory TOT states': people feel that the answer is on the tip of their tongue when it cannot possibly be. Illusory TOT states raise complex issues about the nature of memory, but for the moment, let us just focus on a simple point. Sometimes, when we feel that an answer is on the tip of our tongue, the cause may not be an inability to retrieve information stored in long-term memory, but rather that the information never got stored in the first place. In other words, whether due to encoding failure (we have encountered the information but did not process it adequately) or some other reason, we really may not know the answer, although we think we do. This may help explain why we never resolve some of our TOT states and often turn to other people or reference books to help find an answer.

If you are curious, try reading the three questions above to several friends (give them time to think about each question). Do not expect to trigger a lot of illusory TOT states, but even eliciting one or two would provide an interesting demonstration. Afterwards, be sure to let them know that the questions are unanswerable (so they will not keep thinking about them!) and explain the purpose of the exercise.

CHAPTER NINE
LANGUAGE AND THINKING

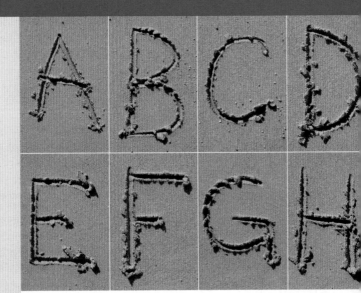

Let language be the divining rod that finds the sources of thought.

KARL KRAUSS

FIGURE 9.1

The successful landing of United Airlines Flight 118 was a tribute to the power of human reasoning, language and problem solving.

For the crew and passengers of United Airlines Flight 118, the skies over Hawaii were about to become the scene of a terrifying test of human resourcefulness, with survival at stake. On a routine flight, 20 000 feet above the Pacific Ocean, the unthinkable happened. With an explosive popping of rivets and a shriek of tearing metal, part of the surface at the front of the plane suddenly ripped away from the rest of the aircraft, exposing the flight deck and forward passenger compartments to the air. Inside, terrified passengers and flight attendants quite literally hung on for dear life as gale-force winds swirled through the cabin and the plane threatened to spin out of control.

The sudden change in the aerodynamics of the plane meant that it could not be flown normally. The captain, an experienced pilot, needed to develop a mental model of the plane in its altered form to keep it from plunging into the ocean. Thanks to his flight experience and his knowledge of the principles under which the aircraft normally responded to its controls, the captain quickly recognized what needed to be done and formulated a plan for doing it.

Yet formulating the plan was not enough. The captain needed his co-pilot's help to execute the appropriate actions. Under normal circumstances this would pose no problem: the captain would simply use spoken language to describe his thoughts, convey the plan and tell the co-pilot what to do. But in a torn-open jetliner flying at several hundred miles per hour, the noise of the engines and the roar of the wind rendered speech useless, so the captain and the co-pilot switched to hand signals to communicate their thoughts and co-ordinate their activities. Through perfect teamwork, they landed the aircraft safely at an auxiliary airfield (Fig. 9.1), a feat described by one aeronautical engineer as 'astonishing'.

Incidents like this illustrate the power of human communication, reasoning and problem solving – cognitive skills that underlie adaptive behaviour. Yet as we shall see, the basic communication procedures and mental operations these aviators used to deal with this life-and-death challenge were really no different from many of the linguistic, reasoning and problem-solving activities that we engage in each day.

We humans are physically puny and relatively defenceless in comparison to some other species, but we dominate our world because we communicate more effectively and think better than do other animals. Humans have a remarkable ability to create *mental representations* of the world and to manipulate them in the forms of language, thinking, reasoning and problem solving (Simon, 1990). **Mental representations** include images, ideas, concepts and principles. At this very moment, through the printed words you are reading, mental representations are being transferred from our minds to yours. Indeed, the process of education is all about transferring ideas and skills from one mind to another.

LANGUAGE

Language has been called 'the jewel in the crown of cognition' (Pinker, 2000) and 'the human essence' (Chomsky, 1972). Much of our thinking, reasoning, and problem solving involves the use of language. In turn, these advanced cognitive processes build on the large store of knowledge that resides in memory, and they provide a foundation for intelligent behaviour.

Language consists of a system of symbols and rules for combining these symbols in ways that can generate an infinite number of possible messages and meanings. To most of us, using our native language comes as naturally as breathing, and we give it about as much thought. Yet using language actually involves a host of complex skills. **Psycholinguistics** is the scientific study of the psychological aspects of language, such as how people understand, produce and acquire language. Before delving into some of these topics, let us consider some adaptive functions and characteristics of language.

ADAPTIVE FUNCTIONS OF LANGUAGE

According to anthropologists who have studied the skulls of prehistoric humans, the brain probably achieved its present form some 50 000 years ago (Pilbeam, 1984). Yet it took another 35 000 years before lifelike paintings began to appear on cave walls and another 12 000 years after that before humans developed a way to store knowledge outside the brain in the form of writing (Kottak, 2000). These time lags tell us that human thought and behaviour depend on more than the physical structure of the brain; although the structure of the brain may not have evolved much over the past 50 000 years, human cognitive and linguistic skills clearly have.

Over the course of evolution, humans adopted a more socially oriented lifestyle that helped them survive and reproduce (Flinn, 1997). Some evolutionary theorists believe that the use of language evolved as people gathered to form larger social units. As the social environment became more complex, new survival problems emerged: the need to create divisions of labour and co-operative social systems, to develop social customs and communicate thoughts, and to pass on knowledge and wisdom. The development of language made it easier for humans to adapt to these environmental demands (Bjorklund and Pellegrini, 2002).

It is no coincidence, then, that every human culture, no matter how isolated or geographically remote, has developed one or more languages. Nor is it a coincidence that the human brain seems to have an inborn capacity to acquire any of the roughly 5000 to 6000 languages spoken across the globe. Humans have evolved into highly social creatures who need to communicate with one another and have the physical characteristics (e.g., a highly developed brain, a vocal tract) that allow them to do so in the most flexible way known: through language (Fig. 9.2).

mental representations
images, ideas, concepts and principles

language
a system of symbols and rules for combining these symbols in ways that can generate an infinite number of possible messages and meanings

psycholinguistics
the scientific study of the psychological aspects of language

Focus 9.1
What are some adaptive functions of language?

Focus 9.2
Describe key properties of language.

FIGURE 9.2

According to many theorists, the development of language was a major milestone in human evolution.

SOURCE: Copyright © 2004 by Sidney Harris. ScienceCartoonsPlus.com. Reprinted with permission.

"GOT IDEA. TALK BETTER. COMBINE WORDS. MAKE SENTENCES."

Language underlies so much of what we do that it is almost impossible to imagine functioning without it. Our conscious thinking usually takes the form of self-talk, or inner speech. Through language, we are also able to share our thoughts, feelings, goals, intentions, desires, needs and memories with other people, and thus interact socially in rich and diverse ways that would not otherwise be possible.

In ways small and big, language also is an extremely powerful learning mechanism. To get to a friend's house for the first time, you do not have to drive or walk all over the area (trial-and-error learning) or wait until someone shows up to lead the way (observational learning). Instead, you simply ask for directions or read a map. More broadly, in oral and written form – through storytelling, books, instruction, mass media and the Internet – language puts the customs and knowledge accrued over generations at your fingertips.

PROPERTIES OF LANGUAGE

What is it that first captures your attention when someone uses a foreign language that you do not speak? Perhaps it is how different that language sounds or looks when written, or simply how incomprehensible it seems to you. Yet what is truly striking about the world's languages is not their differences but the underlying features that they share.

As we noted earlier, language is a system of symbols and rules for combining these symbols in ways that can generate an infinite number of messages and meanings. This definition encompasses four properties that are essential to any language: symbols, structure, meaning and generativity. We also describe a fifth property: displacement.

Language Is Symbolic and Structured

Language uses sounds, written characters or some other system of symbols (e.g., hand signs) to represent objects, events, ideas, feelings and actions. Moreover, the symbols used in any given language are arbitrary. For example, list the words used to represent 'dog' in several languages. None of these written words looks like a dog and, when spoken, there is nothing about how any one of these words sounds that makes it an intrinsically correct choice for representing the concept of 'dog'. In English, *gerk*, *kreg*, *woof*, *zog*, *professor*, or countless other words could be used to represent what we call a *dog*. But they are not (even though 'No Professors Allowed on the Lawn' has a certain ring). Regardless of how the word *dog* came into being, it has an agreed-upon meaning to people who speak English. The same holds true for all the other words we use, although there are some rare exceptions in the form of onomatopoeic words like crash and smash. Formally this is known as *arbitrariness* as outlined in the Hockett's (1960) design features of spoken language.

Language also has a rule-governed structure. A language's **grammar** is the set of rules that dictate how symbols can be combined to create meaningful units of communication. Thus if we ask you whether *zpflrovc* is an English word, you will almost certainly say that it is not. Why? Because it violates the rules of the English language; z is not to be followed by *pf*, and five con-

grammar

the set of rules that dictate how symbols can be combined to create meaningful units of communication

sonants (*z, p, f, l, r*) cannot be put in an unbroken sequence. Likewise, if we ask you whether 'Bananas have sale for I' is an appropriate English sentence, you will shake your head and say 'No. It should read: "I have bananas for sale".' In this case, 'Bananas have sale for I' violates a portion of English grammar called **syntax**, the rules that govern the order of words.

You may not be able to verbalize the formal rules of English that are violated in these examples, but you know them implicitly because they are part of the language you speak. The grammars of all languages share common functions, such as providing rules for how to change present tense ('I am walking the dog') into the past tense ('I walked the dog') or a negative ('I didn't walk the dog'). Yet just as symbols (e.g., words) vary across languages, so do grammatical rules. In English, for example, we say 'green salad' and 'big river', which follow the rule that adjectives almost always come before the noun they modify. In French and Spanish, however, adjectives often follow nouns ('salade verte', 'rio grande'). Although language changes over time, with new words appearing regularly, new words and new phrases need to conform to the basic rules of that language.

Language Conveys Meaning

No matter the arbitrary symbols or grammatical rules used, once people learn those symbols and rules, they are able to form and then transfer mental representations to the mind of another person. Thus you can talk with a friend about your courses, your favourite foods, how you feel, and so on. Based in part on the words you use and how they are organized, both you and your friend will extract meaning – and, it is hoped, the correct or intended meaning – from what is being said. But understanding **semantics**, the meaning of words and sentences, actually is a tricky business. For example, when you ask a friend 'How did you do on the test?' and the reply is 'I nailed it', you know that your friend is not saying 'I hammered the test to the desk with a nail'. Someone who is familiar with English knows from experience not to interpret this expression literally; someone just beginning to learn English might find this expression perplexing.

Language Is Generative and Permits Displacement

Generativity means that the symbols of language can be combined to generate an infinite number of messages that have novel meaning. The English language, for example, has only 26 letters, but they can be combined into over half a million words, which in turn can be combined to create a virtually limitless number of sentences. Thus you can create and understand a sentence like 'Why is that sparrow standing underneath my pancake?' even though you are unlikely to have heard anything like it before.

Displacement refers to the fact that language allows us to communicate about events and objects that are not physically present. In other words, language frees us from being restricted to focusing on events and objects that are right before us in the present. You can discuss the past and the future, as well as people, objects and events that currently exist or are taking place elsewhere. You can even discuss completely imaginary situations, such as a sparrow standing underneath a pancake.

THE STRUCTURE OF LANGUAGE

Psycholinguists describe language as having a *surface structure* and a *deep structure*. They also examine the hierarchical structure of language, in which smaller elements are combined into larger ones. Let us look at both of these issues.

Surface Structure and Deep Structure

When you read, listen to, or produce a sentence, its **surface structure** consists of the symbols that are used and their order. As noted earlier, the syntax of a language provides the rules for

---

syntax
the rules that govern the order of words

semantics
the meaning of words and sentences

generativity
the symbols of language can be combined to generate an infinite number of messages that have novel meaning

displacement
language allows us to communicate about events and objects that are not physically present

Focus 9.3
Differentiate between surface and deep structure. Describe the hierarchy of language.

surface structure
consists of the symbols that are used and their order

deep structure

the underlying meaning of the combined symbols

ordering words properly. In contrast, a sentence's **deep structure** refers to the underlying meaning of the combined symbols, which brings us back to the issue of semantics.

Sentences can have different surface structures but the same deep structure. Consider these examples:

1. Sam ate the cake.
2. The cake was eaten by Sam.
3. Eaten by Sam the cake was.

Each sentence conveys the underlying meaning: that the cake ended up in Sam's stomach. Notice that the syntax of the third sentence is incorrect. English is not spoken this way, except, perhaps, by the fictional *Star Wars* character Yoda. Still, in this case its meaning is clear enough.

Sometimes, a single surface structure can give rise to two deep structures, as happens when people speak or write ambiguous sentences. Consider this example:

The police must stop drinking after midnight.

On the one hand, this sentence could mean that police officers need to enforce a curfew designed to prevent citizens from drinking alcohol after midnight. On the other hand, it could mean that if police officers go out for a few drinks after work, they need to cease drinking by midnight.

In everyday life, when you read or hear speech, you are moving from the surface structure to deep structure: from the way a sentence looks or sounds to its deeper level of meaning. After time you may forget the precise words used in the sentence, but you are likely to recall its essential meaning. In contrast, when you express your thoughts to other people, you must transform deep structure (the meaning that you want to communicate) into a surface structure that others can understand. Eloquent speakers and writers have the ability to convert their deep-structure meanings into clear and pleasing surface-structure expressions.

WHAT DO YOU THINK?

DISCERNING SURFACE AND DEEP STRUCTURES OF LANGUAGE

Figure 9.3 shows a grave marker in the Boothill Graveyard in Tombstone, Arizona, where many notorious outlaws and gunfighters are buried. Analyse the marker carefully in relation to what you have learned about surface structure and deep structure, and then come up with two possible meanings for the inscription. Think about it, then see p. 429.

FIGURE 9.3

This grave marker in Boothill Graveyard illustrates an interesting relation between surface structure and deep structure.

The Hierarchical Structure of Language

Human language has a hierarchical structure, and its most elementary building block is the **phoneme**, the smallest unit of sound that is recognized as separate in a given language. Linguists have identified about 100 phonemes that humans can produce, including the clicking sounds used in some African languages, but no language uses all of these sounds. The world's languages vary considerably in phonemes, some employing as few as 15 and others more than 80. English uses about 40 phonemes, consisting of the various vowel and consonant sounds, as well as certain letter combinations such as *th* and *sh*. Thus sounds associated with *th*, *a* and *t* can be combined to form the three-phoneme word *that*.

Phonemes have no inherent meaning, but they alter meaning when combined with other elements. For example, the phoneme *d* creates a different meaning from the phoneme *l* when it precedes *og* (i.e., *dog* versus *log*). At the next level of the hierarchy, phonemes are combined into **morphemes**, the smallest units of meaning in a language. Thus *dog*, *log* and *ball* are all morphemes, as are prefixes and suffixes such as *pre-*, *un-*, *-ed* and *-ous*. Notice in Fig. 9.4 that morphemes are not always syllables. For example, in English *s* is not a syllable, but the final *s* on a noun is a morpheme that means 'plural'. Thus the word *fans* has one syllable, but two morphemes; *players* has two syllables but three morphemes. In every language, rules determine how phonemes can be combined into morphemes. English's 40 phonemes can be combined into more than 100 000 morphemes.

Morphemes, in turn, are the stuff of which words are formed. English morphemes can be combined into over 500 000 words, words into countless phrases and phrases into an infinite number of sentences. Thus from the humble phoneme to the elegant sentence, we have a five-step language hierarchy (see Fig. 9.4). Beyond this basic hierarchy lies the sixth and most comprehensive level, that of **discourse**, in which sentences are combined into paragraphs, articles, books, conversations, and so forth.

phoneme
the smallest unit of sound that is recognized as separate in a given language

morphemes
the smallest units of meaning in a language

discourse
sentences are combined into paragraphs, articles, books, conversations, and so forth

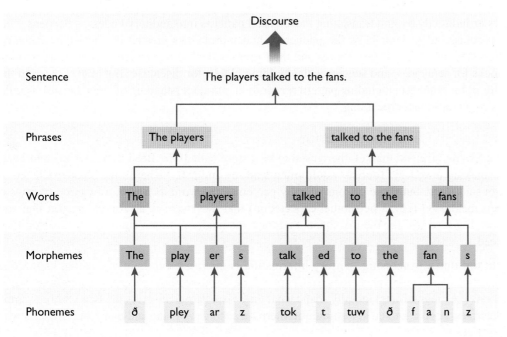

FIGURE 9.4

The hierarchical structure of language.

Human language is structured hierarchically, with phonemes being the most basic unit. The row of phonemes contains symbols used by linguists to denote particular sounds.

UNDERSTANDING AND PRODUCING LANGUAGE

One day after a class discussion on language, a student told us about a humorous incident that had happened the evening before. Her husband answered a phone call, listened for 5 seconds and hung up. 'It was a pre-recorded telemarketing call', he said. 'Some company called

Pressgrits'. 'Pressgrits. That's a really weird name', she said. And then it dawned on her. She was expecting an automated call from a company called Express Scripts to confirm an order. Later, she found out that this had indeed been the confirmation call.

How can a voice on the phone produce the words *Express Scripts* and her husband hear it as 'Pressgrits'? Did he need to clean out his ears? Hardly. He simply failed to perceive the morpheme *Ex*, which left *Press* for the first word. And by saying both words rapidly, as the prerecorded voice did (try it five times, fast), you will realize that phonetically, *pressscripts* and *pressgrits* are not that far apart. Most importantly, her husband had no context for interpreting the message. Later on, when our student listened to a recording of the same message, she heard 'Express Scripts' because she knew what to expect. Context, as you will see, plays a key role in understanding language.

The Role of Bottom-Up Processing

To understand language, your brain must recognize and interpret patterns of stimuli – the sounds of speech, shapes of letters, movements that create hand signs, or tactile patterns of dots used in Braille – that are detected by your sensory systems. And just like other perceptual tasks, extracting information from linguistic stimuli involves the joint influence of bottom-up and top-down processing (concepts that you may recall from Chapter 5). In **bottom-up processing**, individual elements of a stimulus are analysed and then combined to form a unified perception. Analysing the hierarchical structure of spoken language as a set of building blocks that involve the use of phonemes to create morphemes and the combination of morphemes to create words reflects a bottom-up approach.

Likewise, as you read this sentence, specialized cell groups in your brain are (1) analysing the basic elements (e.g., contours, angles of lines) of the visual patterns that are right before your eyes, and (2) feeding this information to other cell groups that lead you to perceive these patterns as letters. We then recognize words either directly by perceiving the visual patterns of letters or indirectly by first translating those visual patterns into auditory codes, as happens when you sound out in your head the phonemes and morphemes created by the letter sequences (Bernstein and Carr, 1996). Words and their grammatical sequence then become the building blocks for sentences, and sentences the building blocks for discourse. But at every step in this bottom-up sequence, including pattern recognition, our understanding of language also is influenced by top-down processing.

The Role of Top-Down Processing

In a Seattle farmers' market, there used to be a store called The Bead Store, which sold beads for making jewellery. Tourists would often walk by and ask, 'Where's the bread?' The store's sign said *Bead*, but these patrons literally perceived the word as *Bread*, a function perhaps of their mental set (i.e., a perceptual expectation) that they were in a farmers' market that sold food. It got so bad for the merchants that they eventually put up a sign saying 'We don't sell bread'.

In **top-down processing**, sensory information is interpreted in light of existing knowledge, concepts, ideas, and expectations. In Chapter 5 we discussed how people's unconscious expectations (i.e., mental sets) literally shape what they visually perceive. As the Bead Store example illustrates, people looked at a stimulus pattern on a store sign that said *Bead*, but *Bread* is what they saw.

Language by its very nature involves top-down processing, because the words you write, read, speak or hear activate and draw upon your knowledge of vocabulary, grammar and other linguistic rules that are stored in your long-term memory. That is why if we write 'Bill g_ve th_ pe_cil to h_s fr__nd', you can probably interpret the words with little difficulty ('Bill gave the pencil to his friend'), despite the absence of several bottom-up elements.

---

bottom-up processing
individual elements of a stimulus are analysed and then combined to form a unified perception

top-down processing
sensory information is interpreted in light of existing knowledge, concepts, ideas, and expectations

Focus 9.4
Explain the role of bottom-up and top-down processes in language. Use speech segmentation and pragmatics as examples.

Let us consider another example of top-down processing. Have you ever listened to someone speak a foreign language in which you are not fluent and found that it was difficult to tell where one word ended and the next began? Even if you have studied that language for a semester or two in school, native speakers may seem to talk so quickly that you cannot distinguish the individual words they are saying. Conversely, they would have the same problem listening to you speak English. Despite all the sophistication of modern computers and software, many still struggle with human voice recognition.

How is it, then, that in your native language this process of **speech segmentation** – perceiving where each word within a spoken sentence begins and ends – seems to occur automatically? When you read a sentence, the spaces between words make segmentation easy. But when people speak, they do not pause in between each pair of words. In fact, when psycholinguists measure the sound energy produced as people utter sentences, they find that the decreases in energy output between words often are smaller than the decreases between segments within the same words. To illustrate, say 'We hope you have a nice day' out loud and at a normal speech rate. Did you distinctly segment each whole word, creating a sound energy break between each one? Or were your segments more like 'We ho pew ha va nice day'? Moreover, in English about 40 per cent of words consist of two or more syllables that are vocally stressed (i.e., emphasized) when spoken (Mattys, 2000). Thus in these and other words, the auditory breaks that we hear in speech often do not correspond well to the physical breaks produced by the spaces in written sentences.

Psycholinguists have discovered that we use several cues to tell when one spoken word ends and another begins (Cunillera et al., 2006). For example, through experience we learn that certain sequences of phonemes are unlikely to occur within the same words, so when we hear these sounds in sequence we are more likely to perceive them as the ending or beginning of an adjacent word.

We also use the context provided by the other words in a sentence to interpret the meaning of any individual word. In two classic experiments, Irwin Pollack and J.M. Pickett (1964) recorded the conversations of four female college students and text passages spoken by four adult men. The researchers then played back one-, two-, three- or four-word segments taken from these recordings to 38 college students. For example, from the words '. . . of the world was covered in ice', the researchers created the segments 'of', 'of the', 'of the world' and 'of the world was' and asked participants to identify the first word in the segment. Remarkably, when participants listened to one-word excerpts, and thus had to identify a word based on its sound alone, they could do so on average only 35 to 62 per cent of the time, depending on the voice of the particular speaker. When participants listened to the four-word segments, they were able to identify the initial word between 70 to 100 per cent of the time, depending on the speaker. In sum, the availability of context made the job of identifying individual words much easier.

> **speech segmentation**
> perceiving where each word within a spoken sentence begins and ends

Pragmatics: The Social Context of Language

Suppose that you call up a friend and someone else answers the phone. You ask, 'Is Bill there?' The person says 'Hang on' and goes to get Bill. Or imagine that a passer-by asks you, 'Do you have the time?' You say '10.20' and part ways. In these cases, the questions really are shorthand for 'Is Bill there, and if so, please go get him and tell him to pick up the phone' and 'I'm not wearing a watch, so please tell me what time it is right now'. You would not expect the person who answered the phone to merely say 'Yes' and then wait until you gave more instructions ('Uh, OK, would you please go get him!'). Nor would you respond to someone's request 'Do you have the time?' merely by saying 'Yes, I do' and then walking away.

Instead, you and the other people involved in these communications understand the social context and rules for how to respond. Likewise, if a friend says 'I need you to explain this material to me. Do you have the time?' you would not say '10.20' and walk away. In this context, you understand that 'Do you have the time?' means 'Can you take a few minutes to help me?'

RESEARCH CLOSE-UP

THE ROLE OF CONTEXT IN READING: EVIDENCE FROM READING TIMES

SOURCE: R.K. Morris (1994) Lexical and message-level sentence context effects on fixation times in reading, *Journal of Experimental Psychology: Learning, Memory and Cognition*, vol. 20 (1), pp. 92–103.

INTRODUCTION

In a series of experiments Robin Morris examined whether the meaning of a sentence speeded up the reading of a target word when sentence meaning was congruent with the target word compared to when it was incongruent. We have already seen that there are top-down influences in language and this experiment was designed to look in detail at these top-down influences. If the meaning of a sentence speeds up, or facilitates, the reading time of a particular word then it would suggest that there is a top-down influence of sentence meaning on word recognition. When Morris conducted their experiment there was already a body of evidence to suggest that context could influence the naming of a word (reading it aloud) but Morris investigated whether this facilitation would also happen when participants were reading silently by examining their eye movements and specifically the length of time participants spent looking at the target word.

METHOD

Morris's experiment was designed to examine whether the meaning of a sentence would influence the reading time of a word embedded in that sentence when participants were reading silently. In order to do this it was necessary to measure where the participants were looking during reading and for how long using eye movement equipment like that shown in Figure 9.5.

FIGURE 9.5

The use of eye movement recording is common in research on reading.

SOURCE: image taken from www.uni-heidelberg.de/university/welcome/behacult.html.

Morris used sentences like:

1. The friend talked as the barber trimmed the *moustache* after lunch.

2. The friend talked to the barber and trimmed the *moustache* after lunch.

3. The friend talked to the person and trimmed the *moustache* after lunch.

The dependent variable was the time taken to read the target word 'moustache' in each sentence. Sentence 1 is a congruent-related sentence because it has meaning that relates to the target word 'barber'. Sentence 2 on the other hand is congruent-altered. This is because it contains the words 'barber' and 'trimmed', hence congruent and yet the meaning of the sentence is altered because it is not the barber that is doing the trimming. Thus for these two sentences the lexical (word-based) information related to moustache is the same in both cases. Finally sentence 3 is a neutral sentence because it does not contain the word 'barber'.

RESULTS

Morris found that there was an effect such that the meaning of the sentence did speed up the processing of the target word. It was found that there was a reduction of reading time in sentences where the message was congruent with the target word compared to similar sentences, in terms of lexical content but where the message was incongruent with the target word. This suggests that the representation of the sentence that the reader is constructing has an influence on the processing of words even while that representation is being constructed.

DISCUSSION

Morris' findings showed that the *meaning* of a sentence is an important influence on the time taken to read a target word embedded in a sentence. When the meaning of the sentence was consistent with the target word then there was a facilitation effect (reading time was faster). When the meaning of the sentence was inconsistent with the target word this facilitation effect disappeared. This was observed even when the lexical content of the two sentence types was almost identical. This suggests that there are influences on lexical access other than just the surrounding words. Findings such as this help to discriminate between competing models of lexical access, some of which suggest that there should not be an influence of the sentence meaning.

The experiment also shows that the use of eye movement data is important in the study of language processing. The recording of eye movement data is now quite common in cognitive psychology (for example, see Ball et al., 2003; Reilly and Radach, 2006; Wilkie and Wann, 2006).

These examples illustrate that it takes more than having a vocabulary and arranging words grammatically to understand language and communicate effectively with others. It also involves **pragmatics**, a knowledge of the practical aspects of using language (Cummings, 2005). Language occurs in a social context, and pragmatic knowledge not only helps you understand what other people are really saying, it helps you make sure that other people get the point of what you are communicating. In essence, pragmatics is another example of how top-down processing influences language use.

Psycholinguists have identified social rules that guide communication between people (Grice, 1975). One rule states that messages should be as clear as possible (Fig. 9.6). Thus, depending on whether you are speaking with an adult who is proficient in your language, a 5-year-old-child, or a foreign visitor who speaks little English, you usually adjust your rate of speech, choice of words and the complexity of your sentences.

Pragmatics also depend on other aspects of the social context. For example, when you write a term paper or go for a job interview, you normally would use a more formal tone than when

> **pragmatics**
> knowledge of the practical aspects of using language

FIGURE 9.6

A breakdown of pragmatics.

Although most of us might understand the underlying meaning of 'Can I see you again', it seems that in this case our suitor made an error in his choice of words.

SOURCE: Copyright © Jim Toomey. Reprinted with special permission of King Features Syndicate.

writing an email or speaking to friends. Thus when a university student sent an email to her lecturer (it was not to one of us) that read 'I cnt find assmnt 4 2moz cud u plz send 2 me? thx m8' the lecturer sternly let the student know about her violation of pragmatics, namely, that the style of the message was completely inappropriate for the context.

Language Functions, the Brain and Sex Differences

Language functions are distributed in many areas of the brain, but the regions shown in Figure 9.7 are especially significant. As discussed in Chapter 4, Broca's area, located in the left hemisphere's frontal lobe, is most centrally involved in word production and articulation (lower-right brain scan). Wernicke's area, in the rear portion of the temporal lobe, is more centrally involved in speech comprehension (upper-left scan). People with damage in one or both areas typically suffer from **aphasia**, an impairment in speech comprehension and/or production that can be permanent or temporary (LaPoint, 2005). The visual area of the cortex is also involved in recognizing written words.

Aphasia can be the result of various forms of damage such as a stroke, head injury or a brain tumour. The range of symptoms and pattern of deficits associated with various aphasias is dependent on the location of the damage that has occurred. For example, Corsten et al. (2007) reported the case of patient 'PS' a 52-year-old German male who suffered a left-hemisphere stroke that resulted in a range of difficulties in language, including speech that included errors such as substituting letters and/or syllables and word finding difficulties. PS also showed difficulty naming pictures of three-syllable items (e.g., 'banana') compared with one-syllable items (e.g., 'cat').

aphasia

an impairment in speech comprehension and/or production

Focus 9.5

What sex differences exist in the brain's language processing?

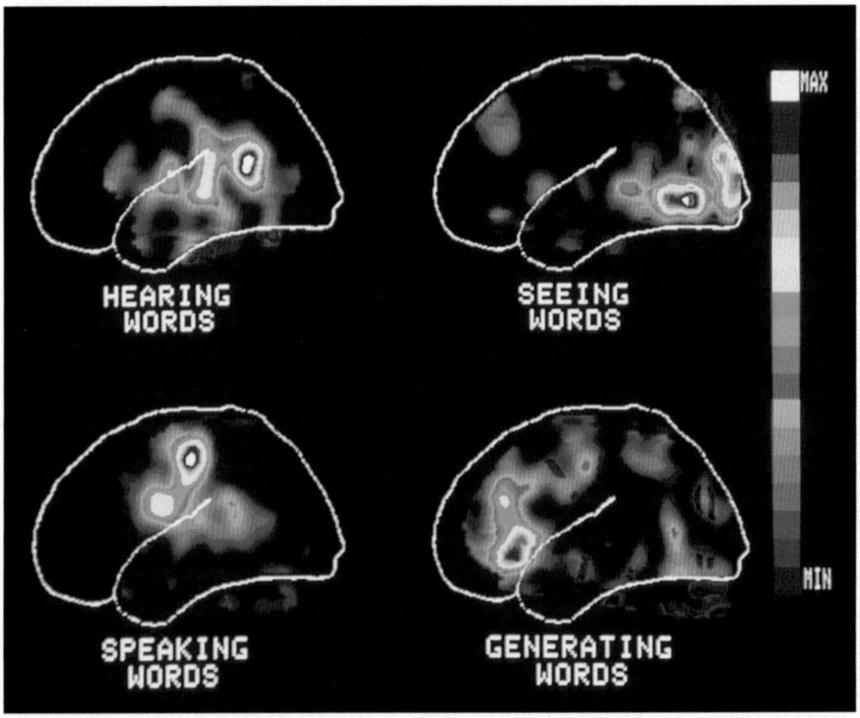

FIGURE 9.7

Brain areas involved in various aspects of language.

In these PET scans, regions of white, red and yellow show the greatest activity. Notice in the upper-left image that Wernicke's area (in the temporal lobe) is especially active when we hear words, and in the lower-right image that Broca's area (located in the frontal lobe) is especially active when we generate words.

Years ago scientists noted that men who suffer left-hemisphere strokes are more likely than women to show severe aphasic symptoms. In female stroke victims with left-hemisphere damage, language functions are more likely to be spared, suggesting that more of their language function is shared with the right hemisphere.

Brain-imaging research by Susan Rossell and co-workers (2002) supports this hypothesis. In their study, men and women engaged in a language task in which words and non words were presented on each side of a computer screen. Participants had to identify which was the real word as quickly as possible by pressing one of two computer keys. Functional MRIs (fMRIs) were recorded during the task and during a non-language control task. As the image in Figure 9.8 shows, men exhibited greater left-hemisphere activation (red areas) during the language task, whereas women's brain activation occurred in both the left and right hemispheres. Maximum activation occurred in regions corresponding to Broca's area and Wernicke's area. Neural systems involved in several aspects of language may be organized differently in women than in men, but because this finding has been successfully replicated in some studies but not others, more research is needed to sort out why these inconsistencies occur (Démonet et al., 2005).

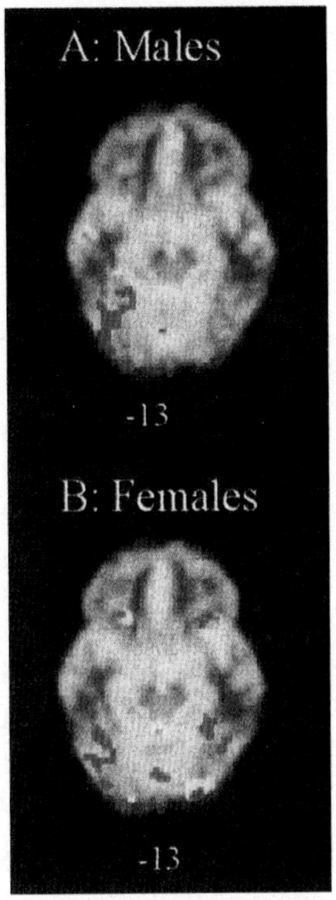

ACQUIRING A FIRST LANGUAGE

Language acquisition is one of the most striking events in human cognitive development. It represents the joint influences of biology (nature) and environment (nurture). Many language experts believe that humans are born linguists, inheriting a biological readiness to recognize and eventually produce the sounds and structure of whatever language they are exposed to (Chomsky, 1965; Pinker 2000).

Biological Foundations

Several facts suggest a biological basis for language acquisition. First, human children, despite their limited thinking skills, begin to master language early in life without any formal instruction. Moreover, despite their differences at the phoneme level, all adult languages throughout the world – including sign languages for the deaf that developed independently in different parts of the world – seem to have common underlying structural characteristics. Language acquisition thus represents the unfolding of a biologically primed process within a social learning environment (Aitchison, 1998; Chomsky, 1987).

Whether born in Toledo, Taiwan or Tanzania, young infants vocalize the entire range of phonemes found in the world's languages. At about 6 months of age, however, they begin to make only those sounds that are specific to their native tongue and abandon those of other languages. For example, Japanese children lose the ability to distinguish between the *r* and *l* sounds because their language does not make this phonetic distinction, but children exposed to English continue to discriminate these sounds as they mature. Likewise, Japanese-speaking children learn the syntactic rule to put the object before the verb ('Ichiro the ball hit'), whereas English-speaking children learn the syntactic rule that the verb comes before the object ('Ichiro hit the ball').

The linguist Noam Chomsky (1987) proposed that humans are born with a **language acquisition device (LAD)**, an innate biological mechanism that contains the general grammatical rules (which he terms 'universal grammar') common to all languages. Among the principles inherent in LAD are that languages contain such things as noun phrases and verb phrases that are arranged in particular ways, such as subjects, predicates, and adjectives. Chomsky likened LAD to a huge electrical panel with banks of linguistic switches that are thrown as children hear the words and syntax of their native language. For example, for a child learning to speak English, the 'switch' that indicates whether to insert a pronoun before a verb (as in '*I* want') is set to yes. But in Spanish, the same switch is set to no, because the applicable verb (in this case, *deseo*) already includes the first-person singular and inserting a pronoun is not necessary. In this manner, universal grammar becomes calibrated to the grammar and syntax of one's native tongue.

FIGURE 9.8

Brain activation, as recorded by fMRI, is shown in the red areas. For males, the left hemisphere is more active than the right hemisphere during this language task. Females' activation patterns are distributed in corresponding areas of both the left and right hemispheres, indicating less lateralization of language functions than in the males' brains. The yellow activation patterns occurred in response to a control (non-language) task.

SOURCE: Rossell et al., 2002.

Focus 9.6

How do biological factors influence language acquisition?

Focus 9.7

How do social learning factors influence language acquisition?

language acquisition device (LAD)

an innate biological mechanism that contains the general grammatical rules (which he terms 'universal grammar') common to all languages

FIGURE 9.9

Language development depends not only on the brain's biological programming device but also on exposure to one's language. Childhood is an important sensitive period for such exposure.

SOURCE: image is from www.cats.org. uk/catcare/cat_books_kiddies.asp.

language acquisition support system (LASS)

factors in the social environment that facilitate the learning of a language

Social Learning Processes

Given the required biological foundation, social learning plays a central role in acquiring a language (Pruden et al., 2006). Early on, mothers and fathers attract their children's attention and maintain their interest by conversing with them in what has been termed *child-directed speech*, a high-pitched intonation that seems to be used all over the world (Fernald et al., 1989). Parents also teach their children words by pointing out objects and naming them, by reading aloud to them and by responding to the never-ending question 'What dat?' (Fig. 9.9).

The behaviourist B.F. Skinner (1957) developed an operant conditioning explanation for language acquisition. His basic premise was that children's language development is strongly governed by adults' positive reinforcement of appropriate language and non-reinforcement or correction of inappropriate verbalizations. However, most modern psycholinguists doubt that operant learning principles alone can account for language development. For one thing, children learn so much so quickly. By grade 2 (age 7–8 years old) in elementary school, children have acquired about 5000 to 6000 words (Biemiller and Slonim, 2001). Moreover, observational studies have shown that parents do *not* typically correct their children's grammar as language skills are developing. Rather, parents' corrections focus primarily on the 'truth value' (or deep structure) of what the child is trying to communicate. Thus, they are less likely to correct a young child who says 'I have two foots' than they are to correct one who says 'I have four feet', even though the latter statement is grammatically correct (Brown, 1973).

As this point also shows, much of children's language is very different from that of their parents, and thus it cannot be explained simply as an imitative process. Nonetheless, social learning is a crucial contributor to language acquisition, and the interplay between biological and environmental factors is a given for most modern theorists. Psychologist Jerome Bruner (1983) proposed the term **language acquisition support system (LASS)** to represent factors in the social environment that facilitate the learning of a language. One could say that when LAD and LASS interact in a mutually supportive fashion, normal language development occurs.

Developmental Timetable and Sensitive Periods

As biological factors (including the maturation of speech-production mechanisms) and experiential factors combine their influences, language acquisition proceeds according to a developmental timetable that is common to all cultures. As shown in Table 9.1, children progress from reflexive crying at birth through stages of cooing, babbling and one-word utterances. By 2 years of age, children are uttering sentences called *telegraphic speech* that at first consist of a noun and a verb (e.g., 'Want cookie'), with non-essential words left out as in a telegraph message. Soon, additional words may be added (e.g., 'Daddy go car'). From that point on, speech development accelerates as vocabulary increases and sentences become more grammatically correct. In the short span of 5 years, an initially non-verbal creature has come to understand and produce a complex language.

In Chapter 5 we saw how the normal development of perceptual abilities requires certain kinds of sensory input early in life. Some linguists are convinced there is also a sensitive period from infancy to puberty during which the brain is most responsive to language input from the environment. Support for a sensitive period comes from studies of children who lived by themselves in the wild or who were isolated from human contact by deranged parents. One such child, found when she was 6 years old, immediately received language training and seemed to develop normal language abilities (Brown, 1958). In contrast, language-deprived children who were found when they were past puberty seemed unable to acquire normal language skills despite extensive training (Clarke and Clarke, 2000; Curtiss, 1977).

The importance of early language exposure applies to any language, not just spoken language. Because sign languages share the deep-structure characteristics of spoken languages, deaf children who learn sign language before puberty develop normal linguistic and cognitive abilities

TABLE 9.1 COURSE OF NORMAL LANGUAGE DEVELOPMENT IN CHILDREN

Age	Speech characteristics
1–3 months	Infant can distinguish speech from non-speech sounds and prefers speech sounds (phonemes). Undifferentiated crying gives way to cooing when happy.
4–6 months	Babbling sounds begin to occur. These contain sounds from virtually every language. Child vocalizes in response to verbalizations of others.
7–11 months	Babbling sounds narrow to include only the phonemes heard in the language spoken by others in the environment. Child moves tongue with vocalizations ('lalling'). Child discriminates between some words without understanding their meaning and begins to imitate word sounds heard from others.
12 months	First recognizable words typically spoken as one-word utterances to name familiar people and objects (e.g., da-da or block).
12–18 months	Child increases knowledge of word meanings and begins to use single words to express whole phrases or requests (e.g., out to express a desire to get out of the crib); primarily uses nouns.
18–24 months	Vocabulary expands to between 50 and 100 words. First rudimentary sentences appear, usually consisting of two words (e.g., more milk) with little or no use of articles (the, a), conjunctions (and) or auxiliary verbs (can, will). This condensed, or telegraphic, speech is characteristic of first sentences throughout the world.
2–4 years	Vocabulary expands rapidly at the rate of several hundred words every 6 months. Two-word sentences give way to longer sentences that, though often grammatically incorrect, exhibit basic language syntax. Child begins to express concepts with words and to use language to describe imaginary objects and ideas. Sentences become more correct syntactically.
4–5 years	Child has learned the basic grammatical rules for combining nouns, adjectives, articles, conjunctions and verbs into meaningful sentences.

even though they never hear a spoken word (Marschark and Mayer, 1998). In contrast, deaf people who are not exposed to sign language before age 12 show language-learning deficits later in life (Morford, 2003).

Can Animals Acquire Human Language?

Non-human species communicate in diverse ways. Chimpanzees grunt, bark, scream and make gestures to other chimps. Dolphins make clicking sounds and high-pitched vocalizations (Fig. 9.10). Many species use special calls to warn of predators and to attract mates (Alcock, 2002).

Communication also abounds in the insect world. Honeybees use a repertoire of body movements – so-called dances – to communicate. When a honeybee discovers nectar, it returns to the hive and performs a turning 'waggle dance' (von Frisch, 1974). The dance's pattern and duration convey information about the nectar's location, which other bees receive by sensing vibrations as they stay in contact behind the dancer. Using this information and odour

Focus 9.8

Does evidence support the view that apes can acquire human language? Why or why not?

FIGURE 9.10

Human scientists debate whether dolphins and other animals use language. Could the opposite also be occurring?

SOURCE: Copyright © 2004 by Sidney Harris. ScienceCartoonsPlus.com. Reprinted with permission.

"Although humans make sounds with their mouths and occasionally look at each other, there is no solid evidence that they actually communicate with each other."

cues, they can zero in on the food source. Honeybees also vibrate their bodies from side to side in a 'grooming invitation dance' that signals other bees to come by and help clean them (Land and Seeley, 2004).

In some species, communication shows interesting parallels to human language. Just as humans have different languages, each songbird species has its own songs. Remarkably, some songbirds also have local dialects, as humans do (Catchpole and Rowell, 1993). Slater (1981) conducted research on chaffinches on one of the Orkney Islands and found that birds in different areas of the island sang slightly different songs, with the song altering slightly from one area to the next until eventually being quite different. Thus it should be possible for an expert to be able to say which part of the island a bird is from just by hearing the song that it produces. And just as humans have a sensitive period in childhood for language acquisition, some songbirds will not sing normally in adulthood unless they hear the songs of their species while growing up (Wilbrecht and Notteebohm, 2003).

Although other species can communicate in intriguing and sophisticated ways, the capacity to use full-fledged language has long been regarded as the sole province of humans. Several decades ago, some scientists attempted to challenge this assumption by teaching apes to use human language.

Washoe: early signs of success   At first, investigators tried to teach chimpanzees to speak verbally, but chimps lack a vocal system that would permit humanlike speech. A breakthrough came in 1966 when Allen Gardner and Beatrice Gardner (1969) took advantage of chimps' hand and finger dexterity and began teaching American Sign Language to a 10-month-old chimp named Washoe. They *cross-fostered* Washoe: they raised her at home and treated her like a human child. By age 5, Washoe had learned 160 signs. More important, at times she combined signs (e.g., 'more fruit', 'you tickle Washoe') in novel ways. For example, when a researcher showed Washoe a baby doll inside a cup and signed 'What that?' Washoe signed back 'Baby in my drink'. Other researchers also had success. A gorilla named Koko learned over 600 signs (Bonvillian and Patterson, 1997), and a chimp named Lana learned to communicate via visual symbols on a specially designed keyboard (Rumbaugh, 1990).

Project Nim: dissent from within   At Columbia University, behaviourist Herbert Terrace (1979) taught sign language to a chimp he named Nim Chimpsky – a play on the name of linguist Noam Chomsky. But after years of work and videotape analysis of Nim's 'conversations', Terrace concluded that when Nim combined symbols into longer sequences, he was either imitating his trainer's previous signs or 'running on' with his hands until he got what he wanted. Moreover, Nim spontaneously signed only when he wanted something, which is not how humans use language. Terrace concluded that Nim had not learned language.

Not surprisingly, some ape-language researchers disputed Terrace's conclusions. They agreed that although apes signed mainly to request things, other types of communication also occurred. For example, Chantek, an orang-utan who had been taught a symbol for 'dirty' in regard to faeces and urine, spontaneously began applying the symbol to spilled food, soiled objects and toilets (Miles et al., 1996). At Central Washington University, Roger Fouts and Deborah Fouts continued working with Washoe and other cross-fostered chimps. They intentionally refrained from signing in front of Loulis, Washoe's adopted son, and found that Loulis acquired over 50 signs by observing other chimps communicate (Fouts et al., 1989). The chimps also signed with each other when humans were not present, and signing occurred across various contexts, such as when they were playing, feeding and fighting (Cianelli and Fouts, 1998).

Kanzi: chimp versus child   Sue Savage-Rumbaugh of Georgia State University has worked extensively with a chimpanzee species called the *bonobo* (Fig. 9.11). At age 1½, a bonobo named Kanzi spontaneously showed an interest in using plastic geometric symbols that were associated with words. By age 4, with only informal training during social interactions, Kanzi

(a)

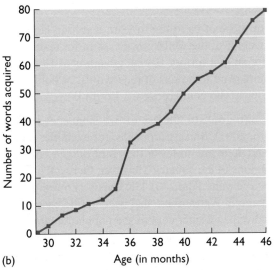

(b)

FIGURE 9.11

Can a chimpanzee acquire language?

(a) Using complex symbols, a bonobo communicates with psychologist Sue Savage-Rumbaugh. (b) This graph shows the rate of Kanzi's symbol acquisition over 17 months of informal training.

SOURCE: adapted from Savage-Rumbaugh et al., 1986.

had learned more than 80 symbols and produced a number of two- and three-word communications. Kanzi typically combined gestures and symbols that he pointed to on a laminated board or typed on a specially designed keyboard. For example, Kanzi created the combinations 'Person chase Kanzi', 'Kanzi chase person' and 'Person chase person' to designate who should chase whom during play. Kanzi also responded readily to spoken English commands.

Savage-Rumbaugh and her co-workers (1993; Segerdahl et al., 2006) also tested Kanzi's ability to understand unfamiliar spoken sentences under controlled conditions. For example, when told 'Give the doggie a shot', Kanzi picked up a toy dog, grabbed a toy hypodermic needle, and gave the dog a shot. Kanzi also appeared to understand syntax. Given slightly different requests, such as 'Make the [toy] snake bite the [toy] doggie' and 'Make the doggie bite the snake', Kanzi responded appropriately. For comparison, one of the researcher's daughters, Alia, was tested under the same conditions between the ages of 2 and 2½. Kanzi correctly responded to 74 per cent of the novel requests and Alia to 65 per cent. In short, Kanzi was comprehending speech at the level of a human toddler.

Is it language?   What should we conclude about apes' language abilities? Recall that human language is (1) symbolic, (2) structured, (3) conveys meaning, (4) generative and (5) permits displacement. Evidence is strongest for the first and third criteria. Apes, undisputedly, are capable of communicating with symbols and hand signs, and they can learn a small vocabulary of several hundred words. However, whether the apes perceive the symbols and signs as words in the sense that humans do is still unclear. As for conveying meaning, realize that just as toddlers can convey meaning by using one- or two-word utterances, apes can convey meaning by using one- or two-symbol communications (e.g., 'banana' or 'give banana'), and they have also produced longer symbol strings that, at least some of the time, convey meaning. As for structure, both sides can point to examples of how apes follow – and violate – rules of grammar. Finally, the evidence for generativity and displacement is limited and controversial.

Critics – even those impressed by Kanzi's feats – are not persuaded. Some believe that ambiguous ape communications are interpreted as language because the researchers erroneously assume what must be going on inside the apes' minds. Conversely, proponents believe the data show that great apes can acquire rudimentary language skills (Segerdahl et al., 2006). If it were anatomically possible, argues Sue Savage-Rumbaugh, Kanzi would be speaking.

At present, neither side in the debate has convinced the other. If nothing else, this intriguing scientific work should remind us to appreciate something that we often take for granted, namely, the seemingly natural ease with which humans acquire a native language.

Focus 9.9

Is there a critical (or sensitive) period for acquiring a second language? Discuss the evidence.

bilingualism

the use of two languages in daily life

Focus 9.10

Discuss the relation between bilingualism and other cognitive abilities. How does the brain process two languages?

BILINGUALISM

For those of us trying to learn a second language, there are models to inspire us. MD Berlitz, inventor of the well-known system for teaching foreign languages, spoke 58 of them. Sir John Bowring, a former British governor of Hong Kong, could speak 100 languages and read 100 more. And some sort of record must be held by the Jesuit missionary Benjamin Schulze (1699–1760), who could recite the Lord's Prayer in 215 languages (Bryan, 1986).

Bilingualism, the use of two languages in daily life, is common throughout the world (Fabbro, 2001). Many Europeans, for example, routinely speak two or more languages. In Switzerland there are no fewer than four *official* languages although they are each specific to different regions of the country. However, there are areas where two languages are both routinely spoken by everyone. The 2001 UK census showed that although English was still the predominant language in Wales, there had been an increase in Welsh speakers over the previous 20 years with more than 21 per cent of the population able to speak Welsh. Not surprisingly, people born in Wales were far more likely to be able to speak, write and understand Welsh (Office for National Statistics, 2001). Bilingualism is common in other areas of Europe too, including Spanish and Catalan in Spain, and French, Dutch and German in Belgium.

In North America, Canada officially is a bilingual country. French is the official language of the province of Quebec, English is the official language elsewhere and the federal government promotes both languages. But individually, only about 18 per cent of Canadians (including 41 per cent of those living in Quebec) report that they speak both English and French (Statistics Canada, 2002).

English is the sole official language in the USA but, as in Canada and other countries, a history of immigration means that many languages and bilingual combinations are spoken. For example, of the 47 million Americans who speak a language at home other than English, the vast majority also speak English well or very well (US Census Bureau, 2005).

Does Bilingualism Affect Other Cognitive Abilities?

In childhood, does learning a second language influence the development of other cognitive abilities or affect acquisition of one's native language? Causation is difficult to establish because researchers typically do not get to randomly assign children to bilingual or monolingual classrooms. Thus, when comparing native-born monolingual children (i.e., children who speak only a first language) to immigrant children who are learning a second language, the two groups may differ on many background factors. Nevertheless, studies in Switzerland, South Africa, Israel and Canada suggest that bilingualism is at least correlated with greater thinking flexibility and higher performance on non-verbal intelligence tests. However, such associations are not likely to appear until both languages are well learned (Lambert et al., 1993).

BENEATH THE SURFACE

LEARNING A SECOND LANGUAGE: IS EARLIER BETTER?

Given that children are language sponges, it seems obvious that a second language would be learned best and spoken most fluently when acquired early in life. Some psycholinguists believe that there is a critical period for learning a second language that ends in childhood or possibly in the early teens. If this is the case, it would not be possible for people who begin to learn a second language in high school or college, or after emigrating as late teens or adults to a foreign country, to achieve the fluency of native speakers. What do you think about this hypothesis?

In one sense, it does appear that the earlier one learns a second language, the better. If you start to learn a second language in childhood, then by the time you reach age 25 to 30, let us say, you will have had many more years of exposure to that language than if you had first started to learn it in your late teens. Thus 'age of acquisition' can easily be confounded with 'years of exposure and practice'. As a critical thinker, realize that to test the biologically based critical period hypothesis, researchers must try to compare the proficiency of people who are 'early' versus 'late' second-language learners yet who also have had a similar amount of overall exposure to that second language.

In one well-known study, Jacqueline Johnson and Elissa Newport (1989) studied university students and faculty members who had emigrated from Korea or China to the USA when they were either 3 to 16 years old ('early arrivals') or 17 to 39 years old ('late arrivals'). Overall, the early- and late-arrival groups had nearly identical years of exposure to English since coming to the USA. Johnson and Newport presented these individuals with 276 English sentences that were either grammatically correct (e.g., 'Every Friday our neighbour washes her car.') or incorrect (e.g., 'Two mouses ran into the house this morning.'). The participants were asked to judge the correctness of each sentence. A sample of native-born Americans also took this grammar test.

The findings strongly supported the critical-period hypothesis. Overall, the early arrivals performed far better than the late arrivals. Moreover, even among the early arrivals, those who had arrived by age 7 mastered English grammar just as well as native-born Americans, whereas immigrants who had arrived between the ages of 8 to 10 and between 11 to 16 did progressively worse on the grammar test (Fig. 9.12). The 17- to 39-year-olds showed the poorest understanding of grammar and, within this age group, breaking down the data by age subgroups made little difference: immigrants who had arrived after age 30 performed as well, for example, as those who had arrived in their late teens (Johnson and Newport, 1989). These findings suggest that because late arrivals had missed a critical period for learning a second language, it mattered little at what age they started to acquire English.

Other findings, however, complicate the picture. David Birdsong and Michelle Molis (2001) used the same grammar test in a study of native Spanish speakers who had emigrated to America at different ages and were now either faculty members, students or employees at a university. Once again, despite having a similar amount of overall exposure to English, early-arriving immigrants (i.e., arrival by age 16) performed much better than late-arriving immigrants (i.e., arrival after age 16). But unlike the previous study, performance among early arrivals generally remained high all the way through age 16 (see Fig. 9.12). And among the late arrivals, age did make a difference. It was not as if some biological second-language acquisition switch got

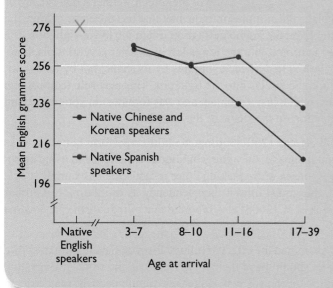

FIGURE 9.12

Age and proficiency of learning a second language.

The X represents the grammar score of native-born Americans. The blue line shows the relation between age of arrival in the USA by Korean and Chinese individuals and their scores on a 276-item test of English grammar, compared with native-born Americans. The red line shows the relation between age of arrival in the USA by native Spanish speakers and their scores on a 274-item version of the same grammar test.

SOURCES: Based on data from Birdsong and Molis, 2001; Johnson and Newport, 1989.

completely turned off by the end of childhood or even by the late teens. Overall, immigrants who arrived in their twenties, though not as proficient as early arrivals, still performed better than those who arrived in their thirties or forties.

Differences in the patterns of findings across studies have led researchers to debate whether there is a biologically based critical period for second-language acquisition and, if so, at what age range it ends. Moreover, some studies suggest that to speak a second language with the fluency and accent of a native speaker people must begin to acquire that language in childhood. Other studies find that even after mid-adolescence, some second-language learners acquire the proficiency (if not quite the perfect accent) of native speakers (Bialystok, 2001; Birdsong and Molis, 2001).

The issue of whether earlier is better – or, more precisely, whether earlier is biologically better – is far from resolved. One study, for example, found that the better grammar proficiency of early- versus late-arriving immigrants to America seemed to be due not to a biological critical period but to the greater amount of formal education in English that the early arrivals had received (Flege et al., 1999). Still, the two studies discussed above, along with most others, support the general principle that it is more difficult to learn a second language in adulthood than in childhood. Overall, at present, the data suggest that there may at least be a *sensitive* (rather than a *critical*) period for learning a second language that extends through mid-adolescence.

FIGURE 9.13

Measuring your ability to ignore irrelevant details.

This figure shows one of the attention-inhibition tasks used by Bialystok and Martin (2004).

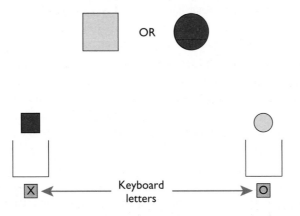

Bilingual children also perform better than monolingual children on perceptual tasks that require them to inhibit attention to an irrelevant feature of an object and pay attention to another feature (Bialystok and Martin, 2004). For example, suppose you sit in front of a computer screen like the one shown in Figure 9.13. There is a box in the lower-left corner with a red square above it and a box in the lower-right corner with a blue circle above it. Next, a stimulus appears at the top of the screen – either a blue square or a red circle. At first, your task is to place the stimulus into the box that has the same colour. If a blue square appears, you hit the letter O on the keyboard to drop it into the lower-right box. If a red circle appears, you hit the X key to drop it into the lower-left box. After several trials, however, we switch the rule. Now your task is to sort each stimulus by its shape, not by its colour: Drop blue squares into the left box and red circles into the right box. This new rule requires you to ignore the colour of each stimulus, which just a moment ago was foremost in your mind, and instead to selectively focus your attention on the shape of the stimulus.

According to psychologist Ellen Bialystok (2001), bilingual children perform better on tasks like this because in learning a second language, they gain continuous experience in using selective attention to inhibit one set of responses while making other responses. For example, while speaking in their second language, they must inhibit their tendency to use the more familiar words of their first language. Bialystok et al. (2004) also reported that bilingualism can slow the process of cognitive decline.

More recently Costa et al. (2008) examined the effect of bilingualism on the attentional ability of young adults whose attention skills should be at their peak. Based on the work of Bialystok, Costa et al. predicted that the ability to control two languages simultaneously may lead to improved performance on attention skills compared to monolinguals. They found that the bilingual adults outperformed the monolingual participants.

Learning a second language also may help children better perceive the unique grammar of their native language and help them realize that the words used to label objects are arbitrary. However, at least in the case of non-English-speaking immigrant children, it appears that they perform best in bilingual educational settings that provide instruction in both their native language and in English. Compared with similar children who are placed in English-only classrooms and left to struggle, those in bilingual classes develop higher self-esteem and exhibit better academic performance and English fluency (Thomas and Collier, 1997).

The Bilingual Brain

Is a second language represented in the same parts of the brain as the native language? One intriguing set of findings comes from studies of bilingual people who experience a brain trauma (e.g., from a tumour or stroke) and subsequently develop an aphasia. In some bilingual patients, the same linguistic ability – such as understanding the meaning of words – may be impaired to different degrees in each language, or impaired in one language and not the other (Fabbro, 2001). Moreover, when brain damage produces similar impairments in both languages, patients may experience some simultaneous recovery in both languages, or recovery in one language but not the other. These findings suggest that there is variability among people in how bilingual abilities are represented in the brain, but also that in some cases, each language is represented by at least partially distinct neural networks.

Brain-imaging studies shed further light on this issue. At the University of Milan, Daniela Perani and her co-workers (1998) used PET scans to measure cortical activation patterns in the brains of English-speaking Italians as they listened to stories read aloud in Italian and in English. People who were highly proficient in English and who had learned this second language before the age of 10 showed representation of the two languages in the same cortical areas. The two languages had, in a sense, become one, accounting for the fluent participants' ability to use the languages interchangeably. In contrast, less fluent Italians who had learned English later in life showed brain activity in different areas depending on whether they listened to stories in Italian or English.

In general, it appears that when people acquire a second language early in life or learn it to a high degree of proficiency later in life, both languages use a common neural network (Démonet et al., 2005). Yet even within this common network, some brain regions become more active when fluent bilinguals use the language to which they have been less extensively exposed (usually the second language). Thus, despite fluency in both languages, this may suggest that the person has to exert more conscious effort to process the less dominant language (Marian et al., 2003). In contrast, people who learn a second language only moderately well later in life show more variability in their patterns of neural activation; at least in certain cases, some of the specific brain areas that process each language are distinct.

LINGUISTIC INFLUENCES ON THINKING

Although many politicians throughout history have demonstrated that a well-developed larynx bears little relation to the capacity for sound thinking, a relation between language and thinking has long been assumed. The linguist Benjamin Lee Whorf (1956) took an extreme position on this matter, contending in his **linguistic relativity hypothesis** that language not only influences but also determines what we are capable of thinking.

If the linguistic relativity hypothesis is correct, then people whose cultures have only a few words for colours should have greater difficulty in perceiving the spectrum of colours than do people whose languages have many colour words. To test this proposition, Eleanor Rosch (1973) studied the Dani of New Guinea, who have only two colour words in their language, one for

> **linguistic relativity hypothesis**
> language not only influences but also determines what we are capable of thinking

bright warm colours and the other for dark cool ones. She found that contrary to what strict linguistic determinism would suggest, the Dani could discriminate among and remember a wide assortment of hues in much the same manner as can speakers of the English language, which contains many colour names. Similarly, in the Amazon, the language of the Mundurukú people contains few words for geometric or spatial concepts, yet Mundurukú children perform as well on many geometric and spatial tasks as American children (Dehaene et al., 2006).

Another research study, however, comparing English children and Himba children from Africa, suggests that colour categories in a given language have a greater influence on colour perception than Rosch's study of the Dani suggested (Davidoff, 2004). The English language contains 11 basic colour terms, whereas the Himba language has only five. Himba children made fewer distinctions among coloured tiles than did English children. For example, Himba children categorized under the colour term *zoozu* a variety of dark colours, such as dark shades of blue, green, brown, purple, red and the colour black. English children distinguished among these colours and remembered the different hues better when retested on which ones they had seen earlier.

Still, most linguists do not agree with Whorf's strong assertion that language *determines* how we think. They would say instead that language can *influence* how we think, how efficiently we can categorize our experiences, and perhaps how much detail we attend to in our daily experience (Newcombe and Uttal, 2006). Language can also colour our perceptions, the decisions we make and the conclusions we draw (Fig. 9.14). Consider, for example, the ability of sexist language to evoke gender stereotypes. In one study, college students read one of the following statements about psychology:

> The psychologist believes in the dignity and worth of the individual human being. He is committed to increasing man's understanding of himself and others.

> Psychologists believe in the dignity and worth of the individual human being. They are committed to increasing people's understanding of themselves and others.

The students then were asked to rate the attractiveness of a career in psychology for men and women. Those who had read the first statement rated psychology as a less attractive profession for women than did the students who read the second statement, written in gender-neutral language (Briere and Lanktree, 1983). Apparently, the first statement implied that psychology is a male profession (when, actually, the majority of psychology doctorates awarded over the past decade went to women). In such ways, language can help create and maintain stereotypes.

Language not only influences *how* we think, but also may influence *how well* we think in certain domains. For example, English-speaking children consistently score lower than children from Asian countries in mathematical skills such as counting, addition and subtraction (Zhou et al, 2005). One reason may be the words and symbols the languages use to represent numbers. Asian languages make it far easier to learn the base-10 number system, particularly the numbers between 10 and 100. For example, in Chinese, the number 11 is 'ten-one', 12 is 'ten-two' and 13 is 'ten-three'. In contrast, English speakers struggle with such words as *eleven, twelve* and *thirteen*, which bear little conceptual relation to a base-10 mode of thinking. Regardless of their counting proficiency, American and British children fail to grasp the base-10 system by age 5; in contrast, by age 5 many Chinese children understand this concept, enabling them to do addition and subtraction with greater ease (Miller and Stigler, 1987). In this manner, the English language appears to hamper the development of skills in using numbers, whereas Asian languages seem to facilitate the development of mathematical skills.

In sum, language provides the foundation of many human behaviours and capabilities, and in this section we have touched on only a few of its complexities. As a central topic of psychological research, it continues to be studied vigorously at the biological, psychological and environmental levels of analysis (Fig. 9.15).

FIGURE 9.14

Sexist language influences our perceptions, our decisions, and the conclusions we draw. Which of these people would you assume is the chairperson of this committee? Might you consider the question differently if we said, 'Which of these people would you assume is the *chairman* of the committee?'

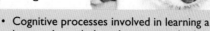

LEVELS OF ANALYSIS   FACTORS RELATED TO LANGUAGE

Biological

- Biological maturation of language-relevant brain structures
- Brain areas involved in understanding and producing language
- Biologically based sensitive periods for language acquisition
- Possible hemispheric lateralization differences between males and females
- Brain modifications created by learning native and new languages at various ages

Psychological

- Cognitive processes involved in learning a language's symbols and grammatical rules
- Bottom-up and top-down processes that influence language recognition
- Ways in which language influences thinking, problem solving and adaptive behaviour
- Relations between deep structure and surface structure in discourse
- Association between bilingualism and cognitive task performance

Environmental

- Early caretaker behaviours in teaching language to children
- Social learning and operant conditioning processes in children's language acquisition
- Effects of cultural variables on language acquisition
- Formal educational experiences that facilitate language development
- Exposure to a monolingual versus bilingual language environment

Language

FIGURE 9.15

Levels of analysis: factors related to language.

IN REVIEW

- Human languages across the globe share the same underlying features. Language is symbolic and structured, conveys meaning, is generative and permits displacement. Language has many adaptive functions, such as facilitating co-operative social systems and allowing people to transmit knowledge to one another. Scientists believe that humans have evolved an innate capacity for acquiring language.

- The surface structure of a language refers to how symbols are combined; the deep structure refers to the underlying meaning of the symbols. Language elements are hierarchically arranged: from phoneme to morpheme to words, phrases and sentences. Discourse involves higher-level combinations of sentences.

- Understanding and producing language – including pattern recognition of words and the hierarchical structure of language – involve bottom-up and top-down processing.

- In infancy, babies can perceive all the phonemes that exist in all the languages of the world. Between 6 to 12 months of age, their speech discrimination narrows to include only the sounds specific to their native tongue. By ages 4 to 5, most children have learned the basic grammatical rules for combining words into meaningful sentences.

- Language development seems to depend heavily on innate mechanisms that permit the learning and production of language, provided that the child is exposed to an appropriate linguistic environment during a sensitive period that extends from early childhood to puberty.

- Researchers have attempted to teach apes to use hand signs or keyboard symbols to communicate in language-like fashion. At best, apes are capable of learning, combining and communicating with symbols at a level similar to that of a human toddler. Sceptics question, however, whether they can learn syntax and generate novel ideas.

- Although research findings are not entirely consistent, it appears that a second language is most easily mastered and fluently spoken if it is learned during a sensitive period that ranges from early childhood possibly through mid-adolescence. Bilingual children tend to perform better than monolingual children on a variety of cognitive tasks.

- In general, it appears that when people acquire a second language early in life or learn it to a high degree of proficiency later in life, both languages share a common neural network.

- Language influences what people think and how effectively they think. Expansion of vocabulary allows people to encode and process information in more sophisticated ways.

THINKING

Can pure thought move mountains? Perhaps not yet, but pure thought can play a video game. In a scene that could be taken right out of a science fiction film, 19-year-old Tristan Lundemo looks at a video screen located next to his hospital bed and, without speaking a word or lifting a finger, makes a red electronic cursor (similar to the paddle in the video game *Pong*) move up, down, to the left, or to the right, merely by thinking it (Paulson, 2004). In this literal mind game, Lundemo tries to move the cursor quickly enough to strike rectangular targets that pop up and then disappear from random locations on the video screen.

THOUGHT, BRAIN AND MIND

Lundemo is a patient with epilepsy who agreed to participate in a brain–computer interface study while undergoing diagnostic tests at Seattle's Harborview Medical Centre (Fig. 9.16a). During a session, the researchers attach 72 electrodes to Lundemo's scalp to record his brain's electrical activity. A computer analyses the patterns and intensity of these brain signals and uses that information to control the movement of the cursor on the video screen. It is not quite that simple, however, as computer and human essentially have to adapt to each other and learn the precise patterns of thought that will make the cursor move. Lundemo was a fast study (as was the computer), and in two days he mastered the task; electric mind over electronic matter.

FIGURE 9.16

The power of pure thought.

(a) With electrodes attached to his scalp underneath the bandage, Tristan Lundemo uses his thoughts to control the movement of a cursor on a video screen. (b) Various brain regions become active when Lundemo moves the cursor in a particular direction.

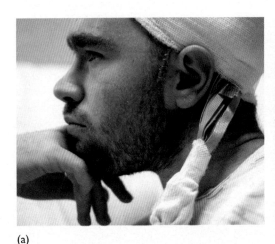

(a)

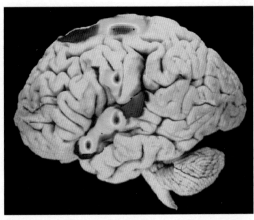

(b)

As Lundemo notes, now 'I just think up, up, up or over left, left, left and it moves' (Paulson, 2004, p. A15). Figure 9.16b shows that several brain regions become most active when Lundemo's thought moves the cursor in a particular direction. The pattern of brain activity changes when he has a thought that moves the cursor in different direction. Researchers hope that this technology eventually will improve the lives of people who have lost limbs or are paralysed.

As we discussed in Chapter 6, according to some neuroscientists, conscious thought arises from the unified activity of different brain areas. In essence, of the many brain regions and connecting circuits that are active at any instant, a particular subset becomes joined in unified activity that is strong enough to become a conscious thought or perception (Koch, 2004). The specific pattern of brain activity that composes this dominant subset varies from moment to moment as we experience different thoughts and respond to changing stimuli. Even altering one's thought from 'move up' to 'move down', 'move left', or 'move right' produces a different pattern of brain activity. Although we are still far from understanding exactly how the brain produces thought, it is clear that from a biological level of analysis, thought exists as patterns of neural activity.

Subjectively, at the psychological level, thinking may seem to be the internal language of the mind – somewhat like 'inner speech' – but it actually includes several mental activities. One mode of thought does indeed take the form of verbal sentences that we say or hear in our minds. This is called **propositional thought** because it expresses a proposition, or statement, such as 'I'm hungry' or 'It's almost time for dinner'. Another thought mode, **imaginal thought**, consists of images that we can see, hear or feel in our mind. A third mode, **motoric thought**, relates to mental representations of motor movements, such as throwing an object. All three modes of thinking enter into our abilities to reason, solve problems and engage in many forms of intelligent behaviour. In this chapter, however, we focus on propositional and imaginal thought.

CONCEPTS AND PROPOSITIONS

Much of our thinking occurs in the form of **propositions**, statements that express ideas. All propositions consist of concepts combined in a particular way. For example, 'university students are intelligent people' is a proposition in which the two concepts 'university students' and 'intelligent people' are linked by the verb *are* (Fig. 9.17). **Concepts** are basic units of semantic memory – mental categories into which we place objects, activities, abstractions (such as 'liberal' and 'conservative') and events that have essential features in common. Every psychological term you are learning in this course is a concept. Concepts can be acquired through explicit instruction or through our own observations of similarities and differences among various objects and events.

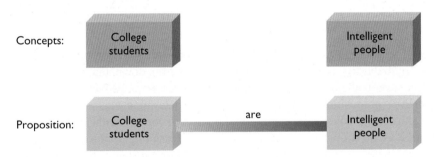

FIGURE 9.17

Concepts are building blocks of thinking and reasoning.

Concepts can be combined into propositions to create simple and complex thoughts, and the propositions can serve as the basis for reasoning and discourse.

Many concepts are difficult to define explicitly. For example, you are quite familiar with the concept 'vegetable', yet you might have difficulty coming up with an explicit definition of what a vegetable is. However, you can quickly think of a good example of a vegetable, such as broccoli or carrots. According to Eleanor Rosch (1977), many concepts are defined by **prototypes**, the most typical and familiar members of a category, or class. Rosch suggests that we often decide which category something belongs to by its degree of resemblance to the prototype.

Consider the following questions:

Is an eagle a bird?
Is a penguin a bird?
Is a bat a bird?

According to the prototype view, you should have come to a quicker decision on the first question than on the last two. Why? Because an eagle fits most people's 'bird' prototype better than does

propositional thought

expresses a proposition, or statement

imaginal thought

images that we can see, hear or feel in our mind

motoric thought

mental representations of motor movements

Focus 9.12

What are concepts, and how do they enter into propositions? How are prototypes involved in concept formation?

propositions

statements that express ideas

concepts

basic units of semantic memory – mental categories into which we place objects, activities, abstractions and events that have essential features in common

prototypes

the most typical and familiar members of a category, or class

a penguin (which is a bird, though it lacks some essential prototypic features, such as the ability to fly) or a bat (which is not a bird, even though it flies). Experiments measuring how quickly participants responded yes or no to the preceding questions have found that it does indeed take most people longer to decide whether penguins or bats are birds (Rips, 1997).

The use of prototypes is perhaps the most elementary method of forming concepts. It requires that we note *only* similarities among objects. Thus children's early concepts are based on prototypes of the objects and people they encounter personally. They then decide if new objects are similar enough to the prototype to be a 'Mummy', a 'biscuit', a 'doggie' and so on (Smith and Zarate, 1992). Because prototypes may differ as a result of personal experience, there is considerable room for arbitrariness and individual differences in prototypic concepts. Thus one person's 'terrorist' can be another person's 'freedom fighter'.

REASONING

One aspect of intelligent thinking is the ability to reason and think logically. Such thinking helps us acquire knowledge, make sound decisions and solve problems. Reasoning helps us avoid the hazards and time-consuming efforts of trial and error. Most of the time, people solve problems by developing solutions in their minds before applying them in the external world. For example, if you decide to build a bookcase, you are unlikely to nail or screw boards together at random in the hope that the finished product will serve your purposes. Instead, you will develop mental representations to guide your efforts, such as a visual image of the finished product and general principles for its successful construction (e.g., 'build from the bottom up').

Deductive Reasoning

deductive reasoning
reason from the top down, that is, from general principles to a conclusion about a specific case

Two types of reasoning underlie many of our attempts to make decisions and solve problems (Fig. 9.18). In **deductive reasoning**, we reason from the top down, that is, from general principles to a conclusion about a specific case. When people reason deductively, they begin with a set of *premises* (propositions assumed to be true) and determine what the premises imply about a specific situation. Deductive reasoning is the basis of formal mathematics and logic. Logicians regard it as the strongest and most valid form of reasoning because the conclusion *cannot be false* if the premises (factual statements) are true. More formally, the underlying deductive principle may be stated: Given the general proposition 'if X then Y', if X occurs, then you can infer Y. Thus, to use a classic deductive argument, or *syllogism*,

If all humans are mortal (first premise), and
if Socrates is a human (second premise),
then Socrates must be mortal (conclusion).

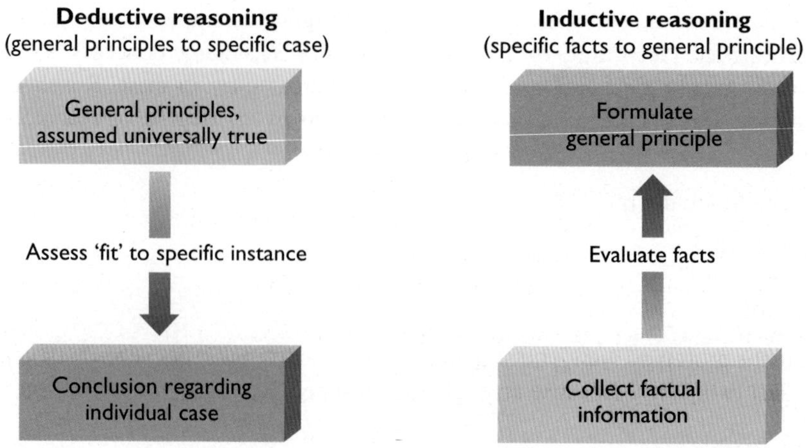

FIGURE 9.18

A comparison of deductive and inductive reasoning.

One form of deductive reasoning – *conditional reasoning* (reasoning about if … then statements) has been extensively studied over the past 40 years using the Wason four-card selection task (Wason, 1966). A form of the original abstract task can be seen in Figure 9.19.

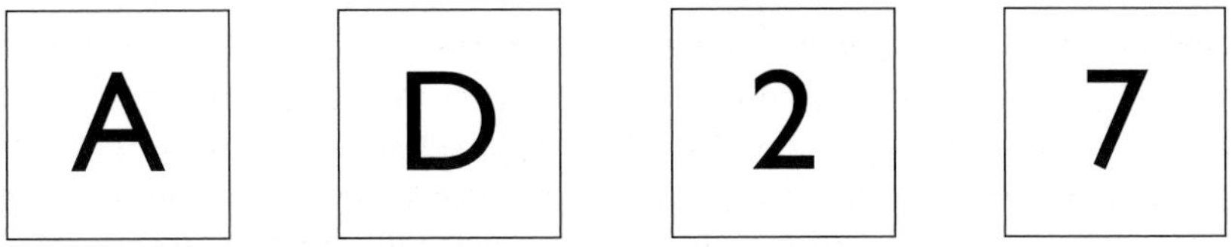

FIGURE 9.19

The Wason four-card selection task.

Participants are told that the cards have a letter on one side and a number on the other and they are given the conditional statement 'if there is an A on one side of the card then there is a 2 on the other side'. They are then asked which of the four cards they would need to turn over to assess whether the rule is true or false.

Although the task appears to be relatively straightforward, performance is generally poor with typically only 10 per cent of participants correctly solving the task. The correct solution is to turn over the A card and the 7 card. This is because these are the only two cards that can show the potentially falsifying combination of an A with a number other than 2. The most common response is to select the A and the 2 cards. Evans and Lynch (1973) demonstrated that participants tend to select the cards that have been mentioned in the rule itself, hence the selection of A and 2 in the example above.

Although this finding would suggest that participants do not reason in accordance with formal logic it appears that the picture is not this straightforward. There are numerous versions of the task that lead to improved performance and hence cloud the issue of whether we reason in accordance with logic or not.

For example, consider the version used by Cheng and Holyoak (1985) in which a scenario was used which involved participants checking the forms of passengers which stated whether passengers were in transit or entering the country on one side and listed the inoculations that a passenger had had on the other side. Participants were told that if the form says 'entering' on one side, then the other side includes cholera among the list of diseases. Participants were required to indicate which of the forms in Figure 9.20 they would need to turn over to check that the rule was not violated.

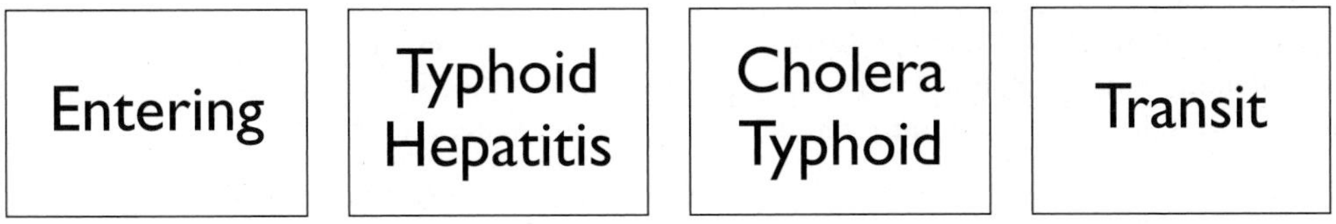

FIGURE 9.20

Cheng and Holyoak's (1985) immigration version of the four-card selection task.

This version of the task has a correct solution rate of about 90 per cent and yet, it could be argued, is logically isomorphic to the abstract task above. It seems that the role of content of a task can have a dramatic effect on how effectively we reason and is one of the aspects of reasoning that any proposed theory must be able to account for. What seems to be crucial here is that this version of the task requires participants to identify what represents a violation of the rule (entering the country when not vaccinated against cholera) rather than testing whether a rule is true or false, which is what is required in the original abstract version of the task. This form of reasoning, reasoning about actions rather than matters of fact is known as deontic reasoning.

Although there is still some debate as to whether the task is purely one of logic or not (Evans and Lynch, 1973; Evans et al., 1993; Oaksford and Chater, 1994) it is clear that the task is central to the psychological study of reasoning and is as widely used now as ever (for example, see, Lucas and Ball, 2005; Manktelow et al., 1995; Manktelow and Over, 1991).

Inductive Reasoning

inductive reasoning
reason from the bottom up,
starting with specific facts
and trying to develop a
general principle

In **inductive reasoning**, we reason from the bottom up, starting with specific facts and trying to develop a general principle. Scientists use induction when they discover general principles, or laws, as a result of observing a number of specific instances of a phenomenon. After Ivan Pavlov observed repeatedly that the dogs in his laboratory began to salivate when approached by the experimenter who fed them, he began to think in terms of a general principle that eventually became the foundation of classical conditioning (repeated CS–UCS pairings produce a CR). A college student who experiences repeated negative consequences when she gets drunk may eventually conclude that binge drinking is a high-risk behaviour to be avoided.

Focus 9.13

Distinguish between deductive reasoning and inductive reasoning. How do irrelevant information and belief bias affect reasoning?

An important difference between deductive and inductive reasoning lies in the certainty of the results. Deductive conclusions are certain to be true *if* the premises are true, but inductive reasoning leads to likelihood rather than certainty. Even if we reason inductively in a flawless manner, the possibility of error always remains because some new observation may disprove our conclusion. Thus you may observe that every person named Jordan you have ever met has blue eyes, but it would obviously be inaccurate to reason that, therefore, all people named Jordan have blue eyes.

In daily life and in science, inductive and deductive reasoning may be used at different points in problem solving and decision making. For example, psychologists often make informal observations (e.g., hearing about crime victims like Kitty Genovese who do not receive help when many bystanders are present). These specific observations may prompt them to construct an initial explanation (e.g., diffusion of responsibility) for the observed phenomenon. This is inductive reasoning, so the explanation could be wrong even if it is consistent with all the known facts. Therefore scientists move to a deductive process in which they design experiments to formally test specific *if–then* hypotheses, moving now from a general explanatory principle to a specific observation (the experiment's results). If the results of these experimental tests do *not* support their hypotheses, they conclude that their explanation or theory cannot be correct and needs to be revised or discarded.

Stumbling Blocks in Reasoning

The ability to reason effectively is a key factor in critical thinking, in making sound decisions, and in solving problems. Unfortunately, several factors may prevent us from selecting the information needed to draw sound conclusions.

Distraction by irrelevant information   Distinguishing relevant from irrelevant information can be challenging. Consider the following problem. As you solve it, analyse the mental steps you take, and do not read on until you have decided on an answer.

> Your drawer contains 19 black socks and 13 blue socks. Without turning on the light, how many socks do you have to pull out of the drawer to have a matching pair?

As you solved the problem, what information entered into your reasoning? Did you take into account the fact that there were 19 black socks and 13 blue ones? If so, you are like many of Robert Sternberg's (1988) Yale University students who did the same thing, thereby making the problem much more difficult than it should be. In this case, all that matters is how many *colours* of socks there are. It would not matter if there were 1000 socks of each colour; once you have selected any three of them, you are bound to have at least two of the same colour. People often fail to solve problems because they simply do not focus on the *relevant* information. Instead, they take into account irrelevant information that leads them astray.

belief bias
the tendency to abandon
logical rules in favour of our
own personal beliefs

Belief bias   Belief bias is the tendency to abandon logical rules in favour of our own personal beliefs. To illustrate, let us consider an experiment in which college students were asked to judge whether conclusions followed logically from syllogisms like the following:

All things that are smoked are good for one's health.
Cigarettes are smoked.
Therefore cigarettes are good for one's health.

What do you think? Is the logic correct? Actually, it is. If we accept (for the moment) that the premises are true, then the conclusion *does* follow logically from the premises. Yet students in one study frequently claimed that the conclusion was not logically correct because they disagreed with the first premise that all things smoked are good for one's health. In this case, their beliefs about the harmful effects of smoking got in the way of their logic. When the same syllogism was presented with a nonsense word such as *ramadians* substituted for *cigarettes*, the errors in logic were markedly reduced (Markovits and Nantel, 1989). Incidentally, we agree that the conclusion that cigarettes are good for one's health is factually false. However, it is false because the first premise is false, not because the logic is faulty. Unfortunately, many people confuse factual correctness with logical correctness. The two are not at all the same.

Emotions and framing When we evaluate problems or make decisions, at times we may abandon logical reasoning in favour of relying on our emotions – 'trusting one's gut' – to guide us (Slovic and Peters, 2006). And even when we try to reason logically, emotions may still creep into the picture.

Reasoning also can be affected by the particular way that information is presented to us, or 'framed'. **Framing** refers to the idea that the same information, problem or options can be structured and presented in different ways. For example, in one classic study, college students who were told that a cancer treatment had a 50 per cent success rate judged the treatment to be significantly more effective and expressed a greater willingness to have it administered to a family member than did participants who were told that the treatment had a 50 per cent failure rate (Kahneman and Tverksy, 1979). Representing outcomes in terms of positives or negatives has this effect because people tend to assign greater costs to negative outcomes (such as losing £100) than they assign value to an equivalent positive outcome (finding £100). The proposition that 'there is a 50 per cent chance of failure' evokes thoughts about the patient's dying and causes the 50–50 treatment to appear riskier (Slovic et al., 1988). Similarly, graphs or other visual displays can be designed to make identical information 'look different' and thus influence people's judgements and decisions (Diacon and Hasseldine, 2007).

Framing influences how we perceive information and can interfere with logical reasoning. This may be especially so when choices are framed to highlight potential positive or negative outcomes, thereby triggering emotions – such as, fear, anger or sadness – that may alter our perceptions of the risks associated with various choice options (Slovic and Peters, 2006). Framing also can enhance reasoning, however, as you will see next, in our closer look at problem solving and decision making.

PROBLEM SOLVING AND DECISION MAKING

Humans have an unmatched ability to solve problems and adapt to the challenges of their world. As illustrated in our chapter-opening vignette, the remarkable problem-solving abilities of the pilot and co-pilot of Flight 118 enabled them to rapidly implement and execute a plan for successfully flying their badly mangled jetliner and saving the lives of the terrified passengers.

Steps in Problem Solving

In accomplishing their astonishing feat, the pilot and co-pilot had to rapidly gain an understanding of the problem they were facing, generate a solution, test that solution, and then evaluate the results. Problem solving typically proceeds through four stages (Fig. 9.21). How well we carry out each of these stages determines our success in solving the problem.

framing
the idea that the same information, problem or options can be structured and presented in different ways

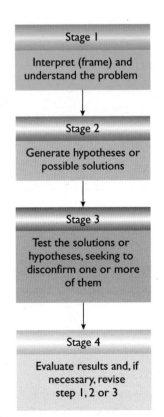

FIGURE 9.21

The stages of problem solving.

Understanding, or framing, the problem   Most of us have had the experience of feeling totally frustrated in our attempts to solve a problem. We may even think that the problem is unsolvable. Then someone suggests a new way of looking at the problem, and the solution suddenly becomes obvious. How we mentally represent, or *frame*, a problem can make a huge difference. Consider the following problem (illustrated in Fig. 9.22):

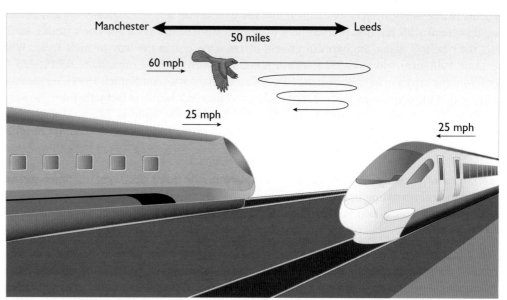

FIGURE 9.22

The crow-and-trains problem.

Train A leaves Manchester for its 50-mile trip to Leeds, at a constant speed of 25 mph. At the same time, train B leaves Leeds, bound for Manchester at the same speed of 25 mph. The world's fastest crow leaves Manchester at the same time as train A, flying above the tracks towards Leeds at a speed of 60 mph. When the crow encounters train B, it turns and flies back to train A, then instantly reverses its direction and flies back to train B. The supercharged bird continues this sequence until trains A and B meet midway between Manchester and Leeds. Try to solve this problem before reading on: what is the total distance the bird will have travelled in its excursions between trains A and B?

Many people approach the problem as a distance problem, which is quite natural because the question is stated in terms of distance. They try to compute how far the bird will fly during each segment of its flight between trains A and B, sometimes filling up several pages with increasingly frenzied computations in the process. But suppose you approach the problem by asking not how far the bird will fly but *how long* it will take the trains to meet. The crow will have flown the same period of time at 60 mph. Now that you have reframed it as a time problem, the problem becomes much easier to solve. (Check your solution against the answer given on p. 428.)

As you can see, our initial understanding of a problem is a key step towards a successful solution. If we frame a problem poorly, we can easily be led into a maze of blind alleys and ineffective solutions. If we frame it optimally, we at least have a chance to generate an effective solution. A knack for framing problems in effective ways that differ from conventional expectations has been called *outside-the-box thinking*, a prized ability in many academic and work environments.

Generating potential solutions   Once we have interpreted the problem, we can begin to formulate potential solutions or explanations. Ideally, we might proceed in the following fashion:

1. Determine which procedures and explanations will be considered.

2. Determine which solutions are consistent with the evidence that has so far been observed. Rule out any solutions that do not fit the evidence.

Focus 9.14

Summarize the four major stages of problem solving. Why are problem framing and mental sets important?

Testing the solutions   Consider the possible solutions that remain. If a solution requires you to choose between specific explanations, ask if there is any test that should give one result if one explanation is true and another result if a different explanation is true. If so, evaluate the explanations again in light of the evidence from that test. In essence, this is what scientists do when they design experiments.

Let us consider a common difficulty in the process of discovering and applying solutions to problems. Consider problem 1 in Figure 9.23:

> You have a 21-cup jug, a 127-cup jug, and a 3-cup jug. Drawing and discarding as much water as you like, how will you measure out exactly 100 cups of water?

Focus 9.15

What are problem-solving schemas? Distinguish between algorithms and heuristics. Describe the means–ends and subgoal analysis heuristics.

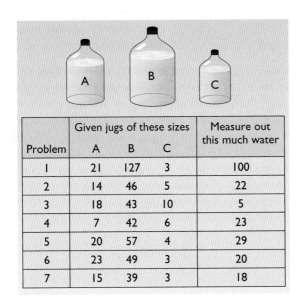

| | Given jugs of these sizes | | | Measure out this much water |
Problem	A	B	C	
1	21	127	3	100
2	14	46	5	22
3	18	43	10	5
4	7	42	6	23
5	20	57	4	29
6	23	49	3	20
7	15	39	3	18

FIGURE 9.23

Luchins's water jugs problems.

Using containers A, B and C with the capacities shown in the table, how would you measure out the volumes indicated in the right-hand column? You may discover a general problem-solving schema that fits all seven problems.

Try to solve all seven problems in Figure 9.23 in order, and write down your calculations for each one before reading on. Does a common solution emerge? If so, can you specify what it is?

As you worked the problems, you probably discovered that they are all solvable by the same formula, namely $B - A - (2 \times C) =$ desired amount. In problem 1, for example, $127 - 21 - (2 \times 3) = 100$. If you discovered this, it gave you a logical formula that you could apply to the rest of the problems. And it worked, did it not? However, by applying this successful formula to problems 6 and 7, you may have missed even easier solutions for these last two problems, namely $A - C$ for problem 6 and $A + C$ for problem 7.

Abraham Luchins (1942) developed the water jugs problems to demonstrate the manner in which a **mental set** – the tendency to stick to solutions that have worked in the past – can result in less effective problem solving. Luchins found that most people who worked on problems 6 and 7 were blinded by the mental set they had developed by working the first five problems. In contrast, people who had not worked on problems 1 to 5 almost always applied the simple solutions to problems 6 and 7. Studies of mental set show how easy it is to become rigidly fixated on one particular approach that has been successful in the past.

Evaluating results   The final stage of problem solving is to evaluate the solutions. As we saw in the water jugs problems, even solutions that prove successful may not be the easiest or the best. Thus after solving a problem, we should ask ourselves, 'Would there have been an easier or more effective way to accomplish the same objective?' This can lead to the development of additional problem-solving principles that may be applicable to future problems.

mental set

the tendency to stick to solutions that have worked in the past

FIGURE 9.24

Experienced snowboarders and skiers learn schemas for various types of snow, which can affect planning and decision making. This boarder might approach a slope covered with 'powder' differently than one covered with 'corn' or 'hardpack' because of their different effects on the board and potentially on the boarder's safety.

problem-solving schemas

mental blueprints or step-by-step scripts for selecting information and solving specialized classes of problems

algorithms

formulas or procedures that automatically generate correct solutions

heuristics

general problem-solving strategies that we apply to certain classes of situations

means–ends analysis

identify differences between the present situation and the desired state, or goal, and then make changes that will reduce these differences

subgoal analysis

formulating subgoals, or intermediate steps, towards a solution

The Role of Problem-Solving Schemas

In solving problems, people often learn to employ short-cut methods that apply to specific situations (Rips, 1997). **Problem-solving schemas** are like mental blueprints or step-by-step scripts for selecting information and solving specialized classes of problems. We have all learned a great many of them, from schemas for cooking dinner to schemas for studying and mastering academic course content (Fig. 9.24). Once we master them, we seem to know what to do without having to engage in step-by-step formal problem-solving procedures.

Algorithms and heuristics   *Algorithms* and *heuristics* are two important strategies for problem solving. **Algorithms** are formulas or procedures that automatically generate correct solutions. Mathematical and chemical formulas are algorithms; if you use them correctly, you will always get the correct answer. Consider another example of an algorithm. If the letters of a word are scrambled in random order to produce an anagram like teralbay, we can identify the word by using a process in which we rearrange the eight letters in all possible combinations – all 40 320 combinations, that is. As you can see, using algorithms can be very time-consuming. You might therefore decide to use some rule-of-thumb strategy, such as trying out only consonants in the first and last positions, because you know that more words begin and end in consonants than in vowels. When we adopt rule-of-thumb approaches like this, we are using heuristics.

Heuristics are general problem-solving strategies that we apply to certain classes of situations. *Means–ends analysis* is one example of a heuristic (Newell and Simon, 1972). In **means–ends analysis**, we identify differences between the present situation and the desired state, or goal, and then make changes that will reduce these differences. Assume, for example, that you have a 30-page paper due at the end of the term and have not begun working on it yet. The present situation is no pages written; the desired end state is a 30-page paper. What, specifically, needs to be done to reduce that discrepancy, and how are you going to do it?

You would be foolish to decide, 'There are 30 days until the paper is due, so all I have to do is write 1 page a day'. This approach is likely to result in a 30-page paper, but it is unlikely to result in one that will earn a passing grade. Instead, you would be wise to use another heuristic known as **subgoal analysis**, formulating subgoals, or intermediate steps, towards a solution. In this case, your expertise as a student will likely lead you to break down the task of writing a paper into subgoals, such as (1) choosing a topic, (2) doing library and Internet research on the topic to get the facts you need, (3) organizing the facts within a general outline of the paper, (4) writing a first draft or specific sections of the paper, (5) reorganizing and refining the first draft, and so on. In so doing, a huge task becomes a series of smaller and more manageable tasks, each with a subgoal that leads you towards the ultimate goal of a quality 30-page paper.

The value of setting subgoals can be seen in the tower-of-Hanoi problem, which is explained in Figure 9.25. Breaking this task into subgoals helps us solve the problem. The first subgoal is to get ring C to the bottom of peg 3. The second subgoal is to get ring B over to peg 3. With these two subgoals accomplished, the final subgoal of getting ring A to peg 3 is quite easy. The solution requires planning (hypothesis formation), checking, and revising hypotheses. The correct seven-step sequence of moves appears on p. 428.

Heuristics enter not only into problem-solving strategies but also into a wide range of decisions and judgements, from judgements about other people to judgements about our own health to decisions about buying products (Katapodi et al., 2005). As we shall see, heuristics can also contribute to errors in judgement.

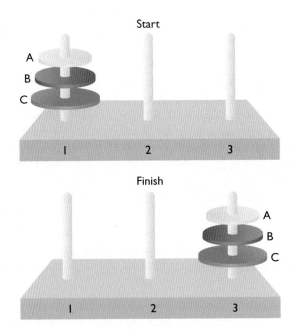

Start

Finish

FIGURE 9.25

The Tower-of-Hanoi problem.

The object is to move the rings one at a time from peg 1 to peg 3 in no more than seven moves. Only the top ring on a peg can be moved, and a larger ring can never be placed on top of a smaller one. (The answer appears on p. 428.)

Uncertainty, Heuristics and Decision Making

Few decisions in everyday life can be made with the absolute certainty that comes from applying some mathematical formula or other algorithm. Typically, the best we can hope for is a decision that has a high probability of a positive outcome. Because we seldom know what the exact probabilities are (for example, how likely it is that the stock market will be up or down when you need your money in the future, or how probable it is that a new dating relationship will become permanent), we tend to apply certain heuristics to form judgements of likelihood.

In daily life, we routinely make decisions about what other people are like. Suppose, for example, you are given the following description of a young woman:

> Linda is 31 years old, single, outspoken, and very bright. She majored in philosophy. As a student, she was deeply concerned with issues of discrimination and social justice, and she also participated in anti-nuclear demonstrations.

Now rate the likelihood that each of the following hypotheses is true. Use 1 to indicate the most likely statement, 8 to indicate the least likely statement, and any number between 2 and 7 to indicate the likelihood of the second most likely statement.

_____Hypothesis A: Linda is active in the feminist movement.

_____Hypothesis B: Linda is a bank clerk.

_____Hypothesis C: Linda is active in the feminist movement and is a bank clerk.

Cognitive psychologists Daniel Kahneman and Amos Tversky (1982) used this problem in a series of experiments that studied the role of heuristics in judgement and decision making. They showed that certain heuristics underlie much of our inductive decision making (drawing conclusions from facts) and that their misuse results in many of our thinking errors. Let us examine how that occurs.

The representativeness heuristic 'What does it look (or seem) like?' This is probably the first decision faced by our perceptual system when it processes incoming stimuli. Earlier, we discussed the importance of prototypes in concept formation. We use the **representativeness heuristic** to infer how closely something or someone fits our prototype for a particular concept, or class, and therefore how likely it is to be a member of that class. In essence, we are asking,

Focus 9.16

What role do uncertainty and heuristics play in decision making? How do the representativeness and availability of heuristics distort probability judgements?

representativeness heuristic

how closely something or someone fits our prototype for a particular concept, or class, and therefore how likely it is to be a member of that class

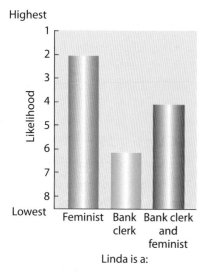

FIGURE 9.26

Illogical judgements.

This graph shows the mean likelihood judgements made by participants on the basis of the description of Linda (top-left column). Overall, people judge it to be more likely that Linda is a bank clerk and a feminist rather than just a bank clerk. Logically, this is impossible.

SOURCE: based on Tversky and Kahneman, 1982.

availability heuristic

causes us to base judgements and decisions on the availability of information in memory

'How likely is it that this [person, object, event] *represents* that class?' In this case, does Linda seem like a feminist? This is a perfectly logical question to ask ourselves. Sometimes, however, our use of representativeness can cause us to make decisions that fly in the face of logic.

For example, what was your order of likelihood judgements concerning Linda? Figure 9.26 shows the mean likelihood estimates that college students attached to each statement (a low number indicating greater likelihood). First, there is a clear tendency to favour hypothesis A (Linda is a feminist). This is not surprising; the description does make her sound like a feminist. However, the significant finding is that hypothesis C (Linda is a feminist bank clerk) was favoured over hypothesis B (Linda is a bank clerk). But this cannot possibly be correct. Why not? Because everyone who is both a feminist and a bank clerk is also *simply* a bank clerk. Furthermore, there are many bank clerks who are not feminists, and Linda could be one of them. Stated differently, any person is more likely to be simply a bank clerk than to be a bank clerk *and* a feminist – or, for that matter, a bank clerk and anything else. People who say that hypothesis C is more likely than hypothesis B (and about 85 per cent of people given this problem do so) violate the logical principle that the combination of two events cannot be more likely than either event alone.

Tversky and Kahneman believe that the reason people make this sort of error is that they confuse representativeness with probability. Linda represents our prototype for a feminist bank clerk better than she fits our prototype for a bank clerk. Therefore, we erroneously think the former is more likely than the latter. Notice how this argument fits with the ideas about memory discussed in Chapter 8 The description of Linda as 'outspoken' and 'concerned with issues of discrimination and social justice' serves a *priming* function, activating the elements in memory that are associated with the concept of 'feminist', so it is hard to think of Linda without thinking of a feminist. On the other hand, there is nothing in Linda's description that would activate the concept of 'bank clerk'. Thus if Linda is to be a bank clerk at all, we think she must be a feminist bank clerk.

However, although Tversky and Kahneman have argued that this is an error, it has been suggested that their findings are a result of the way that the task has been presented. Gigerenzer (1991) cites the version of the problem that was presented to participants by Fielder (1988). In this version of the task, participants are given the same description of Linda as used by Tversky and Kahneman, and then asked the following:

There are 100 persons who fit the description above. How many of them are:
a. bank clerks?
b. bank clerks and active in the feminist movement?

When the task was presented in this form the 'conjunction fallacy' outlined by Tversky and Kahneman almost disappears with only 17 per cent of participants committing the fallacy. Gigerenzer's claims led to a heated debate with Kahneman and Tversky in *Psychological Review* (Gigerenzer, 1996; Kahneman and Tversky, 1996).

The availability heuristic   Another heuristic that can sometimes lead us astray is the **availability heuristic**, which causes us to base judgements and decisions on the availability of information in memory. We tend to remember events that are most important and significant to us. Usually that principle serves us well, keeping important information at the forefront in our memories, ready to be applied. But if something easily comes to mind, we may exaggerate the likelihood that it could occur. For example, consider each of the following pairs and choose the more likely cause of death:

- Murder or suicide?

- Botulism or lightning?

- Asthma or tornadoes?

When Paul Slovic and co-workers (1988) asked people to make these judgements, 80 per cent chose murder over suicide as the more likely cause of death, 63 per cent chose botulism over lightning and 43 per cent chose tornadoes over asthma. In actuality, public health statistics show that people are 25 per cent less likely to be murdered than to kill themselves, that lightning kills 53 times more people than botulism does, and that death by asthma is 21 times more likely than death as a result of a tornado. Yet murder, botulism and tornadoes are more highly and dramatically publicized when they do occur and thus are more likely to come to mind.

A recent memorable event can increase people's belief that they may suffer a similar fate. After the terrorist hijackings of 11 September 2001, airline bookings and tourism declined dramatically within the USA for a significant period. Demand for office space in landmark high-rise buildings also declined and many businesses sought space in less conspicuous suburban settings. Similarly, in the summer of 1975, when Steven Spielberg's film *Jaws* burned into people's memories graphic images of a great white shark devouring swimmers at a New England seaside town, beach attendance all over the country decreased. In fact, *Jaws* was blamed for a drop in tourism on the New England coast so dramatic that in the summer of 1976 many beachfront resorts nearly went bankrupt. The images available in memory – even though the film was clearly fiction – increased people's perceived likelihood that they, too, could become shark bait.

Thus at times the representativeness and availability heuristics can lead us astray by distorting our estimates of how likely an event really is. In other words, they can blind us to the *base rates*, or actual frequencies, at which things occur. In general, it is always best to find out what the actual probabilities are and make judgements on that basis; that is the strategy that allows insurance companies to flourish.

Confirmation Bias and Overconfidence

Sometimes one of the most challenging tasks is obtaining new evidence to test a hypothesis or solution. But what's the best type of evidence? Here is a principle that may seem puzzling to you: The best thing we can do to test our ideas is to seek evidence that will *disconfirm* them, rather than look for evidence that supports them. Why? Because the most informative piece of evidence we can obtain is one that rules out a hypothesis or idea. Disconfirming evidence proves conclusively that our idea *cannot* be true in its current form. In contrast, confirming evidence only supports our idea. It does not prove it with certainty, for it is possible that some future observation will disconfirm it or that another explanation fits the facts even better. Especially in the area of causal beliefs, you can be absolutely sure when you are wrong about something, but you cannot be absolutely sure when you're right because there might be a better explanation or an impending observation that calls your belief into question.

Following this disconfirmation principle is easier said than done, because people are often unwilling to challenge their cherished beliefs. Instead, they are prone to fall into a trap called **confirmation bias**, tending to look for evidence that will confirm what they currently believe rather than looking for evidence that could disconfirm their beliefs. Often, when people have strong beliefs about something – including beliefs about themselves – they are very selective in the kinds of information they expose themselves to (Chen et al., 2006). They seek out like-minded people, compatible mass-media sources and Internet sites, and recall feedback from others that confirms their beliefs about themselves. The fact that people find it difficult or even upsetting to test and challenge their ideas, particularly those to which they are strongly committed, can be a major obstacle to getting the evidence needed to make a correct decision.

Confirmation bias often contributes to a distorted sense of how correct our opinions and beliefs are. **Overconfidence**, the tendency to overestimate one's correctness in factual knowledge, beliefs and decisions, is another reason people do not challenge their beliefs. This tendency, like confirmation bias, is widespread. In one study, college students were asked at the

Focus 9.17
When making decisions, why is disconfirming evidence important? How does overconfidence contribute to confirmation bias?

confirmation bias
tending to look for evidence that will confirm what they currently believe rather than looking for evidence that could disconfirm their beliefs

overconfidence
the tendency to overestimate one's correctness in factual knowledge, beliefs and decisions

beginning of the academic year to make predictions about how likely it was (from 0 per cent to 100 per cent) that they would experience any of a long list of personal events, such as dropping a course, breaking up with a romantic partner, or joining a fraternity or sorority. They also indicated how confident they were in their probability estimates (i.e., how likely it was that they would be correct). At the end of the following semester and at the end of the academic year, they indicated which events had in fact occurred. As shown in Figure 9.27, confidence exceeded accuracy overall, and the difference between the two was equally great when the students were originally 100 per cent confident in their predictions (Vallone et al., 1990). Similar overconfidence effects have been found in studies involving investment professionals, military strategists, weather forecasters and other populations. It apparently stems from people's need to see themselves as knowledgeable and competent (Blanton et al., 2001).

Focus 9.18

Discuss some factors that inhibit and facilitate creative problem solving.

FIGURE 9.27

Displaying overconfidence.

Overconfidence is illustrated in the discrepancy between the accuracy with which students predicted that specific events would occur to them during the coming academic year and the degree of confidence that they had in their predictions. Overall, accuracy was considerably lower than confidence level, even for those events for which the students expressed complete certainty.

SOURCE: based on Vallone et al., 1990.

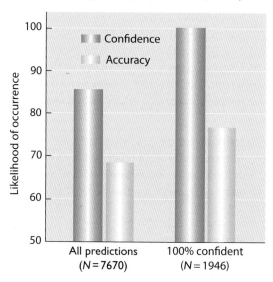

Overconfidence and confirmation bias can be potent adversaries in our search for correct predictions and decisions. When we are confident in the correctness of our views and reluctant to seek evidence that could prove them wrong, we can easily be blinded to the truth.

APPLYING PSYCHOLOGICAL SCIENCE

GUIDELINES FOR CREATIVE PROBLEM SOLVING

creativity

the ability to produce something that is both new and valuable

divergent thinking

the generation of novel ideas that depart from the norm

Creativity is the ability to produce something that is both new and valuable (Sternberg, 2006b). The product may be virtually anything, from a creative painting to a novel approach to solving a problem. In this case, we will be concerned with creative problem solving.

Research on reasoning offers insights into how effective and creative problem solvers think and how they approach problems. In some ways, as experts so often demonstrate, there is no substitute for experience, for it teaches us useful heuristics and problem-solving schemas. Yet one of the marks of creativity is the ability to break out of conventional schemas when the occasion demands it and to engage in **divergent thinking**, the generation of novel ideas that depart from the norm (Guilford, 1959). In part, this means being able to apply concepts or propositions from one domain to another unrelated domain in a manner that produces a new insight. It also means refusing to be constrained by traditional approaches to a problem (Sternberg, 2006b). Creative people are, in this respect, intellectual rebels. The constraints created by the tried and true can be difficult to overcome.

Consider, for example, the nine-dot problem in Figure 9.28. Many people have difficulty solving this problem. Did you? If so, it is probably because you imposed a traditional but unnecessary constraint on yourself and tried to stay within the boundary formed by the dots. But nothing in the statement of the problem forced you to do so. To solve the problem, you have to think outside the box.

FIGURE 9.28

The nine-dot problem.

Without lifting your pencil from the paper, draw no more than four straight lines that will pass through all nine dots. (The answer appears on p. 428.)

Creative problem solvers are often able to ask themselves questions such as the following to stimulate divergent thinking (Simonton, 1999):

1. What would work instead?

2. Are there new ways to use this? How else could it be used if I modified it in some way? By adding, subtracting, or rearranging parts, or by modifying the sequence in which things are done, could I make it more useful?

3. Do the elements remind me of anything else? What else is like this?

Use some of these questions when trying to solve the candlestick problem illustrated in Figure 9.29.

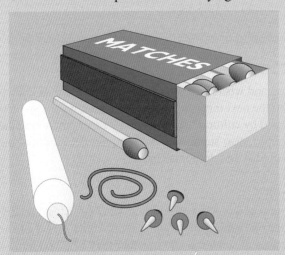

FIGURE 9.29

The candlestick problem.

Using these objects, find a way to mount the candle on a wall so it functions like a lamp. (The answer appears on p. 428.)

Solving the problem requires using some of the objects in unconventional ways. Many people, however, are prevented from doing so because of **functional fixedness**, the tendency to be so fixed in their perception of the proper function of an object or procedure that they are blinded to new ways of using it.

Sometimes creative solutions to problems seemingly appear out of the blue, suddenly popping into our mind in a flash of insight after we have temporarily given up and put the problem aside. **Incubation** is the name given to this phenomenon; it is as if the problem is incubating and being worked on at a subconscious level (Cattell, 1971). Sometimes the best

functional fixedness
the tendency to be so fixed in their perception of the proper function of an object or procedure that they are blinded to new ways of using it

incubation
problem is incubating and being worked on at a subconscious level

approach when we are stymied by a problem is to put it aside for a while and gain a bit of psychological distance from it. Perhaps this causes mental sets and other biases to dissipate somewhat, allowing a new idea to emerge (Anderson, 1985). In addition, as time passes, new internal or external stimuli may activate a different perspective on the problem, aiding its solution.

As you can see, creative problem solving involves many of the principles discussed earlier in the chapter. We see the operation of means–ends reasoning, the testing of hypotheses and the need to overcome biases that may cause us to overestimate or underestimate the likelihood of certain outcomes. Here are some other general problem-solving guidelines:

1. When you encounter a new problem you have not solved before, ask yourself if it is similar to other problems you have solved. Maybe the schema for solving a problem with similar features can be modified to solve this one. Take advantage of the store of knowledge in long-term memory.

2. Make a true effort to test your ideas. Try to find evidence that would disconfirm your ideas, not evidence that would confirm what you already believe. For example, if you are asked to accept statement X as true, see if you can imagine situations in which X would be false. Beware of the human tendency towards confirmation bias.

3. Be careful not to confuse representativeness with probability. The bird you see that looks too big to be a sparrow but just the right size to be a rare Patagonian warbler is probably … a big sparrow; the odds are overwhelmingly in favour of it being a sparrow because there are so many more sparrows (even big ones) than Patagonian warblers.

4. Make use of the means–ends problem-solving heuristic. Ask yourself what you are trying to accomplish, what the present state of affairs is, and what means you have for reducing the discrepancy.

5. Do not be afraid to use pencil and paper. Orderly notes and schematics can substitute for our rather limited working memory and allow us to have more information at hand to work with.

schema

a mental framework, an organized pattern of thought about some aspect of the world

script

a mental framework concerning a sequence of events that usually unfolds in a regular, almost standardized order

Focus 9.19

What roles do schemas play in knowledge acquisition and expertise?

KNOWLEDGE, EXPERTISE AND WISDOM

Knowledge forms a foundation for expertise and wisdom. Each culture passes down its knowledge and world view from one generation to the next through language, instruction and socialization. This vast library of knowledge, shaped by cultural learning and by other environmental experiences (including trial-and-error learning), also supports the reasoning, decision-making and problem-solving skills that we have been discussing in this chapter.

Acquiring Knowledge: Schemas and Scripts

One way to think about knowledge acquisition as a process of building schemas. Most broadly, a **schema** is a mental framework, an organized pattern of thought about some aspect of the world. Concepts and categories represent types of schemas, and together they help you build a mental framework of your world, such as 'interesting versus dull people' or 'easy versus hard examinations'. Algorithms and heuristics also are types of schemas – problem-solving schemas – that provide you with mental frameworks for solving certain types of problems.

Another type of schema, called a **script**, is a mental framework concerning a sequence of events that usually unfolds in a regular, almost standardized order. For example, if we tell you that 'John and Linda went to the cinema', these mere seven words convey a lot of information because 'going to the cinema' is a fairly standardized (i.e., scripted) activity. You can reasonably assume that John and Linda got to the cinema, waited in the ticket line and bought tickets (or bought them online), entered the cinema where someone checked their tickets, then they bought a snack, found seats, and so on. The scripts that you learn – 'attending class', 'shopping', 'driving', and so on – provide knowledge to guide and interpret actions. In sum, your knowledge grows as you acquire new scripts, concepts and other types of schemas; as your existing schemas become more complex; and as you form connections between schemas.

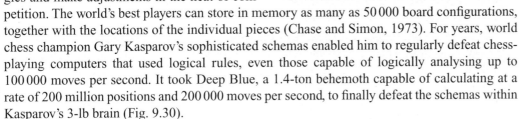

The Nature of Expertise

Schemas help explain what it means to be an expert. Masters and grand masters in chess can glance at a chessboard and quickly plan strategies and make adjustments in the heat of competition. The world's best players can store in memory as many as 50 000 board configurations, together with the locations of the individual pieces (Chase and Simon, 1973). For years, world chess champion Gary Kasparov's sophisticated schemas enabled him to regularly defeat chess-playing computers that used logical rules, even those capable of logically analysing up to 100 000 moves per second. It took Deep Blue, a 1.4-ton behemoth capable of calculating at a rate of 200 million positions and 200 000 moves per second, to finally defeat the schemas within Kasparov's 3-lb brain (Fig. 9.30).

Whether in medicine, science, sports, politics or other fields, experts have developed many schemas to guide problem solving in their field, and just as critically, they are much better than novices at recognizing when each schema should be applied (Montgomery et al., 2005). Applying the correct mental blueprint provides a proven route to solving a problem quickly and effectively.

Williams and Hodges (2005) presented a review of the literature relating to expertise and the development of football skill through training and practice (Fig. 9.31). Although they show that there are benefits to be gained by considering the nature of the practice in which footballers engage, one factor is clearly crucial. No matter how great the innate talent of a player, it is practice that will lead to true expertise, with professional players having done nearly 10 000 hours of practice by their mid-twenties (Helsen et al., 1998).

Expert Schemas and Memory

Consider what the ability to flexibly apply schemas means in terms of what we know about human memory and pattern recognition. As you learned in Chapter 8, schemas reside in long-term memory. Because they rely on learned schemas, experts take advantage of their spacious long-term memory. They can quickly analyse a problem deductively, select the retrieval cues needed to pull the appropriate schema from memory, and apply the schema to solve the problem at hand (Horn and Masunaga, 2000). In contrast, novices who have not yet learned specialized schemas must use general problem-solving methods in working memory, the space-limited blackboard of the mind (Newell and Simon, 1972). In so doing, they tax their working memory – the weakest link in the human mind.

When people develop expertise, their brain functioning changes in ways that increase processing efficiency. This occurs even in animals. Thus as macaque monkeys in one study became experts in categorizing objects, brain recordings revealed quicker and stronger activity in the

FIGURE 9.30

Chess master Gary Kasparov has developed chess schemas that make him a worthy opponent for even the most sophisticated computers, including IBM's Deep Blue.

FIGURE 9.31

Professional footballers like Liverpool's Fernando Torres engage in upwards of 10 000 hours of practice to achieve their levels of expertise.

SOURCE: image from www.football. co.uk/liverpool/players/fernando_ torres_103351.shtml.

specific neurons that responded to the stimulus features of importance in categorizing the stimuli (Sigala and Logothetis, 2002).

What Is Wisdom?

The British journalist Miles Kington suggested that knowledge tells you that a tomato is a fruit, and that wisdom tells you not to put it in a fruit salad. However, defining a concept like wisdom is not always straightforward. The anthropologist Peter Collings (2001) notes that, as in many cultures, the Inuit living in the Arctic of Western Canada accord their elders special status and great respect (Fig. 9.32). Young and old Inuit alike regard wisdom as a key component of ageing successfully. To them, wisdom reflects 'the individual's function as a repository of cultural knowledge and his or her involvement in community life by interacting with younger people and talking to them, teaching them about "traditional" cultural values' (Collings, 2001, p. 146).

Does the Inuit conception of wisdom coincide with yours? If not, how would you define wisdom? Until the past 20 years, relatively few psychologists explored this issue, but their interest in studying wisdom has grown considerably since then (Sternberg, 1998). To German psychologist Paul Baltes and his colleagues, **wisdom** represents a system of knowledge about the meaning and conduct of life (Baltes and Kunzmann, 2004). What, then, are the components – the types of schemas – that make up this system of knowledge? One way to answer this question would be to study the characteristics of people who are widely esteemed for their wisdom. Yet, say Baltes and Kunzmann, this approach is not ideal, because 'Wise persons are approximations to wisdom, but they are not wisdom' (2004, p. 290). Instead, Baltes and his colleagues took another approach, pouring over numerous cultural, historical, philosophical, religious and psychological views of wisdom (Baltes and Staudinger, 2000). They concluded that wisdom has five major components:

1. *Rich factual knowledge about life.* This includes knowledge about human nature and human development, social norms and social relationships, major life events and how one's own well-being is interrelated with the well-being of other people.
2. *Rich procedural knowledge about life.* Such procedural knowledge includes strategies for making decisions, handling conflict, giving advice and weighing the importance of life goals.
3. *An understanding of lifespan contexts.* This understanding includes an awareness that life involves many contexts, such as family, friends, work and leisure. It also involves an awareness that these contexts need to be viewed from a broad temporal perspective that includes the past, present and future.
4. *An awareness of the relativism of values and priorities.* This includes recognizing that values and priorities differ across people and societies.
5. *The ability to recognize and manage uncertainty.* This ability stems from an awareness that the future cannot be fully known and that there are inherent limitations in the ways humans gather and process information.

You can readily see from this discussion that expertise and wisdom, though they may partly intersect, are not the same. For example, being an expert does not guarantee the breadth of qualities and knowledge that comprise wisdom. True wisdom, say Baltes and Staudinger, is hard to achieve, for it combines extraordinary scope with 'a truly superior level of knowledge, judgement, and advice … used for the good or well-being of oneself and that of others' (2000, p. 123).

MENTAL IMAGERY

Having spent most of this chapter discussing language and the types of thought that primarily involve what we subjectively experience as inner speech, let us turn to another mode of thought:

FIGURE 9.32

Among the Inuit of the Canadian Arctic, wisdom involves extensive cultural knowledge, involvement in community life and teaching young people about cultural values.

wisdom

a system of knowledge about the meaning and conduct of life

mental imagery. A **mental image** is a representation of a stimulus that originates inside your brain, rather than from external sensory input. Night-time dreams are among the most common forms of mental imagery. During daydreaming, people may intentionally create and manipulate mental images to get a break from reality or relieve boredom. Many elite athletes receive psychological training in how to effectively use mental imagery to rehearse skills, and people from all walks of life may use mental imagery to help solve problems. By using mental imagery to conduct experiments in their minds, Sir Isaac Newton and Albert Einstein gained insights that led to the discovery of several laws of physics. In a daydream at age 16:

> Einstein imagined himself running alongside a light beam and asked himself the fateful question: what would the light beam look like. Like Newton visualizing throwing a rock until it orbited the earth like the moon, Einstein's attempt to imagine such a light beam would yield deep and surprising results. (Kaku, 2004, p. 43)

Although people have mental images that subjectively involve sounds, tastes, smells, and so on, visual mental images are the most common and most thoroughly researched. Thus, we focus on them here.

Mental Rotation

Take a look at the objects shown in Figure 9.33. In each pair, are the two objects different, or are they the same object that has simply been rotated to a different orientation? This activity is called a *mental rotation task*. Typically, people rotate one object in their mind's eye until it lines up sufficiently with the other object to permit a same–different judgement. By the way, in pairs (a) and (b) the objects are the same. In pair (c) they are different.

In 1971 the journal *Science* published an experiment by psychologists Roger Shepard and Jacqueline Metzler that helped place the study of mental imagery on the scientific map. At a time when cognitive psychology was still in its infancy and emerging from under the shadow of behaviourism's half-century-long dominance, this elegant experiment demonstrated that mental images could be studied by gathering objective data, rather than by relying exclusively on people's subjective self-reports.

Shepard and Metzler presented each participant in their study with 1600 pairs of rotated objects, including the objects shown in Figure 9.33. Upon seeing each pair, participants pulled one of two levers to signal whether the two objects were the same or different, and their speed

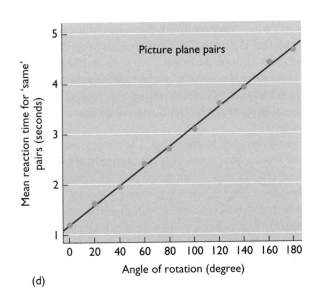

(a)

(b)

(c)

(d)

---

mental image

a representation of a stimulus that originates inside your brain, rather than from external sensory input

Focus 9.20

What are some components of wisdom? How do wisdom and expertise differ?

Focus 9.21

Why was Shepard and Metlzer's mental rotation study important? What did they find?

FIGURE 9.33

Mental rotation. (a, b, c) These are three of the many pairs of objects used in Shepard and Metzler's (1971) mental rotation study. (d) This graph shows the average number of seconds it took participants to decide that the two objects in each pair were similar, as a function of the initial angle of rotation. Factoring in the time that it took to make a physical response, participants' speed of mental rotation was approximately 60 degrees per second.

of response was measured. In 800 of the pairs, the objects within the pair were identical and were rotated from each other at angle of either 0, 20, 40, 60, 80, 100, 120, 140, 160 or 180 degrees. The two objects in pair (a) and pair (b) in Figure 9.33, for example, are rotated 80 degrees from one another. Because the two objects in pair (c) differ from one another, the concept of angle of rotation does not apply.

Subjectively, the participants reported that they were able to mentally rotate the objects as if the objects existed physically in three-dimensional space (i.e., they could rotate the objects vertically, horizontally and from front to back) but that the speed of this mental rotation process was limited. Shepard and Metzler's key finding concerned the pairs in which the two objects were the same. On these trials, the greater the difference in rotation between the two pictured objects, the longer it took participants to reach their decision. Moreover, as Figure 9.33d shows, this relation was linear. Shepard and Metzler (1971) concluded that 'If we can describe this process as some sort of "mental rotation in three-dimensional space," then … the average rate at which these particular objects can be thus "rotated" is roughly 60° per second' (p. 703).

Are Mental Images Pictures in the Mind?

Many researchers believe that mental images, while not literally pictures in the mind, function in ways analogous to actual visual images and are represented in the brain as a type of perceptual code. (Kosslyn et al., 2006) If this is the case, then mental images should have qualities similar to those that occur when we perceive objects and scenes in the real world. For example, if the objects portrayed in Figure 9.33 were real objects, you would be able to physically rotate them in three-dimensional space. Shepard and Metzler's (1971) experiment revealed that mental images likewise can be rotated within mental space.

Mental imagery as perception   Based on studies by Stephen Kosslyn, a leading researcher in the field of mental imagery, let us consider two other examples that illustrate the perceptual nature of mental imagery. For the first example, take a look at the island shown in Figure 9.34, and notice that it contains seven landmarks (e.g., a hut, lake, hill, beach), each of which is marked by a red dot. Suppose that after giving you time to memorize this map, we ask you to close your eyes and focus on a mental image of the map. Next, we ask you to (1) focus on a particular landmark (say, the beach), (2) scan the map until you come to the hill and (3) press a button (which measures your response time) when you find the hill. In another trial, we might ask you to start at the tree and scan the map until you come to the lake. In total, you will end up taking 21 of these mental trips as you scan once between every possible pair of locations.

In the real world, visually scanning between two objects takes longer when they are farther apart. When Stephen Kosslyn and his colleagues (1978) conducted the actual experiment, they found that the greater the distance between the two locations on the mental image of the map, the longer it took participants to scan and find the second location. This supports the view that mental images involve a spatial representation. Kosslyn also conducted experiments (involving mental images of animals rather than walls) that indicated that the size and level of detail of mental images can be changed in ways that correspond to perceiving actual objects.

Mental imagery as language   Some researchers challenge the view that mental images originate from visual codes that are stored in the brain. Instead, they argue that mental imagery is more closely tied to language than to visual perception (Pylyshyn, 2003). According to this view, for example, when you create a mental image of a brick wall, you are not pulling a visual code that represents a brick wall directly out of your long-term memory. Rather, you may subjectively experience a mental image of a brick wall that seems visual, but in reality 'brick wall' is being represented by linguistic concepts that are brought together to form propositions ('brick', 'bonded with', 'mortar', 'stacked', 'vertical', 'spread', 'horizontal').

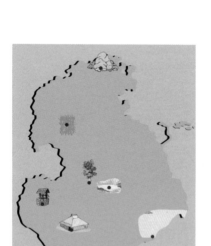

FIGURE 9.34

Imagine an island.

This island is similar to one used in Kosslyn et al.'s (1978) mental imagery scanning study.

Focus 9.22

Does research, including brain research, support the view that mental images are perceptual in nature? Explain.

Mental Imagery and the Brain

If mental imagery is rooted in perception, then people who experience brain damage that causes perceptual difficulties might also be expected to show similar impairments in forming mental images. In most instances this seems to be the case, but there are exceptions. For example, some patients who have damage on one side of the brain (usually, the right hemisphere) suffer from a condition called *visual neglect*: they fail to visually perceive objects on the other side (e.g., the left side) of their visual field. If you showed patients who have left-side visual neglect the picture of the island in Figure 9.34 and asked them to draw a copy, they would draw the right side of the island but fail to copy the left side. However, in some cases, if you were to ask the patients to draw the picture from memory (by calling up a mental image of the picture of the island) rather than to copy it (which relies on direct visual perception), they would be able to draw the entire island (Halligan et al., 2003). Most often, however, damage to brain regions involved in perception also disrupts people's ability to form mental images.

Brain-imaging studies of healthy people reveal that many brain regions that become more active when people perceive actual objects also become more active when people form mental images of those objects (Ganis et al., 2004). Moreover, research found evidence of neurons, which they called *imagery neurons*, that fired in response to a particular stimulus regardless of whether it was visual (a photograph of a fish) or imagined (a mental image of a fish). Altogether, studies of brain functioning suggest that while mental imagery and visual perception do not map onto all of the same neural components, there is a lot of overlap between these two processes (Slotnick et al., 2005).

Recent research into the brain areas involved in mental imagery has revealed some interesting findings. For instance, Sack et al. (2005) asked participants to imagine two clock faces showing different times and they were required to state which time formed the larger angle between the two hands on the clock faces. Sack et al. used transcranial magnetic stimulation which is used to disrupt cortical activity during the completion of a task, thereby helping to investigate the contribution of each hemisphere to the completion of this task. Sack et al. reported that the left parietal lobe was primarily involved in the generation of the image whereas the right parietal lobe was involved in the comparison of the images. They also reported that the right hemisphere was able to compensate and complete the tasks usually performed by the left hemisphere.

METACOGNITION: KNOWING YOUR OWN COGNITIVE ABILITIES

Have you ever had a friend or class-mate say to you after an examination, 'I don't understand why I got this question wrong?' or 'I don't understand how I got such a low grade? I thought I really knew this stuff'. Have you ever felt that way?

Recognizing What You Do and Do Not Know

To cognitive psychologists, the term **metacognition** refers to your awareness and understanding of your own cognitive abilities. For example, *comprehension* has to do with understanding something, such as a concept that you just read about. You may *think* you understand the concept, but in actuality you may or may not understand it. Metacognition has to do with truly knowing whether you do or do not understand the concept. The particular component of metacognition that we are discussing in this case is *metacomprehension*. In other words, people who display good metacomprehension are accurate in judging what they do or do not know, whereas people with poor metacomprehension have difficulty judging what they actually do and do not understand. They may typically think they understand things that, in fact, they do not, or they may often think they do not understand things that they actually do.

Metacomprehension is only one aspect of metacognition. Another component, called *metamemory*, represents your awareness and knowledge of your memory capabilities. For example, suppose that you try to memorize a list of definitions or facts. Your ability to accurately judge how well you will be able to remember those items for an upcoming test reflects one aspect of

Focus 9.23
What is metacognition? Identify two types of metacognition, and provide examples.

metacognition
your awareness and understanding of your own cognitive abilities

metamemory. (Note that being able to remember material, as in the case of rote memorization, does not necessarily mean that you understand it.) Your awareness of how to use various memory strategies (e.g., mnemonic devices) to improve your memory also constitutes part of your metamemory. In this discussion, however, we focus on metacomprehension.

As a student, your ability to effectively monitor what you do and do not know is an important ingredient in studying efficiently (Koriat and Bjork, 2005; Son and Metcalfe, 2000). Some students excel at this. Unfortunately, many studies have found that when it comes to reading text material, students, overall, are only mildly to moderately accurate in judging how well they understand what they are reading. Our 'Research close-up' examines one technique for improving students' metacomprehension.

RESEARCH CLOSE-UP

'WHY DID I GET THAT WRONG?' IMPROVING COLLEGE STUDENTS' AWARENESS OF WHETHER THEY UNDERSTAND TEXT MATERIAL

SOURCE: K.W. Theide and M.C.M. Anderson (2003) Summarizing can improve metacomprehension accuracy, *Contemporary Educational Psychology*, vol. 28, pp. 129–60.

INTRODUCTION

According to psychologists Keith Theide and Mary Anderson, this study is the first to examine whether students' metacomprehension for text material can be enhanced by requiring them to write summaries of that material. Based on other metacognition research, Theide and Anderson hypothesized that students who write delayed summaries of passages of text material will show better metacomprehension than students who write immediate summaries or no summaries. Presumably, the task of writing delayed rather than immediate summaries taps more powerfully into students' long-term memory and provides them with a better opportunity to assess whether they truly understand what they have read.

METHOD

Ethnically diverse samples of 75 and 90 college students taking introductory psychology participated, respectively, in Experiment 1 and Experiment 2. The students in each experiment read six passages of text material, with each passage focusing on a different topic (e.g., black holes, global warming, genetics, intelligence, Norse settlements). In Experiment 1 the passages were each about 220 words long, whereas in Experiment 2 they were much longer (1100 to 1600 words) and more similar in style to material presented in textbooks.

Students in each experiment were randomly assigned to one of three groups. In the no-summary group (control group), they read all six passages and then rated their comprehension of each passage ('How well do you think you understood the passage') on a scale ranging from 1 ('very poorly') to 7 ('very well'). In the immediate-summary group, students summarized each passage immediately after they read it and then, after finishing all six summaries, rated their comprehension of each one. In the delayed-summary group, students read all six passages before summarizing each one and then rating their comprehension of each passage.

Research design (Experiments 1 and 2)	
Question: Will writing summaries of text material that they have read improve college students' accuracy in judging how well they understand that material?	
Type of study: Experiment	
Independent variable	Dependent variables
Writing summaries of text material (random assignment to no summary, immediate summary or delayed summary groups)	• Actual comprehension of material • Students' perceptions of how well they comprehend the material • Metacomprehension accuracy (degree of association between actual and perceived comprehension)

All students, after rating their comprehension, took a multiple-choice comprehension test for each passage that included both factual and conceptual questions. These tests enabled Theide and Anderson to measure how well students' *beliefs* about their comprehension (measured by the rating scales) correlated with their actual comprehension (measured by their test scores).

RESULTS

In all three conditions, there was a positive correlation between students' comprehension ratings and comprehension scores, but in the no-summary and immediate-summary groups, this correlation was only weak to moderate. The critical finding was that in both experiments, students in the delayed-summary group were much more accurate than the other students in judging whether they knew or did not know the material. In other words, the correlation between their comprehension ratings and their comprehension test scores was much stronger (Fig. 9.35).

The data also revealed that, overall, the three groups did not differ in their comprehension ratings or in their test performance. In other words, students in the delayed-summary group did not feel that they knew the material better, and in fact they did not. Rather, summarizing the passages after a time delay helped them become more accurate in distinguishing the material they did know from the material they did not.

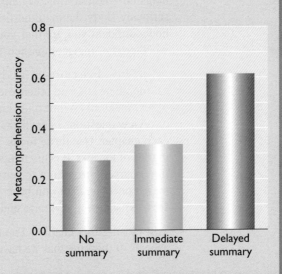

FIGURE 9.35

Writing summaries helps us recognize what we do and do not know.

Students who wrote delayed summaries of text material showed far better metacomprehension than did students who wrote immediate summaries or no summaries.

DISCUSSION

Both experiments supported the researchers' hypothesis: students' ability to accurately determine how well they understood passages of text improved greatly when they summarized that material after a time delay. Because the delayed-summary group did not rate their comprehension higher or perform better on the comprehension tests than the other groups, we want to take special care in making sure that you do *not* reach the wrong conclusion of 'So what if metacomprehension improved; the students didn't do better on the test'.

Realize that the students in this experiment were not allowed to go back and study the text passages again before taking the comprehension tests. Therefore, students in the delayed-summary group did not have the opportunity to act on their superior metacognitive knowledge (i.e., to revise the material that they accurately felt they did not know). But in real-world test situations, students who are better at recognizing what they know and do not know can indeed put that information to efficient use in the days and hours before a test. They can allocate more time to studying the material they have found difficult and less time to the material that they already understand. Students with poor metacomprehension may end up allocating their study time less efficiently, ignoring material that they think they know but truly do not. Indeed, Theide and Anderson found in Experiment 2 that when all the students were asked to identify which passages of text, hypothetically, they would select to restudy for an examination, students in the delayed-summary group were the most likely to accurately select the passages that they had learned least well.

Focus 9.24

Based on the 'Research close-up' and other research, describe some ways to enhance metacomprehension.

Further Advice on Improving Metacomprehension

In Chapter 1's 'Applying psychological science' feature we discussed several study strategies that can enhance your academic performance. As a student, you also want to be able to accurately assess your understanding of how well you know the material *before* it is time to take a test. One way to do this is to take advantage of practice tests, such as those found in study guides. Trying to memorize specific questions and answers from practice tests – as some students do – will do little to help you assess your broader understanding of the material. Instead, seriously study the material first and then try to answer the questions. For each question, rate how confident you are that your answer is right; this may help you develop a better sense of whether your metacomprehension is good.

The 'Research close-up' study found that writing delayed summaries improved students' metacomprehension, and other research finds that writing summaries boosts actual comprehension of text material (Winne and Hadwin, 1998). Many college textbooks provide preview questions or review questions in each chapter. In this textbook there are focus questions in the margins of each chapter. Use these focus, preview or review questions as the basis for writing brief summaries of the text. It is not magic. It takes time and effort. But in writing these summaries, if you find yourself struggling to remember the material or if you have a hard time articulating the main concepts, then you have gained the knowledge that you need to restudy this material or seek assistance in trying to understand it.

In closing this chapter, Figure 9.36 provides a levels-of-analysis summary of some of the aspects of thinking that we have discussed.

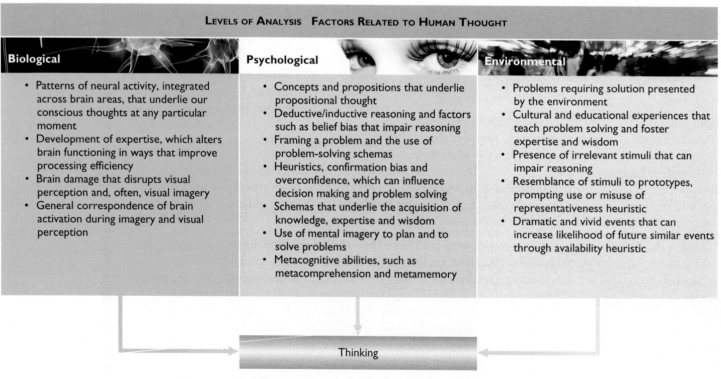

LEVELS OF ANALYSIS   FACTORS RELATED TO HUMAN THOUGHT

Biological

- Patterns of neural activity, integrated across brain areas, that underlie our conscious thoughts at any particular moment
- Development of expertise, which alters brain functioning in ways that improve processing efficiency
- Brain damage that disrupts visual perception and, often, visual imagery
- General correspondence of brain activation during imagery and visual perception

Psychological

- Concepts and propositions that underlie propositional thought
- Deductive/inductive reasoning and factors such as belief bias that impair reasoning
- Framing a problem and the use of problem-solving schemas
- Heuristics, confirmation bias and overconfidence, which can influence decision making and problem solving
- Schemas that underlie the acquisition of knowledge, expertise and wisdom
- Use of mental imagery to plan and to solve problems
- Metacognitive abilities, such as metacomprehension and metamemory

Environmental

- Problems requiring solution presented by the environment
- Cultural and educational experiences that teach problem solving and foster expertise and wisdom
- Presence of irrelevant stimuli that can impair reasoning
- Resemblance of stimuli to prototypes, prompting use or misuse of representativeness heuristic
- Dramatic and vivid events that can increase likelihood of future similar events through availability heuristic

Thinking

FIGURE 9.36

Levels of analysis: factors related to human thought.

IN REVIEW

- At the level of the brain, thoughts are patterns of neural activity. At the level of the mind, thoughts are propositional, imaginal or motoric mental representations.

- Concepts are mental categories, or classes, that share certain characteristics. Many concepts are based on prototypes, the most typical and familiar members of a class. How much something resembles the prototype determines whether the concept is applied to it. Propositional thought involves the use of concepts in the form of statements.

- In deductive reasoning, we reason from general principles to a conclusion about a specific case. Inductive reasoning involves reasoning from a set of specific facts or observations to a general principle. Deduction is the strongest and most valid form of reasoning because the conclusion cannot be false if the premises are true. Inductive reasoning cannot yield certainty.

- Unsuccessful deductive reasoning can result from (1) failure to select relevant information, (2) failure to apply the appropriate deductive reasoning rules, particularly in novel situations, (3) belief bias, the tendency to abandon logical rules in favour of personal beliefs, and (4) emotional reactions and framing effects.

- Problem solving proceeds through several steps: (1) understanding the nature of the problem, (2) establishing initial hypotheses or potential solutions, (3) testing the solutions against existing evidence, and (4) evaluating the results of these tests.

- People use several types of problem-solving schemas. Algorithms are formulas or procedures that guarantee correct solutions. Heuristics are general strategies that may or may not provide correct solutions. Means–ends analysis is a common heuristic. The representativeness heuristic is the tendency to judge evidence according to whether it is consistent with an existing concept or schema. The availability heuristic is the tendency to base conclusions and probability judgements on what is readily available in memory.

- Humans exhibit confirmation bias, a tendency to look for facts to support hypotheses rather than to disprove them. They also suffer from overconfidence, a tendency to overestimate their knowledge, beliefs and decisions.

- In some situations, divergent thinking is needed for generating novel ideas or variations on ideas. Functional fixedness can blind us to new ways of using an object or procedure, thereby interfering with creative problem solving. Sometimes, a period of incubation permits problem solving to proceed on a subconscious level while giving the problem solver psychological distance from the problem.

- Knowledge acquisition can be viewed as a process of building schemas, which are mental frameworks. Scripts, which are one type of schema, provide a framework for understanding sequences of events that usually unfold in a regular, almost standardized order.

- Experts rely heavily on schemas that they have developed from experience. Compared to novices, experts have more schemas to guide problem solving in their field and are much better at recognizing when each schema should be applied. Schemas also enable experts to take greater advantage of long-term memory.

- Wisdom represents a system of knowledge about the meaning and conduct of life. According to one model, wisdom has five major components: rich factual knowledge, rich procedural knowledge, an understanding of lifespan contexts, an awareness of the relativism of values and priorities, and the ability to recognize and manage uncertainty.

- A mental image is a representation of a stimulus that originates inside the brain, rather than from external sensory input. The objective, quantifiable study of mental imagery received a huge boost from research examining people's ability to mentally rotate objects.

- Mental images of objects seem to have properties that are analogous to the properties of actual objects (e.g., you can rotate them, visually scan them). Thus one viewpoint holds that mental images are basically perceptual in nature. A second viewpoint proposes that mental images actually are based on language. Overall, brain research offers more support to the imagery-as-perception view.

Answers to Problems in the Text

Figure 9.22   Manchester and Leeds are 50 miles apart. The trains are travelling at the same speed (25 mph). Hence they will meet at the halfway point, which is 25 miles, after 1 hour of travel time. Since the crow is flying at 60 mph, it will have flown a total of 60 miles when the trains meet.

Figure 9.25   Sequence of moves: A to 3, B to 2, A to 2, C to 3, A to 1, B to 3, A to 3.

Figure 9.28   Here are two solutions to the nine-dot problem. Both require you to think outside the box, literally.

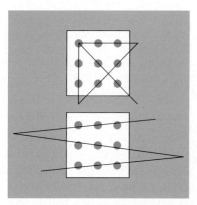

Figure 9.29   Solution to the candlestick problem:

KEY TERMS AND CONCEPTS

Each term has been boldfaced and defined in the chapter on the page indicated in parentheses.

algorithms (p. 412)

aphasia (p. 392)

availability heuristic (p. 414)

belief bias (p. 408)

bilingualism (p. 398)

bottom-up processing
    (p. 388)

concepts (p. 405)

confirmation bias (p. 415)

creativity (p. 416)

deductive reasoning (p. 406)

deep structure (p. 386)

discourse (p. 387)

displacement (p. 385)

divergent thinking (p. 416)

framing (p. 409)

functional fixedness (p. 417)

generativity (p. 385)

grammar (p. 384)

heuristics (p. 412)

imaginal thought (p. 405)

incubation (p. 417)

inductive reasoning (p. 408)

language (p. 383)

language acquisition device
    (LAD) (p. 393)

language acquisition support
    system (LASS) (p. 394)

linguistic relativity
    hypothesis (p. 401)

means–ends analysis
    (p. 412)

mental image (p. 421)

mental representations
    (p. 383)

mental set (p. 411)

metacognition (p. 423)

morphemes (p. 387)

motoric thought (p. 405)

overconfidence (p. 415)

phoneme (p. 387)

pragmatics (p. 391)

problem-solving schemas
    (p. 412)

propositions (p. 405)

propositional thought
    (p. 405)

prototypes (p. 405)

psycholinguistics (p. 383)

representativeness heuristic
    (p. 413)

schema (p. 418)

script (p. 418)

semantics (p. 385)

speech segmentation (p. 389)

subgoal analysis (p. 412)

surface structure (p. 385)

syntax (p. 385)

top-down processing
    (p. 388)

wisdom (p. 420)

WHAT DO YOU THINK?

DISCERNING SURFACE AND DEEP STRUCTURES OF LANGUAGE (p. 386)

The final words on the grave marker ('No Les No More') consist of a single surface structure with two possible deep structures. First, given the preceding words on the tombstone, the phrase 'No Les No More' could be a play on words, which in this case is meant to represent the expression 'No Less, No More'. In other words, Lester Moore was killed by exactly four bullets, no less, no more. Alternatively, the deep structure of 'No Les No More' can be interpreted simply as meaning that Lester is no longer among the living. Thus, like the sentence 'The police must stop drinking after midnight', the inscription on this tombstone has an ambiguous deep structure.

Sometimes, interpreting ambiguous sentences literally can yield humorous results. For example, in a restaurant washroom you might see the sign 'Employees must wash hands'. Should you therefore go back into the restaurant to find an employee who will wash your hands? Similarly, there are signs at the entrances to the escalators in the London Underground that read, 'Dogs must be carried'. Should you conclude that unless you are carrying a dog in your arms, you cannot use the escalator? These examples may strike you as a bit silly, but they illustrate how the existence of ambiguity in language highlights the need to make a distinction between surface and deep structure.

CHAPTER TEN

INTELLIGENCE

CHAPTER OUTLINE

Many highly intelligent people are poor thinkers. Many people of average intelligence are skilled thinkers. The power of a car is separate from the way the car is driven.

EDWARD DE BONO

We know that you highly esteem the kind of learning taught in those colleges.... But you, who are wise, must know that different nations have different conceptions of things: and you will not therefore take it amiss, if our ideas of this kind of education happen not to be the same with yours. We have had some experience of it; several of our young people were formerly brought up at the colleges of the Northern provinces; they were instructed in all your sciences; but, when they came back to us, they were bad runners, ignorant of every means of living in the woods, unable to bear either cold or hunger, knew neither how to build a cabin, take a deer, nor kill an enemy, spoke our language imperfectly, were therefore neither fit for hunters, warriors, nor counsellors; they were totally good for nothing....

We are, however not the less obligated by your kind offer, though we decline accepting it; and to show our grateful sense of it, if the gentlemen of Virginia will send us a dozen of their sons, we will take care of their education, instruct them in all we know, and make men of them. (A Native American leader quoted in Franklin, 1784)

This response to a well-intentioned offer by American colonists to provide Native American boys with access to European educational opportunities reminds us that people have different conceptions of what it means to be clever. In western cultures, being clever is typically thought of as having good mental skills that are instrumental to succeeding in school and in higher-level jobs and occupations. As we shall see, people with good mental skills do indeed do better in school and in jobs in our culture. But if we view intelligence in broader perspective as the ability to respond adaptively to the demands of a particular environment, we can understand why the Native American leader was less impressed with the products of Anglo-Saxon education than were the colonists. It is important to remember, then, that intelligence is not something that has concrete existence; it is, instead, a socially constructed concept (Sternberg, 2004; Fig. 10.1).

FIGURE 10.1

The skills required to adapt successfully to environmental demands may differ from culture to culture, suggesting to some theorists that what constitutes intelligence may be somewhat culture-specific.

In previous chapters, we have explored general principles of human learning, memory, thinking, reasoning and problem solving. In all these areas we have seen that people differ widely in how effectively they learn, remember, think and behave. Is it therefore the case that some people are generally more intelligent than others? If so, can we measure these differences and use the measures to predict success and failure in real-life settings? What is the nature of intelligence, and what factors account for the differences we observe in people's cognitive, emotional and behavioural skills? Attempts to answer these questions have influenced our culture enormously. Today, there exists a multibillion-dollar intelligence-testing industry. Increasing levels of testing in schools demand that we assess the aptitudes and learning outcomes of children in a search for educational accountability. You yourself have undoubtedly taken mental ability tests for educational or occupational reasons. In fact, your results on one or more examinations may have played an important role in your admission to university.

As we shall see, however, even after more than a century of research and theory development, there are still sharp disagreements about what intelligence is. In our discussion, we use the following definition, which accommodates most viewpoints: **Intelligence** is the ability to acquire knowledge, to think and reason effectively, and to deal adaptively with the environment.

intelligence

the ability to acquire knowledge, to think and reason effectively, and to deal adaptively with the environment

Focus 10.1

What is our working definition of intelligence?

Focus 10.2

How did Galton and Binet differ in their approaches to measuring mental abilities?

INTELLIGENCE IN HISTORICAL PERSPECTIVE

Historically, two scientists with entirely different agendas played seminal roles in the study and measurement of mental skills. The contributions of Sir Francis Galton and Alfred Binet set the stage for later attempts to measure intelligence and discover its causes.

SIR FRANCIS GALTON: QUANTIFYING MENTAL ABILITY

Sir Francis Galton was a cousin of Charles Darwin and was strongly influenced by Darwin's theory of evolution (Fig. 10.2). In his book, *Hereditary Genius* (1869), Galton showed through the study of family trees that eminence and genius seemed to occur within certain families. No intellectual slouch himself, young Francis wrote a childhood letter to his sister that contained the following: 'My dear Adele, I am 4 years old, and I can read any English book. I can say all of the Latin substantives and adjectives and active verbs besides 52 lines of Latin poetry.'

Galton's research convinced him that eminent people had 'inherited mental constitutions' that made them more fit for thinking than their less successful counterparts. Exhibiting his own belief bias, Galton dismissed the fact that the more successful people he studied almost invariably came from privileged environments.

Galton then attempted to demonstrate a biological basis for eminence by showing that people who were more socially and occupationally successful would also perform better on a variety of laboratory tasks thought to measure the 'efficiency of the nervous system'. He developed measures of reaction speed, hand strength, and sensory acuity. He even measured the size of people's skulls, believing that skull size reflected brain volume and hence intelligence.

In time, Galton's approach to mental skills measurement fell into disfavour because his measures of nervous-system efficiency proved unrelated to socially relevant measures of mental ability, such as academic and occupational success. Nonetheless, Galton's work created an interest in the measurement of mental abilities, setting the stage for the pioneering work of Alfred Binet.

ALFRED BINET'S MENTAL TESTS

The modern intelligence-testing movement began at the turn of the twentieth century, when the French psychologist Alfred Binet was commissioned by France's Ministry of Public Education to develop the test that was to become the forerunner of all modern intelligence tests (Fig. 10.3). Unlike Galton, with whom he had trained, Binet was interested in solving a practical problem rather than supporting a theory. Certain children seemed unable to benefit from normal public schooling. Educators wanted an objective way to identify these children as early as possible so that some form of special education could be arranged for them.

In developing his tests, Binet made two assumptions about intelligence: First, mental abilities develop with age. Second, the rate at which people gain mental competence is a characteristic of the person and is fairly constant over time. In other words, a child who is less competent than expected at age 5 should also be lagging at age 10.

To develop a measure of mental skills, Binet asked experienced teachers what sorts of problems children could solve at ages 3, 4, 5, and so on, up through the school years. He then used their answers to develop a standardized interview in which an adult examiner posed a series of questions to a child to determine whether the child was performing at the correct mental level for his or her age (Table 10.1). The result of the testing was a score called the *mental age*. For instance, if an 8-year-old child could solve problems at the level of the average 10-year-old, the child would be said to have a mental age of 10. For the French school system, the practical implication was that educational attainment could be enhanced if placement in school were based at least in part on the child's mental age. An 8-year-old child with a mental age of 6 could hardly be expected to cope with the academic demands of a normal classroom for 8-year-olds.

FIGURE 10.2

Sir Francis Galton pioneered the study of intelligence with his studies of hereditary genius.

FIGURE 10.3

Alfred Binet developed the first intelligence test to assess the mental skills of French school children. His test launched the modern intelligence-testing movement.

TABLE 10.1 SAMPLE PROBLEMS FROM THE STANFORD–BINET INTELLIGENCE TEST THAT SHOULD BE ANSWERED CORRECTLY AT PARTICULAR AGES

Age 3 – Child should be able to:	Point to objects that serve various functions such as 'goes on your feet'
	Name pictures of objects such as *chair*, *flag*
	Repeat a list of two words or digits such as *car*, *dog*
Age 4 – Child should be able to:	Discriminate visual forms such as squares, circles and triangles
	Define words such as *ball* and *bat*
	Repeat 10-word sentences
	Count up to four objects
	Solve problems such as 'In daytime it is light; at night it is…'
Age 6 – Child should be able to:	State the differences between similar items such as *bird* and *dog*
	Count up to nine blocks
	Solve analogies such as 'An inch is short; a mile is…'
Age 9 – Child should be able to:	Solve verbal problems such as 'Tell me a number that rhymes with tree'
	Solve simple arithmetic problems such as 'If I buy 4 cents' worth of candy and give the storekeeper 10 cents, how much money will I get back?'
	Repeat four digits in reverse order
Age 12 – Child should be able to:	Define words such as *muzzle*
	Repeat five digits in reverse order
	Solve verbal absurdities such as 'Bill's feet are so big he has to pull his trousers over his head. What is foolish about that?'

SOURCE: Terman and Merrill, 1972.

The concept of mental age was subsequently expanded by the German psychologist William Stern to provide a relative score – a common yardstick of intellectual attainment – for people of different chronological ages. Stern's **intelligence quotient (IQ)** was the ratio of mental age to chronological age, multiplied by 100: IQ = (mental age/chronological age) × 100. Thus a child who was performing at exactly his or her age level would have an IQ of 100. In our previous example, the child with a mental age of 10 and a chronological age of 8 would have an IQ of (10/8 × 100 = 125. A 16-year-old with a mental age of 20 would also have an IQ of 125, so the two would be comparable in intelligence even though their ages differed.

Today's tests no longer use the concept of mental age. Although the concept works pretty well for children, many of the basic skills measured by intelligence tests are acquired by about age 16 through normal life experiences and schooling, so that Stern's quotient is less useful for adults. Moreover, some intellectual skills show an actual decline at advanced ages. If we applied Stern's definition of IQ to a 20-year-old who performed at the typical level of an 80-year-old, we would have to say that the 20-year-old's IQ was 400! To deal with these problems, today's intelligence tests provide an 'IQ' score that is not a quotient at all. Instead, it is based on a person's

intelligence quotient (IQ)

the ratio of mental age to chronological age, multiplied by 100: IQ = (mental age/chronological age) × 100

Focus 10.3

Why do today's intelligence tests no longer use the concept of mental age? How is IQ now defined?

FIGURE 10.4

Lewis Terman imported the intelligence test developed by Binet to the USA and revised it as the Stanford–Binet Scale. The Stanford–Binet became the standard for future individually administered intelligence tests and is still used today.

Focus 10.4

What was Wechsler's concept of intelligence? How do the Wechsler scales reflect this concept?

performance relative to the scores of other people the same age, with a score of 100 corresponding to the average performance of that age group.

BINET'S LEGACY: AN INTELLIGENCE-TESTING INDUSTRY EMERGES

Lewis Terman (Fig. 10.4), a professor at Stanford University, was intrigued by Binet's work. He revised Binet's test for use in the USA, translating it into English and rewriting some of its items to improve their relevance to American culture. Terman's revised test became known as the *Stanford–Binet*. By the mid-1920s, it had become widely accepted in North America as the gold standard for measuring mental aptitude. The Stanford–Binet contained mostly verbal items, and it yielded a single IQ score.

At about the time that the Stanford–Binet test was introduced in 1916, the USA entered the First World War. One of Terman's students at Stanford, Arthur Otis, had been working on a group-administered test of intellectual ability. This test became the prototype for the *Army Alpha*, a verbally oriented test that was used to screen large numbers of US Army recruits for intellectual fitness. Because some recruits were unable to read, a non-verbal instrument using mazes, picture completion problems and digit-symbol tasks was also developed and given the name *Army Beta*. Before the war's end, more than 1.7 million men had been screened for intelligence using these tests.

Inspired by the success of the Army Alpha and Army Beta for measuring the intelligence of large numbers of people in a group setting, educators clamoured for similar instruments to test groups of children. New group tests of intelligence, such as the Lorge–Thorndike Intelligence Test and the Otis–Lennon School Ability Test, soon appeared and became an important part of educational reform and policy. Many schools use these or similar tests (e.g., Cognitive Abilities Tests; Thorndike et al., 1986) routinely, and you are likely to have taken one or more of them during your earlier school years.

Two decades after Terman introduced the American version of Binet's test, psychologist David Wechsler developed a major competitor to the Stanford–Binet. Wechsler believed that the Stanford–Binet relied too much on verbal skills. He thought that intelligence should be measured as a group of distinct but related verbal *and* non-verbal abilities. He therefore developed intelligence tests for adults and for children that measured both verbal and non-verbal intellectual skills. In 1939 the Wechsler Adult Intelligence Scale (WAIS) appeared, followed by the Wechsler Intelligence Scale for Children (WISC) in 1955 and the Wechsler Pre-school and Primary Scale of Intelligence (WPPSI) in 1967. The Wechsler scales have undergone several revisions. Today, the Wechsler tests (WAIS-III and WISC-IV) are the most popular individually administered intelligence tests (MacKintosh, 1998). A new version of the Wechsler test, the WAIS IV, is to be released in 2008 and has updated normative-data and revised measures of working memory and fluid reasoning designed to reflect developments in our understanding of intelligence. Following Wechsler's lead, the Stanford–Binet has also been revised to measure a wider range of mental abilities. Later in the chapter, we have a closer look at the Wechsler tests, as well as other measures that assess various classes of mental skills.

Intelligence has long been a major focus of psychological research, much of which has been inspired by questions that, even after a century of research, continue to evoke disagreement and controversy (Bartholomew, 2005). Should we regard intelligence as a single aptitude or as many specific abilities? Is intelligence an innate mental capacity, or is it a product of our upbringing? What kinds of brain processes underlie mental skills? Are there actually multiple intelligences, including some that may have little to do with mental skills? These and other questions have inspired a fascinating odyssey of scientific discovery. We begin with the most basic question of all: just what is this attribute we call *intelligence*?

IN REVIEW

- Intelligence is the ability to acquire knowledge, to think and reason effectively, and to deal adaptively with the environment. Because cultural environments differ in the skills most important for adaptation, cultural conceptions of intelligence may differ markedly.

- Galton's studies of hereditary genius and Binet's methods for measuring differences in children's mental skills were important historical milestones in the study of intelligence.

THE NATURE OF INTELLIGENCE

Psychologists have used two major approaches in the study of intelligence (Sternberg et al., 2003). The *psychometric approach* attempts to map the structure of intellect and to discover the kinds of mental competencies that underlie test performance. The *cognitive processes approach* studies the specific thought processes that underlie those mental competencies.

THE PSYCHOMETRIC APPROACH: THE STRUCTURE OF INTELLECT

Psychometrics is the statistical study of psychological tests. The psychometric approach to intelligence tries to identify and measure the abilities that underlie individual differences in performance; in essence, it tries to provide a measurement-based map of the mind.

Factor Analysis

Psychometric researchers have long sought to identify the mental abilities of the human mind. How many are there? Are there dozens, or are there perhaps only one or a few basic abilities that underlie performance across diverse tasks? What is the nature of these abilities?

To answer questions like these, researchers administer diverse measures of mental abilities and then correlate them with one another. They reason that if certain tests are correlated highly with one another – if they 'cluster' mathematically – then performance on these tests probably reflects the same underlying mental skill. Further, if the tests within a cluster correlate highly with one another but much less with tests in other clusters, then these various test clusters probably reflect different mental abilities. Thus researchers hope to determine the number of test clusters and to use this information to infer the nature of the underlying abilities.

When large numbers of tests are correlated with one another, many correlation coefficients result, and it is difficult to determine by visual examination the actual patterning of the test scores. Fortunately, a statistical technique called **factor analysis** reduces a large number of measures to a smaller number of clusters, or factors, with each cluster containing variables that correlate highly with one another but less highly with variables in other clusters. A factor allows us to infer the underlying characteristic that presumably accounts for the links among the variables in the cluster.

To illustrate with a highly simplified example the kind of clustering of tests that we are interested in, consider the small correlation matrix in Table 10.2, based on only six different mental ability tests. (There might be as many as 10 to 15 tests in an actual study.) Examination of Table 10.2 reveals two clusters of tests. Tests 1, 2 and 3 correlate highly with one another. Tests 4, 5 and 6 also show high positive correlations with one another. But tests 1, 2 and 3 do not correlate highly with tests 4, 5 and 6. This indicates that the two sets of tests are measuring different abilities. A factor analysis would tell us that there are two different factors.

psychometrics
the statistical study of psychological tests

factor analysis
reduces a large number of measures to a smaller number of clusters, or factors, with each cluster containing variables that correlate highly with one another but less highly with variables in other clusters

TABLE 10.2 CORRELATIONS AMONG SIX COGNITIVE ABILITY TESTS

Test	1	2	3	4	5	6
1	1.00	.84	.79	.46	.39	.43
2		1.00	.87	.51	.48	.54
3			1.00	.47	.50	.48
4				1.00	.88	.91
5					1.00	.82
6						1.00

But what are these two sets of tests measuring? The factor analysis cannot answer this question; it can only identify the clusters for us. It is now up to us to examine the nature of the tests within each cluster and decide what the underlying factors might be. Suppose that test 1 is a measure of vocabulary, test 2 measures reading comprehension and test 3 requires respondents to complete sentences with missing words. Because all three tasks involve the use of words, we might decide to call the underlying factor 'verbal ability'. Inspection of tests 4, 5 and 6 might reveal that all of them involve the use of numbers or mathematical word problems. We might therefore decide to name this factor 'mathematical reasoning'. What matters is that we have now reduced six variables to two variables, based on the correlations among them, and we have arrived at some idea of what the underlying abilities might be.

We should note, however, that the two clusters of tests we have identified are not totally unrelated to one another. The verbal and mathematical scores are also correlated with one another, although at a much lower level than within the clusters. This fact suggests that although the verbal and mathematical factors are clearly distinct from one another, they also share something in common, perhaps a more general mental ability that cuts across both verbal and mathematical abilities. This pattern of results anticipates one of the major controversies in the field of intelligence: is intelligence a general mental capacity, or does it consist of separate and specific mental abilities?

The g Factor: Intelligence as General Mental Capacity

The psychometric argument for intelligence as a general ability was first advanced by the British psychologist Charles Spearman (1923). He observed that school grades in different subjects, such as English and mathematics, were almost always positively correlated but not perfectly. Spearman found the same to be true for different types of Stanford–Binet intelligence test items, such as vocabulary questions, arithmetic reasoning problems and the ability to solve puzzles. Were he to look at the correlation matrix in Table 10.2, he would be impressed by the fact that the verbal ability cluster and the mathematical-reasoning cluster are correlated with one another at about the .40 to .50 level. He would regard these correlations as evidence that verbal and mathematical abilities, while clearly different, also reflect a more basic or general mental capacity that contributes to them.

Spearman concluded that intellectual performance is determined partly by a **g factor**, or general intelligence, and partly by whatever special abilities might be required to perform that particular task. Spearman contended that because the general factor – the g factor – cuts across virtually all tasks, it constitutes the core of intelligence. Thus Spearman would argue that your performance in a mathematics course would depend mainly on your general intelligence but also on your specific ability to learn mathematics.

Today, many theorists continue to believe that the g factor is the core of what we call *intelligence*. Moreover, g matters a great deal as a predictor of both academic and job performance. Nathan

Focus 10.5

How is factor analysis used in the study of intelligence?

Focus 10.6

What kinds of evidence supported the existence of Spearman's g factor?

Focus 10.7

What led Thurstone to view intelligence as specific mental abilities?

g factor
general intelligence

Kuncel and co-workers (2004) performed a meta-analysis of 127 studies involving 20 352 participants in numerous educational and work settings. They concluded that the same general mental ability is significantly related to success in both areas of life. Taking this argument a step further, Frank Schmidt and John Hunter (2004) concluded that measures of the *g* factor predict job success even better than do measures of specific abilities tailored to individual jobs. Summarizing the research evidence, David Lubinski, a prominent intelligence researcher, concluded: '*g* is clearly the most important dimension uncovered in the study of cognitive abilities to date' (2004, p. 100).

Intelligence as Specific Mental Abilities

Spearman's conclusion about the centrality of the *g* factor was soon challenged by Thurstone of the University of Chicago. While Spearman had been impressed by the fact that scores on different mental tasks are correlated, Thurstone was impressed by the fact that the correlations are far from perfect. Thurstone therefore concluded that human mental performance depends not on a general factor but rather on seven distinct abilities, which he called *primary mental abilities* (Table 10.3). Thus Thurstone would focus on the two clusters of test scores shown in Table 10.2 and attach special significance to the high correlations within each cluster. He would expect that performance on a given verbal or mathematical task would be influenced more by the specific skills represented in the relevant cluster than by any *g* factor.

TABLE 10.3 THURSTONE'S PRIMARY MENTAL ABILITIES

Ability name	Description
S – Space	Reasoning about visual scenes
V – Verbal comprehension	Understanding verbal statements
W – Word fluency	Producing verbal statements
N – Number facility	Dealing with numbers
P – Perceptual speed	Recognizing visual patterns
M – Rote memory	Memorization
R – Reasoning	Dealing with novel problems
SOURCE: Thurstone, 1938.	

Following Thurstone's lead, other investigators claimed to have found many more specific cognitive factors. One prominent theorist maintained that there are more than 100 distinct and measurable mental abilities (Guilford, 1967). Other theorists suggest fewer abilities but maintain that intelligence is more complex than a single *g* factor.

For practical reasons, educators tend to find the specific-abilities notion of intelligence more attractive and useful than the general mental ability model (Mayer, 2000). They are more interested in identifying the specific mental skills involved in learning subjects such as reading, mathematics and science. They are also interested in helping children increase the specific mental abilities that are needed for success in various subjects. For such purposes, general mental ability measures such as an overall IQ are less useful than are measures of specific cognitive abilities that can point to a student's areas of strength and weakness. Additionally, it may appear more feasible to enhance specific mental skills than to raise general intelligence.

Crystallized and Fluid Intelligence

Raymond Cattell (1971) and John Horn (1985) proposed a new model of intelligence (Fig. 10.5). They broke down Spearman's general intelligence into two distinct but related subtypes of *g* (with a correlation of about .50). **Crystallized intelligence (g_c)** is the ability to apply

crystallized intelligence (g_c)
the ability to apply previously acquired knowledge to current problems

FIGURE 10.5

Crystallized and fluid intelligence.

Raymond Cattell and John Horn made an important distinction between crystallized and fluid intelligence. Crystallized intelligence is based more strongly on previous learning and experience, whereas fluid intelligence is a more creative type of intelligence.

fluid intelligence (g_f)

the ability to deal with novel problem-solving situations for which personal experience does not provide a solution

Focus 10.8

Differentiate between crystallized and fluid intelligence, and indicate their relation to ageing and types of memory.

three-stratum theory of cognitive abilities

establishes three levels of mental skills – general, broad and narrow – arranged in a hierarchical model

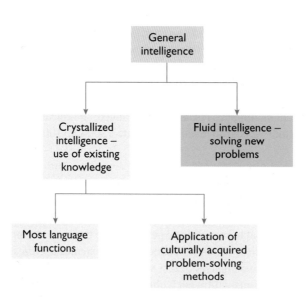

previously acquired knowledge to current problems. Vocabulary and information tests are good measures of crystallized intelligence. Crystallized intelligence, which is the basis for expertise, depends on the ability to retrieve previously learned information and problem-solving schemas from long-term memory (Horn and Masunaga, 2000; Hunt, 1997). It is dependent on previous learning and practice.

Cattell and Horn's second general factor is **fluid intelligence (g_f)**, defined as the ability to deal with novel problem-solving situations for which personal experience does not provide a solution. It involves inductive reasoning and creative problem-solving skills such as those discussed in the previous chapter. Fluid intelligence is dependent primarily on the efficient functioning of the central nervous system rather than on prior experience and cultural context. People high in fluid intelligence can perceive relations among stimulus patterns and draw inferences from relationships. The tower-of-Hanoi and nine-dot problems you worked on in the previous chapter are fluid-intelligence tasks.

Fluid intelligence requires the abilities to reason abstractly, think logically, and manage information in working (short-term) memory so that new problems can be solved on the blackboard of the mind (Hunt, 1997). Thus long-term memory contributes strongly to crystallized intelligence, whereas fluid intelligence is particularly dependent on efficient working memory.

The g_c–g_f model is based in part on what has been learned about intellectual development in adulthood (Berg, 2000). Cattell and Horn concluded that over our lifespan, we progress from using fluid intelligence to depending more on crystallized intelligence. Early in life we encounter many problems for the first time, so we need fluid intelligence to work out solutions. As experience makes us more knowledgeable, we have less need to approach each situation as a new problem. Instead, we simply call up appropriate information and schemas from long-term memory, thereby utilizing our crystallized intelligence. This is the essence of wisdom (Kunzman and Baltes, 2003).

Because long-term memory remains strong even as we age, performance on tests of crystallized intelligence improves during adulthood and remains stable well into late adulthood. In contrast, performance on tests of fluid intelligence begins to decline as people enter late adulthood (Cattell, 1998; Schaie, 1998). The fact that ageing affects the two forms of intelligence differently is additional evidence that they represent different classes of mental abilities (Horn and Noll, 1997; Weinert and Hany, 2003).

Carroll's Three-Stratum Model: A Modern Synthesis

In their attempts to specify the nature of intellect, psychometric researchers have been administering measures of mental abilities for over a century. The many tasks they have used have probably left no cognitive stone unturned. In an attempt to synthesize the results of prior research, John B. Carroll (1993) used factor analysis to re-analyse more than 460 different sets of data obtained by researchers around the world between 1935 and 1980. Carroll's analysis resulted in an integrative model of intelligence that contains elements of Spearman's, Thurstone's and Cattell–Horn's models. The **three-stratum theory of cognitive abilities** establishes three levels of mental skills – general, broad and narrow – arranged in a hierarchical model. As shown in Figure 10.6, at the top, or third stratum, of the model is a *g* factor thought to underlie most mental activity. Below *g* at the second stratum are eight broad intellectual factors arranged from left to right in terms of the extent to which they are influenced by (or correlated with) *g*. Fluid intelligence is most strongly related to (or 'saturated with') *g*, and crystallized intelligence is next, indicating the importance of the Cattell–Horn factors. The other broad abilities at the second stratum involve basic cognitive functions such as memory and learning, perceptual abilities, and speed of mental functioning, some of which resemble Thurstone's primary mental abilities. Finally, at the first stratum of the model are nearly 70 highly specific cognitive abilities that feed into the broader second-stratum factors. On average, these specific ability measures tend to correlate around .30 with one another, reflecting the common *g* factor at the top of the model. Carroll believes that the three-stratum model encompasses virtually all known cognitive abilities and provides the most complete and detailed map of the human intellect derived from the psychometric approach to intelligence.

Focus 10.9
Describe Carroll's three-stratum psychometric model and how it originated. How does it relate to the previously discussed models?

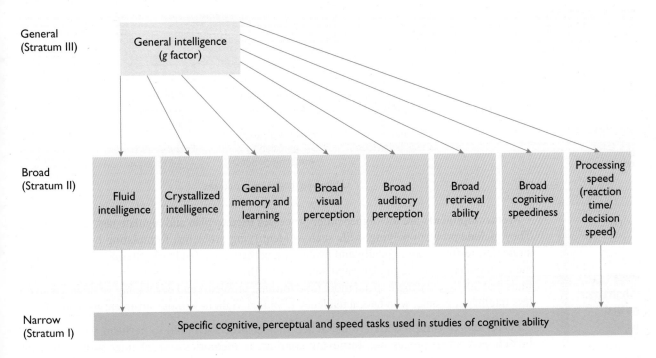

FIGURE 10.6

A modern model of intellect.

John B. Carroll's three-stratum model of cognitive skills is based on a re-analysis of more than 400 data-sets. The model builds upward from specific skills to a *g* factor at its apex. The lengths of the arrows from Stratum III to Stratum II represent the contribution of the *g* factor to each Stratum II ability.

SOURCE: adapted from Carroll, J.B., 1993.

COGNITIVE PROCESS APPROACHES: THE NATURE OF INTELLIGENT THINKING

Psychometric theories of intelligence are statistically sophisticated ways of providing a map of the mind and describing *how* people differ from one another (Birney and Sternberg, 2006). What psychometric theories do not explain is *why* people vary in these mental skills. **Cognitive process theories** explore the specific information-processing and cognitive processes that underlie intellectual ability. Recall that this was the logic behind Galton's early attempts to

cognitive process theories

explore the specific information-processing and cognitive processes that underlie intellectual ability

relate thinking ability to speed of reaction and sensory acuity. Robert Sternberg (1988; 2004) is a leading proponent of the cognitive processes approach to intelligence. His **triarchic theory of intelligence** addresses both the psychological processes involved in intelligent behaviour and the diverse forms that intelligence can take. Sternberg's theory divides the cognitive processes that underlie intelligent behaviour into three specific components (Fig. 10.7).

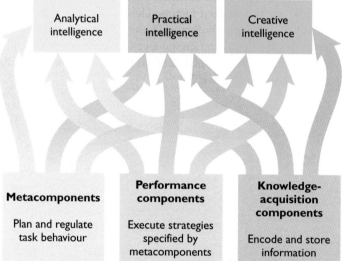

Types of intellectual competence

FIGURE 10.7

Sternberg's triarchic theory.

Sternberg's theory includes three different types of intelligence and three classes of cognitive processes that underlie each type of intelligence.

triarchic theory of intelligence

addresses both the psychological processes involved in intelligent behaviour and the diverse forms that intelligence can take

metacomponents

the higher-order processes used to plan and regulate task performance

performance components

the actual mental processes used to perform the task

knowledge-acquisition components

allow us to learn from our experiences, store information in memory, and combine new insights with previously acquired information

Metacomponents are the higher-order processes used to plan and regulate task performance. They include problem-solving skills such as identifying problems, formulating hypotheses and strategies, testing them logically and evaluating performance feedback. Sternberg believes that metacomponents are the fundamental sources of individual differences in fluid intelligence. He finds that intelligent people spend more time framing problems and developing strategies than do less intelligent people, who have a tendency to plunge right in without sufficient forethought.

Performance components are the actual mental processes used to perform the task. They include perceptual processing, retrieving appropriate memories and schemas from long-term memory, and generating responses. Finally, **knowledge-acquisition components** allow us to learn from our experiences, store information in memory, and combine new insights with previously acquired information. These abilities underlie individual differences in crystallized intelligence. Thus Sternberg's theory addresses the processes that underlie the distinction made by Cattell and Horn between fluid and crystallized intelligences.

Sternberg believes that there is more than one kind of intelligence. He suggests that environmental demands may call for three different classes of adaptive problem solving and that people differ in their intellectual strengths in these areas:

1. *Analytical intelligence* involves the kinds of academically oriented problem-solving skills measured by traditional intelligence tests.

2. *Practical intelligence* refers to the skills needed to cope with everyday demands and to manage oneself and other people effectively.

3. *Creative intelligence* comprises the mental skills needed to deal adaptively with novel problems.

Sternberg has shown that these forms of intelligence, while having a modest underlying *g* factor, are also distinct from one another. Consider, for example, the relationship between academic and practical skills. In one study, adolescents in Kenya were given one set of analytical tests measuring traditional academic knowledge and another set measuring their knowledge of natural herbal medicines used to treat illnesses, a kind of practical knowledge viewed by villagers as important to their survival. The results indicated that the practical intelligence measure of herbal knowledge was unrelated to (and sometimes negatively correlated with) the academic measures (Sternberg et al., 2001). Sternberg also found that Brazilian street-children were very proficient at the mathematics required to carry on their street businesses, despite the fact that many of them had failed mathematics in school (Sternberg, 2004).

Sternberg believes that educational programmes should teach all three classes of skills, not just analytical-academic skills. In studies with elementary school children, he and his colleagues have shown that a curriculum that also teaches practical and creative skills results in greater mastery of course material than does a traditional analytic, memory-based approach to learning course content (Sternberg et al., 1998). As Sternberg's work illustrates, cognitive science is leading us to a focus on understanding and enhancing the mental processes that underlie intelligent behaviour.

BROADER CONCEPTIONS OF INTELLIGENCE: BEYOND MENTAL COMPETENCIES

Traditionally, intelligence has been viewed as *mental competence*. Some psychologists think this is too limited a definition to capture the range of human adaptations. They believe that intelligence may be more broadly conceived as relatively *independent intelligences* that relate to different adaptive demands.

Gardner's Multiple Intelligences

Harvard psychologist Howard Gardner (2003) is one of the strongest proponents of this view. Inspired by his observations of how specific human abilities are affected by brain damage, Gardner advanced a theory of multiple intelligences. The number of intelligences has varied as Gardner's work has progressed; he currently defines eight distinct varieties of adaptive abilities, and a possible ninth variety (Gardner, 2000):

1. *Linguistic intelligence* – the ability to use language well, as writers do
2. *Logical-mathematical intelligence* – the ability to reason mathematically and logically
3. *Visuospatial intelligence* – the ability to solve spatial problems or to succeed in a field such as architecture
4. *Musical intelligence* – the ability to perceive pitch and rhythm and to understand and produce music
5. *Bodily-kinaesthetic intelligence* – the ability to control body movements and skilfully manipulate objects, as demonstrated by a highly skilled dancer, athlete or surgeon
6. *Interpersonal intelligence* – the ability to understand and relate well to others
7. *Intrapersonal intelligence* – the ability to understand oneself
8. *Naturalistic intelligence* – the ability to detect and understand phenomena in the natural world, as a zoologist or meteorologist might.

In recent writings, Gardner (2000) has also speculated about a ninth possible intelligence, which he calls *existential intelligence*, a philosophically oriented ability to ponder questions about the meaning of one's existence, life and death.

Gardner's first three intelligences are measured by existing intelligence tests, but the others are not. Indeed, some of Gardner's critics insist that these other abilities are not really part of the traditional concept of intelligence at all and that some of them are better regarded as talents. However, Gardner replies that the form of intelligence that is most highly valued within a given

Focus 10.11
What three classes of psychological processes and forms of intelligence are found in Sternberg's triarchic theory?

Focus 10.12
What kinds of abilities are included in Gardner's multiple intelligences?

culture depends on the adaptive requirements of that culture. In Gardner's view, the abilities exhibited by Albert Einstein, Tiger Woods and a street-smart gang leader exemplify different forms of intelligence that are highly adaptive within their respective environments (Fig. 10.8). Gardner further suggests that these different classes of abilities require the functioning of separate but interacting modules in the brain. Gardner's approach, though provocative, remains controversial because it goes far beyond traditional conceptions of intelligence as mental skills.

FIGURE 10.8

According to Howard Gardner, these people's abilities exemplify forms of intelligence that are not measured by traditional intelligence tests. John Martyn possesses high musical intelligence, whereas Matt Hayes and Zinedine Zidane exhibit high naturalistic and bodily-kinaesthetic intelligence, respectively.

SOURCES: pictures taken from www.huxrecords.com/john_martyn1.jpg; www.anglersnet.co.uk/files/Matt_Hayes_podcast.jpg; and www.soccer.si/wallpapers/zinedine_zidane.jpg respectively

emotional intelligence
the abilities to read others' emotions accurately, to respond to them appropriately, to motivate oneself, to be aware of one's own emotions, and to regulate and control one's own emotional responses

Emotional Intelligence

Another form of adaptive ability lies within the emotional realm, and some theorists believe that emotional competence is a form of intelligence. According to John Mayer and Peter Salovey, **emotional intelligence** involves the abilities to read others' emotions accurately, to respond to them appropriately, to motivate oneself, to be aware of one's own emotions, and to regulate and control one's own emotional responses (Mayer et al., 2004).

According to Mayer and Salovey, emotional intelligence (EI) includes four components, or branches, as shown in Figure 10.9. The Mayer–Salovey–Caruso Emotional Intelligence Test (MSCEIT) includes specific tasks to measure each branch. *Perceiving emotions* is measured by people's accuracy in judging emotional expressions in facial photographs, as well as the emotional tones conveyed by different landscapes and designs. *Using emotions to facilitate thought*

FIGURE 10.9

The structure of emotional intelligence.

Four specific classes of emotion-detection and control abilities are assumed to underlie emotional intelligence.

SOURCE: based on Mayer et al., 2004.

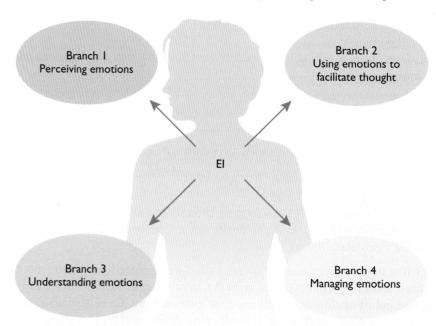

is measured by asking people to identify the emotions that would best enhance a particular type of thinking, such as how to deal with a distressed co-worker or plan a birthday party. To measure *understanding emotions*, people are asked to specify the conditions under which their emotions change in intensity or type; another task measures people's understanding of which basic emotions blend together to create subtle emotions, such as envy or jealousy. Finally, *managing emotions* is measured by asking respondents to indicate how they can change their own or others' emotions to facilitate success or increase interpersonal harmony.

The scoring method for the MSCEIT tasks yields high reliability among expert scorers; it produces scores for each branch, as well as a total emotional-intelligence score. Mayer and Salovey view these tasks as ability measures in the same sense that a Wechsler scale measures mental abilities. As in the case of mental intelligence, it seems important to measure what people can actually do rather than simply asking them how competent they are. Other measures of emotional intelligence, which ask people how competent they are in emotional areas, tend not to correlate highly with the MSCEIT or predict competent behaviours as well (Mayer et al., 2004).

Proponents of emotional intelligence point to the important adaptive advantages of emotional skills in meeting the challenges of daily life, and they believe that the ability to read, respond to and manage emotions has evolutionary roots. Emotionally intelligent people, they suggest, form stronger emotional bonds with others; enjoy greater success in careers, marriage and child-rearing; modulate their own emotions so as to avoid strong depression, anger or anxiety; and work more effectively towards long-term goals by being able to control impulses for immediate gratification. It has been suggested that emotional intelligence may be a crucial aspect of many areas such as nursing (Bellack et al., 2001) and even engineering (Marshall, 2001). In the end, some people who are high in emotional intelligence may enjoy more success in life than do others who surpass them in mental intelligence (Salovey and Pizzaro, 2003). They also tend to use more effective coping strategies (Saklofske et al., 2007).

As is the case with Gardner's multiple intelligences, emotional intelligence has its critics. Some psychologists believe that the concept of intelligence is being stretched too far from its original focus on mental ability (e.g., Matthews et al., 2004). They would prefer a different term, such as *emotional competence*, to distinguish this concept from the traditional mental-skills concept of intelligence. But emotional-intelligence proponents respond that if we regard intelligence as adaptive abilities, we ought not limit ourselves to the purely cognitive realms of human ability. The debate concerning multiple intelligence continues to rage and promises to do so into the future.

So far we have explored the nature of intelligence. Let us now examine more closely how individual differences in intelligence are measured.

Focus 10.13

Describe the four branches of emotional intelligence and how they are measured.

Focus 10.14

How is Wechsler's view of intelligence reflected in the Wechsler tests? What kinds of scores do they provide?

IN REVIEW

- The psychometric approach to intelligence attempts to map the structure of intellect and establish how many different classes of mental ability underlie test performance. A newer approach, the cognitive processes approach, focuses on the specific thought processes that underlie mental competencies.

- Factor analysis can be applied to correlations among test scores to identify clusters of measures that correlate highly with one another and therefore are assumed to have a common underlying factor, such as verbal ability or mathematical reasoning.

- Spearman believed that intelligence is determined both by specific cognitive abilities and by a general intelligence (*g*) factor that constitutes the core of intelligence. Thurstone disagreed, viewing intelligence as a set of specific abilities. Thurstone's position is best supported by observed distinctions between verbal and spatial abilities.

- Cattell and Horn differentiated between crystallized intelligence, the ability to apply previously learned knowledge to current problems, and fluid intelligence, the ability to deal with novel problem-solving situations for which personal experience does not provide a solution. They argued that over our lifespan, we show a progressive shift from using fluid intelligence to using crystallized intelligence as we attain wisdom.

- Carroll's three-stratum model is based on re-analyses of hundreds of data-sets. Mental abilities are represented at three levels, with general intelligence (*g*) at the apex and highly specific cognitive and perceptual skills at its base. Carroll's model may be the most accurate psychometric representation of human cognitive abilities.

- Cognitive process theories of intelligence focus on the elementary information-processing abilities that contribute to intelligence. Sternberg's triarchic theory of intelligence includes a components subtheory that addresses the specific cognitive processes that underlie intelligent behaviour.

- Sternberg and Gardner maintain that there are distinct forms of intelligence beyond the traditional concept. Sternberg differentiates between analytical, practical and creative intelligence, and Gardner proposes nine different kinds of intelligence. The theory of emotional intelligence refers to people's ability to read and respond appropriately to others' emotions, to motivate themselves, and to be aware of and in control of their emotions.

THE MEASUREMENT OF INTELLIGENCE

Today, the Wechsler tests (WAIS-III and WISC-IV) are the most popular individually administered intelligence tests in general use (MacKintosh, 1998). They provide a good illustration of how intelligence is assessed.

Recall that Wechsler believed that intelligence tests should measure a wide array of different mental abilities. His tests reflect that conviction. The WAIS-III consists of a series of subtests that fall into two classes: verbal and performance (Fig. 10.10). A psychologist can therefore plot a profile based on the scores on each of the subtests to assess a person's pattern of intellectual strengths and weaknesses The test yields three summary scores: a *Verbal IQ* based on the sum of the verbal subtests; a *Performance IQ* based on the performance subtests; and a *Full-Scale IQ* based on all of the subtests. For some purposes, it is useful to examine differences between the Verbal IQ and the Performance IQ. For example, individuals from an impoverished environment with little formal schooling might score higher on the performance subtests than on the verbal subtests, suggesting that their overall IQ might be an underestimate of their intellectual potential. Sometimes, too, various types of brain damage are reflected in large discrepancies between certain subtest scores (Goldstein, 2000; Strauss et al., 2006).

INCREASING THE INFORMATIONAL YIELD FROM INTELLIGENCE TESTS

Revisions of both the Stanford–Binet and the Wechsler scales have been responsive to advances in the understanding of the mental processes that underlie intelligence. The original Stanford–Binet yielded a single IQ score based mainly on verbal items, but today's test samples a wider range of abilities and provides, in addition to a composite IQ score, separate scores for Verbal

Wechsler Adult Intelligence Scale (WAIS-III)

Subtest	Description	Example
Verbal Scales		
Information	Taps general range of knowledge	What is steam made of?
Comprehension	Tests understanding of social conventions and ability to evaluate past experience	What is the advantage of keeping money in a bank?
Arithmetic	Tests arithmetic reasoning through verbal problems	Three women divided eighteen golf balls equally among themselves. How many golf balls did each person receive?
Similarities	Asks in what way certain objects or concepts are similar; measures abstract thinking	In what way are an hour and a week alike?
Letter–Number Sequencing	Tests attention and ability to retain and manipulate information in memory; the alternating numbers and letters are presented orally and the subject must repeat first the numbers and then the letters in order of magnitude and alphabetical order, respectively (Alternative to the Digit Span subtest)	Item: 5-J-4-A-1-S Response: 1-4-5-A-J-S
Vocabulary	Tests ability to define increasingly difficult words	What does 'formidable' mean?
Performance Scales		
Digit Symbol	Tests speed of learning through timed coding tasks in which numbers must be associated with drawings of various shapes	Shown: Fill in appropriate symbol: 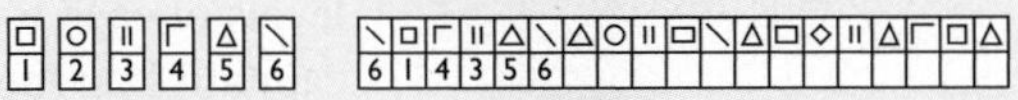
Picture Completion	Tests visual alertness and visual memory through presentation of an incompletely drawn figure; the missing part must be discovered and named	What is missing in this picture? 
Block Design	Tests ability to perceive and analyse patterns by presenting designs that must be copied with blocks	Assemble blocks to match this design: 
Picture Arrangement	Tests understanding of social situations through a series of comic-strip-type pictures that must be arranged in the right sequence to tell a story	Put the pictures in the correct order: 
Object Assembly	Tests ability to deal with part/whole relationships by presenting puzzle pieces that must be assembled to form a complete object	Assemble the pieces into a completed object: 

Note: Sample items courtesy to The Psychology Corporation, 2005.

FIGURE 10.10

The Wechsler Adult Intelligence Scale.

These sample items resemble those found on subscales of the Wechsler Adult Intelligence Scale (WAIS-III).

SOURCE: simulated items similar to those in the Wechsler Adult Intelligence Scale, third edition. Copyright © 2005 by Harcourt Assessment, Inc. Reproduced with permission. All rights reserved.

Reasoning, Abstract/Visual Reasoning, Quantitative Reasoning, and Short-Term Memory. The WISC-IV, used to assess children between ages 6 and 11, provides, in addition to its Full-Scale IQ, separate scores for Verbal Comprehension, Perceptual Organization, Freedom from Distractibility, and Processing Speed. These scores make the tests more useful for understanding test-takers' intellectual strengths and weaknesses, and possibly planning educational interventions for them. Many other tests of specific cognitive skills are currently in use, providing many tools for assessing both children and adults (Bartholomew, 2005; Groth-Marnat, 1999).

THEORY-BASED INTELLIGENCE TESTS

Advances in the theory of intelligence have stimulated the development of new instruments to test the specific abilities dictated by the theories. For example, the Cattell–Horn distinction between crystallized and fluid intelligence has had a strong impact on the field of intelligence testing. Several recently developed tests, such as the Kaufman Adolescent and Adult Intelligence Test and the Woodcock–Johnson Psycho-Educational Battery, are specifically designed to measure fluid and crystallized abilities separately (Kaufman and Kaufman, 1997; Woodcock, 1997). The Kaufman test has three crystallized-ability subscales and three fluid-ability scales, and test results yield separate g_c and g_f IQs, as well as a composite, or full-scale, IQ. The crystallized-intelligence scales require respondents to define words, listen to and answer questions about a detailed news story, and study two sets of words, such as '*animal* and *vampire*' and '*baseball* and *stick*' and then produce a word that relates to both, such as *bat*. The fluid intelligence subtests require respondents to break mystery codes, solve logic problems, and associate words with complex drawings and then 'read' sentences composed only of the drawings. The Kaufman and Woodcock-Johnson tests have become quite popular in educational, job screening, and clinical settings.

Sternberg's triarchic model of intelligence has inspired the development of a new test as well. The Sternberg Triarchic Ability Test (STAT) measures the three forms of intelligence identified in his model – analytic, practical and creative. This test can be useful in identifying students' levels of each of the three types of intelligence so that school curricula can be individualized to capitalize on their strengths and thereby optimize learning and school performance.

SHOULD WE TEST FOR APTITUDE OR ACHIEVEMENT?

Using written tests for selection purposes highlights an issue that Binet faced and that continues to plague test developers today: Should we test a person's abstract 'aptitude for learning', or should we test what a person already knows? Consider an example. In selecting applicants for college, we could give students either an **achievement test** designed to find out how much they have learned so far in their lives, or we could present them with an **aptitude test** containing novel puzzle-like problems that presumably go beyond prior learning and are thought to measure the applicant's potential for future learning and performance.

The argument for achievement testing is that it is usually a good predictor of future performance in a similar situation. If a student learned a lot of academic material in high school (and therefore scored well on the test), he or she is likely to also learn a lot in university. The argument against achievement testing is that it assumes that everyone has had the same opportunity to learn the material being tested. In university selection, for example, a given applicant's test score could depend on whether that person went to a good school rather than on his or her ability to learn in college.

The argument for aptitude testing is that it is fairer because it supposedly depends less on prior knowledge than on a person's ability to react to the problems presented on the test. The argument against aptitude testing is that it is difficult to construct a test that is independent of prior learning. Further, such a test may require an ability to deal with puzzles that is not relevant to success in situations other than the test itself.

In fact, most intelligence tests measure a combination of aptitude and achievement, reflecting both native ability and previous learning (Lubinski, 2004). This has raised major scientific and social issues concerning the meaning of test scores, the extent to which improvement can be fostered by educational experiences, and the usefulness of the measures for describing mental competence and predicting performance in non-test situations.

Tests of mental skills have become a staple of western societies. They are used to make important educational, occupational and clinical decisions, as well as to set social policy. These meas-

Focus 10.15

How have theories of intelligence influenced recently developed tests?

Focus 10.16

Describe the controversy involving aptitude versus achievement tests in relation to the measurement of intelligence.

achievement test

designed to find out how much they have learned so far in their lives

aptitude test

novel puzzle-like problems that presumably go beyond prior learning and are thought to measure the applicant's potential for future learning and performance

ures also have become important scientific tools for cognitive psychologists who study the development, stability, operation and modification of cognitive functions. We will now consider the scientific standards required for psychological tests.

PSYCHOMETRIC STANDARDS FOR INTELLIGENCE TESTS

A **psychological test** is a method for measuring individual differences related to some psychological concept, or construct, based on a sample of relevant behaviour in a scientifically designed and controlled situation. In the case of intelligence testing, intelligence is the *construct* and scores obtained on the test are its *operational definition*. To design a test, we need to decide which specific behaviours serve as indicators of intellectual abilities. Then we need to devise test items that allow us to assess individual differences in those behaviours. We will, of course, need evidence that our sample of items (a sample, because we cannot ask every conceivable question) actually measures the abilities we are assessing. As in designing an experiment (see Chapter 2), we want to collect *a sample of relevant behaviour* under standardized conditions, attempting to control for other factors that could influence responses to the items. To understand how psychologists meet these requirements, we must examine three key measurement concepts: *reliability*, *validity* and *standardization*. We should note that these standards apply to all psychological tests, not just intelligence measures.

Reliability

Reliability refers to consistency of measurement. As shown in Table 10.4, reliability can take several forms when applied to psychological tests. It can refer to consistency of measurement over time, consistency of measurement by the items within the test itself or consistency in scores assigned by different examiners.

TABLE 10.4 TYPES OF RELIABILITY AND VALIDITY IN PSYCHOLOGICAL TESTING

Types of reliability	Meaning and critical questions
Test–retest reliability	Are scores on the measure stable over time?
Internal consistency	Do all of the items on the measure seem to be measuring the same thing, as indicated by high correlations among them?
Interjudge reliability	Do different raters or scorers agree on their scoring or observations?
Types of validity	
Construct validity	To what extent is the test actually measuring the construct of interest (e.g., intelligence)?
Content validity	Do the questions or test items relate to all aspects of the construct being measured?
Criterion-related validity	Do scores on the test predict some present or future behaviour or outcome assumed to be affected by the construct being measured?

One of the most important forms is consistency over time. If you step on your bathroom scales five times in a row, you should expect it to register the same weight each time, unless you have a very unusual metabolism. Likewise, if we assume that intelligence is a relatively stable trait (and virtually all psychologists do), then scores on our measure should be stable, or consistent, over time. Where psychological tests are concerned, this type of measurement stability over

Focus 10.17
Define the three types of test reliability.

psychological test

a method for measuring individual differences related to some psychological concept, or construct, based on a sample of relevant behaviour in a scientifically designed and controlled situation

reliability

consistency of measurement

test–retest reliability

assessed by administering the measure to the same group of participants on two (or more) separate occasions and correlating the two (or more) sets of scores.

internal consistency

consistency of measurement within the test itself

interjudge reliability

consistency of measurement when different people observe the same event or score the same test

validity

how well a test actually measures what it is designed to measure

construct validity

exists when a test successfully measures the psychological construct it is designed to measure, as indicated by relations between test scores and other behaviours that it should be related to

content validity

whether the items on a test measure all the knowledge or skills that are assumed to underlie the construct of interest

criterion-related validity

the ability of test scores to correlate with meaningful criterion measures

time is defined as **test–retest reliability**, which is assessed by administering the measure to the same group of participants on two (or more) separate occasions and correlating the two (or more) sets of scores.

After about age 7, scores on intelligence tests show considerable stability, even over many years (Gregory, 1998). Over a short interval (2 to 12 weeks), the test–retest correlation of adult IQs on the WAIS-III is .96, or nearly perfect (Tulsky et al., 2003). Correlations between IQs at age 9 and age 40 are in the .70 to .80 range (Plomin and Spinath, 2004), indicating a high degree of stability. In a massive Scottish study, in which every child who was present at school on the testing dates was tested, scores on a test of general intelligence administered at age 11 correlated .66 with scores on the same test at age 80 (Deary et al., 2004). Thus, *relative to his or her age group*, a person who achieves an above-average IQ at age 9 or 11 is very likely to also be above the average for 40- or 80-year-olds when he or she reaches those ages. Even while children's cognitive skills are developing rapidly during middle childhood, IQs are quite stable, with test–retest coefficients around .90 (Canivez and Watkins, 1998).

Another form of reliability, **internal consistency**, has to do with consistency of measurement within the test itself. For example, if a Wechsler subtest is internally consistent, all of its items are measuring the same skill, as evidenced by high correlations among the items. In accordance with this requirement, the individual items within the Wechsler subtests correlate substantially with one another (Gregory, 1998).

Finally, **interjudge reliability** refers to consistency of measurement when different people observe the same event or score the same test. Ideally, two psychologists who independently score the same test will assign exactly the same scores. To attain high interjudge reliability, the scoring instructions must be so explicit that trained professionals will use the scoring system in the same way.

Validity

As a general concept, **validity** refers to how well a test actually measures what it is designed to measure. As in the case of reliability, there are several types of validity (see Table 10.4).

As noted earlier, intelligence is a concept, or mental construct. **Construct validity** exists when a test successfully measures the psychological construct it is designed to measure, as indicated by relations between test scores and other behaviours that it should be related to. If an intelligence test had perfect construct validity, individual differences in IQs would be due to differences in intelligence and nothing else. In reality, this ideal is never attained, for other factors such as motivation and educational background also influence test scores.

Two other kinds of validity contribute to construct validity. **Content validity** refers to whether the items on a test measure all the knowledge or skills that are assumed to underlie the construct of interest. For example, if we want the Arithmetic subtest of the WAIS-III to measure general mathematical reasoning skills, we would not want to have only addition problems; we would want the items to sample other relevant mathematical abilities as well, such as subtraction, division and fractions.

If an intelligence test is measuring what it is assumed to measure, the IQ it yields should allow us to predict other behaviours that are assumed to be influenced by intelligence, such as school grades or job performance. These outcome measures are called *criterion measures*, and **criterion-related validity** refers to the ability of test scores to correlate with meaningful criterion measures. A critical issue for intelligence tests is the extent to which they predict the kinds of outcomes we would expect intelligence to influence, such as school and job performance. Let us examine this aspect of validity.

Intelligence and academic performance   Intelligence tests were originally developed to predict academic and other forms of achievement. How valid are they for this purpose? Actually, they do fairly well and far better than personality factors do (Kaia et al., 2007). Correlations of IQ with school grades are in the .60 range for high school students and in the .30 to .50 range for college students (Kuncel et al., 2004). In a large-scale study involving more than 70 000 children, Deary et al. (2007) found that there was a correlation of around 0.8 between a measure of latent intelligence calculated from the Cognitive Abilities Test (the most widely used measure of reasoning ability in the UK) at age and performance on public examinations taken at age 16. In general, then, people who score well on the tests tend to do well academically. Likewise, examinations you took while in high school may be used to predict the criterion of grades in university by assessing verbal and mathematical abilities. Further research in USA has found that scores on the Scholastic Aptitude Test do predict college grades, with correlations slightly below .50 (Willingham et al., 1990). This correlation, which is about the same magnitude as the correlation between people's height and weight, is high enough to justify using the tests for screening purposes but low enough to necessitate the use of other predictors (such as high school grades) in combination with standard assessment task (SAT) scores.

Focus 10.18

What is validity? Describe three kinds of test validity.

Job performance, income and longevity   Intelligence test scores also predict military and job performance. General mental ability predicts both occupational level and performance within one's chosen occupation (Schmidt and Hunter, 2004). Intelligent individuals are far more likely to attain prestigious occupations. One study followed siblings raised together, thereby controlling for home background. When the siblings were in their late twenties, mental ability measures collected during young adulthood were related to their annual adult incomes. Siblings with IQs of 120 or more were, on average, earning $18 000 more than siblings of average intelligence (Murray, 1998). Intelligence correlates .50 to .70 with the level of socio-economic status that people attain (Lubinski, 2004). As long ago as 1945 Harrell and Harrell reported the mean IQ levels of people in various occupations. These ranged from a mean IQ of 128 for lawyers and accountants down to the mid-90s for lorry drivers and farmers.

People with higher intelligence perform better in their jobs, and the more complex the job, the more strongly intelligence is related to performance (Hunter and Hunter, 1984). The relation is particularly striking during the job-training period, when the superior learning ability of highly intelligent people helps them shine (Schmidt and Hunter, 2004). Furthermore, intelligence predicts job performance better than does job experience, specific abilities or personality traits (Schmidt and Hunter, 2004).

Focus 10.19

How well do IQ scores predict academic, job and other life outcomes?

Intelligence predicts other life outcomes as well. People high in intelligence show better recovery from brain injuries (Stern, 2006). Moreover, intelligence literally predicts life and death. One of the most famous and important examinations of the usefulness of IQ in predicting a range of life outcomes was reported in 2004. In 1932 every child in Scotland who had been born in 1921 was administered an intelligence test. These children and another similar-age cohort of children tested in 1947 were followed as their lives unfolded (Deary et al., 2004). Higher childhood intelligence was associated with significantly greater survival to age 76 in both men and women, but the results were particularly striking for women (Fig. 10.11).

How shall we account for these results? Is it possible that cognitive ability is a reflection of general fitness to survive? The researchers suggest the possibility that lower childhood intelligence may in some cases be influenced by pre-natal or post-natal events that also impair later health such as poor living conditions, childhood illnesses and issues around nutrition. Or perhaps good brain development is related to optimal development of other bodily organs as well. But it is also possible that intelligent people are more likely to engage in healthy behaviours and to avoid unhealthy ones, or that higher intelligence allows people to live and work in safer physical environments or to enjoy better nutrition, thereby helping them live longer and healthier lives.

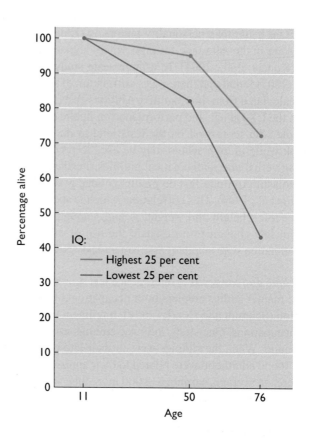

FIGURE 10.11

Does intelligence predict life span?

This graph shows the relation between IQ assessed at age 11 and survival at ages 50 and 76 in women followed in the Scottish Mental Survey.

SOURCE: data from Whalley and Deary, 2001.

standardization

(1) the development of norms, and (2) rigorously controlled testing procedures

norms

test scores derived from a large sample that represents particular age segments of the population

normal distribution

bell-shaped curve with most scores clustering around the centre of the curve

Focus 10.20

What are the two meanings of standardization?

Standardization

The third measurement requirement, **standardization**, has two meanings: (1) the development of norms, and (2) rigorously controlled testing procedures. The first meaning of standardization is especially important in providing a meaningful IQ score. It involves the collection of **norms**, test scores derived from a large sample that represents particular age segments of the population. These normative scores provide a basis for interpreting a given individual's score, just as the distribution of scores in a course examination allows you to determine how well you did relative to your class-mates. Normative data also allow us to recalibrate the distribution of test scores so that an IQ of 100 will remain the 'average' score even if the general population's test performance changes over time.

When norms are collected for mental skills (and for many other human characteristics), the scores usually form a **normal distribution**, a bell-shaped curve with most scores clustering around the centre of the curve. On intelligence tests, the centre of the distribution for each age group from childhood to late adulthood is assigned an IQ score of 100. Because the normal distribution has known statistical properties, we can specify what percentage of the population will score higher than a given score. Thus, as Figure 10.12 shows, an IQ score of 100 cuts the distribution in half, with an equal percentage of the population scoring above and below this midway point. The farther we move from this average score of 100 in either direction, the fewer people attain the higher or lower scores. The figure also shows the percentage of people who score above certain IQ levels. On modern intelligence tests, this method of assigning an IQ score has replaced the original formula of mental age divided by chronological age.

The Flynn effect: are we getting smarter?   The relative nature of the IQ allows its meaning to be preserved even if performance changes within the population. A notable discovery by New Zealand researcher James Flynn (1987; 1998) suggests that much of the world's population is

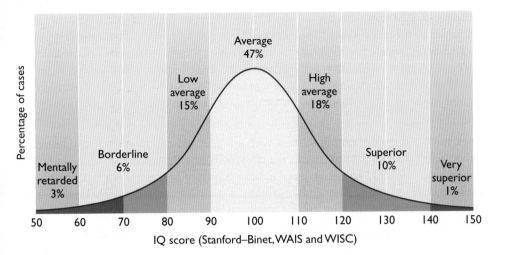

FIGURE 10.12

The bell curve of intelligence.

When administered to large groups of people, intelligence tests yield a normal, or bell-shaped, distribution of IQ scores. The mean of the distribution is set at 100. The range of scores from 90 to 110 is labelled average and includes nearly half of the population.

scoring progressively higher on intelligence tests. This 'rising-curve' phenomenon (also called the *Flynn effect*) has resulted in IQ increases of 28 points in the USA since 1910 and a similar increase in Britain since 1942. On average, IQs in the West have increased about three points per decade, meaning that today's average IQ would be about 115 if the tests were scored according to the norms used in 1955. The increase seems to be occurring to the same degree for both men and women, and for different ethnic groups (Truscott and Frank, 2001).

The reasons underlying the Flynn effect are not clear, but several possibilities have been suggested (Flynn, 1998; Neisser et al., 1998). One possibility is that better nutrition has helped fuel the IQ increase. Height has also increased dramatically over the past century, and it, like increased brain functioning, may be due to nutritional gains. Other explanations focus on the environment. Richer and more complex learning environments that require more complex coping may have increased mental abilities. Likewise, technological advances may have helped shape the kinds of analytical and abstract reasoning skills that boost performance on intelligence tests. For example, Bradmetz and Mathy (2006) suggested that increases in IQ in French children may be due to television and other such media causing an increase in spatial abilities, but that this may have resulted in a decrease in verbal skills. Whatever the reasons, however, the rising-curve phenomenon means that the intelligence score distribution has to be re-calibrated upward periodically if the average IQ is to remain at 100, the traditional midway point of the intelligence range. An interesting study of note here was reported by Teasdale and Owen (2008) who noted that, as has been observed in other western cultures, there had been an increase in IQ scores in Denmark since the 1950s. However, in their study of Danish males they noted that there was a small increase in scores across a range of tests between 1988 and 1998, this being the last time such an increase had been noted, and that between 1998 and 2004 there was a drop in performance on these range of tests equivalent to about 1.5 IQ points, and that on two of the four tests used the levels were down to below that of the 1988 scores.

Testing conditions: static and dynamic testing   Test instructions and procedures are designed to create a well-controlled, or standardized, environment for administering the intelligence test so that other uncontrolled factors will not influence scores. Tests like the Stanford–Binet and Wechsler scales have very detailed instructions that must be closely adhered to, even to the point of reading the instructions and items to the person being tested (Fig. 10.13). The goal is to make sure that all testees are responding to as similar a stimulus situation as possible so that their scores will be solely a reflection of their ability. This traditional approach to testing is called **static testing**.

FIGURE 10.13

When administering intelligence tests, psychologists use consistently applied instructions and procedures in order to create a standardized testing environment.

static testing
traditional approach to testing

Focus 10.21
What is the Flynn effect? What explanations have been suggested?

dynamic testing

the standard testing is followed up with an interaction in which the examiner gives the respondent guided feedback on how to improve performance and observes how the person utilizes the information

Focus 10.22

Explain the nature and value of dynamic testing.

Focus 10.23

How is intelligence assessed in non-western cultures?

Some theorists suggest that the static approach to testing may reveal an incomplete picture of a person's abilities by measuring only the products of previous learning. In **dynamic testing**, the standard testing is followed up with an interaction in which the examiner gives the respondent guided feedback on how to improve performance and observes how the person utilizes the information. This part of the session provides a window to the individual's ability to profit from instruction and improve performance, and may disclose cognitive capacities not revealed by static testing.

Let us look in on a dynamic testing session with a 5-year-old child who is being tested for educational purposes. Daniel is impulsive in the classroom, and the teacher wants to know how best to instruct him. The child has been asked to draw a picture of a person (a task common to several intelligence tests) and has hurriedly scribbled a poorly formed figure that merits a low score. The examiner wants to see how much Daniel can improve with feedback:

> Wow, Daniel. I can really tell that that's a boy. I see a head, two arms, and two legs. He even looks like he could be running, because his legs are kind of bent. Now we're going to work together to see if we can get this picture to look more like a boy. I think we need to think real hard about some more parts that people have and just where they need to go. I also noticed that you did this really fast, and that made this look kind of wobbly. So I'm going to help you slow down a bit so you can make this boy stand really straight. (Lidz, 1997, p. 283)

By testing the limits of Daniel's competencies and his ability to profit from various kinds of feedback, the dynamic tester may gain a fuller picture of his mental skills and may be able to make better educational recommendations. Dynamic testing can be particularly useful when people have not had equal learning opportunities, as occurs in disadvantaged groups. Equally important is the fact that dynamic feedback tends to improve test scores, and these new scores often relate more highly to educational outcomes than do the original test scores (Lidz, 1997). Dynamic testing can be particularly useful and revealing when testing people from cultures that are not accustomed to taking western-style tests (Sternberg, 2004).

ASSESSING INTELLIGENCE IN NON-WESTERN CULTURES

Special challenges await the psychologist who wishes to assess intelligence in non-western cultures. Traditional intelligence tests such as the WAIS and the Stanford–Binet draw heavily on the cognitive skills and learning that are needed to succeed in western educational and occupational settings. They tend to have strong verbal content and to rely on the products of western schooling. Taken into a cultural context where *clever* is defined in different ways and requires other kinds of adaptive behaviour, such tests cannot hope to measure intelligence in a valid fashion. For example, the WAIS does not measure the ability to create herbal medicines, construct shelters or navigate in the open sea. Sternberg (2004) has advanced a *theory of successful intelligence* in which intelligence is whatever is required to meet the adaptive demands of a given culture. Sternberg believes that fundamental mental skills (the metacomponents described earlier) are required for successful behaviour in any culture. These include the ability to mentally represent problems in a way that facilitates their solution, to develop potential solutions and to choose successfully among them, to utilize mental resources wisely and to evaluate the effects of one's action plans. What differs are the kinds of problems to which these basic intellectual skills are applied. People from different cultures may think about the same problem in very different ways (Nisbett, 2003).

Two main approaches have been taken to meet the challenges of cross-cultural intelligence assessment. One is to choose reasoning problems that are not tied to the knowledge base of any culture but that reflect the ability to process and evaluate stimulus patterns. The problem shown in Figure 10.14 resembles one on the Raven Progressive Matrices, a test that is frequently used to measure fluid intelligence (Raven, 1962). On this non-verbal task, you must detect relation-

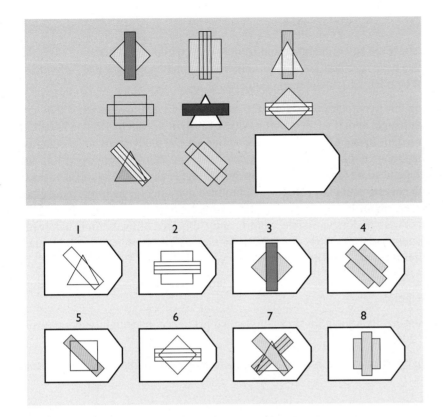

FIGURE 10.14

Culture-fair measurement?

This non-verbal measure tests fluid-intelligence ability, requiring subjects to perceive relationships and decipher the rules underlying the pattern of drawings in the rows and columns of the upper figure and then to select the figure that is the missing entry from the eight alternatives below. (The answer appears on p. 456.)

SOURCE: Carpenter et al., 1990.

ships and then decipher the rules underlying the pattern of drawings in the rows and columns of the upper figure. Finally, you must use this information to select the figure that is the missing entry from the eight alternatives below. The Raven test has been used in many cultures and measures a general mental capacity that is also measured by traditional intelligence tests in our culture (Jensen, 1998). Scores on the Raven correlate positively with measures of IQ derived from traditional tests, yet they seem to be more 'culture fair'.

A second and more challenging approach is to create measures that are tailored to the kinds of knowledge and skills that are valued in the particular culture. Such tests may measure how smart an individual is in terms of the practical skills and adaptive behaviours within that culture. Scores may be unrelated or even negatively correlated with other measures of intelligence, yet, they may predict successful functioning within that culture (Sternberg, 2004). If intelligence is defined as the ability to engage in culture-specific adaptive behaviour, then who is to say that the culture-specific measure is not a valid measure of intelligence in that context?

Focus 10.24

What evidence exists that neural efficiency and brain size underlie high intelligence?

BENEATH THE SURFACE

BRAIN SIZE AND INTELLIGENCE

The brain is clearly the locus of intellectual activities. For a brain to operate more efficiently, it makes sense that having more neurons, or more connections among them, might be advantageous, especially if they were in the areas most involved in processing information. This notion has spurred attempts to relate brain size with intelligence. As noted in Chapter 3, evolutionary evidence indicates a progressive increase in brain size as humanoid species evolved over the ages. Particularly evident is growth in the parts of the brain involved in higher mental functions, especially the cerebral cortex and frontal lobes (Kolb and Whishaw, 2005). Not surprisingly, therefore, scientists have revisited Sir Francis Galton's original hypothesis that individual differences in brain size might be related to intellectual competency.

One intriguing way of testing this hypothesis is to study the brains of dead geniuses to see if they differ from the brains of less brilliant people and, if so, how. After Albert Einstein's death in 1955, a Missouri physician removed and preserved his brain. The brain has undergone several analyses by neuroscientists over the years. The examinations have shown that Einstein's brain was not larger than average overall; in fact, it was actually smaller than average in some regions. But it was indeed bigger in some ways. His parietal lobes were densely packed with both neurons and glial cells, which produce nutrients for neurons and support them. As a result, his parietal lobes were about 15 per cent wider than normal. So densely was this brain area packed that some major fissures were no longer visible. Significantly, this area of the brain is involved in mathematical thinking and visual-spatial functions – precisely the kinds of abilities that seemed to underlie Einstein's creative genius (Witelson et al., 1999).

These findings are intriguing, but before you conclude that the larger your brain is, the more intelligent you are likely to be, consider these points:

- Neanderthals, ancient humans hardly known for their intellectual brilliance, had slightly larger brains than we do (Kolb and Whishaw, 2005).

- Women and men have virtually identical mean IQs, but women's brains are smaller on average (Ankney, 1992).

- Other research, beginning with Galton's, indicates that brain size is minimally related to intelligence, and the meaning of even this weak correlation is not clear. Does larger brain mass cause intelligence, do lots of 'intelligent' interactions with the environment facilitate brain growth, or do other factor(s) cause both brain mass and intelligence?

Most modern neuroscientists believe that it is not how large your brain is, but how efficiently it functions that matters, and it is the efficiency, not size, question that drives today's research. One line of evidence comes from studies of brain metabolism. PET scans of people's brains taken while they engage in problem-solving tasks have shown lower levels of neuronal glucose consumption in people of high intelligence than in those of average or low intelligence, suggesting that intelligent brains work more efficiently and expend less energy (Haier et al., 1993). Some neuroscientists believe that individual differences in *brain plasticity* – the ability of the brain to change by forming new connections among neurons in response to environmental input – may be the key neural factor underlying differences in intelligence. The ability to quickly establish new neural networks would increase processing speed and efficiency, and people with brains capable of greater plasticity would therefore develop better intellectual skills. This suggestion receives support from evidence that there may be a critical period for the growth of new neural circuits that ends at about age 16, the same age period by which crystallized intelligence seems to achieve stability (Garlick, 2002).

Focus 10.25

What evidence supports a genetic contribution to intelligence, and how much IQ group variation is accounted for?

Answer to the Problem in Figure 10.14

The correct choice is geometric form number 5. Can you specify why?

IN REVIEW

- Most modern intelligence tests, such as the Wechsler scales, measure an array of different mental abilities. In addition to a global, or full-scale, IQ, they provide scores for each subtest and summary scores for broader abilities, such as verbal and performance IQs. Some recent tests are derived directly from theories of intelligence. The Kaufman scale provides separate scores for crystallized and fluid intelligence, and Sternberg's STAT measures analytical, practical and creative intelligence.

- Achievement tests measure what has already been learned, whereas aptitude tests are assumed to measure potential for future learning and performance. Most intelligence tests measure combinations of achievement and aptitude, for it is difficult to separate past learning and future learning potential.

- Three important standards for psychological tests are reliability (consistency of measurement over time, within tests, and across scorers), validity (successful measurement of the construct and acceptable relations with relevant criterion measures) and standardization (development of norms and standard testing conditions).

- IQ scores successfully predict a range of academic, occupational and life outcomes, including how long people live. Such findings indicate that intelligence tests are measuring important adaptational skills.

- The Flynn effect refers to the notable rise in intelligence test scores over the past century, possibly due to better living conditions, more schooling or more complex environments.

- In dynamic testing, standard test administration is followed by feedback and suggestions from the examiner and a retaking of the test, thus allowing an assessment of how well the person profits from feedback and how intellectual skills might be coached in the future. Dynamic testing provides information that static testing does not, and retest scores sometimes relate more strongly to criterion measures.

- Intelligence testing in non-western cultures is a challenge. One approach is to use tests that are not tied to any culture's knowledge base. Another approach is to devise tests of the abilities that are important to adaptation in that culture. These culture-specific abilities may bear little relation to the mental skills assessed by western intelligence tests.

- Recent physiological evidence suggests that the brains of intelligent people may function more efficiently. Brain size is not significantly related to intelligence, but the neural networks laid down in the process of brain development may be extremely important. One current theory is that differences in brain plasticity may underlie intelligence.

HEREDITY, ENVIRONMENT AND INTELLIGENCE

Genes and environment both influence intelligence, but they rarely operate independently of one another. The environment can influence how genes express themselves, as when pre-natal factors or malnutrition retard gene-directed brain development. Likewise, genetic factors can influence the effects produced by the environment. For example, genetic factors influence which environments people select for themselves, how they respond to the environment and how the environment responds to the person (Plomin and Spinath, 2004; Scarr and McCartney, 1983).

As we saw in Chapter 3, intelligence clearly has a strong genetic component, with heritability coefficients ranging between .50 and .70 being reported consistently in both twin and adoption studies (Plomin et al., 2007). This indicates that more than half, and perhaps more than two-thirds, of the within-group variation in IQ is attributable to genetic factors. Overall, the pattern is quite clear: The more genes people have in common, the more similar they tend to be in IQ.

In identical twins, the IQ correlation remains at about .80 from age 4 through adulthood. In adulthood, correlations for fraternal twins drop to around .40. Doubling this difference in correlations yields a heritability coefficient of .80 in adulthood, indicating that genetic factors become even more important as we age (Plomin and Spinath, 2004). One reason may be that new genes come on line to affect intelligence as more-advanced cognitive processes emerge during development. Another is that genetic influences snowball during development as people create and select environments that are compatible with their genetic characteristics.

Although genes are important foundations of the g factor (Plomin et al., 2007), there clearly is not a single 'intelligence gene'. The diverse abilities measured by intelligence tests are undoubtedly influenced by large numbers of interacting genes, and different combinations seem to underlie specific abilities (Lykken, 2006; Plomin and Spinath, 2004). The ability now to measure the genome directly has led to a search for specific genes and gene combinations that underlie intelligence. This brings us ever closer to an understanding of the neurological basis for human cognition, and a handful of candidate genes associated with intelligence have already been identified (Posthuma and de Geus, 2006).

Genes are not the whole story, however. As we noted in Chapter 3 (Table 3.2 on p. 96), IQ correlations for identical twins raised together are slightly higher than those for identical twins raised apart. The same is true for other types of siblings raised together and raised apart. This rules out an entirely genetic explanation. Although one's genotype is an important factor in determining intelligence test scores, environment seems to account for 30 to 50 per cent of the IQ variation among people. Both shared and unshared environmental factors are involved. Behaviour-genetic studies indicate that between quarter and a third of the population variability in intelligence can be attributed to shared environmental factors, particularly the family environment (Fig. 10.15). The importance of the home environment is also shown in studies of children who are removed from deprived environments and placed in middle- or upper-class adoptive homes. Typically, such children show a gradual increase in IQ, typically in the order of 10 to 12 points (Scarr and Weinberg, 1977; Schiff and Lewontin, 1986). Conversely, when deprived children remain in their impoverished environments, they either show no improvement in IQ, or they actually deteriorate intellectually over time (Serpell, 2000). Scores on general intelligence correlate around .40 with the socio-economic status of the family in which a child is reared (Lubinski, 2004).

Recall also the Flynn effect – the notable IQ increases that have occurred in western countries during the last century. It is highly unlikely that genetic changes can explain such gains. More likely, they are due to better and longer schooling during the past century, more complex and stimulating environments provided by better educated parents and by technological advances (even television and video games), and better nutrition (Greenfield, 1998). Although the environment we live in may be more complex, fast-paced and stressful than it was a century ago, it is also more conducive to learning the mental skills that are assessed on measures of intelligence.

Focus 10.26

How much do family and school environments contribute to intelligence?

As we might expect, educational experiences can have a significant positive impact on intelligence. Many studies have shown that school attendance can raise IQ and lack of attendance can lower scores (Ceci and Williams, 1997). It appears that the opportunity to practise mental skills like those assessed on cognitive tests is important in solidifying mental skills. Research on intelligence has had a strong impact on educational curricula, and much has been learned about what, when, and how to teach. School-related gains in intelligence are most likely to be observed under the following conditions (Mayer, 2000):

- Rather than 'teaching to' general mental ability, help students learn the specific cognitive skills and problem-solving approaches that underlie success in particular subjects. This is an outgrowth of education's increasing de-emphasis on the g factor and renewed emphasis on the development of specific mental skills.

- Replace the traditional emphasis on repetition and rote learning of facts with instruction in *how* to learn, critically think about and apply course content. In this approach, teachers function as 'mental coaches'.

- Rather than waiting until low-level skills have been mastered before teaching learning tools such as memory-enhancement strategies, apply this 'learning to learn' approach from the very beginning so that the skills are applied to even the most basic course content.

Many children begin their lives in conditions that are not conducive to developing intellectual skills. An important outgrowth of intelligence research is the attempt to intervene early in the lives of such children. Let us examine several of these programmes and what they have accomplished.

Focus 10.27
What effects have been shown in early-intervention programmes for disadvantaged children?

FIGURE 10.15

Shared family environment has a significant influence on intelligence, accounting for between a quarter and a third of IQ variation in children.

APPLYING PSYCHOLOGICAL SCIENCE

EARLY-CHILDHOOD INTERVENTIONS: A MEANS OF BOOSTING INTELLIGENCE?

The belief that early-childhood education can influence the life success of poor children can be found in the eighteenth-century writings of the French social philosopher Jean-Jacques Rousseau. In the USA today, that belief translates into the annual expenditure of more than $10 billion on early-intervention programmes designed to reverse the downward course of cognitive and social development, school dropout rate and joblessness that is so often seen in children from low-income families (Ramey et al., 1998).

In the 1960s, researchers and educators began to design early-childhood intervention programmes such as Head Start in an attempt to compensate for the limited learning environments of disadvantaged children. Head Start began as a summer programme and gradually increased in scope. But even when it was extended to a full school year, Head Start was only a half-day programme that did not begin until age 4. The results were disappointing. Within 2 years, Head Start children were performing in school no better than children who had not attended Head Start (McKey et al., 1985).

What had gone wrong? Was the Head Start programme too little, too late? How much might a more intensive programme begun earlier in life help disadvantaged children? These questions inspired several notable intervention programmes, namely, the Abecedarian Program and the High/Scope Perry Preschool Program.

Participants in the Abecedarian Program were healthy infants born to impoverished families in a southern US community. Many were African-American. The children were randomly assigned to an experimental pre-school programme or to a control group whose families received normal social services. The pre-school group was given an intensive early childhood educational programme beginning when they were 6 months old and continuing until they began kindergarten at 5 years of age. Within an educational child-care setting, highly trained pre-school personnel exposed the children to many stimulating learning experiences designed to foster the growth of cognitive skills (Fig. 10.16). At age 5, the pre-school programme ended, but half of the pre-school children and half of the control children were enrolled in a special home-and-school educational programme during the first three years of school. This experimental design allowed the researchers to test the effects of early versus later intervention.

The long-term effects of the programme have now been evaluated. By the time the children had been in the programme for a year, they tested 18 IQ points higher than the control group. By age 15, the IQ advantage of the children in the pre-school condition had decreased to about five points, but they also had higher scores on standardized tests of reading and mathematics than did the control-group children. Only about half as many had been held back a grade or placed in special education.

FIGURE 10.16

The Abecedarian Program provided intensive pre-school learning experiences for low-income, high-risk children. Here a trainer in an early-intervention programme teaches number concepts to preschool children.

A particularly notable IQ effect was found for children in the pre-school condition whose mothers were classed as having a learning disability, having IQs below 70. In this sample, every one of the children who had the early intervention attained an IQ at least 20 points higher than their mother's, with an average difference of 32 IQ points. No such effect was found in the control group (Landesman and Ramey, 1989). A difference of this magnitude is truly remarkable for children of learning disabled parents, one reason being that such parents are unable to provide much in the way of intellectual stimulation for their children. Apparently, the pre-school programme provided the environmental stimulation needed for normal intellectual development to occur.

What of the control-group children who did not attend the pre-school programme but were exposed to the special programme from 5 to 8 years of age? This delayed training had little effect on any of the outcome measures. Also, the later training had almost no added effects on the children who had been in the pre-school programme. It thus appears that early intervention has a much stronger effect than does later training. By the time disadvantaged children are in school, it may be too late to influence their future cognitive development to any great degree (Ramey and Ramey, 1998).

The Abecedarian Program showed positive intervention effects that were still apparent in adolescence. What effect does early intervention have on later adult functioning? Here, we turn to another programme, the High/Scope Perry Pre-school Program, carried out with African-American children who lived in an impoverished area of Ypsilanti, Michigan. The participants were considered at high risk for educational and social problems. They were 2 or 3 years old when they were matched on IQ and family variables and randomly assigned to either an intensive pre-school programme or to a control group that did not receive the programme. The intervention continued for three years.

The two groups of children have been followed up at age 27, and the results are encouraging. Figure 10.17 compares what happened to the two groups in the 22 years after the programme ended. The early-education group had lower crime rates, required less welfare assistance, exhibited better academic performance and progress, and had higher income and home ownership. A cost–benefit analysis showed that the early-intervention programme provided taxpayers with a return of $7.16 for every dollar invested in the programme (Schweinhart and Weikart, 1998).

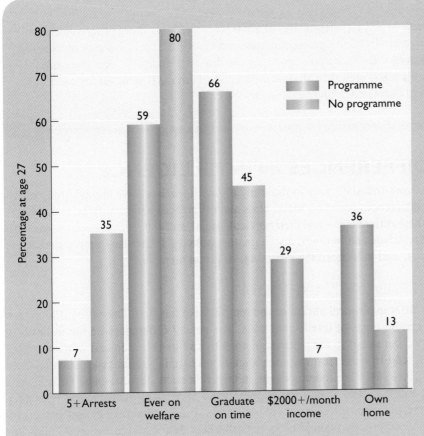

FIGURE 10.17

Effects of early intervention.

This graph shows the differences by age 27 between disadvantaged children who received the High/Scope Perry Preschool Program and matched control children.
SOURCE: Schweinhart and Weikart, 1998.

Does early intervention work? The Abecedarian and High/Scope Perry programmes prove it can provide social, intellectual, educational and psychological dividends if the programme is intensive enough and administered very early in life (Masten and Coatsworth, 1998; Reppucci et al., 1999). A more recent early-intervention programme conducted with low-birth-weight children, also considered at risk for later cognitive impairment and academic failure, showed significant IQ gains of seven to 10 points, but only for those children who had attended the programme for at least 400 days between the ages of 2 and 3 (Hill et al., 2003). We should also note that the positive effects of early-intervention programmes seem to occur only for disadvantaged children, for whom quality programmes offer learning opportunities and support that the children would not experience at home. Such programmes do little for middle- and upper-class children who already have those resources in their homes (Hetherington, 1998).

Such early intervention programmes are not limited to the USA. In 1999 the UK government established the Sure Start programme which was established to tackle poverty and disadvantage in 0–3-year-olds. The Sure Start programme has expanded rapidly, from 210 Sure Start Local Programmes (SSLP) in 2001 to 524 in 2004, and the aim is to have 3500 SSLPs by 2010. Sure Start is an area-based programme and is run in targeted areas rather than being targeted at individual families. The aim of this is to reduce the stigma sometimes associated with such early intervention programmes.

Although the programme is still in the process of expanding there is some evidence to suggest that it is having a positive effect in the communities where it is being implemented. The National Evaluation of Sure Start (NESS, 2004; 2005) reported that in areas where there was an SSLP there was less household chaos reported by mothers of 9-month-old children, and mothers of 36-month-old children were observed as being more accepting of their children. In addition to this the majority of mothers reported that they showed less negative parenting, that there were fewer behavioural problems with their children and that their children showed greater social confidence.

In an evaluation of the effectiveness of SSLPs, Melhuish et al. (2007) reported that those programmes that were assessed as being more effective produced the greatest improvements on child and parenting outcomes, and although the effects were modest they do have implications for the design of future SSLPs. The study found that there were positive benefits associated with an increased sense of empowerment among users and staff as well as better identification of users and strong ethos in the SSLP.

GROUP DIFFERENCES IN INTELLIGENCE

Some of the most controversial issues in the study of intelligence revolve around group differences. There are differences based on social-class and differences between males and females. The meaning of these differences – and their political, social, and educational implications – has often sparked bitter debate and, at times, discriminatory policies. It has also inspired stereotypes about certain groups and influenced the self-image of group members.

SEX DIFFERENCES IN COGNITIVE ABILITIES

Men and women differ in physical attributes and reproductive function. They also differ in their performance on certain types of intellectual tasks. The gender differences lie not in levels of general intelligence but rather in the patterns of cognitive skills that men and women exhibit. Men, on average, tend to outperform women slightly on certain spatial tasks, such as those shown in Figure 10.18. Men are more accurate in target-directed skills, such as throwing and catching objects, and they tend to perform slightly better on tests of mathematical reasoning. Women, on average, perform better on tests of perceptual speed, verbal fluency and mathematical calculation, and on precise manual tasks requiring fine motor co-ordination (Collins and Kimura, 1997; Lippa, 2005). Although typically small, these ability differences have been reported quite consistently by researchers (Halpern, 2004; Hines, 2005). Keep in mind, however, that men and women also vary considerably among themselves in all of these skills, and the performance distributions of males and females overlap considerably.

Deary et al. (2003) reported a large study as part of the Scottish Mental Health survey of 1932. However, despite nearly 90 000 participants being in the study, they found no difference in mean IQ scores, although they did report that there was greater variability of the scores for males with them being over-represented in both the high and low extremes of the cohort. A more recent English study (Strand et al., 2006) reported that there was very little difference between males and females on the Cognitive Abilities Test, although there was a small difference on verbal reasoning, but no difference on qualitative tests or on non-verbal reasoning. Again though, they reported that there was greater variability in the males scores compared with females scores.

This lack of any large difference in ability is particularly interesting given that in UK public examinations taken at age 16 girls consistently outperform boys. The findings of Strand et al. would suggest that this difference is not simply due to ability. It is also worthy of note here that Strand et al. (2006) stressed the notion that, despite the typical differences in examination performance, the fact that there was little, if any, difference in terms of 'ability' it was important that boys are not stereotyped as 'low achievers' (see 'Research close-up' on stereotype threat on p. 464).

Psychologists have proposed explanations for these gender differences, citing both biological and environmental factors. The environmental explanations typically focus on the socialization experiences that males and females have as they grow up, especially the kinds of sex-typed activities that boys and girls are steered into (Crawford and Chaffin, 1997). Prior to the early 1980s, for example, boys were far more likely than girls to play sports that involve throwing and catching balls, which might help account for their general superiority in this ability. Evolution-

Focus 10.28

What sex differences exist in cognitive skills? What biological and environmental factors might be involved?

Focus 10.29

How can teachers' expectations and stereotype threat influence academic performance?

Problem-solving tasks
favouring women

Women tend to perform better than
men on tests of perceptual speed, in
which people must rapidly indentify
matching items – for example, pairing
the house on the far left with its twin.

On some tests of ideational fluency,
for example those in which people
must list objects that are the same
colour, and on tests of verbal fluency,
for example those in which participants
must list words that begin with the
same letter, women also outperform
men.

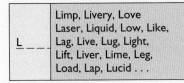

Limp, Livery, Love
Laser, Liquid, Low, Like,
Lag, Live, Lug, Light,
Lift, Liver, Lime, Leg,
Load, Lap, Lucid . . .

L _ _ _

Problem-solving tasks
favouring men

Men tend to perform better than
women on certain spatial tasks. They
do well on tests that involve mentally
rotating an object or manipulating it
in some fashion, such as choosing
which of the three objects at the right
is the same as the one on the left.

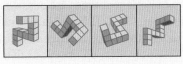

Men are also more accurate than
women in target-directed motor
skills, such as guiding or intercepting
projectiles.

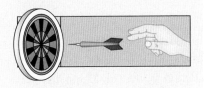

FIGURE 10.18

**Male–female cognitive
differences.**

**Among the most consistent
gender differences in cognitive
abilities reported in the
scientific literature involve
tasks like these.**

SOURCE: adapted from Kimura, 1992.

ary theorists have also weighed in on the differences, suggesting that sex-role specialization developed in ancestral environments. Men's roles, such as navigating and hunting, favoured the development of the visuospatial abilities that show up in sex-difference research. Women's roles, such as child-rearing and tool-making activities, favoured the development of verbal and manual-precision abilities (Joseph, 2000).

Biological explanations have increasingly focused on the effects of hormones on the developing brain (Halpern and Tan, 2001; Hines, 2005). These influences begin during a critical period shortly after conception, when the sex hormones establish sexual differentiation. The hormonal effects go far beyond reproductive characteristics, however. They also alter brain organization and appear to extend to a variety of behavioural differences between men and women, including aggression and problem-solving approaches (Hines, 2005; Lippa, 2005).

Do hormonal factors also influence cognitive performance later in life? Several studies have shown that fluctuations in women's hormonal levels during the menstrual cycle are related to fluctuations in task performance. When women have high levels of the female hormone oestrogen, they perform better on some of the 'feminine-ability' measures while showing declines in performance on some of the 'male-ability' measures (Kimura, 1992; Moody, 1997). However, a more recent study measured a wide range of sex hormones in men and women before they performed a variety of cognitive tasks. Men and women showed the typically reported differences in cognitive skills, but no relations were found between any of the measured hormones and cognitive performance (Halari et al., 2005). Thus the role of sex hormones in adulthood remains unclear.

A study conducted by Ostatnikova et al. (2007) of pre-pubescent children between the ages of 6 and 9 measured the levels of testosterone in saliva of three different groups separated by their IQ scores (gifted, average and mentally challenged). They found that there were significantly lower levels of testosterone in boys in both the gifted and intellectually challenged groups compared with those of average intelligence. They found no difference in testosterone levels in girls in the different IQ groups. It appear then that hormone levels are important in terms of IQ but the role of hormonal factors still needs to be fully explored.

BELIEFS, EXPECTATIONS AND COGNITIVE PERFORMANCE

Cognitive abilities are not the only mental determinants of how well people perform on intellectual and academic measures. Beliefs are also very important. Our beliefs about others' capabilities can affect how we respond to them. For example, many studies have shown that if teachers are told that a particular child has hidden potential or, alternatively, intellectual limitations, they increase or decrease the amount of attention and effort expended on that child, thereby influencing the child's development of cognitive skills (Rosenthal, 1985).

Even more important at times are our own self-beliefs, which tell us who we are and what we can and cannot do. Can self-beliefs and widely held social beliefs about the groups we identify with affect our performance on cognitive tasks? An important line of research, described in the following 'Research close-up', suggests that stereotypes about the capabilities of minorities and women may indeed affect their performance.

RESEARCH CLOSE-UP

STEREOTYPE THREAT AND COGNITIVE PERFORMANCE

SOURCE: C.M. Steele (1997) A threat in the air: how stereotypes shape intellectual identity and performance, *American Psychologist*, vol. 52, pp. 613–29.

INTRODUCTION

Our self-concept is based on numerous experiences that convey to us who we are how valued we are and what we are capable of achieving in our lives. Some of this information comes from observing the consequences of our own behaviour. But our self-concept can also be influenced by our membership of racial and gender groups. If certain stereotypes are widely associated with these groups, we may incorporate them into our self-concept. Once accepted, these self-beliefs may push us to behave in a way that is consistent with our self-concept. But even if not incorporated into the self, group members can experience **stereotype threat** if they believe that certain behaviours on their part would confirm a negative stereotype in the minds of others. Claude Steele believes that stereotype threat evokes anxiety and undermines performance. To test this hypothesis, Steele and his co-workers assessed the academic-performance effects of evoking two widely held stereotypes: (1) that women have less mathematical ability than do men, and (2) that African-Americans have less intellectual ability than do white Americans.

> **stereotype threat**
> they believe that certain behaviours on their part would confirm a negative stereotype in the minds of others

METHOD

Two studies were conducted with students at Stanford University (Spencer et al., 1999; Steele and Aronson, 1995). In the first, men and women who were good in mathematics were given a difficult examination whose items were taken from the advanced mathematics test of the Graduate Record Examination (GRE).

Participants were randomly assigned to one of two experimental conditions designed to either activate the gender stereotype or not. Participants in the stereotype-relevant condition were told that the test generally showed sex differences (expected to activate the stereotype of women as being inferior to men in math). In the other condition, the students were told that scores on the test showed no sex differences. The dependent variable was the students' scores on the mathematics problems.

Research design
Question: Can stereotype threat impair cognitive performance?
Type of study: Experiment

Independent variables	Dependent variable
Experimental manipulation: Experimenter's description of the math and verbal tasks Participant groups: Males and females African Americans, Whites	Measures of task performance by males vs females and African Americans vs Whites in the threat vs non-threat experimental conditions

In the second study, African-American and white American students were tested on the most difficult items from the GRE verbal test. Again, there were two experimental conditions, this time varying the racial relevance of the test. In one condition, the students were told that the test was a measure of intelligence (expected to activate the stereotype of African-Americans as being less intelligent than white Americans). In the other condition, the students were told that the items were part of a laboratory task that was unrelated to general intellectual ability.

RESULTS

The results of the two experiments, shown in Figure 10.19, were strikingly similar. In the first (Fig. 10.19a), women and men performed at an equivalent level on the mathematics problems when they were told there were no sex differences on the test. However, the picture changed dramatically when the task was made relevant to the gender stereotype. Women's performance dropped, and men's performance increased, producing a marked performance difference between the two sexes. In Figure 10.19b, we see a similar pattern of results when the racial stereotype was activated. When the researchers controlled statistically for pre-existing ethnic-group differences in verbal ability by using students' college-entrance SAT scores, the black–white performance difference on the experimental task was far greater if students thought that the task measured intelligence.

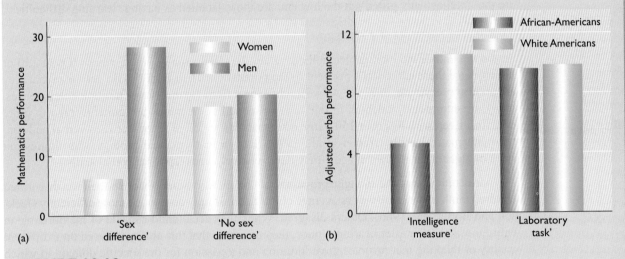

FIGURE 10.19

Effects of stereotype threat on cognitive performance.

(a) The activation of the stereotype that women do less well than men in math was associated with poorer performance by women and enhanced performance by men compared with the control condition, where men and women performed at the same level. (b) Reference to the task as involving intelligence resulted in reduced performance by African-American students.

SOURCE: Steele, 1997.

DISCUSSION

This research illustrates how stereotype-based aspects of the self-concept can affect behaviour, in this case, cognitive performance. Steele (1997) believes that in the stereotype-relevant conditions, the threat of doing poorly on the test and being branded as a 'math-deficient woman' or an 'intellectually inferior African-American' aroused anxiety that lowered performance. Other studies have supported this interpretation and also suggest that stereotype threat creates distracting thoughts that impair performance (Bosson et al., 2004; Croizet et al., 2004).

The results have broad societal implications and might help explain the fact that, over the course of their academic careers, women exhibit less inclination to pursue mathematics, even though, on average, they are slightly superior to men in mathematical calculation skills (Kimura, 1992; Lee, 1998). Later research has shown that the more strongly women are identified with their female sex role, the more susceptible they are to stereotype threat (Schmader et al., 2004). Perhaps stereotype threat also helps account for the fact that African-American children become progressively less identified with, and invested in, academics as they progress through school and that many drop out altogether (Major et al., 1998). In both cases, the sex and females and minorities confront, and perhaps internalize, the stereotypes about their mental abilities may be an important environmental determinant of their performance.

EXTREMES OF INTELLIGENCE

Because of the many genetic and environmental influences on intelligence, there are individuals at both ends of the intelligence distribution who have unusual mental abilities. At the upper end are the 'intellectually gifted'; at the low end are those labelled as having 'learning difficulties'.

THE INTELLECTUALLY GIFTED

At the top end of the intelligence bell curve are the intellectually gifted, whose IQs of 130 or higher place them in the top 1 per cent of the population. Their high IQs do not mean that they are good at everything, however. As we might expect from the theories of multiple intelligences, many are enormously talented in one area of mental competence but quite average in other domains. Even with IQs over 150, large discrepancies are often found between verbal and spatial-mathematical skills (Achter et al., 1996). Thus a mathematical prodigy who figures out rules of algebra on his own at age 3 may have relatively unexceptional verbal skills.

Focus 10.30

What factors allow gifted people to become eminent?

What distinguishes the thought processes of the gifted? Some theorists believe that gifted children think in the same way as average children but simply do it much more efficiently (Jackson and Butterfield, 1986). Others disagree. When they see a child capable of memorizing an entire musical score after hearing it once, they conclude that this ability is based on a different quality of thinking that involves great intuition and a passion for the specific domain in which the child excels (Winner, 2000).

Only a small percentage of gifted children attain true eminence in later life. Eminence seems to be a special variety of giftedness. Joseph Renzulli (2002) has studied this rare group, and he believes that their success is a product of three interacting factors. The first is highly developed mental abilities – not only general intelligence but also specific mental abilities related to one's chosen field. Thus Einstein was blessed with unusual mathematical and spatial abilities (but not exceptional verbal skills). The second factor is the ability to engage in creative problem solving, that is, to come up with novel and unconventional ideas, to judge their potential value, and to apply them to challenging problems (Sternberg and Davidson, 2005). The third factor is motivation and dedication. Eminence involves a great deal of hard work and a determination to attain the highest levels of performance. Studies of eminent scientists, artists, musicians, writers and athletes reveal that they tend to work much harder and to dedicate themselves more strongly to excellence than do their less eminent counterparts (Simonton, 2001). Given that the person has the requisite level of intelligence, these non-intellectual factors become especially important. Many eminent figures, including Sigmund Freud and Charles Darwin, showed no signs of being exceptionally gifted as children, but their motivation and dedication helped them achieve greatness in their professions.

Like children at the low end of the competence continuum, intellectually gifted children often need special educational opportunities. They may become bored in regular classrooms and even drop out of school if they are not sufficiently challenged (Fetterman, 1988). Yet many school systems have de-emphasized programmes for the gifted in the same spirit of egalitarianism that places cognitively challenged children in regular classrooms. Increasingly, parents of gifted children are enrolling their children in special camps and extracurricular programmes to provide the needed intellectual stimulation and exposure to peer groups with common interests and abilities (Winner, 2000).

WHAT DO YOU THINK?

ARE GIFTED CHILDREN MALADJUSTED?

The image of the introverted, socially awkward and unhappy 'nerd' is familiar to all of us. Gifted children are often depicted in the media as unathletic, interested in intellectual activities that do not excite most students, and socially inept. Is there truth in this stereotype? What would you expect research on gifted children to show? Think about your answer, then see p. 471.

Learning Disability

Although it is difficult to give precise figures on the number of people with learning disabilities the Department of Health (DoH) in the UK estimates that there are about 210 000 people with severe and profound learning disabilities. However, the DoH estimates that the occurrence of moderate and mild learning disabilities is around 2.5 per cent or about 1.2 million people in England. The American Psychiatric Association used the criteria outlined in the *Diagnostic and Statistical Manual of Mental Disorders* (2000) to devise a four-level system that classifies learning disabilities as mild, moderate, severe or profound on the basis of IQ scores. Table 10.5 describes these classifications. As you can see, the vast majority are mildly disabled, obtaining IQs between about 50 and 70. Most members of this largest group, given appropriate social and educational support, are capable of functioning adequately in mainstream society, holding jobs and raising families. Progressively greater environmental support is needed as we move towards the profoundly disabled range, where institutional care is usually required.

Mildly disabled children can attend school, but they have difficulties in reading, writing, memory, and mathematical computation. Many of these difficulties result from poorly developed problem-solving strategies. They often have deficiencies in the executive functions discussed in Chapter 4: reasoning, planning and evaluating feedback from their efforts (Molfese and Molfese, 2002).

Learning disability has a variety of causes: some genetic, some owing to other biological factors, and some owing to environmental causes. Genetic abnormalities account for about 28 per cent of all cases (Winnepenninckx et al., 2003). More than 100 different genetic causes of such learning disability have been identified (Brown and Percy, 2007). For example, *Down's syndrome*, which is characterized by mild to severe mental disability, is caused by an abnormal division of the twenty-first chromosome pair.

Heritability plays a different role in mild learning disability than it does in profound cases (Plomin and Spinath, 2004). Cases of profound disability are more likely to be caused by genetic accidents instead of an inherited genotype (Zechner et al., 2001). Therefore, profound learning

Focus 10.31

How do causal factors differ in mild and profound learning disability?

TABLE 10.5 ADAPTIVE CAPABILITIES OF COGNITIVELY CHALLENGED PEOPLE OVER THE LIFESPAN

Category	Percentage of learning disability population	Characteristics from birth to adulthood		
		Birth through age 5	Age 6 through age 20	Age 21 and older
Mild: 50–70 IQ	85	Often not noticed as delayed by casual observer but is slower to walk, feed himself or herself and talk than most children	Can acquire practical skills and master reading and arithmetic to a third- to sixth-grade level with special education. Can be guided towards social conformity	Can usually achieve adequate social, vocational, and self-maintenance skills. May need occasional guidance and support when under unusual social or economic stress
Moderate: 35–50 IQ	10	Noticeable delays in motor development, especially in speech. Responds to training in various self-help activities	Can learn simple communication, elementary health and safety habits, and simple manual skills. Does not progress in functional reading or arithmetic	Can perform simple tasks under sheltered conditions, participate in simple recreation, and travel alone in familiar places. Usually incapable of self-maintenance
Severe: 20–35 IQ	4	Marked delay in motor development. Little or no communication skill. May respond to training in elementary self-help, such as self-feeding	Usually walks, barring specific disability. Has some understanding of speech and some response Can profit from systematic habit training	Can conform to daily routines and repetitive activities. Needs continuing direction and supervision in protective environment
Profound: below 20 IQ	1	Gross disability. Minimal capacity for functioning in sensorimotor areas. Needs nursing care	Obvious delays in all areas of development. Shows basic emotional responses. May respond to skilful training in use of legs, hands and jaws. Needs close supervision	May walk, need nursing care, have primitive speech. Usually benefits from regular physical activity. Incapable of self-maintenance

Reprinted with permission from the *Diagnostic and Statistical Manual of Mental Disorders*, Text Revision. Copyright © 2000, American Psychiatric Association.

disability does not run in families. In one study of 17 000 children, about 0.5 per cent had profound disability. None of these children's siblings had an IQ below 85, and their mean IQ was 103. In contrast, the siblings of the 1.2 per cent who had mild learning disability had mean IQs of 85, and a third of the siblings had IQs below 75 (Nichols, 1984).

Such disabilities can also be caused by accidents at birth, such as severe oxygen deprivation (anoxia); and by diseases experienced by the mother during pregnancy, such as rubella or syphilis. Likewise, drugs and alcohol taken by the mother – especially in the first weeks of pregnancy when a woman is often unaware she is pregnant – can cause neural damage and learning disability. Despite this range of potential causes, in a significant majority (75 to 80 per cent) of those with learning disabilities, no clear biological cause can be found. Experts theorize that these cases may be due to undetectable brain damage, extreme environmental deprivation, or a combination of the two.

In the UK the government has clearly outlined educational policy that is designed to cater specifically for those with learning disabilities. Part of this programme is to ensure that children with learning difficulties have the right to be educated in the mainstream education system. There is a similar situation in the USA where federal law requires that children with learning disabilities, who were formerly segregated into special education classes, be given individual-

ized instruction in the 'least restrictive environment.' This has resulted in the practice of *main-streaming*, or *inclusion programmes*, which allows many cognitively challenged children to attend school in regular classrooms and experience a more normal peer environment (Fig. 10.20). Many schools also provide for individualized instruction for such children so that they can receive the special attention they may require.

A CONCLUDING THOUGHT

In the preceding chapters, we have seen how humans learn, how they remember what they have learned and how they think and solve problems. Language, thinking and intelligent behaviour are intimately related to one another and to the processes of learning and memory. As we have also seen, intelligent behaviour has many causal factors. Some of these factors are summarized in Figure 10.21.

LEVELS OF ANALYSIS FACTORS RELATED TO INTELLECTUAL FUNCTIONING

Biological

- Genetic factors, which account for significant variation in intelligence
- Biological reaction range, which sets broad limits for potential intellectual development
- Neural efficiency that may underlie intellectual differences
- Possible role of sex hormones in certain types of mental abilities

Psychological

- Contribution of a general mental capacity (g factor)
- Specific cognitive and perceptual skills that also underlie intellectual ability
- Adaptive skills that may constitute different types of intelligence
- Beliefs, anxieties and expectations that affect cognitive performance in specific situations (e.g., stereotype threat)
- Motivation to achieve

Environmental

- Learning environments that interact with biological reaction range
- Cultural factors that influence which behaviours are prized and defined as intelligent
- Sex roles, which may influence the abilities that men and women master
- Intelligence measures, which may place culturally different people at a disadvantage

Intellectual functioning

FIGURE 10.21

Levels of analysis: factors related to intellectual functioning.

In today's world, intellectual skills have become increasingly important for successful adaptation. General intelligence, or the *g* factor, captures the kinds of general mental flexibility needed to cope with novelty, read the environment, draw conclusions and choose how and when to act (Lubinski, 2004). In addition to the importance of general mental ability, more specific skills, such as those at the first and second levels of Carroll's three-stratum model, may be needed to cope successfully with more narrowly defined situations and task demands. To an increasing degree, the study of intelligence is focusing on these real-life adaptations and on ways to help people develop and apply their intellectual abilities.

IN REVIEW

- Intelligence is determined by interacting hereditary and environmental factors. Genes account for between 50 and 70 per cent of population variation in IQ. Shared family environment accounts for perhaps one-quarter to one-third of the variance during childhood, but its effects seem to dissipate as people age. Educational experiences also influence mental skills. Heredity establishes a reaction range with upper and lower limits for intellectual potential. Environment affects the point within that range that will be reached.

- Intervention programmes for disadvantaged children have positive effects on later achievement and life outcomes if they begin early in life and are applied intensively. They have little effect when applied after school begins or with middle- or upper-class children.

- Heritability estimates of intelligence can vary, depending on sample characteristics. In impoverished families, shared environment was more important than genes, whereas the opposite was found in affluent families. Twin studies also show that heritability effects on intelligence increase in adulthood.

- Evidence exists for both genetic and environmental determinants.

- Although the differences are not large, there is some evidence to suggest that men tend, as a group, to score higher than women on certain spatial and mathematical reasoning tasks. Women perform slightly better than men on tests of perceptual speed, verbal fluency, mathematical calculation and fine motor co-ordination. Both environmental and biological bases of sex differences have been suggested. Stereotype threat is one potential psychological factor for gender-based performance differences.

- Even people with IQs in the 150s often show discrepancies in specific skills. Those who achieve eminence tend to have, in addition to high IQs, high levels of interest and motivation in their chosen activities.

- Cognitive disability can be caused by a number of factors. Biological causes are identified in only about 28 per cent of cases. Cognitive disability can range from mild to profound. The vast majority of disabled individuals are able to function in the mainstream of society, given appropriate support. Genetic factors seem relatively unimportant in profound learning difficulties, but they seem to play an important role in mild learning difficulties, which is more likely to run in families.

KEY TERMS AND CONCEPTS

Each term has been boldfaced and defined in the chapter on the page indicated in parentheses.

achievement test (p. 448)

aptitude test (p. 448)

cognitive process theories (p. 441)

construct validity (p. 450)

content validity (p. 450)

criterion-related validity (p. 450)

crystallized intelligence (g_c) (p. 439)

dynamic testing (p. 454)

emotional intelligence (p. 444)

factor analysis (p. 437)

fluid intelligence (g_f) (p. 440)

g factor (p. 438)

intelligence (p. 433)

intelligence quotient (IQ) (p. 435)

interjudge reliability (p. 450)

internal consistency (p. 450)

knowledge-acquisition components (p. 442)

metacomponents (p. 442)

normal distribution (p. 452)

norms (p. 452)

performance components (p. 442)

psychological test (p. 449)

psychometrics (p. 437)

reliability (p. 449)

standardization (p. 452)

static testing (p. 453)

stereotype threat (p. 464)

test–retest reliability (p. 450)

three-stratum theory of cognitive abilities (p. 440)

triarchic theory of intelligence (p. 442)

validity (p. 450)

WHAT DO YOU THINK?

ARE GIFTED CHILDREN MALADJUSTED? (p. 467)

Like the cognitively disabled, the gifted are often the victims of stereotypes. Some characterize them as 'geeks' and 'nerds' who are eccentric and socially maladjusted. As is the case with many stereotypes, there is a grain of truth here. A review of the scientific literature on giftedness by Ellen Winner (2000) revealed that nearly a quarter of children with truly exceptional IQs, at the high end of the gifted range (around 180), have social and psychological problems at about twice the rate found in non-gifted children. Such children often have different interest patterns and encounter difficulty finding like-minded peers to relate to, resulting in solitude and loneliness. The research also revealed, however, that the vast majority of these highly intelligent children show adequate adjustment, providing evidence against any stereotype that would be applied to gifted children in general.

Consider also a project begun in the 1920s by Lewis Terman, the psychologist who developed the Stanford–Binet test. Terman identified 1528 California children who had a mean IQ of 150 and began an extensive study of them that has continued for over 70 years. Terman and the researchers who inherited the project found the 'Termites', as they were called, to be above average not only in intelligence but also in height, weight, strength, physical health, emotional adjustment and social maturity. They continued to exhibit high levels of adjustment throughout their adolescent and adult years. By mid-life, the 1528 Termites had authored 92 books, 2200 scientific articles, and 235 patents. Their marriages tended to be happy and successful, and they seemed well adjusted psychologically (Sears, 1977). Nonetheless, some of the Termites underachieved and experienced social and psychological problems. These individuals tended to come from lower socio-economic backgrounds and to have parents who did not emphasize success or convey success expectations. The results were lowered motivation to achieve and a lack of confidence that they could accomplish their goals. Findings such as these show that capitalizing on one's high IQ requires an interest in some domain and the motivation to develop one's gifts.

CHAPTER ELEVEN
MOTIVATION AND EMOTION

CHAPTER OUTLINE

One can never consent to creep when one feels an impulse to soar.

HELEN KELLER

Lal Bahadur Shastri was invested as the Prime Minister of India in 1964. The two years he served as Prime Minister represented the culmination of a long career as an academic, a political activist and a politician. But if we look at how Lal Bahadur started out in life it would very be hard to imagine, let alone predict, his lifetime of achievement.

Lal Bahadur was born at the beginning of the twentieth century, to poor parents living in a town by the river Ganges. His father died when he was very young, and he was brought up by his mother and her family. It is a testament to Lal Bahadur's personal motivations that he was able to overcome these disadvantages to excel in his education, and later become one of the leading politicians of his age

However, the barriers placed before Lal Bahadur went beyond his simple origins. At the time of his birth India was ruled by the British Raj, and much of life was dedicated to the political movement for an independent India. These political efforts were not without their setbacks. Like other prominent activists such as Mahatma Ghandi, Lal Bahadur spent a number of years in prison as a consequence of his outspoken political views. Nonetheless, in the long run it was through the efforts of activists such as Lal Bahadur that the people of India were eventually able to govern themselves in an independent republic (Srivastava, 1995).

…

Sara gained 6.8 kg (15 lbs) during her first year of university thanks to late-night pizza-and-beer parties. She dieted and returned to her normal weight of 52 kilogrammes (8 st 3 lb). Proud of her success, Sara (just over 5 feet [1.52 m] tall) continued dieting and lost 11 more kilogrammes (25 lbs). Her menstrual period stopped, but she was so afraid of gaining weight that she could not bring herself to eat normally. Finally, weighing a mere 36 kilogrammes (5 st 9 lb), she was hospitalized and began psychotherapy.

Lisa also gained weight during her first year at university. Her greater weight made her feel 'like a failure'. She gradually fell into a pattern of eating lightly during the day but bingeing at night on crisps and biscuits. She later began to take laxatives to ward off the effects of the bingeing, such that she was eventually consuming 50 laxatives, along with 10 diet pills, each morning with breakfast. After a laxative-consuming friend suffered a heart attack at age 20, Lisa became scared. Worried about her own eating patterns, Lisa sought professional help (Hubbard et al., 1999).

Focus 11.1

How are motivation and emotion related? How do we define motivation?

Motivation and emotion, two central concepts in psychology, are closely linked. When our motives and goals are gratified, threatened or thwarted, we often experience emotions. Lal Bahadur worked hard in the struggle to free India and felt tremendous pride when he succeeded. Sara also took pride in her success at losing weight. Emotions, in turn, can motivate us to act. Lisa's fear upon seeing a friend nearly die from bingeing and purging prompted her to seek treatment. As we will now see, both our motives and our emotions stem from a confluence of biological, psychological and environmental factors.

MOTIVATION

The term *motivation* often triggers images of people who, like Lal Bahadur, strive to attain success. But to psychologists, motivational issues are broader. What motivates people to eat, have sex and make friends? What motivated Sara's self-starvation?

PERSPECTIVES ON MOTIVATION

Motivation is a process that influences the direction, persistence and vigour of goal-directed behaviour. Psychology's diverse theoretical perspectives view motivation through different lenses.

Evolution, Instincts, and Genes

Darwin's theory of evolution inspired early psychological views that instincts motivate much of our behaviour. An **instinct** (also called a *fixed action pattern*) is an inherited characteristic, common to all members of a species, that automatically produces a particular response when the organism is exposed to a particular stimulus. By the 1920s, researchers had proposed thousands of human instincts (Atkinson, 1964).

Human instinct theories faded because little evidence supported them and they often relied on circular reasoning: why are people greedy? Because greed is an instinct. How do we know that greed is an instinct? Because people are greedy. As we have seen in earlier discussions of scientific thinking, circular reasoning explains nothing.

Scientists now study genetic contributions to motivation more productively. In gene knockout experiments done with animals (see Chapter 3), they disable specific genes and then examine the resulting effects on motivation. Researchers also conduct twin and adoption studies to examine how strongly heredity accounts for differences among people in many aspects of motivated behaviour, such as the tendencies to be outgoing or to behave antisocially. Modern evolutionary psychologists also propose that many human motives have evolutionary underpinnings expressed through the actions of genes (Palmer and Palmer, 2002).

Homeostasis and Drives

Your body's biological systems are delicately balanced to ensure survival. For example, when you are hot, your body automatically tries to cool itself by perspiring. When you are cold, your body generates warmth by shivering. In 1932 Walter Cannon proposed the concept of **homeostasis**, a state of internal physiological equilibrium that the body strives to maintain.

Maintaining homeostasis requires a sensory mechanism for detecting changes in the internal environment, a response system that can restore equilibrium, and a control centre that receives information from the sensors and activates the response system (Fig. 11.1). The control centre functions somewhat like the thermostat in a furnace or

---

motivation

a process that influences the direction, persistence and vigour of goal-directed behaviour

Focus 11.2

Describe the key motivational concepts introduced by biological, cognitive, psychodynamic and humanistic perspectives. What are the BAS and the BIS?

instinct

an inherited characteristic, common to all members of a species, that automatically produces a particular response when the organism is exposed to a particular stimulus

homeostasis

a state of internal physiological equilibrium that the body strives to maintain

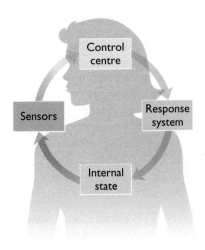

FIGURE 11.1

Homeostatic adaptation.

Your body's internal environment is regulated by homeostatic mechanisms. Sensors detect bodily changes and send this information to a control centre, which in turn regulates a response system that restores bodily equilibrium.

air-conditioning unit. Once the thermostat is set at a fixed temperature, or *set point*, sensors detect temperature changes in either direction. The control unit responds by turning on the furnace or air conditioner until the sensor indicates that the set point has been restored, and then turns it off.

According to Clark Hull's (1943) influential *drive theory of motivation*, physiological disruptions to homeostasis produce **drives**, states of internal tension that motivate an organism to behave in ways that reduce this tension. Drives such as hunger and thirst arise from tissue deficits (e.g., lack of food and water) and push an organism into action. Hull, a learning theorist, proposed that reducing drives is the ultimate goal of motivated behaviour.

Homeostatic models are applied to many aspects of motivation, such as the regulation of hunger and thirst (Woods and Seeley, 2002). But drive concepts are less influential than in the past. For one thing, we often behave in ways that seem to increase rather than reduce states of arousal, as when we skip meals in order to diet or flock to tension-generating horror movies.

Approach and Avoidance Motivation

Motivation impels us towards some things and away from others. We seek to maximize pleasure and minimize pain, gravitate towards rewards and avoid punishment and deprivation. These seemingly universal tendencies reflect the activity of two distinct neural systems in the brain. According to Jeffrey Gray (1991), the **behavioural activation system (BAS)** is roused to action by signals of potential reward and positive need gratification. Activity in this neural system causes the person to begin or to increase movement towards positive goals (the things we want) in anticipation of pleasure. The BAS produces emotions of hope, elation and happiness. Avoidance motivation reflects the activity of the **behavioural inhibition system (BIS)**, which responds to stimuli that signal potential pain, non-reinforcement and punishment. The BIS produces fear, inhibition of behaviour (as when humans and other animals freeze in terror), as well as escape and avoidance behaviours (Fig. 11.2). As we shall see in Chapter 15 on personality, people differ in the degrees to which they demonstrate behavioural activation and inhibition. People high in BAS prefer change and novelty, whereas BIS fosters a preference for the familiar (Quilty et al., 2007).

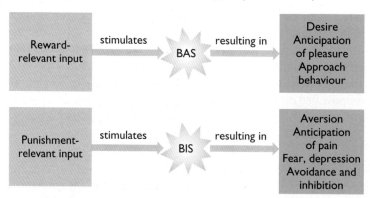

Brain researchers are looking for the specific brain mechanisms underlying the pleasure-seeking and pain-minimizing functions of the BAS and the BIS. These mechanisms involve not only different neurotransmitter systems but also different brain regions. Electroencephalograph and fMRI studies suggest that the prefrontal area in the left hemisphere, a region involved in goal-directed planning and self-regulation, is part of the BAS (Coan and Allen, 2003; Gray and Burgess, 2004). The BIS system is thought to involve several structures of the limbic system and the right frontal lobe (Sutton, 2002). However, there is still much to be learned about the neural underpinnings of the BAS and BIS.

The BAS and BIS are at the forefront of motivational research because they not only address the obviously important distinction between approach and avoidance motivation, but they also

drives

states of internal tension that motivate an organism to behave in ways that reduce this tension

behavioural activation system (BAS)

roused to action by signals of potential reward and positive need gratification

behavioural inhibition system (BIS)

responds to stimuli that signal potential pain, non-reinforcement and punishment

FIGURE 11.2

Approach and avoidance motivation.

Two neurological systems, the behavioural activation system (BAS) and the behavioural inhibition system (BIS) underlie the universal tendencies to maximize pleasure and minimize pain. The BAS regulates approach motivation, whereas the BIS regulates avoidance motivation. The systems also link approach and avoidance motivation with positive and aversive emotions.

help organize the cognitive, physiological and behavioural process involved in seeking pleasure and avoiding pain. These systems tie together motivation and emotion as well, for the BAS links approach motives and desired incentives with positive emotions, and the BIS links avoidance motives with negative emotions, such as fear, depression and guilt.

Cognitive Processes: Incentives and Expectancies

Whereas drives are viewed as internal factors that push an organism into action, **incentives** represent environmental stimuli that pull an organism towards a goal. To a student, anticipating a good degree classification can be an incentive for studying, just as food can be an incentive for someone who is hungry (i.e., someone motivated by the hunger drive).

Why is it, however, that people often respond differently to the same incentive? Consider three students in a mathematics class at school (let us call them Eleanor, James and Pascale). Eleanor, James and Pascale have similar mathematics aptitudes but Eleanor studies hard, while James and Pascale make relatively little effort. According to one cognitive approach, the **expectancy × value theory**, goal-directed behaviour is jointly determined by the strength of the person's expectation that particular behaviours will lead to a goal and by the incentive value the individual places on that goal (Brehm and Self, 1989).

These two factors are multiplied, producing the following equation: motivation = expectancy × incentive value. Eleanor works hard because she believes (expectancy) that the more she studies, the more likely it is she will get an A (incentive), and she values an A highly. James also believes that studying hard will lead to an A, but an A holds little value for him in this subject. In contrast, Pascale values an A but believes that studying hard is unlikely to produce a high grade for her. Therefore, James and Pascale do not study as hard as Eleanor does.

Cognitive theorists also distinguish between **extrinsic motivation**, performing an activity to obtain an external reward or avoid punishment, and **intrinsic motivation**, performing an activity for its own sake – because you find it enjoyable or challenging. In terms of incentives, a student who studies hard solely to get a good mark (rather than to learn) is exhibiting extrinsic motivation.

Psychodynamic and Humanistic Views

The psychodynamic and humanistic perspectives view motivation within a broader context of personality development. Freud (1923) proposed that energy from unconscious motives – especially sexual and aggressive instincts – is often disguised and expressed through socially acceptable behaviours. Thus hidden aggressive impulses may fuel one's motivation to be a trial attorney or an athlete.

Research offers little support for Freud's 'dual-instinct' model, but his work stimulated other psychodynamic theories that highlight motives such as people's desires for self-esteem and social belonging (Kohut, 1977). Modern psychodynamic theorists continue to emphasize that, together with conscious mental processes, unconscious motives guide how we act and feel (Westen, 1998). Cognitive psychologists hold a different (i.e., information-processing) view of the unconscious mind, but their research – together with studies of human social behaviour – indicates that, indeed, people are not always aware of the factors that motivate them to act as they do (Chartrand and Bargh, 2002).

Maslow's hierarchy of needs Abraham Maslow (1954), a humanistic theorist, proposed a broad motivational model. He believed that many of the perspectives taken in psychology ignore a key human motive: our striving for personal growth. He proposed the concept of a *hierarchy of needs*, a progression containing deficiency needs (needs concerned with physical and social survival) at the bottom and uniquely human growth needs at the top (Fig. 11.3). After our basic physiological needs are satisfied, we focus on our need for safety and security. Once that is met,

incentives
environmental stimuli that pull an organism towards a goal

expectancy × value theory
goal-directed behaviour is jointly determined by the strength of the person's expectation that particular behaviours will lead to a goal and by the incentive value the individual places on that goal

extrinsic motivation
performing an activity to obtain an external reward or avoid punishment

intrinsic motivation
performing an activity for its own sake

FIGURE 11.3

A motivational hierarchy.

Maslow proposed that needs are arranged in a hierarchy. After meeting our more basic needs, we experience need progression and focus on needs at the next level. If a need at a lower level is no longer satisfied, we experience need regression and focus once again on meeting that lower-level need.

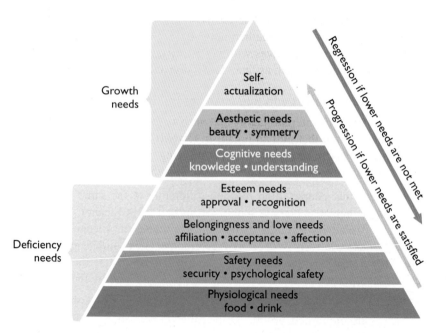

self-actualization

the need to fulfil our potential

self-determination theory

focuses on three fundamental psychological needs: competence, autonomy and relatedness

we then attend to needs at the next higher level, and so on. If situations change and lower-level needs are no longer met, we refocus our attention on them until they are satisfied.

To Maslow, **self-actualization**, which represents the need to fulfil our potential, is the ultimate human motive. It motivates us to perfect ourselves mentally, artistically, emotionally and socially, to explore activities for their intrinsic satisfaction rather than to gain esteem and belongingness, and to live deep and meaningful lives dedicated to the betterment of all people, not just ourselves. Maslow believed that most people become so focused on attaining satisfaction of the needs lower in the hierarchy that they spend little time focused on becoming all they can be. Those rare people who approach self-actualization can, it is argued, make enormous contributions to our world. Examples of such individuals might be Albert Einstein, Mahatma Gandhi, Mother Teresa and Martin Luther King, Jr. Some of these people are thought to achieve a state of *self-transcendence*, moving beyond a focus on self to commit themselves to the welfare of others, spiritual fulfilment and commitment to a cause higher than themselves (Koltko-Rivera, 2006).

Self-determination theory   A more recent humanistic theory of motivation has been advanced by Edward Deci and Richard Ryan (1985; 2002). **Self-determination theory** focuses on three fundamental psychological needs: competence, autonomy and relatedness. People are most fulfilled in their lives when they are able to satisfy these fundamental needs. Competence motivation reflects a human need to master new challenges and to perfect skills. This need motivates much exploratory and growth-inducing human behaviour. In its purest form, the behaviour becomes its own reward, so that it is intrinsically motivated, rather than being done for an extrinsic reward.

The need for autonomy represents an attempt to achieve greater freedom and regulation by the self, rather than by external forces. It leads to greater self-integration, feelings of personal control, and self-actualization. The third basic need, relatedness, refers to the self's desire to form meaningful bonds with others. At first glance, relatedness may seem opposed to autonomy, but the two actually complement one another. When true relatedness is achieved, people often feel freer to be themselves. Adolescents who feel that their autonomy is acknowledged and supported by their parents feel a strong sense of relatedness to their parents (Ryan and Lynch, 1989).

The importance of self-determination theory's three basic needs has been strongly supported by research. They appear to have independent and additive effects on positive outcomes such as psychological well-being, happiness, worker performance and satisfaction, positive social relationships and a sense of meaningfulness in life (Deci and Ryan, 2002; Sheldon et al., 2003). From a humanistic perspective, self-determination theory represents a new model for the elusive concept of self-actualization.

WHAT DO YOU THINK?

IS MASLOW'S NEED HIERARCHY VALID?

Does the concept of a need hierarchy, shown in Figure 11.3, make sense to you? How do you feel about the ordering of needs in Maslow's hierarchy? Think about it, then see p. 525.

IN REVIEW

- Motivation is a process that influences the direction, vigour and persistence of goal-directed behaviour. On several fronts, scientists are actively exploring how heredity influences motivation.

- Homeostatic models view motivation as an attempt to maintain equilibrium in bodily systems. Drive theories propose that tissue deficits create drives, such as hunger, that push an organism from within to reduce that deficit and restore homeostasis.

- Incentive theories emphasize environmental factors that pull people towards a goal. Expectancy × value theory explains why the same incentive may motivate some people but not others.

- Psychodynamic theories emphasize that unconscious motives guide much of our behaviour. Humanist Abraham Maslow proposed that needs exist in a hierarchy, from basic biological needs to the ultimate need for self-actualization. Deci and Ryan's self-determination theory emphasizes the importance of three fundamental needs – competence, autonomy and relatedness – in maximizing human potential.

HUNGER AND WEIGHT REGULATION

As we have seen in the previous section, psychology's diverse perspectives underscore the complexity of studying motivation. Let us now turn to one of our most basic motives: hunger. If you could give up all food for ever and satisfy your nutritional needs with a daily pill, would you? Eating is a necessity, but for many people it also is one of life's delicious pleasures. Numerous biological, psychological and environmental factors regulate our food intake, and hunger can be studied at all three levels of analysis.

The Physiology of Hunger

Eating and digestion supply the body with the fuel it needs to function and survive. **Metabolism** is the body's rate of energy (or caloric) utilization, and several physiological mechanisms keep

metabolism

the body's rate of energy (or caloric) utilization

your body in energy homeostasis by regulating how much you eat. For example, some physiological signals induce hunger and prompt eating, whereas others stop food intake by producing *satiety* (the state in which we no longer feel hungry).

However, it is not the case – as many people believe – that hunger and eating simply occur when we begin to run low on energy and that we feel full when immediate energy supplies are restored (Assanand et al., 1998). Your body monitors its energy supplies, but this information interacts with other factors (e.g., the amount and variety of food) to regulate food intake. Thus hunger and satiety are not necessarily linked to immediate energy needs (Woods and Seeley, 2002). Moreover, homeostatic mechanisms are designed to *prevent* us from running low on energy in the first place. In evolutionary terms, an organism that did not eat until its energy supply started to become low (in any absolute sense) would be at a serious survival disadvantage.

Finally, many researchers believe that there is a **set point**, a biologically determined standard around which body weight (or, more accurately, fat mass) is regulated (Powley and Keesey, 1970). This view holds that if we overeat or undereat, homeostatic mechanisms alter our energy utilization and hunger so as to return us close to our original weight. Other researchers argue that set point theory has limitations. They propose that as we overeat or undereat, homeostatic mechanisms make it harder to keep gaining or losing weight but do not necessarily return us to our original weight. Over time we may settle in at a new weight. Stated differently, in this view 'biology does not determine a fixed body weight, but rather a range or zone of body weight' (Levitsky, 2002, p. 147).

Signals that start and terminate a meal   Do the muscular contractions (hunger pangs) of an empty stomach produce hunger? In an early experiment, A.L. Washburn investigated this question by swallowing a balloon. When it reached his stomach, the balloon was inflated and hooked up to an amplifying device to record his stomach contractions (Fig. 11.4). Washburn then pressed a key every time he felt hungry. The results: Washburn's stomach contractions did indeed correspond with his feelings of hunger (Cannon and Washburn, 1912). But did they *cause* the experience of hunger?

Subsequent research found that hunger does not depend on an empty or twitching stomach, or any stomach at all! Animals display hunger and satiety even if all nerves from their stomachs to their brains are cut, and people who have had their stomachs surgically removed for medical reasons continue to feel hungry and satiated (Brown and Wallace, 1980). Thus other signals must help trigger hunger.

---

set point

a biologically determined standard around which body weight (or, more accurately, fat mass) is regulated

---

Focus 11.3

What physiological factors help regulate hunger, satiety, general appetite, and weight?

FIGURE 11.4

Do stomach sensations regulate hunger?

A.L. Washburn swallowed a balloon and inflated it in his stomach. A machine recorded stomach contractions by amplifying changes in the pressure on the balloon, and Washburn pressed a telegraph key every time he felt a hunger pang. Hunger pangs occurred when the stomach contracted.

SOURCE: based on Cannon and Washburn, 1912.

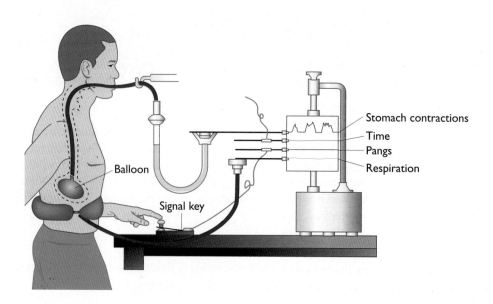

Balloon — Stomach contractions — Time — Pangs — Respiration — Signal key

When you eat, digestive enzymes break down food into key nutrients, such as **glucose**, a simple sugar that is the body's (and especially the brain's) major source of immediately usable fuel. After a meal, some glucose is transported into cells to provide energy, but a large portion is transferred into your liver and fat cells, where it is converted into other nutrients and stored for later use. Sensors in the hypothalamus and liver monitor blood-glucose concentrations. When blood-glucose levels decrease slightly, the liver responds by converting stored nutrients back into glucose, causing blood-glucose levels to rise. Changes in the supply of glucose available to cells provide a signal that helps the brain regulate hunger (Campfield, 1997).

As you eat, several bodily signals cause you to end your meal. Stomach and intestinal distention are satiety signals (French and Cecil, 2001). The walls of these organs stretch as food fills them up, sending nerve signals to the brain. This does not mean, however, that your stomach has to be full for you to feel satiated. As we just noted, patients who have had their stomachs removed continue to experience satiety; this is due not only to intestinal distention but also to chemical signals. For example, **cholecystokinin (CCK)** – a peptide (a type of hormone) that helps produce satiety – and other peptides are released into the bloodstream by the small intestine as food arrives from the stomach. These peptides travel to the brain and stimulate receptors in several regions that decrease food intake (Degen et al., 2001).

Signals that regulate general appetite and weight   **Leptin** is a hormone secreted by fat cells. It enters the bloodstream and reaches the brain, where it decreases appetite and increases energy expenditure.

Leptin is a long-term 'background' signal. It does not make us feel full like CCK and other short-term satiety signals that respond directly to food intake during a meal. Instead, one way leptin may influence appetite is by increasing the potency of these other signals (Woods and Seeley, 2002). Thus as we gain fat and secrete more leptin, we may tend to eat less because mealtime satiety factors make us feel full sooner. As we lose fat and secrete less leptin, it may take a greater accumulation of satiety signals and thus more food to make us feel full. In essence, lower leptin levels may signal a lack of fat tissue and stimulate motivational centres in the brain to direct us towards food. Leptin levels, however, seem to fall more quickly when we lose fat (thus increasing appetite) than they rise when we gain fat. Some researchers suggest that this imbalance served a key adaptive function over the course of evolution; it tilted our ancestral scales in favour of maintaining an adequate fat mass when food was plentiful so that the odds of survival would be increased during times when food was scarce (Jéquier, 2002).

Evidence for leptin's important role grew out of research with genetically obese mice (Zhang et al., 1994). A gene called the *ob* gene (*ob* = obesity) normally directs fat cells to produce leptin, but mice with an *ob* gene mutation lack leptin. As they gain weight, the brain does not receive this 'curb your appetite' signal, and the mice overeat and become obese (Fig. 11.5). Daily leptin injections reduce their appetite, and the mice become thinner. Another strain of obese mice produces ample leptin, but because of a mutation in a different gene (the *db* gene), their brain receptors are insensitive to leptin (Chen et al., 1996). The 'curb your appetite' signal is there, but because they cannot detect it they become obese. Even injecting these mice with additional leptin does not reduce their food intake and weight.

Are these specific *ob* and *db* gene mutations a major source of human obesity? Probably not, for these genetic

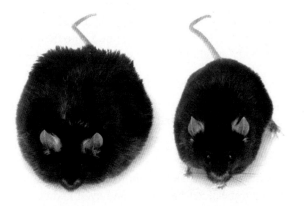

FIGURE 11.5

The mouse on the left has an *ob* gene mutation. Its fat cells fail to produce leptin, and it becomes obese. Leptin injections help such mice return to normal weight.

conditions seem to be rare among humans. However, when these gene mutations do occur, they are associated with extreme obesity, suggesting the importance of normal leptin functioning in human weight regulation.

Might leptin injections be the magic bullet that helps most obese people lose weight? Unfortunately, probably not, because obese people already have ample leptin in their blood owing to their fat mass. It seems, rather, that their brains may be resistant to that information (Ravussin and Gautier, 1999).

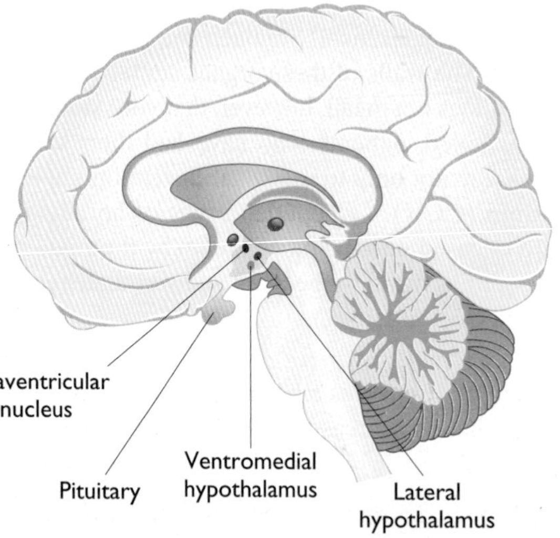

FIGURE 11.6

Motivation and the hypothalamus.

Various structures within the hypothalamus play a role in regulating hunger, thirst, sexual arousal and body temperature. The lateral hypothalamus (LH), ventromedial hypothalamus (VMH) and paraventricular nucleus (PVN) are involved in hunger regulation.

Paraventricular nucleus

Pituitary

Ventromedial hypothalamus

Lateral hypothalamus

Brain mechanisms   Many brain regions – from the primitive brain stem to the lofty cerebral cortex – help regulate hunger and eating (Berthoud, 2002). But is there a master control centre? Early experiments pointed to two regions in the hypothalamus. Areas near the side, called the *lateral hypothalamus (LH)*, seemed to comprise a 'hunger-on' centre (Fig. 11.6). Electrically stimulating a rat's LH would cause it to start eating, and lesioning (damaging or destroying) the LH would cause it to refuse to eat, even to the point of starvation (Anand and Brobeck, 1951).

In contrast, structures in the lower-middle area, called the *ventromedial hypothalamus (VMH)*, seemed to comprise a 'hunger-off' centre. Electrically stimulating the VMH would cause even a hungry rat to stop eating, whereas lesioning the VMH would produce a glutton that ate frequently and doubled or tripled its body weight.

As scientists explored further, they learned that although the LH and VMH play a role in hunger regulation, they are not really hunger-on and hunger-off centres. For example, rats with LH damage stop eating and lose weight in part because they develop trouble swallowing and digesting, and they become generally unresponsive to external stimuli, not just to food. Moreover, axons from many brain areas funnel into the hypothalamus and then fan out again upon leaving it. Cutting these nerve tracts anywhere along their paths – not just within the hypothalamus – duplicates some of the effects of the LH and VMH lesions (Schwartz, 1984).

Researchers are examining how specific neural circuits within the hypothalamus regulate food intake. Many pathways involve the **paraventricular nucleus (PVN)**, a cluster of neurons packed with receptor sites for various transmitters that stimulate or reduce appetite. The PVN appears to integrate several short-term and long-term signals that influence metabolic and digestive processes (Berthoud, 2002). One such signal, a chemical transmitter called *neuropeptide Y*, is a powerful appetite stimulant. Rats in one experiment quickly became obese when they received injections of neuropeptide Y into their PVN for 10 days. Their food intake doubled, and their body weight increased sixfold (Stanley et al., 1986).

paraventricular nucleus (PVN)

cluster of neurons packed with receptor sites for various transmitters that stimulate or reduce appetite

Focus 11.4

Describe how psychological, environmental and cultural factors influence hunger and eating.

Psychological Aspects of Hunger

Eating is positively reinforced by the good taste of food and negatively reinforced by hunger reduction. We develop an expectation that eating will be pleasurable, and this becomes an important motivator to seek and consume food. Indeed, even the mere thought of food can trigger hunger.

Attitudes, habits and psychological needs also regulate food intake. Have you ever felt stuffed during a meal, yet finished it and even had dessert? Beliefs such as 'don't leave food on your plate' and conditioned habits (e.g., eating crisps while watching television) may lead us to eat even when we do not feel hungry. Conversely, countless dieters intentionally restrict their food intake even though they *are* hungry.

Especially for women, such food restriction often stems from social pressures to conform to cultural standards of beauty (Fig. 11.7). Studies of *Playboy* centrefolds, Miss America contestants and fashion models indicate a clear trend towards a thinner and increasingly unrealistic ideal female body shape from the 1950s into the 1990s (Owen and Laurel-Seller, 2000). Given the prevalence of thin models in advertising and cultural media in many parts of the globe, it seems unsurprising that national surveys in these areas have revealed that:

- although most young Australian women are of average, healthy weight, only a fifth are happy with their weight (Kenardy et al., 2001)
- among 12- to 19-year-old female Chinese students, 80 per cent are concerned about their weight and feel fat at least some of the time (Huon et al., 2002)
- compared with male American high school students, female students are less likely to be overweight but much more likely to diet and think of themselves as overweight (Centers for Disease Control and Prevention [CDC], 2002b).

FIGURE 11.7

Throughout much of western history, a full-bodied woman's figure was esteemed, as illustrated by (*left*) Peter Paul Rubens's seventeenth-century painting *The Three Graces* and by (*centre*) actress Lillian Russell, who represented the American ideal of feminine beauty a century ago. In recent decades, the norm of 'thin = beautiful' is illustrated (*right*) by these swimsuit models.

The cultural cause of body dissatisfaction is underlined by studies indicating that: (1), relative to men, women have become increasingly dissatisfied with their body image throughout the second half of the twentieth century (Feingold and Mazzella, 1998), and (2) discrepancies between actual weight and ideal weight are smaller in cultures which have less exposure to western positive values of thinness. For example, Toriola et al. (1996) found that Nigerian women in Britain had a greater dissatisfaction with their weight than Nigerian women in Nigeria.

A classic study by April Fallon and Paul Rozin (1985) suggests an additional reason why this is so. This study showed that women at university overestimated how thin they needed to be to conform to men's preferences, whereas men overestimated how bulky they should be to conform to women's preferences (Fig. 11.8). Women also perceived their body shape as heavier than ideal, whereas men viewed their body shape as close to ideal (see also Carlson and McAndrew, 2004). As Fallon and Rozin noted, 'Overall, men's perceptions serve to keep them satisfied with their figures, whereas women's perceptions place pressure on them to lose weight' (1985, p. 102). It is argued that men's greater propensity to adopt ego-protective perceptions about their body shape occurs across cultures (Demarest and Allen, 2000).

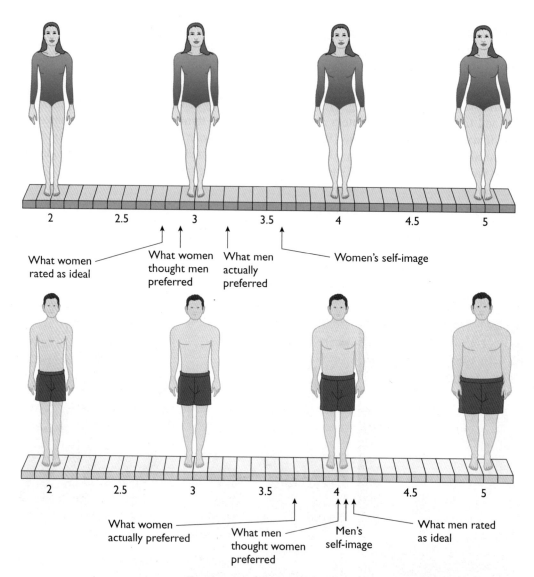

FIGURE 11.8

Preferred body shapes.

When making judgements while viewing body-size drawings, college women overestimated how thin they needed to be to conform to men's preferences, and they viewed their own body shape as heavier than ideal. Men overestimated how bulky or 'buff' they needed to be to conform to women's preferences, but they viewed their body shape as close to ideal.

SOURCE: based on Fallon and Rozin, 1985.

Men too, however, may be influenced by cultural ideals. Men's satisfaction with their bodies decreases when they are exposed to a series of advertisements showing muscular males, but not when the advertisements contain men with average builds (Lorenzen et al., 2004). Male athletes, who value muscle function, believe that women prefer a more muscular body type than their own, and most would prefer to be more muscular than they are (Raudenbush and Meyer, 2003). In general it appears that women typically want to be thin; males who are overweight also want to be thinner, but those who are thin want to be heavier and more 'buff' (Kostanski et al., 2004).

Environmental and Cultural Factors

Food availability is the most obvious environmental regulator of eating. For millions of people who live in poverty or famine-ravaged regions, food scarcity limits consumption. In contrast, abundant high-fat food in many countries contributes to a high rate of obesity (Wadden et al., 2002).

Food taste and variety also regulate eating. Good-tasting food increases food consumption, but during a meal and from meal to meal we can become tired of eating the same thing, causing us to terminate a meal more quickly (Rolls et al., 1981). In contrast, food variety increases consumption, which you may have observed when you eat at a buffet.

Through classical conditioning, we learn to associate the smell and sight of food with its taste, and these food cues can trigger hunger. Eating may be the last thing on your mind until your nose detects the sensuous aroma wafting from a bakery or popcorn machine. Similarly, rats who have recently eaten and do not appear to be hungry (e.g., they ignore available food) will eat again when presented with classically conditioned sounds and lights that they have learned to associate with food (Weingarten, 1983).

Many other environmental stimuli affect food intake. For example, we typically eat more when dining with other people than when we eat alone (deCastro, 2002). Cultural norms influence when, how and what we eat. In Mediterranean countries such as Spain and Greece, people often begin dinner in the late evening (say, around 9 p.m.), by which time most people in the UK have finished supper. And although we like variety, we usually feel most comfortable selecting familiar foods and often have difficulty overcoming our squeamish thoughts about unfamiliar dishes (Fig. 11.9). Figure 11.10 summarizes several factors that help regulate hunger and eating.

Obesity

The heaviest known man and woman in recorded history, both Americans, weighed 635 and 544 kilogrammes (100 st and 85 st 7 lb), respectively (*Guinness Book of Records*, 2000). The *body mass index (BMI)*, which takes height and weight into account, demonstrates that obesity varies substantially between countries. In Europe obesity prevalence varies between 5 and 23 per cent for men and 7 and 36 per cent for women. Percentages of the population who are defined as overweight (but not obese) vary between 27 and 57 per cent for men, and 18 and 43 per cent for women. Uzbekistan and Kazakhstan are among the countries demonstrating the lowest levels of obesity, while the UK and Bosnia and Herzegovina have some of the highest (WHO Summary, 2007).

Obesity places people at greater risk not only for many medical problems but also for being the target of stereotypes and prejudice (Teachman et al., 2003). Obesity is often blamed on a lack of willpower, a dysfunctional way of coping with stress, heightened sensitivity to external food cues (e.g., the sight and aroma of food) and emotional disturbances. Research, however, does not consistently find such psychological differences between obese and non-obese people (Faith et al., 2002; Leon and Roth, 1977).

FIGURE 11.9

Cultural upbringing strongly affects food preferences. Would you like to eat these insect-topped appetizers? Many Europeans and Americans would be squeamish at the thought of eating them. Other foods whose consumption is strongly affected by cultural preferences include reptiles, camel eyes, dog meat and rotten fish.

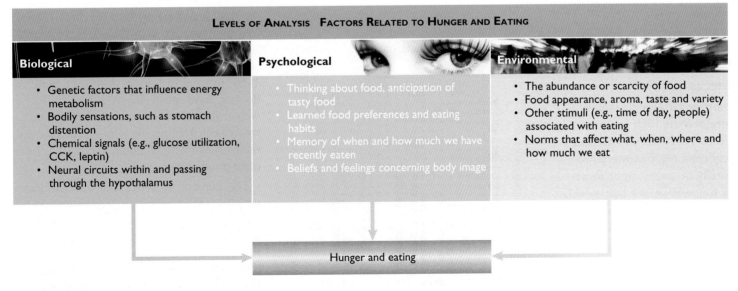

FIGURE 11.10

Levels of analysis: factors related to hunger and eating.

Focus 11.5

Describe biological and environmental factors in obesity and how their interaction affects obesity among the Pima.

Genes and environment   Do you know people who seem to gain weight easily and others who seem to eat as much as they want without adding pounds? Heredity influences one's basal metabolic rate and the tendency to store energy as either fat or lean tissue. Indeed, identical twins raised apart are about as similar in body mass as identical twins reared together. Overall, genetic factors appear to account for about 40 to 70 per cent of the variation in BMI among women and among men (Maes et al., 1997).

More than 200 genes have been identified as possible contributors to human obesity (Comuzzie and Allison, 1998). However, although heredity affects our susceptibility to obesity, so does the environment. Genes have not changed much in recent decades, but obesity rates have increased significantly. According to some experts, the culprits are:

- an abundance of inexpensive, tasty foods that are high in fat and/or carbohydrates
- a cultural emphasis on getting the best value, which contributes to supersizing menu items
- technological advances that decrease the need for daily physical activity (Wadden et al., 2002)
- high levels of dopamine in the brain's 'reward pathways' may make some people especially sensitive to the reinforcing properties of foods (Davis et al., 2007).

The Pima Indians of Arizona in the USA provide a striking example of how genes and environment interact to produce obesity. The Pimas are genetically predisposed to obesity and diabetes, but both conditions were rare among tribe members before the twentieth century. Their native diet and physically active lifestyle prevented their genetic predisposition from expressing itself. But particularly among Pimas born after the Second World War, obesity rates increased dramatically as they adopted a westernized diet and sedentary lifestyle. Today Pimas living in Arizona have one of the highest rates of obesity (and diabetes) in the world. In contrast, Pimas living in north-west Mexico eat a more traditional diet and perform more physical labour, and their obesity rate is much lower than that of their Arizonan counterparts (Esparza et al., 2000).

Dieting and weight loss   Unfortunately for millions of overweight people, being fat primes them to stay fat, in part by altering body chemistry and energy expenditure (Logue, 1991). For example, obese people generally have higher levels of *insulin* (a hormone secreted by the pancreas that helps convert glucose into fat) than do people of normal weight. Substantial weight gain also makes it harder to exercise vigorously, and dieting slows basal metabolism because the body responds to food deprivation with decreased energy expenditure.

Does this mean that diets are doomed to fail? The common adage that '95 per cent of people who lose weight regain it within a few years' evolved from just one study decades ago. According to Albert Stunkard, one of the researchers, 100 obesity patients were 'just given a diet and sent on their way. That was state of the art in 1959' (quoted in Fritsch, 1999). In truth, we do not have good long-term estimates of weight-loss success rates, partly because we rarely hear from people who succeed (or fail) on their own without going to clinics or treatment programmes.

The number of books and advertisements which describe dieting procedures that we can observe day to day is testament to the fact that many people are trying to lose weight. A question of interest concerns whether there are any differences in the number of people engaging in dieting behaviour between gender and ethic groups. Figure 11.11 shows the results of a study in the USA which demonstrated that

FIGURE 11.11

Ethnicity and dieting.

Whether Hispanic, black or white, female high school students in America are less likely than male students to actually be overweight or at risk for overweight but, as this graph shows, they are more likely to be dieting to lose weight. Especially among female students, Hispanics and whites are most likely to diet.

SOURCE: based on CDC, 2002b.

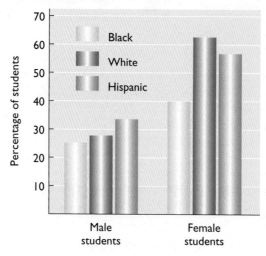

there are significant sex and ethnic differences in dieting that emerge even in adolescence (CDC, 2002b). Health concerns motivate some dieters, but psychological concerns and social pressures to be thin are the primary motivators for many others. Especially among women, what begins as a diet may unfortunately evolve into a health-threatening eating disorder.

Eating Disorders: Anorexia and Bulimia

Sara and Lisa, the first-year university students described at the beginning of the chapter, suffered from eating disorders. Victims of **anorexia nervosa**, like Sara, have an intense fear of being fat and severely restrict their food intake to the point of self-starvation (Fig. 11.12). Despite looking emaciated and weighing less than 85 per cent of what would be expected for their age and height, people with anorexia continue to view themselves as fat. Anorexia causes menstruation to stop, produces bone loss, stresses the heart and increases the risk of death (Neumäker, 2000; Treasure, 2005).

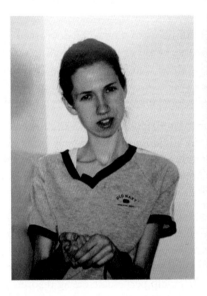 

anorexia nervosa

an intense fear of being fat so that victims severely restrict their food intake to the point of self-starvation

Focus 11.6

What are the major symptoms, health consequences and causes of anorexia and bulimia?

FIGURE 11.12

Anorexia nervosa is a potentially life-threatening disorder in which people virtually starve themselves to be thin. This anorexic woman returned to normal weight after therapy.

bulimia nervosa

a fear of becoming fat, which causes victims to binge-eat and then purge the food

People like Lisa who suffer from **bulimia nervosa** are also afraid of becoming fat, and they binge-eat and then purge the food, usually by inducing vomiting or using laxatives. People with bulimia often consume 2000 to 4000 calories during binges, and in some cases may consume 20000 calories per day (Geracioti et al., 1995). Although most bulimics are of normal body weight, repeated purging can produce severe physical consequences, including gastric problems and badly eroded teeth. Whereas most anorexics do not see their food restriction as problematic, bulimics typically do. Nonetheless, they find it extremely difficult to alter their binge–purge pattern.

About 90 per cent of people with anorexia and bulimia are women. About 7 per cent of anorexics have a previous diagnosis of bulimia, and this group tends to exhibit higher levels of psychological disturbance (Santonastaso et al., 2006). Some surveys indicate that up to 10 per cent of women exhibit symptoms of bulimia, although its general prevalence is 1 to 3 per cent – compared with 0.5 per cent for anorexia (American Psychiatric Association, 1994).

Causes of anorexia and bulimia   What motivates such abnormal eating patterns? Researchers obviously cannot do experiments to manipulate possible causes and see if people become anorexic or bulimic, but they can examine factors associated with the disorders and changes that occur in people when they are successfully treated. Such research suggests that a combination of environmental, psychological and biological factors may be involved.

Anorexia and bulimia are more common in industrialized cultures where thinness is equated with beauty. However, cultural norms alone cannot account for eating disorders, because only a small percentage of women within a particular culture are anorexic or bulimic. Personality factors are another piece of the puzzle. People with anorexia often are perfectionists and high achievers who strive to live up to lofty self-standards, including strict ideals of an acceptably thin body (Tyrka et al., 2002). For them, losing weight becomes a battle for success and control: 'It's me versus food, and I'm going to win.' Their perfectionism and need for control may partly stem from their upbringing. They often describe their parents as disapproving and as setting abnormally high achievement standards. For some anorexic children and teenagers, food refusal may be reinforced by the distress they cause their parents to feel. In essence, self-starvation becomes a way to punish parents and gain some control (Chan and Ma, 2002), as illustrated by the following quotation taken from one young anorexic teenager in a therapy session,

> It was, like, a power thing. I was like, look mum, I don't have to eat. I can piss you off.... That's the last thing your parents want is for you to die.... You can get back at anybody. And I guess ... I need to find a way to forgive her ... because ... I'm killing myself. (*Dying to be Thin*, 2000)

A different pattern emerges for people with bulimia, who tend to be depressed and anxious, exhibit low impulse control and seem to lack a stable sense of personal identity (McElroy et al., 2006). Their food cravings are often triggered by stress and negative mood, and bingeing temporarily reduces their negative emotional state (Waters et al., 2001). But guilt, self-contempt and anxiety follow the binge, and purging may be a means of reducing these negative feelings.

On the biological side, genetic factors appear to predispose some people towards eating disorders. Concordance rates for eating disorders are higher among identical twins than fraternal twins and higher among first-degree relatives (parents and siblings) than second- or third-degree relatives (Kortegaard et al., 2001). Researchers are now searching for specific genes and combinations of genes that contribute to eating disorders.

Anorexics and bulimics also exhibit abnormal activity of serotonin, leptin and other body chemicals (Kaye et al., 2002). Some researchers believe that neurotransmitter and hormonal imbalances help cause eating disorders. Others propose that such chemical changes initially are a *response* to abnormal eating patterns but that once started they *perpetuate* eating and digestive irregularities (Walsh and Devlin, 1998). Other bodily changes also help perpetuate eating disorders. For example, stomach acids expelled into the mouth during vomiting cause bulimics to lose taste sensitivity, making the normally unpleasant taste of vomit more tolerable (Rodin et al., 1990).

IN REVIEW

- Physiological processes attempt to keep the body in energy homeostasis. Changes in the supply of glucose available to cells provide one signal that helps initiate hunger. During meals, hormones such as CCK are released into the bloodstream and help signal the brain to stop eating. Fat cells release leptin, which acts as a long-term signal that helps regulate appetite. The hypothalamus plays an important role in hunger regulation.

- The expected good taste of food motivates eating, and the thought of food can trigger hunger. Our memory, habits and psychological needs affect our food intake.

- The availability, taste, and variety of food powerfully regulate eating. Through classical conditioning, neutral stimuli can acquire the capacity to trigger hunger. Cultural norms affect our food preferences and eating habits.

- Heredity and the environment affect our susceptibility to becoming obese.

- Anorexia and bulimia occur more often in cultures that value thinness and are associated with somewhat different psychological profiles. Heredity predisposes some people towards developing these eating disorders.

Treating eating disorders is difficult and may take years, but with professional help, about half of all anorexic and bulimic patients fully recover (Russell, 2006; Westen et al., 2004). Others are able to eat more normally but maintain their preoccupation with food and weight.

SEXUAL MOTIVATION

Why do people have sex? If you're thinking, 'Isn't it obvious?' let us take a look. Sex often is described as a biological reproductive motive, yet people usually do not have sex to conceive children. A drive to reproduce does not explain why people masturbate or why couples in their seventies and eighties have sex. Pleasure, then, must be the key. Evolution shaped our physiology so that sex feels good; periodically, having sex for pleasure leads to childbirth, through which our genes are passed on. But consider this:

- in a study asking adolescents why they have sex, both genders cited peer pressure more often than sexual gratification (Stark, 1989)
- in the 1920s, British sex researcher Helena Wright found that most women she surveyed viewed sex as an unenjoyable marital duty (Kelly, 2001)
- in America about 10 per cent of men and 20 per cent of women report that sex is not pleasurable (Laumann et al., 1994).

In reality, people engage in sex to reproduce, obtain and give sensual pleasure, express love, foster intimacy, fulfil one's 'duty', conform to peer pressure, and a host of other reasons.

The Physiology of Sex

In 1953 Masters and Johnson began a landmark study in which they examined the sexual responses of 694 men and women under laboratory conditions. In total, they physiologically monitored about 10 000 sexual episodes.

The sexual response cycle   Masters and Johnson (1966) concluded that most people, when sexually aroused, go through a four-stage **sexual response cycle** of excitement, plateau, orgasm and resolution (Fig. 11.13). During the excitement phase, arousal builds rapidly. Blood flow increases to arteries in and around the genital organs, nipples and women's breasts, where it

Focus 11.7

Describe the sexual response cycle. How do hormones influence sex characteristics and sexual behaviour?

sexual response cycle

excitement, plateau, orgasm and resolution

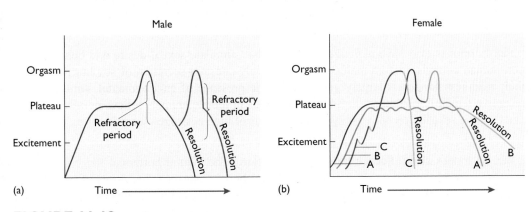

FIGURE 11.13

The human sexual response.

Masters and Johnson discovered a four-stage pattern of sexual response. (a) In males, there is a refractory period after orgasm during which no further response is possible. (b) In females, pattern A represents one or more orgasms followed by resolution, pattern B shows a plateau stage with no orgasm and pattern C shows an orgasm with no preceding plateau stage.

SOURCE: based on Masters and Johnson, 1966.

pools and causes these body areas to swell. The penis and clitoris begin to become erect, the vagina becomes lubricated and muscle tension increases throughout the body. In the *plateau phase*, arousal continues to build until there is enough muscle tension to trigger orgasm.

During the *orgasm phase* in males, rhythmic contractions of internal organs and muscle tissue surrounding the urethra project semen out of the penis. In females, orgasm involves rhythmic contractions of the outer third of the vagina, surrounding muscles and the uterus. In males, orgasm is ordinarily followed by a *resolution phase*, during which physiological arousal decreases rapidly and the genital organs return to their normal condition. During the resolution phase, males enter a *refractory period*, during which they are temporarily incapable of another orgasm. Females may have two or more successive orgasms before the onset of the resolution phase, but Masters and Johnson reported that most women experience only one. Of course, people may experience orgasm on some occasions but not others, and orgasm is not the only goal of all human sexual activity.

Hormonal influences   As with hunger, the hypothalamus plays a key role in sexual motivation. It controls the pituitary gland, which regulates the secretion of hormones called gonadotropins into the bloodstream. In turn, these hormones affect the rate at which the *gonads* (testes in the male and ovaries in the female) secrete *androgens*, the so-called masculine sex hormones such as *testosterone*, and *oestrogens*, the so-called feminine sex hormones such as *oestradiol*. Realize that despite these labels, both men and women produce androgens and oestrogens.

Sex hormones have *organizational effects* that direct the development of male and female sex characteristics (Byer et al., 2002). In the womb, male and female embryos form a primitive gonad that has the potential to develop into either testes or ovaries. If genetically male, the embryo forms testes about eight weeks after conception. Then, as the testes release sex hormones during a key period of pre-natal development, there typically is sufficient androgen activity to produce a male pattern of genital, reproductive, brain and other organ development. Years later, as part of this pattern, the hypothalamus stimulates an increased release of sex hormones from the testes when the male reaches puberty. In contrast, a genetically female embryo does not form testes, and in the absence of sufficient androgen activity during this pre-natal period, a female pattern of development ensues. As part of this pattern, at puberty the hypothalamus stimulates the release of sex hormones from the ovaries on a cyclical basis that regulates the female menstrual cycle.

Sex hormones also have *activational effects* that stimulate sexual desire and behaviour. In non-human animals, mature males have a relatively constant secretion of sex hormones, and their readiness for sex is largely governed by the presence of environmental stimuli (e.g., a receptive female). In contrast, hormonal secretions in female animals follow an *oestrus* cycle, and they are sexually receptive only during periods of high oestrogen secretion (i.e., when they are in heat).

Sex hormones also influence human sexual desire. The natural hormonal surge of puberty increases sexual motivation, as would an artificial boost from receiving doses of testosterone (Tuiten et al., 2000). But in humans, normal short-term hormonal fluctuations have relatively little effect on sexual arousability (Morrell et al., 1984). Desire does not go up and down like a yo-yo as blood levels of sex hormones change, and women may experience high sexual desire at any time during their menstrual cycle. Moreover, in men and women, androgens – rather than oestrogens – appear to have the primary influence on sexual desire (Hyde and DeLamater, 2003).

Focus 11.8

Discuss how psychological, cultural and environmental factors influence sexual behaviour.

The Psychology of Sex

Sexual arousal involves more than physiological responses. It typically begins with desire and a sexual stimulus that is perceived positively (Walen and Roth, 1987). Such stimuli can even be imaginary.

Sexual fantasy is an important component of many people's lives, although studies in Europe, South America and North America indicate that men sexually fantasize more often than women (Martinez and Raul, 2000). Fantasy nicely illustrates how mental processes can affect physiological functioning. Indeed, sexual fantasies alone may trigger genital erection and orgasm in some people and are often used to enhance arousal during masturbation.

Psychological factors can not only trigger sexual arousal but also inhibit it. A person may be engaged in sexual activity and then become turned off by something a partner does. A study in the USA found that about one in three women and one in six men report that they simply lack an interest in sex (Laumann et al., 1994). Other people desire sex but have difficulty becoming or staying aroused. Stress, fatigue and anger at one's partner can lead to temporary arousal problems. **Sexual dysfunction** refers to chronic, impaired sexual functioning that distresses a person. It may result from injuries, diseases and drug effects, but some causes are psychological. Arousal difficulties also may stem from performance anxiety or may be a psychological consequence of sexual assault or childhood sexual abuse (Rumstein and Hunsley, 2001).

sexual dysfunction
chronic, impaired sexual functioning that distresses a person

Cultural and Environmental Influences

Anyone who doubts culture's power to shape human behaviour need only examine sexual customs around the globe. During sex, most westerners probably do not poke a finger into their partner's ear, as do Trukese women of Micronesia, or bite off and then spit out hairs from their partner's eyebrow, as do South American Apinaye women (Hyde and DeLamater, 2003). You may find these practices unusual, but consider how some sexual techniques common in our culture – such as kissing – seem to members of other cultures: 'There are a few societies … in which kissing is unknown. For example, when the Thonga of Africa first saw Europeans kissing, they laughed and said, "Look at them; they eat each other's saliva and dirt"' (Hyde and DeLamater, 2003, pp. 10–11).

More important, the psychological meaning of sex itself depends on cultural contexts. Some societies and religions forbid premarital sex and may also prohibit public dress and behaviour that arouse sexual desire (Fig. 11.14). Many people who view themselves as very religious believe it is important to bring their sexual practices into harmony with their religious beliefs, which may condone sex only within marriage (Janus and Janus, 1993).

FIGURE 11.14

Habits of dress that many people take for granted in western societies, such as wearing bare-midriff shirts and short skirts, are unacceptable in other cultures because they would be considered sexually provocative.

In contrast, some societies openly encourage premarital sex. Among Marquesan Islanders of eastern Polynesia, families sleep together in one room, and children have ample opportunity to observe sexual activity. When boys and girls reach adolescence, a middle-aged adult of the opposite sex instructs them in sexual techniques and has intercourse with them. Having other sexual partners prior to marriage is considered normal (Frayser, 1985). Clearly, what is regarded as proper, moral and desirable varies enormously across cultures.

Environmental stimuli are pervasive and dependable elicitors of sexual desire and behaviour. Such stimuli are prominently displayed both in everyday life and in the media. On a daily basis across Europe and the USA, television shows present explicit scenes and sexual themes that would have been unthinkable half a century ago. The issue is pushed even further by the ready availability of pornography, a multibillion-dollar industry whose primary consumers are men. Social commentators and psychologists have raised the question of whether pornography affects men's sexual attitudes and fosters sexual violence towards women.

Focus 11.9

Describe what is known about the effects of watching violent pornography.

Many pornographic materials model *rape myths*, suggesting that men are entitled to sex and that women enjoy being coerced into sex. Correlational studies paint an ambiguous picture of links between pornography and sexual violence against women. Some countries with high rates of rape have little pornography, whereas others have a great deal. Conversely, in some countries pornography is widely available but rates of rape are low (Bauserman, 1996). Similarly, research with sex offenders shows that they do not differ from other men in amount or earliest age of exposure to pornography, and they are actually *less* aroused by non-violent pornography. Yet they are more aroused by violent pornography and are also more likely to act sexually after viewing violent or even non-violent pornography (Allen et al., 1995; 2000).

Controlled experiments paint a clearer causal picture. In some studies, male university students were randomly assigned to view material whose content was either neutral (i.e., non-sexual), sexually explicit but non-violent (e.g., a couple having consensual sex) or sexually aggressive (e.g., a rape-myth depiction showing a woman who initially resists sexual assault but then becomes a willing participant). Later, the students interacted with another person (a female or male accomplice of the experimenter), who made errors on a learning task. Participants were instructed to punish the person with an electric shock for each error, but they were free to choose the shock intensity and thus the aggression by giving stronger shocks. (The accomplice did not really receive any shock.)

The strongest experimental effects emerged when participants viewed violent pornography (Malamuth et al., 2000). At least temporarily, this increased men's tendency to aggression towards women but not towards other men. However, certain types of people, such as those who reported the greatest attraction to sexual violence, were most strongly affected by viewing it. In addition to its connection with aggression, pornography also promotes a belief that sex is impersonal. An unwelcome side effect is that exposure to pornography decreases viewers' satisfaction with their own sexual partners (Donnerstein and Malamuth, 1997).

Sexual Orientation

sexual orientation

one's emotional and erotic preference for partners of a particular sex

Sexual orientation refers to one's emotional and erotic preference for partners of a particular sex. Determining one's sexual orientation seems simple: Heterosexuals prefer opposite-sex partners, homosexuals prefer same-sex partners, and bisexuals are sexually attracted to members of both sexes. So how would you classify the sexual orientation of these two 25-year-olds?

- Susan feels sexually attracted to men and women, but she has had sex only with men and thinks of herself as heterosexual.

- Keith has had sex with other men twice since puberty, yet he is not attracted to men and views himself as heterosexual.

Some researchers view sexual orientation as a single dimension ranging from 'exclusively heterosexual' to 'exclusively homosexual', with 'equally heterosexual and homosexual' at the midway point. But others argue that sexual orientation has three dimensions: *self-identity*, *sexual attraction* and *actual sexual behaviour* (Kelly, 2001).

Determinants of sexual orientation   Theories about the origins of sexual orientation abound. An early and unsupported biological view proposed that homosexual and heterosexual males differ in their adult levels of sex hormones. Other early theories hypothesized that male homosexuality develops when boys grow up with a weak, ineffectual father and identify with a domineering mother, or that being sexually seduced by an adult homosexual causes children to divert their sex drive towards members of their own sex.

All of these theories have taken a scientific beating. In one study, Alan Bell and co-workers (1981) interviewed nearly 1000 homosexual and over 500 heterosexual men and women. They searched extensively for childhood or adolescent experiences that might predict adult sexual orientation, but only one consistent pattern emerged: even in childhood, homosexual men and women felt that they were somehow different from their same-sex peers and were more likely to engage in *gender-nonconforming behaviours*. Similarly, compared with heterosexual women, homosexual women in Brazil, Peru, the Philippines and the USA were about twice as likely during childhood to be considered tomboys and to be interested in boys' clothes and toys (Whitam and Mathy, 1991). Study after study has obtained similar results (Cohen, 2002).

So why do such patterns arise? Highly publicized studies appeared in the early 1990s reporting anatomical differences in the brains of heterosexual versus homosexual men and identifying a genetic marker shared by some homosexual men. Subsequent research, however, has not consistently replicated these findings (Lasco et al., 2002). Nonetheless, there is growing evidence that heredity influences human sexual orientation. In one study, among gay men who had a brother, the concordance rates for sexual orientation (i.e., the brother was gay also) were 52 per cent among identical twins, 22 per cent among fraternal twins and 11 per cent among adoptive brothers (Bailey and Pillard, 1991). A later study of homosexual women yielded similar results (Bailey et al., 1993). Thus the closer the genetic relatedness, the higher the concordance rates for sexual orientation (Kirk et al., 2000).

Another perspective suggests that the brain develops a neural pattern that predisposes an individual to prefer either female or male sex partners, depending on whether pre-natal sex-hormone activity follows a masculine or feminine path (Rahman, 2005). Experimentally altering animals' pre-natal exposure to sex hormones can influence their sexual orientation. Moreover, in rare cases among humans, some genetically male foetuses are insensitive to their own androgen secretions and some female foetuses experience an atypical build-up of androgens. Studies of these individuals suggest a relation between pre-natal sex-hormone exposure and adulthood sexual orientation (Williams et al., 2000). Of course, the human research is correlational and must be interpreted cautiously. For example, male foetuses who have androgen insensitivity develop the external anatomy of females and are typically raised as girls; socialization could account for their sexual orientation.

What about environmental influences? Even among identical twins, when one is homosexual, often the other is heterosexual. Thus a biological predisposition and socialization experiences may combine to determine sexual orientation. At present, scientists simply do not know what all the factors are. It is also possible, argues Bem (1996; 2001), that heredity affects sexual orientation only indirectly, by influencing children's basic personality style. He proposes that different personality styles then steer children towards gender-conforming or gender-nonconforming activities, causing them to feel similar to or different from same-sex peers. Ultimately, this affects their attraction to same-sex and opposite-sex peers. Bem's theory has mixed support and needs further testing (Bailey et al., 2000; Peplau et al., 1998).

FIGURE 11.15

Homosexuality: the fraternal birth order effect.

The presence of each older brother increases by about one third the relative probability that a later-born male child will be gay. Thus if there is a 2 per cent probability that a man with no older brothers is gay, then the probability for a man with one older brother is about 2.6 to 2.7 per cent, roughly a one-third relative increase.

SOURCE: adapted from Blanchard and Bogaert, 1996.

Finally, there may be multiple paths towards developing a sexual orientation, and the paths for men and women may differ. Consider the intriguing finding shown in Figure 11.15: the greater the number of older brothers (but not older sisters) a newborn boy has, the greater the probability that he will develop a homosexual orientation. In contrast, a woman's sexual orientation is not related to the number of older sisters or brothers in the family. Ray Blanchard (2001), the leading researcher of this *fraternal birth order effect*, has found it in 14 studies, involving over 7000 total participants.

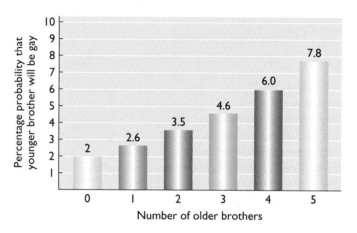

WHAT DO YOU THINK?

FRATERNAL BIRTH ORDER AND MALE HOMOSEXUALITY

Why might having older brothers increase the odds that a later-born male will have a homosexual orientation? Think about possible explanations, then see p. 526.

IN REVIEW

- During sexual intercourse, people often experience a four-stage physiological response pattern consisting of excitement, plateau, orgasm and resolution.

- Sex hormones have organizational effects that guide pre-natal organ development along either a male or female pattern. Sex hormones also have activational effects that influence sexual desire.

- Sexual fantasy can trigger arousal, whereas psychological difficulties can interfere with sexual arousal. Cultural norms help determine the sexual practices and beliefs that are considered proper.

- Environmental stimuli affect sexual desire. Viewing sexual violence reinforces men's belief in rape myths and generally increases men's aggression towards women, at least temporarily.

- Sexual orientation involves dimensions of self-identity, sexual attraction and actual sexual behaviour. Scientists still do not know conclusively what determines an individual's sexual orientation.

SOCIAL MOTIVATION

What makes your life most meaningful? To many people, close relationships are one key. Abraham Maslow (1954) viewed belongingness as a basic psychological need, and considerable research indicates that, indeed, 'the need to belong is a powerful, fundamental, and extremely pervasive motivation' (Baumeister and Leary, 1995, p. 497).

Why Do We Affiliate?

Humans are social beings who affiliate in many ways; in peer groups, in families, with work colleagues and, even, in the bus queue with strangers. Some theorists propose that over the course of evolution, individuals whose biological make-up predisposed them to affiliate were more likely to survive and reproduce than those who were reclusive. By affording greater access to sexual mates, more protection from predators, an efficient division of labour and the passing of knowledge across generations, a socially oriented lifestyle had considerable adaptive value (Kottak, 2000).

> **Focus 11.10**
> Discuss evolutionary and psychological views of affiliation and factors that influence the desire to affiliate.

In today's world, research has shown that positive social relationships are important contributors to life satisfaction (Diener et al., 2006; Haller and Hadler, 2006). Social relationships also help insulate us from stressors in our lives. One recent study showed that simply holding the hand of another person during a stressful event can lower physiological arousal (Coan et al., 2006).

Craig Hill (1987) suggested that we affiliate for four basic psychological reasons:

- to obtain positive stimulation
- to receive emotional support
- to gain attention
- to permit social comparison.

Social comparison involves comparing our beliefs, feelings and behaviours with those of other people. This helps us determine whether our responses are 'normal' and enables us to judge the level of our cognitive and physical abilities (Festinger, 1954).

> **social comparison**
> comparing our beliefs, feelings and behaviours with those of other people

People differ in how strongly they desire friendship. In one study, university students who scored high on a personality test of 'need for affiliation' made more friends during the semester than students who scored low (Byrne and Greendlinger, 1989). In another study, secondary school students wore beepers over a one-week period. They were signalled approximately every two hours, at which time they recorded their thoughts and activities. Participants with a high need for affiliation were more likely than their peers to report that they were thinking about friends and wishing that they could be with people (Wong and Csikszentmihalyi, 1991). Still even people with strong affiliation needs, however, usually desire some time alone. Conversely, people with lower affiliation needs still seek periodic social contact. Some theorists, therefore, view affiliation needs within a homeostatic model (O'Connor and Rosenblood, 1996). They propose that each of us has our own optimal range of social contact. After periods when contact exceeds that range, we compensate by temporarily seeking more solitude. After periods when social contact falls below the optimal range, we increase our effort to be with others. Although some human and animal findings are consistent with this model, it needs much more testing.

Many studies have shown, however, that situational factors influence our tendency to affiliate. For example, fear-inducing situations increase our desire to be with others. During emergencies, as in the aftermath of earthquakes, floods and hurricanes, many people find themselves bonding with strangers. When afraid, we may prefer to be with others who face the same situation we do, which helps us gauge the normalcy of our reactions (Schachter, 1959).

When possible, we seem to desire most strongly to be with others who have already been through the same or similar situations (Kulik and Mahler, 2000). Doing so can provide us with information about what to expect. In one study, hospital patients awaiting open-heart surgery expressed a stronger desire to have room-mates who already had been through surgery than pre-operative room-mates like themselves. In a later study, when patients were actually assigned post-operative rather than pre-operative room-mates, they became less anxious and later recovered from surgery more quickly (Kulik et al., 1996).

Being rejected or excluded from social relationships is a painful event for most people, and exclusion evokes a desire for social reconnection. In one set of experiments, threat of social exclusion caused university students to express greater interest in working with others and making new friends, and to provide more rewards to their new interaction and partners (Maner et al., 2007).

IN REVIEW

- Humans seek to affiliate in many ways. Affiliation has adaptive advantages and allows people to obtain positive stimulation, receive emotional support, gain attention and engage in social comparison.

- People differ in how strongly they need to affiliate, and some theorists view affiliative behaviour as governed by homeostatic principles.

- Situations that induce fear often increase people's tendency to affiliate. When afraid, people often seek the company of others who have been through or are currently experiencing the same or a similar situation.

- Some reliable sex differences occur in people's mating strategies and preferences, such as men's tendency to seek younger women and women's tendency to seek older men.

- Social exclusion is a painful experience for most people, and it often leads to attempts to reconnect socially in new relationships.

ACHIEVEMENT MOTIVATION

In striving to create an independent republic of India, Lal Bahadur exemplified the desire to achieve. As a university student, you are keenly aware of society's emphasis on achievement, and you know that whether in school, sports, music or other fields, some people seek out and thrive on challenges and others do not. In the 1950s, David McClelland, John Atkinson, and their co-workers (1953) began to explore individual differences in **need for achievement**, a positive desire to accomplish tasks and compete successfully with standards of excellence.

need for achievement

a positive desire to accomplish tasks and compete successfully with standards of excellence

Motive for Success and Fear of Failure

McClelland and Atkinson proposed that achievement behaviour can stem from a positively oriented *motive for success* and a negatively oriented motivation to avoid failure, more commonly called *fear of failure*. Need for achievement is the positive orientation towards success. In terms of the behavioural activation and behavioural inhibition systems discussed earlier, motive for success is the part of the BAS that relates to the achievement domain. Fear of failure is a BIS function.

McClelland and Atkinson measured the motive for success with a psychological test that asked participants to write stories in response to a number of pictures, such as the one in

Figure 11.16. The stories were then analysed for achievement-relevant themes using a standardized coding system. The avoidance motive, fear of failure, was measured by psychological tests that asked people to report how much anxiety they experienced in achievement situations. McClelland and Atkinson found that their measures of need for achievement and fear of failure were independent (uncorrelated) dimensions, so that people could be high in both motives, low in both, or high in one and low in the other.

People who have a strong motive for success seek the thrill of victory, whereas those motivated by fear of failure seek to avoid the agony of defeat. Common sense suggests that a strong motive for success combined with a strong fear of failure might lead a person to perform better than someone who is motivated only by a desire for success. But this is not so. The anxiety associated with fear of failure can negate the impact of the need for achievement and can impair performance. In sports, the athlete with a high fear of failure is the one who tends to succumb to pressure (Smith, 1996).

People high in achievement and low in fear of failure, called *high-need achievers*, do not necessarily outperform low-need achievers when conditions are relaxed and tasks are easy. However, when tasks are challenging or the importance of doing well is stressed, high-need achievers outshine low-need achievers. They perform at a higher level, and they are more persistent when they encounter barriers to achievement (McClelland, 1989). In general, high-need achievers are most likely to strive hard for success when they perceive themselves as personally responsible for the outcome, when they perceive some risk of not succeeding, and when there is an opportunity to receive performance feedback (Koestner and McClelland, 1990).

When given a choice of performing a task that is very easy (a high probability of success), moderately difficult (a 40 to 60 per cent probability of success) or very difficult (a low probability of success), which do you predict that high-need achievers will choose? Contrary to what you might expect, they prefer intermediate risks to extremely high or low risks because the outcome – success versus failure – *is most uncertain* (Atkinson and Birch, 1978). In contrast, low-need achievers are more likely to choose tasks that are easy (where success is almost assured) or very difficult (where success is not expected, so that nothing is on the line).

To understand this pattern, realize that it is the individual's *perception* of outcome uncertainty that counts. For most of us, the probability of successfully climbing Mount Everest is virtually zero. But to highly trained mountaineers, the task is neither impossible nor easy. Decades ago, sociologist and mountain climber Dick Emerson (1966) joined a Mount Everest expedition. As he predicted, the team members' communications with one another throughout the long climb struck a balance between optimistic and pessimistic comments about the chances of reaching their goal. This kept the climbers' perceived chance of success or failure close to 50:50 and maintained maximum motivation.

Achievement Goal Theory

Another way to understand achievement motivation is to examine the success goals that people seek to attain in task situations. **Achievement goal theory** focuses on the manner in which success is defined both by the individual and within the achievement situation itself. At the individual level, achievement goal theorists are interested in the achievement goal orientation that people have (Dweck, 1999). They differentiate between a **mastery orientation**, in which the focus is on personal improvement, giving maximum effort and perfecting new skills, and an

FIGURE 11.16

Pictures like this are used to elicit stories that are scored for the motive to succeed. Which of the following two stories, written by different people, reflects a stronger motive to succeed? (1) This young man is sitting in school, but he is dreaming about the day when he will become a doctor. He will study and work harder than anyone else. He goes on to become one of the top medical researchers in the world. (2) The boy is daydreaming about how much he hates being in school. . . . He would like to run away from home and just take it easy on a tropical island. However, he is doomed to be in the rat race the rest of his life.

Focus 11.11
How do the motives and task behaviours of high- versus low-need achievers differ? Describe the achievement goal orientations and motivational climates in achievement goal theory.

achievement goal theory
focuses on the manner in which success is defined both by the individual and within the achievement situation itself

mastery orientation
focus is on personal improvement, giving maximum effort and perfecting new skills

ego orientation

the goal is to outperform others (hopefully, with as little effort as possible)

motivational climate

situation which encourages or rewards either a mastery approach or an ego approach to defining success

ego orientation, in which the goal is to outperform others (hopefully, with as little effort as possible). At the situational level, the theory focuses on the **motivational climate** that encourages or rewards either a mastery approach or an ego approach to defining success (Fig. 11.17).

FIGURE 11.17

Achievement goal theory.

Achievement goal theory focuses on the ways in which success is defined, both by individuals and within achievement environments. Individuals may have mastery or ego goal orientations, and the motivational climate created in achievement situations by significant others may emphasize and support mastery goals, such as effort and skill improvement, or ego definitions of success, such as outperforming others.

Achievement Goal Orientations

Another way to understand achievement motivation is to examine the goals that people seek to attain in task situations. Think for a moment of a class you are taking. On a scale of 1 ('not at true of me') to 7 ('very true of me'), rate statements:

1. I want to learn as much as possible from this class.
2. I am motivated by the thought of outperforming the other students in this class.
3. My goal is to avoid learning less than I possibly could in this class.
4. The main thing is to avoid doing more poorly than the others in this class.

These statements represent four different achievement goals, two of which are approach goals and two of which are avoidance or fear of failure goals (Curry et al., 2006; Elliot and McGregor, 2001). **Mastery-approach goals** (statement 1) focus on the desire to master a task and learn new knowledge or skills, whereas **ego-approach goals** (statement 2) reflect a competitive orientation that focuses on being judged favourably relative to other people. On the avoidance side, **mastery-avoidance goals** (statement 3) reflect a fear of not performing up to one's own standards, whereas **ego-avoidance goals** (statement 4) centre on avoiding being outperformed by others. These four goals are embodied in a 2 (definitions of success) × 2 (approach vs avoidance) framework as different motivational approaches (Fig. 11.17). According to the **2 × 2 achievement goal theory**, each of us can be described in terms of an 'achievement motivation profile' using statements such as the four above. In one sample of university students, Van Yperen (2006) found that 34.4 per cent were highest in mastery-approach, 13.7 per cent in ego-approach, 33.6 per cent in mastery-avoidance and 18.3 per cent in ego-avoidance. Men were twice as likely as women to report ego-avoidance goals and women were more likely than men to report mastery-avoidance goals. No sex differences were apparent in the two approach-goal orientations.

mastery-approach goals

the desire to master a task and learn new knowledge or skills

ego-approach goals

a competitive orientation that focuses on being judged favourably relative to other people

mastery-avoidance goals

a fear of not performing up to one's own standards

ego-avoidance goals

avoiding being outperformed by others

2 × 2 achievement goal theory

each of us can be described in terms of an 'achievement motivation profile'

The 2 × 2 achievement goal framework is relatively new, but already preliminary results indicate that the four motives have different relations to other variables (Schunk et al., 2007). University students' achievement goals for a particular class, measured early in the academic term, help predict their psychological responses to the course as well as their course performance. Students with dominant mastery-approach motivation have higher intrinsic motivation to learn the material, perceive examinations as a positive challenge, and rate the course as more interesting and enjoyable. Students with ego-avoidance motivation show exactly the opposite pattern. They lack intrinsic motivation, perceive examinations as anxiety-provoking threats, report low levels of interest and enjoyment, and perform more poorly than any other motivational group. Interestingly, ego-approach motivation is most strongly associated with high performance, but with less intrinsic motivation and enjoyment than mastery-approach motivation. Finally, in relation to intrinsic motivation, enjoyment, and feelings of competence, mastery-avoidance motivation seems more positive than ego-avoidance motivation and less positive than mastery-approach motivation, but it bears little relation to quality of performance (Curry et al., 2006; Van Yperen, 2006).

By incorporating both desire for success and fear of failure into one theory, the 2 × 2 framework represents a promising approach to understanding the various forms that achievement-related motives can take. Where performance in academic settings is concerned, the optimal motivational pattern may be a combination of mastery-approach and ego-approach goals. The mastery-approach goal enhances enjoyment and interest in the activity, and the ego-approach goal fosters higher performance within the competitive college environment, where grades are often determined by one's performance relative to others (Harackiewicz et al., 2002; McGregor and Elliot, 2002). The same may be true within competitive sports settings (McArdle and Duda, 2002).

Not all people are high on both mastery and ego orientations, however. If you are going to be high on one or the other, which would be preferable? Although both goal orientations contribute to success, in achievement contexts ranging from academic to work and sport settings, research indicates that a mastery goal orientation has several psychological advantages over an ego orientation (Dweck, 1999; McArdle and Duda, 2002). When success is defined as 'being one's best' rather than 'competing with others', people can focus on and enjoy their own improvement and accomplishments. They are more likely to experience intrinsic motivation and enjoyment of the activity, persist in the face of difficulties, select challenging goals and exert maximum effort.

For an ego-oriented person, experiencing personal improvement or knowing that one did one's best would not in itself occasion feelings of success or competence. Indeed, knowing that one tried hard and failed to outperform others would cause an ego-oriented person to feel especially incompetent. If ego-oriented people begin to question their ability to meet performance demands or to compete successfully with others, they are more likely to reduce persistence and avoid the challenge at hand (Nicholls, 1989). This would be especially likely in those high in the avoidance variant of ego orientation (Elliott and Church, 1997). If you turn winning and losing at everyday tasks into life-or-death situations, it seems likely that problems will arise. For one thing, you will be dead a lot.

Motivational climate Besides individual differences in goal orientations, situational factors influence how success is defined. The motivational climate of an achievement setting is influenced by significant others, such as parents, teachers, coaches and supervisors (Ames, 1992; Chi, 2004). In an ego-involving climate, performers are compared with one another, urged to compete to be the best, and those who perform best get special attention. In a mastery-involving climate, effort, enjoyment of the activity and personal improvement are emphasized and rewarded. The assumption is that if people work to achieve their potential and give maximum effort, winning will take care of itself. These differing conceptions of success can have strong effects on participants. In children, they help shape the achievement goal orientation(s) that are internalized.

Mastery-involving achievement environments have been linked to a variety of positive effects in school and sport settings. They foster higher intrinsic motivation and enjoyment of the setting, enhance perceptions of learning and mastery, and bolster self-esteem. Performance anxiety is also lower in such settings because the emphasis is on doing one's best (which is personally controllable) rather than on a win outcome that is dependent in part on how others perform. An ego-involving climate fosters the belief that ability, rather than hard work, leads to success, and satisfaction is gained by outperforming others rather than through skill improvement. At the level of task performance, mastery climates result in better skill development and higher performance levels, due in part to increased effort, greater enjoyment, and lowered anxiety (Dweck, 1999; McArdle and Duda, 2002).

Attempts to influence motivational climate have yielded encouraging results. When youth sport coaches were trained to create a mastery environment, their young athletes showed increased mastery-approach motivation and reduced fear of failure over the course of the sport season (Smith et al., 2007; Smoll et al, 2007).

Family, Culture and Achievement Needs

Focus 11.12

How do family and cultural factors influence achievement motivation?

How does achievement motivation develop? Providing a cognitively stimulating home environment fosters children's intrinsic motivation to perform academic tasks (Gottfried et al., 1998). And when parents or other key caregivers encourage and reward achievement but do not punish failure, they foster a strong motive for success (Koestner and McClelland, 1990). Conversely, fear of failure seems to develop when caregivers take successful achievement for granted but punish failure, thereby teaching the child to dread the possibility of failing (Weiner, 1992). Providing a mastery motivational climate in the home, the school, and the athletic setting also encourages the development of a mastery achievement orientation (Dweck, 1999, McArdle and Duda, 2002).

Cultural norms also shape achievement motivation. Individualistic cultures, such as those in Europe and North America, tend to stress personal achievement. In cultures that nurture collectivism, such as those in China and Japan, achievement motivation more strongly reflects a desire to fit into the family and social group, meet its expectations and work for its goals (Markus and Kitayama, 1991). Chinese secondary school students, for example, typically care more about meeting their parents' expectations for academic success than do American students (Chen and Lan, 1998). In collectivistic Japan, business organizations have traditionally adopted the concept of *kaizen* (continuous improvement), encouraging workers to develop skills and increase productivity (Elsey and Fujiwara, 2000). Such companies assume responsibility for their employees' welfare, promote them gradually and are willing to retain them for life. In turn, the workers are more strongly motivated by loyalty to their managers and to the organization as the company becomes integral to their identities.

At the same time, the human desire to achieve transcends culture and can manifest itself in intriguing ways. Throughout history, some people have left their homelands to seek adventure or better lives elsewhere. Might achievement motivation relate to the desire to emigrate? To answer this question, researchers measured the achievement motivation of university students in Albania, the Czech Republic and Slovenia, and asked students where they would like to live for most of their adult lives. In each sample, students who expressed a desire to emigrate had higher average achievement motivation scores than students who said they wanted to remain in their homeland (Boneva et al., 1998).

IN REVIEW

- High-need achievers have a strong motive for success and relatively low fear of failure. They tend to seek moderately difficult tasks that are challenging but attainable. Low-need achievers are more likely to choose easy tasks, where success is assured, or very difficult tasks where success is not expected.

- Mastery, ego-approach, and ego-avoidance goals are four basic achievement goals. Mastery goals are associated with viewing achievement tasks as a positive challenge, whereas ego-avoidance goals are linked to viewing such tasks as threatening. Ego-approach goals are most strongly linked to eventual course grades for college students, mastery goals to course enjoyment.

- Compared with ego-involving environments, mastery-involving motivational climates foster higher enjoyment and intrinsic motivation, greater feelings of self-determination, lower levels of performance anxiety, and better learning of skills, greater effort and higher performance.

- Child-rearing and cultural factors influence the nature and expression of achievement motivation.

MOTIVATIONAL CONFLICT

Motivational goals sometimes conflict with one another. Our desires to achieve success and to have fun may clash, for example, when we must choose between studying for an examination and attending a party. When something attracts us, we tend to approach it; when something repels us, we tend to avoid it. Different combinations of these tendencies can produce three basic types of conflict.

Approach–approach conflict occurs when we face two attractive alternatives and selecting one means losing the other. Conflict is greatest when both alternatives, such as a choice between two desirable careers, are equally attractive. In contrast, **avoidance–avoidance conflict** occurs when we must choose between two undesirable alternatives (Fig. 11.18). Do I study boring material for an examination, or do I skip studying and fail? **Approach–avoidance conflict** involves being attracted to and repelled by the same goal. A squirrel being offered food by a person on a park bench is motivated by hunger to approach and by fear to keep its distance. A man desires an intimate relationship with a woman but fears the possibility of future rejection.

Approach and avoidance tendencies grow stronger as we get nearer to a desired goal (Miller, 1944). Usually, the avoidance

Focus 11.13

Explain and illustrate three types of motivational conflict.

THE FAR SIDE®   BY GARY LARSON

"C'mon, c'mon—it's either one or the other."

FIGURE 11.18

An unfortunate avoidance–avoidance conflict.

approach-approach conflict

when we face two attractive alternatives and selecting one means losing the other

avoidance–avoidance conflict

when we must choose between two undesirable alternatives

approach–avoidance conflict

being attracted to and repelled by the same goal

tendency increases in strength faster than the approach (Fig. 11.19). Thus at first we may be attracted to a goal and only slightly repelled by its drawbacks, but as we get closer to it the negative aspects become dominant. We may stop, retreat, approach again and continue to vacillate in a state of conflict. However, the general strength of approach and avoidance tendencies differs across people. Behavioural activation system-dominated individuals are more attuned to positive stimuli and the possibility of obtaining desired outcomes, whereas those with strong BIS tendencies are more sensitive to actual and anticipated negative outcomes (Elliot and Thrash, 2002; Sutton, 2002).

FIGURE 11.19

Approach–avoidance conflict.

According to Neal Miller (1944), the tendency to approach and the tendency to avoid grow stronger as one moves closer to the goal. However, the tendency to avoid increases faster than the tendency to approach. Maximum conflict is experienced where the two gradients cross, because at this point the opposing motives are equal in strength.

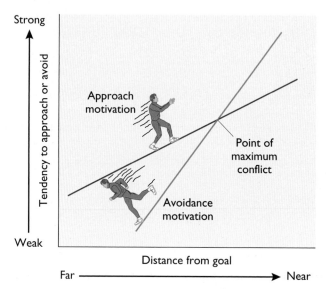

IN REVIEW

- Motivational goals may conflict with one another. Approach–approach conflict occurs when a person has to select between two attractive alternatives, whereas avoidance–avoidance conflict involves choosing between two undesirable alternatives.

- Approach–avoidance conflict occurs when we are attracted to and repelled by the same goal.

EMOTION

emotions

feeling (or affect) states that involve a pattern of cognitive, physiological and behavioural reactions to events

Focus 11.14

In what ways are negative and positive emotions adaptive?

Life without emotion would be bland and empty. Our experiences of love, anger, joy, fear and other emotions energize and add colour to our lives. **Emotions** are feeling (or affect) states that involve a pattern of cognitive, physiological and behavioural reactions to events. Emotion theorist Richard Lazarus (2001) believes that motivation and emotions are always linked, because we react emotionally only when our motives and goals are gratified, threatened, or frustrated (Fig. 11.20).

The intimate relations between motivation and emotion are seen in the strong emotional responses that occur when important goals are either attained or lost.

Emotions have important adaptive functions. Some emotions, such as fear and alarm, are part of an emergency arousal system that increases our chances of survival, as when we fight or flee when confronted by threat or danger. But positive emotions, such as interest, joy, excitement,

FIGURE 11.20

The intimate relations between motivation and emotion are seen in the strong emotional responses that occur when important goals are either attained or lost.

contentment and love, also have important adaptive functions. They help us form intimate relationships and broaden our thinking and behaviour so that we explore, consider new ideas, try out new ways to achieve goals, play and savour what we have (Fredrickson, 1998).

Emotions are also an important form of social communication. By providing clues about our internal states and intentions, emotions influence how other people behave towards us (Isaacs, 1998). Consider, for example, the effects of a baby's crying on adults, who generally respond with caretaking behaviours that have obvious survival value for the infant. Adults' expressions of sadness and distress also evoke concern, empathy and helping behaviour from others.

Positive emotional expressions also pay off. A smiling infant is likely to increase parents' feelings of affection and caring, thereby increasing the likelihood that the child's biological and emotional needs will be satisfied. Happy adults also tend to attract others and to have richer and more supportive relationships (Diener et al., 2006).

Positive emotions are an important part of life satisfaction, and negative emotions foster unhappiness (Diener et al., 2006). Negative emotions also are typically involved in normal stress reactions (Evans-Martin, 2007) and in many psychological disorders (Rottenberg and Johnson, 2007). The ability to self-regulate one's emotions is one mark of psychological adjustment (Denollet et al., 2007; Garber Dodge, 2007).

THE NATURE OF EMOTIONS

Our emotional states share four common features:

1. Emotions are triggered by external or internal *eliciting stimuli*.
2. Emotional responses result from our *appraisals* of these stimuli, which give the situation its perceived meaning and significance.
3. Our *bodies respond physiologically* to our appraisals. We may become physically aroused, as when we feel fear, joy or anger; or we may experience decreased arousal, as when we feel contentment or depression.
4. Emotions include *behaviour tendencies*. Some are *expressive behaviours* (e.g., smiling with joy, crying). Others are *instrumental behaviours*, ways of doing something about the stimulus that evoked the emotion (e.g., studying for an anxiety-arousing test, fighting back in self-defence).

Figure 11.21 illustrates the general relations among these four emotional components. For example, an insulting remark from another person (eliciting stimulus) may evoke a cognitive appraisal that we have been unfairly demeaned, an increase in physiological arousal, a clenching of jaws and fists (expressive behaviour), and a verbal attack on the other person (instrumental

Focus 11.15

Describe the 4 major components of emotion and how they influence one another.

FIGURE 11.21

Components of emotion.

Emotion involves relations between eliciting stimuli, cognitive appraisal processes, physiological arousal, expressive behaviours and instrumental behaviours. Note the reciprocal (two-way) causal relations that exist among the appraisal, physiological arousal and behavioural components. Appraisal influences arousal and expressive behaviours, and the latter affect ongoing appraisals.

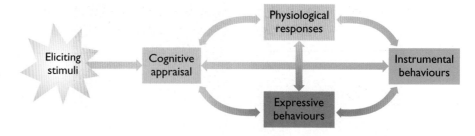

eliciting stimuli

trigger cognitive appraisals and emotional responses

behaviour). As the two-way arrows indicate, these emotional components can affect one another, so that our thoughts influence our feelings and our feelings influence our appraisals (Frijda et al., 2005). They exist in a larger associative network that also includes links to motives, memories, ideas and action tendencies. Stimulation of any of the network's components can trigger other elements, depending on the strengths of the associative links (Berkowitz and Harmon-Jones, 2004). For example, some people can generate strong anger and a tendency towards aggression just by recalling an event in which they were wronged. We will discuss other linkages as well. Thus emotion is a dynamic, ongoing *process*, and any of its four elements can change rapidly in the course of an emotional episode.

Eliciting Stimuli

Emotions do not occur in a vacuum. They are responses to situations, people, objects or events. We become angry *at* something or someone; fearful or proud *of* something; in love *with* someone. Moreover, the **eliciting stimuli** that trigger cognitive appraisals and emotional responses are not always external; they can be internal stimuli, such as a mental image of an upcoming holiday that makes us feel happy or a memory of an unpleasant encounter that arouses anger in us.

Innate biological factors help determine which stimuli have the greatest potential to arouse emotions (Panksepp, 2005). Newborn infants come equipped with the capacity to respond emotionally with either interest or distress to events in their environment (Galati and Lavelli, 1997). Adults, too, may be biologically primed to experience emotions in response to certain stimuli that have evolutionary significance. As we saw in Chapter 7, this may help explain why the majority of human phobias involve 'primal' stimuli such as heights, water, sharks, snakes or spiders, rather than modern threats such as guns, electrical transformers and automobiles (Öhman and Wiens, 2005). A wide variety of aversive stimuli – pain, heat and cold, foul odours – can evoke anger and aggressive tendencies towards people who had nothing to do with creating the discomfort (Berkowitz and Harmon-Jones, 2004).

Learning also influences our emotions. Previous experiences can turn certain people or situations into eliciting stimuli. The mere sight of one's lover can evoke feelings of passion; the sight of a disliked person can trigger instantaneous revulsion that seems almost reflexive. On the broadest level, cultures have different standards for defining the good, the bad and the ugly that affect how we appraise and respond to stimuli. Physical features that provoke sexual arousal and feelings of infatuation in one culture, such as ornamental facial scars, may elicit quite different feelings in another.

The Cognitive Component

Cognitions (thoughts, images, memories, interpretations) are involved in virtually every aspect of emotion. Mental processes can evoke emotional responses. They are part of our inner experience of the emotion, and they influence how we express our emotions and act on them. A situation may evoke pleasure or distress, depending on how we appraise it. For example, a sexual advance may elicit anger, fear or disgust instead of pleasure if it is unwanted or deemed inappropriate. **Cognitive appraisals** are the interpretations and meanings that we attach to sensory stimuli.

cognitive appraisals

the interpretations and meanings that we attach to sensory stimuli

Both conscious and unconscious processes are involved in appraisals (Feldman-Barrett et al., 2007). Often we are not consciously aware of the appraisals that underlie emotional responses. Some appraisals seem to involve little more than an almost automatic interpretation of sensory input based on previous conditioning (Smith and Kirby, 2004). Indeed, most strong emotions are probably triggered initially in this automatic fashion, after which we may appraise the situation in a more reasoning manner. Even at this more 'cognitive' level, however, our habitual ways of thinking can run off in a subconscious shorthand with little or no awareness on our part (Clore and Centebar, 2004; Phelps, 2005). We often fail to appreciate how arbitrarily we interpret 'the way things are'.

The idea that emotional reactions are triggered by cognitive appraisals rather than external situations helps account for the fact that different people (or even the same person at different times) can have different emotional reactions to the same object, situation, or person (Fig. 11.22).

Culture and appraisal   Cross-cultural researchers have asked people in various countries to recall events that triggered certain emotions and to answer questions about how they appraised or interpreted the situations. In one study conducted in 27 different countries, people exhibited strong cross-cultural similarities in the types of appraisals that evoked joy, fear, anger, sadness, disgust, shame and guilt (Wallbott and Scherer, 1988). Whenever any of these emotions occurred, similar appraisals were involved, regardless of the culture.

Despite these cross-cultural commonalities in appraisal, particular situations can evoke different appraisals and emotional reactions, depending on one's culture (Mesquita and Markus, 2005). Consider, for example, the circumstance of being alone. Tahitians often appraise being alone as an opportunity for bad spirits to bother a person, and fear is the most common emotional response. In the close-knit Utku Inuit, an Eskimo culture, being alone signifies social rejection and isolation, triggering sadness and loneliness. In western cultures, being alone may at times represent a welcome respite from the frantic pace of daily life, evoking contentment and happiness (Mesquita et al., 1997). Thus, where appraisals are concerned, there seem to be certain universals but also some degree of cultural diversity in the more subtle aspects of interpreting situations.

FIGURE 11.22

Differences in appraisal can trigger entirely different emotional reactions, as in this instance. What kinds of appraisals are likely occurring in these people?

IN REVIEW

- An emotion is a positive or negative feeling (or affective) state consisting of a pattern of cognitive, physiological and behavioural reactions to events that have relevance to important goals or motives. Emotions further our well-being in several ways: by rousing us to action, by helping us communicate with others, and by eliciting empathy and help.

- The primary components of emotion are the eliciting stimuli, cognitive appraisals, physiological arousal, and expressive and instrumental behaviours. Innate factors and learning play important roles in determining the arousal properties of stimuli.

- The cognitive component of emotional experience involves the evaluative and personal appraisal of the eliciting stimuli. Initial appraisals often occur in an automatic fashion that involves little thinking. The ability of thoughts to elicit emotional arousal has been demonstrated clinically and in experimental research. Cross-cultural research indicates considerable agreement across cultures in the appraisals that evoke basic emotions but also some degree of variation in more complex appraisals.

The Physiological Component

When our feelings are stirred up, one of the first things we notice is bodily changes. Many parts of the body are involved in emotional arousal, but certain brain regions, the autonomic nervous system and the endocrine system play especially significant roles.

Brain structures and neurotransmitters   Emotions involve important interactions between several brain areas, including the limbic system and cerebral cortex (Berridge, 2004; Damasio, 2005). If animals are electrically stimulated in specific areas of the limbic system, they will growl at and attack anything that approaches. Destroying the same sites produces an absence of aggression, even if the animal is provoked or attacked. Other limbic areas show the opposite pattern: lack of emotion when they are stimulated and unrestrained emotion when they are removed.

The cerebral cortex has many connections with the hypothalamus, amygdala and other limbic system structures. Cognitive appraisal processes surely involve the cortex, where the mechanisms for language and complex thought reside. Moreover, the ability to regulate emotion depends heavily on the executive functions of the prefrontal cortex, a region of the brain which lies immediately behind the forehead (Denollet et al., 2007; LeDoux and Phelps, 2000).

Ground-breaking research by psychologist Joseph LeDoux (2000) has revealed that when the thalamus (the brain's sensory switchboard) receives input from the senses, it can send messages along two independent neural pathways, a 'high road' travelling up to the cortex and a 'low road' going directly to the nearby amygdala (Fig. 11.23). The low road enables the amygdala to receive direct input from the senses and generate emotional reactions before the cerebral cortex has had time to fully interpret what is causing the reaction. LeDoux suggests that this primitive mechanism (which is the only emotional mechanism in species such as birds and reptiles) has survival value because it enables the organism to react with great speed before the cerebral cortex responds with a more carefully processed cognitive interpretation of the situation. This may be what occurs when a hiker sees what looks like a snake and jumps out of the way, only to realize an instant later that the object is actually a piece of rope.

The amygdala also seems to function as an early-warning system for threatening social stimuli. Consider a study by Winston et al. (2002) of the amygdala's response to different kinds of

Focus 11.16

According to LeDoux, which brain structures allow emotional responses to occur at two levels of processing?

FIGURE 11.23

Dual emotional pathways.

Parallel neural processes may produce conscious and unconscious emotional responses at about the same time. LeDoux's research suggests that sensory input to the thalamus can be routed directly to the amygdala in the limbic system, producing an 'unconscious' emotional response before cognitive responses evoked by the other pathway to the cortex can occur.

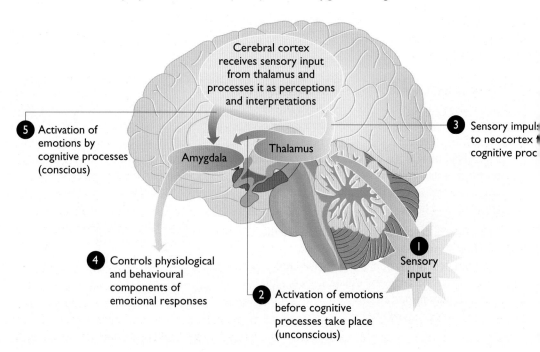

faces. Brain scans using fMRI indicated a burst of activity in the amygdala when people viewed faces they rated as particularly untrustworthy, but showed a much smaller response to faces they judged as particularly trustworthy (Winston et al., 2002). Another fMRI study showed that the amygdala also reacts to stimuli that evoke strong positive emotions (Hamann and Mao, 2002).

The existence of a dual system for emotional processing may help explain some puzzling aspects of our emotional lives. For example, most of us have had the experience of suddenly feeling a strong emotion without understanding why. LeDoux (2000) suggests that not all emotional responses register at the level of the cortex. He also suggests that people can have two simultaneous but different emotional reactions to the same event, a conscious one occurring as a result of cortical activity and an unconscious one triggered by the amygdala. This might help explain instances in which people are puzzled by behavioural reactions that seem to be at odds with the emotion they are consciously experiencing: 'I don't know why I came across as being angry. I felt very warm and friendly.' Some psychodynamic theorists are hailing these discoveries as support for the existence of conscious emotional processes (Westen, 1998). Indeed, there is now little doubt that important aspects of emotional life can occur outside of conscious awareness (Bargh and Chartrand, 1999).

Neuroscientist Candace Pert (1997) argues that because all of the neural structures involved in emotion operate biochemically, it is the ebb and flow of various neurotransmitter substances that activate the emotional programmes residing in the brain. For example, dopamine and endorphin activity appears to underlie some pleasurable emotions, whereas serotonin and norepinephrine play a role in anger and in fear (Damasio, 2005; Depue and Collins, 1999). When the final story of the brain and emotion can at last be told, it will undoubtedly involve complex interactions between brain chemicals and neural structures (Frijda, 2006).

Hemispheric activation and emotion   Decades ago in Italy, psychiatrists who were treating clinically depressed patients with electric shock treatments to either the right or the left hemisphere observed a striking phenomenon. The electric current temporarily disrupted neural activity in the targeted hemisphere. With the left hemisphere knocked out (forcing the right hemisphere to take charge), patients had what physicians termed a 'catastrophic' reaction, wailing and crying until the shock effects wore off. But when they applied shock to the right hemisphere, allowing the left hemisphere to dominate, the patients reacted much differently; they seemed unconcerned, happy and sometimes even euphoric. Researchers noted a similar pattern of emotions in patients in whom one hemisphere had been damaged by lesions or strokes (Gainotti, 1972).

Focus 11.17
What evidence exists that positive and negative emotions involve different patterns of brain activation?

These findings suggest that left-hemisphere activation may underlie certain positive emotions and right-hemisphere functioning negative ones (Sutton, 2002). To test this proposition, Richard Davidson and Nathan Fox (1988) obtained EEG measures of frontal lobe activity as people experienced positive and negative emotions. They found that when people felt positive emotions by recalling pleasurable experiences or watching a happy film, the left hemisphere was relatively more active than the right. But when sadness or other negative emotions were evoked by memories or watching a disgusting film, the right hemisphere became relatively more active. Moreover, this hemispheric pattern seems to be innate. Infants as young as 3 to 4 days old showed a similar pattern of hemispheric activation: left-hemisphere activation when given a sweet sucrose solution, which infants like, and right-hemisphere dominance in response to a citric acid solution, which apparently disgusts them.

Davidson and Fox also found individual differences in typical, or *resting*, hemispheric activation when they recorded people's EEG responses under emotionally neutral conditions. These resting differences predicted the tendency to experience positive or negative emotions. For example, human infants with resting right-hemisphere dominance were more likely to become upset and cry if their mothers later left the room than were those with resting left-hemisphere dominance. In adults, a higher resting level of right-hemisphere EEG activity may be a risk factor for the later development of adult depressive disorders (Tomarken and Keener, 1998).

Autonomic and hormonal processes   You are afraid. Your heart starts to beat faster. Your body draws blood from your stomach to your muscles, and digestion slows to a crawl. You breathe harder and faster to get more energy-sustaining oxygen. Your blood-sugar level increases, producing more nutrients for your muscles. The pupils of your eyes dilate, admitting more light to increase your visual acuity. Your skin perspires to keep you cool and to flush out waste products created by extra exertion. Your muscles tense, ready for action.

Some theorists call this state of arousal the *fight-or-flight response*. It is produced by the sympathetic branch of the autonomic nervous system and by hormones from the endocrine system. The sympathetic nervous system produces arousal within a few seconds by directly stimulating the organs and muscles of the body. Meanwhile, the endocrine system pumps epinephrine, cortisol and other stress hormones into the bloodstream. These hormones produce physiological effects like those triggered by the sympathetic nervous system, but their effects are longer lasting and can keep the body aroused for a considerable length of time.

Do different emotions produce different patterns of arousal? Only subtle autonomic differences occur among basic emotions as different as anger and fear (Cacioppo et al., 2000). Moreover, people differ from one another in their patterns of general arousal, so that we do not all show the same pattern of bodily arousal even when we are experiencing the same emotion. For example, when afraid, some of us might show marked changes in heart rate or blood pressure but only minor changes in muscle tension and respiration. Others would show different patterns. Thus there are no distinctive and universal physiological signatures for the basic emotions.

Focus 11.18

Are autonomic measures of lie detection scientifically defensible? What factors influence their validity?

BENEATH THE SURFACE

THE LIE DETECTOR CONTROVERSY

polygraph

measures physiological responses, such as respiration, heart rate and skin conductance (which increases in the presence of emotion due to sweat gland activity)

Given what you have learned so far about the physiology of emotion, do you think emotional arousal can tell us whether someone is telling the truth or lying? A scientific instrument known as a **polygraph** (Fig. 11.24) measures physiological responses, such as respiration, heart rate and skin conductance (which increases in the presence of emotion due to sweat gland activity). Because we have less control over physiological responses than over numerous other behaviours, many people regard the polygraph as a nearly infallible means of establishing whether someone is telling the truth. However, this approach to detecting lying by increases in emotional arousal is highly controversial (Kleiner, 2002).

Figure 11.24 shows a portion of a polygraph record. Polygraph examiners compare physiological responses to critical questions (e.g., 'Were you present at the French National Bank in Paris when it was robbed on the night of 4 August 2003?') with responses to control questions that make no reference to the crime or crime scene. In this case, note the changes that occurred on the autonomic measures after an emotionally loaded question was asked (point A to point B in Fig. 11.24).

The issue, however, is whether this emotional response to a critical question means that the person was lying. Herein lies one major problem with polygraph tests. Innocent people may appear guilty when doubt, fear or lack of confidence increases their autonomic activity. Even a thought like, 'What if my answer makes me look guilty, even though I'm not?' in response to a critical question could send the polygraph pens into spasms that might suggest a lie. As David Lykken, a leading critic of the lie detector, has noted, 'polygraph pens do no special dance when we are lying' (1981, p. 10).

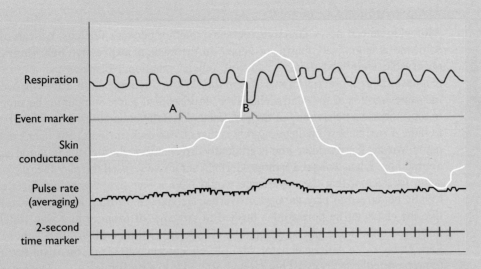

FIGURE 11.24

The lie detector.

The polygraph records physiological changes that are part of emotional responses. Between points A and B, an emotionally loaded question was asked. Within 2 seconds, the effects of the question were visible in the subject's respiration, skin conductance and pulse rate. Does this mean he was lying?

Not only can innocent people appear guilty, but guilty people can also learn to beat the polygraph. For example, by biting their tongue, curling their toes or contracting their anal sphincter when control questions are asked, people can produce an arousal response to those questions, which looks similar to the arousal that occurs when they actually lie on critical questions. William Casey, former director of the US Central Intelligence Agency, used to delight in his ability to fool the lie detector (Carlson and Hatfield, 1992). Fred Fay, a prison convict who had been falsely convicted of murder partly on the basis of a polygraph test, also became an expert at defeating polygraph tests (too late, unfortunately, for his acquittal). On one occasion, Fay coached 27 fellow inmates who were scheduled for polygraph tests. All of the inmates told Fay they were guilty of the relevant crimes. Yet after only 20 minutes of instruction, 23 of the 27 inmates managed to beat the polygraph (Lykken, 1981). Such results sharply contradict the notion of an infallible lie detector.

Misgivings about the validity of polygraph tests are supported by studies in which experienced polygraph examiners were given the polygraph records of suspects known to be either innocent or guilty on the basis of other evidence. The experts were asked to judge the guilt or innocence of the suspects. They usually did quite well in identifying the guilty, attaining accuracy rates of 80 to 98 per cent (Honts and Perry, 1992). However, they were less accurate in identifying the innocent, judging as many as 55 per cent of the truly innocent suspects to be guilty in some studies (Kleinmuntz and Szucko, 1984; Lykken, 1984). These error rates call into question the adage that an innocent person has nothing to fear from a polygraph test.

Largely because of an unacceptably high likelihood that an innocent person might be judged guilty, the American Psychological Association has supported legal challenges to polygraph testing. Congressional testimony by psychologists strongly influenced passage of the Employee Polygraph Protection Act 1988, which prohibits most non-governmental polygraph testing. Moreover, polygraph results alone cannot be used to convict people of crimes in most jurisdictions (Daniels, 2002). Nonetheless, local and federal governments in the USA continue to use polygraph tests in internal criminal investigations and in police officer and security screening, despite the weight of research evidence against their validity for these purposes (Cochrane et al., 2003; Kleiner, 2002).

The Behavioural Component

Although we can never directly experience another person's feelings, we can often infer that someone is angry, sad, fearful or happy on the basis of **expressive behaviours**, the person's observable emotional displays. Indeed, others' emotional displays can even evoke similar responses in us, a process known as *empathy*. While watching a film, have you ever experienced the same emotion as the central character? Professional actors sometimes become so immersed in the expressive behaviours of their characters that the boundaries between self and role begin to fade. A particularly challenging role is that of Woyzeck, in Georg Büchner's play of the same name. Woyzeck is a soldier who is gradually driven insane through the immoral actions of those around him. Klaus Kinski a famous German actor had refused the play the role of Woyzeck on stage for fear of that the experience would have a negative psychological effect upon him. Finally he agreed to play the part in Werner Herzog's 1979 film. Kinski 'found himself much like the character he portrayed – pushed to the edge of insanity in a way which very nearly destroyed him. Some say he never fully recovered' (Knipfel, 2004). In a similar anecdote, by Kirk Douglas, an American actor who played Vincent Van Gogh, the disturbed Dutch painter (who reportedly once cut off his ear and offered it to a prostitute):

> I was close to getting lost in the character of Van Gogh.... I felt myself going over the line, into the skin of Van Gogh.... Sometimes I had to stop myself from reaching my hand up and touching my ear to find out if it was actually there. It was a frightening experience. That way lies madness.... I could never play him again. (Lehmann-Haupt, 1988, p. 2)

Evolution and emotional expression   Where do emotional expressions come from? In his classic work *The Expression of Emotions in Man and Animals* (1965), Charles Darwin argued that emotional displays are products of evolution because they contributed to species survival. Darwin emphasized the basic similarity of emotional expression among animals and humans. For example, both wolves and humans bare their teeth when they are angry (Fig. 11.25). As Darwin explained it, this behaviour makes the animal look more ferocious and thus decreases its chances of being attacked and perhaps killed in a fight. Darwin did not maintain that all forms of emotional expression are innate, but he believed that many of them are.

expressive behaviours
the person's observable emotional displays

Focus 11.19

How do evolutionary and cultural factors influence emotionally expressive behaviour?

FIGURE 11.25

Similarities among species in the expression of certain basic emotions convinced Darwin and other theorists that certain expressive behaviours have an evolutionary origin.

Like Darwin, modern evolutionary theorists stress the adaptive value of emotional expression (Izard, 1989; Plutchik, 1994). They believe that a set of **fundamental emotional patterns**, or innate emotional reactions, are wired into the nervous system (Panksepp, 2005). Their research shows that certain emotional expressions (e.g., rage and terror) are similar across all cultures, suggesting a universal biological basis for them. The fundamental emotional patterns proposed by three evolutionary theorists are shown in Table 11.1. They argue that other emotions are based on some combination of these innate emotions. The evolutionary view does *not* assume that all emotional expressions are innate, nor does it deny that innate emotional expressions can be modified or inhibited as a result of social learning.

fundamental emotional patterns
innate emotional reactions

TABLE 11.1 FUNDAMENTAL OR PRIMARY INNATE EMOTIONS PROPOSED BY THREE LEADING EVOLUTIONARY THEORISTS

Carroll Izard	Silvan Tomkins	Robert Plutchik
Anger	Anger	Anger
Fear	Fear	Fear
Joy	Joy	Enjoyment
Disgust	Disgust	Disgust
Interest	Interest	Anticipation
Surprise	Surprise	Surprise
Contempt	Contempt	
Shame	Shame	
	Sadness	Sadness
	Distress	
Guilt		
		Acceptance

SOURCES: based on Izard, 1982; Tomkins, 1991; Plutchik, 1994.

Facial expression of emotion Most of us are fairly confident in our ability to read the emotions of others. Although many parts of the body can communicate feelings, we tend to concentrate on what the face tells us. Most other species have relatively few facial muscles, so their facial expressions are limited. Only monkeys, apes and humans have the well-developed facial muscles needed to produce a large number of expressions.

The development of sophisticated measuring procedures, such as Ekman and Friesen's (1987) Facial Action Coding System (FACS), have permitted the precise study of facial expressions. The FACS requires a trained observer to dissect an observed expression in terms of all the muscular actions that produced it. It takes about 100 minutes to score each minute of observed facial expression.

Although facial expressions can be valuable cues for judging emotion, even people within the same culture may learn to express the same emotions differently. For example, some people can appear very calm when they are angry or fearful, whereas others express even mild forms of those same emotions in a highly expressive manner. Fortunately, we usually know something about the situation to which people are reacting, and this often helps us judge their emotions. Researchers have found that people's accuracy and agreement in labelling emotions from pictures are considerably higher when the pictures reveal situational cues (Keltner and Ekman,

2000). If a woman is crying, is she weeping because of sadness or because of happiness? A background showing her being declared the winner of a lottery will result in a different emotional judgement than one showing her standing at a graveside.

Across many different cultures, women have proven to be more accurate judges of emotional expressions than men (Zuckerman et al., 1976). Perhaps the ability to read emotions accurately has greater adaptive significance for women, whose traditional role within many cultures has been to care for others and attend to their needs (Buss, 1991). This ability may also result from cultural encouragement for women to be sensitive to others' emotions and to express their feelings openly (Taylor et al., 2000). However, it is worth noting that men who work in professions that emphasize these skills (such as psychotherapy, drama and art) are as accurate as women in judging others' emotional expressions (Rosenthal et al., 1974).

What of Darwin's claim that certain facial expressions universally indicate specific emotions? Do people in different cultures agree on the emotions being expressed in facial photographs? Figure 11.26 shows the results of one study. You can see that there is generally high agreement on these photos of basic emotions, but there are also some cultural variations. Other researchers have found levels of agreement ranging from 40 to 70 per cent across a variety of cultures, well above chance but still far from perfect (Russell, 1994).

   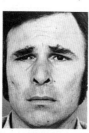 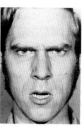 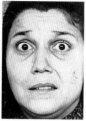

	Happiness	Disgust	Surprise	Sadness	Anger	Fear
United States (N = 99)	97%	92%	95%	84%	67%	85%
Brazil (N = 40)	95%	97%	87%	59%	90%	67%
Chile (N = 119)	95%	92%	93%	88%	94%	68%
Argentina (N = 168)	98%	92%	95%	78%	90%	54%
Japan (N = 29)	100%	90%	100%	62%	90%	66%

FIGURE 11.26

Culture and emotional expression.

Percentages of people from five different cultures who judged each face as expressing the emotions listed beneath the pictures.

SOURCE: Ekman, 1973.

cultural display rules
dictate when and how particular emotions are to be expressed

Cultural display rules   **Cultural display rules** dictate when and how particular emotions are to be expressed (Yrizarry et al., 2001). Certain gestures, body postures and physical movements can convey vastly different meanings in different cultures. For example, gesturing with an upright thumb while hitchhiking in certain regions of Greece could result in decidedly negative consequences, such as tyre tracks on one's body. In those regions, an upright thumb is the equivalent of a raised middle finger in Europe and the USA (Morris et al., 1979). In most cultures, spitting on someone is a sign of contempt. Yet in the traditions of the Masai tribe of East Africa, being spat on is considered a great compliment, particularly if the person doing the spitting is a member of the opposite sex (Wierzbicka, 1986).

More subtle differences exist as well. Ambady and colleagues have shown that people are generally more accurate at judging emotions when the emotions are expressed by members of their own cultural group rather than by members of a different cultural group (Elfenbein and Ambady, 2003). Just as people exhibit linguistic dialects, they also appear to have culturally based emotional behaviour dialects.

An experiment by Ekman et al. (1972) nicely illustrates cultural commonalities and differences in emotional expression. Japanese and American students viewed a gory, stressful film in private. Unbeknown to them, their facial expressions were being videotaped by a hidden camera. The FACS codings of the students' facial displays showed no differences between the Japanese and American students; they expressed negative emotions of disgust and anxiety in the same way and with similar intensity as they watched the film. Afterwards, the students were individually interviewed by a person of their ethnic group concerning their reactions to the film. The Japanese masked their earlier feelings of anxiety and disgust and presented a happy face throughout the interview, whereas the Americans' negative facial expressions closely mirrored those photographed while they watched the stressful movie. Based on such findings, many emotion theorists conclude that innate biological factors and cultural display rules *combine* to shape emotional expression across different cultures.

Instrumental behaviours   Emotional responses are often calls to action, requiring a response to the situation that aroused the emotion. A highly anxious student must find some way to cope with an impending test. A mother angered by her child's behaviour must find a non-destructive way to get her point across. A person in love searches for ways to evoke affection from his or her partner. These are **instrumental behaviours**, directed at achieving some emotion-relevant goal.

People often assume that high emotional arousal enhances task performance, as when athletes try to 'psych' themselves up for competition. Yet as students who have experienced extreme anxiety during examinations could testify, high emotional arousal can also interfere with performance. In many situations, the relation between emotional arousal and performance seems to take the shape of an upside-down, or inverted, U. As physiological arousal increases up to some optimal level, performance improves. But beyond that optimal level, further increases in arousal impair performance. It is thus possible to be either too 'flat' or too 'high' to perform well.

The relation between arousal and performance depends not only on arousal level but also on how complicated the task is and how much precision it requires (Yerkes and Dodson, 1908). Generally speaking, the more complex the task, the lower the optimal arousal level. Thus even a moderate level of arousal can disrupt performance on a highly complex mental or motor task.

Figure 11.27 illustrates this principle and shows that performance drops off less at high levels of arousal for the simplest task than for the others. In fact, even extreme arousal can enhance performance of very simple motor tasks, such as running or lifting something.

> **instrumental behaviours**
> **directed at achieving some emotion-relevant goal**

> **Focus 11.20**
> How do level of arousal and task complexity interact to affect task performance?

FIGURE 11.27

Arousal and performance.

The relation between arousal and performance takes the form of an inverted **U**, with performance declining above and below an optimal arousal level. However, the more complex a task is, the lower the optimal level of arousal for performing it. For which of these figures should the optimal level be lower?

In contrast, high emotionality can interfere with performance on complex mental and physical tasks. People may underachieve on intelligence tests if they are too anxious, and muscle tension can interfere with the skilful execution of complex physical movements (Landers and Arent, 2001). For example, the sport of golf requires precise and complex movements, so the optimal level of arousal is relatively low. Champion golfers often exhibit peak performance in high-pressure competition because they can control their level of arousal and keep it within the optimal range, whereas their opponents succumb to the pressure of a putt worth hundreds of thousands of euros.

IN REVIEW

- Our physiological responses in emotion are produced by the hypothalamus, the limbic system, the cortex and the autonomic and endocrine systems. There appear to be two systems for emotional behaviour, one involving conscious processing by the cortex, and the other unconscious processing by the amygdala.

- Negative emotions seem to reflect greater relative activation of the right hemisphere, whereas positive emotions are related to relatively greater activation in the left hemisphere.

- The validity of the polygraph as a lie detector has been questioned largely because of the difficulty of establishing the meaning of recorded physiological responses.

- The behavioural component of emotion includes expressive and instrumental behaviours. Different parts of the face are important in the expression of various emotions. The accuracy of people's interpretation of these expressions is enhanced when situational cues are also available. Evolutionary theorists propose that certain fundamental emotional patterns are innate but agree that cultural learning can influence emotional expression.

- There is an optimal level of arousal for the performance of any task. This optimal level varies with the complexity of the task; complex tasks have lower optimal levels.

Focus 11.21

Compare the James–Lange and Cannon–Bard explanations for emotional responses.

Focus 11.22

Evaluate scientific evidence that supports the James–Lange and Cannon–Bard theories.

James–Lange theory

our bodily reactions determine the subjective emotion we experience

THEORIES OF EMOTION

Where do emotional experiences come from? For more than 100 years, scientists have explored this question. Several classic theories have guided their efforts.

The James–Lange Somatic Theory

In 1890, the eminent psychologist William James ignited a controversy when he wrote:

> Common sense says … we meet a bear, are frightened, and run; we are insulted by a rival, are angry, and strike. The hypothesis here to be defended says that this order of sequence is incorrect and that the more rational statement is that we feel sorry *because* we cry, angry *because* we strike, afraid *because* we tremble. (James, 1950, p. 451, emphases added)

At about the same time, Danish psychologist Carl Lange reached a similar conclusion. According to the **James–Lange theory**, our bodily reactions determine the subjective emotion we experience. We know we are afraid or in love because our body's reactions tell us so. Today, this theory lives on as the *somatic theory of emotion* (Papanicolaou, 1989).

The Cannon–Bard Theory

It was not long before the James–Lange theory was challenged. In 1927 physiologist Walter Cannon fired back. He pointed out that people's bodies do *not* respond instantaneously to an emotional stimulus; several seconds may pass before signs of physiological arousal appear. Yet people typically experience the emotion immediately. This would be impossible according to the James–Lange theory. Cannon and his colleague L.L. Bard concluded that cognition must be involved as well.

The **Cannon–Bard theory** proposed that the subjective experience of emotion and physiological arousal do not cause one another but instead are independent responses to an emotion-arousing situation. When we encounter such a situation, sensory information is sent to the brain's thalamus, which simultaneously sends messages to the cerebral cortex and to the body's internal organs. The message to the cortex produces the experience of emotion, and the message to the internal organs produces physiological arousal. Figure 11.28 compares the James–Lange and Cannon–Bard theories.

> **Cannon–Bard theory**
> the subjective experience of emotion and physiological arousal do not cause one another but instead are independent responses to an emotion-arousing situation

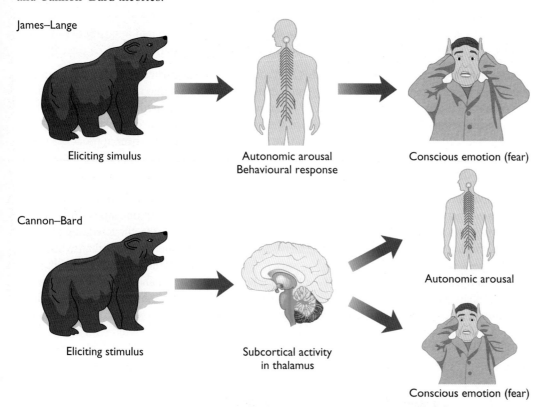

James–Lange

Eliciting simulus → Autonomic arousal / Behavioural response → Conscious emotion (fear)

Cannon–Bard

Eliciting stimulus → Subcortical activity in thalamus → Autonomic arousal / Conscious emotion (fear)

FIGURE 11.28

Two theories of emotion.

Two early theories of emotion continue to influence current-day theorizing. The James–Lange theory holds that the experience of emotion is caused by somatic feedback and physiological arousal. According to the Cannon–Bard theory, the thalamus receives sensory input and simultaneously stimulates physiological responses and cognitive awareness.

The Role of Autonomic Feedback

The James–Lange and Cannon–Bard theories raised intriguing questions about how the various aspects of an emotional experience interact with one another. The theories differ on one crucial point. According to the James–Lange theory, feedback from the body's reactions to a situation tells the brain that we are experiencing an emotion. Without such bodily feedback, there would be no emotional response. In contrast, the Cannon–Bard theory maintains that emotional experiences result from signals sent directly from the thalamus to the cortex, not from bodily feedback. Is there any way to test whether bodily feedback is necessary?

In fact, there is. What if organisms were deprived of sensory feedback from their internal organs? Would they be devoid of emotional reactions? To answer this question, Cannon (1929) carried out experiments with animals in which he severed the nerves that provide feedback from the internal organs to the brain. He found that even after such surgery, the animals exhibited emotional responses, lending support to his theory that direct sensory messages to the brain are the emotional triggers. In like manner, people whose spinal cords have been severed in accidents, and who receive no sensory feedback from body areas below the injury, continue to feel intense emotions – sometimes more intense than those they experienced before their injuries. Moreover, people with upper and lower spinal cord injuries, who differ in the amount of bodily feedback they receive, do not differ in the intensity of their emotions (Chwalisz et al., 1988).

These results appear to cast doubt on the claim that arousal feedback from the body is absolutely necessary for people to experience intense emotions. But let us take this issue one step further.

The Role of Expressive Behaviours

Arousal feedback is not the only kind of bodily feedback considered important by the James–Lange somatic theory. Facial muscles involved in emotional displays also feed messages to the brain, and these muscles are active even in patients with spinal injuries who receive no sensory input from below the neck. According to the **facial feedback hypothesis**, feedback from the facial muscles to the brain plays a key role in determining the nature and intensity of emotions that we experience, as the James–Lange theory would suggest (Adelmann and Zajonc, 1989).

According to the theory, sensory input is first routed to the subcortical areas of the brain that control facial movements. These centres immediately send signals that activate the facial muscles. Sensory feedback from movement of facial muscles is then routed to the cerebral cortex, which produces our conscious experience of the emotion. To return to James's example of the bear, the facial feedback hypothesis says that we are frightened when the bear approaches partly because an automatic expression of terror appears on our face and sends signals from our facial muscles to the cortex, where the subjective feelings of fear are produced.

In support of the facial feedback hypothesis, research shows that feedback from facial muscle patterns can arouse specific emotional reactions (Soussignan, 2002). In one study, Fritz Strack and co-workers (1988) found that when participants held pens in their teeth, activating muscles used in smiling (Fig. 11.29a), they rated themselves as feeling more pleasant than when they held the pens with their lips, activating the muscles involved in frowning (Fig. 11.29b). Participants also rated cartoons as funnier while holding pens in their teeth and activating the 'happy muscles' than while holding pens with their lips (Fig. 11.29c). In another study, researchers compared the subjective experiences of people who pronounced different sounds, such as *eee* and *ooh*. Saying *eee*, which activates muscles used in smiling, was associated with more pleasant feelings than saying *ooh*, which activates muscles involved in negative facial expressions (Zajonc et al., 1989).

facial feedback hypothesis

feedback from the facial muscles to the brain plays a key role in determining the nature and intensity of emotions that we experience

FIGURE 11.29

Facial feedback and emotional experience.

(a) Holding a pencil in the teeth, which activates the muscles used in smiling, evokes more pleasant feelings than (b) holding the pencil in one's lips, which activates muscles associated with negative emotions. (c) The findings shown in this graph provide support for the facial feedback hypothesis.

SOURCE: based on Strack et al., 1988.

  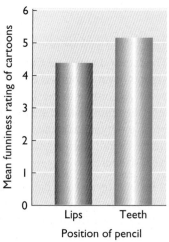

Cognitive-Affective Theories

Nowhere are mind–body interactions more obvious than in the emotions, where thinking and feeling are intimately connected. *Cognitive-affective theories* examine how cognitions and physiological responses interact (Clore et al., 2004; Smith and Kirby, 2004). Historically, Richard Lazarus and Stanley Schachter have been major figures in this approach.

Lazarus (2001) argued that all emotional responses require some sort of appraisal, whether we are aware of that appraisal or not. Schachter was intrigued with the factors that determine our emotional perceptions. According to Schachter's **two-factor theory of emotion**, the intensity of physiological arousal tells us *how strongly* we are feeling something, but situational cues give us the information we need to label the arousal and tell ourselves *what* we are feeling – fear, anger, love or some other emotion (Schachter, 1966).

If appraisal and arousal affect one another in the ways these theories suggest, then by manipulating appraisals we should be able to influence physiological arousal. Moreover, if we can manipulate arousal, we should be able to influence cognitive appraisals of the situation. Let us examine some research that tests these propositions.

two-factor theory of emotion

the intensity of physiological arousal tells us how strongly we are feeling something, but situational cues give us the information we need to label the arousal and tell ourselves *what* we are feeling

Focus 11.23

According to the theories of Lazarus and Schachter, how do appraisal and arousal interact to influence emotions? Describe the two key experiments inspired by these theories.

RESEARCH CLOSE-UP

COGNITION-AROUSAL RELATIONS: TWO CLASSIC EXPERIMENTS

SOURCES: J. Speisman, R.S. Lazarus, A. Mordkoff and L. Davison (1964) Experimental reduction of stress based on ego-defence theory, *Journal of Abnormal and Social Psychology*, vol. 68, pp. 367–80; S. Schachter and L. Wheeler (1962) Epinephrine, chlorpromazine, and amusement, *Journal of Abnormal and Social Psychology*, vol. 65, pp. 121–8.

Two researchers who were at the forefront as appraisal-arousal theories of emotion were being developed in the 1960s were Richard Lazarus and Stanley Schachter. These two experiments are still considered classics in the field of emotion, and they gave impetus to the idea that appraisal and arousal influence one another.

Research design
Question: Can experimentally manipulated cognitive appraisals influence arousal responses to external stimuli?
Type of Study: *Experiment*

Independent variables	Dependent variable
Experimentally manipulated soundtrack conditions	Arousal (skin conductance) responses while viewing the stressful film

LAZARUS: MANIPULATING APPRAISAL TO INFLUENCE AROUSAL

INTRODUCTION

Lazarus and his colleagues at the University of California in the USA examined how differences in cognitive appraisal can influence physiological arousal. To do so, they needed to measure physiological arousal in response to eliciting stimuli, which were held constant for all participants, while influencing the manner in which the eliciting stimuli were appraised. If people in different appraisal conditions showed different arousal responses to the same eliciting stimuli, it would support the notion that arousal is influenced by appraisal.

METHOD

The researchers monitored college students' physiological responses while they watched an anthropology film, *Subincision in the Arunta*, which depicts in graphic detail an aboriginal puberty rite during which the penises of adolescent boys are cut with a jagged flint knife. The film typically elicits a high level of physiological arousal in viewers (and, according to the researchers, many leg-crossing responses in males). The dependent variable, measured by recording electrodes attached to the participants' palms, was changes in electrical skin conductance caused by sweat gland activity.

To study the effects of participants' appraisal of the filmed visual stimuli on arousal, the researchers experimentally varied the film's sound track. Four different sound track conditions were used to manipulate the independent variable:

- A *trauma* soundtrack emphasized the pain suffered by the boys, the danger of infection, the jaggedness of the flint knife, and other unpleasant aspects of the operation.

- A *denial* soundtrack was just the opposite; it denied that the operation was excessively painful or traumatic and emphasized that the boys looked forward to entering adulthood by undergoing the rite and demonstrating their bravery.

- The *intellectualization* soundtrack, also designed to produce a more benign appraisal, ignored the emotional elements of the scenes altogether and focused on the traditions and history of the tribe.

- In a *silent* control condition, the film was shown without any soundtrack at all, leaving viewers to make their own appraisals.

RESULTS

As shown in Figure 11.30, the soundtracks produced markedly different levels of arousal. As predicted, the trauma soundtrack resulted in the highest arousal, followed by the silent film condition, which likely evoked dire appraisals as well. The denial and intellectualization soundtracks, designed to create more benign appraisals, resulted in much lower levels of arousal. This classic study supported Lazarus's contention that appraisal can influence arousal.

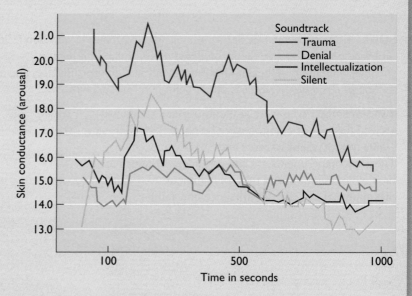

FIGURE 11.30

Does appraisal influence arousal?

Participants who viewed a film showing a painful tribal rite in vivid detail exhibited different levels of physiological arousal, depending on the soundtrack that accompanied the film.

SOURCE: Speisman et al., 1964.

SCHACHTER: MANIPULATING AROUSAL TO INFLUENCE APPRAISAL

INTRODUCTION

Is the reverse also true? Can level of arousal influence people's appraisal of an eliciting stimulus? To test this hypothesis, one must cause people to experience different levels of arousal without knowing the true reason. The level of arousal should then be attributed to whatever eliciting cues are present in the situation.

Research design
Question: Can experimentally manipulated arousal levels influence cognitive appraisal of external stimuli?
Type of Study: *Experiment*

Independent variables	Dependent variable
Arousal-influencing drug conditions (stimulant, tranquilizer, saline control)	Observers' codings of 'amusement' behaviours as participants viewed a comedy film

METHOD

In Schachter's laboratory at Columbia University in the USA, participants were told they were in a study involving the effects of a new vitamin called suproxin on visual perception. The researchers directly manipulated level of physiological arousal by injecting participants with one of three difference 'suproxin' substances. In one condition, participants received adrenaline (sometimes called epinephrine), a hormonal drug that increases arousal. In a second experimental condition, participants received a tranquillizer drug that would decrease arousal. A placebo control group received a saline injection that would have no effects on arousal. The experimenters told all participants that the suproxin injection would have no side effects (when, in fact, the adrenaline and tranquillizer would begin to have immediate and opposite effects on arousal). Then, while presumably waiting for the vitamin to take effect, the participants were shown a short film 'to provide continuous black and white stimulation to the eyes'. The film was a comedy that included a slapstick chase scene. The experimenters hypothesized that the participants in the two drug conditions would attribute their heightened or lowered level of arousal to the funniness (or lack thereof) of the film, because they would know of no other reason why they should feel as they did.

RESULTS

Participants were observed from behind a one-way mirror while they watched the movie. The observers, who were unaware of which participants had received which injections, recorded how frequently the participants smiled, grinned, laughed, threw up their hands, slapped their legs or doubled over with laughter. These behaviours were combined into an 'amusement score' that served as the dependent variable measure of how funny the participants found the film to be.

It appears that arousal cues can indeed influence their appraisal of the situation. As Figure 11.31 shows, the results supported the hypothesis that level of arousal would influence participants' appraisal of the film. The aroused participants in the epinephrine group found the film funnier than the tranquillized participants did, and the placebo control group fell in the middle. Thus, a person injected with adrenaline might think, 'Here I am watching this film and getting all excited. This film's really funny!'

CRITICAL DISCUSSION

These two studies were among the first to experimentally manipulate appraisal and arousal so as to study their effects upon one another. In the first study, even though it was not possible to completely control for participants' own tendencies to appraise situations in certain ways, the four soundtrack conditions did have effects on the arousal responses of participants as they watched the subincision film. When Schachter and Wheeler turned Lazarus's procedure around and manipulated arousal levels with the stimulant and tranquillizing drugs, they found the expected differences in appraisal of the funniness of the films, and they were able to measure these differences in terms of observable behaviour rather than self-report. Thus, these two studies show that appraisal influences arousal and that arousal can influence appraisals, demonstrating the two-way causal relation between cognition and arousal shown in the model of emotion originally presented in Figure 11.31.

FIGURE 11.31

Does arousal influence appraisal?

Participants were injected with either epinephrine, a tranquillizer, or a placebo to affect arousal and then were shown a humorous film. The amount of amusement they displayed varied with their state of arousal.

SOURCE: Schachter and Wheeler, 1962.

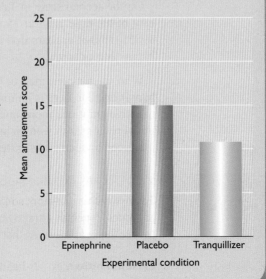

HAPPINESS

For many years, researchers focused primarily on negative emotions such as anxiety, depression and anger. More recently, however, attention has turned to the positive emotions (Aspinwall and Staudinger, 2003; Seligman, 2002). Among psychological researchers, there currently is growing interest in the topic of happiness, or its more technical term **subjective well-being (SWB)**: people's emotional responses and their degree of satisfaction with various aspects of their life (Diener and Seligman, 2002).

> **subjective well-being (SWB)**
>
> **people's emotional responses and their degree of satisfaction with various aspects of their life**

Subjective well-being is typically assessed by self-report ratings of contentment, happiness and satisfaction. Before reading on, please see Table 11.2.

TABLE 11.2 HOW HAPPY ARE YOU?

Here are two measures of subjective well-being. Answer the following questions, then see the text to compare yourself with others.

First, how would you rate your own general life satisfaction on the following scale?

0	1	2	3	4	5	6	7	8	9	10

Most unhappy   *Most happy*

Next, answer the following questions:
What percentage of the time are you happy? _____
What percentage of the time are you neutral? _____
What percentage of the time are you unhappy? _____
(Make sure your percentages add up to 100.)

How Happy Are People?

Diener and Diener (1996) reviewed findings from nearly 1000 representative samples in 43 westernized and developing nations. Across all countries, the mean rating of personal happiness on the 0-to-10 scale was 6.33, indicating mild happiness. Indeed, most of the 43 countries examined demonstrated a level of happiness above neutral, and this general happiness appeared to cut across both westernized (e.g., European states and the USA) and less westernized nations (e.g., Japan, Brazil, Mexico, South Korea and Thailand). In only two economically poor nations, India and the Dominican Republic, did average SWB fall into the unhappy range of the scale. In the USA, all ethnic groups scored well above the neutral point on the happiness scale (Andrews, 1991).

On the second scale in Table 11.2, college students on average reported being happy 65 per cent of the time, neutral 15 per cent and unhappy 20 per cent of the time (Larsen and Diener, 1985). Thus it appears that across many populations, people report living lives that are more happy than unhappy.

Who are happier, men or women? Research shows that the sexes are about equal in global happiness, but there is an important qualifier: Women on average experience *both* positive and negative emotions more intensely than do men (Wood et al., 1989). The more extreme emotional responses of women balance out, resulting in an average level of happiness similar to that produced by men's less extreme highs and lows.

What Makes People Happy?

Focus 11.24

What factors predict and fail to predict happiness?

To answer this question, some researchers have examined the *resources* that might contribute to happiness, such as attractiveness, intelligence, wealth and health. Others have studied internal *psychological processes* that underlie our experiences of happiness.

Personal resources   Is health required for happiness? Not necessarily. On average, individuals with severe and disabling medical conditions such as paralyses do report lower levels of life satisfaction than non-disabled people, yet about two-thirds of disabled people rate their lives as somewhat or very satisfying (Mehnert et al., 1990).

If you had more money, you would be happier? Correct? Well, perhaps not. Although people in affluent countries are happier on average than people who live in abject poverty, such countries differ in many ways besides wealth (e.g., in terms of social and political turmoil) that could also affect SWB. When wealth and SWB are correlated within the same country, whether the country is poor or affluent, wealth is only weakly related to happiness (Diener et al., 1999). Even extreme changes in wealth, such as a big inheritance or winning a lottery, have only a temporary positive impact on SWB (Brickman et al., 1978). Thus where health and wealth are concerned, not having enough of these resources may create unhappiness because important basic needs cannot be met, but once adequate levels are attained, further increases seem to do little to promote lasting happiness.

How about being wise? Overall, intelligence bears little relation to happiness (Seligman, 2002). Educational level does have a weak positive relation to SWB, probably because it helps people avoid poverty and compete for satisfying jobs. Unemployment is one of the strongest predictors of life dissatisfaction, and an adequate educational level can help people avoid this fate (Clark, 1998).

If being healthy, wealthy, and wise will not guarantee happiness, perhaps intimate relationships will. Here researchers consistently find that happy people have more satisfying social relationships (Diener and Seligman, 2002). Additionally, married men and women are significantly happier on average than are single and divorced people. Still, the meaning of these correlational results is not clear. Do social relationships promote greater life satisfaction, or are happier, better-adjusted people more able to establish and sustain good social relationships and stable marriages? Or is there some third variable, such as a personality factor like being more extraverted (i.e., more outgoing), that promotes both happiness and the ability to develop satisfying social relations?

Having a sense of meaning in life also is correlated with happiness. Many people report that their spiritual or religious beliefs contribute to a sense of meaning, and some – though not all – studies find a positive correlation between religiosity and happiness (Diener and Seligman, 2002; Diener et al., 1999). Giving of oneself, such as helping others as a volunteer, contributes to a sense of meaning and life satisfaction (Snyder et al., 2000). But again, causality is difficult to infer. Does a greater sense of meaning promote happiness? Does happiness lead people to feel that their life is more meaningful? Or does some third factor cause both?

Psychological processes   Overall, personal resources and external circumstances account for only about 15 to 20 per cent of the total variability among people in happiness ratings (Argyle, 1999). Perhaps psychological processes, rather than resources, are the keys to happiness. For example, research reveals that feelings of life satisfaction are based on how we compare ourselves and our circumstances with other people and their circumstances and with past conditions we have experienced (Bruunk and Gibbons, 1997). When we engage in **downward comparison**, seeing ourselves as better off than the standard for comparison, we experience increased satisfaction. In contrast, **upward comparison**, when we view ourselves as worse off than the standard for comparison, produces dissatisfaction. In one study, students kept a written record of every time they compared their appearance, grades, abilities, possessions or personality with someone else's over a two-week period. At the same time, they recorded their current mood. Downward comparisons with less fortunate or less talented people were consistently associated with positive moods, and upward comparisons were associated with negative emotional reactions (Wheeler and Miyake, 1992).

Personality factors clearly predispose some people to be happier than others. Individuals who are sociable, optimistic, altruistic, curious and open to new experiences report higher levels of

downward comparison
seeing ourselves as better off than the standard for comparison

upward comparison
when we view ourselves as worse off than the standard for comparison

happiness and are rated by others as happier than are those who have the opposite traits (Larsen and Buss, 2002).

Biological factors may predispose some people to be happier than others. A study of 2310 identical and fraternal twins revealed that the identical twins were far more similar in SWB, regardless of their life circumstances (Lykken and Tellegen, 1996). Perhaps genetic factors contribute in some way to the individual differences in right- and left-hemisphere activation, discussed previously, or perhaps they influence neurotransmitter systems that underlie positive and negative emotions (Hamer and Copeland, 1998).

One's culture may also influence the factors that contribute to happiness. Suh and co-workers (1998) found that in the individualistic 'me' societies of North America and Europe, successes that people can attribute to their own skill and effort contribute to happiness. In collectivistic cultures of Southeast Asia, however, the well-being of the group seems to be a more important factor in personal happiness than one's own emotional life, and people derive more pleasure from accomplishments achieved as part of a group effort (Kitayama et al., 2000).

Happiness thus turns out to be a rather complex phenomenon having biological, psychological and environmental determinants (Fig. 11.32).

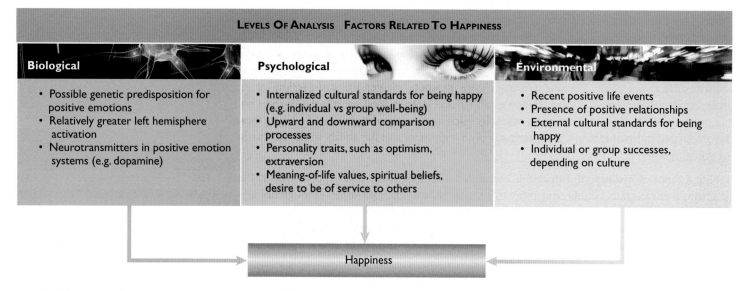

FIGURE 11.32

Levels of analysis: factors related to happiness.

APPLYING PSYCHOLOGICAL SCIENCE

BEING HAPPY: GUIDELINES FROM PSYCHOLOGICAL RESEARCH

As research has accumulated on factors that relate to happiness, psychologists have been able to offer advice based on data rather than intuition (Seligman, 2002; Snyder and Lopez, 2007). Most psychologists believe that happiness, like a good marriage, is something that one must work at (Seligman and Peterson, 2004). Here, then, are some suggestions that may help you maintain and enhance personal happiness.

Focus 11.25

Summarize research-based guidelines for increasing your happiness.

- *Spend time with other people, and work to develop close relationships.* Research consistently suggests that good relationships provide the strongest basis for life satisfaction. Even if you tend to be introverted, form at least a few close relationships and nurture them. Make time for social interactions.

- *Look for ways to be helpful to others, and reach out to the less fortunate.* Try to make a positive difference in the lives of others. Doing so will increase your sense of self-worth, add meaning to your life, and deepen relationships with those whose lives you touch. It will also help put your own problems in perspective and direct your energies away from self-absorption. There is a lot to be said for the proposition that we receive by giving.

- *Seek meaning and challenge in work.* Enjoying one's work is a prime ingredient of happiness. If you feel stuck doing something that provides little gratification, be it your job or your major, consider looking for something more satisfying. Everyone has to make a living, but many people spend their lives doing things they do not derive satisfaction or meaning from – hardly a recipe for a happy life. Even if you love your work, strive for balance between work and personal pursuits. People on their death beds rarely, if ever, express the wish that they had spent more time at the office.

- *Set meaningful personal goals for yourself, and make progress towards them.* Whether in work, school or relationships, engaging in goal-directed activity and seeing yourself moving towards your goals will provide a basis for life satisfaction and foster feelings of being in greater control of your life. Many people find that spiritual development (religiously based or not) confers meaning in their life.

- *Make time for enjoyable activities.* One of the benefits of time-management skills is the ability to schedule everyday activities that provide pleasure around school, work and other obligations. Make time for a hobby, reading, and recreational activities.

- *Nurture physical well-being.* Many studies show that even moderate physical exercise contributes to emotional well-being (Morgan, 1997). Such activities provide a temporary respite from life stressors. When done in a social context, they add the benefits of social interaction as well. People who exercise, get sufficient sleep and practise good dietary habits tend to be more stress resistant and satisfied with themselves and their lives (Taylor, 2006a).

- *Be open to new experiences.* Some of our most pleasurable experiences can occur when we try new things. It is easy to fall into a rut, so whether it is travelling, developing a new hobby or taking a college course on a new subject, be open to doing something you have not done before.

- *Cultivate optimism, and count your blessings.* As we have seen, cognitive appraisals influence emotions, and an upbeat, optimistic approach to life is linked with subjective well-being. Try to look on the positive side of things, to see demanding events as challenges and opportunities rather than threats. Learn to appreciate and be grateful for even the mundane, average day in which nothing bad happens to you. There is a Buddhist saying: 'Happiness is a day without a toothache.' All of us are gifted in ways that we may take for granted. Perhaps we should focus more often on these typically ignored aspects of good fortune.

IN REVIEW

- There are several theories of emotion. The James–Lange theory maintains that we first become aroused and then judge what we are feeling. The Cannon–Bard theory proposes that arousal and cognition are independent and simultaneously triggered by the thalamus. According to Lazarus's cognitive-affective theory, appraisals trigger emotional arousal; in contrast, according to Schachter's two-factor theory of emotion, arousal tells us how strongly we are feeling while cognitions derived from situational cues help us label the specific emotion.

- As the James–Lange theory maintained, expressive behaviours may trigger other aspects of emotions. The facial feedback hypothesis states that feedback from facial muscle patterns associated with innate emotional displays influences cognitive and physiological processes.

- There is a two-way relation between the cognitive and physiological components. It is possible to manipulate appraisals and thereby influence level of arousal, but arousal changes can also influence appraisal of the eliciting stimuli.

- In most countries, the average person is mildly happy. Psychological processes, such as downward comparison and a sense of personal meaning, are more consistently related to subjective well-being than are resources such as wealth, physical attractiveness and high intelligence. Cultural differences may exist in the bases for happiness.

A CONCLUDING THOUGHT

As you have seen in this chapter, motivation and emotion lie at the crossroads of cognition, physiology and behaviour. The diversity of human motives, factors that influence their development and strength, and methods for satisfying them help account for important differences both within and across cultures.

Emotion plays a central role in many aspects of normal and abnormal behaviour. Emotion also illustrates the many fascinating interfaces between evolutionary processes and social learning. It is little wonder, then, that the study of emotion is a major thrust in contemporary psychological research. We still have much to learn about the basic mechanisms that underlie our emotional experiences and about what we can do to self-regulate them in order to amplify pleasurable emotions and dampen those that create distress.

KEY TERMS AND CONCEPTS

Each term has been boldfaced and defined in the chapter on the page indicated in parentheses.

2 × 2 achievement goal
  theory (p. 498)

achievement goal theory
  (p. 497)

anorexia nervosa (p. 487)

approach–approach conflict
  (p. 501)

approach–avoidance conflict
  (p. 501)

avoidance–avoidance
  conflict (p. 501)

behavioural activation
  system (BAS) (p. 476)

behavioural inhibition
  system (BIS) (p. 476)

bulimia nervosa (p. 487)

Cannon–Bard theory
  (p. 514)

cholecystokinin (CCK)
  (p. 481)

cognitive appraisals (p. 504)

cultural display rules
  (p. 512)

downward comparison
  (p. 521)

drives (p. 476)

ego-approach goals (p. 498)

ego-avoidance goals (p. 498)

ego orientation (p. 498)

eliciting stimuli (p. 504)

emotions (p. 502)

expectancy × value theory
  (p. 477)

expressive behaviours
  (p. 510)

extrinsic motivation (p. 477)

facial feedback hypothesis
  (p. 516)

fundamental emotional
  patterns (p. 511)

glucose (p. 481)

homeostasis (p. 475)

incentives (p. 477)

instinct (p. 475)

instrumental behaviours
  (p. 513)

intrinsic motivation (p. 477)

James–Lange theory (p. 514)

leptin (p. 481)

mastery-approach goals
  (p. 497)

mastery-avoidance goals
  (p. 498)

mastery orientation (p. 497)

metabolism (p. 479)

motivation (p. 475)

motivational climate (p. 498)

need for achievement
  (p. 496)

paraventricular nucleus
  (PVN) (p. 482)

polygraph (p. 508)

self-actualization (p. 478)

self-determination theory
  (p. 478)

set point (p. 480)

sexual dysfunction (p. 491)

sexual orientation (p. 492)

sexual response cycle
  (p. 489)

social comparison (p. 495)

subjective well-being (SWB)
  (p. 520)

two-factor theory of emotion
  (p. 517)

upward comparison (p. 521)

WHAT DO YOU THINK?

IS MASLOW'S NEED HIERARCHY VALID? (p. 479)

More than most psychological theories of motivation, Maslow's model appropriately emphasizes that diverse motives influence human behaviour. The concepts of need progression and need regression seem to make intuitive sense. Motives do become stronger and weaker as circumstances change, and it seems logical that when people are starving, finding food becomes more important than contemplating beauty and truth.

Critics, however, have long questioned the validity of the need hierarchy and have argued that the concept of 'self-actualization' is vague and hard to measure (Heylighen, 1992). The ordering of needs seems arbitrary, and the concepts of need progression and regression cannot account for important aspects of motivated behaviour. How does the hierarchy explain why prisoners of war endure torture rather than betray their comrades; why millions of women choose to live in constant hunger to be thin; why political protestors go on hunger strikes or risk their physical safety to defend principles they believe in? Does a need for knowledge and understanding really become prominent only after needs for social belonging and self-esteem are met? Throughout evolution, was seeking esteem and recognition more important and adaptive to our ancestors than acquiring knowledge to help them survive?

Finally, rather than viewing the journey towards self-actualization as a relatively independent striving to maximize one's potential, some modern humanists view the entire process as more relationship oriented (Hanley and Abell, 2002). In their view, healthy social relationships not only satisfy deficiency needs for belonging and esteem, but also are important for achieving and expressing self-actualization.

Despite these drawbacks, by calling attention to the human desire for growth and incorporating diverse motives, the intuitive appeal of Maslow's model has influenced thinking in fields such as philosophy, education and business (Zinovieva, 2001).

FRATERNAL BIRTH ORDER AND MALE HOMOSEXUALITY (p. 494)

Blanchard (2001) estimates that the presence of each older brother increases by about one-third the *relative probability* that a later-born male child will be gay. For example, if there is a 2 per cent probability that a man with no older brothers is gay, then the probability for a man with one older brother is about 2.6 to 2.7 per cent, roughly a one-third relative increase. As Blanchard (2001) notes, 'the probability that a couple's son will be gay rises from 2 to 6 percent for their fifth son. That is a threefold increase. However, 94 percent of fifth sons will still be heterosexual' (p. 108).

So why does this effect occur? Perhaps you thought of one of these explanations: First, it may be that the greater the number of older brothers, the greater the possibility (however small) of having an incestuous sexual encounter with an older male while growing up. However, as Blanchard (2001) notes, evidence does not suggest that such incestuous experiences are linked to adulthood sexual orientation. Second, perhaps if an older brother has a homosexual orientation, awareness of this might influence a younger brother's sexual orientation. A study of gay men with gay brothers, however, found that most were aware of their own homosexual feelings before they became aware of their brother's homosexual orientation (Dawood et al., 2000).

Blanchard (2001) and his co-workers propose a biological explanation, called the *maternal immune hypothesis*. During pregnancy, male (but not female) foetuses contain substances that, as a group, are called *H-Y antigen*, which helps guide the foetal brain towards a male-typical pattern. Sometimes, the H-Y antigen passes from the foetus to the mother's bloodstream, in which case it is a foreign substance to the mother. Thus the mother's immune system responds by producing antibodies (proteins) to combat the H-Y antigen. In turn, these antibodies pass from the mother to the foetus and reach the foetal brain. 'When that happens, these antibodies partly prevent the fetal brain from developing in the male-typical pattern, so that the individual will later be attracted to men rather than women. The probability – or strength – of maternal immunization increases with each male fetus' (Blanchard, 2001, p. 110). Thus a mother with sons is more likely to carry and pass on these antibodies to any new male foetus, altering the H-Y antigen's role in guiding foetal brain development towards a male-typical pattern. Blanchard estimates that for about one-quarter of gay men, the development of their sexual orientation proceeded along this path. Of course, like other current theories, the maternal immune hypothesis needs much more testing.

CHAPTER TWELVE

LIFESPAN DEVELOPMENT I: PHYSICAL AND COGNITIVE DEVELOPMENT

My friend has a baby. I'm recording all the noises he makes so later I can ask what he meant.

STEPHEN WRIGHT

In 1799 three hunters discovered a remarkable child living in the forests of Aveyron, France. Most likely abandoned at a young age, he grew up isolated from human contact, foraging for food and surviving naked in the wild. About 12 years old, he easily climbed trees, ate nuts and roots, scratched and bit people who interfered with him, and made few sounds. He could walk upright yet ran quickly on all fours. Some regarded him as half-human, half-beast, and they called him the 'Wild Boy of Aveyron' (Itard, 1962).

Several medical experts concluded that the boy was incurably 'mentally deficient', but others disagreed, noting that it took intelligence to survive in the wild. They argued that special education and care would enable the child to flower into a normal, civilized adult. In Paris, the boy was placed under the care of a prominent young physician, Jean-Marc Itard, who named him Victor and diligently supervised his training (Fig. 12.1).

At first, Victor was unresponsive to stimuli that most people find aversive. Unfazed, he would stick his hand into boiling kitchen water to grab food or eagerly roll around half-naked on the cold winter ground. Eventually he learned to sense temperature differences, dress himself and perform other self-care behaviours. Victor's emotional responses, which at first fluctuated without reason, began to fit the situation: he laughed in playful situations, shed tears over someone's death and displayed some signs of affection towards Itard. Victor learned to read and write some words, communicate basic needs and perform simple tasks.

Although Victor changed in important ways, as he grew older his progress slowed considerably. He never learned to speak, and after five years of education his cognitive, emotional and social development remained limited. Pessimism over further progress grew, and Itard's 'project' ended. Victor was moved to a nearby home, where a woman cared for him for the rest of his life.

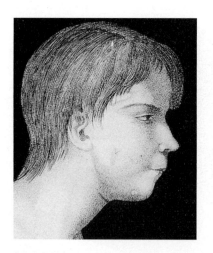

FIGURE 12.1

Victor, the 'Wild Boy of Aveyron'.

In the early 1800s, people expected Victor's case to resolve an intense debate about a key question in developmental psychology; that which asks whether nature or nurture are more important in shaping who we are. But it raised more questions than it answered. For a start, it is very difficult to determine whether Victor was born 'mentally deficient', or whether he had become irreparably harmed by his childhood isolation. If the latter, then why was Itard unable to fully repair the damage done?

Some children exposed to extreme adversity are highly resilient and thrive later in life (Ryff and Singer, 2003). We cannot pinpoint why Victor failed to recover, but his famous historical case begs a fundamental question: Just how does the miracle of human development unfold, and what conditions are required for normal development?

THE SCOPE OF DEVELOPMENTAL PSYCHOLOGY

In this chapter and the next (Chapter 13, 'Lifespan development II: social and emotional development') we explore what developmental psychologists have discovered about the changes which take place across the whole of human development, starting with the newly fertilized ovum and ending in old age. We also identify where researchers have tried to unfold the more difficult question of what factors and processes drive psychological development – the question of how nature interacts with nurture.

We were all young once. It follows that every psychological phenomenon which you can read about in this book has a developmental history. For this simple reason, developmental psychology comprises one of the largest subdivisions within psychology, with huge numbers of scientific papers dedicated to attempting to answer the questions it poses. The journal *Developmental Psychology* receives the second highest number of submitted articles out of all of the American Psychological Association (APA) journals. Because of the sheer volume of research in developmental psychology we have decided to dedicate two chapters to its coverage. In addition to the volume of work which goes on in developmental psychology, the questions which it poses and the methods which it uses to answer these questions are very varied. On the one hand, questions about the development of cognitive abilities are usually addressed with experimental methods in which stimuli and conditions are precisely controlled. On the other hand, questions about social development, by their nature are often best answered with more observational methods in which the scientist attempts to analyse a portion of social behaviour which they have had relatively little influence upon – social behaviour which is ecologically valid. Because of the differences in approach to cognitive and social questions we have divided the two chapters, such that physical and cognitive development is addressed in this chapter (Chapter 12), and social and emotional development, and the development of personality is discussed in Chapter 13.

Linking Social and Cognitive Development

It is, of course, somewhat artificial to separate cognitive and social questions in this way, as both cognitive abilities and social interactions can effect each others' development. It would be very odd to argue, for example, that all cognitive abilities can develop in the absence of social interaction! Likewise, the cognitive 'information-processing' abilities we possess at different stages in development have an important bearing on how we understand and can interact in social situations. After all, our social environment is just another, perhaps more complex, form of 'information'. Because of the importance of social cognitive links in human development, we have highlighted within each chapter where such links have been studied.

MAJOR ISSUES AND METHODS IN DEVELOPMENTAL PSYCHOLOGY

Whether we are interested in cognitive abilities or social interaction, *Developmental Psychology* has two main goals. The first is to examine and describe biological, physical, psychological

Focus 12.1

Describe four major issues and three special research designs often encountered in developmental research.

and behavioural changes that occur as we age. The second, and perhaps more interesting, question is to ask what it is that causes or drives these changes. We now describe four broad issues which arise in most developmental research. The first two issues are concerned with describing developmental change. Issues three and four are concerned with identifying the factors which drive developmental change.

1. *Stability versus change*: do our characteristics remain consistent as we age? This is perhaps the simplest question we can ask in developmental psychology: Is there any development? While both this chapter and the next attempt to describe development across the lifespan, there is a tendency to consider most developmental *changes* to happen in the first years of life, with long periods of *stability* in adulthood. However, as we shall see there are a great number of developmental changes that continue into adulthood and old age.

2. *Continuity versus discontinuity*: is development continuous and gradual, as when a sapling slowly grows into a tree? Or is it discontinuous, progressing through qualitatively distinct stages, as when a creeping caterpillar emerges from its cocoon as a soaring butterfly? As we shall see later, the Swiss psychologist Jean Piaget, who is the most important historical figure in the field of cognitive development, proposed that cognitive development was best characterized as a progression of qualitatively distinct stages.

3. *Nature and nurture*: to what extent is our development the product of heredity (nature) and the product of environment (nurture)? How do nature and nurture interact? Think about Victor, the Wild Boy of Aveyron. Was he different from normal boys because of the social isolation in which he grew up? In other words, is specific environmental experience in the form of human interaction vital for typical development? Or, was Victor just born with an atypical genetic inheritance which caused him to interact differently with people, and perhaps led him to run away into the wilderness? Most developmental psychologists would argue that typical and atypical development are products of an interaction between both nature and nurture, but that the hard task is to determine *how* they interact.

4. *Critical and sensitive periods*: are some experiences especially important at particular ages? A **critical period** is an age range during which certain experiences must occur for development to proceed normally or along a certain path. A **sensitive period** is an optimal age range for certain experiences, but if those experiences occur at another time, normal development is still possible. Consider Victor again. One interpretation of Itard's inability to help Victor catch up with other people of his own age is that he was deprived of important stimuli or human interactions when he was at a *critical period* in his development; a critical period which was over by the time Itard tried to help him. It may have been simply too late to give Victor the experiences he needed to develop normally.

Psychologists often use special research designs to investigate developmental questions (Fig. 12.2). Suppose we wish to study how intellectual abilities change from age 10 to age 60. Using a **cross-sectional design** we would compare people of different ages at the same point in time. Thus in the next month we could administer intellectual tasks to 10-, 20-, 30-, 40-, 50- and 60-year-olds. We would test each person only once and compare how well the different age groups performed. The cross-sectional design is widely used because data from many age groups can be collected relatively quickly, but a key drawback is that the different age groups, called *cohorts*, grew up in different historical periods. For instance, a problem associated with the use of cross-sectional designs in studies of the development of intelligence is that different cohorts may have different average intellectual abilities. If 60-year olds have poorer intellectual abilities than 20-year-olds, we need to ask whether this is due to ageing or possibly to broad environmental differences (e.g., poorer nutrition or medical care or a less stimulating environment) between growing up in the 1940s and 1950s versus the 1980s and 1990s.

To avoid this problem, a **longitudinal design** repeatedly tests the same cohort as it grows older. We could test a sample of 10-year-olds this month and then retest them every 10 years, up to age 60, thus ensuring that everyone is exposed to the same historical time frame. Unfortunately, a lon-

critical period

age range during which certain experiences must occur for development to proceed normally or along a certain path

sensitive period

an optimal age range for certain experiences, but if those experiences occur at another time, normal development is still possible

cross-sectional design

compares people of different ages at the same point in time

longitudinal design

repeatedly tests the same cohort as it grows older

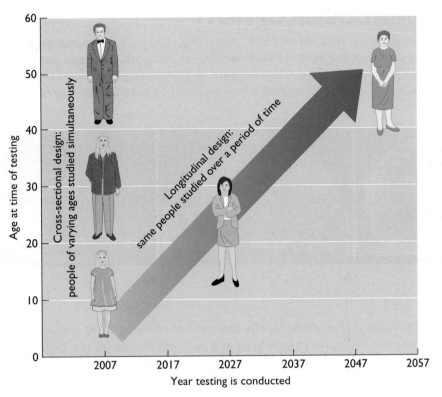

FIGURE 12.2

Developmental research designs.

Using a cross-sectional design we would test different age-groups in the year 2007 and compare their performance. Using a longitudinal design, we would test individuals of one age group and then retest them every 10 years until age 60. Using a sequential design, we would test 10- to 60-year-olds in the year 2007 and then retest them every 10 years until the youngest cohort reached age 60.

gitudinal design can be time-consuming, and as years pass, our sample may shrink as people move, drop out of the study or die. Further, suppose we find that intelligence declines at age 60. Is this really due to ageing or to developmental experiences unique to our particular cohort? Researchers can answer this question by using a **sequential design**, which combines the cross-sectional and longitudinal approaches. For example, we could test 10- to 60-year-olds now, retest them every 10 years and then examine whether the various cohorts followed a similar developmental pattern. This design is the most comprehensive but also the costliest and most time-consuming.

A further advantage of longitudinal approaches is that they allow us to examine differences between individuals in terms of the ways in which they develop (their individual 'developmental trajectories'). Cross-sectional studies lose much of this information by examining the development of aggregated groups of people, rather than individuals.

Now let us turn to the process of human development. We begin with the *pre-natal period*, approximately 266 days during which each of us developed from a single-celled organism barely larger than a pinhead into a wondrously complex newborn human.

> **sequential design**
> combines the cross-sectional and longitudinal approaches

IN REVIEW

- Developmental psychology studies the way in which our psychological abilities change as we get older. It also examines the environmental and genetic factors which drive this development. Questions about the influence of nature and nurture, critical and sensitive periods, continuity versus discontinuity, and stability versus change have guided much developmental research.

- Cross-sectional designs compare different age groups at one point in time. A longitudinal design repeatedly tests the same individuals as they grow older. A sequential design tests several groups at one point in time and then again when they are older.

zygote
fertilized egg

Focus 12.2

Describe the stages of pre-natal development, how sex is determined and the effects of various teratogens.

PRE-NATAL DEVELOPMENT

Pre-natal development consists of three stages (Fig. 12.3). The *germinal stage* comprises approximately the first two weeks of development, beginning when a sperm fertilizes a female egg (*ovum*). This fertilized egg is called a **zygote**, and through repeated cell division it becomes a mass of cells that attaches to the mother's uterus about 10 to 14 days after conception.

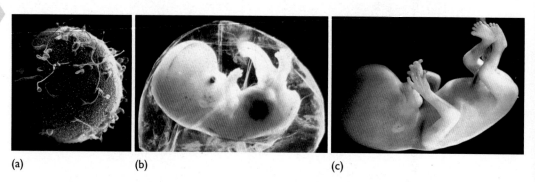

(a)   (b)   (c)

FIGURE 12.3

These remarkable photos show (a) the moment of conception, as one of many sperm cells fertilizes the ovum, (b) the embryo at 6 to 7 weeks, and (c) the foetus at 3 months of age.

embryo

develops from the end of week 2 through to week 8 after conception

foetus

develops from week 9 after conception until birth

The *embryonic stage* is next. The cell mass, now called an **embryo**, develops from the end of week 2 through to week 8 after conception. Two life-support structures, the placenta and umbilical cord, develop at the start of this stage. Located on the uterine wall, the *placenta* contains membranes that allow nutrients to pass from the mother's blood to the umbilical cord. In turn, the *umbilical cord* contains blood vessels that carry these nutrients and oxygen to the embryo and transport waste products back from the embryo to the mother. Supplied with nutrients, embryonic cells rapidly divide and become specialized. Bodily organs and systems begin to form, and by week 8 the heart of the inch-long (2.5 cm-long) embryo is beating, the brain is forming and facial features such as eyes can be recognized.

Finally, during the *foetal stage*, the **foetus** develops from week 9 after conception until birth. Muscles strengthen and other bodily systems develop. At about 24 weeks the eyes open, and by 27 weeks (or, more recently with advances in medical care, several weeks younger) the foetus attains the *age of viability:* it is likely to survive outside the womb in case of premature birth (Subramanian et al., 2002).

GENETICS AND SEX DETERMINATION

Throughout history, many women have been blamed for failing to give birth to a male heir. But, in fact, any father who foolishly feels a need to lay blame should look in the mirror, for it is his genetic contribution that determines the sex of a baby. A female's egg cells and a male's sperm cells each have 23 chromosomes. At conception, an egg and sperm unite to form the zygote, which now contains the full set of 23 *pairs* found in other human cells. The twenty-third pair of chromosomes determines the baby's sex. A genetic female's twenty-third pair contains two X chromosomes (XX), so called because of their shape (Fig. 12.4). Because women carry only X chromosomes, the twenty-third chromosome in the egg is always an X. A genetic male's twenty-third pair contains an X and a Y chromosome (XY). Thus the twenty-third chromosome in the sperm is an X in about half of the cases and a Y in the other half. The Y chromosome contains a specific gene, the *TDF (testis determining factor) gene*, that triggers male sexual development. The union of an egg with a sperm cell having a Y chromosome results in an XY combination and therefore a boy. A sperm containing an X chromosome produces an XX combination and therefore a girl.

How does the Y chromosome determine male sex characteristics? At roughly six to eight weeks after conception, the TDF gene initiates the development of testes. Once formed, the testes secrete sex hormones called *androgens* that continue to direct a male pattern of organ development. If the TDF gene is not present, as happens with an XX combination in the twenty-third pair, testes do not form and – in the absence of sufficient androgen activity during this *pre-natal critical period* – an inherent female pattern of organ development ensues.

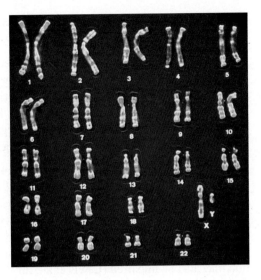

FIGURE 12.4

Most human cells contain 23 pairs of chromosomes. Each pair consists of one chromosome from each parent. The twenty-third pair determines a person's sex. In males, this pair consists of an X chromosome and a Y chromosome. In females, this pair contains two X chromosomes.

ENVIRONMENTAL INFLUENCES

Our genetic blueprint sets forth a path of pre-natal development, but nature and nurture become intertwined even before we are born. **Teratogens** are external agents that cause abnormal pre-natal development. The placenta prevents many dangerous substances from reaching the embryo and foetus, but some harmful chemicals and diseases can pass through. Stress hormones can cross the placenta, and prolonged maternal stress is associated with increased risk of premature birth (Austin and Leader, 2000). If the mother contracts rubella (German measles) – especially when the embryo's eyes, ears, heart and central nervous system are beginning to form early in pregnancy – it can cause blindness, deafness, heart defects and mental retardation in the infant (Plotkin, 2006).

Sexually transmitted diseases can pass from mother to foetus and produce brain damage, blindness and deafness, depending on the disease. Among pregnant women with untreated syphilis, about 25 per cent of foetuses are born dead. Likewise, without treatment during pregnancy or delivery by Caesarean section at birth, about 25 per cent of foetuses born to mothers with the human immunodeficiency virus (HIV) are also infected (Meleski and Damato, 2003).

Mercury, lead, radiation and many other environmental toxins can produce birth defects, as can many drugs. **Foetal alcohol syndrome (FAS)** is a severe group of abnormalities that results from pre-natal exposure to alcohol (Streissguth, 1977; 2001). Foetal alcohol syndrome children have facial abnormalities and small, malformed brains (Fig. 12.5). Psychological symptoms

teratogens

external agents that cause abnormal pre-natal development

foetal alcohol syndrome (FAS)

a severe group of abnormalities that results from pre-natal exposure to alcohol

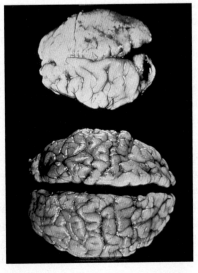

FIGURE 12.5

Children who suffer from foetal alcohol syndrome (FAS) not only look different but also have brains that are underdeveloped and smaller than those of normal children.

include mental retardation, attentional and perceptual deficits, irritability and impulsivity. Other children exposed to alcohol in the womb may display milder forms of these deficits.

The threshold level of alcohol exposure needed to produce FAS is not known. About one-third to one-half of infants born to alcoholic mothers have FAS, but even social drinking or a single episode of binge drinking can increase the risk of pre-natal damage and long-term cognitive impairment (Larroque and Kaminski, 1998). Because no amount of pre-natal alcohol exposure has been confirmed to be absolutely safe, pregnant women and those trying to become pregnant are best advised to completely avoid drinking alcohol (Floyd et al., 2005).

Nicotine is also a teratogen. Maternal smoking increases the risk of miscarriage, premature birth and low birth weight (Kirchengast and Hartmann, 2003). Owing to second-hand smoke ('passive smoking'), regular tobacco use by fathers also has been linked to low infant birth weight and increased risk of respiratory infections (Wakefield et al., 1998). Babies of pregnant mothers who regularly use heroin or cocaine are often born addicted and experience withdrawal symptoms after birth. Their cognitive functioning and ability to regulate their arousal and attention may also be impaired (Lewis et al., 2004).

IN REVIEW

- Pre-natal development involves the germinal, embryonic and foetal stages.

- The twenty-third chromosome in a mother's egg cell is always an X chromosome. If the twenty-third chromosome in the father's sperm cell is an X, the child will be genetically female (XX); if it is a Y, the child will be genetically male (XY).

- Maternal stress, illness, drug use and environmental toxins ('teratogens') can cause abnormal pre-natal development.

INFANCY AND CHILDHOOD

Studying infancy poses unique challenges. Because infants cannot describe their experiences, psychologists must find clever ways to take advantage of behaviours which infants produce readily, such as sucking behaviour and eye movements, to draw inferences about their perceptual and cognitive capabilities. In addition to the special techniques infancy researchers must use, a great deal of patience is required as infants do not always comply with the wishes of experimenters, as adults and even children do. During experiments, as they do outside the laboratory, infants frequently cry, fall asleep or become interested in something completely extraneous, such as their new stripey socks. Infancy research is not easy, but methods developed over the past 40 years have been very successful in demonstrating how well babies of even only a few days old can perceive, understand and interact with their environment.

THE AMAZING NEWBORN

A question that has occupied philosophy for hundreds of years, and psychology since its inception as a scientific field, concerns what perceptual skills we bring with us into the world. Are we born with an ability to perceive the environment around us, or is this a skill which we must learn? William James (1950) took the view shared by the empiricist philosophers of the seventeenth century such as Bishop Berkeley (1656; see Chapter 1); like them, he argued that we bring relatively little with us and that we require to learn how to perceive even simple stimuli. Thus, he famously suggested that after emerging from the womb, the newborn's world is a 'blooming, buzzing confusion'! However, contrary to this long-held view of newborns as helpless and passive, research reveals that they may be surprisingly sophisticated at processing information.

Reflexes and Learning

Neonates require some ways of acting on their environment. Luckily, they are equipped with a number of **reflexes**, automatic, inborn behaviours that occur in response to specific stimuli. Some have obvious adaptive significance. Stroke a baby's cheek, and it will turn its head towards the direction it was touched and open its mouth – the *rooting reflex*. When something is placed in the infant's mouth, it will suck on it – the *sucking reflex*. Together, these reflexes increase the infant's ability to feed. Breathing is another example of a reflex which helps the infant to survive.

However, we cannot have an innate reflex for every action we need in order to interact successfully with our environment. We need learning mechanisms in order to change and adapt our behaviours to new stimuli in the environment. In Chapter 7 we described several ways in which humans and animals learn. Newborns also learn in several ways. One important way in which they learn is through habituation; they decrease their responses to repetitive, non-threatening stimuli. As we shall see shortly, developmental psychologists have used newborns' habituation to gain knowledge about how they perceive their environment. As we described in Chapter 7, habituation is useful as it helps us orient away from the old and towards new information. Newborns can also acquire classically conditioned responses. After a tone (CS) is repeatedly paired with a gentle puff of air to the eye (UCS), they will develop a conditioned eye-blink response to the tone alone (Lipsitt, 1990). Through operant conditioning, newborns learn that they can make things happen. For example, 3-day-old infants can learn to suck a plastic nipple with a certain pattern of bursts to activate a tape-recording of their mother's voice (Moon and Fifer, 1990).

Sensory Capabilities and Perceptual Preferences

The visual preference technique   Just after birth, newborns' eye movements are not well co-ordinated, and this fact among others led early developmental psychologists to assume that we are blind in the first weeks of life. However, in 1961, Robert Fantz conducted a pioneering study which demonstrated that this assumption was wrong. Fantz developed a *preferential looking procedure* to study infants' visual preferences. He placed infants on their backs, showed them two or more stimuli at the same time, and observed their eyes to record how long they looked at each stimulus. Infants preferred complex patterns, such as realistic or scrambled drawings of a human face, to simple patterns and solid colours (Fig. 12.6). The mere fact that very young babies preferred some stimuli over others indicates that they are able to make perceptual discriminations between such stimuli.

The visual habituation technique   But there is a problem with the visual preference procedure, in that if babies have no preference for one stimulus over the other then we will not be able to tell whether they can discriminate between them or not. In order to get around this problem Fantz (1964) also pioneered another method for examining infants' perceptual abilities – the *visual habituation* technique. This technique makes use of the fact that after a period of exposure to visual stimuli, infants begin to habituate to them – they look at them less than they did initially. Correspondingly, when we present infants with stimuli to which they have been habituated and stimuli which are novel, they demonstrate a strong visual preference for the novel stimulus (a 'novelty preference'). Thus, we can use habituation to determine whether infants can discriminate between visual stimuli. If they show a novelty preference when presented with pairs of novel and familiar stimuli (stimuli to which they have been habituated) then we can conclude that they are able to discriminate between those stimuli. Using this technique, Alan Slater at the University of Exeter has shown that newborn infants are able to

Focus 12.3
Describe the newborn's sensory capabilities, perceptual preferences, reflexes and ability to learn.

reflexes
automatic, inborn behaviours that occur in response to specific stimuli

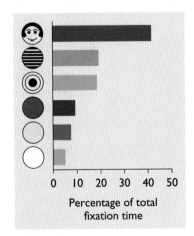

FIGURE 12.6

Infants' visual preferences.

Whether 2 days old or 2 to 3 months old (the data shown here), infants prefer to look at complex patterns more than simple patterns or solid colours.

SOURCE: based on Fantz, 1961.

FIGURE 12.7

Visual habituation in newborns.

If habituated to any one of the four shapes shown here (e.g., the circle), infants only a few days old will demonstrate a novelty preference for any of the other three stimuli (e.g., the cross, the triangle or the square) when they are paired with the habituated stimulus.

SOURCE: based on Slater et al., 1983.

make a wide variety of perceptual discriminations between different visual stimuli. Figure 12.7 shows some of the visual form discriminations which newborns can make.

Despite the success of the visual preference and visual habituation techniques for investigating visual perceptual abilities in very young infants, they are not completely without their complications. One particular problem lies in what we can conclude from a perceptual discrimination. Take, for instance, Slater et al.'s (1983) demonstration of form discrimination (see Fig. 12.7). Do newborn infants discriminate between these stimuli in the same way we might – by comparing the configural shapes of the stimuli? From Slater and colleagues's evidence alone we cannot be sure. It is possible that the infants are focusing on some much more simple perceptual cues, such as the orientation of component lines. For example, they might discriminate the triangle from the other shapes by simply registering that it contains a diagonally oriented line.

RESEARCH CLOSE-UP

FACE PREFERENCES IN THE FIRST MINUTES OF LIFE

SOURCE: M.H. Johnson, S. Dziurawiec, H. Ellis and J. Morton (1991) Newborns' preferential tracking of face-like stimuli and its subsequent decline, *Cognition*, vol. 40, pp. 1–19.

INTRODUCTION

Despite Fantz's (1961) demonstration of a face preference in young infants (between 2 days to 3 months of age), controversy remained concerning whether this visual preference represented an ability to discriminate faces from other stimuli in the environment. One interpretation is that the infants looked longer at schematic faces because of the symmetry of the features. Another interpretation was that the infants preferred the faces as they were more complex than other patterns. Of course, they could also prefer these figures for *both* reasons!

Finally, it is difficult to know what these abilities mean in terms of early development. Do the infants have an innate ability to recognize faces over other stimuli or are they simply attending to a stimulus which they have learned about in the first days and weeks of life? After all, Fantz had tested a group of infants ranging between 2 days and 3 months. It was difficult to determine whether the youngest infants were able to make the discrimination at all. There followed several failures to replicate Fantz's findings with infants who were younger than 2 months of age (Koopman and Ames, 1968; Maurer and Barrera, 1981).

In order to resolve these issues, Mark Johnson and colleagues made use of a straightforward adaptation of the visual preference technique – preferential tracking, in which is measured infants' preferential tendencies to follow a stimulus with their eyes as it is moved through their visual field. In order to examine whether preferences were innate, they tested infants who were only an hour old at the most.

METHOD

Twenty-four newborns of mean gestational age, 280 days, were tested within the first hour after birth. They had been born at and were tested in the Aberdeen Maternity Hospital, Aberdeen, Scotland. Thirteen were male and 11 female.

The newborns were placed on their backs on the experimenter's knee, and shown a single stimulus of the three in Figure 12.8 directly above them and at their midline. The experimenter then moved the stimulus slowly into the periphery of the infant's visual field. The number of degrees though which the infants followed each of the stimuli shown in Figure 12.8 was compared.

Face   Scrambled   Blank

FIGURE 12.8

The stimuli shown to newborn infants, and a newborn being tested in the preferential tracking method.

Will the newborns track face stimuli further than the other stimuli?

SOURCE: Johnson et al., 1991.

RESULTS

Figure 12.9 shows that the infants tracked (with their eyes and head) the face-configured stimuli further into the periphery than both the scrambled stimuli and the blank stimuli. In addition they tracked the scrambled face stimulus further than the blank stimulus. The fact that the infants preferred the face stimulus over the scrambled face stimulus is quite convincing evidence of a preference for faces over other stimuli as both the face stimulus and the scrambled face stimulus contain exactly the same features, and both are symmetrical in their configuration. The only difference is the configural layout of the features.

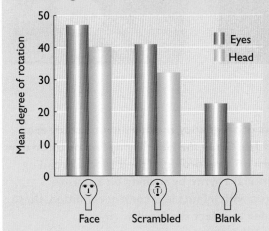

FIGURE 12.9

Newborns preferential tracking of face-like stimuli.

This graph shows the mean number of degrees through which the newborn infants rotated their eyes and heads when following the stimuli.

SOURCE: Johnson et al., 1991.

DISCUSSION

These results demonstrate convincingly that newborn infants can discriminate between faces and other stimuli in their environment, and that they prefer to orient towards faces over other stimuli, even when the other stimuli are of equal complexity. This study is also impressive in demonstrating face preference only a few minutes after birth, and provides compelling evidence that early infant face preferences are innate and not learned in the first days of life. But are you convinced? Can you think of any other reasons why the newborns might have preferred to track the face stimuli further into the periphery?

QUESTION

Do newborn babies prefer face-like stimuli over other stimuli? Type of study: *Experimental*

Independent variables	Dependent variables
Type of stimulus moved past the newborn's eyes (three stimulus types: face-like, scrambled, blank)	Distance the newborn's eyes tracked the stimuli into the periphery
	Distance the newborn's heads tracked the stimuli into the periphery

Newborns' other senses function well at birth also. Just as you would make different facial expressions after tasting sweet, sour or bitter substances, newborns' facial responses tell us that they have a reasonably well-developed sense of taste. Newborns also orient to touch, and can discriminate between different parts of their bodies being touched (Kisilevsky and Muir, 1984). They also distinguish different odours – if exposed to pads taken from inside the bras of several nursing mothers, week-old infants will orient towards the scent of their own mother's pad. Newborns can hear fairly well. They prefer human voices to other sounds and can distinguish their mother's voice from that of a female stranger (DeRegnier et al., 2002). As Figure 12.10 describes, newborns seem to prefer sounds that become familiar to them in their last weeks of foetal development, during which time they can hear sounds transmitted through the womb (DeCasper and Spence, 1986). Thus, in a rudimentary sense, simple forms of learning can occur inside the womb (Gruest et al., 2004).

FIGURE 12.10

Can the foetus learn?

(*Left*) Twice a day during their last six weeks of pregnancy, mothers in one study read out loud the same passage from Dr Seuss's *The Cat in the Hat*. (*Right*) Two or three days after birth, their newborns were able to turn on a recording of their mother reading either *The Cat in the Hat* rhyme or an unfamiliar rhyme by sucking on a sensor-equipped nipple at different rates. Compared with infants in a control condition, these newborns changed their sucking rate in order to select the familiar rhyme.
SOURCE: DeCasper and Spence, 1986.

Perceptual Development in Early Infancy

Even though newborns show surprising competence, some very important developments in perceptual abilities take place in the first year of life across all sensory modalities. In the domain of vision, developments are particularly striking in the way infants make shape discriminations. Cohen and Younger (1984) conducted an elegant habituation-novelty study which demonstrates that infants start off by making shape discriminations on the basis of orientation rather than 'configural' shape (see Fig. 12.11).

In the auditory domain perhaps the most important developments are in infants' abilities to discriminate between phonemes, the sounds of which speech is composed. Werker and Tees (1984) investigated this ability in infants ranging from 6 to 12 months of age with English-speaking parents. They found that the youngest infants were just as competent as the older infants at discriminating speech sounds in English. They also tested the young and older infants on their ability to make speech sound discriminations which are not made in English, but are discriminated in different languages to which they had not been exposed (Hindi, and also

Habituation A B C D

FIGURE 12.11

Can young infants discriminate between acute and obtuse angles?

Cohen and Younger tested this ability by habituating infants to an acute angle (labelled 'habituation'), and then examining whether they would show a novelty preference for each of the test figures A–D. At 1½ months old, infants showed a novelty preference for B and D, both comprising lines which differ in orientation from the habituation stimulus, but they showed no increase in looking towards A and C. It is unsurprising that the infants showed no novelty preference for A which is exactly the same as the habituation stimulus. However, while test C contains exactly the same orientations as the habituation figure, it is a completely new configural shape. Thus, 1½-month-olds discriminate between objects on the basis of orientation and not configural shape. On the other hand, 3½-month-olds showed a novelty preference for C and D, but not for A and B, indicating that by this age they discriminate on the basis of configural shape.

SOURCE: Cohen and Younger, 1984.

Thompson, a language spoken by Salish Native Indians in Canada). When tested on these non-native speech sounds, the youngest 6- to 8-month-old infants performed better than the older 10- to 12-month-olds. This indicates that perceptual development can sometimes follow a process known as perceptual narrowing in which infants lose the ability to make discriminations which they do not need across the first year of life.

Bremner et al. (2008) have recently investigated developments in the ability to localize touch sensations across the first year of life (see Fig. 12.12). They tested two age-groups of infants (6½-month-olds and 10-month-olds), and examined the ability to localize touch stimuli presented to their hands. Both age-groups responded in the correct direction when their hands were in a familiar place (when they were adopting an uncrossed hands posture), but when their hands were crossed over the 6½-month-olds often responded in the wrong direction (they looked at and moved the hand which had not been 'buzzed'). The 10-month-olds were equally good at responding wherever their hands were placed. This research indicates that infants get better at

Uncrossed hands

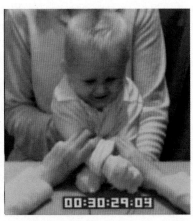

Crossed hands

FIGURE 12.12

Do infants know where touch stimuli come from even when their hands are crossed?

Bremner and colleagues tested this ability by presenting mild tactile 'buzzes' to infants' hands using vibrating 'tactors' – one placed in the palm of each hand.

SOURCE Bremner et al., 2008.

keeping track of tactile locations as they get older – they get better at keeping track of where their limbs are. Interestingly, movement of the limbs across the midline increases between 6 and 10 months also. Perhaps it is this experience which enables the infants to respond correctly across both arm postures.

Human infants thus arrive in the world with a lot of perceptual skills already available to them in all senses. This would suggest a strong role for genetic factors in our perceptual abilities. Nonetheless, there are some important ways in which perceptual skills are honed across the first months of life. Infants have to learn to adapt the structure of their perceptual environment (for example, by honing in on the speech sound discriminations which are important in the language which they hear, and by learning to ignore the distinctions which are only made in other languages). They also have to cope with challenges presented by their increasing motor abilities (for example, they have to learn to track tactile locations around when they become able to move their hands into new positions).

WHAT DO YOU THINK?

THE DEVELOPMENT OF FACE PERCEPTION IN THE FIRST YEAR OF LIFE

Pascalis and colleagues (2003) examined changes in the ability to discriminate between different faces in 6- and 10-month-old infants. Specifically, they examined whether these age-groups could discriminate between different human faces, and between different monkey faces. What do you think they found? Were the infants better at distinguishing human faces than monkey faces? Did they get better at discriminating faces as they got older? Why? Think about it, then see p. 563.

PHYSICAL DEVELOPMENT

Our bodies and movement (motor) skills develop rapidly during infancy and childhood. On average, by our first birthday body weight triples and height increases by 50 per cent. As Figure 12.13 shows, infants vary in the age at which they acquire particular skills, but the sequence in which skills appear is typically the same across children.

Physical and motor development have been characterized as following two direction trajectories. The **cephalocaudal trajectory** is the tendency for development to proceed in a head-to-foot direction. Thus, as you can see in Figure 12.3, the head of a foetus (and infant) is disproportionately large because physical growth concentrates first on the head. In terms of motor skill development, an infant will master the ability to maintain postural balance of the head on the neck, before he or she can sit or stand up. The **proximodistal trajectory** states that development begins along the innermost parts of the body and continues towards the outermost parts. Thus a foetus's arms develop before the hands and fingers. Likewise, infants' arm movements develop before their ability to manipulate objects with their fingers.

The Young Brain

No organ develops more dramatically than the brain. At birth the newborn's brain is far from mature and has reached only about 25 per cent of its eventual adult weight. By age 6 months, however, the brain reaches 50 per cent of its adult weight. As Figure 12.14 shows, neural networks that form the basis for cognitive and motor skills develop rapidly. The first brain areas to mature fully lie deep within the brain and regulate basic survival functions such as heartbeat and

cephalocaudal trajectory
the tendency for development to proceed in a head-to-foot direction

proximodistal trajectory
development begins along the innermost parts of the body and continues towards the outermost parts

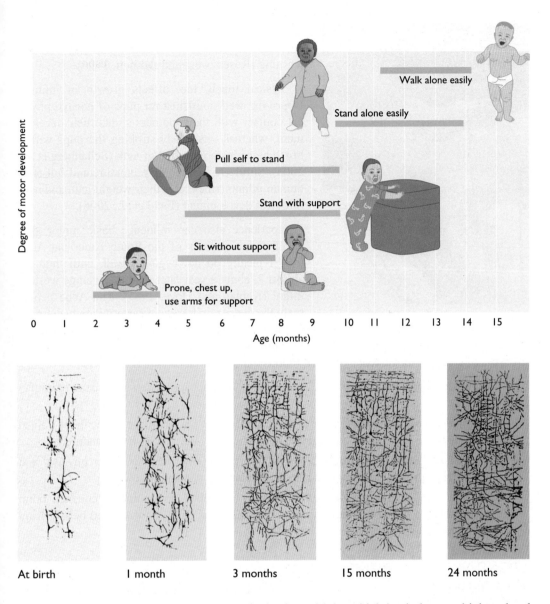

Prone, chest up, use arms for support

Sit without support

Stand with support

Pull self to stand

Stand alone easily

Walk alone easily

Degree of motor development

Age (months)

At birth   1 month   3 months   15 months   24 months

FIGURE 12.13

Infant motor development.

Infant motor development occurs in an orderly sequence, but the age at which abilities emerge varies across children. The left end of each bar represents the age by which 25 per cent of children exhibit the skill; the right end represents the age by which 90 per cent have mastered it.

FIGURE 12.14

The brain matures and adapts.

Increases in the density of neural networks during early development are apparent in these drawings of tissue from the human cerebral cortex.

SOURCE: Reprinted by permission of Harvard University Press from *The postnatal development of the human cerebral cortex, Vols. I–VIII*, by Jesse LeRoy Conel. Copyright © 1939, 1975 by the President and Fellows of Harvard College.

breathing. Among the last areas to mature is the frontal lobe which is vital to our highest-level cognitive functions.

Rapid brain growth during infancy and early childhood slows in later childhood (Sowell et al., 2001). Yet, although 5-year-olds' brains have reached almost 90 per cent of their adult size, brain maturation continues. Neurons become better insulated (through a process called myelination), new synapses form, unnecessary synapses are pruned back and lost, association areas of the cortex mature and the cerebral hemispheres become more highly specialized. The process of brain development continues into adolescence.

Environmental and Cultural Influences

Although guided by genetics, physical development is also influenced by experience. Diet is an obvious example. Chronic, severe malnutrition not only stunts general growth and brain development but also is a major source of infant death worldwide (Pelletier and Frongillo, 2003).

Babies thrive in an enriched environment – one in which the infant has the opportunity to interact with others and to manipulate suitable toys and other objects (Needham et al., 2002). Newborn rats (i.e., pups) raised in an enriched environment develop heavier brains, larger

Focus 12.4

Explain how nature and nurture jointly influence infants' physical growth and motor development.

FIGURE 12.15

At the Parker Ranch in Hawaii, USA, this 2-year-old is learning to ride a horse and use a lasso.

neurons, more synaptic connections and greater amounts of brain neurotransmitters that enhance learning (Rosenzweig and Bennett, 1996).

Physical touch, too, affects growth in infancy. Depriving well-nourished rat pups of normal physical contact with their mothers stunts their development, whereas vigorously stroking the pups with a brush helps restore normal growth (Schanberg et al., 2003). Similarly, massaging premature and full-term human infants accelerates their weight gain and neurological development (Field et al., 2006).

Experience also can influence basic motor skill development. Infants of the South American Ache tribe typically do not begin to walk until they are almost 2, about a year later than the average western infant (Kaplan and Dove, 1987). The Ache people roam the dense rain forests of eastern Paraguay foraging for food. For safety, mothers keep their children in direct physical contact almost constantly until the age of 3, providing them little opportunity to move about. Experience also affects various types of complex movement skills that toddlers and children acquire (Fig. 12.15).

Our discussion of physical growth reinforces three points that apply across the realm of human development:

1. *Biology sets limits on environmental influences*. For example, no infant can be toilet-trained before the nerve fibres that help regulate bladder control have biologically matured.

2. *Environmental influences can be powerful*. Nurturing environments foster physical and psychological growth, and impoverished environments can stunt growth.

3. *Biological and environmental factors interact*. Enriched environments enhance brain development. In turn, brain development facilitates our ability to learn and benefit from environmental experiences.

COGNITIVE DEVELOPMENT

How do the thought processes of a child develop? Swiss psychologist Jean Piaget (e.g., 1926; 1977) spent over 50 years exploring this question.

Piaget's Stage Model

Focus 12.5

Discuss Piaget's concepts of assimilation and accommodation, his four-stage model, and findings that help us evaluate his theory.

Early in his career, Piaget worked for French psychologist Alfred Binet, a pioneer of intelligence testing. Piaget became intrigued when he noticed that children of the same age often made similar errors on test questions. The key to understanding how children think, Piaget believed, was not whether they got the right answers but *how* they arrived at their answers.

Piaget observed children and listened to them reason as they tried to solve problems. He proposed that children's thinking changes *qualitatively* with age and that it differs from the way adults think. Piaget believed that cognitive development results from an interaction of the brain's biological maturation and personal experiences. He viewed children as natural-born scientists who seek to understand their world.

To achieve this understanding, the brain builds **schemas** (or *schemata*), which are organized patterns of thought and action. Think of a schema as a mental framework that guides our interaction with the world. For example, infants are born with a sucking reflex that provides a primitive schema for interacting with physical objects. In other words, sucking is a basic way in which the

schemas

organized patterns of thought and action

infant 'knows' the world. When a child says 'doggie' to describe a family pet, this word reflects a schema – a concept that the child is using to understand this particular experience.

Cognitive development occurs as we acquire new schemas and as our existing schemas become more complex. According to Piaget, two key processes are involved. **Assimilation** is the process by which new experiences are incorporated into existing schemas. When a young infant encounters a new object – a small plastic toy, a blanket, a doll – he or she will try to suck it. The infant tries to fit this new experience into a schema that he or she already has: objects are suckable. Similarly, a child who sees a squirrel for the first time may exclaim 'cat!' After all, a squirrel is nearly as big as a cat, is furry, and has four legs and a tail. The child tries to make sense of this new experience by applying his or her familiar schema: 'cat'.

Accommodation is the process by which new experiences cause existing schemas to change. As the infant tries to suck different objects, he or she will eventually encounter some that are too big or that taste bad. Similarly, the child who calls a squirrel a 'cat' may discover that this 'cat' exhibits some behaviours not found in cats (like eating nuts). This imbalance, or *disequilibrium*, between existing schemas and new experiences ultimately forces those schemas to change. Thus the infant's 'suckability' schema will become more complex: Some objects are suckable, some are not. The child's 'cat' schema also will change, and he or she will begin to develop new schemas for 'dog', 'squirrel', and so on. To the infant and child, this is a fundamental change in their understanding of the world.

Importantly, this change in structure (accommodation) is something which infants and children bring about themselves, by actively assimilating the environment into their schemas. When Piaget introduced these ideas, Psychology was under heavy influence from the behaviourist tradition, which considered skills and knowledge as being passively shaped by the environment. Piaget's assertion that infants and children actively change the structure of their own knowledge was a challenge to the existing behaviourist view, and helped bring about a qualitative change in the development of psychology as a field – from behaviourism to cognitivism (see Chapter 1).

Cognitive growth thus involves a give and take between trying to understand new experiences in terms of what we already know (assimilation) and having to modify our thinking when new experiences do not fit into our current schemas (accommodation). As we have just indicated, qualitative changes in thought processes can continue well into adulthood. However, the biggest changes occur in infancy and childhood. As Table 12.1 shows, Piaget charted four major stages of cognitive growth from birth through to adolescence.

assimilation

the process by which new experiences are incorporated into existing schemas

accommodation

the process by which new experiences cause existing schemas to change

TABLE 12.1 PIAGET'S STAGES OF COGNITIVE DEVELOPMENT

Stage	Age (years)	Major characteristics
Sensorimotor	Birth to 2	• Infant understands world through sensory and motor experiences • Achieves object permanence • Exhibits emergence of symbolic thought
Pre-operational	2 to 7	• Child uses symbolic thinking in the form of words and images to represent objects and experiences • Symbolic thinking enables child to engage in pretend play • Thinking displays egocentrism, irreversibility and centration
Concrete operational	7 to 12	• Child can think logically about concrete events • Grasps concepts of conservation and serial ordering
Formal operational	12 on	• Adolescent can think more logically, abstractly and flexibly • Can form hypotheses and systematically test them

sensorimotor stage
understand their world primarily through sensory experiences and physical (motor) interactions with objects

object permanence
an object continues to exist in a particular place even when it is no longer visible

Sensorimotor stage   From birth to about age 2, infants in the **sensorimotor stage** understand their world primarily through sensory experiences and physical (motor) interactions with objects. Reflexes are infants' earliest schemas, and as infants mature, they begin to explore their surroundings and realize that they can bang spoons, take objects apart and make things happen.

Piaget argued that once objects are 'out of sight' young infants do not understand their continued existence. If you hide 3-month-old Emily's favourite toy from view, she will not search for it, as if the toy no longer exists (Fig. 12.16). But around age 8 months, Emily will search for and retrieve the hidden toy. She now grasps the concept of **object permanence**, the understanding that an object continues to exist in a particular place even when it is no longer visible.

FIGURE 12.16

During the early sensorimotor period, a baby will reach for a visible toy (*left*) but not for one that has been hidden from view while the infant watches (*right*). According to Piaget, the child lacks the concept of object permanence; when something is out of sight, the infant does not understand how it continues to exist.

Infants begin to acquire language after age 1, and towards the end of the sensorimotor period they increasingly use words to represent objects, needs and actions. Thus in the space of two years, infants grow into independent thinkers who form simple concepts, solve some problems and communicate their thoughts.

pre-operational stage
the stage in which children represent the world symbolically through words and mental images but do not yet understand basic mental operations or rules

conservation
the principle that basic properties of objects, such as their volume, mass, or quantity, stay the same (are 'conserved') even though their outward appearance may change

Pre-operational stage   At about age 2, children enter a **pre-operational stage**, in which they represent the world symbolically through words and mental images but do not yet understand basic mental operations or rules. Rapid language development helps children label objects and represent simple concepts, such as that two objects can be the 'same' or 'different'. Children can think about the past ('yesterday') and future ('soon') and can better anticipate the consequences of their actions. Symbolic thinking enables them to engage in make-believe, or pretend, play.

Despite these advances, children's cognitive abilities have major limitations. According to Piaget, the pre-operational child does not understand **conservation**, the principle that basic properties of objects, such as their volume, mass, or quantity, stay the same (are 'conserved') even though their outward appearance may change (Fig. 12.17). For example, 4-year-olds often say that the taller beaker in Figure 12.17c has more liquid than the shorter one. You understand that the liquid can be poured back into the short beaker to return to the original, equal state of affairs, but children's thinking at this age displays *irreversibility*: it is difficult for them to reverse an action mentally. You also pay attention to height and width, recognizing that the liquid is 'taller' because the beaker is narrower. But pre-operational children exhibit *centration*, focusing (centring) on only one aspect of the situation, such as the height of the liquid.

(a) Initial equality

(b) Transformation

(c) Which glass has more juice?

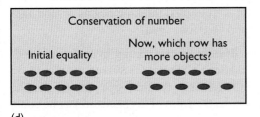

Conservation of number

Initial equality

Now, which row has more objects?

(d)

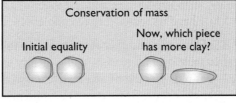

Conservation of mass

Initial equality

Now, which piece has more clay?

(e)

FIGURE 12.17

Conservation tasks.

(a, b, c) Conservation of volume: at the end of this sequence (*from left to right*), when the pre-operational child is asked which beaker contains more liquid, he points to the taller one.

(d) Conservation of number: two rows with an equal number of objects are aligned. After one row is spread out, pre-operational children will say that it has more objects than the other row.

(e) Conservation of mass: pre-operational children watch as one of two identically sized clay balls is rolled into a new shape. They typically will say that the new shape now has more clay.

Pre-operational children often display *animism*, attributing lifelike qualities to physical objects and natural events. When it rains, 'the sky is crying', and stars twinkle at night 'because they're winking at you'. Their thinking also reflects **egocentrism**, difficulty in viewing the world from someone else's perspective. By *egocentrism* Piaget did not mean 'selfishness' but rather that children at this stage believe that other people perceive things in the same way they do (Fig. 12.18).

egocentrism

difficulty in viewing the world from someone else's perspective

FIGURE 12.18

The three-mountain problem.

Piaget used the three-mountain problem to illustrate the egocentrism of young children. Suppose that a pre-operational child named Luke is looking at the mountains just as you are. Another child, Beth, is standing at the opposite (far) side of the table. Luke is asked what Beth sees. Because Luke is able to see the road, he will mistakenly say that Beth also can see it, indicating that he has failed to recognize Beth's perspective as different from his own.

Concrete operational stage   From about ages 7 to 12, said Piaget, children in the **concrete operational stage** can perform basic mental operations concerning problems that involve tangible (i.e., 'concrete') objects and situations. They now grasp the concept of reversibility, display less centration and easily solve conservation problems that baffled them as pre-schoolers.

concrete operational stage

can perform basic mental operations concerning problems that involve tangible (i.e., 'concrete') objects and situations

When concrete operational children confront problems that are hypothetical or require abstract reasoning, however, they often have difficulty or show rigid types of thinking. To demonstrate this, ask a few 9-year-olds, 'If you could have a third eye, where on your body would you put it? Draw a picture'. Then ask them to explain their reasons. David Shaffer (1989) reports that 9-year-olds typically draw a face with a row of three eyes across it. Their thinking is concrete, bound by the reality that eyes appear on the face, and their justifications often are unsophisticated (e.g., 'so I could see you better'). Many find the task silly because 'Nobody has three eyes' (Shaffer, 1989, p. 324).

Formal operational stage   Piaget's model ends with the **formal operational stage**, in which individuals are able to think logically and systematically about both concrete and abstract problems, form hypotheses, and test them in a thoughtful way. Formal thinking begins around ages 11 to 12 and increases through adolescence (Ward and Overton, 1990).

Children entering this stage begin to think more flexibly when tackling hypothetical problems, such as brain-teasers, and typically enjoy the challenge. Shaffer (1989) reports that 11- to 12-year-olds provide more creative answers and justifications in the third-eye problem than do 9-year-old concrete thinkers. One child placed the eye on the palm of his hands so that he could use it to 'see around corners'. Another placed it on top of his head, so that he could 'revolve the eye to look in all directions'. Formal operational children enjoy these hypothetical tasks and often ask for more.

Assessing Piaget's Theory: Stages, Ages and Culture

Tests of Piaget's theory conducted around the world yield several general findings. First, it appears that *the general cognitive abilities associated with Piaget's four stages occur in the same order across cultures* (Berry et al., 1992). For example, children understand object permanence before symbolic thinking blooms, and concrete reasoning emerges before abstract reasoning.

Second, *children acquire many cognitive skills and concepts at an earlier age than Piaget believed* (Bryant, 1974; Donaldson, 1978). In the next section we describe research which demonstrates that even 3½ to 4½ month-olds appear to have a basic grasp of objective permanence when they are tested on special tasks that only require them to look at events rather than physically search for a hidden object. In addition, simple modifications of Piaget's tests of older children's ability appear to reveal logical abilities beyond the stage of development attributed to them by Piaget's theory (see section on 'the social context of cognitive development').

Third, *cognitive development within each stage seems to proceed inconsistently*. A child may perform at the pre-operational level on most tasks yet solve some tasks at a concrete operational level (Siegler, 1986). This challenges the idea that stage-wise development is domain general (i.e., that the advances which children make between stages affect their performance on a wide range of tasks). According to Piaget, development is domain general so a child at a given stage should not show large inconsistencies in solving conceptually similar tasks. Researchers such as Siegler (1986) and Karmiloff-Smith (1992) have argued that rather than being domain-general, cognitive development is 'domain specific'. They argue that stage-wise shifts in ability occur independently in a range of different domains.

Fourth, *culture influences cognitive development*. Later in the chapter we introduce the work of Vygotsky. Vygotsky maintained that the culture in which we live has a profound effect on the way in which we solve cognitive problems. Piaget's western perspective equated cognitive development with scientific-logical thinking, but 'Many cultures … consider cognitive development to be more relational, involving the thinking skills and processes to engage in successful interpersonal contexts' (Matsumoto and Hull, 1994, p. 105). In Africa's Ivory Coast, the Baoulé people most strongly value a type of social intelligence that reflects the skills to get along with others and to be respectful, helpful and responsible (Dasen et al., 1985).

---

formal operational stage

individuals are able to think logically and systematically about both concrete and abstract problems, form hypotheses, and test them in a thoughtful way

Fifth, and most broadly, *cognitive development is more complex and variable than Piaget proposed* (Larivée et al., 2000). Although all children progress from simpler to more sophisticated thinking, they don't all necessarily follow the same developmental path (Siegler, 1996).

In sum, newer research challenges many of Piaget's ideas. Nevertheless, he revolutionized thinking about children's cognitive development, and his work still guides many researchers, often referred to as *neo-Piagetians*, who have modified his theory to account for the issues discussed above (Becker, 2004).

Young Infants' Understanding of the Physical World

We noted above that infants and children acquire many concepts at an earlier age than Piaget proposed. Because infants cannot express their knowledge in words, developmental psychologists have created some ingenious approaches – such as the *violation-of-expectation experiment* – to examine infants' understanding of basic concepts (Baillargeon, 2004). This approach assesses infants' cognitive abilities by taking measures of their attention, in this case, the time they spend looking at a stimulus.

In violation-of-expectation experiments, researchers begin with the hypothesis that young infants possess a certain concept – an expectation – about how the world works. For example, let us make the radical assumption that young infants have an expectation about the addition of very small numbers of objects, such as 'one of a thing' plus 'another one of the thing' equals 'two of the things'. Then researchers expose the infants to an 'impossible event' that violates this expectation and a 'possible event' that does not violate this expectation, as shown in Figure 12.19. If the infants stare longer at the impossible event, then the researchers take this as evidence that the infants understand the concept being tested. In other words, just as you would stare longer at a dropped pencil that suddenly stopped in mid-air than you would at one that fell to the ground, infants pay more attention to events that violate their understanding of the world.

Focus 12.6
Explain violation-of-expectation research. Does this approach represent a valid challenge to Piaget's views?

FIGURE 12.19

A violation-of-expectancy experiment.

Five-month-old infants watch the sequence of events shown in steps 1 to 4. Then in step 5 they witness a 'possible' or 'impossible' event. Infants stare longer at the impossible event, suggesting that they were expecting only one object and are surprised to see two objects still there. In other words, they understand that 2 − 1 should equal 1. In another experiment, in steps 1 to 4, infants watch one object being added to another object. Then the screen is raised and lowered, revealing either two objects ('possible event') or just one object ('impossible event'). Once again, infants stare longer at the impossible event, suggesting that they understand that 1 + 1 should equal 2.

SOURCE: Wynn, 1992.

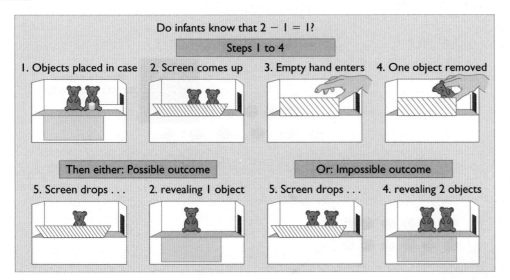

Do infants know that 2 − 1 = 1?

Steps 1 to 4

1. Objects placed in case 2. Screen comes up 3. Empty hand enters 4. One object removed

Then either: Possible outcome Or: Impossible outcome

5. Screen drops . . . 2. revealing 1 object 5. Screen drops . . . 4. revealing 2 objects

These experiments suggest that infants possess basic concepts about the physical properties of objects, such that they continue to exist when out of sight (Baillargeon et al., 1985), much earlier than is claimed by Piaget. Other knowledge infants seem to demonstrate is that two solid objects cannot occupy the same space at the same time (Baillargeon, 1987), and about the addition and subtraction of small numbers of objects, such as $1 + 1 = 2$, $2 + 1 = 3$, and $2 − 1 = 1$ (Spelke, 1994; Wynn, 1998). This approach is not without controversy because, as critics note, researchers are making large inferences about what must be going on inside the infant's head, on the basis of where their eyes are resting (Bremner and Mareschal, 2004; Hood, 2004; Leslie,

2004). Even so, as new research accumulates, it suggests that even 2-month-olds understand more about how the physical world operates than was thought possible just two decades ago (Wang et al., 2005).

The Social Context of Cognitive Development in Early Childhood

A key criticism of Piaget's research was that his studies of children's development did not consider the social context in which children were developing. A number of researchers, in particular Margaret Donaldson, challenged his arguments and findings on these grounds.

A particularly influential criticism was raised by McGarrigle and Donaldson (1975). They argued that Piaget's tasks often lead children into making incorrect responses. Take conservation for example. In the number conservation task the experimenter spreads out one row of counters and asks the child which row has more. Could the children be using the action of spreading out one of the rows as a social cue to respond that the longer row had more counters? In other words it is possible that 4-year-old children might be able to conserve number, but their ability may be masked by their immature understanding of the language which the experimenter is using, and a desire to respond in the way they think the experimenter wants them to. McGarrigle and Donaldson (1975) tested this alternative interpretation, by changing the way in which the transformation was made. They reasoned that if the transformation was made accidentally then the child would ignore the transformation and their true conservation abilities would be revealed. They achieved the accidental transformation by introducing a 'naughty teddy' (a toy manipulated by the experimenter) in the middle of the task. The naughty teddy rampaged across the table and lengthened one of the rows of counters. The experimenter would then take the teddy away and ask the crucial conservation question, 'are the number of counters in the two rows the same or different?' Under these circumstances McGarrigle and Donaldson (1975) found that 4-year-olds responded more accurately, suggesting that pre-operational children do have conservation abilities, but that the social contexts of Piaget's original experiments were leading them into responding inaccurately (see Fig. 12.20).

Focus 12.7

Explain why it is vital to consider social context when studying cognitive development.

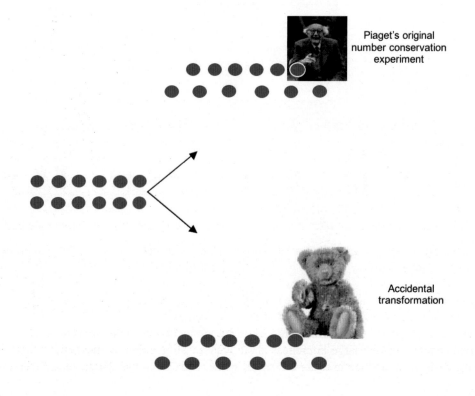

FIGURE 12.20

The 'naughty teddy' experiment.

McGarrigle and Donaldson (1975) adapted Piaget's original conservation of number task to examine whether children would be better able to conserve number following accidental rather than purposeful transformations.

Piaget's conservation experiment has remained controversial, as some other researchers (notably Moore and Fry, 1986) have pointed out that rather than helping children to respond on the basis of what they know, the naughty teddy may actually be distracting children from the transformation so that they answer correctly because they did not notice the change in one of the rows. Nonetheless, McGarrigle and Donaldson's point is well taken. The social context of experiments must be taken into account if we are to know what we are measuring when we place children in an experimental situation. Piaget certainly thought that the conservation experiment measures cognitive abilities, whereas McGarrigle and Donaldson argue that it measures children's sensitivities to the social cues which the experimenter makes (in this case the action of spreading one of the rows might be interpreted as a cue to say that one row has more counters). It is thus vitally important for developmental psychologists to consider the ways in which children of different ages may interpret social cues in the context of an experiment.

Vygotsky's Approach

Social factors however, can clearly play a much larger role in development than simply biasing children's responses in experiments. Russian psychologist Lev Vygotsky (1978) and American psychologist Jerome Bruner (1986) have been the most influential proponents of an approach to developmental psychology in which social context is considered at the core of development. Contrary to Piaget's much more individualistic approach to explaining development, Vygotsky argued that development is driven by the interplay of biological development and sociocultural input. This interplay is very nicely captured in Vygotsky's concept of the **zone of proximal development (ZPD)**: the difference between what a child can do independently and what the child can do with assistance from adults or more advanced peers (Fig. 12.21).

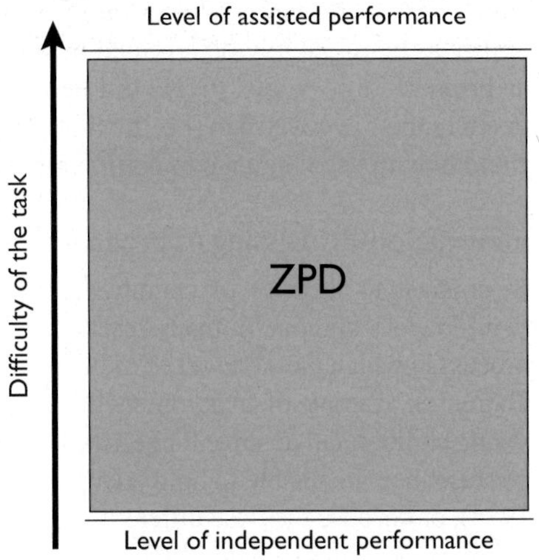

To illustrate, suppose that 3-year-old Joshua is able to build a tower, four blocks tall without assistance. However, with his father's verbal and gestural prompts (like for example prompting him to place the block carefully, or to turn it round the right way) he is able to build a tower eight bricks tall! Vygotsky suggests that for Joshua, the bricks from five to eight are his zone of proximal development.

Level of assisted performance

ZPD

Difficulty of the task

Level of independent performance

FIGURE 12.21

The zone of proximal development (ZPD).

Vygotsky pointed out that an important consideration was the degree to which the collaboration of others could help a child progress forward from the level of performance they were able to attain on their own.

Why is the zone of proximal development important? For one thing, it helps us recognize what children will be able to understand with help. If we consider cognitive development in a social context, this may be as important a measure of ability as a measure which examines what children can do on their own. Humans, and particularly children usually attempt to solve problems with the collaboration of others. Secondly, the ZPD tells us what children may soon be able to do on their own, pointing us towards the appropriate direction to take when attempting to move a child's cognitive development forward. For example, parents who assist a child on scientific tasks may push the child's understanding further along by using age-appropriate but cognitively demanding speech (e.g., introducing scientific concepts), rather than by using only simpler speech which does not challenge their conceptions (Tenenbaum and Leaper, 2003). Also of key importance are the limits of the ZPD (the maximum level to which a child can progress). It is quite clear that if parents talk to their young children as if they were intellectual equals, they might quickly confuse them.

One clear situation in which children are provided with collaborative support within their ZPD, is when they have elder siblings. Older siblings are capable enough to challenge their young brothers' and sisters' misunderstandings of a problem, but they are young enough to be

zone of proximal development (ZPD)
the difference between what a child can do independently and what the child can do with assistance from adults or more advanced peers

able to communicate the correct solution in a way which the younger siblings will understand (Ruffman et al., 1998).

In addition to the help which children get with their cognitive development through the collaboration of others, Vygotsky also emphasized the 'tools' which society gives children to aid or contextualize their development. One of the key tools was language. Vygotsky noted that once language has progressed from being a simple means for communicating needs, young children often begin talking to themselves when undertaking tasks. He argued that this was a progression towards using language to structure their thought, and regulate the way they were doing their task. He argued that by speaking to themselves in this way, children are able to monitor their success and failure, and direct themselves towards new goals. Take for example, Daniel, who is trying to find a toy that his dad has hidden for him in the garden: 'Look in the shed. . . . No! Not there ... how about underneath, or round the back in the flowers? Oops! Not there ... where next?' In this 'monologue' style of early speech, Daniel is monitoring the locations where he is looking, his failure to find the object he desires, and he is also planning what to do next. By 7 years of age, these monologues become less apparent, but Vygotsky argues that they do not stop but rather become internalized as 'inner speech'.

Vygotsky's emphasis on language as structuring cognition is alien to Piaget's approach. Apart from early in his career, Piaget rarely mentioned language in his books, and viewed language ability as being largely determined by an underlying cognitive ability (not the other way round as proposed by Vygotsky). He did note the use of monologues by young children but put this down to their egocentrism (i.e., he thought they spoke to themselves because they did not understand how to use language to communicate with other people).

Information-Processing Approaches

In contrast to theories of cognitive development which argue for stage-wise shifts in ability (e.g., Piaget's approach), many researchers view cognitive development as a continuous, gradual process in which the same set of information-processing abilities become more efficient over time. To give an example of an argument this kind of approach might make, perhaps we might think that young children fail to solve Piaget's tasks, not because they do not understand their logic, but rather because they are unable to hold enough pieces of information in memory simultaneously (Bryant, 1974), or because they use different kinds of attentional (information-search) strategies than older children and adults (Siegler, 1996). Despite the rise of information-processing approaches to cognitive development, the *discontinuity versus continuity* debate (gradual development versus the emergence of distinct stages) is still far from resolved. Some psychologists propose that cognitive development involves both processes. For example, Susan Gathercole (1998) suggests that memory capabilities change qualitatively (i.e., new abilities emerge) between infancy and age 7 but then undergo only gradual quantitative improvements through adolescence. Robbie Case (1987; Case et al., 2001) offered another integrative view, proposing that gradual increases in information-processing capabilities within stages enable children to move qualitatively from one stage of cognitive development to the next. We now describe some of the most important developments in information-processing abilities and strategies which take place during childhood.

Information-search strategies   Look at the two houses in Figure 12.22. Are they identical? This task is easy for you but not for young children. Elaine Vurpillot (1968) recorded the eye movements of 3- to 10-year-olds during tasks like this one. Pre-schoolers often failed to compare each window in the house on the left to the corresponding window in the house on the right, but older children methodically scanned the houses, looking from window to window. In short, older children are better able to search systematically for relevant information (Merrill and Lookadoo, 2004).

Processing speed, attention and response inhibition   As Robert Kail's (1991) review of 72 studies shows in Figure 12.23, the speed with which children process information becomes

Focus 12.8

What are the key developments in memory and information processing during childhood? How do these developments impact on social understanding?

FIGURE 12.22

A visual-search task.

Elaine Vurpillot used stimuli like these to assess visual inspection through filmed eye movements. Pre-schoolers fail to scan the pictures systematically, which often leads them to claim that the two houses are identical.

SOURCE: adapted from Vurpillot, 1968.

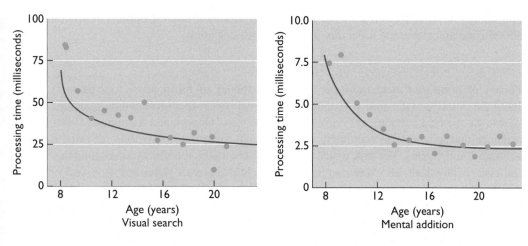

FIGURE 12.23

Information-processing speed quickens during childhood.

These two graphs show how information-processing speed for visual-search and mental-addition tasks becomes faster with age. The relatively rapid rate of change between ages 8 and about 12 slows during adolescence. A similar non-linear pattern also occurs on name-retrieval, mental-rotation and other cognitive tasks.

SOURCE: adapted from Kail, 1991.

faster with age. Notice that processing speed improves continuously and that the relatively rapid rate of change, between ages 8 and about 12, slows during adolescence. Children's attention span and ability to inhibit impulsive responses to distracting stimuli also improve with age. When performing tasks, older children are better able to focus their attention on relevant details and ignore irrelevant information (Luna et al., 2004).

Working memory and long-term memory   Children's working memory improves with age (Gathercole et al., 2004). If you read older children a list of words or numbers or sentences of increasing length, they will be able to store more of that information in working memory and repeat it to you than will younger children. Older children also can retain and manipulate visuospatial information in working memory more effectively than younger children. For example, they can perform mental-rotation tasks (see Fig. 9.33) more easily, and if you asked them to draw you a map to a friend's house several blocks and a few turns away, they would likely have little difficulty. A younger child might be able to lead you to the friend's house but would have difficulty drawing the route.

Older children are also more likely than younger children to use strategies to improve memory (Schneider et al., 2004). In one study, when given lists of words or numbers to remember, preschoolers rarely used rehearsal spontaneously, whereas 8- to 10-year-olds could often be heard rehearsing words or numbers under their breath (Flavell, 1970). More effective rehearsal helps older children to temporarily hold information in working memory for a greater period of time and to process information into long-term memory. Given their more advanced brain maturation, years of additional schooling, and other life experiences, older children also can call upon a larger library of information stored in long-term memory when they need to solve problems or perform tasks.

Memory, language and metacognition   It certainly seems that children get better at remembering information as they grow older. From a biological perspective this can be explained by the increased myelination of neurons in the brain, a process which continues into adolescence. However, there are at least two other factors at play. As discussed earlier, Vygotsky argued that language helps children to structure their thoughts. Language also bestows verbal labels, and use of such verbal labels has been associated with better long-term retention of information (Nelson, 1993). Another important factor which drives memory development is the emergence of an ability to reflect on one's own cognitive processes. Compared to younger children, older children can better judge how well they understand material for a test – they have better meta-memory. In turn, this helps them decide whether they need to study more or ask for help.

An ability to reflect on the effectiveness of one's own cognitive processes is clearly contingent on knowledge of one's own thoughts – metacognition. In the next section we introduce research into the ability to reflect on states of mind, both one's own state of mind, a skill which must underlie metamemory, and reflection on others' states of mind.

Theory of Mind: Understanding Mental States

Theory of mind and metacognition   The term **theory of mind** refers to a person's beliefs about the 'mind' and the ability to understand mental states; an understanding of others' mental states (see the next section) and one's own mental state. Gopnik and Astington (1988) present evidence that an ability to accurately remember and report one's own state of mind develops between 3 and 4 years. The task which they devised to assess this ability was called the 'Smarties' task. In this task, an experimenter shows a child a box of 'Smarties' (a brand of sweets which all children recognized). They ask them, 'What do you think is in this box?' Both 3- and 4-year-olds tend to guess 'Smarties!' Unfortunately for them this is not the case, and when the experimenter opens the box to reveal pencils the children often express dismay. The test of meta-cognition comes in the next question however, when the experimenter asks the children, 'What did you think was in the box when I first showed it to you?' At this point 4-year-olds will typically answer correctly ('Smarties'), but 3-year-olds will often fail to reflect on their past state of mind and answer 'pencils'. As we shall see in the next section this is also the age at which children become able to reflect on other people's states of mind or perspectives – an ability known as 'theory of mind'.

Understanding others' false belief   Consider the following story:

> Angela puts a chocolate bar inside a green box on the table, and then she goes away. Then her mother takes the chocolate bar out of the box and puts it inside a red bag on the bed. Angela does not see her mother do this. Later, Angela comes back and wants to get her chocolate because she is hungry. Where will Angela look for her chocolate bar?

On problems like this, most 2- and 3-year-olds indicate that Angela will look in the red bag, as if she had the same knowledge that they have. But many 4-year-olds say she will choose the green box, recognizing that Angela does not have the information they do. Thus, at some level, they comprehend that Angela's mental state – her 'mind' – is different from theirs (Wimmer and Perner, 1983). Similar studies of young children from African tribal societies, Canada, China, Japan, the UK and the USA yield similar findings (Vinden, 2002).

Interestingly, research has shown that the presence of older siblings in the home environment can speed children's progression from success to failure on false belief tasks. In one study of 2- to 6-year-old English and Japanese children, those over age 3 who grew up with older brothers and sisters performed better on a false belief task than children who grew up alone or with younger brothers and sisters (Ruffman et al., 1998). But children under age 3 performed poorly regardless of how many older siblings they had: the task was simply beyond their cognitive capacity.

There have been some questions raised about the false belief task however. One important question concerns whether the change in children's success at this task is due to developments in understanding other people's minds or whether there is some other artefact driving success, such as children's understanding of the question (Lewis and Osborne, 1990). Lying and deception also provide evidence of theory of mind. They imply an ability to recognize that one person can have information that another does not and therefore that we can influence what other people think by withholding the truth. Researchers find that theory of mind evidenced in attempts at deception emerge earlier than is suggested by Wimmer and Perner's (1983) false belief task. Most 3-year-olds are capable of trying to deceive someone else and recognize the difference between providing someone with false information in the form of a lie and providing false information due to an innocent mistake (Carlson et al., 1998). Perhaps lying and deception are better measures of theory of mind than false belief tasks.

---

theory of mind

a person's beliefs about the 'mind' and the ability to understand mental states

Recent findings suggest that theory of mind may emerge even earlier. Onishi and Baillargeon (2005), using the violation of expectation paradigm have shown that prelinguistic 15-month-old infants appear surprised (look longer) when someone searches successfully for an object when they should have had a false belief (because they were unable to see where an object was finally hidden). Such observations have fuelled speculation that we may be genetically endowed with neural machinery dedicated to telling us about other peoples' minds (Leslie, 2005). Nevertheless, many researchers still believe that developments in conceptual understanding of mental states underpin the shift from failure to success in the false belief task.

Focus 12.9

How does adolescence differ from puberty? Describe psychological consequences of early maturation, and adolescents' brain development.

IN REVIEW

- Newborns distinguish between different visual patterns, sounds, odours and tastes. They display perceptual preferences, learn through classical and operant conditioning, and have a primitive capacity for imitation.

- Perceptual abilities in all sensory modalities develop over the first year of life, as infants learn to attend to the important information for discriminating between objects and stimuli in their environment.

- Biology (e.g., the cephalocaudal and proximodistal principles) and environment (e.g., deprivation and enrichment) jointly steer children's physical and psychological development.

- According to Piaget, cognitive development depends on processes of assimilation and accommodation and occurs in four stages: sensorimotor, pre-operational, concrete operational and formal operational.

- Cognitive development is more complex and variable than Piaget believed. Vygotsky emphasized the sociocultural context of cognitive development. Each child has a zone of proximal development, reflecting the difference between what a child can do independently and what the child can do with assistance from others.

- Information-processing capacities improve with age. Older children search for information more systematically, process it more quickly and display better memory.

- Using false belief tasks, researchers have identified important changes in children's understanding of mental processes between 3 and 4 years of age.

ADOLESCENCE, ADULTHOOD AND OLD AGE

As we know it, the lengthy transition from childhood to adulthood called *adolescence* is largely an invention of eighteenth- to twentieth-century western culture (Valsiner and Lawrence, 1997), and thus many consider it to be a social construction (Spear, 2000). Indeed, we will consider many of the most important developmental aspects of adolescence in the next chapter, on social emotional development (Chapter 13). However, it is important to acknowledge that adolescence differs from **puberty**, a period of rapid maturation in which the person becomes capable of sexual reproduction. These developmental periods overlap, but puberty is a biologically defined period, whereas adolescence is a more socially defined period. However, this is not to say that these periods are unrelated. Adolescence is ushered in and out by changes in thinking, interests, social circumstances, and parental and societal expectations, but puberty may be an important factor in these changes. In research studies, 12- to 18-year olds – give or take a year at each end – are typically considered to be adolescents, but it is essential to keep in mind that the transition into, through and out of adolescence may be gradual (Arnett, 2001).

puberty

a period of rapid maturation in which the person becomes capable of sexual reproduction

PHYSICAL DEVELOPMENT

We now explore some key developmental changes that occur in adolescence and adulthood, beginning with changes in the body's physical processes and capabilities. Note that when we talk about *young adulthood* (approximately 20 to 40 years of age), *middle adulthood* (roughly, one's forties through to early sixties), and *late adulthood* (approximately age 65 and older), these terms – like *adolescence* – represent social constructions rather than distinct biological stages.

Puberty

During adolescence, puberty ushers in important bodily changes as the brain's hypothalamus signals the pituitary gland to increase its hormonal secretions. Pituitary hormones stimulate other glands, speeding up maturation of the *primary sex characteristics* (the sex organs involved in reproduction). Hormonal changes also produce *secondary sex characteristics* (non-reproductive physical features, such as breasts in girls and facial hair in boys).

The pubertal landmark in girls is *menarche*, the first menstrual flow. For boys, it is the production of sperm and the first ejaculation (*spermache*). In North America and Europe, these events occur most often around age 11 to 13 for girls and 12 to 14 for boys (Kaltiala-Heino et al., 2003). Considerable variation, however, occurs among people and cultures. In parts of rural southern Mexico, for example, 50 per cent of girls have their first menstrual period after the age of 13 (Malina et al., 2004).

The physical changes of puberty have psychological consequences. For one thing, hormones that steer puberty also can affect mood and behaviour. Reactions to puberty are also influenced by whether it occurs early or late. Overall, early maturation tends to be associated with fewer negative outcomes for boys than for girls. Early-maturing boys are at somewhat heightened risk of engaging in delinquent behaviour and using drugs (Kaltiala-Heino et al., 2003). However, the physical strength and size that they acquire often contribute to a positive body image, success in athletics and popularity among peers.

In contrast, although some early-maturing girls welcome their changed appearance, the weight gain that comes with puberty results in a negative body image for others. Moreover, early maturation often exposes girls to greater social and sexual pressures from boys. Thus, compared with girls who mature later, early-maturing girls typically feel more self-conscious about their bodies and are more likely to eventually develop eating disorders, problems in school, major depression and anxiety (Graber et al., 2004).

The Adolescent Brain

Compared with infancy and early childhood, overall brain growth slows from late childhood to adolescence (Sowell et al., 2001). Still, 'the adolescent brain is a brain in flux', increasing the myelination of neurons, establishing new neural connections while at the same time pruning away and losing a massive number of the over-abundant synaptic connections formed during earlier years of explosive brain growth (Spear, 2000, p. 438). This insulating and streamlining of neural networks permits more efficient communication between brain regions.

Neural restructuring is especially prominent in the prefrontal cortex and the limbic system, regions that play a key role in planning and co-ordinating behaviours that satisfy motivational goals and emotional urges. Moreover, restructuring within the prefrontal cortex includes an upsurge in activity of dopamine, a neurotransmitter involved in regulating emotional arousal, pleasure and reward, and learning (Spear, 2000). Psychologists are actively exploring how these brain changes provide a biological basis for the increase in drug use, risk taking, sensation seeking and aggression displayed by many adolescents.

Physical Development in Adulthood

As maturation continues, people reach their peak of physical and perceptual functioning in young adulthood. The legs, arms and other body parts typically reach maximum muscle strength at age 25 to 30. Vision, hearing, reaction time and co-ordination peak in the early to mid-twenties (Hayslip and Panek, 1989).

Although many physical capacities decline in the mid-thirties, the changes are not noticeable until years later. After age 40, muscles become weaker and less flexible, particularly in people with sedentary habits. *Basal metabolism*, the rate at which the resting body converts food into energy, also slows, resulting in a tendency to gain weight. Middle age is also the time when many people find their visual acuity declining, especially for close viewing. Women's fertility, which begins to decrease in early adulthood, now drops dramatically as the ovaries produce less oestrogen; this process culminates in *menopause*, the cessation of menstruation, which occurs on average around age 50. Male fertility often persists throughout the lifespan, although it tends to decline after middle age. Despite these declines, many middle-aged adults remain in excellent health and are vigorously active. From crown green bowling to running marathons, they may achieve physical goals beyond those attained by many younger adults.

By late adulthood, physical changes become more pronounced. By age 70, bones become more brittle and hardened ligaments make movements stiffer and slower. But with regular exercise and good nutrition, and barring major disease, many adults maintain physical vigour and an active lifestyle well into old age (Fig. 12.24).

The Adult Brain

During the earliest years of adulthood, the brain's neural networks generally continue to become more efficiently integrated (Luna et al., 2004). But like other parts of the body, the brain declines later in adulthood. In a longitudinal study, Resnick and co-workers (2003) used magnetic resonance imaging to measure the loss of brain tissue among 92 men and women over a four-year period. The participants were 59 to 85 years old at the start of the study, and none of them exhibited abnormal cognitive impairments. On average, over the next four years, they lost tissue at a rate of 5.4 per cent per year in the brain regions studied, with the frontal and parietal lobes showing the greatest loss (Fig. 12.25). Participants who were very healthy experienced less tissue loss than those who experienced medical problems, but still, even among physically and mentally healthy older adults, tissue loss is normal as the brain ages.

FIGURE 12.24

Many older adults maintain a physically active lifestyle.

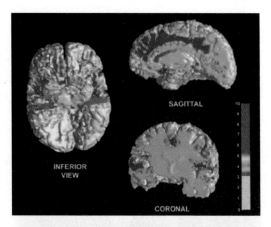

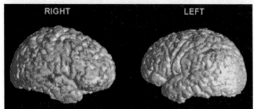

FIGURE 12.25

These photographs portray the average amount of brain-tissue loss that 92 men and women, aged 59 to 85 (who did not have brain disease), experienced over a four-year period. Areas in red had the greatest loss.

SOURCE: Resnick et al., 2003.

COGNITIVE DEVELOPMENT

Supported by continuing brain maturation and learning experiences, cognitive changes during adolescence can be as dramatic as physical ones. Does Figure 12.26 strike a familiar chord? Teenagers can spend a lot of time thinking about themselves and their social circumstances. Such thinking, argues David Elkind (1967), often reflects **adolescent egocentrism**, a self-absorbed and distorted view of one's uniqueness and importance. Elkind proposes that adolescent

Focus 12.10

Describe how physical abilities and the brain change in adulthood.

adolescent egocentrism

a self-absorbed and distorted view of one's uniqueness and importance

ZITS By Jerry Scott and Jim Borgman

Focus 12.11

Discuss the major cognitive changes that occur during adolescence.

egocentrism has two main parts. First, adolescents often overestimate the uniqueness of their feelings and experiences, which Elkind calls the *personal fable*. Examples would be, 'My parents can't possibly understand how I really feel' and 'Nobody's ever felt love as deeply as ours'. Second, many adolescents feel that they are always 'on stage' and that 'everybody's going to notice' how they look and what they do. Elkind calls this oversensitivity to social evaluation the *imaginary audience*.

Adolescents who think more egocentrically are somewhat more likely to engage in risky behaviours, due perhaps in part to a sense of invulnerability (Greene et al., 2000). At the same time, it is not clear that this self-consciousness truly reflects a thinking bias. Some theorists view teenagers' greater self-reflection as a natural outgrowth of the search for individuality and of realistic social consequences that teenagers face (Bell and Bromnick, 2003). They also suggest that young adults, overall, can be just as self-absorbed as adolescents.

Reasoning and Information Processing in Adolescence

Abstract reasoning abilities increase substantially during adolescence. Adolescents can more easily contemplate hypothetical issues, ranging from scientific problems to questions about social justice and the meaning of life (Fig. 12.27a). They reason more flexibly than children and use both the deductive and inductive problem-solving methods described in Chapter 9. Recall that in Piaget's (1970) view, this signifies that adolescents have moved beyond concrete operational thinking and entered a new stage of cognitive development: formal operational thinking.

FIGURE 12.27

Adolescent thinking and the pendulum problem.

(a) When adolescents attain formal operational thought, they can use deductive reasoning to solve scientific problems systematically.
(b) The materials for the pendulum problem used by Inhelder and Piaget include an adjustable string and a set of weights. The problem is to determine which factors influence how long it takes the pendulum to move through its arc. String length is the only relevant factor: the shorter the string, the less time it takes the pendulum to swing back and forth.

SOURCE: adapted from Inhelder and Piaget, 1958.

(a)

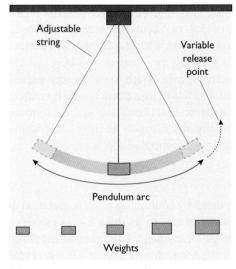

(b)

Consider the pendulum problem in Figure 12.27b. Which variable(s) – length of string, weight of object, how hard it is pushed and release point (height in the arc) – influence(s) how quickly the pendulum oscillates? This problem is best solved by forming and testing an organized set of deductive hypotheses (e.g., '*If* string length is a factor, *then* the swing time with a short versus long string should differ'). Concrete operational children struggle with this task (Inhelder and Piaget, 1958). For example, when they adjust the string length they often adjust the weight as well, making it impossible to draw a conclusion about either variable. In contrast, adolescents think more systematically and manipulate one variable at a time while holding the others constant.

Continued improvements in information-processing capacities help abstract thinking to develop and foster better performance across a wide range of tasks. Although advancing more slowly than during childhood, the speed with which adolescents process information quickens, their working memory becomes more efficient, and they become better able to ignore distracting information, suppress irrelevant responses and stay focused on the task at hand. In one recent study, information-processing speed and visuospatial working-memory abilities began to approach adult-like levels by middle adolescence, and the ability to suppress task-irrelevant responses did so by late adolescence (Luna et al., 2004).

Information Processing in Adulthood

In general, information-processing abilities decline during adulthood, but the age at which they begin to decline can vary substantially. For example, perceptual speed (reaction time) begins to decline steadily in early adulthood, by some estimates as soon as one's early twenties (Salthouse, 2004). As adults grow older, it takes them longer to visually identify and evaluate stimuli, such as when looking at two patterns of lines and deciding whether they are the same. But a loss of perceptual speed may be only part of the reason that older adults perform more slowly on such tasks. By late adulthood, people may process such information more conservatively, essentially trading-off slower response times to gain greater accuracy in their judgements (Ratcliff et al., 2006).

Focus 12.12

How do cognitive and intellectual abilities change in adulthood?

Memory for new factual information also declines. With increasing age, adults generally find it harder to remember new series of numbers, names and faces of new people, and new map directions. On some tasks, such as recalling lists of unrelated words, performance worsens somewhat by the late thirties and then steadily declines after age 50 (Salthouse, 2004). Certain types of verbal memory, however, decline more slowly with age. Thus, the ability immediately to repeat meaningful sentences decreases more slowly than the ability to repeat single, unrelated words. Even in late adulthood, healthy adults do well in recognizing familiar stimuli from long ago, such as the faces of high school class-mates (Bahrick et al., 1975).

The effects of ageing on prospective memory – the ability to remember to perform some action in the future – are less clear (McDaniel et al., 2003). By late adulthood, people generally display poorer prospective memory than young adults in time-based laboratory tasks (e.g., remembering to push a button every 15 minutes). On event-based tasks (e.g., remembering to push a button whenever a light comes on), age differences are less consistent. Moreover, when tested outside the laboratory, older adults may perform as well as young adults, even when the tasks (e.g., simulated pill-taking) are time based. However, when older people remember that they are supposed to execute a task ('Ah, I'm supposed to call Sylvia') and something temporarily delays them from performing it, they will be less likely to remember to perform the task immediately after the delay ends (McDaniel et al., 2003).

Intellectual Changes in Adulthood

How do intellectual abilities change in adulthood? The conclusion from early research seemed clear: After age 30, adults were over the hill. When IQ scores of different age groups were compared in cross-sectional studies, a noticeable decline began between ages 30 and 40 (Doppelt and Wallace, 1955).

However, researchers made an important advance in our understanding by examining separate intellectual abilities rather than overall IQ. They studied *fluid intelligence*, which reflects the ability to perform mental operations (e.g., abstract and logical reasoning, solving spatial problems) and *crystallized intelligence*, which reflects the accumulation of verbal skills and factual knowledge (Horn and Cattell, 1966). Cross-sectional research has typically found that fluid intelligence begins to decline steadily in early adulthood, whereas crystallized intelligence peaks during middle adulthood and then declines in late adulthood (Fig. 12.28a).

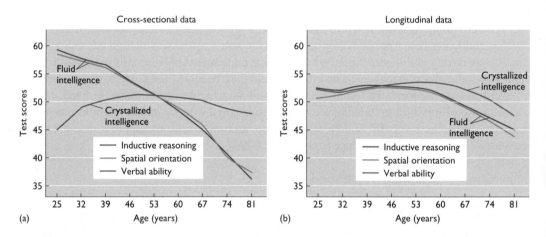

FIGURE 12.28

Intellectual abilities change during adulthood.

(a) Cross-sectional data (ages 25–81) indicate that fluid abilities (reasoning and spatial task performance) begin to decline in young adulthood, whereas crystallized intelligence (verbal ability) begins to decline in late adulthood. (b) However, longitudinal data (ages 25–88) from the same study indicate that both fluid and crystallized intelligence remain fairly stable through young and middle adulthood and do not decline significantly until late adulthood. The longitudinal and cross-sectional data are consistent in showing that crystallized abilities decline at a later age than fluid abilities.

SOURCE: adapted from Schaie, 2005.

Was this early decline in fluid abilities really a function of ageing or instead the result of different experiences encountered by the various generations? The older adults may have had less exposure to scientific problem solving in school or jobs that required less use of abstract intellectual skills. Such factors could have depressed their scores artificially.

To answer this question, K. Warner Schaie of Pennsylvania State University and co-workers (Schaie, 1994; 2005) began a study in 1956 that has now involved several thousand adults. This study uses a sequential design, incorporating longitudinal and cross-sectional components. The longitudinal data do not support an early decline in either fluid or crystallized intelligence. Rather, most abilities are relatively stable throughout early and middle adulthood and do not reliably decline until late adulthood (Fig. 12.28b). But both the cross-sectional and longitudinal data, together with findings from other studies, indicate that fluid intellectual abilities typically begin to decline at an earlier age than crystallized intelligence (Singer et al., 2003).

Is the decline of cognitive abilities that accompanies ageing inevitable? Let us take a closer look 'Beneath the surface'.

Focus 12.13

Critically evaluate the mental exercise hypothesis.

BENEATH THE SURFACE

AGEING AND MENTAL ABILITY: USE IT OR LOSE IT?

When it comes to staying physically fit as we age, experts tell us to 'use it or lose it'. Does this popular advice also apply to mental abilities? Can we prevent or minimize cognitive decline in adulthood by engaging in mentally challenging activities? Let us examine this 'mental exercise hypothesis' (Salthouse, 2006).

To begin, consider that cognitive declines start to occur at different ages and rates for different people. For example, Schaie (1990; 2005) measured five major cognitive abilities (three of which are portrayed in Figure 12.28). He found that between the ages of 60 to 67, about 25 per cent of his participants maintained their levels of functioning for all five abilities, and another 35 per cent maintained their levels of functioning for four of these abilities. Even between ages 74 to 81 years, about 15 per cent of participants maintained their levels of functioning for all five abilities. Importantly, Schaie (1994; 2005) found that people who retained their levels of cognitive functioning for a longer time tended to have above-average education, engaged in cognitively stimulating jobs and personal activities (e.g., reading, travel), and married a spouse with greater intellectual abilities than their own.

This and similar findings from other studies are consistent with the mental exercise hypothesis. But as a critical thinker, you should recognize that such findings are correlational and must be interpreted cautiously in terms of inferring cause and effect. Does engaging in cognitively stimulating activities (variable X) cause people to retain more mental ability (variable Y), or does retaining more mental ability (perhaps due to natural maturation processes) better allow people to engage in cognitively demanding activities? Of course, such bidirectionality problems can be ruled out for some findings: Maintaining better cognitive functioning after age 60 certainly cannot influence the level of education you have achieved earlier in life! Still, remember that in correlational research, it is always possible that other unknown factors – 'third variables' – may be the true cause of why X and Y are associated.

Other evidence comes from many experiments that find older adults' mental abilities can be improved by providing them with cognitively stimulating experiences. In one study of 70- to 91-year-olds, participants' performance at tasks requiring reasoning, visual attention and perceptual-motor speed improved significantly after six one-hour exposures to those tasks (Yang et al., 2006). In another study, Schaie and his co-workers found that 65- to 95-year-old adults' spatial and reasoning abilities could be improved by teaching them strategies for performing such tasks (Saczynski et al., 2002; Willis and Schaie, 1986). For many adults, this training restored their performance to the level it had been 14 years earlier. Moreover, compared with adults who did not receive training, the trained adults were on average still performing better 14 years later. Even playing video games that require fast reaction times seems to boost 70- and 80-year-olds' cognitive abilities (Goldstein et al., 1997).

Based on such findings from many training experiments, shall we conclude that mental exercise reduces the cognitive declines of ageing? Not so fast, says psychologist Timothy Salthouse (2006), a leading researcher on mental ageing: training experiments show that stimulating activities can boost cognitive skills, but they have not reliably shown that those activities change the *rate* (i.e., the slope) at which those skills decline with age.

Consider this hypothetical example. At the start of an experiment, adults in a training group and no training (control) group exhibit the same average score – 70 out of 100 possible points – on a test of abstract reasoning. After the experiment ends, the trained adults' reasoning skills have been boosted by 10 points (average score 80). For the next five years, we find that each group's performance decreases on average by one point per year. Therefore, five years after our experiment, the trained group (average score 75) will still perform better than the untrained group (average score 65) by 10 points, but both groups will have declined cognitively, and at the same rate. Of course, we could repeatedly expose people to the training each year to try to keep their skills up, but with advancing age in late adulthood, the same retraining will likely take longer, or produce smaller improvements (Yang et al., 2006).

Critically examining other types of research as well, Salthouse (2006) believes that at present the mental exercise hypothesis is more a reflection of optimistic hope – a desire to feel that we can control how we age – than reality. Still, he recommends that we should seek out cognitively stimulating activities because they can be enjoyable and because 'there is no evidence that it has any harmful effects' (Salthouse, 2006, p. 84). To this we add that even if research has not yet reliably shown that mental exercise changes rates of cognitive decline, the well-established finding that it can boost people's absolute levels of cognitive skills is no trivial matter.

The Growth of Wisdom?

Even as various mental abilities begin to decline with age, people can still accumulate knowledge that leads to greater wisdom. A common-sense adage says that as we age, we become 'older but wiser'? Do we?

Focus 12.14

Do we become 'older but wiser' during adulthood? Describe senile dementia.

Wisdom includes knowledge about human nature and social relationships, strategies for making decisions and handling conflict, and an ability to manage uncertainty (Baltes and Kunzmann, 2004). To study the growth of wisdom, psychologists present people of different ages with hypothetical social problems or situations (e.g., a 15-year-old girl wants to get married right away) and ask them to provide solutions. Experts blind to the participants' ages then use specific criteria to judge the wisdom of the participants' answers.

Some findings suggest that wisdom rises steadily from age 13 to 25 and then remains relatively stable through to age 75 (Baltes and Staudinger, 2000). Other studies, however, have found that adults in their seventies offer wiser solutions than young adults on some tasks (Happé et al., 1998).

To take a conservative position, it may be that from adolescence through to one's mid-seventies, 'older but wiser' applies only up to a point, beyond which 'older but at least as wise' is more appropriate. Of course, these are averages, and to stereotype elderly adults as 'wise' is just as inappropriate as to stereotype them as 'senile'.

Cognitive Impairment in Old Age

As we noted in Chapter 8, *dementia* is a gradual loss of cognitive abilities that accompanies abnormal brain deterioration and interferes with daily functioning. In people with dementia, an abnormal progressive degeneration of brain tissue occurs as a result of disease or injury.

senile dementia

dementia that begins after age 65

Dementia is most common in late adulthood, and the term **senile dementia** refers to dementia that begins after age 65. Alzheimer's disease (AD), which we previously discussed in Chapter 8 in relation to memory loss, accounts for about two-thirds of senile dementia cases (Grossman et al., 2006). Overall, about 5 to 7 per cent of adults aged 65 years and older have AD, but this percentage increases substantially with age (Hirtz et al., 2007). Parkinson's disease, Huntington's disease and Creutzfeldt-Jakob disease are other common causes of senile dementia, and complications from high blood pressure and stroke may also be causes.

Impaired memory, particularly for very recent events, typically is one of the first symptoms of dementia to appear (Fig. 12.29). Poor judgement, language problems and disorientation may appear gradually or sporadically, and people who develop dementia typically have episodes of distress because they feel confused. Their behaviour may become uninhibited, they may lose the ability to perform familiar tasks, and they may experience significant physical decline in addition to cognitive impairments.

Compared with other adults aged 65 years and older, those who more frequently engage in stimulating cognitive activity show a lower risk for subsequently developing Alzheimer's disease, but whether this truly reflects a causal relation remains to be seen (Wilson and Bennett, 2003). One thing is certain: as people live longer lives, finding a cure for Alzheimer's disease

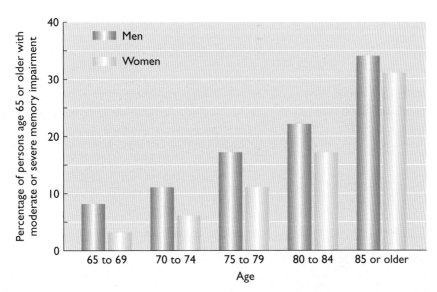

FIGURE 12.29

Impaired memory on a word-recall task.

Participants in this U.S. sample were read a list of 20 words and asked to recall as many as they could. Most healthy adults were able to recall between five and nine words. This graph shows that the percentage of people who recalled four or fewer words increased steadily during late adulthood.

SOURCE: Federal Interagency Forum on Aging-Related Statistics, U.S. 2006.

and other forms of senile dementia becomes more urgent. Until then, many of us can expect our own family members to become Alzheimer's patients.

Unfortunately, being a caregiver for a spouse or for one's elderly parent who has developed dementia is often a stressful and psychologically painful experience (Pinquart and Sörensen, 2003). More than half of the people diagnosed with senile dementia show combinations of depression, anxiety, agitation, paranoid reactions and disordered thinking that may resemble schizophrenia. Ultimately, they may not even be able to walk, talk or recognize close friends or family members.

In-depth studies in Finland, Germany and the USA find that among adults over the age of 65 who do not suffer from dementia, 20 to 25 per cent do have mild cognitive impairment (Unverzagt et al., 2001). Combining cases of mild impairment and dementia, some experts estimate that 79 per cent of 65- to 74-year-olds and 45 per cent of people age 85 and older remain 'cognitively normal' (Unverzagt et al., 2001). These are not pleasant statistics, but they also make clear that even well into old age, cognitive impairment is not inevitable.

Figure 12.30 summarizes some of the diverse factors that affect cognitive development.

FIGURE 12.30

Levels of analysis: factors related to lifespan development.

LEVELS OF ANALYSIS FACTORS RELATED TO LIFESPAN DEVELOPMENT		
Biological	**Psychological**	**Environmental**
• Sex determination and genetic contribution to temperament • Brain maturation underlying cognitive growth in childhood • Pubertal changes, including early and late maturation • Biologically based physical and cognitive changes in adulthood	• Changes in schemas, information processing and intellectual capacities • Development of an understanding of objects in the physical world (including an understanding of numbers and permanence) • Development of an understanding of the mental states of the self and others • Developing use of logical operations, and hypothesis-testing procedures (e.g., in the pendulum task)	• Teratogens that affect pre-natal development • Exercise and lifestyle norms that affect biological functions at all ages • Collaboration of others in cognitive development • Social conceptions of the decline of intelligence in old age

Lifespan development

IN REVIEW

- Adolescence is a socially constructed transition period between childhood and adulthood. Puberty is a major component of adolescence. Generally, early maturation is a more-positive experience for boys than it is for girls.

- Young adults are at the peak of their physical capabilities, but brain functioning undergoes a general decline later in adulthood.

- Adolescents may show egocentrism in their social thinking. Their abstract thinking blossoms and information-processing abilities improve.

- Information-processing speed slows beginning in early adulthood, but many intellectual abilities do not begin to decline reliably until late adulthood. Wisdom appears to increase steadily from early adolescence through the mid-twenties and then level off through the mid-seventies.

KEY TERMS AND CONCEPTS

Each term has been boldfaced and defined in the chapter on the page indicated in parentheses.

accommodation (p. 543)

adolescent egocentrism (p. 555)

assimilation (p. 543)

cephalocaudal trajectory (p. 540)

concrete operational stage (p. 545)

conservation (p. 544)

critical period (p. 530)

cross-sectional design (p. 530)

egocentrism (p. 545)

embryo (p. 532)

foetal alcohol syndrome (FAS) (p. 533)

foetus (p. 532)

formal operational stage (p. 546)

longitudinal design (p. 530)

object permanence (p. 544)

pre-operational stage (p. 544)

proximodistal trajectory (p. 540)

puberty (p. 553)

reflexes (p. 535)

schemas (p. 542)

senile dementia (p. 560)

sensitive period (p. 530)

sensorimotor stage (p. 544)

sequential design (p. 531)

teratogens (p. 533)

theory of mind (p. 552)

zone of proximal development (ZPD) (p. 549)

zygote (p. 532)

WHAT DO YOU THINK?

THE DEVELOPMENT OF FACE DISCRIMINATION IN THE FIRST YEAR OF LIFE (p. 540)

Pascalis et al. (2003) used a visual habituation method in which they exposed infants to a single face and, after a few seconds' exposure, examined whether they would show a preference when presented with the familiar and a novel face paired together. A novelty preference would indicate recognition and discrimination of the familiar from the novel face. They examined 6-month-olds' and 10-month-olds' ability to discriminate between different human faces and different monkey faces. They found that the younger age-group showed a preference for both novel human faces and novel monkey faces. The older age-group however only showed a preference for novel human faces. It seems that face discrimination, like speech sound discrimination, undergoes perceptual narrowing in the first year of life. Infants are initially able to discriminate between faces, whatever species of primate they belong to. However, by 10 months they lose the ability to discriminate between faces of a species they do not usually see in their everyday environment, they undergo perceptual narrowing, homing in on and discriminating only the important information in their environment.

CHAPTER THIRTEEN

LIFESPAN DEVELOPMENT II: SOCIAL AND EMOTIONAL DEVELOPMENT

CHAPTER OUTLINE

There are only two lasting bequests we can hope to give our children. One of these is roots; the other, wings.

HODDING CARTER

FIGURE 13.1

John Bowlby

In 1944 John Bowlby (Fig. 13.1), the famous psychoanalyst, published an article entitled, 'Forty-four juvenile thieves: their characters and home-life'. In this article he reported his observations concerning the psychopathology of 44 juvenile delinquent thieves, and examined the links between their delinquency, their psychopathology and the environment in which they had grown up. In 1940s Britain, theft accounted for nine out of ten criminal cases. Over half of those concerned individuals under the age of 21, and one-sixth concerned children under the age of 14. Bowlby's aim was to discover the causes of this apparent epidemic of criminal behaviour in young people.

The 'forty-four juvenile thieves' ranged from 5 to 17 years of age. All had engaged in some form of theft, be that a single incident or persistent and serious stealing. Their IQ and socio-economic status were normal if not slightly above average for the population. Bowlby identified a variety of mental health problems among them, including depression, mania, impairments in affection, and schizophrenia. But unsatisfied with mental health as an aetiological explanation for the thieves' criminal activity, Bowlby wanted to examine the root causes of both their mental health problems and their antisocial behaviour. He focused specifically on the quality of parental care which the children had received in early life, and found that 17 of the thieves had suffered complete and prolonged separation from their mothers or foster mothers during the first five years of life. Of the other 27 thieves, 17 had mothers who he considered to be hostile towards them, and five had extremely hostile fathers. Perhaps most strikingly he found that prolonged separation from the mother was a strong predictor of the more chronic thieving behaviours among the 44.

The 44 thieves study, among other observations which Bowlby made, led him to propose the 'maternal deprivation hypothesis'; the hypothesis that attachment bonds between infant and parent in the first years of life are vital to ensure well-adjusted socio-emotional development. He thus proposed that *maternal deprivation* led to the maladjusted behaviours of the 44 thieves. While researchers have argued over some of the details of Bowlby's hypothesis, it is quite intuitive to all of us that, on some level, the social bonds we form must have a role in shaping who we are, both in terms of the ways in which we think about the world and in the social bonds we in turn form with others.

As with physical and cognitive development (see Chapter 12), researchers examining social and emotional development tend to consider two main questions. First, how can we describe the changes in emotional and social behaviour which individuals undergo as they progress from newborn to adult and old age? Second, what factors cause these changes? Bowlby's maternal deprivation hypothesis made a strong statement that normal, or well-adjusted social development was determined by the social bonds infants form with their mother in the first years of life. As we shall see, researchers have questioned whether such a large role can be placed on the family environment, and whether in fact, the temperament or personality that an individual's genes bestow upon them, or indeed the social environment outside the home may play just as important roles in our social development. In this chapter we describe what research has shown us so far.

INFANCY AND EARLY CHILDHOOD

Children grow not only physically and mentally but also emotionally and socially. They form attachments and relationships, and each child displays a unique personality – a distinctive yet somewhat consistent pattern of thinking, feeling and behaving.

NEWBORN EMOTIONS AND EMOTIONAL DEVELOPMENT

Emotional responses communicate our inner states to other people and influence how others respond to us (Fig. 13.2). Although infants cannot describe their feelings, Figure 13.2 illustrates that their facial expressions, vocalizations and other behaviours provide a window into their emotional life (Izard, 1982). If you have heard a newborn cry (and cry and cry) or watched a newborn's face after it has been fed, then you know that they can experience distress and contentment. We can also perceive a number of other emotions in young infants. For example, when we see a baby focusing their gaze and staring at objects, this gives a palpable sense that they are interested in the focus of their attention. As infants get older and turn into children, these more basic emotions branch out and divide into more fine-grained distinctions. About six months after birth, infants begin to show joy and surprise ('peekaboo ... I see you!'), and distress branches out into the separate emotions of disgust, anger, fear and sadness (Lewis, 2000). For example, Izard et al. (1987), observed infants between the ages of 2 and 8 months, while they received routine vaccination injections. The younger infants showed a more general distressed response to this unpleasant event, whereas the older infants began to demonstrate expressions of anger.

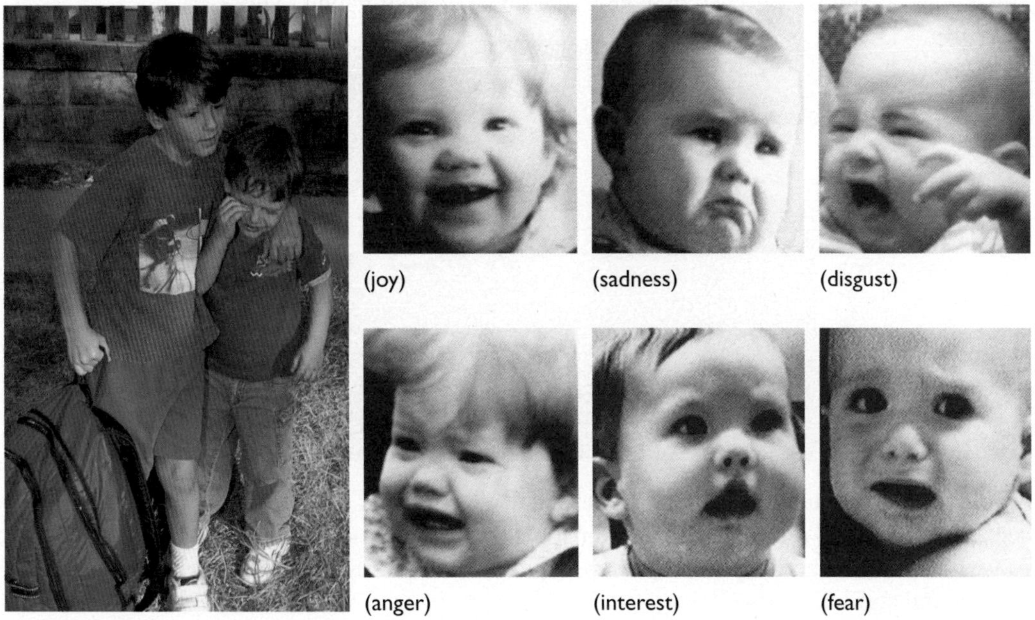

> **Focus 13.1**
> Describe the emotional life of a newborn baby.

(joy) (sadness) (disgust)

(anger) (interest) (fear)

FIGURE 13.2

(*Left*) Emotional responses communicate our internal states, and they can influence how others respond to us, providing us with the aid and comfort we need. (*Right*) Young infants display a variety of emotions.

emotion regulation

the processes by which we evaluate and modify our emotional reactions

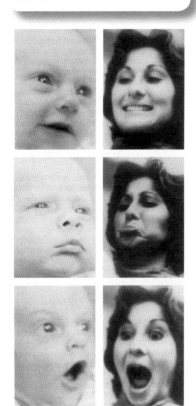

FIGURE 13.3

Emotional imitation in newborn infants.

SOURCE: Field et al., 1982.

FIGURE 13.4

The visual cliff. This experimental apparatus is comprised of a glass tabletop, one side of which sits above a deep 'cliff', and the other side of which sites above a shallow step. Left to their own devices, crawling infants will avoid stepping over the cliff onto the steep side, but what will they do if someone encourages them to do so? Sorce et al. (1985) investigated.

SOURCE: Sorce et al., 1985.

Around 18 months of age, infants begin to develop a sense of self, as illustrated by their ability to recognize themselves in a mirror (Lewis and Brooks-Gunn, 1979). This growing self-awareness sets the stage for envy, embarrassment and empathy to emerge. After age 2, as toddlers learn about performance standards and rules that they are supposed to follow, they begin to display pride and shame. Around the same age, they also display guilt – as evidenced by avoiding eye contact, shrugging shoulders and making facial expressions (Kochanska et al., 1995).

Just as emotional reactions become more diverse with age, so does **emotion regulation**, the processes by which we evaluate and modify our emotional reactions. Young infants may suck their thumb or pacifier, turn their head away from something unpleasant or cling to a caretaker to soothe themselves. To reduce distress, toddlers may seek out a caretaker, cling to a doll or teddy bear, fling unpleasant objects away, and learn to smile, pout or throw a tantrum to get what they want. Once they acquire language, children can reduce distress by talking to themselves and other people.

As children age, their emotional expressiveness and ability to regulate their emotions become part of their overall *emotional competence*, which in turn influences their social behaviour and how well their peers and other people like them. Children who frequently display sadness or who cannot control their anger are less likely to be popular, and emotional competence remains important for well-being as children develop (Eisenberg, 2002).

Importantly, as well as being able to display and regulate their own emotions, infants and children have to be able to recognize emotions in others. Research by Field et al. (1982) has shown that newborn babies will imitate the emotional expressions they see in others (see Fig. 13.3), indicating that they are at least able to distinguish between these facial expressions. But do they recognize the emotions which underlie these; do they feel the emotions themselves through empathy, or are they simply aping? It is difficult to know.

'Social referencing' is a behaviour in which infants or children use the emotions of another person (often the caregiver) to guide their actions. Sorce et al. (1985), undertook an experiment on social referencing using the 'visual cliff' (Fig. 13.4). In this study the infants were placed in front of the cliff, and a parent was positioned on their other side of the cliff and adopted either a happy encouraging expression or a fearful expression. If the mother adopted a happy face, the infants were fairly likely to cross over. Almost none of the infants whose mother adopted the fearful face attempted to. Their actions were guided by their parent's emotions.

Socialization influences children's emotional development, as parents, teachers and peers serve as models and reinforce children for some types of emotional responses (Ahn, 2005). But as we now explore, heredity makes a very important contribution to children's basic emotional-behavioural style.

PERSONALITY DEVELOPMENT

Do babies have personalities? Ask any parent who has had more than one and they will say yes. Some babies appear very docile, and are easy to look after. Some of the most docile babies let their parents sleep for as much as six hours at night! Other babies are a tumultuous bundle of emotions, and seem to have a vocal response to almost everything or everyone they encounter. Developmental psychologists have investigated the individual differences in personality which infants bring with them into the world, and have attempted to describe them. Infant personality is known as temperament.

Infant Temperament

From the moment of birth, infants differ from one another in **temperament**, a biologically based general style of reacting emotionally and behaviourally to the environment. Some infants are calm and happy; others are irritable and fussy. Some are outgoing and active; others are shy and inactive. Indeed, within any age group – children, adolescents or adults – people differ in temperament (Fox et al., 2005; McCrae and Costa, 1990).

In a pioneering study, Alexander Thomas and Stella Chess (1977) asked parents to describe their babies' behaviour. They found that most infants could be classified into three groups. 'Easy infants' ate and slept on schedule, were playful and accepted new situations with little fuss. 'Difficult infants' were irritable, were fussy eaters and sleepers, and reacted negatively to new situations. 'Slow-to-warm-up infants' were the least active, had mildly negative responses to new situations but slowly adapted over time. Subsequently, the difficult infants were most likely to develop emotional and behaviour problems during childhood.

This study was admired but also criticized for relying on parents' reports of their infants' behaviour. Other researchers directly observed infants and identified temperamental styles that differed from those described by Thomas and Chess (1977). Moreover, researchers often found that temperament is only weakly to moderately stable during infancy (Carnicero et al., 2000). Some infants maintain a consistent temperament during their first two years of life, whereas others change.

Consider shyness, which forms part of a more general temperament style called *behavioural inhibition*. Inhibited infants are quiet and timid; they cry and withdraw when exposed to unfamiliar people, places, objects and sounds. Uninhibited infants are more sociable, verbal and spontaneous. Research by Jerome Kagan and co-workers (1988) found that about 20 to 25 per cent of infants displayed this inhibited pattern, which remained moderately stable during infancy. They also studied these infants until age 7½. For the vast majority – those who were only mildly to moderately inhibited or uninhibited between the ages of 1 and 2 years – their temperament did not predict how shy or outgoing they would be as children. But for infants who were *highly* uninhibited or inhibited, the findings were different. Highly uninhibited infants tended to become sociable and talkative 7-year-olds, whereas highly inhibited infants developed into quiet, cautious and shy 7-year-olds (Kagan, 1989).

> **Focus 13.2**
> What individual differences are there in personality in the first year of life?

> **temperament**
> a biologically based general style of reacting emotionally and behaviourally to the environment

WHAT DO YOU THINK?

SHY CHILD, SHY ADULT?

We have just seen that very shy or very outgoing infants tend to retain these traits into early childhood. Do you think that the very shy or outgoing child grows into a shy or outgoing adult? In general, does childhood temperament predict adult behaviour? Think about it, then see p. 597.

Focus 13.3

Describe Erikson's psychosocial theory.

Erikson's Psychosocial Theory

Psychoanalytic psychologist Erik Erikson (1968) believed that personality develops through confronting a series of eight major **psychosocial stages**, each of which involves a different 'crisis' (i.e., conflict) over how we view ourselves in relation to other people and the world (Table 13.1). Each crisis is present throughout life but takes on special importance during a particular age period. Four of these crises occur in infancy and childhood:

1. *Basic trust versus basic mistrust*: depending on how well our needs are met and how much love and attention we receive during the first year of life, we develop a basic trust or basic mistrust of the world.

2. *Autonomy versus shame and doubt*: during the next two years, children become ready to exercise their individuality. If parents unduly restrict children or make harsh demands during toilet training, children develop shame and doubt about their abilities and later lack the courage to be independent.

3. *Initiative versus guilt*: from age 3 to age 5, children display great curiosity about the world. If they are allowed freedom to explore and receive answers to their questions, they develop a sense of initiative. If they are held back or punished, they develop guilt about their desires and suppress their curiosity.

4. *Industry versus inferiority*: from age 6 until puberty, the child's life expands into school and peer activities. Children who experience pride and encouragement in mastering tasks develop *industry* – a striving to achieve. Repeated failure and lack of praise for trying leads to a sense of inferiority.

psychosocial stages

each involves a different 'crisis' (i.e., conflict) over how we view ourselves in relation to other people and the world

TABLE 13.1 ERIKSON'S PSYCHOSOCIAL STAGES

Age (approximate years)	Major psychosocial crisis
Infancy (first year)	Basic trust vs basic mistrust
Toddlerhood (1–2)	Autonomy vs shame and doubt
Early childhood (3–5)	Initiative vs guilt
Middle childhood(6–12)	Industry vs inferiority
Adolescence (12–19)	Identity vs role confusion
Early adulthood (20–30)	Intimacy vs isolation
Middle adulthood(40–64)	Generativity vs stagnation
Late adulthood (65+)	Integrity vs despair

Although critics argue that Erikson's model lacks detail and question its stage approach, the model captures several major issues that developing children confront. As Erikson proposed and as some research supports, successfully resolving each crisis helps prepare us to meet the next (McAdams and de St Aubin, 1998). Because each stage of life creates new opportunities, possibilities for change are ever present. Yet like the early chapters of a novel, themes that emerge in childhood help set the stage for the unfolding story of our lives.

SOCIAL DEVELOPMENT AND ATTACHMENT

The Social Newborn

Focus 13.4

What social abilities do newborn babies have?

As well as their temperaments, infants also bring many social skills with them into the world. Some of the most obvious communicative skills already discussed are smiling and crying. These let the observer know what emotional state the infant is in. As Figure 13.5 demonstrates, smiling occurs before there is anyone present to recognize this (without the help of ultrasound). After birth, newborns smile spontaneously, without reference to any specific environmental stimulus. However, by as early as 3 weeks of age infants begin smiling in specific situations (e.g., on eye contact). Crying is a vocal communication of distress, and often happens a few moments after arriving into the outside world (this is probably quite a distressing event following the comfort and calm of the womb). Crying is an effective communicative signal and, being very difficult for adults to ignore, frequently elicits a response in the caregiver.

As we discussed in Chapter 12, newborn infants prefer to look at faces over most other environmental stimuli (Fantz, 1961; Johnson et al., 1991). This preferential orienting behaviour directs infants' attention towards people and, consequently, social situations. Research by Farroni and colleagues (2002) has demonstrated that newborn infants also prefer to look at faces making direct eye contact with them, as opposed to faces with averted gaze. So newborn infants are also predisposed to attend not just to people, but also to situations in which another person is communicating with them. Researchers such as Csibra and Gergely (2006) have thus argued that we are innately disposed to learn about the world from others. Eibl-Eibesfeld, an ethologist, has also argued that as adults we are programmed to encourage this learning with universal behaviours such as the 'eyebrow flash' (Grammar et al., 1988; see Fig. 13.6).

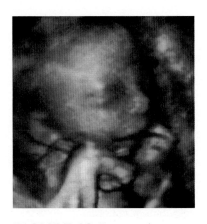

FIGURE 13.5

An ultrasound image of a human foetus smiling *in utero*. We make this communicative expression before there is anyone around to see it.

FIGURE 13.6

A young woman from the Himba tribe (a semi-nomadic tribe in Namibia who have relatively little contact with westerners), makes an eyebrow flash to a young infant. Eibl-Elbesfeld argues that the eyebrow flash occurs in all cultures, suggesting that we do not learn to do it from others, but are genetically predisposed to make this communicative gesture.

Young infants also demonstrate the origins of conversations in their behaviour. Young infants' vocalizations and motor behaviour is often described as showing 'periodicity' or 'burst–pause' patterns. This means that they will vocalize or move a number of times in quick succession, stop for a period and then produce another burst of activity. This periodicity gives other people the chance to communicate back to the infant during the pauses, thus producing prelinguistic conversations ('proto-conversations').

Another early social interaction can be observed in newborns imitation behaviour. As we saw above, newborn infants imitate adults' emotional facial expressions. Meltzoff and colleagues have also shown that newborns will imitate a range of non-emotional facial gestures (Meltzoff, 2002; Fig. 13.7). Researchers are divided about why infants should do this. Some suggests that it helps newborns understand others' perspectives, while Csibra and Gergely (2006) have argued that imitation helps us to learn new skills from others.

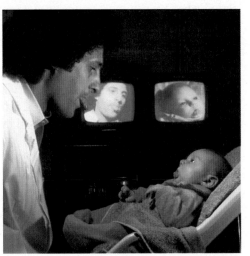

FIGURE 13.7

Young infants have been found to reproduce tongue protrusion after watching an adult model. Here researcher Andrew Meltzoff models the behaviour and records an infant's response.

The newborn infant thus seems to be provided with a set of behaviours which allow him or her to become involved in social interactions. It is likely that the earliest of these interactions will be with their parents or caregivers, at least partly because these people are in closest proximity. However, as they age, infants begin to demonstrate strong preferences for interacting with particular individuals (usually their parents). These social bonds which are formed between infant and adult are referred to as *attachment relationships*.

Attachment

Focus 13.5
Discuss imprinting, Harlow's attachment research, and attachment in humans.

imprinting
a sudden, biologically primed form of attachment

Imagine a single-file procession of ducklings following you around campus and everywhere you went, as if you were their mother. For this to happen, we would only need to isolate the ducklings after they hatched and then expose them to you at a certain time. If they later encountered their real parents, the ducklings would ignore them and continue to follow you (Hess, 1959).

German ethologist Konrad Lorenz (1937) called this behaviour **imprinting**, a sudden, biologically primed form of attachment (Fig. 13.8). It occurs in some bird species, including ducks and geese, and in a few mammals, such as shrews. Imprinting involves a critical period. In mallard ducklings, the strongest imprinting occurs within a day after hatching, and by two days the capacity to imprint is lost (Hess, 1959). Thus, in some species, offspring must be exposed to parents within hours or days after entering the world to attach to them.

FIGURE 13.8

(*Left*) Canadian wildlife sculptor Bill Lishman imprinted Canada geese hatchlings to the sight of his ultralight airplane. Although they have now matured, the ultralight still represents 'mother' to the geese, and they follow it in flight. (*Right*) In humans, infant–caretaker attachment is more complex and forms over a much longer period.

attachment
the strong emotional bond that develops between children and their primary caregivers

In humans, **attachment** refers to the strong emotional bond that develops between children and their primary caregivers (see Fig. 13.8). Human infants do not automatically imprint on a caregiver, and there is not an immediate post-birth critical period during which contact is required for infant–caregiver bonding. Instead, the first few years of life seem to be a sensitive period when we can most easily form a secure bond with caregivers that enhances our adjustment later in life (Sroufe, 2002). Although it may be more difficult to form strong first attachments to caregivers later in childhood or later still in adulthood, it is still possible.

The attachment process   For decades, people assumed that infant–caregiver bonding resulted primarily from the mother's role in satisfying the infant's need for nourishment. Harry Harlow (1958) tested this notion by separating infant rhesus monkeys from their biological mothers shortly after birth. Each infant was raised in a cage with two artificial 'surrogate mothers'. One was a bare-wire cylinder with a feeding bottle attached to its 'chest'. The other was a wire cylinder covered with soft terry cloth without a feeding bottle.

Faced with this choice, the infant monkeys became attached to the cloth mother. When exposed to frightening situations, the infants ran to the cloth figure and clung tightly to it. They even maintained contact with the cloth mother while feeding from the wire mother's bottle (Fig. 13.9). Thus Harlow showed that *contact comfort* – body contact with a comforting object – is more important in fostering attachment than the provision of nourishment.

Around this time, other researchers studied human attachment in African, European and North American societies. Based on this work, and his own observations concerning maternal deprivation (like those in the study of the 44 thieves) John Bowlby (1969) proposed that attachment in infancy develops in five phases:

1. *Indiscriminate attachment behaviour*: newborns cry, vocalize and smile towards everyone, and these behaviours evoke caregiving from adults.

2. *Discriminating attachment behaviour*: around 3 months of age, infants direct their attachment behaviours more towards familiar caregivers than towards strangers.

3. *Specific attachment behaviour*: by 7 or 8 months of age, infants develop a meaningful attachment to specific caregivers. The caregiver becomes a secure base from which the infant can explore his or her environment.

FIGURE 13.9

Infant monkeys, reared with a cloth-covered surrogate and a bare-wire surrogate from birth, preferred contact with the cloth 'mother' even though the wire 'mother' satisfied nutritional needs.

SOURCE: from Harlow, 1958.

4. *Goal-corrected attachment behaviour*: by 3 years of age the child can now take account of the caregiver's needs when expressing attachment. For example they begin to be able to wait alone until the return of the caregiver to allow the mother to achieve something independently. In this sense the attachment relationship becomes more of a 'partnership'.

5. *Lessening of attachment*: at school age, children become happy to spend significant amounts of time further away from the caregiver. At this point Bowlby suggested that the relationship becomes more based upon abstract conceptions of attachment, including trust and affection.

As an infant's attachment becomes more focused, two types of anxiety occur. **Stranger anxiety**, distress over contact with unfamiliar people, often emerges around age 6 or 7 months and ends by age 18 months. When approached by, touched by or handed over to a stranger, the infant becomes afraid, cries and reaches for the caregiver. **Separation anxiety**, distress over being separated from a primary caregiver, typically begins a little later, peaks around age 12 to 16 months and disappears between 2 and 3 years of age. Here the infant becomes anxious and cries when the caregiver is out of sight. Both forms of anxiety show a similar pattern across many cultures (Fig. 13.10).

stranger anxiety
distress over contact with unfamiliar people

separation anxiety
distress over being separated from a primary caregiver

These responses, which coincide with infants' increasing cognitive and physical abilities, may be adaptive reactions shaped through evolution (Bowlby, 1973). At an age when infants master crawling and then learn to walk, fear of strangers and of separation may help prevent them from wandering beyond the sight of caretakers, especially in unfamiliar situations.

Around age 3 to 4 years, as children's cognitive and verbal skills grow, they develop a better understanding of their attachment relationships. According to Bowlby (1969), a stage of *goal-corrected partnership* emerges, in which children and caregivers can describe their feelings to each other and maintain their relationship whether they are together or apart.

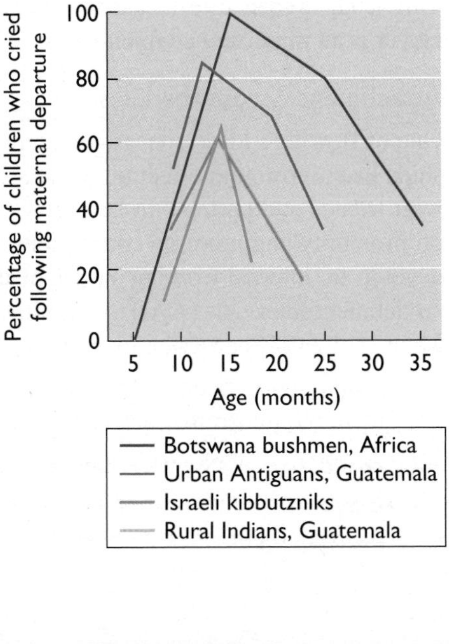

FIGURE 13.10

Separation anxiety across cultures.

The rise and fall of separation anxiety in infancy shows a similar pattern across cultures.

SOURCE: based on Kagan et al., 1978.

Graph: Percentage of children who cried following maternal departure (y-axis, 0–100) versus Age (months) (x-axis, 5–35).

— Botswana bushmen, Africa
— Urban Antiguans, Guatemala
— Israeli kibbutzniks
— Rural Indians, Guatemala

Focus 13.6

Describe types of attachment, how they are measured and how attachment deprivation affects development.

strange situation

a standardized procedure for examining infant attachment

Types of attachment   Infants develop different types of attachments with their caretakers. In order to measure this, Mary Ainsworth and co-workers (1978) developed the **strange situation**, a standardized procedure for examining infant attachment. In the strange situation, the infant, typically a 12- to 18-month-old, first plays with toys in the mother's presence. Then a stranger enters the room and interacts with the child. Soon the mother departs, leaving the child with the stranger. Later the stranger departs, and the child is alone. Finally, the mother returns. The infant's behaviour is observed throughout this procedure.

In the mother's presence, 'securely attached' infants explore the playroom and react positively to the stranger (Ainsworth et al., 1978). They are distressed when the mother leaves and happily greet her when she returns. In contrast, there are two types of 'insecurely attached' infants. 'Anxious-resistant' infants are fearful when the mother is present, demand her attention and are distressed when she leaves. They are not soothed when she returns and may angrily resist her attempts at contact. 'Anxious-avoidant' infants show few signs of attachment, seldom cry when the mother leaves and do not seek contact when she returns.

Across most cultures studied, about one-half to three-quarters of infants are securely attached. But what is the cause of these differences in attachment? Is it the nature of the relationships which the child is exposed to or is it more to do with the temperament of the child him or herself? Mothers who are more sensitive to their babies' needs at home tend to have infants who are more securely attached in the strange situation (Posada et al., 2002). Are the babies more securely attached because of maternal sensitivity, or are the mothers more sensitive to their infants needs because they are influenced by the secure nature of their attachment to the child. This question illustrates an important point. When we talk about attachment we are not just considering the child's behaviour in the relationship, but rather a bidirectional attachment relationship as a whole, including the mother's attachment to the child. Nonetheless behavioural genetics studies (see Chapter 3) indicate only a modest genetic heretability of attachment type (van Ijzendoorn et al., 2000), suggesting that environmental influences are more important in the formation of attachment relationships. But what are these environmental influences? While maternal sensitivity was put forward as a candidate by Ainsworth and colleagues (1978), researchers have more recently suggested that parental consideration of their children's internal emotional states is more important than their responses to the infants' actual behaviour (Meins et al., 2001).

What are the consequences of attachment? It turns out that whether raised by their biological parents or by adoptive parents, securely attached infants seem to be better adjusted socially during childhood. Establishing a secure attachment early in life also may help foster a capacity for compassion and altruism that carries forward into adulthood (Mikulincer and Shaver, 2005). This lends credence to Erikson's view that entering a stable, trusting relationship with a caregiver is an important component of early social development.

Attachment Across the Lifespan

One of Bowlby's ideas concerning attachment was that the nature of early attachment relationships had a profound effect on the ways in which adolescents and adults formed relationships with friends and partners in later life. As children's attachment behaviours become less based on proximity and more on conceptions of love, affection and trust, Bowlby suggests that they develop an 'internal working model' of attachment. Researchers have in fact developed an Adult Attachment Interview (AAI) to examine different kinds of conceptions of attachments in adults. Main et al. (1985) describe four styles of thinking about attachment in adults:

1. *Autonomous*: adults who are able to reflect objectively and openly on their previous attachment relationships, even if these were not always positive experiences.

2. *Dismissive*: adults who dismiss the importance of attachment relationships.

3. *Enmeshed*: adults who think a lot about their dependency on their parents and worry about pleasing them.

4. *Unresolved*: adults who have experienced a traumatic attachment, or loss of an attachment figure, and are still resolving their thoughts on this.

It turns out that there are some relationships between early attachment styles (as measured in the strange situation) and adult attachment classifications as measured by the AAI. Smith et al. (2003) summarize the data as indicating that there is continuity among: (a) secure attachment in infancy and autonomous attachment in adulthood, (b) anxious-avoidant attachment in infancy and dismissive attachment in adulthood, and (c) anxious-resistant attachment in infancy and enmeshed attachment in adulthood.

Theorists such as Belsky (Belsky et al., 1991) have attempted to explain why patterns of attachment should affect the nature of relationships in later life. Belsky et al.'s (1991) point is that our attachment styles are an attempt to make the best of the situation in which we find ourselves. They argue that attachment types are likely to be a product of the environment: an insecure attachment is likely to result from the stressful environment in which infant and child find themselves, whereas a secure attachment is likely to result from a less stressful environment for both. Belsky et al. argue that the evolutionarily adaptive response in the context of a stressful environment is to orient towards maturing and mating at an earlier age and simply passing on ones genes to as many others as is possible (the 'quantity' approach). On the other hand, they argue that the most evolutionarily adaptive response to an unstressful environment is to focus more on personal skills, and the acquisition of resources to prior to childbirth so as to better serve child-rearing (the 'quality' approach). Thus, Belsky and colleagues explain the continuity of attachment styles between infancy and adulthood in terms of two different evolutionary strategies. Their approach has some support from evidence indicating that stressful parent–child relationships lead to faster physical development and earlier menarche in young women (Steinberg, 1988), but it suffers from the problems which all evolutionary accounts have. Their explanation is made after the fact (it is '*post hoc*'), and we have no way of testing it. What do you think? Is their explanation simple and intuitive, or do you feel it has been forced to explain the data?

Attachment Deprivation

If infants and young children are deprived of a stable attachment with a caregiver, how do they fare in the long run? Bowlby's (1944) study of the 44 thieves was influential in making the argument that such early deprivation is harmful to social development. Harry Harlow studied this issue under controlled conditions with monkeys. After rearing 'isolate' monkeys either alone or with artificial surrogate mothers, Harlow returned them to the monkey colony at 6 months of age. Exposed to other monkeys, the isolates were indifferent, terrified or aggressive. When they became adults, some female isolates were artificially inseminated and gave birth, and they were highly abusive towards their firstborns (Harlow and Suomi, 1970). The conclusion: being raised without a secure attachment to a real, interactive caregiver produced long-term social impairment.

A number of cases of extreme deprivation in human infants have been documented. Victor, the Wild Boy of Aveyron (see Chapter 12), was severely impaired after his isolation and showed only limited recovery after intensive remedial training. Did the lack of human contact stunt Victor's development, or was it brain damage, possibly present from birth?

In the 1960s, twin boys in Czechoslovakia were forced by their father and stepmother to live in extreme isolation beginning at 18 months of age. The twins were discovered at age 7, emotionally and socially retarded, with the cognitive development of a 3-year-old and speech skills of a 2-year-old. Jarmila Koluchova (1972; 1991) studied the boys for over 20 years and found that they went on to become happy, sociable and firmly attached to their foster family. Their IQs increased to normal levels, and they became well-adjusted adolescents and young adults.

Why the difference? One reason may be that Victor had some kind of brain damage which was present from birth. However, other explanations for the difference are also plausible. Unlike Victor, the twins had each other's company. Could that have helped prevent long-term harm? However, in other cases even 'lone' isolate children have recovered. Perhaps more important, the twins' isolation ended and their rehabilitation began at a younger age than that of Victor, when their brains' neural plasticity was greater. They were 7; Victor was about 12.

In the 1980s, 100 000 Romanian infants and children were warehoused in orphanages under the most neglectful and squalid conditions imaginable (Fig. 13.11). Despite this horrific neglect, after being adopted about a third of the Romanian infants studied had become securely attached to their adoptive parents (Wilson, 2003).

However, there are a number of problems in drawing strong conclusions about the effects of parental deprivations from all of the studies mentioned so far. As well as being deprived of parental care, all the children and monkeys mentioned above were being deprived of a number of other important stimuli. Harlow and Suomi's monkeys were placed in situations of general social and sensory deprivation. Although many of the Romanian orphans grew up in the proximity of other children, their malnutrition may have prevented them from benefiting from this social input. We can often get better information by examining less extreme circumstances. For example, Barbara Tizard and Jill Hodges (1978) studied children raised in orphanages where the nurses were attentive but high staff turnover prevented the children from forming a stable bond with any caretaker.

FIGURE 13.11

In the 1980s, about 100 000 Romanian infants and children were warehoused in filthy, disease-ridden orphanages where they were often left unattended for days and had no opportunity to bond with caretakers. Studies of Romanian infants who were adopted into American homes before age 2 showed that about a third formed secure attachments, in contrast to the more typical 60 per cent figure found in attachment studies. Still, that so many formed secure attachments is a testament to their resilience in bouncing back from extreme adversity.

Those adopted between ages 2 and 8 years typically formed healthy attachments with their adoptive parents, although in adolescence many had difficulty forming peer relationships because they were viewed as needing 'too much attention' (Hodges and Tizard, 1989). However, Bowlby's ideas, and research like that of Tizard and Hodges (1978) have had important beneficial effect on the standard of institutional care, such that the vast majority of adopted children are nowadays normally adjusted and differ little from children raised by their biological parents (Miller et al., 2000).

In sum, infancy appears to be a sensitive, though not critical, period during which an initial attachment to caregivers forms most easily and facilitates subsequent development. Prolonged attachment deprivation creates developmental risks, but when deprived children are placed into a nurturing environment at a young enough age, many if not most become attached to their caretakers and grow into well-adjusted adults.

The Childcare Controversy

The work of Bowlby, Harlow and Ainsworth has implications that need careful consideration. If deprivation of primary caregivers has negative effects on development, we have to ask how much parental presence should we provide? Over the past decades, the traditional model of maternal care in the home has gradually given way to a more liberal view of parenting and care in which the mother and father may spend the day at work while the child is cared for at home by a nanny, or in a day care centre with other children. Day care is pervasive in Europe and the USA. Important questions to ask concern the effects of the amount of day care which children receive, and the quality of that care. High-quality day care provides a stimulating environment with well-trained caretakers who are responsive to children's needs, few children per caretaker and low staff turnover, whereas poor day care does not (Marshall, 2004).

The most comprehensive investigation of the effects of day care to date has been carried out by psychologists working with the National Institute of Child Health and Human Development (NICHD) Early Child Care Research Network in the USA. These researchers have studied approximately 1400 American children from birth to 12 years of age. Here are some major findings:

1. *Attachment*: overall, as measured by the strange-situation procedure, high-quality day care did not seem to disrupt infants' or very young children's attachment to their parents, even when they attended for several hours a week. However, when the parents were not sensitive to the child in the home, an increased amount of and poorer quality day care increased the risk of insecure attachment (NICHD, 2001a).

2. *Social behaviour*: compared to children with less day care experience, by age 3, children with more experience exhibited better social skills when interacting with peers at day care, although this did not generalize to play situations with friends outside day care (NICHD, 2001b). By age 4, however, children who averaged 30 or more hours a week in day care displayed more behaviour problems (e.g., arguing) than children who spent less than 10 hours a week in childcare (NICHD, 2002). The number of months that children spent in day care before starting school also predicted aggressive behaviour in the class right up to 12 years of age (Belsky et al., 2007).

3. *Cognitive performance*: regardless of their sex or ethnicity or their parents' socio-economic status or parenting quality, 4-year-olds who spent a lot of time in day care centres performed better on several cognitive and linguistic tasks than did peers who spent less time in day care centres (NICHD, 2002). Exposure to high-quality day care was associated with even better cognitive performance. These benefits seemed to persist at least through to 9 years (Vandell et al., 2005), and higher quality of day care predicted higher vocabulary scores at age 12 (Belsky et al., 2007).

Focus 13.7

How do day care, divorce and remarriage affect children's development?

Concerns about disrupted parent–child relationship also surface when parents divorce. Our 'Applying psychological science' feature examines this societally important issue.

APPLYING PSYCHOLOGICAL SCIENCE

UNDERSTANDING HOW DIVORCE AND REMARRIAGE AFFECT CHILDREN

Divorce creates a stressful life transition for parents and their children. Because most divorced parents remarry, they and their children also experience a second major transition: becoming part of a step-family.

Decades ago, there was little scientific information on children of divorce and remarriage, but research now provides us with a better understanding of how these major transitions affect children. With this knowledge, we can attempt to take measures to alleviate some of the negative consequences of divorce on children. Indeed, in the USA, local governments in many of the states require soon to be divorced parents to take classes on helping children cope with divorce.

HOW DOES DIVORCE AFFECT CHILDREN?

Many children report that parental divorce is one of the most painful experiences of their lives. In the short term, they may experience anxiety, fear, anger, confusion, depression and behaviour problems at school.

In the long term, children of divorce remain at greater risk for various difficulties, including academic problems, troubled relationships with family members and peers, low self-esteem and depression (Dawson-McClure et al., 2004). When they become adolescents, children of divorced parents are more likely to drop out of school, be unemployed, use drugs and become unmarried teenage parents. In adulthood, they experience more marital conflict and have a higher divorce rate (Huurre et al., 2006; Wauterickx et al., 2006).

Most of these problems, however, tend to cluster together into an overall pattern of maladjustment. Divorce researcher E. Mavis Hetherington and co-workers (1998) estimate that about 20 to 25 per cent of children in divorced families, versus 10 per cent of children in non-divorced families, experience this cluster of problems. This is a significantly elevated risk for maladjustment, but still, most children of divorced parents grow up to be normally adjusted adults.

SHOULD WE STAY TOGETHER FOR THE SAKE OF THE CHILD?

Many parents considering divorce wonder whether they should stay together for the child's sake. Reviewing 92 studies, Amato and Keith (1991) found that when divorce ends a highly conflictual marriage, children's psychological adjustment typically benefits in the long run. High marital conflict can cause the children to feel 'caught in the middle' in the battle between their parents, and decrease the children's feelings of well-being (Amato and Afifi, 2006). Children living with married but contentious parents have poorer school achievement, lower self-esteem and more behaviour problems than children from divorced families. But many unhappy marriages do not involve extensive conflict, and in those cases divorce usually puts children at greater risk of maladjustment (Booth and Amato, 2001).

HOW CAN DIVORCED PARENTS HELP THEIR CHILDREN?

The major factor affecting a child's adjustment to divorce is the quality of life within the post-divorce family. The period during and after divorce can intensify parents' anger and conflicts. By fighting over their children or trying to enlist them in loyalty battles, parents can damage their children's well-being. In contrast, co-operative and amicable parental behaviours can cushion the negative effects of divorce during this rocky transition (Hetherington and Stanley-Hagan, 2002). By remaining emotionally close to his or her children, the parent who does not have custody (usually the father) can help them adjust to living with the custodial parent (Marsiglio et al., 2000). For children, the lasting problems of divorce often lie in lingering parental conflicts, economic hardships that parents (especially mothers) often experience after divorce, and other factors that destabilize the parents' own lives.

HOW DO CHILDREN RESPOND TO REMARRIAGE AND STEP-FAMILIES?

Forming a step-family temporarily disrupts children's relationships with the remarried custodial parent and typically increases children's problem behaviours in the short term. In turn, such behaviour can increase the risk of marital conflict between the step-parents (Jenkins et al., 2005). It can take several years for parents and children to adjust to their new roles within the step-family. In general, young adolescents seem to have the most difficulty coping with the transition into a step-family.

In remarriages, children may be hostile and reject the step-parent, especially when the step-parent attempts to be a strong disciplinarian. Children usually adjust better to living in a step-family when the custodial parent is warm but firm and has primary responsibility for discipline, and when the step-parent is warm but supports the custodial parent's authority (Bray and Berger, 1993).

Styles of Parenting

Focus 13.8

Identify parenting styles and their associated child outcomes. How do parenting and children's heredity interact?

Beyond divorce and remarriage, how do different child-rearing practices affect children's development? After studying how parents interacted with their pre-school children, Diana Baumrind (1967) identified two key dimensions of parental behaviour. The first is *warmth versus hostility*. Warm parents communicate love and care for the child. Hostile parents express rejection and behave as if they do not care about the child. The second dimension is *restrictiveness versus permissiveness*. Parents differ in the extent to which they make and enforce rules. As Figure 13.12 shows, combining these dimensions yields four parenting styles that are associated with different patterns of child development (Linver et al., 2002).

Authoritative parents are controlling but warm. They establish clear rules, consistently enforce them, and reward children's compliance with warmth and affection. They communicate high expectations, caring and support. This style is associated with the most positive childhood outcomes. Children with authoritative parents tend to have higher self-esteem, are higher achievers in school and have fewer conduct problems.

Authoritarian parents also exert control but do so within a cold, unresponsive or rejecting relationship. Their children tend to have lower self-esteem, be less popular with peers and perform more poorly in school than children with authoritative parents.

Indulgent parents have warm, caring relationships with their children but do not provide the guidance and discipline that help children learn responsibility and concern for others. Their children tend to be more immature and self-centred.

Neglectful parents provide neither warmth nor rules nor guidance. Their children are most likely to be insecurely attached, to have low achievement motivation and disturbed peer relationships, and to be impulsive and aggressive. Neglectful parenting is associated with the most negative developmental outcomes.

Do these findings extend to adolescence? Steinberg et al. (1994) found that overall, authoritative parenting and neglectful parenting were, respectively, associated with the most positive and negative developmental outcomes. Lamborn et al. (1991) have shown that this holds true across a wide variety of ethnicities (Lamborn et al., 1991).

Parenting–Heredity Interactions

Keep in mind that parent–child influences are bidirectional, illustrating once again the interaction of biology and environment in shaping behaviour. For example, children whose biologically based temperament is irritable tend to elicit harsher and less warm parenting behaviours, which in turn can further promote the child's difficult behaviour. Also realize that parents do not mould their children's personality and behaviour like lumps of clay. Parenting makes a difference, but the way children turn out also depends on their heredity, peer and community influences, other experiences, and interactions among these factors (Mezulis et al., 2006).

Antisocial behaviour provides another example of how the family environment and heredity interact. Children of a highly antisocial parent (i.e., a parent with high aggression, irritability and a history of illegal activities) are at increased genetic risk for displaying antisocial behaviour (e.g., lying, fighting, having a hot temper). This genetic risk is present, of course, even if the highly antisocial parent (usually the father) is completely absent from the home and the child is raised by the other parent. However, as Sara Jaffee and co-workers (2003) found, when high-antisocial fathers live at home and are involved in caretaking, this further increases children's antisocial behaviour and risk of developing a conduct disorder. In contrast, when low-antisocial fathers live at home and participate in caretaking, this tends to decrease children's antisocial behaviour. Jaffee and co-workers concluded that children of high-antisocial fathers who are involved in caretaking receive what they call a 'double-whammy' of genetic and environmental contributions to their own antisocial behaviour.

	Warmth/acceptance	Hostility/rejection
Restrictive	Authoritative — Demanding, but caring: good child–parent communication	Authoritarian — Assertion of parental power without warmth
Permissive	Indulgent — Warm towards child, but lax in setting limits	Neglecting — Indifferent and uninvolved with child

FIGURE 13.12

Four styles of child rearing.

Combining two basic dimensions of parental behaviour (warmth–hostility and restrictiveness–permissiveness) yields four different styles of child rearing.

SOURCE: adapted from Maccoby and Martin, 1983.

authoritative parents
controlling but warm

authoritarian parents
exert control but do so within a cold, unresponsive or rejecting relationship

indulgent parents
have warm, caring relationships with their children but do not provide the guidance and discipline that help children learn responsibility and concern for others

neglectful parents
provide neither warmth nor rules nor guidance

Focus 13.9

How does socialization influence children's beliefs about gender?

---

gender identity

a sense of 'femaleness' or 'maleness' that becomes a central aspect of one's personal identity

gender constancy

the understanding that being male or female is a permanent part of a person

sex-typing

treating others differently based on whether they are female or male

---

FIGURE 13.13

Do parents provide more scientific explanations to sons than daughters?

Fathers and mothers provided more explanations to their 1- to 8-year-old sons than to their daughters while engaged with science exhibits at a children's museum. Similar results were obtained regardless of the children's age.

SOURCE: adapted from Crowley et al., 2001.

Gender Identity and Socialization

Parenting also influences children's development in other ways, such as helping children develop a **gender identity**, a sense of 'femaleness' or 'maleness' that becomes a central aspect of one's personal identity. Most children develop a basic gender identity between the ages of 2 and 3 and can label themselves (and others) as being either a boy or a girl, but their understanding of gender is still fragile. They may believe that a boy wearing a dress is a girl and that a girl can grow up to become a man. **Gender constancy**, which is the understanding that being male or female is a permanent part of a person, develops around age 6 to 7 (Szkrybalo and Ruble, 1999).

As gender identity develops, children also acquire *sex-role stereotypes*, which are beliefs about the characteristics and behaviours that are appropriate for boys and girls to possess. Every group, including family and cultural groups, has norms for expected and accepted gender behaviour. Parents, siblings, friends, the mass media and other socializing agents convey these norms to us as we grow up. Ultimately, as we internalize these norms, they become part of our identity (Martin and Ruble, 2004).

Sex-typing involves treating others differently based on whether they are female or male. From infancy onwards, girls and boys are viewed and treated differently. Fathers use more physical and verbal prohibition with their 12-month-old sons than with their daughters, and they steer their sons away from activities that are considered stereotypically feminine (Snow et al., 1983). Even when their sons and daughters display equal interest and aptitude in science, fathers and mothers are more likely to believe that sons have the greater interest and will find science easier (Tenenbaum and Leaper, 2003). Indeed, as Figure 13.13 shows, when parents interact with their 1- to 8-year-olds at science exhibits in a children's museum, they are much more likely to explain the exhibits to their sons than to their daughters – even though the children rarely ask for such explanations (Crowley et al., 2001).

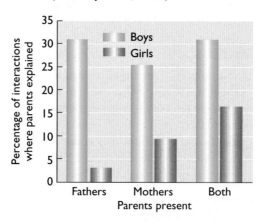

Sex-role stereotypes are also transmitted through observational learning and operant conditioning (Fig. 13.14). Children observe and often attempt to emulate parents, other adults, peers, and television and movie characters (Bandura, 1965). In ways obvious and subtle, others approve of us and reinforce our behaviour when we meet their expectations and disapprove of us when we do not. In turn, this influences the way children think about gender. Some children as young as 2 to 3 years of age display sex-role stereotypes in their ability to identify objects (such as hammers and brooms) and behaviours as 'belonging with' one gender or the other (Campbell et al., 2004). By age 7 or 8, stereotyped thinking is firmly in place; children believe that boys and girls possess different personality traits and should hold different occupations as adults.

As children enter secondary school, they often display more flexible thinking about gender. Some come to believe that traditionally masculine and feminine traits can be blended within a single person – what is called an *androgynous gender identity* – as when a person is both asser-

FIGURE 13.14

In subtle and not so subtle ways, cultures socialize most female and male children in gender-stereotypic ways.

tive and compassionate. During secondary school, some adolescents maintain this view, but overall, gender stereotypes seem to become a little more rigid at this age, so that by early adulthood most people continue to adhere to relatively traditional beliefs (Alfieri et al., 1996).

The Influence of Peers

As well as parents, the peer group has an important effect on children's social development. If you are a child, your 'peers' are children who you know who are of about the same age as yourself, and would often be in the same class as you at school or live in the same neighbourhood. The influence of peers may begin from an early age. Lewis et al. (1975) show that 12- to 18-month-old infants, while they maintain closer proximity to their caregiver, will spend the most time looking at a peer (see Fig. 13.15).

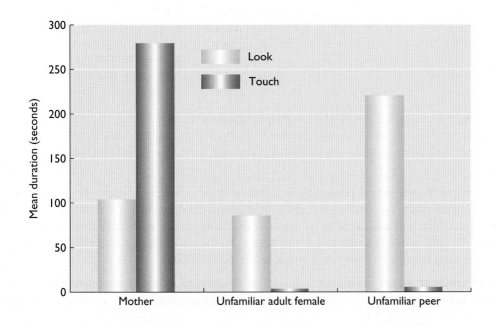

FIGURE 13.15

The average number of seconds (during 15 minutes) which 12- to 18-month-olds infants spent touching and looking at their mother, an unfamiliar adult female and an unfamiliar peer.

Judith Harris is a developmental researcher who has argued that the peer group may have as important, if not more important, a role as parents (or home environment) in shaping our social development. This view has become known as the 'group socialization' theory of development (Harris, 1995). Evidence in favour of Harris's theory comes from behavioural genetics research, including twin and adoption studies. These studies demonstrate that the shared environment of siblings (i.e., the home environment provided by their parents) may have a less substantial effect on development than the 'non-shared environment'. Plomin and Daniels (1987; see also Plomin et al., 2001) demonstrated that children who are born or adopted into the same family show very little similarity in their personalities, and thus environmental influences are concluded to come from environment outside the family. Harris thus suggests that peers may be much more important in shaping our personality. Harris's theory is still under scrutiny however, as non-shared environment can result not just from influences outside the home environment, but also from differences in the ways children's genetic inheritance (e.g., their temperament) interacts with their home environment. As has already been discussed, a happy child is likely to be treated differently by their parents than an irritable child. This is one way in which non-shared environmental differences can arise in the home.

Judity Harris's theory is controversial as it suggests that parents can have little effect on children's development. Michael Rutter, an eminent developmental psychologists has suggested that Harris's theory may apply less in situations where the parental influence is extreme (e.g., when the parents abuse their children). Does Judith Harris's theory of group socialization ring true for you? Do you feel your personality has been more shaped by your parents or your peers?

MORAL DEVELOPMENT

We all have a sense of the difference between right and wrong. At school we can often observe teachers attempting to instil the moral views of society into their students. How does children's moral thinking change as they grow older? What factors cause moral development?

Moral Thinking

Drawing on Piaget's cognitive stage model, and some of Piaget's observations on early morality in children, Lawrence Kohlberg (1963; 1984), a Canadian psychologist, developed an influential theory of moral development across the lifespan. He presented children, adolescents and adults with hypothetical moral dilemmas such as the following:

> Heinz's wife was dying from cancer. There was a rare drug that might save her, but the druggist who made the drug for $200 would not sell it for less than $2000. Heinz tried hard, but he could only raise $1000. The druggist refused to give Heinz the drug for that price even though Heinz promised to pay the rest later. So Heinz broke into the store to steal the drug. What do you think? Should Heinz have stolen the drug? Why or why not?

Kohlberg was interested not in whether people agreed or disagreed with Heinz's behaviour but rather in the *reasons for their judgement*. He analysed responses to various moral dilemmas and identified three main levels of moral reasoning, with two substages within each level (Table 13.2).

Pre-conventional moral reasoning is based on anticipated punishments or rewards. Consider reasons given for stealing the drug. In stage 1, children focus on punishment: 'Heinz should steal the drug because if he lets his wife die he'll get into trouble.' In stage 2, morality is judged by anticipated rewards and doing what is in the person's own interest: 'Heinz should steal the drug because that way he'll still have his wife with him.'

Conventional moral reasoning is based on conformity to social expectations, laws, and duties. In stage 3, conformity stems from the desire to gain people's approval: 'People will think

---

Focus 13.10

Describe Kohlberg's model of moral thinking and factors that influence the development of moral behaviour.

---

pre-conventional moral reasoning

based on anticipated punishments or rewards

conventional moral reasoning

based on conformity to social expectations, laws and duties

TABLE 13.2 KOHLBERG'S STAGES OF MORAL REASONING

Level of moral reasoning	Basis for judging what is moral
Level 1: Pre-conventional morality	*Actual or anticipated punishments or rewards, rather than internalized values*
Stage 1: Punishment-obedience orientation *Stage 2*: Instrumental-hedonistic orientation	Obeying rules and avoiding punishment Self-interest and gaining rewards
Level 2: Conventional morality	*Conformity to the expectations of social groups; person adopts other people's values*
Stage 3: Good-child orientation *Stage 4*: Law-and-order orientation	Gaining approval and maintaining good relationships with others Doing one's duty, showing respect for authority and maintaining social order
Level 3: Post-conventional morality	*Moral principles that have been internalized as part of one's belief and value system*
Stage 5: Social-contract orientation *Stage 6*: Universal ethical principles	General principles agreed on by society that foster community welfare and individual rights; recognition that society can decide to modify laws that lose their social utility Abstract ethical principles based on justice and equality; following one's conscience

SOURCE: adapted from Kohlberg, 1984.

that Heinz is bad if he doesn't steal the drug to save his wife.' In stage 4, children believe that laws and duties must be obeyed simply because rules are meant to be followed. Thus: 'Heinz should steal the drug because it's his duty to take care of his wife.'

Post-conventional moral reasoning is based on well-thought-out, general moral principles. Stage 5 involves recognizing the importance of societal laws but also taking individual rights into account: 'Stealing breaks the law, but what Heinz did was reasonable because he saved a life.' In stage 6, morality is based on abstract, ethical principles of justice that are viewed as universal: 'Saving life comes before financial gain, even if the person is a stranger.'

Kohlberg believed that progress in moral reasoning depends on the development of cognitive ability. Thus, like Piaget (see Chapter 12), he believed that powers of logic underlaid children's competence in a wide variety of domains – including their moral behaviours. Piaget and Kohlberg suggested that cognitive (and moral) development was driven by opportunities to confront moral issues, particularly when such issues can be discussed with someone who is at a higher stage of development.

Culture, Gender and Moral Reasoning

From North, Central and South America to Africa, Asia, Europe and India, studies of moral reasoning indicate that, overall:

- from childhood through adolescence, moral reasoning changes from pre-conventional to conventional levels

- in adolescence and even in adulthood, post-conventional reasoning is relatively uncommon

- a person's moral judgements do not always reflect the same level or stage within levels (Eckensberger and Zimba, 1997).

post-conventional moral reasoning
based on well-thought-out, general moral principles

Critics claim that Kohlberg's theory has a western cultural bias. Fairness and justice are Kohlberg's post-conventional ideals, but in many cultures the highest moral values focus on principles that do not fit easily into Kohlberg's model, such as respect for all animal life, collective harmony and respect for the elderly (Iwasa, 2001).

Carol Gilligan (1982) argues that Kohlberg's emphasis on justice also reflects a male bias. She claims that highly moral women place greater value than do men on caring and responsibility for others' welfare. Overall, however, evidence of gender bias is mixed. Women use justice reasoning when the situation calls for it, and men use reasoning based on caring and relationships when appropriate. Nevertheless, Gilligan's analysis reinforces the key point that the identification of 'high-level' moral reasoning can be based on values other than justice (Gump et al., 2000).

Moral Behaviour and Conscience

Moral reasoning does not necessarily translate into moral behaviour. B.F. Skinner (1971) proposed that we learn which behaviours are 'good' and 'bad' through their association with reinforcement and punishment. Other researchers propose that for children to conform to their culture's moral standards, they must understand that there are moral rules, be able to control their impulses to engage in forbidden behaviour, and experience some negative emotion when they violate these rules.

By the age of 2, children come to understand that there are rules for behaviour, and their emotional expressions suggest that they experience guilt when they break a known rule. Children's ability to stop themselves from engaging in forbidden behaviour develops slowly, but even toddlers can do so at times. This internal regulatory mechanism, often referred to as *conscience*, tends to restrain individuals from acting in destructive or antisocial ways when they are not being monitored by parents or other adults (Kochanska et al., 2005).

Sigmund Freud (1935) believed that children develop a conscience by identifying with their parents. Few developmentalists believe in Freud's theory of how identification occurs (which we discuss in Chapter 15), but they acknowledge that internalizing the societal values transmitted by parents or other caretakers provides the basis of a moral conscience. Children are most likely to internalize parents' values when they have a positive relationship with them, when parents establish clear rules and provide explanations that facilitate children's awareness of parental values, and when discipline is firm but not harsh (Laible and Thompson, 2000).

Children's temperament also enters into the picture. Fearful, inhibited children tend to internalize parental values more easily and at an earlier age than less fearful children, particularly when their parents provide gentle discipline. For relatively fearless, uninhibited children, however, whether discipline is gentle or harsh is less important. A secure attachment with warm parents, rather than fear of punishment, appears to motivate fearless children to internalize their parents' standards. Thus the development of moral behaviour is linked not only to children's moral thinking but also to their emotional development, attachment and temperament (Kochanska et al., 2004).

IN REVIEW

- Children display more types and greater complexity of emotions as they age. The strategies they use to regulate their emotions also become more varied.

- Temperament reflects a biologically based pattern of reacting emotionally and behaviourally to the environment. Extreme temperamental styles in infancy and childhood can predict some aspects of functioning years later.

- Erikson believed that personality development proceeds through eight major psychosocial stages. Each stage involves a major crisis, and how we resolve it affects our ability to meet the challenges of the next stage.

- Infants demonstrate a variety of social behaviours in the first days of life. They prefer to orient towards faces, and direct eye contact. 'Periodicity' in their movements and vocalizations may represent the first conversations between infant and child. Newborns also imitate their parent's facial expressions.

- Infant–caretaker attachment develops in three phases, and infants experience periods of stranger and separation anxiety. Secure attachment is associated with better developmental outcomes than is insecure attachment. For most children, day care does not disrupt attachment. Divorce typically disrupts children's short-term psychological adjustment; for some, it is associated with a long-term pattern of maladjustment.

- Parenting styles vary along dimensions of warmth–hostility and restrictiveness–permissiveness. The children of authoritative parents generally display the best developmental outcomes. Gender identity begins to form early in childhood, and socialization influences children's acquisition of sex-role stereotypes.

- Kohlberg proposed that moral reasoning proceeds through pre-conventional, conventional and post-conventional levels. The development of moral behaviour is linked to children's cognitive, emotional and social development.

ADOLESCENCE, ADULTHOOD AND OLD AGE

We call it Sunrise Dance. It's the biggest ceremony of the White Mountain Apache – when a girl passes from childhood to womanhood.... On Friday evening Godmother dressed me ... Saturday is like an endurance test. Men begin prayer chants at dawn. Godmother tells me to dance.... When the time comes for running, I go fast around a sacred cane.... Next, my father pours candies and corn kernels over me to protect me from famine. My Godfather directs my dancing on Sunday.... Godfather paints me.... On Monday there is more visiting and blessing. (Quintero, 1980, pp. 262–71)

In some cultures, ceremonies like the Sunrise Dance represent *rites of passage* that mark a transition from childhood into adulthood status (Fig. 13.16). But what of **adolescence**, the period of development and gradual transition between childhood and adulthood? Alice Schlegel and Herbert Barry (1991) found that among almost 200 non-industrial societies worldwide, nearly all recognize some type of transition period between childhood and adulthood. Yet in many societies this period is brief and is not marked by a special term analogous to *adolescence*.

As we know it, the lengthy period called *adolescence* is largely an invention of eighteenth- to twentieth-century western culture (Valsiner and Lawrence, 1997). In pre-industrial times,

adolescence

the period of development and gradual transition between childhood and adulthood

FIGURE 13.16

A White Mountain Apache girl participates in the Sunrise Dance, a four-day ceremony that initiates her into womanhood.

Focus 13.11
How does adolescence differ from puberty? Describe psychological consequences of early maturation, and adolescents' brain development.

puberty
the period of rapid maturation in which the person becomes capable of sexual reproduction

biological maturity was a major criterion for adult status. In many cultures, for example, girls were expected to marry once they became capable of bearing children. But as the Industrial Revolution brought new technology and a need for more schooling, recognition of adult status was delayed and the long transition period of adolescence evolved.

Adolescence differs from **puberty**, the period of rapid maturation in which the person becomes capable of sexual reproduction (see Chapter 12). These developmental periods overlap, but puberty is a biologically defined period, whereas adolescence is a broader social construction (Spear, 2000). Puberty is an important aspect of adolescence, but adolescence is also ushered in and out by changes in thinking, interests, social circumstances, and parental and societal expectations. In research studies, 12- to 18-year-olds – give or take a year at each end – are typically considered to be adolescents, but it is essential to keep in mind that the transition into, through and out of adolescence is not always sudden (Arnett, 2001).

SOCIAL-EMOTIONAL DEVELOPMENT IN ADOLESCENCE

G. Stanley Hall (1904), the first psychologist to study adolescence, viewed it as a time of 'storm and stress'. Indeed, adolescents may grapple with difficult issues and experience substantial conflict, yet many find it to be a positive period of life. Thus, Jeffrey Arnett proposes a modified view, noting that 'not all adolescents experience storm and stress, but storm and stress is more likely during adolescence than at other ages' (1999, p. 317).

Adolescents' Search for Identity

'Who am I?' 'What do I believe in?' Erik Erikson (1968) proposed that such questions reflect the pivotal crisis of adolescent personality development: *identity versus role confusion* (see Table 13.1, p. 570). Erikson believed that an adolescent's 'identity crisis' (a term he coined) can be resolved positively, leading to a stable sense of identity, or it can end negatively, leading to confusion about one's identity and values.

Building on Erikson's work, James Marcia (1966; 2002) studied adolescents' and young adults' search for identity. Marcia classified the 'identity status' of each person as follows:

1. *Identity diffusion*: these teens and adults had not yet gone through an identity crisis. They seemed unconcerned or even cynical about identity issues and were not committed to a coherent set of values.
2. *Foreclosure*: these individuals had not yet gone through an identity crisis either, but for a different reason: They committed to an identity and set of values before experiencing a crisis. For example, some automatically adopted peer-group or parental values without giving these values much thought.
3. *Moratorium*: these people wanted to establish a clear identity, were currently experiencing a crisis, but had not yet resolved it.
4. *Identity achievement*: these individuals had gone through an identity crisis, successfully resolved it and emerged with a coherent set of values.

Marcia found that most young adolescents are in identity diffusion or foreclosure; they have not experienced an identity crisis. But during the teen years, people typically begin to think more deeply about who they are, or they reconsider values they had adopted previously. This often leads to an identity crisis, and more than half successfully resolve it by early adulthood.

Identity, of course, is not a simple concept, and our sense of identity has multiple components (Camilleri and Malewska-Peyre, 1997). These include (1) our gender, ethnicity, and other attributes by which we define ourselves as members of social groups ('daughter', 'student', 'athlete'); (2) how we view our personal characteristics ('shy', 'friendly'); and (3) our goals and values. Typically, we achieve a stable identity regarding some components before others, and changing situations may trigger new crises and cause us to re-evaluate prior goals and values.

Focus 13.12
Discuss adolescents' search for identity and their relationships with parents and peers.

Culture plays a key role in identity formation, one that goes beyond the simple idea that we view ourselves as belonging to certain cultural groups. Our cultural upbringing influences the very way we view concepts such as 'self' and 'identity'. Having grown up in an individualistic culture, my sense of identity assumes that I am an autonomous individual with clear boundaries separating me from other people. But in collectivistic cultures, the concept of 'self' is traditionally based more strongly on the connectedness between people (Kagitçibasi, 1997). Thus, the question 'Who am I?' is more likely to be answered in ways that reflect a person's relationships with family members, friends and others. Still, keep in mind that we are talking about relative differences. Across cultures, people's sense of identity incorporates elements that involve autonomy from – and interdependence with – other people (Mascolo and Li, 2004).

Relationships with Parents and Peers

When it comes to teenagers' relationships with their parents, is 'storm and stress' the rule or the exception? A number of studies have suggested that this may be an exaggeration. For example, Moore et al. (2004) report a national survey in the USA, in which about 80 per cent of American teenagers reported thinking highly of, and enjoying spending time with, the parents with whom they lived at home. About two-thirds of the teens reported an overall positive relationship with their parents. In a longitudinal study, Galambos and Almeida (1992) found that conflict over chores, appearance and politeness actually decrease as children enter adolescence. However, they did also note an increase in conflict over money.

Likewise, research in China and the Netherlands, and with various American ethnic groups, suggests that teenager–parent conflict is not as severe as often assumed (Chen et al., 1998). And despite the differences between the family-centred 'collectivistic' cultures of China and the more individualistic style of European and US families, the kinds of conflicts which adolescents have with their parents have a lot in common. For example, Yau and Smetana (1996) found that the children of Chinese families in Hong Kong argue with their parents about choice of activities (e.g., phone conversations, television watching), household chores and homework.

The USA's National Center on Addiction and Substance Abuse (2005) report, however, that most adolescents state that if they face a serious problem, they can confide in one or both parents. Yet many adolescents also feel that for various reasons, including the right to preserve their independence, it is acceptable to lie to their parents at times. As Figure 13.17 shows, in one study most secondary school students said that they had lied to their parents on several issues in the past year (Jensen et al., 2004).

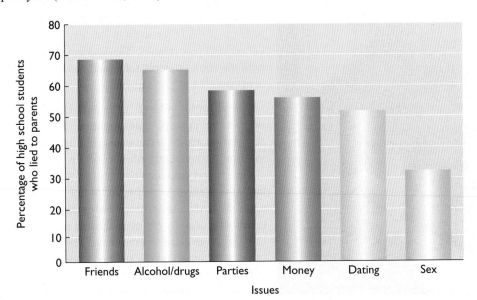

FIGURE 13.17

In one study, 229 students attending a public high school were asked how often they lied to their parents about six issues. For each issue, this graph shows the percentage of students who reported lying to their parents at least once during the past year.

SOURCE: Jensen et al., 2004.

Some parents and teenagers do struggle a lot, and parent–teenager conflict is correlated with other signs of distress. For example, among American, Chinese and Taiwanese teens, those who report more conflict with parents also display higher levels of school misconduct (e.g., skipping school), more antisocial behaviour (e.g., getting into fights), lower self-esteem, more drug use and less life satisfaction (Caughlin and Malis, 2004; Chen et al., 1998). Recalling the principle that correlation does not equal causation, we must consider that although parent–teenager conflict may be a cause of teenagers' psychological problems, it also is likely to be caused *by* such problems.

A typical stereotype of a teenager is someone who likes to spend time hanging out with friends. Peer relationships increase in importance during adolescence, and some studies find that teenagers spend more time with peers than doing almost anything else. But this pattern may be stronger in Europe and North America than in Asia, where people of all ages, teenagers included, generally place a relatively strong emphasis on family relationships (Chen et al., 1998).

Adolescent friendships are typically more intimate than those at previous ages and involve a greater sharing of problems. Peers can strongly influence a teenager's values and behaviours, thereby facilitating the process of separating from parents and establishing one's own identity. For some adolescents, however, experiences with peers increase the risk of misconduct, such as skipping school, damaging property or using drugs (Larson et al., 2006). Fortunately, peer pressure *against* misconduct typically has an even stronger effect, and closeness to parents is an added buffer that helps many teenagers resist peer pressure to do misdeeds (Chen et al., 1998). Despite increased peer influence during adolescence, parental influence remains high on political, religious, moral and career issues. In many ways, the so-called generation gap is narrower than is often assumed.

Emotional Changes in Adolescence

Focus 13.13

How do emotions change during adolescence?

As you progressed from childhood through your teenage years, did you generally become a more or less happy person? Larson et al. (2002) examined changes in teenage emotionality in a creative and powerful way. They randomly selected 328 10- to 14-year-olds from working- and middle-class suburban families. Students carried electronic pagers and paper booklets with them for one week, and the time of year that each student did this was randomly determined. From morning to evening each student was beeped at a random times. On a questionnaire, the students rated how happy or unhappy, cheerful or irritable, and friendly or angry they felt at that moment. The researchers also measured students' self-esteem, depression and the number of major stressful events experienced during the previous six months. This procedure was repeated with the same students four years later, when the students were 14 to 18 years old.

Overall, girls' and boys' daily emotional experiences were more positive than negative. Still, teenagers' daily emotionality became less positive as they moved into and through early adolescence, with changes levelling off and emotions becoming more stable during late adolescence. As they aged, 34 per cent of the teenagers showed a major downward change (less-positive emotions), and 16 per cent showed a major upward change (more-positive emotions). The remaining half of the students showed a smaller amount of change in emotions, although once again, downward changes were twice as common as upward changes (Fig. 13.18).

FIGURE 13.18

Research suggests that emotionality changes during adolescence, with an overall decrease in positive emotions being more likely to occur than an overall increase. By late adolescence, these changes tend to level off.

The study also revealed that students who reported less-positive emotions tended to have lower self-esteem and more frequent major stressful events during the preceding six months.

SOCIAL-EMOTIONAL DEVELOPMENT IN ADULTHOOD

The Transition to Adulthood

In traditional cultures, marriage typically is the key transitional event into adulthood (Arnett, 2001). Through socialization, males develop skills that will enable them to protect and provide for a family of their own, and females learn skills needed eventually to care for children and run a household. Marriage signifies that, in the eyes of the culture, each partner has acquired these skills and is deemed capable of raising a family.

In industrialized societies, how do we know when someone has become an adult? Our 'Research close-up' examines this question.

Focus 13.14

How do people judge whether someone has reached adulthood?

RESEARCH CLOSE-UP

WHAT DOES IT TAKE TO BECOME AN ADULT?

SOURCE: J.J. Arnett (2001) Conceptions of the transition to adulthood: perspectives from adolescence through midlife, *Journal of Adult Development*, vol. 8, pp. 133–43.

INTRODUCTION

If we asked you, 'Have you reached adulthood?', how would you answer? And in your view, just what does it take to be considered an adult? Jeffrey Arnett examined how American adults in various age groups viewed the transition to adulthood. Whereas previous research focused on the viewpoints of adolescents and people in their twenties, this study also examined the viewpoints of older adults.

METHOD

Men and women from a midsized community were recruited to participate. There were 519 participants, representing three age groups: 13- to 19-year-olds, 20- to 29-year-olds and 30- to 55-year-olds. Participants rated ('yes' or 'no') whether each of 38 specific characteristics 'must be achieved before a person can be considered an adult'. These characteristics were presented in random order and represented six general categories of criteria for judging adult status. These categories and some sample items appear below.

General category	Sample of specific characteristics
Individualism	Be responsible for one's actions; determine own values/beliefs; attain financial freedom.
Family capacities	Be capable of caring for and financially supporting a family.
Norm compliance	Refrain from crime, irresponsible sex, drunk driving, illegal drug use.
Biological transitions	Be capable of fathering/bearing children.
Legal/chronological transitions	Reach age 18; reach age 21; obtain driver's licence.
Role transitions	Full-time employment; establish career; finish education, get married.

Each participant also was asked, 'Do you think that you have reached adulthood?' The answer options were 'yes', 'no', and 'in some respects yes, in some respects no'.

RESULTS

What qualities were judged as necessary to be considered an adult? Regardless of age group, about 90 per cent of participants endorsed the importance of accepting responsibility for one's actions. Establishing one's own values and beliefs, seeing oneself as an equal with one's parents, and attaining financial independence were the next most frequently chosen qualities among all age groups. Items such as 'reaching age 18', 'employed full-time', and 'marriage', were endorsed by only 47, 32 and 13 per cent of participants, respectively. In fact, if you look at the six general categories shown in the Methods section, they are listed in the overall order of importance, as determined by the average ratings of all the items in each category. Overall, there was strong consistency in how the various age groups viewed the importance of these characteristics.

Research design
Question: How do people of various ages view the transition to adulthood?
Type of Study: *Correlational*

Independent variables	Dependent variable
Age (Three age groups: 13 to 19, 20 to 29 and 30 to 55 years)	View of transition to adulthood, (e.g., Is this characteristic necessary to be considered an adult? Are you an adult?)

In contrast, substantial age differences emerged in whether participants viewed themselves as having reached adulthood. As Figure 13.19 shows, among adolescents (average age 16 years), fewer than a fifth said that they had reached adulthood. Among people in their twenties (average age 24 years), almost half said that they had reached adulthood. Still, in both of these age groups, the transitional 'yes and no' response was most common. Only among people in mid-life (average age 42 years) did most view themselves as having fully attained adulthood.

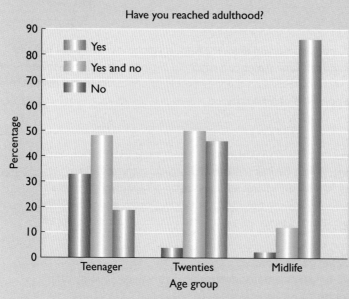

FIGURE 13.19

Have you reached adulthood?

This graph shows the percentage of people in their teens, twenties and thirties to mid-fifties who felt that they had not, partially had or fully had reached adulthood.

SOURCE: Arnett, 2001.

DISCUSSION

This study suggests that on the psychological road to adulthood, biological, legal, chronological, and role transitions take a back seat. *Individualism* – becoming a responsible, independent person – was judged to be the single most important general criterion. Still, in making the transition from adolescence to adulthood, multiple factors appear to come into play for most people.

This study had several strengths. It addressed an interesting question, one likely to assume great personal relevance for many people at some point in their lives. The 38 characteristics for judging adulthood status were carefully chosen on the basis of prior research, and the participants represented a broader age range than in previous studies. All studies have limitations, however, and as a critical thinker you should recognize that this study employed a cross-sectional design. The findings tell us, at a given point in time, how various age groups view the transition to adulthood. It would be interesting to study the same participants using a longitudinal design and thus examine more precisely how people's views of 'becoming an adult' change as they grow older. In addition, most participants in this study (84 per cent) were white Americans. As Arnett notes, although the overall findings were consistent with those of studies conducted elsewhere in the world (see Bynner, 2006), the question of whether the transition to adulthood is viewed differently in different parts of the world, and in different ethic groups, needs careful consideration. What do you think? Do Arnett's findings match up with your evaluation of 'adulthood'. Do they match up with the views of other people you know?

Stages Versus Critical Events in Adulthood

Many researchers view adult social development as a progression through age-related stages (Levinson, 1990). According to Erik Erikson (1980; see Table 13.1), *intimacy versus isolation* is the major developmental challenge of early adulthood (ages 20 to 40). Intimacy is the ability to open oneself to another person and to form close relationships. This is the period of adulthood when many people form close adult friendships, fall in love and marry.

Middle adulthood (ages 40 to 65) brings with it the issue of *generativity versus stagnation*. Through their careers, raising children or involvement in other activities, people achieve generativity by doing things for others and making the world a better place. Certainly, many young adults make such contributions, but generativity typically becomes a more central issue later in adulthood (Slater, 2003).

Late adulthood (age 65 and older) accentuates the final crisis, *integrity versus despair*. Older adults review their life and evaluate its meaning. If the major crises of earlier stages have been successfully resolved, the person experiences integrity: a sense of completeness and fulfilment. Older adults who have not achieved positive outcomes at earlier stages may experience despair, regretting that they had not lived their lives in a more fulfilling way.

Consistent with Erikson's model, many goals increase in importance as people age, and successfully resolving certain life tasks contributes to mastering others (McAdams and de St Aubin, 1998). But critics caution that we should avoid viewing early, middle and late adulthood as strict stages in which one life task takes over while others fade away. Although older adults are more concerned about generativity and integrity than are younger adults, they remain highly concerned about intimacy (Sheldon and Kasser, 2001).

Another way to view adult social development is through the major life events that people experience. Sigmund Freud (1935) once defined psychological adjustment as 'the ability to love and work', and many key life events revolve around these two themes.

Marriage and Family

Around the world, most people marry or form another type of family union at some point in their lives, and family structures can vary widely both across and within different cultures (Fig. 13.20). The 'average' family in many countries across the world has changed in several ways over recent generations. For example, Baby Boomers were born a few years after the end of the Second World War, and their children (born

Focus 13.15
According to Erikson, what are three major developmental challenges of adulthood?

Focus 13.16
Describe research findings on family structure, cohabitation and the course of marital satisfaction.

FIGURE 13.20

These children, from a family of herders in the Republic of Mongolia, are living in an extended family unit that includes parents, grandparents, great-grandparents and other relatives. In more western cultures it is much more common to grow up in a single-parent environment.

in the 1960s through to the early 1980s) became known as Generation X. As Figure 13.21 shows, compared with the families that Baby Boomers grew up in, members of Generation X are more likely to have experienced parental divorce, had two working parents, had a smaller number of siblings and yet maintained a similar level of closeness to their parents (Bengtson, 2001).

FIGURE 13.21

Growing up in different generations.

Baby Boomers were surveyed when they were 18 to 22 years old and asked to identify various characteristics of the families in which they had grown up. A generation later, when the Baby Boomers' children (Generation X) had turned 18 to 22 years old, they answered the same survey questions as their parents had.

SOURCE: Bengtson, 2001.

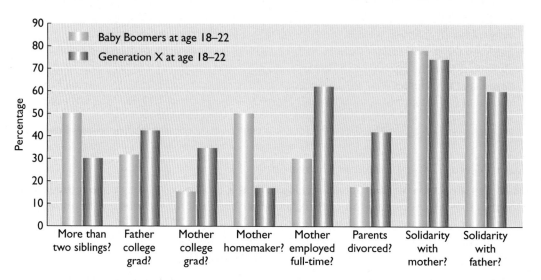

Adults typically expect much from marriage, but a high divorce rate in many countries indicates that marital happiness is by no means automatic. Successful marriages are characterized by emotional closeness, positive communication and problem solving, agreement on basic values and expectations, and a willingness to accept and support changes in the partner (Cordova et al., 2005). On average, marital satisfaction declines over the first few years of the marriage (McNulty and Karney, 2004). This does not mean, however, that most couples are unhappy. They are still satisfied, just less so than they were. In a sense, the honeymoon is over.

The birth of a first baby dramatically alters the way couples spend their time. For many couples, marital satisfaction decreases in the year or two after their first child is born (Cowan and Cowan, 2000). Compared with husbands, wives are more likely to leave their outside jobs, spend more time parenting, and feel that their spouses are not helping enough. Disagreements over the division of labour and parenting are a major contributor to the drop in marital satisfaction (Frisco and Williams, 2003).

Over a broader age period, cross-sectional studies suggest a U-shaped relation between marital satisfaction and progression through major life events. The percentage of couples reporting that they are 'very satisfied' in their marriage typically is highest before or just as the first child is born, drops during child-rearing years and increases after all the children have left home (Orbuch et al., 1996). Contrary to the popular 'empty nest' stereotype, most middle-aged couples do not become significantly depressed or suffer a crisis when their children leave home (Chiriboga, 1989). Couples maintain meaningful relationships with their children but have more time to spend with each other and to pursue leisure activities.

Despite the stresses that accompany marriage and parenthood, studies around the globe find that married people experience greater subjective well-being than unmarried adults (Keyes and Waterman, 2003). They tend to be happier and live longer. Although raising children is demanding, parents often report that having children is one of the best things that has happened in their lives.

Some couples in committed relationships *cohabit* – that is, live together without being married. Some couples cohabit as a permanent alternative to marriage, but many do so as a 'trial marriage' to determine if they are compatible before marrying. In Sweden, premarital cohabitation appears to be the norm (Duvander, 1999).

WHAT DO YOU THINK?

COHABITATION AS A 'TRIAL MARRIAGE'

What would you predict? Do couples who live together before getting married have a lower, higher or similar rate of divorce compared with couples who do not live together before they get married? Why? Think about it, then see p. 597.

Establishing a Career

In the adult world, one of the first questions a new acquaintance typically asks is 'So, what do you do?' A career helps us earn a living and defines part of our identity. Work provides an outlet for achievement, gives us structure and is a significant source of social interactions. Having satisfying relationships at work is especially important in collectivistic countries (Siu, 2003).

According to Donald Super (1957), a pioneer in the field of vocational psychology, from childhood through to our mid-twenties, we first enter a *growth stage* of career interests in which we form initial impressions about the types of jobs we like or dislike, followed by a more earnest *exploration stage* in which we form tentative ideas about a preferred career and pursue the necessary education or training.

From the mid-twenties to mid-forties, people often enter an *establishment phase* during which they begin to make their mark. Initially, they may experience some job instability. After college, for example, many people are likely to change careers at least once. Eventually, careers tend to become more stable, and people enter a *maintenance stage* that continues into late adulthood. Finally, during the *decline stage*, people's investment in work tends to decrease and they eventually retire.

Although this general model is useful, people's career paths vary quite a bit, and this is especially true for women. Joy Schneer and Frieda Reitman (1997) found that among college students who obtained an MBA (master of business administration) degree and then pursued managerial careers, women were more likely than men to experience career gaps by mid-career. Such gaps tended to retard professional advancement and salary level.

Overall, compared with their fathers and mothers at the same age, today's young women hold higher career aspirations (Bengtson, 2001). Still, family responsibilities, which fall disproportionately on women even when their married partners have similar job status, are a major cause of women's work gaps outside the home, reductions to part-time work status or delayed entry into the workforce (Smithson et al., 2004). After raising a family, many women enter the workforce for the first time, reinvigorate an earlier career or return to college to prepare for a new one. Career gaps also occur when adults must temporarily leave the workforce to care for their elderly parents. As in raising children, women disproportionately fill this elder-care role.

Focus 13.17
Discuss the stages of establishing a career and sex differences in career paths.

Mid-life Crisis: Fact or Fiction?

Popular wisdom holds that along the developmental path of career and family, people hit a massive pothole called the *mid-life crisis*. Is it a reality? Daniel Levinson and his co-workers (1978; Levinson, 1986) studied 85 men and women longitudinally and found that many experienced a turbulent mid-life transition between the ages of 40 and 45. They began to focus on their mortality and realized that some of their life's dreams pertaining to career, family and relationships would not come true.

Critics note that Levinson's sample was small and non-representative. In fact, there is considerable evidence that the notion of an inevitable, full-blown mid-life crisis is a myth (Lachman, 2004).

Focus 13.18
Evaluate the concept of mid-life crisis and the view that dying people experience a sequence of psychological stages.

Research conducted around the world shows that happiness and life satisfaction generally do not decrease throughout adulthood (Diener et al., 1999). In one study of adolescents and people in early, middle and late adulthood from eight Western European countries, about 80 per cent of each age group reported they were 'satisfied' or 'very satisfied' with their lives (Ingelhart and Ra-bier, 1986). Moreover, people in their forties do *not* have the highest rates of divorce, suicide, depression, feelings of meaninglessness or emotional instability (Kessler et al., 2004; McCrae and Costa, 1990).

In sum, middle-aged adults surely experience important conflicts, disappointments and worries – and some indeed experience major crises – but so do people of all ages (Wethington, 2000). As Erikson emphasized, there are major goals to achieve, crises to resolve and rewards to experience in every phase of life.

SOCIAL-EMOTIONAL DEVELOPMENT IN OLD AGE
Retirement and the 'Golden Years'

Retirement is an important milestone. Some adults view it as a reminder that they are growing older, but many look forward to leisure and other opportunities they were unable to pursue during their careers. Most retired people do not become anxious, depressed or dissatisfied with life due to retirement itself, although those who have strong work values are most apt to miss their jobs (Hyde et al., 2004).

The decision to retire or keep working typically involves many factors, such as one's feelings about the job, leisure interests, physical health and family relationships. Family income, leisure time and family roles change with retirement, and married couples often experience increased marital stress after a spouse retires, especially if the other spouse is still working. Over time, however, they typically adjust to their new circumstances and marital quality is enhanced (Moen et al., 2001).

Some people, of course, do not have the luxury to choose their work status. They may be forced into retirement by job lay-offs or mandatory retirement ages, or feel compelled to keep working for economic reasons. These circumstances can have a significant impact on well-being. Whether in their fifties, sixties or seventies, adults who are working or retired because this is what *they* prefer report higher life satisfaction and better physical and mental health than adults who are involuntarily working or retired (Shultz et al., 1998). Of course, declining physical and mental health also may be factors that lead people to retire in the first place. Thus, biological, psychological and environmental factors continue to exert their influence on development and jointly shape how people navigate their golden years. Figure 13.22 summarizes some of the diverse factors that affect lifespan development.

FIGURE 13.22

Levels of analysis: factors related to lifespan development.

LEVELS OF ANALYSIS FACTORS RELATED TO LIFESPAN DEVELOPMENT

Biological	Psychological	Environmental
• Sex determination and genetic contribution to temperament	• Changes in schemas, information processing and intellectual capacities	• Teratogens that affect prenatal development
• Brain maturation underlying social-emotional growth in childhood	• Secure or insecure attachment to caregiver, peer relations	• Parenting styles and childhood socialization experiences
• Pubertal changes, including early and late maturation	• Development of gender-identity and sex-role stereotypes	• Major life events (marriage, parenthood, career)
• Biologically based physical and social-emotional changes in adulthood	• Personality formation and resolution of psychological stages	• Exercise and lifestyle norms that affect biological functions at all ages

Lifespan development

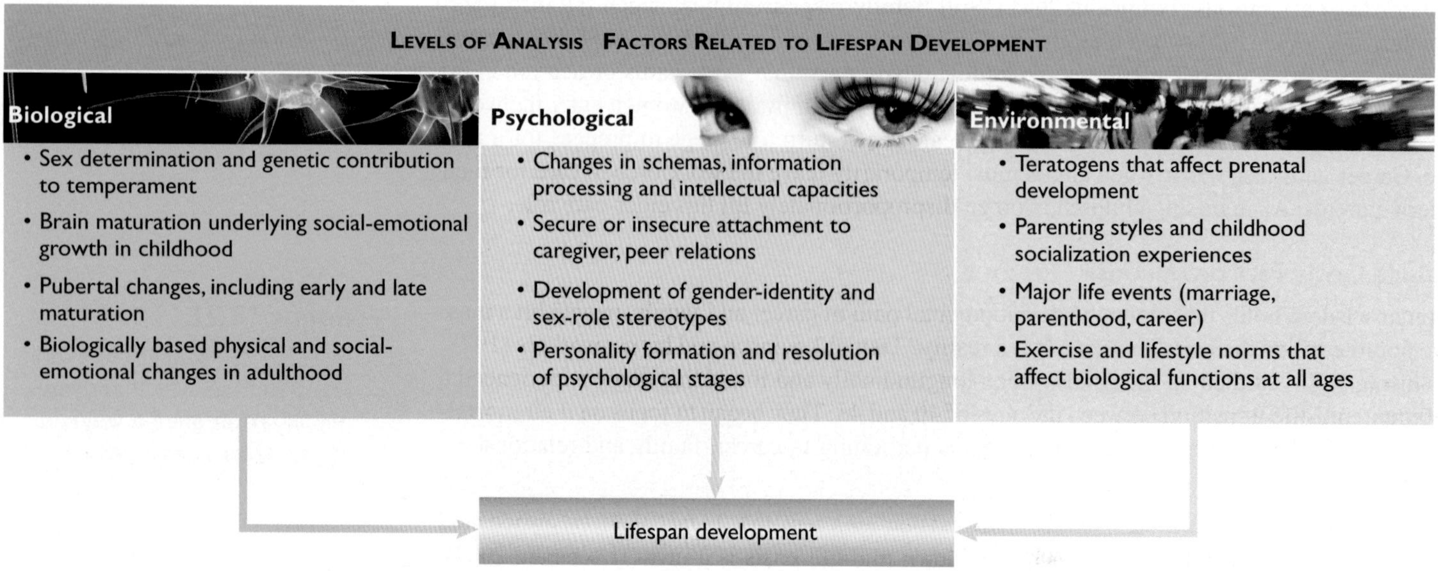

Death and Dying

Jeanne Louise Calment was born in France 10 years after the American Civil War. By age 60, she had lived through the First World War and the invention of the radio, telephone, motion picture, automobile and aeroplane. Still to come was the Second World War, television, space flight, computers and the Internet. Calment rode a bicycle until age 100, and her 120th birthday party was a grand affair. When a reporter asked how her future looked, Jeanne replied with a wry sense of humour, 'Very brief' (Fig. 13.23). Indeed, she died two years later, having lived longer than any human in recorded history.

Part of being human is the fact that we are mortal. Like other aspects of lifespan development summarized in Figure 13.22, death can be viewed at several levels. It is an inevitable biological process, but one with important psychological and environmental components.

In her pioneering work on dying, Elisabeth Kübler-Ross (1969) found that terminally ill patients often experienced five stages as they coped with impending death. *Denial* typically came first, as the person refused to accept that the illness was terminal. Next, denial often gave way to *anger* and then to *bargaining*, such as 'Lord, please let me live long enough to see my grandchild'. *Depression* ushered in the fourth stage, as patients began to grieve. Finally, many experienced *acceptance* and a resigned sense of peacefulness.

It is essential to keep in mind that these stages do not represent a 'normal' or 'correct' way to face death and that terminally ill patients' reactions may not typify those of people facing death under other circumstances (Doka, 1995). Even among terminally ill patients, some move back and forth between stages, do not experience all the stages, or look forward to death. Indeed, some scientists question whether people's psychological responses to their impending death are stage-like at all (Kastenbaum, 2000). Nevertheless, Kübler-Ross's work spurred great interest in understanding and helping people cope with death.

As Figure 13.24 illustrates, beliefs and customs concerning death vary across cultures and among individuals (Werth et al., 2002). To some, death means the complete end of one's existence. Others believe in reincarnation or an afterlife. Death also means different things to people of different ages. By late and even middle adulthood, people typically have lost more friends and loved ones and have thought more about their own eventual death than have younger people.

Understandably, the elderly are more accepting of their own death than any other age group. In the middle of a fatal heart attack, an 81-year-old man we knew reassuringly told his family, 'It's my time. It's been a good life'. We should all wish for this blessing of a fulfilled life's journey.

FIGURE 13.23

Jeanne Louise Calment of Arles, France, was born in 1875 and died in 1997 at the age of 122. Calment's life is the longest that has been verified.

FIGURE 13.24

Many cultures honour a person's death with a ceremony that involves family, friends and the wider community. In some cultures, this traditionally is a sombre occasion; in others it is a more joyous celebration.

IN REVIEW

- Adolescence is a socially constructed transition period between childhood and adulthood.

- During adolescence, peer relationships become more important. Most teenagers maintain good relationships with their parents. Overall, for most teenagers daily emotional experience becomes less positive as they move into and through early adolescence.

- The age at which people think that they have become adults varies widely. Among Americans, it may depend most strongly on viewing oneself as a responsible, independent person.

- Erikson proposed that intimacy versus isolation, generativity versus stagnation, and integrity versus despair are the main crises of early, middle and late adulthood.

- For many couples, marital satisfaction tends to decline in the years following the birth of children but increases later in adulthood.

- Work serves important psychological and social functions. Overall, women experience more career gaps, and their career paths are more variable than men's. Most adults do not experience a full-blown mid-life crisis. Similarly, most retired people do not become more anxious, depressed or lonely due to retirement.

- Many terminally ill patients experience similar psychological reactions as they cope with their impending death, but beliefs and feelings about death vary with culture and age, and there is no 'normal' way to approach death.

KEY TERMS AND CONCEPTS

Each term has been boldfaced and defined in the chapter on the page indicated in parentheses.

adolescence (p. 585)

attachment (p. 572)

authoritarian parents (p. 579)

authoritative parents (p. 579)

conventional moral
   reasoning (p. 582)

emotion regulation (p. 568)

gender constancy (p. 580)

gender identity (p. 580)

imprinting (p. 572)

indulgent parents (p. 579)

neglectful parents (p. 579)

post-conventional moral
   reasoning (p. 583)

pre-conventional moral
   reasoning (p. 582)

psychosocial stages (p. 570)

puberty (p. 586)

separation anxiety (p. 573)

sex-typing (p. 580)

stranger anxiety (p. 573)

strange situation (p. 574)

temperament (p. 569)

WHAT DO YOU THINK?

SHY CHILD, SHY ADULT? (p. 569)

To answer this question, psychologists patiently conduct longitudinal research, measuring people's temperament in childhood and then examining whether it correlates with people's traits or behaviours in adulthood. For example, in America and Sweden, shy, behaviourally inhibited 8- to 12-year-old boys are more likely than non-shy peers to delay marriage and fatherhood when they grow up, possibly reflecting their reluctance to enter new social relationships (Caspi et al., 1988; Kerr et al., 1996). Shy American girls are more likely as adults to quit work after marriage and become homemakers, whereas shy Swedish girls are less likely to complete college than non-shy girls.

What about temperament in early childhood? Denise Newman and co-workers (1997) measured the temperament of 961 New Zealanders at age 3, based on a 90-minute observation of each child. At age 21, participants were studied again. Compared with 3-year-olds with a 'well-adjusted temperament', those who were 'undercontrolled' (i.e., irritable, impulsive, inattentive) reported more antisocial behaviour in adulthood and greater conflict in family and romantic relationships, and they were more likely to have been fired from a job. In contrast, children with an 'inhibited temperament' (i.e., socially shy and fearful) reported having less overall companionship in adulthood.

Most young children are well adjusted and display only mild to moderately strong temperamental traits. Differences in temperament among these children only weakly predict how they will function as adults. But for the remaining children, their strong temperamental traits can provide better insight into adulthood functioning. Still, predicting how any individual child will turn out as an adult is difficult. Many factors influence development, and even during childhood, strong temperaments often mellow (Pfeifer et al., 2002). Even so, it is remarkable that a mere 90-minute observation of children at age 3 can modestly predict different patterns of adjustment 18 years later.

COHABITATION AS A 'TRIAL MARRIAGE' (p. 593)

Large national surveys in several countries, including Canada, Germany, Sweden and the USA, have found that premarital cohabitation is associated with a *higher* risk of subsequent divorce (Heaton, 2002). Many researchers, however, believe that the cohabitation–divorce relationship does not reflect cause and effect. Rather, couples who choose to cohabit before marriage appear to differ psychologically from couples who do not cohabit first. They tend to be less religious and less committed to their partners and to marriage as an institution (Stanley et al., 2004). Taken together, these pre-existing factors would increase the risk of divorce even if these couples had not cohabited before marrying. In some studies, when researchers focus on cohabiting couples who start out with a strong orientation towards marriage, they find that the risk of divorce is no higher and the quality of marital relations is no poorer than among couples who did not cohabit prior to marriage (Bruederl et al., 1997). Still, research does *not* support the view that, overall, cohabitation reduces the risk of subsequent divorce.

CHAPTER FOURTEEN

SOCIAL THINKING AND BEHAVIOUR

CHAPTER OUTLINE

Without the human community, one single human being cannot survive.

THE DALAI LAMA

The prison had become a living hell. Hidden behind their mirrored sunglasses, the guards asserted their total authority over the prisoners. They made the prisoners ask permission to do virtually anything, including going to the toilet. The guards conducted roll calls in the middle of the night to assert their power and disrupt the prisoners' sleep, and they forced prisoners to do push-ups, sometimes with their foot pushing down on the prisoner's back. For their part, the prisoners became increasingly passive and depressed. They hated the guards but were powerless against them. After a few days, one prisoner cracked emotionally. Soon another broke down. Before long, the demoralized prisoners became nothing more than what the guards expected them to be: piteous objects of scorn and abuse.

This prison was not in some brutal dictatorship, the prisoners were not hardened criminals, nor were the guards sadistic psychopaths. Instead, this prison was in the basement of the psychology building at Stanford University, and the guards and prisoners were college students who had volunteered for a study of 'prison life'. Before the study, screening questionnaires, interviews, and psychological tests showed the participants to be well adjusted.

Philip Zimbardo, the social psychologist who designed the study, watched in disbelief as scenes of callous inhumanity unfolded before him. What began as a two-week simulation of prison life had to be halted after only six days. Afterward, Zimbardo and his associates held several sessions with the participants to help them work through their powerful emotional reactions, and they maintained contact over the following year to minimize the risk that participants would experience lasting negative effects.

What transformed normal college students into people they would not have recognized a week earlier? As one guard recalled, 'I was surprised at myself. I made them … clean out the toilets with their bare hands. I practically considered the prisoners cattle' (Zimbardo et al., 1973, p. 42). Decades later, the Stanford prison study remains a landmark for dramatically illustrating a basic concept: behaviour is determined not only by our biological endowment and past learning experiences but also by the power of the immediate social situation (Haney and Zimbardo, 1998).

Human beings are *social* creatures. We spend our days in ever changing social environments where we interact with and think of other people. These other people have a profound impact on our feelings, thoughts and behaviour. Indeed, other people can be said to be the most relevant and emotionally laden stimuli we encounter in our environment. Although we do occasionally feel happy and elated when seeing the beauty of nature and can also feel sad when nature is threatened or destroyed, it is other *individuals* who instigate most of our emotional responses. As social animals, other people are so important that being alone for a long period of time is unbearable for most of us. In our judicial system solitary confinement for example is seen as a form of torture. Indeed, isolating individuals from society by placing them in prison cells is one of the harshest punishments society can think of.

The current chapter explores the field of social psychology, which is particularly interested with the question of how people view, react to and influence other individuals. Gordon W. Allport gave a particularly influential definition of the discipline of social psychology as:

> an attempt to understand and explain how the thought, feeling and behaviour of individuals is influenced by the actual, imagined or implied presence of others. The term 'implied presence' refers to the many activities the individual carries out because of his position (role) in a complex social structure and because of his membership in a cultural group. (Allport, 1954, p. 3).

When you read the above definition, you might have thought, 'I do that all the time!' And you are right; we all try to understand why people behave as they do and why they feel what they feel; in this way we are all social psychologists. While watching other people behave on television, at school, on the streets or in parks, we form ideas about their thoughts and their relationships with others around them. Indeed, the ability to understand our own and other people's behaviour is of great importance for making co-ordinated social life possible. However, are these commonsense assumptions which we derive from our observations always correct? Obviously it is quite difficult to oversee the whole range of influences determining other people's behaviours and indeed our own. Most of the time we can only observe *actual* behaviour, while being completely oblivious as to what others are really thinking. For example, if someone does you a favour, have they done so out of generosity or are they attempting to make you reciprocate in kind? If you like someone, is it because the person is genuinely likeable or is it because this person tries to present himself or herself in a manner which pleases you?

This chapter is divided into three major domains of social psychology. The first question we 'attempt to understand and explain', is that concerning our social thinking; i.e., how we see and what we think of ourselves, and others around us. We ask questions such as, 'How accurate are the ideas we form of others and ourselves?' and 'how strong is the link between what we think and how we act?' The second topic covered in this chapter, is social influence and within-group behaviour. As you can see from Allport's definition, one of the key themes of social psychology has been to understand the way in which other individuals influence the way we think, feel and behave. Indeed, being social *is* to influence and be influenced by others; a process that often occurs within the framework of group membership. Social influence then can be seen as providing a link between 'social thinking' and the third topic of this chapter, 'social relations'. This topic is divided in two domains of interest to social psychologists: *intergroup relations* and *interpersonal* relations. Here we are interested in the way individuals and groups of individuals behave in relation to each other. What leads us to love, hurt, or even kill another person or group of persons? It is important to understand that these three topics, social thinking, social influence and social relations, do not stand for separate bodies of inquiry. All three domains are intricately related, with perceptions *influencing* behaviour, and behaviour *influencing* perceptions.

SOCIAL THINKING

In your judgement, do you think *you* would act in a similarly brutal manner, as did some of the guards in the Stanford prison study? And why did some guards act so brutally? Did you form any impressions of the guards or prisoners as you read about the study? Do you feel that the study was worthwhile? Answers to these questions depend in part on the way you construe reality; that is, individuals do not often respond to so-called 'objective' reality, but respond to their own subjective construction of it. For this reason, is important to understand how individuals think about their surroundings and construe their own reality, or what we call *social thinking*. The above questions about the Stanford prison study focus on four key aspects of social thinking: *attributions*, *impressions*, *self-concept* and *attitudes*.

ATTRIBUTION: PERCEIVING THE CAUSES OF BEHAVIOUR

In everyday life we often make **attributions**, judgements about the causes of our own and other people's behaviour and outcomes (Fig. 14.1). Was my A in the end-of-year examination due to hard work and ability, or was it just an easy test? Did Bill criticize Linda because he is a rude person, or was he provoked? Did the guards' brutal behaviour reflect their personalities or some aspect of the situation? Such attributions can have a profound impact on our own and other people's lives. In the courtroom for example, jurors' attributions about a defendant's behaviour influence their decisions about guilt versus innocence.

Personal versus Situational Attributions

Our attempts to understand why people behave as they do and predict their future behaviour, typically involve either personal attributions or situational attributions (Heider, 1958). *Personal (internal) attributions* infer that people's characteristics cause their behaviour: 'Bill insulted Linda because he is rude.' 'My A in the end-of-year examination reflects my high ability.' *Situational (external) attributions* infer that aspects of the situation cause a behaviour: 'Bill was provoked into insulting Linda.' 'I received an A because the test was easy.'

How do we decide whether a behaviour is caused by personal or situational factors? Suppose you ask Kim for advice on whether to take a particular evening class in 'History of art', and she tells you that the course is terrible. Is the 'History of art' evening-class really poor (a situational attribution), or is it something about Kim (a personal attribution) that led to this response? According to Harold Kelley (1973), three types of information determine the attribution we make: *consistency*, *distinctiveness* and *consensus*. First, is Kim's response consistent over time? If you ask Kim again two weeks later and she still says that the evening-class is terrible, then consistency is high. Second, is her response distinctive? If Kim dislikes only the evening-class in 'History of art', then distinctiveness is high; if she thinks that most of her courses are terrible, then distinctiveness is low. Finally, how do other people respond? If other students agree with Kim that the evening-class in 'History of art' is poor, then consensus is high, but if they disagree with her, then consensus is low.

As Figure 14.2 illustrates, when consistency, distinctiveness and consensus are all high, we are likely to make a situational attribution: 'The course is bad.' But when consistency is high and the other two factors are low, we make a personal attribution: 'Perhaps Kim is overly critical.' Humans, however, are often not so logical. We often take mental short cuts and make snap judgements that bias our attributions.

Attributional Biases

Social psychology teaches us that the immediate social environment profoundly influences behaviour, yet at times we ignore this when making attributions. Instead, we commit a bias called the **fundamental attribution error**: we underestimate the impact of the situation and overestimate the role of personal factors when explaining other people's behaviour (Ross, 2001).

---

attributions
judgements about the causes of our own and other people's behaviour and outcomes

FIGURE 14.1

'He's been under a lot of stress lately.' 'He only thinks about himself. What an idiot!' Depending on which attribution she makes for her husband's outburst, this woman may respond with understanding or anger.

Focus 14.1

What types of information lead us to make situational rather than personal attributions?

fundamental attribution error
we underestimate the impact of the situation and overestimate the role of personal factors when explaining other people's behaviour

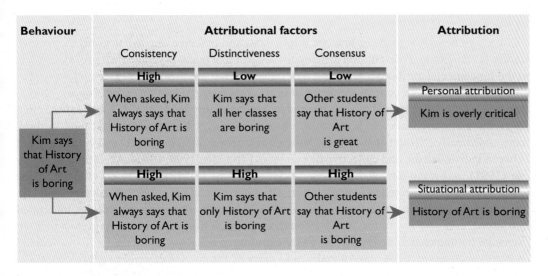

Behaviour	Attributional factors			Attribution
	Consistency	Distinctiveness	Consensus	
	High	**Low**	**Low**	Personal attribution
Kim says that History of Art is boring	When asked, Kim always says that History of Art is boring	Kim says that all her classes are boring	Other students say that History of Art is great	Kim is overly critical
	High	**High**	**High**	Situational attribution
	When asked, Kim always says that History of Art is boring	Kim says that only History of Art is boring	Other students say that History of Art is boring	History of Art is boring

FIGURE 14.2

Forming personal and situational attributions.

Consistency, distinctiveness and consensus information help us determine whether to make personal or situational attributions for someone else's behaviour. Note that in both examples consistency is high. If Kim's behaviour has low consistency (sometimes she says the evening 'History of art' is boring, and other times she says it is interesting), we typically attribute the behaviour to transient conditions (e.g., changes in Kim's mood) rather than to stable personal or situational factors.

SOURCE: based on Kelley, 1973.

Focus 14.2

Describe the fundamental attribution error and the self-serving bias, and discuss how they are affected by culture.

This thinking bias has been found in real-world situations and laboratory experiments (Cowley, 2005).

Imagine that as part of a course assignment you write an essay on whether physicians should be allowed to help terminally ill patients commit suicide. The professor gives you the choice of writing in favour of or against physician-assisted suicide. Your class-mates read the essay, and because they know you had a choice, they logically assume that the essay's content reflects your personal views. Thus if the essay opposes physician-assisted suicide, your class-mates will conclude that you are against this practice.

But suppose instead that the professor assigns you to write a supportive essay or assigns you to write an opposing essay. Your class-mates know that you were not given a choice. Logically, the content of the essay reflects the situation to which you were assigned. After all, perhaps you are against physician-assisted suicide but were told to write an essay in favour of it, or vice versa. Yet experiments indicate that the content of the essay will still influence your class-mates' perception of whether you support or oppose the issue (Jones and Harris, 1967). Similarly, you would be making the fundamental attribution error if – solely on the basis of their professional roles – you expected television and film stars to have the same personal traits as the characters they played.

Psychologists debate what causes the fundamental attribution error, but they agree that it is not inevitable (see Sabini et al., 2001). When people have time to reflect on their judgements or are highly motivated to be careful, the fundamental attribution error is reduced. Moreover, keep in mind that the fundamental attribution error applies to how we perceive other people's behaviour rather than our own. As comedian George Carlin noted, the slow driver ahead of us is a 'moron', and the fast driver trying to pass us is a 'maniac'. Yet we do not think of ourselves as a moron or a maniac when we do these things, perhaps because we are more aware of situational factors (e.g., an unfamiliar road) impinging on us. After the Stanford prison study ended, guards who had treated prisoners cruelly were quick to attribute their behaviour to the role that they had been in rather than to their personal qualities.

Indeed, when it comes to explaining our own behaviour, we often make attributions that protect or enhance our self-esteem by displaying a **self-serving bias**, the tendency to make personal attributions for successes and situational attributions for failures (Ross and Nisbett, 1991). The strength of this bias, however, depends on many factors. For example, a meta-analysis of 266 studies by Amy Mezulis and her co-workers (2004) found that depressed individuals are much less likely than most people to display a self-serving bias. Indeed, depressed people often display the opposite pattern – taking too little credit for successes and too much credit for failures – which helps keep them depressed.

self-serving bias

the tendency to make personal attributions for successes and situational attributions for failures

Culture and Attribution

Culture significantly influences how we think about and perceive our social world. Numerous studies investigating cross-cultural differences suggest that many psychological processes, such as the fundamental attribution error, are not 'universal' but are to a large degree culturally specific (Nisbett, 2003). In general, evidence indicates that East Asians (e.g., China, Japan, Korea) tend to think holistically, and this is reflected in the commonly held belief in these cultures that all events are interconnected. In contrast, westerners (e.g., UK, USA, Canada) tend to think more analytically (Nisbett et al., 2001). Another distinction often made between cultures is that between individualistic and collectivistic countries (Triandis, 1990; 1995). According to Hofstede (1991), *individualism* characterizes 'societies in which the ties between individuals are loose: everyone is expected to look after himself or herself and his or her immediate family' (p. 51), and *collectivism* characterizes 'societies in which people from birth onwards are integrated into strong, cohesive in-groups, which throughout people's lifetime continue to protect them in exchange for unquestioning loyalty' (p. 51). According to this distinction, the English-speaking countries such as the USA and Australia, and parts of Europe (Northern European countries) tend to be high on individualism, whereas some parts of Europe and much of Africa, Asia and Latin America tend to be high on collectivism (e.g., Hofstede, 1980; Triandis, 1994).

One consequence of holistic and collectivistic thinking involves an awareness of complexity, leading East Asians for example to attend more to the context in processing perceptual stimuli (Kitayama et al., 2003). Given the greater weight attached to the context, it is not surprising that our cultural background also affects how we go about making attributions. In one study, participants of varying ages from India and the USA were asked to attribute the cause of other people's behaviour (Miller, 1984). As Figure 14.3 shows, with increasing age, Indians made more situational attributions, whereas Americans made more personal attributions. Accordingly, Incheol Choi and co-workers (2003) predicted and found that compared with European American college students, Korean college students scored higher on measures of holistic thinking and took more information into account when making causal attributions for other people's behaviour. The fundamental attribution error, then, seems much less 'fundamental' than previously thought, leading some authors to refer to the phenomenon as the *correspondence bias* instead (Smith et al., 2006).

Culture not only influences attributions for other people's behaviour, but also influences attributions for our *own* behaviour. Asians living in their homelands are less likely to display a self-serving attributional bias than are Americans or other westerners (Mezulis et al., 2004). Modesty, for example, is highly valued in East Asian collectivistic culture, leading East Asians to take less personal credit for success and accept more responsibility for their failures than do American

FIGURE 14.3

Culture influences attributions.

With increasing age from childhood to adulthood, Americans show a greater tendency to make personal attributions for other people's behaviours. In contrast, participants from India show an increased tendency to make situational attributions.

SOURCE: adapted from Miller, 1984.

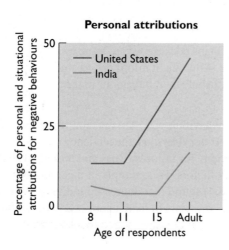

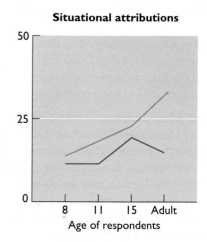

students. Thus, when asked to reflect on their successes and failures, Muramoto (2003) found Japanese students to attribute their successes to others and their failures to themselves. However, she also found her Japanese respondents to believe their friends and family would blame them less for failure and credit them more for success. This indicates that modesty might well be a tool for self-presentation, as a study by Brown and Kobayashi (2001) suggests. Brown and Kobayashi (2001) compared East Asians' and westerners' motivations to achieve a positive self-regard. They found that Japanese respondents rated themselves just as highly on traits they valued most, such as modesty and friendliness, as typically Americans do on *their* most highly valued qualities. This suggests that both East Asians and westerners are motivated to achieve a positive self-regard. This debate regarding the role of modesty and the existence of self-serving biases is important, for it suggests cultures do not differ so much in their 'social thinking', but more in the norms of behaviour they lay down for their group members to conform to.

FORMING AND MAINTAINING IMPRESSIONS

As social beings, we constantly form impressions of other people, just as they form impressions of us. Attributions play a key role: Do you attribute the guards' behaviour in the Stanford prison study to the role they were placed in or to their personal characteristics? Other factors, however, also affect how we form and maintain impressions.

How Important Are First Impressions?

Try this exercise. Tell a few people that you know someone who is 'intelligent, industrious, impulsive, critical, stubborn and envious', and ask them how much they 'like' this person. Repeat the process with a few others, only describe the person as 'envious, stubborn, critical, impulsive, industrious and intelligent'. Solomon Asch (1946) found that the person in the first description is perceived more positively – as more sociable and happier – than the person in the second description, even though both groups received identical information but in reverse order.

When forming impressions, the **primacy effect** refers to our tendency to attach more importance to the initial information that we learn about a person. New information can change our opinion, but it has to 'work harder' for two reasons. First, we tend to be most alert to information we receive first. Second, initial information may shape how we perceive subsequent information. Imagine an athlete who gets off to a great start in training camp. The coach attributes high ability to the athlete. But as time goes on, the athlete's performance declines. To maintain this positive initial impression, the coach may attribute the performance decline to fatigue or a string of bad breaks. First impressions also carry extra weight because they influence our desire to make further contact with a person (Sunnafrank et al., 2004). It is difficult to overcome someone's negative first impression of you if that person subsequently avoids or ignores you.

Primacy is the rule of thumb in impression formation, especially for people who dislike ambiguity and uncertainty (Kruglanski, 2004). We seem to have a remarkable capacity for forming snap judgements based on small amounts of initial information. Indeed, Ambady and Rosenthal's (1992) meta-analysis (for a description of what a meta-analysis is, see Chapter 2) investigating 44 published studies on person perception, showed that snap judgements were just as accurate as longer-term judgements. They showed that a perception of a person after observing him or her for less than half a minute was just as accurate as after an observation period of four to five minutes. Some evolutionary psychologists propose that evaluating stimuli quickly (such as rapidly distinguishing friend from foe) was adaptive for our survival (Krebs and Denton, 1997). But we are not slaves to primacy. Primacy effects decrease – and *recency effects* (giving greater weight to the most recent information) may occur – when we are asked to avoid making snap judgements, reminded to consider the evidence carefully, and made to feel accountable for our judgements (Webster et al., 1996).

primacy effect
refers to our tendency to attach more importance to the initial information that we learn about a person

In-Psych

To learn more about attribution, watch the 'Fundamental Attribution Error' video in Chapter 14 of the In-Psych programme online.

Seeing What We Expect to See

Imagine that we are going to a party and I tell you that the host, George, is a distant, aloof, cold person. You meet him and try to make conversation, but George does not say much and avoids eye contact. A bit later, you say to me, 'You were right, he's really a cold fish'. Now let us rewind this scene. Suppose I describe George as nice but extremely shy. Later when you try to make conversation, he does not say much and avoids eye contact. You say to me, 'You were right, he's really shy'. Same behaviour, different impression. This example reminds us of a basic perceptual principle highlighted in Chapter 5. Whether perceiving objects or people, our *mental set*, which is a readiness to perceive the world in a particular way, powerfully shapes how we interpret a stimulus.

What creates our mental sets? One set of factors that we have discussed throughout the book are *schemas*, mental frameworks that help us organize and interpret information. By telling you that our host is 'cold' or 'shy', I activate a set of concepts and expectations (your schema) for how such a person is likely to behave. The host's behaviour can be interpreted in many ways, but you fit his behaviour into the schema that is already activated.

A **stereotype**, which is a shared belief about person attributes, usually personality traits, but often also behaviours, of a group or category of people, represents a powerful type of schema (Yzerbyt et al., 1997). In one study, participants watched a videotape of a 9-year-old girl named Hannah and then judged her academic potential (Darley and Gross, 1983). They were told either that Hannah came from an upper middle-class environment and had parents with white-collar careers or that she came from a poor neighbourhood and had parents who were blue-collar workers. On the videotape, Hannah displayed average performance, answering some questions correctly and missing others. All participants saw the same performance, but those who thought Hannah came from a poor background rated her as having less ability. This study illustrates how our stereotypes (e.g., about social class) can bias the way we perceive other people's behaviour.

Creating What We Expect to See

Seeing what we expect to see is only one way we confirm our initial impressions. Usually without conscious awareness, a **self-fulfilling prophecy** occurs when people's erroneous expectations lead them to act towards others in a way that brings about the expected behaviours, thereby confirming their original impression. Returning to our party example, if you expect George to be cold and aloof, then perhaps when you meet him you smile less and stand farther away than you would have if I had told you that George was a great guy. Perhaps when he looks at you, you avert your gaze, leading him to perceive you as less likeable (Mason et al., 2005). In any case, his reserved response, in part, could be a reaction to *your* behaviour (Fig. 14.4a).

Self-fulfilling prophecies have been demonstrated in hundreds of studies across different settings, including schools, businesses, sports, close relationships and interactions with strangers (Eden, 2003; Snyder, 2001). When we interact with other people, our initially unfounded expectations can influence how we behave towards them, shaping their behaviour in a way that confirms our expectations (Fig. 14.4b).

SELF-CONCEPT

Just as we form impressions of others, we also have a representation of ourselves – the self-concept. As the ancient Greek saying 'know thyself – and thou shall know all the mysteries of the gods and of the universe' already suggests, the knowledge we have of ourselves is quite similar to knowledge we have of other people around us. And, indeed, if we think about the behaviour of others, we often relate it to how we think *we* would behave. Therefore, having some insight into the self-concept (i.e., where it comes from, what form it takes and how we evaluate it) is important for understanding how we also form impressions of others.

---

stereotype

which is a shared belief about person attributes, usually personality traits, but often also behaviours, of a group or category of people

Focus 14.3

Discuss how the primacy effect, stereotypes and self-fulfilling prophecies influence impression formation.

self-fulfilling prophecy

when people's erroneous expectations lead them to act towards others in a way that brings about the expected behaviours, thereby confirming their original impression

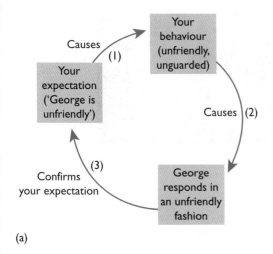

(a)

(b)

FIGURE 14.4

A self-fulfilling prophecy.

(a) Your expectation concerning George may influence your behaviour, and his response to you. (b) What first impressions will these people form of each other? How might these impressions influence their behaviour and possibly create a self-fulfilling prophecy?

Sources of Self-Knowledge

The knowledge we have of ourselves is complex and contains multiple views of the Self. In one situation you may see yourself as a son or daughter, at other times as leader or follower and yet at other times as a scientist or a student. The experience of oneself is highly context dependent and in part linked to the roles we have in society (Markus and Wurf, 1987).

According to self-perception theory, one way in which we might come to understand ourselves is by 'stepping outside ourselves' and observing our own behaviour (Bem, 1972). If you notice yourself raising your hand and asking a question during a lecture, you might reflect on this behaviour and come to see yourself as inquisitive and not afraid to speak in public. Another way through which we can obtain knowledge about ourselves is by a process of social comparison (Festinger, 1954). You might, for example, compare your grades with those of fellow students in order to get an idea of your academic abilities. Indeed, such comparisons are essential for making sense of most of the information we gather about ourselves. Think of the score on an IQ test. Without any knowledge of the range and average score of *other people* on this test (i.e., 100), a score of 120 would be meaningless. Finally, we also come to know ourselves through examining what others think of us (Cooley, 1902; Mead, 1934). So, if a teacher commends you on your excellent paper and remarks you have some talent as a writer, you might come to see yourself as such. This is also known as the **reflected appraisals principle** or the 'looking-glass self', by which we incorporate the views others have of us into our own self-concept.

As we can see, thinking about oneself also involves a great deal of thinking about others' thinking about oneself. According to Carver and Scheier (1981), people's thoughts about themselves, and the self-awareness that comes with this, has two distinct foci: the private self and the public self (Fig. 14.5). A study by Sheldon and Johnson (1993) investigated the frequency with which individuals tended to experience eight different forms of self-awareness during everyday dyadic interaction. They showed that individuals most frequently thought about their private self (their own thoughts and feelings) and about how their interaction partner appeared to them. The self-awareness formed with the next highest frequency however was based on their public self (thoughts of how their interaction partner perceived them).

reflected appraisals principle
we incorporate the views others have of us into our own self-concept

FIGURE 14.5

Private and public selves.

Mirrors trigger one's private self, whereas audiences and cameras trigger the public self (see for example Carver and Scheier, 1978).

self-discrepancy theory

distinguishes among representations of what we currently are (the *actual* self), what we ideally hope to become (the *ideal* self) and what we think we ought to become (the *ought* self).

regulatory focus theory

both future selves are concerned with the pursuit of different types of goals

promotional goals

striving to achieve an ideal state

prevention goals

focusing on what one ought (not) to do

in-groups

groups individuals belong to

out-groups

groups individuals do not belong to individuals' self concept, according to their perceived membership of social groups

social identities

individual's self concept, according to their perceived membership of social groups

self-esteem

an individual's sense of self-worth, or the extent to which the individual appreciates, values or likes him or herself

Forms of Identity

Beyond our own ideas and thoughts of who we 'really' are at this moment, we also have ideas and thoughts of ourselves that are linked to the future. Higgins's (1987) **self-discrepancy theory** distinguishes among representations of what we currently are (the *actual* self), what we ideally hope to become (the *ideal* self) and what we think we ought to become (the *ought* self).

In his subsequent **regulatory focus theory**, Higgins (1997) proposed that both future selves are concerned with the pursuit of different types of goals. Where the ideal self focuses individuals' attention towards **promotional goals**, with individuals striving to achieve an ideal state, the 'ought' self focuses individuals' attention on **prevention goals**, with individuals focusing on what one ought (not) to do. Thus prevention goals are for example concerned with avoiding failure on a particular test, whereas promotional goals are concerned with trying to obtain the highest possible score on this test. These differences in focus can be either chronically or temporarily activated and have a strong impact on people's thoughts and behaviours. Prevention-focused individuals for example are more likely to see negative role models as motivating and inspiring, as they highlight strategies for avoiding failure. Promotion-focused individuals, on the other hand, are more inspired and motivated by positive role models, as they provide information for the individual on how to attain success (Lockwood et al., 2002).

This distinction between the actual, ideal and ought selves focuses mostly on individuals' personal identities, which are based on our personality traits, idiosyncratic characteristics and interpersonal relationships. However, one important feature of social life is that we not only define others and ourselves in terms of personal characteristics, but also in terms of the groups we belong to. People have a strong tendency to group objects and events into meaningful categories. Such categories help guide our daily judgements and enable us to organize and simplify our world (Allport, 1954). Apart from non-social categories and natural categories (such as animals or plants), we also categorize ourselves and other human beings into meaningful groups. This so-called *social categorization* involves classifying individuals in terms of the groups they belong or do not belong to, called **in-groups**, groups individuals belong to, and **out-groups**, groups individuals do not belong to, respectively. *Social identity theorists*, which entails social identity theory (e.g., Tajfel and Turner, 1979) and self-categorization theory (Turner et al., 1987), argue that such social categorizations are *so* important to us as individuals, that our identity is partly based on these group memberships. Social identity theorists have therefore suggested that, besides our personal identities, we also define ourselves in terms of our **social identities**, *derived from the knowledge of belonging to particular groups*. Thus, we are not only intelligent, thoughtful, friends, husbands or spouses, we are also British, European, women and academics.

Evaluating the Self

Individuals have a pervasive tendency to evaluate not only other people but also themselves. Such evaluations of the self lead to a general favourable or unfavourable attitude towards the self, called self-esteem (Rosenberg, 1965). **Self-esteem** refers to an individual's sense of self-worth, or the extent to which the individual appreciates, values or likes him or herself

(Blascovich and Tomaka, 1991). Although we have seen previously that people tend to have unrealistically positive evaluations of themselves (i.e., the self-serving bias), our self-evaluations are also often consistent with what others think of us. For example, Miyamoto and Dornbusch (1956) asked students to rate themselves on four personal attributes (intelligent, self-confident, likeable and physically attractive). They also asked other students belonging to the same groups as the participant to rate him or her on these characteristics. Results showed that people who rated themselves high on these attributes were more likely to be rated high by their fellows than those who rated themselves low on these attributes. Thus, consistent with the reflected appraisals principle, if others think well of you, you tend to think well of yourself.

Consistent with this, Leary and colleagues (1995) suggest that self-esteem is a **sociometer**, or a so-called internal monitor of social acceptance and belonging. According to this view, self-esteem is a thermometer which indicates the extent to which one is successful and accepted by important others. High self-esteem is then an indication that one is successful in this regard.

Not only do we evaluate ourselves on the basis of our personal successes and failures, but we also evaluate the social groups we belong to. Recently, a distinction has been made between personal and **collective self-esteem**, where the latter is a measure of the value one places on one's social groups (Luhtanen and Crocker, 1992). Similar to personal self-esteem, individuals are motivated to positively bias the evaluation of their own groups, thereby enhancing collective self-esteem (Tajfel and Turner, 1979). The self-serving bias for example has also been shown to occur at the group level. Here, people tend to attribute out-group failures and in-group successes to internal properties of the group, whereas in-group failures and out-group successes are attributed to external factors such as luck or chance. This self-serving bias at the group level is called the *ultimate attribution error* (Pettigrew, 1979). As you can see, this is likely to lead to a more positive view of one's own group compared with other groups and helps protect the in-group from negative implications of wrong or immoral actions (Hewstone, 1990).

ATTITUDES AND ATTITUDE CHANGE

Beyond attributions, impressions and our self-concept, much of our social thinking involves the attitudes that we hold towards external stimuli. Indeed, from views on political elections and war to the latest fashion craze, attitudes help steer the course of world events. An **attitude** is a positive or negative evaluative reaction towards a stimulus, such as a person, action, object or concept (Tesser and Shaffer, 1990). Whether agreeing or disagreeing with a political policy or a friend's opinion of a film, you are displaying an evaluative reaction (Fig. 14.6). Our attitudes help define our identity, guide our actions, and influence how we judge people (Fazio and Roskos-Ewoldsen, 2005). In the following paragraphs we take a look at the link between attitudes and behaviour, and whether and how attitudes can be changed.

Do Our Attitudes Influence Our Behaviour?

If we tell you that, according to research, people's attitudes strongly guide their behaviour, you might reply, 'So what? That's just common sense'. But consider a classic study by Richard LaPiere (1934). In the 1930s, he toured the USA with a young Chinese couple, stopping at 251 restaurants, hotels and other establishments. At the time, prejudice against Asians was widespread, yet the couple – who often entered the establishment before LaPiere did – were refused service only once. Later LaPiere wrote to all of these establishments, asking if they would provide service to Chinese patrons. More than 90 per cent of those who responded stated that they would not.

---

sociometer
internal monitor of social acceptance and belonging

collective self-esteem
a measure of the value one places on one's social groups

attitude
a positive or negative evaluative reaction towards a stimulus, such as a person, action, object or concept

FIGURE 14.6

Attitudes represent an important form of social thinking. They help define who we are, and they affect the way people judge one another. Do the attitudes expressed by these protestors influence your impression of them?

Focus 14.4
What is an attitude? Describe three conditions under which people's attitudes best predict their behaviour.

We cannot be sure that the people who expressed negative attitudes in the survey were the same ones who, months earlier, had served the Chinese couple. Yet the discrepancy between prejudicial attitudes and non-discriminatory behaviour seemed overwhelming and called the 'common-sense' assumption of attitude–behaviour consistency into question. Decades of better controlled research, however, indicate that attitudes do predict behaviour (Fazio and Roskos-Ewoldsen, 2005). Three factors help explain why the attitude–behaviour relationship is strong in some cases but weak in others.

First, *attitudes influence behaviour more strongly when situational factors that contradict our attitudes are weak*. For example, conformity pressures may lead us to behave in ways that are at odds with our inner convictions. According to the **theory of planned behaviour** and similar models (Ajzen, 1991), our intention to engage in a behaviour is strongest when we have a positive attitude towards that behaviour, when subjective norms (our perceptions of what other people think we should do) support our attitudes, and when we believe that the behaviour is under our control. Researchers have used this theory to predict successfully whether people will become smokers, exercise regularly, drive safely, donate blood and perform many other behaviours (Victoir et al., 2005).

Second, *attitudes have a greater influence on behaviour when we are aware of them and when they are strongly held*. Sometimes we seem to act without thinking, out of impulse or habit. Attitude–behaviour consistency increases when people consciously think about or are reminded of their attitudes before acting (White et al., 2002).

Third, *general attitudes best predict general classes of behaviour, and specific attitudes best predict specific behaviours*. For example, Martin Fishbein and Icek Ajzen (1974) found almost no relation between people's general attitudes towards religion and 70 specific religious behaviours (such as the frequency of attending services). But when they combined the 70 specific behaviours into a single global index of religious behaviour, the relation between general religious attitudes and overall religious behaviour was substantial.

Does Our Behaviour Influence Our Attitudes?

Under the proper conditions, our attitudes guide our behaviour. But attitude–behaviour consistency is not a one-way street: we also come to develop attitudes that are consistent with how we behave (Cooper et al., 2005). After casting a ballot during elections for example, voters are more convinced that their candidate will win the election then before (Regan and Kilduff, 1988). Similarly, in the Stanford prison study, as the guards slipped into their roles and began mistreating the prisoners, they began to view the prisoners as little more than animals. Why should this be?

Cognitive dissonance Imagine that you volunteer for an experiment, arrive at the laboratory, and repeatedly perform two extremely boring tasks: emptying and filling a tray with spools and turning 48 pegs stuck into holes. After you endure 60 minutes of sheer boredom, the experimenter enters, thanks you for participating and asks for your help: it is important for the next student to begin the study with a positive attitude about the tasks, and all you have to do is tell the student that the boring tasks are interesting. Depending on the condition to which you have been randomly assigned, the experimenter offers to pay you either €1 or €20 for, essentially, lying to the next participant. You agree to do so. Afterwards, you go to the psychology department's main office to collect your money and fill out a 'routine form' that asks how much you enjoyed the tasks in the experiment.

Make a prediction: comparing participants who lied for €1 and who lied for €20 with a control group that simply rated the boring tasks without telling any lie beforehand, which of the three groups rated the task most positively? Why?

Common sense might suggest that participants paid €20 would feel happiest about the experiment and rate the tasks most highly. However, as Leon Festinger and J. Merrill Carlsmith

theory of planned behaviour

our intention to engage in a behaviour is strongest when we have a positive attitude towards that behaviour, when subjective norms (our perceptions of what other people think we should do) support our attitudes, and when we believe that the behaviour is under our control

Focus 14.5

Explain the causes of cognitive dissonance and how it produces attitude change

(1959) predicted in a classic experiment, American participants who were paid $1 gave the most positive ratings. Indeed, they actually rated the boring tasks as 'somewhat enjoyable' (Fig. 14.7)!

According to Festinger's (1957) **theory of cognitive dissonance**, people strive for consistency in their cognitions. When two or more cognitions contradict one another (such as 'I am a truthful person' and 'I just told another student that those boring tasks were interesting'), the person experiences an uncomfortable state of tension, which Festinger calls *cognitive dissonance*, and becomes motivated to reduce this dissonance. The theory predicts that to reduce dissonance and restore a state of cognitive consistency, people will change one of their cognitions or add new cognitions. Participants who received $20 could justify their behaviour by adding a new cognition – 'Who wouldn't tell a little lie for $20?' – and there was little reason for them to change their attitude towards the boring tasks. Those who had lied for only $1 could not use this trivial monetary gain to justify their behaviour. But if they could convince themselves that the tasks actually were enjoyable, then they wouldn't have been lying after all. Thus they changed their attitude about the task to bring it more in line with how they had behaved.

Behaviour that is inconsistent with one's attitude is called *counter-attitudinal behaviour*, and it produces dissonance only if we perceive that our actions were freely chosen rather than coerced. Freely chosen behaviours that produce foreseeable negative consequences or that threaten our sense of self-worth are especially likely to arouse dissonance. Once the behaviour occurs, people start to consider the meaning of what they have done, and this produces dissonance (Cooper et al., 2005). Recall the statement by one of the guards in the Stanford prison study regarding his treatment of the prisoners: 'I was surprised at myself.' If the guard thought of himself as a good, moral person, then his callous behaviour towards the prisoners should have created dissonance. Changing his attitude towards the prisoners – essentially coming to see them as 'cattle' who did not have the same rights as humans – would have reduced dissonance.

Dissonance, however, does not always lead to attitude change. People can reduce dissonance by finding external justifications or by making other excuses (Cooper et al., 2005). In Scandinavian surveys, among people who drank alcohol despite having negative attitudes towards drinking, one rationalization seemed to be 'I may not be perfect, but other people are still worse' (Mäkelä, 1997). Despite the many ways to reduce dissonance, the theory helps explain many interesting aspects of human behaviour (Fig. 14.8).

Not only are people personally motivated to be consistent, inconsistency is also commonly seen as an undesirable personality trait (Allgeier et al., 1979). You can imagine what would happen if people's thoughts did not fit their words or behaviour; it would be very difficult to trust others around us. Indeed, such moral information about other people has a greater impact on our evaluation of others than does information of how competent someone is (Wojciszke et al., 1998). Being accused of being dishonest is much more damaging than being accused of being incompetent.

Self-perception If we see someone campaigning for a political candidate, we will likely assume that this person has a positive attitude towards the candidate. If we see someone exerting great effort to achieve a goal, we will logically judge that the goal is important to that person.

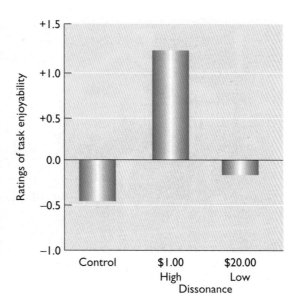

FIGURE 14.7

Cognitive dissonance and external justification.

American participants lied to a fellow student by saying that a boring task was interesting. Those offered $1 to lie later rated the task most positively. Presumably, they reduced their cognitive dissonance about lying by convincing themselves that the task was interesting after all. Participants offered $20 had an external justification to lie, experienced little dissonance and therefore did not need to convince themselves that the task was enjoyable. They and control participants who had not lied rated the boring task less favourably than the $1 group.

SOURCE: based on Festinger and Carlsmith, 1959.

theory of cognitive dissonance

people strive for consistency in their cognitions

FIGURE 14.8

Effort Justification: Every year, tennis fans queue for hours in the hope of gaining tickets for the Wimbledon finals. No doubt a major reason for their positive attitude is that they are committed fans. But might cognitive dissonance have played a role? Experiments show that when people invest a lot of time and energy into achieving a goal, finding out that the goal was not all it was supposed to be creates cognitive dissonance. To justify their effort and thus reduce dissonance, people may convince themselves that the goal (e.g., the tennis match) is more attractive or worthwhile than it really is.

self-perception theory
we make inferences about our own attitudes by observing how we behave

Focus 14.6
Evaluate dissonance versus self-perception theory views of why counter-attitudinal behaviour produces attitude change.

In short, we infer what other people's attitudes must be by watching how they behave. According to Daryl Bem's (1972) **self-perception theory**, we make inferences about our own attitudes in much the same way: by observing how we behave. Knowing that for very little external justification (€1) you have told a fellow student that the boring experimental tasks are enjoyable, you logically conclude that deep down you must feel that the tasks were at least somewhat enjoyable. In Bem's view, your attitude is not produced by a mysterious concept called *cognitive dissonance*; rather you simply observe how you have acted and infer how you must have felt to have behaved in this fashion.

Self-perception theory and cognitive dissonance theory both predict that counter-attitudinal behaviour produces attitude change. How, then, can we determine which theory more accurately explains the reason behind such attitude change? One key difference is that only dissonance theory assumes that we experience heightened physiological arousal (tension produced by dissonance) when we engage in counter-attitudinal behaviour. Do we? At least in some instances it appears so. In one study, college students consumed an unpleasant-tasting drink and were then asked to write a sentence stating that they liked the taste. Students who were given a high degree of choice whether to write this counter-attitudinal statement showed higher arousal (measured by sweat gland activity) and greater attitude change than participants who were simply told to write the statement (Harmon-Jones et al., 1996).

These and other findings indicate that dissonance theory best explains why people change their views after behaving in ways that openly contradict their clearly defined attitudes, especially when such behaviours threaten their self-image (Stone and Cooper, 2003). Lying to someone for a minimal sum of money threatens our self-image of honesty, and acting inhumanely towards prisoners threatens our self-image of being a good, decent person – unless we can somehow justify those actions to ourselves. However, when counter-attitudinal behaviour does not threaten self-worth and we have weak attitudes to begin with, such behaviour is less likely to create significant arousal – yet people may still alter their attitudes to be more consistent with how they have behaved. In this case, self-perception theory may provide the better explanation. Thus both dissonance theory and self-perception theory appear to be correct, but under different circumstances (Tesser and Shaffer, 1990). Both theories, however, agree that *our behaviours can influence our attitudes*.

Persuasion

Persuasion is a fact of everyday life, and it represents the intersection of social thinking and our next topic: social influence. Persuaders try to influence our beliefs and attitudes so that we will vote for them, buy their products, do them favours or otherwise behave as they want us to. Here we examine three aspects of the persuasion process.

The communicator   Communicator credibility – how believable we perceive the communicator to be – is often a key to effective persuasion. In fact, audience members who do not enjoy thinking deeply about issues may pay little attention to the content of a message and simply go along with the opinions of a highly credible source. Credibility has two major components: *expertise* and *trustworthiness* (Hovland et al., 1953). The most effective persuader is one who appears to be an expert and to be presenting the truth in an unbiased manner. We are especially likely to perceive communicators as trustworthy when they advocate a point of view that is contrary to their own self-interest (Petty et al., 2001). Communicators who are physically attractive, likeable, and similar to us (such as in interests or goals) may also gain a persuasive edge, which is why advertisers spend millions of euros hiring attractive, likeable stars to promote their products.

The message   In trying to persuade someone, is it more effective to present only your side of the issue or to also present the opposition's arguments and then refute them? Overall, research indicates that the *two-sided refutational approach* is most effective (Allen, 1991). Especially if an audience initially disagrees with the communicator's viewpoint or is aware that there are two sides to the issue, a two-sided message will be perceived as less biased.

Many messages, such as those in Figure 14.9, attempt to persuade by arousing fear. Does it work? Or do people reduce their fear simply by denying the credibility of the message or the communicator? Overall, fear arousal seems to work best when the message evokes moderate to strong fear and provides people with effective, feasible (i.e., low-cost) ways to reduce the threat (Dillard and Anderson, 2004). High-fear messages accompanied by inadequate information about 'what to do' typically lead to denial.

It might seem logical that we are more easily persuaded by arguments that carry with them a reason for changing our behaviour or attitude. We might be persuaded to stop smoking *because* it causes cancer. It seems however that the word *because* is essential here. This was demonstrated in an experiment in which an experimenter tried to skip ahead of a line of people waiting to make use of a library copy machine. When the experimenter asked: 'Excuse me, I have five pages. May I use the copy machine?', only 60 per cent of those asked, complied to the request. When the experimenter gave a reason for skipping ahead, asking: 'Excuse me, I have five pages. May I use the copy machine because I'm in a rush?', 94 per cent complied with the request. However, when the request was followed by the word *because* and then by an 'empty' reason, something rather obvious: 'Excuse me I have five pages. May I use the copy machine, because I have to make some copies?', a similar percentage (93 per cent) complied to the request (Langer et al., 1978). The word *because* then implies a logical argument to which we automatically react.

---

communicator credibility
how believable we perceive the communicator to be

Focus 14.7
Describe how communicator, message and audience characteristics affect the persuasion process.

FIGURE 14.9

Fear appeals are a common approach to persuasion. They are most effective when people believe that a feared event could occur ('Driving after drinking can increase my risk of an accident'), that the consequences would be aversive ('I could lose my licence or be killed'), that there is an effective way to reduce the risk ('If I drink, I won't drive') and that they can carry out this behaviour without great cost ('Have a designated driver; call a friend').

central route to persuasion

when people think carefully about the message and are influenced because they find the arguments compelling

peripheral route to persuasion

when people do not scrutinize the message but are influenced mostly by other factors such as a speaker's attractiveness or a message's length or emotional appeal

The audience A message loaded with logical arguments and facts may prove highly persuasive to some people yet fall flat on its face with others. One reason is that people differ in their *need for cognition*. Some enjoy analysing issues; others prefer not to spend much mental effort.

According to Richard Petty and John Cacioppo, there are two basic routes to persuasion (Petty and Cacioppo 1986; Petty et al., 2005). The **central route to persuasion** occurs when people think carefully about the message and are influenced because they find the arguments compelling. The **peripheral route to persuasion** occurs when people do not scrutinize the message but are influenced mostly by other factors such as a speaker's attractiveness or a message's length or emotional appeal. Central route persuasion is most likely when individuals are motivated and able to elaborate on the arguments in a message. Attitude change that results from the central route tends to last longer and to predict future behaviour more successfully.

People who have a high need for cognition tend to follow the central route to persuasion. In forming attitudes about consumer services and products, for example, they pay attention to information about the service and product (Wood and Swait, 2002). In contrast, people with a low need for cognition are more strongly influenced by peripheral cues, such as the attractiveness of the person who endorses the product.

IN REVIEW

- Consistency, distinctiveness, and consensus information jointly influence whether we make a personal or situational attribution for a particular act.

- The fundamental attribution error is the tendency to attribute other people's behaviour to personal factors while underestimating the role of situational factors. The self-serving bias is the tendency to attribute one's successes to personal factors and one's failures to situational factors.

- Impressions may change over time, but our first impression generally carries extra weight. Stereotypes and schemas create mental sets that shape our impressions.

- Through self-fulfilling prophecies, our initially false expectations shape the way we act towards someone. In turn, this person responds to our behaviour in a way that confirms our initially false belief.

- Self-knowledge is obtained through observing our own behaviour, through the process of social comparison and through examining what others think of us.

- An individual's identity is partly based on idiosyncratic characteristics, personality traits and interpersonal relationships (personal identity) as well as on the knowledge of belonging to particular groups (social identity).

- Attitudes predict behaviour best when situational influences are weak, when the attitude is strong and when we consciously think about our attitude.

- Behaviour also influences attitudes. Counter-attitudinal behaviour is most likely to create cognitive dissonance when the behaviour is freely chosen and threatens our self-worth or produces foreseeable negative consequences.

- To reduce dissonance, we may change our attitude to become more consistent with how we have acted. When our attitudes are weak and counter-attitudinal behaviour does not threaten our self-worth, we may change our attitudes through self-perception.

- Communicator, message and audience characteristics influence the effectiveness of persuasion. Communicator credibility is highest when the communicator is perceived as expert and trustworthy. Fear-arousing communications may be effective if they arouse moderate to strong fear and suggest how to avoid the feared result. The central route to persuasion works best with listeners who have a high need for cognition; for those with a low cognition need, the peripheral route works better.

SOCIAL INFLUENCE AND BEHAVIOUR IN GROUPS

In the previous section we talked about persuasion and how persuaders might influence our beliefs and attitudes. However, the way in which others influence us takes many forms, not necessarily leading to a change in attitudes. In some instances our behaviour is influenced merely by the presence of others. Imagine Patricia, a novice piano player, who makes more mistakes after her parents enter the room to listen to her practice. At other times people influence our behaviour because we simply do what people ask us to do. This latter form of influence is called *compliance*, which leads to a change in behaviour but not necessarily a change in beliefs or attitudes. Finally, people influence us in a more indirect manner through our tendency to conform to group norms.

THE MERE PRESENCE OF OTHERS

Norman Triplett (1898) helped launch the field of social psychology by testing a deceptively simple hypothesis: the presence of others energizes performance. Triplett analysed the records from numerous bicycle races. In some races, cyclists performed individually against the clock; in other races of similar distance, they performed together in a pack. As Triplett predicted, cyclists' average speed was much faster in group races than in individual races, but from experience he knew that other factors (e.g., racers riding behind one another to cut wind resistance) could also explain this finding. So in a laboratory experiment, Triplett had children perform a simple physical task, either alone or in the presence of another child (called a *co-actor*) who independently performed the same task. Indeed, the children's performance improved when in each other's presence.

Many early studies revealed that the *mere presence* of co-actors or of a silent audience enhanced performance. Even ants carried more dirt with other ants present (Chen, 1937). Yet some research found that the mere presence of others impaired performance on certain tasks.

In 1965 Robert Zajonc proposed a theory to explain this seeming paradox. First, the mere physical presence of another person (or member of the same species) increases our arousal. Second, as arousal increases, we become more likely to perform whatever behaviours happen to be our *dominant responses* (i.e., most typical responses) to that specific situation. When a task is complex and we are first trying to learn it, our dominant responses are likely to be incorrect ones, so we make errors. Therefore, performing in front of other people will impair performance. But when a task is either simple or complex but well learned, our dominant responses usually are correct ones. In these situations, performing in the presence of others will enhance performance (Fig. 14.10).

This phenomenon is called **social facilitation**, an increased tendency to perform one's dominant responses in the mere presence of others. It may be the most basic form of social influence, occurring in species ranging from fruit flies to hens and humans (Thomas et al., 2002), and it has an important practical implication: when learning complex tasks, minimize the presence of other people.

COMPLIANCE

Most of the time, people around us are not strangers 'merely' hanging around. They are important individuals whose opinions of how we should think feel or behave have a strong influence on us, especially when these others are actively trying to influence us.

Compliance Techniques

From telemarketers and salespeople to television and Internet advertisements, would-be persuaders often come armed with special *compliance techniques*, strategies that may manipulate you into saying yes when you really want to say no. By learning to identify these techniques, you will be in a better position to resist them.

Focus 14.8
When does the mere presence of others enhance performance or impair performance? Why?

social facilitation
an increased tendency to perform one's dominant responses in the mere presence of others

Focus 14.9
Identify four common compliance techniques and explain how they work.

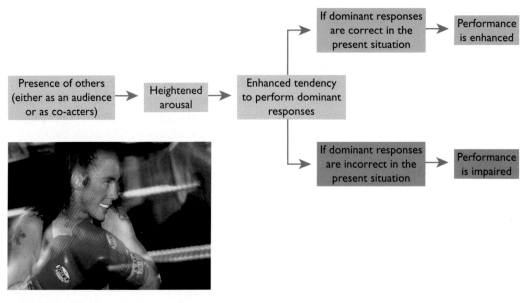

FIGURE 14.10

Social facilitation of dominant responses.

Whether this pool player's performance improves or worsens when other people are watching depends on whether she is highly skilled or a novice (Michaels et al., 1982). Zajonc's (1965) theory of social facilitation proposes that the presence of other people increases our arousal, which then makes us more likely to perform our dominant responses. If a dominant response (e.g., stroking the pool cue in a particular way) happens to be correct – as typically occurs on simple tasks or complex tasks that have been mastered – then performance will be enhanced. But if a dominant response is incorrect – as often occurs when a novice is trying to learn a complex task – then the presence of other people most likely will impair performance.

norm of reciprocity

the expectation that when others treat us well, we should respond in kind

door-in-the-face technique

a persuader makes a large request, expecting you to reject it and then presents a smaller request

FIGURE 14.11

In the 1970s, members of the Hare Krishna Society approached passers-by and gave them a small flower. If a passer-by refused, the member said, 'Please. It is a gift for you'. Reluctantly, people often accepted. Then the member asked for a donation. People felt pressure to reciprocate, donated money and often threw the flower away.

The powerful **norm of reciprocity** involves the expectation that when others treat us well, we should respond in kind. Thus to get you to comply with a request, I can do something nice for you now – such as an unsolicited favour – in the hope that you will feel pressure to reciprocate later when I present you with my request (Cialdini and Sagarin, 2005). As Figure 14.11 illustrates, the Hare Krishna Society (a religious group) cleverly used flower power to manipulate the norm of reciprocity and raise millions of dollars in donations.

Now consider the **door-in-the-face technique**: a persuader makes a large request, expecting you to reject it (you 'slam the door' in the persuader's face), and then presents a smaller request. Telemarketers feast on this technique. Rather than ask you directly for a modest monetary contribution to some organization or cause, they first ask for a much larger contribution, knowing that you will say no. After you politely refuse, they ask for the smaller contribution. In one experiment, after people declined an initial request to donate $25 to a charity, they were more likely to donate $2 than were participants who were directly asked for $2 (Wang et al., 1989). To be effective, the same persuader must make both requests. The persuader 'compromises' by making the second, smaller request, so we feel pressure to reciprocate by complying. Refusing the first request also may produce guilt, and complying with the smaller request may help us reduce guilt or feel socially responsible (Tusing and Dillard, 2000).

Using the **foot-in-the-door technique**, a persuader gets you to comply with a small request first (getting the 'foot in the door') and later presents a larger request. Imagine receiving an email from a stranger who asks for simple advice about a word processing programme. It takes less than a minute to reply, and you do – as did all the participants in an actual experiment (Guéguen, 2002). After you comply, the person sends a second email asking you to help with a class project by filling out a 20-minute online questionnaire. In the experiment, 76 per cent of college students complied, compared with only 44 per cent in a control group that received only the class-project request. Although hypotheses abound, researchers are not sure why the foot-in-the-door technique is effective.

With a final technique, **lowballing**, a persuader gets you to commit to some action and then – before you actually perform the behaviour – he or she increases the 'cost' of that same behaviour. Imagine negotiating to buy a used car for €8000, a 'great price'. The salesperson says, 'I need to confirm this with my manager', comes back shortly, and states, 'I'm afraid my manager says the price is too low. But you can have the car for only €400 more. It's still a great price'. At this point, you are more likely to go through with the deal than you would have been, had the 'real' €8400 price been set at the outset.

Both lowballing and the foot-in-the-door technique involve moving from a smaller request to a larger, more costly request. But with lowballing, the stakes for the *same behaviour* are raised after you commit to it but *before* you consummate the behaviour. Having made a commitment, you may find it easier to rationalize the added costs or may feel obligated to the person to whom you made the commitment (Cialdini and Sagarin, 2005).

By recognizing when compliance techniques are being used to manipulate your behaviour, you are in a better position to resist them. Consider the norm of reciprocity. Robert Cialdini (2001), an expert on influence techniques, suggests that the key is not to resist the initial gift or favour; instead, accept the unsolicited 'favour', but if the person then asks you for a favour in return, recognize this as a manipulative trick. Similarly, if a telemarketer makes a large initial request and then, after you decline, immediately asks for a smaller commitment, respond by thinking or saying, 'I see. It's the door-in-the-face technique'. Of course, you can still choose to comply if you believe it is the right thing to do. The goal is not to automatically reject every social influence attempt but to avoid feeling coerced into doing something you do not want to do.

Influence of Authority: Obedience

Some people do not need all these compliance techniques to get us to obey their every command: legitimate authority figures. One example, cited by Cohen and Davis in their book *Medication Errors: Causes and Prevention* (1981), illustrates a remarkable case of blind obedience to an authority figure. A physician ordered eardrops for a patient with a painful infected right ear. Instead of writing 'place in right ear' the physician wrote on the prescription 'place in R ear'. Upon receiving the medicine, the nurse in attendance mistakenly read Rear, and subsequently applied the eardrops rectally. However absurd it might seem to apply eardrops rectally, neither the nurse *nor* the patient felt anything like suspicious. It was what the doctor had ordered.

Although rectally applying eardrops might be classified as bad, obedience to an authority figure is inherently neither good nor bad. As an aeroplane passenger, you would not be amused if the co-pilot disregarded the pilot's commands simply because he or she did not feel like obeying, putting the flight and your life at risk. Without obedience, society would face chaos.

foot-in-the-door technique
a persuader gets you to comply with a small request first and later presents a larger request

lowballing
a persuader gets you to commit to some action and then – before you actually perform the behaviour – he or she increases the 'cost' of that same behaviour

But obedience can also produce tragic results. After the Second World War, the famous Nuremberg trials were held to judge Nazi war criminals who had slaughtered millions of innocent people in concentration camps. In many instances, the defendants argued that they had only followed orders. No doubt we will continue to hear the cry 'I was just following orders' as accountability is judged for more recent mass atrocities around the globe.

Just as the Nuremberg court did, many of us reject justifications based on obedience to authority as mere rationalizations, secure in our conviction that *we* would behave more humanely in such situations. But would we? Our 'Research close-up' – part of the most famous series of studies ever conducted in social psychology – suggests some provocative answers.

Focus 14.10

Describe Milgram's research, factors that increase and decrease obedience, and implications for society.

RESEARCH CLOSE-UP

THE DILEMMA OF OBEDIENCE: WHEN CONSCIENCE CONFRONTS MALEVOLENT AUTHORITY

SOURCE: S. Milgram (1974) *Obedience to Authority*. New York: Harper and Row.

INTRODUCTION

Fuelled by a scientific interest in social influence and a desire to understand the horrors of the Holocaust, psychologist Stanley Milgram (1974) asked a disturbing question: Would ordinary citizens obey the orders of an authority figure if those orders meant physically harming an innocent person? He conducted 18 studies between 1960 and 1963 to answer this question and to identify factors that increased or decreased obedience to authority. Let us examine one study.

METHOD

Forty men, ranging in age from 20 to 50 and representing a cross-section of occupations and educational backgrounds in the USA, participated in the study. At the laboratory, each participant met a middle-aged man who was introduced as another participant but who was actually a confederate. Participants were told that the experiment examined the effects of punishment on memory. Then through a supposedly random draw (it was rigged), the real participant became the 'teacher' and the confederate became the 'learner'. The teacher presented a series of memory problems to the learner through a two-way intercom system. Each time the learner made an error, the teacher was instructed to administer an electric shock using a machine that had 30 switches, beginning with 15 volts and increasing step-by-step to 450 volts (Fig. 14.12a). As the teacher watched, the experimenter strapped the learner into a chair in an adjoining room and hooked him up to wires from the shock generator (Fig. 14.12b). The learner expressed concern about the shocks and mentioned that he had a slight heart problem.

Returning to the main room, the experimenter gave the teacher a sample shock (45 volts) and then ordered the experiment to begin. Unbeknown to the teacher, the learner intentionally committed many errors, and he did *not* actually receive any shock. The learner made verbal protests that were standardized on a tape recorder, so that they were the same for all participants.

As the learner's errors mounted, the teacher increased the shock. If the teacher baulked at continuing, the experimenter issued one or more escalating commands, such as 'Please continue', 'You must continue' and 'You have no other choice'. At 75 volts, the learner moaned when the teacher threw the switch. At 150 volts, he moaned again and said, 'Experimenter! That's all. Get me out of here. I told you I had heart trouble. My heart's starting to bother me now. Get me out of here, please.... I refuse to go on. Let me out'. Beyond 200 volts, he emitted agonized screams every time a shock was delivered, yelling 'Let me out! Let me out!' At 300 volts, the learner refused to answer and continued screaming to be let out. At 345 volts and beyond, there was only silence. Full obedience was operationally defined as continuing to the maximum shock level of 450 volts.

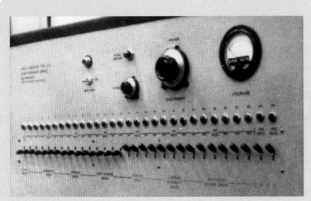

(a)

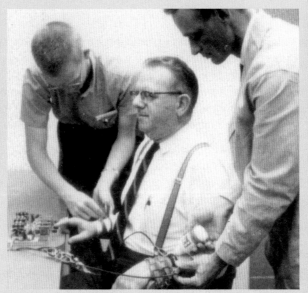

FIGURE 14.12

(a) Switches on the shock generator ranged from 15 volts ('slight shock') to 450 volts ('XXX'). (b) The participant (teacher) saw the learner being strapped into the chair.

(b)

RESULTS

Participants wrestled with a dilemma. Should they continue to hurt this innocent person, as the experimenter commanded, or should they stop the learner's pain by openly disobeying? Most participants became distressed. Some trembled, sweated, laughed nervously or, in a few cases, experienced convulsions. But would they obey? Make a prediction: what percentage of people do you think obeyed to 450 volts?

Before the study, Milgram had asked psychiatrists, professors, university students and middle-class adults to predict the outcome. They said that virtually no one (1 per cent) would obey fully. Indeed, most participants baulked or protested at one time or another and said they would not continue. But ultimately, 26 of the 40 men (65 per cent) obeyed all the way to the end (Fig. 14.13).

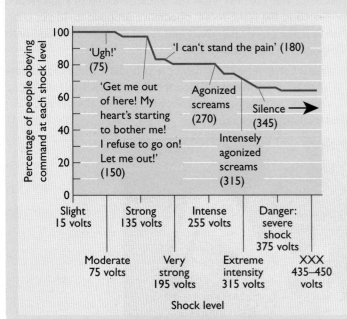

FIGURE 14.13

You must obey.

This graph shows the percentage of male participants who continued to shock the learner through various voltage levels.

SOURCE: based on Milgram, 1974.

DISCUSSION

Milgram's research has generated controversy for decades (Blass, 2002; Miller, 2004). Its ethics were harshly criticized because participants were deceived, were exposed to substantial stress and risked long-lasting negative effects to their self-image (Baumrind, 1964). Milgram countered that the research was so socially significant as to warrant the deception, that participants were carefully debriefed afterwards and that psychiatric follow-ups of a sample of obedient participants suggested no long-term ill effects. Weighing the costs and benefits, do you believe that this research was justified?

Researchers also debate why obedience was high, but many agree with Milgram's view that participants psychologically transferred much of the 'responsibility' for the learner's fate to the experimenter. Participants viewed the experimenter as an expert, a legitimate authority figure (Blass and Schmitt, 2001). While administering the shock, some participants stated that they 'were not responsible' for what happened. Others asked, 'Who is responsible if something happens to the learner?' When the experimenter replied, I am responsible', participants felt greater freedom to continue. Yet they were the ones flipping the switch.

How would you have responded in Milgram's experiment? Almost all of our students say that they would have disobeyed either before or when the victim began protesting at the 150-volt level. Indeed, in one study, students in psychology classes – whether familiar with Milgram's results or not – said that they would stop at around 150 volts (Geher et al., 2002). So suppose we conduct an obedience study today but with real electric shocks and with you as the learner. The teacher will be a randomly selected student from your class. Are you confident that this student will disobey the experimenter and stop giving you shocks when you start yelling in protest? Few of our students or other students express such confidence (Geher et al., 2002). In short, virtually all of us are confident that *we* would disobey early on, but we are less sure about *other* people – and they in turn are not so sure about *us*.

Factors that Influence Obedience

By manipulating the following aspects of the laboratory situation, Milgram and other research-ers obtained obedience rates ranging from 0 to over 90 per cent:

1. *Remoteness of the victim*: obedience was greatest when the learner was out of sight. When the teacher and learner were placed in the same room, obedience dropped to 40 per cent. Further, when the teacher had to make physical contact and force the learner's hand onto a 'shock plate', obedience dropped to 30 per cent (Fig. 14.14).

2. *Closeness and legitimacy of the authority figure*: obedience was highest when the author-ity figure was close by and perceived as legitimate. When the experimenter left the scene and gave orders by phone or when an 'ordinary person' (a confederate) took over and gave the orders, obedience dropped to about 20 per cent.

FIGURE 14.14

In one of Milgram's studies (touch proximity), the teacher was ordered to physically force the learner's hand onto a 'shock plate' after the learner refused to continue. Here, 30 per cent of participants obeyed fully to 450 volts. Although touch proximity strongly reduced obedience, that a significant minority still obeyed raises considerable concern.

3. *Diffusion of responsibility*: when another 'participant' (actually a confederate) flipped the shock switch and the real participants only had to perform another aspect of the task, 93 per cent obeyed. In short, *obedience increases when someone else does the dirty work*. In contrast, when Harvey Tilker (1970) made participants feel fully responsible for the learner's welfare, not a single person obeyed to the end.

4. *Personal characteristics*: Milgram compared the political orientations, religious affiliations, occupations, education, length of military service and psychological characteristics of obedient versus disobedient participants. Differences were weak or non-existent.

Would People Obey Today?

Our students often ask us, 'If Milgram's obedience study were conducted today, would the results be similar?' and for years we have been answering, 'We suspect so'. Here is why. For 25 years after Milgram's research, experiments were conducted in different countries, in 'real-world' settings and laboratories, using a similar 'electric shock' procedure and different obedience procedures, and with children, adolescents and adults as participants. Overall, the findings revealed levels of obedience that were depressingly consistent with Milgram's results (Meeus and Raaijmakers, 1986). We also can add one more piece of information, with the caution that it is from a study that has not yet been published in a scientific journal. Still, it is noteworthy because, for ethical reasons, obedience studies like Milgram's had not been conducted for many years – until this study.

In 2007, the ABC News television programme *Primetime* featured a modified obedience study by social psychologist Jerry Burger (ABC News, 2007). Burger's procedures were reviewed by the American Psychological Association and paralleled Milgram's original approach, but only up to the 150-volt shock level: the point at which the learner protested vigorously, complained of a heart condition and demanded to be released. To avoid exposing participants to too much stress, this was the highest shock level used in Burger's study. The 150-volt level also was a logical point to stop because Milgram had found that participants who continued past this level were very likely to obey all the way to the maximum 450-volt level. Thus, in Burger's study, full obedience meant that after hearing the learner's protests at 150 volts (and if necessary, being ordered to continue by the experimenter), the participant continued with the task of reading the words to the learner, after which the procedure was stopped. Burger found that 65 per cent of the 18 men tested obeyed fully, a high obedience rate consistent with the findings of Milgram's research.

Women also participated in the study. To learn about their results, see the following 'What do you think?' feature.

WHAT DO YOU THINK?

DO WOMEN DIFFER FROM MEN IN OBEDIENCE?

Suppose that the participants in Milgram's featured study had been women. Keeping everything else constant (i.e., the same male experimenter and male learner), would you expect women to be more or less obedient than the men or equally obedient? Why? Think about it, then see p. 657.

Lessons Learned

What lessons shall we draw from this research? Certainly, it is *not* that people are apathetic or evil. Participants became stressed precisely because they did care about the learner's welfare. Neither can we conclude that we are sheep. If we were, obedience would be high across all situations, which is not the case. Rather, Milgram sums up a key lesson as follows:

> It would be a mistake ... to make the simpleminded statement that kindly and good persons disobey while those who are cruel do not ... often, it is not so much the kind of person a man is as the kind of situation in which he finds himself that determines how he will act. (Milgram, 1974, p. 205)

Thus by arranging the situation appropriately, most people – ordinary, decent citizens – can be induced to follow orders from an authority figure they perceive as legitimate, even when doing so contributes to harming an innocent person. The applicability of this principle to the Holocaust and other atrocities seems clear (Blass, 2002). During the Holocaust, obedience was made easier because most of the personnel working at the concentration camps were cogs in a horrendous wheel: They did not pull the switch to flood the chambers with gas but instead performed other tasks. Their victims also were 'remote' at the moment of their murder. Further, to lessen concentration camp workers' feelings of responsibility, Hitler's subordinate, Heinrich Himmler, told them in manipulative speeches that only he and Hitler were personally responsible for what took place (Dawidowicz, 1975).

FIGURE 14.15

Do you remember how this photograph shocked the world? In 2005, US Army reservist Lynndie England faced a court martial for assaulting prisoners in the 2003 Abu Ghraib Iraqi prisoner scandal. Was this the real Lynndie England? Her family said it could not be the same loving person that they knew. Army reservist Charles Graner, the presumed ringleader of the guards involved in the scandal claimed in his own court martial that they were following orders. The military jury rejected the claim. In editorials and news reports, the media turned to the lessons of Milgram's research and the Stanford prison study to try to make sense of the guards' behaviour.

Does obedience research suggest that we are not responsible for following orders? This is a moral and legal question, not a scientific one. But if anything, this research should heighten our responsibility for being aware of the pitfalls of blind obedience and prevent us from being so smug or naive as to feel that such events 'could never happen here'. Beyond obedience, Milgram's research provides yet another powerful example of how social contexts can induce people to behave in ways that they never would have imagined possible (Fig. 14.15).

SOCIAL INFLUENCE IN GROUPS

We have seen how other people can directly persuade us to comply with a request and obey their orders. From early in human evolution, human beings have lived mostly in small, face-to-face groups, where social relationships were highly regulated and social influence occurred mainly in a direct manner, from one individual to another. Only quite recently have people become organized in groups so large that we do not intimately know most people we encounter. So how can we be sure that social influence strategies are still powerful enough to create and maintain shared values in an increasingly complex world? There is another very powerful way in which individuals can exert influence in a more indirect manner, and that is through the medium of social or group norms (Turner, 1991).

Years ago, a professor gave his class an unusual assignment: without doing anything illegal, each student was to violate some unspoken rule of social behaviour and observe how others reacted. One student licked her plate clean at a formal dinner, receiving cold stares from the other guests. Another boarded a nearly empty city bus, sat down next to the only other passenger, and said 'Hi!' The passenger sat up stiffly and stared out the window.

Social norms are shared expectations about how people should think, feel and behave, and they are the glue that binds groups together (Schaller and Crandall, 2004). Some norms are for-

social norms

shared expectations about how people should think, feel and behave

mal laws, but many – as illustrated by the preceding examples – are implicit and unspoken. Such norms regulate daily behaviour without our conscious awareness; we take them for granted until they are violated.

A **social role** consists of a set of norms that characterizes how people in a given social position ought to behave. The social roles of 'college student', 'professor', 'police officer' and 'spouse' carry different sets of behaviour expectations. Because we may wear many hats in our daily life, *role conflict* can occur when the norms accompanying different roles clash. College students who hold jobs and have children often experience role conflict as they try to juggle the competing demands of school, work, and parenthood.

<aside>
social role

a set of norms that characterizes how people in a given social position ought to behave
</aside>

Norm Formation

It is difficult to imagine any society, organization or social group functioning well without norms. In a classic experiment, Muzafer Sherif (1935) found that even randomly created groups develop norms. The task involved an optical illusion called the *autokinetic effect*: when people stare at a dot of light projected on a screen in a dark room, they begin to perceive the dot as moving, even though it really is stationary. When Sherif tested college students individually over several trials, each student perceived the light to move a different amount, from an inch or two (2 to 5 cm) to almost a foot (30 cm).

Later the students were randomly placed into groups of three and made further judgements. As group members heard one another's judgements over several sessions, their judgements converged and a group norm evolved. Interestingly, even when Sherif tested his participants the subsequent day while they were alone, they still conformed to this group norm when judging the movement of the light. Sherif's finding has been replicated in other countries and with different tasks. Whether at a cultural level or in small random groups, humans develop common standards for behaviour and judgement (Arrow and Burns, 2004). The participants in such experiments do not say 'Hey, let's develop a group norm'. It just happens. And, just as norms can vary across cultures, the evolved norm for the autokinetic effect varied from group to group (Fig. 14.16).

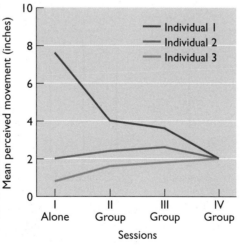

FIGURE 14.16

The evolution of norms across time and cultures.

(*Left*) In 2001, the Netherlands was the first country to allow same-sex marriages. Although still prohibited in most countries, same-sex marriage is increasingly being allowed (Belgium, Spain, Canada, South Africa and Massachusetts, USA), indicating a shift in social norms regarding same-sex marriages. (*Right*) Even randomly created groups spontaneously form norms. In Sherif's experiments, individuals' autokinetic judgements made alone (session I) began to converge when they were made in the presence of two other participants (sessions II, III and IV). Each mean is based on 100 judgements per session. These data are from one of the three-person groups. Notice that the final norm is not simply the average of the original judgements that the group members made while alone. SOURCE: based on Sherif, 1935.

Conformity

Norms can influence behaviour only if people conform to them. Without *conformity* – the adjustment of individual behaviours, attitudes and beliefs to a group standard – we would have social chaos. Although the experiments on the autokinetic effect show us how group norms develop, it does not tell us exactly why and through what process people conform to these norms. Social psychological research has focused mainly on two varieties of conformity. As

FIGURE 14.17

Often we conform to a majority because we believe that their opinion 'must be right'.

"Well, heck! If all you smart cookies agree, who am I to dissent?"

informational social influence

following the opinions or behaviour of other people because we believe that they have accurate knowledge and that what they are doing is right

normative social influence

conforming to obtain the rewards that come from being accepted by other people while at the same time avoiding their rejection

Focus 14.11

Use the concepts of informational and normative social influence to explain how social norms and roles guide behaviour.

Figure 14.17 illustrates, at times we conform due to **informational social influence**, following the opinions or behaviour of other people because we believe that they have accurate knowledge and that what they are doing is right. In the auto-kinetic studies this form of influence would have been present. As there was no 'correct' answer, it is not surprising that participants' own judgements were 'informed' by the judgements of others around them.

We may however also succumb to **normative social influence**, conforming to obtain the rewards that come from being accepted by other people while at the same time avoiding their rejection (Cialdini and Goldstein, 2004; Deutsch and Gerard, 1955). In a series of landmark conformity experiments, Solomon Asch (1951; 1956) tried to rule out informational influence by using stimuli that *could* be answered correctly. In the experimental condition, groups of college students performed several trials of a simple visual task (Fig. 14.18a) in which they were asked – for various sets of lines – which of three comparison lines was the same length as a standard line (line A). Only one member of the group, however, actually was a participant. The rest were accomplices of the experimenter. Group members sat around a table and were called on in order. The real participant sat next to last. According to plan, every accomplice intentionally gave the same wrong answer on some trials. Imagine yourself hearing the first group member choose line 1. (You think to yourself, 'Huh?') Then the next four members also choose line 1. (You're wondering, 'Can this really be?') Now it is your turn.

Would anybody conform to the group's incorrect judgements? Asch found that overall, participants conformed 37 per cent of the time, compared with a mere 1 per cent error rate in a

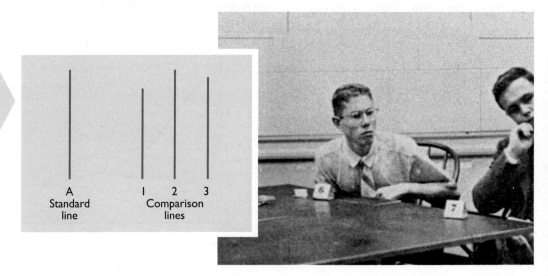

FIGURE 14.18

Asch's classic conformity experiment.

(a) In Asch's (1956) conformity experiments, students were asked to judge which of three comparison lines was the same length as the standard line. They performed this task for multiple trials, using a different set of standard and comparison lines each time. (b) Upon hearing other group members unanimously say that line 1 was the correct match, this participant wondered whether his own judgement (line 2) was correct.

control condition where people judged the lines by themselves. This finding stunned many scientists because the task was so easy and the confederates did not overtly pressure participants to conform. After the task was over, some participants told the experimenter that they felt the group was wrong but went along to avoid making waves and suffering possible rejection. This reflects normative social influence. After several trials, other participants yielded to informational social influence and began to doubt their eyesight and judgement (Fig. 14.18b).

In other experiments, Asch manipulated different variables and measured their effects on conformity. One of the factors that influenced conformity was *group size*. Conformity increased from about 5 to 35 per cent as group size increased from one to about four or five confederates, but contrary to what we might expect, further increases in group size did not increase conformity. Another factor that influenced the extent to which participants conformed was the *presence of a dissenter*. According to plan, one confederate disagreed with the others (e.g., the majority said 'line 3'; the dissenter said 'line 2' or even 'line 1'). This greatly reduced participants' conformity. When someone dissents, this serves as a model for remaining independent from the group.

Turner (1991) recently developed a *third* reason why people might conform to others based on assumptions made in social identity theory (Tajfel and Turner, 1979): **referent informational influence**. Remember that one of the assumptions made by social identity theory is that while the group is external to the self (as the group of confederates in the Asch paradigm) it is also internal to the self (as part of one's self-definition: social identity). So, to the extent that individuals identify with a certain group, they incorporate the group norm as part of the self. This suggests that individuals will be influenced primarily by members of the groups they identify with (i.e., *reference* groups). Indeed, research has demonstrated that individuals are more susceptible to social influence when information is provided by fellow in-group members as compared to out-group members (van Knippenberg and Wilke, 1988).

According to Turner's self-categorization theory, there are several reasons why shared social identity is so important for mutual influence between individuals (Turner, 1991). First, the group forms a link between individuals. Subsequently, if people self-categorize as a member of a particular group, they have the tendency to see themselves as similar to fellow in-group members in attitudes and beliefs. This similarity leads to an expectation of agreement with these others when judging reality. If we *are* the same then we should *think* the same, one might say. Second, such agreement with similar others should produce a sense of *subjective validity* of one's own thoughts and behaviour as being correct or appropriate. Indeed, individuals feel more confident about the correctness of their beliefs and attitudes when they are shared with other in-group members (Bar-Tal, 1998; Spears and Manstead, 1990). Third, disagreeing with similar others should produce uncertainty about the validity of one's thoughts and behaviour. Finally, such uncertainty will motivate individuals to engage in a process of mutual influence in order to reach agreement.

One example might clarify this process. Imagine someone entering a mosque wearing his shoes (which is not allowed). Who do you think will bring about the most vehement reactions, a fellow Muslim or a non-Muslim, say a tourist? Research on the 'black sheep effect' (Marques et al., 1988) suggests that the fellow Muslim will bring about the strongest reaction. This person should know better. Going against an in-group norm brings about uncertainty about the validity of the norm, which will lead to a strong tendency to engage in mutual influence. The tourist, however, might not know about the rules. He is also less likely to be a threat for the in-group's sense of subjective validity. Consistent with this, Hogg and Abrams (1993) suggest that subjective certainty is the primary motivation underlying social identification with a group.

> **referent informational influence**
> individuals will be influenced primarily by members of the groups they identify with (i.e., reference groups)

FIGURE 14.19

Women marching for equal rights. Although initially an unpopular view, thanks to a small active minority (the suffragette movement) in the late nineteenth and early twentieth centuries, women obtained equal voting rights. Women's rights have improved significantly over the past century.

Minority Influence

In his conformity studies, Asch was especially interested in the influence of a majority facing a lone participant. When we look around us, everyday live experience shows us that although majority influence is powerful, in politics, in business, and in other real-world contexts, dissenting information presented by the minority can also be very persuasive (see, for example, Fig. 14.19).

In a first formulation of a theory of minority influence, Moscovici et al. (1969) investigated what happens when a minority tries to influence a majority. Instead of confronting one participant with a majority of confederates, Moscovici and colleagues confronted a majority of naive subjects (six) with a minority of confederates (two). Participants had to judge the colour of a blue slide which varied in intensity. The two confederates responded by saying 'green', either consistently on every trial or on only two-thirds of the trials. Results showed that only 1 per cent of the participants responded with 'green' when the minority was inconsistent in their judgements, whereas 8 per cent of the participants responded with 'green' when the minority consistently gave the answer 'green'.

This line of research culminated in a dual-process theory of social influence (Moscovici, 1976). According to this theory both minorities and majorities can exert strong influence. However, by virtue of its size, majorities are more likely to trigger a need for consensus, with individuals being afraid to publicly disagree with a majority. Majority influence then is more likely to lead to *compliance*, where individuals *publicly* concur to a majority, without necessarily leading to a deeper change of actual attitudes or beliefs. This reflects normative social influence. In contrast, minority influence is more likely to lead to a *private* acceptance and actual attitudinal change or *conversion*, which reflects informational social influence.

One study by Maass and Clark (1983) illustrates this point nicely. In one study, participants were asked to read a summary of a group discussion on gay rights. This discussion had supposedly taken place between five fellow students. In all cases of the discussion, one of the students (minority) had a different opinion regarding gay rights than the four others (majority). In order to avoid possible effects due to the direction of the arguments, half of the participants read a discussion in which the majority was presented as favouring gay rights and the minority as opposing gay rights. For the other half of the participants the roles were reversed, with the minority being presented as favouring gay rights. The participants were subsequently asked to either *publicly* express their attitudes, or express their attitudes in *private*. As can be seen in Figure 14.20, when participants were asked to declare their attitudes in public, they voiced agreement with the majority, regardless of whether or not they had been pro or contra gay rights. In contrast, when asked to express their attitude in private, by writing down their views, participants' attitudes reflected a shift towards the opinion of the minority.

The idea that majority influence is relatively superficial compared with minority influence is to some extent comparable with the distinction between peripheral and central route processing we discussed previously in this chapter (Petty and Cacioppo, 1986). Conversion based on informational social influence is suggested to be the more time-consuming, in need of detailed thought and attention to the information expressed by the minority (Moscovici, 1976). Consistent with this, Nemeth et al. (1990) showed that participants recalled words better when a minority had drawn attention to the words than if a majority had drawn attention to the words. This was presumably because the words had been processed more systematically (i.e., through central route processing) in the minority condition.

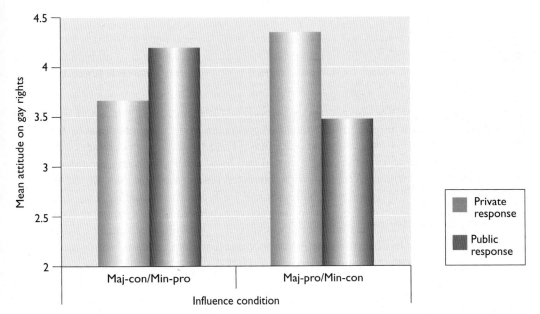

FIGURE 14.20

Participants' attitudes on gay rights on a seven-point scale after reading the group discussion. Higher scores indicate a stronger opposition to gay rights.

SOURCE: Maass and Clark, 1983, study 1.

Dissenting opinions are more likely to sway the majority when they come from several minority members rather than just one (Clark, 2001). Serge Moscovici (1985) proposes that to maximize its influence, the minority must further (1) be highly committed to its point of view, (2) remain independent in the face of majority pressure, yet appear to keep an open mind, (3) disrupt the majority norm, thereby producing uncertainty and doubt, (4) focus attention on itself, make itself visible, (5) show there is an alternative coherent point of view, and (6) convey the necessity for the majority to shift towards the minority as the only means of restoring social stability. Indeed, reviewing almost 100 studies, Wendy Wood and co-workers (1994) found that minority influence is strongest when the minority maintains a highly consistent position over time. However, if the minority appears too unreasonable, deviant, or negative it may cause the majority to become entrenched.

Cultural Differences in Conformity

Social norms lose invisibility not only when they are violated (remember the student boarding a nearly empty city bus and sitting besides the only other passenger) but also when we examine behaviour across cultures and historical periods. In doing so, we see that many social customs we take for granted as 'normal' – from gender roles and child-rearing to views about love, marriage and, even, what constitutes an attractive body shape – are not 'normal' when judged from other cultural perspectives (Tovée et al., 2006). Norms even regulate such subtle aspects of social behaviour as the amount of *personal space* that we prefer when interacting with people (Li, 2001). For example, Japanese sit farther apart when conversing than do Venezuelans, and Americans prefer an intermediate distance (Sussman and Rosenfeld, 1982).

One informative example of how culture influences behaviour, comes from a meta-analysis reporting 134 published studies using Asch's line judgement tasks (Bond and Smith, 1996). Of these 134 studies, 97 of the experiments had been conducted in the USA from 1951 to 1990. Rod Bond and Peter Smith (1996) found that the overall level of conformity decreased slightly over a time period from 1951 to 1990. As can be seen in Figure 14.21, the degree of group influence on conformity responses was found to be lowest in Europe, followed by the USA and the 'rest of the world' (e.g., Japan, Brazil, Kuwait). Individuals from collectivistic countries, then, seem more likely to yield to the majority in the Asch paradigm. This seems to reflect the conceptual difference between individualistic versus collectivistic countries (Triandis, 1990), where individuals in collectivistic countries are assumed to place a higher value on harmony in their interpersonal relationships.

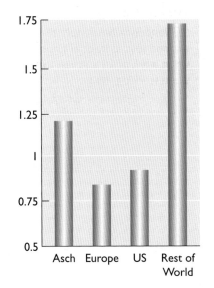

FIGURE 14.21

The amount of conformity found in Asch replication studies around the world.

SOURCE: Bond and Smith, 1996.

BEHAVIOUR IN GROUPS

No man (or woman) is an island. As social animals, we have a need to affiliate with others. Indeed, Baumeister and Leary (1995) suggest that the most fundamental of all human motives is the *need to belong*. Research on *ostracism* (ignoring or excluding someone) suggests that this might well be the case.

Psychologist Naomi Eisenberger and co-workers (2003) measured the brain activity of research participants who played an interactive computer game with, presumably, two other unseen players. In reality, there were no other players and the game was computer-controlled. The game, *Cyberball*, involved tossing a virtual ball back and forth among the three players. After a period during which all three players interacted online, the other two players suddenly ignored the participant by tossing the ball back and forth only to each other. The real participants felt excluded and distressed, and neural activity patterns in their cerebral cortex were 'very similar to those found in studies of physical pain … providing evidence that the experience … of social and physical pain share a common neuroanatomical basis' (Eisenberger et al., 2003, p. 291). Ostracism, or being ignored and excluded, dampens people's moods, decreases their sense of belonging, and – perhaps by heightening their fear of further rejection – makes them more likely to conform to the clearly incorrect judgements of a group.

Because of our strong need to belong and affiliate, much of human behaviour occurs in groups. People often form groups to share interests and activities (play soccer, climb mountains, have fun), to perform tasks and achieve goals that are too complex or demanding to be accomplished by one person (build offices, develop computers) or to provide comfort and reduce uncertainty (support groups). Apart from forming groups, people are also often born in groups that have their own idiosyncratic system of norms and values (families, ethnic groups, nations). However, although groups come in all sorts of shapes and sizes, with different goals and motivations, they share a number of key features. We discuss some of these features below.

> **Focus 14.12**
> Discuss the psychological effects of ostracism.

Social Loafing

> **social loafing**
> the tendency for people to expend less individual effort when working in a group than when working alone

In 1913 Max Ringelmann, a French agricultural engineer, measured the force that men exerted while pulling on a rope as hard as they could. Individually, the men averaged 63 kilograms (kg) of pull. Thus you might expect that eight men pulling in unison would exert a combined force of about 504 kg (i.e., 8 × 63 kg). Surprisingly, group performance was 51 per cent below expectations, and one contributing factor was **social loafing**, the tendency for people to expend less individual effort when working in a group than when working alone. In contrast to social facilitation experiments, in which a person performs a task individually (in front of an audience or with a co-actor) and does not pool her or his effort with anyone, social loafing involves collective performance. Social loafing also occurs on cognitive tasks, as when groups have to evaluate written materials or make decisions. Why does social loafing occur? Steven Karau and Kipling Williams (1993; 2001) propose a *collective effort model*: on a collective task, people will put forth only as much effort as they expect is needed to attain a valued goal. In support of this model, studies reveal that social loafing is *more* likely to occur when:

- the person believes that individual performance within the group is not being monitored
- the task (goal) or the group has less value or meaning to the person
- the person generally displays low motivation to strive for success and expects that co-workers will display high effort (Hart et al., 2004).

Social loafing also depends on gender and culture. It occurs more strongly in all-male groups than in all-female or mixed-sex groups, possibly because women may be more concerned about group outcomes than are men. Participants from individualistic cultures (e.g., Canada, the UK) exhibit more social loafing than people from collectivistic cultures (e.g., China, Japan, Taiwan), in which group goals are especially valued.

Social loafing suggests that in terms of group performance, the whole is less than the sum of its parts. But this is not always the case. Social loafing may disappear when individual performance is monitored or when members highly value their group or the task goal. In fact, to achieve a highly desired goal, some people may engage in **social compensation**, working harder in a group than when alone to compensate for other members' lower output (Hart et al., 2001).

Group Polarization

Key decisions are often entrusted to groups, such as committees, because groups are assumed to be more conservative than individuals and less likely to be irrational. Is this assumption correct? It is, as long as the group is generally conservative to begin with. In such cases, the group's final opinion or attitude will likely be even *more conservative*. But if the group members lean towards a liberal or risky viewpoint to begin with, the group's decision will tend to become *more liberal or riskier*. This principle is called **group polarization**: when a group of like-minded people discusses an issue, the 'average' opinion of group members tends to become more extreme (Moscovici and Zavalloni, 1969).

Why does group polarization occur? One reason, reflecting normative social influence, is that individuals who are attracted to a group may be motivated to adopt a more extreme position to gain the group's approval. A second reason, reflecting informational social influence, is that during group discussions people hear arguments supporting their positions that they had not previously considered (Sia et al., 2002). A final reason, based on referent informational social influence, is that people will conform to the most prototypical position of the group, where the prototype is often more extreme than the actual average of a group (McGarthy et al., 1992).

Groupthink

After the US military ignored warning signs of imminent attack by Japan in 1941, the fleet at Pearl Harbor was destroyed in a 'surprise' attack. In 1961 President Kennedy and his advisers launched the hopelessly doomed Bay of Pigs invasion of Cuba. After analysing these and other historical accounts of disastrous group decisions, Irving Janis (1982) concluded that in each case the decision makers fell victim to a process that he named **groupthink**, the tendency of group members to suspend critical thinking because they are striving to seek agreement.

As shown in Figure 14.22, Janis proposed that groupthink is most likely to occur when a group:

- is under *high stress* to reach a decision
- is *insulated* from outside input
- has a *directive leader* who promotes a personal agenda
- has *high cohesiveness*, reflecting a spirit of closeness and ability to work well together.

Under these conditions, the group is so committed to reaching consensus, and remaining loyal and agreeable, that members suspend their critical judgement. In the business world, groupthink can contribute to poor management decisions that adversely affect the financial value and public reputation of the company (Eaton, 2001).

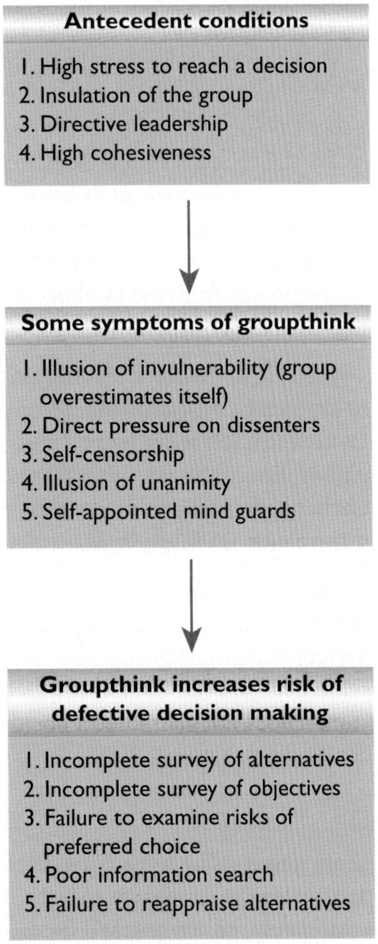

social compensation
working harder in a group than when alone to compensate for other members' lower output

group polarization
when a group of like-minded people discusses an issue, the 'average' opinion of group members tends to become more extreme

groupthink
the tendency of group members to suspend critical thinking because they are striving to seek agreement

Focus 14.13
Describe social loafing, social compensation, and the causes and consequences of group polarization and groupthink.

Antecedent conditions
1. High stress to reach a decision
2. Insulation of the group
3. Directive leadership
4. High cohesiveness

Some symptoms of groupthink
1. Illusion of invulnerability (group overestimates itself)
2. Direct pressure on dissenters
3. Self-censorship
4. Illusion of unanimity
5. Self-appointed mind guards

Groupthink increases risk of defective decision making
1. Incomplete survey of alternatives
2. Incomplete survey of objectives
3. Failure to examine risks of preferred choice
4. Poor information search
5. Failure to reappraise alternatives

FIGURE 14.22

Groupthink.

This diagram illustrates the antecedents, symptoms and negative effects of groupthink on decision making.

SOURCE: adapted from Janis, 1982.

Various symptoms signal that groupthink is at work. Group members who express doubt get *direct pressure* to stop rocking the boat. Some members serve as *mind guards* and prevent negative information from reaching the group. Ultimately, members display *self-censorship* and withhold their doubts, creating an *illusion of unanimity* in which each member comes to believe that everyone else seems to agree with the decision (Fig. 14.23). Overall, the group leader and members who favour the leader's position will have their confidence in the decision reinforced, whereas members who have doubts will feel pressure to go along with the group (Henningsen et al., 2006).

FIGURE 14.23

(*Left*) The illusion of unanimity occurs when group members collectively fail to speak their true minds. (*Right*) The illusion of unanimity contributed to the ill-fated decision to launch the space shuttle *Challenger* on 28 January 1986. The *Challenger* exploded shortly after take-off, killing all the astronauts on board.

"All those in favor say 'aye'."
    "Aye."   "Aye."   "Aye."   "Aye."   "Aye."

Many aspects of groupthink were present during the decision-making process leading up to the fatal launch of the space shuttle *Challenger* in 1986 (Esser and Lindoerfer, 1989). The engineers who designed the rocket boosters opposed the launch, fearing that freezing weather would make the rocket's rubber seals too brittle to contain hot gasses. But the National Aeronautics and Space Administration (NASA) was under high stress, and leadership was directive. This mission was carrying America's first civilian into space, there had been several delays and NASA did not want another. To foster an illusion of unanimity, a key NASA executive excluded the engineers from the final decision-making process (Magnuson, 1986). Thanks to mind guarding, the NASA official who gave the final go-ahead never knew of the engineers' concerns.

In 2003, in the days leading up to the fiery disintegration of the space shuttle *Columbia* as it re-entered Earth's atmosphere, engineers, supervisors and some NASA officials debated whether *Columbia*'s left wing had been damaged during launch. But as the Columbia Accident Investigation Board found, tragically, 'dangerous aspects of NASA's 1986 culture … remained unchanged', such as a 'need to produce consensus at each level' that filtered out dissenting information on safety risks (2003, p. 198).

Can groupthink be prevented? Janis suggested that it might, if the leader remains impartial during discussions, encourages critical thinking, brings in outsiders to offer their opinions, and divides the larger group into subgroups – to see if each subgroup independently reaches the same decision. Of course, while critical debate may enhance the odds of making a good decision, it does not guarantee a positive outcome and in some cases may cause the group to become deadlocked (Kowert, 2002).

Deindividuation

Years ago in New York City, a man sat perched on the ledge of an upper-story window for an hour while a crowd of nearly 500 people on the street below shouted at him to jump. Fortunately, police rescued the man. New York is not alone. When Leon Mann (1981) analysed newspaper reports of incidents in which crowds were present when a person threatened to jump off a building, in 10 of 21 cases the crowd had encouraged the person to jump. Why would people in crowds act this way?

In crowds, people may experience **deindividuation**, a loss of individuality that leads to disinhibited behaviour (Festinger et al., 1952; Zimbardo, 2004). But what is the primary aspect of deindividuation that disinhibits behaviour? Tom Postmes and Russell Spears (1998) meta-analysed 60 deindividuation studies and determined that *anonymity to outsiders* was the key. Conditions that make an individual less identifiable to people *outside* the group reduce feelings of accountability and, slightly but consistently, increase the risk of antisocial actions (Fig. 14.24).

During the Stanford prison study, no names were used and prisoners had to address guards as 'Mr Correctional Officer'. All guards wore identical uniforms and reflecting sunglasses that prevented the prisoners from making direct eye contact. The guards were unaware that their behaviour was being monitored by the experimenters, and antisocial norms evolved from the role of 'tough prison guard' adopted by participants who spontaneously took over leadership roles (Zimbardo et al., 1973). These factors led Zimbardo to conclude that deindividuation was a key factor in the cruelty exhibited by the guards. Reducing anonymity – and thereby increasing public accountability – may be one approach to counteracting deindividuation.

Postmes and Spears (1998) take the explanation, and possible solution of the negative effects as a consequence of deindividuation, a step further in their social identity model of deindividuation effects (SIDE; Spears et al., 2001). They suggest that being anonymous to outsiders enhances the individual's tendency to focus on his or her (social) identity with the group and makes the person more responsive to emerging group norms. One consequence would be that the antisocial effects of deindividuation actually occur not because of a *lack* of norms, but because of the *existence* of norms that actually approve of antisocial behaviour.

Taking a closer look at Zimbardo's Stanford prison experiment, we can see how a group norm was instilled that might explain the antisocial behaviour of the prison guards. Take the following example of the way in which guards where instructed to behave:

> You can create in the prisoners feelings of boredom, a sense of fear to some degree, you can create a notion of arbitrariness that their life is totally controlled by us, by the system, you, me – and they'll have no privacy. They'll have no freedom of action, they can do nothing, say nothing that we don't permit. We're going to take away their individuality in various ways. In general what all this leads to is a sense of powerlessness. (Zimbardo, 1989, cited in Reicher and Haslam, 2006, p. 4).

If anything, the above instructions are a norm that might easily lead to antisocial behaviour from the guards. Indeed, Reicher and Haslam (2006) recently conducted an extensive replication of Zimbardo's Stanford prison experiment without such instructions to the guards. Interestingly, this replication did not lead to extreme antisocial behaviour, more the opposite. An almost egalitarian system was developed under certain circumstances, with guards giving privileges to prisoners and both prisoners and guards getting along rather well. The results of this replication suggest that the way in which individuals behave in groups is more a matter of the norms and values that are attached to their social identity. These norms can either be antisocial *or* pro-social (Jetten et al., 1997). Thus, another way in which antisocial behaviour developing from deindividuation can be counteracted is to make sure that pro-social norms are in place and an integral part of the social group.

Focus 14.14

Describe deindividuation, its main cause, and how conditions in the Stanford prison study may have fostered it.

deindividuation

a loss of individuality that leads to disinhibited behaviour

FIGURE 14.24

Deindividuation can lead to a loss of restraint that causes people to engage in uncharacteristic behaviours.

Focus 14.15

Describe what the role of US Army reservist Lynndie England's superiors might have been. Could they have prevented what happened in the 2003 Abu Ghraib Iraqi prisoner scandal?

IN REVIEW

- People often use special techniques to get us to comply with their requests, such as the norm of reciprocity, the door-in-the-face technique, the foot-in-the-door technique and lowballing.

- Milgram's obedience research raised strong ethical concerns and found unexpectedly high percentages of people willing to obey destructive orders. Such obedience is stronger when the victim is remote and when the authority figure is close by, legitimate and assumes responsibility for what happens.

- A social norm is a shared rule or expectation about how group members should think, feel and behave. A social role is a set of norms that defines a particular position in a social system.

- People conform to a group because of informational social influence, normative social influence and informational referent social influence.

- The size of the majority and the presence or absence of dissenters influence the degree of conformity. Minority influence is strongest when the minority maintains a consistent position over time but does not appear too deviant.

- Ostracism produces negative psychological consequences and activates many of the same brain regions that underlie physical pain.

- Social loafing occurs when people exert less individual effort when working as a group than when working alone. Loafing decreases when the goal is valued highly and when performance within the group is individually monitored.

- When the members of a decision-making group share the same conservative or liberal viewpoint, the group's final decision often becomes more extreme than the average initial opinion of the individual members.

- Cohesive decision-making groups that have directive leaders, are under high stress and are insulated from outside input may display groupthink, a suspension of critical thinking to maintain cohesion and loyalty to the leader's viewpoint.

- Deindividuation refers to a temporary loss of individuality that can occur when a person is immersed in a group. Anonymity to outsiders and the lack of inhibiting social norms within the group appear to be the key factors in producing deindividuation.

SOCIAL RELATIONS: INTERGROUP DYNAMICS

As we have seen, individual behaviour often occurs within groups. However, society consists of an enormous number of different groups and these different groups also interact with each other, forming and maintaining relationships. Sometimes these interactions occur at a major scale, with implications far beyond group boundaries. This is the case with the numerous wars between groups and countries, but also with major formalized interactions between countries such as in the European Union. Other interactions occur at a more minor scale, such as work discussions between departments or competitive team sports, but nonetheless can have a big impact on behaviour. Look again at Figure 14.24 for example. Who do you think the flying chair might be aimed at? Fans supporting his team, or fans supporting a rival team?

Relations between groups can be beneficial, but they also have the potential to change dramatically for the worse. One only has to think of the atrocities that occurred during the Second World War, or more recently the conflict between the Hutus and the Tutsis in Rwanda, the apartheid regime in South Africa, the current terrorist threat, and so on. As a result, social psychology has devoted considerable attention to the study of intergroup relations in order to gain an understanding of such problems as prejudice, discrimination and intergroup conflict.

UNDERSTANDING INTERGROUP RELATIONS

What exactly do we mean by intergroup relations? A classic definition of intergroup situations is given by Sherif (1966: 12): 'Whenever individuals belonging to one group interact, collectively or individually, with another group or its members in terms of their group identification, we have an instance of intergroup behaviour.' This definition makes clear that intergroup relations do not necessarily imply the presence of two large groups standing face to face. Intergroup relations can also occur at the level of two individuals interacting. Thus, a job interview between a female applicant and a male interviewer can be said to be a dyadic situation with two unique individuals interacting. Where the female is applying for a technical job requiring extensive knowledge of mathematics, the interviewer may let his judgement of the applicant, and subsequently his behaviour, be guided by his stereotype of women being poor in mathematics. To the extent that both applicant and interviewer view each other in terms of their different gender identity, one can also see this as an example of intergroup relations.

Earlier in this chapter we discussed how stereotypes (e.g., about social class) can bias the way we perceive other people's behaviour. Stereotypes are not by definition good or bad, they are rather *mental representations of groups and their members*. Such mental representations can refer to personality traits as well as behaviour, and can include positive and negative attitudes towards a group and its members. For example the French are seen by some people as rude and snobby, whereas others might view them as having 'Joie de vivre', generally enjoying life while sipping wine and eating French bread with smelly cheese (Fig. 14.25). Where a negative attitude towards people based on their membership in a group exists, we often refer to this as **prejudice**. Thus we *prejudge* people – dislike them or hold negative beliefs about them – simply because they are female or male, belong to one ethnic group or religion rather than to another, are gay or straight, and so on. This is not to be confused with **discrimination**, which refers to overt behaviour that involves treating people unfairly based on the group to which they belong.

For a more thorough understanding of intergroup relations, we need to consider a constellation of factors. These include historical and cultural norms that legitimize differential treatment of various groups and socialization processes through which parents and other adults transmit values and beliefs to their children. Let us examine several cognitive and motivational processes that are thought to underlie the development of intergroup relations.

Categorization and 'Us–Them' Thinking

In order to organize and simplify our world, we have a tendency to categorize people and objects. At times, this helps us predict other people's behaviour and react quickly to environmental stimuli (Ito and Caci</p>oppo, 2000). But our tendency to categorize people also lays a foundation for intergroup behaviour.

Categorization leads to the perception of in-groups and out-groups, groups to which we do and do not belong, respectively. One important feature of this process of categorization for understanding intergroup relations, is the fact that people have a tendency to exaggerate the difference between categories, called **category accentuation**. This was nicely illustrated in a study by Tajfel and Wilkes (1963). They randomly presented participants with eight lines, varying in length from 16.2 cm to 22.9 cm, and simply asked them to estimate the length of each line. However, for one group of participants these lines were labelled, such that the four smallest lines were labelled 'A' and the four longer lines were labelled 'B'. For the other group no such labelling of lines occurred. Results showed that, in the labelling condition, participants overestimated the difference between the lines labelled 'A' and 'B', such that A essentially meant 'short' where B meant 'long'. This effect was especially marked for the longest line of category A and the shortest line of category B. The perceived differences between these lines (line 1 and 2 in Fig. 14.26) was much greater than the actual difference between the lines. No such exaggerations of perceived difference occurred in the 'no label' condition.

FIGURE 14.25

Joie de vivre!

prejudice

a negative attitude towards people based on their membership in a group

discrimination

overt behaviour that involves treating people unfairly based on the group to which they belong

category accentuation

a tendency to exaggerate the difference between categories

FIGURE 14.26

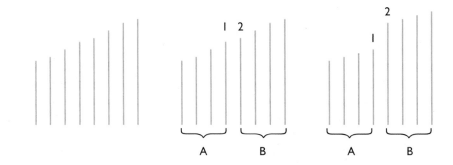

Lines in Tajfel and Wilkes (1963). (*Left*) Lines without labels, (middle) lines with labels, where participants exaggerated the average height of lines labelled 'B' compared with those labelled 'A'. With the biggest perceived difference occurring between lines 1 and 2. (*Right*) An impression of how participants might have perceived the lines in the labelling condition.

out-group homogeneity bias

the tendency of individuals to generally view members of out-groups as being more similar to one another than are members of in-groups

Tajfel and Wilkes (1963) suggested that this accentuation of differences between categories could also explain the exaggeration that occurred between members of different groups. That is, although stereotypes might have some 'kernel of truth', stereotypes are often a simplification of reality and function in a way that exaggerates differences between 'us' and 'them'. This suggests that stereotypes can change depending on the presence or absence of groups that force us to think in terms of 'us' and 'them' (Oakes et al., 1994). Supporting this, a study by Cinnirella (1998) asked British participants to provide stereotype ratings of the British (i.e., reserved) and Italians (i.e., passionate). In one condition participants were asked to provide stereotypes of the British only, in another condition they were asked to provide stereotypes of the Italians only, whereas in a third condition participants were asked to provide stereotypes of both nationalities. Results showed that stereotype ratings of both Italians and British were more pronounced in condition three compared with the first and second condition.

Numerous studies have now provided evidence that in-group versus out-group distinctions spawn several common biases. The **out-group homogeneity bias** for example, refers to the tendency of individuals to generally view members of out-groups as being more similar to one another than are members of in-groups (Brauer, 2001). In other words, we perceive that 'they are all alike' but recognize that 'we are diverse'. The mere fact that we identify people as 'Asian', 'Hispanic', 'black' and 'white' reflects such a bias, because each of these ethnic categories contains many subgroups. In one study, Anglo-American college students were less likely to distinguish among 'Hispanic' subgroups than were Cuban-American, Mexican-American and Puerto Rican-American college students (Huddy and Virtanen, 1995). But just like the Anglo-American students, the Cuban-American, Mexican-American and Puerto Rican-American students also engaged in us–them thinking: They saw their own subgroup as distinct from the others but did not differentiate between the other two Hispanic subgroups.

Categorization, then, enhances the tendency to judge other people based on their perceived group membership rather than their individual characteristics. Whether at a conscious or unconscious level, category labels pertaining to people's race, gender and other attributes seem to activate stereotypes about them (Wheeler and Fiske, 2005). Figure 14.27 illustrates two ways in which racial categorization and gender categorization activate stereotypes and affect our perceptions.

Not all people easily fit into a group or category; some members seem to be a better representative of a category than others. For example, a sheep seems to be a better representative of the category 'mammals' than a dolphin. Similarly, in the example used in the section on social thought, if Hannah would be dressed up according to the latest fashion wearing expensive shoes and accessories, she would not fit well with participants' stereotype of people from a poor neighbourhood. Indeed, categories are often 'fuzzy' or 'ill-defined' concepts, where a person is perceived to be a better representative of the category the more he or she possesses a number of characteristic features that are 'typical' for the group, the so-called *group prototype* (Rosch and Mervis, 1975; Turner et al., 1987).

FIGURE 14.27

Classic experiments on prejudice.

(a) Who is holding the razor knife? Allport and Postman (1947) showed this picture to one person, who then described it while looking at it. A second person listened to this description and was asked to repeat it 'as exactly as possible' to another person, who repeated this description to another person, and so on (up to six or seven tellings). In over half of the trials following this procedure, at some point the black man was erroneously described as holding the knife. (b) Which person contributes most strongly to this research team? When the drawing shows an all-male group, an all-female group or a mixed-gender group with a man at the head of the table (seat 3), participants say that the person in seat 3 is the strongest member. But in this mixed-gender drawing with a woman in seat 3, most male and female participants pick one of the two men.

SOURCE: based on Porter and Geis, 1981.

What happens when we encounter individual members of out-groups whose behaviour clearly contradicts our stereotypes? One possibility is that we may change our stereotype; but if we are motivated to hold on to our prejudiced belief, we may explain away discrepant behaviour in several ways. For example, the out-group member may be seen as an exceptional case or as having succeeded at a task not because of high ability but because of tremendous effort, good luck or special advantage (Pettigrew, 1979). Such attributional biases reflect **in-group favouritism**, which represents the tendency to favour in-group members and attribute more positive qualities to 'us' than to 'them', whereas **out-group derogation** reflects a tendency to attribute more negative qualities to 'them' than to 'us'. Although people may display both biases, especially when they feel threatened, in-group favouritism is usually the stronger of the two (Hewstone et al., 2002).

Motivational Aspects of Intergroup Relations

People's ingrained ways of perceiving the world – categorizing, forming in-groups and out-groups, and so forth – prepare the wheels of prejudice to go into motion, but motivational factors affect how fast those wheels spin. For example, prejudice and stereotyping increase when social motives squarely focus our attention on the fact that people belong to in-groups or out-groups (Wheeler and Fiske, 2005).

Competition and conflict According to **realistic conflict theory**, competition for limited resources fosters prejudice. In the USA and Europe, hostility towards minority groups increases when economic conditions worsen (Pettigrew and Meertens, 1995). Originally, it was believed

in-group favouritism
the tendency to favour in-group members and attribute more positive qualities to 'us' than to 'them'

out-group derogation
a tendency to attribute more negative qualities to 'them' than to 'us'

realistic conflict theory
competition for limited resources fosters prejudice

that a threat to one's personal welfare (as in the fear of losing one's job to a minority worker) was the prime motivator of prejudice, but research suggests that prejudice is triggered more strongly by *a perceived threat to one's in-group*. Among whites, prejudice against blacks is not related to personal resource gains and losses but to the belief that white people as a group are in danger of being 'overtaken' (Bobo, 1988). Likewise, as the Robber's Cave summer camp experiment illustrated in Chapter 1, competition between groups can breed intense hostility towards an out-group (Sherif et al., 1961). Indeed, even when people are angry and know that an out-group did not cause that anger, their implicit prejudice still increases towards the out-group. David DeSteno and co-workers (2004) suggest that the emotion of anger is so closely linked to conflict and competition between groups that it automatically activates feelings of prejudice towards out-groups.

Enhancing self-esteem   According to *social identity theory*, prejudice stems from a need to enhance our self-esteem. Some experiments find that people express more prejudice after their self-esteem is threatened (e.g., receiving negative feedback about their abilities) and that the opportunity to derogate others helps restore self-esteem (Fein and Spencer, 1997). According to social identity theory however, our self-esteem is based on two components: a personal identity and a group identity (Tajfel and Turner, 1986). We can raise self-esteem not only by acknowledging our own virtues but also by associating ourselves with our in-group's accomplishments. Conversely, threats to our in-group threaten our self-esteem and may prompt us to derogate the out-group that constitutes the threat (Perdue et al., 1990).

If people are motivated to enhance their group-based self-esteem, then membership in high-status groups should be desirable, as this may contribute to a positive social identity. Conversely, it might be suggested that members of low-status groups should be motivated to improve their status position in order to attain a more positive social identity. Social identity theory suggests therefore that people in low-status groups are likely to (1) leave their existing group and join a more positive group, a strategy called *individual mobility*, (2) creatively redefine the positivity of their group (i.e., 'black is beautiful'), a strategy known as *social creativity*, or (3) try to attain a higher status by directly competing with another group, also known as *social competition* (Tajfel and Turner, 1979). Which of these *identity management strategies* is chosen by low-status group members to enhance their social identity, is dependent on a number of group characteristics (e.g., Ellemers et al., 1993). For example, if group boundaries are *permeable*, low-status group members are more likely to focus on possibilities of individual mobility. In contrast, if it is impossible for individuals to move over to a higher status group, or when the *status inequality* is seen as *insecure* and likely to change, low-status group members are assumed to engage in social competition in order to change the 'status quo' (Ellemers, 1993; Taylor and McKirnan, 1984).

PREJUDICE AND DISCRIMINATION

Even today, overt prejudice and discrimination are in abundant supply. Armed conflicts based on ethnic or religious divisions continue across the globe; hate crimes persist; and people's race, gender, religion, and sexual orientation spark unfair treatment (Herek, 2000).

Explicit and Implicit Prejudice

In some ways, the most blatant forms of prejudice and discrimination have decreased in many countries. Racial segregation is no longer sanctioned by government policy in the USA or South Africa, and opinion polls indicate that fewer people express prejudiced attitudes towards other (ethnic) groups than was the case decades ago.

Although prejudiced attitudes may have faded a bit, in many ways modern racism, sexism and other forms of prejudice are more difficult to detect. In contrast to **explicit prejudice**, which people express publicly, **implicit prejudice** is hidden from public view. Many people intention-

explicit prejudice
people express publicly

implicit prejudice
hidden from public view

ally hide their prejudices, expressing them only when they feel it is safe or socially appropriate. In other cases, people may honestly believe that they are not prejudiced but still show unconscious biases when tested in sophisticated ways (Fazio et al., 1995).

We can use questionnaires to measure explicit prejudice, but how can we measure implicit prejudice? Some researchers have found that subtle movements of facial muscles involved in smiling (and in some studies, in frowning) can be used to predict people's biases towards members of another ethnic group (Vanman et al., 2004). But most often, measures of implicit prejudice assess people's reaction times at special cognitive tasks (Greenwald et al., 1998; Olson and Fazio, 2003).

To give you a general idea of how an implicit prejudice test might work (they are actually more complicated than this), suppose that a series of word pairs, such as 'black–pleasant' and 'white–pleasant' are flashed on a computer screen. As soon as you see each pair, your task is to press a computer key as quickly as you can, and this represents your reaction time. The principle underlying this task is that people react more quickly when they perceive that the concepts (i.e., the two words in each pair) 'fit' together than when the concepts do not. Thus *without conscious control*, a person prejudiced against blacks will react more slowly to the 'black–pleasant' pair than to the 'white–pleasant' pair. Again, this example is simplified. The actual tests measure how quickly people make judgements about concepts and groups.

Psychologists have found that implicit measures, such as the *Implicit Association Test* (IAT) can reveal many types of unconscious prejudice (Greenwald et al., 2002). These tests also can predict other types of biased responses that explicit measures – which can be easily distorted by people unaware of or trying to hide their prejudice – fail to predict. For example, Kurt Hugenberg and Galen Bodenhausen (2003) used the IAT to measure white college students' implicit prejudice towards blacks; they also used a self-report rating scale to measure explicit prejudice. Finally, they showed the students short, computer-generated movie clips that portrayed the faces of either white or black males making a range of angry, ambiguous and happy expressions. Compared with students who had lower implicit prejudice, those who had higher implicit prejudice were more likely to perceive the ambiguous facial expressions of black males as expressing anger. In contrast, students' reactions to the facial expressions were not related to their explicit prejudice scores.

Focus 14.16

How is implicit prejudice measured? Describe cognitive and motivational roots of prejudice.

How Prejudice Confirms Itself

Self-fulfilling prophecies are one of the most invisible yet damaging ways of maintaining prejudiced beliefs. An experiment by Carl Word and his colleagues (1974) illustrates this point. The researchers began with the premise – supported by research at the time – that whites held several negative stereotypes of blacks. In the experiment, white male college students interviewed white and black high school students who were seeking admission into a special group. The college students used a fixed set of interview questions provided by the experimenter and, unknown to them, each applicant was an accomplice who had been trained to respond in a standard way to the questions. The findings indicated that these white participants sat farther away, conducted shorter interviews, and made more speech errors when the applicants were black. In short, their behaviour was discriminatory.

But this is only half the picture. In a second experiment – a job interview simulation – white male undergraduates served as *job applicants*. Through random assignment, they were treated either as the white applicants had been treated in the first experiment or as the black applicants had been treated. Thus for half the participants, the interviewer sat farther away, held a shorter interview and made more speech errors. The findings revealed that white participants who were treated more negatively performed worse during the job interview, were less composed, made more speech errors and rated the interviewer as less friendly. In short, these experiments suggest that an interviewer's negative stereotypes can lead to discriminatory treatment during a job interview, and this discriminatory behaviour can cause the applicant to perform more poorly – ultimately confirming the interviewer's initial stereotype.

Stanford psychologist Claude Steele (1997) has demonstrated another insidious way that prejudice ends up confirming itself. As described in Chapter 10, his concept of **stereotype threat** proposes that stereotypes create self-consciousness among stereotyped group members and a fear that they will live up to other people's stereotypes. For example, in a study comparing female and male college students who graduate in various fields, women graduating in the traditionally 'male' fields of mathematics, science and engineering reported the highest level of stereotype threat (Steele et al., 2002). They were more likely to feel that they (as well as other women in their field of study) had been targets of sex discrimination and that because of their gender other people (including their professors) expected them to have less ability and do more poorly.

Stereotype threat can occur even if group members do not accept the stereotype themselves, and experiments reveal its debilitating consequences. Given the stereotype that 'blacks are not as intelligent as whites', black college students who take a difficult verbal ability test perform more poorly when it is described as an 'intelligence test' than when it is described merely as a 'laboratory task'. In contrast, the intelligence-test description does not decrease white students' performance. Similar results were found for other stereotypes relating to mathematical ability, namely, 'whites are inferior to Asians', 'Latinos are inferior to whites', and 'women are inferior to men'. When a difficult standardized mathematics test is given in situations that activate these stereotypes, whites, Latinos and women perform more poorly than when the test is presented in a more neutral way (Aronson et al., 1999; Gonzales et al., 2002).

Reducing Prejudice

Psychologists do more than just study the causes of prejudice; they also develop and examine ways to reduce prejudice and its harmful effects. For example, stereotype threat's negative effects on women's mathematics performance can be reduced by allowing them to take mathematics tests without men present and by exposing them to female role models who succeed at such tasks (Marx et al., 2005; McIntyre et al., 2003). We discuss some of the main approaches identified by psychologists as possible suitable ways to reduce prejudice and discrimination.

Intergroup contact   The best-known approaches to prejudice reduction are based on a principle called **equal status contact**: prejudice between people is most likely to be reduced when they (1) engage in sustained close contact, (2) have equal status, (3) work to achieve a common goal that requires co-operation and (4) are supported by broader social norms (Allport, 1954; Fig. 14.28).

---

stereotype threat

stereotypes create self-consciousness among stereotyped group members and a fear that they will live up to other people's stereotypes

Focus 14.17

How do self-fulfilling prophecies and stereotype threat perpetuate prejudice? How can prejudice be reduced?

equal status contact

prejudice between people is most likely to be reduced when they (1) engage in sustained close contact, (2) have equal status, (3) work to achieve a common goal that requires co-operation and (4) are supported by broader social norms

FIGURE 14.28

Reducing prejudice: equal status contact.

Prejudice between two people or groups is most likely to decrease when contact between them occurs under these four conditions.

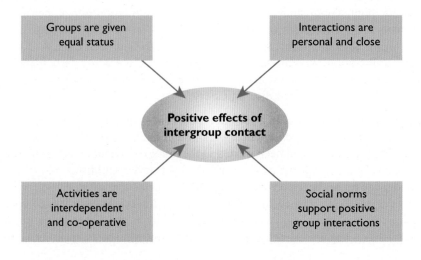

In 1954 the US Supreme Court handed down a momentous decision in the case of *Brown* v. *Board of Education*, ruling that school segregation based solely on race violates the constitutional rights of racial minorities. Providing key testimony, several psychologists stated that segregation contributed to racial prejudice and hostility. Unfortunately, decades later, when Walter Stephan (1990) reviewed more than 80 evaluation studies of desegregation programmes, he concluded that desegregation did not consistently reduce racial prejudice.

Why were the results not more positive? First, the condition of equal-status contact was often not met, and contact when status is unequal serves only to perpetuate both groups' negative stereotypes of one another. Second, in many integrated school situations, close and personal contact between group members did not occur. Black students and white students were sometimes placed in different learning tracks that minimized in-class contact, and they tended to associate only with members of their own ethnic group outside class. Third, classroom experiences focused on individual rather than co-operative learning. Finally, intergroup contact was often not supported by broader social norms; in the early years of desegregation, many white politicians, parents, teachers and school officials militantly opposed school integration.

When intergroup contact takes place under proper conditions, however, prejudice often decreases (Pettigrew and Tropp, 2006). In school settings, *co-operative learning programmes* (such as the 'jigsaw classroom' described in Chapter 1) place children into multiracial learning groups. Contact is close and sustained, each child is accorded equal status, and each has responsibility for learning and then teaching other group members one piece of the information that is needed for the group to succeed in its assignment (Aronson et al., 1978). The children also can forge a common group identity, much as athletes on a team or members of a military unit form a group identity. Overall, such programmes reduce prejudice and promote appreciation of ethnic group differences (Johnson, 2000).

An educational approach to reducing stereotype threat   Michael Johns and his co-workers (2005) asked male and female college students to take a difficult mathematics test. To minimize stereotype threat, one group of randomly assigned students was told that the test was merely an exercise in problem solving. To maximize stereotype threat, a second group and a third group were told that the test assessed mathematical aptitude and that women's and men's scores would be compared. The third group, however, also received educational information about stereotype threat, and the women in this group were told that if they felt anxious during the test, stereotype threat might be the cause.

Would teaching women about stereotype threat make them even more anxious and further impair their mathematical performance, or would it improve their performance by letting them know what to expect and allowing them to make an external attribution (i.e., to the societal stereotype) for their anxiety? As Figure 14.29 shows, compared with the 'mathematics test' condition, the teaching intervention boosted women's performance.

Using simulations to reduce 'shooter bias'   Finally, let us examine another type of racial bias. In several highly publicized cases over the past decade, police officers investigating a crime have shot and killed unarmed black men. The officers, faced with a split-second decision about whether to shoot, mistakenly perceived that these men were either

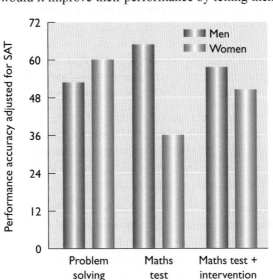

FIGURE 14.29

Reducing stereotype threat.

This graph shows the results of Johns and co-workers' (2005) study of stereotype threat. In the 'mathematics test + intervention' condition, women were told that the task was a mathematics test, but they were also given educational information about stereotype threat. Thus armed, they ended up performing significantly better than the women who were told only that the task was a mathematics test. Moreover, their performance was not significantly poorer than that of the women who were told that the task was merely a problem-solving exercise.

reaching for or holding a weapon. Was the victims' race a factor in these shootings? Social psychologists devised experiments in which college students and other adults had to quickly decide whether to shoot armed and unarmed white and black suspects who appeared on a computer screen during a video simulation. The results revealed a 'shooter bias' in which participants – both white and black participants in some studies – were more likely to shoot unarmed suspects who were black (Correll et al., 2002).

Subsequently, in separate computer simulation experiments with college students and police officers, E. Ashby Plant and co-workers have been able to reduce this shooter bias (Plant and Peruche, 2005; Plant et al., 2005). The shooting simulation programme, like those used in other experiments, was designed so that white and black criminal suspects were equally likely to be armed or unarmed. Over time, with repeated exposure to the simulation programme, the shooter bias that students and police officers displayed on the earlier trials disappeared. As the researchers note, these findings are only a promising first step that await further testing in more rigorous police academy training programmes.

SOCIAL RELATIONS: INTERPERSONAL DYNAMICS

In the previous section we discussed social relations between groups. Because of the tendency to escalate and the implications such relations between groups can have for individuals, social psychology has recently given much attention to this type of relationship. However, as individuals we also form and maintain relationships with other individuals without necessarily having to refer to differing group memberships. Research and theory on *interpersonal* relationships is the focus of the present section.

ATTRACTION: LIKING AND LOVING OTHERS

Commenting on friendship and love, humorist Mason Cooley once quipped, 'Friendship is love minus sex and plus reason. Love is friendship plus sex and minus reason' (Columbia, 1996). Alas, the difference between *liking* and *loving* may not be so simple, but attraction is indeed the first phase of most friendships and romantic relationships. What causes us to connect with some people but not others?

Initial Attraction: Proximity, Mere Exposure and Similarity

People cannot develop a relationship unless they first meet, and proximity (nearness) is the best predictor of who will cross paths with whom. In today's increasingly wired world, friendships and romances sometimes develop after strangers make initial contact through Internet chat rooms or email. Still, *physical proximity* matters. We tend to interact most with people who are physically closer. Residents in married-student apartments are most likely to form friendships with other residents who live close by, and students assigned specific classroom seats are most likely to become friends with students seated nearby.

mere exposure effect
repeated exposure to a stimulus typically increases our liking for it

Proximity increases the chance of frequent encounters, and over 200 experiments in different countries provide evidence of a **mere exposure effect**: repeated exposure to a stimulus typically increases our liking for it. No matter the stimuli – college class-mates, photographs of faces, random geometric shapes, and so on – as long as they are not unpleasant and we are not oversaturated, exposure generally enhances liking (Peskin and Newell, 2004).

After two people meet, then what? When it comes to attraction, folk wisdom covers all the bases. On the one hand, 'opposites attract'. On the other hand, 'birds of a feather flock together'. So which is it? Cross-cultural evidence overwhelmingly supports the role of *similarity*: people most often are attracted to others who are similar to themselves. For psychological attributes, similarity of attitudes and values seems to matter the most (Buss, 1985).

In the laboratory, college students' degree of liking for a stranger can be predicted very accurately simply by knowing the proportion of similar attitudes that they share (Byrne, 1997). Outside the laboratory, researchers matched college students on a brief 30-minute date, pairing people with partners who had either highly similar or dissimilar attitudes (Byrne et al., 1970). Students were more attracted to similar partners and had a stronger desire to date them. One reason we like people with similar attitudes is that they validate our view of the world. Yet even trivial or chance similarities between people also boost attraction (J. Jones et al., 2004).

Do opposites attract? At times, of course. But more often, opposites repel. When choosing potential friends or mates, we typically screen out people who are dissimilar to us. And when dissimilar people do form relationships, they tend not to last as long. Often, when we initially find a dissimilar characteristic of another person appealing, we come to dislike it over time (Felmlee, 1998).

Focus 14.18
Discuss how proximity, mere exposure, similarity and beauty influence initial attraction.

Spellbound by Beauty

It may be shallow and unfair, but most people seem drawn to beauty like moths to a flame. In many studies, when men and women rate the desirability of short-term dating partners, their judgements are influenced most strongly by how good-looking the person is. Indeed, throughout the animal kingdom, species have evolved distinct physical features to attract mates (Fig. 14.30)

In a classic study, Elaine Walster and co-workers (1966) randomly paired over 700 first-year University of Minnesota students on blind dates for a Freshers' week dance. Earlier, the researchers had given all the participants a battery of personality, intelligence and social skills tests, and had other students rate each participant's physical attractiveness. During an intermission at the dance, students rated how desirable they found their partner. Did any of the psychological characteristics predict who would like whom? No. Only one factor did. Women and men with physically attractive partners liked them more and had a stronger desire to date them again. Similarly, among 100 gay men whom researchers paired together for a date, men's liking for their partner and desire to date him again were most strongly influenced by the partner's physical attractiveness (Sergios and Cody, 1985–6).

Facial attractiveness: is 'average' beautiful? Given beauty's power, what makes a face physically attractive? Beauty may be in the eye of the beholder, but within and across cultures, people are seeing through similar eyes; their ratings of facial attractiveness agree strongly (Langlois et al., 2000).

Look at face 3 and face 5 in Figure 14.31. The first thing you need to know is that these people do not exist. These photographs are composites, 'averaged' male and female faces created digitally by blending 16 photographs of young men and 16 photographs of young women (Johnston et al., 2001). Using different sets of photographs, studies in North America, Europe and Asia consistently find that people typically rate 'averaged' male and female faces as more attractive than almost all of the individual faces used to create the composites (Langlois and Roggman, 1990). Moreover, people perceive individual faces as more attractive when those faces are digitally modified to look more like the 'averaged' face (Rhodes et al., 2001). One reason that averaged faces seem more attractive is that they are more symmetrical, and people prefer facial symmetry (B. Jones et al., 2004). However, even when viewing faces from the side, where symmetry is not an issue, averaged faces are still rated as more attractive.

As Gestalt psychologists noted, in visual perception, the whole is more than the sum of its parts. As individual facial features – noses, eyes, lips, and so on – conform more to an 'averaged' norm, we perceive the 'whole face' as more attractive. But keep in mind that some individual faces, which deviate from their composite, are rated the most attractive of all. Moreover, as Figure 14.31 shows, some researchers have taken composite faces and digitally altered them to progressively appear more masculine (e.g., larger jaw and brow ridges) or more feminine

FIGURE 14.30

Many species, such as these frigate birds (male on the left), have evolved distinct features and ritualized mating displays to attract a potential mate's attention.

In-Psych

Watch the 'Attraction and Mate Selection' video in Chapter 14 of the In-Psych programme online to see a lively debate between two prominent researchers in this field.

FIGURE 14.31

Judging beauty.

Which male face do you find most attractive? Which female face? Face 3 and face 5 are 'averaged' composite photographs digitally created by blending photographs of 16 men and 16 women, respectively. These averaged composites were then digitally altered to accentuate either masculine or feminine features. Faces 1 and 7 are extremely masculinized and feminized, respectively; faces 2 and 6, moderately so. Face 4 blends the masculine and feminine features. In actual experiments, masculinization–feminization changes typically are done very gradually, creating many more choices than you see here.

SOURCE: from Johnston et al., 2001, fig. 1. Adapted with permission.

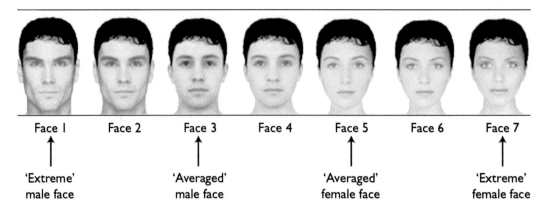

| Face 1 | Face 2 | Face 3 | Face 4 | Face 5 | Face 6 | Face 7 |

'Extreme' male face   'Averaged' male face   'Averaged' female face   'Extreme' female face

(e.g., fuller lips, a narrower jaw). Consistently, people perceive moderately feminized composite faces as the most attractive (Johnston et al., 2001; Perret et al., 1998). In contrast, depending on the study, male faces that have been somewhat masculinized or feminized are rated as the most attractive.

Affiliating with beautiful people   What motivates the desire to affiliate with attractive people? One factor may be the widespread stereotype that 'what is beautiful is good'; we often assume that attractive people have more positive personality characteristics than unattractive people. The popular media reinforce this stereotype. Analysing five decades of top-grossing US movies, Stephen Smith and co-workers (1999) found that good-looking male and female characters were portrayed as more intelligent, moral and sociable than less attractive characters. Because we are often judged by the company we keep, we also may prefer to associate with attractive people to buttress our self-esteem (Richardson, 1991). Evolutionary psychologists propose that we are biologically predisposed to be drawn to attractive people. They point to research showing that newborns prefer to look at attractive faces (Slater et al., 1998) and that 6-month-olds can categorize faces as attractive or unattractive (Ramsey et al., 2004).

Lest you conclude that beauty is the key to happiness, we should note that physical attractiveness during the college years is unrelated to life satisfaction in middle age (Kaner, 1995). And physically attractive people do not necessarily have the highest levels of self-esteem. Beauty is sometimes linked with self-doubt, because highly attractive individuals may attribute the positive responses of others solely to their surface beauty rather than to their inner personal qualities.

Although we are attracted to 'beautiful people', romantic relationships typically reveal a **matching effect**: we are most likely to have a partner whose level of physical attractiveness is similar to our own (Feingold, 1988). In this case, 'birds of equally attractive feathers flock together'. One reason for this is that the most attractive people may match up first and are 'taken', then the next most attractive people match up, and so on. Another factor is that people may refrain from approaching potential dating partners who are more attractive than they are to lessen the risk of rejection.

As Attraction Deepens: Close Relationships

Budding relationships grow closer as people share more diverse and meaningful experiences (Altman and Taylor, 1973). *Self-disclosure* – the sharing of innermost thoughts and feelings – plays a key role (Dindia, 2002). In friendships, dating relationships and marriages, more extensive and intimate self-disclosure is associated with greater emotional involvement and relationship satisfaction. This relation is reciprocal. Self-disclosure fosters intimacy and trust, and intimacy and trust encourage self-disclosure.

Social exchange theory proposes that the course of a relationship is governed by rewards and costs that the partners experience (Thibaut and Kelley, 1959). Rewards include companionship,

matching effect

we are most likely to have a partner whose level of physical attractiveness is similar to our own

social exchange theory

the course of a relationship is governed by rewards and costs that the partners experience

emotional support and the satisfaction of other needs. Costs may include the effort spent to maintain the relationship, arguments, conflicting goals, and so forth. The overall *outcome* (rewards minus costs) in a relationship can be positive or negative.

Outcomes are evaluated against two standards (Fig. 14.32). The first, called the *comparison level*, is the outcome that a person has grown to expect in relationships, and it influences the person's *satisfaction* with the present relationship. Outcomes that meet or exceed the comparison level are satisfying; those that fall below this standard are dissatisfying. The second standard, called the *comparison level for alternatives*, focuses on potential alternatives to the relationship, and it influences the person's degree of *commitment*. Even when a relationship is satisfying, partners may feel low commitment if they perceive that something better is available. In turn, the partners' sense of commitment helps predict whether they will remain together or end their relationship in the future (Sprecher, 2001).

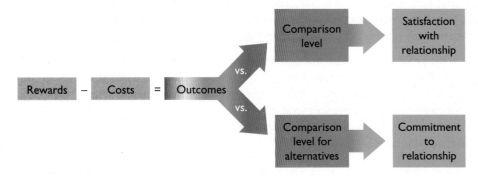

FIGURE 14.32

Social relationships: are you satisfied and committed?

According to Thibaut and Kelley's (1959) social exchange theory, rewards minus costs equal the outcome of a relationship. Comparing our outcomes with two standards, the comparison level and the comparison level for alternatives, determines our satisfaction and commitment to the relationship, respectively.

Sociocultural and Evolutionary Views

According to social exchange theory, a partner's desirable characteristics can be viewed as rewards, whereas undesirable characteristics represent costs. But what specific characteristics do people desire in a partner? In a massive study involving 10 000 men and women from 37 cultures around the world, evolutionary psychologist David Buss and co-workers asked people to identify the qualities they sought in an ideal long-term mate (Buss, 1989; Buss et al., 1990). Overall, for both sexes, mutual attraction/love, dependable character, emotional stability and a pleasing disposition emerged (in that order) as the most highly rated of the 18 characteristics evaluated.

Focus 14.19

Based on social exchange theory, what factors determine whether a relationship will be satisfying and will continue?

The importance attached to many qualities, however, varied considerably across cultures. For example, whereas American men and women viewed refinement/neatness as having only modest importance, Iranian men and women viewed it as the most important quality they desired in a mate. In many cultures, a mate's chastity (no previous experience in sexual intercourse) was viewed as last or near last in importance, but in China and India, men and women viewed chastity as an important quality in a mate.

There also are remarkably consistent sex differences in mate preferences across cultures. Men tend to place greater value on a potential mate's physical attractiveness and domestic skills, whereas women place greater value on a potential mate's earning potential, status and ambitiousness. Men tend to desire a mate who is a few years younger, whereas women desire a mate who is a few years older. Men also are more likely to desire and pursue a greater number of short-term romantic encounters than are women (Schmitt et al., 2001).

As we discussed in detail in Chapter 10, some evolutionary psychologists argue that these sex differences reflect inherited predispositions, shaped by natural selection in response to different adaptive problems that men and women have faced over the ages (Buss and Schmitt, 1993; Schmitt et al., 2001). According to the *sexual strategies theory*, ancestral men who were predisposed to have sex with more partners increased the likelihood of fathering more children

Focus 14.20

Contrast evolutionary and sociocultural explanations for sex differences in mate preferences.

Focus 14.21

Describe types of love, and discuss research-based principles that may help enhance relationship quality.

attachment

a deep bond between two individuals

passionate love

intense emotion, arousal, and yearning for the partner

companionate love

affection and deep caring about the partner's well-being

triangular theory of love

love involves three major components: passion, intimacy and commitment

and passing on their genes. Such men may have perceived a woman's youth and attractive appearance as signs that she was fertile and had many years left to bear children (Buss, 1989). Ancestral women, however, maximized their reproductive success by selecting mates who were willing and able to commit time, energy and other resources (e.g., food, shelter, protection) to the family (Buss, 1989).

Do men and women have different biological wiring when it comes to romantic attraction and relationships? *Social structure theory* proposes that most of these sex differences in mating strategies and preferences occur because society directs men into more advantaged social and economic roles (Eagly and Wood, 1999; Johannesen-Schmidt and Eagly, 2002). As this theory predicts, in cultures with more gender equality, many of the sex differences in mate preferences shrink. Women place less emphasis, for example, on a mate's earning power and status, and men and women seek mates more similar in age. Men's tendency to place more emphasis on a mate's physical attractiveness, however, does not decrease in such cultures. But it is still a leap, say critics, to conclude that sex differences in mating preferences reflect a hereditary predisposition rather than some other aspect of gender socialization that may be consistent across cultures.

This issue is far from settled, but perhaps the most important point for you to realize is that the notion that men and women come from 'different planets' when it comes to attraction, romance and close relationships is more pop psychology than reliable science. Sex differences exist, but cross-cultural differences tend to be stronger. That is, men and women within the same culture are typically more similar to one another than are men from different cultures or women from different cultures (Buss et al., 1990).

Indeed, even some evolutionary theorists disagree with the sexual strategies model. Cindy Hazan and Lisa Diamond (2000) argue that evolution has shaped the human psyche towards seeking **attachment**, a deep bond between two individuals. In their view, the same biological hard-wiring that predisposes infants to bond with a caregiver also steers adult humans towards becoming attached to a mate. As they note: 'The (over)emphasis on sex differences has distracted us from the reality that men and women are basically similar in what they seek in a mate, the processes by which they become attached to a mate, and the benefits that accrue to them as a result of being in a stable pair bond' (Hazan and Diamond, 2000, p. 194).

Love

Love must be powerful, for as a common adage says, 'it makes the world go round'. Indeed, Buss and co-workers (1990) found that mutual attraction/love was highly valued in a mate across cultures. But what is love?

When it comes to romantic relationships, many psychologists identify two basic types of love: *passionate* and *companionate* (Hatfield, 1988). **Passionate love** involves intense emotion, arousal, and yearning for the partner. We may ride an emotional roller coaster that ranges from ecstasy when the partner is present to heartsickness when the person is absent. **Companionate love** involves affection and deep caring about the partner's well-being. At least when studied in westernized countries, both types of love contribute to satisfaction in long-term romantic relationships (Sprecher and Regan, 1998). In general, passionate love is less stable and declines more quickly over time than companionate love, but this does not mean that the flames of passionate love inevitably extinguish.

Psychologist Robert Sternberg (1988; 1997), however, views love as more complex. His **triangular theory of love** proposes that love involves three major components: passion, intimacy and commitment. Passion refers to feelings of physical attraction and sexual desire; *intimacy* involves closeness, sharing, and valuing one's partner; and *commitment* represents a decision to remain in the relationship. Research suggests that these three components do a good job of capturing the way people commonly think about love (Aron and Westbay, 1996).

Figure 14.33 shows that different combinations of these components characterize seven types of love (plus *non-love*, which is the absence of all three). Sternberg proposes that the ultimate form of love between people – *consummate love* – occurs when intimacy, passion and commitment are all present. Clearly, for close relationships to develop and endure, they need more than passion alone. Intimacy and commitment provide a basis for the friendship and trust that sustain and increase love. As our 'Applying psychological science' feature highlights, other behaviours also help make close relationships successful.

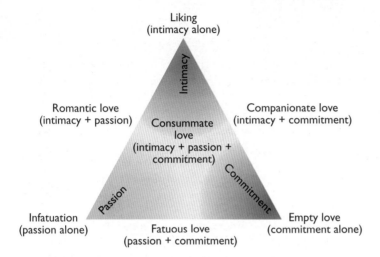

FIGURE 14.33

The complexity of love.

According to Sternberg, different types of love involve varying combinations of intimacy, commitment and passion. Consummate love involves the presence of all three factors, whereas non-love represents the absence of all three.

APPLYING PSYCHOLOGICAL SCIENCE

MAKING CLOSE RELATIONSHIPS WORK: LESSONS FROM PSYCHOLOGICAL RESEARCH

Close relationships go through good times and bad, persisting or dissolving over time. Consider marriage. Although highly intimate, this union is often fragile, and many marriages end in divorce. How can people make their close relationships more satisfying and stable? Research on marriage suggests several answers that also can be applied to dating relationships and friendships.

For decades, most marital research simply asked people about their marriages. But as Figure 14.34 shows, researchers are now bringing couples into laboratories to videotape their interactions and chart their facial reactions, stress hormones and other physiological responses as they discuss emotionally charged issues (Kiecolt-Glaser et al., 2003). Rather than focusing only on unhappy couples to find out what is going wrong in their relationships, researchers are also studying happy couples to discover the secrets of their success.

Using these methods, psychologists have predicted with impressive accuracy whether marriages will last or dissolve. In one laboratory study, John Gottman and co-workers (1998) collected behavioural and physiological data from 130 newly wed couples as they discussed areas of marital conflict (e.g., in-laws, finances, sex) during the first six months of their marriage. Six years later, participants reported whether they were happily married, unhappily married or divorced. Using data collected while the couples were newlyweds, the researchers predicted martial happiness/unhappiness and divorce with 80 per cent accuracy.

Surprisingly, the amount of anger expressed by husbands and wives in their laboratory interactions was not the predictor. Instead, the crucial factor was the manner in which couples dealt with their anger. Four behaviours were particularly important: *criticism*, *contempt*, *defensiveness* and *stonewalling* (listener withdrawal and non-responsiveness).

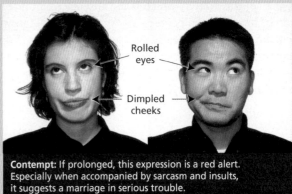

Rolled eyes

Dimpled cheeks

Contempt: If prolonged, this expression is a red alert. Especially when accompanied by sarcasm and insults, it suggests a marriage in serious trouble.

FIGURE 14.34

The 'love lab'.

In Gottman's 'love lab', married couples (husband shown in rear) are filmed while interacting. Researchers record facial expressions, actions, heart rate, breathing rate, perspiration, fidgeting and other responses.

Couples headed for unhappiness or divorce often exhibit these behaviours while discussing conflict, thereby escalating their conflict and negative emotions. When the wife criticizes the husband, he often responds defensively or stonewalls and withdraws from her attempts to reach some resolution. Her resulting frustration leads to stronger emotional displays and criticism, and the interaction degenerates into exchanges of contempt in which the partners tear each other down. Once this negative cycle develops, even positive overtures by one spouse are likely to evoke a negative response from the other.

Happily married couples also experience conflict and anger but keep the spiral of negativity from getting out of control. Instead, they make frequent 'repair attempts' to resolve their differences in a spirit of mutual respect and support. In happy marriages, the wife often introduces the conflict topic gently, rather than with criticism and strong emotion. Next a key factor occurs: the husband responds to the wife's issues with concern and respect, which de-escalates negative emotion. A husband who turns off the television and listens to his wife or who says, 'I can see you're upset, so let us work this out', demonstrates that her concerns are important to him. In happy marriages, after the husbands' responsiveness de-escalates the conflict, couples soothe one another with positive comments and humour, resulting in more emotionally positive interchanges and lowered physiological arousal.

Happily married couples maintain a much higher ratio of positive to negative interactions than couples headed for divorce, and this history provides a positive 'emotional bank account' that helps them repair and recover from their immediate anger and conflict (Wilson and Gottman, 2002). They also strive to get to know each other deeply – their fears, dreams, attitudes and values – and they continually update their knowledge. This allows each partner to be more responsive to the other's needs and to navigate around relationship roadblocks (Gottman and DeClaire, 2002). Such behaviour contributes to an essential aspect of happy marriages: an intimate friendship between the partners. The lessons of happy marriages can be applied to other types of close relationships, and affirmative answers to the questions in Table 14.1 suggest that such relationships are on solid psychological ground.

TABLE 14.1 HOW STRONG IS YOUR RELATIONSHIP?

Answer each question True (T) or False (F):		
I can tell you about some of my partner's dreams.	T	F
We just love talking to each other.	T	F
My partner is one of my best friends.	T	F
My partner listens respectfully, even when we disagree.	T	F
We generally mesh well on basic values and goals in life.	T	F
I feel that my partner knows me pretty well.	T	F
The greater the number of 'True' answers, the stronger your relationship.		

SOURCE: courtesy of John Gottman.

PRO-SOCIAL BEHAVIOUR: HELPING OTHERS

Helping, or *pro-social behaviour*, comes in many forms, from performing heroic acts of bravery to tutoring a class-mate. Acts of violence often dominate the headlines, but we should not lose sight of the mountains of good deeds performed around the world each day (Fig. 14.35).

FIGURE 14.35

Like this rescue worker, many people seek careers or join volunteer organizations that allow them to help other people.

Why Do People Help?

What motivates pro-social behaviour? Biological, psychological and environmental factors all play a role in motivating pro-social behaviour (Dovidio et al., 2006). Let us examine a few of these factors.

Evolution and pro-social behaviour   Pro-social behaviour occurs throughout the animal kingdom. Evolutionary psychologists and sociobiologists (biologists who study species' social behaviour) propose that helping has a genetic basis, shaped by evolution (Hamilton, 1964). According to the principle of **kin selection**, organisms are most likely to help others with whom

kin selection

organisms are most likely to help others with whom they share the most genes, namely, their offspring and genetic relatives

FIGURE 14.36

Spotting a predator, this female ground squirrel may sound an alarm call that warns other squirrels. Is the call truly a pro-social act, much like a human yelling 'Look out!'? Perhaps it simply indicates the squirrel's own sense of alarm, much as we might scream out of fear for our own safety. But if this is the case, why is she more likely to sound this call when her own kin – rather than other squirrels – are nearby?

Focus 14.22

Discuss evolutionary, social learning and empathy-altruism explanations for helping behaviour.

empathy–altruism hypothesis

altruism is produced by empathy – the ability to put oneself in the place of another and to share what that person is experiencing

they share the most genes, namely, their offspring and genetic relatives (Fig. 14.36). By protecting their kin, pro-social individuals increase the odds that their genes will survive across successive generations, and the gene pool of the species increasingly represents the genes of its pro-social members (West et al., 2002). In this manner, over the course of evolution, helping became a biologically predisposed response to certain situations. Sociobiologists note that identical twins are more similar in the trait of helpfulness than are fraternal twins or non-twin siblings (Rushton, 1989).

But what accounts for the abundant helping that humans display towards friends and strangers, and that some animal species display towards nonkin (Clutton-Brock, 2002)? Sociobiologists propose the concept of *reciprocal altruism*: helping others increases the odds that they will help us or our kin in return, thereby enhancing the survival of our genes (Trivers, 1971).

Critics question sociobiologists' generalizations from non-humans to humans, and in some cases kin selection and reciprocal altruism do not adequately explain why people or animals co-operate (Clutton-Brock, 2002). Sociobiologists counter that genetic factors only predispose us to act in certain ways. Experience also shapes helping behaviour.

Social learning and cultural influences   Beginning in childhood, we are exposed to helpful models and taught pro-social norms. The *norm of reciprocity* states that we should reciprocate when others treat us kindly, and the norm of social responsibility states that people should help others and contribute to the welfare of society (De Cremer and van Lange, 2001). We receive approval for adhering to these norms, receive disapproval for violating them and observe other people receiving praise for following these norms. Eventually, we internalize pro-social norms and values as our own.

Studies in Europe, Asia and North America confirm that socialization matters (Eisenberg, 2004). Children are more likely to act pro-socially when they have been raised by parents who have high moral standards, who are warm and supportive, and who encourage their children to develop empathy and 'put themselves in other people's shoes' (Krevans and Gibbs, 1996). However, there also are cross-cultural differences in beliefs about when and why we should help. For example, Joan Miller and co-workers (1990) found that Hindu children and adults in India believe that one has a moral obligation to help friends and strangers, whether their need is serious or mild. In contrast, when a person's need for assistance is mild, American children and adults view helping as more of a choice than an obligation.

Empathy and altruism   C. Daniel Batson (Batson et al., 2004) proposes that pro-social behaviour can be motivated by altruistic as well as egoistic goals. *Altruism* refers to unselfishness, or helping another for the ultimate purpose of enhancing that person's welfare. In contrast, *egoistic goals* involve helping others to improve our own welfare, such as to increase our self-esteem, avoid feeling guilty for not helping, obtain praise or alleviate the distress we feel when seeing someone suffer. Do humans truly have a capacity to help others without any concern for themselves? Batson believes that true altruism exists, and according to his **empathy–altruism hypothesis**, altruism is produced by empathy – the ability to put oneself in the place of another and to share what that person is experiencing (Batson, 1991).

WHAT DO YOU THINK?

DOES PURE ALTRUISM REALLY EXIST?

Do you believe that people ever help one another for purely altruistic reasons? Or is even a small degree of egoism always involved? Think about it, then see p. 658.

When Do People Help?

Ordinary citizens often go to great lengths to help strangers yet at times fail to assist people who are clearly in distress (Fig. 14.37). Recall the infamous Kitty Genovese murder discussed in Chapter 2. Genovese was stabbed and raped by an assailant outside her New York City apartment. It was about 3 a.m., the attack lasted for half an hour, and 38 of her neighbours heard her screams and pleas for help. Yet no one even called the police until it was too late, and Genovese died.

FIGURE 14.37

Why do bystanders sometimes fail to assist a person in need?

What, then, influences whether a bystander will intervene? Many situational and personal factors, such as not being in a hurry, recently observing a pro-social role model, and being in a good mood, increase the odds that we will help someone in need (Eisenberg, 2000).

Bibb Latané and John Darley (1970) view bystander intervention as a five-step process (Fig. 14.38). First, a bystander will not help unless he or she notices the situation. So imagine that as you walk along a street, you hear two people yelling and then hear a scream coming from inside a house. Now what? Many social situations are ambiguous, and step 2 involves deciding whether

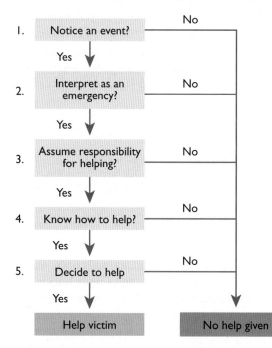

1. Notice an event? — No
   Yes ↓
2. Interpret as an emergency? — No
   Yes ↓
3. Assume responsibility for helping? — No
   Yes ↓
4. Know how to help? — No
   Yes ↓
5. Decide to help — No
   Yes ↓
   Help victim   No help given

FIGURE 14.38

When will a bystander intervene?

Bystander intervention in an emergency situation can be viewed as a five-step process. If the answer at each step is yes, help is given.

SOURCE: based on Latané and Darley, 1970.

this really is an emergency. To answer this question, we often engage in *social comparison*: we look around to see how other people are responding. You might say to yourself, 'No one else seems concerned, so it mustn't be serious'. In Kitty Genovese's murder, some bystanders mistakenly thought that because nobody else intervened they were merely witnessing a 'lovers' quarrel' (Darley and Latané, 1968).

If you conclude that the situation is an emergency, then you move to step 3: assuming responsibility to intervene. If you are the only person to hear someone screaming, then responsibility for helping falls squarely on you. But if others are present, there may be a *diffusion of responsibility* – 'If I don't help, someone else will' – and if each bystander has this thought, the victim will not receive help. In the Kitty Genovese murder, many bystanders who *did* interpret the incident as an emergency failed to intervene because they were certain that someone must already have called the police (Darley and Latané, 1968).

If you do take responsibility, then in step 4 your self-efficacy (confidence in dealing with the situation) comes into play. Sometimes, we fail to help because we do not know how to or believe our help will be ineffective. But even if self-efficacy is high, in step 5 you still may decide not to intervene. For example, you may perceive that the costs of helping outweigh the benefits (Fritzsche et al., 2000).

As this model indicates, the common-sense adage 'there is safety in numbers' is not always true when it comes to receiving help. Many experiments find a **bystander effect**: the presence of multiple bystanders inhibits each person's tendency to help, largely due to social comparison (at step 2) or diffusion of responsibility (at step 3). This inhibition is more likely to occur when the bystanders are strangers rather than friends; it even occurs when communicating over the Internet. Over a 30-day period, P.M. Markey (2000) sent a general request for help ('Can anyone tell me how to look at someone's profile?') to 200 chat groups. Assistance came more slowly from larger chat groups than from smaller ones.

Whom Do People Help?

Some people are more likely to receive help than others, for the following reasons:

1. *Similarity*: whether in attitudes, nationality or other characteristics, perceiving that a person is similar to us increases our willingness to provide help (Dovidio, 1984).
2. *Gender*: male bystanders are more likely to help a woman than a man in need, whereas female bystanders are equally likely to help women and men (Eagly and Crowley, 1986).
3. *Perceived fairness and responsibility*: beliefs about fairness influence people's willingness to help others (Blader and Tyler, 2002). For example, people are more likely to help someone if they perceive that the person is not responsible for causing his or her own misfortune.

Increasing Pro-social Behaviour

Can pro-social behaviour be increased? One approach, consistent with social learning theory, is to expose people to pro-social models. Psychologists have used pro-social modelling as part of a nationwide programme to increase blood donations (Sarason et al., 1991). Students in 66 high schools watched an audio-visual programme showing high school donors giving blood. Compared with a control condition presented with a standard appeal from the local blood bank, the pro-social video increased blood donations by 17 per cent.

Research suggests that developing feelings of empathy and connectedness with others also may make people more likely to help (Eisenberg, 2000), and simply learning about factors that hinder bystander intervention may increase the tendency to help someone in distress. Arthur Beaman and co-workers (1978) exposed some college students to information about the bystander effect. Control participants did not receive this information. Two weeks later, more than half of the students

bystander effect

the presence of multiple bystanders inhibits each person's tendency to help, largely due to social comparison or diffusion of responsibility

Focus 14.23

When and whom are people most likely to help? How can pro-social behaviour be increased?

who had learned about the bystander effect provided aid to the victim of an accident (staged by the researchers), compared with only about one-quarter of the control group participants.

AGGRESSION: HARMING OTHERS

We love. We nurture. We help. But as current events and the history of humankind attest, we also harm. In humans, *aggression* represents any form of behaviour that is intended to harm another person. What causes people to be aggressive?

Biological Factors in Aggression

From barnyard bulls to laboratory rats, animals can be selectively bred to be more or less aggressive (Lagerspetz et al., 1968). In some species, certain aggressive behaviours are reflexively triggered by specific environmental stimuli (Fig. 14.39). Humans do not display such rigid, inborn aggressive responses, but heredity influences why some people are more aggressive than others. Even when raised in different homes, identical twins display more similar patterns of aggression than do fraternal twins (Beatty et al., 2002).

Some theorists propose that, as in other species, a genetic predisposition towards aggression can be traced to evolutionary adaptation. Aggression at the proper time, they argue, helped our ancestors to compete successfully for mates, food and shelter, and to survive against attack. This increased the odds that individuals who were predisposed to such aggression would pass their genes on to the next generation (Rushton, 1989).

There is no single brain centre for aggression, nor one 'aggression chemical'. Electrically stimulate certain neural pathways in a cat's hypothalamus, and it will arch its back and attack. Surgically destroy areas of the amygdala – an approach that has been used with some violent human criminals – and in many species, defensive aggression will decrease (Aggleton, 1993). Especially in humans, aggression also involves activity in the frontal lobes – the seat of reasoning and impulse control. Deficient frontal-lobe activity makes it more difficult to regulate aggressive impulses generated by deeper brain regions (Raine, 2002).

Atypically low levels of serotonin activity appear to play a role in impulsive aggression, as when people lash out from emotional rage (Moore et al., 2002). In many species of mammals, higher levels of the sex hormone testosterone (found in males and females) contribute to greater *social aggression*, acts that establish a dominance hierarchy among members of a species. But in humans and other primates, the association between testosterone and aggression is weaker (O'Connor et al., 2002).

Environmental Stimuli and Learning

Our present environment and past learning experiences also influence aggression. *Frustration*, which occurs when some event interferes with our progress towards a goal, increases the risk of verbal and physical aggression, as do aversive events such as extreme heat, provocation, painful stimuli and crowding. But we do not always respond to frustration by acting aggressively. Inhibited by our internal moral standards, we may simply control ourselves and find non-aggressive ways of dealing with conflict (Anderson and Bushman, 2002).

Aggression, like other behaviours, is influenced by learning. Non-aggressive animals can be trained to become vicious aggressors if reinforcement is arranged so that they are consistently victorious in fights with weaker animals. Such operant conditioning also affects human aggression. Pre-school children become increasingly aggressive when their aggressive behaviour produces positive outcomes for them, such as when they successfully force another child to give up a desired toy (Patterson et al., 1967).

As Albert Bandura's (1965) classic 'Bobo doll' experiments (see Chapter 7) clearly demonstrated, aggression also can be learned by observing others. Children learn how to be aggressive

FIGURE 14.39

Sex and the stickleback: triggers for aggression.

During the mating season, the male stickleback fish develops a red belly. The sight of another red-bellied male – a potential rival for a mate – reflexively triggers an attack by the first male. The key releaser stimulus for this fixed action pattern is the red marking. A male stickleback will not attack a realistic-looking male model that has no red belly, but it will attack unrealistic fish models that have this red marking.

SOURCE: based on Tinbergen, 1951.

Focus 14.24

Describe how biological factors, environmental stimuli, learning and psychological factors influence aggression.

even when they witness an aggressive model being punished. Later, if the punishing agent is not present or if rewards are available for being aggressive, children are likely to reproduce the model's actions. Correlational studies, while not establishing cause and effect, find that aggressive and delinquent children tend to have parents who often behave aggressively (Stormshak et al., 2000).

Psychological Factors in Aggression

Many psychological factors affect whether we behave aggressively in specific situations. From gang violence to rape and war, people may employ several types of *self-justification* to make it psychologically easier to harm other people (Lanier, 2001). Aggressors may blame the victim for imagined wrongs or otherwise convince themselves that the victim 'deserves it'. They may also dehumanize their victims, as the guard in the Stanford prison study did when he began to view the prisoners as 'cattle'.

Our *attribution of intentionality* and degree of empathy also affect how we respond to provocation. When we believe that someone's negative behaviour towards us was intentional, we are more likely to become angry and retaliate (Graham et al., 1992). When someone offends us and then apologizes, whether we forgive the person partly depends on how well we empathize with his or her viewpoint (McCullough et al., 1997).

Sigmund Freud believed that impulses from aggressive instincts build up inside us over time, have to be released, and then build up again in a never-ending cycle. His principle of **catharsis** stated that performing an act of aggression discharges aggressive energy and temporarily reduces our impulse to be aggressive. But how does one do this in a world where violence is punished? Freud proposed that we can channel aggressive impulses into socially acceptable behaviours (such as sports) and discharge aggressive impulses *vicariously* by watching and identifying with other people who behave aggressively.

If people cannot express their aggressive impulses, will the pressures build up and explode? Sometimes, meek or unassertive people do commit shocking and brutal crimes. These people, whom Edwin Megargee (1966) describes as having *over-controlled hostility*, show little immediate reaction to provocations. Instead, they bottle up their anger and, after provocations accumulate, suddenly erupt into violence. The final provocation that triggers their outburst is often trivial. One 10-year-old boy with no prior history of aggression stabbed his sister more than 80 times with an ice pick after she changed the channel during his favourite television show. After the aggressive outburst, such people typically revert to their former passive, unassertive state. Female prison inmates who score high on tests measuring over-controlled hostility are more likely to have committed a one-time violent crime than repeated violent crimes or a non-violent crime (Verona and Carbonell, 2000; Fig. 14.40).

Cases of overcontrolled hostility seem to be consistent with the concept of catharsis, but much research is not. For example, hitting a punching bag while thinking about someone who has just angered them increases – not decreases – people's subsequent aggressive behaviour towards that person (Bushman, 2002). And what about watching violent films and television programmes? Do these activities help people let off steam, as some stars in the entertainment industry claim?

---

catharsis
performing an act of aggression discharges aggressive energy and temporarily reduces our impulse to be aggressive

Focus 14.25
Discuss catharsis and social learning views on effects of media violence. Do violent video games promote aggression?

FIGURE 14.40

Overcontrolled hostility: behind prison bars.

Female inmates at a state prison completed psychological tests that identified whether they had high over-controlled hostility (High O-H) or low over-controlled hostility (Low O-H). Inmates with high over-controlled hostility – but not inmates with low over-controlled hostility – were much more likely to have committed a one-time violent crime than a non-violent crime or multiple violent crimes.

SOURCE: adapted from Verona and Carbonell, 2000.

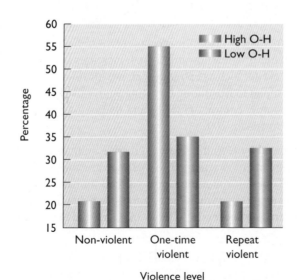

Media (and Video Game) Violence: Catharsis versus Social Learning

Many films and television programmes are saturated with violence. To psychodynamic theorists, media violence should be a cathartic pot of gold. But social learning theorists argue that by providing numerous aggressive models – including many that are reinforced – media violence is more likely to increase viewers' aggressive behaviour than to reduce it.

Headline-making 'copycat' acts of violence clearly illustrate social learning effects. Still, hundreds of millions of people are entertained by media violence, and few commit copycat crimes. What, then, are the more general effects of media violence on aggression? Over the past 30 years, hundreds of experiments and correlational studies have shed light on the 'catharsis versus social learning' debate.

To most experts, the verdict is clear: the evidence favours the social learning view (Johnson et al., 2002). For example, American children who watch greater amounts of television violence are more likely than their peers to display physical aggression when they become young adults (Eron, 1987; Huesmann et al., 2003). This association is not simply due to the fact that children who watch the most television violence are already more aggressive to begin with. Moreover, boys and girls who perceive television violence to be highly realistic and identify strongly with same-sex aggressive television characters are most likely to act aggressively as adults (Huesmann et al., 2003). Experiments in laboratory and field settings reveal a clearer causal link between watching media violence and behaving more aggressively (Leyens et al., 1975).

Media violence appears to exert its effects through multiple avenues (Huesmann, 1997):

- Viewers learn new aggressive behaviours through modelling.
- Viewers come to believe that aggression usually is rewarded, or at least rarely punished.
- Viewers become desensitized to the sight and thought of violence and to the suffering of victims.

Beyond films and television, the question of whether violent video games promote aggression also has raised much public and scientific concern (Fig. 14.41). In 2005 some Washington State legislators drafted a bill to make it easier for parents to sue violent video game manufacturers in cases where playing those games could be linked to the commission of violent crimes (KING Broadcasting Company, 2005). Political reaction or overreaction? What does science have to say?

FIGURE 14.41

Do children who play graphically violent video games become desensitized to violence and more likely to behave aggressively towards other people?

BENEATH THE SURFACE

DO VIOLENT VIDEO GAMES PROMOTE AGGRESSION?

American children and teenagers love violent video games. In one study of Midwestern junior high students, boys reported playing video games for 13 hours a week; girls, for five hours a week. Respectively, 70 per cent and 50 per cent of their favourite games had violent content (Gentile et al., 2004).

Do violent video games breed aggression? Psychologist and retired military officer David Grossman (1996) argues that humans have a natural inhibition against killing. In the Second World War, for example, only 15 per cent of soldiers fired at the enemy when they had a clear shot. This forced modern armies to develop behavioural training programmes that gradually overcome soldiers' reluctance to kill. Violent video games, say Grossman, have a similar effect: they weaken players' inhibition against aggressing towards others.

What does research say? At this point, a link between violent video game exposure and aggressive behaviour seems well established (Buckley and Anderson, 2006). In one intriguing study, male college students completed a questionnaire about their video game usage (Bartholow et al., 2002). Next, their brainwaves were monitored while looking at pictures displaying violent content (e.g., a man holding a knife to a woman's throat), negative but non-violent content (e.g., a baby with a larger tumour on her face) or neutral content (e.g., a man on a bicycle). Later, the students also performed a competitive task. Analysing the results, the researchers focused on a particular type of brainwave response that occurs when people evaluate emotional stimuli. As predicted by the desensitization hypothesis, students who reported greater violent video game exposure had weaker brainwave responses only to the violent images. In turn, students who displayed weaker brainwave responses to the violent images later behaved more aggressively at the competitive task.

Correlational studies of children and adolescents also suggest a link between video game violence and aggression. For example, compared with their peers, youngsters who have greater exposure to violent video games get into more physical fights with other people (Gentile et al., 2004). But as a critical thinker, you should keep in mind that correlation does not necessarily establish causation.

First, violent video games may cause youngsters to get into more fights. Second (the bidirectionality problem), perhaps getting into fights produces consequences (e.g., stress, anger, frustration) that prompt youngsters to play violent video games. Finally (the third-variable problem), perhaps these youngsters have a more hostile, aggressive personality to begin with, which causes them to play more violent video games and also to get into more fights. Indeed, Douglas Gentile and co-workers (2004) found that among young adolescents, those exposed to more violent video games also scored higher on psychological tests of hostility. So, to take this possible confounding factor into account, the researchers conducted special analyses that statistically adjusted for the hostility differences among adolescents. These analyses indicated that violent video game exposure was still correlated – albeit weakly – with a tendency to get into more physical fights.

Experiments in which researchers directly manipulate people's exposure to violent video games provide a clearer causal picture. Roland Irwin and Alan Gross (1995) randomly assigned 60 7- and 8-year-old boys to play either a violent or non-violent video game for 20 minutes. In the violent game, *Double Dragon*, the player assumed the role of a martial arts hero who kicks, punches and uses a rope or chain to whip and defeat ruthless street gang members. In the non-violent game, *Excitebike*, the player raced a motorcycle against the clock.

After playing one of the games, each child engaged in a 10-minute 'free-play' period with another boy (an accomplice). Next, as each participant competed against this boy on a task for a prize, the boy (according to plan) cheated. Compared with participants who had played *Excitebike*, those who had played *Double Dragon* displayed more physical and verbal aggression towards inanimate objects (e.g., toys), more verbal aggression towards the other boy during the free-play period, and more physical aggression towards the other boy during the frustrating competition.

Let us think critically about this result too, because even in experiments there may be confounding variables that provide alternative explanations for the results. For example, did *Double Dragon*'s violent content increase participants' aggression, or was it simply a more exciting game? If so, perhaps it was only greater arousal that led to more aggression? If you were the experimenter, what could you do to rule out this possible confounding factor? Irwin and Gross measured participants' heart rate both before and during the video game play. The result: no heart rate differences between the two video game conditions, strengthening the conclusion that the content of the violent game was the key factor.

To date, most studies employing this procedure have found that children's aggression towards peers increases after playing violent video games. Even among college students, briefly playing a violent video game (*Mortal Kombat*) increased women's and especially men's aggressive behaviour towards a female student (actually a confederate) who had earlier been aggressive towards them (Bartholow and Anderson, 2002).

THE BIG PICTURE

A recent meta-analysis of over 30 experiments and real-world correlational studies on violent video games indicates that:

- the evidence clearly does *not* support the catharsis hypothesis that playing violent video games decreases people's aggression by letting them blow off steam; and, to the contrary

- playing violent video games is linked to increased aggressive behaviour, thoughts and emotions (Anderson, 2004).

The overwhelming majority of children, teenagers and adults who play violent video games do not go out and assault or kill people. But aggression comes in many forms, physical and verbal, obvious and subtle. Still, continued research focusing on long-term effects is needed to pinpoint how strongly children and adults are affected by a world full of *Mortal Kombat* and *Doom*.

As we close this section on social relations, Figure 14.42 highlights some of the biological, psychological and environmental factors that contribute to human aggression.

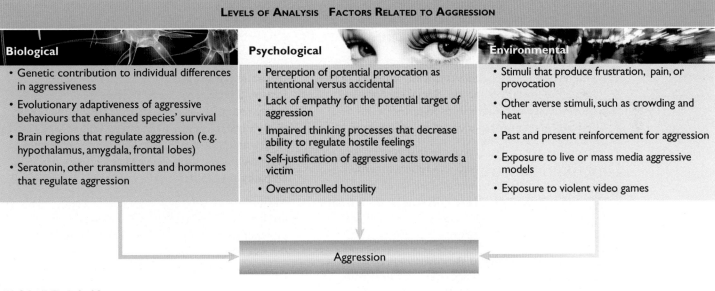

FIGURE 14.42

Levels of analysis: factors related to aggression.

IN REVIEW

- Categorization in in-groups and out-groups enhances the tendency to judge other people based on their perceived group membership rather than their individual characteristics.

- Prejudice stems partly from our tendency to perceive in-groups and out-groups. People typically display in-group favouritism and an out-group homogeneity bias. Perceived threats to one's in-group and a need to enhance one's self-esteem can motivate prejudice.

- People display explicit prejudice publicly. When people conceal or are not consciously aware of their prejudice, they are exhibiting implicit prejudice.

- Prejudice often is reduced when in-group and out-group members work closely together, with equal status, on tasks involving common goals, and under conditions of broader institutional support.

- Proximity, mere exposure, similarity of attitudes, and physical attractiveness typically enhance our attraction towards someone. Social exchange theory analyses relationships in terms of the rewards and costs experienced by each partner.

- Evolutionary theorists propose that gender difference in mate preferences reflect inherited biological tendencies, whereas sociocultural theorists believe that these differences result from socialization and gender inequities in economic opportunities.

- Partners are more likely to remain happily married when they understand each other and deal with conflicts by de-escalating their emotions and providing mutual support.

- Some theorists propose that through kin selection and reciprocal altruism, evolution has shaped a genetic predisposition towards pro-social behaviour among humans. Social learning theorists emphasize how norms, modelling and reinforcement shape pro-social behaviour.

- The presence of multiple bystanders may decrease bystander intervention through social comparison processes and a diffusion of responsibility for helping. We are most likely to help others whom we perceive as similar to us and as not responsible for their plight.

- Pro-social behaviour can be increased by enhancing people's feelings of empathy for victims and providing pro-social models.

- Heredity influences an organism's tendency to aggress. The hypothalamus, amygdala and frontal lobes play central roles in aggression.

- Provocation, heat, crowding and stimuli that cause frustration or pain increase the risk of aggression. Learning experiences help shape a tendency to behave more or less aggressively. People are more likely to be aggressive when they find ways to justify and rationalize their aggressive behaviour, perceive provocation as intentional, and have little empathy for others.

- Most research supports the social learning theory prediction that watching film and television violence and playing violent video games increase the risk that children and adults will act aggressively.

KEY TERMS AND CONCEPTS

Each term has been boldfaced and defined in the chapter on the page indicated in parentheses.

attachment (p. 644)

attitude (p. 609)

attributions (p. 602)

bystander effect (p. 650)

category accentuation (p. 633)

catharsis (p. 652)

central route to persuasion (p. 614)

collective self-esteem (p. 609)

communicator credibility (p. 613)

companionate love (p. 644)

deindividuation (p. 631)

discrimination (p. 633)

door-in-the-face technique (p. 616)

empathy–altruism hypothesis (p. 648)

equal status contact (p. 638)

explicit prejudice (p. 636)

foot-in-the-door technique (p. 617)

fundamental attribution error (p. 602)

group polarization (p. 629)

groupthink (p. 629)

implicit prejudice (p. 636)

informational social influence (p. 624)

in-groups (p. 608)

in-group favouritism (p. 635)

kin selection (p. 647)

lowballing (p. 617)

matching effect (p. 642)

mere exposure effect (p. 640)

norm of reciprocity (p. 616)

normative social influence (p. 624)

out-groups (p. 608)

out-group derogation (p. 635)

out-group homogeneity bias (p. 634)

passionate love (p. 644)

peripheral route to persuasion (p. 614)

prejudice (p. 633)

prevention goals (p. 608)

primacy effect (p. 605)

promotional goals (p. 608)

realistic conflict theory (p. 635)

referent informational influence (p. 625)

reflected appraisals principle (p. 607)

regulatory focus theory (p. 608)

self-discrepancy theory (p. 608)

self-esteem (p. 609)

self-fulfilling prophecy (p. 606)

self-perception theory (p. 612)

self-serving bias (p. 603)

social compensation (p. 629)

social exchange theory (p. 642)

social facilitation (p. 615)

social identities (p. 608)

social loafing (p. 628)

social norms (p. 622)

social role (p. 623)

sociometer (p. 609)

stereotype (p. 606)

stereotype threat (p. 638)

theory of cognitive dissonance (p. 611)

theory of planned behaviour (p. 610)

triangular theory of love (p. 644)

WHAT DO YOU THINK?

DO WOMEN DIFFER FROM MEN IN OBEDIENCE? (p. 621)

After we describe Milgram's research to our own students, one of the first questions they usually ask is, 'Did Milgram study women?' The answer is yes. After conducting the study described in the 'Research close-up', Milgram repeated the identical procedure with 40 women who, like the prior male participants, varied in age and occupation.

What was your hypothesis about sex differences in obedience? A few of our students predict no sex differences, but almost all expect women to differ from men. About half of them predict that women would be more likely to obey the experimenter's orders and keep shocking the learner all the way to the 450-volt level. Their rationale: given the traditional sex-role expectation that men are more dominant than women, and especially given how strong this expectation was at the time of Milgram's research (the early 1960s), women would be less likely to defy the authority of a male experimenter.

The other half of our class usually disagrees, predicting that women would be less obedient because they have more empathy than men for people who are suffering. Thus the learner's screams and pleas to stop would affect women more, and they would stop giving the shocks.

Are either of these hypotheses similar to yours? They both sound plausible, highlighting once again that different people have different 'common sense', leading to opposite predictions that cover all the bases. And what did Milgram find? In the study with men, 26 of 40 (65 per cent) obeyed fully. Among the women, the results were identical: 26 of 40 (65 per cent) obeyed fully.

Using procedures similar to Milgram's, other researchers also failed to find consistent sex differences in obedience rates. Occasionally, a particular study would find that women were more obedient than men, another would show that men were more obedient, while others – including Milgram's – found no sex differences in obedience rates. For example, in the obedience study by Burger that aired on *ABC News Primetime* in 2007, 73 per cent of the 22 women tested obeyed to the highest level – an obedience rate similar to the (65 per cent) among the men. Another study, conducted in Jordan, examined three age groups of boys and girls (6- to 8-year-olds, 10- to 12-year-olds, and 14- to 16-year-olds) who were placed in the role of 'teacher' (Shanab and Yahya, 1977). The experimenter was female, and the 'learner' was a confederate matched in age and sex to each participant (e.g., 10- to 12-year-old girls administered shocks to a similarly aged girl). Overall, 73 per cent of the participants were fully obedient, and neither their sex nor age significantly influenced the results. In sum, the most reasonable conclusion is that there are no consistent sex differences in obedience rates in studies like those conducted by Milgram.

DOES PURE ALTRUISM REALLY EXIST? (p. 649)

Do you believe that people ever help others for purely altruistic reasons? Perhaps your response is, 'Sure. Some Good Samaritans care only about the victim's welfare and even help people at a cost to themselves'. Certainly, people make anonymous donations to charity and help strangers when no one (including the recipient) finds out. In such cases we can seemingly rule out motives for helping based on gaining recognition or others' approval. But still, does not helping someone make us feel good about ourselves?

Moreover, by helping someone, do we not feel better knowing that the person's plight has been reduced? According to the *negative state relief model*, high empathy causes us to feel distress when we learn of others' suffering, so by helping them we reduce our own personal distress – a self-focused, egoistic goal, not an altruistic one (Cialdini et al., 1987).

Batson and many psychologists believe that while egoistic motives account for some pro-social behaviour, at times people do help others for purely altruistic reasons (Batson et al., 2002). Yet other psychologists remain unconvinced, arguing that some negative state relief is always involved (Cialdini et al., 1997).

Recent brain-imaging findings add some provocative fuel to this debate. Empathizing with someone else's pain does not produce the same sensations (i.e., somatosensory cortex activation) that we experience when we are in pain, but it does activate many of the brain areas (e.g., other parts of the cortex, brain stem, thalamus and cerebellum) that process emotional aspects of our own pain (Singer et al., 2004). Moreover, people who feel greater empathy for another's pain experience greater activation in these brain areas. So what do you think? Does this suggest that when helping behaviour stems from empathy, it does indeed involve negative state relief and therefore is not purely altruistic?

CHAPTER FIFTEEN

PERSONALITY

Much of our lives is spent in trying to understand others and in wishing others understood us better than they do.

GORDON ALLPORT

On a hot summer evening in 1966, a University of Texas student wrote the following letter:

I don't really understand myself these days. I am supposed to be an average, reasonable, and intelligent young man. However, lately (I can't recall when it started) I have been the victim of many unusual and irrational thoughts. These thoughts constantly recur, and it requires a tremendous mental effort to concentrate on useful and progressive tasks. In March when my parents made a physical break I noticed a great deal of stress. I consulted a Dr. Cochrum at the University Health Center and asked him to recommend someone that I could consult with about some psychiatric disorders I felt I had. I talked with a doctor once for about two hours and tried to convey to him my fears that I felt overcome by overwhelming violent impulses. After one session I never saw the doctor again, and since then I have been fighting my mental turmoil alone, and seemingly to no avail. After my death I wish that an autopsy would be performed on me to see if there is any visible physical disorder. I have had some tremendous headaches in the past and have consumed two large bottles of Excedrin in the past three months. (Lavergne, 1997, p. 8)

Later that night, Charles Whitman killed his wife and mother, both of whom were lovingly supportive of him. The next morning he carried a high-powered hunting rifle to the top of a 307-foot tower on the busy University of Texas campus in Austin and opened fire on all those passing by below. Within 90 horrifying minutes, he killed 16 people and wounded 30 others before he himself was killed by police.

On the surface, Charles Whitman (Fig. 15.1) seemed as solid and upstanding as the University of Texas tower from which he rained death on unsuspecting strangers. He came from a wealthy, prominent Florida family and was an outstanding student, an accomplished pianist, one of the youngest Eagle Scouts in state history and a former US Marine who had been awarded a Good Conduct Medal and the Marine Corps Expeditionary Medal. He married the woman of his dreams, and the two were seen as an ideal couple. Whitman became a University of Texas student when he was selected by the Marines for a prestigious engineering scholarship. In his spare time, he served as a scoutmaster in Austin.

FIGURE 15.1

(a) Charles Whitman with his wife, whom he later murdered. Few thought this exemplary citizen capable of the heinous acts of violence he committed. (b) Whitman (arrow) fires from the University of Texas tower onto the campus below.

What could have caused this exemplary citizen to commit such extraordinary acts of violence? On 18 December 2001, the Austin History Center opened its records on Charles Whitman to public scrutiny. These records provide important insights into the complexities of Whitman's personality and the turmoil that existed within him. Although the Whitman incident occurred decades ago, it is sadly reminiscent of more recent acts of violence in schools, communities and work places across the world. In this chapter, we consider the factors that triggered Whitman's violence through the lenses of the major personality perspectives. Doing so can help us paint a more complete portrait of Whitman and may further our understanding not only of him but also of others who commit acts of violence and terrorism.

WHAT IS PERSONALITY?

The concept of personality arises from the fascinating spectrum of human individuality. We observe that people differ meaningfully in the ways they customarily think, feel and act. These distinctive behaviour patterns help define one's identity as a person. As one group of theorists noted, each of us is in certain respects like *all other* people, like *some other* people and like *no other* person who has lived in the past or will exist in the future (Kluckhohn and Murray, 1953). Personality researchers attempt to describe these similarities and differences in an informative and predictive way so that we can understand better what it is to be a particular person.

The concept of personality also rests on the observation that a given person seems to behave somewhat consistently over time and across different situations. From this perceived consistency comes the notion of *personality traits* that characterize an individual's customary ways of responding to his or her world. Although only modest stability is found from childhood

Focus 15.1

Which behavioural observations give rise to the concept of personality? Identify three characteristics of 'personality behaviours'.

personality to adult personality, personality becomes more stable as we enter adulthood (Caspi and Roberts, 1999; Terracciano et al., 2006). Nonetheless, even in adulthood, a capacity for meaningful personality change remains (Lewis, 1999; Roberts et al., 2002).

Combining these notions of individuality and consistency, we can define **personality** as the distinctive and relatively enduring ways of thinking, feeling and acting that characterize a person's responses to life situations. Note that this definition refers not only to personal characteristics, but also to situations. Personality psychologists are therefore interested in studying 'person-by-situation' interactions in their efforts to understand the distinctive behaviours of individuals (Robins et al., 2007).

The thoughts, feelings and actions that are seen as reflecting an individual's personality typically have three characteristics. First, they are seen as *behavioural components of identity* that distinguish that person from other people. Second, the behaviours are viewed as being caused primarily by *internal rather than environmental factors*. Third, the person's behaviours seem to have *organization and structure;* they seem to fit together in a meaningful fashion, suggesting an inner personality that guides and directs behaviour (Fig. 15.2).

personality

the distinctive and relatively enduring ways of thinking, feeling and acting that characterize a person's responses to life situations

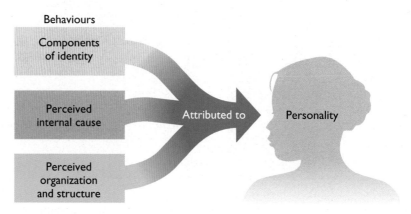

FIGURE 15.2

The behaviours of personality.

Certain perceived characteristics of behaviour are seen as reflecting an individual's personality.

The study of personality has been guided by a number of perspectives; notably, the psychodynamic, humanistic, biological, behavioural, cognitive and sociocultural perspectives. These perspectives often provide quite different conceptions of what personality is and how it functions, and this is summed up in the following quote: 'It seems hard to believe that all the theorists are talking about the same creature, who is now angelic and now depraved, now a black-box robot shaped by reinforcers and now a shaper of its own destiny, now devious ... and now hardheadedly oriented to solid reality' (Stone and Church, 1968, p. 4). It seems likely that this diversity of viewpoints arises partly from the fact that the theorists are describing personality at different levels of analysis (see Chapter 1, and Fig. 15.26), but it may of course also be because they have their own personalities that influence how they perceive and understand themselves and their world. No doubt, you will find some of their theories more in accord with your own life views than you will find others, but bear in mind that the different perspectives are not incompatible. It is possible to make meaningful observations about personality at multiple levels of analysis without contradiction.

Focus 15.2

What three standards determine the scientific usefulness of a personality theory?

Importantly, for personality psychologists, a theory's subjective truth (the degree to which it rings true in your own mind) is less important than its *predictive power*. As discussed in Chapter 2, a scientific theory is useful to the extent that it (1) provides a comprehensive framework within which known facts can be incorporated, (2) allows us to predict future events with some precision, and (3) stimulates the discovery of new knowledge. We evaluate each of the theories we describe in terms of these scientific standards. We consider a number of approaches to the study of personality, beginning with the seminal work of Sigmund Freud, whose psychodynamic theory set the stage for a century of progress in the study of personality.

IN REVIEW

- The concept of personality arises from observations of individual differences and consistencies in behaviour. Personality refers to the distinctive and relatively enduring ways of thinking, feeling and acting that characterize a person's responses to life situations. Behaviours attributed to personality are viewed as establishing an individual's personal identity, having an internal cause, and having a meaningful organization and structure.

- Personality theories differ considerably in their conceptions of what personality is and how it functions. Scientifically useful personality theories organize existing knowledge, allow the prediction of future events and stimulate the discovery of new knowledge.

THE PSYCHODYNAMIC PERSPECTIVE

The first formal theory of personality was advanced by Sigmund Freud in the early years of the twentieth century, and it is the prototype of the psychodynamic approach. Psychodynamic theorists look for the causes of behaviour in a dynamic interplay of inner motivational forces that often conflict with one another. They also suggest that many of these motivational determinants of behaviour are unconscious. Sigmund Freud's psychoanalytic theory of personality is one of the great intellectual contributions of modern times, and it continues to influence western thought today, not just in personality and abnormal psychology, but also in cognitive psychology, to which Freud contributed the notion of separate states of consciousness. Though Freud's approach is still taken by modern psychodynamicists, many psychologists from other disciplines, now have a strong opposition to Freud's ideas. Indeed, opposition to Freud was a stimulus for the development of most of the other theories discussed in this chapter.

FREUD'S PSYCHOANALYTIC THEORY

Freud (1856–1939) spent most of his life in Vienna, where he attended medical school with the intention of becoming a medical researcher (Fig. 15.3). He was particularly interested in brain functioning. A pivotal event in his life occurred when he was awarded a fellowship to study in Paris with the famous French neurologist Jean Charcot. Charcot was treating patients who suffered from a disorder called *conversion hysteria*, in which physical symptoms such as paralysis and blindness appear suddenly and with no apparent physical cause. Freud's experiences in treating these patients convinced him that their symptoms were related to painful memories and feelings that seemed to have been *repressed*, or pushed out of awareness. When his patients were able to re-experience these traumatic memories and unacceptable feelings, which were often sexual or aggressive in nature, their physical symptoms often disappeared or improved markedly.

FIGURE 15.3

Sigmund Freud is shown here with his daughter Anna, who herself became an influential psychoanalytic theorist.

These observations convinced Freud that an unconscious part of the mind exerts great influence on behaviour. He began to experiment with various techniques to unearth the buried contents of the unconscious mind, including hypnosis, *free association* (saying whatever comes to mind, no matter how trivial or embarrassing) and dream analysis. In an attempt to relieve his own painful bouts of depression, Freud also conducted an extensive self-analysis based on his own dreams.

In 1900 Freud published *The Interpretation of Dreams* (Freud, 1953). The book sold only 600 copies in the first six years after its publication, but his revolutionary ideas began to attract followers. His theory also evoked scathing criticism from a Victorian society that was not ready to regard the human being as a seething cauldron of sexual and aggressive impulses. In the words of one commentator,

> It is a shattering experience for anyone seriously committed to the Western tradition of morality and rationality to take a steadfast, unflinching look at what Freud has to say. It is humiliating to be compelled to admit the grossly seamy side of so many grand ideals.... To experience Freud is to partake a second time of the forbidden fruit. (Brown, 1959, p. xi)

Freud based his theory on careful clinical observation and constantly sought to expand it. Over time, psychoanalysis became (1) a theory of personality, (2) an approach to studying the mind, and (3) a method for treating psychological disorders.

Psychic Energy and Mental Events

Inspired by the hydraulic models of nineteenth-century physics, which emphasized exchanges and releases of physical energy, Freud considered personality to be an energy system, somewhat like the steam engines of his day. According to Freud, instinctual drives generate *psychic energy*, which powers the mind and constantly presses for either direct or indirect release. For example, a build-up of energy from sexual drives might be discharged directly in the form of sexual activity or indirectly through such diverse behaviours as sexual fantasies, farming or painting.

Mental events may be conscious, preconscious or unconscious. The *conscious mind* consists of mental events in current awareness. The *preconscious mind* contains memories, feelings, thoughts and images that we are unaware of at the moment but that can be recalled, such as a friend's telephone number or memories of your sixteenth birthday.

Because we can be aware of their contents, we are likely to see the conscious and preconscious areas of the mind as the most prominent ones. But Freud believed that these areas are dwarfed in both size and importance by the *unconscious mind*, a dynamic realm of wishes, feelings, and impulses that lies beyond our awareness. He compared the mind to an iceberg with the unconscious mind represented by the (much larger) part below the surface (see Fig. 15.4). Only when impulses from the unconscious are discharged in one way or another, such as in dreams, slips of the tongue or some disguised behaviour, does the unconscious reveal itself, sometimes with unfortunate consequences. Imagine that in the throes of passion, a young man proclaimed his love for his fiancée

FIGURE 15.4

Freud's model of personality.

Freud's own representation of his three-part conception of personality shows the relation of the id, ego and superego to the unconscious, preconscious, and conscious areas of the mind. Note how relatively small the conscious portion of the mind is compared with the unconscious.

SOURCE: adapted from Smith, 1998.

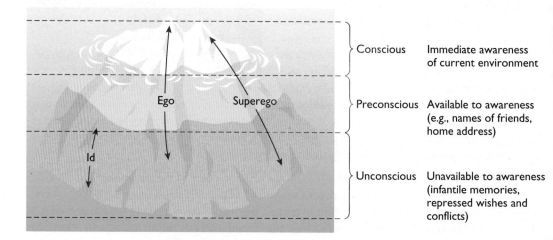

Conscious	Immediate awareness of current environment
Preconscious	Available to awareness (e.g., names of friends, home address)
Unconscious	Unavailable to awareness (infantile memories, repressed wishes and conflicts)

by saying, 'I love you, Alice'. A problem arises if it turns out that his fiancée's name was Amy, and Alice was a former girlfriend. Freud would probably have concluded (as might Amy) that the slip of the tongue was a sign that passionate feelings for Alice, which the man would obviously vehemently deny, were still bubbling within his subconscious mind. Psychoanalysts believe that such verbal slips are holes in our armour of conscious control and expressions of our true feelings.

The Structure of Personality

Freud divided personality into three separate but interacting structures: *id*, *ego* and *superego*. The **id** is the innermost core of the personality, the only structure present at birth and the source of all psychic energy. It exists totally within the unconscious mind (Fig. 15.4). Freud described the id as 'a chaos, a cauldron of seething excitations' (Freud, 1965, p. 73). The id has no direct contact with reality and functions in a totally irrational manner. Operating according to the **pleasure principle**, it seeks immediate gratification or release, regardless of rational considerations and environmental realities. Its dictum: 'Want … take!'

The id cannot directly satisfy itself by obtaining what it needs from the environment because it has no contact with the outer world. In the course of development, a new structure therefore develops. The **ego** has direct contact with reality and functions primarily at a conscious level. It operates according to the **reality principle**, testing reality to decide when and under what conditions the id can safely discharge its impulses and satisfy its needs. For example, the ego would seek sexual gratification within a consenting relationship rather than allowing the pleasure principle to dictate an impulsive sexual assault on the first person who happened to pass by. Freud wrote, 'In popular language, we may say that the ego stands for reason and sanity, in contrast to the id which contains untamed passions' (Freud, 1965, p. 238).

The last personality structure to develop is the **superego**, the moral arm of the personality. Developing by the age of 4 or 5, the superego contains the traditional values and ideals of family and society. These ideals are internalized by the child through identification with his or her parents, who also use reinforcement and punishment to teach the child what is 'right', what is 'wrong', and how the child 'should' be. With the development of the superego, self-control is substituted for external control. Like the ego, the superego strives to control the instincts of the id, particularly the sexual and aggressive impulses that are condemned by society. In a sense the id says 'I want!' and the superego replies 'Don't you dare! That would be evil!' Whereas the ego simply tries to postpone instinctual gratification until conditions are safe and appropriate, the superego, in its blind quest for perfection, tries to block gratification permanently. For the superego, moralistic goals take precedence over realistic ones, regardless of the potential cost to the individual. Thus the superego might cause a person to experience intense guilt over sexual activity even within marriage because it has internalized the idea that 'sex is filthy'.

With the development of the superego, the ego is squarely in the eye of a psychic storm. It must achieve compromises between the demands of the id, the constraints of the superego, and the demands of reality. This balancing act has earned the ego the title 'executive of the personality'.

Conflict, Anxiety and Defence

The dynamics of personality involve a never-ending struggle between instincts and drives in the id striving for release and counter-forces generated by the ego and superego to contain them. Observable behaviour often represents compromises between motives, needs, impulses and defences. When the ego confronts impulses that threaten to get out of control or is faced with dangers from the environment, anxiety results. Like physical pain, anxiety serves as a danger signal and motivates the ego to deal with the problem at hand. In many instances, the anxiety can be reduced through realistic coping behaviours, as when a person who is extremely angry at someone works out the problem through rational discussion instead of murderous assault. However, when realistic strategies are ineffective in reducing anxiety, the ego may resort to

Focus 15.3
Describe Freud's structures of personality, their operating principles, and how they interact with one another.

id
the innermost core of the personality, the only structure present at birth and the source of all psychic energy

pleasure principle
seeks immediate gratification or release, regardless of rational considerations and environmental realities

ego
has direct contact with reality and functions primarily at a conscious level

reality principle,
testing reality to decide when and under what conditions the id can safely discharge its impulses and satisfy its needs

superego
the moral arm of the personality

Focus 15.4

What roles do (1) conflict and defence and (2) psychosexual development play in Freud's theory?

defence mechanisms

unconscious mental operations that deny or distort reality

defence mechanisms, unconscious mental operations that deny or distort reality. Some of the defence mechanisms permit the release of impulses from the id in disguised forms that will not conflict with forces in the external world or with the prohibitions of the superego. The major defence mechanisms are described in Table 15.1.

TABLE 15.1 PSYCHOANALYTIC EGO DEFENCE MECHANISMS

Defence mechanism	Description	Example
Repression	An active defensive process that pushes anxiety-arousing impulses or memories into the unconscious mind	A person who was abused in childhood develops amnesia for the event
Denial	A person refuses to acknowledge anxiety-arousing aspects of the environment. The denial may involve either the emotions connected with the event or the event itself	A man who is told he has terminal cancer refuses to consider the possibility that he will not recover
Displacement	An unacceptable or dangerous impulse is repressed, and then directed at a safer substitute target	A woman who is harassed by her boss experiences no anger at work but then goes home and abuses her husband and children
Intellectualization	The emotion connected with an upsetting event is repressed, and the situation is dealt with as an intellectually interesting event	A person who has been rejected in an important relationship talks in a highly rational manner about the 'interesting unpredictability of love relationships'
Projection	An unacceptable impulse is repressed, then attributed to (projected onto) other people	A woman with strong repressed desires to have an affair continually accuses her husband of being unfaithful to her
Rationalization	A person constructs a false but plausible explanation or excuse for an anxiety-arousing behaviour or event that has already occurred	A student caught cheating in an examination justifies the act by pointing out that the professor's tests are unfair and, besides, everybody else was cheating too
Reaction formation	An anxiety-arousing impulse is repressed, and its psychic energy finds release in an exaggerated expression of the opposite behaviour	A mother who harbours feelings of resentment towards her child represses them and becomes overprotective of the child
Sublimation	A repressed impulse is released in the form of a socially acceptable or even admired behaviour	A man with strong hostile impulses becomes an investigative reporter who ruins political careers with his stories

repression

the ego uses some of its energy to prevent anxiety-arousing memories, feelings and impulses from entering consciousness

sublimation

taboo impulses may even be channelled into socially desirable and admirable behaviours, completely masking the sinister underlying impulses

Psychoanalysts believe that repression is the primary means by which the ego keeps a lid on the id. In **repression**, the ego uses some of its energy to prevent anxiety-arousing memories, feelings and impulses from entering consciousness. Repressed thoughts and wishes remain in the unconscious, striving for release, but they may be expressed indirectly, as in slips of the tongue or in dreams. Through the defence mechanism of **sublimation**, taboo impulses may even be channelled into socially desirable and admirable behaviours, completely masking the sinister underlying impulses. For example, hostile impulses may find expression in becoming a lawyer or a soldier. Although Freud described several defence mechanisms, his primary interest was in repression. His daughter Anna Freud, also a psychoanalyst, extended his ideas and described many of the defence mechanisms shown in Table 15.1.

Defence mechanisms operate unconsciously, so people are usually unaware that they are using self-deception to ward off anxiety. Almost everyone uses defence mechanisms at times, but maladjusted people use them excessively in place of more realistic approaches to dealing with problems.

Psychosexual Development

Freud's clinical experiences convinced him that adult personality traits are powerfully influenced by experiences in the first years of life. He proposed that children pass through a series of **psychosexual stages** during which the id's pleasure-seeking tendencies are focused on specific pleasure-sensitive areas of the body – the erogenous zones. Potential deprivations or overindulgences can arise during any of these stages, resulting in **fixation**, a state of arrested psychosexual development in which instincts are focused on a particular psychic theme. **Regression**, a psychological retreat to an earlier psychosexual stage, can occur in the face of stressful demands that exceed one's coping capabilities.

The first of these stages is the *oral stage*, which occurs during infancy. Infants gain primary satisfaction from taking in food and from sucking on a breast, a thumb or some other object. Freud proposed that either excessive gratification or frustration of oral needs can result in fixation on oral themes of self-indulgence or dependency as an adult.

In the second and third years of life, children enter the *anal stage*, and pleasure becomes focused on the process of elimination. During toilet training, the child is faced with society's first attempt to control a biological urge. According to Freud, harsh toilet training can result in a fixation which produces compulsions, overemphasis on cleanliness, obsessive concerns with orderliness and insistence on rigid rules and rituals (an 'anally retentive' person). In contrast, Freud speculated that extremely lax toilet training results in a fixation which produces a messy, negative and dominant adult personality (and 'anally expulsive' person).

The most controversial of Freud's stages is the *phallic stage*, which begins at 4 to 5 years of age. This is the time when children begin to derive pleasure from their sexual organs. Freud believed that during this stage of early sexual awakenings, the male child experiences erotic feelings towards his mother, desires to possess her sexually and views his father as a rival. At the same time, however, these feelings arouse strong guilt and a fear that the father might find out and castrate him, hence the term *castration anxiety*. This conflictual situation involving love for the mother and hostility towards the father is the **Oedipus complex**, named after the Greek character Oedipus, who unknowingly killed his father and married his mother. Girls, meanwhile, discover that they lack a penis, blame the mother for their lack of what Freud considered the more desirable sex organ, and wish to bear their father's child as a substitute for the penis they lack. The female counterpart of the Oedipus complex was termed the **Electra complex**.

Freud believed that the phallic stage is a major milestone in the development of gender identity, for children normally resolve these conflicts by repressing their sexual impulses and moving from a sexual attachment to the opposite-sex parent to *identification* with the same-sex parent. Boys take on the traits of their fathers and girls those of their mothers. Identification allows the child to possess the opposite-sex parent indirectly, or vicariously, and also helps form the superego as the child internalizes the parent's values and moral beliefs.

As the phallic stage draws to a close at about 6 years of age, children enter the *latency stage*, during which sexuality becomes dormant for about 6 years. Sexuality normally re-emerges in adolescence as the beginning of a lifelong *genital stage*, in which erotic impulses find direct expression in sexual relationships.

psychosexual stages
during which the id's pleasure-seeking tendencies are focused on specific pleasure-sensitive areas of the body – the erogenous zones

fixation
state of arrested psychosexual development in which instincts are focused on a particular psychic theme

regression
psychological retreat to an earlier psychosexual stage

Oedipus complex
conflictual situation involving love for the mother and hostility towards the father

Electra complex
the female counterpart of the Oedipus complex

Focus 15.5

How do neoanalytic and object relations theories depart from and build on Freudian theory?

NEOANALYTIC AND OBJECT RELATIONS APPROACHES

Freud's ideas generated disagreement even within his circle of disciples. **Neoanalytic theorists** were psychoanalysts who disagreed with certain aspects of Freud's thinking and developed their own theories. Among them were Alfred Adler, Karen Horney, Erik Erikson and Carl Jung. The neoanalysts believed that Freud did not give social and cultural factors a sufficiently important role in the development and dynamics of personality. In particular, they believed that he stressed infantile sexuality too much (Kurzweil, 1989). The second major criticism was that Freud laid too much emphasis on the events of childhood as determinants of adult personality. Neoanalytic theorists agreed that childhood experiences are important, but some theorists, such as Erikson, believed that personality development continues throughout the lifespan as individuals confront challenges that are specific to particular phases in their lives.

In contrast to Freud's assertion that behaviour is motivated by inborn sexual and aggressive instincts and drives, Alfred Adler (1870–1937) insisted that humans are inherently social beings who are motivated by *social interest*, the desire to advance the welfare of others. They care about others, co-operate with them, and place general social welfare above selfish personal interests (Fig. 15.5). In contrast, Freud seemed to view people as savage animals caged by the bars of civilization. Perhaps influenced by his own struggles to overcome childhood illnesses and accidents, Adler also postulated a general motive of *striving for superiority*, which drives people to compensate for real or imagined defects in themselves (the *inferiority complex*) and to strive to be ever more competent in life.

Like Adler, Carl Jung (1875–1961) was Freud's friend and associate before he broke away and developed his own theory. Particular points of disagreement between Jung and Freud concerned the nature of the motivational forces underlying the action of the id. While Freud emphasized the sexuality of the id, Jung argued that motivational forces of personality were not specifically sexual, but a more general form of energy which he termed the *libido*. Jung also expanded Freud's notion of the unconscious in unique directions. For example, he believed that humans possess not only a **personal unconscious** based on their life experiences but also a **collective unconscious** that consists of memories accumulated throughout the entire history of the human race. These memories are represented by **archetypes**, inherited tendencies to interpret experiences in certain ways. Archetypes find expression in symbols, myths and beliefs that appear across many cultures, such as the image of a god, an evil force, the hero, the good mother, and the quest for self-unity and completeness (Fig. 15.6). Jung's ideas bear some similarities to those of contemporary evolutionary theorists who emphasize innate cognitive processes.

FIGURE 15.5

In Alfred Adler's theory, people have an inborn social interest that can cause them to put society's welfare above their interests. Mother Teresa's selfless service to others is one striking example.

neoanalytic theorists
were psychoanalysts who disagreed with certain aspects of Freud's thinking and developed their own theories

personal unconscious
based on their life experiences

collective unconscious
consists of memories accumulated throughout the entire history of the human race

archetypes
inherited tendencies to interpret experiences in certain ways

FIGURE 15.6

Shown here is the famous neoanalyst Carl Jung. Behind him is a *mandala* (Sanskrit for 'circle'), which symbolizes wholeness and completion. The *mandala* symbol occurs within numerous cultures and religions of the world, suggesting to Jung that it is a reflection of the collective unconscious.

Following Freud's death in 1939, Melanie Klein (1975), Otto Kernberg (1984), Margaret Mahler (1968) and Heinz Kohut (1971) developed a new psychodynamic emphasis. **Object relations theories** focus on the images or mental representations that people form of themselves and other people as a result of early experiences with caregivers. Whether realistic or distorted, these internal representations of important adults – for example, of the mother as kind or malevolent, the father as protective or abusive – become lenses, or working models, through which later social interactions are viewed, and these relational themes exert an unconscious influence on a person's relationships throughout life (Westen, 1998). People who have difficulties forming and maintaining intimate relationships tend to mentally represent themselves and others in negative ways, expecting painful interactions and attributing malevolence or rejection to others (Kernberg, 1984; Nigg et al., 1992). These working models often create self-fulfilling prophecies, influencing the recurring relationships people form with others.

Adult Attachment Styles

John Bowlby's (1969) attachment theory, discussed in Chapter 13, is an outgrowth of the object relations approach. Correlational research relating early attachment experiences to later adult relationships is yielding provocative results. For example, college students with a history of positive early attachments tend to have longer and more satisfying romances (Shaver and Clark, 1996). In contrast, child-abusing parents often have mental representations of their own parents as punitive, rejecting and abusive (van Ijzendoorn, 1995). Table 15.2 shows descriptive statements that characterize people who manifest 'secure' ('autonomous'), 'avoidant' ('dismissive'), and 'anxious-ambivalent' ('enmeshed') adult attachment styles. These attachment styles are associated with adjustment and well-being. Three studies by Hankin and co-workers (2005) examined the relation between adult attachment dimensions and symptoms of emotional distress (anxiety and depression). Across all three studies, avoidant and anxious-ambivalent attachment predicted depressive symptoms, and anxious attachment was associated with anxiety symptoms. When people with these attachment styles seek treatment for their problems, anxious and avoidant attachment patterns also predict poorer response to psychotherapy because issues involving fear of abandonment and trust complicate the therapeutic relationship (Shorey and Snyder, 2006). Finally, attachment styles affect parenting. In one study, parents with avoidant attachment style reported that they found parenthood more stressful and less satisfying and personally meaningful because of difficulties in developing close and emotionally supportive relationships with their children (Rholes et al., 2006). Such difficulties may also help create an avoidant or anxious attachment style in their children.

> **Focus 15.6**
> What is meant by object relations? Describe three adult attachment styles.
>
> **object relations theories**
> focus on the images or mental representations that people form of themselves and other people as a result of early experiences with caregivers

TABLE 15.2 ATTACHMENT STYLES IN ADULT RELATIONSHIPS

Question: Which of the following best describes your feelings?*
1. I find it relatively easy to get close to others and am comfortable depending on them and having them depend on me. I don't often worry about being abandoned or about someone getting too close to me.
2. I am somewhat uncomfortable being close to others; I find it difficult to trust them completely, difficult to allow myself to depend on them. I am nervous when anyone gets too close, and often, love partners want me to be more intimate than I feel comfortable being.
3. I find that others are reluctant to get as close as I would like. I often worry that my partner doesn't really love me or won't want to stay with me. I want to merge completely with another person, and this desire sometimes scares people away.
NOTE: *The first type of attachment style is described as 'secure', the second as 'avoidant' and the third as 'anxious-ambivalent'.

SOURCE: based on Shaver et al., 1988.

Today, many psychodynamic therapists say that they rely more heavily on object relations concepts than on classical psychoanalytic theory (Jurist et al., 2008; Westen, 1998). The concepts in object relations theories are also easier to define and measure operationally, making them more amenable to research.

Attachment theory predicts that once attachment styles are set down by childhood experiences, they continue to play themselves out in adult relationships. The 'Research close-up' explores the possibility that this can result in abusive romantic relationships.

EVALUATING THE PSYCHODYNAMIC APPROACH

Freud was committed to testing his ideas through case studies and clinical observations. He believed that careful observations of everyday behaviour and clinical phenomena were the best source of evidence. He was opposed to experimental research because he believed that the complex phenomena he had identified could not be studied under controlled conditions (Rosenzweig, 1992). Most modern psychologists do not believe that clinical observations are sufficient proof, but they do acknowledge the difficulty of studying psychoanalytic concepts under controlled laboratory conditions (Carver and Scheier, 2003; Mischel et al., 2004). Indeed, a major shortcoming of psychoanalytic theory is that many of its concepts are ambiguous and difficult to measure or even to define operationally. How, for example, can we measure the strength of an individual's id impulses and unconscious ego defences or study processes that are by definition unconscious and inaccessible to the person? Current psychoanalytic approaches supplement Freud's clinical methods with projective tests of personality such as the *Rorschach Inkblot Test* and the *Thematic Apperceptions Test*. These are explained at the end of the chapter in the section on personality assessment. However, as we shall see, the reliability of these measures is also brought into question.

Although psychoanalytic theory has profoundly influenced psychology, psychiatry and other fields, it has often been criticized on scientific grounds. One reason is that many of its specific propositions have not held up under the scrutiny of research (Fisher and Greenberg, 1996). To some critics, psychoanalytic theory seems to be more science fiction than science. A great drawback of the theory is that it is hard to test, not because it does not explain enough but because it often explains too much to allow clear-cut behavioural predictions (Meehl, 1995). For example, suppose we predict on the basis of psychoanalytic theory that participants in an experimental condition will behave aggressively but they behave instead in a loving manner. Is the theory wrong, or is the aggression being masked by the operation of a defence mechanism such as reaction formation (which produces exaggerated behaviours that are the opposite of the impulse)? The difficulties in making clear-cut behavioural predictions mean that some psychoanalytic hypotheses cannot be disproved, and this detracts greatly from the theory's scientific usefulness.

Freud's emphasis on the unconscious was scorned by a Victorian society that emphasized rationality, and later generations of personality psychologists with a behaviourist orientation condemned it as unscientific. However, research over the past 20 years has vindicated Freud's belief in unconscious psychic events by showing that non-conscious mental and emotional phenomena do indeed occur and can affect our behaviour (Chartrand and Bargh, 2002; Erdelyi, 2001). On the other hand, the unconscious processes that have been demonstrated experimentally are by no means as exotic as the seething cauldron of forbidden wishes and desires described by Freud (Kihlstrom, 1999). Rather, current research is unearthing what one theorist describes as 'a kinder, gentler unconscious' (Greenwald, 1992).

Freud's ideas about psychosexual development are the most controversial feature of his theory. Although many theorists reject Freud's assertions about childhood sexuality and the notion of specific psychosexual stages, there is strong evidence that childhood experiences do indeed influence the development of personality (Lewis, 1999). The previously wide gulf between psychodynamic theories and other psychological perspectives is starting to narrow, due largely to the development of new methods for studying unconscious mental processes.

RESEARCH CLOSE-UP

ATTACHMENT STYLE AND ABUSIVE ROMANTIC RELATIONSHIPS

SOURCE: V. Zayas and Y. Shoda (2007) Predicting preferences for dating partners from past experiences of psychological abuse: identifying the psychological ingredients of situations, *Personality and Social Psychology Bulletin*, vol. 33, pp. 123–48.

INTRODUCTION

Researchers who study abusive romantic relationships have noted that involvement in such relationships tends to repeat itself over time, and that such experiences are more common in women with an anxious-ambivalent attachment style (Dutton, 2006). Does this occur by chance, or is it possible that people with particular personality patterns somehow seek out one another to re-create destructive relationships marked by psychological abuse? One possibility is that adult attachment styles predispose people to prefer romantic partners who fit their working models of intimate relationships (Fig. 15.7). To test this hypothesis, Vivian Zayas and Yuichi Shoda studied the romantic partner preferences of women with a history of victimization and of men with a history of abusing women in romantic relationships within an Internet dating procedure.

FIGURE 15.7

Do adult attachment styles lead some women into abusive relationships?

METHOD

From students in large introductory psychology classes, two groups of women were identified. One group consisted of 32 women who reported being victims of frequent psychological abuse in their most recent long-term romantic relationship. On a 60-item measure of abusive behaviours, these women reported that experiences like the following had often occurred with their romantic partner during a 12-month period: *isolation and emotional control* (e.g., 'My partner tried to keep me from seeing or talking to my family'); undermining self-esteem (e.g., 'My partner treated me like I was stupid'); jealousy (e.g., 'My partner was jealous of my friends'); *verbal abuse* (e.g., 'My partner swore at me'); and *emotional withdrawal* (e.g., 'My partner sulked and refused to talk about a problem'). A comparison group of 33 low-abuse women reported that such experiences occurred seldom or never in their most recent relationship. The women in each group also completed a self-report measure of attachment style, including a scale of attachment anxiety that included items such as 'I worry a lot about my relationships'.

To create a real-life situation to assess romantic partner preference, the women participated in a computer dating procedure in which they indicated how much they would like to date each of 16 different men who provided descriptions of themselves. The self-descriptions of the men comprised statements that had been taken from actual descriptions of themselves given by college men. These statements were rated by a separate sample of women on desirability in a dating partner and potential for being abusive. Statements rated as high in potential for abusiveness reflected a predisposition towards anger (e.g., 'Warning ahead, I do have a very bad temper'), jealousy ('I do admit that I will get jealous if you are always going over to one of your male friends' houses'), themes regarding trust and emotional control (e.g., 'I will treat you like God until you break my trust and then you are just another person'), and possessiveness. The ratings of desirability and abuse potential were used to create potential male dating partners who fell into three categories: (1) potentially abusive (four advertisements); (2) undesirable as a dating partner but not abusive (eight advertisements); and (3) desirable as a dating partner and not abusive (four advertisements).

The high-abuse and low-abuse women viewed each of the 16 personal advertisements on an experimenter-constructed website, where each male's advertisements had a separate web page with his description of himself but no picture. They made four rounds of forced-choice selections. In the first round, they selected eight of the 16 advertisements that were most preferable to them. In the second round, they selected four of the eight, in the third round, two of the four, and in the final round they selected the person they were most interested in getting to know better.

In a second part of the study, college men were administered the psychological abuse questionnaire that the women had completed and were asked how often they had engaged in the abusive behaviours in their previous romantic relationship. The researchers identified 46 men who were abusive and 47 who reported inflicting little or no abuse. These two groups of men engaged in an identical internet dating procedure as the women, except that the personal advertisements of the women were designed to either express high or low levels of attachment anxiety. Eight of the descriptions suggested high attachment anxiety and eight did not. The attachment anxiety statements in the personal advertisements were drawn from the measure used to assess attachment anxiety in the women's portion of the study, and an independent sample of men rated the descriptions of these potential dating partners as indicating higher relationship anxiety.

Research design		
Question:	How is a history of having been psychologically abused or having been the perpetrator of psychological abuse related to preferred characteristics of future dating?	
Type of Study: *Correlational*		

Variable X		Variable Y
Abused vs. non-abused women Abusing vs. non-abusing men	→	Characteristics of most-preferred dating partner

RESULTS

The researchers first examined the relationship between attachment anxiety and past abuse. In agreement with previous research, they found that the high-abuse women were significantly more anxious about their close relationships and fearful of losing them.

Of major interest were the dating preferences of the two groups of women. Table 15.3a shows the percentages of high-abuse and low-abuse women whose top choice from among the 16 was either a desirable, an undesirable or an abusive partner. The low-abuse women overwhelmingly preferred a desirable partner, and very few of them chose one of the potentially abusive men. In striking contrast, the high-abuse women were three times as likely to choose one of the four potentially abusive dating partners, and nearly as likely to choose an abusive partner as a desirable one.

The men's dating preferences are shown in Table 15.3b. Here again, we see a notable contrast. The vast majority of the non-abusive men preferred a woman who was low in attachment anxiety, whereas a majority of the abusive men chose a potential dating partner who was high in the characteristic of attachment anxiety, which this and other studies has shown to be common in women who are victimized by abuse.

TABLE 15.3 PERCENTAGES OF WOMEN AND MEN WHO CHOSE EACH TYPE OF DATING PARTNER

(a) Women's choices

Abuse group	Preferred male dating partner		
	Desirable	Undesirable	Abusive
Low-abuse women	66.7	21.2	12.1
High-abuse women	40.6	21.9	37.5

(b) Men's choices

Abuse group	Preferred female dating partner	
	Low attachment anxiety	High attachment anxiety
Non-abusing men	72.3	27.7
Abusing men	39.1	60.9

DISCUSSION

This study illustrates the potential usefulness of concepts derived from object relations theory in understanding human relationships. The notion that early experiences in intimate relationships produce working models of what is to be expected in future relationships has received considerable research support (Rholes and Simpson, 2006). In this study, we see evidence that people may perpetuate self-injurious and destructive relationship patterns. Women with histories of abuse in romantic relationships might be expected to steer clear of future relationships of this kind. Instead, they are as likely to choose a dating partner who has been judged by others to be impulsive, possessive, jealous, aggressive, hostile, degrading and potentially violent as they are to choose a desirable and non-abusive partner.

Men's personality characteristics also influence their choice of potential romantic partners. Men without a history of abusing women show little desire to relate to insecure, relationship-anxious women. In contrast, abusive men are drawn to these women who are more likely to become dependent on them and therefore tolerate their behaviour as they act out their hostile impulses within the relationship. Clearly, the choices of both men and women are based on 'psychological ingredients' of the situation, which includes the stimulus characteristics of the potential partner.

This study also raises several interesting questions that deserve research attention. The focus here was on psychological abuse, which probably occurs more often than physical abuse. Do these findings generalize to physically abusive relationships? Likewise, this investigation addressed relationships in which men abused women. What are the 'active ingredients' of partners in relationships in which men are psychologically abused by women? Answers to questions like these would increase our understanding of how personality and situational factors interact in destructive interpersonal relationships.

Understanding Charles Whitman

Can the psychodynamic perspective offer possible insights into Charles Whitman's personality and his eventual eruption into violence? Although born into a family of means and showered with material goods, Whitman grew up within a chaotic home environment. His father was a self-made but brutal man who ruled his house with an iron fist and frequently beat his wife. He tolerated no weakness from his sons and viciously belittled them for any perceived failures. Whitman was very close to his mother and deeply resented his father's treatment of her, which, according to Freud, would only enhance any unresolved Oedipal hostility towards the father. In his suicide note, he wrote, 'The intense hatred I feel for my father is beyond description' (Lavergne, 1997, p. 168). Lacking a good paternal model with whom to identify, Whitman seemed to have a poorly developed superego and constantly wrote himself notes about how to behave appropriately, using the notes as a substitute for his tenuous inner controls. A friend describing Whitman said he was 'like a computer. He would install his values into the machine, then program the things he had to do, and out would come the results' (Lavergne, 1997, p. 79).

Object relations theories also have applicability to Whitman. Despite his hatred for his father, his own family experiences caused him to enter his marriage with an internal working model of 'abusive husband' and 'submissive wife'. To his later regret, he beat his own wife on two occasions in the early years of his marriage. He was determined not to repeat this behaviour and kept a journal in which he constantly wrote self-instructions about how to be a good husband. For the most part, these external constraints were effective in keeping his intense hostility under control – until the accumulation of severe life stressors caused his controls to disintegrate. 'Unusual and irrational thoughts' began to intrude into consciousness as his defences were strained to the breaking point, and he eventually exploded into violence. The psychiatrist at the student health centre who interviewed him several months before the tower incident (referred to in Whitman's letter at the opening of this chapter as 'the doctor') found that he 'had something about him that expressed the all-American boy', but 'seemed to be oozing with hostility'. Whitman told the psychiatrist that he had frequent fantasies about 'going up on the tower with a deer rifle and shooting people', but the psychiatrist did not take them seriously because of his non-violent history (Lavergne, 1997, p. 137).

IN REVIEW

- Freud's psychoanalytic theory views personality as an energy system. Personality dynamics involve modifications and exchanges of energy within this system. Mental events may be conscious, preconscious or unconscious.

- Freud divided the personality into three structures: id, ego and superego. The id is irrational and seeks immediate instinctual gratification on the basis of the pleasure principle. The ego operates on the reality principle, which requires it to test reality and to mediate between the demands of the id, the superego and reality. The superego is the moral arm of the personality.

- The dynamics of personality involve continuous conflict between impulses of the id and counterforces of the ego and superego. When dangerous id impulses threaten to get out of control or when the environment poses dangers, the result is anxiety. To deal with threat, the ego may develop defence mechanisms to ward off anxiety and permit instinctual gratification in disguised forms.

- Freud's psychosexual theory of personality development held that adult personality traits are moulded by how children deal with instinctual urges and social reality during the oral, anal and phallic stages.

- Neoanalytic theorists modified and extended Freud's ideas in important ways, stressing social and cultural factors in personality development. Today, object relations theorists focus on the mental representations that people form of themselves, others and relationships.

THE PHENOMENOLOGICAL-HUMANISTIC PERSPECTIVE

The approaches we describe next were in part a reaction to Freud's conception of people as driven by 'those half-tamed demons that inhabit the human beast' (Freud, 1965, p. 202). In contrast to Freud, these theorists believed that our behaviour is not a reaction to unconscious drives and conflicts but rather a response to our immediate conscious experience of self and environment (Kelly, 1955; Rogers, 1951). This emphasis on the primacy of immediate experience is known as **phenomenology**, and it focuses our attention on the present instead of the past. These theorists also regarded themselves as humanists. They embraced a positive view that affirms the inherent dignity and goodness of the human spirit, as well as the individual's creative potential and inborn striving towards personal growth (Fig. 15.8).

GEORGE KELLY'S PERSONAL CONSTRUCT THEORY

> To the humanist every man is a scientist by disposition as well as by right, every subject is an incipient experimenter, and every person is by daily necessity a fellow psychologist. (Kelly, 1966, quoted in Maher, 1979, p. 205)

A theory developed by George Kelly (1905–67) in the 1950s has had a strong and pervasive influence on many other theorists. According to Kelly, people's primary goal is to make sense out of the world, to find personal meaning in it. When they are unable to do so, they experience uncertainty and anxiety. To achieve understanding, they try to explain and understand the events of their lives, and they test this understanding in the same way scientists do: by attempting to anticipate, to predict.

Kelly's primary interest was how people construct reality. They do so by their individual system of **personal constructs**, cognitive categories into which they sort the persons and events in their lives. In Kelly's theory, the personal construct system was the primary basis for individual differences in personality.

As noted in our discussion of concept formation in Chapter 9, all perception involves categorizing. Kelly maintained, that from birth onward, stimuli are categorized, given meaning and reacted to in terms of the categories, or personal constructs, into which they are placed. Every person has her or his own pattern of preferred personal constructs (such as 'good', 'bad', 'successful', 'powerful' and so on), which vary in personal importance. By understanding these constructs, the rules an individual uses to assign events to categories, and her or his hypotheses about how the categories relate to one another, Kelly believed that we can understand the person's psychological world. If we can understand the individual's internal world, then we can understand and predict that person's behaviour.

The same event can be categorized, or perceived, in entirely different ways by different people. For example, suppose that two lovers break up. One observer may construe the event as 'simple incompatibility'; another may think that one person was 'jilted' by the other; another might describe the breakup as the 'result of parental meddling'; another might call it 'a terrible development'; and a fifth might see it as 'a blessing in disguise'.

Rather than evaluating alternative constructions according to whether or not they are true (which we cannot know), Kelly examined the consequences of construing in particular ways.

FIGURE 15.8

The motivations underlying behaviour are much different for humanistic theorists than they are for Freudians. In the view of humanistic theorists like Abraham Maslow and Carl Rogers, creative and artistic accomplishments are a product not of intra-psychiatric conflict and sublimation but rather an expression of an innate tendency towards self-actualization.

phenomenology
study of immediate experience

Focus 15.7
What are personal constructs, and how do they account for personality differences?

personal constructs
cognitive categories into which people sort the persons and events in their lives

For example, if one of the people in the broken relationship interpreted what happened as 'being rejected', Kelly would try to discover the consequences for the person of construing the situation in that way. If the construction led to bad outcomes, such as feelings of worthlessness or the conclusion that 'No one will ever love me, and I'll never get involved again', then the task would be to find a more useful alternative (for example, 'I am someone who hasn't found the right person yet but who will if I keep trying'). Kelly, a clinical psychologist, saw psychotherapy as a way of demonstrating to clients that their constructions are *hypotheses* rather than facts. Once clients realize this, they can be encouraged to test the hypotheses that govern their lives, just as scientists do, and to replace maladaptive ones with more useful ones.

As people seek to understand events within the world, they develop habitual tendencies related to categorization of people and events. Such tendencies can be measured by tasks that determine the extent to which particular categories are used in making such distinctions (Robinson et al., 2004). Kelly developed a measure called the **Role Construct Repertory Test** (or **Rep Test**), to assess individuals' personal construct systems. In taking the Rep Test, you are asked to consider people or events in your life that are important to you. You then consider them in groups of three (for example, father, best friend, romantic partner) and indicate how any two of them are similar to one another and different from the third. In this way, the basic dimensions of similarity and difference that you use to categorize people and events – your personal constructs – will begin to emerge. The Rep Test can also assess other aspects of your construct system, such as the number of different constructs that you use.

In order to help clients experiment with new viewpoints and behaviours, Kelly developed a therapeutic technique called *fixed-role therapy*. He wrote role descriptions and behavioural scripts for his clients that differed from their typical views of themselves. For example, a shy person might be asked to play the role of a more confident and assertive person for two or three days, to think and act like a confident person. Kelly and the client would practise the role within the therapy setting to be certain that the client had a command of the required behaviours and the view of the world that a confident individual would have. Kelly hoped that by trying out the new role, the client might gain a first-hand appreciation for the ways in which different constructions and behaviours could lead to more satisfying life outcomes. Kelly suggested that the willingness to experiment with new roles and ways of thinking can help all of us develop in ways that enhance our lives.

CARL ROGERS'S THEORY OF THE SELF

Carl Rogers (1902–87), a colleague of George Kelly's on the Ohio State University faculty in the 1950s, was one of the most influential humanistic theorists. As a humanist, Rogers believed that the forces that direct behaviour are within us and that when they are not distorted or blocked by our environment, they can be trusted to direct us towards **self-actualization**, the highest realization of human potential.

The Self

The central concept in Rogers's theory is the **self**, an organized, consistent set of perceptions of and beliefs about oneself (Rogers, 1959). Once formed, the self plays a powerful role in guiding our perceptions and directing our behaviour. The self thus has two facets: It is an object of perception (the self-concept) and an internal entity that directs behaviour.

Rather like Piaget (see Chapter 12), Rogers theorized that at the beginning of their lives, children cannot distinguish between themselves and their environment. As they interact with their world, children begin to distinguish between the 'me' and the 'not-me'. The self-concept continues to develop in response to our life experiences, though many aspects of it remain quite stable over time.

Once the self-concept is established, there is a tendency to maintain it, for it helps us understand our relationship to the world around us. We therefore have needs for **self-consistency**, an

Role Construct Repertory Test (or Rep Test)

assesses individuals' personal construct systems

self-actualization

the highest realization of human potential

self

an organized, consistent set of perceptions of and beliefs about oneself

self-consistency

an absence of conflict among self-perceptions

Focus 15.8

Describe the roles of selfconsistency, congruence, threat and conditions of worth in Rogers's self theory.

absence of conflict among self-perceptions, and **congruence**, consistency between self-perceptions and experience. Any experience we have that is inconsistent, or incongruous, with our self-concept, including our perceptions of our own behaviour, evokes **threat**, *or anxiety*. Well-adjusted individuals can respond to threat adaptively by modifying the self-concept so that the experiences are congruent with the self. But other people choose to deny or distort their experiences to remove the incongruence, a strategy that can lead to what Rogers termed 'problems in living.' Thus a person who always attributes interpersonal difficulties to shortcomings in another person will be unlikely to consider the possibility that he or she may have some self-defeating behaviour patterns that deserve attention.

To preserve their self-concepts, people not only interpret situations in self-congruent ways, but also behave in ways that will lead others to respond to them in a self-confirming fashion (Brown, 1998). For example, if Camille has an image of herself as unlovable and certain to be rejected if she lets people get close enough to hurt her, she may behave in ways that distance others. When her behaviour is successful, others pull away from her, confirming in her mind that she is indeed unlovable. As Rogers frequently noted, people are pushed by self-consistency needs to behave in accord with their self-concept (Fig. 15.9).

According to Rogers, the degree of congruence between self-concept and experience helps define one's level of adjustment. The more rigid and inflexible people's self-concepts are, the less open they will be to their experiences and the more maladjusted they will become (Fig. 15.10a). If there is a significant degree of incongruence between self and experience and if the experiences are forceful enough, the defences used to deny and distort reality may collapse, resulting in extreme anxiety and a temporary disorganization of the self-concept.

The Need for Positive Regard

Rogers believed that we are born with an innate **need for positive regard** – for acceptance, sympathy, and love from others. Rogers viewed positive regard as essential for healthy development. Ideally, positive regard received from the parents is unconditional – that is, independent of how the child behaves. **Unconditional positive regard** communicates that the person is inherently worthy of love, regardless of accomplishments or behaviour. In contrast, *conditional positive regard* is dependent on how the child behaves; in the extreme case, love and acceptance are given to the child *only* when the child behaves as the parents want. A study by Assor and co-workers (2004) suggests long-term negative consequences of this child-rearing approach. University students who reported that their mothers and fathers used conditional regard in four domains (emotion control, pro-social behaviour, academics and sports performance) also experienced

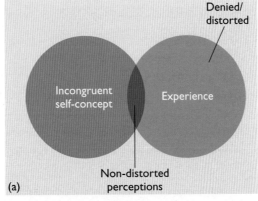

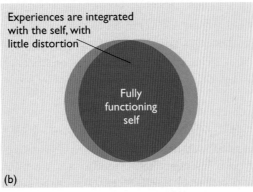

FIGURE 15.9

Tendencies to behave in accordance with one's self-concept can at times have ominous implications.

FIGURE 15.10

Degree of congruence between self-concept and experience.

(a) Maladjustment occurs when a person faced with incongruities between self and experience distorts or denies reality to make it consistent with the self-concept. (b) In contrast, extremely well-adjusted, or fully functioning, people integrate experiences into the self with minimal distortion, so that they are able to profit fully from their experiences.

up-and-down fluctuations in their self-esteem and perceived parental disapproval, and resented their parents as young adults.

People need positive regard not only from others but also from themselves. Thus a **need for positive self-regard**, the desire to feel good about ourselves, also develops. Lack of unconditional positive regard from parents and other significant people in the past teaches people that they are worthy of approval and love only when they meet certain standards. This fosters the development of **conditions of worth** that dictate the circumstances under which we approve or disapprove of ourselves. A child who experiences parental approval when behaving in a friendly fashion but disapproval whenever she becomes angry or aggressive may come to disapprove of her own angry feelings, even when they are justified. As an adult, she may deny in herself all feelings of anger and struggle to preserve a self-image of being totally loving. Rogers believed that conditions of worth can tyrannize people and cause major incongruence between self and experience, as well as a need to deny or distort important aspects of experience. Conditions of worth are similar to the 'shoulds' and 'musts' that make up the Freudian superego.

Fully Functioning Persons

Towards the end of his career, Rogers became particularly interested in **fully functioning persons**, individuals who were close to achieving self-actualization. As Rogers viewed them, such people do not hide behind masks or adopt artificial roles. They feel a sense of inner freedom, self-determination and choice in the direction of their growth. They have no fear of behaving spontaneously, freely and creatively. Because they are fairly free of conditions of worth, they can accept inner and outer experiences as they are, without modifying them defensively to suit a rigid self-concept or the expectations of others. Thus a fully functioning unmarried woman would be able to (1) state quite frankly that her career is more important to her than a role as wife and mother (*if* she truly felt that way), even if others did not approve of her choice, and (2) act comfortably on those feelings. In this sense, she could be true to herself (see Fig. 15.10b).

WHAT DO YOU THINK?

IS SELF-ACTUALIZATION A USEFUL SCIENTIFIC CONSTRUCT?

Self-actualization is a central concept for humanistic theorists such as Maslow and Rogers. Consider what you have learned about formulating a psychological construct and evaluating a theory according to scientific principles. Can you see any problems with establishing the existence of this core motivation from a scientific perspective? Think about it, then see p. 718 for a discussion.

RESEARCH ON THE SELF

By giving the self a central place in his theory, Rogers helped stimulate a great deal of research on the self-concept. Two topics at the forefront are (1) the development of self-esteem and its effects on behaviour, and (2) the roles played by self-verification and self-enhancement motives.

Self-Esteem

Self-esteem, how positively or negatively we feel about ourselves, is a very important aspect of personal well-being, happiness and adjustment (Brown, 1998; Diener, 2000). Table 15.4 shows the types of test items that are used to measure differences in self-esteem. Men and women do not differ in overall level of self-esteem on such measures (Brown, 1998; Maccoby and Jacklin, 1974).

---

need for positive self-regard
the desire to feel good about ourselves

conditions of worth
the circumstances under which we approve or disapprove of ourselves

fully functioning persons
individuals who were close to achieving self-actualization

self-esteem
how positively or negatively we feel about ourselves

TABLE 15.4 ITEMS SIMILAR TO THOSE FOUND ON SELF-ESTEEM SCALES*

1. I believe I am a worthwhile person
2. There are many things I would change about myself if I could. (reverse scored)
3. I approve of myself as a person
4. I have many positive traits
5. I like who I am
6. There are many things I don't like about myself. (reverse scored)

NOTE: *Items are scored on a scale ranging from −3 ('strongly disagree') to +3 ('strongly agree').

Level of self-esteem is quite stable over the lifespan, with correlations of .50 to .70 from childhood to old age (Trzesniewski et al., 2003). High self-esteem is related to many positive behaviours and life outcomes. People with high self-esteem are happier with their lives, have fewer interpersonal problems, achieve at a higher and more consistent level, are less susceptible to social pressure and are more capable of forming satisfying love relationships (Brown, 1998). In contrast, people with poor self-images are less likely to try to make themselves feel better when they experience negative moods in response to perceived failures in their lives (Heimpel et al., 2002). This may be one reason why they are more prone to psychological problems such as anxiety and depression, to physical illness and to poor social relationships and underachievement (Brown, 1998).

People who are low in self-esteem are more reactive to the ups and downs of everyday life. In one study, 15 working couples completed a daily diary and mood ratings during a three-week period. Low self-esteem men and women felt more loved and accepted by their spouses on days when they enjoyed professional successes, but less loved on days when they experienced professional failures. People high in self-esteem were not affected in this manner (Murray et al., 2006).

What conditions foster the development of high self-esteem? Children develop higher self-esteem when their parents communicate unconditional acceptance and love, establish clear guidelines for behaviour, and reinforce compliance while giving the child freedom to make decisions and express opinions within those guidelines (Brown, 1998; Coopersmith, 1967). Beginning in early childhood, success in achieving positive outcomes builds a sense that one is an effective person (Hawley and Little, 2002). Feedback received from other people also has an impact on the child's sense of self. One study showed that when low-self-esteem children were exposed to highly supportive youth sport coaches who gave them large amounts of positive reinforcement and encouragement, the children's self-esteem increased significantly over the course of the sports season (Smoll et al., 1993). Apparently, the positive feedback caused the children to revise their self-concepts in a positive direction.

Focus 15.9

How does self-esteem develop? Describe the roles of self-verification and self-enhancement as motivational forces.

Self-Verification and Self-Enhancement Motives

Rogers proposed that people are motivated to preserve their self-concepts by maintaining self-consistency and congruence. **Self-verification** refers to this need to confirm the self-concept. In one early study of this phenomenon, researchers asked university students to describe themselves in order to measure their self-concepts. In a later and supposedly unrelated experiment, the students interacted with other participants and received fake feedback from them in the form of adjectives that were either consistent or inconsistent with their self-concepts. Later, when the students were asked to recall and identify the adjectives that had been attributed to them, they showed greater recall for the consistent adjectives, suggesting that people selectively attend to and recall self-consistent information (Suinn et al., 1962).

self-verification

the need to confirm the self-concept

Self-verification needs are also expressed in people's tendency to seek out self-confirming relationships. One study found that if people with firmly held negative self-views marry spouses who appraise them favourably, they tend to eventually withdraw from the marriage. Such people are more likely to remain with spouses who agree with the negative image they have of themselves. In contrast, people with positive self-concepts prefer spouses who share their positive views of themselves (Swann et al., 1992).

Rogers (1959) also suggested that people have a need to regard themselves positively, and research confirms the existence of **self-enhancement**, a strong and pervasive tendency to gain and preserve a positive self-image. Self-enhancement needs have been demonstrated across many cultures (Sedikides et al., 2003), and several self-enhancement strategies have been identified. For example, people show a marked tendency to attribute their successes to their own abilities and effort but to attribute their failures to environmental factors. Furthermore, most people rate themselves as better than average on virtually any socially desirable characteristic that is subjective in nature (Leary, 2004). The vast majority of business people and politicians rate themselves as more ethical than the average. In defiance of mathematical possibility, about 80 per cent of secondary school students rate themselves in the top 10 per cent in their ability to get along with others. Even people who have been hospitalized after causing car accidents rate themselves as more skilful than the average driver (Greenberg et al., 1997). People generally view themselves as improving over time, relative to their peers (Ross and Wilson, 2003). Indeed, as evidence on self-serving biases in self-perception continues to accumulate, researchers are concluding that positive illusions of this sort are the rule rather than the exception in well-adjusted people and that these self-enhancement tendencies contribute to people's psychological well-being (Taylor and Brown, 1988; Taylor et al., 2003).

For people low in self-esteem, self-enhancement needs sometimes override self-verification tendencies (Tesser, 2004). In a series of experimental studies, Bernichon and co-workers (2003) found that individuals with low self-esteem have a strong tendency to seek out positive feedback about themselves even when it is not self-verifying. The pervasiveness of self-enhancement tendencies makes one wonder why so many people have low self-esteem. One answer is that although they desire positive self-enhancing feedback from others, people with low self-esteem do not provide much internal positive feedback to themselves. One experiment showed that when people low in self-esteem showed the same level of improvement on a laboratory task as did individuals with high self-esteem, they viewed themselves as improving far less. They also judged themselves more harshly when their performance decreased (Josephs et al., 2003). If one has trouble saying nice things about oneself, the kind of positive input that builds or repairs self-esteem is hard to come by.

EVALUATING THE PHENOMENOLOGICAL-HUMANISTIC APPROACH

What matters most in phenomenological-humanistic approaches is how people view themselves and the world. Some critics believe that the humanistic view relies too heavily on individuals' reports of their personal experiences. For example, psychoanalytic critics maintain that accepting what a person says at face value can easily lead to erroneous conclusions because of the always-present influence of unconscious defences.

Although humanism may indeed seem unscientific to some, Rogers (1959) dedicated himself to developing a theory whose concepts could be measured and whose laws could be tested. One of his most notable contributions was a series of studies on the process of self-growth that can occur in psychotherapy. To assess the effectiveness of psychotherapy, Rogers and his co-workers measured the discrepancy between clients' *ideal selves* (how they would like to be) and their *perceived selves* (their perceptions of what they were actually like). The studies revealed that when clients first entered therapy, the discrepancy was typically large but that it got smaller as

---

self-enhancement

a strong and pervasive tendency to gain and preserve a positive self-image

therapy proceeded, suggesting that therapy may help the client become more self-accepting and perhaps also more realistic. Rogers and his co-workers also discovered important therapist characteristics that either aid or impede the process of self-actualization in therapy. We describe this research in Chapter 18.

Several recent developments have put humanistic concepts back into the scientific spotlight. Deci and Ryan's self-determination theory, described in Chapter 11, has focused new scientific attention on humanistic concepts such as autonomy, competence and relatedness. New methods for measuring brain activation are enabling psychologists to study self-processes as they occur at a biological level (Heatherton et al., 2004). In addition, the positive psychology movement, described in Chapter 1, has redirected many psychologists to the study of human strengths, happiness, virtue and other humanistic concerns (Peterson and Seligman, 2004; Snyder and Lopez, 2007).

Understanding Charles Whitman

What kinds of insights can the phenomenological-humanistic perspective contribute to the Charles Whitman case? The obvious starting point is Whitman's self-concept. Despite the successful façade of achievement and exemplary behaviour erected during his childhood and adolescent years, the abuse and denigration Whitman received from his father took a heavy toll on his self-concept. After years of being belittled, he was eager to prove himself as a man when he enlisted in the Marines. He worked hard and successfully at being a good soldier, but things began to deteriorate after he enrolled at the University of Texas on the Marine Corps scholarship. In the absence of the disciplinary structure provided first by his father and then by the Marines, he began to get into trouble, and his grades suffered to the point that his scholarship was withdrawn. He was ordered to return to his former Marine unit, where he now found military life oppressive. His conduct deteriorated, and he was court-martialled for gambling and for threatening the life of a fellow Marine with a pistol. This proved to be an early indication of his potential for violence.

Eventually, thanks to his father's political influence, Whitman was honourably discharged and returned to the University of Texas. Academic difficulties there left him riddled with self-doubt, and he struggled desperately to reduce the discrepancy between his ideal self and his perceived self. He wrote numerous self-improvement journals filled with instructions designed to programme himself into behaving as a good husband, scholar and citizen. He frequently studied all night and took amphetamines to stay awake, but the drugs made him even less efficient. Soon he began to despair of ever being the person he wanted to be, and failure to live up to his conditions of worth undermined his self-esteem even further. After he killed his wife while she slept, Whitman left a letter on her body in which he professed his love for her and his desire to relieve her of the shame she would surely experience as his wife.

IN REVIEW

- Humanistic theories emphasize the subjective experiences of the individual and thus deal with perceptual and cognitive processes. Self-actualization is viewed as an innate positive force that leads people to realize their positive potential if not thwarted by the environment.

- Kelly's theory addressed the manner in which people differ in their constructions of reality by the personal constructs they use to categorize their experiences.

- Rogers's theory attaches central importance to the role of the self. Experiences that are incongruous with the established self-concept produce threat and may result in a denial or distortion of reality. Conditional positive regard may result in unrealistic conditions of worth that can conflict with self-actualization. Rogers described a number of characteristics of the fully functioning person.

- Rogers's theory helped stimulate a great deal of research on the self-concept, including studies on the origins and effects of differences in self-esteem, self-enhancement and self-verification motives, and self-concept change. Recent humanistic developments include self-determination theory and the character strengths and virtues identified by Peterson and Seligman.

MAPPING THE STRUCTURE OF PERSONALITY

What are the ways in which people differ in personality? People have described others' personalities since time immemorial. This also is one of the main goals of personality psychologists; to describe the basic classes of behaviour that define personality, to devise ways of measuring individual differences in personality, and to use these measures to understand and predict a person's behaviour.

TYPES AND TRAITS OF PERSONALITY

A simple distinction can be drawn between 'type' and 'trait' approaches to describing personality. A type approach attempts to classify people into groups who share the same common personality. An example of this approach can be seen in the earliest documented attempt to define personality. Inspired by the Ancient Greeks, Galen, a second-century physician, proposed four different personality types called: choleric, melancholic, phlegmatic and sanguine (see Fig. 15.11). Galen proposed that people belonged to these personality types by virtue of their having an excess of one particular fluid (or humour) in their body. Choleric people had an excess of 'yellow bile', and were said to be bad tempered and aggressive. Melancholic people had an excess of 'black bile', and were said to be of a pessimistic and mournful disposition. Phlegmatic people had an excess of 'phlegm', and were supposed to be slow and easy-going sorts. Sanguine people had more 'blood' and thus were happy-go-lucky and passionate. While this view that personality types are caused by body fluids is now outmoded, it remains in theories such as that of Freud, who defined personality in terms of fixations at particular stages in development (e.g., an anal retentive or an anal expulsive personality type).

On the other hand, trait theorists attempt to define a person's personality in terms of the *degree to which they possess a particular characteristic*. Rather than the all-or-none (yes or no) classification systems used by type theorists, trait theorists measure where a person sits on a trait *dimension* of personality. An analogy can be used with clothes sizes. Whereas in high-street shops sizes come in small, medium and large (a type system), in an old-fashioned tailor clothes are made to fit a size on a number of different dimensions. The tailor will measure the height, waist size, neck size, and so on. The tailor's system is rather like what trait theorists attempt to do. They try to identify a set of dimensions which can be used to efficiently describe all people.

Personality traits are thus relatively stable cognitive, emotional and behavioural characteristics of people that help establish their individual identities and distinguish them from others. The starting point for the trait researcher is identifying the behaviours that define a particular trait. Years ago, the trait theorist Gordon Allport went through the English dictionary and painstakingly recorded all the words that could be used to describe personal traits. The result: a gigantic list of 17 953 words (Allport and Odbert, 1936). Obviously, it would be impractical, if not impossible, to describe people in terms of where they fall on roughly 18 000 dimensions.

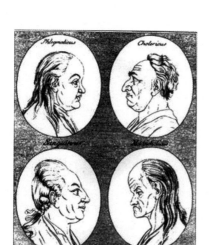

FIGURE 15.11

Personality types.

Clockwise from the top-left: phlegmatic, choleric, sanguine and melancholic. This artist clearly thought that facial appearance as well as behaviour was associated with a personality type.

personality traits

are relatively stable cognitive, emotional and behavioural characteristics of people that help establish their individual identities and distinguish them from others

The trait theorist's goal is thus to condense all of these behavioural descriptors into a manageable number of basic traits that can capture personal individuality.

TRAIT FACTOR ANALYTIC APPROACHES

Psychologists have taken two major approaches to discover and define personality traits. One approach is to propose traits (e.g., 'dominance', 'friendliness', 'self-esteem') on the basis of words or concepts from everyday discourse or from concepts in existing personality theories. This is referred to as the *lexical approach*. A more systematic approach uses the statistical tool of *factor analysis*, the approach described in Chapter 10 that has been used to identify distinct mental abilities. In personality research, **factor analysis** is used to identify clusters of behaviours that are highly correlated (positively or negatively) with one another, but not with behaviours in other clusters. Such behaviour clusters can be viewed as reflecting a basic dimension, or trait, on which people vary. For example, you might find that most people who are socially reserved also avoid parties, enjoy quiet activities and like being alone. At the other end of the spectrum are people who are very talkative and sociable, like parties and excitement, dislike solitary activities such as reading, and constantly seek out new acquaintances. These behavioural patterns define a general factor, or dimension, that we might label *introversion–extraversion* (or simply *extraversion*). At one end of the dimension are highly introverted behaviours, and at the other end are highly extraverted behaviours (Fig. 15.12). Presumably, each of us could be placed at some point along this dimension in terms of our customary behaviour patterns. In fact, as we will see, factor analytic studies have shown introversion–extraversion to be a major dimension of personality.

> **Focus 15.10**
> Describe and compare two models of personality derived from factor analysis.

> **factor analysis**
> used to identify clusters of behaviours that are highly correlated (positively or negatively) with one another, but not with behaviours in other clusters

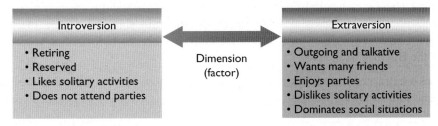

FIGURE 15.12

Describing personality through factor analysis.

Factor analysis allows researchers to reduce many behaviours to a smaller number of basic dimensions, or factors, that are relatively independent of one another. A factor comprises behaviours that are highly correlated with one another (either positively or negatively) and are therefore assumed to have common psychological meaning. Here we see the kinds of behaviours that might fall on the two ends of an introversion–extraversion dimension.

Cattell's Sixteen Personality Factors

If you were asked to describe and compare every person you know, how many different traits would it take to do the job? This is where trait theorists begin to part company. Because factor analysis can be used and interpreted in different ways, trait theorists have cut up the personality pie into smaller or larger pieces. For example, the pioneering trait theorist Raymond B. Cattell (1965) asked thousands of participants to rate themselves on numerous behavioural characteristics; he also obtained ratings from people who knew the participants well. When he subjected this mass of data to factor analysis, he identified 16 basic behaviour clusters, or factors (Fig. 15.13). Using this information, Cattell developed a widely used personality test called the *16 Personality Factor Questionnaire (16PF)* to measure individual differences on each of the dimensions and provide a comprehensive personality description. He was able to develop personality profiles not only for individuals but also for groups of people. For example, Figure 15.13 compares average scores obtained by creative artists and Olympic athletes.

FIGURE 15.13

Cattell's 16 personality factors.

Raymond B. Cattell identified 16 basic personality traits through factor analysis. Here we see personality profiles (mean scores) for Olympic athletes and creative artists on the 16PF, the test developed by Cattell to measure the traits.

SOURCE: Cattell, 1965.

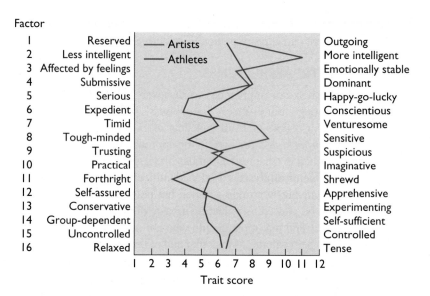

Eysenck's Extraversion-Stability Model

In contrast to Cattell's 16-factor approach, a number of more recent approaches favour a smaller number of personality 'super-traits'. Hans J. Eysenck (1916–97), one of Britain's leading psychologists, suggested that normal personality can be understood in terms of just *two* basic dimensions. These dimensions of introversion–extraversion and stability–instability (sometimes called neuroticism) encompass all of the more specific traits shown in Figure 15.14a. As we shall see, Eysenck's two 'super-traits' are still retained in more recent factor analytic approaches such as 'the Big Five' (see below).

Eysenck's extraversion-stability model is shown in Figure 15.14a. Note that the two basic dimensions intersect at right angles, meaning that they are statistically independent, or uncorre-

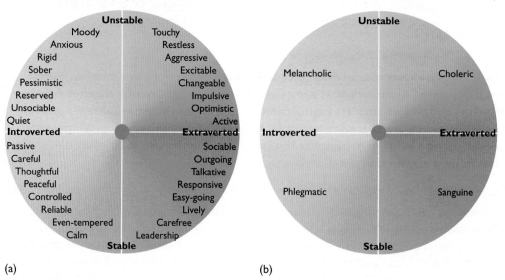

(a)   (b)

FIGURE 15.14

A two-factor model.

According to Hans Eysenck (a), various combinations of two major dimensions of personality, introversion–extraversion and stability–instability (or neuroticism), combine to form more specific traits (b).

SOURCE: Eysenck, 1967.

lated. The secondary traits shown in the circle reflect varying combinations, or mixtures, of the two primary dimensions. Thus we can see that the emotionally stable extravert is a carefree, lively person who tends to be well adjusted and to seek out leadership roles. In contrast, unstable extraverts tend to be touchy, aggressive and restless. The stable introvert is calm, reliable and even-tempered, but the unstable introvert tends to be rigid, anxious and moody. Different combinations of the two basic personality dimensions can thus produce very diverse personality patterns. Interestingly, the various combinations of these dimensions can describe the four types identified by Galen. Thus, someone who is unstable and introverted might be typed melancholic, someone who is unstable and extroverted – choleric, someone who is stable and introverted – phlegmatic, and someone who is stable and extroverted – sanguine (see Fig. 15.14b).

Think about all the different people you know. Does Eysenck's attempt to describe personality in terms of just two 'super-traits' seem a little oversimplifying? More recently, trait theorists have added a few more 'super-traits', to Eysenck's two. Later in his career Eysenck himself saw the need to add a further trait of 'psychoticism'. Psychoticism was proposed to describe the degree to which someone was *aggressive, cold, egocentric, impersonal, impulsive, antisocial, unempathetic, creative* and *tough-minded.* As some of these traits we formerly considered part of extraversion, this entailed some changes to the conceptualization of that super-trait also. More recently, a number of researchers are converging on the opinion that personality is best described by five 'Big' factors.

The Five Factor Model

The 'Big Five' factor model suggests that five higher-order factors, each including several of Cattell's more specific factors, are all that we need to capture the basic structure of personality (McCrae and Costa, 2003). These theorists also propose that these 'Big Five' factors may be universal to the human species, for the same five factors have been found consistently in trait ratings within diverse North American, Asian, Hispanic and European cultures (John and Srivastava, 1999; Trull and Geary, 1997).

The Big Five factors are shown in Table 15.5. (The acronym OCEAN – for openness, conscientiousness, extraversion, agreeableness and neuroticism – may help you remember

TABLE 15.5 THE BIG FIVE PERSONALITY FACTORS AND THE BEHAVIOURAL FACETS THEY INCLUDE

Big Five factors	Behaviours (facets)
E Extraversion versus introversion	Gregariousness (sociable), assertiveness (forceful), activity (energetic), excitement-seeking (adventurous), positive emotions (enthusiastic), warmth (outgoing)
A Agreeableness versus antagonism	Trust (forgiving), straightforwardness (not demanding), altruism (warm), compliance (not stubborn), modesty (not show-off), tender-mindedness (sympathetic)
C Conscientiousness versus lack of direction	Competence (efficient), order (organized), dutifulness (not careless), achievement striving (thorough), self-discipline (not lazy), deliberation (not impulsive)
N Neuroticism versus emotional stability	Anxiety (tense), angry hostility (irritable), depression (not contented), self-consciousness (shy), impulsiveness (moody), vulnerability (not self-confident)
O Openness versus closedness to experience	Ideas (curious), fantasy (imaginative), aesthetics (artistic), actions (wide interests), feelings (excitable), values (unconventional)

SOURCE: based on McCrae and Costa, 2003.

them.) Proponents of the *five factor model* believe that when a person is placed at a specific point on each of these five dimensions by means of a psychological test, behaviour ratings or direct observations of behaviour, the essence of her or his personality has been captured (McCrae and Costa, 2003).

What do you think about that conclusion? If you were sceptical about Eysenck's two (or three) trait models you may not feel much happier about the five factor model. Surely there must be more to individuality than can be captured by only five dimensions. However, we should remember that, as discussed in Chapter 5, the incredible number of colours that the human visual system can distinguish is based on the activity patterns of only *three* types of cones. Thus the many variations that can occur from the blending of five personality dimensions could account for enormous variation in personality patterns.

Trait theorists not only try to describe the basic structure of personality but also attempt to predict real-life behaviour on the basis of a person's traits. Even if a few general traits such as the Big Five seem adequate to describe important features of personality, it is entirely possible that a larger number of specific traits such as Cattell's would capture nuances of behaviour within particular situations and would therefore be better for predictive purposes. Measures of the global Big Five factors seldom correlate above .20 to .30 with real-life behavioural outcomes (e.g., Paunonen, 2003). In recognition of this fact, the Big Five model now includes six subcategories, or *facets* (Table 15.5), under each of the five major factors, and the personality test used to measure the Big Five (the *NEO Personality Inventory*, or *NEO-PI*) now provides scores on each of these facets as well as on the corresponding major factor. For example, scores are obtained not only for the main factor of Extraversion, but also for facets such as activity and positive emotions. These more specific dimensions permit sharper behavioural predictions (McCrae and Costa, 2003). For example, the positive emotions/cheerfulness facet of extraversion is more highly related to life satisfaction than is the total extraversion score based on all six facets (Schimmack et al., 2004). Nonetheless, the ability of even these more specific traits to predict behaviour across varying situations is limited (Cervone, 1999).

Stability of Personality Traits over Time

Focus 15.11

How stable are personality traits across time and situations? What factors decrease consistency across situations?

Because traits are viewed as enduring behavioural predispositions, they should show some degree of stability over time. Yet they should not be unchangeable. As we might expect, the research literature shows evidence for both stability and change (Caspi and Roberts, 1999; Helson et al., 2002). Some personality dimensions tend to be more stable than others. On the one hand, introversion/extraversion, as well as more basic traits such as emotionality and activity level, tend to be quite stable from childhood into adulthood and across the adult years (Eysenck, 1990; Zuckerman, 1991). Self-esteem also shows strong stability (Trzesniewski et al., 2003). On the other hand, both cross-sectional and longitudinal studies indicate that among the Big Five, neuroticism, openness and extraversion exhibit average declines from the late teens to the early thirties, whereas agreeableness and conscientiousness tend to increase (Costa and McCrae, 2002). Likewise, individuals can show developmental changes in many aspects of personality given influential life experiences, including involvement in counselling and psychotherapy.

Certain habits of thought may also be fairly stable. One is our tendency to think optimistically or pessimistically. Melanie Burns and Martin Seligman (1991) coded diaries and letters that elderly people had written approximately 50 years earlier for the tendency to respond either optimistically or pessimistically to life events. The elderly people also completed a personality test that measured their current optimistic–pessimistic tendencies. Although little consistency over time was shown for dealing optimistically or pessimistically with positive events, Burns and Seligman found a stable tendency to respond with optimism or pessimism to negative life events. The authors suggested that the tendency to be pessimistic might constitute an enduring risk factor for depression, low achievement, and physical illness, and they are now studying such linkages. Table 15.6 contains items from the *Life Orientation Test* (Scheier and Carver, 1985), used by personality researchers to measure the trait of optimism–pessimism.

TABLE 15.6 SAMPLE ITEMS FROM A TRAIT MEASURE OF OPTIMISM–PESSIMISM*

1 In uncertain times, I usually expect the best
2. Overall, I expect more good things to happen to me than bad
3. If something can go wrong for me, it will
4. I rarely count on good things happening to me
NOTE: *Items on the Life Orientation Test are answered on a five-point scale ranging from 'strongly disagree' to 'strongly agree'.

SOURCE: adapted from Scheier et al., 1994.

BENEATH THE SURFACE

HOW CONSISTENT IS OUR BEHAVIOUR ACROSS SITUATIONS?

As noted at the beginning of the chapter, one of the reasons we have a concept of personality is because we view people as behaving consistently across situations. Is that assumption of consistency warranted by the data? When Walter Mischel reviewed the evidence in 1968, he came to a surprising conclusion: There was more evidence for inconsistency than for consistency. Even on a trait so central as honesty, people can show considerable behavioural variability across situations. In a classic study done 60 years earlier, Hugh Hartshorne and Mark May (1928) tested the honesty of thousands of children. The children were given opportunities to lie, steal and cheat in a number of different settings: at home, in school, at a party and in an athletic contest. The rather surprising finding was that 'lying, cheating and stealing as measured by the test situations in this study are only very loosely related.... Most children will deceive in certain situations but not in others' (Hartshorne and May, 1928, p. 411). More than a half century later, Mischel (1984) reported similar findings for college students on the trait of conscientiousness. A student might be highly conscientious in one situation (e.g., coming to work on time) without being conscientious in another (e.g., turning in class assignments on time). Many other studies revealed similar behavioural inconsistency across situations.

To some, this called the very concept of personality into question. They reasoned that if behaviour is so inconsistent, maybe only the situation is important and we do not need an internal concept called 'personality' to account for behaviour. This conclusion triggered a lively debate that continued for nearly two decades. Let us consider some of the insights that have arisen from the consistency debate.

FACTORS THAT REDUCE SITUATIONAL CONSISTENCY

Three factors make it difficult to predict on the basis of personality traits how people will behave in particular situations. First, personality traits interact with other traits, as well as with characteristics of different situations. This melding accounts for the incredible richness we see in personality, but it also poses a challenge to psychologists who want to predict behaviour. When two or more traits, such as honesty, dominance and agreeableness, influence a behaviour in a particular situation, our ability to predict on the basis of only one of the traits is bound to be quite limited (Ahadi and Diener, 1989).

Second, the degree of consistency across situations is influenced by how important a given trait is for the person. A person for whom honesty is a cornerstone of the self-concept may show considerable stability in honest behaviours across situations because her or his feelings of self-worth may be linked to living up to moral standards regardless of the circumstances (Kenrick and Funder, 1988).

self-monitoring

attending to situational cues and adapting behaviour to what would be most appropriate

Third, people differ in their tendency to tailor their behaviour to what is called for by the situation. This personality trait is called *self-monitoring* (Table 15.7). People who are high in **self-monitoring** are very attentive to situational cues and adapt their behaviour to what they think would be most appropriate. Extreme self-monitors are behavioural chameleons, who act very differently in various situations. Low self-monitors, on the other hand, tend to act primarily in terms of their internal beliefs and attitudes rather than the demands of the situation. The saying 'What you see is what you get' applies well to low self-monitors, and such people show greater consistency across situations than do high self-monitors (Snyder, 1987).

TABLE 15.7 SAMPLE ITEMS FROM THE SELF-MONITORING SCALE*

1. In different situations and with different people, I often act like very different persons.
2. I am not always the person I appear to be.
3. I have trouble changing my behaviour to suit different people and different situations.
4. I would not change my opinion (or the way I do things) in order to please someone or win their favour.
NOTE: *Items 1 and 2 are keyed 'true' and items 3 and 4 'false' for self-monitoring.

SOURCE: based on Snyder, 1987.

According to some trait theorists, the stability and distinctiveness that we see in personality does not come from the fact that we behave the same way in every situation. Rather, people exhibit different *average* amounts of extraversion, emotional stability, agreeableness, honesty and other traits across many different situations (Epstein, 1983; Kenrick and Funder, 1988). Nonetheless, if they wish to understand more about these interactions among personality traits, situations and behaviour, personality researchers need to define the relevant characteristics of both the person and the situation (Shoda and Mischel, 2000; Zayas and Shada, 2007).

EVALUATING THE TRAIT APPROACH

Despite differences of opinion concerning the nature and number of basic personality dimensions, trait theorists have made an important contribution by focusing attention on the value of identifying, classifying, and measuring stable, enduring personality dispositions. Several challenges confront trait theorists, however. If we are to capture the true complexities of personality, we must pay more attention to how traits combine with one another to affect various behaviours (Ahadi and Diener, 1989; Smith et al., 1990). All too often, researchers try to make specific predictions on the basis of a single measured personality trait without taking into account other personality factors that might also influence the behaviour in question. This approach sells short the complexity of personality.

In evaluating the trait perspective, we must remember the distinction between description and explanation. To say that someone is outgoing and fun-loving *because* she is high in extraversion is merely to describe the behaviour with a trait name, not to explain the inner disposition and how it operates. Traditionally, the trait perspective has been more concerned with describing the structure of personality, measuring individual differences in personality traits and predicting behaviour than with understanding the psychological or biological processes that underlie the traits. For example, a shortcoming of the five factor model is its lack of explanatory power; it tells us nothing about the causal factors that produce extraverted, neurotic or agreeable people's experiences and actions (Cervone, 1999). However, an important exception to this is Hans Eysenck who, as we see later, proposed a biological explanation for his trait theory.

Understanding Charles Whitman

What can the trait perspective tell us about Charles Whitman? Personality psychologists with a trait orientation would be interested in where he falls on a number of relevant personality dimensions. On the Big Five, he likely would have scored high on extraversion and agreeableness (with some notable departures from agreeableness when frustrated), inconsistent on conscientiousness and high on neuroticism. If Whitman had been given a battery of personality tests shortly before the incident, would he have exhibited a profile showing a low level of self-esteem, poor stress-management skills, high hostility and poor impulse control? How would his scores have changed from the period when he was functioning well in adolescence to the period after he was in the Marines? Unfortunately, we will never be able to answer these questions because, to our knowledge, Whitman never took a personality test. It is possible though, that had Whitman been tested in the days preceding his murderous acts, his test results might have served to warn professionals about his potential for violent behaviour.

IN REVIEW

- It is possible to describe personality in terms of types or traits. Type approaches such as those of Galen and Freud classify individuals into specific categories.

- Trait theorists try to identify and measure the basic dimensions of personality. Factor analysis identifies clusters of behaviour that are highly correlated correlated with one another and thus constitute a dimension along which people may vary. Theorists disagree on the number of traits needed to describe personality adequately. Cattell suggested 16 basic traits; other theorists insist that five (or even fewer) may be adequate. Prediction studies indicate that a larger number of more specific traits may be superior for predicting behaviour in specific situations.

- Traits have not proved to be highly consistent across situations, and they also vary in stability over time. Individuals differ in their self-monitoring tendencies, and this variable influences the amount of cross-situational consistency they exhibit in social situations. Traits produce inconsistency by interacting not only with situations but also with one another.

BIOLOGICAL FOUNDATIONS OF PERSONALITY

Both nature and nurture influence the development of personality traits, but their contributions differ according to the trait in question (Plomin and Caspi, 1999). Biological explanations for personality differences focus on three levels. As we saw in Chapter 3, one group of theorists uses evolutionary principles to explain why particular traits exist in the human species (e.g., Buss, 1999). Others seek the genetic bases for trait inheritance (Plomin, 1997). Still others search for differences in the functioning of the nervous system (Heatherton et al., 2004; Pickering and Gray, 1999). Having discussed evolutionary personality theory in Chapter 3, we focus here on genetic and neuroscience approaches.

GENETICS AND PERSONALITY

Have you ever been told that you share a personality trait with a parent or relative? Perhaps you wondered where the presumed similarity originated. Could it possibly have been inherited? Twin studies are particularly informative for studying the role of genetic factors because they

Focus 15.12

What do twin studies reveal about the roles of heredity and environment in personality development?

compare the degree of personality resemblance between monozygotic twins, who have identical genetic make-up, and dizygotic twins, who do not (Lykken, 2006; Rowe, 1999). On a great many psychological characteristics, identical twins are more similar to each other than are fraternal twins, suggesting a role for genetics. However, the issue is clouded by the possibility that identical twins may also have more similar environments than fraternal twins because others are inclined to treat them more similarly.

The ideal solution to this problem would be to compare personality traits in identical and fraternal twins who were raised together and those who were raised apart. If the identical twins who were reared in different families were as similar as those reared together, a more powerful argument could be made for the role of genetic factors. Moreover, this research design would allow us to divide the total variation among individuals on each personality trait into three components: (1) variation attributable to genetic factors; (2) variation due to a shared family environment in those raised together; and (3) variation attributable to other factors, including unique individual life experiences. The relative influence of these sources of variation can be estimated by comparing personality test correlations in twins raised together and apart.

The most comprehensive study (which included the Jim twins described at the beginning of Chapter 3) was conducted by Auke Tellegen and his colleagues at the University of Minnesota. The four groups of twin pairs were administered measures of 14 different personality traits, and the personality variation attributable to genetic, familial environment and unique environment was calculated for each personality characteristic.

As shown in Table 15.8, genetic factors accounted for approximately 40 to 50 per cent of the variance among people in trait scores. In contrast, the degree of resemblance did not differ much whether the twin pairs were reared together or apart, showing that general features of the family environment, such as its emotional climate and degree of affluence, accounted for little variance in any of the traits. However, this does not mean that experience is not important. Rather than the family environment, it was the individual's unique environmental experiences, such as his or her school experiences and interactions with peers, that accounted for considerable personality variance. Even within the same family, individual children have different experiences while growing up. Indeed, as well as outside the home, these may be environmental inside the home, as parents may treat their children differently. It is these unique experiences that help shape personality development.

PERSONALITY AND THE NERVOUS SYSTEM

One logical place to look for biological underpinnings of personality is in individual differences in brain functioning (Canli, 2006; Zuckerman, 2005). Two examples are Hans Eysenck's research and theorizing on extraversion and emotional stability, and more recent work on temperament.

Eysenck and the Biological Basis of Extraversion and Stability

Eysenck (1967) was one of the first modern theorists to suggest a biological basis for major personality traits. He linked introversion–extraversion and stability–instability to differences in individuals' normal patterns of arousal within the brain. He started with the notion that there is an optimal, or preferred, level of biological arousal in the brain. Eysenck believed that extreme introverts are chronically *over-aroused*; their brains are too electrically active, so they try to minimize stimulation and reduce arousal to get down to their optimal arousal level (or 'comfort zone'). In contrast, the brains of extreme extraverts are chronically *under-aroused*, so they need powerful or frequent stimulation to achieve an optimal level of cortical arousal and excitation. The extravert thus seeks social contact and physical arousal, likes parties, takes chances, is assertive and suffers boredom easily.

Whereas introversion–extraversion reflects a person's *customary* level of arousal, stability–instability represents the suddenness with which *shifts* in arousal occur. Unstable people have

Focus 15.13

What biological factors underlie (1) Eysenck's dimensions of extraversion and stability and (2) the behaviours of inhibited children and adults?

TABLE 15.8 ESTIMATES OF THE PERCENTAGES OF GROUP VARIANCE IN 14 PERSONALITY TRAITS ATTRIBUTABLE TO GENETIC AND ENVIRONMENTAL FACTORS

Trait	Genetic	Familial environment	Unique environment
Well-being	.48	.13	.39
Social potency	.54	.10	.36
Achievement	.39	.11	.50
Social closeness	.40	.19	.41
Stress reaction	.53	.00	.47
Alienation	.45	.11	.54
Aggression	.44	.00	.56
Control	.44	.00	.56
Harm avoidance	.55	.00	.45
Traditionalism	.45	.12	.43
Absorption	.50	.03	.47
Positive emotionality	.40	.22	.38
Negative emotionality	.55	.02	.43
Constraint	.58	.00	.42

NOTE: The variance estimates are based on a comparison of the degree of personality similarity in identical and fraternal twins who were reared together or apart.

SOURCE: adapted from Tellegen et al., 1988.

nervous systems that show large and sudden shifts in arousal, whereas stable people show smaller and more gradual shifts (Pickering and Gray, 1999). Eysenck also called this stability dimension *neuroticism* because he found that people with extremely unstable nervous systems are more likely to experience emotional problems that require clinical attention.

Eysenck proposed that the arousal patterns that underlie introversion–extraversion and stability–instability have genetic bases. A growing body of evidence from twin studies supports his view. Identical twins are much more alike on these traits than are fraternal twins, and about half of the variance among people can be attributed to hereditary factors (Loehlin et al., 1988; Plomin, 1997). Eysenck believed that although personality is strongly influenced by life experiences, the ways people respond to those experiences may be at least partly programmed by biological factors. Contemporary research using brain imaging continues to find brain activation patterns related to extraversion and stability. These studies show that the neural bases of these factors go beyond general arousal, involving specific brain structures (Canli, 2004).

An alternative to Eysenck's biological explanation of personality was put forward by eminent UK psychologist, Jeffrey Gray. Rather than starting with the factorial structure of personality as Eysenck did, Gray's (1982) reinforcement sensitivity theory (Corr, 2008) takes the biological level of analysis as its starting point. Reinforcement sensitivity theory proposes that individual differences in personality originate from variations in the sensitivity of biological systems of reward and punishment. In Chapter 4 we described how animals and humans are sensitive to rewards and punishments when they are learning new behaviours (particularly during instrumental conditioning).

FIGURE 15.15

Gray's reinforcement sensitivity theory of personality.

The behavioural approach system (BAS) and the behavioural inhibition system (BIS) dimensions of personality sit at a 30 degree rotation to Eysenck's Extraversion and Stability dimensions.

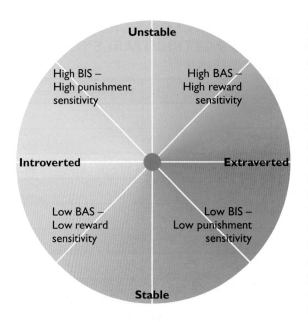

temperament

individual differences in emotional and behavioural styles that appear so early in life that they are assumed to have a biological basis

FIGURE 15.16

Does childhood temperament predict adult personality?

(a) Inhibited temperament expresses itself as shyness and negative reactions to novel situations and people (even Santa Claus) early in life and is assumed to have a biological basis. (b) Adults who were identified as inhibited in childhood showed elevated reactions in the amygdala (a brain region known to initiate and organize fear responses) when exposed to faces they had not seen before, suggesting stability of this temperamental factor into adulthood.

SOURCE: data from Schwartz et al., 2003.

Gray's theory is thus influenced by the behaviourist concepts of learning and reinforcement, but also considers these concepts from a biological level of analysis – suggesting that sensitivity to reward and punishment are determined by some basic biological factors, From this biological starting point, Gray proposes two super-trait factors in personality – the behavioural approach system (BAS), which describes sensitivity to reward, and the behavioural inhibition system (BIS), which describes sensitivity to punishment. These two neural systems map onto the personality space described by Eysenck but the particular dimensions are positioned at a different orientation to the array of specific traits (see Fig. 15.15).

Temperament: Building Blocks of Personality

Temperament refers to individual differences in emotional and behavioural styles that appear so early in life that they are assumed to have a biological basis. Such temperamental factors as emotionality, activity level, sociability and impulsivity are visible even in infancy (Buss and Plomin, 1975; 1984). Temperamental factors are not assumed to be personality traits in their own right, but they are viewed as biological building blocks that influence the subsequent development of personality. The fact that these temperamental factors are more highly correlated in identical than in fraternal twins suggests a genetic link (Buss and Plomin, 1984).

Recent research has focused on biological differences in inhibited and uninhibited people. First identified by Jerome Kagan (1999) on the basis of behavioural observations and biological functioning, inhibited infants and children are shy, restrained in their behaviour, and react to unfamiliar people and situations with distress and avoidance (Fig. 15.16a). In contrast, uninhibited children respond positively to new situations and people and seem to enjoy novelty. About 20 per cent of infants are inhibited, and about 40 per cent are uninhibited. Kagan (1999) found that these temperamental patterns can be identified in the first four months of life and that they persist into later childhood in many (but not all) children. These two groups of children also dif-

(a)

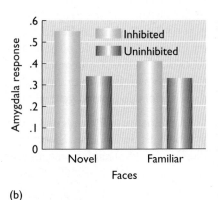

(b)

fer physiologically, with the inhibited children showing higher levels of physiological arousal and stress-hormone secretion in response to unfamiliar situations and people.

Recent research sheds light on brain regions that contribute to inhibited and uninhibited tendencies. One important region is the amygdala, the structure in the limbic system that organizes fear responses. Kagan suggested that the amygdala was involved in the physiological overreactivity he measured in inhibited children. In a more recent study, fMRI brain recordings were taken in young adults who had been categorized as either highly inhibited or as uninhibited when they were 2 years old (Schwartz et al., 2003). Of interest was how their amygdala would react to pictures of familiar and unfamiliar human faces. As shown in Figure 15.16b, those adults who had been uninhibited as children showed relatively low amygdala reactivity to both familiar and novel faces, whereas the formerly inhibited participants showed particularly high reactivity to the novel faces. This study thereby demonstrated a negative response to novel stimuli in inhibited people that extended from childhood to adulthood, as well as a possible biological basis for this tendency.

We should note that temperament is not destiny. Although biological factors are clearly involved, the environment also can bring about some degree of change in temperamental characterics. We should remember that temperamentally based behaviour patterns help create environments that can perpetuate the behaviour patterns. For example, people are unlikely to gravitate towards shy, inhibited individuals, thereby depriving them of positive experiences that might counteract their shyness. Likewise, temperamental traits may need particular kinds of environments to express themselves. Elaine Aron and co-workers (2005) found that adult shyness occurred most predictably when the underlying temperamental characteristic was paired with an adverse childhood environment. Although the link between child temperament and adult personality is far from perfect, there is little doubt that temperament is one building block in personality development.

EVALUATING THE BIOLOGICAL APPROACH

Biological research, spurred by technical advances in measuring nervous system activity and in evaluating genetic influences, is forging new frontiers in personality science. As we learn more about how biological functions are affected by developmental experiences and how they interact with situational factors, new insights about personality development will be achieved.

Behaviour genetics research on personality is moving in some exciting new directions. In the past, twin studies of personality typically have examined degrees of similarity on self-report measures of personality traits. Yet, as we have emphasized, personality characteristics act in combination with situational factors. In a landmark study in Germany, Peter Borkenau and co-workers (2006) studied the role of genes and environment on person-by-situation interaction patterns. The behaviours of 168 identical and 132 fraternal twins were carefully observed and coded as each person reacted to 15 different situations, some involving social encounters and others requiring problem solving. By comparing the degree of similarity in person-by-situation behavioural profiles across the 15 situations in the two types of twin pairs, the researchers established that about 25 per cent of the variation in behavioural profiles could be attributed to genetic factors. As in previous studies, shared-environment effects were negligible. This study shows that genetic factors not only influence what people say about their personality, but how they adjust their behaviour to different situations.

Understanding Charles Whitman

Can the biological perspective offer clues to Charles Whitman's behaviour? In Whitman's letter, we find references to 'tremendous headaches' for which he had been medicating himself and a request that an autopsy be done after his death to see if a 'visible physical disorder' existed. In fact, a post-mortem of his brain detected a fast-growing tumour in the hypothalamus, an area that includes some of the aggression circuitry in the brain (Raine et al., 2000). Medical authorities evaluating Whitman's case differed on the importance of the tumour. If the tumour played a role in his violent acts, it seems unlikely that it was the primary causal factor. However, it could have been a predisposing factor that lowered his inhibitions against violent behaviour.

Another possibility arises from information that Whitman's father had a penchant for violent behaviour and frequently beat his wife and children. Thus a second potential biological factor could be the genes Whitman inherited from his father. Aggression can have a genetic basis (Wasserman and Wachbroit, 2001), and it is possible that a genetic predisposition interacted with environmental factors to increase the potential for violent behaviour.

IN REVIEW

- Biological perspectives on personality traits focus on differences in the functioning of the nervous system, the contribution of genetic factors, and the possible role of evolution in the development of universal human traits and ways of perceiving behaviour.

- Studies comparing identical and fraternal twins reared together and apart indicate that genetic factors may account for as much as half of the variance in personality test scores, with individual experiences accounting for most of the remainder. Evolutionary theories of personality attribute some personality dispositions to genetically controlled mechanisms based on natural selection.

- Eysenck suggested that normal personality differences can be accounted for by variations on the dimensions of introversion–extraversion and stability–instability, both of which are assumed to have a biological basis. In Eysenck's theory, introversion–extraversion reflects a person's customary level of arousal, whereas stability–instability represents the suddenness with which shifts in arousal occur. A more recent biological explanation of personality has been proposed in Jeffrey Gray's reinforcement sensitivity theory.

- Differences in temperament appear early in life and are assumed to have a biological basis. Temperament is assumed to contribute to the development of personality, and there is evidence for stability of temperamental behaviour tendencies during childhood and into adulthood. Inhibited children and adults appear to have a highly reactive amygdala that triggers fear responses to unfamiliar people and situations.

BEHAVIOURAL AND SOCIAL-COGNITIVE THEORIES

Focus 15.14

Describe the major features of social-cognitive theories and the importance of reciprocal determinism.

To understand behaviour, psychodynamic, humanistic and trait theorists emphasize internal personal causes of behaviour, such as unconscious conflicts, self-actualization tendencies and personality traits. In a sense, they account for behaviour from the inside out. In contrast, behaviourists emphasize environmental causes and view humans as reactors to external events (Parker et al., 1998). To them, behaviour is to be explained from the outside in. Behaviourists such as Ivan Pavlov, John Watson and B.F. Skinner were more interested in discovering universal laws of learning than in identifying individual differences in behaviour, and they rejected the notion of an 'internal personality' that directs behaviour. Nonetheless, the laws of learning that they discovered have great relevance for understanding personality. Many behaviours ascribed to personality are acquired through classical and operant conditioning, and the role of life experiences is undeniable.

Despite the power of the environment, however, some behaviourists believed that a purely behavioural account could not fully capture the workings of human personality. They believed that the learner is not simply a passive reactor to environmental forces and that internal processes could not be excluded from an understanding of personality. They viewed the human as perceiver, a thinker and a planner who mentally interprets events, thinks about the past, anticipates the future and decides how to behave. Environmental effects are filtered through these cognitive processes and are influenced – even changed – by them. **Social-cognitive theories** combine the behavioural and cognitive perspectives into an approach to personality that stresses the interaction of a thinking human with a social environment that provides learning experiences. Social-cognitive theorists believe that the debate on whether behaviour is more strongly influenced by personal factors or by the person's environment is basically a meaningless one (Fleeson, 2004). Instead, according to the social-cognitive principle of **reciprocal determinism**, the person, the person's behaviour and the environment all influence one another in a pattern of two-way causal links (Bandura, 1986; Fig. 15.17).

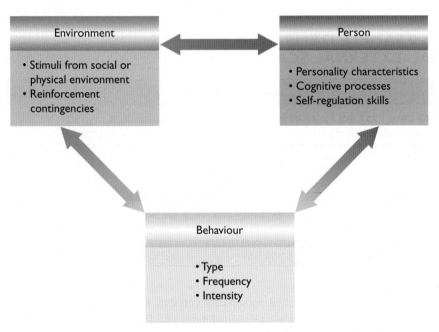

Reciprocal determinism

As an example, let us consider how these interactions or linkages might operate in the case of a hostile and disagreeable man we will call Tom. Tom's disagreeableness trait manifests itself in an irritable, cynical and uncooperative behaviour pattern (his personality influences his behaviour). Tom's disagreeable behaviours tend to evoke negative responses from others (his behaviour causes his social environment to respond to him in kind). These negative social consequences reinforce and strengthen still further his personality trait (including his expectations that others will eventually reject him), and they also strengthen his disagreeable behaviour tendencies (his environment influences both his personality trait and his social behaviour). Thus Tom's personality, his behaviour and his environment all influence one another, much to his detriment, the poor fellow.

JULIAN ROTTER: EXPECTANCY, REINFORCEMENT VALUE AND LOCUS OF CONTROL

In 1954 Julian Rotter (whose name is usually pronounced to rhyme with *motor*) laid the foundation for today's social-cognitive approaches. According to Rotter, the likelihood that we will engage in a particular behaviour in a given situation is influenced by two factors: *expectancy*

---

social-cognitive theories

combine the behavioural and cognitive perspectives into an approach to personality that stresses the interaction of a thinking human with a social environment that provides learning experiences

reciprocal determinism

the person, the person's behaviour and the environment all influence one another in a pattern of two-way causal links

FIGURE 15.17

Reciprocal determinism.

A key concept in social-cognitive theory is reciprocal determinism, in which characteristics of the person, the person's behaviour and the environment all affect one another in reciprocal, or two-way, causal relations.

Focus 15.15

Describe Rotter's concepts of expectancy, reinforcement value and locus of control.

internal–external locus of control

an expectancy concerning the degree of personal control we have in our lives

FIGURE 15.18

Research shows that people with an internal locus of control are more likely to take an active role in social-change movements.

Focus 15.16

Describe four determinants of self-efficacy.

and *reinforcement value*. Expectancy is our perception of how likely it is that certain consequences will occur if we engage in a particular behaviour within a specific situation. Reinforcement value is basically how much we desire or dread the outcome that we expect the behaviour to produce. Thus a student who strongly values academic success and also expects that studying will result in high grades is likely to study (Rotter, 1954). Note that this approach makes use of reinforcement, a central behaviourist concept, but views its effects within a cognitive framework that emphasizes how we think about our behaviour and its expected outcomes.

Locus of Control

One of Rotter's most influential expectancy concepts is **internal–external locus of control**, an expectancy concerning the degree of personal control we have in our lives. People with an *internal* locus of control believe that life outcomes are largely under personal control and depend on their own behaviour (Fig. 15.18). In contrast, people with an *external* locus of control believe that their fate has less to do with their own efforts than with the influence of external factors, such as luck, chance, and powerful others. Table 15.9 contains items from Rotter's (1966) *Internal–External (I–E) Scale*, used to measure individual differences in locus of control. Locus of control is called a *generalized expectancy* because it applies across many life domains as a general world view.

TABLE 15.9 SAMPLE ITEMS FROM ROTTER'S INTERNAL–EXTERNAL SCALE

Choose statement (a) or (b) from each numbered choice.
1. (a) Many times I feel that I have little influence over the things that happen to me (b) It is impossible for me to believe that chance or luck plays an important part in my life
2. (a) The average citizen can have an influence in government decisions (b) The world is run by the few people in power, and there isn't much the person on the street can do about it
3. (a) In the long run, people get the respect they deserve in this world (b) Unfortunately, an individual's worth often passes unrecognized no matter how hard one tries
NOTE: 1b, 2a, and 3a are the internal alternatives.

SOURCE: adapted from Rotter, 1966.

Locus of control is a highly researched personality variable. Quite consistently, people with an internal locus of control behave in a more self-determined fashion (Pervin et al., 2005). In the 1960s, African-Americans who actively participated in the civil rights movement were more internal on the I–E Scale than were those who did not (Rotter, 1966). 'Internal' university students achieve better grades than do 'external' students of equal academic ability, probably because they link their studying to degree of success and work harder. Internals are more likely to actively seek out the information needed to succeed in a given situation (Ingold, 1989). Interpersonally, internals are more resistant to social influence, whereas externals tend to give in to high-status people they see as powerful.

Internal locus of control is positively related to self-esteem and feelings of personal effectiveness, and internals tend to cope with stress in a more active and problem-focused manner than do externals (Jennings, 1990). They are also less likely to experience psychological maladjustment in the form of depression or anxiety (Hoffart and Martinson, 1991).

ALBERT BANDURA: SOCIAL LEARNING AND SELF-EFFICACY

Albert Bandura has made major contributions to the development of the social-cognitive approach. His early studies of modelling, described in Chapter 7, helped combine the psychology of learning with the cognitive perspective. Bandura's social learning analyses of aggression, moral behaviour and behavioural self-control demonstrated the wide applicability of the social-cognitive approach (Bandura, 1986). Perhaps his most influential contribution, however, is his theory and research on self-efficacy.

Self-Efficacy

According to Bandura (1997), a key factor in how people regulate their lives is their sense of **self-efficacy**, their beliefs concerning their ability to perform the behaviours needed to achieve desired outcomes. People whose self-efficacy is high have confidence in their ability to do what it takes to overcome obstacles and achieve their goals.

> **self-efficacy**
> beliefs concerning an ability to perform the behaviours needed to achieve desired outcomes

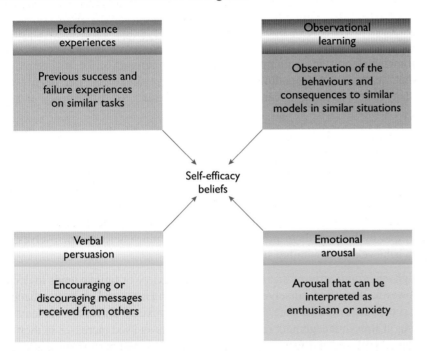

FIGURE 15.19

Self-efficacy beliefs.

Four classes of information affect self-efficacy beliefs.

SOURCE: based on Bandura, 1997.

A good deal of research has been done on the factors that create differences in self-efficacy (Fig. 15.19). Four important determinants have been identified (Bandura, 1997). First and most important is our previous *performance experiences* in similar situations. Such experiences shape our beliefs about our capabilities. For example, as shown in Figure 15.20, university women who felt that they had mastered the martial arts and emotional-control skills taught in a physical self-defence training programme showed dramatic increases in their belief that they could escape from or disable a potential assailant or rapist (Weitlauf et al., 2000).

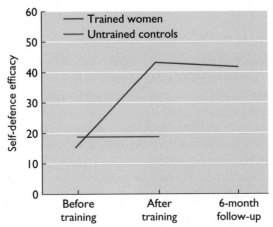

FIGURE 15.20

Effects of self-defence training.

(a) Physical self-defence training has dramatic effects on women's self-efficacy to perform the behaviours needed to defend themselves. (b). The physical defence self-efficacy scores in this study could extend from 6 to 60.

SOURCE: based on Weitlauf et al., 2000.

FIGURE 15.21

The film *Stand and Deliver* depicted the extraordinary accomplishments of math teacher Jaime Escalante, who inspired his inner-city students to exceptional achievement in calculus. His stated faith in their potential and their own performance accomplishments enhanced their sense of self-efficacy.

Bandura stresses that self-efficacy beliefs are always specific to particular situations. Thus we may have high self-efficacy in some situations and low self-efficacy in others. For example, the women who mastered the physical self-defence skills did not feel more capable in all areas of their lives, despite their enhanced self-defence efficacy.

A second determinant of self-efficacy is *observational learning* – that is, observing others' behaviours and their outcomes. If you observe a person similar to yourself accomplish a particular goal, then you are likely to believe that if you perform those same behaviours you will also succeed. A striking example of how powerful such expectations can be comes from the world of sports. At one time, physiologists insisted that it was physically impossible for a human being to run a mile in less than 4 minutes, and no one in the history of track and field had ever done it. When the Englishman Roger Bannister broke the 4-minute barrier in 1954, that limiting belief was shattered. The impact on other runners' performance was immediate and dramatic. In the year following Bannister's accomplishment, 37 other runners broke the barrier, and in the year after that, nearly 300 runners did the 'impossible'. Apparently, a great many people came to believe that 'if he can do it, so can I', and their new sense of self-efficacy enhanced their performance.

Third, self-efficacy can be increased or decreased by *verbal persuasion*. The messages we get from other people who affirm our abilities or downgrade them affect our efficacy beliefs. Thus inspirational teachers who convey high standards and a 'you can do it' conviction can inspire their students to great accomplishments, as exemplified in the true-life story of Jaime Escalante, the mathematics teacher featured in the movie *Stand and Deliver* (Fig. 15.21). By convincing inner-city minority students who had trouble doing simple arithmetic that they were capable of much more, and by helping them prove their hidden competencies to themselves, Escalante helped them achieve award-winning success in calculus.

Fourth, high *emotional arousal* that is interpreted as anxiety or fatigue tends to decrease self-efficacy. However, if we find ourselves able to control such arousal, it may enhance efficacy beliefs and subsequent performance. For example, test-anxious university students who were given training in stress-management relaxation techniques showed increases in their belief that they could remain relaxed and focused during tests, and their test performance and grade point average improved significantly as they controlled anxious arousal (Smith, 1989).

Efficacy beliefs are strong predictors of future performance and accomplishment (Bandura, 1997). They become a kind of self-fulfilling prophecy. The well-known maxim that if you believe you can do something you will succeed certainly has some truth according to Bandura.

APPLYING PSYCHOLOGICAL SCIENCE

INCREASING SELF-EFFICACY THROUGH SYSTEMATIC GOAL SETTING

In Chapter 11 we described motivation as the impetus for goal-directed behaviour. Because positive self-efficacy beliefs are consistently related to success in behaving effectively and achieving goals, Bandura and other social-cognitive theorists have been strongly interested in practical measures for enhancing self-efficacy. When people are successful and when they attribute their success to their own competencies (internal locus of control), their self-efficacy increases and assists them in subsequent goal-directed efforts. Moreover, successful people have usually mastered the skills involved in setting challenging and realistic goals, figuring out what they need to do on a day-to-day basis to achieve them, and making the commitment to do what is required. As they achieve each goal they have set, they become more skilful and increase their sense of personal efficacy (Bandura, 1997).

Not all goal-setting procedures are created equal, and it is important to apply the principles that make goal-setting programmes most effective (Locke and Latham, 2002). Here are some research-derived guidelines for effective goal setting.

1. *Set specific, behavioural and measurable goals.* The first step in changing some aspect of your life is to set a goal. The kind of goal you set is very important, because certain kinds of goals encourage us to work harder, enjoy success, and increase self-efficacy. Studies show that specific and fairly narrow goals are far more effective than general 'do your best' goals (Locke and Latham, 2002). A general goal like 'improve my tennis game' is less helpful than 'increase the number of serves I put in play by 20 per cent'. The latter goal refers to a specific behaviour that you can focus on and measure.

   One of the most important aspects of goal setting is systematically measuring progress towards the goal. This was shown in a study by Bandura and Daniel Cervone (1983) in which participants worked on a strenuous bicycle-pedalling task over a number of sessions. Two independent variables were manipulated: (a) whether the participants were given specific improvement goals before each session after the first (one) and (b) whether the participants were given feedback about their performance during the previous session. A control condition got neither goals nor feedback and provided a basis for evaluating the effects of goals and feedback, alone or in combination. The dependent variable was the speed and power with which the participants pedalled.

   As shown in Figure 15.22, simply having goals was not enough, nor was feedback effective by itself. But having both goals and feedback was a powerful combination. This shows how important it is to measure your progress towards the goal so that you get performance feedback and can see your improvement. Visible movement towards realistic goals builds self-efficacy.

FIGURE 15.22

Goals are not enough.

This graph shows the effects of improvement goals and performance feedback on performance improvement on a gruelling bicycling task. Clearly, the combination of explicit goals *and* performance feedback resulted in greater improvement in performance than did either element by itself.

SOURCE: based on Bandura and Cervone, 1983.

2. *Set behavioural, not outcome, goals.* Many of our goals relate to outcomes in the future, such as getting an A in this course. You are more likely to achieve such goals if you use the means–ends heuristic discussed in Chapter 8 and think about the specific things you must *do* to achieve that outcome goal. Behavioural goals (what one has to do) work better than outcome goals because they keep the focus on the necessary behaviours. A behavioural goal might be 'read and outline the textbook and outline the lecture notes for 1 hour each day'. Achieving this behavioural goal can also be measured quickly and repeatedly, giving you constant feedback. Many people focus on outcome goals and forget what has to be done day-to-day to achieve them. In order for goals to actually be achieved it is vital to focus on the steps required to achieve them.

3. *Set difficult but realistic goals.* Moderately difficult goals challenge and motivate us and give us a sense of hope. When reached, they increase self-efficacy. Easy goals do not provide a sense of accomplishment, and extremely difficult or unattainable goals do not provide the success experiences you need to increase your self-efficacy.

4. *Set positive, not negative, goals.* In Chapter 7 we discussed the advantages of positive reinforcement over punishment. Working towards positive goals, such as 'study for 1 hour before dinner' is better than avoiding a negative consequence, as in 'don't waste time'. Again, positive goals keep you focused on the positive steps that you need to take to achieve them.

5. *Set short-range and long-range goals.* Short-range goals are important because they provide the opportunity for immediate mastery experiences, and they keep you working positively. A long-range goal like 'be fit enough to run a marathon in under 4 hours' can easily be divided into a series of subgoals that you can be working towards right now. Short-range goals are like the steps on a staircase leading to the long-range goal. As each step is accomplished, you enjoy mastery experiences that also lead you towards your ultimate goal.

6. *Set definite time spans for achievement.* To keep your goal-setting programme on track, it is important to specify the dates by which you will meet specific performance goals or subgoals, as well as the behaviours needed to attain them in that time span.

Most of the preceding guidelines can be summarized in the acronym SMART: specific, measurable, action oriented, realistic and time based. The systematic application of these principles of goal setting is a very good way to work towards goals.

Goal setting is a motivational technique that has resulted in remarkable improvements in productivity in many work, social and academic settings (Locke and Latham, 2002). Moreover, for purposes of increasing self-efficacy, it has the added advantage of providing the repeated mastery experiences that are the most powerful sources of efficacy information.

Focus 15.17

Describe the five 'person variables' in Mischel and Shoda's cognitive-affective personality system (CAPS).

WALTER MISCHEL AND YUICHI SHODA: THE COGNITIVE-AFFECTIVE PERSONALITY SYSTEM

Walter Mischel, who studied under George Kelly and Julian Rotter at Ohio State University and was a colleague of Albert Bandura's at Stanford, is a third key figure in social-cognitive theory. Bandura and Mischel became part of the 'cognitive revolution' that occurred among behaviourists during the 1960s. They believed that a more cognitive approach to personality was required, one that takes into account not only the power of situational learning factors but also how people characteristically deal mentally and emotionally with experiences. Mischel set out to identify the important 'person variables' that could help account for individual differences in personality.

In the most recent formulation of social-cognitive theory, Mischel and Yuichi Shoda (1999) describe a **cognitive-affective personality system (CAPS)**, an organized system of five variables that interact continuously with one another and with the environment, generating the distinctive patterns of behaviour that characterize the person (Mischel, 1999). The dynamic interplay among these five variables (encoding strategies, expectancies and beliefs, goals and values, affects, and competencies and self-regulatory processes), together with the characteristics of the situation, accounts for individual differences among people, as well as differences in people's behaviour across different situations. Let us examine these five personality variables.

Encodings and Personal Constructs

We respond to the world as perceived. As Kelly proposed in his theory of personal constructs, discussed earlier in this chapter, people differ greatly in how they customarily *encode* (mentally represent, categorize, interpret) situations. An unkempt man dressed in a caveman-style loincloth who steps into a lift carrying a large snake might be sorted into the personal construct category

cognitive-affective personality system (CAPS)

an organized system of five variables that interact continuously with one another and with the environment, generating the distinctive patterns of behaviour that characterize the person

'dangerous' by one fellow passenger and as 'an intriguing person I'd like to get to know' by another. These different encodings, or appraisals, will affect the other elements of the CAPS, including emotions, expectancies and motivation to exit the lift (Mischel, 1999).

Our encodings determine how we respond emotionally and behaviourally to situations. For example, studies of highly aggressive youths reveal that they have a strong tendency to perceive others as having disrespect and hostile intent towards them. Thus they are primed to interpret ambiguous acts by others, such as being unintentionally brushed against on a stairway at school, as an aggressive act and to react with a violent response (Dodge, 1986). Other individuals tend to encode ambiguous interpersonal events, such as not being greeted by a fellow student, as instances of personal rejection and to become depressed as a result (Downey and Feldman, 1996). As object relations theorists have suggested, the mental representations or working models we have of relationships influence how we perceive (encode) and respond to others in our later relationships. This is an example of how the social-cognitive approach can incorporate concepts and insights from other theories, including psychodynamic ones.

Expectancies and Beliefs

As Rotter emphasized, what we expect will happen if we behave in a particular way is a strong determinant of our behavioural choices. **Behaviour outcome expectancies** represent the 'if–then' links between alternative behaviours and possible outcomes. *If* I take that course in organic chemistry, *then* what will happen to my grade point average? How likely is it that I'll be forgiven *if* I apologize? Will I make enough money to support myself *if* I become a teacher? Different people may have very different answers to such questions and therefore vary in their responses to the same situation.

In addition to behaviour–outcome expectancies, beliefs about our competencies and about the degree of personal control we have influence our actions. Thus the CAPS model also includes Bandura's self-efficacy and Rotter's locus of control as important expectancy variables.

Goals and Values

Motivation plays a central role in attempts to understand behaviour, and it is represented in the CAPS system as goals and values that guide our behaviour, cause us to persist in the face of barriers, and determine the outcomes and situations we seek and our reactions to them (Higgins, 1996). People differ in the goals that are important to them and the values that guide their lives. These differences can cause people to behave very differently in situations that are relevant to these important personality factors.

Affects (Emotions)

Anything that implies important consequences for us, whether beneficial or harmful, can trigger an emotional response (Lazarus, 2001). Once aroused, emotions colour our perceptions and influence our behaviour. For example, if you are already feeling bad due to an argument with a friend and you then get negative feedback in the form of a poor grade on a test, you may feel demoralized for a time. Emotions also affect other CAPS components. Anxiety, for example, can significantly lower outcome expectancies in performance situations (Shepperd et al., 2005).

Research shows that people exhibit stable individual differences in emotionality. For example, people who are high on Eysenck's trait of instability (neuroticism) have a tendency to experience negative *affect*, or emotion, in an intense fashion, a factor that influences many of their perceptions and behaviours. Other people seem predisposed to experience mainly positive affect in their lives (Watson and Clark, 1992).

behaviour outcome expectancies
the 'if–then' links between alternative behaviours and possible outcomes

Competencies and Self-Regulatory Processes

Social-cognitive theorists stress that people extensively control, or regulate, their own behaviour. People's ability to control their own behaviour is a distinguishing aspect of personality, as are the competencies they develop that allow them to adapt to life successfully and pursue important goals. Some of these competencies are cognitive problem-solving methods (such as systematic goal setting) that allow them to plan successful strategies, whereas others involve the ability to exert personal control over thoughts, emotions and behaviours. People who score high on measures of self-esteem tend to have better self-regulation abilities and to enjoy more positive outcomes (Di Paula and Campbell, 2002). These successes undoubtedly contribute to their positive feelings about themselves.

One important way people regulate their own behaviour is through self-administered consequences. **Self-reinforcement processes** refer to internal, self-administered rewards and punishments (Bandura, 1999; Mischel, 1999). In response to our own behaviours, we generate positive evaluations and emotions such as pride, self-approval and the conviction that we did 'the right thing'. In contrast, we may respond with negative responses such as self-reproach, shame and guilt when we violate our personal standards. Self-reinforcement processes often override external consequences, making us more autonomous and self-directed.

Figure 15.23 shows how the CAPS system (represented inside the circle) responds to situations and generates behaviours. Within the circle, solid lines and arrows indicate that a particular unit will stimulate the next one, whereas a dotted line indicates that the next unit will be inhibited. Features of the present situation are perceived and encoded (Enc) as a first step. In this case, assume that the four relevant features are of a potential male partner. In this case, feature 2 (a statement by the person that he has a very bad temper) is encoded as a warning sign. This encoding evokes an expectancy (Exp) that this man might be potentially abusive and the woman experiences a negative emotional response (Aff) and another expectancy (Exp) that this would not be a good relationship to get into. Together, these two expectancies and anxiety about getting into a relationship with this man evoke a competent behavioural script (B) for gracefully declining the date (Behaviour 1). This behaviour should effectively end the encounter (path from Behaviour 1 back to the situation). It is worth noting that if the woman had encoded a different feature of the man (for example, how handsome he is), the lower set of paths might have

---

self-reinforcement processes

internal, self-administered rewards and punishments

FIGURE 15.23

The Cognitive-Affective Personality System (CAPS).

Within the circle are the CAPS variables described in the text, connected in a stable network of relations that characterize the individual's personality functioning. Solid lines represent positive activation in which one CAPS variable activates another. Dotted lines indicate relations in which one unit's activation inhibits the other. Internal CAPS units become activated initially by the encodings of situational features, and network activation patterns result in characteristic patterns of behaviour in response to different situations. In line with social-cognitive theory's principle of reciprocal determinism, output behaviours can, in turn, influence both the situation and the CAPS elements underlying the behavioural responses.

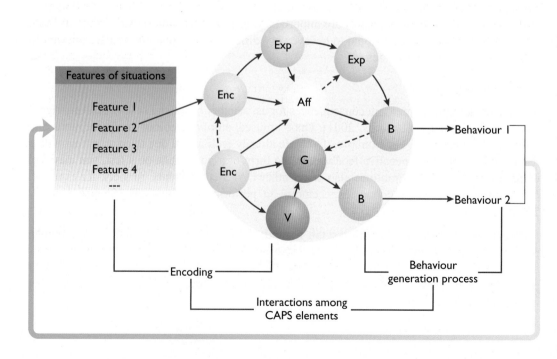

led to Behaviour 2 (accept the date) because she highly values (V) a handsome dating partner, leading to a different situation (involvement in the relationship). We see, therefore, that it is the dynamic relations among the components of the CAPS that account for the links between the 'active ingredients' of situations, personality processes and behaviour, and that our ongoing behaviours feed back into and influence the situation in accordance with the social-cognitive concept of reciprocal determinism. In this manner, the CAPS ties together situations, personality, behaviours and their consequences.

RECONCILING PERSONALITY COHERENCE WITH BEHAVIOURAL INCONSISTENCY

As noted in our earlier discussion of the trait perspective, people's behaviour often shows a notable lack of consistency across situations, a fact that has caused some to question the traditional concept of personality. How can we have a coherent and stable personality yet show such inconsistency across different situations? Does personality really matter? Recent social-cognitive research and theoretical advances may provide the answer to this paradox of personality coherence and inconsistent behaviour by focusing on person-by-situation interactions.

In CAPS theory, personality is defined in terms of the cognitive-affective person variables and the interactions among them. The CAPS system is assumed to be stable and consistent, although it can surely be modified by significant experiences. Behaviour, however, need not be consistent. How a person behaves depends on many factors, including the features of the situation, how these features are encoded, the expectancies and beliefs that are activated, the goals that are relevant, the emotions that might occur and the plans and self-regulatory processes that help determine the behaviour. Thus it is entirely possible for people to behave inconsistently across situations that seem very similar to an outside observer. People will behave similarly in situations that, *to them*, have important characteristics in common, but they may behave inconsistently in situations that differ in ways that evoke different responses from the CAPS (Shoda and Mischel, 2000).

As a result of interactions between situations and the personality system, people exhibit distinctive **behavioural signatures**, consistent ways of responding in particular classes of situations. These behavioural signatures are the outward manifestation of personality that establish a person's unique identity (Mischel et al., 2002). Research shows that people can have very distinctive behavioural signatures. For example, Figure 15.24 shows the behavioural patterns of two verbally aggressive children in a residential summer camp (Shoda et al., 1994). The children's behaviours were systematically observed and coded for more than 150 hours per child. Overall, these two children were quite similar in the overall number of verbally aggressive responses they made. However, inspection of the *situational patterns* of aggression reveals that child A reacted very aggressively towards adults, whether they were behaving towards the child in a warm or a punitive fashion. In contrast, this child consistently showed relatively little aggression towards peers. Child B showed quite a different pattern, consistently reacting with low levels of aggression towards adults or when being teased by peers but showing a consistently high level of aggression when peers approached him in a friendly manner.

The important lesson here is that if we simply averaged the aggressive behaviour counts across the five situations, the two children would look equally aggressive. But in so doing, we would mask the distinctive and consistent behavioural signatures that define each child's individuality. Thus the coherence of personality is shown not at the level of individual behaviours but at the level of behavioural signatures (situation-by-behaviour patterns).

Focus 15.18

How does the concept of behavioural signatures help reconcile the seeming paradox of personality coherence and behavioural inconsistency?

behavioural signatures

consistent ways of responding in particular classes of situations

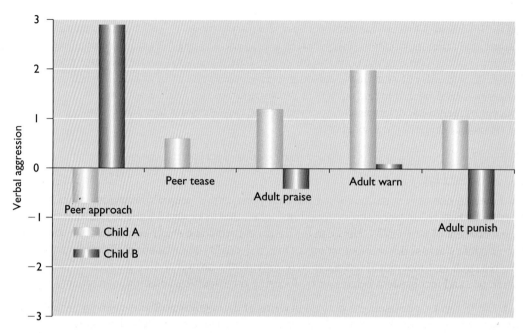

FIGURE 15.24

Stable situation-behaviour patterns.

This chart shows the aggressive responses of two children, A and B, in five different summer camp situations. These data show the children's distinctive behavioural signatures for aggressive responding, even though their aggression scores averaged across the five settings were quite similar. The zero point on the vertical axis represents the average amount of verbal aggression shown in each situation by all the children in the study.

SOURCE: adapted from Shoda et al., 1994.

EVALUATING SOCIAL-COGNITIVE THEORIES

A strength of the social-cognitive approach is its strong scientific base. It brings together two perspectives that have strong research traditions: the behavioural and the cognitive. The constructs of social-cognitive theory can be defined, measured and researched with considerable precision. As a result, the social-cognitive approach has advanced our understanding of how processes within the person and characteristics of the situation interact with one another to influence behaviour. Another strength is its ability to translate insights derived from other perspectives into cognitive-behavioural concepts (Mischel et al., 2004).

Social-cognitive theory also helps resolve an apparent contradiction between the central assumption that personality produces stability in behaviour and research findings that people's behaviour is not very consistent across different situations. Mischel and Shoda's CAPS theory suggests that the inconsistency of a person's behaviour across situations is actually a manifestation of a stable underlying cognitive-affective personality structure that reacts to certain features of situations. However, the ability of the CAPS to predict specific behaviour needs further examination, and it will be challenging to measure the numerous interactions among the CAPS components. Much more needs to be learned about how the CAPS operates, but this question is being explored by many current researchers (Cervone and Shoda, 1999; Mischel et al., 2004). Another major challenge will be to find out what active ingredients of situations cause people to encode them in similar ways, thereby producing the consistencies in behaviour that constitute behavioural signatures (Ten-Berge et al., 2002). The study of abused women and abusive men (Zayas and Shoda, 2007) in this chapter's 'Research close-up' (p. 671) is one attempt to identify the active stimulus ingredients of a situation.

Understanding Charles Whitman

To conclude our analysis of Charles Whitman, let us view him from a social-cognitive perspective. The behavioural aspect of the social-cognitive perspective would focus on past learning experiences that predisposed him to violence. These are not hard to find in his history. First, his father provided an aggressive model during his formative years, controlling his wife and children with physical abuse. His father was also a gun enthusiast, and there were guns hanging in virtually every room of the Whitman home. Family photos show young Charles holding guns when he was only 2 years old, and his father made sure he received plenty of training in using them. Long before he enlisted in the Marines, Whitman was an expert marksman, and the Marines built on this expertise with sniper training that earned him a sharpshooter's badge. As other aspects of his life were crumbling, Whitman's marksmanship was a continuing and positive part of his personal self-identity, and he told several University of Texas acquaintances how easy it would be to pick off people from the tower. His expertise made him a deadly killer as he fired from the tower with stunning accuracy, killing people up to half a mile (800 m) away.

How might Charles Whitman be represented within the CAPS model? At the level of encoding processes, Mischel and Shoda would focus on how he viewed himself and his world. Aggression is fuelled by perceptions that we have been wronged and that the provocation was intentional (Lazarus, 2001). Clearly, Whitman felt victimized both by his father and by the Marines, and he saw the world as so malevolent that he regarded killing his wife and mother as an act of mercy. Moreover, his view of himself became increasingly negative as his life's fortunes declined. His outcome and self-efficacy expectancies became increasingly negative. One source of self-efficacy that remained unchanged was his exceptional marksmanship, and this competency became the medium for the expression of his rage, as well as the means to achieve the death he desired.

Whitman's values involved success in his career, in academics, and as a husband. Success was nowhere in sight, producing feelings of frustration and creating unbearable stress (negative affect) in his life. He felt unworthy of his wife and deeply regretted the two incidents early in their marriage when he had beaten her.

At the level of affect, what also stands out is Whitman's internal rage. In the words of the psychiatrist who saw him shortly before his outburst, he was 'fairly oozing' with generalized hostility. Whitman tried to achieve his goals and exercise self-control with elaborate manuals filled with specific self-instructions about how to act, what to say and how to inhibit his hostility. Eventually, though, in the absence of adequate self-regulation skills, these external controls failed, with tragic consequences.

Applying the concept of behavioural signatures to Charles Whitman, it is clear that Whitman's behaviour differed dramatically across situations. Most of the time, he was an all-American boy, charming, witty, agreeable and a loving husband. However, when under stress, his defences against his inner rage began to crumble and he became hostile and aggressive, capable of abusing his wife and threatening to shoot a fellow Marine. When stress reached a sufficiently severe level, his controls broke down completely and he committed the murderous acts. In the if–then language of behavioural signatures, we might summarize this aspect of his personality as: *if* not under stress, *then* friendly and well controlled; but *if* under stress and facing severe failure, *then* hostile and impulsive.

Having now described the various perspectives on personality, we have seen that each presents us with a different picture of human nature and that each focuses on particular determinants of human individuality. Moreover, each perspective provides us with different pieces of the puzzle that was Charles Whitman.

Figure 15.25 summarizes the determinants emphasized by the various theories at the biological, psychological and environmental levels of analysis.

LEVELS OF ANALYSIS   FACTORS RELATED TO PERSONALITY DIFFERENCES

Biological	Psychological	Environmental
• Personality differences shaped by evolutionary factors (evolutionary personality theory) • Genetic bases for individual differences and temperament (behaviour genetics) • Individual differences in customary level of cortical aurosal and suddenness with which autonomic shifts occur (Eysenck) • Individual differences in biological bases for temperament	• Psychodynamic processes involving impulse, defence, unconscious conflicts and psychosexual factors (Freud) • Differences in object relations and attachment styles • Differences in personal construct systems (Kelly) • Processes involving the self-concept and striving for self-actualization (Rogers) • Personality dispositions to act, think and feel in particular ways (trait theorists) • Cognitive social learning variables that interact with situational factors (Bandura, Rotter, Mischel)	• Early relationship experiences (psychodynamic theories) • Environmental factors that support or stifle self-actualization (humanistic theorists) • Past social learning experiences and current environmental factors that interact with social cognitive person variables (social-cognitive theorists)

Personality differences

FIGURE 15.25

Levels of analysis: factors related to personality differences.

IN REVIEW

- Social-cognitive theories are concerned with how social relationships, learning experiences and cognitive processes jointly contribute to behaviour. A key concept is reciprocal determinism, relating to two-way causal relations between people, their behaviour and the environment.

- Rotter's theory viewed behaviour as influenced by expectancies and the reinforcement value of potential outcomes. His concept of locus of control is a generalized belief in the extent to which we can control the outcomes in our life.

- Bandura's concept of self-efficacy relates to our self-perceived ability to carry out the behaviours necessary to achieve goals in a particular situation. It is influenced by past performance attainments, verbal persuasion, observation of others' attainments and perceived emotional arousal. Self-efficacy can be enhanced through the application of systematic goal-setting procedures.

- According to Mischel and Shoda, situational features activate the person's cognitive-affective personality system (CAPS). The CAPS involves individual differences in encoding strategies, expectancies and beliefs, goals and values, affects, and competencies and self-regulatory processes. The CAPS interacts with features of the environment, helping to explain why people have specific behavioural signatures and do not necessarily behave consistently across situations.

CULTURE, GENDER AND PERSONALITY

As we have seen, personality is a product of interacting biological and environmental influences. Children inherit different biologies that influence how their environment, including culture, affects them (Kagan and Fox, 2006).

Environment exists at many different levels, ranging from the physical surroundings in which we develop to the increasingly global social contexts shown in Figure 15.26. Among the most important environmental influences is the culture in which we develop. We are often unaware of these influences because they serve as an amorphous background against which the specific events of our lives unfold. Culture encompasses unstated assumptions (including assumptions about the very nature of reality), norms, values, sex roles, and habitual ways of behaving that are shared by members of a social group. It influences what we perceive, how we perceive, how we relate to ourselves and others, and how we behave.

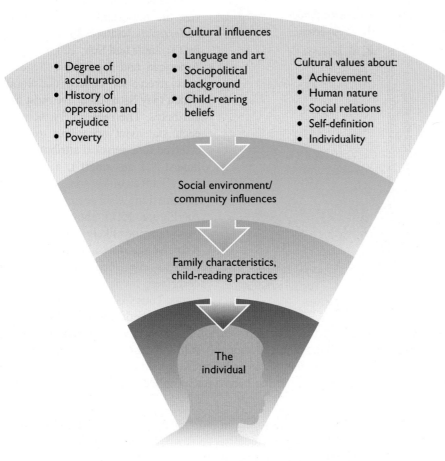

Cultural influences

- Degree of acculturation
- History of oppression and prejudice
- Poverty

- Language and art
- Sociopolitical background
- Child-rearing beliefs

Cultural values about:
- Achievement
- Human nature
- Social relations
- Self-definition
- Individuality

Social environment/ community influences

Family characteristics, child-reading practices

The individual

FIGURE 15.26

Culture and personality.

This model shows how cultural elements are transmitted to the individual through the medium of social environment and family influences.

SOURCE: based on factors cited by Locke, 1992; Sue and Sue, 1990.

CULTURE DIFFERENCES

Cultures differ along a number of dimensions that can affect personality development (Triandis and Suh, 2002). One dimension is *complexity*. Consider how much more complex a western information-age culture is than a hunter-gatherer culture in a remote region of an undeveloped country. Consider also how much more potential for diversity and conflict of values and behavioural norms exists in a highly complex culture.

A second cultural dimension is *interdependence*. Markus and Kitayama (1991) proposed that cultures differ profoundly in the extent to which they weight interdependence. So-called 'western cultures' including Western Europe and the USA, are argued to be rather independent, with an emphasis on individual choice. On the other side of the coin, Markus and Kitayama argue

Focus 15.19

In what three ways can cultures differ, thereby influencing personality? What personality and gender differences occur within individualistic and collectivistic cultures?

that non-western cultures such as China and Japan are highly interdependent, and the emphasis is placed on the choices and decisions of groups of people. If we are to consider personality in this light, it seems reasonable to expect that adolescents in 'independent' cultures would show greater diversity and feelings of individuality than those in 'interdependent' cultures. However, adolescents in independent cultures might also experience more conflicts in deciding which values to embrace and what type of person they want to be. These hypothesized cultural differences have found some support in the literature. For example, Markus and Kitayama (1998) describe large differences between Japanese and European-American students' endorsements of descriptions of themselves as 'ordinary'. Whereas only 18 per cent of the European-American students endorsed, this, 84 per cent of the Japanese students did. On the other hand, when asked if they would describe themselves as special, 55 per cent of Japanese students endorsed this, compared with 96 per cent of European-American students.

FIGURE 15.27

Cultural differences in the self-concept.

This graph shows the percentages of personal identity and social/relational self-attributes given by Japanese and American college students as key aspects of their self-concepts.

SOURCE: adapted from Cousins, 1989.

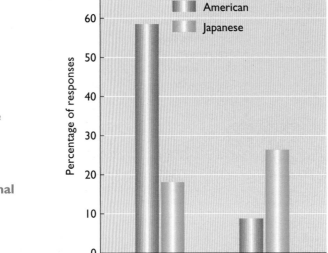

Other researchers have chosen to emphasize the importance of *individualistic* vs *collectivistic* cultures in shaping personality (Triandis and Suh, 2002). In one study, American and Japanese college students were given a self-concept questionnaire on which they listed their five most important attributes. The researchers then classified each statement according to whether it referred to a personal attribute (e.g., 'I am honest', 'I am smart'), a social identity (e.g., 'I am an oldest son', 'I am a student'), or something else, such as a physical trait. As Figure 15.27 shows, the Americans were far more likely than the Japanese to list personal traits, abilities or dispositions, whereas the Japanese more frequently described themselves in social identity terms. Thus Cousins (1989) argued that the social embeddedness of the collectivistic Japanese culture was reflected in their self-perceptions, as was cultural individualism in the Americans' self-concepts. Interestingly, personality trait measures do not predict behaviour as well in collectivistic cultures as they do in individualistic cultures, possibly because environmental factors play a stronger role in the behaviour of collectivistic individuals (Church and Katigbak, 2000).

Self-enhancement needs are equally strong in individualistic and collectivistic cultures, but they are satisfied in different ways. Individualists enhance the self through personal successes, whereas collectivists feel better about themselves when their group succeeds (Sedikides et al., 2003). In individualistic cultures, personal success also serves to increase people's motivation, whereas in collectivistic cultures, motivation increases after failure, as the person attempts to change the self and conform to the demands of the situation (Heine et al., 2000). Even emotional lives differ. In a study of cultural differences in experienced emotions, Americans reported more self-oriented positive emotions, such as self-pride and personal happiness, whereas Japanese reported more interpersonally oriented positive emotions, such as closeness, friendliness and respect (Kitayama et al., 2000). On self-esteem measures, Japanese score lower than Americans. Kitayama and Markus (1999) explain that in Japanese culture, self-criticism is not bad, for it serves the valuable function of encouraging self-improvement that can benefit the individual and society. In western cultures, self-criticism is predictive of depression, but this is not the case in Japan.

However, there are a number of criticisms that can be laid against research examining cultural differences in personality. First, it is uncertain whether the personality differences captured in cross-cultural studies are caused by the collectivistic and individualistic nature of their respective cultures. In fact, on average, only about 40 per cent of people within a particular culture strongly embrace individualistic or collectivistic goals. Second, the cross-cultural effects do not seem to be as robust as has often been claimed. In a meta-analysis of studies comparing individualistic and collectivistic values across several cultures, Oyserman et al. (2002), found that although European-Americans were less collectivistic than the Chinese, they were no less collectivistic than the Japanese or Koreans (cultures traditionally thought to be highly collectivistic in organization). Finally, as pointed out by Matsumoto (1999), very little evidence has examined cultural differences in collectivism and individualism outside of comparisons between European-Americans and East Asians. Can we be sure that these proposed effects of culture on personality will bear out in Europe, Africa, South America and Australasia?

GENDER SCHEMAS

Gender-role socialization provides us with **gender schemas**, organized mental structures that contain our understanding of the attributes and behaviours that are appropriate and expected for males and females (Bem, 1981). Within a given culture, gender schemas tell us what the typical man or woman should be like. In western cultures, men tend to prize attributes related to achievement, emotional strength, athleticism and self-sufficiency, whereas women prize interpersonal competencies, kindness and helpfulness to others (Beyer, 1990; Marsh, 1990). In this sense, men in western cultures tend to develop more of an individualistic self-concept, emphasizing achievement and separateness from others, whereas women's self-concepts tend to be more collectivistic, emphasizing their social connectedness with others (Kashima et al., 1995). Nonetheless, as with differences in cultures, we should keep in mind that significant individual differences exist within each gender group, with many women being individualists and many men collectivists (Triandis and Suh, 2002).

gender schemas
organized mental structures that contain our understanding of the attributes and behaviours that are appropriate and expected for males and females

IN REVIEW

- Cultures differ along several important dimensions, including complexity, interdependence and individualism–collectivism, all of which can affect personality development.

- People in collectivistic cultures tend to see the environment as fixed (i.e., having rigid rules and expectations) and themselves as changeable, with a capacity to fit in. In contrast, members of individualistic cultures are more likely to see themselves and their personalities as relatively stable and the environment as malleable.

- Culture influences self-concept development. People from individualistic cultures tend to describe themselves in terms of personal traits, abilities or dispositions, whereas those from collectivistic cultures are more likely to describe themselves in social identity terms.

- The proposed effects of culture on personality have not been universally accepted. There is widespread variation in the extent to which the cultural values supposed to affect personality are taken up by individuals. Furthermore, most research has been limited to only the USA and East Asia. Can we be sure that culture affects personality in the same way elsewhere in the world?

- Gender schemas are organized mental structures that contain our understanding of the attributes and behaviours that are appropriate and expected for males and females. In western cultures, men tend to value achievement, emotional strength and self-sufficiency, whereas women prize interpersonal skills, kindness and helpfulness to others.

PERSONALITY ASSESSMENT

If you were to be introduced to Jennifer, a woman you had never met before, and given one week to provide a complete personality description of her, what would you do? The chances are, that you would seek information in a variety of ways. You might start by interviewing Jennifer and finding out as much as you could about her. Based on your knowledge of the theories we have discussed, what questions would you ask? Would you ask about early childhood experiences and dream; about how she sees herself and others? Would you be interested in the kinds of traits embodied in the Big Five model or in Eysenck's dimension of introversion–extraversion? Would you want to know how Jennifer customarily feels and responds in various situations? Your answers to these questions and your other assessment decisions would in some sense reflect your own theory of what is important in describing personality.

You probably would not be content simply to interview Jennifer. You might also decide to interview other people who know her well and get their views of what she is like. You might even ask them to rate her on a variety of traits, and you could ask Jennifer to rate herself on the same measures to see if her self-concept agrees with how others see her.

Finally, you might decide that it would be useful to actually observe how Jennifer behaves in a variety of situations. You would want to observe her in a way that would allow you to get as natural and characteristic a sample of her behaviour as possible. This information, together with that obtained from Jennifer and from those who know her best, might provide a reasonable basis for a personality description.

Figure 15.28 shows the major methods that psychologists use to assess personality characteristics. As you can see, they use some of the same methods you might have chosen: the interview, trait ratings and behaviour reports, as well as behavioural assessment or direct observation and measurement of the subject's behaviour. In addition, psychologists have developed several types of tests, including objective self-report measures and projective tests that ask respondents to interpret ambiguous stimuli, such as inkblots or pictures. Finally, physiological measures can be used to measure various aspects of personality, such as emotional reactivity or levels of cortical arousal.

The task of devising valid and useful personality measures is anything but simple, and it has taxed the ingenuity of psychologists for nearly a century. To be useful from either a scientific or a practical perspective, personality tests must conform to the standards of reliability and validity discussed in Chapter 10. *Reliability*, or consistency of measurement, takes several forms.

Focus 15.20

Describe two characteristics that personality measures must have in order to be scientifically and practically useful.

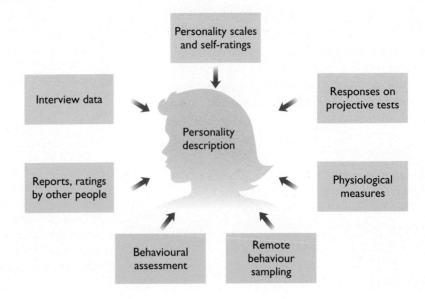

FIGURE 15.28

Measurement approaches used to assess personality.

A test that measures a stable personality trait should yield similar scores when administered to the same individuals at different times (test–retest reliability). Another aspect of reliability is that different professionals should score and interpret the test in the same way (inter-judge reliability).

Validity refers to the most important question of all: Is the test actually measuring the personality variable that it is intended to measure? A valid test allows us to predict behaviour that is influenced by the personality variable being measured. Research on test reliability and validity is an important activity of personality psychologists, and good measures of personality are an absolute must for scientific research on personality and for ethical clinical application (Domino, 2000).

In general, current personality assessment tests perform as well as measures in a variety of other health service areas, as shown in the findings of 125 meta-analyses and 800 comparative studies (Meyer et al., 2001). These include electrocardiograms, mammography, smear tests, serum cholesterol tests, PET scans and MRIs. That is the good news. The bad news is that neither the psychological nor the medical tests have as much validity as one would like.

INTERVIEWS

Interviews are one of the oldest methods of assessment. Long before the invention of writing, people undoubtedly made judgements about others by observing them and talking with them. Interviewers can obtain information about a person's thoughts, feelings and other internal states, as well as information about current and past relationships, experiences and behaviour. This assessment method is particularly popular among psychodynamic and phenomenological-humanistic workers.

Structured interviews contain a set of specific questions that are administered to every participant. An attempt is made to create a standardized situation so that interviewees' responses to more-or-less identical stimuli can be interpreted and compared. Such interviews are frequently used to collect research data or to make a psychiatric diagnosis. Other interviews are unstructured, with interviewers tailoring their questions to the particular individual and situation.

Good interviewers do not limit their attention to what an interviewee says; they also look at how she or he says it. They note interviewees' general appearance and grooming, their voice and speech patterns, the content of their statements, and their facial expressions and posture. Sometimes, attitudes that are not expressed verbally can be inferred from behaviour, as in this instance:

> During the interview she held her small son on her lap. The child began to play with his genitals. The mother, without looking directly at the child, moved his hand away and held it securely for a while.... Later in the interview the mother was asked what she ordinarily did when the child masturbated. She replied that he never did this – he was a very 'good' boy. She was evidently entirely unconscious of what had transpired in the very presence of the interviewer. (Maccoby and Maccoby, 1954, p. 484)

The interview is valuable for the direct personal contact it provides, but it has some limitations. First, characteristics of the interviewer may influence how the interviewee responds and thus affect the validity of the information. In addition, the validity of information obtained depends on the interviewee's desire to co-operate, to respond honestly, and to report accurately what the interviewer is trying to assess.

Despite its limitations, the face-to-face interview is essential for certain purposes. For example, a clinical psychologist needs to observe and converse with a person who is being considered for admission to a mental hospital. Interviews are often used in research as well. The challenge is to design and conduct interviews in ways that maximize the validity of the data obtained from the respondent.

Focus 15.21
How are interviews, behavioural assessment and remote behavioural sampling used to assess personality?

structured interviews
a set of specific questions that are administered to every participant

BEHAVIOURAL ASSESSMENT

Personality psychologists can sometimes observe the behaviours they are interested in rather than asking people about them. In **behavioural assessment**, psychologists devise an explicit coding system that contains the behavioural categories of interest. Then they train observers until they show high levels of agreement (inter-judge reliability) in using the coding categories to record behaviour. Assessors may code the behaviour in live settings, or they made code videotaped behaviour sequences. A staple of behaviourists, behavioural assessment can provide valuable information about how frequently and under what conditions certain classes of behaviour occur (Hersen, 2006). Social-cognitive researchers used this method to measure the behavioural signatures of the verbally aggressive children in the summer camp environment discussed earlier.

Behavioural assessment requires precision in defining the behaviours of interest and the conditions under which they occur. For example, observers studying a young child who is having problems in school do not simply say, 'Claude is disruptive'. Instead, they try to answer the question, 'What, specifically, does Claude *do* that causes disruption?' Once they have identified Claude's specific behaviours, the next questions are, 'How often and under what conditions does the disruptive behaviour occur?' and 'What kinds of outcomes do the behaviours produce?' Answers to these questions can be particularly important not only in measuring differences in people's personality characteristics but also in identifying potential situational causes of their behaviour (Greene and Ollendick, 2000; Haynes, 2000).

REMOTE BEHAVIOUR SAMPLING

It is not practical or possible for behavioural assessors to follow people around from situation to situation on a daily basis. In addition, assessors are frequently interested in unobservable events, such as emotional reactions and thinking patterns, that may shed considerable light on personality functioning. Through **remote behaviour sampling**, researchers and clinicians can collect self-reported samples of behaviour from respondents as they live their daily lives. A tiny computerized device resembling a mobile phone is used. The device pages respondents at randomly determined times of the day (Fig. 15.29). When the beeper sounds, respondents rate or record their current thoughts, feelings, or behaviours, depending on what the researcher or therapist is assessing (Stone et al., 2000). Respondents may also report on aspects of the situation they are in so that situation–behaviour interactions can be examined. Remote sampling procedures can be used over weeks or even months to collect a large behaviour sample across many situations. This approach to personality assessment holds great promise, for it enables researchers and clinicians to detect patterns of personal functioning that might not be revealed by other methods.

FIGURE 15.29

In remote behaviour sampling, a computerized device resembling a mobile phone is used to collect responses from participants – such as ratings of their mood at a certain time – as they live their daily lives.

PERSONALITY SCALES

Personality scales, or inventories, are widely used for assessing personality in both research and clinical work. They are considered *objective* measures because they include standard sets of questions, usually in a true–false or rating-scale format, that are scored using an agreed scoring key (Nezami and Butcher, 2000). Their advantages include (1) the ability to collect data from many people at the same time, (2) the fact that all people respond to the same items, and (3) ease of scoring. Their major disadvantage is the possibility that some people will choose not to answer the items truthfully, in which case their scores will not be valid reflections of the trait being measured. To combat this threat to validity, some widely used tests have special *validity scales* that detect tendencies to respond in a socially desirable manner or to present an overly negative image of oneself.

The items on personality scales are developed in two major ways. In the **rational-theoretical approach**, items are based on the theorist's conception of the personality trait to be measured. For example, to develop a measure of introversion–extraversion, we would ask ourselves what introverts and extraverts often say about themselves, and then we would write items that captured those kinds of self-descriptions (e.g., 'I love to be at large social gatherings' or 'I'm very content to spend time by myself'). One frequently used measure of this kind is the NEO Personality Inventory (NEO-PI), which measures the Big Five personality traits of openness, conscientiousness, extraversion, agreeableness and neuroticism (Costa and McCrae, 1992). Other scales developed according to the rational approach are the measures of optimism-pessimism, self-monitoring and locus of control shown in Tables 15.6, 15.7 and 15.9.

A different approach to developing personality scales is the **empirical approach**, in which items are chosen not because their content seems relevant to the trait on rational grounds, but because each item has been answered differently by groups of people (for example, introverts and extraverts) known to differ in the personality characteristic of interest. The Minnesota Multiphasic Personality Inventory-2 (MMPI-2) is a widely used personality test developed according to the empirical approach. The MMPI was originally designed to provide an objective basis for psychiatric diagnosis. Its 567 true–false items consist of statements that were answered by groups of patients diagnosed with specific psychiatric disorders (e.g., hysteria, paranoia and schizophrenia) in ways different from the answers given by respondents in a non-psychiatric comparison sample. The items vary widely in content; some are concerned with attitudes and emotions, others relate to overt behaviour and symptoms, and still others refer to the person's life history.

The MMPI-2 has 3 validity scales and 10 clinical scales (Table 15.10). The validity scales are used to detect tendencies to present either an overly positive picture or to exaggerate the degree of psychological disturbance. Though the scales were originally intended to measure severe personality deviations such as schizophrenia, depression and psychopathic personality, the *profile* of scores obtained on the various scales also reveals important aspects of personality functioning even in people who do not display such disorders (Graham, 2006). Thus the MMPI-2 is used not only as an aid to psychiatric diagnosis but also for personality description and as a screening device in industrial and military settings.

PROJECTIVE TESTS

Freud and other psychodynamic theorists emphasized the importance of unconscious factors in understanding behaviour. By definition, however, people are unaware of unconscious dynamics, so they cannot report them to interviewers or on self-report tests like the NEO-PI or the MMPI-2. Other methods were therefore needed to assess them.

Projective tests present subjects with ambiguous stimuli and ask for some interpretation of them. The assumption is that because the meaning of the stimulus is unclear, the subject's interpretation will have to come from within, reflecting the projection of inner needs, feelings and ways of viewing the world onto the stimulus.

The stimuli that people are asked to respond to include inkblots and pictures. The Rorschach test consists of 10 inkblots. The person being tested is shown each one in succession and asked,

---

Focus 15.22
Compare the rational-theoretical and empirical approaches to developing personality scales.

rational-theoretical approach
items are based on the theorist's conception of the personality trait to be measured

empirical approach
items are chosen not because their content seems relevant to the trait on rational grounds, but because each item has been answered differently by groups of people known to differ in the personality characteristics of interests

Focus 15.23
How do projective tests differ from objective measures? Describe and compare two projective tests.

projective tests
present subjects with ambiguous stimuli and ask for some interpretation of them

TABLE 15.10 THE VALIDITY AND CLINICAL SCALES OF THE MINNESOTA MULTIPHASIC PERSONALITY INVENTORY-2 (MMPI-2) AND THE BEHAVIOURAL CHARACTERISTICS ASSOCIATED WITH HIGH SCORES ON THE SCALES

Scale	Abbreviation	Behavioural correlates
Validity scales		
Lie	L	Lies or is highly conventional
Frequency	F	Exaggerates complaints, answers haphazardly
Correction	K	Denies problems
Clinical scales		
Hypochondriasis	Hs	Expresses bodily concerns and complaints
Depression	D	Is depressed, pessimistic, guilty
Hysteria	Hy	Reacts to stress with physical symptoms, lacks insight into negative feelings
Psychopathic deviate	Pd	Is impulsive, in conflict with the law, involved in stormy relationships
Masculinity, femininity	Mf	Has interests characteristic of the opposite sex
Paranoia	Pa	Is suspicious, resentful
Psychasthenia	Pt	Is anxious, worried, high-strung
Schizophrenia	Sc	Is confused, disorganized, disoriented and withdrawn from others
Hypomania	Ma	Is energetic, active, restless
Social introversion	Si	Is introverted, with little social contact

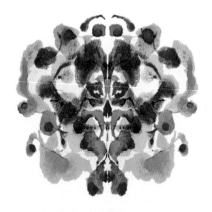

FIGURE 15.30

During a Rorschach test administration, the person being tested is shown a series of inkblots similar to this one and is asked to indicate what each resembles and what feature of the stimulus (for example, its shape or its colour) makes it appear that way.

'What does this look like? What might it be?' (Fig. 15.30). After responding, the person is asked to explain what specific feature of the inkblot (e.g., its shape or its colour) makes it seem that way. Examiners categorize and score responses in terms of the kinds of objects reported, the features attended to (e.g., the whole blot, coloured portions, tiny details) and the emotional tone of particular types of responses (Erdberg, 2000).

Interpretations made by Rorschach examiners are often based on what the responses seem to symbolize. For example, people who see peering eyes and threatening figures in the inkblots are likely to be viewed as projecting their own paranoid fears and suspicions onto the stimuli. One drawback of the Rorschach is that different examiners may interpret the same response very differently, producing unreliability among examiners. In an attempt to minimize clinician subjectivity in interpreting Rorschach responses, John Exner (1991) developed a scoring system with specific coding categories and scoring criteria. Although this system created greater uniformity in scoring, many of the personality interpretations derived from the Rorschach lack research support (Lilienfeld et al., 2000). Nonetheless, many psychodynamic clinicians maintain their faith in the Rorschach, insisting that they find it useful for gaining insight into unconscious processes, and the test seems to be especially valuable in detecting psychotic thought disorders (Society for Personality Assessment, 2005).

The Thematic Apperception Test (TAT) consists of a series of pictures derived from paintings, drawings, and magazine illustrations. In general, the pictures are less ambiguous than the Rorschach inkblots, but they still require an interpretation. To illustrate, look at the picture in Figure 15.31, and then write a story that addresses the following questions:

1. What is happening? Who are the people involved?
2. What has led up to this situation?
3. What is being thought, felt and wanted, and by whom?
4. What will happen? How will the story turn out?

FIGURE 15.31

A picture from the Thematic Apperception Test.

Subjects are asked to make up a story about the picture, covering specific points, such as those listed in the text. The stories are analysed for recurrent themes that are assumed to reflect significant aspects of personality.

SOURCE: Reprinted by permission of the publisher from Henry A. Murray, *Thematic Apperception Test,* Plate 12F. Cambridge, MA: Harvard University Press. Copyright © 1943 by the president and fellows of Harvard College; Copyright © 1971 by Henry A. Murray.

The stories told in response to a set of 10 to 20 pictures are analysed for recurrent themes that are assumed to reflect important aspects of the respondent's personality. These might include the kinds of personal relationships depicted in the stories, the types of motives and feelings that are attributed to the characters, whether positive or negative outcomes occur, and factors that produce these outcomes such as personal weaknesses or forces in the environment. (Langan-Fox and Grant, 2006).

The TAT, like the Rorschach, typically relies on the subjective interpretation of test responses, which can result in different interpretations of the same stories. Since not everyone can be right, the possibility of erroneous interpretations is obvious. Where specific systems have been developed to score stories, however, the TAT has proven to be a useful and valid test (Atkinson, 1958). Scoring of stories told to TAT pictures is used by researchers to measure achievement motivation (see Chapter 11). The TAT appears to provide a more valid measure of this and other motives, such as power, than do objective self-report measures of the same motives, showing stronger relations with motivated behaviour (Ferguson, 2000). Despite such exceptions, however, objective measures of personality have generally been found to have better reliability and validity than projective measures (Lilienfeld et al., 2000; Nezami and Butcher, 2000).

IN REVIEW

- Methods used by psychologists to assess personality include the interview, behavioural assessment, remote behaviour sampling, objective personality scales and projective tests.

- The major approaches to constructing personality scales are the rational approach, in which items are written on an intuitive basis, and the empirical approach, in which items discriminate between groups known to differ on the trait of interest. The NEO-PI, reflecting the rational approach, measures individual differences in the Big Five factors. The MMPI-2 is the best-known test developed with the empirical approach.

- Projective tests present ambiguous stimuli to people. It is assumed that interpretations of such stimuli give clues to important internal processes. The Rorschach inkblot test and the Thematic Apperception Test are the most commonly used projective tests.

KEY TERMS AND CONCEPTS

Each term has been boldfaced and defined in the chapter on the page indicated in parentheses.

archetypes (p. 668)

behaviour-outcome expectancy (p. 701)

behavioural assessment (p. 712)

behavioural signatures (p. 703)

cognitive-affective personality system (CAPS) (p. 700)

collective unconscious (p. 668)

conditions of worth (p. 678)

congruence (p. 677)

defence mechanisms (p. 666)

ego (p. 665)

Electra complex (p. 667)

empirical approach (p. 713)

factor analysis (p. 683)

fixation (p. 667)

fully functioning persons (p. 678)

gender schemas (p. 709)

id (p. 665)

internal–external locus of control (p. 696)

need for positive regard (p. 677)

need for positive self-regard (p. 678)

neoanalytic theorists (p. 668)

object relations theories (p. 669)

Oedipus complex (p. 667)

personal constructs (p. 675)

personal unconscious (p. 668)

personality (p. 662)

personality traits (p. 682)

phenomenology (p. 675)

pleasure principle (p. 665)

projective tests (p. 713)

psychosexual stages (p. 667)

rational-theoretical approach (p. 713)

reality principle (p. 665)

reciprocal determinism (p. 695)

regression (p. 667)

remote behaviour sampling (p. 712)

repression (p. 666)

Role Construct Repertory Test (or Rep Test) (p. 676)

self (p. 676)

self-actualization (p. 676)

self-consistency (p. 676)

self-efficacy (p. 697)

self-enhancement (p. 680)

self-esteem (p. 678)

self-monitoring (p. 688)

self-reinforcement processes (p. 702)

self-verification (p. 679)

social-cognitive theory (p. 695)

structured interview (p. 711)

sublimation (p. 666)

superego (p. 665)

temperament (p. 692)

threat (p. 677)

unconditional positive regard (p. 677)

WHAT DO YOU THINK?

IS SELF-ACTUALIZATION A USEFUL SCIENTIFIC CONSTRUCT? (p. 678)

Self-actualization is a centrepiece of some humanistic theories, but it is troublesome from a scientific perspective. Some critics believe that it is impossible to define an individual's actualizing tendency except in terms of the behaviour that it supposedly produces. This would be an example of circular reasoning: why did the person achieve such success? Because of self-actualization. How do we know self-actualization was at work? Because the person achieved great success.

Unless a construct can be operationally defined in a manner independent of the phenomena it is supposed to cause, it is not scientifically useful. A construct must also be measurable. While it is true that concepts related to the self-actualization motive (such as people's beliefs that they are fulfilling their potential) could potentially be measured, most psychologists suggest that rather than being a scientific construct, self-actualization is better considered a philosophical concept.

CHAPTER SIXTEEN

HEALTH PSYCHOLOGY: ADJUSTING TO LIFE

CHAPTER OUTLINE

Life is largely a process of adaptation to the circumstances in which we exist.

HANS SELYE

Sarah, now 18, had anything but an idyllic childhood. She grew up in an impoverished suburban home with an alcoholic father who physically and sexually abused her and her younger sister. Sarah's mother, too helpless and fearful to protect her children, was hospitalized twice for 'nervous breakdowns'. When Sarah was 8 years old, a neighbour who suspected the sexual abuse reported the father to Child Protective Services. Upon being notified of the impending investigation, Sarah's father called his family together in the living room and told them, 'You drove me to this'. He then put a gun to his head and committed suicide as his wife and children watched in horror. From that point on, Sarah had to work after school to help support her family. For a time, the family was homeless and lived in a shelter. Her mother became increasingly disturbed and sometimes beat her.

Given her life circumstances, how could Sarah become anything except an unhappy, maladjusted person, her emotional life dominated by anxiety, anger and depression? Instead, she grew into a delightful and popular young woman who was emotionally well adjusted, a talented singer, and an honours student who was awarded a scholarship to an Ivy League university.

…

In his book *Persuasion and Healing*, psychiatrist Jerome Frank (1961) describes a treatment performed by the German physician Hans Rheder on three bedridden patients. One patient had an inflamed gall bladder and chronic gallstones. The second was having difficulty recovering from pancreatic surgery and had experienced such severe weight loss that Rheder described her as 'skeletal'. The third patient was dying from a painful uterine cancer that had spread throughout her body.

Since conventional medicine had done all that was possible for the women, Rheder decided to try the unconventional: he told the women that he had discovered a powerful faith healer who could cure with remarkable success simply by directing his healing power to a particular place. Rheder told each woman that he had arranged for this healing power to be projected to her room on a specific day and hour. In truth, he had already tried the healer without telling the women, and there had been no change in their conditions.

Within a few days after the appointed healing date, the patient with gallstones lost all of her symptoms, returned home and remained symptom-free for a year. The woman who had been wasting away began to eat and subsequently gained 30 pounds. The patient with cancer was already a terminal case, but her bloated body soon excreted excess fluids, she gained strength and her blood count improved. She was able to return home and lived for three months in relative comfort.

These cases illustrate some of the intriguing phenomena studied in an area known as *health psychology*. Children like Sarah have been termed 'invulnerable' or 'resilient' youngsters because they somehow develop normally, or even exceptionally, in the face of great adversity (Garmezy, 1983; Masten, 2001). What allows resilient people to rise above extraordinarily stressful environments while other individuals, blessed with more benign life histories, collapse under the weight of relatively minor stresses? And what are we to think of the dramatic physical changes that followed Rheder's invocation of the faith healer's curative powers? How can mind triumph over matter to such a degree? Can a simple belief that one will be healed stop illness in its tracks? The answers to these questions will show us that adapting to the demands and challenges in our lives involves complex interactions between the person, the environment, and behaviour. Figure 16.1 previews some of the biological, psychological and environmental factors that influence our health and well-being.

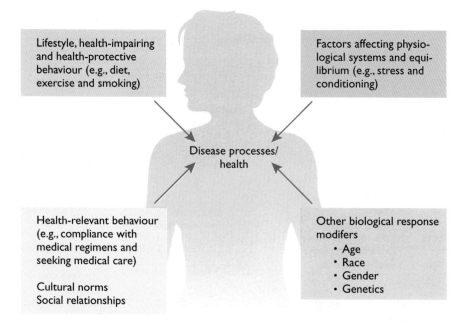

FIGURE 16.1

Biological, psychological and environmental factors that contribute to disease processes and health.
SOURCE: adapted from Baum, 1994.

Health psychology addresses factors that influence well-being and illness, as well as measures that can be taken to promote health and prevent illness. It therefore confronts many of the leading problems of our times. For example, because stress has negative effects on both physical and psychological well-being, the study of stress and coping is a central focus of health psychology. Pain is another important topic because it is a central feature of many illnesses and a major stressor. Health psychologists explore factors that influence pain perceptions and develop psychological interventions to reduce people's suffering. As we shall see, they also develop and evaluate health-promotion and disease-prevention programmes.

STRESS AND WELL-BEING

The term *stress* appears regularly in our everyday discourse. It is also a leading topic of study in psychology. What, exactly, is stress?

Psychologists have viewed stress in three different ways: as a stimulus, as a response and as an ongoing interaction between an organism and its environment. Some scientists define stress as events that place strong demands on us. These demanding or threatening situations are **stressors**. We refer to stress as a *stimulus* when we make statements such as, 'I've got a lot of stress in my life right now. I have three examinations next week, I lost my class notes, my fiancé just announced a vow of eternal celibacy, and my car broke down'.

health psychology
addresses factors that influence well-being and illness, as well as measures that can be taken to promote health and prevent illness

stressors
demanding or threatening situations

Stress can also be a *response* that has cognitive, physiological and behavioural components. Thus a person might say, 'I'm feeling all stressed out. I'm tensed up, I'm having trouble concentrating on things, and I've been flying off the handle all week'. The presence of negative emotions is an important feature of the stress response and links the study of stress with the field of emotion (Zautra, 2003).

A third way of thinking about stress combines the stimulus and response definitions into a more inclusive model. Here stress is viewed as a *person–situation interaction* or, more formally, as an ongoing transaction between the organism and the environment (Lazarus, 1991; 1998). This conception of stress is the basis for the model shown in Figure 16.2, and it will guide our discussion of stress. From this perspective, **stress** can be defined as a pattern of cognitive appraisals, physiological responses and behavioural tendencies that occur in response to a perceived imbalance between situational demands and the resources needed to cope with them.

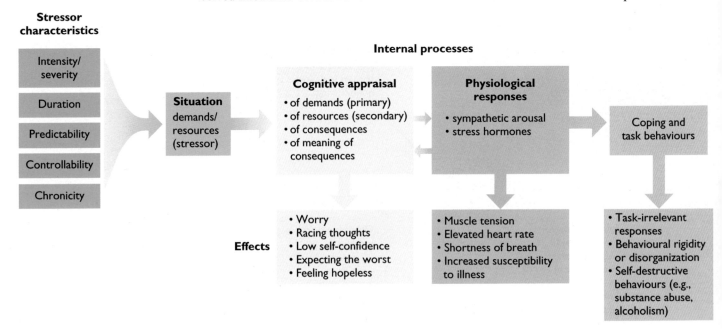

FIGURE 16.2

The nature of stress.

Stress involves complex interactions among situational (stressor) characteristics, cognitive appraisal processes, physiological responses and behavioural attempts to cope with the situational demands. Stressor characteristics that influence stress responses are shown. The lower panels show potential cognitive, physiological and behavioural stress responses that can interfere with well-being.

To explore the topic of stress, we begin by describing different types of stressors, as well as the methods that scientists have developed to measure life stress. Then we explore the mind–body interaction that constitutes our response to stressors and the manner in which stress affects our psychological and physical health. Next we examine factors that influence the relations between stress and health. Finally, we describe the process of coping with stress.

STRESSORS

Let us begin with the situational component of stress. Stressors are specific kinds of stimuli. Whether physical or psychological, they place demands on us that endanger our well-being and require us to adapt in some manner. The more the demands of a situation outweigh the resources we have to deal with them, the more stressful a situation is likely to be.

Stressors differ in their severity (Fig. 16.3). They can range from *microstressors* – the daily hassles and minor annoyances, such as difficult colleagues, traffic jams and academic deadlines – to more severe stressors. *Major negative events*, such as the death or loss of a loved one, an academic or career failure, a serious illness or being the victim of a serious crime, place strong demands on us and require major efforts to cope. *Catastrophic events* tend to occur unexpectedly and typically affect large numbers of people (Resick, 2005). They include traumatic natural disasters such as the Indian Ocean tsunami of 2004, acts of war or terrorism and physical or psychological torture. All three classes of stressors can have significant negative effects on psychological and physical well-being (van Praag, 2004; Zautra, 2003).

FIGURE 16.3

Stressful life events can vary from catastrophic ones, such as 2004's train bombing in Madrid, to micro-stressors, or daily inconveniences. Both classes of stressor take their toll on physical and psychological well-being.

In addition to intensity or severity, other characteristics that make situations more or less stressful are listed at the far left of Figure 16.2. In general, events over which a person has little or no control, which occur suddenly and unpredictably, and which have an impact on a person over a long period of time seem to take the greatest toll on physical and psychological well-being (Lazarus and Folkman, 1984; Taylor, 2006a).

Measuring Stressful Life Events

Researchers have attempted to study the relation between life events and well-being. Sometimes we may know that a person has lived through a natural disaster or lost a loved one to death. In other cases, researchers may have to rely on people's self-reports, using *life-event scales* to quantify the amount of life stress that a person has experienced over a given period of time (e.g., the past three months or the past year). The life-event scale shown in Table 16.1 asks people to indicate not only whether a particular event occurred but also whether the event was positive or negative and whether it was a major event (defined as having a significant and long-term impact on the person's life) or a minor event (Smith et al., 1990). We can thus score the scale for the number of specific kinds of events that occurred (for example, 'minor negative', 'major negative', 'major positive'). We can obtain additional information by asking respondents to rate the predictability, controllability and duration of each event they experienced, permitting an analysis of these factors as well. Life-event scales have been widely used in life-stress research. Like other self-report measures, however, we know that they are subject to possible distortion and failures of memory (R.E. Smith et al., 1999).

Some early theorists considered a stressor to be any life event that requires significant life adjustments, whether a negative event such as those described above or a positive one such as a job promotion (Holmes and Rahe, 1967; Selye, 1976). Because later research showed that only negative life changes consistently predicted adverse health and behavioural outcomes, most modern researchers now define stress in terms of negative life changes only (Cohen et al., 1995; Lazarus, 1998). Indeed, positive life events sometimes counter or even cancel out the impact of negative events (Thoits, 1983).

TABLE 16.1 SAMPLE ITEMS FROM A SELF-REPORT MEASURE OF POSITIVE AND NEGATIVE LIFE EVENTS FOR ADOLESCENTS

Experience	Happened in last 6 months?		Good or bad?		'Minor' or 'major'?	
Parents discover something you did not want them to know	No	Yes	Good	Bad	Minor	Major
Pressures or expectation by parents	No	Yes	Good	Bad	Minor	Major
Receiving a gift	No	Yes	Good	Bad	Minor	Major
Having plans fall through (not going on a trip, etc.)	No	Yes	Good	Bad	Minor	Major
Losing job (quitting, getting fired, laid off, etc.)	No	Yes	Good	Bad	Minor	Major
Making honour roll or other school achievement	No	Yes	Good	Bad	Minor	Major
Making love or sexual intercourse	No	Yes	Good	Bad	Minor	Major
Something good happens to a friend	No	Yes	Good	Bad	Minor	Major
Work hassles (rude customers, unpleasant jobs, etc.)	No	Yes	Good	Bad	Minor	Major
Death of a friend or family member	No	Yes	Good	Bad	Minor	Major

SOURCE: adapted from Smith et al., 1990.

stress response

has cognitive, physiological and behavioural components

primary appraisal

interpreting the situation as either benign, neutral/irrelevant or threatening in terms of its demands and its significance for your well-being

secondary appraisal

appraising your perceived ability to cope with the situation, that is, the resources you have to deal with it

THE STRESS RESPONSE: A MIND–BODY LINK

Let us now consider how people respond to stressors. Like the emotional responses discussed in Chapter 10, the **stress response** has cognitive, physiological and behavioural components.

Cognitive Appraisal

We respond to situations as we perceive them. The starting point for the stress response is therefore our cognitive appraisal of the situation and its implications for us. As Figure 16.2 indicates, four aspects of the appraisal process are particularly significant:

1. Appraisal of the *nature and demands* of the situation (*primary appraisal*)
2. Appraisal of the *resources* available to cope with it (*secondary appraisal*)
3. Judgements of what the *consequences* of the situation could be
4. Appraisal of the *personal meaning*, that is, what the outcome might imply about us

Let us apply these appraisal steps to a real-life situation. You are about to have an important job interview. According to Richard Lazarus (1991), a leading stress researcher, you will first engage in a **primary appraisal**, interpreting the situation as either benign, neutral/irrelevant or threatening in terms of its demands (how difficult the interview will be) and its significance for your well-being (how badly you want or need the job). At the same time, through the process of **secondary appraisal**, you will be appraising your perceived ability to cope with the situation, that is, the resources you have to deal with it. Coping resources include your knowledge and

Focus 16.2

What four types of appraisals occur in response to a potential stressor? Contrast primary and secondary appraisal.

abilities, your verbal skills and your social resources such as people who will give you emotional support and encouragement. If you believe that the demands of the interview greatly exceed your resources, you will likely experience stress.

You will also take into account *potential consequences* of failing to cope successfully with the situation, including both the seriousness of the consequences and the likelihood that they will occur. Will you be able to pay your rent or tuition if you perform poorly in the interview and do not get the job? How likely is it that you will fail? Appraising the consequences of failing as very costly and very likely to occur increases the perceived stressfulness of the situation.

Finally, the *psychological meaning of the consequences* may be related to your basic beliefs about yourself or the world. Certain beliefs or personal standards can make people vulnerable to particular types of situational demands. For example, if your feelings of self-worth depend on how successful you are in situations like this, you may regard doing poorly during the interview as evidence that you are a worthless failure.

Distortions and mistaken appraisals can occur at any of the four points in the appraisal process, causing inappropriate stress responses. People may overestimate the difficulty of the demands, they may underestimate their own resources, they may exaggerate the seriousness of the consequences and the likelihood that they will occur, or they may have irrational self-beliefs that confer inappropriate meaning on the consequences (e.g., 'If I don't succeed at this, it means I am a total loser and always will be'). The fact that appraisal patterns can differ so greatly from person to person helps us understand why people respond differently to the same event or situation and why some people are particularly vulnerable to certain types of demands.

Physiological Responses

As soon as we make appraisals, the body responds to them (Kemeny, 2004; Steckler et al., 2005). Although appraisals begin the process, appraisals and physiological responses affect one another (Sun, 2005). Sensory feedback from our body's response can cause us to reappraise how stressful a situation is and whether our resources are sufficient to cope with it. Thus if you find yourself trembling and your heart pounding as you enter the interview room, you may appraise the situation as even more threatening than you did initially. The two-way arrows between the cognitive and physiological elements in Figure 16.2 illustrate this.

Endocrinologist Hans Selye (1976) was a pioneer in studying the body's response to stress. He described a physiological response pattern to strong and prolonged stressors. The **general adaptation syndrome (GAS)** consists of three phases: alarm, resistance and exhaustion (Fig. 16.4).

In response to a physical or psychological stressor, organisms exhibit an immediate increase in physiological arousal as the body mobilizes itself to respond to the threat. This *alarm reaction* occurs because of the sudden activation of the sympathetic nervous system and the release of stress hormones by the endocrine system. The alarm stage cannot last indefinitely, however, and the body's natural tendency to maintain the balanced internal state of homeostasis causes activity in the parasympathetic nervous system, which reduces arousal. The body continues to remain on red alert, however, responding with the second stage, resistance.

During *resistance*, the body's resources are mobilized by the continued outpouring of stress hormones by the endocrine system, particularly the adrenal glands. Resistance can last for a relatively long time, but the body's resources are being depleted and immune system functioning is being partially suppressed by the stress hormones (Chiappelli, 2000). If the stressor is intense and persists too long, the body will eventually reach a stage of *exhaustion*, in which there is increased vulnerability to disease and, in some extreme cases, collapse and death. Selye theorized that whichever body system is weakest (e.g., cardiovascular, respiratory, gastrointestinal) will be the one most affected.

general adaptation syndrome (GAS)

consists of three phases: alarm, resistance and exhaustion

Focus 16.3

Describe the three stages of Selye's GAS and their effects on health.

FIGURE 16.4

Hans Selye's general adaptation syndrome.

When a person is exposed to a stressor, the body's resistance is temporarily reduced by a state of shock until the alarm reaction mobilizes the body's resources. During the stage of resistance, stress hormones maintain the body's defensive changes, and the body reactions characteristic of the alarm reaction virtually disappear. But if the stress persists over a long time, the body's resources become depleted, and exhaustion occurs; the organism can no longer cope and is highly vulnerable to breakdown.

SOURCE: Selye, 1976.

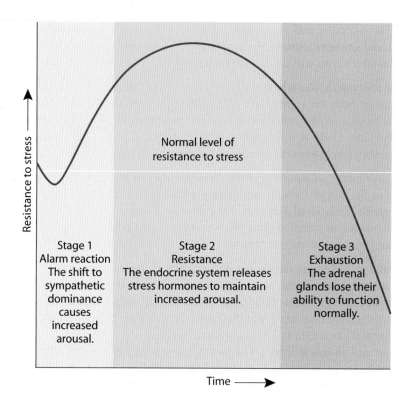

EFFECTS OF STRESS ON WELL-BEING

From a biological perspective, it seems that a high-arousal fight-or-flight biological mechanism sculpted by evolution to help us survive life-threatening *physical* stressors may be maladaptive for dealing with the *psychological* stressors of modern life. In terms of survival, taking a final examination or sitting in rush-hour traffic is not equivalent to an attack by a hungry sabre-toothed tiger, where high arousal could facilitate fighting or fleeing. In Selye's view, our physiological responses may thereby take an unnecessary toll on our physical and psychological well-being. Selye's work inspired a generation of psychological and medical researchers to explore the effects of stress on psychological and physical well-being.

Stress and Psychological Well-Being

Effects of stress on psychological well-being are clearest and most dramatic among people who have experienced catastrophic life events. Anthony Rubonis and Leonard Bickman (1991) surveyed the results of 52 studies of victims of catastrophic floods, hurricanes and fires. In the wake of natural disasters, they found an average increase of 17 per cent in rates of psychological disorders such as anxiety and depression.

Some stressors are so traumatic that they can have a strong and long-lasting psychological impact (Resick, 2005). More than 50 years after the horrors of the Holocaust, psychological scars remain for Jewish survivors of Nazi concentration camps (Nadler and Ben-Slushan, 1989; Valent, 2000). Many survivors are still troubled by high levels of anxiety and recurrent nightmares about their traumatic experiences. Those who were children and lost their families continue to experience sudden fears that something terrible will happen to their spouses or children whenever they are out of sight. Depression and crying spells are also common, as are feelings of insecurity and difficulties in forming close relationships. As one researcher reported, 'child survivors (now in their 50s and 60s) ... despite their outward normalcy, remain entrapped in this survival mode' (Valent, 1998, p. 751).

Long-lasting psychological symptoms have also been found among soldiers who experienced the trauma of combat. Twenty years after the 1982 Lebanon war, Israeli soldiers who had seen combat reported more psychological, social and health problems than did a matched group of veterans who had not experienced combat (Zahava et al., 2006). Some women who experience the trauma of rape have psychological scars that are intense and long-lasting. In one long-term study of female rape victims, a quarter of the women felt that they had not recovered psychologically six years after the rape (Meyer and Taylor, 1986). Even more common stressors such as unemployment leave scars. In a 15-year longitudinal study of German workers, unemployment led to significant declines in subjective well-being and, even after regaining employment, the workers never returned to their previous level of life satisfaction (Lucas et al., 2004).

Many researchers have examined relations between self-reported negative life events and measures of psychological well-being. Findings consistently show that the more negative life events people report on measures such as the one shown in Table 16.1, the more likely they are to also report symptoms of psychological distress, which include anxiety, depression and unhappiness (Holahan and Moos, 1990; Monroe and Peterman, 1988). Many medical and psychological researchers have therefore concluded that stress causes distress, and this conclusion has been widely accepted among the general public and in the mass media.

Focus 16.4
What links exist between stress and psychological well-being?

WHAT DO YOU THINK?

DO STRESSFUL EVENTS CAUSE PSYCHOLOGICAL DISTRESS?

A consistent statistical relation has been shown between stressful life events and psychological distress; the greater the number of stressful events people have experienced, the more distress they are likely to report. Based on these results, are you willing to accept the conclusion that life stress causes distress, or can you think of other possible reasons for this relation? Think about it, then see p. 773 for a commentary.

Stress and Illness

There are indications that stress can combine with other physical and psychological factors to influence the entire spectrum of physical illnesses, from the common cold to cancer, heart disease, diabetes and sudden death (Lovallo, 2005; Suls and Wallston, 2003). Sometimes the effects are immediate. On the day of the 1994 Northridge, California earthquake, the number of sudden deaths due to heart attacks in the greater Los Angeles area nearly tripled from an average of 35.7 per day during the previous seven days to 101 (Leor et al., 1996).

Focus 16.5
Describe physiological and behavioural mechanisms through which stress can contribute to illness.

Other effects of major stressors on physical well-being are less immediate but no less severe. Within one month following the death of a spouse, bereaved widowers and widows begin to show a higher mortality rate than married people of the same age who have not lost a spouse (Kaprio et al., 1987), and within one year of spousal death, about two-thirds of bereaved people decline in health (Irwin et al., 1987). A notably increased rate of mortality is found in men, who tend to respond to the death of their spouse with relatively greater distress and health declines than do women (Stroebe et al., 2001). Stressful life events have also been linked to a higher risk of developing cancer (Sklar and Anisman, 1981). People who experience the chronic stress that attends caring for a spouse with Alzheimer's disease have significantly increased risk of health problems (Vitaliano et al., 2004).

A traumatic life event can worsen an already existing medical condition, as in this case of a 7-year-old African-American girl with sickle-cell anaemia:

This little girl was bused to a new elementary school in a white neighbourhood.... She and other black children were met with cries by angry whites to 'go back to where you belong!' The little girl was quite upset by the incident. After some time at the school she went to the principal's office crying and complaining of chest pains. She died later that day in the hospital, apparently from a sickle-cell crisis brought on by stress. As she died, she kept repeating 'go back where you belong.' (Friedman and DiMatteo, 1989, p. 169)

Linkages between long-term stress and illness are not surprising, for physiological responses to stressors can directly harm other body systems. For example, the secretion of stress hormones, such as epinephrine, norepinephrine and cortisol, is a major part of the stress response. These hormones affect the activity of the heart, and excessive secretions can damage the lining of the arteries. By reducing fat metabolism, the stress hormones can also contribute to the fatty blockages in arteries that cause heart attacks and strokes (Lovallo and Gerin, 2003; Willenberg et al., 2000).

Stress can also contribute to health breakdowns by causing people to behave in ways that increase the risk of illness. For example, people with diabetes can frequently control their disease through medication, exercise and diet. When under stress, however, diabetics are less likely to regulate their diets and take their medication, resulting in an increased risk of serious medical consequences (Brantley and Garrett, 1993). People are also more likely to quit exercising when under stress, even if the primary reason they began exercising in the first place was to reduce stress (Stetson et al., 1997). Stress may also lead to smoking, alcohol and drug use, sleep loss, undereating or overeating, and other health-compromising behaviours. Poor dietary and sleep patterns in students studying for final examinations may increase risk of illness and help ruin the semester break.

Stress and ageing

Sometimes, people who are under intense, chronic stress seem to age before our eyes. Scientists have long suspected that stress can accelerate the ageing process, but only recently has a physiological mechanism been identified. Elissa Epel and her co-workers (2004) studied 39 mothers who experienced the constant stress of caring for a child who suffered from a serious chronic illness, such as infantile paralysis or autism, and 19 similar women who had healthy children. The researchers examined structures called *telomeres* that are found at the tips of chromosomes. Every time a cell divides, telomeres become shorter. When the telomeres become too short, the cell can no longer divide and it dies. Cell death produces the effects of ageing as muscles weaken, skin becomes wrinkled, hearing and eyesight fade, organs fail and cognitive abilities decline. Fortunately, the body has an enzyme called *telomerase* that helps counter telomere shortening. This enzyme can slow the ageing process.

When Epel and co-workers examined the white blood cells of the two groups of women, they made a startling discovery. The mothers with the disordered children had significantly shorter telomeres and lower levels of the enzyme telomerase, and the more stressful the women rated their lives as being, the more pronounced these effects were. Women with the highest levels of perceived stress had telomeres equivalent to women 10 years older. Although the mechanisms whereby stress produces these effects are currently unknown, it is possible that chronically elevated levels of stress hormones such as cortisol damage the telomeres and lower telomerase levels, thereby speeding the ageing process.

Whereas stress can accelerate the ageing process, ageing *itself* can also be a stressor, in turn contributing to health breakdowns. One longitudinal study on respiratory mortality by Levy and Meyers (2005) demonstrated this. In this study, elderly people between 50 and 87, who held negative individual beliefs about their own ageing, were more likely to die of respiratory causes than were elderly people holding positive beliefs about their own ageing. This was even the case after taking into account such factors as age, loneliness, functional health and socio-economic status.

Stress and the Immune System

Considerable evidence suggests that life stress can weaken immune functioning (Suls and Wallston, 2003; Taylor, 2006a). Research by Ronald Glaser, Janet Kiecolt-Glaser and their co-workers has shown that reduced immune system effectiveness is one possible reason for increased risk of illness (Kiecolt-Glaser et al., 2002; Marsland et al., 2001). In one study, researchers closely followed medical students over a one-year period. They collected blood samples from the students during three stressful academic examination periods in order to measure immune cell activity. The researchers found that immune system effectiveness was reduced during the stressful examination periods and that this reduction was linked to the likelihood of becoming ill. Other studies have shown that stress hormones released into the bloodstream by the adrenal glands can suppress the activity of specific immune system cells, increasing the likelihood of illness (Cohen and Herbert, 1996; Maier and Watkins, 1999).

Research has shown that external stressors can 'get into' the immune system in several ways. Fibres extending from the brain into lymph tissues can release a wide variety of chemicals that bind to receptors on white blood cells, thus influencing immune functions. As noted earlier, stress hormones such as cortisol and epinephrine also bind to cells in the immune system and influence their functions. Third, people's attempts to cope with stressors sometimes lead them to behave in ways (e.g., substance use or not sleeping enough) that impair immunity (Taylor, 2006a).

Although stress can affect immune functions, the relations are far from simple. As shown in a major meta-analysis by Suzanne Segerstrom and Gregory Miller (2004), which combined the statistical results of more than 300 studies, effects depend on the nature of the stressor and the specific immune functions of the body.

There are two kinds of immune reactions. *Natural immunity* occurs quickly (often within minutes) of an immune challenge and is relatively non-specific in nature. One type of natural immunity is inflammation, in which certain immune cells congregate at the site of an infection and release toxic substances that kill invaders. One class of molecules released by immune cells are **cytokines**, which help produce fever and inflammation, promote healing of injured tissue and activate and direct other immune cells. Natural killer (NK) cells are also part of the natural defence team. These cells attack invaders, as well as tumours, and help keep invaders at bay during the early stages of infection. From an evolutionary perspective, natural immunity is an adaptive feature of the fight-or-flight response to an acute physical stressor that could produce injury and the entry of pathogens into the body through wounds.

Specific immunity is a much more targeted process and takes longer to occur, sometimes up to several days. One common specific immunity response is the identification of the specific properties of the invader and the development of specific antibodies that can neutralize bacteria, kill cancerous cells or bind to viruses to prevent their entry into healthy cells.

Like immune reactions, stressors can differ in a number of ways, including how they occur and how long they last. Segerstrom and Miller found that acute, time-limited stressors, such as participating in a stressful job interview, actually enhance natural immunity. The number of natural killer cells in the blood increases and the immune system readies itself for a protective-infection response. Specific immunity does not increase, however, probably because the stressor is very brief. Longer-lasting stressors, such as the days in preparation for an important examination, are associated with a different pattern of immune response, created largely by different types of cytokines. Some cytokines suppress cellular immune responses against viruses, whereas others enhance immune responses against bacteria and parasites. Thus, brief naturalistic stressors of this type might make you more susceptible to a viral infection, but probably not to a bacterial one.

Some stressors, such as the death of a parent or a natural disaster, produce a whole series of consequences as one tries to pick up the pieces and move on. One consistent finding is that the

cytokines

help produce fever and inflammation, promote healing of injured tissue and activate and direct other immune cells

death of a spouse is associated with declines in the fast-acting natural immune response against invading pathogens. Natural disasters do not seem to have this effect. Finally, the many studies reviewed by Segerstrom and Miller showed that chronic stressors, such as caring for a spouse with Alzheimer's disease, severe marital conflict or unemployment, were the most damaging, having suppressive effects on both types of immunity. Finally, stressors from the distant past (five years or more) bore no relation to current immune function.

Focus 16.6

How do various kinds of stressors affect immune functioning?

Overall, research results support a *biphasic model* in which acute stress enhances the immune response, whereas chronic stress suppresses it (Dhabhar and McEwen, 2001). Over an extended period of time, chronic stress taxes the body, eventually resulting in impaired immunity and increasing vulnerability to illness.

IN REVIEW

- Various theorists view stress as a stimulus; as a response having cognitive, physiological and behavioural components; or as an interaction (i.e., transaction) between the person and the environment. The latter view incorporates the stimulus and response conceptions into a more dynamic model.

- Stressors are events that place physical or psychological demands on organisms. The stressfulness of a situation is defined by the balance between demands and resources. Life events vary in terms of how positive or negative they are and how intense they are. Other dimensions that affect their impact include duration, predictability, controllability and chronicity.

- Cognitive appraisal processes play an essential role in people's responses to stressors. People appraise the nature of the demands, the resources available to deal with them, the possible consequences of the situation, and the personal meaning of these consequences. Distortions at any of these levels can result in inappropriate stress responses.

- The physiological response to stressors is mediated by the autonomic and endocrine systems and involves a pattern of arousal that mobilizes the body to deal with the stressor. Selye described a general adaptation syndrome (GAS), which involves the stages of alarm, resistance and exhaustion.

- Measures of both major negative life events and microstressors are associated with negative psychological outcomes, such as anxiety and depression. Life stress also is related to negative health changes. It can worsen pre-existing medical conditions and increase the risk of illness and death. Reduced immune system functioning may underlie some negative health effects caused by stress.

FACTORS THAT INFLUENCE STRESS–HEALTH RELATIONS

As we saw with Sarah at the opening of the chapter, some highly resilient individuals seem to tolerate extremely demanding stressors over a long period of time without negative effects. Others appear to quickly fall prey to relatively minor stressors. The fact that people differ so dramatically in their responses to stressful events has prompted many health psychologists to search for personal and environmental factors that make people more or less reactive to stressful events. **Vulnerability factors** increase people's susceptibility to stressful events. They include low social support, poor coping skills, tendencies to become anxious or pessimistic, excessive bot-

vulnerability factors

increase people's susceptibility to stressful events

tling-up of feelings, and other factors that reduce stress resistance. In contrast, **protective factors** are environmental or personal resources that help people cope more effectively with stressful events. They include physiological reactivity, social support, effective coping skills, and personality factors such as hardiness, coping self-efficacy, optimism and an ability to find meaning in stressful events.

protective factors
environmental or personal resources that help people cope more effectively with stressful events

Social Support

Social support is one of the most important environmental resources (Suls and Wallston, 2003). The knowledge that we can rely on others for help and support in a time of crisis helps blunt the impact of stress (Fig. 16.5). In contrast, lack of social support is a significant vulnerability factor. Studies carried out in the USA, Finland and Sweden carefully tracked the well-being of some 37 000 people for up to 12 years. Even after taking into account medical risk factors such as age, smoking, high blood pressure, high cholesterol levels, obesity and lack of physical exercise, the researchers found that people with weak social ties were twice as likely to die during the period of the study as those with strong ties to others (House et al., 1988). The relation between social isolation and poor health was stronger for men than for women.

FIGURE 16.5

Social support is one of the strongest protective factors against stress.

Focus 16.7

In what ways can social support protect against stressful events?

One way that social support protects against stress is by enhancing immune system functioning. Robert Baron and his co-workers (1990) studied people whose spouses were being treated for cancer and who were experiencing psychological distress. When they were exposed to an antigen, spouses who rated themselves as high in social support produced more immune cells, particularly at high levels of the allergen, than did those who indicated lower social support in their lives. These results may help explain why people who have high levels of social support are more disease-resistant when they are under stress (House et al., 1988).

Many other studies show that social support decreases psychological distress in people who are dealing with stressful life events of all kinds (Holahan and Moos, 1986; 1990; Holland and Holahan, 2003; Schwarzer, 1998). In one such study, 86 women undergoing breast cancer treatment at Stanford Medical School in the USA were randomly assigned either to a weekly psychotherapy group designed to increase social support and strengthen their coping skills or to a control condition that received just the medical centre's regular cancer treatment. As shown in Figure 16.6, those in the therapy groups survived nearly twice as long as did the controls (Spiegel et al., 1989). A later study using a similar intervention failed to find greater longevity among breast cancer patients, but it did find significant quality-of-life benefits, such as lowered depression, feelings of closeness with other group members and a positive reordering of life priorities (Goodwin et al., 2001). Peer support groups appear especially helpful to breast cancer victims who lack support from their spouses and physicians (Helgeson et al., 2000).

Besides enhancing immune system functioning, social support has a number of other stress-buffering benefits. People who feel that they are part of a social system experience a greater sense of identity and meaning in their lives, which in turn results in greater psychological well-being (Cohen, 1988; Rodin and Salovey, 1989). Social networks also reduce exposure to other risk factors, such as loneliness. Third, having the backing of others can increase one's sense of control over stressors. Finally, true friends can apply social pressure to prevent people from coping with stressors in maladaptive ways (e.g., through alcohol or drug use).

Social support benefits the giver as well as the recipient. In one five-year longitudinal study of elderly people, Stephanie Brown and co-workers (2003) found that those who gave help and support to friends, relatives and family members had lower mortality rates than those who did

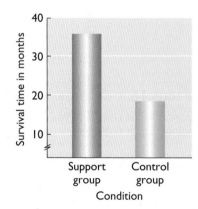

FIGURE 16.6

The effect of coping and social support.

This graph shows the mean survival time for breast cancer patients who received a coping-skills and social-support intervention compared with control patients who received normal cancer treatment.

SOURCE: based on Spiegel et al., 1989.

not, even when health and other quality-of-life variables were statistically controlled. Likewise, highly sociable people are more resistant to infectious diseases, despite their greater exposure to other people who might be contagious (Cohen et al., 2003).

As the previous discussion makes clear, considerable evidence suggests that high levels of social support can have beneficial effects on health and well-being. There are, however, a number of studies reporting contradictory findings. Social support has been associated with, for example, adverse effects on well-being (Buunk and Verhoeven, 1991), and has even been shown to aggravate the effects of stressors (Kaufman and Beehr, 1986). One explanation for the sometimes equivocal relationship between social support and decreased psychological distress, comes from a study by Dunbar et al. (1998). Their data showed that receiving social support was associated with distress among a sample of 'disabled' individuals, because receiving support threatened the equitable balance of their social relationships. In other words, the distress resulted from people wondering if they could ever 'pay back' the donor of social support.

Physiological Reactivity

Responses of the autonomic and endocrine systems appear to underlie many of the negative psychological and health consequences of stress (McEwen, 2001). The fact that people differ widely in the pattern and intensity of their physiological responses makes people more or less vulnerable to stressors. As we saw in Chapter 15, people high in neuroticism, who tend to have intense and prolonged autonomic responses, seem more vulnerable to stress than are people low in this personality factor (Eysenck, 1990; Snyder, 2001). People whose autonomic and endocrine systems are wired for high reactivity have increased risk for a wide range of diseases, including hypertension and coronary disease (Lovallo and Gerin, 2003; Taylor, 2006a).

Two types of stress hormones, catecholamines and cortisol, are important links between physiological reactivity and health. Both mobilize the body's fight-or-flight response in the face of stressors, but they have somewhat different effects on the body. Cortisol's arousal effects last much longer and seem to be more damaging than those produced by the catecholamines (unless the catecholamines are secreted at high levels over a long period of time). Cortisol reduces immune system functioning and helps create fatty deposits in the arteries that lead to heart disease. In contrast, catecholamine secretion increases immune system functioning (Taylor, 2006a). Increased vulnerability to bodily breakdowns occurs when the person responds to stress with high levels of cortisol instead of catecholamines. The fact that physical exercise creates catecholamine-produced arousal may help account for its health-enhancing effects and its ability to promote stress resistance (Ehrman, 2003; Morgan, 1997).

Type A Behaviour Pattern

The Type A behaviour pattern was discovered by an upholsterer working on the chairs in the office of a physician who specialized in treating heart-attack victims. The upholsterer noticed an unusual wear pattern at the front of the seats, not the back, indicating that the patients were constantly sitting on the edges of their seats and moving about.

This edge-of-the-seat pattern typifies the behaviours seen in people with the **Type A behaviour pattern**, who tend to live under great pressure and demand much of themselves and others. Many Type A people are workaholics, continually striving to get more done in less time. Type A people are also characterized by high levels of competitiveness and ambition, which can foster aggressiveness and hostility when things get in their way (Fig. 16.7). In contrast, people labelled Type B show the opposite pattern of patience, serenity and lack of time urgency.

Several large-scale studies suggest that even when other physical risk factors, such as obesity and smoking, are taken into account, Type A men and women have about double the risk for coronary heart disease (CHD) compared with less driven people (Rosenman et al., 1975). However, research indicates that not all components of the Type A pattern increase vulnerability to

Focus 16.8
Describe the role of stress hormones in well-being.

Focus 16.9
Describe the Type A behaviour pattern and how it can contribute to coronary heart disease.

Type A behaviour pattern
live under great pressure and demand much of themselves and others

CHD. The Type A person's fast-paced, time-conscious lifestyle and high ambition apparently are not the culprits. Rather, the crucial component seems to be negative emotions, particularly anger. The Type A behaviour pattern virtually guarantees that these people will encounter many stressful situations, such as time pressures of their own making and frustrations that anger them (see, for example, van Ijzendoorn et al., 1998). A cynical hostility marked by suspiciousness, resentment, frequent anger, distrust and antagonism is likely to alienate others, produce interpersonal stress and conflict, and reduce the amount of social support the person receives. In addition, Type A people tend to overreact physiologically to stressful events and take longer to recover, a biological factor that may contribute to their tendency to develop heart disease (Taylor, 2006a). John Hunter, an eighteenth-century pioneer in cardiovascular medicine, recognized his own vulnerability when he said, 'My life is in the hands of any rascal who chooses to put me in a passion'. Hunter's statement was all too prophetic; he died of a heart attack during an angry debate at a hospital board meeting.

Mind as Healer or Slayer

The mind as well as the body can make people more or less vulnerable to stressors. Considering the important role that appraisal processes play in emotions and stress, we should not be surprised that our beliefs about situations and ourselves are significant protective and vulnerability factors.

Hardiness   In the 1970s, Suzanne Kobasa of the University of Chicago began an intensive study of 200 executives who worked in highly stressful jobs. She found that some of them responded to their circumstances with psychological distress and physical illness, whereas others continued to function well both physically and psychologically. How did the two groups differ? The answer came in the form of three beliefs, comprising a stress-protective factor that she termed **hardiness**. The three Cs of hardiness are commitment, control, and challenge.

Hardy people are committed to their work, their families and their other involvements, and they believe that what they are doing is important. Second, they view themselves as having control over their outcomes, as opposed to feeling powerless to influence events. Finally, they appraise the demands of the situations as challenges, or opportunities, rather than as threats. As a result, demanding situations not only become less stressful, but they can actually stimulate higher levels of performance (Kobasa et al., 1985), and in the end may contribute to general well-being (Smith et al., 2004).

Of these three hardiness components, perceived control is apparently the strongest in buffering stress (Funk, 1992; Steptoe, 2000). A five-year longitudinal study showed that women who felt in control of their lives did not show increases in future illness when stress increased, whereas those low in perceived control did (Lawler and Schmied, 1992).

Coping self-efficacy   When confronted by a stressor, one of the most significant appraisals we make is whether we have sufficient resources to cope with the demands (Bandura, 1997). Small wonder, then, that **coping self-efficacy** – the belief that we can perform the behaviours necessary to cope successfully – is an important protective factor (Bandura, 1989). As hardiness research shows, even events that are appraised as extremely demanding may generate little stress if we believe that we have the skills to deal with them.

Self-efficacy is always specific to the particular situation: 'Can I handle *these* demands?' As noted in Chapter 15, previous successes in similar situations increase efficacy; failures undermine it (Bandura, 1997). People can also increase efficacy expectancies by observing others

FIGURE 16.7

Studies of the hard-driving Type A behaviour pattern have shown that the most damaging aspect is the negative emotions, particularly anger and hostility, that these people experience.

In-Psych

Does your personality type more closely reflect a Type A or a Type B behaviour pattern? Try the interactive video exercise, 'Type A Behaviour', in Chapter 16 of the In-Psych programme online to find out.

Focus 16.10

How do hardiness, coping self-efficacy, optimism/pessimism and spiritual beliefs affect stress outcomes?

hardiness

three beliefs on commitment, control and challenge, that comprise a stress-protective factor

coping self-efficacy

the belief that we can perform the behaviours necessary to cope successfully

cope successfully and through social persuasion and encouragement from others. The teacher who befriended Sarah constantly gave her the message, 'I believe in you. You can do it!' Finally, experiencing a low level of physiological arousal in the face of a stressor can convey a sense of strength and ability to cope, demonstrating another way in which arousal can affect appraisal.

Feelings of self-efficacy may fortify our bodies as well as our minds against stressful events, reducing psychological distress and increasing well-being over time (Chesney et al., 2006). An intriguing finding came from a laboratory study in which people with phobias confronted a feared object. When participants reported high self-efficacy while confronting the stressful situation, their immune systems actually began to function more effectively. In contrast, those who reported low coping efficacy showed a drop in immune system functioning (Wiedenfeld et al., 1990).

Optimistic expectations and positive attitudes   Our optimistic or pessimistic beliefs about how things are likely to turn out also play an important role in dealing with stressors. Whereas coping self-efficacy denotes an individual's belief to be able to handle the *specific* demands of a particular situation, optimism is better characterized by a general feeling of being able to cope with *any* situation. Recent research indicates that optimistic people are at lowered risk for anxiety and depression when they confront stressful events. Edward Chang (1998) found that people with optimistic beliefs felt less helpless in the face of stress and adjusted better to negative life events than did pessimists. Optimistic women in high-risk pregnancy, for example, experienced lower levels of distress, partly because they evaluated their high-risk pregnancy as controllable compared to less optimistic women (Lobel et al., 2002). In one year-long study, optimists had about half as many infectious illnesses and visits to doctors as did pessimists (Peterson and Seligman, 1987). In another study, researchers followed women who came to the National Cancer Institute for breast cancer treatment for five years. On average, women who were optimistic about their recovery lived longer than pessimists, even when the physical severity of the disease was the same at the beginning of the five-year period (Levy et al., 1988).

The process of ageing is a background stressor in many people's lives. People's reactions differ considerably as their hair thins, wrinkles deepen, physical and sexual capacity diminish, health declines, acquaintances begin to die and a sense of mortality becomes more salient. Some dread the ageing process, whereas others accept or even find value in it. In one study (Levy et al., 2002), researchers assessed attitudes towards ageing in a large community sample of men and women who were over 50 years of age and then followed them up over a 23-year period. Statistically controlling for age, physical health and loneliness, the researchers found that attitudes towards ageing predicted how long people lived even better than their physical health did (Fig. 16.8). On average, people with positive attitudes towards their ageing lived an average of 7.6 years longer than did their counterparts with negative attitudes. This survival advantage existed whether the

FIGURE 16.8

Ageing attitudes and longevity.

Research has shown a relation between positive or negative self-perceptions of one's ageing and subsequent longevity. These survival curves show the likelihood that a randomly selected group member will still be alive in a given year after the beginning of the study. The median number of years until death was 15 in the group with negative self-attitudes and 22.6 among positive-attitude participants.

SOURCE: adapted from Levy et al., 2002.

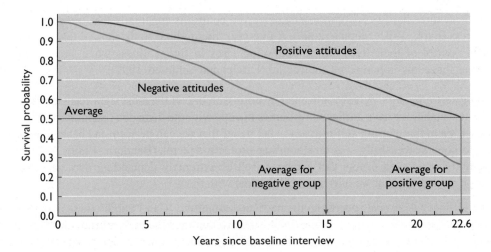

positive-attitude people were in their fifties, sixties, seventies and eighties when the study began. Clearly, attitude makes a difference, and perhaps a life-or-death difference.

Finding meaning in stressful life events   Humanistic theorists emphasize the human need to find meaning in one's life and the psychological benefits of doing so (May, 1961; Watson and Greenberg, 1998). Some people find personal meaning through spiritual beliefs, which can be a great comfort in the face of crises. Daniel McIntosh and co-workers (1993) studied 124 parents who had lost their babies to sudden infant death syndrome. They found that grieving parents whose religious beliefs provided some higher meaning to their loss experienced greater well-being and less distress 18 months later. In another study, researchers found that people who were able to find meaning in the death of a family member experienced less distress during the year following the loss. Finding a sense of meaning from their own process of coping with the loss (e.g., the sense that the event helped them grow spiritually) had even longer-term positive effects (Davis et al., 1998).

Religious beliefs can be a two-edged sword, however: They can either decrease or increase stress, depending on their nature and the type of stressor to which they are applied. In one study of elderly people with medical problems, poorer physical and psychological adjustment occurred in patients who viewed God as punishing them; saw themselves as the victims of demonic forces; expressed anger towards God, clergy or church members; or questioned their faith (Koenig et al., 1998). Religious beliefs may have positive effects in dealing with some types of stressors but not with others. Such beliefs seem to help people cope more effectively with losses, illnesses and personal setbacks. In contrast, they can increase the negative impact of other stressors such as marital problems and abuse, perhaps by inducing guilt or placing internal pressures on individuals to remain in the stressful relationship (Strawbridge et al., 1998).

Resilient Children: Superkids or Ordinary Magic?

At the beginning of this chapter we described Sarah, a child who grew up in a terrible home environment with a psychotic mother, and a father who abused her and committed suicide in her presence. Somehow, despite these experiences, Sarah grew into a highly successful young woman. Since the 1970s, psychologists such as Emmy Werner have been studying children who are somehow resilient to highly stressful environments (Werner and Smith, 1982).

Focus 16.11

What factors create stress resilience in children?

What factors matter in the lives of resilient children like Sarah, who rise far above what their environments would predict for them? Are they 'superkids', as a *New York Times* writer referred to them? After reviewing many studies of unusually resilient children and adolescents, Ann Masten (2001) concluded that such children are a monument to the ordinary adaptive processes that occur in the lives of most children, factors she termed 'ordinary magic'. Masten and J. Douglas Coatsworth (1998) found that these children have certain characteristics that contribute to a positive outcome even in the face of stressful life events (Table 16.2). These characteristics include adequate intellectual functioning, social skills, self-efficacy and faith (optimism and hope), as well as environmental factors such as a relationship with at least one caring, pro-social adult.

To be resilient, a child need not have all of the characteristics listed in Table 16.2, but he or she must have some of them. Good intellectual functioning and a supportive relationship with a caring adult seem to be the most important (Masten and Coatsworth, 1998). In Sarah's case, this positive adult relationship did not exist with either parent. Instead, the critical relationship was provided by a loving elementary school teacher who befriended, encouraged, and guided her during the critical formative period of middle childhood. This key relationship, combined with Sarah's obvious intelligence, allowed her to develop self-esteem, a belief in her own capabilities and the will to nurture her talents.

However, it is not enough to *hope* that children have enough characteristics that will help them cope with severe adversity. It is also important to *help* them cope. Unfortunately, data on the utilization of factors found to enhance resilience in clinical intervention programmes are still

TABLE 16.2 PERSONAL AND ENVIRONMENTAL FACTORS THAT CONTRIBUTE TO STRESS RESILIENCE IN CHILDREN

Source	Characteristic
Individual	Good intellectual functioning Appealing, sociable, easy-going disposition Self-efficacy, self-confidence, high self-esteem Talents Faith
Family	Close relationship to caring parent figure Authoritative parenting: warmth, structure, high expectations Socio-economic advantages Connections to extended supportive family networks
Extra-familial context	Bonds to pro-social adults outside the family Connections to pro-social organizations Attending effective schools

SOURCE: Masten and Coatsworth, 1998.

scarce (Coyne and Racioppo, 2000). Waaktaar and colleagues derived important therapeutic principles based on four resilience factors (e.g., self-efficacy). They showed, for example, that clinical intervention programmes focused on creating pro-social, supportive interactions with same-age peers, assisting them in attaining self-relevant goals and encouraging them to create a meaningful understanding of their past, present and future lives, might prove potent in helping youths to cope with stressful experiences. In Sarah we have an example of what can happen even in the face of great adversity when certain critical protective factors are present. As Masten (2001) concluded: 'What began as a quest for the extraordinary has revealed the power of the ordinary. Resilience does not come from rare and special qualities, but from the everyday magic of ordinary, normative human resources in the minds, brains, and bodies of children, in their families and relationships, and in their communities' (p. 235).

FIGURE 16.9

Levels of analysis: factors related to the stress response.

As we have now seen, a variety of biological, cognitive and environmental factors influence stress and its effects on us. Figure 16.9 summarizes these important influences.

LEVELS OF ANALYSIS   FACTORS RELATED TO THE STRESS RESPONSE

Biological
- Evolutionary mechanisms for responding to stressors
- Physiological responses of autonomic and endocrine systems to situational stressors
- Stress effects on immune system
- Individual differences in physiological reactivity to stressors (e.g., physiological toughness)

Psychological
- Cognitive appraisal of environmental demands, resources, potential consequences and personal meaning of consequences
- Personality factors, such as optimism and hardiness, that affect responses to stressors
- Coping strategies and the skill with which they are applied
- Self-efficacy and expectations of available social support

Environmental
- Number, intensity and duration of the stressful events
- Predictability, controllability and chronicity of stressors
- Availability of social support
- Cultural factors that teach one how to respond to stressors

Stress response

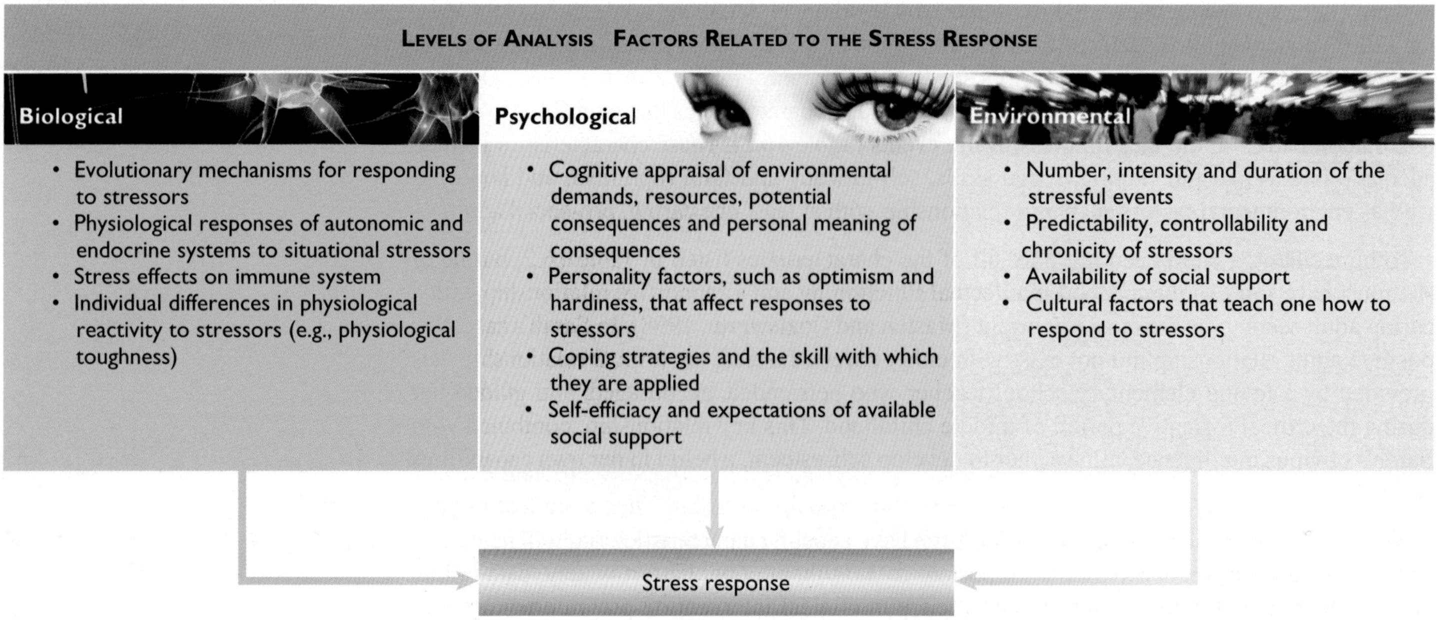

IN REVIEW

- Vulnerability and protective factors make people more or less susceptible to stressors. Social support is an important protective factor, having both direct and buffering effects that help people cope with stress.

- Individual differences in physiological reactivity also affect well-being. People who exhibit strong and prolonged arousal responses are more susceptible to negative psychological and health effects. Physiological reactivity can predispose people to health problems, particularly if they respond with high levels of cortisol. The Type A behaviour pattern increases vulnerability to coronary heart disease.

- Hardiness is a protective factor against stress. Hardy individuals are committed, have feelings of personal control and tend to perceive stressful situations as challenges. Other cognitive protective factors are self-efficacy and optimism. Spiritual beliefs often help people cope more effectively with stressful life events, but certain religious beliefs seem capable of increasing stress.

- Studies of highly resilient children reveal important characteristics that contribute to positive outcomes as children mature, such as good intellectual functioning, social skills, self-efficacy and hope, usually nurtured by social support from at least one caring adult in the child's life.

COPING WITH STRESS

My courage sank, and with each succeeding minute it became less possible to resist this horror. My cue came, and on I went to that stage where I knew with grim certainty I would not be capable of remaining more than a few minutes.... I took one pace forward and stopped abruptly. My voice had started to fade, my throat closed up and the audience was beginning to go giddily round. (Aaron, 1986, p. 24)

This account of stage fright was given not by a novice actor in his first play but by Sir Laurence Olivier (1907–89), considered by many the greatest actor of his generation, appearing in more than 120 stage roles, nearly 60 films and more than 15 television productions. Few people were aware that for most of his career, Olivier experienced a private hell before every performance. His audiences saw only what happened once he stepped onto the stage: another flawless performance. Olivier had a remarkable ability to purge the terror from his mind, relax his body and concentrate fully on his role once showtime arrived (Aaron, 1986).

Although there are countless ways people might respond to a stressor, coping strategies can be divided into the three broad classes shown in Figure 16.10. **Problem-focused coping** strategies attempt to confront and directly deal with the demands of the situation or to change the situation so that it is no longer stressful. Examples of problem-focused strategies might include studying for a test, going directly to another person to work out a misunderstanding, or signing up for a course to improve one's time-management skills.

Rather than dealing directly with the stressful situation, **emotion-focused coping** strategies attempt to manage the emotional responses that result from it. Olivier was obviously able to control his paralysing fear once he stepped on stage. Some forms of emotion-focused coping involve appraising the situation in a manner that minimizes its emotional impact. A person might deal with the stress from an interpersonal conflict by denying that any problem exists. Other forms involve avoidance or acceptance of the stressful situation. Thus a student might decide to deal with anxiety about an upcoming test by going to a party and forgetting about it. Informed that he has a terminal illness, a man might decide that nothing can be done about the situation and simply accept this unwelcome reality – or he might use the avoidance strategy of

problem-focused coping
strategies to confront and directly deal with the demands of the situation or to change the situation so that it is no longer stressful

Focus 16.12
Describe the three major classes of coping strategies. How does stressor controllability influence their outcomes?

emotion-focused coping
strategies to manage the emotional responses that result from it

FIGURE 16.10

Ways of coping.

Coping strategies fall into three general categories: (1) problem-focused coping, actively attempting to respond to situational demands; (2) emotion-focused coping, directed at minimizing emotional distress; and (3) seeking or accepting social support.

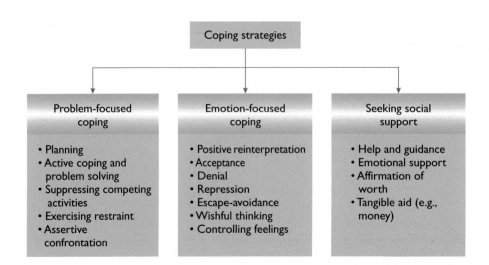

seeking social support

turning to others for assistance and emotional support in times of stress

discontinuing medical treatment and keeping the illness a secret, even from close family members.

A third class of coping strategies involves **seeking social support**, that is, turning to others for assistance and emotional support in times of stress. Thus the student might seek the help of a class-mate in preparing for the test, and the man with the terminal illness might choose to join a support group for the terminally ill. Sarah accepted and benefited from the social support provided by the teacher who befriended her.

EFFECTIVENESS OF COPING STRATEGIES

Which of the three general classes of coping strategies would you expect to be most generally effective? Whenever we ask this question in our classes, the majority of our students vote for problem-focused coping. This response is understandable, for many people, particularly in western cultures, approach problems with the attitude that if something needs fixing, we should fix it.

What does the research literature say? Charles Holahan and Rudolf Moos (1990) studied coping patterns and psychological outcomes in more than 400 California adults over a one-year period. Although people often used several coping methods in dealing with a stressor, problem-focused coping methods and seeking social support were most often associated with favourable adjustment to stressors. In contrast, emotion-focused strategies that involved avoiding feelings or taking things out on other people predicted depression and poorer adjustment. Other studies have yielded similar results. In children and adults and across many different types of stressors, emotion-focused strategies that involve avoidance, denial and wishful thinking seem to be related to less effective adaptation (Snyder, 2001). On the other hand, there are adaptive emotion-focused strategies, such as identifying and changing irrational negative thinking and learning relaxation skills to control arousal. When you are transgressed against by someone else for example, people often think negatively about this person, reacting by experiencing unforgiveness. One emotion-focused strategy that has been shown to reduce stressful reactions to such transgression is by forgiving the other person, thereby changing negative thinking (Worthington and Scherer, 2004). Such emotion-focused strategies can thus be effective methods for reducing stress responses without avoiding or distorting reality (DeLongis, 2000; Meichenbaum, 1985).

CONTROLLABILITY AND COPING EFFICACY

Despite the evidence generally favouring problem-focused coping, attempting to change the situation is not always the most adaptive way to cope with a stressor. Problem-focused coping works best in situations where there is some prospect of controlling the stressor (Park et al., 2004). However, there are situations that we cannot influence or modify, and in those cases problem-focused coping may do more harm than good. Instead, emotion-focused coping may be the most adaptive approach we can take, for while we cannot master the situation, we may be able to prevent or control maladaptive emotional responses to it (Auerbach, 1989). Of course, reliance on emotion-focused coping is likely to be maladaptive if it prevents us from acting to change situations in which we actually *do* have control.

Thomas Strentz and Stephen Auerbach (1988) demonstrated the effectiveness of emotion-focused coping in adapting to a stressful situation with limited personal control. As part of a US Federal Bureau of Investigation (FBI) programme to deal with potential airline hijackings, airline employees volunteered to participate in a training exercise. The employees were randomly assigned to one of two experimental conditions or to a control condition. In one experimental condition, employees were trained in problem-focused techniques that hostages can use to actively deal with their situation. They were shown how to interact with captors and maintain a façade of dignity and composure through appearance and behaviour. They also learned ways of supporting one another non-verbally and communicating with one another by using a prisoner-of-war tap code.

Training for the second experimental group focused on the emotional reactions the hostages would likely experience and techniques they could use to minimize their stress responses. These emotion-focused techniques included deep breathing, muscle relaxation, stopping unwanted thoughts and generating pleasant fantasies. Employees in the control condition were given no coping skills training.

Weeks later, the employees were unexpectedly abducted by FBI agents posing as terrorists and held hostage for four days under very realistic and stressful conditions. During their captivity, the hostages completed self-report measures of emotional distress and psychiatric symptoms. In addition, trained observers rated the adaptiveness of their behaviour. Results indicated that the hostage groups trained in either problem-focused or emotion-focused strategies fared better than did the untrained employees on both the self-report and the behavioural measures. However, employees who had received emotion-focused training adapted better to the largely uncontrollable conditions of captivity than did those who had received problem-focused coping instruction (Fig. 16.11).

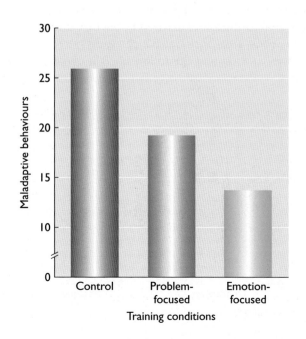

FIGURE 16.11

Coping with captivity.

These data show the behavioural ratings of participants in a mock airline-hostage crisis. Participants who received instruction in emotion-focused coping fared better than did those in the problem-focused and control conditions.

SOURCE: based on Strentz and Auerbach, 1988.

The important conclusion from this and many other studies is that no coping strategy or technique is equally effective in all situations. Instead, effectiveness depends on the characteristics of the situation, the appropriateness of the technique and the skill with which it is carried out. People are likely to adapt well to the stresses of life if they have mastered a variety of coping techniques and know how and when to apply them most effectively. The importance of controllability in the choice of techniques recalls the wisdom in theologian Reinhold Niebuhr's famous prayer that asks for the courage to change those things that can be changed, the forbearance to accept those that cannot be changed, and the wisdom to discern the difference.

TRAUMA DISCLOSURE AND EMOTIONAL RELEASE

Is there any truth to the popular wisdom that when we are stressed out and upset, it is good to talk with someone about it? James Pennebaker (1995; 1997) conducted several studies in which college students talked about past traumas to an experimenter in an adjoining room or they tape-recorded or wrote about the experiences. Many tearfully recounted incidents of personal failure, family tragedies, shattered relationships, sexual or physical abuse, and traumatic accidents. Participants in a control group were asked to talk or write about trivial everyday matters. A comparison of blood samples taken from the students before and after their sessions indicated enhanced immune system functioning in those who had purged themselves of negative emotions but not in those who had not. Moreover, the students who had disclosed the traumatic incidents had 50 per cent fewer visits to the campus health centre over the next six months compared with the control group. A study by Panagopoulou et al. (2006) on pre-operative psychological distress demonstrates however that it is not the *quantity* or number of times individuals have the opportunity to share emotions that leads to the strongest decrease in distress. Instead the perceived *quality* of the disclosure, such as the supportiveness, understanding or appropriateness of the sharing partner, seemed more important for predicting decreased preoperative distress as a function of social sharing.

In another study, Denise Sloan and Brian Marx (2004) used the written-disclosure procedure with college students who had reported experiencing a traumatic event in their lives. The students completed measures of stress symptoms, depression and number of days they had been sick since the beginning of the school term. In an experimental condition, participants were then asked to write about the traumatic event, whereas the control condition did an unrelated task. Physiological arousal was recorded as the participants performed the tasks. One month later, the students again completed the measures of psychological symptoms and sick days. The students had not differed on any of these measures at baseline, but they differed strongly afterwards (Fig. 16.12). Those who had written about their traumas showed lowered stress and depression scores. They also reported fewer sick days at the follow-up. The more physiologically aroused the

Focus 16.13

How do trauma disclosure and emotional constraint affect well-being?

FIGURE 16.12

Does trauma disclosure help?

These data show the effects of written disclosure concerning a previous traumatic life event on (a) subsequent stress symptoms, depression, and (b) number of self-reported sick days.

SOURCE: based on Sloan and Marx, 2004.

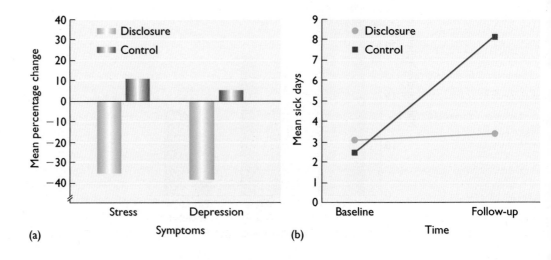

participants in the written-disclosure group became while they wrote about their traumatic events, the healthier they looked physically and psychologically a month later. The researchers concluded that writing or talking about traumatic events affords exposure to the situational cues that accompanied the trauma and now function as conditioned stimuli that trigger distress. Exposure allows extinction to occur, thus reducing the stimuli's emotional impact.

BOTTLING UP FEELINGS: THE HIDDEN COSTS OF EMOTIONAL CONSTRAINT

You can probably think of several people in your life who differ greatly in how they express their negative emotions in response to stress. While constantly venting strong negative feelings may not be a good way to make friends and influence people, an inability to express negative feelings can also have its costs. Some studies have reported relations between cancer development and the use of denial or repressive coping strategies, but others have not (McKenna et al., 1999). In order to understand the sometimes equivocal results on the relation between negative health outcomes and the inhibition of expression, it is important to notice that negative effects on health are most likely when individuals *simultaneously* experience high levels of negative affect *and* inhibit their expression of it. This emotional reaction pattern has been linked to, for example, recurrence of cardiac events and higher mortality risk for patients with coronary heart disease (Denollet et al., 1997). In this sense, denial may also lead to a decrease in experienced negative emotions, thereby undermining the association between inhibition of expression and negative health outcomes.

In one long-term European study, people who were experiencing high stress levels but were too emotionally restrained to express negative feelings, even when appropriate, had a significantly higher likelihood of developing cancer than did highly stressed people who were not so emotionally restrained. Seeking to reduce this potential vulnerability factor, the researchers designed a treatment programme to help stress-ridden but emotionally constrained people who had not yet developed cancer. The programme focused on teaching participants how to express their emotions in an adaptive fashion and to build stress-coping skills to manage their feelings without bottling them up. A control group of similar people did not receive the training. Thirteen years later, a follow-up study revealed that 90 per cent of the trained participants were still alive, whereas 62 per cent of the control group participants had died from cancer and other ailments (Eysenck, 1994; Eysenck and Grossarth-Marticek, 1991).

The question of whether there is indeed a 'cancer-prone personality' remains a topic of scientific study and debate (Suls and Wallston, 2003; Taylor, 2006a). Nonetheless, in the eyes of many researchers, there is enough evidence to suggest that a rigid pattern of emotional constraint can have negative effects on health. One impressive example of this comes from two studies by Cole and colleagues (1996a; 1996b). During a five-year period they followed a normal population of gay men and found that participants who concealed the expression of their homosexual identity experienced higher incidence of several infectious diseases like bronchitis and pneumonia, as well as a higher incidence of cancer compared with participants who did not conceal the expression of their homosexual identity. A second study furthermore showed that for HIV-positive gay men who concealed the expression of their homosexuality, the HIV infection advanced more rapidly. These studies provide some strong evidence of the association between bottling up one's feelings and future health outcomes.

The question of whether or not it is better to purge one's feelings or bottle them up, is not that easy however. As in the earlier discussion of coping strategies, the best outcomes may occur if we have the flexibility to do either, depending on the situation. George Bonnano and co-workers (2004) studied New York City college students shortly after the 11 September terrorist attacks. In a series of laboratory tasks, participants were required to either openly express emotional responses or suppress them. The researchers found that the students who were most able to engage in either expression or suppression reported less distress about the terrorist attacks and less general life distress two years later than did participants who were less flexible in their emotional responses.

GENDER, CULTURE AND COPING

Focus 16.14

How do gender and cultural factors affect the tendency to use particular coping strategies?

Many factors, including gender roles and culture, influence our tendency to favour one coping strategy over another. Although men and women both use problem-focused coping, men are more likely to use it as the first strategy when they confront a stressor (Ptacek et al., 1992). Women, who tend to have larger support networks and higher needs for affiliation than men, are more likely than men to seek social support (Billings and Moos, 1984; Schwarzer, 1998). Women also are somewhat more likely than men to use emotion-focused coping (Carver et al., 1989; Pearlin and Schooler, 1978).

This general pattern of coping preferences is consistent with the socialization that boys and girls traditionally experience. In most cultures, boys are pushed to be more independent, assertive and self-sufficient, whereas girls are expected to be more emotionally expressive, supportive and dependent (Eccles, 1991; Lytton and Romney, 1991). In the words of stress researcher Shelley Taylor (2006a), the common male response is 'fight or flight', whereas women are more likely than men to 'tend and befriend'. *Tending* involves nurturant activities designed to protect the self, offspring and significant others. These behaviours promote safety and reduce distress. *Befriending* is the creation and maintenance of social networks that may aid in this process. Taylor (2000b) speculates that the tend-and-befriend pattern is a product of biological mechanisms that underlie attachment and caregiving behavioural tendencies in women. The female hormone oxytocin, acting in conjunction with female reproductive hormones and endorphin mechanisms, may be a key player in this biological system.

The importance of support received from a spouse in reducing women's negative emotional responses to threat was assessed in a recent study by Coan et al. (2006). In this study women were exposed to threatening stimuli (the possibility of receiving an electric shock), while their brain responses were monitored by a brain scanner (fMRI). Support occurred in the form of having one's hand held during the procedure, a behaviour that is used to express soothing and support in both humans and primates under conditions of threat. In one block of trials, the wife held the hand of her spouse. In a second block of trials, an anonymous and unseen male experimental assistant held the woman's hand. In the third block, no one held the woman's hand. At the end of each trial block, the woman rated how unpleasant the situation was and how much fear arousal she was experiencing. As expected, the fMRI recordings of brain activation yielded dramatic proof that social support, particularly from a spouse, reduces the brain's response to threat. That is, the spouse's hand-holding was associated with the lowest physiological arousal. One other important finding occurred. Despite the fact that all of the couples were in satisfying marriages, the researchers found that even in this restricted marital-satisfaction group, satisfaction scores were significantly correlated with reduced brain activation on the threat trials when the spouse was holding the woman's hand. This relation did not occur when the woman's hand was being held by a stranger. The question of whether the same findings would occur if husbands were being shocked and the wife was doing the hand-holding is as of yet unresolved and awaits further investigation.

Apart from differences between men and women, researchers have also found cultural differences in coping. North Americans and Europeans show a tendency to use problem-focused coping more than do Asian and Hispanic people, who tend to favour emotion-focused coping and social support (Essau and Trommsdorff, 1996; Jung, 1995). Asians also show a greater tendency to avoid stressful situations involving interpersonal conflict, perhaps reflecting their culture's emphasis on interpersonal harmony (Chang, 1996). In a study of how American married couples deal with marital stress, African-Americans reported a greater tendency than Caucasian-Americans to seek social support (Sistler and Moore, 1996). The manner in which particular coping strategies affect well-being under differing cultural conditions is an important topic for future research.

WHAT DO YOU THINK?

WHY DO WOMEN OUTLIVE MEN?

In the USA, women live an average of about 5.2 years longer than men do (National Center for Health Statistics, 2004). A leading news magazine suggested that this difference is probably caused by the fact that men live more stressful lives. Given what you have learned so far, can you think of alternative explanations for the longevity difference? What would you need to know in order to rule out the life-stress explanation? Think about it, then see the discussion on p. 773.

STRESS-MANAGEMENT TRAINING

Because stress takes a toll on people's physical and psychological well-being, much effort has gone into developing methods for reducing stress. The model shown in Figure 16.2 suggests that we can reduce stress by modifying any of its major components (Linden, 2005). Thus we can change the situation that constitutes the stressor, modify cognitive appraisals that trigger the rest of the stress response, or learn ways to control the physiological arousal. Finally, we can adopt more effective behaviours for meeting the demands of the situation.

In many coping-skills programmes, people learn to modify habits of thought that trigger inappropriate emotional responses and to control physiological arousal responses through relaxation skills (Barlow et al., 2001; Greenberg, 2005). Figure 16.13 previews the most common stress-management techniques taught by psychologists.

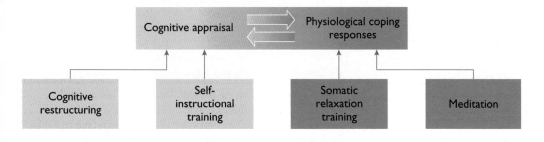

Cognitive Coping Skills

Because cognitive appraisal processes play a central role in generating stress, Richard Lazarus, Albert Ellis and other cognitive theorists maintain that the most powerful means of regulating feelings is by controlling how we think about stressful situations and about ourselves. Ellis (1962) suggests that a relatively small number of irrational core beliefs lie at the root of most maladaptive negative feelings. For example, we tell ourselves that we *must* achieve and be approved of in virtually every respect if we are to consider ourselves worthwhile people; that it is terrible, awful and *catastrophic* when life or other people are not the way that we demand they be; that people who do not behave as we wish are bad and therefore deserving of punishment. In Ellis's terms, these '*must*urbation' and 'catastrophizing' tendencies, together with other irrational ideas, generate unnecessary anxiety, despair and anger. When people use the technique of **cognitive restructuring** to systematically detect, challenge and replace these irrational ideas, their feelings can change dramatically, as in the following case:

Focus 16.15

Which stress-management/ coping-skills training procedures are used to control cognitive and physiological stress responses?

FIGURE 16.13

Stress-management training.

Many stress-management/ coping-skills programmes teach self-modification techniques, such as cognitive restructuring and self-instructional training to alter stress-producing cognitive appraisals. Relaxation techniques such as progressive relaxation and meditation help counter physiological arousal.

cognitive restructuring

systematically detect, challenge and replace these irrational ideas

Whenever I find myself getting guilty or upset, I immediately tell myself that there must be some silly sentence that I am saying to myself to cause this upset; and almost immediately … I find this sentence…. [It] invariably takes the form of 'Isn't it terrible that…' or 'Wouldn't it be awful if…' And when I look at and question these sentences and ask myself, 'How is it really terrible that…?' or 'Why would it actually be awful if…?' I always find that it isn't terrible or wouldn't be awful, and I get over being upset very quickly…. I can hardly believe it, but I seem to be getting to the point, after so many years of worrying over practically everything and thinking I was a slob no matter what I did, of now finding that nothing is so terrible or awful, and I now seem to be recognizing this in advance rather than after I have seriously upset myself. (Ellis, 1962, pp. 31–2)

Another approach to changing cognitions does not involve attacking irrational ideas that cause disturbance. In **self-instructional training**, people learn to talk to themselves and guide their behaviour in ways that help them cope more effectively (Meichenbaum, 1985). They prepare different self-instructions to use at four critical stages of the stressful episode: preparing for the stressor, confronting the stressor, dealing with the feeling of being overwhelmed and appraising coping efforts after the stressful situation. Table 16.3 provides examples of self-instructions that can be used at these stages of the coping process.

self-instructional training

people learn to talk to themselves and guide their behaviour in ways that help them cope more effectively

TABLE 16.3 SELF-INSTRUCTIONAL TRAINING: EXAMPLES OF ADAPTIVE SELF-STATEMENTS THAT CAN BE APPLIED AT VARIOUS STAGES OF THE COPING PROCESS

Phase of coping process	Self-statements
Preparing for the stressor	• What do I have to do? • I can work out a plan to deal with it. • Remember, stick to the issues and don't take it personally. • Stop worrying. Worrying won't help anything.
Confronting and handling the stressor	• As long as I keep my cool, I'm in control of the situation. • I can meet this challenge. This tenseness is just a cue to use my coping techniques. • Don't think about stress, just about what I have to do. • Take a deep breath and relax. Ah, good.
Coping with the feeling of being overwhelmed	• Keep my focus on the present. What is it I have to do? • Relax and slow things down. • Don't try to eliminate stress totally; just keep it manageable. • Let's take the issue point by point.
Evaluation and self-reinforcement	• OK, what worked and what didn't? • I handled it pretty well. • It didn't work, but that's OK. I'll do better next time. • Way to go! You did it!

SOURCE: adapted from Meichenbaum, 1985.

Relaxation Techniques

Coping-skills training can also help people control their physiological responses in stressful situations. Because relaxation is incompatible with arousal, **somatic relaxation training** provides a means of voluntarily reducing or preventing high levels of arousal. To learn this skill, people typically tense the various muscle groups of their body and pair tension release with a trigger word (e.g., 'Relax') and the exhalation (relaxing) phase of the breathing cycle. The goal is to condition relaxation to the trigger word and to exhalation so that a state of relaxation can be immediately produced in stressful situations by exhaling and mentally saying the trigger word.

somatic relaxation training

a means of voluntarily reducing or preventing high levels of arousal

Most people can learn this technique with about a week of practice. Somatic relaxation training is a cornerstone of most stress-management training programmes, and evidence suggests that this type of intervention has a positive impact on adjustment, well-being and medical utilization (e.g., Brantley and Jones, 1993). In a study on adult asthmatics for example, tape-recorded relaxation training led to a decrease in number of reported asthma symptoms and negative mood (Smyth et al., 1999).

Another type of relaxation can be produced through meditation. Meditation not only relaxes the body but also produces **cognitive relaxation**, a peaceful, mind-clearing state. In one approach, the person sits quietly in a comfortable position with eyes closed and mentally concentrates on the word *one* with each exhalation. This procedure is continued for about 20 minutes and, when mastered, quickly relaxes both body and mind (Benson and Klipper, 1976). One key difference between meditation and somatic relaxation is that the latter can be applied at any time during the stressful situation, whereas meditation is best done in a quiet, private space. Many people who meditate practise their technique daily as a means of counteracting ongoing stressors in their lives and preventing short-term stressors from taking a toll.

cognitive relaxation
a peaceful, mind-clearing state

IN REVIEW

- Three major ways of coping with stressors are problem-focused coping, emotion-focused coping and seeking social support. Problem-focused coping and seeking social support generally relate to better adjustment than emotion-focused coping. However, in situations involving low personal control, emotion-focused coping may be the most appropriate and effective strategy.

- Trauma disclosure has shown positive effects on physical and psychological well-being. Severe emotional constraint may be a risk factor for cancer and perhaps other disorders. Flexibility in emotional expression and suppression seems desirable.

- Stress-management training teaches people adaptive coping skills for handling stressful situations. Cognitive restructuring and self-instructional training can be used to develop adaptive cognitive coping responses; somatic relaxation training and meditation can be used to develop greater control of physiological arousal.

PAIN AND PAIN MANAGEMENT

Physical pain surely is one of the most unpleasant realities of life, and most of us do our best to avoid it. Hundreds of thousands seek relief from unbearable pain, and one-third of all people experience pain that requires medical attention at some time in their lives. Half of all adult Americans suffer from back pain and 10 per cent from severe headaches. Pain is a significant feature of many illnesses, and some form of pain is responsible for 80 per cent of all medical complaints in North America and Europe (National Center for Health Statistics, 2004; Salovey et al., 2000).

Pain, however, is a two-edged sword. Despite its unpleasantness, pain also has important survival functions. It serves as a warning signal when the body is being threatened or damaged, and it can trigger a variety of behavioural reactions that help us cope with the threat, such as jerking back from a hot skillet or going to see a doctor (Fig. 16.14).

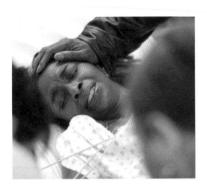

FIGURE 16.14

Although pain is an aversive state, it also is adaptive. Pain signals that something is wrong in the body, and it motivates behaviours, such as seeking medical aid, that promote healing and survival.

gate control theory

the experience of pain results from the opening and closing of gating mechanisms in the nervous system

Focus 16.16

How does gate control theory explain pain perception and control? How are glial cells and cytokines involved?

On the surface, we might think that pain is a purely sensory phenomenon and wonder why it is of interest to psychologists. When we examine it more carefully, however, we see that pain is a complex perceptual phenomenon that involves the operation of numerous psychological processes. For example, it is possible for people to experience excruciating pain in the absence of tissue damage (Melzack, 1998). Conversely, people may suffer severe physical damage and experience no pain, as has occurred in soldiers engaged in combat who were unaware for several hours that they had been wounded (Fordyce, 1988).

BIOLOGICAL MECHANISMS OF PAIN

Pain receptors are found in all body tissues with the exception of the brain, bones, hair, nails and non-living parts of the teeth. Free nerve endings in the skin and internal organs respond to intense mechanical, thermal or chemical stimulation and then send nerve impulses into the spinal cord, where sensory tracts carry pain information to the brain. Once in the brain, the sensory information about pain intensity and location is relayed by the thalamus to the somatosensory and frontal areas of the cerebral cortex (Fields, 2005). Other tracts from the thalamus direct nerve impulses to the limbic system, which is involved in motivation and emotion. These tracts seem to control the emotional component of pain (Melzack, 1998). Thus pain has both a sensory and an emotional component. *Suffering* occurs when both painful sensations and a negative emotional response are present (Fordyce, 1988; Turk, 2001).

Spinal and Brain Mechanisms

Gate control theory, developed by Canadian psychologist Ronald Melzack and physiologist Patrick Wall (1982), was a major advance in the study of pain. **Gate control theory** proposes that the experience of pain results from the opening and closing of gating mechanisms in the nervous system. Events in the spinal cord can open a system of spinal cord 'gates' and allow the nerve impulses to travel towards the brain. However, other sensory input can partially or completely close the gates and blunt our experiencing of pain. For example, rubbing a bruise or scratching an itch can produce relief. Gate control theorists also suggest that acupuncture achieves its pain-relieving effects because the acupuncture needles stimulate mostly tactile receptors that close the pain gates.

From a psychological perspective, perhaps the most intriguing feature of gate control theory is that nerve impulses in fibres descending from the brain can also influence the spinal gates, thereby increasing or decreasing the flow of pain stimulation to the brain. This *central control mechanism* allows thoughts, emotions and beliefs to influence the experience of pain and helps explain why pain is a psychological phenomenon as well as a physical phenomenon. Gate control theory has been valuable in suggesting techniques for pain control and in stimulating research on psychological factors in pain (Turk and Melzack, 2001).

Gate control and other theorists have traditionally viewed pain as reflecting solely the action of neurons. However, the immune system also plays a role in pain. Recent research has shown that glial cells, which structurally support and service neurons within the spinal cord, are involved in the creation and maintenance of pathological pain (Watkins and Maier, 2003). These glial cells become activated by immune challenges (viral or bacterial infection) and by substances released by neurons within the pain pathway. They then amplify pain by releasing cytokines (messenger molecules) that promote inflammation. This may help account for that 'ache all over' sensation that many of us experience when we are ill.

The Endorphins

In 1680 an English physician wrote, 'Among the remedies which it has pleased Almighty God to give man to relieve his suffering, none is so universal and so efficacious as opium' (quoted in Snyder, 1977). Opiates (such as opium, morphine and heroin) have been used for centuries to relieve pain, and they strongly affect the brain's pain and pleasure systems. In the 1970s, scientists discovered that opiates produce their effects by locking into specific receptor sites in brain regions associated with pain perception.

But why would the brain have built-in receptors for opiates unless there was some natural chemical in the brain for the receptor to receive? Later research disclosed what had to be true: The nervous system has its own built-in analgesics (painkillers) with opiate-like properties. These natural opiates were named **endorphins** (meaning endogenous, or internally produced, morphines). Endorphins exert some of their painkilling effects by inhibiting the release of neurotransmitters involved in the synaptic transmission of pain impulses from the spinal cord to the brain (Fields, 2005). Some endorphins are enormously potent. One of the brain endorphins isolated by scientists is more than 200 times more powerful than morphine (Franklin, 1987). Endorphins are of great interest to psychologists because they may help explain how psychological factors 'in the head' can have such strong effects on pain and suffering.

In 2001 John-Kar Zubieta and co-workers published a landmark study that showed the endorphins in action within the brain. They injected a radioactive form of an endorphin into volunteer participants, then stimulated them with painful injections of salt water into the jaw muscles. Brain scans allowed the researchers to see which areas of the brain lit up from endorphin activity and to relate this activity to pain reports given by the participants every 15 seconds. The scans revealed a surge of endorphin activity within several brain regions, including the thalamus (the sensory switchboard), the amygdala (an emotion centre) and a sensory area of the cortex. As the endorphin surge continued over 20 minutes of pain stimulation, participants reported decreased sensory and emotional ratings of pain.

Two other findings were noteworthy. First, people differed in their pain experiences despite identical pain stimulation. Second, these differences were linked to variations in (1) the number of opioid receptors the participants had for the endorphins to bind to and (2) their own ability to release endorphins. Thus biological factors seem to be an important determinant for understanding differences in people's ability to tolerate pain (Zubieta et al., 2001).

Acupuncture is a pain-reduction technique that may ultimately be understood in terms of endorphin mechanisms. Injections of naloxone, a drug that counteracts the effects of endorphins, greatly decrease the pain-reducing effects of acupuncture (Oleson, 2002). This suggests that acupuncture normally releases endorphins (Fig. 16.15).

Another phenomenon attributable to endorphins is **stress-induced analgesia**, a reduction in – or absence of – perceived pain that occurs under stressful conditions. For example, research has shown that about 65 per cent of soldiers wounded during combat report having felt no pain at the time of their injury (Warga, 1987). Likewise, people involved in accidents are sometimes unaware of serious injuries until the crisis is over. This analgesic response could be highly adaptive. In a life-threatening situation, fight-or-flight defensive behaviour must be given immediate priority over normal responses to pain, which typically involve immobility. By reducing or preventing pain sensations through the mechanism of endorphin release, stress-induced analgesia helps suppress these pain-related behaviours so that the person or animal can perform the actions needed for immediate survival, such as fleeing, fighting or getting help (Fanselow, 1991). As an example, consider the report of a man who was so severely bitten during an attack by a grizzly bear that he required more than 200 stitches:

> I had read the week before about someone who was killed and eaten by a grizzly bear. So I was thinking that this bear was going to eat me unless I got away. I did not have time for pain. I was fighting for my life. It was not until the next day that I started feeling pain and fear. (Kolb and Whishaw, 2001, p. 386)

The release of endorphins seems to be part of the body's natural response to stress, but we may pay a price for this temporary relief from pain. It appears that chronically high levels of

Focus 16.17
How do endorphins influence pain perception and physical well-being?

endorphins
endogenous, or internally produced, morphines

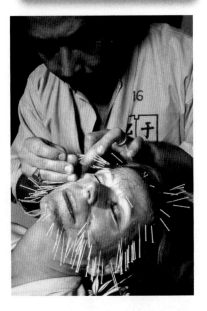

FIGURE 16.15
Acupuncture is a proven pain-reduction procedure. Gate control theory attributes its effects to the stimulation of sensory fibres that close sensory gates in the pain system. In addition, there is evidence that acupuncture stimulates endorphin release.

stress-induced analgesia
a reduction in – or absence of – perceived pain that occurs under stressful conditions

endorphin release help block the activity of immune system cells that recognize and selectively kill tumour cells. This may be one way in which stress makes us more susceptible to serious illnesses such as cancer (Shavit, 1990).

CULTURAL AND PSYCHOLOGICAL INFLUENCES ON PAIN

As a complex perception, pain is influenced by numerous factors. Cultural learning, meanings attributed to pain, beliefs, and personality factors all affect our experiences of pain.

Cultural Factors

Our interpretation of pain impulses sent to the brain depends in part on our experiences and beliefs, and both of these factors are influenced by the culture in which we develop (Rollman, 1998). Consider, for example, the experience of childbirth. This event is widely perceived as a painful ordeal in western cultures, and many women express considerable anxiety about going through it (Blechman and Brownell, 1998). Yet in some cultures, women show virtually no distress during childbirth. Indeed, in one culture studied by anthropologists, it was customary for the woman's husband to get into bed and groan as if he were in great pain while the woman calmly gave birth to the child. The husband stayed in bed with the baby to recover from his terrible ordeal while the mother returned to work in the fields almost immediately (Kroeber, 1948).

Certain societies in India practise an unusual hook-hanging ritual. A holy person, chosen to bless children and crops, travels from village to village on a special ceremonial cart. Large steel hooks, attached by ropes to the top of the cart, are shoved under the skin and muscles on each side of the holy person's back. At the climax of the ceremony, he leaps from the cart and swings free, hanging only by the hooks embedded in his back (Fig. 16.16). Incredibly, though hanging from the hooks with his entire body weight, the celebrant shows no evidence of pain during the ritual; on the contrary, he appears to be in a state of ecstasy. When the hooks are removed, the wounds heal rapidly and are scarcely visible within two weeks (Kosambi, 1967).

Although ethnic groups do not appear to differ in their ability to discriminate among pain stimuli, members of different cultural groups may differ greatly in their interpretation of pain and the amount of suffering they experience (Rollman, 1998; Zatzick and Dimsdale, 1990). In the Indian hook-hanging ceremony, for example, the religious meanings attached to the act seem to transform the interpretations and meaning of the sensory input from the hooks. Likewise, childbearing mothers in cultures where the pain of childbirth is not feared do not attach strong negative emotions to the associated sensations, and they therefore suffer far less.

The role of cultural factors in pain perception is found even within modern western subcultures. In Massachusetts, researchers studied pain perception in 372 medical patients who represented six different ethnic groups: 'Old Americans' (at least third-generation US-born Caucasians who identified with no ethnic group except 'Americans'), Hispanic-Americans, Italian-Americans, Irish-Americans, French-Canadians and Polish-Americans. All of the patients suffered from chronic pain conditions that had persisted for at least three months and were beyond the point of healing. The patients completed self-report measures about their pain experiences.

The ethnic groups did not differ overall in type of physical affliction, how long they had had it or the kinds of treatments and medications they were receiving. They did differ, however, in the pain levels they reported, and these differences were associated with different attitudes and beliefs about their pain. The Hispanic-American and Italian-American patients believed most strongly that they had no control over their pain, reported feeling worried and angry about it, and believed that they would be unhappy as long as they experienced it. They also believed that it is appropriate to express one's pain openly. These two ethnic groups reported the highest levels of pain and suffering. In contrast, the Old American and Polish-American patients felt it best to suppress the outward expression of pain, reported feeling less upset about their pain sensa-

Focus 16.18
How do cultural factors influence pain experience and behaviour?

FIGURE 16.16

Cultural beliefs and pain tolerance.

Illustrated here is a hook-swinging ceremony practised in remote villages in India. After blessing all the children and farm fields in a village, the celebrant leaps from the cart and hangs suspended by the hooks embedded in his back in a state of ecstasy, showing no sign of pain.

SOURCE: adapted from Kosambi, 1967.

tions, and believed that they had greater personal control over their lives. These attitudinal differences were associated with much lower levels of reported suffering (Bates et al., 1993).

Meanings and Beliefs

Differences exist not only between cultural groups but also within them, as physician Henry Beecher (1959) observed while working at Anzio Beachhead in the Second World War and later at Massachusetts General Hospital. At Anzio, Beecher found that only about 25 per cent of the severely wounded soldiers he observed required pain medication, compared with 80 per cent of civilian men who had received similarly serious 'wounds' from surgeons at Massachusetts General. Why the difference? Beecher concluded that for the soldiers, the wounds had a fundamentally positive meaning: they spelled evacuation from the war zone and a socially acceptable ticket back home to their loved ones. For the civilian surgical patients, on the other hand, the operations meant a major life disruption and possible complications. The different meanings attributed to the pain stimuli resulted in very different levels of suffering and, consequently, different needs for pain relief (Fig. 16.17).

FIGURE 16.17

The amount of pain a wounded soldier experiences may be influenced by the meaning it has for him. Does the wound represent a ticket home to his loved ones, or does it herald a lifetime of pain and disability?

Perhaps nowhere is the influence of belief on pain perception more evident than in the effects of **placebos**, physiologically inert substances that have no medicinal value but are thought by the patient to be helpful (Shapiro and Shapiro, 1997). At the beginning of this chapter we described the observations made by German physician Hans Rheder, whose female patients responded with startling improvements in their symptoms to the news that he had invoked the healing powers of a faith healer. Similar observations have been made in pain research. In one classic study by Henry Beecher (1959), either a placebo or a morphine injection was given to 122 surgical patients who were suffering postoperative pain. All were told they were receiving pain medication. Of those who received morphine, 67 per cent reported relief, but 42 per cent of those given placebos reported equal relief. More recent medical studies of placebo effects have yielded even higher rates of pain relief, as high as 100 per cent in some studies (Turner et al., 1994). However, it is also clear that placebos work only if people *believe* they are going to work. Research using PET-scan technology at the Karolinska Institute in Sweden indicates that given a positive belief in the placebo's effectiveness, the brain sends messages that result in the release of endorphins to reduce pain (Petrovic et al., 2002).

Where pain is concerned, the statement 'I can control it' may be more than an idle boast or an empty reassurance. In one experiment, patients suffering from the prolonged pain of a

placebos

physiologically inert substances that have no medicinal value but are thought by the patient to be helpful

bone-marrow transplant were randomly assigned to one of two conditions. One group was allowed to directly control the amount of pain medication that they received intravenously. The other patients were given prescribed amounts of the same medication by the hospital staff (and told they could request additional medication if needed). The patients who had direct control over their medication not only rated their pain as less intense but also gave themselves less pain medication (Zucker et al., 1998). As in the case of placebo effects, beliefs about personal control apparently exert their effects by increasing endorphin release. Naloxone injections, which counteract endorphin activity, sharply reduce the ability of people to endure intensely painful stimuli, no matter how high their confidence in their pain tolerance (Bandura et al., 1987).

Personality Factors and Social Support

Focus 16.19

How do cognitive and personality factors affect people's responses to pain stimuli?

Beginning with Sigmund Freud, personality theorists have suggested that emotional and personality factors can play a role in experiencing and responding to pain. Pain and suffering can be a way of attaining certain goals. For some bitter and deprived people, pain can be a way of dramatizing their unhappiness; eliciting caring, sympathy or guilt from others, or gaining favours. Pain may also be a way of escaping from or avoiding threatening situations. For example, an athlete who dreads the possibility of failing may avoid the feared competition by experiencing severe pain that prevents participation. This coping process, different from consciously faking being hurt, occurs at an unconscious level (May and Sieb, 1987).

People who have the personality trait of neuroticism, the tendency to experience negative emotions such as anxiety and depression, report higher levels of physical pain, both in relation to medical conditions and in controlled laboratory administrations of painful stimuli such as heat, cold, electrical shock or pressure (Turner and Aaron, 2001). In contrast, personality styles that include optimism and a sense of personal control over one's life are associated with lower pain perception and less suffering (Pellino and Ward, 1998). Moreover, patients with chronic pain conditions who are able to simply accept the pain rather than bemoaning their fate and responding emotionally to it have less disability, better social adjustment and higher work performance (McCracken, 1998). Thus it seems clear that psychological factors play important roles in pain perception and adaptation.

A person does not function in a social vacuum however. A study by Holtzman and colleagues, for example, showed that rheumatoid arthritis (RA) patients' coping with daily pain was associated with reported satisfaction of social support. That is, social support enabled patients to more effectively use coping strategies such as cognitive reframing in order to cope with the daily pain among patients with RA (Holtzman et al., 2004). Further evidence that one's emotional state and social support network are associated with one's experience of pain comes from a study by Carmen Alonso and Christopher Coe (2001). In a sample of 184 college women, the researchers found that self-reported depression and anxiety were strongly associated with ratings of menstrual pain. More significantly, perhaps, the greatest pain and distress occurred in women who had recently lost a significant source of social support.

Does life stress increase pain experiences? Many studies with medical patients have suggested that it does (Fields, 2005). Linda Watkins and Steven Maier (2003) explain how this might occur. Normally, sensory nerves cannot respond to stress hormones because they have no receptors for them. After nerve damage resulting from injury, however, receptors for stress hormones begin to appear on the surface of sensory nerves. These new receptors increase the excitability of damaged nerves when stress hormones are present, therefore allowing life stress to increase pain.

Focus 16.20

Describe cognitive, informational and behavioural interventions for pain reduction.

The fact that psychological processes are so central to the experience of pain has stimulated many health psychologists to research methods that can be used to control or reduce pain and suffering. The following 'Applying psychological science' feature highlights this important area of application.

APPLYING PSYCHOLOGICAL SCIENCE

PSYCHOLOGICAL TECHNIQUES FOR CONTROLLING PAIN AND SUFFERING

We all occasionally experience physical pain, and for some people, pain is a never-ending nightmare. In recent years, psychological pain-control strategies have received increasing attention from health psychologists (Gatchel, 2005; Turk, 2001).

COGNITIVE STRATEGIES

Recent attention has focused on two classes of cognitive strategies known as *dissociation* and *association*. A *dissociative strategy* involves dissociating, or distracting, oneself from the painful sensory input. This can be done in a variety of ways: by directing your attention to some other feature of the external situation, by vividly imagining a pleasurable experience or by repeating a word or thought to yourself. Research has shown that dissociative strategies are most effective when they require a great deal of concentration or mental activity, thereby directing attention away from the painful stimuli.

If you are a recreational jogger or a long-distance runner, you may be familiar with the discomfort of extending yourself. Endurance running seems an ideal real-life task to use in the study of cognitive strategies. William Morgan and co-workers (1983) gave this simple dissociative strategy to participants who were running on a treadmill to exhaustion: 'Focus your attention on a spot in front of you on the treadmill and say "Down" each time your right foot comes down on the treadmill.' A control group also ran the treadmill but did not receive the strategy. Although the two groups did not differ physiologically while running the treadmill, the mental-strategy group was able to tolerate the discomfort of treadmill running 32 per cent longer than the control group.

A more dramatic, high-tech dissociative strategy is being tested in the burns centre at the Harborview Medical Center in Seattle, Washington. There children and adults with burns covering up to 60 per cent of their bodies are donning virtual-reality goggles during the often agonizing processes of wound cleansing and physical therapy. The goggles take patients into a visually compelling world of shapes and colours. Pain ratings are significantly lower when these patients are immersed in virtual reality than when they are in a non-distracted condition (Hoffman et al., 2001).

Associative strategies are the opposite of dissociative strategies. Here you focus your attention on the physical sensations and study them in a detached and unemotional fashion, taking care not to label them as painful or difficult to tolerate. It appears that when pain is intense, associative strategies become more effective than dissociative ones (McCaul and Malott, 1984). There seems to be a point at which pain stimuli become too intense to ignore and dissociative strategies become ineffective. Thus one strategy is to use dissociation as long as possible and then shift to an associative mode.

Combined dissociative and associative strategies can be effective in dealing with acute pain. In one study, participants' pain tolerance was tested by measuring how long they could keep their hand immersed in ice water. One group of participants was then trained and practised a number of dissociative coping strategies (such as attention diversion and the use of distracting imagery) and associative strategies (such as imagining that the hand immersed in the ice water was detached from the body and focusing non-emotionally on the pain sensations). Two control groups equated in initial pain tolerance were given either no strategies or a placebo pain reducer. Then their ice-water pain tolerance was tested a second time. As shown in Figure 16.18, the cognitive skills training resulted in a large increase in pain tolerance (Bandura et al., 1987).

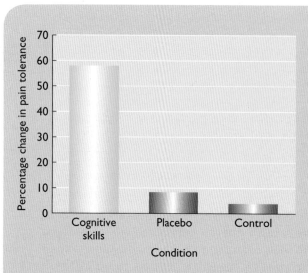

FIGURE 16.18

Coping strategies and pain tolerance.

These data show the increases in pain tolerance in an ice-water/hand-immersion task exhibited by a cognitive-skills training group, a placebo condition and a control group that repeated the task with no intervention.

SOURCE: based on Bandura et al., 1987.

HOSPITAL INTERVENTIONS: GIVING PATIENTS INFORMATIONAL CONTROL

Having relevant information about a challenging environment and event is also a kind of cognitive control, since it tells us what to expect. In the medical setting of the past, doctors typically gave patients no more information than needed about a specific medical procedure and its aftermath. However, psychological research on how certain types of information reduce anxiety and contribute to positive medical outcomes has ushered in a new era in many medical settings. Imagine that you are in the hospital for major surgery. You know that this surgical procedure entails risk and that your recovery will be painful. What kinds of information would help you cope and recuperate more easily?

You might profit from *sensory information* about what you will feel after the operation. Knowing, for example, that patients often have shooting pains in their stomach after the surgery could prevent surprise or fear if it occurred to you. You would see the pain as a normal consequence of the surgery and the recovery process rather than as a sign of danger.

Second, *procedural information* on the surgery itself would help you understand what exactly is going to be done and why. You might be shown a model of the body part to demonstrate what will be done in the surgery, or you may see a video describing the procedure. This kind of information would give you a sense of predictability and control, and reassure you that precautions were being taken to anticipate and reduce possible hazards.

Third, you could profit from *coping guidance* about handling the pain or other complications from the surgery. For example, you might learn breathing exercises designed to reduce pain by helping you relax (Tollison et al., 2002). You might also be taught some of the cognitive strategies previously described to get through sieges of acute pain during the recovery process.

Informational interventions have proved helpful in many medical settings. Surgical patients show a better course of recovery and require less pain medication than those treated in a traditional fashion (Faust, 1991). Such interventions have proven remarkably successful in decreasing distress in hospitalized children, who are likely to find major medical procedures particularly frightening (Christopherson and Mortweet, 2001).

A KEY BEHAVIOURAL STRATEGY: BECOMING ACTIVE AGAIN

Recovering patients who avoid activity and become overly protective of an injured body part are at risk for developing a chronic pain condition (Turk, 2001). It is important to return to activity after an injury as soon as the healing process will allow (Fig. 16.19). A key to successfully treating chronic pain patients who have 'shut themselves down' is to decrease their guarding and resting behaviours and to modify their belief that their pain signals body damage. Such interventions produce significant decreases in patient disability (Jensen et al., 2001). Wilbert Fordyce (1988), a leader in the behavioural treatment of pain, emphasizes the negative effects that unnecessary rest and disuse of a body part can have on recovery:

The lavish prescription of rest virtually ensures adverse disuse effects. With disuse in the musculoskeletal system, movement then becomes painful. But pain from disuse risks being interpreted by patient and professional as an indication of lack of healing. The result may become more prescribed rest or practical disuse and yet more pain with movement.... Pain problems originating in tissue injury but in which healing has occurred are made better by use. Patients must be helped to understand the dictum 'To make it better, use it.' ... People who have something better to do don't suffer as much. (p. 282)

FIGURE 16.19

A key to preventing chronic pain and disability is to begin physical activity again as soon as possible.

Pain is an intriguing and complex biological, psychological, and social phenomenon. Figure 16.20 provides a levels-of-analysis summary of the factors we've discussed.

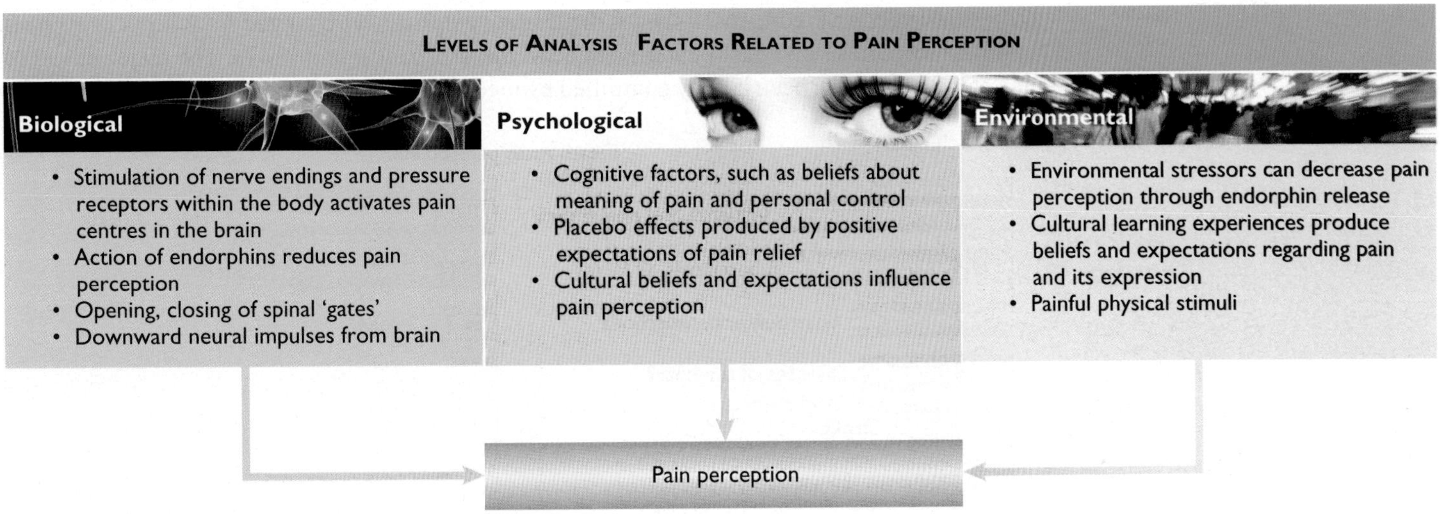

LEVELS OF ANALYSIS   FACTORS RELATED TO PAIN PERCEPTION

Biological
- Stimulation of nerve endings and pressure receptors within the body activates pain centres in the brain
- Action of endorphins reduces pain perception
- Opening, closing of spinal 'gates'
- Downward neural impulses from brain

Psychological
- Cognitive factors, such as beliefs about meaning of pain and personal control
- Placebo effects produced by positive expectations of pain relief
- Cultural beliefs and expectations influence pain perception

Environmental
- Environmental stressors can decrease pain perception through endorphin release
- Cultural learning experiences produce beliefs and expectations regarding pain and its expression
- Painful physical stimuli

Pain perception

FIGURE 16.20

Levels of analysis: factors related to pain perception.

IN REVIEW

- Pain is a complex perception influenced by biological, psychological and sociocultural factors. At the biological level, the major pain receptors appear to be free nerve endings. Gate control theory attributes pain to the opening and closing of gates in the spinal cord and to influences from the brain. Glial cells and cytokines are also involved in pain. The nervous system contains endorphins, which play a major role in pain reduction.

- Expectations of relief produced by placebos can markedly reduce medical symptoms and pain. Cultural factors also influence the appraisal and response to painful stimuli, as do control beliefs. Negative emotional states increase suffering and decrease pain tolerance.

- Psychological techniques for pain control include (1) cognitive strategies, such as dissociative and associative techniques; (2) providing medical patients with sensory and procedural information to increase cognitive control and support; and (3) increasing activity level to counter chronic pain.

HEALTH PROMOTION AND ILLNESS PREVENTION

In 1979 the Surgeon General of the USA issued a landmark report entitled *Healthy People* (US Public Health Service, 1979). The report concluded that improvements in the health of Americans are more likely to result from efforts to prevent disease and promote health than from new drugs and medical technologies. Two recent US government reports, *Healthy People 2010* (2005) and *Health, United States 2004* (2004) provide strong evidence for that assertion.

Consider the leading causes of death in the USA and Europe in comparison with the leading killers in 1900. As Figure 16.21 shows, the leading culprits have changed from influenza, pneumonia, tuberculosis and gastroenteritis to heart disease, cancer and stroke. The major killers of the early 1900s have been largely controlled by medical advances. In contrast, the death rate has

FIGURE 16.21

Causes of death, 1900 versus 2002.

Modern causes of death are far more attributable to health-endangering behaviours.

SOURCES: based on Murphy, 2000; Sexton, 1979; US Centers for Disease Control, 2002a; National Center for Health Statistics, 2004.

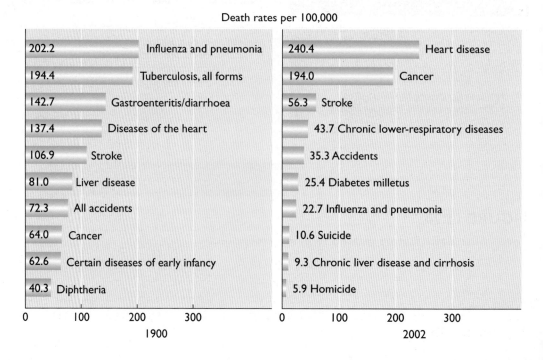

Death rates per 100,000

1900	
202.2	Influenza and pneumonia
194.4	Tuberculosis, all forms
142.7	Gastroenteritis/diarrhoea
137.4	Diseases of the heart
106.9	Stroke
81.0	Liver disease
72.3	All accidents
64.0	Cancer
62.6	Certain diseases of early infancy
40.3	Diphtheria

2002	
240.4	Heart disease
194.0	Cancer
56.3	Stroke
43.7	Chronic lower-respiratory diseases
35.3	Accidents
25.4	Diabetes milletus
22.7	Influenza and pneumonia
10.6	Suicide
9.3	Chronic liver disease and cirrhosis
5.9	Homicide

almost doubled for heart disease and tripled for cancer since 1900. As shown in Table 16.4, these diseases and today's other killers are strongly influenced by behavioural factors. Health authorities estimate that half of all cases of early mortality (deaths occurring prior to the life-expectancy age within a culture) from the 10 leading causes of death can be traced to risky behaviours, such as cigarette smoking, excessive alcohol consumption, insufficient exercise, poor dietary habits, use of illicit drugs, failure to adhere to doctors' instructions, unsafe sex practices and failure to wear car seat belts (Mokdad et al., 2004).

Recognition of the crucial role that behaviour plays in health maintenance has prompted much research in the field of health psychology. Psychologists have helped identify many of the psychological and social causes for risky health behaviours, and the clear need for lifestyle interventions has spurred attempts around the world to promote positive changes in such behaviours (Suls and Wallston, 2003; Taylor, 2006a). Modifying people's health behaviours as a form of illness prevention can reduce medical costs and avert the physical and psychological distress that illness produces.

Health-related behaviours fall into two main categories. *Health-enhancing behaviours* serve to maintain or increase health. Such behaviours include exercise, healthy dietary habits, safe sexual practices, regular medical check-ups, and breast and testicular self-examination. *Health-impairing behaviours* promote the development of illness. They include tobacco use, fatty diets, a sedentary lifestyle and unprotected sexual activity. Psychologists have developed programmes that focus on both classes of behaviour (Schneiderman, 2004).

TABLE 16.4 BEHAVIOURAL RISK FACTORS FOR THE LEADING CAUSES OF DEATH IN THE USA

Disease	Risk factors
Heart disease	Tobacco, obesity, elevated blood pressure, cholesterol, sedentary lifestyle
Cancer	Tobacco, improper diet, alcohol, environmental exposure
Cerebrovascular disease (stroke)	Tobacco, elevated blood pressure, cholesterol, sedentary lifestyle
Accidental injuries	Safety belt non-use, alcohol, home hazards
Chronic lung disease	Tobacco, environmental exposure

SOURCE: based on McGinnis, 1994.

HOW PEOPLE CHANGE: THE TRANSTHEORETICAL MODEL

In order to increase health-enhancing behaviours and reduce health-impairing ones, we need to understand the processes that underlie behaviour change in general. The most commonly known approach for understanding underlying processes in behaviour change is so-called stage-based approach. Stage theories (e.g., Prochaska and DiClemente, 1984; Schwarzer, 1992; Weinstein and Sandman, 1992) suggest that behavioural change is not a continuous process, but something that passes between distinctly different stages. The implication of such theories is that, in order to be effective, interventions should be tailored to the specific stage an individual is currently in. The most widely used stage model was developed in the 1980s, by psychologists James Prochaska and Carlo DiClemente. They began to study the process that occurs as people modify their thoughts, feelings, and behaviours in positive ways, either on their own or with professional help. Their research resulted in a **transtheoretical model** that identified six major stages in the change process (DiClemente, 2003; Prochaska and DiClemente, 1984):

transtheoretical model
identified six major stages in the change process

1. *Precontemplation*: the person does not perceive a health-related problem, denies that it is something that endangers well-being, or feels powerless to change.

2. *Contemplation*: the person perceives a problem or the desirability of a behaviour change but has not yet decided to take action. Thus some smokers are well aware of the health risks of their habit, yet they are not ready to make a decision to quit. Until the perceived benefits of changing outweigh the costs or effort involved, contemplators will not take action.

3. *Preparation*: the person has decided to change the behaviour, is making preliminary plans to do so, and may be taking preliminary steps such as cutting down on the number of cigarettes per day.

4. *Action*: the person actively begins to engage in behaviour change, perhaps stopping smoking altogether. Success at this stage hinges on the behaviour-control skills necessary to carry out the plan of action. The action stage requires the greatest commitment of effort and energy.

5. *Maintenance*: the person has been successful in avoiding relapse and has controlled the target behaviour for at least six months. This does not mean that the struggle is over. Many people lapse back into their former behaviour pattern at various times, but they reinstate their change efforts, as would be expected when one is trying to change deeply ingrained habits. It typically takes smokers three to five cycles through the action stage before they finally beat the habit, and New Year's resolutions are typically made for five or more consecutive years before they are finally carried out successfully (Prochaska et al., 1994; Schachter, 1982).

6. *Termination*: the change in behaviour is so ingrained and under personal control that the original problem behaviour will never return.

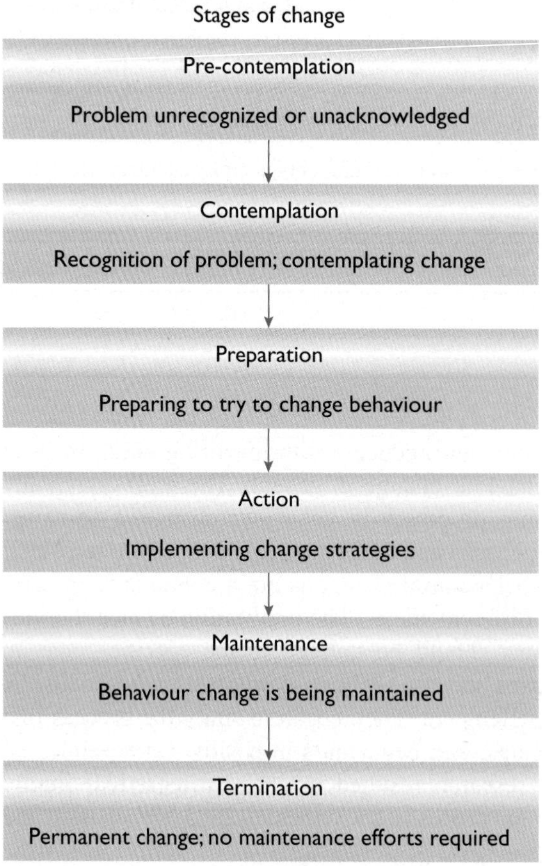

Focus 16.21

Describe the transtheoretical model and the rationale for stage-matched interventions.

FIGURE 16.22

Stages of change.

The transtheoretical model identifies a series of stages through which people pass as they modify their behaviour. People may move up and down through the stages several times before they reach the final stage of termination.

SOURCE: Prochaska et al., 1998.

Stages of change

Pre-contemplation
Problem unrecognized or unacknowledged

Contemplation
Recognition of problem; contemplating change

Preparation
Preparing to try to change behaviour

Action
Implementing change strategies

Maintenance
Behaviour change is being maintained

Termination
Permanent change; no maintenance efforts required

The transtheoretical model, shown in Figure 16.22, does not assume that people go through the stages in a smooth sequence. Longitudinal studies have shown that many people move forwards and backwards through the stages as they try to change their behaviour over time, and many people make repeated efforts to change before they finally succeed (Davidson, 1998; Evers et al., 1998). However, failure at a given stage is likely to occur if the previous stages have not been mastered.

The transtheoretical model helps us understand how people change, and it has important applied implications. For example, we know that different intervention procedures are needed for people at various stages. Psychologists have therefore developed ways of determining what stage people are in so that they can apply *stage-matched interventions* designed to move the person towards the action, maintenance and termination stages. Pre-contemplators need consciousness raising information that finally convinces them that there is a problem, as well as social support to change (DeVries et al., 1998). Contemplators often need a wake-up emotional experience that increases their motivation to change or causes them to re-evaluate themselves in relation to the behaviour. For example, a serious car accident while intoxicated may finally convince a problem drinker that his or her behaviour has to change. In the preparation stage, the person needs to develop a specific plan (ideally based on the goal-setting procedures described in Chapter 15) and have the skills to carry it out before action is likely to be successful. Only when the person is ready for the action stage are change techniques, however powerful, likely to have their intended effect.

Unfortunately life is not always as easy as a model would suggest. Despite the popularity of the transtheoretical model, a recent review suggests that there is only limited evidence of the effectiveness of interventions based on this model (Bridle et al., 2005). This might partly be due to the difficulty in accurately classifying the stage an individual is in, as well as methodological weaknesses or lack of details given regarding both methodology and intervention in the studies. These recent doubts as to the effectiveness of interventions based on stage models is a clear indications of how difficult it can be to change actual behaviour through interventions.

INCREASING BEHAVIOURS THAT ENHANCE HEALTH

During the 1970s, the role of behaviour in maintaining health and living longer became evident as researchers began to study the effects of lifestyle. Figure 16.23 shows the results of one longitudinal study of nearly 7000 adults. The researchers studied the relation of seven good health practices to life expectancy. These included sleeping seven to eight hours per day, eating breakfast, not smoking, rarely eating between meals, being at or near one's prescribed body weight, engaging in regular physical activity and drinking only small to moderate amounts of alcohol. For men and women alike, these behaviours predicted a longer life. A higher mortality rate among those with poor health practices began to appear in men between the ages of 45 and 64 and in women between 55 and 64 (Belloc, 1973). Let us examine some of these health-enhancing behaviours and what can be done to encourage them.

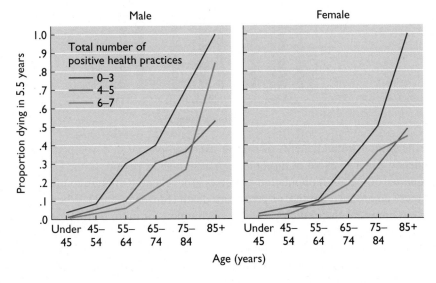

FIGURE 16.23

Healthy habits and longevity.

These data show the relation between the number of positive health practices and longevity in men and women. Those who adhered to few of the health practices experienced earlier mortality, with the pattern appearing earlier in men than in women.

SOURCE: adapted from Belloc, 1973.

Exercise

The couch potato lives! (But apparently not as long.) A sedentary lifestyle is a significant risk factor for health problems, including coronary heart disease and obesity (Rodin and Salovey, 1989; Taylor, 2006a). Despite this widely publicized fact, about 70 per cent of Americans are inactive (Baum et al., 1997; Ehrman, 2003). As fewer people now engage in vigorous manual labour, inactivity has helped double the rate of obesity since 1900, despite a 10 per cent decrease in daily caloric intake over the same period (Friedman and DiMatteo, 1989).

aerobic exercise
sustained activity that elevates the heart rate and increases the body's need for oxygen

Aerobic exercise is sustained activity, such as jogging, swimming, and bicycling, that elevates the heart rate and increases the body's need for oxygen. This kind of exercise has many physical benefits. In a body that is well conditioned by regular aerobic exercise, the heart beats more slowly and efficiently, oxygen is better utilized, slow-wave sleep increases, cholesterol levels may be reduced, faster physiological adaptation to stressors occurs and more calories are burned (Baum and Posluszny, 1999; deGeus, 2000).

Exercise is associated with physical health and longevity (Fig. 16.24). A study that followed 17 000 Harvard undergraduates into middle age revealed that death rates were one-quarter to one-third lower among moderate exercisers than among those in a less active group of the same age. Surprisingly, perhaps, extremely high levels of exercise were not associated with enhanced health; instead, moderate exercise (burning 2000 to 3500 calories per week) on a regular basis produced the best health benefits (Paffenbarger et al., 1986). Performing at 70 to 85 per cent of maximal heart rate non-stop for 15 minutes three times a week significantly reduces risk for coronary heart disease (Dishman, 1982). Such exercise also has positive psychological effects, reducing depression and anxiety (Morgan, 1997).

FIGURE 16.24

Aerobic exercise and health.

Aerobic exercise is an important health-enhancing behaviour, contributing to physical well-being. Significantly higher death rates occur for both men and women who are low in physical fitness.

SOURCE: data from Blair et al., 1989.

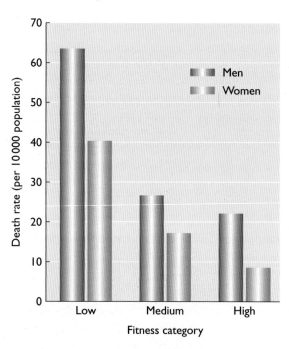

Despite the demonstrated benefits of regular exercise, people in developed countries have a strong tendency either to avoid or discontinue it after a short period. In the USA, for example, only one-quarter of the adult population exercises at levels high enough to maintain cardiorespiratory fitness and reduce the risk of premature death (Ehrman, 2003). When employers offer exercise programmes to their employees, it is uncommon for more than 30 per cent to participate, and dropout rates of 50 per cent within six months are found in virtually all exercise programmes that have been studied (Chenoweth, 2002; Dishman, 1994). On the other hand, people who are able to persist for three to six months are likely to continue, as exercise becomes a healthy habit (McAuley, 1992).

What factors predict dropout? This is an important research question, for if we can identify the risk factors, we can take measures to counteract them. Research has shown that general attitudes towards physical fitness do *not* predict adherence or dropout; the exercise-related attitudes of dropouts and people who adhere to their exercise programmes are equally favourable (Suls and Wallston, 2003). However, low self-efficacy for success in exercising regularly ('I can't do this'), Type A behaviour pattern ('Sorry, too busy to exercise'), inflated estimates of current

Focus 16.22

What is aerobic exercise? What evidence exists that it promotes health and longevity?

physical fitness ('I'm already in great shape from walking from my couch to the refrigerator') and inactive leisure pursuits (such as watching television and walking to the refrigerator) all predict dropout (Martin and Dubbert, 1985; Wilcox and Storandt, 1996). The strongest social-environmental factor related to dropout is lack of social support from friends, family, or other exercisers (Ehrman, 2003).

Psychologists have been able to increase compliance by helping exercisers identify these impediments and prepare specific strategies to deal with them before they occur (Rosen, 2000; Simkin and Gross, 1994). For example, a person who anticipates feeling too tired to work out at the end of the day might prepare a set of self-statements about how much better he or she will feel after exercising. If the person is not receiving social support and encouragement from others, he or she could also arrange for a pleasurable activity after each workout to positively reinforce his or her exercising (Courneya, 1995).

Weight Control

Obesity (being more than 20 per cent overweight) is becoming an increasingly urgent problem. Since 1960, the incidence of obesity among for example American adults has increased from 13 to 34 per cent. In 2005 an estimated 400 million adults and at least 20 million children under the age of 5 were obese worldwide (World Health Organization, 2008). Although the incidence of obesity is steadily rising everywhere, Europe now has one of the highest average Body Mass Index (BMI: weight in kilograms divided by the square of a person's height in metres) worldwide (World Health Report, 2002). Indeed, the prevalence of obesity in many European countries has risen threefold since 1980. In 2005, 130 million adults were estimated to be obese and, if the upward trend continues, an estimated number of 150 million European adults will be obese in 2010 (a rise of 4 million each year). The rise in obesity is especially alarming among children. In the USA, 19 per cent of children 6–11 years of age are overweight, compared with only 7 per cent in 1980, and the corresponding figure among 12- to 19-year-olds has more than tripled, from 5 per cent to 17 per cent (National Center for Health Statistics, 2006). Similarly, in France 16 per cent of children below 15 years of age are overweight compared to 3 per cent in 1960. If current trends continue, obesity's death toll will soon exceed 500 000 each year in the USA alone (Mokdad et al., 2004; Fig. 16.25).

Obesity is a risk factor for a variety of chronic diseases, such as cardiovascular disease, kidney disease and diabetes. Women who are 30 per cent overweight are more than three times more likely to develop heart disease than normal-weight women (Manson et al., 1990). For reasons yet unknown, fat that is localized in the abdomen is a far greater risk factor for cardiovascular disease, diabetes and cancer than is excessive fat in the hips, thighs or buttocks (Taylor, 2006a). Accumulation of abdominal fat is increased by yo-yo dieting that results in big weight fluctuations. Such dieting markedly increases the risk of dying from cardiovascular disease, an excellent reason to avoid this practice (Hafen and Hoeger, 1998; Rodin et al., 1990).

Were you to enrol in a behavioural intervention programme for weight loss, here is what would happen: the programme would begin with a period of self-monitoring, during which you would keep careful records of what, how much and under what circumstances you eat. This is designed to make you more aware of your eating habits and to identify situational factors (antecedents) that affect your food intake. You would then learn to take control of those antecedents. For example, you would learn to make low-calorie foods such as raw vegetables freely available and to limit high-calorie foods in the house. You would then learn stimulus-control techniques, such as confining your eating to one location in the house and eating only at certain times of the day. Because overeaters tend to wolf down their food and overload their stomachs, you would also learn to slow down your eating by putting down eating utensils until each bite is chewed and swallowed, and you would learn to pause between mouthfuls. These behaviours reduce food intake and help you learn to pay attention to how full you are. You would also be told to savour

Focus 16.23

How large are exercise dropout rates? What factors do and do not predict dropout?

FIGURE 16.25

An alarmingly large percentage of adults and children are overweight, increasing health risks. Obesity contributes annually to nearly 500 000 deaths in the USA alone.

SOURCE: Mokdad et al., 2004.

Focus 16.24

What are the behaviour-change techniques used in behavioural weight-control programmes?

each mouthful of food. The goal is to eat less but enjoy it more. Finally, you would learn to chart the amount of food you eat to provide constant feedback, and you would arrange to positively reinforce yourself for successful performance. These behavioural practices would be combined with nutritional guidelines to help you eat a healthier diet. Table 16.5 shows specific guidelines from a highly successful weight-reduction programme developed by psychologist Kelly Brownell (1994).

TABLE 16.5 A SAMPLE OF EFFECTIVE BEHAVIOURAL WEIGHT-CONTROL TECHNIQUES

Keep an eating diary	Keep problem foods out of sight
Examine your eating patterns	Serve and eat one portion at a time
Prevent automatic eating	Use gradual shaping for behaviour change
Examine triggers for eating	Distinguish hunger from cravings
Do nothing else while eating	Focus on behaviour, not weight loss
Eat in one place	Cope positively with slips, lapses
Put fork down between bites	Keep an exercise diary
Pause during the meal	Understand benefits of exercise
Shop on a full stomach	Know calorie values of various exercise activities
Buy foods that require preparation	Programme exercise activity

SOURCE: based on Brownell, 1994.

Research shows that the addition of an exercise programme increases the positive effects of behavioural eating-control programmes (Avenell et al., 2004; Wadden et al., 1997). High levels of physical activity are associated with initial weight loss and its maintenance, and exercise adds to the effectiveness of other weight-loss methods, such as dietary change. Research indicates that many overweight people are able to attain gradual weight loss of about 2 pounds per week for up to 20 weeks and to keep the weight off for two years and beyond (Jackson et al., 1999; Taylor, 2003).

Lifestyle Changes and Medical Recovery

Teaching people how to control their health-related programmes can have dramatic benefits even for those who are already afflicted with serious illnesses. William Haskell and co-workers (1994) randomly divided a sample of patients suffering from coronary artery disease into two groups. Both groups received the usual high-quality medical care from their physicians at Stanford University Medical School. In addition, the experimental group received a behavioural self-regulation programme that targeted health factors such as smoking, exercise, weight, nutrition and medication adherence.

A four-year follow-up revealed dramatic results. Those receiving the usual medical care showed either no improvement or a worsening of their condition, and their health habits had not improved. In contrast, those who also received the behavioural self-regulation programme showed significant positive changes in their health habits. They reduced their intake of dietary fat, lowered their bad (LDL) cholesterol and raised their good (HDL) cholesterol, increased their exercise and raised their cardiovascular capacity. The programme also influenced the progression of the disease, as the self-management group had 47 per cent less build-up of blockage material on artery walls. During the four-year follow-up period, 45 per cent of the control patients either died or had non-fatal heart attacks or other cardiac emergencies, compared with only 24 per cent in the behaviour self-regulation group. This study, like the others we have discussed, demonstrates the value of psychologically based health-promotion efforts.

REDUCING BEHAVIOURS THAT IMPAIR HEALTH

We now turn our attention to several types of health-impairing behaviours. We begin with a class of behaviours that two decades ago was not considered a major health threat. Although a number of serious diseases can be transmitted through sexual contact, the majority of them can be successfully treated. In the early 1980s, however, a mysterious and lethal sexually transmitted disease emerged.

Psychology and the AIDS Crisis

On 5 June 1981, the Centers for Disease Control reported the first case of *acquired immune deficiency syndrome (AIDS)*. In the decades that followed, AIDS grew from an unknown disease into a devastating worldwide epidemic for which no medical cure has been found. According to the World Health Organization (2004), about 16 000 new infections occur each day. Worldwide, one in every 100 adults between the ages of 15 and 49 is infected with the HIV virus that causes AIDS, and the disease has so far claimed the lives of nearly 20 million people. Forty-five per cent of the HIV-positive are women. Of the 3.1 million people who died from AIDS in 2004, 37 per cent were women and 20 per cent were children. In some countries of southern Africa, 25 to 40 per cent of the population is infected, including a third of all pregnant women. Globally, only 5 to 10 per cent of the cases now occur in homosexual men (the population typically identified with the affliction), and women now make up half of all HIV cases (United Nations, 2002). In the early 2000s, the rates of infection began to rise again among homosexual men in North America, Europe and Australia owing to increases in risky sexual behaviour (CDC, 2003). The AIDS epidemic threatens to overwhelm the world's health-care financing and delivery systems.

AIDS is caused by the *human immunodeficiency virus (HIV)*, which cripples the immune system. The patient then becomes vulnerable to invading viruses, bacteria and tumours, which are the actual killers. Because the HIV virus evolves rapidly, vaccines are at present ineffective in preventing its spread. Moreover, the incubation period between initial HIV infection and the appearance of AIDS symptoms may be as long as 10 years, meaning that an infected person may unknowingly pass the virus on to many other people. The major modes of transmission are direct exposure to infected semen, vaginal fluids and blood through either heterosexual or homosexual contact, the sharing of infected needles in intravenous drug use, and exposure to infected blood through transfusion or in the womb. Breast milk is also a major means of transmission through which many women have unknowingly transmitted the HIV virus to their children.

In the absence of a vaccine or cure, the only existing means of controlling the AIDS epidemic is by changing the high-risk behaviours that transmit the virus. In this respect, AIDS is as much a psychological problem as a medical one. Prevention programmes are typically designed to (1) educate people concerning the risks that attend certain behaviours, such as unprotected sex; (2) motivate people to change their behaviour and convince them that they can do so; (3) provide specific guidelines for changing the risky behaviours and teach the skills needed for change; and (4) give support and encouragement for the desired changes (O'Leary et al., 2001).

Early AIDS interventions were directed at homosexual men, who were originally the major at-risk group. In this population, a primary mechanism of HIV transmission is anal intercourse without the use of a condom. In one successful prevention study (Kelly et al., 1989), 42 homosexual men went through a programme that instructed them on the risks accompanying unprotected intercourse, helped them develop and rehearse strategies for avoiding high-risk situations

Focus 16.25

Describe the nature and effectiveness of behaviour-change techniques used in AIDS prevention projects.

FIGURE 16.26

Effects of an AIDS prevention programme.

An AIDS prevention programme for homosexual men increased their use of condoms during sexual activity. The programme educated the men on the risks involved in sexual behaviours (especially unprotected sex), promoted the use of condoms and taught them coping skills to deal with high-risk situations.

SOURCE: based on Kelly et al., 1989.

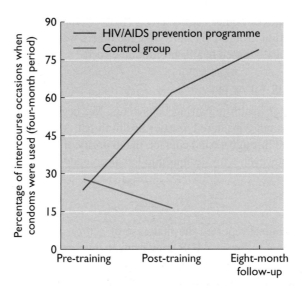

(such as sexual relations with strangers) and taught them how to be more assertive in refusing to engage in high-risk behaviours. Another group of 43 homosexual men also completed the programme after initially serving as an untreated control group.

Both groups were assessed before and after the first group went through the programme and then were followed for eight months after completing the programme to assess long-term behaviour changes. As Figure 16.26 shows, the intervention programme resulted in a substantial and lasting increase in the use of condoms during sexual activity. Similar programmes are now being conducted with adolescent populations, where unprotected heterosexual intercourse is resulting in a surge of new infections (Jemmott et al., 1998). Another target for interventions is heterosexual women, who not only are the fastest-growing segment of the HIV population but also have the potential to infect their babies if they become pregnant.

With something as urgent as AIDS prevention, it is important to recognize that research has shown that the success of prevention programmes depends on the extent to which the individual's social system supports the desired changes. Although the principles of health behaviour change are thought to be universal, and can be useful across cultures, the implementations of such principles than need to take into account local cultural contexts (Bell et al., 2007). Issues such as existing stigmas surrounding the relevant risky behaviours (e.g., Varga et al., 2006), population literacy (Carstens et al., 2006) and specific substance abuse (Sawyer et al., 2006) for example are important factors in determining the effectiveness of HIV/AIDS prevention interventions. When sexual abstinence or the use of condoms runs contrary to the values of an individual or cultural group, people may continue to engage in high-risk behaviours even though they have been informed of the dangers involved (Herdt and Lindenbaum, 1992; Huff and Kline, 1999). Likewise, within both homosexual and heterosexual populations, and particularly among adolescents and young adults, many individuals continue to have an irrational sense of invulnerability to infection, and this belief contributes to a failure to abstain from sex or to engage in protected sexual practices (Kelly, 2001). Counteracting these barriers to safe sexual behaviour is a major challenge for health psychologists.

Although much of the previous research on HIV/AIDS prevention has been conducted in developed countries, the high prevalence of HIV in developing countries (see Table 16.6), together with the differences in local social and cultural contexts and beliefs about the nature of disease, has directed researchers' attention more and more to the application of intervention programmes in developing countries. One successful approach to this problem was a programme described in the Chapter 7 'Research close-up', in which modelling procedures were transmitted through an engaging radio drama to promote safe sex in Tanzania (Bandura, 2000). Given the high prevalence of AIDS in African countries, the following 'Research close-up' will take a closer look at how cultural beliefs may determine the success of HIV/AIDS intervention programmes.

TABLE 16.6 LEADING CAUSES OF DEATH: DEVELOPING VERSUS DEVELOPED COUNTRIES

Developing countries	Number of deaths	Developed countries	Number of deaths
1. HIV/AIDS	2 678 000	1. Ischaemic heart disease	3 512 000
2. Lower respiratory infections	2 643 000	2. Cerebrovascular disease	3 346 000
3. Ischaemic heart disease	2 484 000	3. Chronic obstructive pulmonary disease	1 829 000
4. Diarrhoeal diseases	1 793 000	4. Lower respiratory infections	1 180 000
5. Cerebrovascular disease	1 381 000	5. Trachea/bronchus/lung cancers	938 000
6. Childhood diseases	1 217 000	6. Road traffic accidents	669 000
7. Malaria	1 103 000	7. Stomach cancer	657 000
8. Tuberculosis	1 021 000	8. Hypertensive heart disease	635 000
9. Chronic obstructive pulmonary disease	748 000	9. Tuberculosis	571 000
10. Measles	674 000	10. Self-inflicted	499 000

NOTE: Countries grouped by WHO mortality stratum.

SOURCE: World Health Report 2002.

RESEARCH CLOSE-UP

THE INFLUENCE OF INDIGENOUS BELIEFS ON ATTITUDES TO AIDS PRECAUTIONS

SOURCE: C. Liddell, L. Barrett and M. Bydawell (2006) Indigenous beliefs and attitudes to AIDS precautions in a rural South African community: an empirical study, *Annals of Behavioral Medicine*, vol. 32, pp. 218–25.

INTRODUCTION

How do indigenous belief systems influence people's attitudes towards HIV/AIDS prevention? Several studies have suggested that indigenous practices and beliefs with regards to reproduction and sexuality may play an important role in understanding the sustained AIDS epidemic in Africa. However, more general indigenous beliefs about the origin and spreading of illness and diseases may also play a pivotal role in the likelihood of people taking AIDS precautions. Epidemics and sexually transmitted diseases (STD's) for example are commonly attributed to witchcraft and sorcery in African traditional belief systems. In this sense, STD infection is often associated with supernatural routes, where an infected person may *choose* to infect a lover or spouse when this person behaves unreasonably towards his or her partner, or may infect a lover or spouse through mystical pollutants or sorcery. On the other hand, people's traditional beliefs about the role of ancestral protection against disease and other misfortunes may similarly play an important role in determining the effectiveness of HIV/AIDS prevention programmes.

METHOD

In a remote mountainous area of KwaZulu Natal (KZN), South Africa, an area identified as having the highest prevalence of HIV infection in Southern Africa, 407 participants were recruited to participate in the study. The selection of participants was based on their age-group, as the researchers suggested that age differences may influence the extent to which indigenous beliefs influenced people's attitudes and behaviours. 206 participants (109 males and 97 females) between 18 and 24 years old, and 201 participants (87 males and 114 females) between the age of 35 and 45 years old, completed questionnaires measuring attitudes to AIDS precautions (e.g., the use of condoms), traditional beliefs about illness (e.g., 'women are able to give men medicines that persuade the men to love them'; TBAI) and ancestral protection (e.g., 'provided that I do not upset them, my ancestors can protect me from harm'; AP), as well as general indigenous knowledge (IK) pertaining to traditional dress, foods, etc.

RESULTS

In general both old and young individuals in Kwazulu Natal held strong traditional beliefs about illness and disease and strongly endorsed a belief in ancestral protection, as well as being very familiar with indigenous practices and customs. In contrast, all participants were fairly negative about AIDS precautions. More importantly, beliefs in ancestral protection predicted these negative attitudes to AIDS precautions, such that stronger beliefs led to more negative attitudes. This pattern was however only significant for the older group of participants. Interestingly, a stronger endorsement of traditional beliefs among the older participants about the causes of illness and disease was also associated with attitudes to AIDS precautions, but in an unexpected direction. That is, the stronger older people endorsed traditional beliefs, the *less* negative they were about AIDS precautions. An explanation for this unexpected result was given by the researchers who suggested that condom use might 'fit harmoniously with the traditional views of infectious substances, and how these can be avoided' (Liddell et al., 2006, p. 223). To test this explanation, the researchers extracted five items from the 'attitudes to AIDS precaution' questionnaire that explicitly dealt with condom use and summed them to yield a factor on 'attitudes to condoms'. Results confirmed the idea that condoms fitted with the traditional views of protection from pollutants. Thus, older participants' traditional beliefs about illness were strongly correlated with their attitudes to condoms, but not with the rest of the items of the 'attitudes to AIDS precaution' questionnaire. For the younger participants no such correlation between traditional beliefs and attitudes to condoms was found.

DISCUSSION

The results of this study suggest that, although both younger and older individuals show equally strong endorsements of traditional beliefs about illness and ancestral protection, the attitudes to AIDS protection for younger individuals shows a much weaker association with these beliefs than for older individuals. This suggests that for younger people decision-making around safe sex is less dependent on traditional beliefs. Furthermore, the results indicate that traditional belief systems are not inevitably at odds with western medicine and HIV/AIDS prevention programmes. Instead, indigenous belief systems are highly complex and can consist of conflicting constructs. It seems important therefore to take into account relevant indigenous belief systems and identify the important key aspects that might hinder or benefit the development of effective HIV/AIDS prevention programmes and education campaigns. It may, however, turn out to be a daunting task to acquire in-depth specialist knowledge of a culture, especially as small communities change rapidly in a world with fast-moving changes in public attitude and behaviour.

Combating Substance Abuse

Substance abuse exacts a fearsome toll on society. Tobacco use harms smokers and those who breathe their second-hand smoke. Smoking ranks as the single largest cause of preventable death, currently killing more than 5 million people a year worldwide (World Health Organization, 2008). Because of this, several countries (e.g., Ireland, Norway, the UK, Sweden, South Africa, Italy) have recently introduced smoking bans in indoor public places. Interestingly, several recent studies demonstrate a significant short-term reduction in hospital admissions for acute myocardial infarction following these bans (Barone-Adesi et al., 2006; Sargent et al., 2004). However, although tobacco use has levelled off in Western European countries, tobacco products have been aggressively marketed in other countries, and sales have nearly doubled over the past 15 years. The coming decades will therefore witness an appalling increase in the diseases caused by smoking, particularly in developing countries that are ill equipped to provide good medical treatment.

With a global per capita consumption of 5.1 litres of pure alcohol per year (period 1961–2001), alcohol abuse also contributes enormously to human suffering. Although in general alcohol consumption is relatively stable per capita from the 1980s, there is a trend that young people in Europe are more frequently intoxicated than their elders (Leifman et al., 2002). In the USA alone, alcohol abuse costs over $100 billion a year in decreased work productivity and treatment costs and $13.8 billion in alcohol-related car accidents (National Center for Health Statistics, 2004). Alcohol is implicated in half of all fatal automobile accidents and is a leading factor in industrial and farm accidents (Fig. 16.27). Alcohol abuse is also highly damaging to one's health. Death rates among those who abuse alcohol are two to four times higher for men and three to seven times higher for women, depending on the disease in question. Life expectancy is 10 to 12 years less (CDC, 2002a). Recent studies show, for example, an increased risk from even moderate alcohol consumption of specific kinds of cancer such as cancer of the stomach, colon, breast, rectum and ovaries (Bagnardi et al., 2001; Single et al., 1999). Alcohol affects the welfare of others as well. Some children are born with foetal alcohol syndrome, and others are subjected to disrupted family relationships, including domestic violence. For every person who has a problem with alcohol, an average of four other people's lives are adversely affected on a daily basis (Levinthal, 1996).

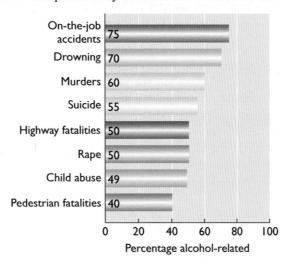

FIGURE 16.27

Societal costs of alcohol abuse.

This graph shows the percentage of common negative events that are alcohol related.

SOURCE: based on Carroll, 1993.

Other varieties of substance abuse also have adverse effects. Many crimes are committed by users of illicit drugs in order to support their habits (Kendall, 1998). Moreover, substance abuse is highly associated with psychological disorders, often being part of a larger pattern of maladjustment in both adolescents and adults (Miller and Brown, 1997).

Psychological principles discussed in earlier chapters have been successfully applied to the treatment of smoking, problem drinking and drug use (Taylor, 2006a). As the transtheoretical model has shown, however, even the best programmes are unlikely to be utilized effectively by people until they are ready to change. In recent years, there has been an emphasis on bringing pre-contemplators and contemplators to the point where they are ready to engage themselves in a change process.

Motivational interviewing   If smokers, problem drinkers, drug abusers and others who practise self-defeating behaviours are to change, they must increase their awareness of their problems,

motivational interviewing

leads the person to his or her own conclusion by asking questions that focus on discrepancies between the current state of affairs and the individual's ideal self-image, desired behaviours and desired outcomes

In-Psych

Why do some people become addicted to alcohol while others do not? Watch the video, 'Neurochemical Basis of Addiction', in Chapter 16 of the In-Psych programme online to learn some compelling answers.

Focus 16.26

What are the major goals and techniques in motivational interviewing?

Focus 16.27

What kinds of behaviour-change procedures are employed in multimodal treatments for substance abuse?

multi-modal treatments

often include biological measures with psychological measures

have a desire to take action and believe that they can change (Miller and Rollnick, 2002; Miller, 1996). Rather than confronting the person with his or her problem (which often drives away people who need help), the technique of **motivational interviewing** leads the person to his or her own conclusion by asking questions that focus on discrepancies between the current state of affairs and the individual's ideal self-image, desired behaviours and desired outcomes. Focusing on these discrepancies may help motivate change. Consider the following exchange:

Client: I really don't believe I have a drinking problem.
Counsellor: You're the best judge of that. May I ask how many drinks you have a day?
Client: Oh, it varies. Probably five or six.
Counsellor: Is that about what you'd like to be drinking?
Client: Well, I'd probably be better off if I cut down a little – maybe to three or four.
Counsellor: How would that be helpful to you?
Client: Well, I could study better and reduce the arguments with my room-mate. I can get pretty nasty when I'm buzzed. I hate being nasty. I'm not that kind of person. Our relationship is going downhill, and I'd hate to lose a friend.
Counsellor: Well, you know, you don't have to have a big problem in order to want to make a change. I'm sure you could do so if you really want to.
Client: I can see that I'd be more the person I want to be if I worked on this.
Counsellor: And I'd be happy to help you make your change.

Following a client's decision to pursue behaviour change, the counsellor helps the client set specific goals and select from a menu of behaviour change strategies those he or she would like to employ. Thereafter, the counsellor provides feedback and support for the client's efforts. Motivational interviewing has proven to be an effective and low-cost treatment approach for substance abusers (Miller and Rollnick, 2002). In one large-scale study of alcohol-abuse patients, a four-session motivational interviewing intervention proved to be as effective as a 12-session programme modelled on Alcoholics Anonymous (Project MATCH Research Group, 1997). More than 20 other studies have demonstrated the effectiveness of motivational interviewing with problem drinkers (Vasilaki et al., 2006).

Multi-modal treatment approaches   All substance abuse behaviours are resistant to change, and for good reason. Some people may be more vulnerable than others because of genetic factors (Crabbe, 2002). Craving, caused by either psychological need or physical dependence, is a huge barrier to overcome. Negative emotions, such as anxiety, irritability or depression, are temporary results of abstinence that cause many who quit successfully to have relapses. Past conditioning may create stimuli that trigger the behaviour in certain common situations. For example, coffee drinking or social situations are linked with smoking for many individuals, thus encouraging lapses in behavioural control when those stimuli are present. The numerous factors that encourage smoking, drinking or drug abuse make these behaviours very hard to change. Psychologists are therefore willing to combine anything that has proven effective into what they hope will be a more powerful behaviour change package to apply when people are ready to make a change. These **multi-modal treatments** often include biological measures (for example, the use of nicotine patches to help smokers quit), with psychological measures such as the following:

- aversion therapy, in which the undesired behaviour is associated with an aversive stimulus, such as electric shock or a nausea-producing drug, in an attempt to create a negative emotional response to the currently pleasurable substance

- relaxation and stress-management training, which help the person adapt to and deal with stressful situations

- self-monitoring procedures that help the person identify the antecedents and consequences of the abuse behaviours

- coping and social-skills training for dealing with high-risk situations that trigger abuse
- marital and family counselling to reduce conflicts and increase social support for change
- positive-reinforcement procedures to strengthen change.

This broad-based multi-modal approach appears to produce favourable outcomes for many people who have substance addictions. For example, in one of the more successful multi-modal treatment outcome studies, 427 alcoholic patients were followed for 12 to 20 months after completing an in-patient programme that included aversion therapy (using a drug that produces nausea when alcohol is consumed), personal counselling and coping-skills training. Follow-up assessments revealed that 65 per cent were totally abstinent for one year after treatment. The best outcome occurred in cases where the urge to drink had been eliminated (presumably by aversion therapy) and alternate coping skills were increased through the use of cognitive-behavioural techniques such as those just described (Smith and Frawley, 1993). Despite these encouraging results, typical treatment results are less favourable: long-term maintenance of behaviour changes often occurs in fewer than 30 per cent of treated individuals, whether the target behaviour is smoking, drinking or some other substance abuse (Ockene et al., 2000). The goal of many researchers is therefore to develop more effective treatment packages.

> **Focus 16.28**
>
> How serious are the consequences of heavy drinking among college students?

BENEATH THE SURFACE

COLLEGE-AGE DRINKING: HARMLESS FUN OR RUSSIAN ROULETTE?

The harmful problems that result from the behaviours of alcoholics and drug addicts are self-evident. But because college students view themselves as different from these populations, many fail to realize the extent to which they place themselves in harm's way through their use of alcohol. Many students view heavy-drinking parties as a natural part of college life, like going to classes or athletic events. Studies have found that many heavy-drinking students, who average 40 to 50 drinks per week, do not view their behaviour as either abnormal or problematic (Marlatt, 1998). One consequence is that heavy-drinking college students neither recognize the need to reduce their alcohol intake, nor intend to change their drinking habits (Wechsler and Kuo, 2000; Vik et al., 2000).

Beneath this surface of complacency lies evidence that heavy-drinking students are placing themselves at considerable risk. Although the term 'binge drinking' is used ambivalently in the literature, two main definitions can be identified (Gmel et al., 2003): (1) Having more than x number of drinks on one occasion leading to intoxication, and (2) a recurrent pattern of heavy drinking over an extended period of time for the purpose of intoxication (Gmel et al., 2003). In one national study carried out in the USA, for example, binge drinking was defined as having more than four (for women) or five (for men) drinks at a time on at least three occasions during the previous two weeks (Wechsler et al., 1994). Data from 18 000 students at 140 US colleges revealed that 50 per cent of the males and 40 per cent of the women met this bingeing criterion, yet fewer than 1 per cent saw themselves as having an alcohol problem. However, the dangerous consequences of their drinking became clear when binge drinkers were asked about alcohol-related problems.

Frequent binge drinkers were seven to 10 times more likely than moderate drinkers to engage in unplanned and unprotected sexual intercourse, to suffer injuries, to drive under the influence of alcohol, to damage property and to get in to trouble with the law. At schools with the highest alcohol consumption rates, non-drinkers and moderate drinkers were two to three times more likely to report physical assault, sexual harassment, destruction of their property, and interruption of their sleep and studying by heavy drinkers. Some college women (sound sleepers, apparently) complained that they woke up Sunday after Sunday to find a strange man in bed with their room-mate (and all too frequently the heavy-drinking room-mate did not know him either). So, while common belief may have it that heavy drinking is harmless fun, scientific findings suggest otherwise.

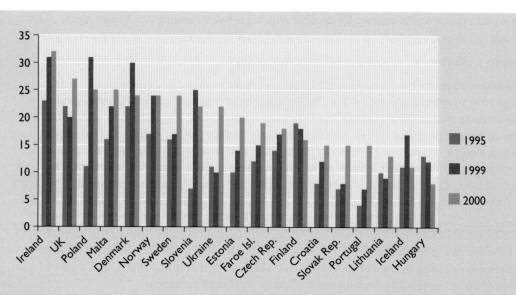

FIGURE 16.28

Changes between 1995 and 2003 in the proportion of students between 15 and 16 years old, who have reported 'binge drinking' three times or more during past 30 days. Data sorted by all students 2003
SOURCE: Hibell., 2004.

The necessity of prevention efforts regarding binge drinking seems evident, especially given recent data suggesting that the percentage of students binge drinking is still increasing. A survey (Hibell et al., 2004) among more than 100 000 European students between 15 and 16 years old showed that, on average, binge drinking in most European countries increased between the period of 1995 and 2003 (Fig. 16.28). Interestingly, heavy-drinking events are most likely when beer and spirits are consumed, whereas wine consumption does not seem to trigger binge drinking (Clapp and Shillington, 2001). Binge drinking, furthermore, seems to vary with adult and adolescent drinking culture, where binge-drinking is less likely in countries in which alcohol consumption is an integrated part of everyday life. Most bingeing can be found in northern, eastern and western parts of Europe, compared with central and southern parts. This pattern is indirectly supported by epidemiological studies showing that drink-related problems such as accidents and cardiovascular problems were most strongly associated with alcohol intake in northern and eastern European countries (Gmel et al., 2003; see Kuntsche et al., 2004).

Harm-Reduction Approaches to Prevention

harm reduction

prevention strategy that is designed not to eliminate a problem behaviour but, rather, to reduce the harmful effects of that behaviour when it occurs

Substance abuse not only has negative effects on physical well-being but often results in other severe consequences, such as self-defeating sexual and aggressive behaviours. **Harm reduction** is a prevention strategy that is designed not to eliminate a problem behaviour but, rather, to reduce the harmful effects of that behaviour when it occurs (MacCoun, 1998; Weingardt and Marlatt, 1998). In the area of drug abuse, harm-reduction approaches include needle and syringe exchange programmes to reduce the spread of HIV infections. Another example is methadone maintenance programmes for heroin addicts, which are targeted at reducing addicts' need to engage in criminal activity to feed their heroin habit. The reasoning is that even if an addictive behaviour cannot be eliminated, it is possible to modify how often and under what conditions it occurs and thereby minimize its harmful effects on the person and society. Harm-reduction programmes have enjoyed considerable success in several European countries (Heather, 2006).

The harm that can befall college students who abuse alcohol has inspired a new generation of intervention programmes focused on helping problem drinkers control how much and under what circumstances they drink. The goal is to reduce harmful consequences to the problem drinkers and others (Marlatt et al., 2001). In one harm-reduction project carried out at a large western-US university, incoming freshmen were screened for alcohol problems before they arrived on campus (Marlatt et al., 1998). Once on campus, those identified as problem drinkers were randomly assigned either to an intervention condition or to a no-treatment control condition. Over the next two years, the students in both conditions regularly reported on their alcohol consumption and alcohol-related problems. People who knew them well also furnished reports, and high agreement between the two sources of data indicated that the students were being truthful and accurate.

The intervention, occurring in the winter of the freshman year, was a brief one based on the motivational-interviewing approach described earlier. The goal was to prevent or reduce harmful consequences of drinking by increasing motivation to make constructive changes, rather than to stop students' drinking. Clinical psychologists met with each student individually for one session. The interviewer reviewed the drinking data submitted by the student over the previous academic term and gave individualized feedback in graphic form. The graph compared his or her drinking rate with college student averages, which were invariably much lower. The interviewers listed the potential risks for heavy college drinkers (such as those discussed in 'Beneath the surface') and discussed environmental risk factors, such as being in a fraternity or sorority or having heavy-drinking friends, if relevant. The interviewers were never confrontational but instead helped students evaluate their situation ('What do you make of this? Are you surprised?'), to think about present and possible future problems ('Would you be worried about something like this happening to you? What impact would it have on your life?'), and to consider the possibility of change. Specific goals of behaviour change were left to the student and not imposed by the interviewer.

At the end of two years, the students in the intervention group were still drinking more than the average college student, and although they continued to have more alcohol-related problems than the average student, they had far fewer alcohol-related problems than did students in the untreated high-risk group (Fig. 16.29). Thus despite the lack of an explicit focus on reducing drinking, the brief one-session intervention had significant positive effects. In particular, students learned to moderate their drinking in potentially hazardous situations, thereby reducing harmful consequences.

Focus 16.29

What is a harm-reduction approach, and how does it differ from an abstinence-based one?

Focus 16.30

Which factors increase or decrease relapse? How does relapse-prevention training address these factors?

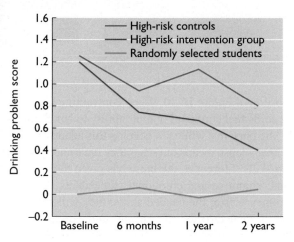

FIGURE 16.29

Effects of a brief intervention on alcohol-related problems.

At one year and two years after the intervention, high-risk drinkers who underwent the harm-reduction programme still reported more alcohol-related problems than the average college student, but fewer than the high-risk drinkers in the control group.

SOURCE: adapted from Marlatt et al., 1998.

RELAPSE PREVENTION: MAINTAINING POSITIVE BEHAVIOUR CHANGE

Despite the availability of effective methods for changing behaviour, high dropout rates and failure to maintain positive behaviour changes are a major problem in every health-relevant behaviour we have discussed, from exercise maintenance to weight control to ending substance

relapse prevention

designed to reduce the risk of relapse

abstinence violation effect

the person becomes upset and self-blaming over the lapse and views it as proof that he or she will never be strong enough to resist temptation

FIGURE 16.30

Relapse and relapse prevention.

Relapse is most likely to occur as a result of inadequate coping skills for dealing with high-risk situations, a focus on anticipated positive effects of engaging in the behaviour, and a resulting abstinence violation effect that causes the person to feel incapable of successful change and to abandon attempts at behaviour control.

SOURCE: Marlatt and Gordon, 1985.

abuse. Why do people relapse into their problem behaviours, and what can be done to prevent this? Research on these questions has led to a better understanding of the relapse process and an intervention known as **relapse prevention** that is designed to reduce the risk of relapse (Marlatt and Gordon, 1985). Research with substance abusers shows that most *relapses* (a full-fledged return to the undesirable behaviour pattern) tend to occur after the person has suffered one or more *lapses* (occasional 'slips') in response to high-risk situations. High-risk situations include stressful events, interpersonal conflicts, social pressure to perform the undesirable behaviour, being in the company of other individuals using the substance and experiencing negative emotions (Marlatt, 1996).

The path to relapse is shown in the bottom portion of Figure 16.30. Increased likelihood of relapse occurs when people have not developed strong enough coping skills to deal successfully with the high-risk situations. As a result, they experience low self-efficacy, believing that they are not strong enough to resist the temptation, or they allow expected positive benefits (such as enjoyment of the substance or anticipated stress reduction) to influence their decision to perform the undesirable behaviour. A lapse then occurs, followed by a critically important reaction called the **abstinence violation effect**, in which the person becomes upset and self-blaming over the lapse and views it as proof that he or she will never be strong enough to resist temptation. This sense of hopelessness places people at great risk to abandon all attempts to change, and in many cases a total relapse will occur. In one study of relapses in dieting, the abstinence violation effect was more strongly associated with relapse episodes than were temptations (Carels et al., 2004).

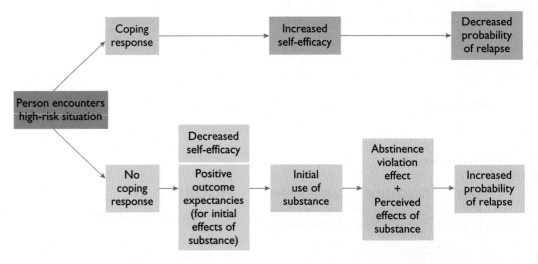

Relapse resistance is shown in the upper portion of Figure 16.30. When confronting high-risk situations, people who have effective coping skills feel confident in their ability to handle them and are far less likely to relapse, even if they slip once in a while. To develop this adaptive process, relapse prevention specialists tell people that a lapse means only that they have encountered a situation that exceeded their current coping skills. Moreover, the lapse has given them valuable information about the specific situational, cognitive and emotional antecedents that they must learn to handle more effectively. When they master the needed skills, they will be better able to resist high-risk situations. Attention is then directed at learning and practising the required skills so that self-efficacy improves. The continuing focus is on 'progress, not perfection'.

Relapse prevention training is increasingly being incorporated into many behaviour change programmes. It has proven effective in changing many problematic behaviours, including overeating, smoking, cocaine and marijuana abuse, and sexual offending (Witkiewicz and Marlatt, 2004). Relapse prevention is also an important complement to the transtheoretical model, which tells us that many people regress from the action and even maintenance stages into a previous stage because they are not prepared to deal with the lapses that almost inevitably occur as they try to alter ingrained behaviour patterns. Being prepared for occasional lapses helps people move more smoothly from the preparation stage to the action and maintenance stages (DiClemente, 2003).

IN REVIEW

- The transtheoretical model identifies six stages through which people may move during the process of successful long-term behavioural change: pre-contemplation, contemplation, preparation, action, maintenance and termination. The model has inspired stage-matched interventions focused on the individual's current stage, with the intent of moving the person to the action, maintenance and termination stages.

- Exercise is an important health-enhancing behaviour that affects both physical and psychological well-being. Numerous behavioural interventions have been developed to promote exercise, but many people fail to adhere to exercise programmes. One factor that influences adherence is social support. People who are able to stick with an exercise programme for three to six months have a better chance of adhering to it thereafter.

- About a third of the American population is obese, as are one in six children and adolescents. Behavioural weight-control programmes feature self-monitoring, stimulus-control procedures, and eating procedures designed to help people eat less but enjoy it more. The addition of an exercise programme to weight-control procedures enhances weight loss.

- Because HIV infection is caused by high-risk sexual and drug-abuse behaviours (e.g., sharing needles), a prevention approach is essential. Behavioural changes have been accomplished in homosexual populations, and efforts are centring on high-risk heterosexual populations, such as teenagers. Cultural factors sometimes conflict with safe-sex practices, increasing the challenges of reducing health-endangering behaviours.

- Substance abuse is highly associated with other disorders and is often part of a larger pattern of maladjustment. Multi-modal treatments combine a number of techniques, including aversion training, stress-management and coping-skills training and positive reinforcement for change. A promising new approach is motivational interviewing, a non-confrontational procedure designed to engage the person's own motivation to change self-defeating behaviours.

- Harm-reduction approaches attempt to reduce the negative consequences that behaviour produces rather than to focus on stopping the behaviour itself. Examples include needle exchange programmes for drug addicts and programmes designed to reduce the destructive consequences of binge drinking in college students.

- Relapse prevention is designed to keep lapses from becoming relapses by building effective coping skills to deal with high-risk situations and countering the abstinence violation effect when lapses occur. This approach enhances the effects of many behaviour-change programmes

A CONCLUDING THOUGHT

The enterprise of living involves a constant process of adjusting to environmental demands. When those demands exceed our personal and social resources, we experience stress and may attempt to reduce it by changing our environment or our own behaviour. Thus stress can be a catalyst for growth and change, or it can drag us down physically and psychologically, depending on how effectively we respond to it. Psychologists have been at the forefront of stress research and have developed interventions to help people cope more effectively.

We have also seen that people's behaviour contributes strongly to both illness and physical well-being. The field of health psychology focuses on psychological and behavioural processes that affect physical well-being. Health psychologists have made important contributions to helping people reduce health-impairing behaviours and acquire healthier lifestyles, but many challenges remain.

Unfortunately, people do not always have the resources to cope with life's demands. As a result, they may engage in thought processes, emotional responses and behaviours that are hurtful to themselves or to society. In the next chapter, we will consider the behaviour disorders that can result from failures to adapt successfully.

KEY TERMS AND CONCEPTS

Each term has been boldfaced and defined in the chapter on the page indicated in parentheses.

abstinence violation effect (p. 770)

aerobic exercise (p. 758)

cognitive relaxation (p. 745)

cognitive restructuring (p. 743)

coping self-efficacy (p. 733)

cytokines (p. 729)

emotion-focused coping (p. 737)

endorphins (p. 747)

gate control theory (p. 736)

general adaptation syndrome (GAS) (p. 725)

hardiness (p. 733)

harm reduction (p. 768)

health psychology (p. 721)

motivational interviewing (p. 766)

multi-modal treatments (p. 766)

placebos (p. 749)

primary appraisal (p. 724)

problem-focused coping (p. 737)

protective factors (p. 731)

relapse prevention (p. 770)

secondary appraisal (p. 724)

seeking social support (p. 738)

self-instructional training (p. 744)

somatic relaxation training (p. 744)

stress (p. 722)

stress response (p. 724)

stress-induced analgesia (p. 747)

stressors (p. 721)

transtheoretical model (p. 755)

Type A behaviour pattern (p. 732)

vulnerability factors (p. 730)

WHAT DO YOU THINK?

DO STRESSFUL EVENTS CAUSE PSYCHOLOGICAL DISTRESS? (p. 727)

As we noted, the relation between stress and distress is correlational. Now let us think critically and challenge the causal interpretation. Certainly, it is possible that life stress causes psychological distress – and there are other kinds of evidence to suggest that it does. But it is also possible that distress may be the causal factor instead of the effect. That is, distressed people may be more likely than non-distressed people to remember and report negative things that have happened to them. Or they may tend to view more events as negative, resulting in higher negative life-change scores. Moreover, psychological distress could actually cause people to behave in ways that produce more negative events. For example, research has shown that anxious and depressed people often evoke negative reactions from others because of their gloomy outlook and their tendency to frustrate others' attempts to help them feel better.

And that is not all: a third causal possibility is that some other variable causes both negative life events *and* psychological distress to go up or down, thus creating the relation between them. The Big Five personality trait of neuroticism, discussed in Chapter 15, might be such a third variable. We know that people who are high in neuroticism have a tendency to experience lots of negative emotions *and* to get themselves into stressful situations through their self-defeating behaviours. Differences in neuroticism could thus cause the relation between stress and distress. These different causal possibilities remind us that stressful life events are part of a network of causal relations and that stressful life events can function as either a cause or an effect.

WHY DO WOMEN OUTLIVE MEN? (p. 743)

According to the World Health Organization, women live an average of five to eight years longer than men in most industrialized countries. Only in underdeveloped countries, where many women die in childbirth, do men live longer. Is stress the reason? This popular media interpretation is contradicted by research results showing that women report as many stressful events as men do and are, in fact, more susceptible to a variety of stress-related psychological disorders. So, what other factors could be at work?

One possibility is that women are simply more biologically fit than men are. Although more males than females are conceived, more male children are miscarried or stillborn, and more males die in infancy and at every age thereafter. Some biological survival factors may be genetic, some hormonal. One possibility is that females' XX chromosomal structure may protect them against certain diseases that afflict males. Another suggestion is that the female hormones oestrogen and prolactin may help protect them against some major diseases, including heart disease.

Other explanations focus on behavioural and social differences between the sexes. Men engage in more risky and health-impairing behaviours. They are more likely to die in accidents and to smoke and drink heavily. In fact, smoking differences may account for as much as 40 per cent of the mortality difference between adult men and women. Finally, men are more likely to have physically hazardous occupations than are women.

At the environmental level, explanations focus on the important protective functions of social support on health and well-being. On average, women have larger and more active social support networks and more intimate relationships than do men. Whether this difference contributes to women's greater longevity is not known. Once again, however, we see the usefulness of considering potential causal factors at biological, psychological and environmental levels of analysis.

Which of these sex differences do you think might be particularly important? Can you think of other differences that might matter? Finally, do you think that the diminishing differences in sex roles, which place increasingly more women into traditionally male work settings and lifestyles, might reduce the longevity difference in coming decades?

CHAPTER SEVENTEEN

PSYCHOLOGICAL DISORDERS

CHAPTER OUTLINE

Why is it that when we talk to God we're praying, but when God talks to us we're schizophrenic?

THOMAS SZASZ, PSYCHIATRIST

Mark has been depressed for several years, but things are even worse now. He feels totally inadequate and inferior. The future looks hopeless, and he cannot sleep at night. During the day, he can barely function, and his moods alternate between deadening depression and intense anxiety. A friend has suggested that he seek professional counselling, but Mark is convinced that he has slipped too deeply into the black hole of despair to ever feel good again. He wonders how long he wants to go on living in his private hell.

…

Anna-Maria was walking across campus the first time it happened. Suddenly, her heart began pounding and skipping beats. She grew weak and shaky, began sweating profusely and felt an indescribable sense of impending doom. She was sure she was either going insane or was about to die on the spot. Gathering all her strength, she made it to her room in her hall of residence and began to feel better. Now, after several such incidents while on campus, she is afraid to leave her room.

…

Unwashed, unshaven, and wearing tattered clothes, Johannes lives in the centre of his city. He often sits in a park mumbling to himself. Occasionally, he covers his ears and yells, 'Shut up!' to try to still the voices in his head. Some nights he eats and sleeps at a shelter, but more often he rolls himself in a filthy blanket and sleeps under a bridge. Johannes has been committed to a mental hospital more than 10 times. In the hospital, he responds quickly to antipsychotic drugs and begins to behave more normally. But soon after being released back into the community, he stops taking his medication and gradually slides once again into a deteriorated mental state. Today a social services caseworker notices him and asks how he's feeling. Staring vacantly into space, he replies, 'Life is trouble, bubble, double, zubble'.

These three people could very well live in your city or town. Mark or Anna-Marie could be students at your college. Many people are unaware of how common psychological disorders are. According to UK and World Heath Authority statistics:

- it is estimated that 450 million people worldwide suffer with mental health problems
- at any given time, one in six people in the UK are suffering from a diagnosable mental health problem
- one in four people in the UK suffer from a diagnosable mental health problem in any one year
- psychological disorders are the second leading cause of disability, after heart disease
- medications used to treat anxiety and depression are among the most frequently prescribed drugs in Europe
- one adolescent in the USA commits suicide every 90 seconds.

These cold statistics, startling though they may be, cannot possibly capture the intense suffering that they reflect. They cannot communicate the confusion and alienation felt by the person with schizophrenia whose psychological world is distorted in episodes, the often intense personal misery of a depressed person who feels hopelessness all around him or her, the intermittent terror experienced by someone with a panic disorder or the frustration endured by the families and friends of those who have psychological disorders.

This chapter is therefore not just about the problems of 'someone else'. Even if you are fortunate enough never to experience a psychological disorder in your lifetime, statistics suggest that you will almost surely have a family member, friend or acquaintance who will.

HISTORICAL PERSPECTIVES ON DEVIANT BEHAVIOUR

Psychological disorders are not just a modern problem. The pages of history are filled with accounts of prominent people who suffered from psychological disorders. The eighteenth-century French philosopher Jean-Jacques Rousseau developed marked paranoid symptoms in the later part of his life and was plagued by fears of secret enemies. Mozart was convinced he was being poisoned during the time he was composing his *Requiem*. Abraham Lincoln suffered recurrent bouts of depression throughout his life and was, on one occasion, so depressed that he failed to show up for his own wedding. Winston Churchill also periodically suffered from severe depression, referring to it as his 'black dog' (Fig. 17.1).

These dysfunctional states may manifest themselves as dysfunctional behaviours which do not go unnoticed. Throughout history, human societies have explained and responded to abnormal behaviour in different ways at different times, based on their values and assumptions about human life and behaviour. The belief that abnormal behaviour is caused by supernatural forces

FIGURE 17.1

Abraham Lincoln and Winston Churchill suffered from severe depression during their lifetimes. Knowing about your problem does not stop you suffering from it.

goes back to the ancient Chinese, Egyptians and Hebrews, all of whom attributed deviance to the work of the devil. One ancient treatment was based on the notion that bizarre behaviour reflected an evil spirit's attempt to escape from a person's body. In order to release the spirit, a procedure called *trephination* was carried out. A sharp tool was used to chisel a hole in the skull about 2 centimetres (¾ inch) in diameter (Fig. 17.2). It seems likely that in many cases trephination successfully eliminated abnormal behaviour by putting an end to the patient's life.

FIGURE 17.2

An early treatment for disordered behaviour was trephination, in which a hole was chiselled through the skull to release the evil spirit thought to be causing the abnormal behaviour. Some people survived the operation, but many died from it.

In medieval times, the demonological model of abnormality held that disturbed people either were possessed involuntarily by the devil or had voluntarily made a pact with the forces of darkness (Fig. 17.3). The killing of witches was justified on theological grounds, and various 'diagnostic' tests were devised. One was to bind a woman's hands and feet and throw her into a lake or pond. Based on the notion that impurities float to the surface, a woman who sank and drowned could be posthumously declared pure. Of course, a woman who floated was in *real* trouble. During the sixteenth and seventeenth centuries, more than 100 000 people with psychological disorders were identified as witches, hunted down and executed.

Centuries earlier, in about the fifth century BC, the Greek physician Hippocrates suggested that mental health problems are diseases just like physical disorders. Anticipating the modern viewpoint, Hippocrates believed that the site of a mental health problem was the brain. By the 1800s, western medicine had returned to viewing mental disorders as biologically based and was attempting to extend medical diagnoses to them. The biological emphasis was given impetus by the discovery that *general paresis*, a disorder characterized in its advanced stages by mental deterioration and bizarre behaviour, resulted from massive brain deterioration caused by the sexually transmitted disease syphilis. This was a breakthrough – the first demonstration that a psychological disorder was caused by an underlying physical malady.

In the early 1900s, Sigmund Freud's theory of psychoanalysis ushered in psychological interpretations of disordered behaviour. As we shall see, psychodynamic theories of abnormal behaviour were soon joined by other models based on behavioural, cognitive and humanistic conceptions. These various conceptions focus on different classes of causal factors and help capture the complex determinants of abnormal behaviour. The importance of cultural factors has also received increasing attention. Although many questions remain, these perspectives have given us a deeper understanding of how biological, psychological and environmental factors can combine to cause psychological disorders.

Today, many psychologists find it useful to incorporate these factors into a more general framework. According to the **vulnerability-stress model (**also known as the **diathesis-stress model**) (Fig. 17.4), each of us has some degree of vulnerability, or diathesis (ranging from very low to very high) for developing a psychological disorder, given sufficient stress. The *vulnerability (diathesis)*, or predisposition, can have a biological basis, such as our genotype, over- or

FIGURE 17.3

This painting by Francisco de Goya reflects the widespread belief that disordered people were possessed by the devil. *Sabbath* portrays the weekly gathering of Satan and the witches he possessed.

vulnerability-stress model (also known as the diathesis-stress model)

each of us has some degree of vulnerability, or diathesis (ranging from very low to very high) for developing a psychological disorder, given sufficient stress

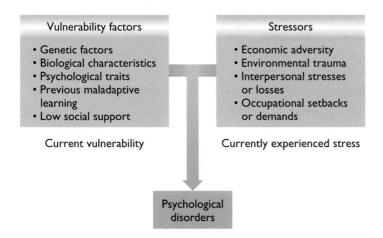

FIGURE 17.4

The vulnerability-stress model, also known as the diathesis-stress model.

This popular conception attributes behaviour disorders to interactions between personal vulnerability factors and life stressors. Personal vulnerability factors contribute to maladaptive efforts to cope with life's challenges.

Focus 17.1

Describe the demonological, behavioural, cognitive, humanistic and sociocultural perspectives on abnormal behaviour.

under-activity of a neurotransmitter system in the brain, an extremely active autonomic nervous system or a hormonal factor. It could also be due to a personality factor, such as low self-esteem or extreme pessimism, or to previous environmental factors, such as poverty or a severe trauma or loss earlier in life. Likewise, cultural factors can create vulnerability to certain kinds of disorders (Ingram and Price, 2001).

But vulnerability is only part of the equation. In most instances, a predisposition creates a disorder only when a *stressor* – some recent or current event that requires a person to cope – combines with a vulnerability to trigger the disorder (van Praag, 2004). Thus a person who has a genetic predisposition to depression or who suffered a traumatic loss of a parent early in life may be primed to develop a depressive disorder *if* faced with the stress of a loss later in life. As we shall see, the biological, psychological and environmental levels of analysis have all contributed to the vulnerability-stress model and to our understanding of behaviour disorders and how they develop. One key point of the diathesis-stress model is that the bigger the diathesis (so to speak) the less stress required to trigger a disorder; the smaller the diathesis, the more stress is required.

DEFINING AND CLASSIFYING PSYCHOLOGICAL DISORDERS

So far, we have discussed historical and contemporary accounts of abnormal behaviour without actually defining what we mean by *abnormal*. Doing so is not as easy as it might at first appear.

WHAT IS 'ABNORMAL'?

Defining what is normal and what is abnormal is problematic. Judgements about where the line between normal and abnormal should be drawn differ depending on the time and the culture. For example, cannibalism has been practised in many cultures around the world (Walker, 2001). In contemporary western culture, however, such behaviour would be viewed as extraordinarily pathological, although, as we shall see, it is not completely unheard of even now. On 25 May 1895, Oscar Wilde was imprisoned for 'acts of gross indecency', or homosexuality. Being gay or acting on your sexual desires if gay was illegal at that time, and Wilde was by no means the only person to fall foul of the law. It was considered a crime, and also a form of mental health problem. The law, making homosexuality legal, has changed in most countries now, following Denmark's lead in 1932. However, it was not until 1992 that the World Health Organization removed its definition of homosexuality as a mental health problem. Other countries then followed their lead, removing the mental health label from their laws. This removal of homosexuality as a mental health problem was surely the quickest and most widespread cure in the history

Focus 17.2

How does the vulnerability-stress model illustrate person–situation interactions?

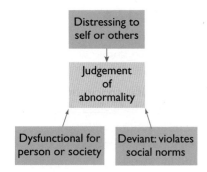

FIGURE 17.5

Deviance as a social construct.

Whether a behaviour is considered abnormal involves a social judgement made on the basis of the three Ds: distress, dysfunction and deviance.

Focus 17.3

Cite the three Ds that typically underlie judgements that behaviour is abnormal.

abnormal behaviour

behaviour that is personally distressing, personally dysfunctional and/or so culturally deviant that other people judge it to be inappropriate or maladaptive

reliability

clinicians using the system should show high levels of agreement in their diagnostic decisions

validity

the diagnostic categories should accurately capture the essential features of the various disorders

of psychiatry. Despite this formal change in the psychiatric status of this sexual orientation, some people in our society continue to view homosexuality as an indicator of psychological disturbance, illustrating to some the arbitrary nature of abnormality judgements. The role of psychiatry can be likened to a form of social control. If something is identified by authorities as deviant or abnormal, then it becomes mistrusted and unacceptable to society.

Despite the arbitrariness of time, place and value judgements, three criteria – *distress*, *dysfunction* and *deviance* – seem to govern decisions about abnormality, and one or more of them seem to apply to virtually any behaviour regarded as abnormal (Fig. 17.5). First, we are likely to label behaviours as abnormal if they are intensely *distressing* to the individual. People who are excessively anxious, depressed, dissatisfied or otherwise seriously upset about themselves or about life circumstances might be viewed as disturbed, particularly if they seem to have little control over these reactions. On the other hand, personal distress is neither necessary nor sufficient to define abnormality. Some seriously disturbed individuals with mental health problems are so out of touch with reality that they seem to experience little distress, and yet their bizarre behaviours are considered very abnormal. And although all of us experience suffering as a part of our lives, our distress is not likely to be judged abnormal unless it is disproportionately intense or long-lasting relative to the situation.

Second, most behaviours judged abnormal are *dysfunctional* either for the individual or for society. Behaviours that interfere with a person's ability to work or to experience satisfying relationships with other people are likely to be seen as maladaptive and self-defeating, especially if the person seems unable to control such behaviours. Some behaviours are labelled as abnormal because they interfere with the well-being of society. But even here, the standards are not completely settled. For example, is a suicide bomber who detonates a bomb in a public market psychologically disturbed, a criminal or a patriot?

The third criterion for abnormality is society's judgements concerning the *deviance* of a given behaviour. Conduct within every society is regulated by *norms*, behavioural rules that specify how people are expected to think, feel and behave. Some norms are explicitly codified as laws, and violation of these norms defines criminal behaviour. Other norms, however, are far less explicit. For example, it is generally expected in our culture that one should not carry on animated conversations with people who are not present, nor should one face the rear of an elevator and stare intently into the eyes of a fellow passenger (do not try this unless you want to see an elevator empty out quickly). People are likely to be viewed as psychologically disturbed if they violate these unstated norms, especially if the violations make others uncomfortable and cannot be attributed to environmental causes.

To summarize, both personal and social judgements of behaviour enter into considerations of what is abnormal. Thus we may define **abnormal behaviour** as behaviour that is personally distressing, personally dysfunctional and/or so culturally deviant that other people judge it to be inappropriate or maladaptive.

DIAGNOSING PSYCHOLOGICAL DISORDERS

Classification is a necessary first step towards introducing order into discussions of the nature, causes and treatment of psychological disorders. To be scientifically and practically useful, a classification system must meet standards of diagnostic reliability and validity. **Reliability** means that clinicians using the system should show high levels of agreement in their diagnostic decisions. Because professionals with different types and amounts of training – including psychologists, psychiatrists, social workers and physicians – make decisions which lead directly or indirectly to diagnoses, the system should be couched in terms of observable behaviours that can be reliably detected in order to minimize subjective judgements. **Validity** means that the diagnostic categories should accurately capture the essential features of the various disorders. Thus if research and clinical observations show that a given disorder has four behavioural characteristics, the diagnostic category for that disorder should also have those four features. More-over, the diagnostic categories should allow us to differentiate one psychological disorder from another.

There are two major classification systems in use around the world. The *World Health Organization International Classification of Diseases – 10th Edition* (ICD-10; World Health Organization, 1993) and the *Diagnostic and Statistical Manual of Mental Disorders, Fourth Edition, Text Revision* (DSM-IV-TR; American Psychiatric Association, 2000). The ICD-10 covers mental health problems (described in ICD-10 as mental illnesses) and other disorders, and as such is a more complete diagnostic classification system. The DSM covers only mental health problems, but is very widely used around the world, and is included here for that reason. The subcategories of ICD-10 that deal with mental health problems are shown in Table 17.1. Table 17.2 samples the range of DSM-IV-TR categories.

Reflecting an awareness of interacting personal and environmental factors, the DSM allows diagnostic information to be represented along five dimensions, or *axes*, that take both the person and their life situation into account. Axis I, the primary diagnosis, represents the person's primary clinical symptoms, that is, the deviant behaviours or thought processes that are occurring at the present time. Axis II reflects long-standing personality disorders, or mental 'retardation'. which can influence the person's behaviour and response to treatment. It is worth noting that the term 'mental retardation' is used in the DSM, and might be better understood and perhaps more appropriately termed mental 'handicap', although this term also has negative connotations associated with disability. The word 'retardation' is extremely negative, but it is used in the DSM and as such it is used here in our description of the manual. Axis III notes any medical conditions that might be relevant, such as high blood pressure or a recent concussion. Reflecting the vulnerability-stress model discussed earlier, the clinician also rates the intensity of psychosocial or environmental problems in the person's recent life on Axis IV and the person's coping resources, as reflected in recent adaptive functioning, on Axis V. Figure 17.6 shows how the axes are represented in a sample DSM-IV diagnosis.

Although the reliability and validity of DSM-IV-TR are still being evaluated, the highly specific behavioural criteria in the diagnostic categories clearly have improved Axis I reliability

Focus 17.4
What is meant by diagnostic reliability and validity?

Focus 17.5
Describe the five axes of the DSM-IV-TR.

TABLE 17.1 CHAPTER V OF THE ICD-10 – 'MENTAL DISORDERS'

Categories F00–F09: Organic, including symptomatic mental disorders
Categories F10–F19: Mental and behavioural disorders due to psychoactive substance misuse
Categories F20–F29: Schizophrenia, schizotypal and delusional disorders
Categories F30–F39: Mood (affective) disorders
Categories F40–F49: Neurotic, stress-related and somatoform disorders
Categories F50–F59: Behavioural syndromes associated with physiological disturbances and physical factors
Categories F60–F69: Disorders of adult personality and behaviour
Categories F70–F79: Mental 'retardation' (the phrase mental handicap might be used here)
Categories F80–F89: Disorders of psychological development
Categories F90–F98: Behavioural and emotional disorders with onset usually occurring in childhood and adolescence
Category F99: Unspecified mental disorders

TABLE 17.2 A SAMPLE OF MAJOR DIAGNOSTIC CATEGORIES IN THE DSM-IV-TR

1. *Anxiety disorders*: intense, frequent or inappropriate anxiety, but no loss of reality contact; includes phobias, generalized anxiety reactions, panic disorders, obsessive-compulsive disorders and post-traumatic stress disorders

2. *Mood (affective) disorders*: marked disturbances of mood, including depression and mania (extreme elation and excitement)

3. *Somatoform disorders*: physical symptoms, such as blindness, paralysis or pain, that have no physical basis and are assumed to be caused by psychological factors; also, excessive preoccupations and worry about health (hypochondriasis)

4. *Dissociative disorders*: psychologically caused problems of consciousness and self-identification, including amnesia and multiple personalities (dissociative identity disorder)

5. *Schizophrenic and other psychotic disorders*: severe disorders of thinking, perception and emotion that involve loss of contact with reality and disordered behaviour

6. *Substance-abuse disorders*: personal and social problems associated with the use of psychoactive substances, such as alcohol, heroin or other drugs

7. *Sexual and gender identity disorders*: inability to function sexually or enjoy sexuality (sexual dysfunctions); deviant sexual behaviours, such as child molestation and arousal by inappropriate objects (fetishes); strong discomfort with one's gender accompanied by the desire to be a member of the other sex

8. *Eating disorders*: includes anorexia nervosa (self-starvation) and bulimia nervosa (patterns of bingeing and purging)

9. *Personality disorders*: rigid, stable and maladaptive personality patterns, such as antisocial, dependent, paranoid and narcissistic disorders

SOURCE: based on American Psychiatric Association, 2000.

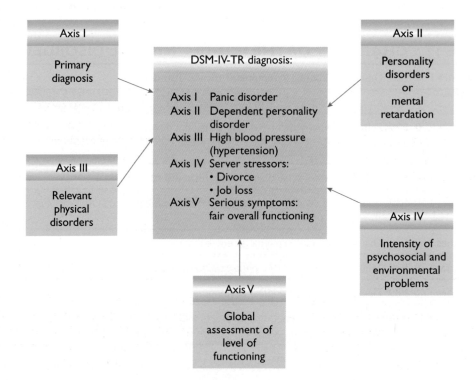

FIGURE 17.6

The DSM classification system.

The DSM-IV-TR uses a five-axis system to arrive at a comprehensive diagnosis that takes into account not only deviant behaviours, but also other relevant personal and environmental factors.

SOURCE: based on American Psychiatric Association, 2000.

over earlier versions (Brown et al., 2001; Nathan and Lagenbucher, 1999). One trade-off, however, is that the criteria are so detailed and specific that many people do not fit neatly into the categories. Moreover, debate continues over the reliability and validity of certain categories, particularly some of the Axis II personality disorders, whose characteristics overlap extensively with one another and with some Axis I disorders (Beutler and Malik, 2002). Such overlap leads to diagnostic disagreements and validity concerns about how different these disorders really are from one another (Widiger and Sankis, 2000). An important goal in the development of the next version of the DSM is to develop categories with less overlap (Helzer and Hudziak, 2002).

The history of the ICD-10 is relevant here. This diagnostics manual is widely used by the members of the World Health Organization and is truly an international resource. The earliest edition was produced as long ago as 1850, and was called the 'International Causes of Death'. It is, then very wrong to think of the ICD-10 as another diagnostics manual, as it covers all general medical problems. It also includes valuable health-management information about different populations around the world. The ICD-10 provides information on the prevalence of different diseases for instance, and how they may interact with other medical conditions. At the time of writing, the ICD is in its 'tenth' revision (hence ICD-10) but we are all waiting for ICD-11, which is due for initial release in 2008.

Differences between the ICD and the DSM

In their latest revisions the classifications systems strive to use the same classification numbers. However, there are some differences that differentiate the two. The major difference has already been identified, in that the ICD-10 extends to cover all medical problems. The mental disorders subsection, however, is equivalent in many ways to the DSM. If you look at the two closely, you will find that *personality disorders* feature on the same axis as other mental health problems, but the DSM keeps them separate. There are more subtle differences, however, such as how the two manuals deal with things like *substance abuse*. Alcohol dependence syndrome has been used in the development of both manuals' definitions of substance abuse, and as such there are close similarities in these two components of the texts. In both manuals, a list of 'symptoms' is provided for practitioners to use. If their 'client' or 'patient' suffers with a certain number of these 'symptoms' then the practitioner can diagnose a case of 'substance abuse and dependence'. The list of 'symptoms' has some common ground in both manuals, but there are also some differences. The potential problem here is very clear. A person suffering with a drug or alcohol problem may be diagnosed appropriately if their practitioner consults the DSM but not if they consult the ICD. So, someone in Europe (where the ICD is used, and the DSM is used less widely) suffering from drug abuse may not be identified as such, but an identical case in the USA, where the DSM is used almost exclusively, would be. There are issues here of both under-diagnosis and possible over-diagnosis. Here the practitioners run the risk of identifying a problem where there may not be one at all, and therefore diagnosing treatments (both medical and psychological) that may be both costly and of no use to the person concerned. These differences are being identified and hopefully dealt with in the new editions of the diagnostic manuals.

CONSEQUENCES OF DIAGNOSTIC LABELLING

Beyond their clinical and scientific utility, diagnostic labels can have important personal, social and legal consequences for people who receive them.

Social and Personal Consequences

Once a diagnostic label is attached to a person, it becomes all too easy to accept the label as an accurate description of the *individual* rather than of the *behaviour*. It then becomes difficult to look at the person's behaviour objectively, without preconceptions about how he or she will act. It is also likely to affect how we will interact with that person. Consider how you might react if you were told that your new next-door neighbour had been diagnosed as a paedophile. It would be surprising indeed if this label did not influence your perceptions and interactions with that person, whether or not the label was accurate.

In one famous study, eight normal individuals, including psychologist David Rosenhan (1973), got themselves admitted to psychiatric hospitals in five different states by telling mental health workers that they were hearing strange voices. Not surprisingly, they received diagnoses of schizophrenia upon admission. Once in the hospitals, however, they acted completely normally for the duration of their stay. When they were discharged after intervals ranging from seven to 52 days, they typically received the diagnosis 'schizophrenia, in remission.' This label means that even in the absence of deviant behaviour, the disorder was still presumed to be present, though not currently active. Once attached (understandably in this case, given their reports of hearing strange voices), diagnostic labels are not easily shed even when the disordered behaviours are no longer present.

Psychiatrist Thomas Szasz (1963; 2004) has long been an outspoken critic of psychiatric diagnosis. Indeed, he argues that the concept of mental illness is itself a myth, a poor analogy to physical illness. In contrast to physical illness diagnoses, there are no clear physical criteria for mental illness. According to Szasz, the deviations that psychiatry calls *mental illness* are better viewed as 'problems in living' rather than 'inner disorders'. He suggests that society invented the concept of mental illness to make it easier to control or change people whose behaviour upsets or threatens the existing social order. Although many mental health experts disagree with Szasz's extreme argument, they readily acknowledge the arbitrary elements in judgements of deviance.

Diagnostic labels may also play a role in creating or worsening psychological disorders. An analogy that is often used is that of the person sent to prison. They find themselves identified with the label of 'ex-convict'. The way they are now treated by people around them and the prejudice many have towards them because of ignorance and mistrust could very well lead them to live a life of crime even though they might have the initial desire not to. When people become aware that a psychiatric label has been applied to them, they may accept the new identity implied by the label and develop the expected role and outlook. Because psychiatric labels often carry degrading and stigmatizing implications, the effects on morale and self-esteem can be devastating. Moreover, in some cases (not all by any means) a person may despair of ever changing and therefore give up trying to deal with life circumstances that may be responsible for the problems. In this way, the expectations that accompany a label may result in a self-fulfilling prophecy, in which expectation becomes reality. Many people with psychological disorders do not seek treatment because of the stigma attached to 'mental illness'. In some cases people may welcome a diagnosis. For instance, many countries have limited resources to be spent on often expensive facilities that are designed carefully to help those children diagnosed with autism. Parents often describe their huge frustration at knowing that something is out of the ordinary with their child, but medics have difficulty identifying it in many cases. Autism is a spectrum disorder, which means that children can range from very mildly autistic to severely so. As such, identifying a borderline case as something that merits intervention is a very difficult and often lengthy procedure. It takes a strong parent to maintain vigilance, and drive to continue the process of medical checks and psychological investigations that precede a diagnosis. Often, it is only with an appropriate diagnosis that the correct help, including access to appropriate schooling, for a child can be obtained. In this case, a label may be welcomed.

Focus 17.6

How can psychiatric labels affect social and self-perceptions?

Legal Consequences

Psychiatric diagnoses also have important legal consequences. Individuals judged to be dangerous to themselves or others may be involuntarily committed to mental institutions under certain circumstances. Most people held against their will are held because they are a danger to themselves as a result of neglect or other actions. Some are held because they are a danger to those around them. When so committed, they lose some of their civil rights and may be detained indefinitely if their behaviour does not improve. It should be noted that in most cases the section is revoked relatively quickly, and many appeal successfully against the section. The law though, is not as black and white as we might like; as in all things, individual differences and circumstances must be considered. The laws in different countries differ, if not significantly, then certainly in part.

In all cases, though, the law tries to take into account the mental status of individuals accused of crimes. The definitions associated with this area of law must be carefully considered. In US law, two particularly important legal concepts are *competency* and *insanity*. **Competency** refers to a defendant's state of mind at the time of a judicial hearing (not at the time the crime was committed). A defendant judged to be too disturbed to understand the nature of the legal proceedings may be labelled 'not competent to stand trial' and institutionalized until judged competent.

Insanity relates to the presumed state of mind of the defendant at the time the crime was committed. Defendants may be declared 'not guilty by reason of insanity' if they are judged to have been so severely impaired when they committed a crime that they lacked the capacity either to appreciate the wrongfulness of their acts or to control their conduct. It is important to understand that insanity is a legal term, not a psychological one.

Elsewhere, in the UK for instance, the definitions are a little different. The phrase 'not fit to stand trial' is used in UK law rather than 'not competent to stand trial' and similar wording is used elsewhere. Also, we have to be careful about what the law accepts as a definition of insanity. If the person does not realize that their act was wrong, then, the person can be described as insane. However, in UK law a second definition is also accepted as a definition of insanity. If the person did 'not know the nature and quality of their actions'. For instance, if the person thinks that they are using a knife to cut up a scarecrow, or a snowman when really they are using the knife on a real person. This is different from the US definition which relates to the control of your actions. Another concept that is slightly different is that in the UK at least, the law says that the insanity must be a result of a 'disease of the mind'. This allows the law to distinguish between insanity caused by mental problems and behaviour caused by taking mind-altering drugs.

Despite the fact that the insanity plea is entered in relatively few US cases and that in most cases the prosecution agrees that the person was indeed insane, the so-called 'insanity defence' has long been hotly debated in may countries around the world. The 'insanity defence' is slightly different in the UK than it is in the USA. In the UK 'diminished responsibility' is a defence which relates to those who are designated as insane. For instance, a schizophrenic may commit a violent act, which results in the death of a person. Rather than murder, the person would be charged with manslaughter because of 'diminished responsibility'.

1. In March 2000, a Russian Colonel, Yuri Badanov, was tried for murdering a woman in Chechnya. He claimed temporary insanity, and that he was not in control of his mind during the crime in which he kidnapped, raped and strangled the 18-year-old woman. He was convicted of her murder and sentenced to 10 years.

2. In September 2004, Phiona Davies was sent to Broadmoor Security Hospital in the South of England. The 25-year-old had killed her great-grandmother and her ex-boyfriend. She told the court that she believed her boyfriend was a robot and her grandmother was the devil and was found not guilty of murder due to insanity. She can never be freed without explicit permission from the government.

3. In 2006 Daniel Gonzalez was accused of murdering four people. He reportedly indicated that he wanted to become a notorious serial killer. The court heard testimony that he was a schizophrenic and had once attempted to bite himself to death while being held for trial in Broadmoor security hospital. He was convicted of the murders, and sent for treatment in Broadmoor where staff have said that he is the most unpredictable patient there.

competency
a defendant's state of mind at the time of a judicial hearing

insanity
the presumed state of mind of the defendant at the time the crime was committed

4. In September 2006 an Oxford student, William Jaggs, killed Lucy Braham, a design student. He stabbed her to death before stabbing himself repeatedly in the chest and falling into a coma. It took a week before police could talk to him. He pleaded guilty on the grounds of diminished responsibility and the plea was accepted by the judge. The court heard that Jaggs had a history of LSD and cocaine abuse while at university, which, he said, caused violent and sexual hallucinations. He was sent to a secure hospital indefinitely, the judge adding 'It may never be safe to release you'.

5. On 14 July 2007 Robert Torto, a schizophrenic with religious and grandiose delusions, was detained indefinitely at Broadmoor Secure Hospital for firebombing shops and killing two people. He reportedly had a hate list identifying people who he wanted to kill, and these included homosexuals, those of faiths other than Christianity and those who go to off-licences and nightclubs.

FIGURE 17.7

Armin Miewes advertised for a willing victim. Berndt Jurgen Brandes responded to this advert and was killed, butchered and subsequently eaten by Miewes who was found guilty of manslaughter and sent to prison for 8½ years.

These examples show that even though a crime may, on the surface, seem to be the result of a person suffering from a mental disorder, society and the law may deal with it differently. In 2004, Armin Miewes (Fig. 17.7) confessed to killing and subsequently eating 43-year-old Berndt Juergen Brandes at his home near Rotenburg. The dead man replied to an advertisement Miewes had posted on the Internet asking for a volunteer. Miewes said he regretted the crime and that he would never feel the need to do it again. The court convicted him of manslaughter because there were no 'base motives' for the crime, and sentenced him to eight and a half years in prison. The case of Armin Miewes, on the surface, can be seen as a clear case of mental illness; how could any sane person kill and eat another man? The court, however, decided that Miewes was in control of his mind, and because the person volunteered for death (a form of mercy killing as his defence lawyer put it) then he should be dealt with by the prison system under a manslaughter charge. This case is unusual (thank goodness!) in many ways, but is interesting in that it involves two people whose mental state must be considered. Both Miewes and his victim entered into a complex and peculiar relationship, willing killer and willing victim. The mental state of both could, and should, be questioned in this case.

Focus 17.7

Contrast the legal concepts of competency and insanity. What is the current burden of proof in insanity hearings?

To balance punishment for crimes with concerns about a defendant's mental status and possible need for treatment, Canada and an increasing number of US jurisdictions have adopted a verdict of 'guilty but mentally ill'. This verdict imposes a normal sentence for a crime but sends the defendant to a mental hospital for treatment. Defendants who are considered to have recovered before serving out their time are sent to prison for the remainder of the sentence. This is similar to the verdict of 'diminished responsibility' offered by UK courts. It seems then that the problem of definition of abnormality extends to the law. Moral decisions taken by an organization charged with maintaining order and punishing those who commit crimes are made extremely difficult by those whose mental health falls outside the 'norm'. It is good to see, however, than the law in some of the most powerful nations or regions in the world seems to be developing to take mental illness into consideration when passing verdicts over those whose actions are significantly influenced by often terrible illnesses.

WHAT DO YOU THINK?

'DO I HAVE THAT DISORDER?'

When people read descriptions of disorders, whether physical or psychological, they often see some of those symptoms or characteristics in themselves. In medical education, this is sometimes termed 'medical students' disease'. If you experience such concerns as you read about the various psychological disorders in this chapter, how should you decide whether you have a problem worthy of professional attention? After thinking about this, compare your standards with those discussed on p. 836.

IN REVIEW

- Abnormality is largely a judgement made by society. Behaviour that is judged to reflect a psychological disorder typically is (1) distressing to the person or to other people; (2) dysfunctional, maladaptive or self-defeating; and/or (3) socially deviant in a way that arouses discomfort in others and cannot be attributed to environmental causes.

- Among the important issues in psychiatric diagnosis are the potential negative effects of labelling on social perceptions and self-perceptions. Legal implications of competency, fitness to stand trial and insanity judgements are also receiving attention around the world.

- The major psychiatric classification systems in use around the world are the DSM-IV-TR and the ICD-10. The DSM-IV-TR describes the current status of the individual using five different dimensions, or axes, that capture personal and environmental factors. Reliability (diagnostic agreement) and validity are important issues in diagnostic classification systems. The ICD-10 describes all illnesses but has a chapter specifically relating to mental illnesses. It is organized similarly to the DSM but there are some differences. These differences are being identified and dealt with in a new edition of the ICD which is due for initial viewing in 2008 and publication in 2011.

ANXIETY DISORDERS

We have all experienced **anxiety**, the state of tension and apprehension that is a natural response to perceived threat. In **anxiety disorders**, the frequency and intensity of anxiety responses are out of proportion to the situations that trigger them, and the anxiety interferes with daily life.

Anxiety responses have four components: (1) a *subjective-emotional* component, including feelings of tension and apprehension; (2) a *cognitive* component, including worrisome thoughts and a sense of inability to cope; (3) *physiological* responses, including increased heart rate and blood pressure, muscle tension, rapid breathing, nausea, dry mouth, diarrhoea and frequent urination; and (4) *behavioural* responses, such as avoidance of certain situations and impaired task performance (Barlow, 2002; Fig. 17.8). Anxiety disorders take a number of different forms, including phobic disorder, generalized anxiety disorder, panic disorder, obsessive-compulsive disorder and post-traumatic stress disorder.

Prevalence refers to the number of people who have a disorder during a specified period of time. Alonso et al. (2004) indicate that just under 14 per cent of the very large number of people

anxiety
the state of tension and apprehension that is a natural response to perceived threat

anxiety disorders
the frequency and intensity of anxiety responses are out of proportion to the situations that trigger them, and the anxiety interferes with daily life

Focus 17.8
Describe the four components of anxiety.

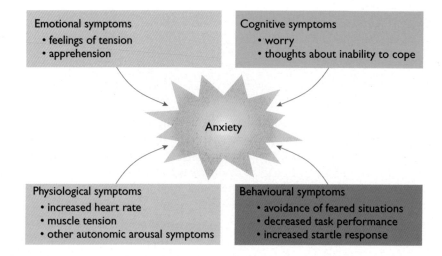

FIGURE 17.8

Components of anxiety.

Anxiety consists of subjective-emotional, cognitive, physiological and behavioural components.

from six European countries asked identified that they have suffered from an anxiety disorder of some kind during their lifetime. The study used DSM-IV diagnosis criteria. Figure 17.9 shows lifetime prevalence rates for the various anxiety disorders in the USA, where overall prevalence of anxiety disorder were identified by Kessler et al. (1994) and Robins and Regier (1991) as being at 17.6 per cent, a little higher than in Europe. Each of the anxiety disorders occurs more frequently in females than in males. In more than 70 per cent of cases, anxiety disorders are considered *clinically significant*, meaning that they interfere significantly with life functions or cause the person to seek medical or psychological treatment (Narrow et al., 2002).

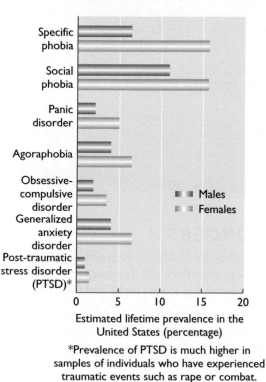

FIGURE 17.9

Prevalence rates for anxiety disorders.

This graph shows the lifetime prevalence rates for anxiety disorders in men and women. All of the anxiety disorders occur more frequently in women.

SOURCES: based on Kessler et al., 1994; Robins and Regier, 1991.

PHOBIC DISORDER

Gabriella's fear of the water dates back to her childhood. She recalls that on several occasions her mother, who had a similar fear, vividly described seeing a friend from her school drown while swimming in the local pool. Gabriella's fear of water intensified after she inhaled some water and panicked when playing with a friend at the swimming pool. She panicked and was sure she was going to drown, until a lifeguard pulled her to safety. Although she took swimming lessons as a child, she now dreads the thought of swimming or even paddling. For the past 15 years, Gabriella has avoided outings that would take her near the ocean, a lake or even a pool. She once turned down a free trip to Hawaii because of the anxiety she knew she would experience flying over the ocean.

Phobias are strong and irrational fears of certain objects or situations. The word is derived from *Phobos*, the Greek god of fear, whose likeness was painted on masks and shields to frighten enemies in battle. Today's phobic individual fights a different kind of battle, with fears of a less realistic but no less intense nature.

People with phobias realize that their fears are out of proportion to the danger involved, but they feel helpless to cope with these fears. Instead, they make strenuous efforts to avoid the phobic situation or object. Among the most common phobias in western society are **agoraphobia**, a fear of open or public places from which escape would be difficult; **social phobias**, excessive fear of situations in which the person might be evaluated and possibly embarrassed; and **specific phobias**, such as a fear of dogs, snakes, spiders, aeroplanes, lifts, enclosed spaces, water, injections or germs. Animal fears are more common among women; fear of heights, among men (Curtis et al., 1998). Phobias can develop at any point in life, but many of them arise during childhood, adolescence and early adulthood. Once phobias develop, they seldom go away on their own, and they may broaden and intensify over time (Stein and Hollander, 2002).

The degree of impairment produced by a phobia depends in part on how often the phobic stimulus is encountered in the individual's normal activities. For example, fear of flying is an extremely common phobia. An aeroplane phobia may be a relatively minor inconvenience for a person who never needs to fly, but it would be a serious handicap for an executive whose job requires extensive travel. These phobias can be extremely inconvenient. Muhammad Ali, apparently, was afraid of flying (aerophobic) as is Whoopi Goldberg. Some phobias are less awkward but can still be difficult to deal with; for instance, Napoleon was apparently afraid of cats (ailurophobia) and Andre Agassi has a fear of spiders (arachnophobia) (Fig. 17.10).

---

phobias
strong and irrational fears of certain objects or situations

agoraphobia
fear of open or public places from which escape would be difficult

social phobias
excessive fear of situations in which the person might be evaluated and possibly embarrassed

specific phobias
such as a fear of dogs, snakes, spiders, aeroplanes, lifts, enclosed spaces, water, injections or germs

Focus 17.9
Describe the features of phobic, generalized anxiety, panic and obsessive-compulsive disorders.

FIGURE 17.10

People who suffer from phobic disorders cope in different ways. The focus of their anxiety is easier to avoid for some people than others. Napoleon, for instance, probably found it relatively easy to banish cats from his home, but Mohammad Ali may have found travelling long distances between engagements difficult without addressing the object of his fear.

generalized anxiety disorder

a chronic (ongoing) state of diffuse, or free-floating, anxiety that is not attached to specific situations or objects

panic disorders

occur suddenly and unpredictably, and they are much more intense

GENERALIZED ANXIETY DISORDER

As its name implies, **generalized anxiety disorder** is a chronic (ongoing) state of diffuse, or free-floating, anxiety that is not attached to specific situations or objects. The anxiety may last for months, with the signs almost continually present. Emotionally, Fabian feels jittery, tense and constantly on edge. Cognitively, he expects something awful to happen but doesn't know what. Physically, Fabian sweats constantly under his arms, his stomach is usually upset, he has diarrhoea, and he is unable to attain a refreshing level of sleep.

As we might expect, this disorder can markedly interfere with daily functioning, even if the symptoms are not continually present for the six months required for a formal diagnosis. The person may find it hard to concentrate, to make decisions and to remember commitments. One large-scale study found that 4.3 per cent of people aged 15 and above reported having experienced the symptoms of generalized anxiety disorder (Kadri et al., 2007). Onset tends to occur in childhood and adolescence (Wittchen et al., 1994).

PANIC DISORDER

In contrast to generalized anxiety disorder, which involves chronic tension and anxiety, **panic disorders** occur suddenly and unpredictably, and they are much more intense. The symptoms of panic attacks can be terrifying. As in the case of Anna-Maria, the university student described at the beginning of the chapter, it is not unusual for victims to believe that they are dying.

> Ms. Watson reported that until the onset of her current problems two years ago, she had led a normal and happy life. She was returning from work one night when suddenly she felt that she couldn't catch her breath. Her heart began to pound, and she broke out into a cold sweat. Things began to seem unreal, her legs felt leaden, and she became sure she would die or faint before she reached home. She asked a passerby to help her get a taxi and went to a nearby hospital emergency room. (Spitzer et al., 1983, pp. 7–8)

As in Anna-Maria's and Ms Watson's cases, panic attacks usually occur unexpectedly and in the absence of any identifiable stimulus. It is this unpredictable quality that makes panic attacks so mysterious and terrifying to their victims. About 60 per cent of people with daytime panic disorders also experience attacks during their sleep. Their symptoms awaken them, and they fear that they are dying (Craske and Rowe, 1997). Most often, however, the issue is much less dramatic, with the person experiencing a fear of collapsing or making a fool of themselves, not dying.

Many people who suffer recurrent panic attacks develop agoraphobia, an aversion to public places, because they fear that they will have an attack in public. In extreme cases, they may fear leaving the familiar setting of the home, and some have been known to remain housebound for years at a time because of their 'fear of fear' (Milrod et al., 1997). Ms Watson developed an agoraphobic pattern:

> As the attacks continued, Ms. Watson began to dread going out of the house alone. She feared that while out she would have an attack and would be stranded and helpless. She stopped riding the subway to work out of fear she might be trapped in a car between stops when an attack struck, preferring instead to walk the 20 blocks between her home and work. Social and recreational activities, previously frequent and enjoyed, were severely curtailed because an attack might occur. (Spitzer et al., 1983, p. 8)

Formal diagnosis of a panic disorder requires recurrent attacks that do not seem tied to environmental stimuli, followed by psychological or behavioural problems. These typically involve persistent fear of future attacks or agoraphobic responses. Panic disorders with or without agoraphobia tend to appear in late adolescence or early adulthood and in Europe affect about 1.8 per cent of the population in any one 12-month period.

OBSESSIVE-COMPULSIVE DISORDER

A 38-year-old mother of one child had been obsessed by fears of contamination during her entire adult life. Literally hundreds of times a day, thoughts of being infected by germs would occur to her. Once she began to think that either she or her child might become infected, she could not dismiss the thought. The constant concern about infection resulted in a series of washing and cleaning rituals that took up most of her day. Her child was confined to one room only, which the woman tried to keep entirely free of germs by scrubbing it – floor to ceiling – several times a day. Moreover, she opened and closed all doors with her feet, in order to avoid contaminating her own hands. (Rachman and Hodgson, 1980)

This woman was diagnosed as having an *obsessive-compulsive disorder* (OCD). Such disorders usually consist of two components, one cognitive, the other behavioural, although either can occur alone. **Obsessions** are repetitive and unwelcome thoughts, images or impulses that invade consciousness, are often abhorrent to the person and are very difficult to dismiss or control. This mother was tyrannized by thoughts and images of contamination. **Compulsions** are repetitive behavioural responses – like the woman's cleaning rituals – that can be resisted only with great difficulty. Compulsions are often responses that function to reduce the anxiety associated with the intrusive thoughts (Clark and O'Connor, 2005; De Silva and Rachman, 1998). Once the mother performed her compulsive cleaning acts, she was relatively free from anxiety, at least until the thoughts of contamination intruded once more.

In this case, the woman's germ obsession clearly interfered with her life, as well as her daughter's. One man's obsession resulted in a far more favourable outcome: Louis Pasteur's discovery of a process for eliminating destructive micro-organisms and limiting fermentation in milk, beer and other liquids. His tireless work on this invention was fuelled in part by his own obsession about contamination and infection. Pasteur refused to shake hands with others and had a ritual of vigorously wiping his plate and glass before dining (Asimov, 1997).

Behavioural compulsions are extremely difficult to control. They often involve checking things repeatedly (for example, whether the door was locked or the gas burners on the stove were turned off), cleaning or hand washing, and repeating tasks endlessly. If the person does not perform the compulsive act, he or she may experience tremendous anxiety, perhaps even a panic attack. Like phobic avoidance responses, compulsions are strengthened through a process of negative reinforcement because they allow the person to avoid anxiety.

Torres et al. (2006) estimated prevalence of OCD as being approximately 1.1 per cent. Obsessive-compulsive disorder is a complicated problem, with significant co-morbidity (happens at the same time) with other problems. Torres et al. go on to indicate that in their sample, co-morbidity was as high as 62 per cent in those they found with OCD.

POST-TRAUMATIC STRESS DISORDER

Post-traumatic stress disorder (PTSD) is a severe anxiety disorder that can occur in people who have been exposed to traumatic life events (Fig. 17.11). Four major symptoms commonly occur in this anxiety disorder (Falsetti et al., 2005; Wilson and Keane, 2004):

1. The person experiences severe symptoms of anxiety, arousal and distress that were not present before the trauma.

2. The victim relives the trauma recurrently in flashbacks, in dreams and in fantasy.

obsessions

repetitive and unwelcome thoughts, images or impulses that invade consciousness, are often abhorrent to the person and are very difficult to dismiss or control

compulsions

repetitive behavioural responses that can be resisted only with great difficulty

post-traumatic stress disorder (PTSD)

a severe anxiety disorder that can occur in people who have been exposed to traumatic life events

FIGURE 17.11

The devastation and loss of life caused by the 2004 Indian Ocean tsunami traumatized millions of people in 11 countries. One effect of the trauma was the development of post-traumatic stress disorder in many people, particularly those who were personally affected by the destruction.

3. The person becomes numb to the world and avoids stimuli that serve as reminders of the trauma.

4. The individual experiences intense survivor guilt in instances where others were killed and the individual was somehow spared.

The PTSD category arose in part from studies of soldiers who had been subjected to the horrors of war. One study found the incidence of PTSD to be seven times more likely for Vietnam veterans who spent significant time in combat and were wounded than for other Vietnam-era veterans (CDC, 1988). Another study reported a 12-month PTSD rate of 27.8 per cent following combat exposure (Prigerson et al., 2002). Civilian war victims may be even more vulnerable than soldiers. Amy Ai and co-workers (2002) found a PTSD rate of 60.5 per cent in a sample of refugees from the bloody civil war in Kosovo. Roth and Ekland (2006) followed the Kosovar evacuees in a longitudinal study and showed that the prevalence of PTSD increased significantly as years following their terrible experiences went by. On average, the refugees reported having experienced 15 war-related traumatic events. Traumas caused by human actions, such as war, rape and torture, tend to precipitate more severe PTSD reactions than do natural disasters, such as hurricanes or earthquakes (Corales, 2005; O'Donohue and Elliot, 1992). Compared with men, women exhibit twice the rate of PTSD following exposure to traumatic events (Kimerling et al., 2003).

Terrorist acts can exact a heavy toll in PTSD. Interviews with 1008 adult residents of Manhattan revealed that 7.5 per cent experienced symptoms consistent with a PTSD diagnosis in the five to eight weeks following the 11 September 2001 attacks. In those living closest to the World Trade Center, the PTSD rate was 20 per cent (Galea et al., 2002).

The psychological wreckage caused by PTSD may increase vulnerability to the later development of other disorders. One study found that women who experienced PTSD had double the risk of developing a depressive disorder and three times the risk of developing alcohol-related problems in the future (Bresalau et al., 1997). Such findings highlight the importance of prompt post-trauma intervention aimed at preventing the development of PTSD (Litz, 2004). Do not make the mistake of thinking that PTSD can result only from terrorist attacks, war or natural disasters. Post-traumatic stress disorder can result from any trauma if not dealt with appropriately. Being involved in a car crash, for instance, might be enough to cause significant harm which may result in a diagnosis of PTSD, and this point cannot be made strongly enough. An experience of a violent crime, as an observer as well as a 'victim' could possibly result in PTSD, as well as any number of events not nearly as dramatic or obviously harrowing as the experiencing war or the atrocities we have become to associate with conflict.

CAUSAL FACTORS IN ANXIETY DISORDERS

Anxiety is a complex phenomenon having biological, psychological and environmental causes. Within the vulnerability-stress model presented earlier, any of these factors can create predispositions to respond to stressors with an anxiety disorder.

Biological Factors

Genetic factors may create a vulnerability to anxiety disorders (Jang, 2005). Where clinical levels of anxiety are concerned, identical twins have a concordance rate (i.e., if one twin has it, so does the other) of about 40 per cent for anxiety disorders, compared with a 4 per cent concordance rate in fraternal twins (Carey and Gottesman, 1981). Although such findings indicate a genetic predisposition, the concordance rate even in identical twins is far from 100 per cent, indicating that psychological and environmental factors have an important role to play.

Psychologist David Barlow (2002), a leading expert on anxiety disorders, suggests that genetically caused vulnerability may take the form of an autonomic nervous system that overreacts

Focus 17.10

Describe the four major features of PTSD.

Focus 17.11

What biological factors seem involved in anxiety disorders?

to perceived threat, creating high levels of physiological arousal. Hereditary factors may also cause over-reactivity of neurotransmitter systems involved in emotional responses (Mineka et al., 1998). One such transmitter is GABA (gamma-aminobutyric acid), an inhibitory transmitter that reduces neural activity in the amygdala and other brain structures that trigger emotional arousal. Some researchers believe that abnormally low levels of inhibitory GABA activity in these arousal areas may cause some people to have highly reactive nervous systems that quickly produce anxiety responses to stressors (Bremner, 2000). In support of this hypothesis, brain scans show that clients with a history of panic attacks have a 22 per cent lower concentration of GABA in the occipital cortex than age-matched controls without panic disorder (Goddard et al., 2001). Such people could also be more susceptible to classically conditioned phobias because they already have a strong unconditioned arousal response in place, ready to be conditioned to new stimuli. Other transmitter systems might also be involved in the anxiety disorders.

As noted earlier, women exhibit anxiety disorders more often than do men. In a large-scale study of adolescents, Peter Lewinsohn and co-workers (1998) found that this sex difference emerges as early as 7 years of age. Even when the researchers applied statistical methods to control for sex differences in 11 psychosocial factors (including negative life events, self-esteem and social support), a large sex difference in anxiety disorders remained. Such findings suggest a sex-linked biological predisposition for anxiety disorders, but social conditions that give women less power and personal control may also contribute (Craske, 2003). As in other instances of sex differences, it seems likely that biological, psychological and environmental factors combine in complex ways.

Psychological Factors

Psychodynamic theories   Anxiety is a central concept in psychoanalytic conceptions of abnormal behaviour. Freud referred to anxiety-based disorders as neuroses. According to Freud, **neurotic anxiety** occurs when unacceptable impulses threaten to overwhelm the ego's defences and explode into consciousness or action. How the ego's defence mechanisms deal with neurotic anxiety determines the form of the anxiety disorder. Freud believed that in phobic disorders, neurotic anxiety is displaced onto some external stimulus that has symbolic significance in relation to the underlying conflict. For example, in one of Freud's most celebrated cases, a 5-year-old boy named Hans suddenly developed a fear of horses and the possibility of being bitten. Seeing a horse fall down near his home worsened his fear, and little Hans began to dread leaving his home. To Freud, the phobia resulted from the boy's unresolved Oedipus complex. The powerful horse represented Hans's father, and the fear of being bitten symbolized Hans's unconscious fear of being castrated by his father if he acted on his sexual desire for his mother; the falling horse symbolized Hans's forbidden triumph over his father.

Psychoanalysts believe that obsessions and compulsions are also ways of handling anxiety. According to Freud, the obsession is symbolically related to, but less terrifying than, the underlying impulse. A compulsion is a way of taking back, or undoing, one's unacceptable urges, as when obsessive thoughts about dirt and compulsive hand-washing are used to deal with one's 'dirty' sexual impulses. Finally, generalized anxiety and panic attacks are thought to occur when one's defences are not strong enough to control or contain neurotic anxiety but are strong enough to hide the underlying conflict.

Cognitive factors   Cognitive theorists stress the role of maladaptive thought patterns and beliefs in anxiety disorders. People with anxiety disorders catastrophize about demands and magnify them into threats. They anticipate that the worst will happen and feel powerless to cope effectively (Clark, 1988; Mineka et al., 1998). Intrusive thoughts about the previous traumatic event are a central feature of post-traumatic stress disorder, and the presence of such thoughts after the trauma predicts the later development of PTSD (Falsetti et al., 2005).

neurotic anxiety
occurs when unacceptable impulses threaten to overwhelm the ego's defences and explode into consciousness or action

Focus 17.12
Compare psychoanalytic and cognitive explanations of anxiety disorders.

Cognitive processes also play an important role in panic disorders. Clark (1986; 1988) describes panic disorders as a resulting from *catastrophic misinterpretation*. By this he means that the, at first, subtle changes in sensation, which may include a raised heart rate, etc., are interpreted as indicating a physical threat. This makes the person anxious. The result is a vicious circle. The anxiety experienced produces more of the physical sensations that led to the anxiety in the first place, causing more anxiety, and the circle continues, resulting in a 'catastrophic misinterpretation' of physical signals, a panic attack (Fig. 17.12). At first the person becomes *hypervigilant* where their sensitivity to physical changes is increased. Next, the person engages in what Clarke called *avoidance*, where the person does everything he or she can to avoid these sensations, and stop them getting worse. For instance, if the person feels that being in the sun will cause him or her to develop a skin cancer, then he or she might avoid going out in the sun. This avoidance makes the person more vigilant, and more anxious of the 'stressor', and avoiding it does not provide him or her with any evidence that experiencing sunshine does not (usually) result in a cancer at all. McNally (1994) says that generalizing panic like this is not appropriate. Some clients report that they do not engage in catastrophic misinterpretation at all, whereas others may feel that the physical sensations they experience may indeed lead to death, and they will are hard to convince otherwise. Helping those with panic problems replace such mortal-danger appraisals with more benign interpretations of their bodily symptoms (e.g., 'It's only a bit of anxiety, not a heart attack') results in a marked reduction in panic attacks (Barlow, 1997; Craske, 1999).

FIGURE 17.12

What causes panic attacks?

Cognitive explanations of panic attacks describe a process in which normal manifestations of anxiety are appraised catastrophically, increasing anxiety to a level that ultimately results in a full-blown panic attack.

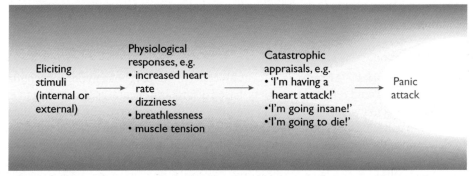

The role of learning   From the behavioural perspective, classical conditioning, observational learning or operant conditioning can contribute to the development of an anxiety disorder. Some fears are acquired as a result of traumatic experiences that produce a classically conditioned fear response (Rachman, 1998). For example, a person who has suffered a traumatic fall from a high place may develop a fear of heights (a conditioned response – CR) because the high place (the conditioned stimulus – CS) was associated with the pain and trauma of the fall (the unconditioned stimulus – UCS).

Classical conditioning cannot be the whole story, however, because many phobic people have never had a traumatic experience with the phobic object or situation that they now fear (Bruce and Sanderson, 1998; Menzies and Clarke, 1995). Most people who are afraid to fly have never been in an aeroplane crash. So how did they learn their fear? Clearly, phobias can also be acquired through observational learning. For example, televised images of aeroplane crashes evoke high levels of fear in some people. Yet most people do not develop phobias under these conditions, so there must be still more going on. It may be that biological dispositions and cognitive factors help determine whether a person develops a phobia from observing or even hearing about a traumatic event. Recall, for example, how Gabrilla's fear of the water began with her mother's description of a drowning. Thus if a person has a biological disposition towards intense fear, experiences traumatic scenes vicariously and comes to believe that 'the same thing could happen to me', the likelihood of developing a phobia on the basis of observational learning may increase.

Once anxiety is learned, either classically or vicariously, it may be triggered either by cues from the environment or by internal cues, such as thoughts and images (Pitman et al., 2000). In phobic reactions, the cues tend to be external ones relating to the feared object or situation. In panic disorders, the anxiety-arousing cues tend to be internal ones (Clark, 1986; 1988), such as bodily sensations (e.g., one's heart rate) or mental images (such as the image of collapsing and having a seizure in a public place; Craske, 1999).

In addition to classical conditioning and observational learning, operant conditioning also plays a role. People are highly motivated to avoid or escape anxiety because it is such an unpleasant emotional state. Behaviours that are successful in reducing anxiety, such as compulsions or phobic avoidance responses, become stronger through negative reinforcement. Thus the obsessive-compulsive mother's scrubbing ritual reduces anxiety about contamination, and Gabrilla's avoidance of swimming prevents her from experiencing anxiety. In the case of agoraphobia, remaining at home also serves as a *safety signal*, a place where the person is unlikely to experience a panic attack (Seligman and Binik, 1977). Again, anxiety reduction reinforces the response of staying at home (Fig. 17.13). Unfortunately, successful avoidance prolongs the problem because it prevents the learned anxiety response from being extinguished, which would occur eventually if these people exposed themselves to the feared stimuli enough times without experiencing the feared consequence.

Focus 17.13
Explain anxiety disorders in terms of classical conditioning, observational learning and operant conditioning.

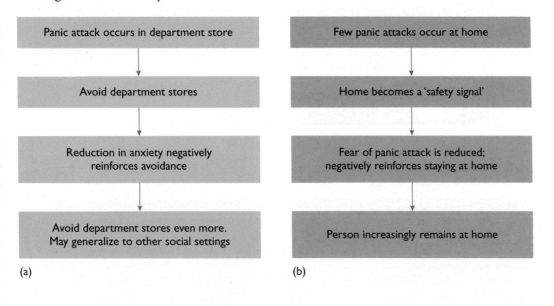

(a)   (b)

FIGURE 17.13

Panic and agoraphobia.

This diagram illustrates how panic disorders contribute to the development of agoraphobia. Negative reinforcement through anxiety reduction fosters avoidance of feared situations (a), as well as an attraction to safety signals, such as one's own home (b), where panic does not occur.

Sociocultural Factors

Social and cultural factors also play a role in the development of anxiety disorders (Lopez and Guarnaccia, 2000). The role of culture is most dramatically shown in **culture-bound disorders** that occur only in certain locales. One such disorder found in Japan is a social phobia called *Taijin Kyofushu* (Tanaka-Matsumi, 1979). People with this disorder are pathologically fearful of offending others by emitting offensive odours, blushing, staring inappropriately or having a blemish or improper facial expression. Taijin Kyofushu has been attributed to the Japanese cultural value of extreme interpersonal sensitivity and to cultural prohibitions against expressing negative emotions or causing discomfort in others (Kleinknecht et al., 1997). Another culture-bound disorder is *koro*, a South-east Asian anxiety disorder in which a man fears that his penis is going to retract into his abdomen and kill him. This is also known as *genital retraction syndrome* (GRS) and is an example of a mass hysteria, with outbreaks happening in waves and often large groups as in Singapore in 1967. Treatment is by removing reminders of the anxiety, by ordering news and media black-outs on reporting of the issue and sometimes by treating with anti-anxiety drugs.

culture-bound disorders
occur only in certain locales

Western culture also spawns culture-specific anxiety reactions. Although formally classified as an eating disorder, anorexia nervosa has a strong phobic component, namely the fear of getting fat. It also has obsessive-compulsive elements. This eating disorder is found almost exclusively in developed countries, where being thin has become a cultural obsession (Becker et al., 1999).

As we have seen, the causes of anxiety disorders are complex. They often interact with one another and can be viewed at biological, psychological and environmental levels of analysis (Fig. 17.14).

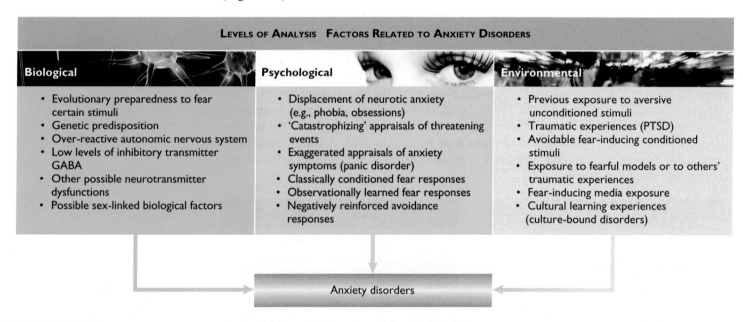

LEVELS OF ANALYSIS FACTORS RELATED TO ANXIETY DISORDERS

Biological
- Evolutionary preparedness to fear certain stimuli
- Genetic predisposition
- Over-reactive autonomic nervous system
- Low levels of inhibitory transmitter GABA
- Other possible neurotransmitter dysfunctions
- Possible sex-linked biological factors

Psychological
- Displacement of neurotic anxiety (e.g., phobia, obsessions)
- 'Catastrophizing' appraisals of threatening events
- Exaggerated appraisals of anxiety symptoms (panic disorder)
- Classically conditioned fear responses
- Observationally learned fear responses
- Negatively reinforced avoidance responses

Environmental
- Previous exposure to aversive unconditioned stimuli
- Traumatic experiences (PTSD)
- Avoidable fear-inducing conditioned stimuli
- Exposure to fearful models or to others' traumatic experiences
- Fear-inducing media exposure
- Cultural learning experiences (culture-bound disorders)

Anxiety disorders

FIGURE 17.14

Levels of analysis: factors related to anxiety disorders.

IN REVIEW

- Anxiety involves four components: (1) subjective-emotional feelings of tension and discomfort; (2) cognitive processes involving worry, perceptions of threat and lack of control; (3) excessive physiological arousal; and (4) behaviours that reflect the anxious state and others that are designed to escape or avoid the feared object or situation.

- Anxiety disorders include phobic disorder (an irrational fear of a specific object or situation), generalized anxiety disorder (recurrent anxiety reactions that are difficult to link to specific environmental stimuli), panic disorder, obsessive-compulsive disorder (which involves uncontrollable and unwelcome thoughts and repetitive behaviours) and post-traumatic stress disorder.

- Biological factors in anxiety disorders include both genetic and biochemical processes, possibly involving the action of neurotransmitters, such as GABA, within parts of the brain that control emotional arousal. The greater prevalence of anxiety disorders in women has been explained in both biological and sociocultural terms.

- Psychoanalytic theorists believe that neurotic anxiety results from the inability of the ego's defences to deal with internal psychological conflicts. The cognitive perspective stresses the role of cognitive distortions, including the tendencies to magnify the degree of threat and danger and, in the case of panic disorder, to misinterpret normal anxiety symptoms in ways that can evoke panic.

- The behavioural perspective views anxiety as a learned response established through classical conditioning or vicarious learning. The avoidance responses in phobias and compulsive disorders are seen as operant responses that are negatively reinforced through anxiety reduction.

- Sociocultural factors are also involved in anxiety disorders, as illustrated by certain culture-bound anxiety disorders.

SOMATOFORM AND DISSOCIATIVE DISORDERS: ANXIETY INFERRED

The anxiety disorders just considered involve anxiety and stress reactions that are vividly experienced by the sufferer and, often, are externally observable. In some other disorders, however, underlying anxiety is largely inferred, or assumed to be present, rather than outwardly expressed. In somatoform and dissociative disorders, for example, the person may not consciously feel any anxiety because the function of the disorders is to protect the person from strong psychological conflict (Rosenhan and Seligman, 1989). Psychodynamic theorists believe that whatever distress the person may experience in such disorders is less stressful than the underlying anxiety that is being defended against.

SOMATOFORM DISORDERS

Somatoform disorders involve physical complaints or disabilities that suggest a medical problem but that have no known biological cause and are not produced voluntarily by the person (Finell, 1997). In **hypochondriasis**, people become unduly alarmed about any physical symptom they detect and are convinced that they have or are about to have a serious illness. People with **pain disorder** experience intense pain that either is out of proportion to whatever medical condition they might have or for which no physical basis can be found.

Somatoform disorders differ from *psychophysiological disorders*, in which psychological factors cause or contribute to a real medical condition, such as migraine headaches, asthma, hypertension (chronic high blood pressure) or cardiac problems. Perhaps the most fascinating of the somatoform disorders is **conversion disorder**, in which serious neurological symptoms, such as paralysis, loss of sensation, or blindness, suddenly occur. In such cases, electrophysiological recordings and brain imaging indicate that sensory and motor pathways in the brain are intact (Black et al., 2004). People with conversion disorders often exhibit *la belle indifference*, a strange lack of concern about their symptom and its implications (Pajer, 2000). In some cases, the complaint itself is physiologically impossible. An example is *glove anaesthesia*, in which a person loses all sensation below the wrist. As Figure 17.15 shows, the hand is served by nerves that also provide sensory input to the wrist and arm, making glove anaesthesia anatomically impossible.

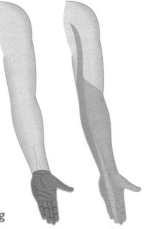

Glove anaesthesia   Actual nerve innervation

FIGURE 17.15

An impossible conversion symptom.

Glove anaesthesia is a conversion disorder in which all feeling is lost below the wrist. The skin areas served by nerves in the arm make this symptom physiologically impossible.

Focus 17.14

Describe three kinds of somatoform disorders. What causal factors might be involved?

somatoform disorders

physical complaints or disabilities that suggest a medical problem but that have no known biological cause and are not produced voluntarily by the person

hypochondriasis

people become unduly alarmed about any physical symptom they detect and are convinced that they have or are about to have a serious illness

pain disorder

experience intense pain that either is out of proportion to whatever medical condition they might have or for which no physical basis can be found

conversion disorder

serious neurological symptoms, such as paralysis, loss of sensation, or blindness, suddenly occur

FIGURE 17.16

A physician examines a Cambodian refugee who appears to be suffering from psychologically induced blindness. There is nothing wrong with his eyes, but he cannot see.

Focus 17.15

What is the central feature of dissociative disorders? Describe the three major dissociative disorders.

Although *psychogenic blindness* is rare in the general population, researchers discovered the largest known civilian group of people in the world with trauma-induced blindness. They were Cambodian refugees who escaped from their country and settled in southern California. These survivors of the 'killing fields' of Cambodia were subjected to unspeakable horror at the hands of the Khmer Rouge in the years following the Vietnam War (Cooke, 1991). More than 150 of them became functionally blind, even though their eyes appeared intact and electrophysiological monitoring showed that visual stimuli registered in their visual cortex (Fig. 17.16). Many of the victims reported that their blindness came on suddenly after they witnessed traumatic scenes of murder. Were the sights from the outer world so painful that the visual system involuntarily shut down? An intriguing but as yet unanswered question is how cultural factors might have affected the development of this response to trauma.

To Freud, conversion symptoms were a symbolic expression of an underlying conflict that aroused so much anxiety that the ego kept the conflict in the unconscious by converting the anxiety into a physical symptom. In one of Freud's cases, a young woman who was forced to take care of her hostile, verbally abusive and unappreciative father suddenly developed paralysis in her arm. According to Freud, this occurred when her repressed hostile impulses threatened to break through and cause her to strike him using that arm (Freud, 1935). Contemporary psychodynamic theorists continue to accept explanations consistent with Freud's beliefs (Phillips, 2001).

A predisposition to somatoform disorders may involve a combination of biological and psychological vulnerabilities. Somatoform disorders tend to run in families, though it is not clear whether this reflects the role of genetic factors, environmental learning and social reinforcement for bodily symptoms, or both (Trimble, 2003). Additionally, some people may experience internal sensations more vividly than others, or they may focus more attention on them. People with somatoform disorders are also very suggestible. One study found them to be far more responsive to hypnotic suggestions than were matched controls, and conversion clients' hypnotic susceptibility scores were significantly correlated with the number of conversion symptoms they reported (Roelofs et al., 2002).

The incidence of somatoform disorders tends to be much higher in cultures that discourage open discussion of emotions or that stigmatize psychological disorders (Tanaka-Matsumi and Draguns, 1997). Within western culture, there are subgroups, such as the police and military, where open discussion of feelings and self-disclosure of psychological problems are frowned on. In such settings, somatic symptoms may be the only acceptable outlet for emotional distress. The same may occur in people who are so emotionally constricted that they cannot acknowledge their emotions or verbally communicate them to others (Trae and Deighton, 2000).

DISSOCIATIVE DISORDERS

dissociative disorders

a breakdown of normal personality integration, resulting in significant alterations in memory or identity

psychogenic amnesia

a person responds to a stressful event with extensive but selective memory loss

Ordinarily, personality has unity and coherence, and the many facets of the self are integrated so that people act, think, and feel with some degree of consistency. Memory plays a critical role in this integration, for it connects past with present and provides a sense of personal identity that extends over time. **Dissociative disorders** involve a breakdown of normal personality integration, resulting in significant alterations in memory or identity. Three forms that such disorders can take are *psychogenic amnesia*, *psychogenic fugue* and *dissociative identity disorder*.

In **psychogenic amnesia**, a person responds to a stressful event with extensive but selective memory loss. Some people can remember nothing about their past. Others can no longer recall specific events, people or places, although other contents of memory, such as cognitive, language and motor skills remain intact.

Psychogenic fugue is a more profound dissociative disorder in which a person loses all sense of personal identity, gives up his or her customary life, wanders to a new faraway location and establishes a new identity. Usually the fugue (derived from the Latin word *fugere*, 'to flee') is triggered by a highly stressful event or trauma, and it may last from a few hours or days to several years. Some adolescent runaways have been found to be in a fugue state, and married fugue victims may marry someone else and start a new career (Loewenstein, 1991). Typically the fugue ends when the person suddenly recovers his or her original identity and 'wakes up', mystified and distressed at being in a strange place under strange circumstances.

Dissociative Identity (Multiple Personality) Disorder

In **dissociative identity disorder (DID)** (formerly called multiple personality disorder), two or more separate personalities coexist in the same person. Dissociative identity disorder is the most striking and widely publicized of the dissociative disorders, and several celebrated cases have been the topic of books and movies, such as *Sybil*, *The Three Faces of Eve* and *Psycho* (Fig. 17.17). In DID, a primary personality, or *host personality*, appears more often than the others (called *alters*), but each personality has its own integrated set of memories and behaviours. The personalities may or may not know about the existence of the others. They can differ in age and gender. The personalities can differ not only mentally and behaviourally but also physiologically, as in the following case.

> A 38-year-old woman named Margaret was admitted to a hospital with paralysis of her legs following a minor car accident. During the course of her interview the woman, a member of an ultra-religious sect, reported that she sometimes heard a strange voice inside her threatening to 'take over completely.' The physician suggested that she let the voice 'take over.' Here is his report of what happened:
>
> The woman closed her eyes, clenched her fists, and grimaced for a few moments during which she was out of contact with those in the room. Suddenly she opened her eyes and one was in the presence of another person. Her name, she said, was 'Harriet.' Whereas Margaret had been paralysed, and complained of fatigue, headache, and backache, Harriet felt well and she at once proceeded to walk around the room unaided. She spoke scornfully of Margaret's religiousness, her invalidism, and her puritanical life, professing that she herself liked to drink and 'go partying' but that Margaret was always going to church and reading the Bible.... At length, at the interviewer's suggestion, Harriet reluctantly agreed to 'bring Margaret back' and after more grimacing and fist clenching, Margaret reappeared paralyzed, complaining of her headache and backache, and completely amnesic for the brief period of Harriet's release from her prison. (Nemiah, 1978, pp. 179–80)

Mental health workers and researchers have reported dramatic differences among the 'alter' personalities of those with DID, including physical health differences, voice changes and even changes in right- and left-handedness. Some clients have severe allergies when one personality is present but no allergies when the others are active. One client nearly died of a violent allergic

psychogenic fugue
is a more profound dissociative disorder in which a person loses all sense of personal identity, gives up his or her customary life, wanders to a new faraway location and establishes a new identity

dissociative identity disorder (DID)
two or more separate personalities coexist in the same person

FIGURE 17.17

In one celebrated depiction of dissociative identity disorder, motel clerk Norman Bates is shocked to discover the body of a woman murdered in her shower by his mother (actually his 'alter' personality) in the movie *Psycho*.

Focus 17.16
Summarize the trauma-dissociation theory of DID. On what grounds do critics challenge and explain DID?

reaction to a bee sting; a week later, when an 'alter' personality was active, another sting produced no reaction. Females with DID frequently have different menstrual cycles for each female personality; one woman had three periods per month. Others need spectacles with different prescriptions for different personalities; one may be far-sighted, another near-sighted (Miller et al., 1991). Those people with epilepsy and DID often have their seizures in one personality but not another (Drake et al., 1988).

What Causes DID?

According to Frank Putnam's **trauma-dissociation theory**, the development of new personalities occurs in response to severe stress. For the vast majority of clients, this begins in early childhood, frequently in response to physical or sexual abuse. Putnam (1989) studied the life histories of 100 diagnosed DID cases and found that 97 of them reported severe abuse and trauma in early and middle childhood, a time when children's identities are not well established and it is quite easy for them to dissociate. Putnam believes that in response to the trauma and their helplessness to resist it, children may engage in something akin to self-hypnosis and dissociate from reality. They create an alternate identity to detach themselves from the trauma, to transfer what is happening to someone else who can handle it, and to blunt the pain. Over time, it is theorized, the protective functions served by the new personality remain separate in the form of an alternate personality rather than being integrated into the host personality (Meyer and Osborne, 1987; Putnam, 2000).

Dissociative identity disorder has become a controversial diagnosis. Friedl and Draijer (2000) looked at Dutch psychiatric clients and 2 per cent of the clients they saw over 12 months were identified as having DID, significantly lower than many similarly made US-based estimates. Some critics question how often it actually occurs, and others question its very existence (Beahrs, 1994; Spanos, 1994). Prior to 1970, only about 100 cases had been reported worldwide, and even today DID is virtually unknown in many cultures, including Japan (Takahashi, 1990). But after the disorder was highly publicised in popular books and films, many additional cases appeared, numbering in the tens of thousands by the mid-1990s. The number of alternate personalities also had increased from two or three to an average of about 15 (Spanos, 1994). Could this dramatic increase in the prevalence of DID and number of alters be the result of publicity and client or therapist expectations? As we noted in our discussion of hypnosis in Chapter 6, people can become so immersed in an imagined role (such as an 'alter' personality) that it becomes quite real to them, and they act accordingly (Spanos, 1996). The controversy that swirls around DID is inspiring research that may advance our understanding of factors that can produce alterations in memory, physiological responses and behaviour.

WHAT DO YOU THINK?

DID: DISSOCIATION OR ROLE PLAYING?

Suppose you knew of several experimental studies that convincingly demonstrated that average people could, by means of role-playing, produce all of the DID phenomena described in this section. What would this tell you about the validity of the DID cases described by mental-health workers? Think about it, then see the discussion on p. 836.

IN REVIEW

- Somatoform disorders involve physical complaints that do not have a physiological explanation. They include hypochondriasis, pain disorders and conversion disorders.

- Familial similarities in somatoform disorders may have a biological basis, or they may be the result of environmental shaping through attention and sympathy. Somatoform clients may be highly vigilant and reactive to somatic symptoms. Such disorders tend to occur with greater frequency in cultures that discourage open expression of negative emotions.

- Dissociative disorders involve losses of memory and personal identity. The major dissociative disorders are psychogenic amnesia, psychogenic fugue and dissociative identity disorder (DID).

- The trauma-dissociation theory holds that DID emerges when children dissociate to defend themselves from severe trauma or sexual abuse. This model has been challenged by other theorists who believe that multiple personalities result from role immersion and therapist expectations.

MOOD DISORDERS

Another set of emotion-based disorders are **mood disorders**, which include depression and mania (excessive excitement). Together with anxiety disorders, mood disorders are the most frequently experienced psychological disorders. There is high *comorbidity* (co-occurrence) involving anxiety and mood disorders. About half of all depressed people also experience an anxiety disorder.

DEPRESSION

Almost everyone has experienced depression, at least in its milder and more temporary forms. Loss and pain are inevitable parts of life, and when they occur, most of us feel sad, discouraged, apathetic and passive. The future looks bleak, and some of the zest goes out of living. Such reactions are not unheard of and usually fade after the event has passed or as the person becomes accustomed to the new situation.

In clinical depression, however, the frequency, intensity and duration of depressive symptoms are out of proportion to the person's life situation. Some people may respond to a minor setback or loss with **major depression**, an intense depressed state that leaves them unable to function effectively in their lives. Mark, the young man described at the beginning of the chapter, suffers from a major depression. Other people exhibit **dysthymia**, a less intense form of depression that has less dramatic effects on personal and occupational functioning. Dysthymia, though less intense, is a more chronic and longer-lasting form of misery, occurring for years on end with some intervals of normal mood that never last more than a few weeks or months.

The *negative mood state* is the core feature of depression. Alonso et al. (2004) reported that in Europe, 14 per cent of people they looked at indicate that they have suffered from a mood disorder of some kind. When depressed people are asked how they feel, they most commonly report sadness, misery and loneliness. Whereas people with anxiety disorders retain their capacity to experience pleasure, depressed people lose it (Mineka et al., 1998). Activities that used to bring satisfaction and happiness feel dull and flat. Even biological pleasures, such as eating and sex, lose their appeal.

Although depression is primarily a disorder of emotion or mood, there are three other types of symptoms: cognitive, motivational and somatic (physical) (Fig. 17.18). *Cognitive symptoms* are

mood disorders
include depression and mania (excessive excitement)

major depression
an intense depressed state that leaves them unable to function effectively in their lives

dysthymia
a less intense form of depression that has less dramatic effects on personal and occupational functioning

Focus 17.17
Describe the four classes of symptoms that characterize depression. What is bipolar disorder?

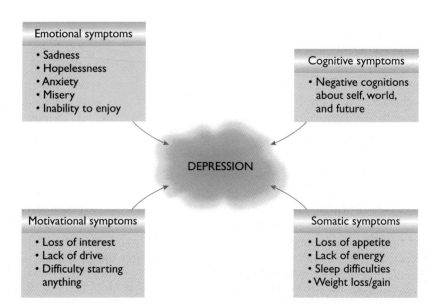

FIGURE 17.18

Facets of depression.

Depression includes emotional, cognitive, motivational and somatic features.

a central part of depression. Depressed people have difficulty concentrating and making decisions. They usually have low self-esteem, believing that they are inferior, inadequate and incompetent. When setbacks occur in their lives, depressed people tend to blame themselves; when failure has not yet occurred, they expect that it will and that it will be caused by their own inadequacies. Depressed people almost always view the future with great pessimism and hopelessness (Clark et al., 1999).

Motivational symptoms in depression involve an inability to get started and to perform behaviours that might produce pleasure or accomplishment. A depressed student may be unable to get out of bed in the morning, let alone go to class or study. Everything seems too much of an effort. In extreme depressive reactions, the person may have to be prodded out of bed, clothed and fed. In some cases of severe depression, the person's movements slow down and he or she walks or talks slowly and with excruciating effort.

Somatic (bodily) *symptoms* often include loss of appetite and weight loss in moderate and severe depression, whereas in mild depression, weight gain sometimes occurs as a person eats compulsively. Sleep disturbances, particularly insomnia, are common. Sleep disturbance and weight loss lead to fatigue and weakness, which tend to add to the depressed feelings. Depressed people also may lose sexual desire and responsiveness.

BIPOLAR DISORDER

When a person experiences only depression, the disorder is called *unipolar depression*. In a **bipolar disorder**, depression (which is usually the dominant state) alternates with periods of **mania**, a state of highly excited mood and behaviour that is quite the opposite of depression. In a manic state, mood is euphoric and cognitions are grandiose. The person sees no limits to what he or she can accomplish and fails to consider negative consequences that may ensue if grandiose plans are acted on. At a motivational level, manic behaviour is hyperactive. The manic person engages in frenetic activity, be it in work, in sexual relationships or in other areas of life. The nineteenth-century composer Robert Schumann produced 27 works during a one-year manic phase, but his productivity ground to a halt when he sank back into the depressive phase of his bipolar disorder (Jamison, 1995). Manic people can become very irritable and aggressive when their momentary goals are frustrated in any way. Stephen Fry, the writer and actor, has suffered with a bipolar disorder for many years, which he has described as playing a significant role in his expulsion from school, and a well publicized disappearance from a West End play some years ago.

bipolar disorder

depression (which is usually the dominant state) alternates with periods of mania

mania

a state of highly excited mood and behaviour that is quite the opposite of depression

In-Psych

Watch the video, 'Bipolar Disorder', in Chapter 17 of the In-Psych programme online for insights into one man's lifelong struggle to overcome bipolar disorder.

In a manic state, speech is often rapid or pressured, as if the person must say as many words as possible in the time allotted. With this flurry of activity comes a greatly lessened need for sleep. A person may go for several days without sleeping, until exhaustion inevitably sets in and the mania slows down. The following case illustrates a severe manic episode:

> Robert B, a 56-year-old dentist, awoke one morning with the idea that he was the most gifted dental surgeon in his area; his mission then was to provide service for as many persons as possible so that they could benefit from his talents. Consequently, he decided to enlarge his 2-chair practice to a 20-chair one, and his plan was to reconstruct his two dental offices into 20 booths so that he could simultaneously attend to as many clients. That very day he drew up the plans for this arrangement and telephoned a number of remodelers and invited them to submit bids for the work.
>
> Toward the end of that day he became irritated with the 'interminable delays' and, after he attended to his last client, rolled up his sleeves and began to knock down the walls of his dental offices. When he discovered that he couldn't manage this chore with the sledge hammer he had purchased for this purpose earlier, he became frustrated and proceeded to smash his more destructible tools, washbasins, and X-ray equipment. He justified this behavior in his own mind by saying, 'This junk is not suitable for the likes of me; it'll have to be replaced anyway.'
>
> He was in perpetual motion and his speech was 'overexcited.' When Robert was later admitted to a hospital, he could not sit in his chair; instead he paced the office floor like a caged animal. (Kleinmuntz, 1980, pp. 309–10)

PREVALENCE AND COURSE OF MOOD DISORDERS

Epidemiological studies in Europe suggest that at this moment, 8.5 per cent of people are suffering from a depressive disorder (Ayuso-Mateos et al. 2001). No age group is exempt from depression. It appears in infants as young as 6 months who have been separated from their mothers for prolonged periods. In some studies the rate of depressive symptoms in children and adolescents is as high as the adult rate (c.f. Essau and Petermann, 1999). The National Institute for Health and Clinical Excellence estimates that up to 75 per cent of cases of depression may be undetected, so the incidence in young people is much higher than the numbers that have been diagnosed suggests (Fig. 17.19).

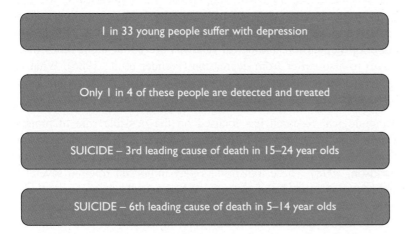

FIGURE 17.19

Depression in young people and children.

These statistics highlight the very high prevalence of depression in our communities, and the importance of detecting it. It is clear that many cases go undetected and in this vulnerable group, treatment.

SOURCE: National Institute of Health and Clinical Excellence, 2004.

Prevalence of depressive disorders is similar across socio-economic and ethnic groups, but there is a major sex difference in our culture. Although men and women do not differ in prevalence of bipolar disorder, women appear to be about twice as likely as men to suffer unipolar depression (Fig. 17.20). Women are most likely to suffer their first episode of depression in their twenties, men in their forties (Keyes and Goodman, 2006).

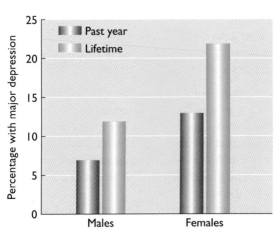

FIGURE 17.20

Sex differences in depression.

This graph shows the prevalence rates for major depression in men and women.

SOURCE: based on Kessler et al., 1994.

FIGURE 17.21

What follows major depression?

One of three outcomes may follow a major depressive episode. About 40 per cent never have a recurrence, perhaps 50 per cent have a recurrence and about 10 per cent suffer chronic (ever-present) depression.

Focus 17.18

What evidence exists for genetic and biochemical factors in depression and mania?

Many people who suffer depressive episodes never seek treatment. What is likely to happen to such people? Perhaps the one positive thing that can be said about depression is that it usually dissipates over time. After the initial episode, which typically comes on suddenly after a stressful experience, depression typically lasts an average of five to 10 months when untreated (Tollefson, 1993).

Once a depressive episode has occurred, one of three patterns may follow. In perhaps 40 per cent of all cases, clinical depression will not recur following recovery. Many other cases show a second pattern: recovery with recurrence. On average, these people will remain symptom-free for perhaps three years before experiencing another depressive episode of about the same severity and duration. The interval between subsequent episodes of depression tends to become shorter over the years (Rubin, 2000). Finally, about 10 per cent of people who have a major depressive episode will not recover and will remain chronically depressed (Fig. 17.21).

Manic episodes, though less common than depressive reactions, are far more likely to recur. Fewer than 1 per cent of the population experiences mania, but those who do are very likely to experience a recurrence of the reaction. Whether the reaction has occurred before or not is an extremely good indicator here of whether it will again (Di Marzo et al., 2006).

CAUSAL FACTORS IN MOOD DISORDERS

As in the case of anxiety disorders, the mood disorders are a product of interacting biological, psychological and environmental factors.

Biological Factors

Both genetic and neurochemical factors have been linked to depression (Donaldson, 1998). Genetic factors surface in both twin and adoption studies (McGuffin et al., 2005). Identical twins have a concordance rate of about 67 per cent for experiencing clinical depression, compared with a rate of only 15 per cent for fraternal twins (Gershon et al., 1989). Among adopted people who develop depression, biological relatives are about eight times more likely than adoptive relatives to also suffer from depression (Wender et al., 1986). What is likely to be inherited is a predisposition to develop a depressive disorder, given certain kinds of environmental factors such as significant losses and low social support (Barondes, 1999; Jang, 2005).

Increasingly, biological research has focused on the possible role of brain chemistry in depression. One influential theory holds that depression is a disorder of motivation caused by underactivity in a family of neurotransmitters that include norepinephrine, dopamine and serotonin (Davidson, 1998). These transmitters play important roles in several brain regions involved in experiencing reward and pleasure. When neural transmission decreases in these brain regions, the result is the lack of pleasure and loss of motivation that characterize depression (Donaldson, 1998; White and Milner, 1992). Also in support of this theory, several highly effective antidepressant drugs operate by increasing the activity of these neurotransmitters, thereby further stimulating the neural systems that underlie positive mood and goal-directed behaviour. A study by Lescia Tremblay and co-workers (2002) tested the amount of reward experienced by depressed clients when these centres were activated by a stimulant drug. As shown in Figure 17.22, severely depressed individuals showed a much stronger pleasure response to the drug, supporting the hypothesis of a 'pleasure deficit' in the brain. Later research by Ian

Gotlib and co-workers (2004a) using fMRI readings of emotion areas of the brain showed low levels of neuron responsiveness to both happy and sad scenes, as if the emotion response systems had shut down. This may account for the lack of positive emotionality and the 'emptiness' of the depressive emotional experience.

Bipolar disorder, in which depression alternates with less frequent periods of mania, has been studied primarily at the biological level because it appears to have a stronger genetic basis than does unipolar depression (Young and Joffe, 1997). Among both men and women, the lifetime risk of developing a bipolar disorder is just below 1 per cent. Yet about 50 per cent of clients with bipolar disorder have a parent, grandparent or child with the disorder (Barondes, 1999; Rubin, 2000). The concordance rate for bipolar disorder is five times higher in identical twins than in fraternal twins, suggesting a genetic link.

Manic disorders may stem from an overproduction of the same neurotransmitters that are underactive in depression. This might explain the symptom picture that is quite the opposite of that seen in depression. Significantly, lithium chloride, the drug most frequently used to calm manic disorders, works by decreasing the activity of these transmitters in the brain's motivational/pleasure activation system (LeMoal, 1999; Robinson, 1997).

Psychological Factors

Biological factors seem to increase vulnerability to certain types of psychological and environmental events that can then trigger the disorders. Other perspectives specify what those events might be.

Personality-based vulnerability   Psychoanalysts Karl Abraham (1911) and Sigmund Freud (1957) believed that early traumatic losses or rejections create vulnerability for later depression by triggering a grieving and rage process that becomes part of the individual's personality (Fig. 17.23). Subsequent losses and rejection reactivate the original loss and cause a reaction not only to the current event but also to the unresolved loss from the past.

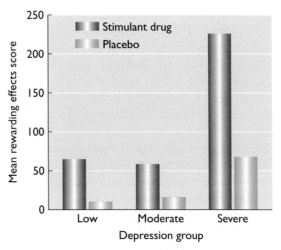

FIGURE 17.22

An underactive reward system?

This graph shows an increase in pleasure ratings produced by a stimulant drug or a placebo in non-depressed, moderately depressed and severely depressed males and females. The magnitude of the increase in pleasure reported by severely depressed people suggests a normally underactive reward system in the brain.

SOURCE: adapted from Tremblay et al., 2002.

Focus 17.19

Describe the cognitive triad, the depressive attributional pattern and learned helplessness in relation to depression.

FIGURE 17.23

Psychoanalysts believe that early catastrophic losses increase vulnerability to later depressive disorders.

Were he alive today, Freud would surely point to research by sociologists George Brown and Terrill Harris (1978) to support his theory of early loss. Brown and Harris interviewed women in London and found that the rate of depression among women who had lost their mothers before age 11 and who had also experienced a severe recent loss was almost three times higher than that among women who had experienced a similar recent loss but had not lost their mothers before age 11. Experiencing the death of a father during childhood is also associated with increased risk of later depression (Barnes and Prosen, 1985; Bowlby, 2000).

Cognitive processes According to Aaron Beck (1976), depressed people victimise themselves through their own beliefs that they are defective, worthless and inadequate. They also believe that whatever happens to them is bad and that negative things will continue happening because of their personal defects (Clark et al., 1989). This **depressive cognitive triad** of negative thoughts concerning (1) the world, (2) oneself and (3) the future seems to pop into consciousness automatically, and many depressed people report that they cannot control or suppress the negative thoughts (Wenzlaff et al., 1988). Depressed people also tend to recall most of their failures and few of their successes, and they tend to focus much of their attention on their perceived inadequacies (Clark et al., 1999; Haaga et al., 1991). Depressed people also detect pictures of sad faces at lower exposure times and remember them better than do non-depressed people (Gotlib et al., 2004b), indicating a perceptual and memory sensitivity to the negative.

As noted in the discussion of self-enhancement tendencies in Chapter 14, most people tend to take personal credit for the good outcomes in their lives and to blame their misfortunes on factors outside themselves, thereby maintaining and enhancing their self-esteem. According to Beck, depressed people do exactly the opposite: They exhibit a **depressive attributional pattern**, attributing successes or other positive events to factors outside the self while attributing negative outcomes to personal factors (Fig. 17.24). Beck believes that taking no credit for successes but blaming themselves for failures helps depressed people maintain low self-esteem and their belief that they are worthless failures. Quite literally, they cannot win, even when they do!

Glossary (margin)

depressive cognitive triad
negative thoughts concerning (1) the world, (2) oneself and (3) the future

depressive attributional pattern
attributing successes or other positive events to factors outside the self while attributing negative outcomes to personal factors

learned helplessness theory
depression occurs when people expect that bad events will occur and that there is nothing they can do to prevent them or cope with them

FIGURE 17.24

The depressive attributional pattern.

Cognitive theorists believe that the attributional patterns of depressed people are the opposite of the self-enhancing patterns that characterize non-depressed people. In the depressive attributional pattern, people attribute negative outcomes to themselves and positive outcomes to factors outside themselves.

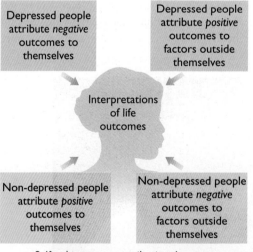

Depressive attributional pattern

Depressed people attribute *negative* outcomes to themselves

Depressed people attribute *positive* outcomes to factors outside themselves

Interpretations of life outcomes

Non-depressed people attribute *positive* outcomes to themselves

Non-depressed people attribute *negative* outcomes to factors outside themselves

Self-enhancement attributional pattern (non-depressed people)

Another prominent cognitive account of depression, **learned helplessness theory**, holds that depression occurs when people expect that bad events will occur and that there is nothing they can do to prevent them or cope with them (Abramson et al., 1978; Seligman and Isaacowitz, 2000). The depressive attributional pattern plays a central role in the learned helplessness model, but learned helplessness theorists take it a step further by specifying what the negative attributions for failures are like. They suggest that chronic and intense depression occurs as the result of negative attributions for failures that are personal ('It's all *my* fault'), stable ('I'll *always* be this way') and global ('I'm a *total* loser'). Thus people who attribute negative events in their lives to factors such as low intelligence, physical repulsiveness or an unlovable personality tend to believe that their personal defects will render them helpless to avoid negative events in the future, and their sense of hopelessness places them at significantly greater risk for depression.

Learning and environmental factors   The behavioural perspective also has important things to say about depression. Peter Lewinsohn and his colleagues (1985) believe that depression is usually triggered by a loss, by some other punishing event or by a drastic decrease in the amount of positive reinforcement that the person receives from his or her environment. As the depression begins to take hold, people stop performing behaviours that previously provided reinforcement, such as hobbies and socializing. Moreover, depressed people tend to make others feel anxious, depressed and hostile (Joiner and Coyne, 1999). Eventually, these other people begin to lose patience, failing to understand why the person does not snap out of it. This diminishes social support still further and may eventually cause depressed people to be abandoned by those who are most important to them (Nezlek et al., 2000). Longitudinal studies show that reductions in social support are a good predictor of subsequent depression (Burton, 2004). Figure 17.25 shows the cyclical course of depression.

Focus 17.20

How does Lewinsohn's learning theory explain the spiralling-downward course that occurs in depression?

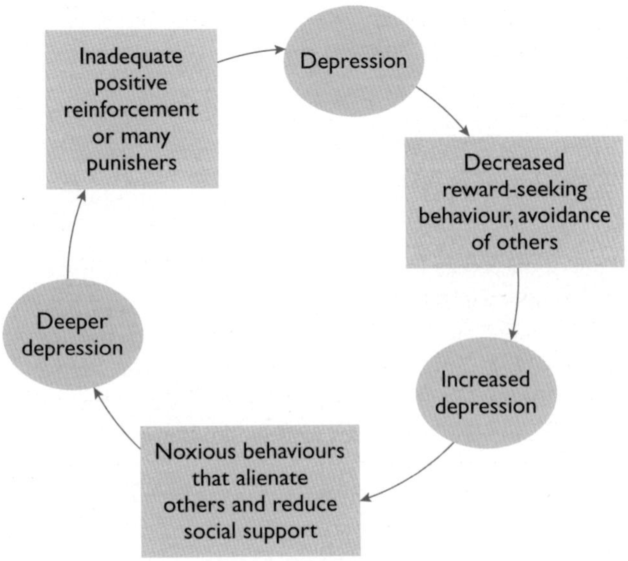

FIGURE 17.25

Lewinsohn's behavioural model of depression.

Behaviourists focus on the environmental causes and effects of depression. Depression results from loss of positive reinforcement and produces further declines in reinforcement and social support in a vicious-cycle fashion.

Behavioural theorists believe that to begin feeling better, depressed people must break this vicious cycle by initially forcing themselves to engage in behaviours that are likely to produce some degree of pleasure. Eventually, positive reinforcement produced by this process of *behavioural activation* will begin to counteract the depressive affect, undermine the sense of hopelessness that characterizes depression, and increase feelings of personal control over the environment (Martell et al., 2004).

Environmental factors may also help explain why depression tends to run in families. Constance Hammen (1991) studied the family histories of depressed people and concluded that children of depressed parents often experience poor parenting and many stressful experiences as they grow up. As a result, they may fail to develop good coping skills and a positive self-concept, making them more vulnerable later in life to stressful events that can trigger depressive reactions. This conclusion is supported by findings that children of depressed parents exhibit a significantly higher incidence of depression and other disorders as adolescents and young adults (Lieb et al., 2002).

Sociocultural Factors

Although depression exists in virtually all cultures, its prevalence, symptom pattern and causes reflect cultural variation (Lopez and Guarnaccia, 2000). For example, the prevalence of depressive disorders is far lower in Hong Kong and Taiwan than in western nations. People in these societies tend to have strong social support from family and other groups, which helps reduce the negative impact of loss and disappointments when they occur (Tseng et al., 1990).

Focus 17.21

How are sociocultural factors related to prevalence, manifestations and sex differences in depression?

Focus 17.22

What are the major motives and risk factors for suicide? Describe four guidelines for helping a suicidal person.

Cultural factors also can affect the ways in which depression is manifested. Feelings of guilt and personal inadequacy seem to predominate in North American and Western European countries, whereas somatic symptoms of fatigue, loss of appetite and sleep difficulties are more often reported in Latin, Chinese and African cultures (Manson, 1994).

Finally, cultural factors may influence who develops depression. As noted earlier, women are about twice as likely as men to report feeling depressed in technologically advanced countries such as Canada, the USA and other western nations (Keyes and Goodman, 2006). Yet this sex difference is not found in developing countries (Culbertson, 1997; Nolen-Hoeksema, 1990). At present, we do not know why this pattern occurs, but attempts are under way to learn more about how the cultural environment influences the development of depression.

At one time or another, many depressed people consider suicide as a way to escape from the unhappiness of their lives. We now examine suicide, its causes and what can be done to prevent this tragic event.

APPLYING PSYCHOLOGICAL SCIENCE

UNDERSTANDING AND PREVENTING SUICIDE

suicide

the wilful taking of one's own life

Suicide is the wilful taking of one's own life. The World Health Organization (WHO) estimates that worldwide, nearly 500 000 people commit suicide each year – almost one per minute. Ten times that number engage in non-fatal suicide attempts. Gudjón Magnusson, the director for Europe in charge of mental health with the WHO told a ministerial summit on mental health that the suicide rate for Europe was 17.5 per every 100 000 (Fig. 17.26). This is extremely high and above the world average of 16 per 100 000. Of the 873 000 suicides worldwide, Europe has 163 000.

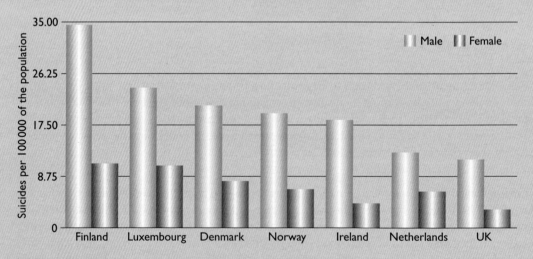

FIGURE 17.26

Suicide rates in countries in Western Europe.

SOURCE: World Health Organization, 2007.

Women attempt suicide about three times more often than men, but men are, on average, three times more likely to actually kill themselves. These differences may be due to (1) a higher incidence of depression in women and (2) men's choice of more violent and lethal methods, such as shooting themselves or jumping off buildings. The suicide rate for both men and women is higher among those who have been divorced or widowed. Women's suicides are more likely to be triggered, although not certain to be triggered by any means, by failures in love relationships, whereas career failure more often prompts men's suicides (Shneidman, 1976). A history of sexual or physical abuse significantly increases the likelihood of later suicide attempts (Garnefski and Arends, 1998).

Depression is one of the strongest predictors of suicide. About 15 per cent of clinically depressed individuals will eventually kill themselves, a rate that is 22 to 36 times higher than the suicide rate for the general population. An estimated 80 per cent of suicidal people are significantly depressed (Yen et al., 2003). It is noteworthy, however, that suicides do not usually occur when depression is deepest. Instead, suicide often occurs unexpectedly as a depressed person seems to be emerging from depression and feeling better. The lifting of depression may provide the energy needed to complete the suicidal act but not reduce the person's underlying sense of hopelessness and despair.

MOTIVES FOR SUICIDE

There appear to be two fundamental motivations for suicide: the desire to end one's life and the desire to manipulate and coerce other people into doing what the suicidal person wants (Beck et al., 1979; Shneidman, 1998). Those who wish to end their lives have basically given up. They see no other way to deal with intolerable emotional distress, and in death they see an end to their problems. In one study, 56 per cent of suicide attempts were classified as having been motivated by the desire to die (Beck, 1976). These attempts were accompanied by high levels of depression and hopelessness, and they tended to be more lethal than other suicide attempts. In some instances, a suicide decision is based on a desire to stop being a burden to others. High levels of impetuosity in the individual is also a factor in whether they may engage in a suicide attempt.

The second primary motivation for 'suicide' is manipulation of others. Many *parasuicides* (suicide attempts that do not end in death) are cries for help or attempts to coerce people to meet one's needs. Trying to prevent a lover from ending a relationship, induce guilt in others or dramatize one's suffering are manipulative motives. Manipulative suicide attempters tend to use less lethal means (such as drug overdose or wrist slashing) and to make sure help is available. In the study cited earlier (Beck, 1976), 13 per cent of the suicide attempts were classified as manipulative. The remaining 31 per cent combined the two types of motivation. A small minority of suicides result from altruistic decisions to sacrifice one's life for the survival of others; examples include the soldier who dives on a hand grenade to save his comrades' lives or the mother who elects to give birth rather than aborting her baby, knowing that she will die in the process.

WARNING SIGNS FOR SUICIDE

The best predictor of suicide attempts in both men and women is a verbal or behavioural threat to commit suicide, and such threats should always be taken seriously. One of the most destructive myths about suicide is that people who talk openly about suicide are just seeking attention and do not actually intend to carry out the act. Yet research shows that a high proportion of suicide attempts – perhaps 80 per cent – are preceded by some kind of warning (Bagley and Ramsay, 1997). Sometimes the warning is an explicit statement of intent, such as 'I don't want to go on living' or 'I won't be a burden much longer'. Other times, the warnings are more subtle, as when a person expresses hopelessness about the future, withdraws from others or from favourite activities, gives away treasured possessions, or takes unusual risks. Other important risk factors are a history of previous suicide attempts and a detailed plan that involves a lethal method (Chiles and Strossahl, 1995; Shneidman, 1998). Substance use and abuse also increase suicide risk (Yen et al., 2003).

SUICIDE PREVENTION: WHAT YOU CAN DO

Scientific research has taught us much about the dynamics and prevention of suicide. These findings provide the following guidelines for preventing this tragic answer to life's problems and for helping potentially suicidal people:

1. Another myth about suicide is that broaching the topic with a potentially suicidal person may prompt the person to carry out the act. In truth, the best first step if you suspect that someone may be suicidal is to ask the person directly whether he or she is considering suicide: 'Have you thought about hurting yourself or ending your life?' If the person responds affirmatively, try to find out if he or she has a plan or a time frame in mind. Do not be hesitant to approach the person. *Diffusion of responsibility* (discussed in Chapters 2 and 11) could result in your assuming that someone else is helping the person when in fact no one is (Goldsmith, 2003). Your ultimate goal should be to help the person receive assistance from a qualified professional as soon as possible, not to treat the person yourself. Nonetheless, you can take some immediate steps that may be helpful.

2. Many suicidal people feel alone in their misery. It is important to provide social support and empathy at this critical juncture. An expression of genuine concern can pave the way for other potentially helpful interventions (Barnett and Porter, 1998). For example, a frank discussion of the problem that is foremost in the person's life can be helpful. Suicidal people often feel totally overwhelmed by life, and focusing on a specific problem may help the person realize that it is not unsolvable and need not cloud his or her total perception of life.

3. When people are distressed and hopeless, their time orientation tends to narrow and they have difficulty seeing beyond their current distress. Try to help the person see his or her present situation within a wider time perspective and to consider positive possibilities that might exist in the future. In particular, discuss reasons for continuing to live, and focus on any doubts the person might have about electing suicide. For example, if the person indicates that his or her family will suffer greatly from the suicide, adopt this as one of your arguments for finding a different solution to the problem. Many suicidal people would like to feel that they do not have to commit suicide. Capitalise on such feelings.

4. If a person is suicidal, stay with him or her and seek professional assistance. Most cities have suicide-prevention centres that offer 24-hour services, including telephone and direct counselling. These centres are usually listed under *suicide* or *crisis* in the phone book.

IN REVIEW

- Mood disorders include several depressive disorders and bipolar disorder, in which intermittent periods of mania (intense mood and behaviour activation) occur. Depression has four sets of symptoms: emotional, cognitive, motivational and somatic. The symptoms of negative emotions and thoughts, loss of motivation and behavioural slowness are reversed in mania.

- Both genetic and neurochemical factors have been linked to depression. One prominent biochemical theory links depression to an underactivity of neurotransmitters (norepinephrine, dopamine and serotonin) that activate brain areas involved in pleasure and positive motivation. Drugs that relieve depression increase the activity of these transmitters. Bipolar disorder seems to have an even stronger genetic component than does unipolar depression.

- Psychoanalytic theorists view depression as a long-term consequence of traumatic losses and rejections early in life that create a personality vulnerability pattern.

- Cognitive theorists emphasize the role of negative beliefs about the self, the world and the future (the depressive cognitive triad) and describe a depressive attributional pattern, in which negative outcomes are attributed to personal causes and successes to situational causes. Seligman's theory of learned helplessness suggests that attributing negative outcomes to personal, stable and global causes fosters depression.

- The behavioural approach focuses on the vicious cycle in which depression-induced inactivity and aversive behaviours reduce reinforcement from the environment and thereby increase depression still further.

- Manipulation and a desire to escape distress are the two major motives for suicide. The risk for suicide increases if the person is depressed and has a lethal plan and a past history of parasuicide.

SCHIZOPHRENIA

Of all the psychological disorders, schizophrenia is the most bizarre and, in many ways, the most puzzling. It is also one of the most challenging disorders to treat effectively (Hogarty, 2003). Despite many theories of schizophrenia and thousands of research studies, a complete understanding of this disorder continues to elude us. **Schizophrenia** includes severe disturbances in thinking, speech, perception, emotion and behaviour (Herz and Marder, 2002). Schizophrenia is one of a family of *psychotic* disorders, all of which involve some loss of contact with reality, as well as bizarre behaviours and experiences.

The term *schizophrenia* was introduced by the Swiss psychiatrist Eugen Bleuler in 1911, but had been identified as a mental illness as early as 1887, by German physician Emile Kraepelin. Literally, schizophrenia means 'split mind', which has often led people to confuse schizophrenia with dissociative identity disorder ('split personality') or with a Dr Jekyll–Mr Hyde phenomenon. But multiple personalities are not what Bleuler had in mind when he coined the term. Instead, he intended to suggest that certain psychological functions, such as thought, language and emotion, which are normally integrated with one another, are somehow split apart or disconnected in schizophrenia.

CHARACTERISTICS OF SCHIZOPHRENIA

Schizophrenic disorders are identified, generally by the way that the sufferer has problems, or distortions of perception and thinking, and by the way that they show inappropriate or less-clear emotions. The person may hallucinate, both visually and auditorily, but most notably the latter. The person may share their most delicate and personal thoughts with others, where they would ordinarily not do so. Sounds and colours may seem out of the ordinary, appearing more vivid or altered in some way. There is often a belief that everyday situations have a meaning that they do not. These meanings are usually directed towards the sufferer, and may have a sinister quality to them. The mood of the sufferer is also severely affected, with the impression that the person could not care less about what is going on around them sometimes. Other mood variations may be present. The person may, sometimes appear to be catatonic. The onset of the problem may be acute, or it may occur gradually over time, the person developing odd thinking and conduct during this process. Sometimes people recover completely with treatment, and sometimes they do not. The gender split is approximately equal for men and women. (c.f. ICD-10).

The schizophrenic thought disorder sometimes entails **delusions**, false beliefs that are sustained in the face of evidence that normally would be sufficient to destroy them. A schizophrenic person might believe that his brain is being turned to glass by ray guns operated by his enemies from outer space (a *delusion of persecution*) or that Jesus Christ is one of his special agents (a *delusion of grandeur*). Several aspects of thought disorder were described by a schizophrenic client during a period of recovery:

> The most wearing aspect of schizophrenia is the fierce battle that goes on inside my head in which conflicts become unresolvable. I am so ambivalent that my mind can divide on a subject, and those two parts subdivide over and over until my mind feels like it is in pieces, and I am totally disorganized. At other times, I feel like I am trapped inside my head, banging against its walls, trying desperately to escape while my lips can utter only nonsense. (*New York Times*, 1986, p. C12)

---

schizophrenia
severe disturbances in thinking, speech, perception, emotion and behaviour

Focus 17.23
What is meant by the term schizophrenia? What are its major cognitive, behavioural, emotional and perceptual features?

delusions
false beliefs that are sustained in the face of evidence that normally would be sufficient to destroy them

(a)   (b)

FIGURE 17.27

(a) Clients diagnosed with schizophrenia are tormented by bizarre and intrusive thoughts and images. (b) This picture, drawn by a client diagnosed with schizophrenia, may offer insights into his subjective world.

hallucinations

false perceptions that have a compelling sense of reality

Perceptual disorganization and disordered thought become more pronounced as people progress in schizophrenia (McKenna and Oh, 2003). Unwanted thoughts constantly intrude into consciousness (Morrison, 2005). What the world might come to look like from inside the schizophrenic mind is illustrated in art created by schizophrenic clients during periods of disturbance (Fig. 17.27b). Some experience **hallucinations**, false perceptions that have a compelling sense of reality. Auditory hallucinations (typically voices speaking to the client) are most common, although visual and tactile hallucinations may also occur. This person describes his hallucinations:

> Recently, my mind has played tricks on me, creating The People inside my head who sometimes come out to haunt me and torment me. They surround me in rooms, hide behind trees and under the snow outside. They taunt me and scream at me and devise plans to break my spirit. The voices come and go, but The People are always there, always real. (*New York Times*, 1986, p. C12)

The language of people with schizophrenia is often disorganized, and it may contain strange words. 'I am here from a foreign university ... and you have to have a "plausity" of all acts of amendment to go through for the children's code ... and it is no mental disturbance or "putenance" ... it is an "amorition" law ... it is like their "privatilinia"' (Vetter, 1969, p. 189). Clients' language sometimes contains word associations that are based on rhymes or other associations rather than meaning. Consider the following conversation between a psychologist and a hospitalized schizophrenic:

> After two weeks, the psychologist said to him: 'As you say, you are wired precisely wrong. But why won't you let me see the diagram?' Carl answered: 'Never, ever will you find the lever, the eternalever that will sever me forever with my real, seal, deal, heel. It is not on my shoe, not even on the sole. It walks away.' (Rosenhan and Seligman, 1989, p. 369)

Schizophrenia can affect emotions in a number of ways. Many people with schizophrenia have *blunted affect*, manifesting less sadness, joy and anger than most people. Others have *flat affect*, showing almost no emotions at all. Their voices are monotonous, their faces impassive. *Inappropriate affect* can also occur, as in the following case:

The psychologist noted that Carl 'smiles when he is uncomfortable, and smiles more when in pain. He cries during television comedies. He seems angry when justice is done, frightened when someone compliments him, and roars with laughter on reading that a young child was burned in a tragic fire.' (Rosenhan and Seligman, 1989, p. 369)

SUBTYPES OF SCHIZOPHRENIA

Schizophrenia has cognitive, emotional and behavioural facets that can vary widely from case to case. The DSM-IV-TR differentiates among four major subtypes of schizophrenia:

1. **Paranoid schizophrenia**, whose most prominent features are delusions of persecution, in which people believe that others mean to harm them, and delusions of grandeur, in which they believe they are enormously important. Suspicion, anxiety, or anger may accompany the delusions, and hallucinations may also occur in this subtype.

2. **Disorganized schizophrenia**, whose central features are confusion and incoherence, together with severe deterioration of adaptive behaviour, such as personal hygiene, social skills and self-care. Thought disorganization is often so extreme that it is difficult to communicate with these individuals. Their behaviour often appears silly and childlike, and their emotional responses are highly inappropriate. People with disorganized schizophrenia are usually unable to function on their own.

3. **Catatonic schizophrenia**, characterized by striking motor disturbances ranging from muscular rigidity to random or repetitive movements. People with catatonic schizophrenia sometimes alternate between stuporous states, in which they seem oblivious to reality, and agitated excitement, during which they can be dangerous to others. While in a stuporous state, they may exhibit *waxy flexibility*, in which their limbs can be moulded by another person into grotesque positions that they will then maintain for hours (Fig. 17.28).

4. **Undifferentiated schizophrenia**, a category assigned to people who exhibit some of the symptoms and thought disorders of the above categories but who do not have enough of the specific criteria to be diagnosed in those categories.

Focus 17.24

Describe the four major subtypes of schizophrenic disorders. What are positive and negative symptoms and their significance?

In-Psych

What is it like for a mathematical genius and his similarly talented son to live with schizophrenia? View the video, 'Beautiful Minds: An Interview with John Nash and Son', in Chapter 14 of the In-Psych programme online to find out.

Focus 17.25

Describe the evidence for genetic, neurological, and biochemical factors in schizophrenia.

paranoid schizophrenia

most prominent features are delusions of persecution, in which people believe that others mean to harm them, and delusions of grandeur, in which they believe they are enormously important

disorganized schizophrenia

central features are confusion and incoherence, together with severe deterioration of adaptive behaviour, such as personal hygiene, social skills and self-care

catatonic schizophrenia

characterized by striking motor disturbances ranging from muscular rigidity to random or repetitive movements

undifferentiated schizophrenia

a category assigned to people who exhibit some of the symptoms and thought disorders of the above categories but who do not have enough of the specific criteria to be diagnosed in those categories

FIGURE 17.28

The woman pictured here exhibits catatonic rigidity. She might hold this position for several hours. If someone were to move her limbs into another position, she would maintain that position, a phenomenon known as *waxy flexibility*.

positive symptoms
bizarre behaviours such as delusions, hallucinations, and disordered speech and thinking

negative symptoms
an absence of normal reactions, such as lack of emotional expression, loss of motivation and an absence of speech

In addition to these formal categories, many mental health workers and researchers divide schizophrenic reactions into two main categories on the basis of two classes of symptoms. One type is characterized by a predominance of **positive symptoms**, bizarre behaviours such as delusions, hallucinations, and disordered speech and thinking. These symptoms are called *positive* because they represent pathological extremes of normal processes. The second type features **negative symptoms** – an absence of normal reactions, such as lack of emotional expression, loss of motivation and an absence of speech (Herz and Marder, 2002).

The distinction between positive- and negative-symptom subtypes (first identified by Bleuler) seems to be an important one. Researchers have found differences in brain function between schizophrenics having positive symptoms and those with primarily negative symptoms (Gur et al., 1998; Zakzanis, 1998). The subtypes also show differences in life history and prognosis. Negative symptoms are likely to be associated with a long history of poor functioning prior to diagnosis and with a poor outcome following treatment (McGlashan and Fenton, 1992). In contrast, positive symptoms, especially those associated with a diagnosis of paranoid schizophrenia, are associated with good functioning prior to breakdown and a better prognosis for eventual recovery, particularly if the symptoms came on suddenly and were preceded by a history of relatively good adjustment (Fenton and McGlashan, 1991a; 1991b).

The data for prevalence is not at all clear. Some studies have it as low as 0.5 per 1000 and some as high as 17 per 1000. Generally, the agreed figure is something between three and 10 per 10 000 people worldwide, and this equates to approximately 0.5 per cent of the world's population. Staggeringly, the prevalence of schizophrenia is approximately twice that of Alzheimer's disease, and approximately six times that of (insulin-dependent) diabetes. However, schizophrenic clients occupy a greater proportion of beds in mental hospitals than their prevalence would suggest they might. Many who are not hospitalized have serious difficulty functioning. About 10 per cent of people with schizophrenia remain permanently impaired, and 65 per cent show intermittent periods of normal functioning. The ICD-10 indicates that the rest, approximately 25 per cent recover from the disorder fully.

CAUSAL FACTORS IN SCHIZOPHRENIA

Because of the seriousness of the disorder and the many years of anguish and incapacitation that its victims are likely to experience, schizophrenia has long been a focus of research. There is a growing consensus that schizophrenia results from a biologically based vulnerability factor that is set into motion by psychological and environmental events (Herz and Marder, 2002; McGuffin et al., 2005).

Biological Factors

Genetic predisposition   Strong evidence exists for a genetic predisposition to schizophrenia, though the specific genes involved and their roles in creating the disposition are still unknown (Jang, 2005; McGuffin et al., 2005). As Figure 17.29 shows, the more closely one is related to a person diagnosed with schizophrenia, the greater is the likelihood of developing the disorder during one's lifetime. Twin studies show that identical twins have higher concordance rates than fraternal twins, and adoption studies show much higher concordance with biological parents than with adoptive parents (Kety, 1988; Wahlberg et al., 1997). But, again, genetics do not by themselves account for the development of schizophrenia. If they did, the concordance rate in identical twins would be 100 per cent, not 48 per cent.

Brain abnormalities   Brain scans have indicated a number of structural abnormalities in the brains of schizophrenic clients. According to the *neurodegenerative hypothesis*, destruction of neural tissue can cause schizophrenia (Weinberger and McClure, 2002). Magnetic resonance imaging (MRI) studies have shown mild to moderate *brain atrophy*, a general loss or deterioration of neurons in the cerebral cortex and limbic system, together with enlarged ventricles

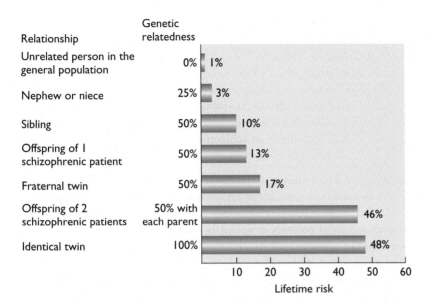

Relationship	Genetic relatedness
Unrelated person in the general population	0% — 1%
Nephew or niece	25% — 3%
Sibling	50% — 10%
Offspring of 1 schizophrenic patient	50% — 13%
Fraternal twin	50% — 17%
Offspring of 2 schizophrenic patients	50% with each parent — 46%
Identical twin	100% — 48%

Lifetime risk

FIGURE 17.29

Genes and schizophrenia.

The degree of risk for developing schizophrenia in one's lifetime correlates highly with the degree of genetic relationship with someone who has that disorder. These data summarize the results of 40 concordance studies conducted in many countries.
SOURCE: based on Gottesman, 1991.

(cavities that contain cerebrospinal fluid; Fig. 17.30). The atrophy is centred in brain regions that influence cognitive processes and emotion, which may help explain the thought disorders and inappropriate emotions that are seen in such clients. Likewise, MRI images of the thalamus, which collects and routes sensory input to various parts of the brain, reveal abnormalities (Williamson, 2006). This may help account for the disordered attention and perception reported by those with schizophrenia whose cerebral cortex might be getting garbled or unfiltered information from the thalamus (Andreason et al., 1994). All these structural differences are more common in clients who exhibit the negative-symptom pattern (Herz and Marder, 2002). As we have seen, these clients have a poorer chance of recovery than those with the positive-symptom pattern. Most recently, Job et al. (2006) have used MRI to show that the density of grey matter and how it changes over time is a useful predictor of whether someone is at risk of schizophrenia. The research, carried out in Edinburgh, looked at people with relatives with schizophrenia, and who were therefore deemed 'at risk'. Job and his team predicted whether the person scanned would develop schizophrenia and they were correct on an amazing 90 per cent of occasions.

Biochemical factors and food   Dopamine, a major excitatory neurotransmitter, may play a key role in schizophrenia. According to the **dopamine hypothesis**, the symptoms of schizophrenia – particularly positive symptoms – are produced by overactivity of the dopamine system in

dopamine hypothesis
the symptoms of schizophrenia – particularly positive symptoms – are produced by overactivity of the dopamine system in areas of the brain that regulate emotional expression, motivated behaviour and cognitive functioning

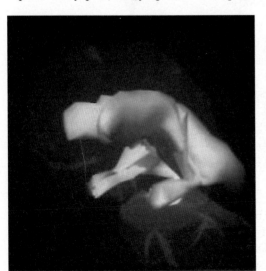
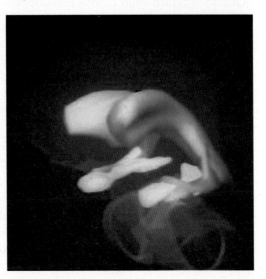

FIGURE 17.30

Schizophrenia and the brain.

One difference between the brains of schizophrenics and non-schizophrenics is enlarged ventricles (the butterfly-shaped spaces seen in the middle of the MRIs) in the schizophrenic brain (right). Findings like these support the position that brain abnormalities play a role in schizophrenia.

areas of the brain that regulate emotional expression, motivated behaviour and cognitive functioning (Heinrichs, 2001). People diagnosed with schizophrenia have more dopamine receptors on neuron membranes than do non-schizophrenics, and these receptors seem to be overreactive to dopamine stimulation (Black et al., 1988; Wong et al., 1986). Additional support comes from the finding that the effectiveness of antipsychotic drugs used to treat schizophrenia is positively related to their ability to reduce dopamine-produced synaptic activity (Creese et al., 1976; Green, 1997). Other neurotransmitter systems are probably involved in this complex disorder as well. The serotonin (5-HT) hypothesis of schizophrenia for instance, indicates the possible role of this particular neurotransmitter in schizophrenia.

The biochemical and brain findings concerning schizophrenia are intriguing. What is not clear is whether they cause the disorder or are caused by it. Work from the Institute of Psychiatry's neurochemical imaging team is showing further links between schizophrenia and the dopamine system, and most recently a deficit in schizophrenics in the NDMA (N-methyl-d-asparte) system using a technique called SPET (Single Photon Emission Tomography) (Pilowsky et al. 2006). Future research is almost certain to reveal other biological bases for the complex disorders of schizophrenia. The relationship between food and schizophrenia is under investigation. Christensen and Christensen (1988) suggest that diet may be a factor in schizophrenia, particularly fat consumption, and Peleg et al. (2004) have shown a possible relationship between the consumption of gluten and schizophrenia.

Interestingly, the degenerative hypothesis and dopamine hypothesis have recently been described as one (Walker and Diforio, 1997). Increasing the quantity of dopamine can indeed result in the person developing positive symptoms. However, larger concentrations of dopamine are neurotoxic, and neurons are destroyed, which results in a degeneration of the brain, which in turn results in a reoccurrence of the original symptoms.

Psychological Factors

Freud and other psychoanalytic thinkers viewed schizophrenia as a retreat from unbearable stress and conflict. For Freud, schizophrenia represented an extreme example of the defence mechanism of **regression**, in which a person retreats to an earlier and more secure (even infantile) stage of psychosocial development in the face of overwhelming anxiety. Other psychodynamic thinkers, focusing on the interpersonal withdrawal that is an important feature of schizophrenia, view the disorder as a retreat from an interpersonal world that has become too stressful to deal with. Although Freud's regression explanation has not received much direct research support (Fisher and Greenberg, 1996), the belief that life stress is a causal factor is generally accepted today (Crook and Copolov, 2000).

Some cognitive theorists believe that people with schizophrenias have a defect in the attentional mechanism that filters out irrelevant stimuli, so that they are overwhelmed by both internal and external stimuli (Hemsley, 1996). Sensory input thus becomes a chaotic flood, and irrelevant thoughts and images flash into consciousness. The stimulus overload produces distractability, thought disorganization, and the sense of being overwhelmed by disconnected thoughts and ideas. As one schizophrenic noted, 'Everything seems to come pouring in at once … I can't seem to keep anything out' (Carson et al., 1988, p. 329). The recent MRI findings of thalamic abnormalities described previously may help explain how this stimulus overload could occur through a malfunction of the brain's switchboard.

Environmental Factors

Stressful life events seem to play an important role in the emergence of schizophrenic behaviour. These events tend to cluster in the two or three weeks preceding the 'psychotic break', when the acute signs of the disorder appear (Day et al., 1987). Stressful life events seem to interact with biological or personality vulnerability factors. A highly vulnerable person may

---

regression

a person retreats to an earlier and more secure (even infantile) stage of psychosocial development in the face of overwhelming anxiety

Focus 17.26

How do psychoanalytic and cognitive theorists explain the symptoms of schizophrenia?

require little in the way of life stress to reach the breaking point (van Praag, 2004). In one study, psychotic and non-psychotic people rated their emotional responses as they encountered stressful events in their daily lives. Psychotic individuals reacted to their stressors with more intense negative emotions, suggesting that emotional over-reactivity may be a vulnerability factor (Myin-Germeys et al., 2001).

Family dynamics have long been a prime suspect in the origins of schizophrenia, but the search for parent or family characteristics that might cause the disorder has been largely unsuccessful. Significantly, children of biologically normal parents who are raised by schizophrenic adoptive parents do *not* show an increased risk of developing schizophrenia (Kety, 1988). Although persons with schizophrenia often come from families with problems, the nature and seriousness of those problems are not different from those of families in which non-schizophrenics are raised.

This does not mean that family dynamics are not important; rather, it may mean that an individual must have a biological vulnerability factor in order to be damaged by stressful family events to such a degree. Indeed, there is evidence that this vulnerability factor may appear early in life. In one study, researchers analysed home movies showing pre-schizophrenic children (those who were later to develop schizophrenic behaviours) and their non-schizophrenic brothers and sisters. Even at these early ages – sometimes as young as 2 years old – pre-schizophrenic children tended to show more odd and uncoordinated movements and less emotional expressiveness, especially for positive emotions (Grimes and Walker, 1994). These behavioural oddities may not only reflect a vulnerability factor, but they may also help to create environmental stress by evoking negative reactions from others.

Although researchers have had difficulty pinpointing family factors that contribute to the *initial* appearance of schizophrenia, one consistent finding is that previously hospitalized schizophrenics are more likely to relapse if they return to a home environment that is high in a factor called *expressed emotion* (Vaughn and Leff, 1976). **Expressed emotion** involves high levels of criticism ('All you do is sit in front of that television'), hostility ('We're getting sick and tired of your craziness'), and over-involvement ('You're not going out unless I go with you'). One review of 26 studies showed that within nine to 12 months of their return home, an average relapse rate of 48 per cent occurred in clients whose families were high in expressed emotion, compared with a relapse rate of 21 per cent when families were low in this factor (Kavanagh, 1992).

Before we conclude that high expressed emotion causes clients to relapse, however, we should note a finding from another study in which researchers videotaped actual interactions involving clients and their families (Rosenfarb et al., 1995). Analyses of the videotapes revealed that families high in expressed emotion did indeed make more negative comments to clients when they engaged in strange behaviours, but they also showed that the clients in these families engaged in about four times as many strange and disruptive behaviours, clouding the issue of what causes what. Thus high expressed emotion may be either a cause of or a response to clients' disordered behaviours. Because individuals with schizophrenia may be overly sensitive to stress, even mildly negative family reactions may trigger underlying biological vulnerabilities that could result in relapse (Hooley, 2004).

Sociocultural Factors

Sociocultural factors are undoubtedly linked to schizophrenia (Murray et al., 2003). Many studies have found that the prevalence of schizophrenia is highest in lower-socio-economic populations (Fig. 17.31). Why is this? Is poverty a cause of schizophrenia, or is it an effect of the disorder? Two views give opposite answers. The **social causation hypothesis** attributes the higher prevalence of schizophrenia to the higher levels of stress that low-income people experience, particularly within urban environments. In contrast, the **social drift hypothesis** proposes

expressed emotion
involves high levels of criticism, hostility and over-involvement

social causation hypothesis
attributes the higher prevalence of schizophrenia to the higher levels of stress that low-income people experience

social drift hypothesis
proposes that as people develop schizophrenia, their personal and occupational functioning deteriorates, so that they drift down the socio-economic ladder

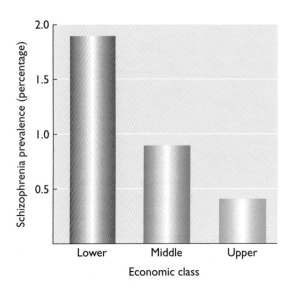

FIGURE 17.31

Social class and schizophrenia.

This graph shows the relation between economic status and prevalence of schizophrenia. Is economic status a cause or an effect of schizophrenia? Or does some other factor cause both?

SOURCE: based on Keith et al., 1991.

that as people develop schizophrenia, their personal and occupational functioning deteriorates, so that they drift down the socio-economic ladder into poverty and migrate to economically depressed urban environments. Perhaps social causation and social drift are both at work, for the factors that link poverty, social and environmental stressors, and schizophrenia are undoubtedly complex.

In contrast to most of the disorders we have described so far, schizophrenia may be a culture-free disorder. A worldwide epidemiological study sponsored by the World Health Organization indicated that the prevalence of schizophrenia is not dramatically different throughout the world (Jablensky et al., 1992). However, researchers have found that the likelihood of recovery is greater in developing countries than in the developed nations of North America and Western Europe. This may reflect a stronger community orientation and greater social support extended to disturbed people in developing countries (Tanaka-Matsumi and Draguns, 1997).

Schizophrenia reflects complex interactions among biological, psychological, and environmental factors. Figure 17.32 presents prominent causal factors identified at these levels of analysis.

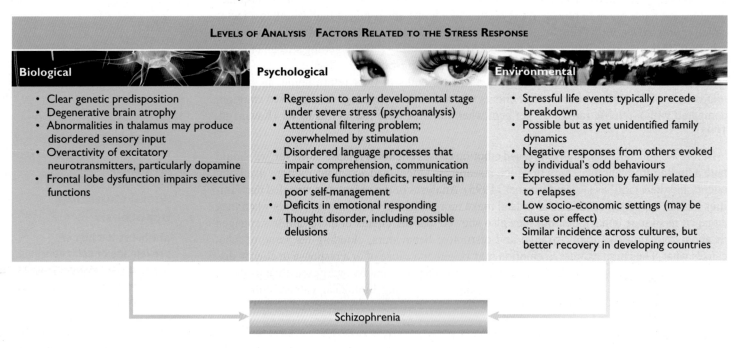

FIGURE 17.32

Levels of analysis: factors related to schizophrenia.

IN REVIEW

- Schizophrenia is a psychotic disorder featuring disordered thinking and language; poor contact with reality; flat, blunted or inappropriate emotion; and disordered behaviour. The cognitive portion of the disorder can involve delusions (false beliefs) or hallucinations (false perceptions).

- Schizophrenias have been categorized in a number of ways. The DSM-IV-TR lists four subtypes: paranoid, disorganized, catatonic and undifferentiated. Another categorization is based on the nature of the symptoms: positive versus negative. Positive symptoms, such as delusions or hallucinations, predict a better outcome than negative symptoms, such as lack of emotional expression.

- Psychoanalytic theorists regard schizophrenia as a profound regression to a primitive stage of psychosocial development in response to unbearable stress, particularly within the family. Stressful life events do often precede a schizophrenic episode, but researchers have not been successful in identifying a family pattern related to the onset of schizophrenia. However, expressed emotion is a family variable related to relapse among formerly hospitalized schizophrenic individuals.

- There is strong evidence for a genetic predisposition to schizophrenia that makes some people particularly vulnerable to stressful life events. The dopamine hypothesis states that schizophrenia involves overactivity of the dopamine system, resulting in too much stimulation.

- Cognitive theorists focus on the thought disorder that is central to schizophrenia. One idea is that people with schizophrenia have a defect in their attentional filters, so that they are overwhelmed by internal and external stimuli and become disorganized. Deficiencies may also exist in the executive functions needed to organize behaviour.

- Sociocultural accounts of the higher incidence of schizophrenia at lower socio-economic levels include the social causation hypothesis, which attributes schizophrenia to the higher levels of life stress that poor people experience, and the competing social drift hypothesis, which attributes the relation to the downward drift into poverty as the disorder progresses. Schizophrenia does not appear to differ in prevalence across cultures.

PERSONALITY DISORDERS

People diagnosed with **personality disorders** exhibit stable, ingrained, inflexible and maladaptive ways of thinking, feeling and behaving. In some situations these traits may are not only acceptable but desirable. For instance, stable, ingrained and inflexible thinking might describe a solid, reliable and driven thinker. However, when those suffering with a personality disorder encounter situations in which their typical behaviour patterns do not work, they are likely to intensify their inappropriate ways of coping, their emotional controls may break down and unresolved conflicts tend to re-emerge (Lenzenweger and Clarkin, 2005; Millon et al., 2004).

Personality disorders are an important part of the DSM system because they increase the likelihood of acquiring several Axis I (symptom) disorders, particularly anxiety, depression and substance-abuse problems. They are also associated with a poorer course of recovery from these disorders. Ann Massion and co-workers (2002) followed people suffering from anxiety disorders for five years and found that those also diagnosed with personality disorders were 30 to 40 per cent less likely to recover from their anxiety disorders.

Table 17.3 briefly describes the 10 personality disorders in Axis II of DSM-IV-TR. The disorders are divided into three clusters that capture important commonalities: dramatic and impulsive behaviours, anxious and fearful behaviours, and odd and eccentric behaviours.

> **personality disorders**
> exhibit stable, ingrained, inflexible and maladaptive ways of thinking, feeling and behaving

TABLE 17.3 DSM-IV-TR PERSONALITY DISORDERS AND THEIR MAJOR FEATURES

Dramatic/impulsive cluster

Antisocial personality disorder: severe irresponsible and antisocial behaviour beginning in childhood and continuing past age 18; impulsive need gratification and lack of empathy for others; often highly manipulative and seem to lack conscience

Histrionic personality disorder: excessive, dramatic emotional reactions and attention seeking; often sexually provocative; highly impressionable and suggestible; out of touch with negative feelings

Narcissistic personality disorder: grandiose fantasies or behaviour, lack of empathy, and oversensitivity to evaluation; constant need for admiration from others; proud self-display

Borderline personality disorder: pattern of severe instability of self-image, interpersonal relationships and emotions, often expressing alternating extremes of love and hatred towards the same person; high frequency of manipulative suicidal behaviour

Anxious/fearful cluster

Avoidant personality disorder: extreme social discomfort and timidity; feelings of inadequacy and fearfulness of being negatively evaluated

Dependent personality disorder: extreme submissive and dependent behaviour; fears of separation from those who satisfy dependency needs

Obsessive-compulsive personality disorder: extreme perfectionism, orderliness and inflexibility; preoccupied with mental and interpersonal control

Odd/eccentric cluster

Schizoid personality disorder: indifference to social relationships and a restricted range of experiencing and expressing emotions

Schizotypal personality disorder: odd thoughts, appearance, and behaviour, and extreme discomfort in social situations

Paranoid personality disorder: an unwarranted tendency to interpret the behaviour of other people as threatening, exploiting or harmful

SOURCE: based on DSM-IV-TR, American Psychiatric Association, 2000.

As many as 10 to 15 per cent of adults in the Europe may have personality disorders. A study in Norway found a rate of 13.4 per cent, equally distributed among men and women. The most frequently encountered were avoidant, paranoid, histrionic and obsessive-compulsive personality disorders (Torgerson et al., 2001).

Among the personality disorders, the most destructive to society is the *antisocial personality disorder* (Livesley, 2003). This personality disorder has received by far the greatest attention from clinicians and researchers over the years (Reich, 2006). A second personality disorder that is attracting a great deal of current attention is the *borderline personality disorder*. We focus on these two disorders.

ANTISOCIAL PERSONALITY DISORDER

In the past, individuals with antisocial personality disorder were referred to as *psychopaths* or *sociopaths*; those terms are still in use today, though not for formal diagnostic purposes, and they are probably wrong even though clinicians still use them. There is a debate as to whether antisocial personality disorder (also known as sociopathy) and psychopathy are subtly different. Many people use the diagnostic criteria laid out by Hare (1991) even though they disagree with the DSM. The sociopath is characterized as performing antisocial criminal acts, whereas the psychopath is characterized additionally by a lack of empathy and a degree of remorselessness. Hare says 'thrill seeking' and 'an inability to process emotional information'. So, there may also be a different aetiology to the disorder to antisocial disorder (a social/biological versus neurological aetiology). Koch introduced the phrase 'psychopathic inferiority' in 1889 and such people were then sometimes referred to as 'moral imbeciles'. People with antisocial personality

Focus 17.27

Describe the major characteristics of the antisocial personality disorder.

disorder are among the most interpersonally destructive and emotionally harmful individuals. Males outnumber females by approximately three to one in this diagnostic group. In a large study carried out in Oslo, Torgersen et al. (2001) estimate prevalence as being approximately 0.7 per cent in the general population.

People with **antisocial personality disorder** exhibit a lack of emotional attachment to other people, as suggested in this report by a man diagnosed as having an antisocial personality disorder:

> When I was in high school my best friend got leukemia and died and I went to his funeral. Everybody else was crying ... (but) ... I suddenly realised I wasn't feeling anything at all.... That night I thought about it some more and found I wouldn't miss my mother and father if they died and that I wasn't too nuts about my brothers and sisters for that matter. I figured there wasn't anybody I really cared for but, then, I didn't need any of them anyway so I rolled over and went to sleep. (McNeil, 1967, p. 87)

A lack of capacity to care about others can make antisocial individuals a danger to society (Black, 1999). Although antisocial individuals often verbalise feelings and commitments with great sincerity, their behaviours indicate otherwise. They often appear very intelligent and charming, and they have the ability to rationalize their inappropriate behaviour so that it appears reasonable and justifiable. Consequently, they are often virtuosos at manipulating others and talking their way out of trouble.

The characteristics we have discussed can be reflected in psychological test responses as well as in social behaviour. Figure 17.33 shows the Minnesota Multiphasic Personality Inventory (MMPI) profile of notorious serial killer Jeffrey Dahmer. You may not be very familiar with his name, as his terrible crimes were committed in the USA between 1989 and 1991, although other crimes were committed earlier, but his psychology is of relevance here, and the data are interesting. In summary, over the 1989–91 period, he killed and dismembered at least 17 male victims. He slept with the dead bodies, engaged in sex acts with them, stored body parts in jars and cannibalized many of them. He was convicted of the serial murders and sentenced to 1070 years in prison.

antisocial personality disorder

a lack of emotional attachment to other people

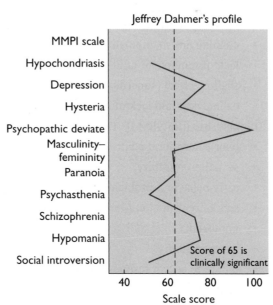

FIGURE 17.33

A serial killer's MMPI.

The Minnesota Multiphasic Personality Inventory (MMPI) profile of serial killer Jeffrey Dahmer reveals severe antisocial tendencies. Scores beyond the dotted line are assumed to reflect pathological tendencies. Dahmer's extraordinarily elevated score on the psychopathic deviate scale reflects a callous disregard for other people and is consistent with his pattern of unrestrained and vicious victimisation of others.

SOURCE: Caldwell, 1994.

According to Caldwell (1994), several aspects of this MMPI profile help explain Dahmer's bizarre and destructive behaviour. The extraordinarily high score on the psychopathic deviate scale reflects an extreme antisocial impulsiveness coupled with a total lack of capacity for compassion and empathy. His victims were in all likelihood regarded as little more than objects to satisfy his perverse needs. Caldwell viewed the marked discrepancy between the depression and psychasthenia (anxiety) scales – rarely seen on the MMPI – as reflecting Dahmer's sense of being fated or doomed to repeat his acts until he would be caught (the high depression score), together with an absence of fear that, in normal people, might inhibit murderous behaviour (the low psychasthenia score). Although the profile clearly indicates Dahmer's high level of psychological disturbance, it also reflects an ability to mask his pathology under the normal façade that for years fooled law enforcement officials. Indeed, Dahmer's general demeanour looked so normal that despite the horror of his acts and the level of psychopathology shown in his test results, his plea of not guilty by reason of insanity was rejected by the jury. Instead, he went to prison, where he was murdered by another inmate.

People with antisocial personalities also display a perplexing failure to respond to punishment. Because of their lack of anxiety (seen, for example, in Dahmer's MMPI profile), the threat of punishment does not deter them from engaging in self-defeating or illegal acts again and again. As a result, some of them develop imposing prison records.

To be diagnosed with antisocial personality disorder, a person must be at least 18 years of age. However, the diagnostic criteria also require substantial evidence of antisocial behaviour before the age of 15, including such acts as habitual lying, early and aggressive sexual behaviour, excessive drinking, theft, vandalism and chronic rule violations at home and in school. Thus antisocial personality disorder is the culmination of a deviant behaviour pattern that typically begins in childhood (Kernberg, 2000).

Robert Hare (1991), has identified a number of traits in the psychopath, and has developed the Psychopath Check List (revised) (PCL-R). The PCL-R comes in two parts, an interview, where a clinician uses a 'semi-structured' style to identify ratings on a number of levels, and a review of the person's records and history. The Traits that the PCL-R assesses are as follows:

- glib and superficial charm
- grandiose (exaggeratedly high) estimation of self
- need for stimulation
- pathological lying
- cunning and manipulativeness
- lack of remorse or guilt
- shallow affect (superficial emotional responsiveness)
- callousness and lack of empathy
- parasitic lifestyle
- poor behavioural controls
- sexual promiscuity
- early behaviour problems
- lack of realistic long-term goals
- impulsivity
- irresponsibility
- failure to accept responsibility for own actions
- many short-term marital relationships
- juvenile delinquency
- revocation of conditional release
- criminal versatility.

The practitioner gives each of the 20 traits a score out of two. The fully psychopathic individual would, then, score 40.

Causal Factors

Biological factor   Biological research on antisocial personality disorder has focused on both genetic and physiological factors. Evidence for a genetic predisposition is shown in consistently higher rates of concordance for antisocial behaviour among identical twins than among fraternal twins (Rutter, 1997). Adoption studies suggest a similar conclusion. When researchers compared the criminal records of men who had been adopted early in life with those of their biological fathers and their adoptive fathers, they found that the criminality rate was nearly twice as high if the biological father had a criminal record and the adoptive father did not, clearly suggesting the operation of genetic factors (Cloninger and Gottesman, 1989).

How might genetic factors predispose individuals to engage in antisocial behaviour? One clue might lie in the relative absence of anxiety and guilt that seems to characterize antisocial personality disorder. Many researchers have suggested that the physiological basis for the disorder might be some dysfunction in brain structures that govern emotional arousal and behavioural self-control (Blair, 2005). This results in behavioural impulsiveness and a chronically underaroused state that impairs avoidance learning, causes boredom and encourages a search for excitement (Arnett, 1997; Ishikawa et al., 2001). In support of a physiological basis, both children and adults with antisocial behaviour patterns have lower heart rates, particularly when under stress (Ortiz and Raine, 2004). Magnetic resonance imaging also reveal that antisocial individuals have subtle neurological deficits in the prefrontal lobes – the seat of executive functions such as planning, reasoning and behavioural inhibition; these neurological deficits are associated with reduced autonomic activity (Raine et al., 2000). It thus appears, as long suspected, that severely antisocial individuals may indeed be wired differently at a neurological level, responding with less arousal and greater impulsiveness to both pleasurable and unpleasant stimuli (Verona et al., 2004). Damasio (2000) urges caution in reading too much into these data on neurological differences between those with antisocial personality disorder (APD) and other groups. Raine et al.'s (2000) research on brain volume does indeed show a difference of approximately 11 per cent between the frontal lobes of those with APD and others. However, we should not conclude that this deficit causes the APD. The relationship between the lower capacity of the frontal lobes can be understood only when we take other factors, namely the interaction of the frontal lobes and other areas of the brain, into consideration.

Psychological and environmental factors   Psychodynamic theorists regard antisocial personalities as people without a conscience. Psychoanalytic theorists suggest that such people lack anxiety and guilt because they did not develop an adequate superego (Gabbard, 1990). In the absence of a well-developed superego, the restraints on the id are reduced, resulting in impulsive and hedonistic behaviour. The failure to develop a strong superego is thought to result from inadequate identification with appropriate adult figures because these figures were either physically or psychologically unavailable to the child (Kernberg, 2000). In support of this position, the absence of the father from the home is related to a higher incidence of antisocial symptoms in children, even when socio-economic status is equated (Pfiffner et al., 2001).

Cognitive theorists believe that an important feature in antisocial individuals is their consistent failure to think about or anticipate the long-term negative consequences of their acts. As a result, they behave impulsively, thinking only of what they want at that moment (Bandura, 1997). From this perspective, a key to preventing these individuals from getting into trouble is to help them develop the cognitive controls (i.e., the executive functions) needed to think before acting.

Learning through modelling may also play an important role. Many antisocial individuals come from homes where parents exhibit a good deal of aggression and are inattentive to their children's needs (Rutter, 1997). Such parents provide role models for both aggressive behaviour and disregard for the needs of others. Another important environmental factor is exposure to deviant peers. Children who become antisocial often learn some of their deviant behaviours from peer groups that both model antisocial behaviour and reinforce it with social approval (Bandura, 1997). It is easy to see how such environmental factors, combined with a possible genetic predisposition for antisocial behaviour, would encourage the development of deviant behaviour patterns.

Like some biological theories, learning explanations suggest that persons with antisocial personality disorder lack impulse control. Learning theorists believe that poor impulse control

Focus 17.28
How do biological, psychoanalytic and behavioural theorists account for antisocial personality disorder?

occurs in these individuals because of an impaired ability to develop conditioned fear responses when punished. This results in a deficit in avoidance learning. Hans Eysenck (1964) maintained that developing a conscience depends on the ability to learn fear and inhibitory avoidance responses, and people who fail to do so will be less able to inhibit their behaviour.

Focus 17.29

How does the Schachter–Latané study support the arousal-deficit theory of antisocial personality disorder.

In accord with this hypothesis, Adrian Raine and co-workers (1996) did a 14-year follow-up of males who had been subjected at age 15 to a classical conditioning procedure in which a soft tone was used as the CS and a loud, aversive tone as the UCS. Conditioned fear was measured by the participant's skin conductance response when the CS occurred after a number of pairings with the loud UCS. The researchers found that men who accumulated a criminal record by age 29 had shown much poorer fear conditioning at age 15 than had those with no criminal record.

RESEARCH CLOSE-UP

FEAR, AVOIDANCE LEARNING AND PSYCHOPATHY

SOURCE: S. Schachter and B. Latané (1964) Crime, cognition, and the autonomic nervous system, in D. Levine (ed.), *Nebraska Symposium on Motivation – 1964*. Lincoln, NE: University of Nebraska Press.

INTRODUCTION

In antisocial personality disorder, punishment seems to have little effect on future destructive behaviour. As we have seen, one explanation for this is a deficit in fear arousal, which serves to inhibit antisocial behaviour in normal people (Blair, 2005). This lack of fear arousal contributes to poor avoidance learning, so that such people get into trouble repeatedly.

What would happen if it were possible to make people with antisocial personality disorder more physiologically reactive, or fearful? Would their avoidance-learning deficit disappear? Stanley Schachter and Bibb Latané set out to answer this important question.

METHOD

Schachter and Latané selected two groups of inmates at state prisons on the basis of psychologists' diagnoses and life-history data. One group consisted of 'psychopaths'. These prisoners were described by prison psychologists as being free from any symptoms of anxiety, lacking a sense of responsibility or shame, being habitual liars and manipulators, able to commit antisocial acts without guilt or remorse, lacking insight and unable to profit from negative experiences. Most, if not all, of these prisoners would meet current diagnostic criteria for antisocial personality disorder. A normal (non-'psychotic') group consisted of prisoners matched in age and intelligence who did not exhibit this behavioural pattern. Life-history data showed that the psychopaths had been arrested more often (8.3 versus 3.3 arrests) and had spent more of their adult lives in prison (36.2 per cent versus 18.1 per cent).

The two groups of prisoners were recruited as paid participants in an investigation of 'a newly developed hormone thought to enhance learning'. The researchers used an experimental apparatus that required participants to learn a complicated mental maze. It consisted of a metal cabinet on which was mounted a counter, two pilot lights and four switches. The maze consisted of 20 choice points. At each choice point, the participant selected one of the four switches. If it was the correct one, a green light flashed and the learner advanced to the next choice point. If one of the three incorrect switches was selected, a red light flashed and an error was recorded on the counter visible to the participant. When the twentieth choice point was reached, the procedure began again from the start. The learner repeated the maze 21 times, the objective being to learn the correct response at each choice point so as to minimize the total number of errors.

To study avoidance learning, one of the three incorrect switches at each choice point not only activated the red light and recorded an error, but it also resulted in a moderately painful electric shock to the learner. Thus the learner would do well to learn not only the correct switch at each point but also to avoid the one that delivered a shock (i.e., to do good *and* avoid evil).

To manipulate emotional arousal, the prisoners were given an injection of the 'experimental hormone, Suproxin', being tested to see if it enhanced learning ability. They were told that this hormone would have no side effects. The injection was used to manipulate autonomic arousal. It contained either adrenalin, which would increase arousal, or a placebo, which would not. Each participant worked until he learned two different mental mazes, one while under the influence of adrenalin and the other while under the placebo. Half received adrenalin on the first maze and then received the placebo for the second maze; the other half received injections in the reverse order.

RESULTS

The two groups of prisoners did not differ in their overall learning of the two mazes; they made similar numbers of correct responses and errors. Thus the psychopaths did not differ in their ability to learn the positively reinforced 'correct' responses. Of major interest, then, was the avoidance-learning measure, that is, the ability to learn to avoid choosing the switch at each choice point that would result in electric shock. The dependent variable here was the percentage of incorrect responses made by each participant that resulted in electric shock. The lower the percentage of shocked incorrect responses, the better the avoidance learning over trials through each maze.

Figure 17.34a shows avoidance learning under the placebo condition, in which the psychopathic and normal prisoners experienced their normal levels of arousal. As you can see, the normal prisoners made a lower percentage of shocked responses during their later trips through the maze, indicating avoidance learning. In contrast, the psychopaths showed almost no evidence of learning. On their later trials through the maze, they were still as likely to select the shocked switch as they were in their early trials.

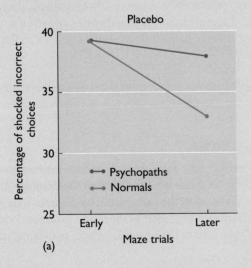 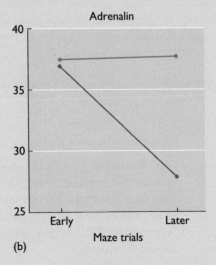

FIGURE 17.34

Avoidance learning in psychopathic and non-psychopathic prisoners.

The avoidance ratio is the percentage of errors in which the incorrect choice resulted in electric shock. Performance is shown on early and later trials on each mental maze. Under placebo conditions (a), normal prisoners showed avoidance learning but psychopaths did not. However, increasing arousal with an adrenaline injection (b) resulted in successful avoidance learning in the psychopaths.

If lack of fear underlies the psychopaths' lack of conditioning, what would happen if one artificially increased their level of arousal? In Figure 17.34b, we see the effect of doing so. When injected with adrenalin, the psychopaths showed dramatic evidence of avoidance learning. Indeed, they actually performed better than the normal prisoners, whose performance on this complex task may have been somewhat impaired by increasing their already-existing fear responses.

CRITICAL DISCUSSION

This study, done nearly a half-century ago, is still considered a classic. Schachter and Latané cleverly tested a clinical explanation for a behaviour disorder under controlled laboratory conditions. They not only demonstrated the avoidance-learning deficit presumed to underlie antisocial behaviour, but they also showed that this deficit could be reversed if it were possible to experimentally create the physiological arousal that psychopaths lack. Indeed, the increase in arousal produced by the adrenalin injection had an especially notable effect on the psychopaths, who learned to avoid even better than the normal prisoners did in the placebo condition. This may be because the psychopaths' arousal in this fear-inducing situation was so different from their normal experience.

It is important to rule out other possible explanations for the results. For example, what if the pain experiences of the prisoner groups were affected differently by the injections, thereby affecting motivation to avoid the shock? The researchers were able to rule this out by showing that the two groups of prisoners rated the pain as equally unpleasant under both injection conditions. Therefore, the psychopathic and normal prisoners apparently experienced equal pain when shocked. As in this case, it is important to anticipate factors that could affect results and make sure that they are measured.

This study exemplifies a research area known as *experimental psychopathology*. Researchers bring clinical populations into the laboratory to study processes assumed to underlie a particular disorder under controlled conditions, using state-of-the-art science techniques from other areas of psychology, such as cognitive psychology, social psychology and behavioural neuroscience. This kind of research helps identify the mechanisms that contribute to behaviour disorders. It also allows researchers to test hypotheses derived from existing theories of psychopathology and, sometimes, to directly pit competing theories against one another. In this manner, clinical observation informs science, and science helps inform clinical understanding and, it is hoped, the treatment of behaviour disorders.

BORDERLINE PERSONALITY DISORDER

The borderline personality disorder has become the focus of intense interest among clinical researchers because of its chaotic effects on those who suffer from the disorder, their families and their therapists. The prevalence is disputed in the literature. The disorder may occur in 3 to 5 per cent of the general population (Clarkin et al., 1992; Frances and Widiger, 1986), but Torgersen et al. (2001) have it nearer to 0.7 per cent in their sample. About two-thirds of those diagnosed are women.

borderline personality disorder (BPD)

a collection of symptoms characterized primarily by serious instability in behaviour, emotion, identity and interpersonal relationships

Before 1980 the term *borderline* referred to an intermediate level of disturbance between neurotic and psychotic. Now, however, **borderline personality disorder (BPD)** refers to a collection of symptoms characterized primarily by serious instability in behaviour, emotion, identity and interpersonal relationships. Borderline individuals have intense and unstable personal relationships and experience chronic feelings of extreme anger, loneliness and emptiness, as well as momentary losses of personal identity. They are inclined to engage in impulsive behaviour such as running away, promiscuity, binge eating and drug abuse, and their lives are often marked by repetitive self-destructive behaviours, such as self-mutilation and suicide attempts that seem designed to call forth a 'saving' response from other people in their lives. The complex nature of the borderline disorder is shown in the following case:

> A 27-year-old woman was married and had two small children. She had had a stormy adolescence, having been forced into sexual relations with a brother 6 years her senior whom she at first idolized and later feared. Their relationship continued until just before she left home for college, when she told her parents of it. In the ensuing emotional turmoil, she made a gesture of suicide (overdose of aspirin) but was not hospitalized.... Outwardly flirtatious, although inwardly shy and ill at ease, she felt intensely lonely and went through a period of mild alcohol abuse and brief sexual affairs in an effort to cope with her anxiety and sense of inner emptiness. At age 19, she married a class-mate and dropped out of school.
>
> Fairly at ease in the first years of her marriage, she became anxious, bored, and given to fits of sadness and tearfulness after the birth of her second child. Her mood fluctuated widely from hour to hour and day to day, but negative feelings were greatly intensified on the 3 or 4 days before her period. Her husband had grown less attentive as the family expanded, in response to which she became increasingly irritable, provocative, and at times abusive (smashing plates, hurling insults). Her husband began to carry on an extramarital relationship, which she eventually discovered. At that point, she became seriously depressed, lost sleep and appetite, began to abuse alcohol and sedatives, and made several gestures of suicide, including one instance of cutting her wrist. On two occasions she hid for several nights in motels without informing anyone where she was. (Stone, 1986, p. 210)

Borderline personality disorder is highly associated with a number of other disorders, including mood disorders, PTSD and substance-related disorders. In one study, the BPD symptoms of emotional instability and impulsivity predicted recurrent problems in academic achievement and social relationships two years later (Bagge et al., 2004). One intensive study of 57 people diagnosed with BPD revealed a total of 42 suicide threats, 40 drug overdoses, 36 instances of self-mutilation and cutting, 38 episodes of drug abuse, 36 instances of promiscuity with near-strangers, and 14 accidents, mainly caused by reckless driving.

The chaos that marks the lives of borderline clients extends to their relationships with their psychotherapists. They are considered to be among the most difficult clients to treat because of their clinging dependency, their irrational anger and their tendency to engage in manipulative suicide threats and gestures as efforts to control the therapist (Linehan, 1993). Many borderline individuals, perhaps 6 to 9 per cent, eventually do kill themselves, either by miscalculation or by design (Davis et al., 1999).

Focus 17.30
Describe the major features of BPD and the hypothesized causes of the disorder.

Causal Factors

Borderline clients tend to have chaotic personal histories marked by interpersonal strife, abuse and inconsistent parenting. This history is sometimes reflected in their earliest memories. In one study, borderline and normal participants were asked to describe their earliest memories in life. When the researchers analysed the content of the memory reports, they found that the borderlines reported six times more events in which someone had treated them in a malevolent manner or had injured them emotionally or physically. Borderline individuals also viewed potential helpers as far less helpful to them (Nigg et al., 1992). Parents of many borderline individuals are described as abusive, rejecting and non-affirming, and some theorists suggest that an early lack of acceptance by parents may cripple self-esteem and lead to clinging dependency and an inability to cope with separation (Cardasis et al., 1997). As they mature, the behaviours of borderlines tend to evoke negative reactions and rejection from others, affirming their sense of worthlessness and their view of the world as malevolent.

Psychoanalyst Otto Kernberg has focused on the dramatic changes that borderlines exhibit in their relationships with others (Kernberg, 1984; Kernberg and Caligor, 2005). Their sudden and

splitting
the failure to integrate positive and negative aspects of another's behaviour

FIGURE 17.35

Actress Glenn Close's portrayal of Alex in the film *Fatal Attraction* illustrated the tendency of people with borderline personality disorder to show dramatic shifts in their relationships. During her affair with the man played by Michael Douglas, Alex went from consuming love to a homicidal rage in which she tried to murder her lover with a butcher's knife when he tried to end the relationship.

vitriolic shifts from extreme love and clinging dependence to intense hatred or feelings of abandonment reflect a cognitive process that he calls **splitting**, the failure to integrate positive and negative aspects of another's behaviour (for example, a parent who is usually accepting but sometimes voices disapproval) into a coherent whole. As a result, the borderline may react as if the other person has two separate identities, one deserving of love and the other of hatred. Whichever of these seemingly independent images the borderline individual is reacting to at the moment totally determines how she or he relates or feels (Fig. 17.35). Together with severe problems in emotional control, splitting makes for chaotic and unpredictable relationships.

Biological factors also seem to be at work (Depue and Lenzenweger, 2005). Close relatives of those with BPD are five times more likely than those in the general population to also have the disorder (Torgerson, 2000). The emotional explosiveness and impulsivity of borderlines may also reflect some biological abnormality in neurotransmitter systems or areas of the brain that contribute to emotional self-regulation (Gurvitz et al., 2000). It seems entirely possible that BPD reflects an interaction between biological factors and an early history of trauma, rejection and psychological if not physical abandonment. Finally, sociocultural factors may also contribute. Cases of BPD seem to increase in societies that are unstable and rapidly changing, leaving some of its members with a sense of emptiness, problems of identity and fears of abandonment (Paris, 1993).

BENEATH THE SURFACE

HOW DANGEROUS ARE PEOPLE WITH PSYCHOLOGICAL DISORDERS?

When they occur, violent acts committed by mentally ill people or those who have formerly suffered with mental health problems often are sensationalized in the media. Fictional depictions of psychologically disturbed individuals often involve violent behaviour. One analysis of prime-time television programmes revealed that 73 per cent of mentally ill characters committed violent acts, compared with 40 per cent of normal characters (Gerbner et al., 1981). In the climactic scene of the movie *Fatal Attraction*, a woman resembling a borderline individual attempts to murder her former lover when he abandons her. Part of the stigma attached to psychological disorders is the widespread belief that such people are especially prone to commit violent acts (Monahan, 1992). How valid are such concerns?

The preceding discussion of antisocial personality disorder notes characteristics that can make such people prone to violence. Individuals such as Fred and Rosemary West, Jeffrey Dahmer and Ian Brady represent extreme examples of how destructive a mentally ill individual can be. Other subgroups with elevated violence potential are people with paranoid and catatonic schizophrenia who have stopped taking their medications (Torrey and Zdanowicz, 2001). The fact is, however, that the vast majority of people with psychological disorders do not fall into these categories. The two largest diagnostic groups, people with anxiety disorders and depression, are likely to be no more dangerous than the average person, and severely depressed people in particular are of greater danger to themselves than they are to others.

As we have seen, severe disorders such as schizophrenia are more common in lower socio-economic groups, and violent behaviour is also more common at lower socio-economic levels. In a study designed to control for this factor, people with mental disorders were followed for one year following their discharge from psychiatric hospitals (Steadman et al., 1998). The frequency with which they, family members or police records revealed violent acts was compared with the frequency of similar acts in 'normal' people from the same lower socio-economic neighbourhoods where the former clients lived.

As shown in Figure 17.36, former clients without substance-abuse problems differed little in violence rates from other members of the community (comparison group) without substance-abuse problems during the year-long period. However, substance abuse (which occurred more often among the former clients) was associated with a significant increase in the mean number of violent acts in both the client and comparison groups. The researchers also found that violent acts by the former mental health clients were most frequently directed towards family members and acquaintances. Those in the comparison group were actually more likely than former clients to commit the kinds of violent acts outside the home that most frighten the public.

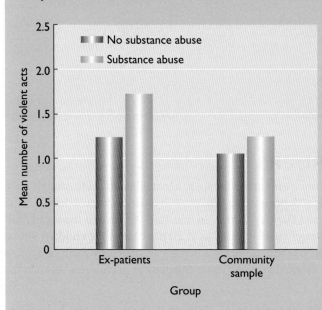

FIGURE 17.36

Challenging a popular stereotype.

This graph shows the mean number of violent acts committed by former psychiatric clients during the year following their discharge from hospital, as compared with similar acts committed by a comparison group living in their lower-socioeconomic neighbourhoods. No difference was found between former clients and other community members when neither group engaged in substance abuse; however, when substance abuse was a factor, it was associated with more violence in both client and comparison samples.

SOURCE: based on Steadman et al., 1998.

Based on this and other research, the following conclusion by two prominent mental health researchers appears reasonable:

To date, nearly every modern study indicates that public fears are way out of proportion to the empirical reality. The magnitude of the violence risk associated with mental illness is comparable to that associated with age, educational attainment, and gender and is limited to only some disorders and symptom constellations. Furthermore, because serious mental illness is relatively rare and the excess risk modest, the contribution of mental illness to overall levels of violence in our society is miniscule. (Link and Steuve,

IN REVIEW

- Personality disorders are rigid, maladaptive patterns of behaviour that persist over a long time. They fall on Axis II of the DSM-IV-TR. Personality disorders can contribute to the development of Axis I disorders and reduce the chances of recovery from those disorders.

- Antisocial personality disorder is the most studied of the Axis II disorders. It is characterized by an egocentric and manipulative tendency towards immediate self-gratification, a lack of empathy for others, a tendency to act impulsively and a failure to profit from punishment.

- Research on antisocial personality disorder suggests that genetic and physiological factors that result in underarousal may contribute to the disorder's causes. Psychoanalysts view the disorder as a failure to develop the superego, which might otherwise restrain the individual's impulsive self-gratification.

- Learning explanations focus on the failure of punishment to inhibit maladaptive behaviours and exposure to aggressive, uncaring models.

- Borderline personality disorder is characterized by serious instability in behaviour, emotions, interpersonal relationships, and personal identity, as well as impulsive and self-destructive behaviours.

- It appears that the majority of people with psychological disorders are not a danger to others. Research is identifying the subgroups that are more dangerous, and substance abuse is an important risk factor.

CHILDHOOD DISORDERS

Focus 17.31

Describe the major features and causal factors in ADHD and autistic disorder, as well as implications for adult functioning.

Psychological disorders can occur at any point in the lifespan. Mental health professionals have observed symptoms resembling clinical depression in infants, and older children exhibit a wide range of problem behaviours (Mash and Barkley, 2003). In one study of several thousand children between the ages of 2 and 5, researchers diagnosed over 20 per cent of the children with a DSM-IV disorder and considered half of these to be significantly impaired by their symptoms (Lavigne et al., 1996). Similar levels of incidence and impairment exist in children between the ages of 9 and 17 (Satcher, 1999).

Other studies show that only about 40 per cent of children with psychological disorders receive professional attention, and only half of this group is seen by qualified mental health professionals (Satcher, 1999). In contrast, 74 per cent of children with physical handicaps receive professional treatment (US Office of Behavior Technology, 1990). Failure to treat childhood behaviour disorders not only results in needless distress for children and families, but such disorders tend to continue into adulthood as psychological problems. In one New Zealand study, four in five adults with diagnosed DSM disorders had histories of childhood or adolescent problems that also met DSM criteria (Newman et al., 1996).

Although many childhood disorders are the subject of current research, two are receiving particular attention. *Attention deficit/hyperactivity disorder* is of interest because it is the most frequently diagnosed childhood disorder. *Autism* is being scrutinized because it is becoming more common and is one of the most baffling disorders.

ATTENTION DEFICIT/HYPERACTIVITY DISORDER

In **attention deficit/hyperactivity disorder (ADHD)**, problems take the form of inattention, hyperactivity/impulsivity, or a combination of the two. Ratings by teachers and parents indicate that 7 to 10 per cent of American children meet DSM-IV-TR criteria for the disorder, with Faraone et al. (2003) suggesting that in non-US populations the incidence is at least as high. This makes ADHD the most common childhood disorder. Faraone et al. (2003) go on to say that the diagnosis may depend on the criteria used, with those provided by the DSM, used almost exclusively in the USA, providing the highest number of diagnoses. The disorder occurs at least four times more frequently in boys than in girls. Boys are more likely to exhibit aggressive and impulsive behaviours, whereas girls are more likely to be primarily inattentive. Some professionals believe that the ADHD diagnosis is applied too liberally, since normal children also exhibit the behaviours in question. They worry that some children may be inappropriately labelled and medicated (Carlson, 2000).

It may be tempting to assume that children routinely outgrow ADHD, but follow-up studies of individuals diagnosed with the disorder suggest that for 50 to 80 per cent, the problems persist into adolescence and, for 30 to 50 per cent, into adulthood (Biederman, 1998). Overall, adults with ADHD have more occupational, family, emotional and interpersonal problems.

Despite many years of research, the precise causes of ADHD are unknown. Genetic factors are probably involved, as concordance rates are higher in identical than fraternal twins. In adoption studies of ADHD children, the children's biological parents are more likely to have ADHD than the adoptive parents (Smalley et al., 2000). Experts have long suspected that the disorder has a biological basis, but EEG studies of electrical brain activity and imaging studies of brain structures and neurotransmitters have failed to reveal consistent differences between people with ADHD and control groups (Green, 1999). This may be due to the fact that ADHD is a multifaceted disorder with several subcategories of biological patterns. Environmental factors, such as inconsistent parenting, are also involved, perhaps in complex combinations with biological factors.

There is a contention that the disorder does not exist at all. Wright (2005) regards ADHD as a 'fad' diagnosis that is currently popular and in fashion but one that will eventually fall from favour. He suggests that these 'diagnoses' are guilty of elevating symptoms to descriptions of symptoms into disorders, and once so described, these result in often serious over-diagnoses and medication. Either way, the diagnosis is there, and is being used. It is useful for the reader to be aware that even though the current status quo is of the mind that a problem is real, and merits treating, there are alternative views that might be considered.

AUTISTIC DISORDER

One of the most mysterious and perplexing of all disorders is autism. First identified by the American psychiatrist Leo Kanner in 1943, **autistic disorder** is a long-term disorder characterized by extreme unresponsiveness to others, poor communication skills, and highly repetitive and rigid behaviour patterns. Autism affects about five in every 10 000 children, about 80 per cent of them boys (American Psychiatric Association, 2000). Typically appearing in the first three years of life in the form of unresponsiveness and lack of interest in others, autism tends to be a lifelong disorder. Approximately 70 per cent remain severely disabled into adulthood and cannot lead independent lives. More than two-thirds are mentally retarded, having IQs below 70 and frequently below 35. The rest have normal to above-average intelligence. But even the highest-functioning adults with autism have problems in communication, restricted interests and activities, and difficulty relating to others. Simon Baron-Cohen's research in Cambridge is part of the forefront of research in the area and his autism research is a rich and dynamic resource for this fascinating and often perplexing issue. Baron-Cohen has been instrumental in

---

attention deficit/ hyperactivity disorder (ADHD)

problems take the form of inattention, hyperactivity/ impulsivity, or a combination of the two

autistic disorder

a long-term disorder characterized by extreme unresponsiveness to others, poor communication skills, and highly repetitive and rigid behaviour patterns

identifying issues and patterns in autism, and developing tests and methods of identifying and measuring it in children. In 1992, Baron-Cohen et al. published CHAT (the Checklist for Autism in Toddlers) that provides practitioners with a method of identifying autism in young children. The checklist is a series of questions, and observation guidelines used by a family doctor at the 18-month check-up. Parents are asked a number of things, including 'Does your child enjoy playing peek-a-boo/hide and seek?' and 'Does your child ever pretend, for example, to make a cup of tea using a toy cup and teapot, or pretend other things?'. Doctors note down whether the child made eye contact during the session, or if they could be encouraged to point to items around them using their index finger (declarative pointing). The completed checklist gives the doctor a guide as to whether further investigation is warranted.

Lack of social responsiveness to others is a central feature of autism. Autistic infants typically do not reach out to or even make eye contact with their parents. They seem not to recognize or care who is around them. Autistic children do not engage in normal play with either adults or peers. They do not include others in their play and often do not even acknowledge their presence.

Language and communication difficulties are also common, with half of autistic people not developing language. The language that does develop is often strange, involving repetition of words or phrases with little recognition of meaning. Many engage in *echolalia*, the exact echoing of phrases spoken by others.

Sameness and routine are very important, and autistic children become extremely upset at even minute changes. The movement of a piece of furniture even slightly or the change of one word in a song may evoke a tantrum. Some theorists believe that sameness is an attempt to avoid over-stimulation, but nobody knows for sure.

FIGURE 17.37

People with autism often engage in odd and repetitive stereotyped behaviours. For example, an autistic child may manipulate an object for hours at a time, showing no interest in playing with other children or relating to adults.

Autistic individuals have repetitive and stereotyped behaviour patterns and interests (Fig. 17.37). They may spend their time spinning objects, playing with objects like jar tops, flicking their fingers, or rocking their bodies. Some engage in self-injurious behaviours, such as banging their heads against sharp objects or biting chunks of flesh out of their bodies, and these children may have to be physically restrained.

Some autistic people, such as the man portrayed by Dustin Hoffman in *Rain Man*, exhibit extraordinary *savant* (from the French word for 'wise', or 'learned') abilities. A common savant skill is calendar calculation. An autistic person with this ability could tell you in an instant what day of the week your birthday will fall on in 2039. Others can perfectly reproduce any song or commercial after hearing it once. Sometimes, these skills give the impression of superior intelligence, even in people who have learning difficulties. The savant is rather rare though, and only one in 10 autistics exhibit these abilities, so one should be careful not to stereotype autism in this way. Nevertheless, they do exist, and their abilities are often outstanding and beyond belief. Stephen Wiltshire, now a man in his thirties, with a gallery in one of the most exclusive areas of London, draws scenes in incredible detail from memory.

Causal Factors

Leo Kanner (1943), who first described childhood autism, offered a psychodynamic explanation. He speculated that these children had been driven into their own worlds by a cold and ungiving family environment during infancy. Parents (particularly the mother) were described as 'refrigerator parents' who had thawed out just long enough to conceive a child. These were purely theoretical statements, and no evidence for such a family pattern has ever existed, but generations of parents who were exposed to this hypothesis suffered the agony of thinking they had caused their child's autistic disorder.

Today, it is widely accepted that autism has a biological basis (Kabot et al., 2003). What that might be remains undetermined, however. Widespread anomalies in the structures and functioning of the brain have been found in autistic children. For example, brain-imaging studies show that the brains of autistic children are larger than average, reflecting abnormal brain growth during the first year of life, and they also reveal abnormal development in the cerebellum, which co-ordinates movement and is involved in shifting attention (Courchesne et al., 2003).

Genetic factors have been linked to autism. Siblings of autistic children are 200 times more likely to have the disorder than are children in the general population, and concordance is highest in identical twins (Piven et al., 1997). No single gene seems involved; instead, there may be multiple interacting genes. One notable finding is that many relatives of autistic children, though not manifesting the disorder themselves, have unusual personality characteristics that parallel autism, including aloofness and very narrow and specialized interests (Rutter, 2000).

Another line of research is examining autism from the *theory of mind* perspective. As discussed in Chapter 12, theory of mind refers to an awareness of what others are thinking and how they may be reacting internally. Children usually become aware of some characteristics of other people's thinking by age 3 or 4 (Ritblatt, 2000). Autistic people seem to have poorly developed skills in this area, making it difficult for them to communicate with others or understand how other people might be internally reacting to them (Heerey et al., 2003). Autistic children also show poor comprehension of others' emotional responses, such as expressions of distress (Dawson et al., 2004). Theory of mind deficits could severely impair language and social development, and they are a strong focus of current research on autism.

Baron-Cohen (1985; 1995) has identified a number of issues of importance that relate to theory of mind in autism. He indicates that the autistic is lacking a mechanism for identifying gaze direction (the Eye Direction Detector – EDD) and also a mechanism for being able to share attention with someone else (the Shared Attention Mechanism – SAM). The SAM is an extremely important issue in those with a theory of mind, where the intentions and perspectives of others can be perceived by the individual. Identifying whether a person has a theory of mind is possible with the 'Sally–Ann task' described in Figure 17.38. However, care must be taken here. Adults

FIGURE 17.38

The Sally–Ann task.

In this task, two dolls, a basket and a box are used. A child watches the scene as it unfolds, acted out with dolls by the researcher, or possibly described in pictures like those in the figure. The doll on the left in our picture is Sally; the one on the right is Ann. Sally takes an object (a ball perhaps) and places it in the covered basket, then leaves the scene. Ann then moves the object into the box. On Sally's return, the child is asked 'Where will Sally look for her ball?' Children with a 'theory of mind' will know that Sally was not present when the ball was moved, and as such will return to her covered basket where she left her ball. Those who show less theory of mind will think that Sally has exactly the same information as themselves. They know that the ball is in the box, and so they think Sally will look there. A simple and elegant task.

with autism can, often pass theory of mind tasks that a 6-year old may fail, but this does not indicate that they are performing in the normal range.

Another test that Baron-Cohen has used to great effect is the 'eyes test' (Baron-Cohen et al., 1997). The task involves the participant to look at an image of a pair of eyes, and match it to either a simple or complex description of the person's state of mind. A simple state might be 'happy' or 'sad' and a more complex state might be 'reflective' or 'scheming'. The data are quite striking and can be seen in Figure 17.39. Baron-Cohen et al. used a third participant group as a control, all of whom had Tourette's syndrome. Statistics show that the Tourette's group and the 'normal' groups show the same level of performance, while the autistic group is significantly worse than both. In this 'higher functioning' test of theory of mind, autistics do indeed show a deficit.

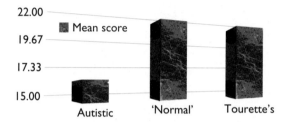

FIGURE 17.39

The eyes test.

In the 'eyes test' participants match a description of a state of mind with an image of a pair of eyes. The graph shows the number of correct responses for each of three groups. Statistics show that the autistic group is reliably and significantly worse at this task than the other two groups

SOURCE: data redrawn from Baron-Cohen et al., 1997.

In addition to this, Baron-Cohen has identified and extended a theory that relates to the 'maleness' of the autistic brain (2003). Here he indicates that autistic children are extremely male-like in their systematic behaviour, and not female-like in their lack of empathy. This theory was developed in 2005 where Baron-Cohen et al. looked at how social development can be significantly influenced by testosterone levels in the amniotic fluid during gestation. These behaviour patterns include the things we know as influenced in autism, including eye contact, language development, empathy and the quality of social relationships. It is clear from this research that there is a biological mechanism that plays a role in the development of autistic spectrum disorders.

IN REVIEW

- Psychological disorders can occur at any point in the lifespan, and epidemiological data show that both children and adolescents exhibit a variety of disorders. Moreover, many childhood disorders are precursors for psychological disorders in adulthood.

- Attention deficit/hyperactive disorder (ADHD) and autistic disorder originate in childhood and often persist into adulthood. ADHD can involve inattention, hyperactivity or a combination of the two.

- Autistic disorder is a severe disorder that involves extreme unresponsiveness to others, poor communication skills, and highly repetitive and rigid behaviour. Both disorders appear to have biological underpinnings, but the nature of these causal factors is not fully understood.

A CLOSING THOUGHT

All of us do the best we can to adapt to the many demands we face during the course of our lives. In this chapter, we have seen the intense personal and societal suffering that occurs when biologically and experientially produced vulnerabilities combine with stressful demands to create psychological disorders. It is our hope that this discussion has increased your understanding and compassion for those who suffer from these disorders. No one wants to be dysfunctional and miserable, and everyone deserves the opportunity to live a meaningful and fulfilling life. In the next chapter we focus on what can be done through psychological and biological treatments to ease the suffering that results from psychological disorders.

KEY TERMS AND CONCEPTS

Each term has been boldfaced and defined in the chapter on the page indicated in parentheses.

abnormal behaviour (p. 780)

agoraphobia (p. 789)

antisocial personality disorder (p. 821)

anxiety (p. 787)

anxiety disorders (p. 787)

attention deficit/hyperactivity disorder (ADHD) (p. 831)

autistic disorder (p. 831)

bipolar disorder (p. 802)

borderline personality disorder (BPD) (p. 826)

catatonic schizophrenia (p. 813)

competency (p. 785)

compulsions (p. 791)

conversion disorder (p. 797)

culture-bound disorders (p. 795)

delusions (p. 811)

depressive attributional pattern (p. 806)

depressive cognitive triad (p. 806)

disorganized schizophrenia (p. 813)

dissociative disorders (p. 798)

dissociative identity disorder (DID) (p. 799)

dopamine hypothesis (p. 815)

dysthymia (p. 801)

expressed emotion (p. 817)

generalized anxiety disorder (p. 790)

hallucinations (p. 812)

hypochondriasis (p. 797)

insanity (p. 785)

learned helplessness theory (p. 806)

major depression (p. 801)

mania (p. 802)

mood disorders (p. 801)

negative symptoms (p. 814)

neurotic anxiety (p. 793)

obsessions (p. 791)

pain disorder (p. 797)

panic disorders (p. 790)

paranoid schizophrenia (p. 813)

personality disorders (p. 819)

phobias (p. 789)

positive symptoms (p. 814)

post-traumatic stress disorder (PTSD) (p. 791)

psychogenic amnesia (p. 798)

psychogenic fugue (p. 799)

regression (p. 816)

reliability (p. 780)

schizophrenia (p. 811)

social causation hypothesis (p. 817)

social drift hypothesis (p. 817)

social phobias (p. 789)

somatoform disorders (p. 797)

specific phobias (p. 789)

splitting (p. 828)

suicide (p. 808)

trauma-dissociation theory (p. 800)

undifferentiated schizophrenia (p. 813)

validity (p. 780)

vulnerability-stress model (diathesis-stress model) (p. 778)

WHAT DO YOU THINK?

'DO I HAVE THAT DISORDER?' (p. 787)

Wondering if you have a psychological disorder when reading about their features is quite understandable. We all experience problems in living at various times, and we might react in ways that bear similarities to the disorders described in this chapter. Logically, seeing such a similarity does not necessarily mean that you have the disorder at a clinically significant level. On the other hand, if you find that maladaptive behaviours such as those described in this chapter are interfering with your happiness or personal effectiveness, then you should not hesitate to seek professional assistance in changing these behaviours. In addition to the three Ds discussed earlier (distress, dysfunction and deviance), you will want to consider the frequency with which the particular behaviours or experiences occur, as well as their intensity and their duration. When problem behaviours occur frequently, are intense, and/or last for a long time, they are more likely to be clinically significant. In such a case, it is important not to let any stigma you might attach to having a psychological problem keep you from acting in your best interest and discussing your problem with a mental health professional.

DID: DISSOCIATION OR ROLE-PLAYING? (p. 800)

If a person asked to role-play different people could exhibit radically different behavioural and physiological features, could we conclude that the trauma-dissociation model of DID is disproven or that DID does not exist? A critical thinker will reframe this as follows: does the fact that one explanation of a given phenomenon is supported prove that all other potential explanations are impossible? Not at all, as supporters of the trauma-dissociation theory would correctly maintain. Indeed, a compelling depiction of an autistic adult by a skilled actor such as Dustin Hoffman in *Rain Man* does not imply that autistic disorder involves nothing more than acting. However, from a scientific perspective, the principle of parsimony dictates that if two different theories can each account for *all* the phenomena, then we should choose the simpler of the two theories. Although intriguing, our view is that the role theory explanation has not yet achieved the scientific support needed to displace other DID theories.

CHAPTER EIGHTEEN

TREATMENT OF PSYCHOLOGICAL DISORDERS

*It is a process, a thing-in-itself, an experience, a
relationship, a dynamic.*

CARL ROGERS

There is no doubt in my mind that therapy helped me.... For so long I wondered why my therapist insisted on talking about my relationship with him. He was not my problem; the problem was my life – my past, my fears, what I was going to do tomorrow, how I would handle things, sometimes just how to survive.... It took a long time, but finally I saw why it was important to explore my relationship with my therapist – it was the first real relationship I had ever had: that is, the first I felt safe enough to invest myself in. I rationalized that it was all right because I would learn from this relationship how to relate to other people and maybe even one day leave behind the isolation of my own world.... I often felt at odds with my therapist until I could see that he was a real person and he related to me and I to him, not only as patient and therapist, but as human beings. Eventually I began to feel that I too was a person, not just an outsider looking in on the world.

Medication or superficial support is not a substitute for the feeling that one is understood by another human being. For me, the greatest gift came the day I realized that my therapist really had stood by me for years and that he would continue to stand by me and help me achieve what I wanted to achieve. With that realization, my viability as a person began to grow. ('A recovering patient', 1986, pp. 68–70)

In this poignant account, written by a person who had suffered from schizophrenia for much of her life, we see that even in this most serious of behaviour disorders, humans can reach out and help one another. This chapter explores the many approaches that are being taken to treat psychological disorders, as well as the critical issue of their effectiveness. Although first-person reports, like the one above, suggest that many people derive considerable benefit from psychotherapy, psychologists demand much more in the way of evidence. Nearly 60 years of research on psychological treatments has taught us that the question of efficacy, or treatment outcome, is a tremendously complex one that has no simple answers. Yet as we shall see, much has been learned about the effectiveness of these various therapeutic approaches and about the factors that influence treatment outcome.

PSYCHOLOGICAL TREATMENTS

The basic goal of all psychotherapy, whatever the approach, is to help people change maladaptive thoughts, feelings and behaviour patterns so that they can live happier and more productive lives. As the remarks of the 'recovering patient' suggest, the relationship between the client and the person providing help is a prime ingredient of psychotherapeutic success (Binder and Strupp, 1997; Gabbard et al., 2005). Within that helping relationship, therapists use a variety of treatment techniques to promote positive changes in the client. These techniques vary widely, depending on the therapists' own theories of cause and change, and they may range from biomedical approaches (such as administering psychoactive drugs) to a wide variety of psychological treatments. Both of these elements – relationship and techniques – are important to the success of the treatment enterprise (Figs 18.1 and 18.2).

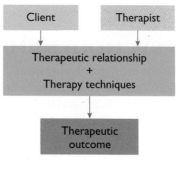

FIGURE 18.1

The process of therapy involves a relationship between a client and a therapist, who applies the techniques dictated by his or her approach to treatment.

PROFESSIONAL BODIES AND ORGANIZATIONS

The role of professional bodies is very important in this area. In an earlier chapter we described these bodies as responsible for overseeing that psychological teaching and research is done ethically, each with their own, but similar, guidelines in this area. These professional bodies also guide and accredit the provision of these therapy and counselling qualifications. There are other organizations that psychologists themselves belong to, and as members they agree to abide by rules and guidelines for professional conduct laid down by those societies. These societies include the British Psychological Association, the Danish Psychologists Association, Suomen Psyckologinen Seura in Finland, The Malta Union of Professional Psychologists, Nederlands Instituut van Psychologen, the Norwegian Psychological Association, the Psychological Society of South Africa and the Swedish Psychological Association.

Focus 18.1

How do client, therapist and treatment techniques combine in the process of therapy?

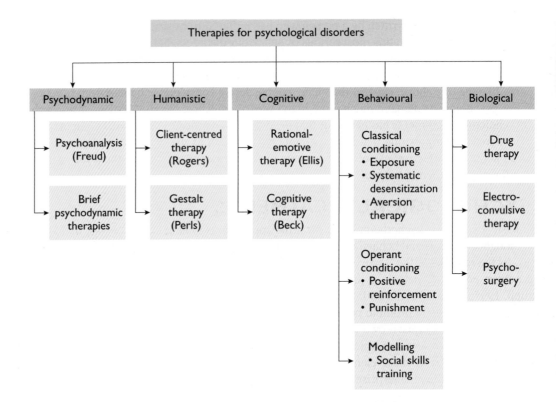

FIGURE 18.2

Major approaches to treatment.

This diagram gives an overview of the major treatment approaches to behaviour disorders.

PSYCHODYNAMIC THERAPIES

Of the many psychotherapeutic approaches, psychodynamic treatments have the longest tradition. Their historical roots lie in Sigmund Freud's psychoanalytic theory. Although both the theory and the techniques of therapy were later modified by his followers and by those who defected to pursue rival approaches, the psychodynamic principles underlying Freud's approach continue to exert a major influence today (Alexander, 2004). Psychodynamic approaches have in common a focus on internal conflicts and unconscious factors that underlie maladaptive behaviour.

PSYCHOANALYSIS

The term *psychoanalysis* refers not only to Freud's theory of personality but also to the specific approach to treatment that he developed. The goal of psychoanalysis is to help clients achieve **insight**, the conscious awareness of the psychodynamics that underlie their problems. Such awareness permits clients to adjust their behaviour to their current life situations, rather than repeating the maladaptive routines learned in childhood. Analysts believe that as the client repeatedly encounters and deals with long-buried emotions, motives and conflicts within and outside therapy, the psychic energy that was previously devoted to keeping unconscious conflicts under control can be released and redirected to more adaptive ways of living (Gabbard, 2004). We now consider the methods and concepts that Freud developed to achieve the end product of successful therapy: 'Where there was id, there shall ego be' (Freud, 1923, p. 148).

Free Association

Freud believed that mental events are meaningfully associated with one another, so that clues to the contents of the unconscious can be found in the ongoing stream of thoughts, memories, images and feelings that we experience. In the technique of **free association**, clients verbally report without censorship any thoughts, feelings or images that enter their awareness. Analysts sit out of sight behind the client so that the client's thought processes will be determined primarily by internal factors (Fig. 18.3).

The analyst does not expect that free association will necessarily lead directly to unconscious material but, rather, that it will provide clues concerning important themes or issues (Hoffer and Youngren, 2004). For example, a client's stream of thoughts may suddenly stop after she mentions her father, suggesting that she was approaching a salient topic that activated repressive defences

FIGURE 18.3

In classical Freudian psychoanalysis, the client reclines on a couch while the analyst sits out of view to minimize external stimuli that might influence the client's thought processes.

Focus 18.2
What is the major therapeutic goal in psychoanalysis?

Focus 18.3
Describe the roles of free association, dream analysis, resistance, transference and interpretation in psychoanalysis.

Dream Interpretation

Psychoanalysts believe that dreams express impulses, fantasies and wishes that the client's defences keep bottled up in the unconscious during waking hours (Glucksman, 2001). Even in dreams, which Freud termed 'the royal road to the unconscious', defensive processes usually disguise the threatening material to protect the dreamer from the anxiety that the material might evoke. In dream interpretation, the analyst helps the client search for the unconscious material contained in the dreams. One means of doing so is to ask the client to free-associate to each element of the dream. The analyst then helps the client arrive at an understanding of what the symbols in the dream might really represent (Fig. 18.4).

"HAVE A COUPLE OF DREAMS, AND CALL ME IN THE MORNING."

FIGURE 18.4

Dream analysis is a central technique in psychoanalysis.
SOURCE: Copyright © 2003 by Sidney Harris: ScienceCartoonsPlus.com. Reprinted with permission.

Resistance

Although clients come to therapists for help, they also have an unconscious investment in maintaining the status quo. After all, underlying their problems are unconscious conflicts so threatening and painful that the ego has resorted to maladaptive defensive patterns to deal with them. These avoidance patterns emerge in the course of therapy as **resistance**, defensive manoeuvres that hinder the process of therapy. Resistance can appear in many different forms. A client may suddenly experience difficulty in free-associating, arrive late at a therapy session or 'forget' about it altogether, or avoid talking about certain topics. Resistance is a sign that anxiety-arousing material is being approached. An important task of analysis is to explore the reasons for resistance, both to promote insight and to guard against the ultimate resistance: the client's decision to drop out of therapy prematurely.

resistance
defensive manoeuvres that hinder the process of therapy

Transference

As noted earlier, the analyst sits out of view of the client and reveals nothing to the client about himself or herself. Eventually, Freud discovered, clients begin to project onto the 'blank screen' of the therapist important perceptions and feelings related to their underlying conflicts. **Transference** occurs when the client responds irrationally to the analyst as if he or she were an important figure from the client's past. Transference is considered a most important process in psychoanalysis, for it brings into the open repressed feelings and maladaptive behaviour patterns that both the therapist and client can discover and explore.

Transference takes two basic forms. *Positive transference* occurs when a client transfers feelings of intense affection, dependency or love to the analyst, whereas *negative transference* involves irrational expressions of anger, hatred or disappointment. Analysts believe that until transference reactions are analysed and resolved, there can be no full resolution of the client's problems. In the following excerpt from a psychoanalytic session, a client traces her transference reaction to its source and then recognizes the operation of similar reactions in other relationships.

> *Client*: I have conflicting emotions about you. Sometimes I like you too much and sometimes I get mad at you for no reason. I often can't think of you, even picture you.... Yes, I don't want to like you. If I do, I won't be able to help myself. I'll get hurt. But why do I feel or insist that I'm in love with you?
>
> *Therapist*: Are you?
>
> *Client*: Yes. And I feel so guilty and upset about it. At night I think of you and get sexual feelings and it frightens me.
>
> *Therapist*: Do I remind you of anyone?
>
> *Client*: Yes. (Pause) There are things about you that remind me of my brother.
>
> (Laughs) I realize this is silly.
>
> *Therapist*: Mmhmm.
>
> *Client*: My brother Harry, the one I had the sex experiences with when I was little. He made me do things I didn't want to.... I'm afraid of you taking advantage of me. If I tell you I like you, that means you'll make me do what you want.
>
> *Therapist*: Just like Harry made you do what he wanted.
>
> *Client*: Yes. I didn't want to let him do what he did, but I couldn't help myself. I hated myself. That's why. I know it now because there is no reason why I should feel you are the same way. That's why I act that way with other people too.... I don't like to have people get too close to me. The whole thing is the same as happens with you. It's all so silly and wrong. You aren't my brother and the other people aren't my brother. I never saw the connection until now. (Wolberg, 1967, pp. 660–1)

In this interchange, we see both positive and negative transference reactions based on an important past relationship. The client's feelings about her brother continue to play out in her fear of getting close to others and being exploited once again.

Interpretation

How can analysts help clients detect and understand resistances, the meaning of dream symbols, and transference reactions? The analyst's chief therapeutic technique for these purposes is **interpretation**, any statement by the therapist that is intended to provide the client with insight into his or her behaviour or dynamics. An interpretative statement confronts clients with something that they have not previously admitted into consciousness, for example, 'It's almost as if you're angry with me without realizing it'.

---

transference

occurs when the client responds irrationally to the analyst as if he or she were an important figure from the client's past

interpretation

any statement by the therapist that is intended to provide the client with insight into his or her behaviour or dynamics

A general rule in psychoanalytic treatment is to interpret what is already near the surface and just beyond the client's current awareness (McWilliams, 2004). Offering 'deep' interpretations of strongly defended unconscious dynamics is considered poor technique because, even if they are correct, such interpretations are so far removed from the client's current awareness that they cannot be informative or helpful. This is one reason that even after the analyst fully understands the causes of the client's problems, psychoanalysis may require several more years of treatment. It is the client who must eventually arrive at the insights, then translate them into behaviour changes within important life domains and relationships.

BRIEF PSYCHODYNAMIC AND INTERPERSONAL THERAPIES

Classical psychoanalysis as practised by Freud (and by a declining number of contemporary analysts) is an expensive and time-consuming process, for the goal is no less than rebuilding the client's personality. In classical psychoanalysis, it is not uncommon for a client to be seen five times a week for five years or more. Today, however, many therapists consider this level of client–therapist commitment both impractical and unnecessary. Their conclusion is supported by psychotherapy studies in which researchers and clients rated the degree of improvement that occurred by the end of therapy. Figure 18.5 plots the amount of improvement in relation to the number of sessions the clients were seen for treatment (Howard et al., 1986). As you can see, about half of the clients improved markedly within eight sessions, and most therapeutic effects as rated by researchers occurred within 26 sessions. Other studies have also shown sudden gains early in treatment (Stiles et al., 2003).

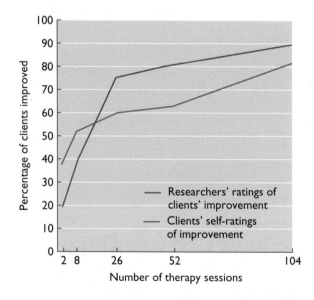

FIGURE 18.5

How quickly does improvement occur?

These data, based on researchers' and clients' ratings, suggest that many psychotherapy clients improve within eight months and that most improvement occurs within the first 26 sessions.

SOURCE: adapted from Howard et al., 1986.

To an increasing extent, psychodynamic therapists are adopting briefer and more economical approaches. Like psychoanalysis, brief psychodynamic psychotherapies focus on understanding the maladaptive influences of the past and relating them to current patterns of self-defeating behaviour. Many of these brief therapies utilize basic concepts from psychoanalysis, such as the importance of insight and the use of interpretation, but they employ them in a more focused and active fashion (Binder, 2004). The therapist and client are likely to sit facing each other and conversation typically replaces free association. Clients are seen once or twice a week rather than daily, and the goal is typically limited to helping the client deal with specific life problems rather than attempting a complete rebuilding of the client's personality. Therapy is therefore more likely to focus on the client's current life situations than on past childhood experiences, and may involve teaching the client specific interpersonal and emotion-control skills (Benjamin, 2003).

Focus 18.4

How do brief psychodynamic and interpersonal therapies differ from classical psychoanalysis? Which research results support their use?

interpersonal therapy
focuses almost exclusively on clients' current relationships with important people in their lives

One brief therapy, **interpersonal therapy**, focuses almost exclusively on clients' current relationships with important people in their lives (Weissman and Markowitz, 1994). This therapy, designed in part for research on the treatment of depression, is highly structured and seldom takes longer than 15 to 20 sessions. Therapeutic goals include resolving role disputes such as marital conflict, adjusting to the loss of a relationship or to a changed relationship, and identifying and correcting deficits in social skills that make it difficult for the client to initiate or maintain satisfying relationships. The therapist collaborates very actively with the client in finding solutions to these problems and may invite the client to link issues in current relationships with those in important past relationships, thereby showing that what happened in the past need not be carried into the present. In controlled outcome studies, interpersonal therapy has proven effective for several disorders, particularly depression (Chambless and Hollon, 1998; DeRubeis and Crits-Christoph, 1998). Its relative brevity appeals not only to clinicians but also to insurance companies and health maintenance organizations that are interested in reducing therapy costs.

IN REVIEW

- The client, the therapist and the techniques used by the therapist combine to influence the outcomes of psychotherapy.

- Psychodynamic therapists view maladaptive behaviours as symptoms of an underlying conflict that needs to be resolved if behaviour is to change.

- The goal of Freudian psychoanalysis is to help clients achieve insight into the unconscious dynamics that underlie their behaviour disorders so that they can deal adaptively with their current environment.

- The therapist's chief means for promoting insight in psychoanalysis is the interpretation of the client's free associations, dream content, resistance and transference reactions.

- Brief psychodynamic therapies have become increasingly popular alternatives to lengthy psychoanalysis. Their goal is also to promote insight, but they tend to focus more on current life events. Interpersonal therapy is a structured therapy that focuses on addressing current interpersonal problems and enhancing interpersonal skills.

HUMANISTIC PSYCHOTHERAPIES

Focus 18.5

How does the goal of humanistic therapies differ from that of psychodynamic therapies?

In contrast to psychodynamic theorists, who view behaviour as a product of unconscious processes, humanistic theorists view humans as capable of consciously controlling their actions and taking responsibility for their choices and behaviour. These theorists also believe that everyone possesses inner resources for self-healing and personal growth, and that disordered behaviour reflects a blocking of the natural growth process. This blocking is brought about by distorted perceptions, lack of awareness about feelings, or a negative self-image.

When these assumptions about human nature are applied to psychotherapy, they inspire treatments that are radically different from psychoanalysis. Humanistic psychotherapy is seen as a human encounter between equals. The therapist's goal is to create an environment in which clients can engage in self-exploration and remove the barriers that block their natural tendencies towards personal growth (Greenberg and Rice, 1997). These barriers often result from childhood experiences that fostered unrealistic or maladaptive standards for self-worth. When people try to live their lives according to the expectations of others rather than their own desires and feelings, they often feel unfulfilled and empty and unsure about who they really are.

In contrast to classical psychoanalytic therapy, humanistic approaches focus primarily on the present and future instead of the past. Therapy is directed at helping clients to become aware of feelings as they occur rather than to achieve insights into the childhood origins of those feelings.

CLIENT-CENTRED THERAPY

The best-known and most widely used humanistic therapy is the *client-centred* (now sometimes called *person-centred*) *approach* developed by Carl Rogers (1959; 1980; Fig. 18.6). In the 1940s, Rogers began to depart from psychoanalytic methods. He became convinced that the important active ingredient in therapy is the relationship that develops between client and therapist, and he began to focus his attention on the kind of therapeutic environment that seemed most effective in fostering self-exploration and personal growth (Bozarth et al., 2002). Rogers's research and experiences as a therapist identified three important and interrelated therapist attributes:

1. **Unconditional positive regard** is communicated when the therapist shows that he or she genuinely cares about and accepts the client, without judgement or evaluation. The therapist also communicates a sense of trust in the client's ability to work through his or her problems. In part, this sense of trust is communicated in the therapist's refusal to offer advice or guidance.

2. **Empathy**, the willingness and ability to view the world through the client's eyes, is a second vital factor. In a good therapeutic relationship, the therapist comes to sense the feelings and meanings experienced by the client and communicates this understanding to the client. The therapist does this by *reflecting* back to the client what she or he is communicating – perhaps by rephrasing something the client has just said in a way that captures the meaning and emotion involved.

3. **Genuineness** refers to consistency between the way the therapist feels and the way he or she behaves. The therapist must be open enough to express his or her own feelings honestly, whether positive or negative. In the case of negative feelings, this may seem to be contradictory to the attribute of unconditional positive regard, but that is not necessarily the case. Indeed, the most striking demonstrations of both attributes occur when a therapist can express displeasure with a client's behaviour and at the same time communicate acceptance of the client as a person. For example, a therapist might say, 'I feel frustrated with the way you handled that situation because I want things to work out better than that for you.'

Rogers believed that when therapists can express these three key therapeutic attributes, they create a climate in which the client feels accepted, understood, and free to explore basic attitudes and feelings without fear of being judged or rejected. Within such a climate, the client experiences the courage and freedom to grow. These therapeutic attitudes are exhibited in the following excerpt from one of Rogers's therapy sessions:

Client: I cannot be the kind of person I want to be. I guess maybe I haven't the guts or the strength to kill myself, and if someone else would relieve me of the responsibility or I would be in an accident, I – just don't want to live.

Rogers: At the present time things look so black that you can't see much point in living. (Note the use of empathic reflection and the absence of any criticism.)

Client: Yes, I wish I'd never started this therapy. I was happy when I was living in my dream world. There I could be the kind of person I wanted to be. But now there is such a wide, wide gap between my ideal and what I am.... (Notice how the client responds to reflection with more information.)

Rogers: It's really tough digging into this like you are and at times the shelter of your dream world looks more attractive and comfortable. (Reflection.)

FIGURE 18.6

'Psychotherapy is the releasing of an already existing capacity in a potentially competent individual, not the expert manipulation of a more or less passive personality' (Carl Rogers).

unconditional positive regard

communicated when the therapist shows that he or she genuinely cares about and accepts the client, without judgement or evaluation

empathy

the willingness and ability to view the world through the client's eyes

genuineness

consistency between the way the therapist feels and the way he or she behaves

Focus 18.6

What three therapist attributes did Rogers find to be crucial to therapeutic success?

Client: My dream world or suicide.... So I don't see why I should waste your time coming in twice a week – I'm not worth it – what do you think?

Rogers: It's up to you.... It isn't wasting my time. I'd be glad to see you whenever you come, but it's how you feel about it.... (Note the genuineness in stating an honest desire to see the client and the unconditional positive regard in trusting her capacity and responsibility for choice.)

Client: You're not going to suggest that I come in oftener? You're not alarmed and think I ought to come in every day until I get out of this?

Rogers: I believe you're able to make your own decision. I'll see you whenever you want to come. (Trust and positive regard.)

Client: (Note of awe in her voice.) I don't believe you are alarmed about – I see – I may be afraid of myself but you aren't afraid for me. (She experiences the therapist's confidence in her.)

Rogers: You say you may be afraid of yourself and are wondering why I don't seem to be afraid for you. (Reflection.)

Client: You have more confidence in me than I have. I'll see you next week, maybe. (Based on Rogers, 1951, p. 49) [The client did not attempt suicide.]

Rogers believed that as clients experience a constructive therapeutic relationship, they exhibit increased self-acceptance, greater self-awareness, enhanced self-reliance, increased comfort with other relationships, and improved life functioning (Rogers, 1959). Research does indicate that therapists' characteristics have a strong effect on the outcome of psychotherapy. Therapy is most likely to be successful when the therapist is perceived as genuine, warm and empathic (Sachse and Elliott, 2002).

GESTALT THERAPY

Frederick S. (Fritz) Perls, a psychoanalyst who was trained in Gestalt psychology, developed another humanistic approach to treatment. As noted in Chapter 5, the term *gestalt* ('organized whole') refers to perceptual principles through which people actively organize stimulus elements into meaningful 'whole' patterns. Ordinarily, whatever we perceive, whether external stimuli, ideas, or emotions, we concentrate on only part of our whole experience – the figure – while largely ignoring the background against which the figure appears. For people who have psychological difficulties, that background includes important feelings, wishes, and thoughts that are blocked from ordinary awareness because they would evoke anxiety. Gestalt therapy's goal is to bring them into immediate awareness so that the client can be whole once again.

Focus 18.7

What is the goal of gestalt therapy?

Gestalt therapy, often carried out in groups, entails a variety of imaginative techniques to help clients 'get in touch with their inner selves'. These methods are much more active and dramatic than client-centred approaches and sometimes even confrontational. Therapists often ask clients to role-play different aspects of themselves so that they may directly experience their inner dynamics. In the *empty-chair technique*, a client may be asked to imagine his mother sitting in the chair, then carry on a conversation in which he alternatively role-plays his mother and himself, changing chairs for each role and honestly telling her how he feels about important issues in their relationship. These techniques can evoke powerful feelings and make clients aware of unresolved issues that affect other relationships in their lives as well. Recent research on the empty-chair technique indicates that it does indeed help clients resolve 'unfinished business' with significant others from their pasts (Greenberg and Malcolm, 2002). Although Perls died in 1970, Gestalt therapy remains a vital force, and its principles and techniques are being incorporated into non-humanistic therapies as well (Burley and Freier, 2004; Cain and Seeman, 2002).

IN REVIEW

- Humanistic psychotherapies attempt to liberate the client's natural tendency towards self-actualization by establishing a growth-inducing therapeutic relationship.

- Rogers's client-centred therapy emphasizes the importance of three therapist characteristics: unconditional positive regard, empathy and genuineness.

- The goal of Gestalt therapy is to remove blockages to clients' awareness of the wholeness of immediate experience by making them more aware of their feelings and the ways in which they interact with others.

COGNITIVE THERAPIES

As we saw in the previous chapter, many behaviour disorders, including anxiety, mood and schizophrenic disorders, involve maladaptive ways of thinking about oneself and the world. Cognitive approaches to psychotherapy focus on the role of irrational and self-defeating thought patterns, and therapists who employ this approach try to help clients discover and change the cognitions that underlie their problems.

In contrast to psychoanalysts, cognitive therapists do not emphasize the importance of unconscious psychodynamic processes. They do, however, point out that because our habitual thought patterns are so well-practised and ingrained, they tend to 'run off' almost automatically, so that we may be only minimally aware of them and may simply accept them as reflecting reality (Clark et al., 1999). Consequently, clients often need help in identifying the beliefs, ideas, and self-statements that trigger maladaptive emotions and behaviours. Once identified, these cognitions can be challenged and, with practice and effort, changed. Albert Ellis and Aaron Beck are the most influential figures in the cognitive approach to therapy.

ELLIS'S RATIONAL-EMOTIVE THERAPY

Albert Ellis originally trained as a psychoanalytic therapist, but became convinced that irrational thoughts, rather than unconscious dynamics, were the most immediate cause of self-defeating emotions. In the 1960s, his new approach of rational emotive therapy helped launch the cognitive revolution in clinical psychology.

Ellis's theory of emotional disturbance and his rational-emotive therapy are embodied in his ABCD model (Fig. 18.7).

- *A* stands for the *activating event* that seems to trigger the emotion.
- *B* stands for the *belief system* that underlies the way in which a person appraises the event.
- *C* stands for the emotional and behavioural *consequences* of that appraisal.
- *D* is the key to changing maladaptive emotions and behaviours: *disputing*, or challenging, an erroneous belief system.

Ellis points out that people are accustomed to viewing their emotions (C) as being caused directly by events (A). Thus a young man who is turned down for a date may feel rejected and depressed. However, Ellis would insist that the woman's refusal is *not* the true reason for the emotional reaction. Rather, the young man's depression is caused by his irrational belief that 'Because she doesn't want to be with me, I'm worthless, and no one will ever want me'. If the young man does not want to feel depressed and rejected, this belief must be countered and

Focus 18.8

How is the ABCD model used in rational-emotive therapy? Which disorders respond well to Beck's cognitive therapy?

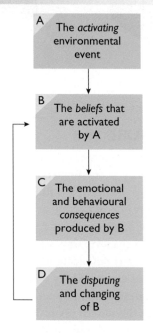

FIGURE 18.7

Ellis's ABCD model.

Albert Ellis's ABCD model describes his theory of the cause – and remediation – of maladaptive emotional responses and behaviours. In rational-emotive therapy, the goal is to discover, dispute, and change the client's maladaptive beliefs.

replaced by a more rational interpretation (e.g., 'It would have been nice if she had accepted my invitation, but I don't need to turn it into a catastrophe. It doesn't mean other women will never care about me').

Rational-emotive therapists introduce clients to commonly held irrational beliefs (Table 18.1) and then train them to ferret out the particular ideas that underlie their maladaptive emotional responses (Fig. 18.8). Clients are given homework assignments to help them analyse and change self-statements. They may be asked to place themselves in challenging situations and practice control over their emotions by using new self-statements. For example, a shy person might be required to go to a party and practice rational thoughts that counteract social anxiety. Ellis reports that he overcame his own fears of women's rejection by going to Central Park in New York, practicing anxiety-reducing self-statements and striking up conversations with more than 100 different women. He reports that he got only one date, but he overcame his anxiety without being either assaulted or arrested. By learning and practicing cognitive coping responses, clients can eventually modify underlying belief systems in ways that enhance wellbeing (Dryden, 2002).

TABLE 18.1 IRRATIONAL IDEAS THAT CAUSE DISTURBANCE AND ALTERNATIVES THAT MIGHT BE OFFERED BY A RATIONAL-EMOTIVE THERAPIST

Irrational belief	Rational alternative
It is a dire necessity that I be loved and approved of by virtually everyone for everything I do	Although we might prefer approval to disapproval, our self-worth need not depend on the love and approval of others. Self-respect is more important than giving up one's individuality to buy the approval of others
I must be thoroughly competent and achieving to be worthwhile. To fail is to be a failure	As imperfect and fallible human beings, we are bound to fail from time to time. We can control only effort; we have incomplete control over outcome. We are better off focusing on the process of doing rather than on demands that we do well
It is terrible, awful and catastrophic when things are not the way I demand that they be	Stop catastrophizing and turning an annoyance or irritation into a major crisis. Who are we to demand that things be different from what they are? When we turn our preferences into dire necessities, we set ourselves up for needless distress. We had best learn to change those things we can control and accept those that we cannot control (and be wise enough to know the difference)
Human misery is externally caused and forced on us by other people and events	Human misery is produced not by external factors but rather by what we tell ourselves about those events. We feel as we think, and most of our misery is needlessly self-inflicted by irrational habits of thinking
Because something deeply affected me in the past, it must continue to do so	We hold ourselves prisoner to the past because we continue to believe philosophies and ideas learned in the past. If they are still troubling us today, it is because we are still propagandizing ourselves with irrational nonsense. We can control how we think in the present and thereby liberate ourselves from the 'scars' of the past

BECK'S COGNITIVE THERAPY

Like Ellis, Aaron Beck's goal is to point out errors of thinking and logic that underlie emotional disturbance and to help clients identify and reprogramme their overlearned automatic thought patterns (Fig. 18.9). In treating depressed clients, a first step is to help clients realize that their thoughts, and not the situation, cause their maladaptive emotional reactions. This sets the stage for identifying and changing the self-defeating thoughts:

FIGURE 18.8

'The essence of effective therapy according to rational-emotive therapy is full tolerance of people as individuals combined with a ruthless campaign against their self-defeating ideas.... These can be easily elicited and demolished by any scientist worth his or her salt; and the rational-emotive therapist is exactly that: an exposing and nonsense-annihilating scientist' (Albert Ellis).

Client: I get depressed when things go wrong. Like when I fail a test.

Beck: How can failing a test make you depressed?

Client: Well, if I fail, I'll never get into law school.

Beck: So failing a test means a lot to you. But if failing a test could drive people into clinical depression, wouldn't you expect everyone who failed a test to have a depression? Did everyone who failed get depressed enough to require treatment?

Client: No, but it depends on how important the test was to the person.

Beck: Right, and who decides the importance?

Client: I do.

Beck: Now what did failing mean?

Client: (Tearful) That I couldn't get into law school.

Beck: And what does that mean to you?

Client: That I'm just not smart enough.

Beck: Anything else?

Client: That I can never be happy.

Beck: And how do those thoughts make you feel?

Client: Very unhappy.

Beck: So it is the *meaning* of failing a test that makes you very unhappy. In fact, believing that you can never be happy is a powerful factor in producing unhappiness. So you get yourself into a trap – by definition, failure to get into law school equals 'I can never be happy.' (Beck et al., 1979, pp. 145–6, emphasis added)

Beck's contributions to understanding and treating depression have made his cognitive therapy a psychological treatment of choice for that disorder (Moorey, 2003). Cognitive therapy has also been applied to the treatment of anxiety and personality disorders (Beck et al., 2004; Clark, 2004).

Cognitive behaviour therapies (as they have become known) deserve a little more of the spotlight. The rise in use and acceptance of cognitive behaviour therapy of the last few years has been nothing short of extraordinary. In the UK, for instance, it has now risen to be one of the dominant treatments offered by the National Health Service (NHS). Its use is backed by both mental-health policy makers and the politicians who help make the law. The impact of this treatment is very significant indeed. As we have described, the therapies have their roots in cognition and the premise that the problem the client has can be alleviated through carefully helping them modify their thoughts and, importantly, their behaviours. In doing this the clinician influences the client's emotions. It was Arnold Lazarus (1971) who first used the term 'behaviour therapy' in this context, and to some extent might be regarded as the founding father of this enormously popular style of therapy.

The therapy can be used for a very wide spectrum of problems, including depression, general anxiety disorders and obsessive-compulsive disorder. It is used with adults and with children and adolescents, and can be combined with drug therapy. When combined with drugs, research has shown it to be even more effective in helping those with depression (Leahy and Holland, 2000). It is wide ranging, flexible, relatively cheap and has been shown in very many cases to works. The popularity of cognitive behaviour therapy (CBT) seems set to rise and rise. A very interesting development in CBT is the development and introduction of computerized sessions. The British National Health Service (Department of Health, 2007) continues to show its support of CBT by backing a project aimed to provide computerized CBT (CCBT) via the NHS. The *Delphi Poll* is a survey carried out every 10 years, begun by Norcross and Prochaska in 1982. The survey asks some of the most prominent psychotherapists around the world to predict the direction psychotherapy might take. When first surveyed in 1982, the *Delphi Poll* correctly predicted that the popularity of CBT would rise over the decade that followed. In fact, the popularity of CBT has continued to rise and rise, in each of the three decades following the first

FIGURE 18.9

'The formula for treatment may be stated in simple terms: The therapist helps the patient to identify his warped thinking and to learn more realistic ways to formulate his experience' (Aaron Beck).

Focus 18.9

Which classical and operant conditioning principles underlie exposure therapy? What problems is it applied to?

Delphi Poll. Merrick and Dattilio (2006) indicate that it is now described as the number one 'theoretical orientation', meaning that, out of all forms of therapy, more therapists regard themselves as cognitive therapists than anything else. Soon we will be provided with access to CBT online. The ease of access to some forms of this therapy should ensure its popularity for years to come.

BEHAVIOUR THERAPIES

In the 1960s, behavioural approaches emerged as a dramatic departure from the assumptions and methods that characterized psychoanalytic and humanistic therapies. The new practitioners of behaviour therapy denied the importance of inner dynamics. Instead, they insisted that (1) maladaptive behaviours are not merely symptoms of underlying problems but rather *are* the problem; (2) problem behaviours are learned in the same ways normal behaviours are; and (3) maladaptive behaviours can be unlearned by applying principles derived from research on classical conditioning, operant conditioning and modelling. Behaviourists demonstrated that these learning procedures could be applied effectively to change the behaviours of schizophrenia, to treat anxiety disorders, and to modify many child and adult behaviour problems that seemed resistant to traditional therapy approaches (Hersen, 2002).

Classical conditioning procedures have been used in two major ways. First, they have been used to reduce, or decondition, anxiety responses. Second, they have been used in attempts to condition aversive emotional responses to a particular class of stimuli, such as alcohol or inappropriate sexual objects. The most commonly used classical conditioning procedures are *exposure therapies*, *systematic desensitization* and *aversion therapy*.

EXPOSURE: AN EXTINCTION APPROACH

From a behavioural point of view, phobias and other fears result from classically conditioned emotional responses. The conditioning experience is assumed to involve a pairing of the phobic object (the neutral stimulus) with an aversive unconditioned stimulus (UCS). As a result, the phobic stimulus becomes a conditioned stimulus (CS) that elicits the conditioned response (CR) of anxiety. According to the two-factor learning theory (Mowrer, 1947) discussed in Chapter 7, avoidance responses to the phobic situation are then reinforced by anxiety reduction (operant conditioning based on negative reinforcement). Thus a person who is bitten by a dog may subsequently be afraid of dogs. Moreover, each time he avoids a dog, his avoidance response is strengthened through anxiety reduction.

exposure
to the feared CS in the absence of the UCS

response prevention
to keep the operant avoidance response from occurring

FIGURE 18.10

A behaviour therapist guides and supports a client with a dog phobia during an *in vivo* exposure therapy session. As a result of exposure, the man's anxiety will extinguish and he will be able to interact more comfortably with this animal and with other dogs.

According to this formulation, the most direct way to reduce the fear is through a process of classical extinction of the anxiety response. This requires **exposure** to the feared CS in the absence of the UCS while using **response prevention** to keep the operant avoidance response from occurring. This is the theoretical basis for the exposure approach (Marks, 1991; Zinbarg et al., 1992). The client may be exposed to real-life stimuli (Fig. 18.10) or asked to imagine scenes involving the stimuli. These stimuli will, of course, evoke considerable anxiety, but the anxiety will extinguish in time if the person remains in the presence of the CS and the UCS does not occur (Rosqvist and Hersen, 2006). The process may need repeating over time.

Some critics of exposure treatment are concerned that the intense anxiety created by the treatment may worsen the problem or cause clients to flee from treatment (Bruce and Sanderson, 1998). In a study of women being treated for post-traumatic stress disorder with exposure created by imaging the traumatic event, 15.4 per cent of the women did indeed show a temporary increase in PTSD symptom intensity when exposure began.

However, this increase did not impair treatment effectiveness or increase the likelihood of withdrawal from treatment (Foa et al., 2002).

Exposure has proved to be a highly effective technique for extinguishing anxiety responses in both animals and humans (Roth and Fonagy, 2005; Spiegler and Guevremont, 2003). Both real-life (*in vivo*) and imaginal exposure are effective. An additional advantage is that clients can administer exposure treatment to themselves under a therapist's direction with high success rates (Marks, 1991).

Computer technology has provided a new method for delivering exposure treatments by bringing the external environment into the therapy room. **Virtual reality (VR)** involves the use of computer technology to create highly realistic virtual environments that simulate actual experience so vividly that they evoke many of the same reactions that a comparable real-world environment would. Observers typically wear helmets containing two small video monitors (one for each eye) attached to a high-speed computer. The image to each eye is slightly different, producing binocular depth perception cues that result in a three-dimensional image. With the aid of position-tracking devices, the computer monitors the person's physical movements and adjusts the images and sounds accordingly (Fig. 18.11). Observers thus have a vivid sense of being 'present' in a different place when navigating through the virtual world. Virtual reality is increasingly being applied to the treatment of anxiety disorders, particularly phobias (Wiederhold and Wiederhold, 2005). The following 'Research close-up' describes the use of VR in treating patients with a fear of flying.

> **virtual reality (VR)**
> the use of computer technology to create highly realistic virtual environments that simulate actual experience so vividly that they evoke many of the same reactions that a comparable real-world environment would

FIGURE 18.11

This woman with a spider phobia views a virtual 'spider world' inside the helmet. She also handles a realistic toy spider whose movements inside the virtual environment are linked to her manipulation of the toy. The monitor shows the scene being experienced by the client.

RESEARCH CLOSE-UP

EXPOSURE TREATMENT FOR FEAR OF FLYING USING VIRTUAL REALITY

SOURCE: B.O. Rothbaum, L. Hodges, P.L. Anderson, L. Price and S. Smith (2002) Twelve-month follow-up of virtual reality and standard exposure therapies for the fear of flying, *Journal of Consulting and Clinical Psychology*, vol. 70, pp. 428–32.

INTRODUCTION

Approximately 25 million Americans suffer from a fear of flying in aeroplanes. They cope with their fear by flying under the influence of drugs or alcohol, or by avoiding flying altogether. These coping methods can have negative medical, social and occupational consequences.

Exposure therapy based on classical extinction principles offers a proven anxiety-reduction approach. In this study, exposure therapy using VR was compared with a standard exposure approach having in vivo and imaginal components and with a waiting-list control condition that did not immediately receive treatment. If effective, VR can be an economical method for treating people with a variety of fear-based conditions, for the stimuli can be easily tailored to the specific problem and client.

METHOD

Forty-nine people who replied to an advertisement offering treatment for severe fear of flying were randomly assigned to three conditions: VR exposure therapy, a standard exposure therapy and a waiting-list control group that was offered its choice of the two exposure therapies after the exposure groups were treated. Forty-five completed the study.

The VR and standard exposure treatments consisted of eight individual sessions over a six-week period. In the first 4 sessions, clients were oriented to the programme and learned to reduce anxiety using deep breathing and to counter irrational thoughts, such as 'This plane is going to crash. I'm doomed.'

Exposure therapy was carried out in the final four sessions. In the VR condition, clients donned a head-mounted display like that shown in Figure 18.11 and sat in specially equipped aeroplane seats. Stereo earphones piped in realistic recorded sounds of take-offs and landings and of flying in both clear and stormy weather. Woofers under the seats provided realistic sounds and vibrations to simulate flight stimuli and turbulence. The therapist encouraged the clients to continue their exposure to the stimuli until their anxiety diminished.

In the standard exposure condition, clients were taken to the Atlanta airport and went through ticketing and security checks, rode a train to a remote gate, sat in the gate area with passengers, and then boarded an empty airliner where they were seated and asked to imagine scenes like those experienced by the VR clients.

After the clients in the two exposure conditions completed their treatment, all clients in the three groups were offered the opportunity to take a round-trip commercial flight from Atlanta to Houston. Later, clients in the waiting-list control condition were offered their choice of the two exposure treatments. All but one of the 15 control clients chose the VR treatment.

RESULTS

After randomly assigning participants to experimental and control conditions, the researchers assessed the clients before treatment began, at the end of the exposure treatments, and 12 months after the completion of treatment. Outcome measures included both a self-report measure of fear of flying and a behavioural measure of actually flying in an airliner.

Figure 18.12 shows the intensity of clients' fear of flying at the three assessment periods. At the end of treatment, both exposure groups showed significant fear reduction as compared to the waiting-list clients, who had not yet received treatment. Treatment gains in the exposure clients were maintained over the next 12 months, indicating that the treatment provides long-term benefits. After the control clients received treatment, they exhibited similar improvement on the fear measure.

On the behavioural measure of flying, eight of 15 VR clients, 10 of 15 standard exposure clients and only one of 15 waiting-list clients accepted the invitation to take the post-treatment flight. By the 12-month follow-up, however, over 90 per cent of the clients in the two exposure conditions had taken at least one commercial airline flight. No differences were found between the exposure groups on overall self-ratings of improvement or on satisfaction with the treatments they received.

DISCUSSION

This study confirms the usefulness of short-term exposure treatments for anxiety-based problems, an effect shown in many previous studies (Rosqvist and Hersen, 2006). More significantly, results indicate that VR was similar in effectiveness to the traditional *in vivo* and imaginal exposure treatment, both in its initial effects at post-treatment and in the maintenance of therapy gains over the following 12 months. This was the first VR outcome study to conduct a follow-up assessment of treatment gains over such an extended period of time.

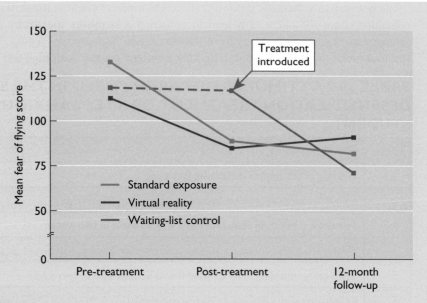

FIGURE 18.12

Effects of exposure treatment on self-reported fear of flying.

Exposure was carried out in two ways. Standard exposure involved *in vivo* and imaginal exposure, whereas virtual reality presented airline-related stimuli. Both exposure methods resulted in significant fear reduction that was maintained over a 12-month period. The waiting-list control group showed similar improvement when given the treatment.

SOURCE: based on Rothbaum et al., 2002.

Conducting exposure treatment using VR may have some practical advantages. If the VR programme is standardized for a particular fear, as in this study, then once the software has been developed, many therapists can apply the treatment to clients in their offices. Standard exposure treatments may require the therapist to leave the office and accompany the client to remote sites, an added treatment expense. With VR, a client may be able to experience many take-offs and landings per hour, whereas repeated experiences on real aeroplanes would be prohibitively expensive. Another advantage of VR is the degree of stimuli control; in the real world, specific stimuli are not always available on demand. On the other hand, customizing stimuli for a client may require extensive VR programming that could be very expensive. It thus appears that standardized VR presentations for specific fears (e.g., driving, heights, exposure to various animals) may be most feasible at this time. Future research is certain to provide more information about the effectiveness, advantages, and possible limitations of VR for a variety of other disorders.

SYSTEMATIC DESENSITIZATION: A COUNTER-CONDITIONING APPROACH

In 1958 Joseph Wolpe introduced **systematic desensitization**, a learning-based treatment for anxiety disorders. Wolpe also presented impressive outcome data for 100 phobic patients he had treated with the technique. Systematic desensitization remains a widely used treatment today. In many controlled studies, its success rate in treating a wide range of phobic disorders has been 80 per cent or better (Rachman, 1998; Spiegler and Guevremont, 2003).

Wolpe viewed anxiety as a classically conditioned emotional response. His goal was to eliminate the anxiety by using a procedure called **counter-conditioning**, in which a new response that is incompatible with anxiety is conditioned to the anxiety arousing CS. The difference between extinction and counter-conditioning is that extinction requires only exposure to the CS; it does not require a substitute response to counter the anxiety response.

systematic desensitization

a learning-based treatment for anxiety disorders

counter-conditioning

a new response that is incompatible with anxiety is conditioned to the anxiety arousing CS

stimulus hierarchy

10 to 20 scenes arranged in roughly equal steps from low-anxiety to high-anxiety scenes

The first step in systematic desensitization is to train the client in the skill of voluntary muscle relaxation. Next the client is helped to construct a **stimulus hierarchy** of 10 to 20 scenes arranged in roughly equal steps from low-anxiety to high-anxiety scenes. Table 18.2 shows a stimulus hierarchy that was used in treating a college student with high test anxiety.

TABLE 18.2 A STIMULUS HIERARCHY USED IN THE SYSTEMATIC DESENSITIZATION TREATMENT OF A TEST-ANXIOUS COLLEGE STUDENT

Scene	Hierarchy of anxiety-arousing scenes
1	Hearing about someone else who has a test
2	Instructor announcing that a test will be given in three weeks
3	Instructor reminding class that there will be a test in two weeks
4	Overhearing class-mates talk about studying for the test, which will occur in one week
5	Instructor reminding class of what it will be tested on in two days
6	Leaving class the day before the examination
7	Studying the night before the examination
8	Getting up the morning of the examination
9	Walking towards the building where the examination will be given
10	Walking into the testing room
11	Instructor walking into the room with the tests
12	Tests being passed out
13	Reading the test questions
14	Watching others finish the test
15	Seeing a question I cannot answer
16	Instructor waiting for me to finish the test

Focus 18.10

How does systematic desensitization differ from exposure in terms of its underlying principle and techniques?

In the desensitization sessions, the therapist deeply relaxes the client and then asks the client to vividly imagine the first scene in the hierarchy (the least anxiety-arousing one) for several seconds. The client cannot be both relaxed and anxious at the same time, so if the relaxation is strong enough, it replaces anxiety as the CR to that stimulus – the counter-conditioning process. When the client can imagine that scene for increasingly longer periods without experiencing anxiety, the therapist proceeds to the next scene. When low-arousal scenes have been deconditioned, some of the total anxiety has been reduced and the person is now ready to imagine more anxiety-arousing scenes without becoming anxious. Therapists can also accomplish desensitization through carefully controlled exposure to a hierarchy of real-life situations (e.g., having a person with a phobia of heights actually stand on a step stool and, eventually, walk across a suspension bridge while voluntarily relaxing). Both imaginal and real-life desensitization approaches are highly effective in reducing anxiety (Hersen, 2003).

Although both exposure therapy based on extinction and systematic desensitization are very effective in reducing fear responses, there are practical trade-offs. Systematic desensitization is sometimes preferred over exposure therapy because it produces far less anxiety for the client during the treatment. Exposure, however, often achieves the desired reduction in anxiety with a briefer course of therapy than does systematic desensitization (Bruce and Sanderson, 1998).

WHAT DO YOU THINK?

ARE CONDITIONING TECHNIQUES COMPATIBLE WITH PSYCHOANALYTIC THEORY?

Conditioning techniques such as exposure and systematic desensitization are highly effective in treating fears and phobias. Assume, however, that you are a psychoanalyst who believes that the phobia is the result of an underlying unconscious conflict. From your theoretical perspective, what concerns would you have about using these behavioural techniques? Think about it, then see the discussion p. 887.

AVERSION THERAPY

For some clients, the therapeutic goal is not to reduce anxiety but actually to condition anxiety to a particular stimulus that triggers deviant behaviour. In **aversion therapy**, the therapist pairs a stimulus that is attractive to the client (the CS) with a noxious UCS in an attempt to condition an aversion to the CS. For example, aversion treatment for alcoholics might involve injecting the client with a nausea-producing drug and then having him or her drink alcohol (the CS) as nausea (the UCS) develops. Electric shock may also be paired with alcohol ingestion. Similarly, paedophiles have undergone treatment in which strong electric shocks are paired with slides showing children similar to those the offenders sexually abused (Fig. 18.13). To measure the effects of the treatment for males, therapists can use a physiological recording device that measures penile blood-volume responses to the slides; the therapists can then compare the readings before and after treatment (Sandler, 1986).

aversion therapy
the therapist pairs a stimulus that is attractive to the client (the CS) with a noxious UCS in an attempt to condition an aversion to the CS

Focus 18.11
Which learning principles underlie aversion therapy? What are its limitations, and how can its effects be enhanced?

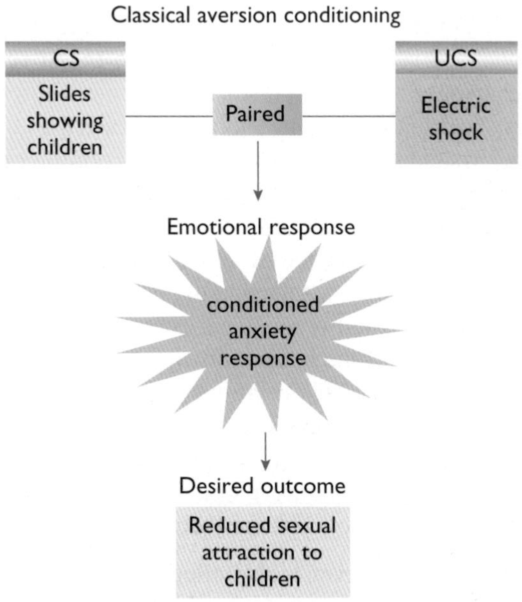

Classical aversion conditioning

CS		UCS
Slides showing children	Paired	Electric shock

Emotional response

conditioned anxiety response

Desired outcome

Reduced sexual attraction to children

FIGURE 18.13

Aversion therapy.

The classical conditioning that occurs in aversion therapy is illustrated in the treatment of paedophiles who receive electric shocks as they view pictures of children. The goal of the treatment is the development of a conditioned aversion in order to reduce sexual attraction to children.

Aversion therapies have been applied to a range of disorders, with variable results. In one study of 278 alcoholics who underwent aversion therapy, 190 (63 per cent) were still abstinent a year after treatment had ended. Three years later, a third of the patients were still abstinent, an impressive result given the traditionally high relapse rate in chronic alcoholic individuals (Wiens and Menustik, 1983). Unfortunately, treatment gains from aversion therapies often fail to generalize from the treatment setting to the real world. A recovering alcoholic or drug addict who goes to a party where friends abuse the substance is likely to have difficulty resisting the temptation to relapse. Some experts believe that aversion therapy is most likely to succeed if it is part of a more comprehensive treatment programme in which the client also learns specific coping skills for avoiding relapses (Marlatt and Gordon, 1985).

OPERANT CONDITIONING TREATMENTS

The term **behaviour modification** refers to treatment techniques that apply operant conditioning procedures in an attempt to increase or decrease a specific behaviour. These techniques may use any of the operant procedures for manipulating the environment that we discussed in Chapter 7: positive reinforcement, extinction, negative reinforcement or punishment.

The focus in behaviour modification is on externally observable behaviours. The behaviours targeted for change are measured throughout the treatment programme, allowing the therapist to track the progress of the treatment programme and to make modifications if behaviour change begins to lag.

Behaviour modification techniques have been successfully applied to many different behaviour disorders. They have yielded particularly impressive results when used in populations that are difficult to treat with more traditional therapies, such as hospitalized schizophrenic patients, profoundly disturbed children and those with learning difficulties. (Ayllon and Azrin, 1968; DeRubeis and Crits-Christoph, 1998; Lovaas, 1977). We now consider the use of positive reinforcement and punishment in two of these populations.

Positive-Reinforcement Techniques

One of the dangers of long-term psychiatric hospitalization is the gradual loss of social, personal care, and occupational skills needed to survive outside the hospital. Such deterioration is common among chronic schizophrenic patients who have been hospitalized for an extended period. Verbal psychotherapies have very limited success in rebuilding such skills.

In the 1960s, Teodoro Ayllon and Nathan Azrin (1968) introduced a revolutionary approach to the treatment of hospitalized schizophrenic patients. The **token economy** is a system for strengthening desired behaviours – such as personal grooming, appropriate social responses, housekeeping behaviours, working on assigned jobs, and participation in vocational training programmes – through the systematic application of positive reinforcement. Rather than being given reinforcers such as food or grounds privileges directly, patients earn a specified number of plastic tokens for the performance of each desired behaviour listed on a kind of menu. Patients can then redeem the tokens for a wide range of tangible reinforcers, such as a private room, exclusive rental of a radio or television set, selection of personal furniture, freedom to leave the ward and walk around the grounds, and recreational activities. The long-term goal of token-economy programmes is to jump-start the behaviours that the patient will need to get along in the world outside the hospital. The tangible reinforcers used in these programmes eventually come under the control of social reinforcers and self-reinforcement processes (such as self-pride). When this begins to occur, the tokens can be phased out and the desired behaviours will continue (Kazdin, 2003). Using this technique, Ayllon and Azrin reported remarkable increases in adaptive behaviour in patients for whom change seemed hopeless.

Token-economy programmes have proven highly effective with some of the most challenging populations. In one study, a token-economy programme was carried out over a four-year period with severely disturbed schizophrenic patients who had been hospitalized for an average of more than 17 years. During the course of the programme, 98 per cent of the patients from the behavioural treatment programme were able to be released from the hospital (most to shelter-care facilities in the community), compared with only 45 per cent of a control group that received the normal hospital treatments (Paul and Lentz, 1977). Token economies have also been applied

---

behaviour modification

treatment techniques that apply operant conditioning procedures in an attempt to increase or decrease a specific behaviour

---

token economy

a system for strengthening desired behaviours through the systematic application of positive reinforcement

---

In-Psych

Watch the 'Alcohol Addiction' video in Chapter 18 of the In-Psych programme online for a personal perspective on treatment for alcoholism.

successfully within business, school, prison and home environments to increase desirable behaviours (Sullivan and O'Leary, 1990).

In one study in the USA, researchers used a positive reinforcement programme to reduce cocaine and opium use among drug addicts receiving methadone treatment. Patients received weekly urine tests for drug detection. Those who had negative tests were eligible to draw a piece of paper from a bowl. Half of the papers earned them prizes ranging in value from $1 to $100. Bonus draws were given for extended periods of abstinence (for example, two consecutive weeks of negative urine tests earned six bonus draws). The patients randomly assigned to the positive-reinforcement programme had a significantly higher percentage of negative urine tests over the 12-week period. By abstaining from drugs, the patients had a greater opportunity to build coping responses to avoid relapse following treatment (Petry and Martin, 2002).

Focus 18.12

How are positive reinforcement and punishment used therapeutically? What evidence exists for their effectiveness?

Therapeutic Application of Punishment

As we saw previously in this book, punishment is the quickest way to stop a behaviour from occurring, but most psychologists regard it as the least preferred way to control behaviour because of its aversive qualities and potential negative side effects. Therefore, before deciding to use punishment as a therapy technique, therapists ask themselves two important questions. (1) Are there alternative, less painful approaches that might be effective? (2) Is the behaviour to be eliminated sufficiently injurious to the individual or to society to justify the severity of the punishment?

Sometimes the answers to these questions lead to a decision to use punishment. For example, some of the most startling self-destructive behaviours occur in certain severely disturbed autistic children. Such children may strike themselves repeatedly, bang their heads on sharp objects, bite or tear pieces of flesh from their bodies, or engage in other self-mutilating behaviours. O. Ivar Lovaas (1977), a psychologist who pioneered the use of operant conditioning techniques in the treatment of such children, successfully eliminated such behaviours with a limited number of contingent electric shocks. One 7-year-old boy had been self-injurious for five years and had to be kept in physical restraints. During one 90-minute period when his restraints were removed, he struck himself more than 3000 times. With the consent of his parents, shock electrodes were attached to the boy, and he was given a painful electric shock each time he struck himself. Only 12 shocks were needed to virtually eliminate the self-destructive behaviour. In another case, 15 shocks eliminated self-destructive behaviour in a severely disturbed girl with a history of banging her head against objects. Punishment is never employed without the consent of the client or the client's legal guardian in cases when the client is a minor or is mentally incompetent to give consent.

social skills training

clients learn new skills by observing and then imitating a model who performs a socially skilful behaviour

MODELLING AND SOCIAL SKILLS TRAINING

Modelling is one of the most important and effective learning processes in humans, and modelling procedures have been used to treat a variety of behavioural problems. One of the most widely used applications is designed to teach clients social skills that they lack.

In **social skills training**, clients learn new skills by observing and then imitating a model who performs a socially skilful behaviour. In the following example, a therapist served as a model for his client, a socially anxious college student who had great difficulty asking women for dates. The client began by pretending to ask for a date over the telephone:

> *Client*: By the way (pause), I don't suppose you want to go out Saturday night?
> *Therapist*: Up to actually asking for the date you were very good. However, if I were the girl, I might have been offended when you said, 'By the way.' It's like asking her out is pretty casual. Also, the way you posed the question, you are kind of suggesting to her that she doesn't want to go out with you. Pretend for the moment I'm you. Now, how does this sound: 'There's a movie at the Varsity Theater that I want to see. If you don't have other plans, I'd very much like to take you.'

Focus 18.13

How is modelling used in social skills training? How is self-efficacy involved in its effectiveness?

Focus 18.14

What is eclecticism? Give two examples of new treatment approaches.

Client: That sounded good. Like you were sure of yourself and like the girl, too.
Therapist: Why don't you try it? (Rimm and Masters, 1979, p. 74).

Social skills training has been used with many populations, including individuals who have minor deficits in social skills, delinquents who need to learn how to resist negative peer pressures and, even, hospitalized schizophrenic patients who need to learn social skills in order to function adaptively outside the hospital (Bellack et al., 2004). It is often used in conjunction with other psychological or biological treatments to jump-start new adaptive behaviours that can then be strengthened by natural reinforcers in the client's everyday environment.

Research demonstrates that increased self-efficacy is a key factor in the effectiveness of social skills training. When clients come to believe that they are capable of performing the desired behaviours, they are more likely to be successful in doing so (Bandura, 1997; Maddux, 1999). Observing successful models also increases self-efficacy by encouraging the view, 'If she can do that, so can I'.

INTEGRATING AND COMBINING THERAPIES

We have now surveyed a variety of therapeutic orientations. To an increasing extent, clinicians are embracing **eclecticism**, a willingness to combine treatments and use whatever orientations and therapeutic techniques seem appropriate for the particular client they are treating (Lazarus, 1995; Snyder and Ingram, 2000). In a recent survey of practising clinical psychologists, 45 per cent reported using concepts and methods from multiple therapeutic orientations (Holloway, 2003). Many therapists now label themselves *cognitive-behavioural therapists* because their techniques include elements of both perspectives. In recent years, Albert Ellis and other rational-emotive therapists have renamed their technique *rational-emotive behaviour therapy* (Dryden, 2002).

In part, this tendency towards eclecticism reflects a responsiveness to research findings that certain approaches to therapy are well suited for some problems and ill suited for others. For example, Gestalt techniques are highly effective for helping people discover underlying feelings, but a behavioural approach would be the treatment of choice for treating a phobia. Cognitive-behaviour therapy is highly effective for depression, but so are interpersonal therapy and a behavioural approach called **behavioural activation treatment**, designed to counter depression by helping clients develop action plans that increase the amount of positive reinforcement they experience in their lives (Jacobson et al., 2001). A broadly trained therapist could choose to use any combination of techniques for a client who has depression or multiple problems. One national survey of eclectic therapists revealed that 72 per cent included psychodynamic principles within their version of treatment, 54 per cent included cognitive approaches, 45 per cent used behavioural techniques and a smaller percentage used various humanistic techniques (Jensen et al., 1990).

The move towards eclecticism has resulted in some integrations that are tailored to address particular disorders. One such integrative approach that has been used in treating personality disorders. Cognitive analytic therapy (CAT) finds its origins in the psychoanalytic and cognitive approaches. Cognitive analytic therapy says that social interactions with important people in our world help us to form our views of ourselves and the world around us. Important people may include our mother. If the mother helps the child reflect on their thoughts and interactions then development will be more likely to be self-aware. This provides the beginnings of a moral framework that is developed through further interaction with society. These multiple interactions help the child develop, but making mistakes in the interactions or making incorrect assumptions can cause difficulties. Open, welcoming conversations provide a basis for development of the relationship. On the other hand, of there is suspicion, the child reacts by avoiding further interaction. How the person responds in a relationship is dependent

eclecticism

a willingness to combine treatments and use whatever orientations and therapeutic techniques seem appropriate for the particular client they are treating

behavioural activation treatment

designed to counter depression by helping clients develop action plans that increase the amount of positive reinforcement they experience in their lives

on a number of issues, including their expectations of the intentions of the people with whom they are interacting and their past experiences. Therapy progresses by gathering information about the individual and 'reformulation' where the therapist describes to the client their view of the problem. In the next stage, the therapist encourages the client to reflect on how they approach relationships, and how the decisions made about the interactions they have may be faulty. The client may be encouraged to keep a diary that allows them to reflect on the different interactions they have. Finally, the therapy process reaches a final stage, where the relationship with the therapist is brought to an end. Summaries are made, with the therapist indicating to the client what progress has been made and any areas that they feel need further attention.

Another integrative approach is **dialectical behaviour therapy (DBT)**, developed by Marsha Linehan (Fig. 18.14) for the treatment of borderline personality disorder. As described in Chapter 17, this complex disorder is characterized by chaotic interpersonal relationships, poor emotional control, self-destructive behaviours and low self-esteem. The word *dialectic* describes the contradictions in emotional and interpersonal behaviour, thinking, and self-concept that characterize the borderline client's life (Linehan, 1993). Dialectical behaviour therapy includes elements from cognitive, behavioural, humanistic and psychodynamic therapies to address the many aspects of this disorder. It is intensive in nature, with clients seen in both individual and group sessions by multiple therapists. Behavioural techniques are used to help clients learn interpersonal, problem-solving and emotion-control skills. Cognitive approaches are employed to help clients learn more adaptive thinking about the world, relationships and themselves. A psychodynamic element traces the history of early deprivation and rejection that created many of the problems. A humanistic emphasis on acceptance of thoughts and feelings has now been added to help clients better tolerate unhappiness and negative emotions as they occur. A major goal early in treatment is to bring self-destructive behaviours, such as suicide attempts and self-mutilation, under control, and this is approached in a very direct manner throughout treatment. Linehan describes other goals of DBT:

> Many borderline patients react to themselves with extreme loathing, bordering on self-hate. All but a few feel enormous shame in general, and shame about their own abuse history, the troubles they have caused, and their present emotional activity in particular. Cherishing oneself is the opposite of these emotional reactions. Thus, the therapist must target the self-hate, the self-blame, and the sense of shame.... The therapist must ultimately pull back and relentlessly reinforce within the therapeutic relationship self-validation, self-care, self-soothing, and problem-solving. (Linehan, 1993, p. 160)

dialectical behaviour therapy (DBT)
developed by Marsha Linehan for the treatment of borderline personality disorder

FIGURE 18.14

Marsha Linehan's dialectical behaviour therapy approach is an eclectic blend of principles and techniques from cognitive, behavioural, humanistic and short-term psychodynamic treatments.

IN REVIEW

- Cognitive and behaviour therapies are among the most popular and effective approaches to psychological treatment.

- Ellis's rational-emotive therapy and Beck's cognitive therapy focus on discovering and changing maladaptive beliefs and logical errors of thinking that underlie maladaptive emotional responses and behaviours.

- Behavioural treatments based on classical conditioning are directed at modifying emotional responses. Exposure to a CS and prevention of avoidance responses promote extinction. Exposure may be provided *in vivo* (real life), through imagination, or through virtual reality (VR) technology.

- Modelling is an important component of social skills training programmes, which help clients learn and rehearse more effective social behaviours.

- Systematic desensitization is designed to countercondition a response to anxiety-arousing stimuli that is incompatible with anxiety, such as relaxation. Aversion therapy is used to establish a conditioned aversion response to a stimulus that triggers deviant behaviour.

- Operant procedures have been applied successfully in many behaviour modification programmes. The token economy is a positive reinforcement programme designed to strengthen adaptive behaviours. Punishment has been used to reduce self-destructive behaviours in disturbed children.

- Psychotherapy today shows a growing trend towards eclecticism – the combination of various theoretical perspectives and the development of new, more effective, therapeutic techniques.

GROUP, FAMILY AND MARITAL THERAPIES

Most of the therapeutic approaches we have discussed so far can be carried out with groups of clients as well as with individuals (Brabender et al., 2004). Therapy groups typically include six to eight clients and a single therapist. Within a group, clients can experience acceptance, support and a sense of belonging. They soon see that other people also struggle with problems, a realization that helps counter feelings of isolation and deviance. Clients can also observe how others approach problems, and the interpersonal relations that develop within the group can be a training ground for learning new interpersonal skills. Furthermore, clients can gain insight into how they are perceived by others.

FAMILY THERAPY

Focus 18.15

What principles underlie family and marital therapy? What is the importance of acceptance in marital therapy?

Sometimes the group being treated is a family. Family therapy arose from the clinical observation that many clients who had shown marked improvement in individual therapy – often in institutional settings – suffered relapses when they returned home and began interacting with their families. This observation led to an important concept in the field of psychotherapy, namely, that the disorder shown by the 'identified patient' might reflect dysfunctional relationships within the family system and that permanent change in the client may require that the entire family system be the focus of therapy (Minuchin, 1974). Family therapists therefore help the family understand how it functions and how its unique patterns of interaction contribute to conflicts and to the problems of one or more members (Fig. 18.15):

> In one family, Jessica, an anorexic 14-year-old girl, was the identified patient. However, as the therapist worked with the family, he saw a competitive struggle for the father's attention and observed that the girl was able to compete and get 'cuddly' affection from

her father only when she presented herself to him as a 'sick' person. To bring the hidden dynamics out into the open, the therapist worked at getting the family members to express their desires more directly – in words instead of through hidden behavioural messages. In time, Jessica became capable of expressing her need for affection directly to her father, and her anorexia disappeared. (Based on Aponte and Hoffman, 1973)

MARITAL THERAPY

Today's soaring divorce rate is a stark reflection of the difficulties that exist in many marriages. Nearly half of all first marriages end in divorce, and the divorce rate is even higher among people who remarry (Hetherington, 1998). Couples frequently seek marital therapy because they are troubled by their relationship or because they are contemplating separation or divorce. Typically, the therapist works with both partners together, and therapy focuses on clarifying and improving the interactions between them (Harway, 2005). Research has shown that happily married couples differ from distressed couples in that they talk more to one another, keep channels of communication open, show more sensitivity to each other's feelings and needs, and are more skilled at solving problems (Gottman and Levinson, 1992). Marital therapy targets improvement in these areas.

FIGURE 18.15

Family therapists focus on the total pattern of family interactions, and they include the entire family in treatment

Distressed couples frequently have faulty communication patterns, as demonstrated in the following case:

Husband: She never comes up to me and kisses me. I am always the one to make the overtures.
Therapist: Is this the way you see yourself behaving with your husband?
Wife: Yes, I would say he is the demonstrative one. I didn't know he wanted me to make the overtures.
Therapist: Have you told your wife you would like this from her – more demonstration of affection?
Husband: Well, no. You'd think she'd know.
Wife: No, how would I know? You always said you didn't like aggressive women.
Husband: I don't, I don't like dominating women.
Wife: Well, I thought you meant women who make the overtures. How am I to know what you want?
Therapist: You'd have a better idea if he had been able to tell you. (Satir, 1967, pp. 72–3)

An important recent addition to marital therapy is a focus on *acceptance* (Jacobson and Christensen, 1996). This addition was based on findings that in well-functioning couples, as well as in those who profit from treatment, partners make a decision to accept those aspects of the partner's behaviour that probably are too ingrained to change. For example, it makes little sense to demand that a person with a highly introverted personality style suddenly become a social gadfly and the life of the party. The therapeutic emphasis is on helping couples work towards change in those areas where change is possible and helping them learn to accept aspects of the partner and the relationship that seem unlikely to change. Doing so reduces frustration, lessens demands on the other spouse, and allows the couple to focus on and enjoy the positive aspects of their relationship. The addition of acceptance training to the other elements of marital therapy has improved treatment outcomes (Jacobson et al., 2000).

CULTURAL AND GENDER ISSUES IN PSYCHOTHERAPY

Psychological treatments reflect the cultural context in which they develop. Within the dominant cultures of Western Europe and North America, personal problems are seen as originating within people in the form of dysfunctional thinking, conflict and stress responses. People are assumed to be capable of expressing their feelings and taking personal responsibility for improving themselves. We can easily see these values and assumptions reflected in the therapies we have discussed. Psychodynamic, humanistic and cognitive treatments all focus on changing these internal factors.

These values are not shared by all cultures and ethnic groups, however. For example, people from some Asian cultures might view the 'therapeutic' expression of hostility towards one's parents as unthinkable (Hall and Okazaki, 2003). Likewise, the suggestion that assertiveness training would be helpful in competing more successfully with others and standing up for one's rights might be appalling to a person from a collectivistic culture (Cooper and Denner, 1998). Given diverse cultural norms and values, we should not be surprised that some individuals from non-western cultures view psychotherapy as a totally inappropriate, and even shameful, option for the solution of their problems in living (Foulks et al., 1995).

CULTURAL FACTORS IN TREATMENT UTILIZATION

Recent large-scale epidemiological studies suggest that rates of mental health problems. differ among ethnic groups. For instance, in the USA, Stanley Sue and June Chu (2003) concluded that African-Americans appear to have low rates despite a history of prejudice, discrimination and the resulting stress. American Indians and Alaska Natives have high rates, and Mexican-Americans and Asian-American and Pacific Islanders show slightly lower or very similar rates compared with non-Hispanic whites. Even more clear, however, is the fact that members of minority groups use mental health services far less than does the majority white population (Fearon et al, 2006; Wang et al., 2002).

Even when minority group members seek out mental health services, they often fail to stay in treatment. As a result, many problems that could benefit from psychological treatment go untreated (Sue, 1998; Wang et al., 2002). These data indicate broad differences between cultures and subcultures in their use of treatment. Other research is more specific and highlights how the frequency of mental illnesses differs between cultures. In a World Health Organization review (1983) symptoms associated with depression across cultures revealed that depressed people across the survey shared many symptoms (sadness, anxiety, tension, etc.) but the presence of some symptoms differed widely. Guilt, for instance, was lowest in Iran and highest in Switzerland, with 22 and 68 per cent (respectively) responding that they did indeed feel guilt. Also, the incidence of mental health differed within cultures, with different cities in the same country suffering different levels of depression. Nagasaki, for instance, had a higher incidence of depression than did Tokyo. Jablenski et al. (1992), on the other hand, looked at the incidence of schizophrenia in 10 different countries, including Denmark and the UK, and found comparable levels in each. It is clear, then that there are cultural differences in the diagnoses of different mental illnesses, but the reasons why treatment may not be taken up are still a little unclear. Why might people refuse treatment, or not seek it out?

Sue and Sue (1990) have identified several barriers to treatment among minority groups. One of them is a cultural norm against turning to professionals outside one's own culture for help. Instead these individuals turn to family, clergy, acupuncturists, herbalists and folk healers for assistance. Moreover, for many minority group members, a history of frustrating experiences with white bureaucracies makes them unwilling to approach a hospital or mental health centre. There may also be language barriers.

Sometimes access to treatment is a major problem. In certain parts of the world, access is restricted by financial issues and the requirement for health insurance. Because many minority groups suffer high rates of unemployment and poverty, they may lack the ability to pay for appropriate health insurance – and be unable to afford therapy. Likewise, many community mental health agencies and professional therapists are located outside the areas where the underserved populations live. But even within organized health systems, minorities do not receive

Focus 18.16

What barriers to therapy exist for ethnic minorities? What characteristics are found in culturally competent and gender-sensitive therapists?

equal treatment. In one study of individuals 65 years or older with medical insurance research-ers assessed the percentage of members receiving mental health services, rates of follow-up after hospitalization for mental illness, the number of practitioner contacts for antidepressant medication management, and the number of referrals to effective treatments. On all of these measures, elderly members of minority groups received poorer treatment than did whites (Virnig et al., 2004).

But according to Sue and Zane (1987), the biggest problem of all is the shortage of skilled counsellors who can provide culturally responsive forms of treatment. Therapists often have lit-tle familiarity with the cultural backgrounds and personal characteristics of ethnic groups other than their own. For example, a therapeutic goal that emphasizes the direct and assertive expres-sion of negative feelings may conflict with the cultural norms of a client from a culture not their own. Sometimes, as well, therapists operate on the basis of inaccurate stereotypes that result in unrealistic and possibly inappropriate goals and expectations, as well as great difficulty in estab-lishing the positive client–therapist relationship that has been shown to be a powerful factor in therapeutic success.

What can be done to increase access of culturally diverse groups to psychological treatment? One answer is to take therapy to the people. Studies have shown that establishing mental health service agencies in minority population areas increases utilization of mental health services, particularly if agencies are staffed by culturally skilled counsellors (Sue, 1998). Another solu-tion might be to train more therapists from these ethnic groups. Stanley Sue and his co-workers (1991) found that dropout rates fell and the number of therapy sessions increased when cli-ents saw ethnically similar therapists. However, for clients who elect to remain in therapy, it has *not* been demonstrated that treatment outcomes are better for clients who work with therapists from their own ethnic group. What seems more important than an ethnic match is for the thera-pist and client to form a good relationship and to share similar viewpoints regarding goals for treatment and preferred means for resolving problems (Fig. 18.16).

FIGURE 18.16

Research suggests that the outcome of therapy with minority populations is affected more by the cultural sensitivity and competency of the therapist than it is by the ethnic similarity of therapist and client.

culturally competent therapists

use knowledge about the client's culture to achieve a broad understanding of the client

Sue (1998) suggests that **culturally competent therapists** are able to use knowledge about the client's culture to achieve a broad understanding of the client. At the same time, they are attentive to how the client may differ from the cultural stereotype, thereby balancing cultural understanding with the individual characteristics and needs of the client. They are also able to introduce *culture-specific elements* into the therapy. Thus a therapist might draw on some of the techniques used by folk healers within that culture (e.g., prayer or a specific ritual) to effect changes in the client. Obviously, this would require a good working knowledge of the client's culture, plus a willingness to take advantage of what is therapeutically effective for promoting positive changes in that culture (Mishne, 2002). When therapists receive cultural competence training, they are able to work more effectively with members of other cultures, and clients are more likely to remain in treatment (Wade and Bernstein, 1991).

GENDER ISSUES IN THERAPY

Even within the same culture, the lives of men and women can differ in many ways, as can the life demands they must cope with. As we saw in Chapter 17, psychological disorders, particu-larly those involving anxiety and depression, occur more frequently among women in western cultures. This may reflect the impact of specific stressors that women face, such as poverty (women are over-represented at the poverty level); lack of opportunity fostered by sexism;

strains created by the demanding multiple roles of mother, worker and spouse among married women; and the violence and histories of abuse that many women experience. In many instances, psychological problems arise not so much from internal problems and conflicts but from oppressive elements in the family, social and political worlds. As women strive for more egalitarian relationships with men and for equal opportunity to develop their potential, they often meet external barriers that are deeply embedded in their culture's traditional sex roles and, in some cultures, religious traditions.

feminist therapy

focuses on women's issues and strives to help women achieve greater personal freedom and self-determination

Feminist therapy focuses on women's issues and strives to help women achieve greater personal freedom and self-determination (Brown, 1994; Worell and Remer, 2003). It is not a specific therapeutic technique but rather an orientation that takes into account issues that affect women's lives. In the eyes of many therapists, it may be more important to focus on what can be done to change women's life circumstances than to help them adapt to sex-role expectations that constrain them (Brown, 1994).

It is important for therapists to support people in making choices that meet their needs, whether it be a man who wishes to stay at home and care for children or a woman who wants a career in the military. Whether the therapist is a man or a woman, what seems most important is the therapist's sensitivity to gender issues.

IN REVIEW

- Group approaches offer clients a number of advantages, including opportunities to form close relationships with others, to gain insights into how they interact with others and are perceived by them, and to observe how others approach problems.

- Family therapy is based on the notion that individuals' problems are often reflections of dysfunctional family systems. Such systems should be treated as a unit.

- Marital therapies help couples improve their communication patterns and resolve difficulties in their relationships. The recent addition of acceptance training has improved outcomes.

- Research has shown that members of minority groups underutilize mental health services. Barriers include lack of access to therapists who can provide culturally responsive forms of treatment. More important to outcome than an ethnic match is a therapist who can understand the client's cultural background and has a similar viewpoint on therapy goals and the means to achieve them. Culturally competent therapists take into account both cultural and individual factors to understand and treat the client.

- For female clients, the most helpful therapist is one who is aware of oppressive environmental conditions and is willing to support life goals that do not necessarily conform to gender expectations. Whether the therapist is a man or a woman seems less important to outcome than gender sensitivity.

EVALUATING PSYCHOTHERAPIES

specificity question

'which types of therapy administered by which kinds of therapists to which kinds of clients having which kinds of problems produce which kinds of effects?'

Given the human suffering created by psychological disorders, the effects of psychotherapy have both personal and societal implications. Practising clinicians and clinical researchers want to know which approaches are most effective against which kinds of problems and what the effective active ingredients of each treatment are.

Today the basic question 'Does psychotherapy work?' is viewed as a gross oversimplification of a much more involved question known as the **specificity question**: 'Which types of therapy administered by which kinds of therapists to which kinds of clients having which kinds of problems produce which kinds of effects?' After nearly a half century of psychotherapy research involving many hundreds of studies, this complex question is still not fully answered (Roth and Fonagy, 2005). Nonetheless, for many reasons, this question demands answers. Selecting and administering the most appropriate kind of intervention is vital in human terms. It is also important for economic reasons. A huge amount of money is spent each year on psychological treatments by increasingly stretched health services worldwide. As the need and demand for psychological services increase, the overall costs can only do the same, and those who bear the financial burden, such as taxpayers, and insurance companies who may provide access to private services, increase their demands for accountability and for demonstrations that the treatments they are paying for are useful.

EYSENCK'S GREAT CHALLENGE

In the 1930s and 1940s, individual case studies provided most of the psychotherapy outcome data. Indeed, Freud and other psychoanalysts opposed the use of experimental methods to evaluate psychoanalysis, insisting that case studies left no doubt regarding its effectiveness (Fisher and Greenberg, 1996). They assumed that without therapy, patients would not improve, and they saw plenty of people who did improve in treatment.

In 1952 British psychologist Hans Eysenck mounted a frontal assault on this assumption. Using recovery data from insurance companies on people who applied for disability because of psychological problems, Eysenck (1952) concluded that the rate of **spontaneous remission** – symptom reduction in the absence of any treatment – was as high as the success rates reported by psychotherapists. He therefore concluded that troubled people who receive psychotherapy are no more likely to improve than are those who go untreated. He also pointed out, quite correctly, that virtually all of the existing outcome data were based on therapists' evaluations of their clients' improvement, and he suggested that these evaluations could be biased by therapists' needs to see themselves as competent and successful.

Eysenck's conclusions sparked intense debate – even outrage – among clinicians, but they provided an important wake-up call that could not be ignored. Eysenck's challenge triggered a vigorous increase in psychotherapy research and stimulated the development of more sophisticated methods for evaluating treatment outcomes.

PSYCHOTHERAPY RESEARCH METHODS

Conducting good psychotherapy research is one of the most challenging tasks in all of psychology because there are so many variables that cannot be completely controlled. In contrast to laboratory studies, in which the experimental conditions can be highly standardized, therapist–client interactions are by their nature infinitely varied. Another difficulty involves measuring the effects of psychotherapy. Figure 18.17 shows some of the typical ways of measuring change. These measures differ in the outcome variable assessed (thoughts, emotions or behaviours) and in the source of the data (the therapist, the client or other informants). Which measures of change are most important or valid? What if one set of measures indicates improvement, another indicates no change and a third suggests that the client is worse off than before treatment? How should we evaluate the effects of the therapy? These are just a few of the vexing issues that can arise in psychotherapy research.

A variety of methods have been used to assess the effects of psychotherapy. The individual case study can provide useful information, particularly if objective data are collected throughout and following therapy. However, it can be difficult to generalize conclusions from the individual case. One remedy to this problem is to present multiple case studies of people who have received similar treatment (Kazdin, 2003).

A second approach is to survey large numbers of people who have been in therapy and measure their reactions to their experience. This provides us with information about what is happening

Focus 18.17
What is the specificity question in psychotherapy research? How did Eysenck challenge beliefs about therapeutic effectiveness?

spontaneous remission
symptom reduction in the absence of any treatment

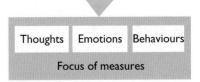

Source of data

- Therapist's ratings
- Client's self-reports
- Ratings of client by acquaintances
- Client's self-monitoring of behavior
- Behavioural observations

Thoughts	Emotions	Behaviours

Focus of measures

FIGURE 18.17

Psychotherapy outcome measures.

The measures used to assess the outcome of psychotherapy may come from a variety of data sources, and they may measure different aspects of the client's functioning.

randomized clinical trial

clients are randomly assigned to treatment or control conditions, and the treatment and control groups are compared on outcome measures

Focus 18.18

What were the major findings of the *CR* survey? On what bases can Seligman's conclusions be challenged?

in the world of clinical practice. A third method is the experimental approach as embodied in the **randomized clinical trial**, in which clients are randomly assigned to treatment or control conditions, and the treatment and control groups are compared on outcome measures.

Survey Research

A good example of the survey approach is a study carried out by the periodical *Consumer Reports* (*CR*; Seligman, 1995). One form of *CR*'s 1994 annual survey, mailed to 184 000 randomly selected subscribers, contained a section on stress and mental health. Readers were asked to complete the mental health section if they had sought help for emotional problems in the past three years. A total of 22 000 readers responded to the questionnaire – a 13 per cent response rate that is typical of *CR* surveys. Of these, 35 per cent reported that they had a mental health problem, and 40 per cent (approximately 2900 respondents) of this group reported that they had sought professional help from a psychologist, psychiatrist, social worker or marriage counsellor. The respondents were asked to indicate how much they improved as a result of treatment and how satisfied they were with the treatment they received.

As shown in Figure 18.18, the majority of clients said that they had improved as a result of treatment and that they were satisfied with their therapy. No overall outcome differences were found among mental health professionals, but clients were less satisfied with marriage counsellors than with psychologists, psychiatrists and social workers. The *CR* survey found no effectiveness differences between the various types of psychotherapy the clients said they had received. Seligman concluded that '*CR* has provided empirical validation of the effectiveness of therapy' (1995, p. 974). Further, he concluded that the survey method used in this study might actually have provided data that are more representative of real-life outcomes than data yielded by highly controlled clinical trials.

FIGURE 18.18

The *Consumer Report* study.

These graphs show the ratings of (a) self-perceived improvement and (b) satisfaction with therapy outcome made by 2900 subscribers of *Consumer Reports* who had been in psychotherapy for the treatment of psychological disorders.

SOURCE: based on Seligman, 1995.

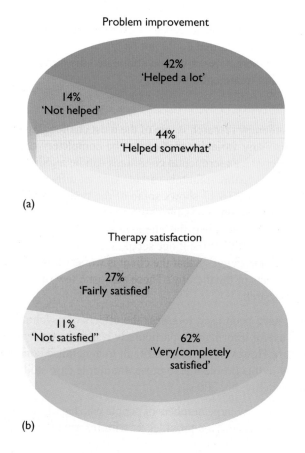

Problem improvement

42% 'Helped a lot'

14% 'Not helped'

44% 'Helped somewhat'

(a)

Therapy satisfaction

27% 'Fairly satisfied'

11% 'Not satisfied'

62% 'Very/completely satisfied'

(b)

WHAT DO YOU THINK?

DO SURVEY RESULTS PROVIDE AN ACCURATE PICTURE OF TREATMENT EFFECTIVENESS?

Based on what you have already learned about research methods, do you agree with Seligman's conclusion that the *CR* data may be a more valid reflection of therapy success than data from randomized clinical trials? Can you think of any aspects of the *CR* methods that might limit your ability to conclude how effective psychotherapy is? Compare your thoughts with the issues discussed on p. 887.

Meta-Analysis: A Look at the Big Picture

As discussed in Chapter 2, the technique of **meta-analysis** allows researchers to combine the statistical results of many studies to arrive at an overall conclusion. In the psychotherapy research literature they can compute an effect size statistic that represents a common measure of treatment effectiveness. The **effect size** tells researchers what percentage of clients who received therapy had a more favourable outcome than that of the average control client who did not receive the treatment.

In 1977 Smith and Glass used meta-analysis to combine the effects of 375 studies of psychotherapy involving 25 000 clients and 25 000 control participants. These studies differed in many ways, but they all compared a treatment condition with a control condition. The results indicated that the average therapy client had a more favourable outcome than 75 per cent of the untreated cases. These results prompted Smith and Glass to dispute Eysenck's earlier conclusion, maintaining that therapy does indeed have positive effects beyond spontaneous remission. More recent therapy meta-analyses support this conclusion. Glass and Smith also concluded that psychodynamic, client-centred and behavioural approaches were quite similar in their effectiveness. This finding of similar efficacy for widely differing therapies has been termed the **dodo bird verdict,** after the dodo bird's statement in *Alice in Wonderland* that 'Everybody has won and all must have prizes' (Luborsky et al., 2002). Other researchers challenge this conclusion, maintaining that lumping together studies involving different kinds of clinical problems may mask *differential effectiveness*, i.e., the fact that specific therapies might be highly effective for treating some clinical disorders but not others (Beutler, 2002; Westen and Morrison, 2001). Later meta-analyses have tended to focus on specific disorders and the treatments that are most effective for them. Table 18.3 shows the results of recent meta-analyses of the application of drugs that have previously been tested and trialled (**empirically supported treatments**) for several disorders (Westen et al., 2004).

In evaluating the results of meta-analyses, we should remember that the studies lumped together in a meta-analysis can differ in many ways, including the nature and severity of the problems that were treated, the outcome measures that were used and the quality of the methodology. Psychotherapy researchers point out that combining good studies with less adequate ones can produce misleading results (Kazdin, 2003). When studies that meet rigorous research standards are compared in meta-analyses with less rigorous studies, the rigorous studies tend to yield more favourable outcomes for therapy conditions (Matt and Navarro, 1997). Apparently, the rigorous methods used in such studies allow effective therapies to show their true effects.

meta-analysis

allows researchers to combine the statistical results of many studies to arrive at an overall conclusion

effect size

tells researchers what percentage of clients who received therapy had a more favourable outcome than that of the average control client who did not receive the treatment

dodo bird verdict

similar efficacy for widely differing therapies

empirically supported treatments

meta-analyses of the application of drugs that have previously been tested and trialled

Focus 18.19
What have meta-analyses shown about the effectiveness of therapies?

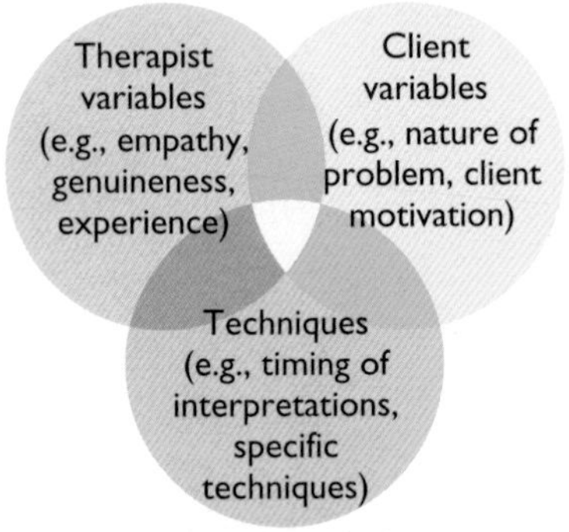

FIGURE 18.19

Determinants of therapy outcome.

Research on factors that influence therapy outcome has focused on three sets of interacting variables: client variables, therapist variables, and technique variables.

Focus 18.20

What client, therapist, technique and common factors influence treatment outcome?

openness

clients' general willingness to invest themselves in therapy and take the risks required to change themselves

self-relatedness

clients' ability to experience and understand internal states such as thoughts and emotions, to be attuned to the processes that go on in their relationship with their therapist, and to apply what they learn in therapy to their lives outside of treatment

TABLE 18.3 META-ANALYSES OF IMPROVEMENT AND RECOVERY RATES FOR EMPIRICALLY SUPPORTED TREATMENTS APPLIED TO VARIOUS ADULT DISORDERS

Disorder	Percentage improved or recovered*
Obsessive-compulsive disorder	66.7
Panic disorder	63.3
Generalized anxiety disorder	52.1
Major depression	50.8
Bulimia	50.0

NOTE: *Improvement* typically means at least a 30 to 50 per cent reduction in symptoms; recovery means total symptom reduction. The data for bulimia are for recovery only. The number of randomized clinical trials summarized range from seven to 26 for the various disorders.

SOURCES: adapted from Thompson-Brenner et al., 2003; Westen et al., 2004; Westen and Morrison, 2001.

FACTORS AFFECTING THE OUTCOME OF THERAPY

Clearly, not everyone who enters therapy profits from it. There is even evidence that some clients – perhaps 10 per cent – may get worse as a result of treatment (Binder and Strupp, 1997; Lambert et al., 1986). What, then, are the factors that influence treatment outcome? Research to answer this question has focused on three sets of variables: client variables, therapist variables and technique variables (Fig. 18.19). The American Psychological Association (APA) task force on empirically supported principles has identified variables that make a difference within each of these categories (Castonguay and Beutler, 2005).

Where client variables are concerned, three important factors are the client's openness to therapy, self-relatedness and the nature of the problem (Castonguay and Beutler, 2005). **Openness** involves clients' general willingness to invest themselves in therapy and take the risks required to change themselves. **Self-relatedness** refers to clients' ability to experience and understand internal states such as thoughts and emotions, to be attuned to the processes that go on in their relationship with their therapist, and to apply what they learn in therapy to their lives outside of treatment (Howard et al., 1993). The third important client factor is the nature of the problem and its degree of fit with the therapy being used. For example, specific problems such as phobias may respond best to a behavioural anxiety-reduction treatment such as systematic desensitization or exposure, whereas a more global problem, such as a search for self-discovery and greater meaning in life, may respond better to a psychodynamic, cognitive or humanistic approach. Patient age, gender, ethnicity and intelligence do not seem to affect outcome (Castonguay and Beutler, 2005).

Among therapist variables, perhaps the most important is the quality of the relationship that the therapist is able to establish with the client (Castonguay and Beutler, 2005). Carl Rogers's emphasis on the importance of therapist qualities such as empathy, unconditional acceptance of the client as a person and genuineness has been borne out in a great many studies. An empathic, trusting and caring relationship forms the foundation on which the specific techniques employed by the therapist can have their most beneficial effects.

When therapists do not manifest these behaviours, the effects of therapy are not simply null; clients can actually get worse. For example, hostile interchanges between therapist and client can contribute to a *deterioration effect* in therapy (Binder and Strupp, 1997).

Assuming the therapy relationship is a positive one, there is still the consideration of technique variables. A therapist needs to be skilled and knowledgeable in selecting and implementing the appropriate techniques for each client and situation. The correctness of the interpretations made by psychoanalytic therapists, as measured by expert ratings, is related to more positive treatment outcome (Crits-Christoph et al., 1988). Likewise, in a detailed analysis of the audiotaped therapy sessions of 21 psychotherapists, Jones et al. (1988) found that the most effective therapists adjusted their techniques to the specific needs of their clients. They concluded that 'general relationship factors, such as therapeutic alliance, are closely bound with the skillful selection and application of psychotherapeutic techniques' (p. 55).

Despite dramatic differences in the techniques they employ, various therapies tend to enjoy similar success rates, perhaps because people who differ on the client variables are lumped together within studies. This finding has led many experts to search for **common factors,** characteristics shared by these diverse forms of therapy that might contribute to their success. These common factors include:

- clients' faith in the therapist and a belief that they are receiving help
- a plausible explanation for clients' problems and an alternative way of helping them look at themselves and their problems
- a protective setting where clients can experience and express their deepest feelings within a supportive relationship
- an opportunity for clients to practice new behaviours
- clients' achieving increased optimism and self-efficacy.

How important these common factors are in comparison with specific therapeutic techniques is currently unknown, and the dodo bird verdict described earlier may reflect a failure to identify specific factors that underlie therapeutic success (Beutler, 2002). The complexities of psychotherapy pose a formidable challenge for clinical researchers. Despite decades of research on the efficacy of psychotherapy techniques, there is still much to learn. We know that some techniques are very effective for certain problems. Yet in the words of the British psychotherapist Isaac Marks, 'Little is known about which treatment components produce improvement, how they do so, and why they do not help all sufferers' (Marks, 2002, p. 200).

common factors
characteristics shared by these diverse forms of therapy that might contribute to their success

IN REVIEW

- The *Consumer Reports* survey of therapy clients suggested high levels of improvement and client satisfaction with their treatment. Meta-analyses of treatment outcome studies found more improvement in therapy clients than in 75 per cent of control clients and little difference in effectiveness among various therapies (the so-called dodo bird verdict).

- Three sets of interacting factors affect the outcome of treatment: client characteristics (including the nature of the problem), therapist characteristics and therapy techniques.

- Client variables that contribute to therapy success include openness, self-relatedness and a good match between the nature of the problem and the kind of therapy being received.

- A crucial factor in the success of various therapies is the quality of the relationship that the therapist establishes with the client. The three therapist characteristics suggested by Rogers – empathy, unconditional positive regard and genuineness – are particularly important.

- Factors common to many therapies, such as faith in the therapist, a protected environment for self-exploration, and the ability to try out new behaviours, contribute to therapeutic outcome.

BIOLOGICAL APPROACHES TO TREATMENT

In the previous chapter, we found that biological factors play an important role in many psychological disorders. Thus a medical approach designed to alter the brain's functioning is an alternative (or an addition) to psychological treatment.

DRUG THERAPIES

Drug therapies are the most commonly used biological interventions. Discoveries in the field of *psychopharmacology* (the study of how drugs affect cognitions, emotions and behaviour) have revolutionized the treatment of the entire range of disorders. Each year a huge and growing number of prescriptions for drugs that affect mood, thought and behaviour are prescribed around the world. The most commonly prescribed drugs fall into three major categories: antipsychotic drugs, anti-anxiety drugs and antidepressant drugs. Effective drugs (e.g., lithium) also exist for the treatment of mania. Many experts recommend using such drugs in conjunction with psychotherapy to achieve a higher level of long-term success (Hollon, 1996; Thase et al., 1997).

Antipsychotic Drugs

Perhaps the most dramatic effects of drug therapy have occurred in the treatment of severely disordered people, permitting many of them to function outside of the hospital setting (Shorter, 1998). This is shown very vividly if we look at the USA as a test case. As shown in Figure 18.20, a sharp decline in the number of inpatients in public mental hospitals has occurred since 1955, when antipsychotic drugs were first introduced to American in-patients on a wide scale.

FIGURE 18.20

Effects of antipsychotic drugs.

Antipsychotic drugs have revolutionized the treatment of severely disturbed individuals, allowing many of them to leave mental hospitals. Note the decline that occurred following the introduction of antipsychotic drugs in the mid-1950s.

SOURCE: United States National Institute of Mental Health, 1992.

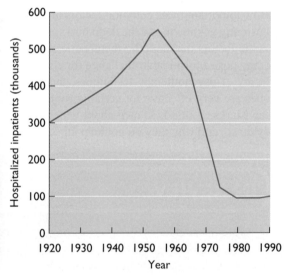

Focus 18.21

What is tardive dyskinesia, and what causes it?

The revolution in drug therapy for severe psychological disorders began in the early 1950s, when it was accidentally discovered that *reserpine*, a drug derived from the root of the snakeroot plant, calmed psychotic patients. The use of reserpine has been discontinued largely because of some side effects, but is still used to help treat problems of high blood-pressure, because of its action on how the body deals with norepinephrine (noradrenaline). The discovery of reserpine resulted in the development of synthetic *antipsychotic drugs* (also called *major tranquillizers*), used today to treat schizophrenic disorders. The primary effect of the major tranquillizers is to decrease the action of dopamine, the neurotransmitter whose overactivity is thought to be involved in schizophrenia (Schatzberg et al., 2002). These drugs dramatically reduce positive symptoms, such as hallucinations and delusions. However, they have little effect on negative symptoms, such as apathy and withdrawal, and 20 to 40 per cent of people with schizophrenia get little or no relief from them (Tamminga, 1997). Antipsychotic drugs are now so widely used that nearly all schizophrenic patients living in Western Europe, the USA and Canada, and have received them at one time or another. It is common practice to continue the medication indefinitely once the individual has returned to the community because patients often relapse very quickly if they stop taking the drugs.

Antipsychotic drugs have reduced the need for padded cells, straitjackets and other restraints that were formerly used to control the disordered behaviour of hospitalized patients. Although they allow many patients to be released from hospitals, these drugs can produce **tardive dyskinesia,** a severe movement disorder (Kane, 1992). Uncontrollable and grotesque movements of the face and tongue are especially prominent in this disorder, and sometimes the patient's arms and legs flail uncontrollably. Tardive dyskinesia can be more debilitating than the psychotic symptoms that prompted the drug treatment, and it appears to be irreversible once it develops. One study found that within four years of beginning antipsychotic medications, 18.5 per cent of young adults and 31 per cent of those over 55 developed tardive dyskinesia symptoms (Saltz et al., 1991).

Researchers are working to develop new drugs that can control schizophrenic symptoms without producing side effects, such as the devastating symptoms of tardive dyskinesia. A drug called *clozapine* (also called Clozaril, Leponex and Fazalco) reduces not only positive symptoms but negative ones as well, and it appears not to produce tardive dyskinesia (Marangell, 2002). Unfortunately, it produces a fatal blood disease (agranulocytosis) in 1 to 2 per cent of people who take it, requiring expensive weekly blood tests for patients who use the medication, and for this reason its use was banned soon after it was introduced in the early 1970s. It has now been reintroduced because it really is very effective at helping reduce the risk of suicide in schizophrenic patients

Antipsychotic drugs can often be used in conjunction with psychotherapy. For example, drugs may be used to bring psychotic symptoms under control so that the patient can benefit from other approaches such as social skills training, family therapy and group therapy. This two-pronged approach is extremely popular, ad can be extremely effective.

Anti-anxiety Drugs

The use of anti-anxiety or tranquillizing drugs such as diazapam (marketed as Valium) is widespread. These drugs are designed to reduce anxiety as much as possible without affecting alertness or concentration. Sometimes anti-anxiety drugs are used in combination with psychotherapy to help clients cope successfully with problematic situations (Stahl, 1998). A temporary reduction in anxiety from the use of a drug may allow a client to enter anxiety-arousing situations and learn to cope more effectively with them

Anti-anxiety drugs work by slowing down excitatory synaptic activity in the nervous system. *Bisopirone* (marketed as BuSpar or Axoren), for instance has a simpler effect to diazipam, and functions by blocking receptors of the excitatory transmitter serotonin and by enhancing the postsynaptic activity of GABA, an inhibitory transmitter that reduces neural activity in areas of the brain associated with emotional arousal (Gorman, 2002; Pies, 1998).

Anti-anxiety drugs can have a variety of undesirable side effects, such as drowsiness, lethargy and concentration difficulties. A more serious drawback is psychological and physical dependence that can result from their long-term use. People who have developed physiological dependence can experience characteristic withdrawal symptoms, such as intense anxiety, nausea and restlessness when they stop taking the drug (Lieberman, 1998). In addition, anxiety symptoms often return when people stop taking the drugs.

Antidepressant Drugs

Antidepressant drugs fall into three major categories: *tricyclics* (e.g., amitryptyline, brand name *Elavil*, imipramine, brand name *Tofranil*), *monoamine oxidase (MAO) inhibitors* (e.g., phenelzine,

Focus 18.22
How do anti-anxiety drugs work, and how effective are they? Do they have any drawbacks?

tardive dyskinesia
a severe movement disorder

Focus 18.23
How do antidepressant drugs achieve their effects? What concerns have been raised about them?

brand name *Nardil*, tranylcypromine, brand name *Parnate*), and *selective serotonin re-uptake inhibitors* or *SSRIs* (e.g., fluoxetine, brand name *Prozac*). The first two classes increase the activity of the excitatory neurotransmitters norepinephrine and serotonin, whose lowered level of activity in brain regions involved in positive emotion and motivation is related to depression. The tricyclics work by preventing re-uptake of the excitatory transmitters into the pre-synaptic neurons, allowing them to continue stimulating postsynaptic neurons. The MAO inhibitors reduce the activity of monoamine oxidase, an enzyme that breaks down the neurotransmitters in the synapse. Other drugs include *serotonin-norepinephrine re-uptake inhibitors* (*SNRIs*) such as Venlafaxine and Duloxetine

Monoamine oxidase inhibitors have more severe side effects than the tricyclics. They can cause dangerous elevations in blood pressure when taken with certain foods, such as cheeses and some types of wine. Many patients have abandoned their antidepressant medications because of severe side effects. The SSRIs were designed to decrease side effects by increasing the activity of just one transmitter, serotonin (Marangell, 2002). Like the other antidepressants, however, SSRIs do have side effects. For example, about 30 per cent of patients on Prozac report nervousness, insomnia, sweating, joint pain or sexual dysfunction (Hellerstein et al., 1993). Nonetheless, the SSRIs are gradually replacing the tricyclics because, in addition to milder side effects, they reduce depressive symptoms more rapidly and reduce anxiety symptoms that often accompany depression (Lieberman, 1998). Figure 18.21 shows how the SSRIs produce their effects.

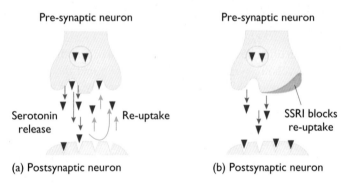

FIGURE 18.21

SSRI mechanisms.

(a) When a presynaptic neuron releases serotonin into the synaptic space, a re-uptake mechanism begins to pull neurotransmitter molecules back into the 'sending' neuron, limiting the stimulation of the postsynaptic neuron. (b) Selective serotonin re-uptake inhibitors (SSRIs) allow serotonin, whose activity is reduced in depressed clients, to continue its stimulation of postsynaptic neurons by inhibiting the reuptake of serotonin into the presynaptic neuron.

Increasingly, depression researchers are studying the effects of combining drugs and psychotherapy. A meta-analysis of such studies revealed that recovery rates for psychotherapy and the combined treatments did not differ for less severely depressed people. However, the combination of psychotherapy and drug treatment yielded the best recovery rates in more severe cases of depression (Thase et al., 1997).

In-Psych

Are antidepressants over-prescribed? Watch the video on 'Depression Theories and Treatments' in Chapter 15 of the In-Psych programme online for some thoughts.

BENEATH THE SURFACE

SOME DEPRESSING FACTS ABOUT ANTIDEPRESSANT DRUGS

Antidepressant drugs have become a treatment of choice for depression in both adults and children. As a less expensive form of treatment than psychotherapy, they are especially attractive to insurers and managed-care providers, and with good reason. Clinicians often observe dramatic improvements in people given SSRIs and other antidepressants. In recent years, however, increasing concerns have been raised about their efficacy and about potential side effects.

PLACEBO EFFECTS

When compared with no-treatment control conditions, antidepressant medication (ADM) effects are quite impressive. But when **placebo control groups** are introduced in randomized clinical trials, the picture can change dramatically. If those taking the placebo simply believe they are receiving an antidepressant, they frequently show improvement that rivals drug effects. By dividing the amount of change shown in the placebo group by the magnitude of change shown by the drug group, one can estimate how much of the drug effect is truly attributable to the pharmacological effects of the drug. For example, in two clinical trials of the SSRI sertraline hydrochloride (sold as *Zoloft and Xydep*), in depressed children and adolescents, placebo patients showed 85 per cent as much improvement as those who received sertraline. Both groups showed notable decreases in self-reported depression, but the difference between sertraline and placebo groups was so small as to be of no practical significance (Wagner et al., 2003).

> **placebo control groups**
> no-treatment control conditions

An overview of research where clinicians rated their clients' depression symptoms while unaware of whether the person was taking a drug or a placebo showed interesting results. As shown in Figure 18.22, improvement rates in the placebo conditions ranged from 68 to 89 per cent of those shown in the antidepressant medication conditions, suggesting that expectancies and beliefs account for much of the drugs' effects and that the actual pharmacological effects of the drugs are quite small. Indeed, the data on (brand names) Paxil, Zoloft and Celexa actually underestimate placebo effects because in nine other trials where no significant differences were found between the drugs and placebos, the investigators did not provide depression change scores (Kirsch et al., 2002). In such studies, the placebo effect could account for as much as 100 per cent of patient improvement, so what the placebo effect means for those drugs would be even higher than those shown in Figure 18.22. Even where statistically significant differences were found between drug and placebo conditions on depression ratings, the actual differences were typically too small to be of any clinical significance

The strength of placebo effects may also be underestimated in many studies because of the practice of dropping from clinical trials any patient in the placebo condition who shows 20 per cent or more improvement in the first week or two of the trial. Such patients are called *placebo washouts*. In contrast, patients in the drug condition who show similar levels of improvement are retained in the study. Obviously, this practice loads the dice in favour of the drug condition. Another factor favouring drug effects is the selective publication of results. Although the drug companies (who conduct or sponsor much of the research on their drugs) are required to submit the raw data from all trials to the Food and Drug Administration (FDA), studies that do not show significant drug effects may not find their way into the published literature (Antonuccio et al., 2003). In contrast though, work from Geller et al. (2003) took an overview of research (a meta-analysis) which looked at the use of SSRIs with children with obsessive-compulsive disorders and showed that all SSRIs were effective, and that all were more effective than the placebo. As with many areas of research, data exists to support each side of the argument, and a careful reading of the available literature is needed to draw (if possible) a firm conclusion.

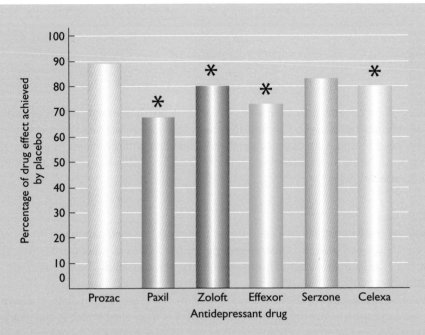

FIGURE 18.22

Placebo effects and antidepressant (SSRI) drugs.

These data were derived by dividing the magnitude of improvement shown by placebo controls by the magnitude of change shown by the drug group. They suggest that, on average, around 79 per cent of the drug effects may be attributable to patient expectations that they will be helped by the drug, rather than to pharmacological effects. The asterisks (*) indicate drugs for which depression improvement scores were not submitted because the drug and placebo groups did not differ significantly, suggesting even stronger placebo effects for those drugs.

SOURCE: adapted from Kirsch et al., 2002.

DO THE BENEFITS OUTWEIGH THE DANGERS?

Given the small treatment effects that can be attributed to pharmacological factors, some are questioning whether the benefits achieved through antidepressant drug treatment outweigh possible costs. Despite the fact that SSRIs have less severe side effects than older antidepressants, such side effects do exist. Even when patients have shown improvement on the drugs, they sometimes abandon them because of these effects. In a study of 161 patients who gave up taking SSRIs conducted by Bolling and Kohlenberg (2004), 46 per cent complained of having experienced a narrowed range of emotions, 32.9 per cent of 'not feeling like myself', 24 per cent of a loss of creativity, 18 per cent of apathy, 17 per cent of concentration difficulties and 13 per cent of increased anger. When people stop taking SSRIs, about 25 per cent experience a *discontinuation syndrome*, which can include severe sensory, somatic, gastrointestinal and sleep problems, as well as irritability and anxiety. Some patients report that these discontinuation symptoms are worse than the original depression. Finally, reports of suicidal thoughts and behaviours in patients on SSRIs have raised concerns. One study compared suicide attempts and suicides of adults in randomized clinical trials comparing SSRIs with placebos (Healy, 2004). Overall, one in 80 of all SSRI recipients attempted or committed suicide, compared with one in 200 of all placebo patients. In children, the risk may be even greater (Jureidini et al., 2004). At the urging of the British Medical Association, the UK Committee on Safety in Medicines has banned the use of all SSRIs with the exception of Prozac for patients under 18 years of age. The European Medical Agency followed in 2005, with the ruling that special care should be taken with the prescription of SSRIs to children and adolescents, recommending strong warnings. The link between SSRIs and suicide risk is still a subject of debate, but recent research from Gibbons et al. (2005) seems to suggest that not medicating leaves the individual at greater risk. Hall (2006) concluded that the benefits certainly outweighed the risks, with a meta-analysis that led him to conclude that any suicide risk is very small, and probably not limited to SSRIs, but that risk is outweighed by the benefit, certainly when adult data are taken into account.

Clearly, the results of ongoing studies of the efficacy, side effects, and cost/benefit aspects of antidepressants have enormous clinical and economic implications. Meanwhile, research continues on the development of new drugs that are more effective and have fewer side effects.

ELECTROCONVULSIVE THERAPY

Another biologically based treatment, *electroconvulsive therapy (ECT)*, was based on the observation by a Hungarian physician that schizophrenia and epilepsy rarely occur in the same person. (Apparently, he did not stop to consider the fact that the probability of epilepsy and *any* other disorder occurring together is very low.) The physician therefore suggested that seizure induction might be useful in the treatment of schizophrenia. In 1938 two Italian physicians, Ugo Cerletti and Lucio Bini, began to treat schizophrenic patients by attaching electrodes to their skulls and inducing a seizure by means of an electric current administered to the brain. In early applications of ECT, a wide-awake patient was strapped to a table, electrodes were attached to the patient's scalp, and a current of roughly 100 volts was applied to the brain, producing violent convulsions and loss of consciousness. Sometimes the seizures were so violent that patients fractured their arms or legs.

Today the procedure is quite different (Fig. 18.23). A patient is first given a sedative and a muscle relaxant to prevent injuries from the convulsions. The patient is then placed on a well-padded mattress, and electrodes are attached to his or her scalp. A modified procedure in which electrodes are placed on only one side of the head is often used. The duration of the shock is less than a second, causing a seizure of the central nervous system. There is little observable movement in the patient, other than a twitching of the toes and a slight facial grimace. The patient wakes up 10 to 20 minutes after ECT, possibly with a headache, sore muscles and some confusion. Recently, scientists have been able to calibrate the amount of electric current a patient needs so that treatments can be individualized, and research is being carried out to determine whether certain drugs can further reduce seizure-induced confusion and amnesia.

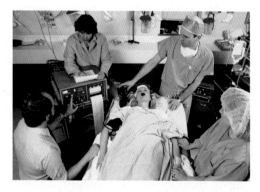

FIGURE 18.23

A severely depressed and possibly suicidal patient is prepared for an ECT session. The patient has been sedated and given a muscle relaxant to minimize limb movements during the brief electrical stimulation of the brain. The rubber object in her mouth prevents her from biting her tongue or damaging her teeth during the convulsion.

When ECT was first introduced in the 1930s, it was applied to a wide range of disorders, but later research revealed that it cannot relieve anxiety disorders and is of questionable value for schizophrenic patients (Herrington and Lader, 1996). However, ECT can be useful in treating severe depression, particularly if there is a high risk of suicide. In such cases, the use of antidepressant drugs may be impractical because they will likely take several weeks to begin reducing the depression. In contrast, the effects of ECT can be immediate. Controlled studies indicate that 60 to 70 per cent of severely depressed people given ECT improve, but no one knows why ECT works (Rey and Walter, 1997).

Electroconvulsive therapy has many critics. Some note that even when the effects are dramatically positive, the possibility of a depressive relapse is high, perhaps 85 per cent (Swartz, 1995).

Concerns have been raised about the safety of ECT because in some instances permanent memory loss has been reported, and there are also concerns about the possibility of permanent brain damage when ECT is used repeatedly. Today the number of ECT treatments is limited to fewer than 10, and scientific evidence suggests that today's ECT is a safer treatment than previous forms were. For example, MRI studies of patients who received brief pulse treatment to both sides of the brain revealed no evidence of brain damage (Coffey et al., 1991).

The professional psychology bodies and government departments and committees that advise on clinical treatments review the arguments for and against treatments such as ECT and set out guidelines for their use. The National Institute for Clinical Excellence (NICE, 2003) in the UK indicates clearly that ECT should only be used if other treatments have proved ineffective. Electroconvulsive therapy may also be used in conditions where the patient's condition is considered to be potentially life-threatening, such as those with severe depression, catatonia or those that suffer with prolonged or severe manic episodes. Even when ECT is sanctioned for use, NICE make it very clear that the decision should not be taken lightly, all records must be carefully checked and all risks should be considered. Consent should be given by the patient through careful discussion, with risks clearly indicated. If an informed discussion cannot take place, then the patient's advocate and/or carer should be consulted. In Italy, however, where it all began, ECT has all but been abolished, with its use reserved for extreme cases of life-threatening diseases in government hospitals only.

PSYCHOSURGERY

Psychosurgery refers to surgical procedures that remove or destroy brain tissue in an attempt to change disordered behaviour. It is the least used of the biomedical procedures, but such was not always the case. In the 1930s, before the advent of antipsychotic drugs, Portuguese surgeon Egas Moniz reported that cutting the nerve tracts that connect the frontal lobes with subcortical areas of the brain involved in emotion resulted in a calming of psychotic and uncontrollably violent patients. The operation eliminated emotional input from the limbic system into the areas of the brain connected with executive functions of planning and reasoning. Walter Freeman developed a 10-minute *lobotomy* operation called a *spike-lobotomy* performed by inserting an ice pick-like instrument with sharp edges through the eye socket into the brain, then wiggling it back and forth to sever the targeted nerve tracts. During the 1930s and 1940s, tens of thousands of patients underwent the operation. Moniz received a Nobel Prize for his discovery.

Initial enthusiasm for lobotomy was soon replaced by a sober recognition that the massive neural damage it caused had severe side effects on mental and emotional functioning. Seizures, stupor, memory and reasoning impairments, and listlessness occurred frequently. With the development of antipsychotic drugs in the 1950s, the frequency of lobotomies decreased, and they are hardly ever used today. However, more precise and limited psychosurgery procedures are sometimes used in the most extreme cases and when every other avenue has been tried. One procedure called *cingulotomy* involves cutting a small fibre bundle near the corpus callosum that connects the frontal lobes with the limbic system. Cingulotomy has been used successfully in treating severe depressive and obsessive-compulsive disorders that have failed to improve with drug treatment or psychotherapy. However, even this more limited procedure can also produce side effects, including seizures (Pressman, 1998). Appropriately, cingulotomy and other forms of psychosurgery are considered to be last-resort procedures. In England and Wales in the UK, a panel of three representatives appointed by the Mental Health Act Commission is required to assess that the person is providing full consent to the operation and that they are likely to benefit from it.

Focus 18.24
Which disorders do and do not respond favourably to ECT and psychosurgery? What are their drawbacks?

psychosurgery
surgical procedures that remove or destroy brain tissue in an attempt to change disordered behaviour

MIND, BODY AND THERAPEUTIC INTERVENTIONS

The impact of drug and electroconvulsive therapies on psychological disorders illustrates once again the important interactions between biological and psychological phenomena. In the final analysis, both psychological and biological treatments affect brain functioning in ways that can change disordered thoughts, emotions, and behaviour. Moreover, they may constitute different routes to the same changes, as illustrated in a study by Tomas Furmark and co-workers (2002) at Uppsala University in Sweden. The researchers randomly assigned patients with social phobia to nine-week treatments that involved either drug therapy with an SSRI or a course of cognitive and behavioural psychotherapy involving exposure to feared social situations and cognitive modification of anxiety-arousing thoughts. Before and after treatment, the participants received PET scans while they gave a hastily prepared speech to a group of six to eight people standing around the scanner bed. They also provided subjective ratings of their anxiety during the procedure. Uniformly high anxiety scores were reported by all participants prior to treatment.

In general, both treatments were effective, although overall, the psychological treatment produced a stronger reduction in fear and social phobia symptoms than did the drug treatment. Nonetheless, when the researchers compared the pre- and post-treatment PET scans of those participants who responded to the two treatments with reduced social anxiety, the psychotherapy and drug groups showed basically the same changes in cerebral blood flow from the first speech situation to the second. These changes involved reduced neural activity in an 'anxiety circuit' involving the amygdala, the hippocampus and areas of the temporal cerebral cortex (Fig. 18.24). Treatment non-responders did not show these brain changes. Thus different forms of therapy, whether psychological or biological, may result in similar changes at a neurological level and, ultimately, at a behavioural level.

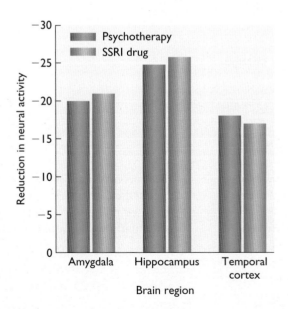

FIGURE 18.24

Drug and therapy effects on the brain.

Clients treated for social phobia received either psychotherapy or drug therapy. Those clients who responded to their respective treatments with reduced anxiety showed nearly identical changes in PET-scan recordings of neural activity in three areas of the brain whose activation is thought to underline anxiety.

SOURCE: based on Furmark et al., 2002.

An important factor to keep in mind is that drug treatments, however effective they may be in modifying some disordered behaviours in the short term, do not cure the disorder. They suppress symptoms but do not teach the client coping and problem-solving skills to deal with stressful life situations (DeLongis, 2000; Nezu et al., 2000). They may even prevent people from taking steps to confront the real causes of their problems. Many therapists believe that one of the major benefits of psychological treatments is their potential not only to help clients deal with current problems, but also to increase their personal resources so that they might enjoy a higher level of adjustment and life satisfaction in the future (Hollon, 1996).

We have now considered a wide spectrum of approaches to treating abnormal behaviour. Figure 18.25 summarizes biological, psychological and environmental mechanisms for therapeutic change.

LEVELS OF ANALYSIS   FACTORS RELATED TO THERAPEUTIC BEHAVIOUR CHANGE

Biological
- Changes in neurotransmitter, autonomic, or hormonal activity brought about by drug treatment, psychotherapy or surgical procedures
- Structural changes in brain circuitry and synaptic networks produced by cognitive, emotional and behavioural changes

Psychological
- Cognitive and emotional changes brought about by cognitive therapies
- Modification of conditioned emotional responses by deconditioning procedures such as exposure desensitization and aversion therapy
- Behavioural changes produced by operant procedures
- Self-concept changes brought about by psychotherapy (e.g. client-centred, Gestalt therapy)
- Insight into unconscious dynamics and development of more mature defences brought about by short- and long-term psychodynamic therapies

Environmental
- Life-situation changes resulting from constructive behaviour changes learned in therapy or produced by biological means
- Exposure to specific therapeutic techniques administered by a mental health expert
- A positive therapeutic relationship that helps promote change and allows therapy techniques to be effective
- Cultural factors that affect access to therapy, type of therapy and exposure to a culturally competent therapist

Therapeutic behaviour change

FIGURE 18.25

Levels of analysis: factors related to therapeutic behaviour change.

IN REVIEW

- Drugs have revolutionized the treatment of many behaviour disorders and have permitted many hospitalized patients to function outside institutions. Drugs and psychotherapy may be combined to hasten the relief of symptoms while establishing more effective coping responses to deal with the sources of a disorder. Drug treatments exist for anxiety, depression, schizophrenia and mania. Some of these drugs have undesirable side effects and can be addictive. All of them affect neurotransmission within the brain, and they work on specific classes of neurotransmitters.

- Electroconvulsive therapy is used less frequently than in the past, and its safety has been increased. It is used primarily to treat severe depression, particularly when a strong threat of suicide exists.

- Psychosurgery techniques have become more precise, but they are still generally used only after all other treatment options have failed.

- Studies have shown that successful therapeutic treatments, whether involving drugs or psychotherapy, are associated with similar alterations of brain functioning.

PSYCHOLOGICAL DISORDERS AND SOCIETY

Since the days of insane asylums, first established in the sixteenth century to segregate the mentally ill from society, severe behaviour disorders have been treated in institutional settings. Many private and government funded institutions were built. The rise in patients being treated in these facilities increased significantly. It became apparent to mental health experts that although there were some high-quality institutions, many mental hospitals were not fulfilling their intended role as treatment facilities. They were overcrowded, understaffed and underfunded. Many of them could provide little more than minimal secure care and a haven from the stresses and demands of the outside world. Moreover, people who were admitted to such hospitals often sank into a chronic 'sick' role in which passive dependence and typically 'insane' behaviour were not only tolerated but expected (Goffman, 1961; Scheff, 1966). They lost the self-confidence, motivation and skills needed to return and adapt to the outside world, and had little chance of surviving outside the hospital.

DEINSTITUTIONALIZATION

There is a significant movement towards **deinstitutionalization**. The idea is to transfer the primary focus of treatment from the hospital to the community. The World Health Organization indicates that in many of the countries in Europe the number of beds available in mental health institutions, and indeed the number of mental health institutions themselves, have fallen dramatically. Some countries such as Holland and the UK have deinstitutionalized to a greater extent than other countries, but the trend is certainly there. Traditional psychiatric care is being moved slowly but surely into a more public mental health approach, which is shown, in most cases, to give a better quality of life, and encourage social inclusion rather than exclusion.

In the UK, asylum care was the usual method of dealing with the mentally ill until the mid-1950s, but gradually, a more community-based system began to replace this institutionalization. In the 1980s the number of asylums and hospital beds set aside for those with mental health problems actually decreased, and deinstitutionalization was increased. Turner warns that because of regular and unwanted, often violent, problems with some being cared for 'in the community', which all too often are picked up by the press, re-institutionalization may well take place in the future. Indeed Aerhart Treichel (2005) says that there are already signs of this re-institutionalization of those with mental health problems. The data from this study can be seen in Figure 18.26. However, Aerhart-Treichel goes on to say that although the number of beds has fallen, the number of involuntary admissions to hospital have not followed this trend. In some countries they have actually risen, especially in Germany. It is accepted that these data may only reflect a rise in short-term admissions, not necessarily proof of 're-institutionalization'. However, the increase is relevant, and is something to monitor. The research also identifies the additional cost of moving people from institutions. The number of residential care places has dramatically increased, up 15 per cent in Sweden, and as much as 256 per cent in Italy.

The concept of community treatment is a good one, for it allows people to remain in their social and work environments and to be treated with minimal disruption of their lives. However, it requires the availability of high-quality mental health care in community clinics, halfway houses, sheltered workshops and other community facilities. When these facilities are available, deinstitutionalization can work. Unfortunately, the funding for these support systems is hard to come by. As a result, many patients are

deinstitutionalization
to transfer the primary focus of treatment from the hospital to the community

Focus 18.25
What is the rationale for deinstitutionalization? What prevents the achievement of its goals?

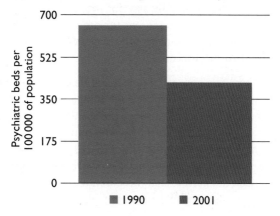

FIGURE 18.26

Number of beds.

The number of conventional psychiatric hospital beds has fallen in all countries looked at except Italy.

SOURCE: data from England, Germany, Italy, Netherlands, Spain and Sweden. Redrawn from Priebe et al., 2005.

FIGURE 18.27

The revolving-door phenomenon created by inadequate funding of community-based treatment facilities has produced a large population of disturbed homeless people who often live on our streets.

Focus 18.26

What therapeutic issues exist in managed-care environments?

being released into communities that are ill prepared to care for their needs. The result is a *revolving-door phenomenon* involving repeated re-hospitalizations. The majority of all hospital admissions involve formerly hospitalized patients.

This revolving door has produced a growing population of disturbed and homeless people who have nowhere to go for help (Fig. 18.27). In large urban populations, the largest mental wards very often exist not in hospitals but on city streets.

MENTAL HEALTH TREATMENT IN A MANAGED HEALTH-CARE ENVIRONMENT

Rising costs and changes in demand have swelled altered the mental health treatment landscape dramatically over recent years. Rising populations means rising burdens on health-care systems. The desire to contain health costs very often translates into a strong preference for drug treatments and short-term versus more costly long-term forms of psychotherapy, as well as the use of less expensive counsellors who charge lower fees that psychotherapists. Even then, the demand for mental-health support is often so great that waiting lists to see appropriate practitioners are extremely long. How health care is funded depends on where you live in the world. In some countries, health-care provision is almost entirely private and, as a consequence, often very expensive, so an insurance policy that can be drawn on at times of medical emergency is advised. Of course, insurance policies are, themselves, not inexpensive, so those that cannot afford them find themselves in terrible debt once they fall ill, or worse. If unable to afford mental-health care, a problem may persist and worsen. The consequences of this can be dire. In a report on public health systems, the World Health Organization (2000) indicates that health expenditure increased from 3 per cent of the world's gross domestic product in 1945 to almost 8 per cent in 1997. More money is being spent, but by whom? Health-care organizations and governments are looking at ways to ensure that health financing is in place to ensure that everyone, not just those that can afford it, has access to a decent level of care.

Some countries have an organized system of health care which people pay for through taxation and through some form of national insurance contribution, such as the National Health Service in the UK. Others, as we have heard, rely very heavily on private insurance. In the Netherlands, health care is essentially provided by a number of competing health funds, who each provide funds into a pool, which is spent exclusively on the care of the less affluent in society thus providing for all citizens in one way or another. A similar situation exists in South Africa, which has recently moved to making access to mental-health facilities easier for those that need it. The South African Mental Health Act that became law in 2004, provided regulations directing private health-care providers in their duty of care to patients requiring both regular medical care and mental-health care. This means that even those without insurance can now gain access to at least some of the services that those wealthy enough to pay for themselves enjoy.

Private health care remains an extremely important part of the health-care system worldwide. Those who eventually pay for the health care are, quite rightly, demanding evidence that the treatments they are paying for are effective. These pressures have had some positive results, including the stimulation of research on treatment outcomes and the development of some effective short-term therapies.

There are, however, some negative effects as well. To many psychologists, the most serious is that many decisions about the type and duration of therapy to be provided are being made by representatives of insurance companies rather than by the client or a trained mental-health professional. In some instances, the number of sessions permitted may be woefully inadequate to treat a serious disorder (Fig. 18.28). Although many psychologists concede that some of the more effective treatments are short-term cognitive-behavioural and interpersonal therapies, they do not believe that these treatments are best for every problem and client. It depends on the disorder, and the treatment, but current data suggest that about 12 to 18 sessions are required to achieve a 50 per cent recovery rate for most disorders (Hansen et al., 2002). Managed-care plans frequently limit payment to fewer sessions than this, so that many managed-care subscribers do not receive the level of care that they need. Likewise, the preference for drug treatments that require minimal contact between the patient and a professional may provide short-term improvement at the cost of a more satisfactory long-term result that could occur with psychological treatments that allow the development of better coping skills. Moreover, as we have seen in this chapter's 'Beneath the surface' feature, drug therapy has its own negative consequences.

" IT'S YOUR INSURANCE COMPANY, THEY SAY YOU'RE CURED. "

FIGURE 18.28

In environments where private health insurance is required, treatment decisions may be made by untrained representatives of an insurance company instead of a health-care professional.
SOURCE: cartoon by Ron Delgado, *The Wall Street Journal*, 1997. By permission of Cartoon Features Syndicate.

PREVENTATIVE MENTAL HEALTH

Up to now, we have focused entirely on what can be done to help people once they have developed a behaviour disorder. Successful treatment is one way to reduce the toll of human suffering produced by failures to adapt. Another way is to try to *prevent* the development of disorders through psychological intervention. In terms of economic and personal costs, and the costs to society it may be the case that a small amount of time and money spent on prevention will yield much greater benefits. If current efforts to enhance personal well-being and to slow the rise of health-care costs are to be successful, the prevention of behaviour disorders must be a focal point of social policy. In some cases, this may involve treating psychological disorders during childhood in an attempt to prevent their continuation into adult life. Jané-Llopis and Anderson (2006) looked at how mental-health prevention is being tackled by members of the European Union. Sweden, in particular was praised for a long tradition of preventative work in many areas of health provision. The Swedish attitude and preventative drive to combat alcoholism was singled out as extremely worthy of praise in its influence on more positive mental health. Sweden has a long history of careful supervision of alcohol consumption and instruction of the dangers associated with it, which began at the start of the twentieth century. In addition to this, the Swedish Health Care Act sets out a number of areas which should be targeted by money set aside for preventative measures of health care. Interestingly though, the policy makes it clear that these targeted areas are not, in themselves, the areas we may be concerned with. For instance, 'mental health' does not feature as an item to be targeted. Rather, and interestingly, the items include issues such as 'safe and good conditions in which to grow up' and 'participation and influence in the community'. It is thought that by targeting these areas general health, including mental health, will improve. Elsewhere, more direct action such as school-based intervention programmes have proven effective in preventing and reducing antisocial and often aggressive behaviours in children (Wilson et al., 2003)

People may become vulnerable to psychological disorders as the result of situational factors, personal factors, or both. Thus prevention can be approached from two perspectives (Fig. 18.29). **Situation-focused prevention** is directed at either reducing or eliminating the environmental causes of behaviour disorders or enhancing situational factors that help prevent the development of disorders. Programmes designed to enhance the functioning of families, reduce stress within organizations, provide better educational opportunities for children, and develop a sense of connection to other people and the community at large all have the potential to help prevent the development of behaviour disorders (Albee, 1997; Taylor and Wang, 2000). One community

Focus 18.27

Describe two major approaches to prevention, and provide an example of each.

situation-focused prevention

directed at either reducing or eliminating the environmental causes of behaviour disorders or enhancing situational factors that help prevent the development of disorders

FIGURE 18.29

Preventive mental health.

Two approaches to the prevention of psychological disorders are based on the principle that deviant behaviour represents the interaction of personal and situational factors. Situation-focused approaches increase situational protective factors or reduce vulnerability factors in the environment. Competency-focused approaches reduce personal vulnerability factors or strengthen personal competencies and coping skills.

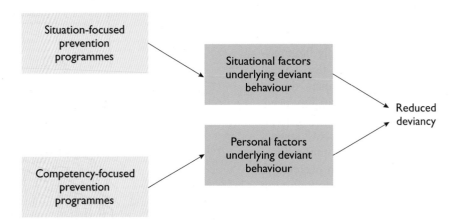

competency-focused prevention

designed to increase personal resources and coping skills

intervention programme was designed to prevent the development of antisocial personality disorder in a high-risk inner-city environment. Between the ages of 3 and 5 years, children randomly assigned to the experimental group participated in an intensive nutritional, physical exercise and educational programme. Children exposed to this programme had lower scores on measures of antisocial personality disorder at age 17 and lower criminal records at age 23 compared with a control group (Raine et al., 2003).

The personal side of the equation is addressed by **competency-focused prevention,** designed to increase personal resources and coping skills. Such programmes may focus on strengthening resistance to stress, improving social and vocational competencies, enhancing self-esteem and helping people gain the skills needed to build stronger social support systems. One illustrative programme, developed by Edna Foa and her co-workers (1995), focused on preventing post-traumatic stress disorder (PTSD) in women who had recently been raped or assaulted.

FIGURE 18.30

Preventing PTSD.

A competency-based prevention project was designed to prevent PTSD in women who were victims of rape and assault. The programme, which combined a number of behavioural and cognitive therapy techniques to increase stress-management coping skills, sharply reduced the likelihood of developing PTSD.

SOURCE: Foa et al., 1995.

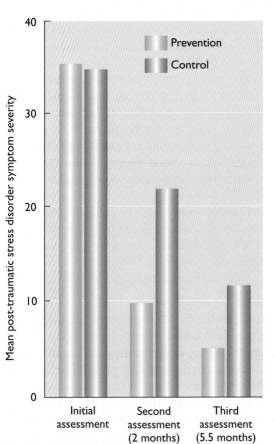

The victims were randomly assigned to either a treatment condition or to an untreated control condition. In hourly sessions over a four-week period, the women in the treatment group learned about the common psychological reactions to being raped, helping them to realize that their responses were understandable, given what they had experienced. They relived their trauma through guided imagery to help defuse their lingering fears through exposure. The women also learned stress-management coping skills such as relaxation, and they went through a cognitive therapy procedure to replace stress-producing cognitions with more realistic appraisals.

The results of the prevention programme are shown in Figure 18.30. The women exposed to the prevention treatment had less severe symptoms at both the 2-month and 5.5-month assessments. Moreover, two months after their trauma, diagnostic interviews with the women in the two groups revealed that 70 per cent of the women in the control condition met the DSM-IV criteria for PTSD compared with only 10 per cent of the women who had received the prevention programme. Thus for many of the women, an efficient four-week programme prevented what might have been a PTSD disorder that would have created tremendous personal misery and required a far more expensive and time-consuming course of therapy.

Although many mental-health experts believe that more resources need to be focused on the prevention of maladaptive behaviour, they also recognize that prevention presents its own challenges. For example, we cannot develop an intervention programme until we understand the causes of the disorder we want to reduce. Even when causal factors are known, we also need to understand what kinds of interventions will be successful in modifying them. This requires careful research into which types of programmes are most effective in preventing which types of problems in which types of people – our old specificity question.

Another practical problem is that the effects of prevention are usually not immediately obvious. It may take years for their effects to become evident. Moreover, their effects (which usually involve the *absence* of a disorder) can be hard to measure. For these reasons, prevention programmes can be difficult to justify when funding priorities are being set, even though the programmes may, in the long run, have greater positive impact than programmes that focus on treating disorders that have already developed.

Having described the nature and benefits of treatments, we end this chapter with some research derived guidelines for seeking and benefiting from therapy.

APPLYING PSYCHOLOGICAL SCIENCE

WHEN AND WHERE TO SEEK THERAPY

No one is immune to the problems of living. Every day, each of us does the best we can to balance our personal and social resources against the demands created by our life circumstances. We all have certain vulnerabilities, and if environmental demands and our vulnerabilities combine to exceed our resources, we may experience psychological problems for which professional assistance would be helpful. Here are some general guidelines for seeking such help and profiting from it.

WHEN TO SEEK HELP

First is the issue of when to seek help. In general terms, you should consider seeking professional assistance if any of the following apply:

- You are experiencing serious emotional discomfort, such as feelings of depression or anxiety, that are adversely affecting your personal, work or family life.

- You are encountering a serious problem or life transition that you feel unable to handle on your own.

- A problem that has interfered with your life or personal happiness in the past is worsening or has suddenly resurfaced.

- You have experienced some traumatic event, either in the past or recently, that you find yourself frequently thinking about, dreaming about or responding to with negative emotions.

- You are preoccupied with your weight or body image and are taking extreme steps, such as not eating or purging yourself by vomiting or taking laxatives.

- You have severe and recurring conflicts with other people.

- You hear voices telling you what to do, or you feel that others are controlling your thoughts.

WHERE TO SEEK HELP

How does one go about getting help in dealing with psychological problems? Help may be sought at a college, or university counselling or student-welfare centre, at a community agency, or from a professional, either your local doctor or in private practice. The university centres are often a good place for a student to start, for they can provide direct help or an appropriate referral to a reputable mental-health professional. If you are at a larger university that has a course in clinical or counselling psychology, there may also be an on-campus psychology training clinic administered by that department. There you would typically work with a graduate student who is being closely supervised by a licensed clinician.

How expensive is treatment? For students it is often offered free at a campus facility or as part of your country's health-care arrangements. If you are paying, then community mental-health providers typically have a sliding-fee scale based on the client's income, so financial considerations need not be a barrier to seeking professional assistance. A private practitioner may charge as much as medical doctors, dentists and lawyers. As a prospective client, you should always ask beforehand about the fee. If you have a health insurance policy you should check the mental-health benefits it provides, including what kinds of treatments and the number of sessions it covers and whether it will reimburse your chosen treatment provider.

WHAT TO LOOK FOR IN A THERAPIST

In choosing a therapist, what should you look for? It is important that your therapist be well trained and competent. Ask the therapist about his or her degree, licence, training, therapeutic orientation and the problems in which he or she specializes. This chapter has provided an overview of the major theoretical orientations, and one or more of them may seem especially attractive to you or suited to the problems you wish to address.

As we have seen, the relationship between client and therapist is of the utmost importance. You will want a therapist who can create a good working relationship with you. The degree of 'value similarity' between you and the therapist can be important. Timothy Kelly and Hans Strupp (1992) found that the most positive therapeutic outcomes were achieved when the client and therapist were neither very similar nor very dissimilar in values. High similarity may result in a failure to explore value-related issues, whereas too much dissimilarity may interfere with building a good therapeutic relationship. One exception to this general rule may occur in the area of religious values. Clients who have strong and committed religious values may profit most from a therapy that supports those values and uses them to help change problem behaviours (Probst et al., 1992).

Some clients prefer to work with either a male or female therapist, or one who is heterosexual or gay or lesbian, depending in part on the nature of the personal issues that have caused them to seek counselling. As we have seen, research has shown that personal warmth, sincere concern and empathy are important therapist characteristics. You should like and feel comfortable with your therapist, and you should feel at ease with the methods the therapist uses. Under no circumstances should your therapeutic relationship involve physical intimacy of any kind (even hugging). If a therapist should ever engage in such behaviour, you should immediately terminate treatment with that therapist and notify the appropriate professional organization, such as the state psychological or medical association. Such conduct is a serious breach of professional ethics and cannot be condoned under any circumstances.

WHAT CAN YOU EXPECT?

You and your therapist should have explicit, agreed-on goals for the treatment programme. If therapy proceeds well, you will experience beneficial changes that indicate movement towards your goals. It may take some time for these changes to occur, however, since long-standing personal vulnerabilities are not easily changed, and significant change seldom occurs overnight. If you do not see any progress after several months or if you seem to be functioning less well than before, you should discuss your progress with the therapist. The therapist may be more satisfied with your progress than you are. However, if you continue to be dissatisfied with your progress or with the therapeutic relationship, you may at some point decide to terminate it. This should not prevent you from seeking help from another therapist.

Entering a helping relationship is a courageous step, and resolving problems in living may involve taking risks and experiencing pain. However, many clients look back on the pain and risks and feel that the process was a valuable one that enabled them to live happier lives than they otherwise could have. Here is a reflection by Dr Sandra L. Harris, a prominent clinical psychologist, on the course of therapy she undertook as a college student:

> When I think about the girl I was in my freshman year at the University of Maryland and the young woman I was when I graduated four years later, it is clear that it was not only the issues Jim and I discussed, but how we talked that made the difference. The intangibles of trust, respect, and caring were at least as important as the active problem solving that transpired in our weekly meetings. It was not a dramatic transformation, rather it was a slight shifting of a path by a few degrees on the compass. Over the years that shift has had a cumulative effect and I walk a very different road than I would have without him. (Harris, 1981, p. 3)

IN REVIEW

- The introduction of drug therapies that normalize disturbed behaviour, as well as concerns about the deterioration of life skills during hospitalization, has helped stimulate a move towards deinstitutionalization – the treatment of people in their communities.

- Research has shown that deinstitutionalization can work when adequate community treatment is provided. Unfortunately, many communities have been unable to fund the needed facilities, resulting in a revolving door of release and re-hospitalization, as well as a new generation of homeless people who live on the streets and do not receive needed treatment.

- Managed care is requiring therapists to demonstrate the efficacy of their techniques and to develop shorter, more economical treatments. An issue of concern is that decisions about the type and duration of treatment are increasingly being taken out of the hands of trained professionals.

- Prevention programmes may be either situation focused or competency focused, depending on whether they are directed at changing environmental conditions or personal factors.

KEY TERMS AND CONCEPTS

Each term has been boldfaced and defined in the chapter on the page indicated in parentheses.

aversion therapy (p. 855)

behaviour modification (p. 856)

behavioural activation treatment (p. 858)

common factors (p. 869)

competency-focused prevention (p. 882)

counter-conditioning (p. 853)

culturally competent therapists (p. 863)

deinstitutionalization (p. 879)

dialectical behaviour therapy (DBT) (p. 859)

dodo bird verdict (p. 867)

eclecticism (p. 858)

effect size (p. 867)

empathy (p. 845)

empirically supported treatments (ESTs) (p. 867)

exposure (p. 850)

feminist therapy (p. 864)

free association (p. 840)

genuineness (p. 845)

insight (p. 840)

interpersonal therapy (p. 844)

interpretation (p. 842)

meta-analysis (p. 867)

openness (p. 868)

placebo control group (p. 873)

psychosurgery (p. 876)

randomized clinical trial (p. 866)

resistance (p. 841)

response prevention (p. 850)

self-relatedness (p. 868)

situation-focused prevention (p. 881)

social skills training (p. 857)

specificity question (p. 864)

spontaneous remission (p. 865)

stimulus hierarchy (p. 854)

systematic desensitization (p. 853)

tardive dyskinesia (p. 871)

token economy (p. 856)

transference (p. 842)

unconditional positive regard (p. 845)

virtual reality (VR) (p. 851)

WHAT DO YOU THINK?

ARE CONDITIONING TECHNIQUES COMPATIBLE WITH PSYCHOANALYTIC THEORY? (p. 855)

Behaviourists and psychoanalytic theorists have very different viewpoints about psychological symptoms, such as a phobia. For the behaviourist, the phobia *is* the problem, period. Decondition it and the problem is resolved. In contrast, the psychodynamic view is based on a 'medical model' analogy that distinguishes between symptoms and underlying causes. As noted in Chapter 17, a psychoanalyst would view a phobia as a behavioural manifestation of some underlying, probably unconscious conflict. Simply treating the observed symptom does nothing to resolve the psychodynamic issues assumed to cause it, in much the same way that reducing a malaria victim's fever with aspirin does nothing to cure the underlying disease. The analyst would therefore maintain that the goal of therapy should be to treat the underlying dynamics, after which the phobia should disappear on its own. Even if the phobia were successfully treated with behavioural conditioning therapies, the underlying problem would remain unresolved, and some new symptom might well appear in place of the phobia. This prediction of *symptom substitution* was frequently raised by psychodynamic critics of behaviour therapies, but no indisputable evidence of new symptoms popping up after behaviour therapy treatment has ever materialized (Paul, 2001). In instances when new symptoms appeared, they could be attributed to new post-treatment learning experiences.

DO SURVEY RESULTS PROVIDE AN ACCURATE PICTURE OF TREATMENT EFFECTIVENESS? (p. 867)

Seligman's conclusion that the *CR* survey provides a realistic appraisal of treatment effects is thought-provoking, but before you accept this conclusion, you should consider some of the survey's shortcomings. First, consider the nature of the *CR* sample. Only 1.6 per cent of the original 184 000 people contacted described their therapy experience. Is it possible that among the other 98.4 per cent are a significant number of people who had been in therapy with unfavourable results and chose not to share their experiences? If so, the effectiveness of therapy could be exaggerated in this self-selected sample.

Second, what about the nature and quality of the data? We have only global, after-the-fact reports from clients. There is no way to corroborate respondents' reports with other sources of data. How do we know that they are not biased by memory distortions or by rationalizing their investment ('If I spent that much time and money, I must have got better')? Rationalization could also account for the apparent superiority of long-term therapy, where more time and money were expended, as well as the tendency to return the questionnaire and share the success story.

Third, what has the *CR* study told us about the more important specificity question? We do not know if some matches of clinical problems with specific forms of therapy yielded better outcomes than others. In fact, we cannot even be sure what kinds of therapy were administered because respondents did not describe their treatments in detail.

Fourth, how about the absence of a control group? Can we rule out spontaneous remission of symptoms? As we saw in Chapter 17, many mental health problems (e.g., depression and anxiety) fluctuate or improve with time. People who are assessed at their low points, when they are most likely to seek therapy, are almost certain to improve, with or without therapy (Mintz et al., 1996). Could this factor alone explain the respondents' perceptions that they had improved? As Seligman himself conceded, 'Because there are no control groups, the *CR* ... study cannot tell us directly whether talking to sympathetic friends or merely letting time pass would have produced just as much improvement as treatment by a mental-health professional' (1995, p. 972).

Despite the interpretive challenges that attend community studies like this, psychotherapy researchers agree that it is critically important to see how well the treatment principles and techniques identified in controlled studies work in the real world (Westen et al., 2004). One way to accomplish this is by systematically measuring the variables of interest within individual cases being seen by practising therapists in the community. A large number of single-client case studies containing such measurement can provide important data on the effectiveness of specific therapies and the factors that influence those outcomes (Goldfried and Eubanks-Carter, 2004).

References

'A Recovering Patient.' (1986). 'Can we talk?' The schizophrenic patient in psychotherapy. *American Journal of Psychiatry*, *143*, 68–70.

Aaron, S. (1986). *Stage fright*. Chicago: University of Chicago Press.

ABC News (2007). Basic instincts: The science of evil. *ABC News Primetime*. Retrieved online on 3/14/2007 from http://abcnews.go.com/Primetime/story?id=2765416&page=1

Abel, T., & Kandel, E. (1998). Positive and negative regulatory mechanisms that mediate long-term memory storage. *Brain Research Reviews, 26,* 360–378.

Abraham, K. (1911). Notes on the psychoanalytic investigation and treatment of manic-depressive insanity and allied conditions. In *Selected papers of Karl Abraham*. New York: Basic Books, 1968.

Abramov, I., & Gordon, J. (1994). Color appearance: On seeing red—or yellow, or green, or blue. *Annual Review of Psychology, 45,* 451–485.

Abramson, L. Y., Seligman, M. E. P., & Teasdale, J. D. (1978). Learned helplessness in humans: Critique and reformulation. *Journal of Abnormal Psychology, 87,* 49–74.

Achter, J., Lubinski, D., & Benbow, C. P. (1996). Multipotentiality among the intellectually gifted: 'It was never there and already it's vanishing.' *Journal of Counseling Psychology, 43,* 65–76.

Adams, P. R., & Cox, K. J. A. (2002). Synaptic Darwinism and neocortical function. *Neurocomputing, 42,* 197–214.

Adelmann, P. K., & Zajonc, R. B. (1989). Facial efference and the experience of emotion. *Annual Review of Psychology*, *40,* 249–280.

Ader, R. (2001). Psychoneuroimmunology. *Current Directions in Psychological Science, 10,* 94–98.

Ader, R., & Cohen, N. (1975). Behaviorally conditioned immunosuppression. *Psychosomatic Medicine, 37,* 333–340.

Ader, R., & Cohen, N. (1982). Behaviorally conditioned immunosuppression and murine systemic lupus erythematosus. *Science, 215*(4539), 1534–1536.

Adrés, P. (2003). Frontal cortex as the central executive of working memory: Time to revise our view. *Cortex, 39,* 871–895.

Aggleton, J. P. (1993). The contribution of the amygdala to normal and abnormal emotional states. *Trends in Neurosciences, 16,* 328–333.

Agnew, H. W., Jr., Webb, W. B., & Williams, R. L. (1967). Comparison of stage four and 1-REM sleep deprivation. *Perceptual and Motor Skills, 24,* 851–858.

Ahadi, S., & Diener, E. (1989). Multiple determinants and effect size. *Journal of Personality and Social Psychology, 56,* 398–406.

Ahn, H. J. (2005). Child care teachers' strategies in children's socialization of emotion. *Early Child Development & Care, 175,* 49–61.

Ai, A. K., Peterson, C., & Ubelhor, D. (2002). War-related trauma and symptoms of posttraumatic stress disorder among adult Kosovar refugees. *Journal of Traumatic Stress, 15,* 157–160.

Ainsworth, M., Blehar, M. C., Waters, E., & Wall, S. (1978). *Patterns of attachment: A psychological study of the strange situation*. Hillsdale, NJ: Erlbaum.

Aitchison, J. (1998). *The articulate mammal: An introduction to psycholinguistics*. Florence, KY: Taylor & Francis/Routledge.

Aitken, S., & Bower T. G. (1982). Intersensory substitution in the blind. *Journal of Experimental Child Psychology, 33,* 309–323.

Ajzen, I. (1991). The theory of planned behavior. *Organizational Behavior and Human Decision Processes, 50,* 179–211.

Alanko, L. O., Laitinen, J. T., Stenberg, D., & Porkka-Heiskanen, T. (2004). Adenosine Al receptor-dependent G-protein activity in the rat brain during prolonged wakefulness. *Neuroreport: For Rapid Communication of Neuroscience Research, 15,* 2133–2137.

Albee, G. W. (1997). Speak no evil? *American Psychologist, 52*, 1143–1144.

Alcock, J. (2002). *Animal behavior: An evolutionary approach*. New York: Sinauer.

Aldridge, S. (1998). *The thread of life: The story of genes and genetic engineering*. New York: Cambridge University Press.

Alexander, F. (2004). A classic in psychotherapy integration revisited: The dynamics of psychotherapy in the light of learning theory. *Journal of Psychotherapy Integration, 14*, 347–359.

Alfieri, T., Ruble, D. N., & Higgins, E. T. (1996). Gender stereotypes during adolescence: Developmental changes and the transition to junior high school. *Developmental Psychology, 32*, 1129–1137.

Allen Institute for Brain Science (2006, September 6). *Allen Institute for Brain Science Completes Brain Atlas*. Retrieved September 8, 2006 from http://www.alleninstitute.org

Allen, M. (1991). Meta-analysis comparing the persuasiveness of one-sided and two-sided messages. *Western Journal of Speech Communication, 55*, 390–404.

Allen, M., D'Alessio, D., & Brezgel, K. (1995). A meta-analysis summarizing the effects of pornography: II. Aggression after exposure. *Human Communication Research, 22*, 258–283.

Allen, M., D'Alessio, D., & Emmers-Sommer, T. M. (2000). Reactions of criminal sexual offenders to pornography: A meta-analytic summary. In M. Roloff (Ed.), *Communication Yearbook 22*. Thousand Oaks, CA: Sage.

Allgeier, A. R., Byrne, D., Brooks, B., & Revnes, D. (1979). The waffle phenomenon: Negative evaluations of those who shift attitudinally. *Journal of Applied Social Psychology, 9*, 170–182.

Allport, G. W. (1954). *The nature of prejudice*. Oxford and Reading, MA: Addison-Wesley.

Allport, G. W., & Odbert, H. S. (1936). Trait names: A psycho-lexical study. *Psychological Monographs, 47*(Whole No. 211).

Alonso, C., & Coe, C. J. (2001). Disruptions of social relationships accentuate the association between emotional distress and menstrual pain in young women. *Health Psychology, 20*, 411–416.

Alonso, J., Angermeyer, M. C., Bernert, S., Bruffaerts, R., Brugha, T. S., Bryson, H., de Girolamo, G., Graaf, R., Demyttenaere, K., Gasquet, I., Haro, J. M., Katz, S. J., Kessler, R. C., Kovess, V., Lépine, J. P., Ormel, J., Polidori, G., Russo, L. J., Vilagut, G., Almansa, J., Arbabzadeh-Bouchez, S., Autonell, J., Bernal, M., Buist-Bouwman, M. A., Codony, M., Domingo-Salvany, A., Ferrer, M., Joo, S. S., Martínez-Alonso, M., Matschinger, H., Mazzi, F., Morgan, Z., Morosini, P., Palacín, C., Romera, B., Taub, N., & Vollebergh, W. A., ESEMeD/MHEDEA 2000 Investigators, European Study of the Epidemiology of Mental Disorders (ESEMeD) Project (2004). Prevalence of mental disorders in Europe: results from the European Study of the Epidemiology of Mental Disorders (ESEMeD) project. *Acta Psychiatrica Scandinavica Supplement,* (420), 21–27.

Altman, I., & Taylor, D. A. (1973). *Social penetration: The development of interpersonal relationships*. New York: Holt, Rinehart & Winston.

Altman, J., & Bayer, S. A. (1996). *Development of the cerebellar system: In relation to its evolution, structure and functions*. Boca Raton, FL: CRC-Press.

Amato, P. R., & Afifi, T. D. (2006). Feeling caught between parents: Adult children's relations with parents and subjective wellbeing. *Journal of Marriage and Family, 68*, 222–235.

Amato, P. R., & Keith, B. (1991). Parental divorce and the well-being of children: A meta-analysis. *Psychological Bulletin, 110*, 26–46.

Ambady, N., & Rosenthal, R. (1992). Thin slices of expressive behaviour as predictors of interpersonal consequences: A meta-analysis. *Psychological Bulletin, 111*, 256–274.

American Psychiatric Association (1994). *Diagnostic and statistical manual of mental disorders* (4th ed.). Washington, DC: American Psychiatric Association.

American Psychiatric Association. (2000). *The diagnostic and statistical manual of mental disorders, fourth edition, text revision (DSMIV)*. Washington, DC: Author.

Ames, C. (1992). Achievement goals and adaptive motivation patterns: The role of the environment. In G. Roberts (Ed.), *Motivation in sport and exercise*. Champaign, IL: Human Kinetics.

Anand, B. K., & Brobeck, J. R. (1951). Hypothalamic control of food intake in rats and cats. *Yale Journal of Biology and Medicine, 24,* 123–140.

Anderson, C. A. (2004). An update on the effects of playing violent video games. *Journal of Adolescence, 27,* 113–122.

Anderson, C. A., & Bushman, B. J. (2002). Human aggression. *Annual Review of Psychology, 53,* 27–51.

Anderson, J. R. (1985). *Cognitive psychology and its implications* (2nd ed.). New York: Freeman.

Anderson, M. C., & Neely, J. H. (1996). Interference and inhibition in memory retrieval. In E. L. Bjork & R. A. Bjork (Eds.), *Memory: Handbook of perception and cognition* (2nd ed.). San Diego: Academic Press.

Anderson, N. D., & Craik, F. I. M. (2000). Memory in the aging brain. In E. Tulving & F. I. M. Craik (Eds.), *The Oxford handbook of memory.* New York: Oxford University Press.

Andreason, N. C., Arndt, S., Swayze, V., Cizadlo, T. et al. (1994). Thalamic abnormalities in schizophrenia visualized through magnetic resonance image averaging. *Science, 266,* 294–298.

Andrews, F. M. (1991). Stability and change in levels and structure of subjective well-being: USA 1972 and 1988. *Social Indicators Research, 25,* 1–30.

Ankney, C. D. (1992). Sex differences in relative brain size: The mismeasure of women, too? *Intelligence, 16,* 329–336.

Anthony, J. C., Warner, L. A., & Kessler, R. C. (1997). Comparative epidemiology of dependence on tobacco, alcohol, controlled substances, and inhalants: Basic findings from the National Comorbidity Survey. In G. A. Marlatt & G. R. VandenBos (Eds.), *Addictive behaviors: Readings on etiology, prevention and treatment.* Washington, DC: American Psychological Association.

Anton, R. F. (2001). Pharmacologic approaches to the management of alcoholism. *Journal of Clinical Psychiatry, 62,* 11–17.

Antonuccio, D. O., Danton, W. G. et al. (2003). Psychology in the prescription era: Building a firewall between marketing and science. *American Psychologist 58,* 1028–1043.

Antrobus, J. (1991). Dreaming: Cognitive processes during cortical activation and high afferent thresholds. *Psychological Review, 98,* 96–121.

APA Monitor (1997, December). *Author, 28*(12).

Aponte, H., & Hoffman, L. (1973). The open door. A structural approach to a family with an anorectic child. *Family Process, 12,* 1–44.

Arendt, J., Skene, D.J., Middleton, B. et al. (1997). Efficacy of melatonin in jet lag, shift work and blindness. *Journal of Biological Rhythms, 12,* 604–617.

Argyle, M. (1999). Causes and correlates of happiness. In D. Kahneman, E. Diener, & N. Schwarz (Eds.), *Well-being: The foundations of hedonic psychology.* New York: Russell Sage Foundation.

Ariznavarreta, C., Cardinali, D. P., Villanua, M. A., Granados, B., Martin, M., Chiesa, J. J. et al. (2002). Circadian rhythms in airline pilots submitted to long-haul transmeridian flights. *Aviation, Space, and Environmental Medicine, 73,* 445–455.

Arnett, J. J. (1999). Adolescent storm and stress, reconsidered. *American Psychologist, 54,* 317–326.

Arnett, J. J. (2001). Conceptions of the transition to adulthood: Perspectives from adolescence through midlife. *Journal of Adult Development, 8,* 133–143.

Arnett, P. A. (1997). Autonomic responsivity in psychopaths: A critical review and theoretical proposal. *Clinical Psychology Review, 17,* 903–936.

Aron, A., & Westbay, L. (1996). Dimensions of the prototype of love. *Journal of Personality and Social Psychology, 70,* 535–551.

Aron, E., Aron, A., & Davies, K. M. (2005). Adult shyness: The interaction of temperamental sensitivity and an adverse childhood environment. *Personality and Social Psychology Bulletin, 31*, 181–197.

Aronson, E., Stephan, C., Sikes, J., Blaney, N., & Snopp, M. (1978). *The jigsaw classroom.* Beverly Hills, CA: Sage.

Aronson, J., Lustina, M. J., Good, C., Keough, K., Steele, C. M., & Brown, J. (1999). When White men can't do math: Necessary and sufficient factors in stereotype threat. *Journal of Experimental Social Psychology, 35*, 29–46.

Arrow, H., & Burns, K. L. (2004). Self-organizing culture: How norms emerge in small groups. In M. Schaller, & C. S. Crandall (Eds.), *The psychological foundations of culture.* Mahwah, NJ: Erlbaum.

Asch, S. E. (1946). Forming impressions of personality. *Journal of Abnormal and Social Psychology, 41*, 258–290.

Asch, S. E. (1951). Effects of group pressure upon the modification and distortion of judgment. In H. Guetzkow (Ed.), *Groups, leadership, and men.* Pittsburgh: Carnegie Press.

Asch, S. E. (1956). Studies of independence and conformity: A minority of one against a unanimous majority. *Psychological Monographs, 70*, 416.

Asimov, I. (1997). *Isaac Asimov's book of facts.* New York: Random House/Wings Books.

Aspinwall, L. G., & Staudinger, U. M. (Eds.) (2003). *A psychology of human strengths: Fundamental questions and future directions for a positive psychology.* Washington, DC: American Psychological Association.

Assanand, S. P., John, P. J., & Lehman, D. R. (1998). Teaching theories of hunger and eating: Overcoming students' misconceptions. *Teaching of Psychology, 25*, 44–46.

Assor, A., Roth, G., & Deci, E. L. (2004). The emotional costs of parents' conditional regard: A self-determination theory analysis. *Journal of Personality, 72*, 47–88.

Atkinson, J. W. (1964). *An introduction to motivation.* Princeton, NJ: Van Nostrand.

Atkinson, J. W. (Ed.). (1958). *Motives in fantasy, action, and society.* Princeton, NJ: Van Nostrand.

Atkinson, J. W., & Birch, D. (1978). *An introduction to motivation.* New York: Van Nostrand.

Atkinson, R. C., & Shiffrin, R. M. (1968). Human memory: A proposed system and its control processes. In K. W. Spence & J. T. Spence (Eds.), *Advances in the psychology of learning and motivation: Research and theory* (Vol. 2). New York: Academic Press.

Auerbach, S. M. (1989). Stress management and coping research in the health care setting: An overview and methodological commentary. *Journal of Consulting and Clinical Psychology, 57*, 388–395.

Austin, M., & Leader, L. (2000). Maternal stress and obstetric and infant outcomes: Epidemiological findings and neuroendocrine mechanisms. *Australian and New Zealand Journal of Obstetrics and Gynaecology, 40*, 331–337.

Avenell, A., Brown, T. J., McGee, M. A., Campbell, M. K. et al. (2004). What interventions should we add to weight reducing diets in adults with obesity? A systematic review of randomized controlled trials of adding drug therapy, exercise, behaviour therapy or a combination of these interventions. *Journal of Human Nutrition and Dietetics, 17*, 293–316.

Ayllon, T., & Azrin, N. H. (1968). *The token economy: A motivational system for therapy and rehabilitation.* New York: Appleton-Century-Crofts.

Ayres, J. J. B. (1998). Fear conditioning and avoidance. In W. T. O'Donohue (Ed.), *Learning and behavior therapy.* Boston: Allyn & Bacon.

Ayuso-Mateos, J. L., Vázquez-Barquero, J. L., Dowrick, C. et al. (2001). Depressive disorders in Europe: prevalence figures from the ODIN study. *British Journal of Psychiatry, 179*, 308–316.

Baars, B. J. (1997). In the theatre of consciousness: Global workspace theory, a rigorous scientific theory of consciousness. *Journal of Consciousness Studies, 4*, 292–309.

Baars, B. J. (2002). The conscious access hypothesis: Origins and recent evidence. *Trends in Cognitive Sciences, 6*, 47–52.

Backhaus, W. G., Kliegl, R., & Werner, J. S. (Eds.). (1998). *Color vision: Perspectives from different disciplines.* New York: Walter de Gruyter.

Baddeley, A. D. (1990). *Human memory: Theory and practice.* Boston: Allyn & Bacon.

Baddeley, A. D. (2002). Is working memory still working? *European Psychologist, 7,* 85–97.

Baddeley, A. D., & Hitch, G. J. (1974). Working memory. In G. H. Bower (Ed.), *The psychology of learning and motivation* (Vol. 8). New York: Academic Press.

Baddeley, A. D., Gathercole, S. E., & Papagno, C. (1998). The phonological loop as a language learning device. *Psychological Review, 105,* 158–173.

Baddeley, A. D., Thompson, N., & Buchanan, M. (1975). Word length and the structure of short-term memory. *Journal of Verbal Learning and Verbal Behavior, 14,* 575–589.

Baehr, E. K. (2001). Circadian phase-delaying effects of nocturnal exercise in older and young adults. *Dissertation Abstracts International: Section B: The Sciences and Engineering, 62*(4-B), 2105.

Bagge, C., Nickell, A., Stepp, S., Durrett, C., Jackson, K., & Trull, T. J. (2004). Borderline personality disorder features predict negative outcomes 2 years later. *Journal of Abnormal Psychology, 113,* 279–288.

Bagley, C., & Ramsay, R. (1997). *Suicidal behaviour in adolescents and adults: Research, taxonomy and prevention.* Aldershot: Ashgate Publishing.

Bagnardi, V., Blangiardo, M., LaVecchia, C., & Corrao, G. (2001). A Meta-analysis of alcohol drinking and cancer risk. *British Journal of Cancer, 85,* 1700–1705.

Bahrick, H. P. (1984). Semantic memory content in permastore: Fifty years of memory for Spanish learned in school. *Journal of Experimental Psychology: General, 113,* 1–29.

Bahrick, H. P. (2005). The long-term neglect of long-term memory: Reasons and remedies. In A. F. Healy (Ed.), *Experimental cognitive psychology and its applications: Decade of behavior.* Washington, DC: American Psychological Association.

Bahrick, H. P., Bahrick, P. O., & Wittlinger, R. P. (1975). Fifty years of memory for names and faces: A cross-sectional approach. *Journal of Experimental Psychology: General, 104,* 54–75.

Bahrick, H. P., Hall, L. K., & Berger, S. A. (1996). Accuracy and distortion in memory for high school grades. *Psychological Science, 7,* 265–271.

Bailey, J. M., & Pillard, R. C. (1991). A genetic study of male sexual orientation. *Archives of General Psychiatry, 48,* 1089–1096.

Bailey, J. M., Dunne, M. P., & Martin, N. G. (2000). Genetic and environmental influences on sexual orientation and its correlates in an Australian twin sample. *Journal of Personality and Social Psychology, 78,* 524–536.

Bailey, J. M., Pillard, R. C., Neale, M. C., & Agyei, Y. (1993). Heritable factors influence sexual orientation in women. *Archives of General Psychiatry, 50,* 217–223.

Baillargeon, R. (1987). Object permanence in 3½- and 4½-month-old infants. *Developmental Psychology, 23,* 655–664.

Baillargeon, R. (2004). Infants' physical world. *Current Directions in Psychological Science, 13,* 89–94.

Baillargeon, R., Spelke, E. S., & Wasserman, S. (1985). Object permanence in five-month-old infants. *Cognition, 20,* 191–208.

Ball, L. J., Lucas, E. J., Miles, J. N. V., & Gale, A.G. (2003). Inspection times and the selection task: What do eye-movements reveal about relevance effects? *Quarterly Journal of Experimental Psychology, 56A,* 1053–1077.

Baltes, P. B., & Kunzmann, U. (2004). The two faces of wisdom: Wisdom as a general theory of knowledge and judgment about excellence in mind and virtue vs. wisdom as everyday realization in people and products. *Human Development, 47,* 290–299.

Baltes, P., & Staudinger, U. M. (2000). Wisdom: A metaheuristic (pragmatic) to orchestrate mind and virtue toward excellence. *American Psychologist, 55,* 122–136.

Bandura, A. (1965). Influence of models' reinforcement contingencies on the acquisition of imitated responses. *Journal of Personality and Social Psychology, 1,* 589–595.

Bandura, A. (1969). *Principles of behavior modification.* New York: Holt, Rinehart & Winston.

Bandura, A. (1986). *Social foundations of thought and action: A social-cognitive theory.* Englewood Cliffs, NJ: Prentice Hall.

Bandura, A. (1989). Social cognitive theory. *Annals of Child Development, 6,* 3–58.

Bandura, A. (1997). *Self-efficacy: The exercise of control.* New York: W. H. Freeman.

Bandura, A. (1999). Social cognitive theory of personality. In D. Cervone & Y. Shoda (Eds.), *The coherence of personality.* New York: Guilford Press.

Bandura, A. (2000). Health promotion from the perspective of social cognitive theory. In P. Norman, C. Abraham, & M. Conner (Eds.), *Understanding and changing health and behaviour.* Reading: Harwood.

Bandura, A. (2002a). Environmental sustainability by sociocognitive deceleration of population growth. In P. Schmuck & W. P. Schultz (Eds.), *Psychology of sustainable development.* Dordrecht, Netherlands: Kluwer.

Bandura, A. (2002b). Growing primacy of human agency in adaptation and change in the electronic era. *European Psychologist, 7,* 2–16.

Bandura, A. (2004). Social cognitive theory for personal and social change by enabling media. In A. Singhal, M. J. Cody, E. M. Rogers, & M. Sabido (Eds.), *Entertainment, education and social change: History, research, and practice.* Mahwah, NJ: Erlbaum.

Bandura, A., & Cervone, D. (1983). Self-evaluative and self-efficacy mechanisms governing the motivational effects of goal systems. *Journal of Personality and Social Psychology, 45,* 1017–1028.

Bandura, A., O'Leary, A., Taylor, C., et al. (1987). Perceived self-efficacy and pain control: Opioid and nonopioid mechanisms. *Journal of Personality and Social Psychology, 53,* 563–571.

Banyard, P., & Hunt, N. (2000). Reporting research: Something missing? *Psychologist, 13*(2), 68–71.

Barber, J. (1998). The mysterious persistence of hypnotic analgesia. *International Journal of Clinical and Experimental Hypnosis, 46,* 28–43.

Barber, T. X. (1961). Death by suggestion. *Psychosomatic Medicine, 23,* 153–155.

Bardo, M. T. (1998). Neuropharmacological mechanisms of drug reward: beyond dopamine in the nucleus accumbens. *Critical Review of Neurobology, 12,* 37–67.

Bargh, J. A., & Chartrand, T. L. (1999). The unbearable automaticity of being. *American Psychologist, 54,* 462–479.

Barlow, D. H. (1997). Cognitive-behavioral therapy for panic disorder: Current status. *Journal of Clinical Psychiatry, 58*(Suppl. 2), 32–36.

Barlow, D. H. (2002). *Anxiety and its disorders.* New York: Guilford Press.

Barlow, D. H., Rapee, R. M., & Reisner, L. C. (2001). *Mastering stress 2001: A lifestyle approach.* Dallas, TX: American Health.

Barnes, G. E., & Prosen, H. (1985). Parental death and depression. *Journal of Abnormal Psychology, 94,* 64–69.

Barnett, J. E., & Porter, J. E. (1998). The suicidal patient: Clinical and risk management strategies. In L. VandeCreek & S. Knapp (Eds.), *Innovations in clinical practice: A source book* (Vol. 16). Sarasota, FL: Professional Resource Press.

Baron, A., & Perone, M. (2001). Explaining avoidance: Two factors are still better than one. *Journal of the Experimental Analysis of Behavior, 75,* 357–361.

Baron, R. S., Cutrona, C. E., Hicklin, D., Russell, D. W., & Lubaroff, D. M. (1990). Social support and immune responses among spouses of cancer patients. *Journal of Personality and Social Psychology, 59,* 344–352.

Baron-Cohen, S. (1995). From attention-goal psychology to belief desire psychology: the development of a theory of mind and its dysfunction. In O. Liverta Sempio, & A. Marchetti (Eds.), *Il Pensiero Dell'Altro.* Rafaello Cortina Editore. Reprinted from *Understanding other minds: perspectives from autism.* Oxford: Oxford University Press.

Baron-Cohen, S. (2003) The male and female brain. *Cambridge Medicine, 18,* 20–21.

Baron-Cohen, S. Wheelwright, S., & Jolliffe, T., (1997). Is there a 'language of the eyes'? Evidence from normal adults and adults with autism/Asperger's syndrome. *Visual Cognition, 4,* 311–331.

Baron-Cohen, S., Allen, J., & Gillberg, C. (1992). Can autism be detected at 18 months? The needle, the haystack, and the CHAT. *British Journal of Psychiatry, 161,* 839–843.

Baron-Cohen, S., Knickmeyer, R., & Belmonte, M. (2005). Sex differences in the brain: implications for explaining autism. *Science, 310,* 819–823.

Baron-Cohen, S., Leslie, A.M., & Frith, U. (1985). Does the autistic child have a 'theory of mind?' *Cognition, 21,* 37–46.

Barondes, S. H. (1999). *Mood genes: Hunting for origins of mania and depression.* New York: Oxford University Press.

Barone-Adesi, F., Vizzini, L., Merletti, F., & Richiardi, L. (2006). Short-term effects of Italian smoking regulation on rates of hospital admission for acute myocardial infarction. *European Heart Journal, 27,* 2468–2472.

Barrow, C. J. (2003). *Environmental change and human development: The place of environmental change in human evolution.* New York: Oxford University Press.

Bar-Tal, D. (1998). Group beliefs as an expression of social identity. In D. Paez, J-C. Deschamps, S. Worchel & J. F. Morales (Eds.), *Social Identity: International Perspectives* (pp. 93–113). Thousand Oaks, CA: Sage Publications.

Bartholomew, D. L. (2005). *Measuring intelligence: Facts and fallacies.* New York: Cambridge University Press.

Bartholow, B. D., & Anderson, C. A. (2002). Effects of violent video games on aggressive behavior: Potential sex differences. *Journal of Experimental Social Psychology, 38,* 283–290.

Bartlett, F. C. (1932). *Remembering: A study in experimental and social psychology.* New York: Cambridge University Press.

Basedow, H. (1925). *The Australian aboriginal.* Adelaide, Australia: F. W. Preece.

Bates, M. S., Edwards, W. T., & Anderson, K. O. (1993). Ethnocultural influences on variation in chronic pain perception. *Pain, 52,* 101–112.

Bateson, W. (1909). *Mendel's Principles of Heredity.* Cambridge: Cambridge University Press.

Batson, C. D. (1991). *The altruism question: Toward a social-psychological answer.* Hillsdale, NJ: Erlbaum.

Batson, C. D., Ahmad, N., & Stocks, E. L. (2004). Benefits and liabilities of empathy-induced altruism. In A. G. Miller (Ed.), *The social psychology of good and evil.* New York: Guilford Press.

Batson, C. D., Ahmad, N., Lishner, D. A., & Tsang, J. A. (2002). Empathy and altruism. In C. R. Snyder & S. J. Lopez (Eds.), *Handbook of positive psychology.* London: Oxford University Press.

Bauer, R. M. & Verfaellie, M. (1988). Electrodermal discrimination of familiar but not unfamiliar faces in prosopagnosia. *Brain and Cognition, 8,* 240–252.

Baum, A. (1994). Disease processes: Behavioral, biological, and environmental interactions in disease processes. In S. J. Blumenthal, K. Matthews, & S. M. Weiss (Eds.), *New research frontiers in behavioral medicine: Proceedings of the national conference.* Washington, DC: NIH Publications.

Baum, A., & Posluszny, D. M. (1999). Health psychology: Mapping biobehavioral contributions to health and illness. *Annual Review of Psychology, 50,* 137–164.

Baum, A., Krantz, D. S., & Gatchel, R. J. (1997). *An introduction to health psychology* (3rd ed.). Boston: McGraw-Hill.

Baumeister, R. F., & Leary, M. R. (1995). The need to belong: Desire for interpersonal attachments as a fundamental human motivation. *Psychological Bulletin, 117,* 497–529.

Baumeister, R. F., & Tice, D. M. (1990). Anxiety and social exclusion. *Journal of Social and Clinical Psychology, 9,* 165–195.

Baumeister, R. F., Catanese, K. R., & Vohs. K. D. (2001). Is there a gender difference in strength of sex drive? Theoretical views, conceptual distinctions, and a review of relevant evidence. *Personality and Social Psychology Review, 5,* 242–273.

Baumrind, D. (1964). Some thoughts on ethics of research: After reading Milgram's behavioral study of 'obedience.' *American Psychologist, 19,* 421–423.

Baumrind, D. (1967). Child care practices anteceding three patterns of preschool behavior. *Genetic Psychology Monographs, 75,* 43–88.

Baumrind, D., Larzelere, R. E., & Cowan, P. A. (2002). Ordinary physical punishment: Is it harmful? Comment on Gershoff (2002). *Psychological Bulletin, 128,* 580–589.

Bauserman, R. (1996). Sexual aggression and pornography: A review of correlational research. *Basic and Applied Social Psychology, 18,* 405–427.

Bayley, T. M., Dye, L., Jones, S., DeBono, M., & Hill, A. J. (2002). Food cravings and aversions during pregnancy: Relationships with nausea and vomiting. *Appetite, 38,* 45–51.

Beahrs, J. O. (1994). Dissociative identity disorder: Adaptive deception of self and others. *Bulletin of the American Academy of Psychiatric Law, 22,* 223–237.

Beaman, A. L., Barnes, P. J., Klentz, B., & McQuirk, B. (1978). Increasing helping rates through information dissemination: Teaching pays. *Personality and Social Psychology Bulletin, 4,* 406–411.

Beatty, M. J., Heisel, A. D., Hall, A. E., Levine, T. R., & La France, B. H. (2002). What can we learn from the study of twins about genetic and environmental influences on interpersonal affiliation, aggressiveness, and social anxiety? A meta-analytic study. *Communication Monographs, 69,* 1–18.

Beauchamp, G. K., & Bartoshuk L. (Eds.). (1997). *Tasting and smelling.* Philadelphia: Academic Press.

Beck, A. T. (1976). *Cognitive therapy and the emotional disorders.* New York: International Universities Press.

Beck, A. T. (2002). Cognitive patterns in dreams and daydreams. *Journal of Cognitive Psychotherapy, 16,* 23–28.

Beck, A. T., Freeman, A., & Davis, D. D. (2004). *Cognitive therapy of personality disorders* (2nd ed.). New York: Guilford.

Beck, A. T., Rush, A. J., Shaw, B. F., & Emery, G. (1979). *Cognitive therapy of depression.* New York: Guilford Press.

Becker, A. E., Grinspoon, S. K., Klibanski, A., & Herzog, D. B. (1999). Current concepts: Eating disorders. *New England Journal of Medicine, 340,* 1092–1098.

Becker, J. (2004). Reconsidering the role of overcoming perturbations in cognitive development: Constructivism and consciousness. *Human Development, 47,* 77–93.

Beecher, H. K. (1959). Generalization from pain of various types and diverse origins. *Science, 130,* 267–268.

Begg, I. M., Needham, D. R., & Bookbinder, M. (1993). Do backward messages unconsciously affect listeners? No. *Canadian Journal of Experimental Psychology, 47*(1), 1–14.

Beilcock, S. L., & Carr, T. H. (2001). On the fragility of skilled performance: What governs choking under pressure? *Journal of Experimental Psychology: General, 130,* 701–725.

Békésy, G. von. (1957). The ear. *Scientific American, 230,* 66–78.

Bell, A. P., Weinberg, M. S., & Hammersmith, S. K. (1981). *Sexual preference: Its development in men and women.* Bloomington, IN: Indiana University Press.

Bell, C. C., Bhana, A., McKay, M., & Petersen, I. (2007). A commentary on the Triadic Theory of Influence as a guide for adapting HIV prevention programs for new contexts and populations: The CHAMP-South Africa story. *Social Work in Mental Health, 5,* 241–267.

Bell, J. H., & Bromnick, R. D. (2003). The social reality of the imaginary audience: A ground theory approach. *Adolescence, 38,* 205–219.

Bellack, A. S., Mueser, K. T., Gingerich, S., & Agresta, J. (2004). *Social skills training for schizophrenia* (2nd ed.). New York: Guilford Press.

Bellack, J. P., Morjikian, R., Barger, S., Strachota, E., Fitzmaurice, J., Lee, A., Kluzik, T., Lynch, E., Tsao, J., & O'Neil, E. H. (2001). Developing BSN leaders for the future: The Fuld Leadership Initiative for Nursing Education (LINE). *Journal of Professional Nursing, 17,* 23–32.

Belloc, N. B. (1973). Relationship of health practices and mortality. *Preventive Medicine, 2,* 67–81.

Belsky, J., Steinberg, L., & Draper, P. (1991). Childhood experience, interpersonal development and reproductive strategy: An evolutionary theory of socialization. *Child Development, 62,* 647.670.

Belsky, J., Vandell, D., Burchinal, M., Clarke-Stewart, K.A., McCartney, K., Owen, M. & The NICHD Early Child Care Research Network (2007). Are there long-term effects of early child care? *Child Development, 78,* 681–701.

Bem, D. J. (1972). Self-perception theory. In L. Berkowitz (Ed.), *Advances in Experimental Social Psychology, Vol. 6,* (pp.1–63). NY: Academic Press.

Bem, D. J. (1996). Exotic becomes erotic: A developmental theory of sexual orientation. *Psychological Review, 103,* 320–335.

Bem, D. J. (2001). Exotic becomes erotic: Integrating biological and experiential antecedents of sexual orientation. In A. R. D'Augelli & C. J. Patterson (Eds.), *Lesbian, gay, and bisexual identities and youth: Psychological perspectives.* London: Oxford University Press.

Bem, D. J., & Honorton, C. (1994). Does psi exist? Replicable evidence for an anomalous process of information transfer. *Psychological Bulletin, 115,* 4–18.

Bem, S. L. (1981). Gender schema theory: A cognitive account of sex typing. *Psychological Review, 88,* 354–364.

Benedito-Silva, A. A., Menna-Barreto, I. S., Cipolla-Neto, J., Marques, N., & Tenreiro, S. (1989). A self-evaluation questionnaire for the determination of morningness-eveningness types in Brazil. *Chronobiologia, 16,* 311.

Bengtson, V. L. (2001). Beyond the nuclear family: The increasing importance of multigenerational bonds. *Journal of Marriage and the Family, 63,* 1–16.

Benjamin, A. S., & Bjork, R. A. (2000). On the relationship between recognition speed and accuracy for words rehearsed via rote versus elaborative rehearsal. *Journal of Experimental Psychology: Learning, Memory, and Cognition, 26,* 638–648.

Benjamin, L. S. (2003). *Interpersonal reconstructive therapy: Promoting change in nonresponders.* New York: Guilford Press.

Bennett, H. L. (1983). Remembering drink orders: The memory skills of cocktail waitresses. *Human Learning, 2,* 157–169.

Benson, H., & Klipper, M. Z. (1976). *The relaxation response.* New York: Morrow.

Berg, C. A. (2000). Intellectual development in adulthood. In R. J. Sternberg (Ed.), *Handbook of intelligence.* New York: Cambridge University Press.

Berkowitz, L., & Harmon-Jones, E. (2004). Toward an understanding of the determinants of anger. *Emotion, 4,* 107–130.

Bernichon, T., Cook, K. E., & Brown, J. D. (2003). Seeking self-evaluative feedback: The interactive role of global self-esteem and specific self-views. *Journal of Personality and Social Psychology, 84,* 194–204.

Bernstein, S. E., & Carr, T. H. (1996). Dual-route theories of pronouncing printed words: What can be learned from concurrent task performance? *Journal of Experimental Psychology: Learning, Memory, and Cognition, 22,* 86–116.

Berntsen, D. (2001). Involuntary memories of emotional events: Do memories of traumas and extremely happy events differ? *Applied Cognitive Psychology, 5,* S135–S158.

Berridge, K. C. (2004). Motivation concepts in behavioral neuroscience. *Physiology and Behavior, 81,* 179–209.

Berry, J. W., Poortinga, Y. H., Segall, M. H., & Dasen, P. (1992). *Cross-cultural psychology: Research and application.* New York: Cambridge University Press.

Berthoud, H. R. (2002). Multiple neural systems controlling food intake and body weight. *Neuroscience and Biobehavioral Reviews, 26,* 393–428.

Best, S. J., Krueger, B., Hubbard, C., & Smith, A. (2001). An assessment of the generalizability of Internet surveys. *Social Science Computer Review, 19,* 131–145.

Beutler, L. E. (2002). The dodo bird is extinct. *Clinical Psychology: Science and Practice, 9,* 30–34.

Beutler, L. E., & Malik, M. L. (2002). *Rethinking the DSM: A psychological perspective.* Washington, DC: American Psychological Association.

Beyer, S. (1990). Gender differences in the accuracy of self-evaluations of performance. *Journal of Personality and Social Psychology, 59,* 960–970.

Bialystok, E. (2001). *Bilingualism in development: Language, literacy, and cognition.* New York: Cambridge University Press.

Bialystok, E., & Martin, M. M. (2004). Attention and inhibition in bilingual children: Evidence from the dimensional change card sort task. *Developmental Science, 7,* 325–339.

Bialystok, E., Craik, F. I. M., Klein, R., & Viswanathan, M. (2004). Bilingualism, aging, and cognitive control: evidence from the Simon task. *Psychology and Aging, 19*(2), 290–303.

Biederman, I. (1987). Recognition-by-components: A theory of human image understanding. *Psychological Review, 94,* 115–147.

Biederman, I. (1990). Higher-level vision. In Osherson, D. N., Kosslyn, S. M., & Hollerbach, J. M. (Eds.), *Visual Cognition and Action.* Cambridge, MA: MIT Press.

Biederman, J. (1998). Attention-deficit/hyperactive disorder: A life-span perspective. *Journal of Clinical Psychology, 59,* 1–13.

Bieling, P. J., Israeli, A. L., & Antony, M. M. (2004). Is perfectionism good, bad, or both? Examining models of the perfectionism construct. *Personality and Individual Differences, 36,* 1373–1385.

Biemiller, A., & Slonim, N. (2001). Estimating root word vocabulary growth in normative and advantaged populations: Evidence for a common sequence of vocabulary acquisition. *Journal of Educational Psychology, 93,498–520.*

Biller, J., Brazis, P., & Masdeu, J. C. (2006). *Localization in clinical neurology.* Philadelphia: Lippincott, Williams, & Wilkins.

Billings, A. G., & Moos, R. H. (1984). Coping, stress, and social resources among adults with unipolar depression. *Journal of Personality and Social Psychology, 46,* 877–891.

Binder, J. L. (2004). *Key competencies in brief dynamic psychotherapy.* New York: Guilford Press.

Binder, J. L., & Strupp, H. H. (1997). 'Negative process': A recurrently discovered and underestimated facet of therapeutic process and outcome in the individual psychotherapy of adults. *Clinical Psychology: Science and Practice, 4,* 121–139.

Birdsong, D., & Molis, M. (2001). On the evidence for maturational constraints in second-language acquisition. *Journal of Memory and Language, 44,* 235–249.

Birney, D. P., & Sternberg, R. J. (2006). Intelligence and cognitive abilities as competencies in development. In E. Bialystok & F. I. M Craik (Eds.), *Lifespan cognition: Mechanisms of change.* New York: Oxford University Press.

Bjorklund, D. F., & Pellegrini, A. D. (2002). Evolutionary perspectives on social development. In P. K. Smith & C. H. Hart (Eds.), *Blackwell handbook of childhood social development.* Malden, MA: Blackwell.

Black, D. N., Seritan, A. L., Taber, K. H., & Hurley, R. A. (2004). Conversion hysteria: Lessons from functional imaging. *Journal of Neuropsychiatry & Clinical Neurosciences, 16,* 245–251.

Black, D. W. (1999). *Bad boys, bad men: Confronting antisocial personality disorder.* New York: Oxford University Press.

Black, D. W., Yates, W. R., & Andreason, N. C. (1988). Schizophrenia, schizophreniform disorder, and delusional paranoid disorders. In J. A. Talbott, R. E. Hales, & S. C. Yudofsky (Eds.), *Textbook of psychiatry.* Washington, DC: American Psychiatric Press.

Blader, S. L., & Tyler, T. R. (2002). Justice and empathy: What motivates people to help others? In M. Ross & D. T. Miller (Eds.), *The justice motive in everyday life.* New York: Cambridge University Press.

Blair, J. (2005). *Development of the psychopath: Emotion and the brain.* St. Louis, MO: Blackwell.

Blair, S. N., Kohl, H. W., III, Paffenbarger, R. S., et al. (1989). Physical fitness and all-cause mortality: A prospective study of healthy men and women. *Journal of the American Medical Association, 262,* 2395–2401.

Blakemore, C., & Cooper, G. G. (1970). Development of the brain depends on visual environment. *Nature, 228,* 477–478.

Blanchard, R. (2001). Fraternal birth order and the maternal immune hypothesis of male homosexuality. *Hormones and Behavior, 40,* 105–114.

Blanchard, R., & Bogaert, A. F. (1996). Homosexuality in men and number of older brothers. *American Journal of Psychiatry, 153,* 27–31.

Blanke, O., Ortigue, S., Landis, T., & Seeck, M. (2002). Stimulating illusory own-body perceptions. *Nature, 419* (6904), 269–270.

Blanton, H., Pelham, B., DeHart, T., & Carvallo, M. (2001). Overconfidence as dissonance reduction. *Journal of Experimental Social Psychology, 37,* 373–385.

Blascovich, J., & Tomaka, J. (1991). Measures of self-esteem. In L. Wrightsman, J. P. Robinson & P. R. Shaver (Eds.), *Measures of Personality and Social Psychological Attitudes* (pp. 115–160). San Diego, CA: Academic Press.

Blass, T. (2002). Perpetrator behavior as destructive obedience: An evaluation of Stanley Milgram's perspective, the most influential social-psychological approach to the Holocaust. In L. S. Newman & R. Erber (Eds.), *Understanding genocide: The social psychology of the Holocaust.* London: Oxford University Press.

Blass, T., & Schmitt, C. (2001). The nature of perceived authority in the Milgram paradigm: Two replications. *Current Psychology: Developmental, Learning, Personality, Social, 20,* 115–121.

Blechman, E., & Brownell, K. D. (1998). *Behavioral medicine and women: A comprehensive handbook.* New York: Guilford Press.

Blessing, W. W. (1997). *The lower brainstem and bodily homeostasis.* New York: Oxford University Press.

Blodgett, H. C. (1929). The effect of the introduction of reward on the maze performance of rats. *University of California Publications in Psychology, 4*(8), 114–126.

Bloomfield, K., Greenfield, T. K., Kraus, L., & Augustin, R. (2002). A comparison of drinking patterns and alcohol-related problems in the United States and Germany, 1995. *Substance Use and Misuse, 37,* 399–428.

Bobo, L. (1988). Attitudes toward the black political movement: Trends, meaning, and effects of racial policy preferences. *Social Psychology Quarterly, 51,* 287–302.

Boehm, S. L., Reed, C. L., McKinnon, C. S., & Phillips, T. J. (2002). Shared genes influence sensitivity to the effects of ethanol on locomotor and anxiety-like behaviors, and the stress axis. *Psychopharmacology, 161,* 54–63.

Boesch, C. (1991). Teaching in wild chimpanzees. *Animal Behaviour, 41*(3), 530–532.

Bolles, R. C., & Beecher, M. D. (Eds.). (1988). *Evolution and learning.* Hillsdale, NJ: Erlbaum.

Bolling, M. Y., & Kohlenberg, R. J. (2004). Reasons for quitting serotonin reuptake inhibitor therapy: Paradoxical psychological side effects and patient satisfaction. *Psychotherapy and Psychosomatics, 73*(6), 380–385.

Bonanno, G. A., Papa, A., Lalande, K., Westphal, M., & Coifman, K. (2004). The importance of being flexible. *Psychological Science, 15,* 482–487.

Bond, R., & Smith, P. B. (1996). Culture and conformity: A meta-analysis of studies using Asch's (1952b, 1956) line judgment task. *Psychological Bulletin, 119,* 111–137.

Boneva, B., Frieze, I. H., Ferligoj, A., Pauknerova, D., & Orgocka, A. (1998). Achievement, power, and affiliation motives as clues to (e)migration desires: A four countries comparison. *European Psychologist, 3,* 247–254.

Bonnel, A. M., & Hafter, E. R. (1998). Divided attention between simultaneous auditory and visual signals. *Perception & Pychophysics, 60,* 179–190.

Bonvillian, J. D., & Patterson, F. G. P. (1997). Sign language acquisition and the development of meaning in a lowland gorilla. In C. Mandell & A. McCabe (Eds.), *The problem of meaning: Behavioral and cognitive perspectives.* Amsterdam: North-Holland/Elsevier Science.

Booth, A., & Amato, P. R. (2001). Parental predivorce relations and offspring postdivorce well-being. *Journal of Marriage and the Family, 63,* 197–212.

Bootzin, R. R. (2002). Cognitive-behavioral treatment of insomnia: Knitting up the ravell'd sleeve of care. In D. T. Kenny, J. G. Carlson, F. J. McGuigan, & J. L. Sheppard (Eds.), *Stress and health: Research and clinical applications.* Amsterdam: Harwood.

Borkenau, P., Riemann, R., Spinath, F. M., & Angleitner, A. (2006). Genetic and environmental influences on person x situation profiles. *Journal of Personality, 74,* 1451–1480.

Borod, J. C. (2000). *The neuropsychology of emotion.* New York: Oxford University Press.

Boschker, M. S., Baker, F. C., & Michaels, C. F. (2002). Memory for the functional characteristics of climbing walls: Perceiving affordances. *Journal of Motor Behavior, 34,* 25–36.

Bosson, J. K., Haymovitz, E. L., & Pinel, E. C. (2004). When saying and doing diverge: The effects of stereotype threat on self-reported versus non-verbal anxiety. *Journal of Experimental Social Psychology, 40,* 247–255.

Bouchard, T. J. (2004). Genetic influence on human psychological traits. *Current Directions in Psychological Science 13,* 148–151.

Bouchard, T. J., & McGue, M. (1981). Familial studies of intelligence: A review. *Science, 212,* 1055–1059.

Bouchard, T. J., Lykken, D. T., McGue, M., Segal, N. L., & Tellegen, A. (1990). Sources of human psychological differences: The Minnesota study of twins reared apart. *Science, 250,* 223–228.

Boulos, Z. (1998). Bright light treatment for jet lag and shift work. In R. Lam & W. Raymond (Eds.), *Seasonal affective disorder and beyond: Light treatment for SAD and non-SAD conditions.* Washington, DC: American Psychiatric Press.

Boutros, N. N., Gelernter, J., Gooding, D. C., Cubells, J., Young, A., Krystal, J. H., & Kosten, T. (2002). Sensory gating and psychosis vulnerability in cocaine-dependent individuals: Preliminary data. *Biological Psychiatry, 51,* 683–686.

Bower, G. H., Clark, M. C., Lesgold, M. A., & Winzenz, D. (1969). Hierarchical retrieval schemes in recall of categorized word lists. *Journal of Verbal Learning and Verbal Behavior, 8,* 323–343.

Bowlby, J. (1944). Forty-four juvenile thieves: Their character and home-life. *International Journal of Psychoanalysis, 25,* 19–52.

Bowlby, J. (1969). *Attachment and loss: Vol. 1. Attachment.* New York: Basic Books.

Bowlby, J. (1973). *Attachment and loss: Vol. 2. Separation: Anxiety and anger.* London: Hogarth.

Bowlby, J. (2000). *Loss: Sadness and depression.* New York: Basic Books.

Boyd, R., & Richerson, P. J. (2005). *The origin and evolution of cultures.* New York: Oxford University Press.

Bozarth, J. D., Zimring, F. M., & Tausch, R. (2002). Client-centered therapy: The evolution of a revolution. In D. J. Cain (Ed.), *Humanistic psychotherapies: Handbook of research and practice.* Washington, DC: American Psychological Association.

Brabender, V., Fallon, A. E., & Smolar, A. I. (2004). *Essentials of group therapy.* New York: Wiley.

Bradmetz, J., & Mathy, F. (2006). An estimate of the Flynn effect: Changes in IQ and subtest gains of 10-yr-old French children between 1965 and 1988. *Psychological Reports, 99*(3), 743–746.

Brandon, S., Boakes, J., Glaser, D., & Green, R. (1998). Recovered memories of childhood sexual abuse: Implications for clinical practice. *British Journal of Psychiatry, 172*, 296–307.

Bransford, J. D., & Johnson, M. K. (1972). Contextual prerequisites for understanding: Some investigations of comprehension and recall. *Journal of Verbal Learning & Verbal Behavior, 11*, 717–726.

Brantley, P. J., & Jones, G. N. (1993). Daily stress and stress-related disorders. *Annals of Behavioral Medicine, 15*, 17–25.

Brantley, P., & Garrett, V. D. (1993). Psychobiological approaches to health and disease. In B. Sutker & H. E. Adams (Eds.), *Comprehensive handbook of psychopathology* (2nd ed.). New York: Plenum.

Brauer, M. (2001). Intergroup perception in the social context: The effects of social status and group membership on perceived out-group homogeneity and ethnocentrism. *Journal of Experimental Social Psychology, 37*, 15–31.

Bray, J. H., & Berger, S. H. (1993). Developmental issues in Step Families Research Project: Family relationships and parent-child interactions. *Journal of Family Psychology, 7*, 76–90.

Brazel, C. Y., & Rao, M. S. (2004). Aging and neuronal replacement. *Ageing Research Reviews, 3*, 465–483.

Brehm, J. W., & Self, E. A. (1989). The intensity of motivation. *Annual Review of Psychology, 40*, 109–131.

Breland, K., & Breland, M. (1961). The misbehavior of organisms. *American Psychologist, 16*, 681–684.

Breland, K., & Breland, M. (1966). *Animal behavior.* New York: Macmillan.

Bremner, A. J., & Mareschal, D. (2004). Reasoning . . . what reasoning? *Developmental Science, 7*, 419–421.

Bremner, A. J., Mareschal, D., Lloyd-Fox, S., & Spence, C. (2008). Spatial localization of touch in the first year of life: Early influence of a visual spatial code and the development of remapping across changes in limb position. *Journal of Experimental Psychology: General, 137*, 149–162.

Bremner, J. D. (2000). Neurobiology of posttraumatic stress disorder. In G. Fink (Ed.), *Encyclopedia of stress.* San Diego, CA: Academic Press.

Bremner, J. D. (2005). *Brain imaging handbook.* New York: Norton.

Breslau, N. S., Davis, G. C., Andreski, P., Peterson, E. L., & Schultz, L. R. (1997). Sex differences in post-traumatic stress disorder. *Archives of General Psychiatry, 54*, 1044–1048.

Brewin, C. R. (2004). Commentary on McNally 'Is traumatic amnesia nothing but psychiatric folklore?' *Cognitive Behaviour Therapy, 33*, 102–104.

Brickman, P., Coates, D., & Janoff-Bulman, R. (1978). Lottery winners and accident victims: Is happiness relative? *Journal of Personality and Social Psychology, 36*, 917–927.

Bridle, C., Riemsma, R. P., Pattenden, J., Sowden, A. J., Mather, L., Watt, I. S., & Walker, A. (2005). Systematic review of the effectiveness of health behavior interventions based on the transtheoretical model. *Psychology and Health, 20*, 283–301.

Briere, J., & Lanktree, C. (1983). Sex role-related effects of sex bias in language. *Sex Roles, 9*, 625–632.

Broadbent, D. E. (1958). *Perception and communication.* London: Pergamon Press.

Broberg, D. J., & Bernstein, I. L. (1987). Candy as a scapegoat in the prevention of food aversions in children receiving chemotherapy. *Cancer, 60*, 2344–2347.

Bronzaft, A. L., Ahern, K. D., McGinn, R., O'Connor, J., & Savino, B. (1998). Aircraft noise: A potential health hazard. *Environment & Behavior, 30*, 101–113.

Brown, E., Deffenbacher, K., & Sturgill, W. (1977). Memory for faces and the circumstances of encounter. *Journal of Applied Psychology, 62*, 311–318.

Brown, G. W., & Harris, T. O. (1978). *Social origins of depression.* London: Tavistock Press.

Brown, I., & Percy, M. (Eds.) (2007). *A comprehensive guide to intellectual and developmental disabilities.* Baltimore, MD: Paul H. Brookes Publishing Company.

Brown, J. A. (1958). Some tests of the decay theory of immediate memory. *Quarterly Journal of Experimental Psychology, 10,* 12–21.

Brown, J. D. (1998). *The self.* Boston: McGraw-Hill.

Brown, J. D., & Kobayashi, C. (2001). Self-enhancement in Japan and America. *Asian Journal of Social Psychology, 5,* 145-167.

Brown, L. S. (1994). *Subversive dialogues: Theory in feminist therapy.* New York: Basic Books.

Brown, N. O. (1959). *Life against death.* New York: Random House.

Brown, R. (1973). *A first language: The early stages.* Cambridge, MA: Harvard University Press.

Brown, R., & Kulik, J. (1977). Flashbulb memories. *Cognition, 5,* 73–99.

Brown, S. L., Nesse, R. M., Vinokur, A. D., & Smith, D. M. (2003). Providing social support may be more beneficial than receiving it: Results from a prospective study of mortality. *Psychological Science, 14,* 320–327.

Brown, T. A., Di-Nardo, P. A., Lehman, C. L., & Campbell, L. A. (2001). Reliability of DSM-IV anxiety and mood disorders: Implications for the classification of emotional disorders. *Journal of Abnormal Psychology, 110,* 49–58.

Brown, T. S., & Wallace, P. (1980). *Physiological psychology.* New York: Academic Press.

Brownell, K. D. (1994). *The LEARN program for weight control.* Dallas, TX: American Health.

Bruce, T. J., & Sanderson, W. C. (1998). *Specific phobias: Clinical applications of evidence-based psychotherapy.* Northvale, NJ: Aronson.

Bruce, V., Henderson, Z., Newman, C., & Burton, A. M. (2001). Matching identities of familiar and unfamiliar faces caught on CCTV images. *Journal of Experimental Psychology: Applied, 7,* 207–218.

Bruce, V., Valentine, T., & Baddeley, A. (1987). The basis of the 3/4 view advantage in face recognition. *Applied Cognitive Psychology, 1,* 109–120.

Bruck, M., Ceci, S. J., & Hembrooke, H. (1998). Reliability and credibility of young children's reports: From research to policy and practice. *American Psychologist, 53,* 136–151.

Bruederl, J., Diekmann, A., & Engelhardt, H. (1997). Erhoeht eine Probeehe das Scheidungrisiko? Eine empirische Untersuchung mit dem Familiensurvey [Does a trial marriage increase divorce risk? Empirical study of the Families Survey]. *Koelner Zeitschrift fuer Soziologie und Sozialpsychologie, 49,* 205–222.

Bruner, J. (1983). *Child's talk.* New York: Norton.

Bruunk, B., & Gibbons, F. X. (Eds.). (1997). *Health, coping, and well-being: Perspectives from social comparison theory.* Mahwah, NJ: Erlbaum.

Bryan, J., III. (1986). *Hodgepodge: A commonplace book.* New York: Ballantine.

Bryant, P. E. (1974). *Perception and understanding in young children: An experimental approach.* London: Methuen.

Buck, L., & Axel, R. (1991). A novel multigene family may encode odorant receptors: A molecular basis for odor recognition. *Cell, 65,* 175–187.

Buckley, K. E., & Anderson, C. (2006). A theoretical model of the effects and consequences of playing video games. In P. Vorderer & J. Bryant (Eds.), *Playing video games: Motives, responses, and consequences.* Mahwah, NJ: Erlbaum.

Bullier, J. (2002). Neural basis of vision. In H. Pashler & S. Yantis (Eds.), *Steven's handbook of experimental psychology: Vol. 1. Sensation and perception* (3rd ed.). New York: Wiley.

Burgess, C. A., & Kirsch, I. (1999). Expectancy information as a moderator of the effects of hypnosis on memory. *Contemporary Hypnosis, 16,* 22–31.

Burgwyn-Bailes, E., Baker-Ward, L., Gordon, B. N., & Ornstein, P. A. (2001). Children's memory for emergency medical treatment after one year: The impact of individual difference variables on recall and suggestibility. *Applied Cognitive Psychology, 15,* S25–S48.

Burley, T., & Freier, M. C. (2004). Character structure: A gestalt-cognitive theory. *Psychotherapy: Theory, Research, Practice, Training, 41*, 321–331.

Burns, M. O., & Seligman, M. E. P. (1991). Explanatory style, helplessness, and depression. In C. R. Snyder & D. R. Forsyth (Eds.), *Handbook of social and clinical psychology: The health perspective.* New York: Pergamon Press.

Burnstein, E., Crandall, C., & Kitayama, S. (1994). Some neo-Darwinian decision rules for altruism: Weighing cues for inclusive fitness as a function of the biological importance of the decision. *Journal of Personality and Social Psychology, 67*, 773–789.

Burton, A. M., Bruce, V., & Dench, N. (1993). What's the difference between men and women? Evidence from facial measurement. *Perception, 22*, 153–176.

Burton, A. M., Bruce, V., & Hancock, P. J. B. (1999). From pixels to people: a model of familiar face recognition. *Cognitive Science, 23*, 1–31.

Burton, E., Stice, E., & Seeley, J. R (2004). A prospective test of the stress-buffering model of depression in adolescent girls: No support once again. *Journal of Consulting and Clinical Psychology, 72*, 689–697.

Busey, T. A., Tunnicliff, J. J., Loftus, G. R., & Loftus, E. F. (2000). Accounts of the confidence-accuracy relation in recognition memory. *Psychonomic Bulletin and Review, 7*, 26–48.

Bushman, B. J. (2002). Does venting anger feed or extinguish the flame? Catharsis, rumination, distraction, anger and aggressive responding. *Personality and Social Psychology, 28*, 724–731.

Bushman, B. J., & Bonacci, A. M. (2002). Violence and sex impair memory for television ads. *Journal of Applied Psychology, 87*, 557–564.

Buske-Kirschbaum, A., Kirschbaum, C., & Hellhammer, D. H. (1994). Conditioned modulation of NK cells in humans: Alteration of cell activity and cell number by conditioning protocols. *Psychologische Beitraege, 36*, 100–111.

Buske-Kirschbaum, A., Kirschbaum, C., Stierle, H., & Lehnert, H. (1992). Conditioned increase of natural killer cell activity (NKCA) in humans. *Psychosomatic Medicine, 54*, 123–132.

Buss, A., & Plomin, R. (1975). *A temperament theory of personality development.* New York: Wiley.

Buss, A., & Plomin, R. (1984). *Temperament: Early developing personality traits.* Hillsdale, NJ: Erlbaum.

Buss, D. M. (1985). Human mate selection. *American Scientist, 73*, 47–51.

Buss, D. M. (1989). Sex differences in human mate preferences: Evolutionary hypotheses tested in 37 cultures. *Behavioral and Brain Sciences, 12*, 1–49.

Buss, D. M. (1991). Evolutionary personality theory. *Annual Review of Psychology, 42*, 459–491.

Buss, D. M. (1995). Evolutionary psychology: A new paradigm for psychological science. *Psychological Inquiry, 6*, 1–30.

Buss, D. M. (1999). Human nature and individual differences: The evolution of human personality. In L. A. Pervin & O. P. John (Eds.), *Handbook of personality: Theory and research.* New York: Guilford Press.

Buss, D. M. (2005). *The handbook of evolutionary psychology.* New York: Wiley.

Buss, D. M. (2007). *Evolutionary psychology. The new science of the mind.* Boston: Allyn & Bacon.

Buss, D. M., & Schmitt, D. P. (1993). Sexual Strategies Theory: An evolutionary perspective on human mating. *Psychological Review, 100*, 204–232.

Buss, D. M., Abbott, M., Angleitner, A., Asherian, A., Biaggio, A., Blanco-Villasenor, A., et al. (1990). International preferences in selecting mates: A study of 37 cultures. *Journal of Cross-Cultural Psychology, 21*, 5–47.

Buunk, B. P., & Verhoeven, K. (1991). Companionship and support at work: A microanalysis of the stress-reducing features of social interaction. *Basic and Applied Social Psychology, 12*, 243–258.

Byer, C. O., Shainberg, L. W., & Galliano, G. (2002). *Dimensions of human sexuality* (6th ed.). Boston: McGraw-Hill.

Byrne, D. (1997). An overview (and underview) of research and theory within the attraction paradigm. *Journal of Social and Personal Relationships, 14,* 417–431.

Byrne, D., & Greendlinger, V. (1989). *Need for affiliation as a predictor of classroom friendships.* Unpublished manuscript, State University of New York at Albany.

Byrne, D., Ervin, C. R., & Lamberth, J. (1970). Continuity between the experimental study of attraction and real-life computer dating. *Journal of Personality and Social Psychology, 16,* 157–165.

Bywaters, M. J., Andrade, J., & Turpin, G. (2004). Determinants of the vividness of delayed recall, stimulus affect and individual differences. *Memory, 12,* 479–488.

Cabeza, R., Nyberg, L., & Park, D. C. (2005). *Cognitive neuroscience of aging: Linking cognitive and cerebral aging.* New York: Oxford University Press.

Cacioppo, J. T., Berntson, J. T., Poehlmann, K. M., & Ito, T. A. (2000). The psychophysiology of emotion. In M. Lewis & J. M. Haviland-Jones (Eds.), *Handbook of emotions* (2nd ed.). New York: Guilford Press.

Cain, D. J., & Seeman, J. (Eds.). (2002). *Humanistic psychotherapies: Handbook of research and practice.* Washington, DC: American Psychological Association.

Cairns, H. (1952). Disturbances of consciousness in lesions of the mid-brain and diencephalon. *Brain, 75,* 107–114.

Caldwell, A. B. (1994). *The profile of Jeffrey Dahmer* [Videotape]. Los Angeles: Caldwell Report.

Camilleri, C., & Malewska-Peyre, H. (1997). Socialization and identity strategies. In J. W. Berry, P. R. Dasen, & T. S. Saraswathi (Eds.), *Handbook of cross-cultural psychology: Basic processes and human development: Vol. 2. Handbook of cross-cultural psychology* (2nd ed.). Boston: Allyn & Bacon.

Campbell, A., Shirley, L., & Candy, J. (2004). A longitudinal study of gender-related cognition and behaviour. *Developmental Science, 7,* 1–9.

Campfield, L. A. (1997). Metabolic and hormonal controls of food intake: Highlights of the last 25 years: 1972–1997. *Appetite, 29,* 135–152.

Canivez, G. L., & Watkins, M. W. (1998). Longterm stability of the Wechsler Intelligence Scale for Children—Third Edition. *Psychological Assessment, 10,* 285–291.

Canli, T. (2004). Functional brain mapping of extraversion and neuroticism: Learning from individual differences in emotion processing. *Journal of Personality, 72,* 1105–1132.

Canli, T. (Ed.) (2006). *Biology of personality and individual differences.* New York: Guilford.

Cannon, W. B. (1927). The James-Lange theory of emotion: A critical examination and an alternative theory. *American Journal of Psychology, 39,*106–124.

Cannon, W. B. (1929). *Bodily changes in pain, hunger, fear, and rage.* New York: Appleton-Century.

Cannon, W. B. (1932). *Wisdom of the body.* New York: Norton.

Cannon, W. B. (1942). 'Voodoo' death. *American Anthropologist, 44,* 169–181.

Cannon, W. B., & Washburn, A. L. (1912). An explanation of hunger. *American Journal of Physiology, 29,* 441–454.

Cardasis, W., Hochman, J. A., & Silk, K. R. (1997). Transitional objects and borderline personality disorder. *American Journal of Psychiatry, 154,* 250–255.

Cardeña, E., Lynn, S. J., & Krippner, S. (2000). Introduction: Anomalous experiences in perspective. In E. Cardeña, S. J. Lynn, & S. Krippner (Eds.), *Varieties of anomalous experience: Examining the scientific evidence.* Washington, DC: American Psychological Association.

Carels, R. A., Douglass, O. M., & Cacciapaglia, H. M. (2004). An ecological momentary assessment of relapse crises in dieting. *Journal of Consulting and Clinical Psychology, 72,* 341–348.

Carey, G., & Gottesman, I. I. (1981). Twin and family studies of anxiety, phobic, and obsession disorders. In D. F. Klein & J. Rabkin (Eds.), *Anxiety: New research and changing concepts.* New York: Raven Press.

Carlson, C. (2000). ADHD is overdiagnosed. In R. L. Atkinson, R. C. Atkinson, E. E. Smith, D. J. Bem, & S. Nolen-Hoeksema, *Hilgard's introduction to psychology* (13th ed.). Ft. Worth, TX: Harcourt Brace.

Carlson, E. A., & McAndrew, F. T. (2004). Body shape ideals and perceptions of body shape in Spanish and American college students. *Perceptual and Motor Skills, 99,* 1071–1074.

Carlson, J. G., & Hatfield, E. (1992). *Psychology of emotion.* Ft. Worth, TX: Harcourt Brace Jovanovich.

Carlson, S. M., Moses, L. J., & Hix, H. R. (1998). The role of inhibitory processes in young children's difficulties with deception and false belief. *Child Development, 69,* 672–691.

Carney, L. H. (2002). Neural basis of audition. In H. Pashler & S. Yantis (Eds.), *Steven's handbook of experimental psychology: Vol. 1. Sensation and perception* (3rd ed.). New York: Wiley.

Carnicero, J. A. C., Perez-Lopez, J., Salinas, M. D. C. G., & Martinez-Fuentes, M. T. (2000). A longitudinal study of temperament in infancy: Stability and convergence of measures. *European Journal of Personality, 14,* 21–37.

Carpenter, P. A., Just, M. A., & Shell, P. (1990). What one intelligence test measures: A theoretical account of the processing in the Raven Progressive Matrices Test. *Psychological Review, 97,* 404–431.

Carpenter, R., & Robson, J. (Eds.). (1999). *Vision research: A practical guide to laboratory methods.* New York: Oxford University Press.

Carroll, C. R. (1993). *Drugs in modern society.* Madison, WI: Brown & Benchmark.

Carroll, J. B. (1993). *Human cognitive abilities: A survey of factor-analytic studies.* New York: Cambridge University Press.

Carson, R. C., Butcher, J. N., & Coleman, J. C. (1988). *Abnormal psychology and modern life* (8th ed.). Glenview, IL: Scott, Foresman.

Carstens, A., Maes, A., & Gangla, B. L. (2006). Understanding visuals in HIV/AIDS education in South Africa: Differences between literate and low-literate audiences. *African Journal of AIDS Research, 5,* 221–232.

Carter, S. J., & Cassaday, H. J. (1998). State dependent retrieval and chlorpheniramine. *Human Psychopharmacology: Clinical and Experimental, 13,* 513–523.

Cartwright, R. D. (1977). *Night life: Explorations in dreaming.* Englewood Cliffs, NJ: Prentice Hall.

Carver, C. S., & Scheier, M. F. (1978). Self-focusing effects of dispositional self-consciousness, mirror presence, and audience presence. *Journal of Personality and Social Psychology, 36,* 324–332.

Carver, C. S., & Scheier, M. F. (1981). Self-consciousness and reactance. *Journal of Research in Personality, 15,* 16-29.

Carver, C. S., & Scheier, M. F. (2003). *Perspectives on personality* (5th ed.). Boston: Allyn & Bacon.

Carver, C. S., Scheier, M. F., & Weintraub, J. K. (1989). Assessing coping strategies: A theoretically based approach. *Journal of Personality and Social Psychology, 56,* 267–283.

Case, R. (1987). The structure and process of intellectual development. *International Journal of Psychology, 22,* 571–607.

Case, R., Demetriou, A., Platsidou, M., & Kazi, S. (2001). Integrating concepts and tests of intelligence from the differential and developmental traditions. *Intelligence, 29,* 307–336.

Caspi, A., & Roberts, B. W. (1999). Personality continuity and change across the life course. In L. A. Pervin & O. P. John (Eds.), *Handbook of personality: Theory and research.* New York: Guilford Press.

Caspi, A., Elder, G. H., & Bem, D. J. (1988). Moving away from the world: Life course patterns of shy children. *Developmental Psychology, 24,* 824–831.

Caspi, A., McClay, J., Moffitt, T. E., Mill, J., Martin, J., Craig, I. W., Taylor, A., & Poulton, R. (2002). Role of genotype in the cycle of violence in maltreated children. *Science, 297,* 851–853.

Castonguay, L. G., & Beutler, L. E. (2005). *Principles of therapeutic change that work.* New York: Oxford University Press.

Catania, A. C. (2001). Positive psychology and positive reinforcement. *American Psychologist, 56,* 86–87.

Catania, C. A. (1998). *Learning* (4th ed.). Upper Saddle River, NJ: Prentice Hall.

Catchpole, C. K., & Rowell, A. (1993). Song sharing and local dialects in a population of the European wren *Troglodytes troglodytes. Behaviour, 125,* 67–78.

Cattabeni, F., Colciaghi, F., & Di Luca, M. (2004). Platelets provide human tissue to unravel pathogenic mechanisms of Alzheimer disease. *Progress in Neuro-Psychopharmacology & Biological Psychiatry, 28,* 763–770.

Cattell, R. B. (1965). *The scientific analysis of personality.* Chicago: Aldine.

Cattell, R. B. (1971). *Abilities: Their growth, structure, and action.* Boston: Houghton Mifflin.

Cattell, R. B. (1998). Where is intelligence? Some answers from the triadic theory. In J. J. McArdle & R. W. Woodcock (Eds.), *Human cognitive abilities in theory and practice.* Mahwah, NJ: Lawrence Erlbaum Associates.

Caughlin, J. P., & Malis, R. S. (2004). Demand/withdraw communication between parents and adolescents: Connections with selfesteem and substance use. *Journal of Social and Personal Relationships, 21,* 125–148.

Ceci, S. J., & Williams, W. M. (1997). Schooling, intelligence, and income. *American Psychologist, 52,* 1051–1058.

Ceci, S. J., Bruck, M., & Battin, D. B. (2000). The suggestibility of children's testimony. In D. F. Bjorklund (Ed.), *False-memory creation in children and adults: Theory, research, and implications.* Mahwah, NJ: Erlbaum.

Centers for Disease Control and Prevention. (1988). *Posttraumatic stress disorders.* Atlanta, GA: Author.

Centers for Disease Control and Prevention (CDC). (2002a). *Causes of death in the United States.* Atlanta, GA: Author.

Centers for Disease Control and Prevention (CDC). (2002b). Youth risk behavior surveillance—United States, 2001. *Morbidity and Mortality Weekly Report, 51*(SS04), 1–64. Washington, DC: Author.

Cervone, D. (1999). Bottom-up explanation in personality psychology: The case of cross-situational consistency. In D. Cervone & Y. Shoda (Eds.), *The coherence of personality.* New York: Guilford Press.

Cervone, D., & Shoda, Y. (1999). *The coherence of personality: Social-cognitive bases of consistency, variability, and organization.* New York: Guilford Press.

Chalmers, D. J. (1995). The puzzle of conscious experience. *Scientific American, 273*(6), 80–86.

Chambless, D. L., & Hollon, S. D. (1998). Defining empirically supported therapies. *Journal of Consulting and Clinical Psychology, 66,* 7–18.

Chan, Z. C. Y., & Ma, J. L. C. (2002). Family themes of food refusal: Disciplining the body and punishing the family. *Health Care for Women International, 23,* 49–58.

Chandler, M. J., Lacritz, L. H., Cicerello, A. R., Chapman, S. B., Honig, L. S., Weiner, M. F., & Cullum, C. M. (2004). Three-word recall in normal aging. *Journal of Clinical and Experimental Neuropsychology, 26,* 1128–1133.

Chang, E. C. (1996). Cultural differences in optimism, pessimism, and coping: Predictors of subsequent adjustment in American and Caucasian American college students. *Journal of Counseling Psychology, 43,* 113–123.

Chang, E. C. (1998). Dispositional optimism and primary and secondary appraisal of a stressor:

Controlling for confounding influences and relations to coping and psychological and physical adjustment. *Journal of Personality and Social Psychology, 74,* 1109–1120.

Chappell, M., & Humphreys, M. S. (1994). An auto-associative neural network for sparse representations: Analysis and application to models of recognition and cued recall. *Psychological Review, 101,* 103–128.

Chartrand, T. L., & Bargh, J. A. (2002). Nonconscious motivations: Their activation, operation, and consequences. In A. Tesser, D. A. Stapel, & J. V. Wood (Eds.), *Self and motivation: Emerging psychological perspectives.* Washington, DC: American Psychological Association.

Chartrand, T. L., Bargh, J. A., & van Baaren, R. (2002). *Consequences of automatic evaluation for mood.* Manuscript submitted for publication.

Chase, J. H. (1950). *The Marijuana Mob.* London: Robert Hale.

Chase, W. G., & Simon, H. A. (1973). Perception in chess. *Cognitive Psychology, 4,* 55–81.

Chee, M. W., & Choo, W. C. (2004). Functional imaging of working memory after 24 hr of total sleep deprivation. *Journal of Neuroscience, 24,* 4560–4567.

Chen, C., Greenberger, E., Lester, J., Dong, Q., & Guo, M. S. (1998). A cross-cultural study of family and peer correlates of adolescent misconduct. *Developmental Psychology, 34,* 770–781.

Chen, H., & Lan, W. (1998). Adolescents' perceptions of their parents' academic expectations: Comparison of American, Chinese-American, and Chinese high school students. *Adolescence, 33,* 385–390.

Chen, H., Charlat, O., Tartaglia, L. A., Woolf, E. A., Weng, X., & Ellis, S. J. (1996). Evidence that the diabetes gene encodes the leptin receptor: Identification of a mutation in the leptin receptor gene in db/db mice. *Cell, 84,* 491–495.

Chen, S. C. (1937). Social modification of the activity of ants in nest-building. *Physiological Zoology, 10,* 420–436.

Chen, S., English, T., & Peng, K. (2006). Selfverification and contextualized self-views. *Personality and Social Psychology Bulletin, 32,* 930–942.

Cheng, P. W., & Holyoak, K. J. (1985). Pragmatic reasoning schemas. *Cognitive Psychology, 17,* 391–416.

Chenoweth, D. (2002). *Evaluating worksite health promotion.* Champaign, IL: Human Kinetics.

Cherry, E. C. (1953). Some experiments on the recognition of speech, with one and with two ears. *Journal of the Acoustical Society of America, 25*(5), 975–979.

Chesney, M. A., Neilands, T. B., Chambers, D. B., Taylor, J. M., & Folkman, S. (2006). A validity and reliability study of the coping self-efficacy scale. *British Journal of Health Psychology, 11,* 421–437.

Chi, L. (2004). Achievement goal theory. In T. Morris & J. Summers (Eds.), *Sport psychology: Theories, applications, and issues* (2nd ed.). Sydney, Australia: Wiley.

Chiappe, D., & MacDonald, K. (2005). The evolution of domain-general mechanisms in intelligence and learning. *Journal of General Psychology, 132,* 5–40.

Chiappelli, F. (2000). Immune suppression. In G. Fink (Ed.), *Encyclopedia of stress.* San Diego, CA: Academic Press.

Chiles, J. A., & Strossahl, K. D. (1995). *The suicidal patient: Principles of assessment, treatment, and case management.* Washington, DC: American Psychiatric Press.

Chiriboga, D. A. (1989). Mental health at the midpoint: Crisis, challenge, or relief? In S. Hunter & M. Sundel (Eds.), *Midlife myths: Issues, findings, and practice implications.* Newbury Park, CA: Sage.

Choi, I., Dalal, R., Kim Prieto, C., & Park, H. (2003). Culture and judgement of causal relevance. *Journal of Personality and Social Psychology, 84,* 46–59.

Chomsky, N. (1965). *Aspects of a theory of syntax.* Cambridge, MA: MIT Press.

Chomsky, N. (1972). *Language and mind.* New York: Harcourt.

Chomsky, N. (1987). Language in a psychological setting. *Sophia Linguistic Working Papers in Linguistics, 22,* Sophia University, Tokyo.

Christiansen, O., & Christiansen, E. (1988). Fat consumption and schizophrenia. *Acta Psychiatrica Scandanavica, 78,* 587–591.

Christianson, S. A., & Nilsson, L. G. (1989). Hysterical amnesia: A case of aversively motivated isolation of memory. In T. Archer & L. G. Nilsson (Eds.), *Aversion, avoidance, and anxiety: Perspectives on aversively motivated behavior.* Hillsdale, NJ: Erlbaum.

Christopherson, E. R., & Mortweet, S. L. (2001). *Treatments that work with children: Empirically supported strategies for managing childhood problems.* Washington, DC: American Psychological Association.

Chrousos, G. P., Kaltsas, G. A., & Mastorakos, G. (2006). *Neuroimmunodulation: Neuroendocrine and immune crosstalk.* London: Blackwell.

Church, A. T., & Katigbak, M. S. (2000). Trait psychology in the Philippines. *American Behavioral Scientist, 44,* 73–94.

Chwalisz, K., Diener, E., & Gallagher, D. (1988). Autonomic arousal feedback and emotional experience: Evidence from the spinal cord injured. *Journal of Personality and Social Psychology, 54,* 820–828.

Chwilla, D. J., & Kolk, H. H. J. (2002). Three step priming in lexical decision. *Memory and Cognition, 30,* 217–225.

Cialdini, R. (2007). *Influence: The psychology of persuasion.* New York: Harper Collins.

Cialdini, R. B. (2001). *Influence: Science and practice* (4th ed.). Boston, MA: Allyn & Bacon.

Cialdini, R. B., & Goldstein, N. J. (2004). Social influence: Compliance and conformity. *Annual Review of Psychology, 55,* 591–621.

Cialdini, R. B., & Sagarin, B. J. (2005). Principles of interpersonal influence. In T. C. Brock & M. C. Green (Eds.), *Persuasion: Psychological insights and perspectives* (2nd ed.). Thousand Oaks, CA: Sage.

Cialdini, R. B., Brown, S. L., Lewis, B. P., & Luce, C. (1997). Reinterpreting the empathyaltruism relationship: When one into one equals oneness. *Journal of Personality and Social Psychology, 73,* 481–494.

Cialdini, R. B., Schaller, M., Hoolihan, D., Arps, K., Fultz, J., & Beaman, A. L. (1987). Empathy-based helping: Is it selflessly or selfishly motivated? *Journal of Personality and Social Psychology, 52,* 749–758.

Cianelli, S. N., & Fouts, R. S. (1998). Chimpanzee to chimpanzee American Sign Language. *Human Evolution, 13,* 147–159.

Cigales, M., Field, T., Lundy, B., Cuadra, A., & Hart, S. (1997). Massage enhances recovery from habituation in normal infants. *Infant Behavior and Development, 20,* 29–34.

Cinnirella, M. (1998). Manipulating stereotype rating tasks: Understanding questionnaire context effects on measures of attitudes, social identity and stereotypes. *Journal of Community and Applied Social Psychology, 8,* 345–362.

Clancy, S. A., McNally, R. J., Schacter, D. L., Lenzeweger, M. F., & Pitman, R. K. (2002). Memory distortion in people reporting abduction by aliens. *Journal of Abnormal Psychology, 111,* 455–461.

Claparède, E. (1911). Recognition et moïté. *Archives de Psychologies, 11,* 79–90.

Clapp, J. D., & Shillington, A. M. (2001). Environmental predictors of heavy episodic drinking. *American Journal of Drug and Alcohol Abuse, 27,* 301–313.

Clark, A. E. (1998). *The positive externalities of higher unemployment: Evidence from household data.* Working paper, Université d'Orléans, Orléans, France.

Clark, D. A. (2004). *Cognitive-behavioral therapy for OCD.* New York: Guilford Press.

Clark, D. A., & O'Connor, K. (2005). Thinking is believing: Ego-dystonic intrusive thoughts in obsessive-compulsive disorder. In D. A. Clark (Ed.), *Intrusive thoughts in clinical disorders: Theory, research, and treatment.* New York: Guilford Press.

Clark, D. A., Beck, A. T., & Alford, B. A. (1999). *Scientific foundations of cognitive theory and therapy of depression.* New York: Wiley.

Clark, D. A., Beck, A. T., & Brown, G. (1989). Cognitive mediation in general psychiatric outpatients: A test of the content-specificity hypothesis. *Journal of Personality and Social Psychology, 56,* 958–964.

Clark, D. M. (1986). A cognitive approach to panic. *Behaviour Research and Therapy, 24,* 461–470.

Clark, D. M. (1988). A cognitive model of panic attacks. In S. Rachman & J. D. Maser (Eds.), *Panic: Psychological perspectives.* Hillsdale, NJ: Erlbaum.

Clark, K. B., & Clark, M. P. (1947). Racial identification and preference in Negro children. In T. N. Newcomb & E. L. Hartley (Eds.), *Readings in Social Psychology.* New York: Holt.

Clark, R. D. (1990). The impact of AIDS on gender differences in willingness to engage in casual sex. *Journal of Applied Social Psychology, 20,* 771–782.

Clark, R. D., III, & Hatfield, E. (1989). Gender differences in willingness to engage in casual sex. *Journal of Psychology and Human Sexuality, 2,* 39–55.

Clark, R. D., III. (2001). Effects of majority defection and multiple minority sources on minority influence. *Group Dynamics, 5,* 57–62.

Clark, W. R., & Grunstein, M. (2005). *Are we hardwired?: The role of genes in human behavior.* New York: Oxford University Press.

Clarke, A. M., & Clarke, A. D. B. (2000). *Early experience and the life path.* London: Kingsley.

Clarkin, J. F., Marziali, E., & Munroe-Blum, H. (1992). *Borderline personality disorder: Clinical and empirical perspectives.* New York: Guilford Press.

Clifford, B. R. (2004). Levels of processing 30 years on: A special issue of memory: Book review. *Applied Cognitive Psychology, 18,* 486–489.

Cloninger, C. R., & Gottesman, I. I. (1989). Genetic and environmental factors in antisocial behavior disorders. In S. Mednick, T. Moffitt, & S. Strack (Eds.), *The causes of crime: New biological approaches.* Cambridge: Cambridge University Press.

Clore, G. L., & Centerbar, D. (2004). Analyzing anger: How to make people mad. *Emotion, 4,* 139–144.

Clutton-Brock, T. (2002). Breeding together: Kin selection and mutualism in cooperative vertebrates. *Science, 296,* 69–72.

Coan, J. A., & Allen, J. (2003). Frontal EEG asymmetry and the behavioral activation and inhibition systems. *Psychophysiology, 40,* 106–114.

Coan, J. A., Schaefer, H. S., & Davidson, R. J. (2006). Lending a hand: Social regulation of the neural response to threat. *Psychological Science, 17,* 1032–1039.

Cochrane, R. E., Tett, R. P., & Vandecreek, L. (2003). Psychological testing and the selection of police officers: A national survey. *Criminal Justice and Behavior, 30,* 115–120.

Coffey, C. E., Weiner, R. D., Djang, W. T., et al. (1991). Brain anatomic effects of electroconvulsive therapy: A prospective magnetic resonance imaging study. *Archives of General Psychiatry, 48,* 1013–1020.

Coffey, C., Carlin, J. B., Degenhardt, L., Lynskey, M., Sanci, L., & Patton, G. C. (2002). Cannabis dependence in young adults: An Australian population study. *Addiction, 97,* 187–194.

Cohen, K. M. (2002). Relationships among childhood sex-atypical behavior, spatial ability, handedness, and sexual orientation in men. *Archives of Sexual Behavior, 31,* 129–143.

Cohen, L. B., & Younger, B. A. (1984). Infant perception of angular relations. *Infant Behavior and Development, 7,* 37–47.

Cohen, M., & Davis, N. (1981). *Medication errors: Causes and prevention.* Philadelphia: G. F. Stickley.

Cohen, S. (1988). Psychosocial models of the role of social support in the etiology of physical disease. *Health Psychology, 7,* 269–297.

Cohen, S. I. (1985). Psychosomatic death: Voodoo death in a modern perspective. *Integrative Psychiatry, 3,* 46–51.

Cohen, S., & Herbert, T. B. (1996). Health psychology: Psychological factors and physical disease from the perspective of human psychoneuroimmunology. *Annual Review of Psychology, 47,* 113–142.

Cohen, S., Doyle, W. J., Turner, R., Alper, C. M., & Skoner, D. P. (2003). Sociability and susceptibility to the common cold. *Psychological Science, 14,* 389–395.

Cohen, S., Kessler, R. C., & Gordon, L. U. (1995). *Measuring stress.* New York: Oxford University Press.

Cole, S. W., Kemeny, M. E., Taylor, S. E., & Visscher, B. R. (1996a). Elevated physical health risk among gay men who conceal their homosexual identity. *Health Psychology, 15,* 243–251.

Cole, S. W., Kemeny, M. E., Taylor, S. E., Visscher, B. R., & Fahey, J. L. (1996b). Accelerated course of human immunodeficiency virus infection in gay men who conceal their homosexual identity. *Psychosomatic Medicine, 58,* 219–231.

Collings, P. (2001). If you got everything, it's good enough: Perspectives on successful aging in a Canadian Inuit community. *Journal of Cross-Cultural Gerontology, 16,* 127–155.

Collins, A. M., & Loftus, E. F. (1975). A spreading activation theory of semantic processing. *Psychological Review, 82,* 407–428.

Collins, D. W., & Kimura, D. (1997). A large sex difference on a two-dimensional mental rotation task. *Behavioral Neuroscience, 111,* 845–849.

Columbia Accident Investigation Board. (2003). *Report* (Vol. 1). Retrieved October 2, 2003 from http://www.nasa.gov/columbia/home/ index.html

Columbia. (1996). *The Columbia world of quotations.* Retrieved March 21, 2003, from http://www.bartleby.com

Comuzzie, A. G., & Allison, D. B. (1998). The search for human obesity genes. *Science, 280,* 1374–1377.

Conrad, R. (1964). Acoustic confusions in immediate memory. *British Journal of Psychology, 55,* 75–84.

Conway, M. A., & Rubin, D. C. (1993). The structure of autobiographical memory. In A.F. Collins, S.E. Gathercole, M.A. Conway, & P.E. Morris (Eds.), *Theories of memory.* Hove: Psychology Press.

Conway, M. A., Anderson, S. J., Larsen, S. F., Donnelly, C. M., McDaniel, M. A., McClelland, A. G. R., Rawles, R. E., & Logie, R. H. (1994). The formation of flashbulb memories. *Memory and Cognition, 22*(3), 326–343.

Cooke, P. (1991, June 23). They cried until they couldn't see. *New York Times Magazine, 25,* 43.

Cooley, C. H. (1902). *Human Nature and the Social Order.* New York: Charles Scribner's.

Cooper, C. R., & Denner, J. (1998). Theories linking culture and psychology: Universal and community-specific processes. *Annual Review of Psychology, 49,* 559–584.

Cooper, J., Mirabile, R., & Scher, S. J. (2005). Actions and attitudes: The theory of cognitive dissonance. In T. C. Brock & M. C. Green (Eds.), *Persuasion: Psychological insights and perspectives* (2nd ed.). Thousand Oaks, CA: Sage.

Coopersmith, S. (1967). *The antecedents of selfesteem.* San Francisco: Freeman.

Corales, T. A. (Ed.). (2005). *Focus on posttraumatic stress disorder research.* Hauppauge, NY: Nova Science.

Cordova, J. V., Gee, C. B., & Warren, L. Z. (2005). Emotional skillfulness in marriage: Intimacy as a mediator of the relationship between emotional skillfulness and marital satisfaction. *Journal of Social and Clinical Psychology, 24,* 218–235.

Corr, P. J. (2008). *The reinforcement sensitivity theory of personality.* Cambridge: Cambridge University Press.

Correll, J., Park, B., Judd, C. M., & Wittenbrink, B. (2002). The police officer's dilemma: Using ethnicity to disambiguate potentially threatening individuals. *Journal of Personality and Social Psychology, 83,* 1314–1329.

Corsten, S., Mende, M., Cholewa, J., & Huber, W. (2007). Treatment of input and output phonology in aphasia: A single case study. *Aphasiology, 21*(6/7/8), 587–603.

Cosmides, L., & Tooby, J. (2002). Unraveling the enigma of human intelligence: Evolutionary psychology and the multimodular mind. In R. J. Sternberg & J. C. Kaufman (Eds.), *The evolution of intelligence.* Mahwah, NJ: Erlbaum.

Costa, A., Hernandez, M., & Sebastian-Galles, N. (2008). Bilingualism aids conflict resolution: Evidence from the ANT task. *Cognition,106*(1), 59–86.

Costa, P. T., & McCrae, R. R. (1992). The five-factor model of personality and its relevance to personality disorders. *Journal of Personality Disorders, 6,* 343–359.

Costa, P. T., & McCrae, R. R. (2002). Looking backward: Changes in the mean levels of personality traits from 80 to 12. In D. Cervone & W. Mischel (Eds.), *Advances in personality science.* New York: Guilford Press.

Couey, J. J., Meredith, R. M., Spijker, S., Poorthuis, R. B., Smit, A. B., Brussaard, A. B., & Mansvelder, H. D. (2007). Distributed network actions by nicotine increase the threshold for spike-timing-dependent plasticity in prefrontal cortex. *Neuron, 54,* 73–87.

Courchesne, E., Carper, R., & Aksboomoff, N. (2003). Evidence of brain overgrowth in the first year of life. *Journal of the American Medical Association, 290,* 337–344.

Courneya, K. S. (1995). Understanding readiness for regular physical activity in older individuals: An application of the theory of planned behavior. *Health Psychology, 14,* 80–87.

Cousins, S. D. (1989). Culture and selfperception in the United States and Japan. *Journal of Personality and Social Psychology, 56,* 124–131.

Cowan, C. P., & Cowan, P. A. (2000). *When partners become parents: The big life change for couples.* Mahwah, NJ: Erlbaum.

Cowley, E. (2005). Views from consumers next in line: The fundamental attribution error in a service setting. *Journal of the Academy of Marketing Science, 33,* 139–152.

Coyne, J. C., & Racioppo, M. W. (2000). Never the twain shall meet? Closing the gap between coping research and clinical intervention research. *American Psychologist, 55,* 655–664.

Crabbe, J. C. (2002). Genetic contributions to addiction. *Annual Review of Psychology, 53,* 435–462.

Craik, F. I. M., & Lockhart, R. S. (1972). Levels of processing: A framework for memory research. *Journal of Verbal Learning and Verbal Behavior, 11,* 671–684.

Craik, F. I. M., & Tulving, E. (1975). Depth of processing and the retention of words in episodic memory. *Journal of Experimental Psychology: General, 104,* 268–294.

Craske, M. (1999). *Anxiety disorders: psychological approaches to theory and treatment.* Boulder, CO: Westview Press.

Craske, M. (2003). *Origins of phobias and anxiety disorders: Why more women than men?* New York: Elsevier Science.

Craske, M. G., & Rowe, M. K. (1997). Nocturnal panic. *Clinical Psychology: Science and Practice, 4,* 153–174.

Crawford, M., & Chaffin, R. (1997). The meanings of difference: Cognition in social and cultural context. In P. J. Caplan & M. Crawford (Eds.), *Gender differences in human cognition. Counterpoints: Cognition, memory, and language.* New York: Oxford University Press.

Creese, I., Burd, D. R., & Snyder, S. H. (1976). Dopamine receptor binding predicts clinical and pharmacological potencies of antischizophrenic drugs. *Science, 192,* 481–483.

Crits-Christoph, P., Cooper, A., & Luborsky, L. (1988). The accuracy of therapists' interpretations and the outcome of dynamic psychotherapy. *Journal of Consulting and Clinical Psychology, 56,* 490–495.

Croizet, J.-C., Despres, G., Gauzins, M.-E., Huguet, P., Leyens, J.-P., & Meot, A. (2004). Stereotype threat undermines intellectual performance by triggering a disruptive mental load. *Personality and Social Psychology Bulletin, 30,* 721–731.

Crook, J. M., & Copolov, D. L. (2000). Schizophrenia. In G. Fink (Ed.), *Encyclopedia of stress.* San Diego, CA: Academic Press.

Crowe, L. C., & George, W. H. (1989). Alcohol and human sexuality: Review and integration. *Psychological Bulletin, 105,* 374–386.

Crowley, K., Callanan, M. A., Tenenbaum, H. R., & Allen, E. (2001). Parents explain more often to boys than to girls during shared scientific thinking. *Psychological Science, 12,* 258–261.

Csibra, G., & Gergely, G. (2006). Social learning and social cogniton: The case for pedagogy. In Y. Munakata, & M. H. Johnson (Eds.), *Processes of Change in Brain and Cognitive Development. Attention and Performance XXI.* Oxford: Oxford University Press.

Culbertson, F. M. (1997). Depression and gender: An international review. *American Psychologist, 52,* 25–31.

Cull, W. L. (2000). Untangling the benefits of multiple study opportunities and repeated testing for cued recall. *Applied Cognitive Psychology, 14,* 215–235.

Cummings, L. (2005). *Pragmatics: A multidisciplinary perspective.* Mahwah, NJ: Erlbaum.

Cunillera, T., Toro, J. M., Sebastian-Galles, N., & Rodriguez-Fornells, A. (2006). The effects of stress and statistical cues on continuous speech segmentation: An event-related brain potential study. *Brain Research, 1123,* 168–78.

Curry, F., Elliot, A. J., Fonseca, D. D., & Moller, A. C. (2006). The social-cognitive model of achievement motivation and the 2 x 2 achievement goal framework. *Journal of Personality and Social Psychology, 90,* 666–679.

Curtis, G. C., Magee, W. J., Eaton, W. W., Wittchen, H.-U., & Kessler, R. C. (1998). Specific fears and phobias: Epidemiology and classification. *British Journal of Psychiatry, 173,* 112–117.

Curtiss, S. (1977). *Genie: A psychological study of a modern day 'wild child.'* New York: Academic Press.

Cytowic, R. E. (2002). *Synesthesia: A union of the senses* (2nd ed.). Boston: MIT Press.

Dalton, P. (2002). Olfaction. In H. Pashler & S. Yantis (Eds.), *Steven's handbook of experimental psychology: Vol. 1. Sensation and perception* (3rd ed.). New York: Wiley.

Daly, M., & Wilson, M. (1988). *Homicide.* New York: Aldine de Gruyter.

Damasio, A. R. (2005). Emotions and feelings: a neurobiological perspective. In A. S. R. Manstead, N. H. Frijda, A. H. Fischer, & K. Oatley (Eds.), *Feelings and Emotions: The Amsterdam Symposium.* New York: Cambridge University Press.

Damasio, A.R. (2000). A neural basis for sociopathy. *Archives of General Psychiatry, 57,* 128–129.

Daniels, C. W. (2002). Legal aspects of polygraph admissibility in the United States. In M. Kleiner (Ed.), *Handbook of polygraph testing.* San Diego, CA: Academic Press.

Darley, J. M., & Gross, P. H. (1983). A hypothesis-confirming bias in labeling effects. *Journal of Personality and Social Psychology, 44,* 20–33.

Darley, J. M., & Latané, B. (1968). Bystander intervention in emergencies: Diffusion of responsibility. *Journal of Personality and Social Psychology, 8,* 377–383.

Darwin, C. (1859). *On the origin of species by means of natural selection.* London: Murray.

Darwin, C. (1877). A biographical sketch of an infant. *Mind, 2,* 285–294.

Darwin, C. (1965). *The expression of emotion in man and animals.* Chicago: University of Chicago Press. (Original work published 1872)

Dasen, P. R., Barthélémy, D., Kan, E., Kouamé, K., Daouda, K., Adjéi, K. K., & Assandé, N. (1985). N'glouele, l'intelligence chez les Baoulé [N'glouele, intelligence according to the Baoulé]. *Archives de Psychologie, 53,* 293–324.

Davidoff, J. (2004). Coloured thinking. *Psychologist, 17,* 570–572.

Davidson, R. J. (1998). *Neuropsychological perspectives on affective and anxiety disorders.* Chicago: Psychology Press.

Davidson, R. J., & Fox, N. A. (1988). Cerebral asymmetry and emotion: Developmental and individual differences. In D. L. Molfese & S. J. Segalowitz (Eds.), *Brain lateralization in children: Developmental implications.* New York: Guilford Press.

Davidson, R. J., Pizzagalli, D., Nitschke, J. B., & Putnam, K. M. (2002). Depression: Perspectives from affective neuroscience. *Annual Review of Psychology, 53*, 545–574.

Davis, C. G., Nolen, H. S., & Larson, J. (1998). Making sense of loss and benefiting from the experience: Two construals of meaning. *Journal of Personality and Social Psychology, 75*, 561–574.

Davis, C., Patte, K., Levitan, R., Reid, C., Tweed, S., & Curtis, C. (2007). From motivation to behaviour: A model of reward sensitivity, overeating, and food preferences in the risk profile for obesity. *Appetite, 48*, 12–19.

Davis, T., Gunderson, J. G., & Myers, M. (1999). Borderline personality disorder. In D. G. Jacobs (Ed.), *The Harvard Medical School Guide to suicide assessment and intervention.* San Francisco: Jossey-Bass.

Dawidowicz, L. S. (1975). *The war against the Jews, 1933–1945.* New York: Holt, Rinehart & Winston.

Dawkins, R. (2006) *The selfish gene* (revised edition). New York: Oxford University Press.

Dawood, K., Pillar, R. C., Horvath, C., Revelle, W., & Bailey, J. M. (2000). Familial aspects of male homosexuality. *Archives of Sexual Behavior, 29*, 155–163.

Dawson, G., Toth, K., Abbott, R., Osterling, J., Munson, J., Estes, A., & Liaw, J. (2004). Early social attention impairments in autism: Social orienting, joint attention, and attention to distress. *Developmental Psychology, 40*, 271–283.

Dawson-McClure, S. R., Sandler, I. N., Wolchik, S. A., & Millsap, R E. (2004). Risk as a moderator of the effects of prevention programs for children from divorced families: A six-year longitudinal study. *Journal of Abnormal Child Psychology, 32*, 175–190.

Day, R., Nielsen, J. A., Korten, A., et al. (1987). Stressful life events preceding the acute onset of schizophrenia. *Culture, Medicine, and Psychiatry, 11*, 123–205.

De Cremer, D., & van Lange, P. A. M. (2001). Why prosocials exhibit greater cooperation than proselfs: The roles of social responsibility and reciprocity. *European Journal of Personality, 15*, 5–18.

De Silva, P., & Rachman, J. (1998). *Obsessivecompulsive disorders.* New York: Oxford University Press.

De Weerd, A. W., & van den Bossche, R. A. S. (2003). The development of sleep during the first months of life. *Sleep Medicine Reviews, 7*, 179–191.

De Weerd, A. W., van den Bossche, R. A. S., & Peeters, E. A. J. (2003). Late in- and out of bed in teenagers. *Sleep, 26* (suppl.), A132–133.

De Zeeuw, C. I., & Cicirata, F. (Eds.) (2005). *Creating coordination in the cerebellum.* St. Louis: Elsevier Sciences/Mosby.

Deary, I. J., Strand, S., Smith, P., & Fernandes, C. (2007). Intelligence and educational achievement. *Intelligence, 35*(1), 13–21.

Deary, I. J., Thorpe, G., Wilson, V., Starr, J. M., & Whalley, L. J. (2003). Population sex differences in IQ at age 11: The Scottish mental survey 1932. *Intelligence, 31*, 533–542.

Deary, I. J., Whiteman, M. C., Starr, J. M., Whalley, L. J., & Fox, H. (2004). The impact of childhood intelligence on later life: Following up the Scottish Medical Surveys of 1932 and 1947. *Journal of Personality and Social Psychology, 86*, 130–147.

DeCasper, A. J., & Spence, M. J. (1986). Prenatal maternal speech influences newborns' perceptions of speech sounds. *Infant Behavior and Development, 9*, 133–150.

deCastro, J. M. (2002). Age-related changes in the social, psychological, and temporal influences on food intake in free-living, healthy, adult humans. *Journals of Gerontology: Series A. Biological Sciences and Medical Sciences, 57A*, 368–377.

Deci, E. L., & Ryan, R. M. (1985). *Intrinsic motivation and self-determination in human behavior.* New York: Plenum Press.

Deci, E. L., & Ryan, R. M. (2002). *Handbook of selfdetermination theory research.* Rochester, NY: University of Rochester Press.

Deese, J. (1959). Influence of inter-item associative strength upon immediate free recall. *Psychological Reports, 5,* 305–312.

Degen, L., Matzinger, D., Drewe, J., & Beglinger, C. (2001). The effect of cholecystokinin in controlling appetite and food intake in humans. *Peptides, 22,* 1265–1269.

deGeus, E. J. C. (2000). Aerobics in stress reduction. In G. Fink (Ed.), *Encyclopedia of stress.* San Diego, CA: Academic Press.

Dehaene, S., & Naccache, L. (2001). Towards a cognitive neuroscience of consciousness: Basic evidence and a workspace framework. *Cognition, 79,* 1–37.

Dehaene, S., Izard, V., Pica, P., & Spelke, E. (2006). Core knowledge of geometry in an Amazonian indigene group. *Science, 311,* (5759), 381–384.

Dekker, E., & Groen, J. (1956). Reproducible psychogenic attacks of asthma. *Journal of Psychosomatic Research, 1,* 56–67.

DeLongis, A. (2000). Coping skills. In G. Fink (Ed.), *Encyclopedia of stress.* San Diego, CA: Academic Press.

Demarest, J., & Allen, R. (2000). Body image: Gender, ethnic, and age differences. *Journal of Social Psychology, 140,* 465–472.

Dement, W. C. (1974). *Some must watch while some must sleep.* San Francisco, CA: W. H. Freeman.

Démonet, J. F., Thierry, G., & Cardebat, D. (2005). Renewal of the neurophysiology of language: Functional neuroimaging. *Physiological Reviews, 85,* 49–95.

DeMoranville, B. M., Jackson, I., Ader, R., Madden, K. S., Felten, D. L., & Bellinger, D. L. (2000). Endocrine and immune systems. In B. S. Fogel, R. B. Schiffer, & S. M. Rao (Eds.), *Synopsis of neuropsychiatry.* Philadelphia: Lippincott-Raven.

Denollet, J. (1997). Personality, emotional distress and coronary heart disease. *European Journal of Personality, 11,* 343–357.

Denollet, J., Nyklicek, I., & Vingerhoets, A. (Eds.) (2007). *Emotional regulation: Conceptual and clinical issues.* New York: Springer.

Denzin, N. K., & Lincoln, Y. S. (Eds.). (2005). *The Sage Handbook of Qualitative Research.* Thousand Oaks, CA: Sage Publications.

Department of Health (DoH) (2007). *Improving access to psychological therapies (IAPT) programme: Computerised cognitive behavioural therapy (cCBT) implementation guidance.* London: DoH.

Depue, R. A., & Collins, P. F. (1999). Neurobiology of the structure of personality: Dopamine, facilitation of incentive motivation, and extraversion. *Behavioral and Brain Sciences, 22,* 491–569.

Depue, R. A., & Lenzenweger, M. F. (2005). A neurobehavioral dimensional model of personality disorders. In M. F. Lenzenweger & J. F. Clarkin (Eds.), *Major theories of personality disorder.* New York: Guilford Press.

DeRegnier, R. A., Wewerka, S., Georgieff, M. K., Mattia, F., & Nelson, C. A. (2002). Influences of postconceptional age and postnatal experience on the development of auditory recognition memory in the newborn infant. *Developmental Psychobiology, 41,* 216–225.

Deregowski, J. B. (1989). Real space and represented space: Cross-cultural perspectives. *Behavior and Brain Sciences, 12,* 51–119.

DeRubeis, R. J., & Crits-Christoph, P. (1998). Empirically supported individual and group psychological treatments for adult mental disorders. *Journal of Consulting and Clinical Psychology, 66,* 37–52.

DeStefano, D., & LeFevre, J. (2004). The role of working memory in mental arithmetic. *European Journal of Cognitive Psychology, 16,* 353–386.

DeSteno, D., Dasgupta, N., Bartlett, M. Y., & Cajdric, A. (2004). Prejudice from thin air: The effect of emotion on automatic intergroup attitudes. *Psychological Science, 15,* 319–324.

Deutsch, M., & Gerard, H. B. (1955). A study of normative and informational social influence upon individual judgment. *Journal of Abnormal and Social Psychology, 51,* 629–636.

DeVries, H., Mudde, A. N., Dijkstra, A., & Willemsen, M. C. (1998). Differential beliefs, perceived social influences, and self-efficacy expectations among smokers in various motivational phases. *Preventive Medicine, 27,* 681–689.

Dhabhar, F. S., & McEwen, B. S. (2001). Bidirectional effects of stress and glucocorticoid hormones on immune function: Possible explanations for paradoxical observations. In R. Ader, D. L. Feiten, & N. Cohen (Eds.), *Psychoneuroimmunology* (Vol. 1). San Diego, CA: Academic Press.

Di Marzo, S., Giordano, A., Pacchiarotti, I., Colom, F., Sánchez-Moreno, J., & Vieta, E. (2006). The impact of the number of episodes on the outcome of bipolar disorder. *European Journal of Psychiatry, 20*(1), 21–28.

Di Paula, A., & Campbell, J. D. (2002). Selfesteem and persistence in the face of failure. *Journal of Personality and Social Psychology, 83,* 711–724.

Diacon, S., & Hasseldine, J. (2007). Framing effects and risk perception: The effect of prior performance presentation format on investment fund choice. *Journal of Economic Psychology, 28, 31–52.*

Diaz, J. (1997). *How drugs influence behavior: A neuro-behavioral approach.* Upper Saddle River, NJ: Prentice Hall.

DiClemente, C. C. (2003). *Addiction and change: How addictions develop and addicted people recover.* New York: Guilford Press.

Diener, E. (2000). Subjective well-being: The science of happiness and a proposal for a national index. *American Psychologist, 55,* 34–43.

Diener, E., & Diener, C. (1996). Most people are happy. *Psychological Science 7,* 181–185.

Diener, E., & Seligman, M. (2004). Beyond money: Toward an economy of well-being. *Psychological Science in the Public Interest, 5,* 1–31.

Diener, E., & Seligman, M. E. P. (2002). Very happy people. *Psychological Science, 13,* 81–84.

Diener, E., Suh, E., Lucas, R. E., & Smith, H. L. (1999). Subjective well-being: Three decades of progress. *Psychological Bulletin, 125,* 276–302.

Diener, E., Tamir, M., & Scollon, C. N. (2006). Happiness, life satisfaction, and fulfillment: The social psychology of subjective wellbeing. In P. A. M. Van Lange (Ed.), *Bridging social psychology: Benefits of transdisciplinary approaches.* Mahwah, NJ: Erlbaum.

Dillard, J. P., & Anderson, J. W. (2004). The role of fear in persuasion. *Psychology & Marketing, 21,* 909–926.

Dimberg, U. (1997). Psychophysiological reactions to facial expressions. In U. C. Segerstrale et al. (Eds.), *Nonverbal communication: Where nature meets culture.* Mahwah, NJ: Erlbaum.

Dindia, K. (2002). Self-disclosure research: Knowledge through meta-analysis. In M. Allen, R. W. Preiss, B. M. Gayle, & N. A. Burrell (Eds.), *Interpersonal communication research: Advances through meta-analysis.* Mahwah, NJ: Erlbaum.

Dinges, D. F., Pack, F., Williams, K., Gillen, K. A., Powell, J. W., Ott, G. E., Aptowicz, C., & Pack, A.I. (1997). Cumulative sleepiness, mood disturbance, and psychomotor vigilance performance decrements during a week of sleep restricted to 4–5 hours per night. *Sleep, 20,* 267–277.

Dinges, D., & Kribbs, N. (1991). Performing while sleepy: effects of experimentally-induced sleepiness. In T. Monk (Ed.), *Sleep, sleepiness, and performance.* New York: John Wiley & Sons.

Dishman, R. K. (1982). Compliance/adherence in health-related exercise. *Health Psychology, 1,* 237–267.

Dishman, R. K. (1994). *Advances in exercise adherence.* Champaign, IL: Human Kinetics.

Dixon, N. F. (1981). *Preconscious processing.* New York: Wiley.

Dodge, K. A. (1986). A social information processing model of social competence in children. *Cognitive perspectives on children's social behavioral development. The Minnesota symposium on child psychology, 18,* 77–125.

Doka, K. J. (1995). Coping with life-threatening illness: A task model. *Omega: Journal of Death and Dying, 32,* 111–122.

Dolezal, H. (1982). *Living in a world transformed: Perceptual and performatory adaptation to a visual distortion.* New York: Academic Press.

Domhoff, G. W. (1999). Drawing theoretical implications from descriptive empirical findings on dream content. *Dreaming: Journal of the Association for the Study of Dreams, 9,* 201–210.

Domhoff, G. W. (2001). A new neurocognitive theory of dreams. *Dreaming: Journal of the Association for the Study of Dreams, 11,* 13–33.

Domino, G. (2000). *Psychological testing.* Upper Saddle River, NJ: Prentice Hall.

Domjan, M. (2000a). *The essentials of conditioning and learning* (2nd ed.). Belmont, CA: Wadsworth/Thomson.

Domjan, M. (2000b). General process learning theory: Challenges from response and stimulus factors. *International Journal of Comparative Psychology, 13,* 101–118.

Donaldson, D. (1998). *Psychiatric disorders with a biochemical basis.* New York: Parthenon.

Donaldson, M. (1978). *Children's minds.* New York: Norton.

Donnerstein, E., & Malamuth, N. (1997). Pornography: Its consequences on the observer. In L. B. Schlesinger & E. Revitch (Eds.), *Sexual dynamics of anti-social behavior* (2nd ed.). Springfield, IL: Charles C Thomas.

Doppelt, J. E., & Wallace, W. L. (1955). Standardization of the Wechsler Adult Intelligence Scale for older persons. *Journal of Abnormal and Social Psychology, 51,* 312–330.

Dossenbach, M., & Dossenbach H. D. (1998). *All about animal vision.* Chicago: Blackbirch Press.

Dovidio, J. F. (1984). Helping behavior and altruism: An empirical and conceptual overview. In L. Berkowitz (Ed.), *Advances in experimental social psychology* (Vol. 17). New York: Academic Press.

Dovidio, J. F., Piliavin, J. A., Schroeder, D. A., & Penner, L. (2006). *The social psychology of prosocial behavior.* Mahwah, NJ: Erlbaum.

Downey, G., & Feldman, S. L. (1996). Implications of rejection sensitivity for intimate relationships. *Journal of Personality and Social Psychology, 70,* 1327–1343.

Drake, M. E., Pakalnis, A., & Denio, L. C. (1988). Differential diagnosis of epilepsy and multiple personality: Clinical and EEG findings in 15 cases. *Neuropsychiatry, Neuropsychology, and Behavioral Neurology, 1,* 131–140.

Driscoll, I., McDaniel, M. A., & Guynn, M. J. (2005). Apolipoprotein E and prospective memory in normally aging adults. *Neuropsychology, 19,* 28–34.

Driskell, J. E., Willis, R. P., & Copper, C. (1992). Effect of overlearning on retention. *Journal of Applied Psychology, 77,* 615–622.

Drukin, K. (1998). Implicit content and implicit processes in mass media use. In K. Kirsner et al. (Eds.), *Implicit and explicit mental processes.* Mahwah, NJ: Erlbaum.

Dryden, W. (Ed.). (2002). *Handbook of individual therapy.* Thousand Oaks, CA: Sage.

Duffy, J. F., Rimmer, D. W., Czeisler, C. A. (2001). Association of intrinsic circadian period with morningness-eveningness, usual wake time, and circadian phase. *Behavioral Neuroscience, 115,* 895–899.

Dunbar, M., Ford, G., & Hunt, K. (1998). Why is the receipt of social support associated with increased psychological distress? An examination of three hypotheses. *Psychology & Health, 13,* 527–544.

Dunbar, R. (1993). Coevolution of neocortical size, group size and language in humans. *Behavioural and Brain Sciences, 16,* 681–735.

Duncan, H. J., & Seiden, A. M. (1995). Long-term follow-up of olfactory loss secondary to head trauma and upper respiratory tract infection. *Arch Otolaryngol Head Neck Surgery, 121,* 1183–1187.

Duncan, P. M., Alici, T., & Woodward, J. D. (2000). Conditioned compensatory response to ethanol as indicated by locomotor activity in rats. *Behavioural Pharmacology, 11,* 395–402.

Dunn, J., & Plomin, R. (1990). *Separate lives: Why siblings are so different.* New York: Basic Books.

Durrant, J. E. (2000). Trends in youth crime and well-being since the abolition of corporal punishment in Sweden. *Youth and Society, 31,* 437–455.

Dutton, D. G. (2006). *The abusive personality: Violence and control in intimate relationships.* New York: Guilford Press.

Duvander, A. Z. E. (1999). The transition from cohabitation to marriage: A longitudinal study of the propensity to marry in Sweden in the early 1990s. *Journal of Family Issues, 20,* 698–717.

Dweck, C. (1999). *Self theories: Their role in motivation, personality, and development.* Philadelphia: Psychology Press/Taylor and Francis.

Dying to be thin. (2000). *Nova* [Television series]. Boston: WGBH.

Eacott, M. J., & Crawley, R. A. (1998). The offset of childhood amnesia: Memory for events that occurred before age 3. *Journal of Experimental Psychology: General, 127,* 22–33.

Eagles, J. M. (2003). Seasonal affective disorder. *British Journal of Psychiatry, 182,* 174–176.

Eagly, A. H., & Crowley, M. (1986). Gender and helping behavior: A meta-analytic review of the social psychological literature. *Psychological Bulletin, 100,* 283–308.

Eagly, A. H., & Wood, W. (1999). The origins of sex differences in human behavior: Evolved dispositions versus social roles. *American Psychologist, 54,* 408–423.

Eagly, A. H., & Wood, W. (2006). Three ways that data can misinform: Inappropriate partialling, small samples, and, anyway, they're not playing our song. *Psychological Inquiry, 17,* 131–137.

Eaton, J. (2001). Management communication: The threat of groupthink. *Corporate Communications, 6,* 183–192.

Ebbinghaus, H. (1964). *Über das Gedächtnis: Untersuchungen Zur Experimentellen Psychologie [Memory: A contribution to experimental psychology]* (H. A. Ruger & C. E. Bussenius, Trans.). New York: Dover. (Original work published 1885)

Eccles, J. (1991). Gender-role socialization. In R. M. Baron, W. G. Graziano, & C. Stangor (Eds.), *Social psychology.* Ft. Worth, TX: Holt, Rinehart & Winston.

Eckensberger, L. H., & Zimba, R. F. (1997). The development of moral judgment. In J. W. Berry, P. R. Dasen, & T. S. Saraswathi (Eds.), *Handbook of cross-cultural psychology* (2nd ed., Vol. 2). Boston: Allyn & Bacon.

Eden, D. (2003). Self-fulfilling prophecies in organizations. In J. Greenberg (Ed.), *Organizational behavior: The state of the science* (2nd ed.). Mahwah, NJ: Erlbaum.

Edser, S. J. (2002). Hypnotically facilitated counter conditioning of anticipatory nausea and vomiting associated with chemotherapy: A case study. *Australian Journal of Clinical Hypnotherapy and Hypnosis, 23,* 18–30.

Edwards, A. E. (1962). A demonstration of the long-term retention of a conditioned galvanic skin response. *Psychosomatic Medicine, 24,* 459–463.

Ehrman, J. (2003). *Clinical exercise psychology.* Champaign, IL: Human Kinetics.

Eisenberg, N. (2000). Emotion, regulation, and moral development. *Annual Review of Psychology, 51,* 665–697.

Eisenberg, N. (2002). Emotion related regulation and its relation to quality of social functioning. In W. Hartup & R. A. Weinberg (Eds.), *Child psychology in retrospect and prospect: In celebration of the 75th anniversary of the Institute of Child Development. The Minnesota symposia on child psychology* (Vol. 32). Mahwah, NJ: Erlbaum.

Eisenberg, N. (2004). Prosocial and moral development in the family. In T. A. Thorkildsen & H. J. Walberg (Eds.), *Nurturing morality. Issues in children's and families' lives.* New York: Kluwer Academic/Plenum Press.

Eisenberger, N. I., Lieberman, M. D., & Williams, K. D. (2003). Does rejection hurt? An fMRI study of social exclusion. *Science, 302,* 290–292.

Ekman, P. (1973). Cross-cultural studies of facial expression. In P. Ekman (Ed.), *Darwin and facial expression.* San Diego, CA: Academic Press.

Ekman, P., & Friesen, W. V. (1967). Hand and body cues in the judgement of emotion: A reformulation. *Perceptual and Motor Skills, 24,* 711–24.

Ekman, P., & Friesen, W. V. (1969). The repertoire of nonverbal behaviour: Categories, origins, usuage and coding. *Semiotics, 1,* 49–98.

Ekman, P., & Friesen, W. V. (1971). Constants across cultures in the face and emotion. *Journal of personality and Social Psychology, 17,* 124–129.

Ekman, P., & Friesen, W. V. (1987). *Facial Action Coding System.* Palo Alto, CA: Consulting Psychologists Press.

Ekman, P., Friesen, W. V., & Ellsworth, P. (1972). *Emotion in the human face: Guidelines for research and an integration of findings.* Oxford: Pergamon Press.

Elbert, T., Pantev, C., Wienbruch, C., Rockstroh, B., & Taub, E. (1995). Increased cortical representation of the fingers of the left hand in string players. *Science, 270,* 305–307.

Elfenbein, H. A., & Ambady, N. (2003). Universals and cultural differences in recognizing emotions. *Current Directions in Psychological Science, 12,* 159–164.

Eliassen, J. C., Souza, T., & Sanes, J. N. (2003). Experience-dependent activation patterns in human brain during visual-motor associative learning. *Journal of Neuroscience, 23,* 10540–10547.

Elkind, D. (1967). Egocentrism in adolescence. *Child Development, 38,* 1025–1034.

Ellemers, N. (1993). The influence of socio-structural variables on identity management strategies. In W. Stroebe, & M. Hewstone (Eds.), *European review of social psychology* (Vol. 4, pp. 27–57). Chichester: Wiley.

Ellemers, N., Wilke, H., & Van Knippenberg, A. (1993). Effects of the legitimacy of low group or individual status on individual and collective status-enhancement strategies. *Journal of Personality and Social Psychology, 64,* 766–778.

Elliot, A. J., & Church, M. A. (1997). A hierarchical model of approach and avoidance achievement motivation. *Journal of Personality and Social Psychology, 72,* 218–232.

Elliot, A. J., & McGregor, H. A. (2001). A 2 × 2 achievement goal framework. *Journal of Personality and Social Psychology, 80,* 501–519.

Elliot, A. J., & Thrash, T. M. (2002). Approach-avoidance motivation in personality: Approach and avoidance temperaments and goals. *Journal of Personality and Social Psychology, 82,* 804–818.

Ellis, A. (1962). *Reason and emotion in psychotherapy.* New York: Lyle Stuart.

Elsey, B., & Fujiwara, A. (2000). Kaizen and technology transfer instructors as workbased learning facilitators in overseas transplants: A case study. *Journal of Workplace Learning, 12,* 333–342.

Emerson, R. M. (1966). Mount Everest: A case study of communication feedback and sustained group goalstriving. *Sociometry, 29,* 213–227.

Emlen, S. T. (1975, August). The stellar orientation system of a migratory bird. *Scientific American,* 102–111.

Epel, E. S., Blackburn, E. H., Lin, J., Dhabhar, F. S., Adler, N. E., et al. (2004). Accelerated telomere shortening in response to life stress. *Proceedings of the National Academy of Sciences, 101*(49), 17312–17315.

Epstein, M. A., & Bottoms, B. L. (2002). Explaining the forgetting and recovery of abuse and trauma memories: Possible mechanisms. *Child Maltreatment: Journal of the American Professional Society on the Abuse of Children, 7,* 210–225.

Epstein, R., Kirshnit, C. E., Lanza, R. P., & Rubin, L. C. (1984). 'Insight' in the pigeon: Antecedents and determinants of an intelligent performance. *Nature, 308,* 61–62.

Epstein, S. (1983). Aggregation and beyond: Some basic issues on the production of behavior. *Journal of Personality, 51,* 360–392.

Erdberg, P. (2000). Rorschach assessment. In G. Goldstein & M. Hersen (Eds.), *Handbook of psychological assessment* (3rd ed.). New York: Elsevier.

Erdelyi, M. H. (2001). Defense processes can be conscious or unconscious. *American Psychologist, 56,* 761–762.

Ericsson, K. A., & Chase, W. G. (1982). Exceptional memory. *American Scientist, 70,* 607–615.

Ericsson, K. A., & Polson, P. G. (1988). An experimental analysis of the mechanisms of a memory skill. *Journal of Experimental Psychology: Learning, Memory, and Cognition, 14,* 305–316.

Ericsson, K. A., Chase, W. G., & Faloon, S. (1980). Acquisition of a memory skill. *Science, 208,* 1181–1182.

Ericsson, K. A., Delaney, P. F., Weaver, G., & Mahadevan, R. (2004). Uncovering the structure of a memorist's superior 'basic' memory capacity. *Cognitive Psychology, 49,* 191–237.

Ericsson, K. A., Krampe, R. T., & Tesch R. C. (1993). The role of deliberate practice in the acquisition of expert performance. *Psychological Review, 100,* 363–406.

Erikson, E. H. (1968). *Identity, youth and crisis.* New York: Norton.

Erikson, E. H. (1980). *Identity and the life cycle.* New York: Norton. (Original work published 1959)

Eron, L. D. (1987). The development of aggressive behavior from the perspective of a developing behaviorism. *American Psychologist, 42,* 435–442.

Eron, L. D. (2000). A psychological perspective. In V. B. Van Hasselt & M. Hersen (Eds.), *Aggression and violence: An introductory text.* Boston: Allyn & Bacon.

Esparza, J., Fox, C., Harper, I. T., Bennett, P. H., Schulz, L. O., Valencia, M. E., & Ravussin, E. (2000). Daily energy expenditure in Mexican and USA Pima Indians: Low physical activity as a possible cause of obesity. *International Journal of Obesity and Related Metabolic Disorders, 24,* 55–59.

Essau, C., & Petermann, F. (1999). *Depressive disorders in children and adolescents: Epidemiology, risk factors, and treatment.* Northvale, NJ: Aronson.

Essau, C., & Trommsdorff, G. (1996). Coping with university-related problems: A crosscultural comparison. *Journal of Cross-Cultural Psychology, 27,* 315–328.

Esser, J. K., & Lindoerfer, J. S. (1989). Groupthink and the space shuttle Challenger accident: Toward a quantitative case analysis. *Journal of Behavioral Decision Making, 2,* 167–177.

Estes, T. H., & Vaughn, J. L. (1985). *Reading and learning in the content classroom: Diagrams and instructional strategies* (3rd ed.). Boston: Allyn & Bacon.

Eurocare (2003). http://ec.europa.eu/health-eu/news_alcoholineurope_en.htm

Evans, J. St. B. T., & Lynch, J. S. (1973). Matching bias in the selection task. *British Journal of Psychology, 64,* 391–397.

Evans, J. St. B. T., Over, D. E., & Manktelow, K. I. (1993). Reasoning, decision-making and rationality. *Cognition, 49,* 165–187.

Evans-Martin, F. F. (2007). *Emotion and stress.* New York: Facts on File.

Evers, K. E., Harlow, H. L., Redding, C. A., & LaForge, R. G. (1998). Longitudinal changes in stages of change for condom use in women. *American Journal of Health Promotion, 13,* 19–25.

Exner, J. E. (1991). *The Rorschach—A comprehensive system: Assessment of personality and psychopathology* (Vol. 2). New York: Wiley.

Eysenck, H. J. (1952). The effects of psychotherapy: An evaluation. *Journal of Consulting Psychology, 16,* 319–324.

Eysenck, H. J. (1964). *Crime and personality.* Boston: Houghton Mifflin.

Eysenck, H. J. (1967). *The biological basis of personality.* Springfield, IL: Charles C. Thomas.

Eysenck, H. J. (1990). Biological dimensions of personality. In L. A. Pervin (Ed.), *Handbook of personality: Theory and research.* New York: Guilford Press.

Eysenck, H. J. (1994). Cancer, personality, and stress: Prediction and prevention. *Advances in Behaviour Research and Therapy, 16,* 167–215.

Eysenck, H. J., & Grossarth-Marticek, R. (1991). Creative novation behavior therapy as a prophylactic treatment for cancer and coronary heart disease: II. Effects of treatment. *Behavior Research and Therapy, 29,* 17–31.

Fabbro, F. (2001). The bilingual brain: Bilingual aphasia. *Brain & Language, 79,* 201–210.

Fagley, N. S. (1987). Positional response bias in multiple-choice tests of learning: Its relation to testwiseness and guessing strategy. *Journal of Educational Psychology, 79,* 95–97.

Faith, M. S., Matz, P. E., Jorge, M.A. (2002). Obesity depression associations in the population. *Journal of Psychosomatic Research, 53,* 935–942.

Fallon, A. E., & Rozin, P. (1985). Sex differences in perceptions of desirable body shape. *Journal of Abnormal Psychology, 94,* 102–105.

Falsetti, S. A., Monnier, J., & Resnick, H. S. (2005). Intrusive thoughts in posttraumatic stress disorder. In D. A. Clark (Ed.), *Intrusive thoughts in clinical disorders: Theory, research, and treatment.* New York: Guilford Press.

Fanselow, M. S. (1991). Analgesia as a response to aversive Pavlovian conditional stimuli: Cognitive and emotional mediators. In M. R. Denny (Ed.), *Fear, avoidance, and phobias: A fundamental analysis.* Hillsdale, NJ: Erlbaum.

Fanselow, M. S., & Poulos, A. M. (2005). The neuroscience of mammalian associative learning. *Annual Review of Psychology, 56,* 207–234.

Fantz, R. L. (1961, May). The origin of form perception. *Scientific American, 204,* 66–72.

Fantz, R. L. (1964). Visual experience in infants: Decreased attention to familiar patterns relative to novel ones. *Science, 146,* 668–670.

Faraone, S. V., Sergeant, J., Gillberg, C., & Biederman, J. (2003). The Worldwide Prevalence of ADHD: Is it an American Condition? *World Psychiatry, 2,* 104–113.

Farroni, T., Csibra, G., Simion, F., & Johnson, M. H. (2002). Eye contact detection in humans from birth. *Proceedings of the National Academy of Sciences of the United States of America, 99,* 9602–9605.

Faust, J. (1991). Same-day surgery preparation: Reduction of pediatric patient arousal and distress through participant modeling. *Journal of Consulting and Clinical Psychology, 59,* 473–478.

Fazio, R. H., & Roskos-Ewoldsen, D. R. (2005). Acting as we feel: When and how attitudes guide behavior. In T. C. Brock & M. C. Green (Eds.), *Persuasion: Psychological insights and perspectives* (2nd ed., pp. 41–62). Thousand Oaks, CA: Sage.

Fazio, R. H., Jackson, J. R., Dunton, B. C., & Williams, C. J. (1995). Variability in automatic activation as an unobstrusive measure of racial attitudes: A bona fide pipeline? *Journal of Personality and Social Psychology, 69,* 1013–1027.

Fearon, P., Kirkbride, J. B., Morgan, C., Dazzan, P., Morgan, K., Lloyd, T., Hutchinson, G., Tarrant, J., Fung, W. L., Holloway, J., Mallett, R., Harrison, G., Leff, J., Jones, P. B., & Murray, R. M., AESOP Study Group. (2006). Incidence of schizophrenia and other psychoses in ethnic minority groups: results from the MRC AESOP Study. *Psychological Medicine, 36*(11), 1541–50.

Federal Interagency Forum on Aging-Related Statistics (2006). *Older Americans update 2006: Key indicators of well-being.* Retrieved February 20, 2007 from http://www.agingstats.gov/update2006/Health_Status.pdf.

Fein, S., & Spencer, S. J. (1997). Prejudice as selfimage maintenance: Affirming the self through derogating others. *Journal of Personality and Social Psychology, 73,* 31–44.

Feingold, A. (1988). Matching for attractiveness in romantic partners and same-sex friends: A meta-analysis and theoretical critique. *Psychological Bulletin, 104,* 226–235.

Feingold, A., & Mazzella, R. (1998). Gender differences in body image are increasing. *Psychological Science, 9,* 190–195.

Feldman-Barrett, L., Niedenthal, P. M., & Winkielman, P. (Eds.) (2007). *Emotion and consciousness.* New York: Guilford Press.

Felmlee, D. H. (1998). 'Be careful what you wish for . . .': A quantitative and qualitative investigation of 'fatal attractions.' *Personal Relationships, 5,* 235–253.

Felton, D. L., & Maida, M. E. (2000). Neuroimmunomodulation. In G. Fink (Ed.), *Encyclopedia of stress.* San Diego, CA: Academic Press.

Fenichel, G. (2006). *Neonatal neurology.* St. Louis: Mosby.

Fenton, W. S., & McGlashan, T. H. (1991a). Natural history of schizophrenia subtypes: I. Longitudinal study of paranoid, hebephonic, and undifferentiated schizophrenia. *Archives of General Psychiatry, 48,* 969–977.

Fenton, W. S., & McGlashan, T. H. (1991b). Natural history of schizophrenia subtypes: II. Positive and negative symptoms and long-term course. *Archives of General Psychiatry, 48,* 978–986.

Ferguson, E. D. (2000). *Motivation: A biosocial and cognitive integration of motivation and emotion.* New York: Oxford University Press.

Fernald, A., Taeschner, T., Dunn, J., Papousek, M., De Boysson-Bardies, B., & Fukui, I. (1989). A cross-cultural study of prosodic modification in mothers' and fathers' speech to preverbal infants. *Journal of Child Language, 16,* 477–501.

Ferster, C. B., & Skinner, B. F. (1957). *Schedules of reinforcement.* Englewood Cliffs, NJ: Prentice Hall.

Festinger, L. (1954). A theory of social comparison processes. *Human Relations, 2,* 117–140.

Festinger, L. (1957). *A theory of cognitive dissonance.* Stanford, CA: Stanford University Press.

Festinger, L., & Carlsmith, J. M. (1959). Cognitive consequences of forced compliance. *Journal of Abnormal and Social Psychology, 58,* 203–210.

Festinger, L., Pepitone, A., & Newcomb, T. (1952). Some consequences of deindividuation in a group. *Journal of Abnormal Psychology, 47,* 382–389.

Fetterman, D. M. (1988). *Excellence and equality: A qualitatively different perspective on gifted and talented education.* Albany, NY: State University of New York Press.

Fiedler, K., Nickel, S., Muehlfriedel, T., & Unkelbach, C. (2001). Is mood congruency an effect of genuine memory or response bias? *Journal of Experimental Social Psychology, 37,* 201–214.

Field, T. (2000). Infant massage therapy. In C. H. Zeanah, Jr. (Ed.), *Handbook of infant mental health* (2nd ed.). New York: Guilford Press.

Field, T. (2001). Massage therapy facilitates weight gain in preterm infants. *Current Directions in Psychological Science, 10,* 51–54.

Field, T. M., Schanberg, S. M., Scafidi, F., Bauer, C. R., Vega-Lahr, N., Garcia, R., Nystrom, J., & Kuhn, C. M. (1986). Tactile/kinesthetic stimulation effects on preterm neonates. *Pediatrics, 77,* 654–658.

Field, T., Diego, M.A., Hernandez-Reif, M., Deeds O., & Figuereido, B. (2006). Moderate versus light pressure massage therapy leads to greater weight gain in preterm infants. *Infant Behavior & Development, 29,* 574–578.

Field, T.M., Woodson, R., Greenberg, R., & Cohen, D. (1982). Discrimination and imitation of facial expression by neonates. *Science, 218,* 179–181.

Fields, H. L. (2005). *Pain: Mechanisms and management.* New York: McGraw-Hill.

Fishbein, M., & Ajzen, I. (1974). Attitudes toward objects as predictors of single and multiple behavioral criteria. *Psychological Review, 81,* 59–74.

Fisher, C., Kahn E., Edwards, A., Davis, D. M., & Fine, J. (1974). A psychophysiological study of nightmares and night terrors: III. Mental content and recall of stage 4 night terrors. *Journal of Nervous and Mental Disease, 158,* 174–188.

Fisher, S., & Greenberg, R. P. (1996). *Freud scientifically reappraised: Testing the theories and therapy.* New York: Wiley.

Flavell, J. H. (1970). Developmental studies of mediated behavior. In H. W. Reese and L. P. Lipsett (Eds.), *Advances in child development and behavior* (Vol. 5). New York: Academic Press.

Fleeson, W. (2004). Moving personality beyond the person-situation debate. *Current Directions in Psychological Science, 13*, 83–87.

Flege, J. E., Yeni-Komshian, G. H., & Liu, S. (1999). Age constraints on second-language acquisition. *Journal of Memory & Language, 41*, 78–104.

Flinn, M. V. (1997). Culture and the evolution of social learning. *Evolution and Human Behavior, 18*, 23–67.

Flohr, H. (2000). NMDA receptor-mediated computational processes and phenomenal consciousness. In T. Metzinger (Ed.), *Neural correlates of consciousness: Empirical and conceptual questions*. Cambridge, MA: The MIT Press.

Floyd, R. L., O'Connor, M. J., Sokol, R. J., Bertrand, J. , & Cordero, J. F. (2005). Recognition and prevention of fetal alcohol syndrome. *Obstetrics & Gynecology, 106*, 1059–1064

Flynn, J. R. (1987). Massive IQ gains in 14 nations: What IQ tests really measure. *Psychological Bulletin, 101*, 171–191.

Flynn, J. R. (1998). IQ gains over time: Toward finding the causes. In U. Neisser et al. (Eds.), *The rising curve: Long-term gains in IQ and related measures*. Washington, DC: American Psychological Association.

Foa, E. B., Riggs, D. S., & Gershuny, B. S. (1995). Arousal, numbing, and intrusion: Symptom structure of posttraumatic stress disorder following assault. *American Journal of Psychology, 152*, 116–120.

Foa, E. B., Zoellner, L. A., Feeny, N. C., Hembree, E. A., & Alvarez-Conrad, J. (2002). Does imaginal exposure exacerbate PTSD symptoms? *Journal of Consulting and Clinical Psychology, 70*, 1022–1028.

Folkard, S., & Tucker, P. (2003). Shift work, safety and productivity. *Occupational Medicine, 53*(2), 95–101.

Fordyce, W. E. (1988). Pain and suffering: A reappraisal. *American Psychologist, 43*, 276–283.

Fosse, R., Stickgold, R., & Hobson, J. A. (2001). Brain-mind states: Reciprocal variation in thoughts and hallucinations. *Psychological Science, 2001, 12*, 30–36.

Foulkes, D. (1982). REM-dream perspectives on the development of affect and cognition. *Psychiatric Journal of the University of Ottawa, 7*, 48–55.

Foulks, F. F., Bland, I. J., & Shervington, D. (1995). Psychotherapy across cultures. *Review of Psychiatry, 14*, 511.

Fouts, R. S., Fouts, D. H., & Van Cantfort, T. E. (1989). The infant Loulis learns signs from other cross-fostered chimpanzees. In R. A. Gardner, B. T. Gardner, & T. E. Van Cantfort (Eds.), *Teaching sign language to chimpanzees*. Albany: State University of New York Press.

Fox, D. K., Hopkins, B. L., & Anger, W. K. (1987). The long-term effects of a token economy on safety performance in open-pit mining. *Journal of Applied Behavior Analysis, 20*, 215–224.

Fox, N. A., Henderson, H. A., Marshall, P. J., Nichols, K. E., & Ghera, M. M. (2005). Behavioral inhibition: Linking biology and behavior within a developmental framework. *Annual Review of Psychology, 56*, 235–262.

Frances, A., & Widiger, T. A. (1986). Methodological issues in personality disorder diagnosis. In T. Millon & G. L. Klerman (Eds.), *Contemporary directions in psychopathology: Toward the DSM-IV*. New York: Guilford Press.

Frank, J. (1961). *Persuasion & healing: A comparative study of psychotherapy*. Baltimore: John Hopkins University Press.

Frank, N. C., Spirito, A., Stark, L., & Owens- Stively, J. (1997). The use of scheduled awakenings to eliminate childhood sleepwalking. *Journal of Pediatric Psychology, 22*, 345–353.

Franklin, B. *Remarks Concerning the Savage of North America*. (1784).

Franklin, J. (1987). *Molecules of the mind: The brave new science of molecular psychology*. New York: Atheneum.

Franklin, T. R., Acton, P. D., Maldjian, J. A., Gray, J. D., Croft, J. R., Dackis, C. A., O'Brien, C. P., & Childress, A. R. (2002). Decreased gray matter concentration in the insular, orbitofrontal, cingulate, and temporal cortices of cocaine patients. *Biological Psychiatry, 51,* 134–142.

Frayser, S. G. (1985). *Varieties of sexual experience: An anthropological perspective on human sexuality.* New Haven, CT: HRAF.

Fredrickson, B. L. (1998). What good are positive emotions? *Review of General Psychology, 2,* 300–319.

French, S. J., & Cecil, J. E. (2001). Oral, gastric and intestinal influences on human feeding. *Physiology and Behavior, 74,* 729–734.

Freud, S. (1923). *The ego and the id.* New York: Norton.

Freud, S. (1935). *A general introduction to psychoanalysis.* New York: Washington Square Press.

Freud, S. (1953). The interpretation of dreams. In J. Strachey (Ed.), *The standard edition of the complete psychological works of Sigmund Freud* (Vols. 4 and 5). London: Hogarth. (Original work published 1900)

Freud, S. (1957). Mourning and melancholia. In J. Strachey (Ed.), *The standard edition of the complete psychological works of Sigmund Freud,* (Vol. 14). London: Hogarth. (Original work published 1917)

Freud, S. (1965). *The interpretation of dreams.* New York: Avon. (Original work published 1900)

Friedl, M. C., and Draijer, N. (2000). Dissociative disorders in Dutch psychiatric inpatients. *American Journal of Psychiatry, 157,* 1012–1013.

Friedman, H., & DiMatteo, M. R. (1989). *Health psychology.* New York: Prentice Hall.

Frijda, N. (2006). *The laws of emotion.* Mahwah, NJ: Erlbaum.

Frijda, N. H., Manstead, A. S. R., & Bem, S. (Eds.). (2005). *Emotions and beliefs: How feelings influence thoughts.* New York: Cambridge University Press.

Frisby, J. P. (1980). *Seeing: Illusion, brain and mind.* Oxford: Oxford University Press.

Frisco, M. L., & Williams, K. (2003). Perceived housework equity, marital happiness, and divorce in dual earner households. *Journal of Family Issues, 24,* 51–73.

Fritsch, J. (1999, May 25). 95% Regain Lost Weight. Or Do They? *New York Times,* p. F7.

Fritzsche, B. A., Finkelstein, M. A., & Penner, L. A. (2000). To help or not to help: Capturing individuals' decision policies. *Social Behavior and Personality, 28,* 561–578.

Funk, S. C. (1992). Hardiness: A review of theory and research. *Health Psychology, 11,* 335–345.

Furmark, T., Tillfors, M., Marteinsdottir, I., Fischer, H., Pissiota, A., Langstroem, B., Fredrikson, M. (2002). Common changes in cerebral blood flow in patients with social phobia treated with citalopram or cognitivebehavioral therapy. *Archives of General Psychiatry, 59,* 425–433.

Gabbard, G. O. (1990). *Psychodynamic psychiatry in clinical practice.* Washington, DC: American Psychiatric Press.

Gabbard, G. O. (2004). *Long-term psychodynamic psychotherapy.* Washington, DC: American Psychiatric Publishing.

Gabbard, G. O., Beck, J., & Holmes, J. (2005). *Oxford textbook of psychotherapy.* New York: Oxford University Press.

Gabrieli, J. D. E. (1998). Cognitive neuroscience of human memory. *Annual Review of Psychology, 49,* 87–115.

Gabrieli, J. D. E., Desmond, J. E., Demb, J. B., & Wagner, A. D. (1996). Functional magnetic resonance imaging of semantic memory processes in the frontal lobes. *Psychological Science, 7,* 278–283.

Gainotti, G. (1972). Emotional behavior and hemispheric side of lesion. *Cortex, 8,* 41–55.

Galambos, N. L., & Almeida, D. M. (1992). Does parent adolescent conflict increase in early adolescence? *Journal of Marriage and the Family, 54,* 737–748.

Galanter, E. (1962). Contemporary psychophysics. In R. Brown (Ed.), *New directions in psychology*. New York: Holt, Rinehart & Winston.

Galati, D., & Lavelli, M. (1997). Neonate and infant emotion expression perceived by adults. *Journal of Nonverbal Behavior, 21,* 57–83.

Galea, S., Ahern, J., Resnick, H., Kilpatrick, D., Bucuvalas, M., Gold, J., & Vlahov, D. (2002). Psychological sequelae of the September 11 terrorist attacks in New York City. *New England Journal of Medicine, 346,* 982–987.

Gallup, G. G. (1970). Chimpanzees: Self-recognition. *Science, 167*(3914), 86–87.

Galton, F. (1869). *Hereditary genius.* London: Macmillan.

Gangestad, S. W., Haselton, M. G., & Buss, D. M. (2006). Evolutionary foundations of cultural variation: Evoked culture and mate preferences. *Psychological Inquiry, 17,* 75–95.

Gangestad, S.W., Thornhill, R., & Garver-Apgar. C. E. (2005) Adaptations to ovulation: Implications for sexual and social behavior. *Current Directions in Psychological Science, 14,* 312–316.

Ganis, G., Thompson, W. L., & Kosslyn, S. M. (2004). Brain areas underlying visual mental imagery and visual perception: An fMRI study. *Cognitive Brain Research, 20,* 226–241.

Garbarino, S., Beelke, M., Costa, G., Violani, C., Lucidi, F., Ferrillo, F. et al. (2002). Brain function and effects of shift work: Implications for clinical neuropharmacology. *Neuro-psychobiology, 45,* 50–56.

Garber, J., & Dodge, K. A. (Eds.) (2007). *The development of emotional regulation and dysregulation.* New York: Cambridge University Press.

Garcia, J., & Koelling, R. A. (1966). The relation of cue to consequence in avoidance learning. *Psychonomic Science, 4,* 123–124.

Garcia, J., Lasiter, P. S., Bermudez, R. F., & Deems, D. A. (1985). A general theory of aversion learning. *Annals of the New York Academy of Sciences, 443,* 8–21.

Gardner, H. (2000). *Multiple intelligences: The theory in practice.* New York: Basic Books.

Gardner, H. (2003). Three distinct meanings of intelligence. In R. J. Sternberg, J. Lautrey, & T. I. Lubart (Eds.), *Models of intelligence: International perspectives.* Washington, DC: American Psychological Association.

Gardner, R. A., & Gardner, B. T. (1969). Teaching language to a chimpanzee. *Science, 165,* 664–672.

Garlick, D. (2002). Understanding the nature of the general factor of intelligence: The role of individual differences in neural plasticity as an explanatory mechanism. *Psychological Review, 109,* 116–136.

Garmezy, N. (1983). *Stress, coping and development in children.* New York: McGraw-Hill.

Garnefski, N., & Arends, E. (1998). Sexual abuse and adolescent maladjustment: Differences between male and female victims. *Journal of Adolescence, 21,* 99–107.

Gatchel, R. J. (2005). *Clinical essentials of pain management.* Washington, DC: American Psychological Association.

Gathercole, S. E. (1998). The development of memory. *Journal of Child Psychology and Psychiatry and Allied Disciplines, 39,* 3–27.

Gathercole, S. E., Pickering, S. J., Knight, C., & Stegmann, Z. (2004). Working memory skills and educational attainment: Evidence from national curriculum assessments at 7 and 14 years of age. *Applied Cognitive Psychology, 18,* 1–16.

Gazzaniga, M. S., & Smylie, C. S. (1983). Facial recognition and brain asymmetries: Clues to underlying mechanisms. *Annals of Neurology, 13,* 536–540.

Geary, D. C. (2005). *The origin of mind: Evolution of brain, cognition, and general intelligence.* Washington, DC: American Psychological Association.

Geher, G., Bauman, K. P., Hubbard, S. E. K., & Legare, J. R. (2002). Self and other obedience estimates: Biases and moderators. *Journal of Social Psychology, 142,* 677–689.

Geller, D. A,, Biederman, J., Stewart, S. E., Mullin, B., Martin, A., Spencer, T., & Faraone, S. V.

(2003). Which SSRI? A meta-analysis of pharmacotherapy trials in pediatric obsessive-compulsive disorder. *American Journal of Psychiatry, 160*(11), 1919–1928.

Gentile, D. A., Lynch, P. J., Linder, J. R., & Walsh, D. A. (2004). The effects of violent video game habits on adolescent hostility, aggressive behaviors, and school performance. *Journal of Adolescence, 27,* 5–22.

George, W. H., Stoner, S. A., Norris, J., Lopez, P. A., & Lehman, G. L. (2000). Alcohol expectancies and sexuality: A self-fulfilling prophecy analysis of dyadic perceptions and behavior. *Journal of Studies on Alcohol, 61,* 168–176.

Geracioti, T. D., Loosen, P. T., Ebert, M. H., & Schmidt, D. (1995). Fasting and postprandial cerebrospinal fluid glucose concentrations in healthy women and in an obese binge eater. *International Journal of Eating Disorders, 18,* 365–369.

Gerbner, G., Gross, L., Morgan, M., & Signiorelli, N. (1981). Health and medicine on television. *New England Journal of Medicine, 305,* 901–904.

Gergen, K. (2000). *An invitation to social constructivism.* Thousand Oaks, CA: Sage.

Gershoff, E. T. (2002a). Corporal punishment by parents and associated child behaviors and experiences: A meta-analytic and theoretical review. *Psychological Bulletin, 128,* 539–579.

Gershon, E. S., Berrettini, W. H., & Golden, L. E. (1989). Mood disorders: Genetic aspects. In H. I. Kaplan & B. J. Sadock (Eds.), *Comprehensive textbook of psychiatry/V.* Baltimore: Williams & Wilkins.

Gerwirtz, J. C., & Davis, M. (2000). Using Pavlovian higher-order conditioning paradigms to investigate the neural substrates of emotional learning and memory. *Learning & Memory, 7,* 257–266.

Ghetti, S., Qin, J., & Goodman, G. S. (2002). False memories in children and adults: Age, distinctiveness, and subjective experience. *Developmental Psychology, 38,* 705–718.

Gibbons, R. D., Hendricks Brown, C., Hur, K., Marcus, S. M., Bhaumik, D. K., Erkens, J. A., Herings, R. M. C., & Mann, J. J., (2007). Early evidence on the effects of regulators' suicidality warnings on SSRI Prescriptions and suicide in children and adolescents. *American Journal of Psychiatry, 164,* 1356–1363.

Gibson, E., & Walk, R. D. (1960). The visual cliff. *Scientific American, 202,* 80–92.

Gibson, J. J. (1979). *The ecological approach to visual perception.* Boston: Houghton Mifflin.

Gigerenzer, G. (1991). How to make cognitive illusions disappear: Beyond 'heuristics and biases'. In W. Stroebe & M. Hewstone (Eds.), *European Review of Social Psychology*, Vol. 2 . Chichester: Wiley.

Gigerenzer, G. (1996). On narrow norms and vague heuristics: A reply to Kahneman and Tversky (1996). *Psychological Review, 103,* 592–596.

Gilbert, P. (2001) Evolutionary approaches to psychopathology: the role of natural defences. *Australian and New Zealand Journal of Psychiatry, 35*(1), 17–27.

Gilligan, C. (1982). *In a different voice: Psychological theory and women's development.* Cambridge, MA: Harvard University Press.

Glanzer, M. (1972). Storage mechanisms in recall. In G. H. Bower (Ed.), *The psychology of learning and motivation: Advances in research and theory* (Vol. 5). New York: Academic Press.

Glanzer, M., & Cunitz, A. R. (1966). Two storage mechanisms in free recall. *Journal of Verbal Learning and Verbal Behavior, 5,* 351–360.

Glaser, R., & Bassock, M. (1989). Learning theory and the study of instruction. *Annual Review of Psychology, 40,* 631–666.

Glucksman, M. L. (2001). The dream: A psychodynamically informative instrument. *Journal of Psychotherapy Practice and Research, 10,* 223–230.

Gmel, G., Rehm, J., & Kuntsche, E.N. (2003). Binge drinking in Europe: Definitions, epidemiology, and consequences. *Sucht, 49,* 105–116.

Gobet, F., & Simon, H. A. (2000). Five seconds or sixty? Presentation time in expert memory. *Cognitive Science, 24,* 651–682.

Goddard, A. W., Mason, G. F., Almai, A. et al. (2001). Reductions in occipital cortex GABA levels in panic disorder detected with sup- 1H-magnetic resonance spectroscopy. *Archives of General Psychiatry, 58,* 556–561.

Godden, D. R., & Baddeley, A. D. (1975). Context-dependent memory in two natural environments: On land and under water. *British Journal of Psychology, 66,* 325–332.

Goffman, E. (1961). *Asylums: Essays on the social situation of mental patients and other inmates.* New York: Doubleday.

Goldberg, L. R. (1981). Unconfounding situational attributions from uncertain, neutral, and ambiguous ones: A psychometric analysis of descriptions of oneself and various types of others. *Journal of Personality and Social Psychology, 41,* 517–552.

Golden, C., Golden, C. J., & Schneider, B. (2003). Cell phone use and visual attention. *Perceptual and Motor Skills, 97,* 385–389.

Goldfried, M. R., & Eubanks-Carter, C. (2004). On the need for a new psychotherapy research paradigm: Comment on Westen, Novotny, & Thompson-Brenner. *Psychological Bulletin, 139,* 669–673.

Goldsmith, S. K. (2003). *Reducing suicide: A national imperative.* Washington, DC: National Academy Press.

Goldstein, B. (2002). *Sensation and perception* (6th ed.). Belmont, CA: Wadsworth.

Goldstein, E. B. (2007). *Sensation and perception* (7th ed.). Belmont, CA: *Sensation and perception.* Wadsworth.

Goldstein, G. (2000). Comprehensive neuropsychological assessment batteries. In G. Goldstein & M. Hersen (Eds.), *Handbook of psychological assessment* (3rd ed.). New York: Elsevier.

Goldstein, J. H., Cajko, L., Oosterbroek, M., Michielsen, M., Houten, O., & Salverda, F. (1997). Video games and the elderly. *Social Behavior and Personality, 25,* 345–352.

Gonzales, P. M., Blanton, H., & Williams, K. J. (2002). The effects of stereotype threat and double minority status on the test performance of Latino women. *Personality and Social Psychology Bulletin, 28,* 659–670.

Goodale, M. A. (1995). The cortical organization of visual perception and visuomotor control. In S. Kosslyn & D. N. Osheron (Eds.), *Visual cognition: An invitation to cognitive science* (2nd ed.). Cambridge, MA: MIT Press.

Goodale, M. A. (2000). Perception and action in the human visual system. In M. S. Gazzaniga (Ed.), *The new cognitive neurosciences* (2nd ed.). Cambridge, MA: MIT Press.

Goodall, J. (1986). *The chimpanzees of Gombe: Patterns of behavior.* Cambridge, MA: Harvard University Press.

Goode, W. J. (1959). The theoretical importance of love. *American Sociological Review, 24,* 38–47.

Goodman, W. (1982, August 9). Of mice, monkeys and men. *Newsweek,* 61.

Goodwin, P. J., Leszcz, M., Ennis, M. et al. (2001). The effect of group psychosocial support on survival in metastatic breast cancer. *New England Journal of Medicine, 34,* 1719–1726.

Gopnik, A., & Astington, J. W. (1988). Children's understanding of representational change and its relation to the understanding of false belief and the appearance–reality distinction. *Child Development, 59,* 26–37.

Gorman, J. M. (2002). Treatment of generalized anxiety disorder. *Journal of Clinical Psychiatry, 63*(Suppl. 8), 17–23.

Gosling, S. D., Vazire, S., Srivastava, S., & John, O. P. (2004). Should we trust web-based studies? A comparative analysis of six preconceptions about Internet questionnaires. *American Psychologist, 59,* 93–104.

Gotlib, I. H., Kasch, K. L, Traill, S., Joormann, J., Arnow, B. A., & Johnson, S. L. (2004a). Coherence and specificity of informationprocessing biases in depression and social phobia. *Journal of Abnormal Psychology, 113,* 386–398.

Gotlib, I. H., Krasnoperova, E., Yue, D. N., & Joormann, J. (2004b). Attentional biases for negative interpersonal stimuli in clinical depression. *Journal of Abnormal Psychology, 113,* 127–135.

Gottesman, I. I. (1991). *Schizophrenia genesis: The origins of madness.* New York: Freeman.

Gottfried, A. E., Fleming, J. S., & Gottfried, A. W. (1998). Role of cognitively stimulating home environment in children's academic intrinsic motivation: A longitudinal study. *Child Development, 69,* 1448–1460.

Gottman, J. M., & DeClaire, J. (2002). *The relationship cure: A five-step guide to strengthening your marriage, family, and friendships.* New York: Three Rivers Press.

Gottman, J. M., & Levenson, R. (1992). Marital processes predictive of later dissolution: Behavior, psychology and health. *Journal of Personality and Social Psychology, 63,* 221–233.

Gottman, J. M., Coan, J., Carrere, S., & Swanson, C. (1998). Predicting marital happiness and stability from newlywed interactions. *Journal of Marriage and the Family, 60,* 5–22.

Goulding, A. (2005). Participant variables associated with psi Ganzfeld results. *European Journal of Parapsychology, 20,* 50–64.

Graber, J. A., Seeley, J. R., Brooks-Gunn, J., & Lewinsohn, P. M. (2004). Is pubertal timing associated with psychopathology in young adulthood? *Journal of the American Academy of Child & Adolescent Psychiatry, 43,* 718–726.

Gracely, R. H., Farrell, M. J., & Grant, M. A. B. (2002). Temperature and pain perception. In H. Pashler & S. Yantis, (Eds.), *Steven's handbook of experimental psychology: Vol. 1. Sensation and perception* (3rd ed.). New York: Wiley.

Graham, J. R. (2006). *MMPI-2: Assessing personality and psychopathology.* New York: Oxford University Press.

Graham, S., Hudley, C., & Williams, E. (1992). Attributional and emotional determinants of aggression among African-American and Latino young adolescents. *Developmental Psychology, 28,* 731–740.

Grammer, K., Schiefenhövel, W., Schleidt, M., Lorenz, B., & Eibl-Eibesfeldt, I. (1988). Patterns on the face: The eyebrow flash in crosscultural comparison. *Ethology, 77,* 279–299.

Grant, H. M., Bredahl, L. C., Clay, J., Ferrie, J., Groves, J. E., McDorman, T. A., & Dark, V. J. (1998). Context-dependent memory for meaningful material: Information for students. *Applied Cognitive Psychology, 12,* 617–623.

Graw, P., Werth, E., Kraeuchi, K., Gutzwiller, F., Cajochen, C., & Wirz-Justice, A. (2001). Early morning melatonin administration impairs psychomotor vigilance. *Behavioural Brain Research, 121,* 167–172.

Gray, J. A. (1982). *The neuropsychology of anxiety: An enquiry into the functions of the septohippocampal system.* Oxford: Oxford University Press.

Gray, J. A. (1991). Neural systems, emotions, and personality. In J. Madden IV (Ed.), *Neurobiology of learning, emotion, and affect.* New York: Raven Press.

Gray, J. R., & Burgess, G. C. (2004). Personality differences in cognitive control? BAS, processing efficiency, and the prefrontal cortex. *Journal of Research in Personality, 38,* 35–36.

Green, A. R., Sanchez, V., O'Shea, E., Saadat, K. S., Elliott, J. M., & Colado, M. I. (2004). Effect of ambient temperature and a prior neurotoxic dose of 3,4-methylenedioxymethamphetamine (MDMA) on the hyperthermic response of rats to a single or repeated ('binge' ingestion) low dose of MDMA. *Psychopharmacology, 173,* 264–269.

Green, D. M, Swets, J. A (1974). *Signal detection theory and psychophysics.* New York: Wiley.

Green, J. T., & Woodruff-Pak, D. S. (2000). Eyeblink classical conditioning: Hippocampal formation is for neutral stimulus associations as cerebellum is for association-response. *Psychological Bulletin, 126,* 138–158.

Green, M. (1999). Diagnosis of attention-deficit/ hyperactivity disorder. *Technical Review Number 3, Publication No. 99–0050.* Rockville, MD: Agency for Health Care Policy and Research.

Green, M. F. (1997). *Schizophrenia from a neurocognitive perspective: Probing the impenetrable darkness.* Boston: Allyn & Bacon.

Greenberg, J. S. (2005). *Comprehensive stress management*. New York: McGraw-Hill.

Greenberg, J., Solomon, S., & Pyszynski, T. (1997). Terror management theory of selfesteem and cultural worldviews: Empirical assessments and conceptual refinements. In M. P. Zanna (Ed.), *Advances in experimental social psychology* (Vol. 29). San Diego, CA: Academic Press.

Greenberg, L. S., & Malcolm, W. (2002). Resolving unfinished business: Relating process to outcome. *Journal of Consulting and Clinical Psychology, 70,* 406–416.

Greenberg, L. S., & Rice, L. N. (1997). Humanistic approaches to psychotherapy. In P. L. Wachtel & S. B. Messer (Eds.), *Theories of psychotherapy: Origins and evolution.* Washington, DC: American Psychological Association.

Greene, K., Krcmar, M., Walters, L. H., Rubin, D. L. & Hale, J. L. (2000). Targeting adolescent risk-taking behaviors: The contribution of egocentrism and sensation seeking. *Journal of Adolescence, 23,* 439–461.

Greene, R. L. (1992). *Human memory: Paradigms and paradoxes.* Hillsdale, NJ: Erlbaum.

Greene, R. W., & Ollendick, T. H. (2000). Behavioral assessment of children. In G. Goldstein & M. Hersen (Eds.), *Handbook of psychological assessment* (3rd ed.). New York: Elsevier.

Greenfield, P. M. (1998). The cultural evolution of IQ. In U. Neisser (Ed.), *The rising curve: Long-term gains in IQ and related measures.* Washington, DC: American Psychological Association.

Greenleaf, E. (1973). 'Senoi' dream groups. *Psychotherapy: Theory, Research and Practice, 10,* 218–222.

Greenwald, A. G. (1992). New look 3: Unconscious cognition reclaimed. *American Psychologist, 47,* 766–779.

Greenwald, A. G., & Banaji, M. R. (1995). Implicit social cognition: Attitudes, self-esteem, and stereotypes. *Psychological Review, 102,* 4–27.

Greenwald, A. G., Banaji, M. R., Rudman, L. A., Farnham, S. D., Nosek, B. A., & Mellott, D. S. (2002). A unified theory of implicit attitudes, stereotypes, self-esteem, and self-concept. *Psychological Review, 109,* 3–25.

Greenwald, A. G., McGhee, D. E., & Schwartz, J. (1998). Measuring individual differences in implicit cognition: The implicit association test. *Journal of Personality and Social Psychology, 74,* 1464–1480.

Greenwald, A. G., Spangenberg, E. R., Pratkanis, A. R., & Eskenazi, J. (1991). Double-blind tests of subliminal self-help tapes. *Psychological Science, 2,* 119–122.

Gregory, R. J. (1998). *Foundations of intellectual assessment: The WAIS-III and other tests in clinical practice.* Boston: Allyn & Bacon.

Gregory, R. L. (1966). *Eye and brain.* New York: McGraw-Hill.

Gregory, R. L. (2005). *Illusion: The phenomenal brain.* New York: Oxford University Press.

Gregory, R. L., & Gombrich, E. H. (1973). *Illusion in nature and art.* London: Duckworth.

Grice, H. P. (1975). Logic and conversation. In P. Cole & J. L. Morgan (Eds.), *Syntax and semantics: Vol. 3. Speech acts.* New York: Seminar.

Grigorenko, E. L. (2003). Selected links between nutrition and the mind. In R. J. Sternberg, J. Lautrey, & T. I. Lubart (Eds.), *Models of intelligence: International perspectives.* Washington, DC: American Psychological Association.

Grimes, K., & Walker, E. F. (1994). Childhood emotional expressions, educational attainment, and age at onset of illness in schizophrenia. *Journal of Abnormal Psychology, 103,* 784–790.

Gross, A.M., Bennett, T., Sloan, T., Marx, B., & Juergens, J. (2001). The impact of alcohol and alcohol expectancies on male perception of female sexual arousal in a date rape analogue. *Experimental & Clinical Psychopharmacology.9*(4), 380–388.

Grossberg, S., Finkel, L., & Field, D. (Eds.). (2005). *Vision and brain: How the brain sees: New approaches to computer vision.* St. Louis: Elsevier.

Grossman, D. (1996). *On killing: The psychological cost of learning to kill in war and society.* Boston: Little, Brown.

Grossman, H., Bergmann, C., & Parker, S. (2006). Dementia: A brief review. *The Mount Sinai Journal of Medicine, 73,* 985–992.

Groth-Marnat, G. (1999). *Handbook of psychological assessment.* New York: Wiley.

Groves, P. M., & Thompson, R. F. (1970). Habituation: a dual-process theory. *Psychological Review, 77,* 419–450.

Gruest, N., Richer, P., & Hars, B. (2004). Emergence of long-term memory for conditioned aversion in the rat fetus. *Developmental Psychobiology, 44,* 189–198.

Grünbaum, A. (1986). Précis of the foundations of psychoanalysis: A philosophical critique. *Behavioral and Brain Sciences, 9,* 217–284.

Guéguen, N. (2002). Foot in the door technique and computer mediated communication. *Computers in Human Behavior, 18,* 11–15.

Guilford, J. P. (1959). Three faces of intellect. *American Psychologist, 14,* 469–479.

Guilford, J. P. (1967). *The nature of human intelligence.* New York: McGraw-Hill.

Guilleminault, C., Poyares, D., Abat, F., & Palombini, L. (2001). Sleep and wakefulness in somnambulism: A spectral analysis study. *Journal of Psychosomatic Research, 51,* 411–416.

Guinness book of records. (2000). Stamford, CT: Guinness Media.

Gulevich, G., Dement, W., & Johnson, L. (1966). Psychiatric and EEG observations on a case of prolonged (264 hours) wakefulness. *Archives of General Psychiatry, 15,* 29–35.

Gump, L. S., Baker, R. C., & Roll, S. (2000). Cultural and gender differences in moral judgment: A study of Mexican Americans and Anglo-Americans. *Hispanic Journal of Behavioral Sciences, 22,* 78–93.

Gupta, P., & Cohen, N. J. (2002). Theoretical and computational analysis of skill learning, repetition priming, and procedural memory. *Psychological Review, 109,* 401–448.

Gur, R. E., Cowell, P., Turetsky, B. I., Gallacher, F., Cannon, T., Bilker, W., & Gur, R. B. (1998). follow-up magnetic resonance imaging study of schizophrenia: Relationship of neuroanatomical changes to clinical and neurobehavioral measures. *Archives of General Psychiatry, 55,* 145–152.

Gurvitz, I. G., Koenigsberg, H. W., & Siever, L. J. (2000). Neurotransmitter dysfunction in patients with borderline personality disorder. *Psychiatric Clinics of North America, 23,* 27–40.

Gustavson, C. R., Garcia, J., Hankins, W. G., & Rusiniak, K. W. (1974). Coyote predation control by aversive conditioning. *Science, 184,* 581–583.

Guthrie, J. P., Ash, R. A., & Bendapudi, V. (1995). Additional validity evidence for a measure of morningness. *Journal of Applied Psychology, 80,* 186–190.

Guthrie, R. V. (1976). *Even the rat was white: A historical view of psychology.* New York: Harper & Row.

Haaga, D. A. F., Dyck, M. J., & Ernst, D. (1991). Empirical status of cognitive theory of depression. *Psychological Bulletin, 110,* 215–236.

Hafen, B. Q., & Hoeger, W. W. K. (1998). *Wellness: Guidelines for a healthy lifestyle.* Englewood, CO: Morton.

Haier, R. J., Siegel, B. V., Crinella, F. M., & Buchsbaum, M. S. (1993). Biological and psychometric intelligence: Testing an animal model in humans with positron emission tomography. In D. K. Detterman (Ed.), *Individual differences and cognition: Current topics in human intelligence* (Vol. 3). Norwood, NJ: Ablex.

Hailman, J. P. (1967). The ontogeny of an instinct. *Behaviour Supplements, 15,* 1–159.

Hailman, J. P. (1969). How an instinct is learned. *Scientific American, 221,* 98–106.

Haines, R. F. (1991). A breakdown in simultaneous information processing. In G. Obrecht & L. W. Stark (Eds.), *Presbyopia research.* New York: Plenum Press.

Halari, R., Hines, M., Kumari, V., Mehrotra, R., Wheeler, M., Ng, V., & Sharma, T. (2005). Sex differences and individual differences in cognitive performance and their relationship to endogenous gonadal hormones and gonadotropins. *Behavioral Neuroscience, 119,* 104–117.

Hall, C. S., & Van de Castle, R. (1966) *The content analysis of dreams.* New York: Appleton-Century-Crofts.

Hall, G. C. N., & Okazaki, S. (2003). *Asian American psychology: The science of lives in context.* Washington, DC: American Psychological Association.

Hall, G. S. (1904). *Adolescence* (Vols. 1 and 2). New York: Appleton-Century-Crofts.

Hall, W. (2006). How have the SSRI antidepressants affected suicide risk? *The Lancet, 367*(9527), 1959–1962.

Haller, M., & Hadler, M. (2006). How social relations and structures can produce happiness and unhappiness: An international comparative analysis. *Social Indicators Research, 75,* 169–216.

Halligan, P. W., Fink, G. R., Marshall, J. C., & Vallar, G. (2003). Spatial cognition: Evidence from visual neglect. *Trends in Cognitive Sciences, 7,* 125–133.

Halpern, B. (2002). Taste. In H. Pashler & S. Yantis (Eds.). *Steven's handbook of experimental psychology: Vol. 1. Sensation and perception* (3rd ed.). New York: Wiley.

Halpern, D. F. (2004). *Sex differences in cognitive abilities* (3rd ed.). Mahwah, NJ: Erlbaum.

Halpern, D. F., & Tan, U. (2001). Stereotypes and steroids: Using a psychobiosocial model to understand cognitive sex differences. *Brain and Cognition, 45,* 392–414.

Hamann S., & Mao, H. (2002). Positive and negative emotional verbal stimuli elicit activity in the left amygdala. *Neuroreport, 13*(1), 15–19.

Hamer, D. H., & Copeland, P. (1998). *Living with our genes: Why they matter more than you think.* New York: Doubleday.

Hamilton, R. J. (1985). A framework for the evaluation of the effectiveness of adjunct questions and objectives. *Review of Educational Research, 55,* 47–85.

Hamilton, W. D. (1964). The genetical theory of social behaviour, I, II. *Journal of Theoretical Biology, 12,* 12–45.

Hammen, C. (1991). *Depression runs in families: The social context of risk and resilience in children of depressed mothers.* New York: Springer-Verlag.

Haney, C., & Zimbardo, P. (1998). The past and future of U.S. prison policy: Twenty-five years after the Stanford Prison Experiment. *American Psychologist, 53,* 709–727.

Hankin, B. L., Kassel, J. D., & Abela, R. Z. (2005). Adult attachment dimensions and specificity of emotional distress symptoms: Prospective investigations of cognitive risk and interpersonal stress generation as mediating mechanisms. *Personality and Social Psychology Bulletin, 31,* 136–151.

Hanley, S. J., & Abell, S. C. (2002). Maslow and relatedness: Creating an interpersonal model of self-actualization. *Journal of Humanistic Psychology, 42,* 37–56.

Hansen, C. H., & Hansen, R. D. (1988). Finding the face in the crowd: An anger superiority effect. *Journal of Personality and Social Psychology, 54,* 917–924.

Hansen, N. B., Lambert, M. J., & Forman, E. M. (2002). The psychotherapy dose-response effect and its implications for treatment delivery services. *Clinical Psychology: Science and Practice, 9,* 329–343.

Happé, F. G. E., Winner, E., & Brownell, H. (1998). The getting of wisdom: Theory of mind in old age. *Developmental Psychology, 34,* 358–362.

Harackiewicz, J. M., Barron, K. E., Tauer, J. M., & Elliot, A. J. (2002). Predicting success in college: A longitudinal study of achievement goals and ability measures as predictors of interest and performance from freshman year through graduation. *Journal of Educational Psychology, 94,* 562–575.

Hare, R. D. (1991). *The Hare Psychopathy Checklist.* Toronto: Multi-Health Systems.

Harley, K., & Reese, E. (1999). Origins of autobiographical memory. *Developmental Psychology, 35,* 1338–1348.

Harlow, H. F. (1958). The nature of love. *The American Psychologist, 13,* 673–685.

Harlow, H. F., & Suomi, S. J. (1970). The nature of love-simplified. *American Psychologist, 25,* 161–168.

Harlow, J. M. (1868). Recovery from the passage of an iron bar through the head. *Massachusetts Medical Society, 2,* 327.

Harlow, J., & Roll, S. (1992). Frequency of day residue in dreams of young adults. *Perceptual and Motor Skills, 74,* 832–834.

Harmon-Jones, E., Brehm, J. W., Greenberg, J., Simon, L., & Nelson, D. E. (1996). Evidence that the production of aversive consequences is not necessary to create cognitive dissonance. *Journal of Personality and Social Psychology, 70,* 5–16.

Harrell, T. W., & Harrell, M. S. (1945). Army General Classification Test scores for civilian occupations. *Educational and Psychological Measurement, 5,* 229–239.

Harris, C. (2002, August 27). Amazing memory for digits still loses track of car keys. *Naples Daily News.*

Harris, J. R. (1995). Where is the child's environment? A group socialization theory of development. *Psychological Review, 102,* 458–489.

Harris, S. L. (1981). A letter from the editor on loss and trust. *Clinical Psychologist, 34*(3), 3.

Harrison, J. E., & Baron-Cohen, S. C. (1997). Synaesthesia: A review of psychological theories. In S. C. Baron et al. (Eds.), *Synaesthesia: Classic and contemporary readings.* Oxford: Blackwell.

Hart, J. W., Bridgett, D. J., & Karau, S. J. (2001). Coworker ability and effort as determinants of individual effort on a collective task. *Group Dynamics, 5,* 181–190.

Hart, J. W., Karau, S. J., Stasson, M. F., & Kerr, N. A. (2004). Achievement motivation, expected coworker performance, and collective task motivation: Working hard or hardly working ? *Journal of Applied Social Psychology, 34,* 984–1000.

Hartmann, E., Kunzendorf, R., Rosen, R., & Grace, N. G. (2001). Contextualizing images in dreams and daydreams. *Dreaming: Journal of the Association for the Study of Dreams, 11,* 97–104.

Hartshorne, H., & May, A. (1928). *Studies in the nature of character: Vol. 1. Studies in deceit.* New York: Macmillan.

Hartwell, L. H., Hood, L., Goldberg, M. L., Reynolds, A. E., Silver, L. M., & Veres, R. C. (2008). *Genetics: From genes to genomes.* (3rd ed.). New York: McGraw-Hill.

Harway, M. (2005). *Handbook of couples therapy.* New York: Wiley.

Hasher, L., & Zacks, R. T. (1979). Automatic and effortful processes in memory. *Journal of Experimental Psychology: General, 108,* 356–388.

Haskell, W. L., Alderman, E. L., Fair, J. M. et al. (1994). Effects of intensive multiple risk factor reduction on coronary atherosclerosis and clinical cardiac events in men and women with coronary artery disease. *Circulation, 89,* 975–990.

Hatfield, E. (1988). Passionate and companionate love. In R. J. Sternberg & M. L. Barnes (Eds.), *The psychology of love.* New Haven, CT: Yale University Press.

Hauri, P. (1982). *The sleep disorders* (2nd ed.). Kalamazoo, MI: Upjohn.

Hawley, P., & Little, T. D. (2002). Evolutionary and developmental perspectives on the agentic self. In D. Cervone & W. Mischel (Eds.), *Advances in personality science.* New York: Guilford Press.

Haynes, S. N. (2000). Behavioral assessment of adults. In G. Goldstein & M. Hersen (Eds.), *Handbook of psychological assessment* (3rd ed.). New York: Elsevier.

Hayslip, B., & Panek, P. E. (1989). *Adult development and aging.* New York: Harper & Row.

Hazan, C., & Diamond, L. M. (2000). The place of attachment in human mating. *Review of General Psychology, 4,* 186–204.

Health, United States 2006. (2006). Hyattsville, MD: National Center for Health Statistics.

Healthy People 2010. (2005). Retrieved April 17, 2005, from http://www.healthypeople.gov

Healy, D. (2004). *Let them eat Prozac: The unhealthy relationship between the pharmaceutical industry and depression.* New York: New York University Press.

Hearold, S. (1986). A synthesis of 1043 effects of television on social behavior. In G. Comstock (Ed.), *Public communications and behavior* (Vol. 1). New York: Academic Press.

Heath, A. C., Bucholz, K. K., Madden, P. A. F., Dinwiddie, S. H., Slutske, W. S., Bierut,

L. J., Statham, D. J., Dunne, M. P., Whitfield, J. B., & Martin, N. G. (1997). Genetic and environmental contributions to alcohol dependence risk in a national twin sample: consistency of findings in women and men. *Psychological Medicine, 27,* 1381–1396.

Heath, A. C., Kendler, K. S., Eaves, L. J., & Martin, N. G. (1990). Evidence for genetic influences on sleep disturbance and sleep pattern in twins. *Sleep, 13,* 318–335.

Heath, R. G. (1972). Pleasure and brain activity in man. *Journal of Nervous and Mental Disease, 154,* 3–18.

Heather, N. (2006). Controlled drinking, harm reduction and their roles in the response to alcohol-related problems. *Addiction Research and Theory, 14,* 7–18.

Heatherton, T. F., Macrae, C. N., & Kelley, W. M. (2004). What the social brain sciences can tell us about the self. *Current Directions in Psychological Science 13,* 190–193.

Heaton, T. B. (2002). Factors contributing to increasing marital stability in the U.S. *Journal of Family Issues, 23,* 392–409.

Hebb, D. O. (1949). *The organization of behavior.* New York: Wiley.

Heerey, E. A., Keltner, D., & Capps, L. M. (2003). Making sense of self-conscious emotion: Linking theory of mind and emotion in children with autism. *Emotion, 3,* 394–400.

Heider, F. (1958). *The psychology of interpersonal relations.* New York: Wiley.

Heimpel, S. A., Wood, J. V., Marshall, M. A., & Brown, J. D. (2002). Do people with low self-esteem really want to feel better? Self-esteem differences in motivation to repair negative moods. *Journal of Personality and Social Psychology, 82,* 128–147.

Heine, S. J., Kitayama, S., Lehman, D. R., Takata, T., Ide, E. et al. (2000). *Divergent consequences of success and failure in Japan and North America: An investigation of self-improving motivations and malleable selves.* Vancouver: University of British Columbia.

Heinrichs, R. W. (2001). *In search of madness: Schizophrenia and neuroscience.* New York: Oxford University Press.

Helgeson, V. S., Cohen, S., Schultz, R., & Yasko, J. (2000). Group support interventions for women with breast cancer: Who benefits from what? *Health Psychology, 19,* 107–114.

Heller, M. A., & Schiff, W. (Eds.). (1991). *The psychology of touch.* Hillsdale, NJ: Erlbaum.

Hellerstein, D., Yankowitch, P., Rosenthal, J. et al. (1993). Arandomized double-blind study of fluoxetine versus placebo in the treatment of dysthymia. *American Journal of Psychiatry, 150,* 1169–1175.

Helsen, W. F., Starkes, J. L., & Hodges, N. J. (1998). Team sports and the theory of deliberate practice. *Journal of Sport and Exercise Psychology, 20,* 12–34.

Helson, R., Jones, C., & Kwan, V. S. Y. (2002). Personality change over 40 years of adulthood: Hierarchical linear modeling analyses of two longitudinal samples. *Journal of Personality and Social Psychology, 83,* 752–766.

Helzer, J. E., & Hudziak, J. J. (Eds). (2002). *Defining psychopathology in the 21st century: DSM-V and beyond.* Washington, DC: American Psychiatric Publishing.

Hemsley, D. R. (1996). Schizophrenia: A cognitive model and its. implications for psychological intervention. *Behaviour. Modification, 20,* 139–169.

Hennessey, T. M., Rucker, W. B., & McDiarmid, C. G. (1979). Classical conditioning in paramecia. *Animal Learning & Behavior, 7,* 417–423

Henningsen, D. D., Henningsen, M. L. M., Eden, J., & Cruz, M. G. (2006). Examining the symptoms of groupthink and retrospective sensemaking. *Small Group Research, 37,* 36–64.

Herdt, G., & Lindenbaum, S. (Eds.). (1992). *Social analysis in the time of AIDS.* Newbury Park, CA: Sage.

Herek, G. M. (2000). The psychology of sexual prejudice. *Current Directions in Psychological Science, 9,* 19–22.

Hernandez, L. M., & Blazer, D. G. (2007). *Genes, behavior, and the social environment: Moving beyond the nature/nurture debate.* Washington, DC: National Academies Press.

Herrington, R., & Lader, M. H. (1996). *Biological treatments in psychiatry* (2nd ed.). New York: Oxford University Press.

Hersen, M. (2002). *Clinical behavior therapy: Adults and children*. New York: Wiley.

Hersen, M. (2003). *Effective brief therapies*. New York: Academic Press.

Hersen, M. (2006). *Clinician's handbook of adult behavioral assessment*. New York: Academic Press.

Herz, M., & Marder, S. (2002). *Schizophrenia: A comprehensive text*. New York: Williams & Wilkins.

Herzog, H. A. (2005). Dealing with the animal research controversy. In C. K. Akins, S. Panicker, & C. L. Cunningham (Eds.), *Laboratory animals in research and teaching: Ethics, care, and methods*. Washington, DC: American Psychological Association.

Hess, E. H. (1959). Imprinting. *Science, 130,* 133–141.

Hess, W. R. (1965). Sleep as phenomenon of the integral organism. In K. Akert, C. Bally, & J. P. Schade (Eds.), *Sleep mechanisms*. New York: Elsevier.

Hetherington, E. M. (1998). Relevant issues in developmental science: Introduction to the special issue. *American Psychologist, 53,* 93–94.

Hetherington, E. M., & Stanley-Hagan, M. (2002). Parenting in divorced and remarried families. In M. H. Bornstein (Ed.), *Handbook of parenting: Being and becoming a parent* (2nd ed., Vol. 3). Mahwah, NJ: Erlbaum.

Hetherington, E. M., Bridges, M., & Insabella, G. M. (1998). What matters? What does not? Five perspectives on the association between marital transitions and children's adjustment. *American Psychologist, 53,* 167–184.

Hewstone, M. (1990). The 'ultimate attribution error'? A review of the literature on intergroup causal attribution. *European Journal of Social Psychology, 20,* 311–335.

Hewstone, M., Rubin, M., & Willis, H. (2002). Intergroup bias. *Annual Review of Psychology, 53,* 575–604.

Heylighen, F. (1992). A cognitive-systemic reconstruction of Maslow's theory of selfactualization. *Behavioral Science, 37,* 39–58.

Hibell, B., Andersson, B., Bjarnason, T., Ahlström, S., Balakireva, O., Kokkevi, A., & Morgan, M. (2004). *The ESPAD report 2003: alcohol and other drug use among students in 35 European countries*. Stockholm: Swedish Council for Information on Alcohol and Other Drugs.

Higgins, E. T. (1987). Self-discrepancy: A theory relating self and affect. *Psychological Review, 94,* 319–340.

Higgins, E. T. (1996). The 'self digest': Selfknowledge serving self-regulatory functions. *Journal of Personality and Social Psychology, 71,* 1062–1083.

Higgins, E. T. (1997). Beyond pleasure and pain. *American Psychologist, 52,* 1280–1300.

Higher Education Statistics Agency (HESA) (2003). *Standard Occupational Classfication (SOC) psychology graduates*. www.HESA.ac.uk

Hilgard, E. R. (1977). *Divided consciousness: Multiple controls in human thought and action*. New York: Wiley.

Hilgard, E. R. (1991). A neodissociation interpretation of hypnosis. In S. J. Lynn & J. W. Rhue (Eds.), *Theories of hypnosis: Current models and perspectives*. New York: Guilford Press.

Hill, C. A. (1987). Affiliation motivation: People who need people but in different ways. *Journal of Personality and Social Psychology, 52,* 1008–1018.

Hill, J. L., Brooks-Gunn, J., & Waldfogel, J. (2003). Sustained effects of high participation in an early intervention for low-birth-weight premature infants. *Developmental Psychology, 2003,* 730–744.

Hill, M. M., Dodson, B. B., Hill, E. W., & Fox, J. (1995). An infant sonicguide intervention program for a child with a visual disability. *Journal of Visual Impairment and Blindness, 89,* 329–336.

Hill, W. F. (1963). *Learning: A survey of psychological interpretations*. San Francisco: Chandler.

Hillman, D. C., Siffre, M., Milano, G., & Halberg, F. (1994). Free-running psycho-physiologic circadians and three-month pattern in a woman isolated in a cave. *New Trends in Experimental and Clinical Psychiatry, 10,* 127–133.

Hines, M. (2005). *Brain gender*. New York: Oxford University Press.

Hirtz, D., Thurman, D. J., Gwinn-Hardy, K., Mohamed, M., Chaudhuri, A. R., & Zalutsky, R. (2007). How common are the 'common' neurologic disorders? *Neurology, 68*, 326–337.

Hobson, J. A., Pace-Schott, E. F., & Stickgold, R. (2000). Dreaming and the brain: Toward a cognitive neuroscience of conscious states. *Behavioral and Brain Sciences, 23*, 793–842.

Hockett, C. F. (1960). The origin of speech. *Scientific American, 203*, 89–96.

Hodges, J., & Tizard, B. (1989). Social and family relationships of ex-institutional adolescents. *Journal of Child Psychology and Psychiatry, 30*, 77–97.

Hoffart, A., & Martinson, E. W. (1991). Mental health locus of control in agoraphobia and depression: A longitudinal study of inpatients. *Psychological Reports, 68*, 1011–1018.

Hoffer, A., & Youngren, V. R. (2004). Is free association still at the core of psychoanalysis? *International Journal of Psychoanalysis, 85*, 1489–1492.

Hoffman, H. G., Patterson, D. R., Canougher, G. J., & Sharar, S. R. (2001). Effectiveness of virtual reality-based pain control with multiple treatments. *Clinical Journal of Pain, 17*, 229–235.

Hofmann, S. G., Moscovitch, D. A., & Heinrichs, N. (2004). Evolutionary mechanisms of fear and anxiety. In P. Gilbert (Ed.), *Evolutionary theory and cognitive therapy* (pp. 119–136). New York: Springer.

Hofstede, G. (1980). *Culture's consequences: International differences in work-related values*. Beverly Hills, CA: Sage.

Hofstede, G. (1991). Empirical models of cultural differences. In N. Bleichrodt & P. J. D. Drenth (Eds.), *Contemporary issues in cross-cultural psychology* (pp. 4–20). Lisse: Swets & Zeitlinger.

Hogan, R. (1983). A socioanalytic theory of personality. In M. Page & R. Dienstbier (Eds.), *Nebraska Symposium on Motivation, 1982*. Lincoln: University of Nebraska Press.

Hogg, M. A., & Abrams, D. (1993). Towards a single-process uncertainty-reduction model of social motivation in groups. In D. Abrams & M. A. Hogg (Eds.), *Group motivation: Social psychological perspectives* (pp. 173–190). Hemel Hempstead: Harvester Wheatsheaf.

Hogue, M. E., Beaugrand, J. P., & Lauguee, P. C. (1996). Coherent use of information by hens observing their former dominant defeating or being defeated by a stranger. *Behavioural Processes, 38*, 241–252.

Holahan, C. J., & Moos, R. H. (1986). Personality, coping, and family resources in stress resistance: A longitudinal analysis. *Journal of Personality and Social Psychology, 51*, 389–395.

Holahan, C. J., & Moos, R. H. (1990). Life stressors, resistance factors, and improved psychological functioning: An extension of the stress resistance paradigm. *Journal of Personality and Social Psychology, 58*, 909–917.

Holden, G. W. (2002). Perspectives on the effects of corporal punishment: Comment on Gershoff (2002). *Psychological Bulletin, 128*, 590–595.

Holland, K. D., & Holahan, C. K. (2003). The relation of social support and coping to positive adaptation to breast cancer. *Psychology & Health, 18*, 15–29.

Hollon, S. D. (1996). The efficacy and effectiveness of psychotherapy relative to medications. *American Psychologist, 51*, 1025–1030.

Holloway, J. D. (2003). Snapshot from the therapy room: In session strategies are not limited by overall theoretical orientation, finds Practice- Net survey. *APA Monitor, 34*(11), 23.

Holmes, D. S. (1990). The evidence for repression: An examination of sixty years of research. In J. L. Singer (Ed.), *Repression and dissociation*. Chicago: University of Chicago Press.

Holmes, T. H., & Rahe, R. H. (1967). The Social Readjustment Rating Scale. *Journal of Psychosomatic Research, 11*, 213–218.

Honts, C. R., & Perry, M. V. (1992). Polygraph admissibility: Changes and challenges. *Law and Human Behavior, 16*, 357–379.

Hood, B. (2004). Is looking good enough or does it beggar belief? *Developmental Science, 7*, 415– 417.

Hooley, J. M. (2004). Do psychiatric patients do better clinically if they live with certain kinds of families? *Current Directions in Psychological Science, 13*(5), 202–205.

Hooper, J., & Teresi, M. (1986). *The three-pound universe.* New York: Macmillan.

Horn, J. (1985). Remodeling old models of intelligence. In B. B. Wolman (Ed.), *Handbook of intelligence: Theory, measurement, and application.* New York: Wiley.

Horn, J. L., & Cattell, R. C. (1966). Refinement and test of the theory of fluid and crystallized general intelligences. *Journal of Educational Psychology, 57,* 253–270.

Horn, J. L., & Masunaga, H. (2000). On the emergence of wisdom: Expertise development. *Understanding wisdom: Sources, science, & society.* Philadelphia: Templeton Foundation Press.

Horn, J. L., & Noll, J. (1997). Human cognitive capabilities: Gf-Gc theory. In D. P. Flanagan, J. L. Genshaft, & P. L. Harrison (Eds.), *Contemporary intellectual assessment: Theories, tests, and issues.* New York: Guilford Press.

Hornstein, S. L., Brown, A. S., & Mulligan, N. W. (2003). Long-term flashbulb memory for learning of Princess Diana's death. *Memory, 11*(3), 293–306.

Houpt, T. A., Boulos, Z., Moore, E., & Martin, C. (1996). MidnightSun: Software for determining light exposure and phaseshifting schedules during global travel. *Physiology and Behavior, 59,* 561–568.

House, J. S., Landis, K. R., & Umberson, D. (1988). Social relationships and health. *Science, 241,* 540–545.

Hovland, C. I., Janis, I., & Kelley, H. H. (1953). *Communication and persuasion.* New Haven, CT: Yale University Press.

Howard, I. P. (2002). Depth perception. In H. Pashler & S. Yantis (Eds.), *Steven's handbook of experimental psychology: Vol. 1. Sensation and perception* (3rd ed.). New York: Wiley.

Howard, K. I., Kopta, S. M., Krause, M. S., & Orlinsky, D. E. (1986). The dose-effect relationship in psychotherapy. *American Psychologist, 41,* 159–164.

Howard, K. I., Lueger, R. J., Maling, M. S., & Martinovich, Z. (1993). A phase model of psychotherapy outcome: Causal mediation of change. *Journal of Consulting and Clinical Psychology, 61,* 678–685.

Hubbard, K., O'Neill, A. M., & Cheakalos, C. (1999, April 12). Out of control. *People, 52*–72.

Hubel, D. H., & Wiesel, T. N. (1979). Brain mechanisms of vision. *Scientific American, 241,* 150–162.

Hubel, D. H., & Wiesel, T. N. (2005). *Brain and visual perception: The story of a 25-year collaboration.* New York: Oxford University Press.

Hublin, C., Kaprio, J., Partinen, M., & Koskenvuo, M. (2001). Parasomnias: co-occurrence and genetics. *Psychiatric Genetics, 11,* 65–70.

Hublin, C., Kaprio, J., Partinen, M., Heikkila, K., & Koskenvuo, M. (1997). Prevalence and genetics of sleepwalking: A population based twin study. *Neurology, 48,* 177–181.

Huddy, L., & Virtanen, S. (1995). Subgroup differentiation and subgroup bias among Latinos as a function of familiarity and positive distinctiveness. *Journal of Personality and Social Psychology, 68,* 97–108.

Hudson, W. (1960). Pictorial depth perception in sub-cultural groups in Africa. *Journal of Social Psychology, 52,* 183–208.

Huesmann, L. R. (1997). Observational learning of violent behavior: Social and biosocial processes. In A. Raine, P. A. Brennan, D. P. Farrington, & S. A. Mednick (Eds.), *Biosocial bases of violence.* New York: Plenum Press.

Huesmann, L. R., Moise-Titus, J., Podolski, C. L., & Eron, L. D. (2003). Longitudinal relations between children's exposure to TV violence and their aggressive and violent behavior in young adulthood: 1977–1992. *Developmental Psychology, 39,* 201–221.

Huettel, S. A., Song, A. W., & McCarthy, G. (2005). *Functional magnetic resonance imaging.* New York: Sinauer.

Huff, R. M., & Kline, M. V. (Eds.) (1999). *Promoting health in multicultural populations: A handbook for practitioners.* Thousand Oaks, CA: Sage.

Hugdahl, K., & Davidson, R. A. (Eds.) (2005). *The asymmetrical brain*. Boston: MIT Press.

Hugenberg, K., & Bodenhausen, G. V. (2003). Facing prejudice: Implicit prejudice and the perception of facial threat. *Psychological Science, 14,* 640–643.

Hull, C. L. (1943). *Principles of behavior: An introduction to behavior theory.* New York: Appleton-Century.

Human Genome Project. (2007). Retrieved May 16, 2007, from http://www.genome.gov/

Humphreys, G. W., & Riddoch, M. J. (1987). *To see but not to see: A case of visual agnosia.* Hove: Erlbaum.

Hunt, E. (1997). The status of the concept of intelligence. *Japanese Psychological Research, 39,* 1–11.

Hunter, J. E., & Hunter, R. F. (1984). Validity and utility of alternative predictors of job performance. *Psychological Bulletin, 96,* 72–98.

Huon, G. F., Mingyi, Q., Oliver, K., & Xiao, G. (2002). A large-scale survey of eating disorder symptomatology among female adolescents in the people's Republic of China. *International Journal of Eating Disorders, 32,* 192–205.

Huttenlocher, P. R. (1979). Synaptic density in human frontal cortex: Developmental changes and effects of aging. *Brain Research, 163,* 195–205.

Huttenlocher, P. R. (2002). *Neural plasticity.* Cambridge, MA: Harvard University Press.

Huurre, T., Junkkari, H., & Aro, H. (2006). Longterm psychosocial effects of parental divorce: A follow-up study from adolescence to adulthood. *European Archives of Psychiatry and Clinical Neuroscience, 256,* 256–263.

Hyde, J. S., & DeLamater, J. (2003). *Understanding human sexuality* (8th ed.). Boston: McGraw-Hill.

Hyde, M., Ferrie, J., Higgs, P., Mein, G., & Nazroo, J. (2004). The effects of pre-retirement factors and retirement route on circumstances in retirement: Findings from the Whitehall II study. *Ageing & Society, 24,* 279–296.

Hyman, R. (1994). Anomaly or artifact? Comments on Bem and Honorton. *Psychological Bulletin, 115,* 19–24.

Ikemi, Y., & Nakagawa, A. (1962). A psychosomatic study of contagious dermatitis. *Kyushu Journal of Medical Science, 13,* 335–350.

Ingelhart, R., & Rabier, J. R. (1986). Aspirations adapt to situations—but why are the Belgians so much happier than the French? A cross-cultural study of the quality of life. In F. M. Andrews (Ed.), *Research on the quality of life.* Ann Arbor, MI: Institute for Social Research, University of Michigan.

Ingold, C. H. (1989). Locus of control and use of public information. *Psychological Reports, 64,* 603–607.

Ingram, R. E., & Price, J. M. (2001). *Vulnerability to psychopathology: Risk across the lifespan.* New York: Guilford Press.

Inhelder, B., & Piaget, J. (1958). *The growth of logical thinking from childhood to adolescence.* New York: Basic Books.

International Union of Psychological Sciences (IUPsyS). (2005). Members in IUPsyS. Retrieved March 13, 2005, from http://www.am.org/iupsys/ members.html

Intraub, H. (2002). Anticipatory spatial representation of natural scenes: Momentum without movement? *Visual Cognition, 9*(1–2), 93–119.

Intraub, H., Gottesman, C. V., Willey, E. V., & Zuk, I. J. (1996). Boundary extension for briefly glimpsed photographs: Do common perceptual processes result in unexpected memory distortions? *Journal of Memory and Language, 35,* 118–134.

Irie, M., Maeda, M., & Nagata, S. (2001). Can conditioned histamine release occur under urethane anesthesia in guinea pigs? *Physiology and Behavior, 72,* 567–573.

Irwin, A. R., & Gross, A. M. (1995). Cognitive tempo, violent video games, and aggressive behavior in young boys. *Journal of Family Violence, 10,* 337–350.

Irwin, J. R., & McCarthy, D. (1998). Psychophysics: Methods and analyses of signal detection.

In K. A. Lattal & M. Perone (Eds.), *Handbook of research methods in human operant behavior: Applied clinical psychology.* New York: Plenum Press.

Irwin, M., Daniels, M., & Weiner, H. (1987). Immune and neuroendocrine changes during bereavement. *Psychiatric Clinics of North America, 10,* 449–465.

Isaacs, K. S. (1998). *Uses of emotion: Nature's vital gift.* New York: Praeger.

Isaacson, R. L. (2002). Unsolved mysteries: The hippocampus. *Behavioral and Cognitive Neuroscience Reviews, 1,* 87–107.

Ishikawa, S. L., Raine, A., Lencz, T., Bihrle, S., & Lacasse, L. (2001). Autonomic stress reactivity and executive functions in successful and unsuccessful criminal psychopaths from the community. *Journal of Abnormal Psychology, 110,* 423–432.

Ishti, H., Jiro. G., Kamachi, M., Mukaida, S., & Akamatsu, S. (2004). Analyses of facial attractiveness on feminised and juvenilised faces. *Perception,33*(2), 135–145.

Itard, J. M. G. (1962). *The wild boy of Aveyron* (G. Humphrey & M. Humphrey, Trans.). New York: Appleton-Century-Crofts. (Original work published 1894)

Ito, K., Momose, T., Oku, S., Ishimoto, S.-I., Yamasoba, T., Sugasawa, M., & Kaga, K. (2004). Cortical activation shortly after cochlear implantation. *Audiology & Neurotology, 9,* 282–293.

Ito, T. A., & Cacioppo, J. T. (2000). Electrophysiological evidence of implicit and explicit categorization processes. *Journal of Experimental Social Psychology, 36,* 660–676.

Itti, L., & Rees, G. (2005). *Neurobiology of attention.* St. Louis: Elsevier.

Iwasa, N. (2001). Moral reasoning among adults: Japan U.S. comparison. In H. Shimizu & R. A. LeVine (Eds.), *Japanese frames of mind: Cultural perspectives on human development.* New York: Cambridge University Press.

Iwawaki, S., & Sarmany-Schuller, I. (2001). Cross-cultural (Japan-Slovakia) comparison of some aspects of sleeping patterns and anxiety. *Studia Psychologica, 43,* 215–224.

Izard, C. (Ed.). (1982). *Measuring emotions in infants and children.* Cambridge: Cambridge University Press.

Izard, C. E. (1989). The structure and functions of emotions: Implications for cognition, motivation, and personality. In I. S. Cohen (Ed.), *The G. Stanley Hall Lecture Series* (Vol. 9). Washington, DC: American Psychological Association.

Izard, C. E., Hembree, E. A., & Huebner, R. R. (1987). Infants' emotion expressions to acute pain: Developmental change and stability of individual differences. *Developmental Psychology, 23,* 105–113.

Jablensky, A., Sartorius, N., Enberg, C., Anker, M., Korten, A. et al. (1992). Schizophrenia: Manifestation, incidence, and course in different cultures: A World Health Organization ten country study. *Psychological Medicine Monograph Supplement 20.* Cambridge: Cambridge University Press.

Jackson, A., Morrow, J., Hill, D., & Dishman, R. (1999). *Physical activity for health and fitness.* Champaign, IL: Human Kinetics.

Jackson, N., & Butterfield, E. (1986). A conception of giftedness designed to promote research. In R. J. Sternberg & J. E. Davidson (Eds.), *Conceptions of giftedness.* New York: Cambridge University Press.

Jacobs, B. L (2004). Depression: The brain finally gets into the act. *Current Directions in Psychological Science, 13,* 103–106.

Jacobson, N. S., & Christensen, A. (1996). *Integrative couple therapy: Promoting acceptance and change.* New York: Norton.

Jacobson, N. S., Christensen, A., Prince, S. E., Cordova, J., & Eldridge, K. (2000). Integrative couple behavior therapy: An acceptance-based, promising new treatment for couple discord. *Journal of Consulting and Clinical Psychology, 68,* 351–355.

Jacobson, N. S., Martell, C. R., & Dimidjian, S. (2001). Behavioral activation therapy for depression: Returning to contextual roots. *Clinical Psychology: Science and Practice, 8,* 255–270.

Jaffee, S. R., Moffitt, T. E., Caspi, A., & Taylor, A. (2003). Life with (or without) father: The benefits of living with two biological parents depend on the father's antisocial behavior. *Child Development, 74,* 109–126.

James, W. (1879). Are we automata? *Mind, 4,* 1–22.

James, W. (1950). *Principles of psychology* (Vol. 2). New York: Dover. (Original work published 1890)

Jamison, K. (1995, February). Manic-depressive illness and creativity. *Scientific American,* 63–67.

Jané-Llopis, E., & Anderson, P. (Eds.). (2006). *Mental Health Promotion and Mental Disorder Prevention Across European Member States: A Collection of Country Stories.* Luxembourg: European Commission.

Jang, C.-G., Lee, S.-Y., Yoo, J.-H., Yan, J.-J., Song, D.-K., Loh, H. H., & Ho, I. K. (2003). Impaired water maze learning performance in mu-opioid receptor knockout mice. *Molecular Brain Research, 117,* 68–72.

Jang, K. (2005). *The behavioral genetics of psychopathology: A clinical guide.* Hillsdale, NJ: Erlbaum.

Janis, I. L. (1982). *Groupthink: Psychological studies of policy decisions and fiascos* (2nd ed.). Boston: Houghton Mifflin.

Jansma, J. M., Ramsey, N. F., Slagter, H. A., & Kahn, R. S. (2001). Functional anatomical correlates of controlled and automatic processing. *Journal of Cognitive Neuroscience, 13,* 730–743.

Janus, S. S., & Janus, C. L. (1993). *The Janus report on sexual behavior.* New York: Wiley.

Jemmott, J. B., Jemmott, L. S., & Fong, G. T. (1998). Abstinence and safer sex HIV risk reduction interventions for African American adolescents. *Journal of the American Medical Association, 279,* 1529–1536.

Jenkin, M., & Harris., L. (2005). *Seeing spatial form.* New York: Oxford University Press.

Jenkins, J., Simpson, A., Dunn, J., Rasbash, J., & O'Connor, T. G. (2005). Mutual influence of marital conflict and children's behavior problems: Shared and nonshared family risks. *Child Development, 76,* 24–39.

Jennings, B. M. (1990). Stress, locus of control, social support, and psychological symptoms among head nurses. *Research in Nursing & Health, 13,* 393–401.

Jensen, A. R. (1998). The g factor and the design of education. In R. J. Sternberg & W. M. Williams (Eds.), *Intelligence, instruction, and assessment: Theory into practice.* Mahwah, NJ: Erlbaum.

Jensen, J. P., Bergin, A. E., & Greaves, D. W. (1990). The meaning of eclecticism: New survey and analysis of components. *Professional Psychology: Research and Practice, 21,* 124–130.

Jensen, L. A., Arnett, J. J., Feldman, S. S., & Cauffman, E. (2004). The right to do wrong: Lying to parents among adolescents and emerging adults. *Journal of Youth and Adolescence, 33,* 101–112.

Jensen, M. P., Turner, J. A., & Romano, J. M. (2001). Changes in beliefs, catastrophizing, and coping are associated with improvement in multidisciplinary pain treatment. *Journal of Consulting and Clinical Psychology, 69,* 655–662.

Jéquier, E. (2002). Pathways to obesity. *International Journal of Obesity and Related Metabolic Disorders, 26,* 12–17.

Jetten, J., Spears, R., & Manstead, A. S. R. (1997). Strength of identification and differentiation: The influence of group norms. *European Journal of Social Psychology, 27,* 603-609.

Jimenez, L., & Mendez, C. (2001). Implicit sequence learning with competing explicit cues. *Quarterly Journal of Experimental Psychology: Comparative and Physiological Psychology, 54,* 345–369.

Job, D. E., Whalley, H. C., McIntosh, A. M., Owens, D. G. C., Johnstone, E. C., & Lawrie, S. M. (2006). Grey matter changes can improve the prediction of schizophrenia in subjects at high risk. *BMC Medicine, 4,* 29.

Johannesen-Schmidt, M. C., & Eagly, A. H. (2002). Another look at sex differences in preferred mate characteristics: The effects of endorsing the traditional female gender role. *Psychology of Women Quarterly, 26*, 322–328.

John, O. P., & Srivastava, S. (1999). The Big Five trait taxonomy: History, measurement, and theoretical perspectives. In L. A. Pervin & O. P. John (Eds.), *Handbook of personality: Theory and research.* New York: Guilford Press.

Johns, M., Schmader, T., & Martens, A. (2005). Knowing is half the battle: Teaching stereotype threat as a means of improving women's math performance. *Psychological Science, 16*, 175–179.

Johnson, A. M., Wadsworth, J., Wellings, K., & Bradshaw, S. (1992). Sexual lifestyles and HIV risk. *Nature, 360*, 410–412.

Johnson, D. W. (2000). Cooperative learning processes reduce prejudice. In S. Oskamp (Ed.), *Reducing prejudice and discrimination.* Mahwah, NJ: Erlbaum.

Johnson, J. G., Cohen, P., Smailes, E. M., Kasen, S., & Brook, J. S. (2002). Television viewing and aggressive behavior during adolescence and adulthood. *Science, 295*, 2468–2471.

Johnson, J. L., & Newport, E. L. (1989). Critical period effects in second language learning: The influence of maturational state on the acquisition of English as a second language. *Cognitive Psychology, 21,* 60–99.

Johnson, M. H., Dziurawiec, S., Ellis, H., & Morton, J. (1991). Newborns' preferential tracking of face-like stimuli and its subsequent decline. *Cognition, 40*, 1–19.

Johnston, M. S., Kelley, C. S., Harris, F. F., & Wolf, M. M. (1966). An application of reinforcement principles to development of motor skills of a young child. *Child Development, 37*, 379–387.

Johnston, V. S., Hagel, R., Franklin, M., Fink, B., & Grammer, K. (2001). Male facial attractiveness: Evidence for hormone-mediated adaptive design. *Evolution and Human Behavior, 22*, 251–267.

Joiner, T. E., & Coyne, J. C. (Eds.). (1999). *The interactional nature of depression: Advances in interpersonal approaches.* Washington, DC: American Psychological Association.

Jones, B. C., Little, A. C., Feinberg, D. R., Penton- Voak, I. S., Tiddeman, B. P., & Perrett, D. I. (2004). The relationship between shape symmetry and perceived skin condition in male facial attractiveness. *Evolution and Human Behavior, 25*, 24–30.

Jones, E. E., & Harris, V. A. (1967). The attribution of attitudes. *Journal of Experimental Social Psychology, 3*, 2–24.

Jones, E. G. (2006). *The thalamus.* New York: Cambridge University Press.

Jones, E., Cumming, J. D., & Horowitz, M. J. (1988). Another look at the nonspecific hypothesis of therapeutic effectiveness. *Journal of Consulting and Clinical Psychology, 56*, 48–55.

Jones, J. T., Pelham, B. W., Carvallo, M., & Mirenberg, M. C. (2004). How do I love thee? Let me count the Js: Implicit egotism and interpersonal attraction. *Journal of Personality and Social Psychology, 87*, 665–683.

Jones, M. C. (1924). A laboratory study of fear: The case of Peter. *Pedagogical Seminary, 31*, 308–315.

Joseph, R. (2000). The evolution of sex differences in language, sexuality, and visualspatial skills. *Archives of Sexual Behavior, 29*, 35–66.

Josephs, R. A., Bosson, J. K., & Jacobs, C. G. (2003). Self-esteem maintenance processes: Why self-esteem may be resistant to change. *Personality and Social Psychology Bulletin, 29*, 920–933.

Julien, R. M. (2005). *A primer of drug action: A comprehensive guide to the actions, uses, and side effects of psychoactive drugs* (10th ed.). New York: Worth.

Jung, J. (1995). Ethnic group and gender differences in the relationship between personality and coping. *Anxiety, Stress & Coping: An International Journal, 8*, 113–126.

Jureidini, J. N., Doecke, C. J., Mansfield, P. R., Haby, M. M., Menkes, D. B., & Tonkin,

A. L. (2004). Efficacy and safety of antidepressants for children and adolescents. *British Medical Journal, 328*(7444), 879–883.

Jurist, E. L., Slade, A., & Bergner, S. (2008). *Reflecting on the future of psychoanalysis: Mentalization, internalization, and representation.* New York: Other Press.

Kabot, S., Masi, W., & Segal, M. (2003). Advances in the diagnosis and treatment of autism spectrum disorders. *Professional Psychology: Research and Practice, 34,* 26–33.

Kadri, N., Agoub, M., El Gnaoui, S., Berrada, S., & Moussaoui, D. (2007). Prevalence of anxiety disorders: a population-based epidemiological study in metropolitan area of Casablanca, Morocco. *Annals of General Psychiatry, 6,* 6.

Kagan, J. (1989). Temperamental contributions to social behavior. *American Psychologist, 44,* 668–674.

Kagan, J. (1999). The concept of behavioral inhibition. In L. A. Schmidt & J. Schulkin (Eds.), *Extreme fear, shyness, and social phobia: Origins, biological mechanisms, and clinical outcomes.* New York: Oxford University Press.

Kagan, J., & Fox, N. A. (2006). Biology, culture, and individual differences. In N. Eisenberg, Nancy W. Damon, & R. M. Lerner (Eds.). *Handbook of child psychology: Vol. 3, Social, emotional, and personality development* (6th ed.). Hoboken, NJ: Wiley.

Kagan, J., Kearsley, R. B., & Zelazo, P. (1978). *Infancy: Its place in human development.* Cambridge, MA: Harvard University Press.

Kagan, J., Reznick, S., & Snidman, N. (1988). Biological bases of childhood shyness. *Science, 240,* 167–171.

Kagitçibasi, C. (1997). Individualism and collectivism. In J. W. Berry, M. H. Segall, & C. Kagitçibasi (Eds.), *Handbook of cross-cultural psychology* (Vol. 3). Boston: Allyn & Bacon.

Kahneman, D., & Tversky, A. (1979). Prospect theory: An analysis of decisions under risk. *Econometrica, 47,* 263–291.

Kahneman, D., & Tversky, A. (1982). On the study of statistical intuitions. *Cognition, 11,* 123–141.

Kahneman, D., & Tversky, A. (1996). On the reality of cognitive illusions : A reply to Gigerenzer's critique. *Psychological Review, 103,* 582–591.

Kaia, L., Pullmann, H., & Allik, J. (2007). Personality and intelligence as predictors of academic achievement: A cross-sectional study from elementary to secondary school. *Personality and Individual Differences, 42,* 444–451.

Kail, R. (1991). Developmental change in speed of processing during childhood and adolescence. *Psychological Bulletin, 109,* 490–501.

Kaku, M. (2004). *Einstein's cosmos: How Albert Einstein's vision transformed our understanding of space and time.* New York: Norton.

Kaltiala-Heino, R., Marttunen, M., Rantanen, P., & Rimpela, M. (2003). Early puberty is associated with mental health problems in middle adolescence. *Social Science & Medicine, 57,* 1055–1064.

Kamin, L. J. (1968). 'Attention-like' processes in classical conditioning. In M.R. Jones (Ed.), *Miami symposium on the prediction of behavior: Aversive stimulation.* Miami: University of Miami Press.

Kamin, L. J. (1969). Predictability, surprise, attention, and conditioning. In B.A. Campbell, & R. M. Church (Eds.), *Punishment and aversive behavior.* New York: Appleton-Century-Crofts.

Kampmann, K. M., Volpicelli, J. R., Mulvaney, F., Rukstalis, M., Alterman, A. I., Pettinati, H. et al. (2002). Cocaine withdrawal severity and urine toxicology results from treatment entry predict outcome in medication trials for cocaine dependence. *Addictive Behaviors, 27,* 251–260.

Kandel, E. R. (2001). The molecular biology of memory storage: A dialogue between genes and synapses. *Science, 294,* 1030–1038.

Kandel, E. R. (2004). Nobel Lecture: The molecular biology of memory storage: A dialogue between genes and synapses. *Bioscience Reports, 24,* 477–522.

Kane, J. M. (Ed.). (1992). *Tardive dyskinesia: A task force report of the American Psychiatric Association.* Washington, DC: American Psychiatric Press.

Kaner, A. (1995). Physical attractiveness and women's lives: Findings from a longitudinal study. *Dissertation Abstracts International: Section B. The Sciences and Engineering, 56,* 2942.

Kanfer, F. H., & Goldstein, A. P. (Eds.). (1991). *Helping people change: A textbook of methods* (4th ed.). New York: Pergamon Press.

Kanner, L. (1943) Autistic disturbance of affective contact. *Nervous Child, 12,* 17–50.

Kanwisher, N. (1998). The modular structure of human visual recognition: Evidence from functional imaging. In M. Sabourin et al. (Eds.), *Advances in psychological science: Vol. 2. Biological and cognitive aspects.* Hove: Psychology Press/Erlbaum.

Kaplan, H., & Dove, H. (1987). Infant development among the Ache of eastern Paraguay. *Developmental Psychology, 23,* 190–198.

Kaprio, J., Koskenvu, M., & Rita, H. (1987). Mortality after bereavement: A prospective study of 95,647 widowed persons. *American Journal of Public Health, 77,* 283–287.

Karau, S. J., & Williams, K. D. (1993). Social loafing: A meta-analytic review and theoretical integration. *Journal of Personality and Social Psychology, 65,* 681–706.

Karau, S. J., & Williams, K. D. (2001). Understanding individual motivation in groups: The collective effort model. In M. E. Turner (Ed.), *Groups at work: Theory and research: Applied social research.* Mahwah, NJ: Erlbaum.

Karmiloff-Smith, A. (1992). Beyond modularity: A developmental perspective on cognitive science. Cambridge, MA: MIT Press.

Karon, B. P. (2002). Psychoanalysis: Legitimate and illegitimate concerns. *Psychoanalytic Psychology 19,* 564–571.

Kashima, Y., Yamaguchi, S., Kim, U., Choi, S., Gelfand, M., & Yuki, M. (1995). Culture, gender, and self: A perspective from individualism-collectivism research. *Journal of Personality and Social Psychology, 69,* 925–937.

Kastenbaum, R. (2000). *The psychology of death* (3rd ed.). New York: Springer.

Katapodi, M. C., Facione, N. C., Humphreys, J. C., & Dodd, M. J. (2005). Perceived breast cancer risk: Heuristic reasoning and search for a dominance structure. *Social Science & Medicine, 60,* 421–432.

Katz, J., & Melzack, R. (1990). Pain 'memories' in phantom limbs: Review and clinical observations. *Pain, 43,* 319–336.

Kaufman, A. S., & Kaufman, N. (1997). The Kaufman Adolescent and Adult Intelligence Test. In D. P. Flanagan, J. L. Genshaft, & P. L. Harrison (Eds.), *Contemporary intellectual assessment: Theories, tests, and issues.* New York: Guilford Press.

Kaufmann, G. M., & Beehr, T. A. (1986). Interactions between job stressors and social support: Some counterintuitive results. *Journal of Applied Psychology, 71,* 522–526.

Kavanagh, D. (1992). Schizophrenia. In P. H. Wilson (Ed.), *Principles and practice of relapse prevention.* New York: Guilford Press.

Kay, L. (1982). *Spatial perception through an acoustic sensor.* Christchurch, New Zealand: University of Canterbury Press.

Kaye, W. H., Strober, M., & Klump, K. L. (2002). Serotonin neuronal function in anorexia nervosa and bulimia nervosa. In F. Lewis Hall et al. (Eds.), *Psychiatric illness in women: Emerging treatments and research.* Washington, DC: American Psychiatric Publishing.

Kazdin, A. E. (Ed.). (2003). *Methodological issues and strategies in clinical research* (3rd ed.). Washington, DC: American Psychological Association.

Keith, S. J., Regier, D. A., & Rae, D. S. (1991). Schizophrenic disorders. In L. N. Robins & D. A. Regier (Eds.), *Psychiatric disorders in America: The Epidemiological Catchment Area Study.* New York: Free Press.

Keller, H. (1955). *The story of my life.* New York: Doubleday.

Kelley, H. H. (1973). The process of causal attribution. *American Psychologist, 28,* 107–128.

Kelly, G. (1955). *The psychology of personal constructs.* New York: Norton.

Kelly, G. F. (2001). *Sexuality today: The human perspective* (6th ed.). Boston: McGraw-Hill.

Kelly, J. A., St. Lawrence, J. S., Hood, H. V., & Brasfield, T. L. (1989). Behavioral intervention to reduce AIDS risk activities. *Journal of Consulting and Clinical Psychology, 57,* 60–67.

Kelly, T. A., & Strupp, H. H. (1992). Patient and therapist values in psychotherapy: Perceived changes, assimilation, similarity, and outcome. *Journal of Consulting and Clinical Psychology, 60,* 34–40.

Keltner, D., & Ekman, P. (2000). Facial expression of emotion. In M. Lewis & J. M. Haviland-Jones (Eds.), *Handbook of emotions* (2nd ed.). New York: Guilford Press.

Kemeny, M. E., (2004). The psychobiology of stress. *Current Directions in Psychological Science, 12,* 124–129.

Kempermann, G. (2005). *Adult neurogenesis: Stem cells and neuronal development in the adult brain.* New York: Oxford University Press.

Kenardy, J., Brown, W. J., & Vogt, E. (2001). Dieting and health in young Australian women. *European Eating Disorders Review, 9,* 242–254.

Kendall, D. (1998). *Social problems in a diverse society.* Boston: Allyn & Bacon.

Kendler, K. S., Gatz, M., Gardner, C. O., & Pedersen, N. L. (2006). A Swedish national twin study of lifetime major depression. *American Journal of Psychiatry, 163,* 109–114.

Kenrick, D. T., & Funder, D. C. (1988). Profiting from controversy: Lessons from the person-situation debate. *American Psychologist, 43,* 23–34.

Kensinger, E. A., Ullman, M. T., & Corkin, S. (2001). Bilateral medial temporal lobe damage does not affect lexical or grammatical processing: Evidence from amnesic patient H. M. *Hippocampus, 11,* 347–360.

Kernberg, O. F. (1984). *Severe personality disorders: Psychotherapeutic strategies.* New Haven, CT: Yale University Press.

Kernberg, O. F. (2000). *Personality disorders in children and adolescents.* Poulsbo, WA: H-R Press.

Kernberg, O. F., & Caligor, E. (2005). A psychoanalytic theory of personality disorders. In M. F. Lenzenweger & J. F. Clarkin (Eds.), *Major theories of personality disorder.* New York: Guilford Press.

Kerr, M., Lambert, W. W., & Bem, D. J. (1996). Life course sequelae of childhood shyness in Sweden: Comparison with the United States. *Developmental Psychology, 32,* 1100–1105.

Kessler, R. C., Gilman, S. E., Thornton, L. M., & Kendler, K. S. (2004). Health, well-being, and social responsibility in the MIDUS twin and sibling subsamples. In O. G. Brim, C. D. Ryff, & R. Kessler (Eds.), *How healthy are we? A national study of well-being in midlife.* Chicago: University of Chicago Press.

Kessler, R. C., McGonagle, K. A., Zhao, S., Nelson, C. et al. (1994). Lifetime and 12-month prevalence of DSM-III-R psychiatric disorder in the United States. *Archives of General Psychiatry, 51,* 8–19.

Ketellar, T. (1995). *Emotion as mental representations of fitness affordances: I. Evidence supporting the claim that the negative and positive emotions map onto fitness costs and benefits.* Paper presented at the annual meeting of the Human Behavior and Evolution Society, Santa Barbara, CA.

Kety, S. S. (1988). Schizophrenic illness in the families of schizophrenic adoptees: Findings from the Danish national sample. *Schizophrenia Bulletin, 14,* 217–222.

Kety, S. S., Rosenthal, D., Wender, P. H., Schulsinger, F., & Jacobson, B. (1978). The biological and adoptive families of adopted individuals who become schizophrenic: Prevalence of mental illness and other characteristics. In L. C. Wynne, R. L. Cromwell, & S. Matthysse (Eds.), *The nature of schizophrenia: New approaches to research and treatment.* New York: Wiley.

Keyes, C. L. M., & Waterman, M. B. (2003). Dimensions of well-being and mental health in adulthood. In. M. H. Bornstein, L. Davidson, C. L. M. Keyes, & K. A. Moore (Eds.),

Well-being: Positive development across the life course: Crosscurrents in contemporary psychology. Mahwah, NJ: Erlbaum.

Keyes, L. M., & Goodman, S. H. (2006). *Women and depression: A handbook for social, behavioral, and biomedical sciences.* New York: Cambridge University Press.

Kiecolt-Glaser, J., Bane, C., Glaser, R., & Malarkey, W. B. (2003). Love, marriage, and divorce: Newlyweds' stress hormones foreshadow relationship changes. *Journal of Consulting and Clinical Psychology, 71,* 176–188.

Kiecolt-Glaser, J., McGuire, L., Robles, T. F., & Glaser, R. (2002). Emotions, morbidity, and mortality: New perspectives from psychoneuroimmunology. *Annual Review of Psychology, 53,* 83–107.

Kihlstrom, J. F. (1998). Dissociations and dissociation theory in hypnosis: Comment on Kirsch and Lynn. *Psychological Bulletin, 123,* 186–191.

Kihlstrom, J. F. (1999). The psychological unconscious. In L. A. Pervin & O. P. John (Eds.), *Handbook of personality: Theory and research.* New York: Guilford Press.

Kimerling, R., Ouimette, P., & Wolfe, J. (2003). *Gender and PTSD.* New York: Guilford Press.

Kimura, D. (1992). Sex differences in the brain. *Scientific American, 267*(3), 119–195.

Kimura, K., Tachibana, N., Aso, T., Kimura, J., & Shibasaki, H. (1997). Subclinical REM sleep behavior disorder in a patient with corticobasal degeneration. *Sleep, 20,* 891–894.

KING Broadcasting Company. (2005, March 2). 5 P.M. Evening News. Seattle, WA.

King, N. J., Dudley, A., Melvin, G., Pallant, J., & Morawetz, D. (2001). Empirically supported treatments for insomnia. *Scandinavian Journal of Behaviour Therapy, 30,* 23–32.

Kirchengast, S., & Hartmann, B. (2003). Nicotine consumption before and during pregnancy affects not only newborn size but also birth modus. *Journal of Biosocial Science, 35,* 175–188.

Kirk, K. M., Bailey, J. M., & Martin, N. G. (2000). Etiology of male sexual orientation in an Australian twin sample. *Psychology, Evolution, and Gender, 2,* 301–311.

Kirkham, T. C. (2004). Cannabinoids and medicine: eating disorders, nausea and emesis. In V. Di Marzo (Ed.), *Cannabinoids.* New York: Kluwer Academic/Plenum Publishers.

Kirsch, I. (2001). The response set theory of hypnosis: Expectancy and physiology. *American Journal of Clinical Hypnosis, 44,* 69–73.

Kirsch, I., & Braffman, W. (2001). Imaginative suggestibility and hypnotizability. *Current Directions in Psychological Science, 10,* 57–61.

Kirsch, I., Moore, T. J., Scoboria, A., & Nicholls, S. S. (2002). The emperor's new drugs: An analysis of antidepressant medication data submitted to the U.S. Food and Drug Administration. *Prevention & Treatment, 5,* 262–279.

Kisilevsky, B. S., & Muir, D. W. (1984). Neonatal habituation and dishabituation to tactile stimulation during sleep. *Developmental Psychology, 20,* 367–373.

Kitayama, S., & Markus, H. (1999). The yin and yang of the Japanese self. In D. Cervone & Y. Shoda (Eds.), *The coherence of personality.* New York: Guilford Press.

Kitayama, S., Duffy, S., Kawamura, T., & Larsen, J. T. (2003). Perceiving an object and its context in different cultures: A cultural look at New Look. *Psychological Science,* 14, 201-206.

Kitayama, S., Markus, H. R., & Kurokawa, M. (2000). Culture, emotion, and well-being: Good feelings in Japan and the United States. *Cognition and Emotion, 14,* 93–124.

Kleim, J. A., Barbay, S., Cooper, N. R., Hogg, T. M., Reidel, C. N., Remple, M. S., & Nudo, R. J. (2002). Motor learning-dependent synaptogenesis is localized to functionally reorganized motor cortex. *Neurobiology of Learning & Memory, 77,* 63–77.

Klein, M. (1975). *The writings of Melanie Klein.* London: Hogarth Press.

Klein, S. B., & Mowrer, R. R. (1989). *Contemporary learning theories: Vol I. Pavlovian conditioning and the status of tradition.* Hillsdale, NJ: Erlbaum.

Kleiner, M. (Ed). (2002). *Handbook of polygraph testing.* San Diego, CA: Academic Press.

Kleinknecht, R. A., Dinnel, D. L., Kleinknecht, E. E., Hiruma, N. et al. (Eds.) (1997). Cultural factors in social anxiety: A comparison of social phobia symptoms and Taijin Kyofusho. *Journal of Anxiety Disorders, 2,* 157–177.

Kleinman, A. (2004). Culture and depression. *New England Journal of Medicine, 351,* 951–953.

Kleinmuntz, B. (1980). *Essentials of abnormal psychology* (2nd ed.). New York: Harper & Row.

Kleinmuntz, B., & Szucko, J. J. (1984). Lie detection in ancient and modern times: A call for contemporary scientific study. *American Psychologist, 39,* 766–776.

Kleitman, N. (1963). *Sleep and wakefulness* (2nd ed.). Chicago: University of Chicago Press.

Kluckhohn, C., & Murray, H. A. (1953). Personality formation: The determinants. In C. Kluckhohn, H. A. Murray, & D. M. Schneider (Eds.), *Personality in nature, society, and culture.* New York: Knopf.

Kluft, R. P. (1999). True lies, false truths, and naturalistic raw data: Applying clinical research findings to the false memory debate. In L. M. Williams & V. L. Banyard (Eds.), *Trauma and memory.* Thousand Oaks, CA: Sage.

Knauth, E. (1996). Designing better shift systems. *Applied Ergonomics, 27,* 39–44.

Knauth, P. (1996). Designing better shift systems. *Applied Ergonomics, 27,* 39–44.

Knipfel, J. (2004). *Herzog Kinski: A film legacy.* Anchor Bay Entertainment.

Knoblauch, K. (2002). Color vision. In H. Pashler & S. Yantis (Eds.), *Steven's handbook of experimental psychology: Vol. 1. Sensation and perception* (3rd ed.). New York: Wiley.

Knopik, V. S., Heath, A. C., Madden, P., Bucholz, K. K., Slutske, W. S., Nelson, E. C., Statham, D., Whitfield, J. B., & Martin, N. G. (2004). Genetic effects on alcohol dependence risk: Re-evaluating the importance of psychiatric and other heritable risk factors. *Psychological Medicine, 34,* 1519–1530.

Kobasa, S. C., Maddi, S. R., Puccetti, M. C., & Zola, M. A. (1985). Effectiveness of hardiness, exercise and social support as resources against illness. *Journal of Psychosomatic Research, 29,* 525–533.

Koch, C. (2004). *The quest for consciousness: A neurobiological approach.* Denver, CO: Roberts.

Koch, J. L. A. (1889). *Leitfaden der Psychiatrie* (2nd ed.). Ravensburg: Dornschen Buchhandlung.

Kochanska, G., Aksan, N., Knaack, A., & Rhines, H. M. (2004). Maternal parenting and children's conscience: Early security as moderator. *Child Development, 75,* 1229–1242.

Kochanska, G., Casey, R. J., & Fukumoto, A. (1995). Toddlers' sensitivity to standard violations. *Child Development, 66,* 643–656.

Kochanska, G., Forman, D. R., Aksan, N., & Dunbar, S. B. (2005). Pathways to conscience: Early mother-child mutually responsive orientation and children's moral emotion, conduct, and cognition. *Journal of Child Psychology and Psychiatry, 46,* 19–34.

Koenig, H. G., Pargament, K. L., & Nielsen, J. (1998). Religious coping and health status in medically ill hospitalized older adults. *Journal of Nervous and Mental Disease, 186,* 513–521.

Koestner, R., & McClelland, D. C. (1990). Perspectives on competence motivation. In L. A. Pervin (Ed.), *Handbook of personality theory and research.* New York: Guilford Press.

Kogi, K. (1985). Introduction to the problems of shift work. In S. Folkard & T. H. Monk (Eds.), *Hours of work.* West Sussex: Wiley.

Kohlberg, L. (1963). The development of children's orientations toward a moral order: I. Sequence in the development of moral thought. *Human Development, 6,* 11–33.

Kohlberg, L. (1984). *The psychology of moral development: Essays on moral development* (Vol. 2). New York: Harper & Row.

Köhler, W. (1925). *The mentality of apes* (Trans. from the 2nd rev. ed. by Ella Winter). New York: Harcourt.

Kohut, H. (1971). *Analysis of the self.* New York: International Universities Press.

Kohut, H. (1977). *The restoration of self.* New York: International Universities Press.

Kolb, B., & Whishaw, I. Q. (2001). *An introduction to brain and behavior.* New York: Worth.

Kolb, B., & Whishaw, I. Q. (2003). *Fundamentals of human neuropsychology* (5th ed.). New York: Worth.

Kolb, B., & Whishaw, I. Q. (2005). *An introduction to brain and behavior* (2nd ed.). New York: Worth.

Kollar, E. J., & Fisher, C. (1980). Tooth induction in chick epithelium: Expression of quiescent genes for enamel synthesis. *Science, 207,* 993–995.

Koltko-Rivera, M. (2006). Rediscovering the later version of Maslow's hierarchy of needs: Self-transcendence and opportunities for theory, research, and unification. *Review of General Psychology, 10,* 302–317.

Koluchova, J. (1972). Severe deprivation in twins: A case study. *Journal of Child Psychology and Psychiatry, 13,* 107–114.

Koluchova, J. (1991). Severely deprived twins after 22 years of observation. *Studia Psychologica, 33,* 23–28.

Koopman, P. R., & Ames, E. W. (1968). Infants' preferences for facial arrangements: A failure to replicate. *Child Development, 39,* 481–487.

Koriat, A., & Bjork, R. A. (2005). Illusions of competence in monitoring one's knowledge during study. *Journal of Experimental Psychology: Learning, Memory, and Cognition, 31,* 187–194.

Koriat, A., Goldsmith, M., & Pansky, A. (2000). Toward a psychology of memory accuracy. *Annual Review of Psychology, 51,* 481–537.

Kortegaard, L., Hoerder, K., Joergensen, J., Gillberg, C., & Kyvik, K. O. (2001). A preliminary population-based twin study of self-reported eating disorder. *Psychological Medicine, 31,* 361–365.

Kosambi, D. D. (1967). Living prehistory in India. *Scientific American, 216,* 105.

Kosslyn, S. M., Ball, T. M., & Reiser, B. J. (1978). Visual images preserve metric spatial information: Evidence from studies of image scanning. *Journal of Experimental Psychology: Human Perception and Performance, 4,* 47–60.

Kosslyn, S. M., Thompson, W. L., & Ganis, G. (2006). *The case for mental imagery.* New York: Oxford University Press

Kosslyn, S. M., Thompson, W. L., Costantini- Ferrando, M. F., Alpert, N. M., & Spiegel, D. (2000). Hypnotic visual illusion alters color processing in the brain. *American Journal of Psychiatry, 157,* 1279–1284.

Kostanski, M., Fisher, A., & Gullone, E. (2004). Current conceptualisation of body image dissatisfaction: Have we got it wrong? *Journal of Child Psychology and Psychiatry, 45,* 1317–1325.

Kottak, C. P. (2000). *Cultural anthropology* (8th ed.). Boston: McGraw-Hill.

Kowert, P. A. (Ed.). (2002). *Groupthink or deadlock: When do leaders learn from their advisors? SUNY series on the presidency.* New York: State University of New York Press.

Kraft, C. L. (1978). A psychophysical contribution to air safety: Simulator studies of illusions in night visual approaches. In H. L. Pick, Jr., H. W. Leibowitz, J. E. Singer, A. Steinschneider, & H. W. Stevenson (Eds.), *Psychology: From research to practice.* New York: Plenum Press.

Krasnegor, N. A., Lyon, G. R., & Goldman, R. P. S. (1997). *Development of the prefrontal cortex: Evolution, neurobiology, and behavior.* Baltimore, MD: Paul H. Brookes.

Krebs, D. L., & Denton, K. (1997). Social illusions and self-deception: The evolution of biases in person perception. In J. A. Simpson & D. T. Kenrick (Eds.), *Evolutionary social psychology.* Mahwah, NJ: Erlbaum.

Krevans, J., & Gibbs, J. C. (1996). Parents' use of inductive discipline: Relations to children's empathy and prosocial behavior. *Child Development, 67,* 3263–3277.

Kribbs, N. B. (1993). Siesta. In M. A. Carskadon (Ed.), *Encyclopedia of sleep and dreaming.* New York: Macmillan.

Kroeber, A. L. (1948). *Anthropology.* New York: Harcourt Brace Jovanovich.

Krosnick, J. A., Betz, A. L., Jussim, L. J., & Lynn, A. R. (1992). Subliminal conditioning of attitudes. *Personality and Social Psychology Bulletin, 18,* 152–162.

Kruger, J., Wirtz, D., & Miller, D. T. (2005). Counterfactual thinking and the first instinct fallacy. *Journal of Personality and Social Psychology, 88,* 725–735.

Kruglanski, A. W. (2004). *The psychology of closed mindedness.* New York: Psychology Press.

Kryger, M. H., Walid, R., & Manfreda, J. (2002). Diagnoses received by narcolepsy patients in the year prior to diagnosis by a sleep specialist. *Sleep: Journal of Sleep and Sleep Disorders Research, 25,* 36–41.

Ksir, C. J., Hart, C. I., & Ray, O. S. (2008). *Drugs, society, and human behavior.* New York: McGraw-Hill.

Kübler-Ross, E. (1969). *On death and dying.* New York: Macmillan.

Kulik, J. A., & Mahler, H. I. M. (2000). Social comparison, affiliation, and emotional contagion under threat. In J. Suls & L. Wheeler (Eds.), *Handbook of social comparison: Theory and research.* Dordrecht, Netherlands: Kluwer.

Kulik, J. A., Mahler, H. I. M., & Moore, P. J. (1996). Social comparison and affiliation under threat: Effects of recovery from major surgery. *Journal of Personality and Social Psychology, 66,* 301–309.

Kuncel, N. P., Hezlett, S. A., & Ones, D. S. (2004). Academic performance, career potential, and job performance: Can one construct predict them all? *Journal of Personality and Social Psychology, 86,* 148–161.

Kuntsche, E.N., Rehm, J., & Gmel, G. (2004). Characteristics of binge drinkers in Europe. *Social Science and Medicine, 59,* 113–127.

Kunzendorf, R. G., Hartmann, E., Cohen, R., & Cutler, J. (1997). Bizarreness of the dreams and daydreams reported by individuals with thin and thick boundaries. *Dreaming: Journal of the Association for the Study of Dreams, 7,* 265–271.

Kunzman, U., & Baltes, P. B. (2003). Beyond the traditional scope of intelligence: Wisdom in action. In R. J. Sternberg, J. Lautrey, & T. I. Lubart (Eds.), *Models of intelligence: International perspectives.* Washington, DC: American Psychological Association.

Kurzweil, E. (1989). *The Freudians: A comparative perspective.* New Haven, CT: Yale University Press.

LaBar, K. S., & Phelps, E. A. (1998). Arousal-mediated memory consolidation: Role of the medial temporal lobe in humans. *Psychological Science, 9,* 490–493.

Lachman, M. E. (2004). Development in midlife. *Annual Review of Psychology, 55,* 305–331.

Lagerspetz, K. Y., Tirri, R., & Lagerspetz, K. M. (1968). Neurochemical and endocrinological studies of mice selectively bred for aggressiveness. *Scandinavian Journal of Psychology, 9,* 157–160.

Laible, D., & Thompson, R. A. (2000). Motherchild discourse, attachment security, shared positive affect, and early conscience development. *Child Development, 71,* 1424–1440.

Lambert, M. J., Shapiro, D. A., & Bergin, A. E. (1986). The effectiveness of psychotherapy. In L. Garfield & A. E. Bergin (Eds.), *Handbook of psychotherapy and behavior change* (3rd ed.). New York: Wiley.

Lambert, W. E., Genesee, F., Holobow, N., & Chartrand, L. (1993). Bilingual education for majority English-speaking children. *European Journal of Psychology of Education, 8,* 3–22.

Lamborn, S. D., Mounts, N. S., Steinberg, L., & Dornbusch, S. M. (1991). Patterns of competence and adjustment among adolescents from authoritative, authoritarian, indulgent, and neglectful families. *Child Development, 62,* 1049–1065.

Land, B. B., & Seeley, T. D. (2004). The grooming invitation dance of the honey bee. *Ethology, 110,* 1–10.

Landers, D. M., & Arent, S. (2001). Arousal-performance relations. In J. M. Williams (Ed.), *Applied sport psychology: Personal growth to peak performance* (4th ed.). Boston: McGraw-Hill.

Landesman, S., & Ramey, C. T. (1989). Developmental psychology and mental retardation: Integrating scientific principles with treatment practices. *American Psychologist, 44,* 409–415.

Lane, R. D., Reiman, E. M., Ahern, G. L., & Schwartz, G. E. (1997). Neuroanatomical correlates of happiness, sadness, and disgust. *American Journal of Psychiatry, 154,* 926–933.

Lane, S. D., Cherek, D. R., Lieving, L. M., & Tcheremissine, O. V. (2005). Marijuana effects on human forgetting functions. *Journal of the Experimental Analysis of Behavior, 83,* 67–83.

Langan-Fox, J., & Grant, S. (2006). The Thematic Apperception Test: Toward a standard measure of the Big Three motives. *Journal of Personality Assessment, 87,* 277–291.

Langer, E. (1989). *Mindlessness.* Reading, MA: Addison-Wesley.

Langer, E. J., Blank, A., & Chanowitz, B. (1978). The mindlessness of ostensibly thoughtful actions: The role of 'placebic' information in interpersonal interaction. *Journal of Personality and Social Psychology, 36,* 635-642.

Langlois, J. H., & Roggman, L. A. (1990). Attractive faces are only average. *Psychological Science, 1,* 115–121.

Langlois, J. H., Kalakanis, L., Rubenstein, A. J., Larson, A., Hallam, M., & Smoot, M. (2000). Maxims or myths of beauty? A meta-analytic and theoretical review. *Psychological Bulletin, 126,* 390–423.

Lanier, C. A. (2001). Rape accepting attitudes: Precursors to or consequences of forced sex. *Violence Against Women, 7,* 876–885.

LaPiere, R. T. (1934). Attitudes and actions. *Social Forces, 13,* 230–237.

LaPointe, L. L. (2005). *Aphasia and related neurogenic language disorders* (3rd ed.). New York: Thieme New York.

Larivée, S., Normandeau, S., & Parent, S. (2000). The French connection: Some contributions of French language research in the post Piagetian era. *Child Development, 71,* 823–839.

Larroque, B., & Kaminski, M. (1998). Prenatal alcohol exposure and development at preschool age: Main results of a French study. *Alcoholism: Clinical and Experimental Research, 22,* 295–303.

Larsen, R., & Buss, D. M. (2002). *Personality psychology: Domains of knowledge about human nature.* Boston, MA: McGraw-Hill.

Larsen, R., & Buss, D. M. (2007). *Personality psychology: Domains of knowledge about human nature* (3rd ed.). Boston MA: McGraw-Hill.

Larsen, R., & Diener, E. (1985). A multitraitmultimethod examination of affect structure: Hedonic level and emotional intensity. *Personality and Individual Differences, 6,* 631–636.

Larson, R. W., Hansen, D. M., & Moneta, G. (2006). Differing profiles of developmental experiences across types of organized youth activities. *Developmental Psychology, 42,* 849–863.

Larson, R. W., Moneta, G., Richards, M. H., & Wilson, W. (2002). Continuity, stability, and change in daily emotional experience across adolescence. *Child Development, 73,* 1151–1165.

Lasco, M. S., Jordan, T. J., Edgar, M. A., Petito, C. K., & Byne, W. (2002). A lack of dimorphism of sex or sexual orientation in the human anterior commissure. *Brain Research, 936,* 95–98.

Lashley, K. S. (1950). In search of the engram. *Symposia of the Society for Experimental Biology, 4,* 454–482.

Latané, B., & Bourgeois, M. J. (2001). Successfully simulating dynamic social impact: Three levels of prediction. In J. P. Forgas & K. D. Williams (Eds.), *Social influence: Direct and indirect processes. The Sydney symposium of social psychology.* Philadelphia, PA: Psychology Press.

Latané, B., & Darley, J. M. (1970). *The unresponsive bystander: Why doesn't he help?* New York: Appleton-Century-Crofts.

Laumann, E. O., Gagnon, J. H., Michael, R. T., & Michaels, S. (1994). *The social organization of sexuality: Sexual practices in the United States.* Chicago: University of Chicago Press.

Lavergne, G. M. (1997). *A sniper in the tower: The Charles Whitman murders.* Denton: University of North Texas Press.

Lavie, P. (2000). Sleep-wake as a biological rhythm. *Annual Review of Psychology, 52,* 277–303.

Lavie, P., Pratt, H., Scharf, B., Peled, R., & Brown, J. (1984) Localized pontine lesion: Nearly total absence of REM sleep. *Neurology, 34,* 118–20.

Lavigne, J. V., Gibbons, R. D., Christoffel, K. K., & Arend, R. (1996). Prevalence rates and correlates of psychiatric disorders among preschool children. *Journal of the American Academy of Child & Adolescent Psychiatry, 35,* 204–214.

Lawler, K. A., & Schmied, L. A. (1992). A prospective study of women's health: The effects of stress, hardiness, locus of control, Type A behavior, and physiological reactivity. *Women and Health, 19,* 27–41.

Lazarus, A. A. (1971). *Behavior therapy and beyond.* New York: McGraw-Hill.

Lazarus, A. A. (1995). Multimodal therapy. In R. J. Corsini & D. Wedding (Eds.), *Current psychotherapies* (5th ed.). Itasca, IL: Peacock.

Lazarus, R. S. (1991). Progress on a cognitivemotivational- relational theory of emotion. *American Psychologist, 46,* 819–834.

Lazarus, R. S. (1998). *Fifty years of the research and theory of R. S. Lazarus: An analysis of historical and perennial issues.* Mahwah, NJ: Erlbaum.

Lazarus, R. S. (2001). Relational meaning and discrete emotions. In B. K. Scherer et al. (Eds.), *Appraisal processes in emotion: Theory, methods, research.* New York: Oxford University Press.

Lazarus, R. S., & Folkman, S. (1984). *Stress, appraisal, and coping.* New York: Springer.

Leahy, R. L., & Holland, S. J. (2000).*Treatment plans and interventions for depression and anxiety disorders.* New York: Guilford Press.

Leary, M. R. (2004). The self we know and the self we show: Self-esteem, selfpresentation, and the maintenance of interpersonal relationships. In M. B. Brewer & M. Hewstone (Eds.), *Emotion and motivation: Perspectives on social psychology.* Malden, MA: Blackwell.

Leary, M. R., Tambor, E. S., Terdal, S. K., & Downs, D. L. (1995). Self-esteem as an inter-personal monitor: The sociometer hypothesis. *Journal of Personality and Social Psychology, 68,* 518–530.

LeDoux, J. E. (1998). *The emotional brain.* New York: Simon & Schuster.

LeDoux, J. E. (2000). Emotion circuits in the brain. *Annual Review of Neuroscience, 23,* 155–184.

LeDoux, J. E., & Phelps, E. A. (2000). Emotional networks in the brain. In M. Lewis & J. M. Haviland-Jones (Eds.), *Handbook of emotions* (2nd ed.). New York: Guilford Press.

Lee, J. D. (1998). Which kids can 'become' scientists? Effects of gender, self-concepts, and perceptions of scientists. *Social Psychology Quarterly, 61,* 199–219.

Lehmann-Haupt, C. (1988, August 4). Books of the times: How an actor found success, and himself. *New York Times,* p. 2.

Leichtman, M. D., & Ceci, S. J. (1995). The effects of stereotypes and suggestions on preschoolers' reports. *Developmental Psychology, 31,* 568–578.

Leifman, H., Österberg, E., & Ramstedt, M. (2002). *Alcohol in postwar Europe, ECAS II: A discussion of indicators on alcohol consumption and alcohol-related harm.* Stockholm: National Institute of Public Health.

LeMoal, H., (1999). *Dopamine and the brain: From neurons to networks.* New York: Academic Press.

Lenzenweger, M. F., & Clarkin, J. F. (Eds.). (2005). *Major theories of personality disorder.* New York: Guilford Press.

Leon, G. R., & Roth, L. (1977). Obesity: Psychological causes, correlations, and speculations. *Psychological Bulletin, 84,* 117–139.